Management Basics for Information Professionals

SECOND EDITION

G. Edward Evans & Patricia Layzell Ward

Neal-Schuman Publishers, Inc.
New York   London

A companion Web page keeps this text up to date.
www.neal-schuman.com/managementbasics

Published by Neal-Schuman Publishers, Inc.
100 William St., Suite 2004
New York, NY 10038

Copyright © 2007 by Neal-Schuman Publishers, Inc.

Printed and bound in the United States of America.

The paper used in this publication meets the minimum requirements of American National Standard for Information Sciences - Permanence of Paper for Printed Library Materials, ANSI Z39.48-1992.

Library of Congress Cataloging-in-Publication Data

Evans, G. Edward, 1937-
    Management basics for information professionals / G. Edward Evans, Patricia Layzell Ward. — 2nd ed.
        p. cm.
    Includes bibliographical references and indexes.
    ISBN: 978-1-55570-586-2 (alk. paper)
1. Library administration—United States. 2. Information services—United States—Management. I. Layzell Ward, Patricia. II. Title.
Z678.E9 2007
025.1—dc22

                                        2007012843

From Edward Evans to two fine grandsons—

Travis and Trenton

Table of Contents

List of Figures

List of Tables

Foreword

Management *must* be taught in the Library and Information Science field. It is at the core of everything that needs to be done in this profession, that is, managing resources, facilities, people, and most importantly, ourselves.

The authors of this second edition, G. Edward Evans and Patricia Layzell Ward, state their belief that "good managers are made, not born" and give readers a practical grounding in the managerial and philosophical concepts of getting the job done. The new edition is organized into four sensible content areas—Background; Knowledge and Skills; Managing Resources; Career Development and Your Future—which divides and conquers vast amounts of information using a user-friendly writing style.

The authors present some difficult concepts in an approachable way to help readers understand why strong management skills and abilities are required.

New additions include: Examples of major employment legislation; discussions on unionization and collective bargaining; contracts and licensing; using volunteers; issues and corrective actions dealing with discipline; potential lawsuit issues such as sexual harassment.

Students will no longer keep a list of "things I didn't learn during professional training." The facilities chapter includes risk management, health, safety and security and disaster management but it also includes something as basic as housekeeping.

It is enough of an introduction to each of these topics to ensure their importance in the operations of information organizations but not enough to overwhelm. And the inclusion of the last chapter on career development was a capstone.

The second edition of *Management Basics for Information Professionals* is a "one-stop shopping place" for all things management. My hats (the many hats of a manager) are off to the authors. It is obvious they have worked hard to make this a thoughtful and comprehensive text.

Dr. Pat Feehan
Associate Professor
School of Library and Information Science
College of Mass Communication and
   Information Studies
University of South Carolina

Preface

One might well question the need for a new edition of a book entitled *Management Basics for Information Professionals*. When we started working on this project, we knew we had to make changes in a few areas and updates in others. It quickly became clear, however, that a great deal had changed in less than ten years. The result is this second edition with very different content. Readers will find two entirely new chapters: "Managing Diversity" (Chapter 4) and "Career Development" (Chapter 19). Every other chapter contains a substantial amount of new material, and what remains of the old material has been rewritten. To reflect our belief that all types of information services have a management core, we have included examples from a variety of such services (including archives, information brokers, libraries, and records management).

Clearly the pace of change in management thought and practice in general, and for information services in particular, has been increasing. In many ways, information services currently face more new challenges than at any time in the past. We will mention three areas here, but many more are discussed throughout the text.

Many information service providers receive the majority of their operating funds from public sources. Such organizations currently face a change in public attitude toward funding "social services"—an attitude of support has shifted to an attitude of grave doubt regarding the value received for moneys expended. As a result of this trend, services must demonstrate their benefits, be accountable in more transparent ways, and sometimes even find additional funding from alternative sources.

Technology is also creating management challenges for services. Sometimes service managers must make difficult decisions as they confront swiftly changing basic technologies (such as computers, telecommunications, and funding) and the training issues associated with those changes. In addition, new technologies that are introduced may or may not be longlasting, and deciding whether or when to adopt the new approach is often a complex process. Finally, new competitors often vie for the attention and support of information users. Projects from commercial Internet content providers are examples of the ever-growing competition.

Our final example of a new challenge relates to the demographics of the information workforce. Managers must address both cultural and generational issues effectively in order to provide the high-quality programs and services that their users expect and demand. To be successful, an information service manager must focus on the user/client/patron/customer. Our basic philosophy is that management should be people-centered. We believe that management can be defined in one sentence (albeit one that hides great complexity): Management is the accomplishment of things with, through, and for people.

Like its predecessor, this second edition provides a comprehensive introduction to the management of information services. We wish to emphasize the word *introduction*. Acquiring the basic management background and skills to oversee the operation of a dynamic information service organization today is a complex challenge. Our text is intended for students in archive, library, and related information programs, as well as for information professionals seeking a regular update of relevant sources of literature related to library and information center management.

Management Basics for Information Professionals, Second Edition, is organized in a fashion that parallels the arrangement of many management and administration courses. The text is divided into four parts. Part I, "Background," contains four chapters addressing the essential concepts, definitions, and perspectives needed to comprehend and discuss the "science" of management. The ten chapters in Part II, "Management: Knowledge and Skills," collectively cover the skills and knowledge needed by beginning managers. Topics include such basics as the planning process; understanding the differences (and connections) among power, authority, and responsibility; delegation; motivation; and leadership. Part III, "Managing Resources," covers the four areas that require the bulk of most library and information center managers' time: personnel, fiscal, technological, and facilities management. Part IV, "Career Development and Your Future," looks at career development and briefly addresses what we believe the future will hold for incoming managers.

We have arranged for this book's contents to be updated and supplemented by material housed on the Web. This material can be found at www.neal-schuman.com/managementbasics.html. We urge you to investigate this Web site, which will include regular reviews of the library and information science management literature. Keeping up to date in the field is vitally important. Making a habit of scanning such journals as *American Archivist, Harvard Business Review, Journal of the Society of Archivists, Library Management,* and *Library Administration & Management* on a regular basis will aid that process. Logging on to such sites as www.ipl.org/div/subject/ to browse for archive and records management information is also an easy way to keep up with the field. Joining the management interest group of relevant local, national, and international professional bodies, and attending program events at conventions will provide valuable networking and mentoring opportunities.

While this text—like most classes—uses a linear approach to the very broad and abstract world of management, the topics are, of course, interrelated in complex ways. A basic knowledge (from Part I) of management informs planning; managers must have some specific knowledge (from Part II) of the planning cycle and communication in order to manage; and both planning and communication skills are needed when one sets out to manage technology (covered in Part III). To underscore these connections, we provide a variety of brief text boxes (examples include "For Further Thought," "Tips," and "Check This Out") in each chapter. Most of the chapters also include "Key Points to Remember," which help bring all the pieces together. Each chapter concludes with a "Launching Pad"—a selected list of recent items that will help readers explore chapter ideas in depth.

There will always be differing views about what management is and what managers should do. While there is agreement among many library and information science educators about the discipline's fundamental concepts, the way in which management is practiced changes from time to time, depending on the current operating environment. Since most readers who use this book are likely to manage during both good and bad times, we offer a set of principles, illustrated by practice, that provides an introduction to the topics based on our many years of managerial experience in a wide range of information settings.

Management is a mix of integrated activities that, when successfully carried out, leaves people with almost no sense of having been managed. Some writers in the field call this accomplishment "seamless management." Whatever one calls the mix, there is one certainty: Good managers must expect, and be prepared, to manage change. The most successful managers consider all conceivable occurrences in their realms of responsibility.

Keep in mind that managerial skills are transferable. A sound knowledge of both the theory and practice of management, as well as a successful management track record and a powerful focus on quality service, will allow you to "spread your wings" beyond information services.

We believe that good managers are made, not born. To be made, two ingredients are required: the motivation to learn and develop knowledge and skills, and the gift of support and the opportunity to grow. We urge you to use *Management Basics for Information Professionals, Second Edition*, as one of many such opportunities.

G. Edward Evans, Flagstaff, Arizona, USA
Patricia Layzell Ward, Penrhyndeudraeth, Wales

Part I

Background

1

Introduction

"If the boss presents his solution first and asks for opinions about it, a vote of approval will follow almost every time."
George Odiorne

"Bosses nearly always overestimate their importance to the organization."
Maurice Line

Organizations are a central fact of modern life. Some are commercial in nature, some are not; some are voluntary in membership, some are not. Whatever their character, organizations share several characteristics—they have an impact on our lives, they are run by people like ourselves, and the better they are run the more positive their influence on our lives. The way organizations are run changes over time as the societies in which they exist evolve. Today most societies are changing fast and the rate of change seems to be accelerating with each passing day.

Politics has also always been a factor in change. Clearly there are consequences when the controlling political party believes it should play an active role in social and economic activities, just as there are consequences when the party in power believes the opposite. Shifting political fortunes and the attendant shifts in priorities usually mean shifting fortunes for libraries and information centers. We see this trend in concerns about public spending, and, with such concerns, a growing pressure for libraries to find new sources of funding and to engage in collaborative activities.

As the economy moves through its cycles of highs and lows, *economic issues* play an important role, both positive and negative, on change. Globalization of the economy means that far distant economic events can have a major impact on the local economy and organizations. Although most libraries and information centers serve a localized population and operate

---

Explore These:

Take some time to explore the Web sites for two examples of the world-wide growing emphasis for expanding collaborative activities among cultural organizations:

- United States Institute of Museum and Library Services (www.imls.gov)
- Museums, Libraries and Archives Council (www.mla.gov.uk)

---

within the local economy, they are no longer insulated from economic "shocks" occurring halfway around the world. A good example is the impact of increased fuel costs on library mobile services.

A number of factors push the changes, and we will mention just a few of the more significant ones. New patterns of demographics and a variety of lifestyles are important factors today. Different generational groups—"Veterans," "Boomers," "Gen Xers," and "Millenniums"—all exist in organizations and their disparate values and "world views" impact organizational operations (see Chapters 4 and 12 for a discussion of the differences). Declining birth rates and aging populations cause shifts in social and government spending on services and basic priorities. Increasing global migration results in more diverse societies and workforces. That in turn has implications for organizational management and operations and activities such as resource sharing.

Technology is probably the most discussed agent of change. Information and communication technologies (ICT) have led to an amazing degree of global connectivity in the space of just 20 years. What the future holds is impossible to predict with any accuracy, beyond the fact that it will bring more change more quickly. There are at least two major issues for organizations and technology. First, and foremost, technology will continue to influence how organizations operate, how they are structured, and how they are staffed. Second, the cost of maintaining a responsible level of organizational technology becomes an ever-growing concern. Technology has certainly made it easier, if not less costly, for information services to collaborate with one another. Technology provides many benefits, but it also creates some divides. An obvious divide exists in some developing countries where the infrastructure can present enormous challenges, even for meeting basic human needs. There is also the well-observed divide within developed countries where some people cannot afford the technology and have difficulty gaining free or inexpensive access to it. Another divide is less frequently discussed in the United States—the divide in the information services area between the United States and the rest of the world. For example, OCLC has become the de facto world bibliographic utility; in the field of full-text commercial databases, the U.S. market drives decision making. In both cases, the United States needs tend to dominate what happens and how it happens. Finally, there is a growing divide between those organizations that are able to keep up-to-date technologically and those that are not. The more well-to-do organizations are able to increase their influence and support often to the detriment of those less fortunate.

Closing the Divide:

One day the cost of gaining access to the very basic ICT may become less of an issue for less well-off people and countries. A news note (*Economist*, 2005) reported that a group led by Nicholas Negroponte plans on displaying a computer priced at $100 at a United Nations summit late in 2005. The group's goal is to develop a basic computer that will help address the information needs of poor people and countries. At the time of the report the group had gotten the cost down to $130. By the time the summit started, the cost had dropped to $100, and by the end of 2006, they were manufacturing and distributing the computers.

All these factors, as well as many others, have an influence on how organizations are run or managed. Libraries, information centers, and archives must be managed, and the people who do this must have an understanding of what "management" means. It is important to understand that while organizations change and operate, the underlying basics of management remain in place. The following chapters address those basics.

WHAT IS MANAGEMENT?

Management, at its most basic level, is the process of accomplishing things through people. This simple definition belies the complexity of management, which we will explore throughout this book. The exploration begins with Chapter 2 covering some of the history of general managerial thought and practice as well as their reflection in library and information center operations. One obvious reason for such a chapter is that the management of libraries and other information organizations draws upon general management practice and thought. A second, less obvious, reason is that there is a tendency for people to focus on the latest "in" solution to management challenges. What you usually find when closely examining the latest "in" solution is that it is some new mix of the "old" basics, repackaged and with a new twist. Much of what past scholars in management fundamentals said is as valid today as it was 75 or more years ago.

Yale economist Charles Lindblom described management as "the science of 'muddling' through" (1959). People will engage in a little "muddling" regardless of their training; however, the amount of muddling decreases as the amount of training increases. Information organizations, not-for-profit (NFP) organizations, and government organizations have been rather slow to see the need for formal training in management. In fact, such formal training as a "core" subject in educational programs for information professionals is relatively recent.

Formal training programs in business schools focus on profit and loss as well as on precisely defined products and markets. Information services and libraries deal in imprecisely defined services (access to information) to what is most often a very heterogeneous population/market. Lacking precise goals and measures of achievement (such as a profit), in the past they saw little need for formal training in management.

The old notion that any information professional could be a manager has shifted to a recognition that such professionals should have some formal training in management. Formal training provides an understanding of the basic elements of managerial activities since over the years managers and researchers have accumulated a large body of literature about what leads to successful or unsuccessful performance.

One reflection of the changing views regarding management education for information professionals occurred way back in 1983 at a conference of educators from the International Federation of Library Associations and Institutions, the Federation Internationale de Documentation, and the International Council on Archives. The purpose of the meeting was to explore the possibilities of identifying a universal "core" for the education of information professionals in management. This book's authors participated in that conference. By the end of the conference it was agreed (a) that it is absolutely essential to provide all information professionals with management training, and (b) that there is a core set of topics that the information professional should know.

Since that time the archives, information, knowledge, library, museums, and records sectors have been increasingly working together in partnership. At the management level there is more mobility between these fields. For this reason we have chosen, in general, to refer to "information professionals" or "information services" as generic terms, unless reference is being made to a specific field.

Another matter concerns semantics. At different times there has been a fashion to talk of "clients," "customers," or "users." We have chosen the term "users," for it means that reference can be made to "nonusers"— "nonclients" or "noncustomers" somehow doesn't sound quite right.

Throughout this book, there are several terms to keep in mind: manager, administrator, executive, leader, and supervisor. *Manager* is the term on which we will focus in this book. *Administrator* is the term often used as a synonym for manager in reference to the public sector or not-for-profit organizations (hospital administrator, academic administrator, or library administrator). *Executive* usually means a top manager of an organization—the chief executive officer (CEO), the president, a vice president, the library director. *Leader* is used for a person, at any level in an organization in today's work environment, who is able to get other staff to follow him or her in some work activities. *Supervisor* generally refers to someone in the first level of management—job titles such as department head and unit head are common at this level—who directs and controls the day-to-day activities of the majority of organizational employees.

Perhaps the shortest definition of management is one attributed to Mary Parker Follett (1941): "management is the art of getting things done through people." A less charitable definition is "getting others to do *your* work." A longer and more balanced definition is Daniel Wren's "management is an activity essential to organized endeavors that perform certain functions to obtain the effective acquisition, allocating, and utilization of human efforts and physical resources for the purpose of accomplishing some goal" (1979: 3). There are literally hundreds of other definitions of the term. Almost every one contains two elements: a mention of people and activities, and a reference to formal organizations.

For Further Thought:

Check two other definitions of "management." Now compare the four. What do they have in common? How do they differ?

Managers direct and facilitate the work of others. There is generally something of a pyramid shape to any organization, with more people involved in nonmanagerial activities than there are in performing managerial duties. Organizations almost always consist of a "top" (few people), a "middle" (several people), and a "bottom" (many people). In recent years, organizations have flattened their structures, and so the ratios at the different levels have changed and will continue to do so; however, almost all organizations still have some form of these three levels, which may appear to be much of a hierarchy. Even in more or less fully team-based organizations there is some type of management team, team leaders, and team members.

We believe that, just because people are at the top or middle, it does not mean they are exempt from performing bottom functions at times. In fact, it is often very useful for everyone when tops and middles do some of the work of the bottom levels. One of our professional mottos is "Everyone *must* get their hands dirty from time to time." This means that when a major task comes up, the *entire* staff does the work. Having tops and middles pushing book trucks, shifting materials in the stacks, or whatever, results in everyone feeling they are part of a team and there is mutual support whenever needed.

Such mixing of top and bottom activities provides tops with a firsthand sense of what bottoms face on a day-to-day basis. It also makes sure that the middles and tops have the technical background and skills to perform, as well as direct, bottom activities. We will show, in Chapter 14, that one element of leadership is the staff's belief in the technical abilities of their "leader."

Just what *do* managers do? There are many answers to that question, but the question actually contains two issues: management function and behavior. Some managerial functions are planning, directing, or budgeting, while behavioral aspects involve the roles filled, such as negotiator or group spokesperson. Writers tend to emphasize one side or the other. This book is organized according to functions; however, we also explore behavioral aspects and place great emphasis on user needs.

What Do Managers Do?:

Try this experiment to gain an idea of what managers do. Approach a person known to be a manager. Ask the person to describe what he or she does. The response will be something like, "Well, I'm head of the reference department," or, "I'm assistant director for technical services," or, "I'm the director of the archives." This vague definition will require further probing, so say, "But tell me what you actually do during a typical work day." More often than not, the answer will be some variation of "I attend lots of uninteresting meetings, write letters, reports, and memos, and listen to complaints. It seems like I never get anything done." Another response might be, "I spend most of my day solving little problems and putting out brush fires." Seldom will the answer be, "Oh, I direct, plan, control, delegate, budget, and hire and fire people."

Often a manager/supervisor will say something like, "I never get my real work done." Usually the person is referring to some of the classical concepts of the functions of a manager. One set of labels for these functions appeared in a classic paper by Gulick and Urwick (1937). In it, they coined the acronym POSDCoRB, which stands for the following functions:

Planning	Coordinating
Organizing	Reporting
Staffing	Budgeting
Directing	

POSDCoRB functions underlie, in one form or another, all management behavior; however, they do not describe the work of a manager. They merely identify the objectives of a manager's work. At least one management writer claims that, because the labels fail to describe what a manager actually does, they are of little use (Mintzberg, 1973). This is too harsh a judgment, for if we do not know where we are going (that is, if we do not have objectives), how shall we know when we get there? By studying POSDCoRB concepts a person can gain an understanding of what good management attempts to accomplish.

For Further Thought:

POSDCoRB—Think of an example of each of these functions. Remember that they are *objectives*, not a description of the work of the manager.

We have used the concept of tops, middles, and bottoms several times. A reasonable question to ask is, "Do all levels engage in the same activities?" A short answer is "yes," but such an answer obscures many important differences, especially in terms of the skills employed (see Figure 1.1). Tops tend to devote more time to planning than do the others, and planning calls for a major use of conceptual skills. Tops also tend to devote more time to interacting with a variety of people internal and external to the information service. This level of interaction calls for very strong interpersonal-relations skills. Finally, tops engage in very little production/service work, and thus they make limited use of the technical skills they once employed when they first entered the field.

A particularly good discussion of such difference in skills at varying levels of managerial responsibility is in Robert Katz's *Skills of an Effective Administrator* (1974). A variation on this concept, time spent on various activities, showed a similar difference from bottoms to tops (Mahoney, Jardee, and Carroll, 1964). For bottoms, the emphasis is almost a mirror opposite of the tops: great emphasis on technical skills, a strong component of human-relations skills, and only limited use of conceptual skills. As always, middles are in between: less use of technical skills than bottoms but more than tops, and a greater need for conceptual skills among middles than for bottoms, but less than for tops. You can envision these differences in terms

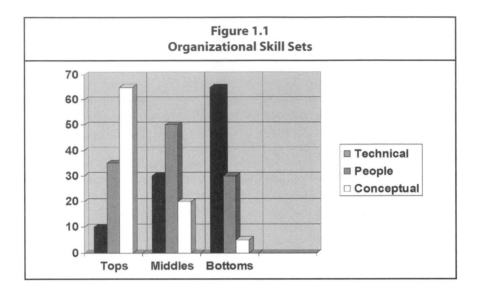

Figure 1.1
Organizational Skill Sets

of percentages. For a bottom, perhaps 60 to 70 percent of the emphasis is on technical skills, 20 to 30 percent on human relations, and the balance on conceptual abilities. Middles would perhaps be 20 to 30 percent technical, 10 to 50 percent human relations, and the balance conceptual. Conceptual abilities would be 40 to 50 for tops, with technical skills at 10 percent or less, and the balance involving human relations.

Perhaps the author who had the greatest general influence in the area of managerial behavior/work was Henry Mintzberg (1971, 1973, 1975). He criticizes the "functions" approach to management as not being reflective of what managers do on a day-to-day basis. Rather, he suggests looking at the roles played. His concept employs ten roles divided among three categories: interpersonal roles, informational roles, and decisional roles. Under interpersonal there are three roles: figurehead, leader, and liaison. Under informational he lists the roles of nerve center, disseminator, and spokesperson. Decisional activities include the roles of entrepreneur, disturbance handler, resource allocation, and negotiator. We suggest that there is perhaps a fourth role under informational: politician. To some extent such a role is part of being a figurehead, leader, negotiator, and spokesperson. However, given the changes that have taken place since the 1970s when Mintzberg carried out his research, the political role has become more important. We think it ought to be considered as a separate role.

Without question, Mintzberg's work added substantially to our understanding of what managers actually do. For teaching/learning purposes, however, the approach does not work very well because the research on which he based his concept focused on top managers and, to a lesser extent, middle managers, and it focused on observable activities rather than the reasons for the activity. Also, it does not represent a full picture of a manager's work; as we noted, the role of politician is not clearly delineated. Because of these deficiencies, the classical "functions" approach is still the most useful method for newcomers to conceptualize managerial responsibilities. We will, at various points in later chapters, note how roles as described by Mintzberg come into play.

As with many fields, there is a question of whether management is an art or a science. Our belief is that, despite elements of science, management is an art. Although a person can learn the basic concepts, principles, functions, and techniques such as those described by Mintzberg and others, each management situation is unique. While two situations may appear similar, the individuals involved will be different. Even when faced with similar situations and the same personnel, the management situations are unique. The passage of time causes each person to be just a little different from the last time the situation arose. Thus, what worked yesterday may or may not work today. One's ability to assess degrees of change and make appropriate adjustments is the real art of management.

PREPARING YOURSELF FOR THE FUTURE

As teachers in library schools and as teachers of management, we often heard questions or statements that implied, "I have no interest in management and see no reason to study the subject." It is true many students do not see themselves as ever becoming a manager and they have little interest in the area; however, the fact is that one may very quickly find oneself becoming a "manager." Given today's tight economic conditions in most information service organizations, staffing is limited and people are called on to perform in unexpected areas. A very common first "management" responsibility is to supervise one or more part-time people, frequently volunteers rather than paid staff. Whatever their pay status, they deserve good supervision, direction, control, assistance, and support. Normally the supervisor has scheduling responsibility. There may be a need to project time, equipment, and even funding needs. These are some of the things of "management." You are better served, as are those you will first supervise, if you have some grounding in the basics of effective management.

Sometimes front-line staff and supervisors forget they have a multiplier effect on organizational performance—that is, each individual's good performance generates a positive value for the organization. On the other hand, a poor performance will far outweigh dozens of good performances. Essentially the multiplier effect means that the combined good efforts of people far exceed what any one person can accomplish and that one poor performance has a much greater impact than several good performances. When it comes to management performance the ratio is even greater. The multiplier effect is one reason for individuals to have a sound grasp of good management practices.

Almost everyone who enters library/information service does so, in part, because of a strong drive to serve or help people. What many beginners, who say they have no interest in management, are unaware of is there are real psychological rewards from being a good manager. At the most basic level, there is the satisfaction that comes from assisting a staff member perform more effectively or achieve a goal. Another source of satisfaction can arise from developing and achieving a new goal for the organization. Even the respect of those whom one works with is a psychological plus; that respect develops in large measure from being an effective performer oneself. Yet another source of satisfaction is from working with others to develop a "big picture" for the library/information center. Yes, there are frustrations, setbacks, and problems, but being a good manager is also satisfying. One cannot be a good manager without having an understanding of the principles of management.

USING THIS TEXTBOOK

A number of features throughout the book will help you learn how to manage. "For Further Thought" and "Try This" boxes help relate an idea or concept with professional practice. The "Tips" come from experience— our own and that of other managers. "Check This Out" draws attention to useful texts that expand study of the topic being discussed.

Additionally, the authors maintain a Web site (accessible at www.neal-schuman.com/managementbasics.html or www.lmu.edu/mbiF) that updates the references provided in the text. The literature of management in general, and of the management of information services in particular, is expanding at a rapid rate. Regular updating aims at saving time for the reader—a value, set down by Ranganathan, that we feel remains relevant today.

Check This Out:

S. R. Ranganathan was a major figure in Indian and International librarianship in the twentieth century. Among his many practical writings was his *Book Selection* (New Delhi, Indian Library Association, 1952), in which he proposed five basic "laws":
- books are for use
- every reader his book
- every book its reader
- save the reader's time
- a library is a growing organism

Although he was writing about last-century's books and readers, it is easy to see how his "laws" still apply in the twenty-first century.

REFERENCES

Follett, Mary Parker. 1941. *Dynamic Administration.* London: Pitman.

Gulick, Luther, and Lyndall Urwick. 1937. *Papers on the Science of Administration.* New York: Institute of Public Administration, Columbia University.

Katz, Robert. 1974. "Skills of an Effective Administrator." *Harvard Business Review* 52 (September/October): 90–102.

Lindblom, Charles. 1959. "The Science of 'Muddling Through.'" *Public Administration Review* 19: 78–88.

Luthans, Fred. 1973. "Contingency Theory of Management: A Path Out of the Jungle." *Business Horizons* 6 (June): 62–72.

Mahoney, Thomas, Thomas Jardee, and Stephen Carroll. 1964. "The Job(s) of Management." *Industrial Management* 4 (February): 97–110.

Mintzberg, Henry. 1971. "Managerial Work: Analysis from Observation." *Management Science* (October): B97–B110.

Mintzberg, Henry. 1973. *The Nature of Managerial Work.* Englewood Cliffs, NJ: Prentice-Hall.

Mintzberg, Henry. 1975. "The Manager's Job: Folklore and Fact." *Harvard Business Review* 53, no. 5 (July/August): 49–61.

"New-Look Passports." 2005. *Economist* 274, no. 8414: 75.

Wren, Daniel. 1979. *The Evolution of Management Thought.* 2nd Ed. New York: Wiley.

LAUNCHING PAD

Bazillion, Richard J. 2001. "Academic Libraries in the Digital Revolution." *EDUCAUSE Quarterly* 4, no. 1 (April): 51–55.

Cox, Richard J. 2005. *Archives and Archivists in the Information Age.* New York: Neal-Schuman.

Fisher, Donna M. 2004. "Flying Solo." *Information Outlook* 8, no. 9 (September): 23–24.

Hunter, Gregory S. 2007. *Records Management.* New York: Neal-Schuman.

Nuckolls, Karen A. 2005. "Change in a Small Law Library: How We Moved Our Department into the 21st Century." *Information Outlook* 9, no. 4 (April): 23–24.

Roberts, Sue, and Jennifer Rowley. 2004. *Managing Information Services.* New York: Neal-Schuman.

Ryan, David. 2005. "The Future of Managing Electronic Records." *Records Management Journal* 15, no. 3: 128–130.

Simon, Carol. 2005. "How Can You Be a Manager? You're a Solo." *Information Outlook* 9, no. 3 (March): 13–14.

2

Management Concepts

"The information we have is not what we want.
The information we want is not what we need.
The information we need is not available."
                                    John Peers

"Principles are more important than rules."
                                    Maurice Line

INTRODUCTION

Anyone looking into management literature quickly discovers that, although people have been managing organizations for thousands of years,
only within the last 125 years or so has there been serious interest in what
it takes to have a successful operation. Furthermore, only in the past 60-
plus years has there been widespread research into management operations and activities. In this chapter, we explore the development of
management thought in general and how that was reflected in information
service operations. The fundamental reason for including these topics is to
help illustrate our point that the successful fundamentals of management
have a substantial history. Another reason is provide you with a sound base
for assessing the latest management idea put forward by consultants and
others who make their living by churning out "secrets" to organizational
success. The real secrets lie in understanding the fundamentals and their
thoughtful application. As we noted earlier, most of the "new" approaches
are merely repackaged.

EARLY CONTRIBUTORS TO MANAGEMENT THOUGHT

Until well into the nineteenth century, all one needed to be a "manager" was authority. Exceptions existed, of course, but heavy reliance on unchallenged authority was the norm. Certainly some remarkable feats of organization and human efforts to modify the environment took place. Works such as Egyptian and Middle American pyramids attest to this fact. It is likely that these early major building efforts were largely dependent on authority and some significant use of force. The results are spectacular, but the limited number of such sites attests to one of the weaknesses of the approach— there was seldom any cooperation between the manager and the managed.

Certainly, many of today's managerial techniques have their roots in this period. For example, during Nebuchadnezzar's reign in Babylonia, organizations employed the concepts of color coding for production and inventory control and employed the notion of piecework wages—an idea later widely credited to Frederick W. Taylor. In China (B.C. 500), Sun-Tzu identified the necessity of such basic management concepts as planning, organizing, controlling, and directing.

The Renaissance also contributed its share to management thought and practice. For example, the operation of the arsenal of Venice employed assembly lines, standardized parts, cost accounting, merit rating, and even "wine breaks" for workers. Machiavellian ideas about management are still employed by some managers today.

Check This Out:

A good book that explores the relationship between management and Machiavelli is Anthony Jay's 1996 *Management and Machiavelli: A Prescription for Success in Your Business* (Englewood Cliffs, NJ: Prentice Hall).

The rise of industrialism brought with it the first glimmer of thinking in terms of teaching and learning management skills. Factory operations led to a need for more middle and top managers who understood how to manage. Key issues were coordinating activities, planning, productivity, and decision making. Open conflict became a feature of the employer-employee relationship, control became the issue for successful factory operation, and profits became the primary concern. Capital investments in all phases of operation increased sharply, with control of expenditures, output, and income requiring careful coordination.

Power and authority were still important, as the owner/manager held the economic "whip," and laborers were well aware of this fact. Nevertheless, very few companies that relied solely on authority succeeded during this period. Elements such as planning, the ability to select good workers, and the ability to retain their services were also important. It was only a matter of time before someone would combine several of the repeatedly successful methods into a unified form. Robert Owen, in the early 1800s, focused on the need for better personnel practices and improved working conditions because he believed people were the key to achieving better productivity.

The development of scientific management rests on the ideas and work of people like James Mill and Charles Babbage. Mill's work in the 1820s on analyzing and synthesizing human motions was a cornerstone for the later nineteenth-century efforts to improve productivity. Babbage added to Mill's work in the 1830s, placing an emphasis on work specialization, division of labor, time, motion studies, and cost accounting.

Prior to the mid-1930s, most libraries operated with a strong authoritarian, paternalistic (or, at least, highly directive) approach to management. Change came about slowly. Directors made decisions in almost all phases of operation with little or no staff input. As the organizations tended to be small, this management style was usually possible. Even in large organizations (such as the Library of Congress or British Museum Library), where directors had to delegate some authority, emphasis was still on following past practice and comparing outcomes with what others were doing.

Turning to later development in management thinking, we discuss eight approaches:

- scientific
- administrative
- behavioral
- management science/quantitative
- systems
- contingency
- quality
- composite

To some degree the following discussion also reflects a chronology of the development of management thinking. There are, of course, overlaps between the approaches that we cover, but the categories represent the most common groupings used by writers on the development of management thought.

Scientific Management

The keyword for the scientific management approach is mechanistic. Emphasis was on the organizational aspects of work, especially those related to the production of goods. Frederick Winslow Taylor, Frank and Lillian Gilbreth, and Henry Gantt were leading figures in developing and promoting "scientific management." Taylor generally receives the credit for being the father of scientific management, in part because of the book he wrote about the concept.

Taylor emphasized the importance of production and developed methods to assess what workers could accomplish under the best working conditions. Because of his concern with maximum production, Taylor gained the reputation of being antiworker, but his attitude toward the job situation is evident from the following: "When a naturally energetic man works for a few days beside a lazy one, the logic of the situation is unanswerable: Why should I work hard when that lazy fellow gets the same pay that I do and does only half as much work?" (Taylor, 1947: 31). Taylor believed that the very common conflict between labor and management arose from the definition of a "fair day's work"; he believed that with objective standards, managers would have what they wanted (high production) and workers would strive to achieve a given production level (because they would receive more pay). Toward this end, Taylor employed time-and-motion studies to define a "fair day's work" for a given task.

A second element in Taylor's system was a new compensation plan—one using incentive pay. He knew workers would not be willing to do more work for the same amount of money, so he created what he called "*differential piecework*." Workers received one rate when they met the established standard, but a higher rate when they surpassed the standard (owners could afford this model because of increased productivity).

Many people contributed to the field of scientific management. Henry Gantt was a protégé of Taylor's; they worked together early in Gantt's career. Gantt's task and bonus plan has led some people to view Gantt as more humanitarian than Taylor. Gantt's major contribution was developing charting techniques that still carry his name.

Perhaps two of the best-known followers of Taylor were Frank and Lillian Gilbreth (of *Cheaper by the Dozen* fame). The Gilbreths' many refinements in work-motion study methodology were their major contribution to the field. They also were among the first to emphasize an organization's need to "develop" employees to improve employee morale and effectiveness.

An Interesting Fact:

An interesting side note is that Lillian Gilbreth's doctoral dissertation appeared in book form (she was the first woman to receive a Ph.D. in psychology in the United States) with the title *Psychology of Management* (Gilbreth, 1914). The publisher insisted on listing the author as L. M. Gilbreth to hide the fact that a woman wrote the book!

Another person we wish to mention in the area of scientific management is Harrington Emerson of efficiency engineering fame. His main advice to his consulting clients was "eliminate wanton, wicked waste." He published a book that outlined his 12 principles of efficiency (Emerson, 1912). His first five principles are really general management in nature: having clearly defined goals, using common sense in decision making, seeking advice from competent people, applying any rules and regulations fairly and consistently, and dealing honestly and fairly with employees. The remaining seven principles applied to scientific management and efficiency.

Several library science doctoral dissertations produced in the late 1930s began the period of scientific management for information services, at least in the United States. Studies using cost analysis to examine technical services, cataloging, and the use of edge-notched cards appeared at this time. Information professionals began investigating scientific management to see whether some techniques were applicable in their organizations.

Following World War II, information providers began applying a combination of scientific management ideas and some of the mathematical/operations-research techniques developed during that war. Dougherty and Heinritz's *Scientific Management of Library Operations* (1982) is representative of the concern during this period with efficient operation. Most of the work during this period tended to focus on activities and objects rather than on people (in contrast to Taylor's work, which did consider people).

Key Points to Remember:

Some of the key beliefs of the early practitioners of scientific management are:
- Economic issues are workers' primary motivation factor.
- Organizations, because they control economic rewards, can direct worker behavior through those rewards.
- The distrust between workers and management and the lack of understanding about what was a "fair day's work" could be removed by using scientific (rational) studies.
- A rationalized work activity would to lead to an acceptable basis of compensation (task plus bonus) that would be beneficial for both worker and management.

The scientific management period contributed several concepts to general management practice. One concept was the need for developing specialized tasks and designating people to handle those tasks. Another concept was the need for efficient and effective work flow/design. Yet another, which is often overlooked, is a concern for developing well-trained staff.

This is not to say that library management had become antipeople, but simply that the concern was not with matching people and tasks.

Administrative Approach

Followers of the scientific approach focused on production and workers while others looked at the overall operation of the organization. The earliest figures in the administrative approach wrote at about the same time as the "time and motion" advocates were most active. Two of the proponents of this approach were Henri Fayol and Max Weber; other notable figures are Lyndal Urwick, and Chester Barnard.

Henri Fayol was both a practitioner/manager and a thinker about management. His successful career as a manager spanned the nineteenth and twentieth century in a variety of organizations. He believed his success was due to skills he developed over the years as well as his ideas about what it took to be an effective manager. He published his "principles" in 1916 in *Administration Industrielle et Generale* (Fayol, 1962). One of his ideas was that management is a skill one can learn, rather than a talent received at birth. Today, his views are incorporated into most management thinking.

Fayol divided organizational activities into five major groups: *technical,* or production, aspects; *commercial* aspects (buying, selling, and exchanging goods); *financial* aspects (the search for, securing of, and efficient use of money); *security* (protecting the safety of employees and property alike); and *accounting* (fiscal and administrative accountability). Fayol identified 14 principles of management. We have summarized his major points for each principle below:

- Division of labor—workers perform best (are most productive) when they specialize.
- Authority and Responsibility—giving orders and being responsible must go together.
- Discipline—arises from having clearly defined policies and rules for staff.
- Unity of command—employees must have only one supervisor.
- Unity of direction—units must operate in a unified effort to achieve organizational goals.
- Subordination of individual to general interest—employees must focus on organizational rather than personal interests while on the job.
- Remuneration—wages for staff must be appropriate and fair.
- Centralization—authority should be "reasonably" centralized to assure overall organizational direction.
- Scalar chain—an organization must have a formalized structure for authority and communication.

- Order—relationships between units should be logical and assure a timely flow of information and materials.
- Equity—employee treatment should be fair and equitable.
- Stability of tenure—high employee retention is a hallmark of a well-managed organization.
- Initiative—managers should encourage employee initiative, especially in terms of how they might improve their work performance.
- Esprit de corps—managers should strive to achieve high morale and team spirit in their units.

For Further Thought:

Now that you have read about Fayol's principles, give one example of how each is demonstrated in an information or library setting. How would these principles vary in a team setting?

Lyndall Urwick was perhaps one of the first and strongest English-speaking supporters of Fayol's concepts. He was a British management consultant who emphasized a "Fayolian" approach. His book, *Elements of Administration*, attempted to integrate all the work of leading management thinkers and was his greatest contribution to the field (Urwick, 1943).

Another British executive, Oliver Sheldon, is an important person in the administrative approach. While accepting Fayol's principles, he added two of his own. In 1923 Sheldon published *The Philosophy of Management*, in which he suggested management had both a technical and ethical aspect. He set forth a philosophy that tried to demonstrate how a manager might seek/find technical efficiency and still be socially responsible (Sheldon, 1923). There are still occasions when it appears as if not all managers and organizations totally accept the idea that there must be an element of social responsibility in management activities or ethical behavior. Just think about the various recent corporate scandals. Sheldon was well ahead of his time.

Max Weber, with his classic work on bureaucracy, became a key figure in management thinking. Although his study was of how governments operate, most of his findings apply to almost any large organization. His approach to the study of organizations is widely accepted among individuals who study nongovernment organizations.

Not-for-profit organizations, especially government agencies or those dependent on government funds, tend to exhibit the characteristics that Max Weber labeled "bureaucratic." For many, the words bureaucracy and bureaucratic have only negative connotations suggesting red tape and delay. This type of organizational behavior is not what Weber was describing: one or two people who seem to thrive on creating "red tape" and other delaying tactics can exist in any organization. In popular usage, such behavior is usually labeled "bureaucratic" but is not necessarily a function of organizational type or structure.

Weber identified the following traits as characteristic of an "ideal" bureaucracy:

1. A continuous organization of official functions bound by rules.
2. A specific sphere of competence. This involves a sphere of obligations to perform functions that have been marked off as part of a systematic division of labor, involves the provision of the incumbent with the necessary authority to carry out these functions, and requires that the necessary means of compulsion are clearly defined and that their use is subject to definite conditions.
3. The organization of offices follows the principle of hierarchy; that is, each lower office is under the control and supervision of a higher one.
4. The rules that regulate the conduct of an office may be technical rules or norms. In both cases, if their application is to be fully rational, specialized training is necessary. It is thus normally true that only a person who has demonstrated an adequate technical training is qualified to be a member of the administrative staff.
5. It is a matter of principle that the members of the administrative staff should be completely separated from ownership of the means of production or administration.
6. A complete absence of appropriation of their official position by incumbents.
7. Administrative acts, decisions, and rules are formulated and recorded in writing. (Weber, 1947: 330–332)

Naturally, one ought to read Weber's entire book on this subject in order to fully understand his "ideal" bureaucracy because it has become a classic in the study of organizations and how they function. The summary above is, however, an adequate base for determining how most information services do or do not fit Weber's model. Although today's environment is changing, especially with flatter structures and teams, information services do still share most of the above characteristics.

Rules, both internal and external, represent significant limitations on how an organization operates. Certainly for archives and libraries there are rules regarding a variety of operations, if one is going to follow professional association standard practices. (Cataloging rules are an example.) Furthermore, services themselves often formulate regulations about local access, for example. Finally, the organization or government jurisdiction of which the service is a part will have many of its own rules, regulations, and laws that govern the way in which the service is to function.

Information and library services have *specific spheres* in which to operate (Weber's second point), and, in many cases, they have a legal obligation to provide services to a specified group. They seldom lack adequate authority to perform their basic services; but occasionally, when they attempt to expand services, problems arise. For example, offering a new service that might be in competition with a commercial enterprise might require the local municipal officials to resolve the question of spheres of operation.

Weber's third point about organizational *hierarchy* is an area of increasing disparity between information services and Weber's "classic bureaucracy." Many information and library services now employ management approaches that reduce the number of layers in the service. However, almost every organization has a small number of persons (top management) who have the final say on how their organization operates. Below them is a larger group of persons "in the middle" who have a certain amount of decision-making responsibility. Finally, there is the majority of staff members, the "bottoms." With a top, middle, and bottom, the service still resembles a hierarchy, at least in terms of number of people at each level. We know of no library or service that does not have a person identified as the chief officer (regardless of the actual title given the position). In some countries, such as the Nordic countries, the top person often has the title "library leader," which reflects the fact that the management style is democratic, or group oriented. Nevertheless, one person is ultimately responsible for the overall performance of the service.

Some of the rules governing the operation of an information and library service are technical, and there are many *professional norms* (Weber's fourth point). The effective application and understanding of these rules and norms requires formal (specialized) training in their use. Active involvement in planning and coordinating professional information activities demands professional education and knowledge.

As to Weber's fifth trait, there is no question but that the administrative staff has no *"ownership"* of the means of production and administration. The ultimate means of production are the operational moneys. These moneys come from agencies outside the control of the managerial staff; in fact, the staff is accountable to the funding body. For most services there is both an annual budget and an annual accounting.

Weber's sixth trait, *appropriation*, rarely arises in libraries and information services, although it does occasionally occur. When someone, generally the most senior manager, misuses organizational resources for personal gain the governing body or outside group steps in. In a few instances, the behavior may result in criminal or civil legal action. More often than not, the matter is handled by dismissing the person from his or her position.

Finally, information and library services are prime examples of organizations that record their acts, decisions, plans, procedures, rules, and regulations *in writing* (Weber's seventh point). This tendency arises in part from the nature of the field: dealing with the preservation and distribution of information. To some degree, a major portion of the negative feelings concerning bureaucracies arises from paperwork, forms, and books of rules and regulations that occasionally overwhelm persons seeking a simple goal. It is not the records that are a problem, but rather their use that generates problems.

Having reviewed Weber's seven characteristics of a bureaucracy, we see that the "typical" library or information service more or less fits the model. Whether or not an individual organization fits the positive or negative image of a bureaucracy depends on its managers and staff. When run properly, a classic bureaucratic organization provides effective, efficient, rational, and humane service. No organization is good or bad in itself. The people who run an organization determine its positive and negative characteristics.

A later figure in the administrative approach is Chester Barnard. Barnard was the leading proponent of examining management in terms of the 20th-century profit organizations. His book *Functions of Management* is perhaps the most insightful of any written on the character of organizations (Barnard, 1938). He based his book on a combination of practical experience and an extensive study of sociology, psychology, and philosophy. Questions such as "Why do people form organizations, join, and remain with an organization?" served as his starting point in developing his views on the nature of the "organization." His definition of an organization was very broad. His three universal elements of an organization were a willingness to cooperate, sharing one or more common goals, and communication. He stressed that managers were present not to do the work of the organization, but rather to keep it running.

Key Points to Remember:

The administrative approach:

- focuses on organizational issues in a holistic manner
- recognizes that managers, not just workers, need training/development
- focuses on activities that are still relevant in today's organizations
- provides a solid basis for thinking about organizational structure and its operational implications

Behavioral Approach

Humanism is the term that best characterizes the behavioral approach, as psychologists interested in workplace behavior played a major role in defining its characteristics. There is a connection between the scientific management behavioral approaches. As noted above, Lillian Gilbreth's book was on industrial psychology not scientific management.

Hugo Munsterberg is probably the best candidate for the founder of the behavioral approach to management. His book *Psychology and Industrial Efficiency* makes the case for applying psychology to the workplace (Munsterberg, 1913). He proposed three major foci: identifying the person with the proper characteristics to perform the job (skills, attitudes, physical abilities), developing methods to identify the ideal psychological condition for engaging in a task, and creating optimal motivational influences on the worker. He drew on scientific methods, specifically conducting experiments to accomplish the field's goals. In essence, his work led to the development of preemployment skills testing.

Another early practitioner in the field was Walter Dill Scott, an academic much like Munsterberg. His research interest was worker attitudes and the impact of those attitudes on work motivation and productivity. Scott also coauthored one of the first personnel management textbooks (Scott and Clothier, 1923).

Most management textbooks published in the United States devote considerable space to the work of Elton Mayo. Mayo led a research team from Harvard's Graduate School of Business Administration that undertook a long-term study of worker fatigue and productivity at Western Electric's Hawthorne, Illinois, plant. Starting in 1927, the purpose of that study was to determine the validity of a suggestion (by the Gilbreths) that brief rest periods would improve production. Having observed the workers beforehand and having kept careful production records, the researchers then requested volunteers for the study. They moved the volunteers to a separate work area identical in equipment arrangement to the area that the workers used previously.

Thus began the now famous series of experiments. Short rest periods, longer and less frequent rests, a light lunch in the morning and afternoon—the team tried all these variations. The experiments concluded with a return to the original system. No matter what changes took place, production improved. Sick time and tardiness dropped to about one-third the level for the other employees, and management reduced supervision to a minimum because they could depend on good performance from the experimental group.

Mayo's major contribution to management theory was to provide a sociological perspective to the work situation. The results at Hawthorne, as

---

The Hawthorne Effect:

Researchers today know what happened at Western Electric's Hawthorne plant, but at the time no one realized what had occurred. The so-called Hawthorne effect is common in all studies of human behavior. In essence, the Hawthorne effect is a result of an observer's presence and the subject's awareness of it. The observed person will not perform in a typical manner for some time, if ever, because of the presence of the observer. Also, there is no way to know exactly what the effect will be: workers may become nervous and perform very badly, they may work harder than they normally do, or they may see the observer as a threat and therefore respond with the type of performance most likely to cancel the perceived danger. Work analysis is necessary to manage any work unit effectively, but the manager must be fully aware of any potential problems.

---

well as other studies, convinced Mayo that management should reject the long-held notion of the "rabble hypothesis." This hypothesis held that workers were a disorganized group of individuals, each of whom acted only out of self-interest. When managers accept that hypothesis, they seek to appeal to that self-interest to increase production. Mayo's work demonstrated the importance of the group in work motivation.

Mayo's research confirmed Robert Owen's concept that an honest concern for workers pays dividends. He also highlighted the fact that a manager's style was an important factor in employee motivation, and ultimately in productivity. Finally, Mayo's work made it clear that productivity and its improvement was more complex than believed—far more so than Taylor's "rational-economic person." Mayo is usually credited with being the founder of industrial sociology-psychology and of the human-relations theories of management.

Key Points to Remember:

The behavioral approach focuses on:
- worker motivation as a primary factor in effective productivity
- social interaction factors as an equally, if not more, important issue than economic factors in employee motivation
- self-actualization as a workplace issue and something that almost all the people have and act upon
- research in the field of human behavior in search of concepts applicable in the workplace

From the mid-1960s to 1980, libraries and archives began shifting away from the director-controlled management approach to one involving at least the professional staff, if not the entire staff. "Human relations" management approach in libraries usually means democratic administration, participative administration, use of committees, and involvement (or apparent involvement) of staff in decision making. However, the way in which some administrators used the human-relations approach resulted in an emphasis on some of the more difficult aspects of human relations. For example, real involvement in the decision-making process by the staff will unquestionably make the decisions more palatable to everyone. All too often, however, outside factors limit the scope of real involvement. This limitation, in turn, can cause the staff to take a skeptical view of the process; managers must be careful when and how they use this approach. We see this problem even in today's team-oriented environments.

All of the approaches are, to some degree, bridges between scientific, administrative, and human-relations types of management. They draw on the work of early management writers, such as Fayol, and on such later scholars as Gulick, Sheldon, and Urwick. The essential characteristics of most of the approaches rest upon four ideas:

- A manager can identify, define, and study the basic functions of management (planning, budgeting, motivating, and so forth).
- There are fundamental "features" about organizations and management, and by knowing and studying such truths a manager may improve managerial practice.
- Principles derived from the study of management are the starting points for management research, and such studies should produce even more useful management theory.
- In the end, management is an art not a science; therefore, no amount of research will completely resolve all of the issues in managing an organization.

Management Science/Quantitative Approach

There are a variety of subfields, or labels, for the management science/quantitative approach—operations research, decision analysis, simulation, forecasting, game theory, mathematical modeling, management information systems, project management, and data mining are but a few of the variations. The above labels provide a good sense of the areas of interest for this approach. Certainly one can see that scientific management was a forerunner of management science. Mathematical analysis underlies almost all of these fields to some degree and, today, all rely on ever-increasing computing power. Given the breadth of interest it is not surprising that many academic institutions have a department devoted to management science. For many managers it is more a tool than a method for structuring or leading an organization. We explore this approach in more depth in Chapters 7 and 11.

Like scientific management, management science can trace its roots back to such people as Charles Babbage and his 1835 book *On the Economy of Machinery and Manufactures* (London: Knight). His focus on practical science and the use of higher mathematics when confronting commercial/industrial problems is often echoed in today's management science activities.

A major figure in management in general and management science in particular was Herbert A. Simon. He was an early leader in the fields of quantitative modeling of human behavior, artificial intelligence, and problem-solving strategies (simulation). His book *Administrative Behavior* (Simon, 1947) focused on the behavioral and cognitive process involved when people engage in rational decision making. Any decision involves a choice selected from a number of alternatives; through modeling the process and alternative choices the organization can and should make a better decision.

Two other individuals who, to some degree, collaborated with Simon, are Richard Cyert and James G. March. Their seminal work, *A Behavioral Theory of the Firm* (Englewood Cliffs, NJ: Prentice-Hall, 1963), explored organizational decision making. They challenged the idea that organizations always operate "rationally" and in their own best interests. Although they concluded that organizations intend to operate rationally, the reality is rather different. They suggest a variety of variables, both internal and external, that cause decisions and actions to occur that are at odds with rationality. March and Simon co-authored an important book, *Organizations* (New York: Wiley, 1958) which further expanded on rational decision making.

Key Points to Remember:

Management science/quantitative approaches focus on:
- rational/logical approach to organizational issues
- employing mathematical modeling for the purpose of predicting alternative outcomes and results and thus improve decision making
- modeling decision/actions that lead to better solutions
- using the approach for complex or unstructured problems/situations
- application of computing power as the key to successful modeling

Systems Approach

General systems theory (GST) draws on the concept that everything is part of a larger system. A system regardless of type (biological or social) consists of interdependent parts with four basic components—input, transformation, output, and feedback. Ludwig von Bertalanffy, a biologist, is the person most writers credit with founding GST (1950). His purpose was to develop a theoretical framework that would apply to any academic discipline. In its simplest form, the theory holds that all organizations exist in an environment (see Chapter 3); it takes "inputs" (people, resources, money) from the environment, processes (transforms) the inputs, and produces outputs that go back to the environment with a constant feedback taking place. Flow studies examine the inputs, throughputs, and outputs, while feedback studies focus on the control mechanisms that are in place to ensure organizational success.

Russell L. Ackoff is a significant figure in the fields of operations research and systems theory. He coauthored, with C. West Churchman and Leonard Arnoff, *Introduction to Operations Research* (New York: Wiley, 1957) which helps define the field. Another early contributor is Jay W. Forrester with his focus on dynamic systems and simulations, especially in terms of business cycles (1961, 1968). He later applied his ideas to social problems (1969).

Perhaps one of today's best-known "systems approach" people is Peter M. Senge, who has made the concept of the "learning organization" (1990) so well known. His "cornerstone" discipline in the *Fifth Discipline* is systems thinking, which leads to a holistic approach to organizations and the people who work in them. The five "component technologies" of a learning organization are:

- systems thinking
- personal mastery
- mental models
- building shared visions
- team learning

Key Points to Remember:

The systems approach emphasizes:
- the need to think about the interdependency of all the parts of an organization
- interdependency thinking focuses attention on the fundamentals—input, transformation, output, and feedback
- systems thinking makes it clear that organizations are complex rather than simple in character and thus require complex thinking and planning

---

Senge's work puts systems theory to work in a very practical manner. One of his key points is that much of what is done in the name of management is too simplistic and fails to recognize organizations as complex systems (a focus on parts rather than the whole). We will explore Senge's ideas in greater depth in the sections on leadership and the team environment.

Contingency Theory

This concept of contingency theory holds that there are no universal answers in management. Rather, the manager must view each situation as unique and determine what steps are appropriate on a situation-by-situation basis. What effective managers must do, according to this approach, is to assure there is a fit between an organization's structure, its size, and its technology and environmental requirements. In this approach, "size" encompasses more than the number of people; it includes outputs as well as resources (facilities and capital). Some of the ideas regarding size (the percentage of the organization involved in "overhead" activities, increased structuring, and decreasing power concentrations) are being rethought in today's flatter structures and smaller staff numbers.

Followers of this approach view technology as tightly linked to structure. An example, in organizations that deal in one-of-a-kind services (such as libraries and archives), technology, in itself, tends to be less important than the skill of the people using it. They also tend to have fewer layers (flatter structure) and low spans of control. As we discuss in Chapter 3, organizations that do not monitor and adapt to their environment generally perform poorly and often fail.

Mary Parker Follett was one of the first women to be recognized for her contributions to management theory (Graham, 1995). This was a result of her explorations of a wide variety of management topics in the 1920s—leadership, power and authority, conflict management, empowerment, teams, and what she termed the "law of the situation." Her background was in philosophy and social work, and while most of her career occurred during the scientific management period and while she agreed with some of its principles, she believed there was undue emphasis on authority/control. By suggesting that good performance arises from working *with* someone, not *under* someone, she emphasized worker control rather than supervisor control. One of her major contributions was developing the idea that management leadership should not, and cannot, come from the power of formal authority, but rather from a manager's knowledge and expertise. She delivered a series of highly influential lectures to business leaders at Oxford University and the London School of Economics, as well as offering the first U.S. executive development seminars in New York City. We believe she would very much find herself at home with today's emphasis on empowerment and self-managed teams.

Fred Luthans, one of the more prolific writers and researchers on contingency management, suggests that one needs to specify *upon which* and *in what ways* the situation depends (Luthans, 1973; Luthans and Stewart, 1977). For example, sometimes in one environment, tightly defined jobs with "close" authoritarian supervision can result in high productivity and employee satisfaction, while in another environment such an approach would be disastrous. He also places a strong emphasis on leadership.

Tom Peters, a widely published and read management "guru," places a strong emphasis on empowerment and the necessity of managers to be flexible and adaptable. Likewise, he believes strongly in the need to monitor the environment and make adjustments as circumstances change. His first highly popular book appeared in 2002 (*In Search of Excellence*) while a more recent title (2003) is *Re-Imagine! Business Excellence In a Disruptive Age.* Both titles make the point that change is constant and successful organizations adjust with the times.

Two important researchers in the field are Tom Burns and George Stalker. They explored how the environment impacts an organization, its structure, and operations. They identified two types of environment—stable and innovative. (Later researchers took Burns and Stalkers' concept and expanded it to four such environments—Fred Emery and Eric Trist, 1965.)

Another researcher, Joan Woodward, conducted research on how technology affects organizational structure in addition to the environmental factors. She employed a three-part classification system for technology—custom (small batch, high worker skill), mass production (large batch, moderate worker skill), and continuous production (process, little worker involvement). Her work (1965) demonstrated a relationship between technology, organizational structure, span of control, and employee skill levels.

Key Points to Remember:

The contingency approach has several features:
- Managers need to employ a variety of strategies/techniques when dealing with people and activities—no one approach is always "right."
- Selecting the appropriate strategy/technique calls for a solid knowledge of research into organizational theory as well as an assessment of the environment.
- Environmental scanning is a key component of this approach.
- "Diagnosis" of situations a skill manager should develop—selecting actions that fit the circumstances.

Quality Approach

A fairly recent approach suggests that managers should emphasize customer satisfaction by providing high-quality goods and services as a means of achieving long-term viability. Some of the labels for the quality approach are quality control, quality assurance, quality circles, and total quality management (TQM). In the United States, interest in "quality" developed in the late 1970s and early 1980s as Japan's economy became a world leader. Individuals who helped transform the perception of quality of Japanese goods, and ultimately the economy as well, became quality gurus for U.S. business leaders. The concept of *kaizen* (Japanese for "improvement") became part of the U.S. managers' lexicon. (It is important to note that the concept went beyond "quality"—it includes "just-in-time" delivery of resources and services, the right equipment/technology for the job, and eliminating waste, for example.)

While many individuals place emphasis on this approach (Phil Crosby, Armand Feigenbaum, David Garvin, Kaoru Ishikawa, and Genichi Taguchi, for example), there are two early figures in the field—W. Edwards Deming and Joseph Juran. Both of these men went to Japan soon after World War II and assisted in the transformation of the methods of production/quality and, in the long run, the economy.

Deming was invited to Japan by industrial leaders and engineers to help counteract the negative perception of the quality of Japanese products. Rather quickly his "14 Points" of management became a basis for operating a great many Japanese firms, and they soon moved to the forefront as producers of quality goods, a reputation that remains strong today. The points are:

- maintain constancy of purpose
- adopt a new philosophy—waste, delays, and poor quality are unacceptable
- cease dependence on mass inspection
- stop using lowest price as the sole factor in accepting bids from suppliers
- improve every process
- institute on-the-job training
- eliminate arbitrary numerical goals
- permit/encourage pride of workmanship
- lead with the aim of helping people do the best possible job
- drive out fear—solve the problem rather than looking for who to blame
- break down barriers between units and people
- encourage and support self-improvement and educational goals of staff

- clearly define top management in terms of quality and productivity
- eliminate slogans, exhortations, and targets asking for zero defects on new levels of productivity

Joseph Juran arrived in Japan in the mid-1950s to conduct a series of executive seminars addressing such topics as planning, organizational issues, management's responsibility in maintaining quality goods and services, and goal setting. He published his ideas in *Managerial Breakthrough* (Juran, 1995). There were three key pieces to this approach—quality planning, quality improvement, and quality control. Another feature of his thinking was the importance of the internal customer as well as the outside consumer of the goods or services.

The concept of quality service to the "end user/customer" has an important role to play in the management of information services. Our sole purpose is to provide service, and anything but quality services should be unacceptable. Certainly, limited funding and staffing creates challenges and, all too often, makes it impossible to do all we wish we could. However, such challenges should not deter us from thinking about and attempting to do the very best we can.

Key Points to Remember:

Quality approaches to management suggest:
- Successful organizations are ones that have satisfied customers.
- Satisfied customers are developed and retained by receiving high-quality goods or services from an organization.
- Maintaining high-quality goods or services requires a staff that is committed to quality.
- Staff commitment is best achieved through staff involvement in teamwork, planning, and decision making.

COMPOSITE APPROACHES

We end this brief review of management approaches with a discussion of three thinkers—Peter Drucker, Harry Mintzberg, and Harold Koontz. Each has had a long and distinguished career as a scholar and teacher of management. They are not associated with any particular management approach, but rather they draw from the vast array of options available to contemporary managers. If anything, they are closest to the contingency approach. Also, they draw on ideas, concepts, and theories from any academic discipline that offers something for managers to ponder and, in some cases, implement. Certainly you will find frequent references to these scholars throughout this book, as their wide-ranging approach also reflects our views about managing.

Key Points to Remember:

The contemporary manager realizes that:
- Management is a multidimensional activity.
- Useful management concepts are found in almost every academic discipline.
- Effective managers do not restrict themselves to a single approach.
- Effective managers read on a regular basis about a wide variety of topics beyond management.

Figure 2.1
Major Figures in Approaches to Management

Scientific	Administrative	Behavioral	Management Systems
Taylor	Weber	Follett	Babbage
Gilbreths	Fayol	Mayo	Simon
Gantt	Gulick	Munsterburg	Cyert
Emerson	Urwick	Dill Scott	March
	Barnard	L. Gilbreth	
	Sheldon	Owen	

System	Contingency	Quality	Comtemporary
Bertalanffy	Follett	Deming	Drucker
Ackoff	Luthans	Juran	Mintzberg
Churchman	Peters	Taguchi	Koontz
Arnoff	Burns & Stalker	Crosby	
Senge	Woodard	Garvin	

Something to Ponder:

Think about your present or most recent place of employment. Which management approach do you think most closely matches what you experienced/observed there? Would another approach have been more effective? If so, why?

PERSONAL STYLE OF MANAGEMENT

If the concept of management as an art is accepted, it goes without saying that there is a need to develop one's own style. Furthermore, in moving from one management role to another, slight variations will emerge in that style. If the basic approach of this book is shared—that is, that people are the most important resource of an organization—it is necessary to recognize that each person is unique. As such, individuals do not respond to everyone in the same way. The management style must change as situations and the persons involved change. A corollary of the statement that management is an art is that there is no such thing as a "correct" style. Many of us have had the opportunity to observe two persons of differing personalities and styles of management effectively manage the same organization. Such an experience is the clearest demonstration that a variety of management styles can be effective in the same work situation.

The beginning manager needs to start by assessing her or his personal strengths and weaknesses. As a starting point, consider such questions as:

- "What don't I like done to me?"
- "What type of direction or supervision do I like?"
- "What type of directions am I comfortable giving?"
- "Can I (and how do I) tell someone that he or she has done a good or a bad job?"

As you develop answers to such questions, you will be developing your own style of management.

Changes in personal style draw ideas about how managers approach management. In this chapter, you have read about several approaches that may provide you with ideas regarding your individual approach to a style of management. We employed the word "approach" throughout the chapter as a generic label for ideas, concepts, philosophies, schools, and styles. One problem commonly found in the literature is that writers use such terms as "school," "style," or "philosophy" in various ways. You may find one writer using the term "school" while another uses the word "philosophy" when both are discussing the same concept or theory. We use the word "approach"

For Further Thought:

Scan several recent issues of two or three general management journals, such as *Harvard Business Review* or *The Professional Manager*. What are the trends in management thought today?

because all the ideas discussed in this chapter represent a way of viewing and approaching the field of management.

KEY POINTS TO REMEMBER

- The key to managerial success is a firm understanding of management thinking as well as its practices.
- Be aware of the major approaches to management and some of the major thinkers.
- Know how information services fit into the larger management picture.
- Understand the options available and begin to develop your own style.
- Don't get locked into just one approach.
- Circumstance/environments change and flexibility is the cornerstone to successful managing.

REFERENCES

Barnard, Chester. 1938. *Functions of the Executive.* Cambridge, MA: Harvard University Press.

Blau, Peter M. 1955. *Dynamics of a Bureaucracy.* Chicago: University of Chicago Press.

Bowen, Howard Rothman. 1953. *Social Responsibility of the Businessman.* New York: Harper & Row.

Burns, Thomas, and George Stalker. 1961. *The Management of Innovation.* London: Tavistock.

Carroll, Archie B. 1979. "A Three-Dimensional Concept of Corporate Performance." *Academy of Management Review* 4 (October): 497–505.

Carroll, Archie B. 1981. *Business and Society.* Boston, MA: Little, Brown & Co.

Dougherty, Richard M., and Fred J. Heinritz. 1982. *Scientific Management of Library Operations,* 2nd ed. Metuchen, NJ: Scarecrow Press.

Drucker, Peter. 1973. *Management: Tasks, Responsibilities, and Practices.* New York: Harper & Row.

Emerson, Harrington. 1912. *Twelve Principles of Efficiency.* New York: Engineering Magazine.

Emery, Fred, and Eric Trist. 1965. "Causal Texture of Organizational Environments." *Human Relations* 18 (February): 21–31.

Fayol, Henri. 1962. *Administration Industrielle et Generale.* Paris: Dunnod.

Follett, Mary Parker. 1940. *Dynamic Administration: The Collected Papers of Mary Parker Follett.* Edited by Henry Metcalf and Lyndall Urwick. New York: Harper.

Forrester, Jay W. 1961. *Industrial Dynamics.* Cambridge, MA: M.I.T. Press.

_____. 1968. *Principles of Systems.* Cambridge, MA: M.I.T. Press.

_____. 1969. *Urban Dynamics.* Cambridge, MA: M.I.T. Press.

Gilbreth, Lillian. 1914. *Psychology of Management*. New York: Sturgis & Walton.

Graham, Pauline, ed. 1995. *Mary Parker Follett—Prophet of Management: A Celebration of Writings from the 1920s*. Boston, MA: Harvard Business School Press.

Gulick, Luther, and Lyndall Urwick. 1937. *Papers on the Science of Administration*. New York: Institute of Public Administration, Columbia University.

Haire, Mason. 1964. *Psychology in Management*. New York: McGraw-Hill.

Jay, Anthony. 1996. *Management and Machiavelli: A Prescription for Success in Your Business*. Englewood Cliffs, NJ: Prentice-Hall.

Juran, Joseph. 1995. *Managerial Breakthrough*. New York: McGraw-Hill.

Koontz, Harold. 1980. "The Management Theory Jungle Revisited." *Academy of Management Review* 5, no. 2 (April):175–188.

Luthans, Fred. 1973. "Contingency Theory of Management: A Path Out of the Jungle." *Business Horizons* 6 (June): 62–72.

———. 1976. *Introduction to Management: A Contingency Approach*. New York: McGraw-Hill.

Luthans, Fred, and Todd I. Stewart. 1977. "A General Contingency Theory of Management." *Academy of Management Review* 2 (April): 181–195.

Mayo, Elton. 1933. *The Human Problems of an Industrial Civilization*. Salem, NH: Ayer.

Mintzberg, Henry. 1973. *The Nature of Managerial Work*. Englewood Cliffs, NJ: Prentice-Hall.

———. 1989. *Mintzberg on Management: Inside Our Strange World of Organizations*. New York: Free Press.

Munsterberg, Hugo. 1913. *Psychology and Industrial Efficiency*. New York: Houghton Mifflin.

Ouchi, William. 1981. *Theory Z*. Reading, MA: Addison-Wesley.

Pascale, Richard, and Anthony Athos. 1981. *Art of Japanese Management*. New York: Warner Books.

Peters, Thomas, and Robert Waterman. 2002. *In Search of Excellence*. New York: Harper Business Essentials.

———. 2003. *Re-Imagine! Business Excellence in a Disruptive Age*. London: Dorling-Kindersley.

Schmidt, Warren H., and B. Posner. 1982. *Managerial Values and Expectations*. New York: American Management Association.

Scott, Walter, and R. C. Clothier. 1923. *Personnel Management: Principles, Practices and Point-of-View*. Chicago: A. W. Shaw.

Senge, Peter. 1990. *The Fifth Discipline*. New York: Random House.

Sheldon, Oliver. 1923. *Philosophy of Management*. London: Isaac Pitman & Sons.

Simon, Herbert. 1947. *Administrative Behavior*. New York: Macmillan.

Taylor, Fredrick. 1947. *Principles of Scientific Management*. New York: Harper.

Urwick, Lyndall. 1943. *Elements of Management*. New York: Harper & Bros.

von Bertalanffy, Ludwig. 1950. "Theory of Open Systems in Physics and Biology." *Science* 3 (January): 23–29.

Weber, Max. 1947. *The Theory of Social and Economic Organizations*. Translated by A. M. Henderson and Talcott H. Parsons. New York: Free Press of Glencoe.

Woodward, Joan. 1965. *Industrial Organization: Theory and Practice*. London: Oxford University Press.

LAUNCHING PAD

Christensen, Clayton M., and Michael E. Raynor. 2003. "Why Hard-Nosed Executives Should Care About Management Theory." *Harvard Business Review* 81 no. 9 (September): 66–74.

Gane, Nicholas. 2006. "Speed Up or Slow Down? Social Theory in the Information Age." *Information, Communication & Society* 9 (1 February): 20–38.

Hamel, Gary. 2006. "The Why, What, and How of Management Innovation." *Harvard Business Review* 84, no. 2 (February): 72–84.

Harris, Martin. 2006. "F. W. Taylor and the Legacies of Systemization." *Information, Communication & Society* 9 (1 February): 109–120.

3

The Operating Environment

"If we want things to stay as they are, things have to change."
Giuseppi di Lampedusa

"Those at the top of the tree should remember they depend on the roots."
Maurice Line

INTRODUCTION

Some management writers suggest that a manager can learn a great deal from reading Sun-Tzu's *The Art of War*. Although we don't fully agree that the book can be the basic guide, it does have concepts that can be useful. Perhaps one of the most useful concepts comes from the opening of the first chapter: "Warfare is a great matter to a nation, . . . it is the way of survival and of destruction and must be examined" (Last accessed February 2007. Available: www.sonshi.com/sun1.html). By substituting two words, one has the focus of this chapter: "Environment is a great matter to an organization. . . ."

In the modern world, we are surrounded by organizations of one type or another, both formal and informal. Some we join by choice, and we are members of others just by being alive. To a large degree our environment is composed of organizations that influence what we do and how we do it. Both individuals and organizations share and react to an ever-changing environment. They also have internal and external environments in common.

For libraries and other information service organizations there is a tripartite environment. Few information services exist as independent entities; rather they are part of a larger organization—a city, a university, a school district, or a corporation. Thus, library and information service managers have an internal environment, over which they have or should have reasonably good control. There is the environment within the parent organization, over which the information professional may have some, if small, influence. And finally, there is the environment beyond the parent institution, over which the information professional has no control. All three environments require monitoring and responds if the library or information service is to be successful rather than fail. A good article that explores the reason for examining the environment of a nonprofit organization is by Andrews, Boyne, and Walker (2006).

FORMAL ORGANIZATIONS

Chester Barnard (1956) identified five elements of an organization: size, interdependence, input, throughput, and output. Using his concepts, any grouping of two or more people (size) who recognize they can accomplish some mutual goal by working together (interdependence), who also contribute resources (input)—such as money, material, labor, or time—and then employ those resources in some activities (throughput) to generate the desired end (output), constitutes an organization.

Try This:

For each of Barnard's five basic elements, try to provide two additional examples that relate to an information or library service of your choice.

Individuals join an organization because, to some the degree, its mission and goals represent them personally and/or professionally. As an organization grows and changes, so do its objectives. Organizational objectives will change over time, often to such an extent that the founders would have difficulty recognizing "their" old organizations. Organizations are rather like people; once they attain an objective, they seek out new objectives. Organizational objectives expand and contract as a result of successes and failures as well as from responding to changes in the environment.

Key Points to Remember:

- Organizations exist to accomplish specific objectives.
- Objectives evolve or change over the lifetime of the organization.
- Organizations try to be self-sustaining, changing objectives in response to a changing environment.

As an organization becomes more complex, its objectives may be in conflict with one another. In a complex society, organizations often have objectives that conflict with other organizations' objectives. Then there is the inevitable conflict between staff members' personal objectives and those of the organization. Handling such conflicts becomes a fact of managerial life.

People may belong to many formal organizations, including place of employment, subgroups within the organization (such as a staff association or a women's discussion group), the community and professional groups. We are also involved in informal groups (such as a Thursday-night concert group). Thus, with so many organizations, we must handle conflicting goals and objectives on a personal level as well.

Management writers have addressed this "conflict control." They look at a series of interpersonal and interorganizational interactions that constantly occur:

- Individuals interact with the environment.
- Individuals interact with one another.
- Individuals interact with organizations.
- Organizations interact with other organizations.
- Organizations interact with the environment.

In the past, management's tendency was to focus on internal issues, such as improving operations to achieve organizational goals more efficiently and effectively. This focus usually meant looking at technology/equipment, people, tasks, and structure rather than examining what was taking place in the environment. Today, if their organizations are to succeed, managers must devote significant time to studying what is in place in the world around them.

Before turning to the primary topic of this chapter, we must pause to discuss the nature of not-for-profit (NFP) organizations, such as libraries and information centers, as this discussion does matter when it comes to studying the surrounding environment. Managing an NFP has several managerial implications. Two of the most important implications are:

- Financial resources are generally derived from outside funding sources (such as taxes, grants, and private benefactors) rather than from sales of services.
- Many NFP organizations are public rather than private and are thereby subject to public scrutiny in ways for-profits are not scrutinized.

Profit-making organizations have a clear indicator of effectiveness—profit or loss—and a long period of loss leads to failure. For NFPs, lacking such a clear indicator, poor performance may pass unnoticed for some time. Failing to secure adequate operating funds may be the first indication of a serious performance problem. However, as we all know, economic conditions and political decisions are also a leading cause of low funding. Knowing what is taking place in the environment is the key to identifying the real cause of the funding problems.

Something to Think About:

Reflect on the differences between managing in the for-profit sector and the not-for-profit sector. For each, list three advantages and three disadvantages that the manager may encounter.

With the exception of those in the for-profit- sectors, most libraries and information services depend on tax moneys derived from a government jurisdiction (community, county, state, or national) for operating funds. Government funding means that political issues become very important in deciding when and where to spend taxes. As a result, the fund allocation process, both external and internal, is also a political activity.

Politics (not partisan politics but the politics of decision making)and the political process are part of maintaining a publicly funded information system. The word "politics" has many definitions and connotations, most of which cover the following: the acquisition and maintenance of power, competition and conflict over scarce resources, allocation of resources, and determination of who gets what, when, why, and how. Aside from the first point, libraries constantly find themselves involved in these "political" areas. Taxpayer "revolts," a global trading environment, and varying economies demonstrate that politics can dramatically affect funding for library operations and underscore the constant need to monitor the world around us.

Every information service (with the exception of a few private libraries) is part of a larger organization. As part of a larger organization, the manager must also be aware of what the "whole" does and must recognize that the whole needs to have some say in what the service does.

An excellent article by Beverly Lynch (1974) describes four very important factors to consider when studying the library/information service environment:

- the nature of the environment itself
- the relationship among the libraries within a set of organizations (it is also useful to study the relationships among the other organizations making up the environment)

- the characteristics of the exchanges that take place among libraries (again it is of use to study the exchanges between the other organizations, both among themselves and the library)
- the impact that the environment has upon the libraries' internal structure and operations

Something to Think About:

What are the characteristics of information and library services that affect the management function? Try to identify six characteristics, drawing on this text and your experience as a customer.

Environment and the Organization

Today's managers *must* develop methods that allow them to handle a changing environment effectively. The external environment has several major dimensions: sociocultural, technological, political/legal, economic, and institutional. In addition, there exist many subvariables of the major dimensions that the manager must also consider, including dimensions on local, regional, national, and international levels. Other subvariables, such as customers, suppliers, competitors, and sources of funding, all become key factors in developing an effective service organization.

Emery and Trist's classic paper (1965) on organizational environments identified four organizational environments: placid, placid-random, disturbed, and turbulent. Each environment has implications for the manager. The first two listed are relatively stable; "dangers" are relatively few, except economic ones; few, if any, competitors exist; goals are long-term. Services that operate in a more-or-less stable environment are archives and national libraries.

A "disturbed" environment is probably the most commonly seen in libraries today. This environment has competing organizations and changing laws, expectations, and technologies that require the manager to monitor the external environment constantly in order to anticipate and respond effectively to change.

Information and communication technologies (ICTs) are a major issue in today's environment. Governmental change (election outcomes) can produce policies and regulations that affect, for example, the management of staff. Political change can also produce the possibility of additional funding if governments can be persuaded of the benefits of investing in library and information services. Managers working in countries that have a volatile exchange rate should keep a close watch on economic developments that may benefit—or limit—their spending power. These are just some of the reasons why managers need to scan the environment for developments that may affect their services, seeking opportunities and benefits as well as watching for threats and impending problems.

"Turbulent" environments are not common for information services. One potential example, though, would be within research and development organizations. Competitors exist, competition is often fierce, and, occasionally, organizational survival is at stake. Goals tend to be short-term, and sometimes change overnight, and significant organizational resources go into monitoring the external environment.

As mentioned in Chapter 2, Burns and Stalker (1961) identified two organizational systems that help match structure to the environment: "mechanistic" and "organic." Mechanistic systems emphasize specialization and a hierarchical organizational structure. This approach creates a stable organization that tends to change slowly, which is most suitable for placid environments. Organic systems typically emphasize work groups and a flat structure. Such systems work well in turbulent environments. Based on their research, Burns and Stalker suggested that some combination of mechanistic/organic systems was most effective in the disturbed environment. Lawrence and Lorsch (1967) further extended this work by looking at the relationship between departmental/unit values and goals and the environment. They found that organizations operating in changing environments had highly differentiated units and made use of committees, task forces, and a flat structure to achieve intra-unit coordination.

There are any number of ways to apply the concepts of Burns and Stalker to today's organizations. Martin Harris (2006) drew upon their concepts in a paper exploring innovation and organizational structure. His study's finding suggested that a "bureaucratic" structure may not have as negative an impact as some writers, with a "post-bureaucratic organizational" view, have contended. Ingrid Bonn (2005) explored methods for improving strategic thinking and relationships between environmental issues and organizations. The concepts of Burns and Stalker played a significant role in her analysis.

Something to Consider:

In terms of libraries and information services, compare the differences and similarities between Emery and Trist's concepts and those of Burns and Stalker.

ENVIRONMENTAL SCANNING

"Environmental scanning" is a very useful concept and process for any manager at any level. Essentially, it is a process for gathering information about activities, trends, relationships, competitors, potential dangers, and any other factor in the environment that could impact the organization. Data collected can feed into a variety of management activities, but they are essential in planning and decision making. Some other library information center usages include budgeting and collection management. With a formalized scanning process in place, managers can avoid pitfalls or being "blindsided." Lacking such a process, the chances for long-term viability decline (Albright, 2004). In today's rapidly changing world, monitoring the environment is very important for any organization. We will explore this topic again in Chapter 8; here we will only touch on the major points.

Check This Out:

You will find an excellent detailed discussion of environmental scanning in John D. Stoffel's 1994 *Strategic Issues Management: A Comprehensive Guide to Environmental Scanning* (Tarrytown, NY: Elsevier Science).

Some combination of external issues/concerns is important to every organization. However, most organizations would want to consider examining some "typical" factors on a regular basis. Some of the common variables are:

- **Customers**—User behavior and needs are the foundation upon which one should build information services.
- **Competitors/market**—Libraries and information services face competition from one another as well as from other services.
- **Funding sources**—Funding is crucial for effective information and library service, and knowing what factors are affecting the source(s) is the key to successful planning.
- **Suppliers**—Two key categories of suppliers are firms that provide information materials services (jobbers and publishers, for example) and those that handle library/information service technologies. Factors impacting such firms will impact both the library/information services and the end users.
- **Labor issues**—An important ongoing concern is the availability of qualified people for positions in information services, both professional and support staff.

- **Legal/regulatory factors**—Legal, regulatory, and legislative factors impact managerial actions in many ways, from facilities to staffing. A worldwide example of a legal concern for libraries and information services is copyright.
- **Economic trends**—Economic factors affect information services in two primary ways: what one can buy with available funds, and how much money will be available to spend.
- **Technology**—Technology is a critical variable for information services, as we will discuss in some depth in the chapter on managing technology.
- **Political changes/trends**—Any information service that derives a significant portion of its operating funds from public sources must monitor political trends. Thinking about the potential implications of a changing scene is very useful when developing short-term and medium-term plans.
- **Sociocultural factors**—By sociocultural factors, we mean the values, attitudes, demographics, historic context, and customs of the society in which the organization operates. All of the factors have obvious implications for information services.

Tip:

Keeping up with the economic, political, and social factors can be done easily by regularly scanning such weekly journals as *Newsweek*, *Time*, *Economist*, and *The Bulletin*. Naturally local, regional, and national newspapers also key in to monitoring activities.

Try This:

Consider a public library in a rural area, a large private university, and an information service in a large law firm. List and compare their common institutional variables.

FORECASTING THE ENVIRONMENT

One reason for monitoring the environment is to assess the potential future impact (forecast) of changes in that environment. There is a saying about forecasts: "The only certainty is the forecast will be wrong." While it holds true rather often, a forecast does not have to be "100 percent right" to be useful. If nothing else, scanning causes managers to consider possible changes in the environment and to think about how to respond if change does occur. (Being proactive is almost always better than being reactive.) In essence, scanning and forecasting provide highly valuable data for the planning process.

Normally, forecasting focuses on factors that are critical to the organization. Some such factors may be controllable to an extent, while others are beyond the organization's control, (such as population, birth rate, and high school graduation rate). Often, the data needed for forecasting are already available in the library, but some data will be available from the parent organization or obtained from such external sources as government agencies. Forecasts can be qualitative or quantitative in character. We will explore forecast methods in more detail in Chapter 8.

Something to Think About:

Think about the future, then list four changes that are most likely to impact a service of your choice. Rate changes as *most likely*, *possible*, or *probable* in terms of next year, in five years, and in ten years. How difficult was it to identify the potential changes? How satisfied are you with your predictions? Persuade a colleague to do the exercise and then compare results.

ANTI-ENVIRONMENTAL VIEWS

Not all writers on management agree that the external operating environment plays a significant role in management actions. Perhaps the most thoughtful "anti-environment" writer was Child (1972). He raised three arguments against the idea that the environment plays a dominating role in how an organization operates. According to Child, the decision makers have more autonomy than expected even if one assumes that the environment is a determining factor. His position was that decision makers may select from a range of viable alternatives, and choose the type of operating environment that they consider most suitable for their organization. Thus, the environment does not unduly constrict actions. Although his point may be valid for profit-oriented organizations, few information services are free to change their operating environment; however, we certainly agree there are usually a number of viable alternative courses of action.

Child's second point is that organizations are not always passive reactors to the environment. Certainly many influences are beyond the control of the organization, but there are also some that the organization can try to modify or influence. For example, one library environmental factor that one could influence is the funding authority's view of the importance of library services.

His third argument states that having an environmentally deterministic point of view blurs the distinction between real environmental characteristics and the *perception* and *evaluation* of these characteristics by senior management. We completely agree with this argument, as it is essential to base action on reality rather than perception.

CONFLICT IN THE OPERATING ENVIRONMENT

Conflict has many sources, and the ability to recognize the major causes helps a manager perform more effectively. A major source of conflict is competition for resources. No matter how "well off" others may think an organization is, within the organization there is a finite pool of resources to distribute. During any given period, some resources may be more available than others and the pattern of availability and demand fluctuates. In the 1950s libraries worried about material resources, physical facilities, and funds to support intellectual freedom. During the 1960s the big resource problem was personnel. In the 1970s and 1980s it was financial support. Since the 1990s libraries have faced the burden of having adequate funding for Information Communication Technology (ICT) equipment and electronic resources. While the specifics vary, the conflict over resources remains a constant.

Competition for scarce resources takes place both inside and outside the organization, and competition between similar organizations can be very strong. Because most library and information services are publicly supported, these organizations find themselves in a yearly struggle for funds. Generally the process involves requesting an increase that will keep pace with inflation. All agencies in the jurisdiction compete for at least last year's allocation, as well as a claim for greater support. Each agency will attempt to seek support and justify all requested increases. The total money requested by all agencies usually far exceeds the available funds; therefore, conflict arises as each agency tries to prove that it is more worthy of support than other agencies. Resource competition also takes place within the organization. Perhaps the library secured only one of the six requested new positions. The six requesting department heads will, in all likelihood, attempt to show their staffing need as the primary one. Just as with interagency conflict, the ultimate decision maker must realize that the final decision will probably result in some lasting tension(s). Competition for resources forces the issue, and it is the role of the manager to limit the long-term effects of such conflicts.

Whatever the source, managers must have a tolerance for conflict. Methods of dealing with conflict situations range from using personal judgment to negotiation to the all-too-popular process of "muddling through."

ORGANIZATIONAL CULTURE

Like societies, every organization has a culture that its members learn, or should learn, in order to be an effective member. That culture plays a very significant role in how the organization operates. Unless someone acts in a manner contrary to the cultural norm, it is common for staff members to be unaware of its influence on their actions—"learning" the culture is seldom a formalized process.

Just what is "organizational culture"? As Kell and Carrott noted, "Corporate culture, like personal character, is an amorphous quality that exerts a powerful influence" (2005, p. 22). They go on to note both the positive and negative aspects of organizational culture. Although we acknowledge that the concept is rather amorphous, some elements are generally agreed upon. One such element is that members of the organization (consciously or not) share a set of values, assumptions, and expectations regarding what the organization is "about," how things should be done, and what is important and acceptable. Staff acts on these views even though the culture is rarely articulated, much less recorded. One learns it, as one learns social culture, through observation and through making mistakes. Although it is an internal "environment," it can and does change as the result of changes in the external environment. Managers who ignore this internal environment do so at their peril—understanding the culture can make all the difference when it comes time for the organization to make adjustments due to external factors.

While we will discuss this concept in more depth in Chapter 6, we will briefly outline here a few of the significant sources of organizational culture. According to Bloor and Dawson (1994) organizational culture arises from interactions among five elements:

- operating and cultural systems (dynamic/ongoing interaction)
- historical factors (founder[s] vision, for example)
- societal context (external to organization)
- external organizational environment (competition)
- professional external environment (association values, practices)

Jassawalla and Sashittal (2002) took a different tack, and suggested that people learn organizational culture through:

- heroes (people past and present who made significant contributions to the organization)
- stories (tales told about the good and bad of the past)
- slogans ("the virtual library," "24/7 service")
- symbols (name tags, pins, signs)
- ceremonies (birthday parties, years of service)

It seems very likely that all of the above factors play some role in the learning process. What is significant is that culture does matter. In our view, organizational culture constitutes a major environmental situation for the staff and the organization. It is incumbent on managers to assess and understand that culture.

Check This Out:

Edgar Schein's 1990 "Organizational Culture" (*American Psychologist* 45, no. 2: 109–119) offers a very good basic overview on that topic.

Something to Think About:

Consider your current or most recent place of employment. Did you realize it had a special culture? If so, what elements, experiences helped you learn and absorb that culture? Do you think that culture helped or hindered change?

PEOPLE-FRIENDLY ORGANIZATIONS

As long as the manager remains fully aware of the ramifications inherent in managing organizations and people, and as long as the manager tries to maintain a balance between the needs of the two, people control the organization. When the balance tips in favor of activities, people are no longer in control. An organizational threat to individual freedom and dignity cannot exist in a balanced situation. Gellerman (1973: 13) summed up the situation with the following:

> Thus we return to the dilemma that organizations have always faced, and always will, as long as they are comprised of individuals. The organization exists, thrives, and survives by harnessing the talents of individuals. Its problem is to do so without hobbling those talents or turning them against itself. This perpetual balancing act is the responsibility of management,

especially those members of management in the lower echelons, whose influence upon employees is most direct.

Very few people deny that every formal organization has anti-people elements; nevertheless, when someone threatens the entire organizational structure, many others rush to the defense of the status quo. If, however, managers direct some of their attention toward correcting the anti-people elements and developing a balance between people and things, then almost everyone in an organization will help with the process.

KEY POINTS TO REMEMBER:

- Organizations—formal and informal—play a key role in our working and personal lives.
- Organizations are pervasive.
- Most libraries and information centers operate as nonprofit organizations (public support and scrutiny).
- How organizations operate and survive is in large part determined by their highly complex environments.
- Information service managers must recognize the need to assess three environments—one external and two internal (Internal to the service itself and the internal environment of its parent organization).
- Managers who fail to monitor, assess, and adjust to the changing environments risk failure for themselves and their organizations (environmental scanning).
- Organizational culture plays a major role in an organization's internal environment.
- Understanding the organizational culture is essential for everyone on the staff.

REFERENCES

Albright, Kendra. 2004. "Environmental Scanning: Radar for Success." *Information Management Journal* 38, no. 3 (May–June): 38–42, 45.

Andrews, Rhys, George Boyne, and Richard Walker. 2006. "Strategy Content and Organizational Performance." *Public Administration Review* 66, no. 1 (January–February): 52–64.

Barnard, Chester. 1956. *Organization and Management*. Cambridge, MA: Harvard University Press.

Bloor, Geoffrey, and Patrick Dawson. 1994. "Understanding Professional Culture in the Organizational Context." *Organization Studies* 15, no. 2: 241–275.

Bonn, Ingrid. 2005. "Improving Strategic Thinking: A Multilevel Approach." *Leadership & Organization Development Journal* 26, no. 5: 336–354.

Burns, Tom, and G. M. Stalker. 1961. *Management of Innovation.* London: Tavistock.

Child, John. 1972. "Organization Structure, Environment, and Performance—The Tale of Strategic Choice." *Sociology* 6, no. 1 (January): 1–22.

Emery, Fred, and Eric Trist. 1965. "Causal Texture of Organizational Environments." *Human Relations* 18, no. 1 (February): 21–31.

Gellerman, Saul. 1973. *Management of Human Resources.* Hinsdale, IL: Dryden Press.

Harris, Martin. 2006. "Technology, Innovation, and Post-Bureaucracy: The Case of the British Library." *Journal of Organizational Change Management* 19, no. 1: 80–92.

Jassawalla, Avan, and Hemet Sashittal. 2002. "Cultures that Support Product Innovation Processes." *Academy of Management Executive* 16, no. 4 (November): 42–54.

Kell, Thomas, and Gregory Carrott. 2005. "Culture Matters Most." *Harvard Business Review* 83, no. 5 (May): 22.

Komolafe, Helen Olubunkola. 1994. "Promoting Nigeria's Health Care Delivery System Through Effective Library and Information Services." *African Journal of Library, Archives, and Information Science* 4 (October): 139–141.

Lawrence, Paul, and Jay Lorsch. 1967. *Organization and Environment.* Homewood, IL: Irwin.

Lynch, Beverley. 1974. "The Academic Library and Its Environment." *College & Research Libraries* 35, no. 2 (March): 127.

Schein, Edgar. 1990. "Organizational Culture." *American Psychologist* 45, no. 2: 109–119.

Schneider, Karen, ed. 1998. "Outsourcing." *The Bottom Line* 11, no. 3: 97–121.

Stoffel, John D. 1994. *Strategic Issues Management: A Comprehensive Guide to Environmental Scanning.* Tarrytown, NY: Elsevier Science.

Sun-Tzu. *The Art of War.* Available: www.sonshi.com/sun1.html (accessed February 2007).

LAUNCHING PAD

Calvert, Philip, Daniel Dorner, and G. E. Gorman. 2006. *Analysing What Your Users Need.* New York: Neal-Schuman.

Day, George S., and Paul J. H. Schoemaker. 2005. "Scanning the Periphery." *Harvard Business Review* 83, no. 11 (November): 135–148.

Dilevko, Juris, and Kisa Gottleib. 2004. *The Evolution of Library and Museum Partnerships.* Westport, CT: Libraries Unlimited.

Hough, Jill R., and Margaret A. White. 2004. "Scanning Actions and Environmental Dynamism." *Management Decision* 42, no. 6: 781–793.

Nastanski, Michael. 2004. "The Value of Active Scanning to Senior Executives." *Journal of Management Development* 23 no. 5 (June): 426–436.

Westbrook, Lynn. 2000. *Identifying and Analyzing User Needs.* New York: Neal-Schuman.

4

Managing Diversity

*"We have become not a melting pot but a beautiful mosaic. Different people,
different beliefs, different yearnings, different hopes, different dreams."*

Jimmy Carter

*"We all live with objective of being happy; our lives are all different and yet
the same."*

Anne Frank

INTRODUCTION

Western society has moved on from the time when discrimination in the
workplace was a major issue. In the past, racial and sexual discrimination
could affect the recruitment and promotion of staff and approaches to
management. The introduction of anti-discriminatory legislation sensitized
society to these social injustices and brought about changes in attitudes.
With increasing mobility in the international community, linked to the
globalization of business, benefits have emerged from a growing understanding of the value of cultural diversity in the workplace.

Needless to say, a diverse workplace requires managers who are sensitive to the issues that surface from time to time. Legislation brought benefits, but cultural differences influence the way that we, as individuals,
approach diversity. Culture influences the way that people interact—sometimes consciously, sometimes unconsciously. Cultural diversity touches on
many managerial responsibilities relating both to the workforce and the
community served. Effective managers who are responsible for planning
and operating services take diversity into account to comply with the law
and draw on a breadth of talents, viewpoints, and experience to improve
problem solving, decision making, and, most importantly, service delivery.

There are good reasons for factoring in diversity:

- First, there is the very human reason that it affects everyone who interacts with the service—the staff and the members of the community served. Everyone has a need to achieve their individual goals. For staff, the goals may relate to their career or personal life. For the users, they need to gain the greatest possible benefit from the service.
- Second, it makes good sense to create a collegial environment in which people are viewed as individuals. This encourages staff to become members of a team, and users are welcomed as valued members of the community. It optimizes both the potential of individuals and their productivity.
- Third, diversity is a factor in attracting and retaining the best talent among the staff. Staff turnover carries both visible and invisible costs.
- Fourth, when staff members know they are valued and take pride in the quality of their work, it influences how they interact with the community, which, in turn, increases the comfort level of users and raises the overall performance of the service. As business discovered, investing in good practice brings benefits for everyone and makes good sense. Equity is important.

Check This Out:

Winston, M. D. 2001. "The Importance of Leadership Diversity: The Relationship Between Diversity and Organizational Success in the Academic Environment." *College & Research Libraries* 62, no. 6 (November): 517–526.

With increasing globalization, cultural diversity assumes even greater importance. Information professionals have a long track record of cooperating closely with colleagues around the world. International co-operation increased as technology enabled services to provide 24/7 access by working across the globe to take advantage of time differences. Many businesses in the private sector operate on a global basis, for example in the legal and mining sectors. Within the information professions members contribute to the work of international committees to enhance collaboration, or to transborder information organizations such as OCLC, and too, being mobile professionals, need to understand the complexities of diversity.

This chapter defines diversity, considers the legal framework, discusses management issues relating to strategic planning, the governance of the service, staffing, and the provision of effective service to a diverse community.

Check This Out:

Dewey, Barbara I., and Loretta Parham, eds. 2006. *Achieving Diversity: A How-To-Do-It Manual for Librarians*. New York: Neal-Schuman.

DEFINING DIVERSITY

Diversity is a complex topic that has been defined in a number of ways. Some writers and organizations take a narrow view, relating diversity mainly to racial or sexual discrimination. Reflecting on our experiences, we prefer the broader view described by Hofstede who indicates why it is a complex issue:

> Every person carries within him or herself patterns of thinking, feeling, and potential acting which were learned throughout their lifetime. Much of it has been acquired in early childhood.... As soon as certain patterns ... have established themselves ... he [sic] must unlearn these before being able to learn something different, and unlearning is more difficult than learning for the first time (Hofstede, 1997: 4).

By thinking about the way in which beliefs are formed and the crucial issue of "unlearning," it becomes easier to understand why the subject is complex and sensitive. The range of issues influenced by cultural diversity is easier to identify when Hofstede distinguishes between the several layers of culture that people carry within them as "mental programming." They are:

- a national level, according to one's country (or countries for people who migrated during their lifetime)
- a regional, ethnic, religious, and/or linguistic affiliation level, as most nations are composed of culturally different regions and ethnic, religious, and/or language groups
- a gender level, according to whether a person is female or male
- a generation level, which separates grandparents from parents from children
- a social class level, associated with educational opportunities and with a person's occupation or profession
- for those who are employed, an organizational or corporate level according to the way employees have been socialized by their work organization (Hofstede, 1997: 10).

Check These Out:

Hofstede, Geert. 1997. *Cultures and Organizations: Software of the Mind.* New York: McGraw-Hill. His Web site (www.geert-hofstede.com) is also worth perusing.

National Level

Each country develops its own unique immigration policies. Some encourage assimilation, while others encourage integration. Either response can influence the provision of information services, particularly in the public sector.

Consider This:

In Scandinavia, there has been debate concerning the role of the public library in the integration of immigrants (Skot-Hansen, 2002). Should they follow the political and social integration government policies or encourage cultural and artistic diversity?

The United States has experienced high levels of immigration, and most large cities are microcosms of the world. This is illustrated in maps derived from the 2000 Census of Population.

Check This Out:

The map of a city close to you:
Mapping Census 2000: The Geography of U.S. Diversity.
(www.census.gov/population/www/cen2000/atlas.html)

Regional, Ethnic, Religious or Linguistic Affiliation Levels

Regional differences often exist within national boundaries, for example: Latino and Spanish-speaking communities are widespread within the United States; Singapore has four official languages (Mandarin Chinese, Malay, Tamil, and English); Canada has two official languages (French and English); and Wales also has two official languages (Welsh and English). Moving within national boundaries from one part of a country to another can produce culture shock, even if the same language is used, for there may be a strong local dialect.

Within communities, members of religious groups generally maintain close ties. Religious affiliation and the observance of holy days may not follow the established pattern within a country.

Reflect on:

Consider the community in which you live and the cultural characteristics that are visible, and those that are "hidden." Do you see any differences? How does this affect the information service?

Gender Level

Hofstede considered the gender level of birth as a boy or girl, but there are other gender-based groups that are included in the charge of the Diversity Council of the American Library Association—the gay, lesbian, bisexual, and transgender communities.

Generational Level

Society is sensitive to generational issues and the ways in which life experience shapes the values and attitudes of the individual and how, in turn, this process affects an individual's thoughts and behavior patterns. Impacts on staff and users are apparent as people live to a greater age, remain more active in the community, and there is no mandatory age for retirement. The workplace is likely to consist of four generations working side by side with workers ranging from older volunteers to younger interns. Ensuring the different generations work together effectively calls for a greater understanding on the part of both individuals and managers.

Zemke, Raines, and Filipczak (1999) identified four cohorts born since the 1930s. Veterans born before 1946 are now generally retired from paid work but often contribute to the volunteer workforce (*Retired and Inspired*, 2006). Raised in times that were economically difficult and experiencing the effects of several wars, they became survivors who make a commitment to their work. They are respectful, put duty before pleasure, have worked in a hierarchical organization, and want to return some of the benefits they feel they have received. They may be past-oriented.

Baby Boomers born after World War II experienced more affluent times and had greater educational opportunities than the veterans. Joining the workforce during a labor shortage, they often received rapid promotion to high positions. They tend to be optimistic, believe in consensus, and have a love/hate view of financial prosperity. Having experienced the introduction of computers and newer approaches to management, they are accustomed to change. However they may find themselves caught in a "sandwich"—having raised a family, they may now have a responsibility to care for elderly relatives. As this generation retires, a significant shortage of experienced qualified staff has emerged.

Gen X, born between 1966 and 1976, grew up in the information society, entering the workforce as major changes were occurring partly as a result of tougher economic times. They are happy, self-reliant, skeptical, unimpressed by authority and thus preferring competence-based leadership, and think about the job, not the hours. Tensions can arise in the workplace between the Baby Boomers and Gen X.

Several labels have been applied to the next generation—Gen Yers, Nexters or N-Geners. This is the first group to have experienced interactive and distributed communication and the capability to direct their own learning. They are very independent, have emotional and intellectual openness, hold strong views, and are optimistic, pragmatic risk takers. With changes in technology and the way that business operates, it is natural that this generation has the capability and attitude to develop knowledge management within organizations.

The label most frequently given to the youngest generation is the Millennial Generation. Members of this group are experiencing more challenging economic times and the threat of terrorism. As a result they are aware of the fragile nature of society.

Managing a team of paid and volunteer staff comprised of the different generations is challenging but very rewarding if strengths and different talents are recognized and used to benefit service provision. Managers have the responsibility to ensure that everyone understands and respects the views of others to avoid potential tension.

Social Class Level

Social class can affect the potential use of a service, particularly in the public sector. If social class were to be perceived to be linked to educational level, then challenges may well arise. Potential users of public libraries or record offices may need but be hesitant to ask for information. They can be discouraged by having to enter an unfamiliar, imposing building. Think of how forbidding and authoritarian a library or archives can appear if it is housed in a grand building. A potential user may not speak the common community language. Other groups that can be disadvantaged in trying to access public services include travelers and people who do not have a permanent address.

Work Socialization Level

The experiences of working in another organization or using other services are naturally carried over to a new employer or different service. As discussed in Chapter 3, however, all organizations carry their own culture and "the way we do it here." It is not always easy to pick up on any differences instantly, and there is also that question of "unlearning" that Hofstede referred to. Expectations of the job or service may not be matched by reality. It takes a perceptive person to recognize that a new staff member or user, when confronted with a new set of circumstances, is not being fully understood. Managers who have not experienced organizational culture shock or have not had to adapt to a different situation are disadvantaged. If newcomers are to feel comfortable, socialization to the workplace and its service requires thoughtfully planned and phased induction programs, with built-in checks to assess progress.

Disability

Another disadvantaged group does not fit into any of Hofstede's categories but can face discrimination in the workplace and in using services. That group is people who have any form of disability. This discussion is necessary because, while a physical disability may present challenges, society does not always recognize when it is unintentionally discriminating against employment or the use of services for disabled people. It is important to note that many forms of disability might affect staff members or users, and each disability requires a different response.

HOW DO YOU VIEW CULTURAL DIVERSITY?

One way to begin to understand the complexity of cultural diversity is to discover your own viewpoint by examining the concept of ten lenses proposed by Williams (2001). Taking the analogy of a lens, he identifies the ways we approach race, culture, nationality, and ethnicity. The approach was validated in a large-scale Gallup poll.

Williams labeled each lens as follows:

- *assimilationist* favors nationalistic and patriotic ideals
- *colorblind* views people as individuals (ignoring race and color has an equalizing effect)
- *culturalcentrist* improves welfare by accentuating history and identity
- *elitist* believes in the superiority of the upper class (keeps advantages through social ties)

- *integrationist* believes in breaking down barriers by having people live and work together
- *meritocratist* believes dreams will come true if you have the abilities and work hard
- *multiculturalist* celebrates diversity and its contribution to national character and history
- *seclusionist* wants to protect oneself (different groups should live and work apart)
- *transcendent* focuses on the human spirit (diversity contributes to the richness of humanity)
- *victim/caretaker* feels one is suffering from oppression and deserves compensation

Taking the test to determine your lens may bring surprises. Remember: self-awareness is a building block in emotional intelligence.

While attention has been focused on political correctness, there is a certain level of recognition that this awareness may inhibit the development of cultural diversity.

Check This Out:

"Sensitivity to race, religion, or gender is a good thing, but too often it is driven by fear. Rather than walk on eggshells, managers can learn to develop more productive, meaningful relationships at work" (Ely, Meyerson, and Davidson, 2006: 79).

MANAGERIAL RESPONSIBILITY

Managers have the responsibility to:

- create an organizational culture that values diversity in all its manifestations
- ensure that everyone has, and demonstrates, respect for the views and experiences of others
- implement practices based on sound policies ensuring that diversity brings benefits to the service—both staff members and users.

The key to success is to make flexibility a central component that will both support and retain staff and users.

Try This:

Think about the ways that society is changing. For example, the nuclear family is no longer the norm—there are women heads of households, unmarried couples, same-sex partners, and single parents who have children at school. Add to the list and consider how these changes affect staff and users.

THE LEGAL FRAMEWORK

Over time, a considerable body of legislation has been introduced covering equal opportunity, equal pay, and discrimination, including racial, sexual, age, and disability. Each country, and sometimes each state, has a different approach to legislation. Knowing the detail of every change simply is not realistic for managers, but most will be working in, or attached to, parent organizations that have, human resources and legal staff to provide information and advice. Our experience indicates that managers need to keep up with major changes but seek an authoritative opinion if in doubt about any aspect of the law.

However, the enactment of legislation does not always immediately bring the expected outcomes, and national agencies are charged with responsibilities to raise awareness, disseminate information, provide advice, allocate financial support for action projects, and identify areas where legislation needs to be revised. Feedback provided to the agencies refines, improves, and updates legislation.

Action Point:

To understand the work of such a regulatory agency, check out the one that has responsibility for equal opportunity in your country or state. Examine the relevant legislation to ensure that you are aware of the main points as they affect employment and education. Identify other agencies whose responsibilities cover other aspects of diversity. See how many you can find. Visit the Web sites of these agencies regularly to keep updated with developments.

Institutional Discrimination

In some organizations, discrimination has been identified at the institutional level, and it generally takes time and legal action to change the situation. For example, many women experienced sex discrimination in the past in both the not-for-profit and private sectors. Institutional discrimination resulted in barriers to promotion if top management preferred to promote men to senior posts. Legal cases were pursued by women, and some paid a price, finding themselves labeled "trouble makers" and, if promoted, subtle ways were found to ensure that their work role was limited.

Carlson, Kacmar and Whitten (2006) followed up research carried out in 1965, finding that female respondents indicated steady support for the concept of women in management, and a favorable attitude on the part of men had increased from 35 percent to 88 percent. In spite of attempts to level the playing field when it came to abilities, however, only 32 percent of men thought women had to be exceptional to succeed, in contrast to 70 percent of women feeling that way. The researchers were unsure whether men actually were not seeing the barriers for women's advancement anymore or simply providing politically correct responses.

In the academic library sector, women hold the majority of directorships, and in some cases their compensation exceeds that of men in similar posts (Deyrup, 2004).

INDIVIDUAL RESPONSIBILITY

Everyone working within the service at any level has a personal responsibility to recognize and value differing attitudes and patterns of behavior of the different people with whom they interact. Many readers will have visited a foreign country, moved to the U.S., or perhaps lived in another part of the country and experienced some degree of culture shock.

Earlier we noted that individual values may differ among people, which creates different expectations when it comes to interactions. Unlike language, some differences are more subtle. For example, attitudes toward time vary; some people are more relaxed about time, while others are more rigid, which can cause conflicts. The rituals in meeting another person may vary from the warm smile, friendly handshake, and use of first names to the use of greater formality and presentation of gifts. The pattern of the working day also varies in different parts of the world.

Check These Out:

Americans at Work: A Guide to the Can-Do People (Sorti, 2004) and *Watching the English: The Hidden Rules of English Behaviour* (Fox, 2004), are the two volumes we have enjoyed reading. They illustrate some of the cultural differences between Americans and the English.

Having an experience of living in a different society helps you understand the degree of culture shock that can be experienced by a new colleague or user. Rituals and symbols can be confusing to anyone but are grasped more quickly by those who have lived in the society for a while and observed daily life. For a newcomer, the challenge lies in identifying and understanding the values of the community. These values are not obvious or stated, and the newcomer has much to learn before adaptation takes place.

If You Haven't Experienced Culture Shock:

Margaret Child is an American preservation consultant who went to Malaysia on a three-month fellowship. Her reaction to the local situation provides a graphic impression of the experience of the culture gap between the United States and Malaysia (Child, 1997).

We stress the concept of culture shock because every staff member needs to understand how newcomers and new users feel during the process of acculturation. Everyone can experience frustration, helplessness, and perhaps hostility when faced with a new environment, as they compare the old and familiar life or organization with the new one. Remember that you don't have to move from one geographic location to another—the shock can happen simply in changing jobs. First comes a short period of euphoria—the time when everything is new and thrilling. This is followed by a period of shock, as differences become more obvious. A sense of isolation from the new community emerges and it seems impossible to grasp the subtleties of the new situation. Hopefully newcomers move to a third stage of acculturation as they learn to operate in the new society or organization and acquire the norms of behavior which result in self-confidence and integration. It takes time.

Tip:

Although newcomers to the staff will have an orientation program, it is also good to link them with someone who will explain things, answer their questions—in an informal way—and make them feel at home. New users should have someone to turn to who has an understanding of their information needs and the experience of using other services. Remember that the small points are what can confuse newcomers, and they may feel too embarrassed to ask questions.

The worst experience for a newcomer occurs when the question of culture shock is ignored by the manager. In such cases, the newcomer cannot hope to meet expectations and also may face hostility within the work team. New users also may encounter this experience.

Wynn (1992) outlined steps that assist in working through the process of understanding:

- becoming aware of the commonalties and differences among and between various cultures: Taking a look
- recognizing that yours may not be the "right or only" way: Taking a perspective
- investing yourself: Taking a part
- developing positive relationships with people of different cultures: Taking a hand
- confronting the prejudice in others and ourselves: Taking a stand
- evolving bridge-building projects: Taking a step
- sharing the cultural bridges vision: Sharing the dream

Although the steps were designed to bridge national cultural differences, we feel they can be applied to other areas of diversity.

THE ROLE OF PROFESSIONAL ASSOCIATIONS

The information sector has some professional bodies, such as the International Council on Archives and the International Federation of Library Associations and Institutions, operating at the international level. Members meet at conferences and use the Internet to exchange ideas, building bridges across cultures and professional practices.

At a national level, the American Library Association (ALA) vigorously pursues programs to increase equal opportunity in the library workforce. Starting with a conference on women in the early 1970s, the ALA recognized that people of color were under-represented in the profession at large and adopted a leadership role to recruit and retain staff. Meetings and training sessions have been held at the national, regional, and state levels to exchange ideas and experiences about ways to improve the situation. A Spectrum Initiative offers scholarships, mentoring and leadership training, and at the ALA annual conference a Diversity Fair offers stalls and displays that demonstrate good practice in services large and small. Despite these efforts, the 2000 U.S. Census data indicated that

[about] 25 percent of Americans were non-white, compared with 11 percent of credentialed librarians for example African Americans made up 5 percent of the profession but 12.3 percent of the population. Academic

librarians were slightly more ethnically diverse than their counterparts in public and school libraries, with a representation of 15 percent non-white (January 2007. Available: www.ala.org/diversitycounts).

Check These Out:

The American Library Association's Office of Diversity (www.ala.org/ala/diversity/diversity.htm) offers a full range of activities and resources.
Wheeler, Maurice. 2005. *Unfinished Business: Race, Equity and Diversity* in Library and Information Science Education. Lanham, MD: Scarecrow Press.

STRATEGIC PLANNING

The majority of information services have a parent organization that holds the responsibility for developing a mission statement and policies to ensure that it meets statutory requirements. The responsibility of managers is to ensure that these organizational policies are embedded in the strategic planning at the service level, and to work with supervisors to ensure that good practice is being observed. The manager is accountable to the parent organization. Two other responsibilities of the parent body are to commit funding to implement policies and to monitor goals for diversity.

In free-standing services, the manager may need to develop policies. One factor to consider is the state of readiness of the service to engage in a comprehensive diversity initiative. Royse, Conner, and Miller (2006) discussed the design, methodology, and outcomes of a climate assessment survey that produced benchmarks for measuring the progress and success of its diversity programs. The American Library Association provides examples of plans from large and small services that could be adapted to other types of information services.

Kendall (1994) made a number of valuable points about making a successful transition to a hospitable working environment, which includes:

- Top management must genuinely and seriously commit to an ongoing examination of its attitudes, as well as its policies and procedures.
- The organization must view diversity as a long-term, multifaceted, continual process, not as an event or a quick fix.
- The organization must expect and be willing to deal with discomfort and resistance.

- The organization must not avoid discussions on institutional racism when addressing diversity and multicultural environments.
- The organization must develop a core staff willing to commit time and energy to bringing about a hospitable work environment for all people.
- The organization must know that its diversity activities will mirror its other activities.

And there will be challenges in evaluating the process:

- difficulties measuring changes in attitude
- the lack of a discrete beginning and ending to the task
- stress caused by other events in the library manifesting itself as resistance to diversity (Kendall, 1994)

We stress that performance must be monitored. Data on recruitment, promotion, and retention will be available. To this can be added qualitative information gathered from exit interviews, appraisal interviews, or surveys assessing the health of the service. Feedback can be obtained from users and non-users through the use of questionnaires, focus groups, and one-on-one interviews.

Tip:

One way to assess progress and identify potential problems is to adopt a commercial diversity/inclusion tool. An example is available at: www.promosaic.org

---

GOVERNANCE

Appointments to governing boards or advisory groups should reflect the composition of the community served. It may sound like a statement of the obvious, but it can be tricky to achieve a balanced membership. It is often easy to identify regular users or those known to be supporters of the service, but it is essential also to have representatives from groups who make little use of the services or who do not use them at all. This is one facet of the manager's role where benefit is gained by being visible and known within the whole community, ensuring that recruitment to the board or group is well publicized. Political and social skills and networking help to achieve the vital balance.

> **Check This Out:**
>
> Donna Howell (2004) suggests that the type of people who become trustees may not reflect the diversity of the population as a whole. She holds that this tendency can create a fertile ground for power games.

LEADERSHIP

Success in managing diversity rests on the leadership skills of the manager. Turock (2003) sets this within four streams of research and theory. She identifies the feminist perspective, the historical conceptualization of leadership over time, factors impacting the recruitment of minority groups, and the interdependence of educators and practitioners as being keys to improving the current situation.

> **Check This Out:**
>
> Alire, Camila. 2001. "Diversity and Leadership: The Color of Leadership." *Journal of Library Administration* 32, nos. 3/4: 95–109.

Leaders face a difficult challenge if they have been recruited from outside the community in which the service is located. Their local knowledge and contacts are likely to be limited. Their previous work experience may be in organizations that operated in very different ways, yet from the start they will be expected to perform as anticipated by their new colleagues.

Leadership styles can be culturally dependent, ranging from the autocratic to the quasiautocratic, democratic, or participative. There is a body of literature that draws upon international experiences of aspects of management; for example, West, Tjosvold and Smith (2005) write about teamwork

STAFFING ISSUES

Recruitment

In an ideal situation, a service will be staffed by people who together reflect on the diverse composition of the community served. The reality, however, is more likely to be that this is a goal rather than an achievement. The manager needs to profile the diversity of the total potential user community in order to determine if it is matched by the current staff profile.

As a result of past recruitment to the professional schools, the profile of graduates is generally not representative of the community at large. There may be fewer minority graduates in the pool of potential recruits. It can extend to the question of identifying staff for promotion if there are, for example, fewer members of minority groups ready for the next step. It takes time to achieve diversity goals, and tokenism is a risk.

Tokenism presents challenges both for a person who may be seen as a "token" appointment, and for his or her colleagues. Careful managing is necessary. In the past, women promoted to senior posts could be unpopular with male colleagues who believed they had been unjustly passed over for promotion. A token appointment can present challenges beyond resentment, since there may not be ready acceptance into a peer group within the organization.

A staff profile indicates levels of attainment, years in the current post, and attrition rates for all staff members. It may reveal that people in certain groups have not been promoted at the average rate of the staff, or it may show that people recruited from minority groups have not held positions as long as the staff as a whole. This difference can happen for either negative or positive reasons. Sometimes staff members from minority groups do not find the organizational climate hospitable. Conversely, they may be highly sought after in the labor marketplace.

In addition to collecting data and other information for assessing progress on cultural diversity at the macro level, one can use the data to assist decisions about staffing policies at the micro level. Qualitative information supplements hard data and gives, for example, clues as to why people leave. It can be difficult to articulate reasons or issues except within a sensitive exit interview. The aim is to create a climate that supports diversity and aids retention.

Position or job descriptions can discriminate in a way that may not be obvious, and so it is essential that they be written with care. The requirements for the post must not disadvantage any one group and the selection criteria must be scrutinized. Advertisements for vacancies should be widely publicized in order to attract people from a diverse community. The local media and the organization's Web site can draw attention to the positive diversity work that is taking place, and thereby be used to attract the attention of potential candidates.

In selecting the short list of candidates, care must be taken to avoid any discrimination. The process of selection can be carried out more smoothly if representatives of minority groups are members of the committee which will interview candidates.

Cohen (1994) provides guidelines to assist in reviewing recruitment and retention policies and comments that issues surrounding retention are not easy to describe. (See Chapter 15 for further information on staffing issues.)

Training

Regular training programs help ensure that existing staff—both paid and volunteer—are receptive to cultural diversity. Everyone must understand the code of acceptable behavior, and that breaking the code will bring forth consequent action.

For newcomers from minority groups, there should be an in-service program designed to meet their needs. In larger organizations this will be a corporate responsibility provided to cover general matters, such as the goals of the organization, its values, operating policies and practices, and expectations of new staff members. Such a program provides support for participants and assists networking. Within the service, a program of training may need to be developed for staff recruited from overseas. Although many operating practices are common around the world, some differ, with these differences possibly relating to classification and cataloging schemes, technical practices, and the software used within the service. A custom-designed training program may need to be prepared after consultation with the new colleague. Progress can be assessed periodically to ensure that training needs and the needs of the organization have been met.

Mentoring

The process of adapting to a new working situation can be greatly helped if a mentor is nominated, preferably someone who has moved through similar experiences. With a mentor, the newcomer will be motivated and encouraged to raise questions and concerns that may seem trivial but that are essential to understand if they are not to appear to be "different." Unwritten customs—the dress code, birthday teas, and the like—are best conveyed through mentoring. Having someone who can assist the process of learning and adaptation speeds up the process of assimilation and helps overcome the isolation that the newcomer may experience.

Check These Out:

Bonnette, Ashley E. 2004. "Mentoring Minority Librarians Up the Career Ladder." *Library Administration & Management* 18, no. 3 (Summer): 134–139.

Thomas, David A. 2001. "The Truth About Mentoring Minorities: Race Matters." *Harvard Business Review* 79, no. 4 (April): 98–107.

A Diversity Committee

Some services have set up a diversity or equal opportunity committee, which can take either a narrow or broad focus. Such a committee keeps an informal watch over the range of activities within the service as they affect both users and staff, and often organizes informal events to bring people together.

SUPERVISING A DIVERSE STAFF

Communication

Communication is a word that appears frequently in this volume. It appears here because it is important not only that communication must take place, but that it should be effective. In a culturally diverse organization, it is essential for managers to ensure that their messages are fully understood by staff members. In some ways, it is easier to communicate with someone who has a different native tongue, because both parties are well aware of the linguistic difference. The danger comes when two staff members come from countries that use the same language, because there can be subtle, or not so subtle, differences of meaning. The idiomatic use of language is a good example. In Australia, an invitation to a barbecue accompanied by "bring a plate" means you come with a contribution to the meal—not an empty plate. It makes entertaining easy, but is a social pitfall for the new migrant. Thankfully, Australians have a sense of humor.

It is vital to ensure that communication, both written and spoken, is performed without upsetting the self-confidence of the newcomer, particularly if that person is learning a new dialect or language and is trying hard to become assimilated.

Communication differs between cultures in other ways. Using the skills of observation helps one assess the comfort level of colleagues and users. Consider the contrasts between the Japanese and the American approaches to communication. The Japanese may communicate by not stating matters directly, while Americans communicate in a very direct way. In some cultures, it is not usual to question the words of a "superior" person, even for trivial matters. If a person fails to question a request she or he has not fully understood, mistakes may occur, which may affect both parties, whether they are staff or users. It can be particularly challenging for frontline staff who are unsure whether a user has received the right answer to a request. Making assumptions about the level of awareness of local practices and customs is not the wisest course of action. (See Chapter 12 for a further discussion of communication issues.)

Check This Out:

Beamer, Linda, and Iris Varner. 2005. *Intercultural Communication in the Global Workplace*. 3rd ed. New York: McGraw-Hill.

Multinational businesses face considerable challenges that must be overcome if they are to be successful. Patricia de Pablos (2004) has examined knowledge flow transfers and the influence of four human resource management models—exported, adapted, hybrid, and open—that influence the transferability of organizational knowledge within the organizational and national culture.

Sensitivity

One sensitive issue that managers must handle is that of leave. Taking everyone's preferences into account can be a challenge. If there are no policies in place at the level of the parent organization, or if there are varying circumstances within the service (such as extended hours of operation), then policies should be developed, in consultation with the staff, to guide practice. Create awareness and clearly indicate any non-negotiable points.

Family obligations of some staff members can cause resentment among those who do not have such responsibilities. A similar issue is that of religious observances and national holidays. The organization may prefer that everyone conform to the holidays and dominant religious festivals of the country, but this practice can be a hardship for those having other religious beliefs or who observe other holidays. A positive approach that allows flexibility often works in services open to the public. For example, within multicultural communities, some staff may be quite willing to trade holidays, thus allowing for more flexible service hours. It can be a win-win situation.

Check These Out:

Montgomery, Jack G. 2002. "A Most Delicate Matter: Religious Issues and Conflict in the U.S. Library Workplace." *Library Management* 23, nos. 8/9: 422–434.
Montgomery, Jack G., and Eleanor I. Cook. 2005. *Conflict Management for Libraries: Strategies for a Positive, Productive Workplace*. Chicago: American Library Association.

The process of achieving diversity is often slower than anyone would like; it is complex, and requires sensitivity, patience, time, and monitoring by management.

For Further Thought:

List four or five factors that supervisors must be sensitive to in a culturally diverse workgroup.

PROVIDING SERVICE TO A DIVERSE COMMUNITY

User Experience and Motivation

Managerial responsibilities also ensure that the service is delivered in a culturally sensitive manner. Users will base their expectations about the nature and quality of the service provided to them on previous experience. Some will have experienced very sophisticated services and have excessive expectations as a result. Others may have lower expectations. Services may not have been a natural part of everyday life, or users may have lived in a rural area with poor access to small information services. Some may not have a good command of the local language or of information technology.

Liu and Redfern (1997) surveyed students at San Jose State University, where the minorities accounted for 51 percent of the total student population. They found that for 60 percent of minorities, English was their second language, over half coming from an Asian country. Statistical analyses indicated that the student's level of success in using the library was related to English-language proficiency, frequency of library use, and the frequency of reference desk inquiries. Among those who were less successful, the reasons for not asking for help at the reference desk were as follows:

- afraid of asking stupid questions
- afraid that their English was not good enough
- afraid of not understanding the answers well enough
- did not think of asking questions
- do not know the role of the reference librarian (Liu and Redfern, 1997)

These findings are likely to be common in any culturally diverse community.

Users have to overcome difficulties if they are to gain the information they need; students, for example, are highly motivated to succeed with their education. This is also the case for users of archives and other specialized library collections. However, the barriers to use can be greater in the case of a public library or archives where the degree of motivation for use may be less. Public libraries and archives may be forbidding to those who do not speak the language of the community, especially if they are first-time users. Instruction and coaching are likely to be needed in the use of computers and accessing catalogs and databases.

Check This Out:

Neely, Teresa Y., and Kuang-Hwei Lee-Smeltzer. 2001. "Diversity Now: People, Collections and Services in Academic Libraries." *Journal of Library Administration* 33, nos. 1 and 2.

Collection Development

The majority of services will have an acquisitions policy, but not every service may have fully addressed the question of diversity.

Check These Out:

Mason, Karen M. 2002. "Fostering Diversity in Archival Collections: The Iowa Women's Archives." *Collection Management* 27, no. 2: 23–31.
Neal, Kathryn M. 2002. "Cultivating Diversity." *Collection Management* 27, no. 2: 33–42.

The process of making changes to a collections policy can be met with a reaction from those who have been well served by the former policy, since changing directions is not always accompanied by an injection of additional funding. Providing an enhanced service to one group may mean a reduction in that provided to another group. This happened when the National Library of Australia determined that, as part of its strategic planning, the library would have to reduce its acquisition of overseas materials substantially. The collection policy was shifted to emphasize national identity, multiculturalism, and the Asia-Pacific region. In this example, the dissenters were academics who had looked to the National Library of Australia to augment the collections held in their universities, principally the universities in Canberra where the National Library is situated (Macintyre, 1997).

Ways to augment document collections include setting up exchange agreements with services serving similar ethnic groups, or developing cooperative acquisitions policies to build a shared circulating collection. This practice can be welcomed by users of public and school library services where a limited collection can quickly be "read out" by enthusiastic readers.

In building collections for indigenous communities there may well be sensitivities about access, and the rights of the indigenous communities must take precedence over the broader policy.

ACCESS TO THE COLLECTIONS

Subject Headings

The multicultural archive or library must be sensitive to the ways in which it provides access to its collections. Moorcroft (1992) drew attention to ethnocentrism in subject headings by discussing the field of Australian Aboriginal Studies, and similar examples can be found in other countries that use Library of Congress Subject Headings. Headings can be long and convoluted; Moorcroft quotes, as an example, "Aborigines, Australian—Australia, Northern-History-Congresses." Some headings can be value-laden, such as "Mixed Blood." Another example, which shows how Aboriginal people are regarded as "others," lies in the headings used for *Aboriginal Adolescence: Maidenhood in an Australian Community*, which could not be found under the general heading of "Adolescence," but rather under "Aborigines, Australian—Social Life and Customs" and "Aborigines, Australian—Northern Territory—Arnhem Land—Social Life and Customs." Moorcroft (1992) makes the point that "librarians have a social responsibility to ensure that information is easily accessible to all groups regardless of whether the content is politically uncomfortable to the dominant paradigm."

Multilingual Signage and OPACS

Making the collections accessible extends to installing signage in languages other than the dominant language used within the community. Multilingual OPACs allow users to work in the language in which they are most comfortable. The use of different languages to describe how to search the catalog and the collections helps users to increase their skills in retrieving documents and information.

> **A Good Example:**
>
> Visit the Web site of the National Library of New Zealand—Te Puna Mātauranga o Aotearoa (www.natlib.govt.nz) for a well-designed and informative resource in the Maori and English languages.

Marketing

Interacting with the diverse groups in the community will be easier for staff or users who are members of or affiliated with the groups. These people become ambassadors for the service by talking to groups, either formally or informally, working with the media, and reviewing aspects of service that can be improved to increase access.

> **Check This Out:**
>
> The Web site for the United Kingdom's National Archives (www.nationalarchives.gov.uk) provides a wealth of information for people wanting to trace their family history. Many are not experienced users of archives but are encouraged to visit Kew (where the archives are located) and learn more. It is very effective marketing for the service.

Displays and Exhibitions

Exhibitions and displays are effective ways to create awareness of the range of resources available to users. They make a visual statement about the scope of the collection, drawing attention to its multicultural nature and providing a talking point between users and staff. Displays also can draw community groups into the archives or library. Offering a display facility in a public place brings out community pride, provides information to the community at large, and increases the awareness of available services.

> **For Further Thought:**
>
> Reflect on the difficulties that someone who has lived in another part of the world might face in using an archives or library service. Identify six areas in which action can be taken to help them.

KEY POINTS TO REMEMBER:

- Cultural diversity touches on many of the manager's responsibilities.
- Cultural diversity affects everyone who interacts with the information service.
- We each have a lens through which we view diversity.
- There are laws and regulations to be observed.
- Everyone has the responsibility to value and recognize differences in society.
- We need to understand culture shock.
- An acknowledgment of cultural diversity must be embedded in planning.
- Staffing and supervising a diverse staff presents challenges.
- Cultural diversity affects service to users.

REFERENCES

Carlson, Dawn S., K. Michele Kacmar, and Dwayne Whitten. 2006. "What Men Think They Know About Executive Women." *Harvard Business Review* 84, no. 9 (September): 28–29.

Child, Margaret. 1997. "Taking Preservation Across Cultural Frontiers." *Libri* 47, no. 3: 139–146.

Cohen, Lucy. 1994. "Employment Practices." In *Cultural Diversity in Libraries*, edited by Donald E. Riggs and Patricia A. Tarin (65–74). New York: Neal-Schuman.

de Pablos, Patricia Oronez. 2004. "Knowledge Flow Transfers in Multinational Corporations: Knowledge Properties and Implications for Management." *Journal of Knowledge Management* 8, no. 6: 105–116.

Deyrup, Marta Mestrovic. 2004. "Is the Revolution Over? Gender, Economic, and Professional Parity in Academic Library Leadership Positions." *College & Research Libraries* 65, no. 3 (May): 242–250.

Ely, Robin, Debra E. Meyerson and Martin N. Davidson. 2006. "Rethinking Political Correctness." *Harvard Business Review* 84, no. 9 (September): 78–87.

Fox, Kate. 2004. *Watching the English: The Hidden Rules of English Behaviour.* London: Hodder & Stoughton.

Hofstede, Geert. 1991. *Cultures and Organizations: Software of the Mind.* New York: McGraw-Hill.

Howell, Donna W. 2004. "The Politics of Public Library Boards." *Rural Libraries* 24, no. 1: 15–24.

Kendall, Frances E. 1994. "Creating a Multicultural Environment in the Library." In *Cultural Diversity in Libraries*, edited by Donald E. Riggs and Patricia A. Tarin (76–91). New York: Neal-Schuman.

Liu, Mengxiong, and Bernice Redfern. 1997. "Information-Seeking Behavior of Multicultural Students: A Case Study at San Jose State University." *College & Research Libraries* 58, no. 4 (July): 348–354.

Macintyre, Stuart. 1997. "Whose Library? Whose Culture? The Library as Cultural Custodian." *Australian Library Journal* 46, no. 2 (May): 118–124.

Moorcroft, Heather. 1992. "Ethnocentrism in Subject Headings." *Australian Library Journal* 41, no. 1 (February): 40–45.

"Retired and Inspired: After Leaving Their Jobs These Librarians Find Themselves Busier—and Happier—Than Ever." 2006. *American Libraries* 37, no.10 (November): 32–37.

Royse, Molly, Tiffani Conner, and Tamara Miller. 2006. "Charting a Course for Diversity: An Experience in Climate Assessment." *Portal: Libraries and the Academy* 6, no. 1 (January): 23–45.

Skot-Hansen, D. 2002. "The Public Library between Immigration and Cultural Diversity." *Scandinavian Public Library Quarterly* 35, no. 1: 12–13.

Sorti, Craig. 2004. *Americans at Work: A Guide to the Can-Do People.* Yarmouth, ME: Intercultural Press, Inc.

Turock, Betty. 2003. "Developing Diverse Professional Leaders." *New Library World* 104, nos. 11/12: 491–498.

West, Michael A., Dean Tjosvold, and Ken G. Smith, eds. 2005. *Essentials of Teamworking: International Perspectives.* Chichester, UK: John Wiley & Sons Ltd.

Williams, Mark. 2001. *The Ten Lenses: Your Guide to Living and Working in a Multicultural World.* Sterling, VA: Capital Books.

Wynn, Michael. 1992. *Don't Quit.* South Pasadena, CA: Rising Sun Publishing.

Zemke, Ron, Claire Raines, and Bob Filipczak. 1999. *Generations at Work: Managing the Clash of Veterans, Boomers, Xers, and Nexters in Your Workplace.* New York: AMACOM.

LAUNCHING PAD

Darby, Lakeshia. 2005. "Abolishing Stereotypes: Recruitment and Retention of Minorities in the Library Profession." *Rural Libraries* 25, no. 1: 7–17.

Hankin, Harriet. 2004. *The New Workforce: Five Sweeping Trends That Will Shape Your Company's Future.* New York: AMACOM.

Hankins, Rebecca, Michele Saunders, and Ping Situ. 2003. "Diversity Initiatives vs. Residency Programs." *College & Research Libraries News* 64, no. 5 (May): 308–310, 315.

Hewlett, Sylvia Ann, Carolyn Buck Luce, and Cornel West. 2005. "Leadership in Your Midst: Tapping the Hidden Strengths of Minority Executives." *Harvard Business Review* 83, no. 11 (November): 74–82.

Howland, J. S. 2001. "Challenges of Working in a Multicultural Environment." *Journal of Library Administration* 33, nos. 1/2: 105–123.

Mason, Karen M. 2002. "Fostering Diversity in Archival Collections: The Iowa Women's Collection." *Collection Management* 27, no. 2: 23–31.

Morison, Robert, Tamara Erickson, and Ken Dytchwald. 2006. "Managing Middlescene." *Harvard Business Review* 84, no. 3 (March): 78–86.

Ocholla, Denis N. 2002. "Diversity in the Library and Information Workplace: A South African Perspective." *Library Management* 23, nos. 1/2: 59–67.

Tannen, Deborah. 1996. *Gender and Discourse.* New York: Oxford University Press.

Thistlethwaite, P. 2001. "Recruit, Recruit, Recruit: Organizing Benefits for Employees with Unmarried Families." *Journal of Library Administration* 33, nos. 1/2: 31–44.

Voelck, Julie. 2003. "Directive and Connective: Gender-Based Differences in the Management Styles of Academic Library Managers." *Portal: Libraries and the Academy* 3, no. 3 (July): 393–418.

Winston, M.D. 2001. "The Importance of Leadership Diversity: the Relationship between Diversity and Organizational Success in the Academic Environment." *College & Research Libraries*, 62, no. 6 (November): 517–526.

Zemon, Mickey, and Alice Harrison Bahr. 2005. "Career and/or Children: Do Female Academic Librarians Pay a Price for Motherhood?" *College & Research Libraries* 66, no. 5 (September): 394–405.

Part II

Management:
Knowledge and Skills

5

Marketing

"Don't forget that your service or product is not differentiated until the customer understands the difference."

Tom Peters

"If you keep your head well down, you may not be shot at, but you may be trampled on."

Maurice Line

INTRODUCTION

Marketing and information services, do they actually go together? Is marketing of information services appropriate? As Jennifer Rowley (2003: 13) noted, for many information professionals in the past, "marketing was regarded as an alien commercial process, inconsistent with the values of public service." In 2004, Shontz, Parker, and Parker published the results of an attitude survey of U.S. public librarians regarding the concept of marketing. Overall they found there were generally favorable views regarding marketing and a recognition of a need for the activity to some degree. They did note that "administrators and public service librarians had more positive attitudes than did reference and technical service librarians" (Shontz et al., 2004: 74). An interesting finding was the more library experience one had, the more positive the view held. Unsurprisingly, those who had attended a workshop or taken formal coursework in marketing were the most positive about the process.

We firmly believe that in today's highly competitive information world, information services must market themselves. Even without the competition, it would still be critical for long-term success. The general public has yet to fully appreciate what library and archive services can and are capable of doing. When funding is difficult, being able to draw upon a knowledge-able, satisfied user community can make all the difference between suc-cess and failure. Market analysis and marketing programs will help build such a base.

Successful service depends upon accurately determining population de-mographics (such as mentioned in Chapter 3), community information wants and needs, and how people use the information supplied. Knowing these and other characteristics assists managers in a variety of activities, such as planning, programming, and fund allocation.

Market analysis, and some of the related methods for assessing needs that employ similar techniques, can provide managers with vital data about a variety of topics, such as:

- when and how services are used
- who does and does not use the services
- what new services are desired
- what information is desired
- what formats are desired
- what image of the service is held in the minds of the community served

We make a distinction between marketing and public relations. In the broadest sense, both processes are concerned with "selling" something. However, they differ in significant ways. *Public relations* build a relationship between a service and its stakeholders, using the skills of communications management. The service reaches out to win support from policy makers, providers of funding from internal and external sources, and the commu-nity within which it operates. Communications management uses the media, staff interacting with the service community on a daily basis, pub-lished guides on how to use services, Web pages, catalogs, annual reports, and exhibitions mounted within the facility to gain the support of stake-holders. Frank Jefkins defined public relations as "the planned and sus-tained effort to establish and maintain goodwill and mutual understanding between an organization and its public" (Jefkins, 1994: 7). It is both an art and science through which the service informs and persuades its stake-holders to be aware of, and support, its activities. On the other hand, *mar-keting* tends to focus on identifying and meeting customer needs for services or products.

For many years libraries, archives, and information services in general did not see much, if any, need to market their products and services. They expected users to know about services, but they took little action to create awareness and persuade the service community that the service could offer something of value. In the 1980s a number of texts on marketing appeared that focused on information services (Cronin, 1992; Kies, 1987; McNeal, 1992; Rowley, 2001; Savard, 2000; Walters, 1992; Weingand, 1998; Wood and Young, 1988). We fully agree with Richard Leventhal's view that in today's environment "an effective marketing effort is based upon information which can be used in terms of developing sound business strategies, . . . allow for more successful innovation, lead to better branding efforts, increase the effectiveness of your promotional efforts and strengthen your web marketing" (2005: 3).

WHAT IS MARKETING?

There are several ways to view marketing. One definition that originally dates from 1991 is "the management process for identifying, anticipating, and satisfying customer requirements profitably" (Chartered Institute of Marketing, 2006). Darlene Weingand related the topic to the field of library science by defining marketing as "a process of exchange and a way to foster the partnership between the library and its community"(Weingand, 1995: 296). Elam and Palcy stated, "Marketing is a total system of interacting business activities designed to plan, price, promote, and distribute want-satisfying products and services to organizational and household users at a profit in a competitive environment" (1992: 7). More recently the definition has introduced the concept of exchange, which is the transfer of a service in return for something of value and this is incorporated in Philip Kotler's definition of marketing as being "the process of planning and executing the conception, pricing, promotion, and distribution of ideas, goods and services to create exchanges that satisfy individual and organizational goals" (August 2006. Available: http://wps.prenhall.com/wps/media/objects/ 2170/222134/bp_kotler_mm12_glossary.pdf).

Something to Ponder:

The term "marketing" is interpreted in a number of ways. We have given five. Check dictionaries and Web sites for two more examples. Scan the six definitions that you have. Which do you feel best describes what you understand as "marketing"? Note the sources and put the definition in a safe place for future reference.

The Web site for Kotler's definition gives a comprehensive glossary of marketing terms.

Another approach is strategic marketing. This approach is an excellent example of the integration of management activities that we view as critical for a successful manager. Essentially, the approach draws on methods of strategic planning (see Chapter 8) and combines them with marketing methods. Over the past 30 years, Phillip Kotler developed the idea that non-profit marketing differs from for-profit marketing in important ways. He has published six editions of his text on nonprofit marketing (Andreasen and Kotler, 2003). The first three editions emphasized the methods of market-ing such organizations. Starting with his fourth edition, he added the strategic planning aspects to the approach. In the fifth edition (1996), a strong international element was added as well as social marketing.

There are some important similarities in the above definitions. All of them mention the customer/user as being a key element in the process. They also suggest that people's needs are the focal point of marketing. When employing some form of user-oriented marketing, success will come to the organization that best determines the perceptions, needs, and wants of its target markets and that satisfies these needs through the design, com-munication, pricing, and delivery of appropriate and competitively viable offerings (Andreasen and Kotler, 2003).

Some services, particularly those that are publicly funded, need to em-phasize the sales aspect and employ social marketing. Social marketing grew out of efforts by Kotler and others at a time when a number of non-profit groups with relatively narrow interests began to engage in sales-oriented marketing. Some examples of such nonprofit groups are health care and environmental or consumer protection organizations. Frequently, these organizations have a special aspect, or "cause," that they want to sell to the general public. Take the example of public libraries, which often have programs/activities that are social in the sense of social marketing—adult literacy programs, after-school storytelling, or programs for "latchkey" children. In a sense, this approach employs marketing techniques to gen-erate support for and perhaps move forward certain social causes or agen-das. Social marketing for information services is sometimes difficult to differentiate from public relations activities. The difference, as stated by Andreasen and Kotler, is that "social marketing seeks to influence social be-havior not to benefit the marketer but *to benefit the target audience and the general society*" (2003: 46). (Emphasis in the original.)

So far we have focused on external marketing (that is marketing to users and funding bodies, for example). But there are other stakeholders who together form the internal market—senior management and, most im-portant, the staff of the service—and we will return to this point.

Why Market Information Services?

A well-planned marketing program can provide data for a variety of activities. A few examples include collection building, providing optimum service hours and optimum staffing of service points, and developing desirable new services. There are four key reasons why one should consider developing a marketing program. First and foremost, almost all archives and libraries face either a decreasing resource base or stronger competition for existing resources while needing to provide an increasing range of services. Second, as a result, user convenience usually decreases—shorter service hours, fewer public service staff, and reductions in the number of locally owned information resources are some examples. Third, frequently each year the services reach a smaller and smaller percentage of the total service population. (Actual numbers of interactions and customers may increase over the previous year, but when the overall service population increases sharply there can be a drop in the percentage served.) Finally, all information services face competition, and, in some cases, a decrease in the role of transferring information from the creators/producers to the end-consumer. Just consider the growth in access to the Web—it is a competitor.

One question to consider when creating a marketing program is "Why is a nonuser a nonuser?" The following general statements about noncustomers of for-profit organizations apply equally to information services:

- **The person does not know your product.** Many surveys ask "Does your community or organization have an archive or library service?" and it is surprising how often the response is "no" when one does exist.
- **The person cannot find your product or it is not available when needed.** Service location and hours are always an issue. There is always a "cost" to a person even when there is no monetary exchange required. Fine (1990) identified four types of "social price" in using nonprofit service organizations: time, effort, lifestyle, and psyche. The first two are the ones that managers normally consider in their planning activities. Lifestyle is, in part, related to effort, in that service hours or locations may require people to adjust the way they live in order to use the service. Too much adjustment usually results in potential users becoming nonusers. Psyche "price" is one of the areas where, for many individuals, the service's price is too high. Although our online catalogs and databases are substantially easier to use than those that existed just 20 years ago, people must still learn how the system functions and face changes as the system is upgraded. Many people can find a service to be intimidating or have difficulty asking for assistance. Very often, these potential users become nonusers because of such factors as self-esteem, pride, fear of loss of privacy, or the need to depend on others for assistance.
- **The person does not need your product.** In the case of information services, this statement may not apply, since everyone needs some

information to carry out necessary activities. Nevertheless, the service may not have the specific information that the user needs.

- **The person prefers a different brand of product.** In many ways, this is probably the fastest-growing factor for all types of information services. Increased home and office access to high-speed Internet services has demonstrated that people prefer convenience when it comes to finding and using information. Also the psyche price is very low—no one else will know you could not spell this or that word or did not know this or that fact. Control, self-esteem, privacy, and so forth cease being issues.

- **The person does not understand what your product can do.** For archives and libraries, this is frequently the case—many people perceive them as offering at best a limited range of documents or print materials. The idea that an archive or library is an information service is only just becoming appreciated and understood by some individuals outside the field.

- **The person believes the cost of your product is too high or the value for the cost is too low.** For this to be a factor, the nonuser should have used your product at least once in order to form an opinion. Many people generalize about libraries and archives based on one or two experiences, often in their youth, rather than a recent experience. Learning the basis for the nonuser's judgment is important when planning a marketing program.

- **The person has had difficulty using your product.** In the past, libraries and archives were not people-friendly. In the days of card catalogs and complex filing rules, it was difficult to gain access to materials in the collection. If a user did not understand the rules, he or she was completely dependent upon staff assistance, and that might be difficult if not impossible to secure. Someone who has not gone to a library or archive service since the arrival of online catalogs may well have memories of it being a difficult place to use.

- **The person does not expect good service.** While it is impossible to please everyone all the time, displeasing too many people is disastrous. A question to answer is: "For many people, how often, and in what situations did problems develop?" The goal is to reduce the problems as much as possible to retain existing customers; it is not to create a cadre of dissatisfied former users who may discourage potential others from becoming users.

A sound marketing program provides the staff with data (market intelligence) that help them address the above issues and develop a plan to increase both the number of customers and the percentage of total target population (market share).

Something to Think About:

Consider a marketing program for an information service of your choice. Target three activities that would be part of your program, identify the type of data that would be needed, and indicate how it could be obtained, noting the sources.

Market intelligence is data that are secured from four broad areas: environmental, activity type, customers, and competitors (Fine, 1990). Data from the operating environment are essential in planning and goal setting, so the manager should have much of these data already collected for use in other management activities. All of the environmental factors we discussed earlier apply to any marketing program. Activity data are really subsets of information about the operational environment, such as vendor activities, technological developments, and competitors. Users are a logical source of demographic data—level of use, age, and major responsibilities (researcher, teacher, and administrator) are some examples. Likewise, competitors provide more useful data when thought of in terms of subsets, such as market share, distribution methods, and price range.

Tip:

It can be expensive and time-consuming to collect the data needed for a marketing plan. Information services are not always good at estimating internal costs—principally staff time—of carrying out projects. It is worthwhile checking with a market research organization to get a quote for their services. They have experience to bring to the task and may be able to meet your information needs by piggybacking your survey with other data-collection exercises. Their fees might not be as high as you would expect.

Some of the marketing data require collection directly from the source. Direct collecting is often expensive and time-consuming. Building some of that collecting into the normal operational routines will reduce overall costs. When the data collecting becomes part of the operational routine, it is almost cost-free. For instance, organizations often already collect a wealth of data about existing users (registration data, collection usage reports, and data from document delivery services). Such data provide the staff with profiles of what are, at the very least, semisatisfied users. That information can be beneficial in choosing the most cost-effective services to offer to people with similar profiles. Another example would be deciding how to reach out to a very different segment of the population. When developing a marketing plan, managers would draw heavily on such data.

THE MARKETING PROCESS

Michael Porter (1979) suggested that, from a strategic point of view, planners need to locate a potentially profitable niche, develop products to meet the needs of customers in that niche, and create a defensive plan for dealing with possible competitors. Philip Kotler's strategic marketing process for not-for-profit organizations has three major elements: analysis, strategy, and implementation (Andreason and Kotler, 2003). Much of their process involves the steps of strategic planning. The steps are:

1. generic product definition
2. target group definition
3. differential marketing analysis
4. customer behavior analysis
5. differential advantages analysis
6. multiple marketing approaches
7. integrated market planning
8. continuous market feedback
9. marketing audit

Generic Product Definition

A key to the long-term success of any organization is a realistic answer to the question, "What is our business?" Every organization produces at least one of the following: physical products (tangible), services (intangible), persons (press agents), the organization itself (political parties or professional organizations), or ideas (population control or human rights). Often, the answer to the above question is product-oriented rather than customer-oriented. When that happens, the outcome limits the organization's growth potential. Thinking about the organization in terms of the user tends to broaden the scope of possible activities. Rather than being in the railroad business, think in terms of transportation—soap becomes cleaning, movies become entertainment, and documents become information. For information services, increasing the user base is very important to long-term survival.

Target Group Definition

The generic or user-based product definition usually results in identifying a wide market. Looking at such a market can lead to the creation of a marketing program so broad that it fails to produce the desired results. Dividing the large market into smaller units usually produces more cost-effective marketing. A market "segment"

- comprises units with similar or related characteristics
- comprises units with common needs and wants
- comprises units with similar responses to like motivations
- accepts a service/product that fulfills these needs at a reasonable price

Segmenting a market takes time and effort, but it will pay off in a better response to any marketing effort targeted to a particular market segment.

Take the example of a library that is part of a university. What are some of the potential market segments? The most obvious segments are the faculty and students; however, even those groups are probably too large to fit our definition of a market segment. There are likely to be more useful segments if you think in terms of subject interest and degree of interest in the subject. Such a segment might group doctoral students with faculty, instead of grouping them with general students. Another way to divide students would be into undeclared-major lower-division undergraduates, declared-major lower-division undergraduates, undeclared upper-division, undergraduates, declared upper-division undergraduates, master's degree students, and doctoral-level students.

Check These Out:

Debra Lee's 2004 article "Market Segmentation and Libraries" (*Library Administration & Management* 18, no. 1: 47–48) explores segmenting in more depth. Another useful article is Charles Forrest's 2005 "Segmenting the Library Market" (*Georgia Library Quarterly* 42, no. 1: 4–7). The principles can be translated into other information settings.

Other types of information services have equally diverse markets, and so each of the larger markets can be analyzed and grouped into smaller more homogenous units. There is never enough money to address all the potential marketing areas; however, having smaller homogenous units to consider helps managers make the difficult decision of where to expend the available marketing funds. Thinking about each segment and asking questions such as the following will help:

- What are the common needs/wants of this group?
- Which, if any, of those needs do we now serve?
- What do we know about their behavior patterns?
- How much benefit do they currently receive from our services?
- What is the potential gain from meeting more of this group's needs and wants?

- What type of message is the most effective for reaching this group?
- What do we know about their perceptions of the service?
- Compared to other market segments, how important is this group for the service?
- Who is our competition?

The answer to the last question should facilitate ranking the various market segments. (These rankings will vary over time as the situation and the operating environment change.) Some of the other questions may indicate that the need to collect more data before a final decision is reasonable. All of the answers will help determine which group(s) will be the target(s).

Differential Marketing Analysis

Different segments require different approaches, and thus differentiated marketing. While most services have three basic product lines—collections, services, and programs—the mix in emphasis or importance for a particular market segment will vary. Using the for-profit terminology, each product line consists of several different, specific products. To take the example of a university library, specific collection products might be defined by dividing the collection into instructional, secondary, and primary research materials. Services might be document delivery and online searching. Program products might be electronic search methods instruction and dissertation format assistance. As the specific products are examined, it will be seen how different packages would have greater or lesser interest to various market segments. For-profit organizations learned long ago that when serving more than one target population, differentiating products and communications about the products in terms of each target population produces the maximum results.

Thinking about the packages in terms of what costs and benefits a person accrues from using the package provides marketing planners with two useful perspectives. First, it offers a complete picture of what the package consists of and the interrelationship between the component parts. Second, it gives planners some sense of how the person perceives, or will perceive, the package. This latter element is very important because nonprofit organizations tend to believe that their service or package is vital.

Customer Behavior Analysis

For many years, individuals responsible for developing collections knew that it was vital to understanding the service community's information needs and lifestyles (sometimes referred to in the information field as community analysis, information audit, or needs analysis). Asking questions about what topics are of interest, "product" usage, when and where people usc information, and when and where they would *prefer* to use it allows staff to structure services and programs more effectively. Such information is helpful in determining the most effective approaches to marketing existing services as well as in promoting new services. Focus groups can be a highly effective method for gathering answers to such questions.

Check These Out:

A good general discussion of the focus group method is David Morgan's 1998 *Planning Focus Groups* (Thousand Oaks, CA: Sage).

Some examples of focus groups in library/information service settings are Marilyn Von Seggern and Nancy J. Young's 2003 "The Focus Group Method in Libraries" (*References Services Review* 31, no. 3: 272–284), Andrew Large and Jamshid Behesti's 2001 "Focus Groups with Children: Do They Work?" (*Canadian Journal of Information and Library Science* 26, nos. 2/3: 77–79), and K. C. Elhard and Qiang Jin's 2004 "Shifting Focus: Assessing Cataloging Service Through Focus Groups" (*Library Collections, Acquisitions, and Technical Services* 28, no. 2: 196–204)).

Differential Advantages Analysis

Once you understand the behaviors and needs of the various segments, it is possible to identify differential advantages for each segment. A differential advantage is one that exploits the reputation, services, or programs by creating or enhancing a special value in the minds of potential users. An example in an academic library would be a special document delivery service for professors and doctoral candidates that provides, within 48 hours, materials not locally available. By providing quick assistance, the library reinforces the value that the institution places on research activities. For service organizations such as libraries and archives, it is essential to reinforce the values and/or needs of the service community and the parent organization.

Multiple Marketing Approaches

In planning a marketing effort, it is advantageous, if not essential, to employ several different marketing tools. The selected tools (such as Web sites, newsletters, flyers, advertisements, and annual reports) should be those that best fit the lifestyle of the target segment. Receptions or open houses can be effective promotional tools, especially when there is a new service or product to demonstrate. In the case of a public library attempting to reach new immigrants, using the native languages of the target population is essential. One caution when preparing material in another language: it is imperative to have the material reviewed by a native speaker who understands both formal and colloquial usage.

Integrated Market Planning and Continuous Feedback

When an organization implements an ongoing marketing program, there is the chance that, over time, different components of the program will be working at cross-purposes. An integrated program is the best insurance against ineffective use of marketing funds. One element in achieving an integrated plan is to have one person responsible for coordinating all marketing and promotional activities. Only the very largest libraries/information services have the resources to allocate one or more full-time persons to work solely on marketing or promotional activities. In the past, such positions often carried the title "public relations officer." Today, more often than not the title is "marketing director." Even when the level of staffing will not allow for a full-time marketing position, only one person (or, a lesser second choice, a committee) should be responsible for coordinating all marketing and promotional activities. To make the work manageable, there must be a strategic marketing plan for the managers to review and update on a regular basis.

Marketing Audit

Monitoring activities are a part of a market auditing. An audit also draws on feedback from the service community, service staff, and governing boards. Looking at what worked and why, what did not work and why, how the environment and community base has or has not changed, and what changes have taken place within the organization (staff, services, resources, facilities) all become important aspects in adjusting and maintaining a viable marketing program. Other elements include assessing the resources available to carry out the program, how well the people responsible for carrying out the program have performed, and assessing how effective the program is in achieving long-term organizational mission goals and objectives.

Darlene Weingand suggests:

> the audit should also develop a "futures screen" that identifies trends and projections in both external and internal environments in order to develop contingency plans that will relate to alternative future scenarios. The futures screen places considerable emphasis on securing data on what "may be" in the next five years (and beyond); objectives can then be developed to reflect that informed projection. (1995: 303)

Additional issues for an audit involve how certain factors have or have not changed since the program's inception. For instance, if the time frame is five years, organizational staff members probably will have changed.

Perhaps services are slightly different and this change is not reflected in the marketing program. Another factor is that small variations in organizational resources over the years may, in totality, be significant. A careful review of the operating environment may reveal that new or different competitors exist for the service. In essence, one should examine *all* relevant changes, both internal and external.

Such an analysis often helps to increase service usage (quantitatively or qualitatively), to increase attendance at important events, or build a following for a valued program. The problem is that managers may be tempted to initiate promotional efforts on an ad hoc basis to meet a particular need independent of larger or competing priorities. If such efforts succeed, they may become annual activities; the cumulative effect is a hodgepodge of disparate marketing efforts, which can consume massive amounts of time and energy but in total bear little resemblance to the strategic agenda of the institution as a whole.

FOUR KEY STRATEGIES

Once management accepts the concept of strategic marketing, the question becomes, "What kinds of strategies lend themselves to institutional marketing and promotion?" Four strategic platforms stand out as having a particularly good fit to the typical needs of a library. These are positioning, segmentation, targeting, and the quality approach.

Positioning is defined by Andreasen and Kotler as "the act of designing the organization's image and value offer so that . . . customers understand and appreciate what the organization stands for in relation to its competitors" (Andreasen and Kotler, 2003: 205). From an ethical standpoint, the most desirable image is the most authentic. These are values to which good marketers subscribe, but on which marketing itself has little to say. From the purely utilitarian perspective of marketing, it "is not important whether your product is the best of its kind. What is important is whether people think it is best" (Nash, 1986: 216).

In applying the general positioning principle to an information service market, its position is the image it projects in the minds of potential users in relation to competitive institutions. In concentrating on the perceptions of the prospect, a positioning strategy looks for windows in the mind (Wright, 1973: 63). It is then simply a matter of "determining what someone is really buying when they buy your product or service and then conveying those impressions and motivations to the buyer" (Ries and Trout, 1986: 12).

Segmentation is the process of identifying discrete divisions of potential customers according to demographic, geographic, psychographic, and psychometric characteristics (McCormack, 1980: 123). This process allows a better use of limited resources by applying them only to potential users. As noted by Evans and Berman, "a market segmentation approach aims at a narrow, specific consumer group (market segment) through one, specialized marketing plan that caters to the needs of that segment" (Evans and Berman, 1985: 210).

Targeting is closely related to segmentation. It is a strategic method by which an organization sets out to tailor its message so well and deliver it so close to the prospect's interest and sphere of attention that the message cannot miss. Target markets consist of those users whom the library can attract effectively (strategy) and efficiently (tactics). Kotler and Andreasen view this method as being "a style of marketing appropriate to a customer-oriented organization. In it the organization distinguishes between the different segments making up the market" (Kotler and Andreasen, 1996: 167). The key to targeting is found not only in the unique characteristics of the segment, but also in the ability to evaluate it. As Peter Drucker noted, "only if targets are defined can resources be allocated to their attainment, priorities and deadlines set and somebody be held accountable for results" (Drucker, 1974: 140).

Quality of service is always an issue that demands attention. Research at Arizona State University's First Interstate Center for Services Marketing relates how organizations face this issue as they move to instill a more service-oriented culture. It is simply not enough to meet the expectations of prospective users; the organization ought to *exceed* those expectations.

Information services must make a commitment to quality service and user satisfaction, and this commitment must begin at the senior level. Commitment must manifest itself in the actions of those in the highest positions and those with the greatest visibility. A service that follows a quality strategy will find it necessary to decentralize authority, if it hopes to succeed in the 21st century.

A Tactical Framework

Once the institution establishes the direction it wishes to follow (strategy), and has decided to mount an integrated promotional effort, managers have a proper frame of reference for the selection of tactics.

As mentioned previously, tactics are the specific actions designed to accomplish objectives which the strategy has defined. The tactical arena is the scene of highest expenditures as well as highest casualties. There is more

---

Check This Out:

For a practical overview of strategic marketing concepts, read Dale Fodness' 2005 "Rethinking Strategic Marketing" (*Journal of Business Strategy* 26, no. 3: 20–34).

debate, and less knowledge, applied to marketing tactics than to almost any endeavor in libraries.

BRANDING

Between marketing and promotion is the concept of branding. At its simplest, branding is the process of developing a symbol (often a logo) that embodies the essence of a product, service, or organization. Deborah Lee (2006: 94) defined branding as "a marketing concept that identifies a good or service through the use of a name, phrase, design or symbol." Libraries have a generic logo, originally developed by the American Library Association, to draw upon when thinking about developing a brand: @your library[R]. This logo has been translated into many languages.

> **Check This Out:**
>
> The American Library Association's @your library[R] logo is a registered trademark. Visit their Web site to see the different ways it can be used. (Available: www.ala.org/ala/pio/campaign/downloadlogos/your library.htm [accessed October 2006].)

Branding is not always just a matter of a local service, as evidenced by the headline of a story in *American Libraries:* "Britain Launches Campaign to Transform Libraries' Image" (2006).

Corporations spend large sums of money each year to maintain a brand they have created. Information services may not have much, if any money to maintain their brands. However, at least two aspects of a brand can be

> **Check These Out:**
>
> The following resources are useful for addressing branding concepts:
> Miller, Jon, and David Muir. 2004. *The Business of Branding.* Hoboken, NJ: Wiley.
> Olins, Wally. 2003. *On Brand.* London: Thames & Hudson.
> Interesting and useful Web sites related to branding are:
> "Brand Strategy" (May 2006). Available: www.brandstrategy.co.uk
> "What Makes a Great Logo" (May 2006). Available:
>   www.code-interactive.com/thinker/a112.html
> "Logo Design Services Directory" (May 2006). Available: www.logoterra.com

maintained without the expenditure of funds. Brands invoke both a physical and a psychological experience. When a powerful sense of service is developed in the staff, a manager/supervisor can be confident that users will experience a positive psychological experience in almost every case and assure as good a physical experience as the facilities allow. Both will be significant assets in establishing and maintaining a service's brand.

INTERNAL MARKETING

Management is not a set of separate processes: the processes are interrelated and overlap. Internal marketing along with performance or service quality provide an example of the effect of one activity upon another. Experience indicates that we remember poor service more often than good service, and the staff is the factor that can make the difference. Ensuring that staff members are well informed about the service should increase user satisfaction. While managers prepare mission statements, strategic plans, and goals and objectives, these efforts may not be effectively conveyed to the frontline staff. They have to know and understand changes in policy. If, for example, a policy change includes "good news," informed staff members can convey the news to users. Updates and changes to the service Web site also need to be conveyed to all staff. If they are not, staff at any level may be told by an outsider of an internal change.

One technique to judge the effectiveness of internal marketing is to conduct an employee satisfaction survey. The results will indicate the state of staff satisfaction and the organizational climate within the service.

Internal marketing to senior management keeps them in touch with service developments. They need to be aware of both the "good news" and the "less good news." The "less good news" might be an incident (such as an influential user being upset by what he or she considered to be poor service) and service disruptions. Be sure to deliver such news with care, emphasizing how the situation is being positively addressed.

PROMOTION

Promotion should be part of any marketing mix. Kotler defines the marketing mix as consisting of price, promotion, and product (Kotler, 1980: 89). Promotion refers to a cluster of techniques to communicate, inform, persuade, stimulate, and remind the service community of the merits of the services and programs available. The goal of promotion is to modify or reinforce existing behavior. The successful approach will blend selective activities to reach and recruit potential users.

The basic forms of promotion, according to McDaniel (1996: 8), are advertising, personal selling, sales promotion, and publicity. Relatively few information services employ a wholehearted advertising approach—partly due to cost, but also because, traditionally, advertising was thought to be somewhat inappropriate and too impersonal for the type of services offered. Another reason for its low use has been the thought that advertising was unnecessary. Today, we know that this is wishful thinking.

Check This Out:

The Cerritos (Calif.) Public Library hosts Clioinstitute (Available: http://clioinstitute. info [accessed May 2006]), a great Web site for ideas and examples of library and information service promotion activities. Its goal is to inspire "libraries to inspire communities." It includes an online tutorial on promoting activities, a blog, and special topics and trends.

Sales/Promotion

Some of the efforts that libraries call promotion are referred to in the profit sector as sales promotion. Alexander defined sales promotion as consisting "of activities other than personal selling, advertising, and publicity that stimulate consumer purchasing and dealer effectiveness such as displays, shows, and exhibitions, demonstrations, and various non-recruitment efforts not in the ordinary routine" (1961: 20).

Looking at information services as if they were a company, sales promotion can consist of discounts (such as volume discounts on copying), use of coupons, samples (for example, limited free access to a fee-based service), toll-free numbers, films/videos (self-paced bibliographic instruction), catalogs and guides, decals, calendars, and other tactics normally used in the commercial world. Catalogs, view books, and films/videos are also obvious promotional materials. Public libraries can and do make use of decals and posters prepared by state or national professional associations, as well as locally developed items.

Other Options

There are additional options to consider when building one's marketing mix. Certainly the service's Web pages are a powerful tool. They convey not only basic information about the services offered, but also reflect its image and culture. The service may have a free-standing Web site, or it may have pages within the Web site of the broader organization. Naturally you must carefully consider what to cover (putting too much information on a page is as bad as having too little). Think about such issues as page indexing, links to other relevant sites, design, and layout—users should be able to navigate the site quickly to find the information they are seeking. Remember that the information provided needs to be updated regularly—a site that is not updated gives a very bad impression of the service. Pictures, video, and sound can enhance the site, but they can be expensive, and they can cause frustration for the visitor with a low-end computer. Maintain a balance between ease and speed of access and the use such enhancements as images and sound.

Preprinted advertising inserts and circulars can be used to publish service offerings, schedules, or a calendar of events. A library can have these inserted into weekly community newspapers or in bulk mailers to home and work addresses. Some libraries have a weekly column in the local newspaper.

Canvassing is the marketing category for a technique better known in public libraries as outreach activities. If used discriminatingly—choosing events and locations where real prospects are likely to be concentrated—this tactic has its place in most strategies. If overused, it will drain resources from more cost-efficient alternatives.

Brochures can be the keystone elements in a well-orchestrated sequence of varied communications efforts—if they are written, designed, and distributed at the right time in the cycle and if they are aimed at carefully targeted populations.

Billboards and print advertising are mass-media options that typically are expensive mass-media options for trying to reach thousands of nonusers. On occasion, however, these tactics can lend key support. For example, such options are an appropriate means to promote a special event by identifying time, place, and the specific benefit to the target population. One obvious occasion to consider using this approach is during a bond issue campaign.

Signs are often considered too humdrum a subject for creative marketers. For prospective users, however, effective signs and clear directions can make the difference between a positive experience with the service or extreme frustration. Libraries, especially public libraries, are often surprised to discover, after a survey of community members, how many people do not know if there is a library in their region or how many cannot identify the nearest branch.

Newspaper, magazine, television, and radio are all mass-media formats well suited to targeting or segmentation, but they must be used with care. Certain sections of newspapers in targeted zip codes and certain radio or television programs may or may not fit the profile of the targeted population. If so, these media should be evaluated on the basis of cost per contact. This may be one of the few ways to effectively reach noncustomers. In the end, regardless of which tactics are chosen, the institution must "decide what it wants to say and how (by what media) it wants the message delivered" (McDaniel, 1996: 377).

For Further Thought:

Think about your local public library. Which tactics could it employ? Rank them in the order of their likely cost and effectiveness.

Tip:

Most national library associations have awards for various categories of promotional activities. In the United States, these are the John Dana Cotton Awards. Look at the prize-winning entries each year. Some good examples can stimulate thinking about how to promote your service. At the ALA midwinter meeting, many libraries offer copies of their promotional materials. Sharing these materials with your colleagues can lead to some creative thinking.

PUBLIC RELATIONS

We made the distinction earlier between public relations and marketing. We include public relations in this chapter, however, because of its origins in the promotion and marketing campaigns that were employed in the 1890s to promote the expansion of railways in the United States. Over time, the techniques have become more sophisticated, and today information services adopt public relations practices to build relationships with their stakeholders. In recent years there has been criticism of "spin," but if handled in a professional and ethical way, communications management is an essential tool for information services.

Public relations is a profession with its own set of core values and ethics. The core values of the Public Relations Society of America are advocacy, honesty, expertise, independence, loyalty, and fairness. The ethical code provisions are free flow of information, competition, disclosure of information, safeguarding confidences, conflicts of interest, and enhancing the profession. These are sound principles to follow in undertaking any public relations project.

Few information services are able to employ a professional communications manager or publicist. Within larger or for-profit organizations, internal expertise may be available. Support in the library sector is provided by the American Library Association. Larger services may retain a public relations consultant on an as-needed basis.

Check These Out:

The American Library Association's Advocacy Resource Center (Available: www. ala.org/ala/issues/issuesadvocacy.htm [accessed August 2006]) carries advice, message templates, and tools that can be used in public relations campaigns. Materials are drafted for different types of service and in the English and Spanish languages. Elsie Finch's 2006 *Advocating Archives: An Introduction to Public Relations for Archivists* (Lanham, MD: Scarecrow Press and American Society of Archivists) is also a good resource.

As mentioned earlier, public relations is concerned with building relationships, One vital relationship is that between the service and either the public relations professional within the organization or the external consultant. Unless a strong relationship is developed, any public relations activity will be less effective. Rather than engaging a specialist for a specific project, regard the specialist as a member of the team. Work together to carry out a situational analysis and prepare a public relations plan. A specialist's expertise may be needed to maintain a high profile in the user community, lobby for improvements in funding or facilities, launch a new building, promote a new service, introduce a new senior staff member, or publicize a success story. Public relations specialists aim to keep their clients in the public eye and present a positive image.

The most frequently used communications tool is a media release. If it concerns a major event, a media conference can be arranged with the local press, and radio and television stations, and a media release can be distributed by mail, fax, e-mail or the Internet. This is a form of indirect promotion, and it is in many ways the most powerful. From the promotion or marketing communications mix point of view, it is also the least controllable of all the techniques. To paraphrase Kotler, publicity is nonpaid communication about a company or its products appearing in the media as news. As a result "the seller pays nothing for the news coverage" (Kotler, 1980: 469). Communication about staff, services, or a special category of customer appearing in the media can be legitimate news, but it also serves as a form of promotion—as long as the news is good.

Tip:

Claudia O'Keefe provides excellent guidance on how to create an effective press release in her 2005 article "Publicity 101" (*American Libraries* 36, no. 6 [June]: 52–54).

Unfortunately, negative publicity seems easier to get than positive press. Based on experience, we know that academic libraries can expect to see a negative story once or twice a year in the student-run newspaper. Any allegation of fiscal mismanagement or labor problems easily makes the local evening news, the morning newspaper, or some Web site. In early 1997 articles appeared in national newspapers and magazines about problems at the San Francisco Public Library. What is unfortunate, but typical, is that none of the major publications ever published anything on the resolution of the problems. At the time of writing, it seemed likely that such would also be the fate for the Boston Public Library, as the news headline "Boston PL Defends Reputation in Wake of Scathing Report" (2006) was picked up in various publications. When negative stories hit the media, fast action is necessary and a good relationship with a public relations expert is essential. Such an expert will have contacts and the experience to counteract the bad news.

Check This Out:

In her 2005 "Sensemaking a Public Library's Internet Policy Crisis," Mary Cavanagh (*Library Management* 26, nos. 6/7: 351–360) describes how a library board and library management resolved a public controversy led by staff and a community newspaper. The controversy centered on the right of the library staff to be protected from reviewing Internet pornography and the community's reaction to the issue of protecting children's Internet access, versus the library's commitment to intellectual freedom online.

Public relations advisors will have the expertise to target segments of the stakeholders tailoring messages to specific groups, and perhaps arranging events for them to carry a message about a new service or development. By identifying influential people in the user community and organizing an event in which they are likely to be interested, both the users and the service may benefit. For example, an exhibition is organized for a migrant group within the community and representatives from that group are invited to an opening. The opening receives publicity tailored both for the group and the community at large—in the media. This event will incur a cost, but a public relations professional probably has contacts who would consider sponsoring such an event. The sponsor and the service could be in a win-win situation. Businesses within local communities know that they benefit from demonstrating community involvement, and the senior management of organizations recognize that obtaining sponsorship is beneficial. Other forms of sponsorship can include prizes for events organized for young people. In turn, an information service may be able to offer sponsorship, incurring a small, visible cost by making a room available for a one-time community event.

Support is probably most needed when the service lobbies politicians and funding agencies about funding issues. Since politicians and agencies receive a large volume of mail and phone calls, skill and experience are necessary to catch their attention and make a convincing case. The American Library Association Web site provides templates for letters, which are very useful for small services with limited funding. In addition, it is always useful to know a friendly public relations person who might at times offer some pro bono advice.

Positive publicity requires patient cultivation and serious effort to package, which cost time and money. Publicity may be unpaid, but it's not free. Large public relations budgets do not always produce better results unless the outcomes are monitored and evaluated. Ideally, everyone on the staff acts as a salesperson or a press agent by being positive and highlighting the many worthwhile and fascinating activities which, after all, are characteristic of the service's operations. That is the essence of internal marketing that precedes external marketing.

KEY POINTS TO REMEMBER:

- Marketing is an essential element in the strategic plan of a successful information service.
- Marketing, in common with all managerial activities, requires time and careful thought.
- A sound marketing plan is based on generic product definition, target group definition, differential analysis, user behavior analysis, differential advantage analysis, multiple approaches, integration, feedback, and auditing.
- Internal marketing is essential.
- Branding a service is an important activity for projecting quality service.
- Public relations and communications management are related to, but different from, marketing activities.
- All marketing, promotion, and public relations activities should be monitored and evaluated.

REFERENCES

Alexander, Ralph S. 1961. *Marketing Definitions.* Chicago: American Marketing Association.

Andreasen, Allen, and Philip Kotler. 2003. *Strategic Marketing for Nonprofit Organizations.* 6th ed. Englewood Cliffs, NJ: Prentice-Hall.

"Boston PL Defends Reputation in Wake of Scathing Report." 2006. *American Libraries* 37, no. 5 (May): 19.

"Britain Launches Campaign to Transform Libraries' Image." 2006. *American Libraries* 37, no. 5 (May): 22.

Cavanagh, Mary. 2005. "Sensemaking a Public Library's Internet Policy Crisis." *Library Management* 26, nos. 6/7: 351–360.

Chartered Institute of Marketing. "Knowledge Hub: Marketing." (August 2006). Available: www.cim.org.uk/cim/ser/html

Cronin, Blaise, ed. 1992. *Marketing of Library and Information Services.* 2nd ed. London: Aslib.

Drucker, Peter. 1974. *Management Responsibilities: Practices.* New York: Harper & Row.

Elam, Houston, and Norton Paley. 1992. *Marketing for Nonmarketers.* New York: American Management Association.

Evans, Joel, and Barry Berman. 1985. *Marketing.* New York: Macmillan.

Fine, Seymour. 1990. *Social Marketing: Promoting the Causes of Public and Nonprofit Agencies.* Needham Heights, MA: Allyn and Bacon.

Fodness, Dale. 2005. "Rethinking Strategic Marketing," *Journal of Business Strategy* 26, no. 3: 20–34.

Forrest, Charles. 2005. "Segmenting the Library Market." *Georgia Library Quarterly* 42, no. 1: 4–7.

Gronroos, Christian. 1988. *Assessing Competitive Edge in the New Competition of the Service Economy.* Working Paper, no. 9. First Interstate Center for Services Marketing. Tempe, AZ: Arizona State University.

Jefkins, Frank. 1994. *Public Relations Techniques.* 2nd ed. Oxford. Butterworth Heinemann.

Kies, Cosette. 1987 *Marketing and Public Relations for Libraries.* Metuchen, NJ: Scarecrow Press.

Kotler, Philip. 1980. *Marketing Management Analysis: Planning and Control.* 4th ed. Englewood Cliffs, NJ: Prentice-Hall

Kotler, Philip, 1994. *Marketing Management Analysis: Planning and Control.* 8th ed. Englewood Cliffs, NJ: Prentice-Hall.

Kotler, Philip, and Allen Andreasen. 1996. *Strategic Marketing for Nonprofit Organizations.* 5th ed. Englewood Cliffs, NJ: Prentice-Hall.

Lee, Deborah. 2006. "Check Out the Competition: Marketing Lesson from Google." *Library Administration & Management* 20, no. 2 (Spring): 94–95.

Lee, Debra. 2004. "Market Segmentation and Libraries." *Library Administration and Management* 18, no. 1: 47–48.

Leventhal, Richard. 2005. "The Importance of Marketing." *Strategic Directions* 21, no. 6: 3–4.

McCormack, Mary J. 1980. *Marketing of Public Issues as Private Troubles.* Ann Arbor, MI: University Microfilms.

McDaniel, Carl D. 1996. *Contemporary Marketing Research*. 3rd ed. St. Paul, MN: West Publishing.

McNeal, James U. 1992. *Kids as Customers: A Handbook of Marketing to Children*. New York: Macmillan.

Morgan, David. 1998. *Planning Focus Groups*. Thousand Oaks, CA: Sage.

Nash, E. L. 1986. *Direct Marketing: Strategy, Planning, and Execution*. 2nd ed. New York: McGraw-Hill.

O'Keefe, Claudia. 2005. "Publicity 101." *American Libraries* 36, no. 6 (June): 52–54.

Porter, Michael. 1979. "How Competitive Forces Shape Strategy." *Harvard Business Review* 57, no. 3 (March–April): 137.

Ries, Al, and Jack Trout. 1986. *Marketing Warfare*. New York: McGraw-Hill.

Rowley, Jennifer. 2001. *Information Marketing*. Ashgate, UK: Aldershot.

Rowley, Jennifer. 2003. "Information Marketing: Seven Questions." *Library Management* 24, nos. 1/2: 13–19.

Savard, Rejean. 2000. *Adapting Marketing to Libraries in a Changing and World-Wide Environment*. Munich: K. G. Sauer.

Shontz, Marilyn, Jon C. Parker, and Richard Parker. 2004. "What Do Librarians Think About Marketing?" *Library Quarterly* 74, no. 1: 63–84.

Von Seggern, Marilyn, and Nancy J. Young. 2003. "The Focus Group Method in Libraries." *References Services Review* 31, no. 3: 272–284.

Walters, Suzanne. 1992. *Marketing: A How-to-Do-It Manual for Librarians*. New York: Neal-Schuman.

Weingand, Darlene. 1995. "Preparing for the New Millennium: The Case for Using Market Strategies." *Library Trends* 43, no. 3 (Winter): 296.

Weingand, Darlene. 1998. *Future-Driven Library Marketing*. Chicago: American Library Association.

Wood, Elizabeth J., and Victoria L. Young. 1988. *Strategic Marketing for Libraries*. New York: Greenwood Press.

Wright, Peter L. 1973. *Analyzing Consumer Judgment Strategies*. Urbana, IL: College of Commerce and Business Administration, University of Illinois at Urbana-Champaign.

LAUNCHING PAD

Broady-Preston, Judy, and Lucy Steel. 2002. "Internal Marketing Strategies in LIS." *Library Management* 23, nos. 6/7: 294–301.

Fisher, Patricia H., and Marseille M. Pride. 2005. *Blueprint for Our Library Marketing Plan: A Guide to Help You Survive and Thrive*. Chicago: American Library Association.

Gupta, Dinesh, Christie Koontz, Angela Massisimo, and Réjean Savard, eds. 2006. *Marketing Library and Information Services*. Munich: K.G. Saur.

Imhoff, Kathleen R., and Ruithie Maslin. 2006. *Library Contests: A How-To-Do-It Manual*. New York: Neal-Schuman.

Osif, Bonnie. 2006. "Branding, Marketing, and Fundraising." *Library Administration & Management* 20, no. 1: 39–43.

Padovan, Gabriella, and Daniel Nzekwu. 2006. "Marketing Libraries Services in a Global Corporate Environment." *Information Outlook* 10, no. 3 (March): 23–24.

Sen, Barbara. 2006. "Market Orientation: A Concept for Health Libraries." Health Information and Libraries Journal 23, no. 1: 23–31.

Thenell, Jan. 2004. *Library's Crisis Communications Planner: A PR Guide for Handling Every Emergency.* Chicago: American Library Association.

Varaprasad, N., Paul Johnson, and Lena Kua. 2006. "Gaining Mindshare and Timeshare: Marketing Public Libraries in Singapore." *Australian Public Libraries and Information Services* 19, no. 1: 31–38.

Yankelovich, Daniel, and David Meer. 2006. "Rediscovering Market Segmentation." *Harvard Business Review* 84, no. 2 (February): 122–131.

6

Change and Innovation

"The value of an idea lies in using it."

Thomas Alva Edison

"Tell me and I'll forget, show me and I may remember, involve me and I'll understand."

Chinese proverb

INTRODUCTION

Change and innovation relate, in one way or another, to almost every topic in this book. Change is inevitable in one's personal and work life. People, technology, plans, organizational structure, and culture environment all change. The list could go on and on, but the point is that change is pervasive. Its pace varies—sometimes it happens rapidly, sometimes slowly—but change happens. Effectively handling change is of one a manager's more challenging tasks that is never finished.

One truth about today's organizational environment is that change is ubiquitous and constant. Another truth is that successful organizations address change head-on in a proactive manner. As we stated in Chapter 3, monitoring the operating environment is a key to anticipating what changes may surface and allows the opportunity to think about what organizational adjustments might be necessary. Part of your responsibility is to assist staff in accepting and effectively handling change. At times an organization will face a situation that calls for innovative/creative ideas to make a sharp break with the past. Just as managers should foster a work environment that is accepting of change, they should also create an atmosphere that promotes and encourages innovation and creative thinking.

107

NATURE OF CHANGE

"There is nothing more difficult to take in hand, more perilous to conduct, or more uncertain in its success than to take the lead in the introduction of a new order of things" (Machiavelli, 1952: 52). Organizational change takes place across a continuum from incremental to radical. "New orders" (radical) factors may be present for organizations as conditions change. On the other hand, every day small incremental changes occur as the external and internal environments change. Staff members deal with change on a daily basis and without realizing they are doing so. The vast majority of the changes are so small as to be unnoticeable. It is change beyond the midpoint that creates the challenge. In this chapter, we address both the management of change and ways in which to generate changes working within the organizational framework.

Leslie Szamosi and Linda Duxbury (2002: 186) explored the continuum of change and defined radical change as something that:

- interrupts the status quo
- happens quickly or abruptly
- is fundamental and all encompassing
- brings something that is dramatically different from what used to be

Clearly such change does not happen often in an organization, but obviously it would challenge the skill of almost any manager. Most changes are at a lesser level. However, even at the incremental stage, staff may need support during the change process. Some examples of incremental change are the resignation and hiring of a replacement staff member, an adjustment in the work schedule, a shift in the timing of work activities, and the appointment of a new department head. Such changes are natural and as important to organizational success as larger scale changes, and they require thought and attention to make them not appear as "a change" to the staff.

Beyond the character of change (incremental to radical) you can fit almost all organizational change into one of four broad categories—people, technology, structure, and strategy. Some changes may represent a

---

Something to Ponder:

What are some of the change areas in technology, structure, and strategy for information services? Thinking about your current or recent work experience, what forces of change did you observe?

single type while others are combinations; the more categories in a change situation, the more complex the change process becomes. A few examples of the areas where "people change" occurs are skills, activities/performance, attitudes, perceptions, and of course replacement (including transfer, promotion, resignation, and retirement, etc.).

MANAGING CHANGE

Moran and Brightman (2001: 111) defined change management as "the process of continually renewing the organization's direction, structure, and capabilities to serve the ever-changing needs of external and internal customers." An interesting article by Brown and Mark (2005: 73), reporting on focus group sessions with librarians regarding organizational change suggests librarians are well aware of the need to manage change: "It is particularly interesting to note that the study's participants spoke consistently in positive terms about successful change mechanisms." It takes little thought to understand how McWilliam and Ward-Griffin's (2006: 119) opening statement applies to libraries and information services: "Declining resources and organizational restructuring distract attention from efforts to develop more client-centered, empowering partnership approaches to health and social services."

Research into organizational change has brought to light the notion that nearly 70 percent of change programs fail to achieve all or most of their objectives (for example, Kotter, 1990; Higgs and Rowland, 2000). That figure is surprising at first glance and almost unbelievable; however, when you think about it, how many times does one read about failures compared to announcements of success? Few of us like to announce a failed effort. Also, remember the statistic covers "all or most" of the objectives; thus a partial success counts as a failure as defined. Regardless of what the count of failures should or should not include, why is total success difficult to achieve?

Part of the answer is, of course, people's resistance to change (more about that later in the chapter). Perhaps an equally significant factor lies with the traditional way in which managers are taught to think about change. Recent research suggests that long-standing models (Lewin's and Kotter's, for example) are no longer fully sufficient for managing change (for example, Higgs and Rowland, 2005; Burnes, 2004; Black, 2000; Fitzgerald, 2002). The sense is that, at best, managers have an understanding of how to address complicated change, as opposed to complex change.

Senior (2006) outlined three categories of change (rate of occurrence, what triggers it, and its scale) that help gain a sense of the complexity of change. In the past, there was a view that successful/effective organizations were highly stable (infrequent change). Clearly, in today's world just the opposite is the case. Success comes from ongoing monitoring of the operating environment and making appropriate adjustments.

A review of the total body of change literature shows it to be dominated (obviously due to the high number of older items) by discussions of planned and emergent change (rate of occurrence). However, the area of planned and emergent change is where change management models were developed, such as Lewin's (1951) classic model. No one disagrees that planned change is desirable or possible in many cases, nor is there disagreement regarding the desirability of understanding the "states" an organizations goes through in order to achieve such change. However, some important limits do exist regarding the models' utility.

Before exploring the limits, it is useful have some knowledge of the three most widely discussed models for planned change: Lewin, Kotter, and Bullock and Batten. Kurt Lewin's change model (1951) was one of the first and it is certainly the most commonly thought of when it comes to change management. His forced-field analysis has become a classic model for thinking about organizational change. Most changes are to be permanent or at least exist for a specified period (planned long-term). Presenting a change to the staff as "an experiment" is a good way to cause it to fail. "Why bother with an experiment? Doesn't management know what they're doing?" are very common reactions. Lewin, a sociologist, noted in many cases in his research that change often lasted only a brief time before people reverted, as much as possible, to their former ways. Lewin suggested that if a person's behavior is to change, three interrelated conditions must occur: unfreezing, changing, and refreezing.

Unfreezing is the process of creating a readiness to acquire or learn new behaviors. For managers planning change, this means assisting staff in recognizing the ineffectiveness of the current behavior in terms of the area of the planned change. It also means pointing out how the change will be more effective. Unfreezing staff may be very time-consuming, and without gaining their active participation, it is very, very difficult. Not only do people need to adjust, in many cases so does the organizational culture.

Changing is the period when staff begins to work with the new behavior pattern. There will be a testing period while they make their assessment of the new pattern. Managers must be watchful during this period as staff may begin to slip back into the old pattern. Managers also should be even more supportive than normal to encourage people to make the adjustments.

Refreezing takes place when the staff internalizes the new pattern and it becomes part of the organizational culture. Rewards for implementing the new pattern are a key factor in achieving refreezing.

Lewin developed these three conditions from his forced-field analysis concept. The concept involves a person, unit, or organization and how he/she/it must overcome the status quo or state of equilibrium in order to

Figure 6.1 Lewin's Forced-Field Concept		
Change	Status Quo	No Change
Driving Forces $\rightarrow$	Equilibrium $\leftarrow$	Restraining Forces

change. He suggested that two sets of forces are at work to maintain the equilibrium: driving forces and restraining forces (see Figure 6.1). For changes to occur, the driving forces must be greater than the restraining forces.

John Kotter (1990) expanded Lewin's three-phase model by breaking each condition down into smaller steps/activities. During the unfreezing process he suggested that managers should establish a sense of urgency, create a "guiding" coalition, develop a vision and strategy for the change, and finally communicate the vision and strategy. His subconditions for the change phase are empower a broad base for action, identify/create some short-term "wins" for people, and consolidate gains (don't declare victory too soon). The only difference for the refreezing stage is that Kotter points out that it may take years for change(s) to be anchored and become a part of the organizational culture.

Bullock and Batten (1985) put forward a four-phase model for planned change: exploration, planning, action, and integration. Their model looks at the process and phases of change and what an organization must do in order to achieve a successful transition.

Something to Ponder:

Think about successful and unsuccessful change(s) you have experienced in an organization. What factors can you identify that led to either the success or failure? Did the manager(s) employ elements of the change models?

As we indicated, planned change models have a long history, and are generally viewed as having value in managing some forms of change within certain limits. Perhaps the most significant limit is that they focus on small-scale or incremental change, and thus are of limited value at the other end of the change spectrum. Second, there is an assumption that the organization's operational environment is relatively stable and therefore would make a smooth transition from one stable state to another. Such an assumption seems less and less valid in today's world. Third, the models do not apply well, if at all, to crisis situations where consultation, widespread involvement, and the like are neither possible nor appropriate. Finally, critics suggest that the approach does not give adequate weight to staff resistance and instead gives too much to the notion of staff agreement/acceptance.

We should note a newer, related approach: "emergent change." The essential point in the emergent model is that one should not think of change as a linear process through time. Rather, one should think in terms of an open-ended process in which unexpected turns/events are normal (the unpredictability factor). Thinking this way, say advocates (for example, Burnes, 2004; Bamford and Forrester, 2003), allows one to cope more effectively with complexity and uncertainty. Another aspect of the concept is the need to have a staff that is open to learning.

Returning to the last of Senior's three categories of change—scale—there is less difference of opinion. Scale is the variation along the change continuum. A commonly accepted way to think about scale is as four distinct points: fine tuning, incremental adjustments, modular transformation, and corporate/organizational transformation. The first two points are easy to understand; the difference between modular and organizational transformation is that the former refers to a single component of an organization.

Rune Todnem (2005: 378) summed up the case regarding a high failure rate for change efforts:

> This may indicate a basic lack of a valid framework of how to successfully implement and manage organizational change since what is currently available is a wide range of contradictory and confusing theories and approaches.

Check This Out:

A good recent guide to change management in libraries is by Susan Curzon's 2006 *Managing Change: A How-To-Do-It Manual for Librarians* (New York: Neal-Schuman Publishers).

RESISTANCE TO CHANGE

One fact managers must keep in mind is that, while resistance to change is inevitable, there is no definite means of knowing who will resist and how strong that resistance will be. Some people seem to thrive on change, and some prefer never to change. Occasionally, people switch roles, creating an unexpected challenge for the manager. Knowing exactly what circumstances and what type of change will trigger acceptance or resistance is difficult at best.

What are some of the issues in resistance? When faced with a greater-than-incremental change, people normally go through a four-stage process:

denial, resistance, exploration, and commitment. Denial may take the form of "It will not impact me." Another common response is either "Why is this necessary?" or "This is unnecessary." When people realize that change will take place, some will actively resist, some will unknowingly resist, and a few will move on to the next stage on their own. Exploration is the first phase of actively accepting the need to change and starting to look at how it will impact personal activities. The final phase is actively working toward making the process a success.

People resist change for a number reasons that are all some variation of fear. An obvious variation relates to job or wage security ("What will happen to my job?"). Change generally brings uncertainty that goes well beyond one's job. Today's status quo is known and is, to a greater or lesser degree, comfortable (the unknown can be worrisome). "What will happen to my work relationships?" is a common issue. Possible loss of control may play a role for some people (for example, one's status, power, and future prospects).

Change often calls for new duties that may require learning new skills. Learning anxiety is a very real issue for many people ("Can I learn what is required?" "Will I look incompetent in front of my peers?"). The anxiety can lead to serious resistance when something like a new software package is introduced.

Kegan and Lahey (2001: 85) describe a form of resistance that is frequently unrecognized because it occurs with people who appear to be committed to change. "Many people are unwittingly applying productive energy toward a hidden *competing commitment*" (emphasis in original). One example the authors give is a project manager who is "dragging his feet" on a project due to a stronger and unrecognized competing commitment (avoidance)—the fear that the next project will be beyond his capabilities. They acknowledge that overcoming such hidden commitments is difficult because "it challenges the very psychological foundation upon which people function" (Kegan and Lahey, 2001: 86). Kegan and Lahey's article is well worth reading before you undertake a major change.

Something to Ponder:

Think about the ways that people demonstrate resistance to change; then consider a change situation you experienced. What, if any, forms of resistance did you feel and/or engage in?

Lack of information, or poor communication, is another cause of resistance. The more you explain the exact nature of change and listen to staff concerns, the less likely the staff are to resist actively. Open and honest communication is a key component to achieving a successful change.

People who understand the change and its necessity are more accepting of change than those who do not understand. Related to that understanding is the sense of having a say about the change. Managers must realize that some valid resistance develops when people identify flaws in the proposed change. Pointing out potential or perceived problem areas is not always a method for passively resisting or delaying a change. It may identify an important, but overlooked problem area.

Basic Steps for Addressing Resistance to Change:

- develop a plan
- communicate the need to change and communicate the plan
- build trust (use existing trust)
- identify potential benefits
- openly acknowledge any potential drawbacks
- empower people by securing their input and modifications to the plan
- provide active encouragement, support training, and resources to ensure success

---

John Kotter and Leonard Schlesinger (1979) provided four realistic suggestions for managing resistance to change. In fact, the four points are good management tools for almost any purpose:

- education plus communication
- participation plus involvement
- facilitation plus support
- negotiation and agreement

If implemented, these points allow access to information that only the staff may have, commitment to a change that they helped design, and acceptance of necessary compromises that they helped to reach.

IMPLEMENTING CHANGE

Because organizational change is inevitable, managers must understand more about change than just how to overcome resistance. One useful concept in the field is organizational developmen, a method for generating both individual and organizational change. Organizational development is a planned change technique, however, so it does have limits.

> **Check This Out:**
>
> The classic text on organizational development is Richard Beckhard's 1969 *Organization Development: Strategies and Models* (Reading, MA: Addison-Wesley).

Organizational development's primary focus is on people who are or will be undergoing an organizational change process. Some of the most frequent uses of organizational development are assisting with mergers, managing conflict, and revitalizing organizations. Although information services may not be for-profit, at times they may engage in merger-like activities—for example, merging departments, such as serials and acquisitions. It is not uncommon for conflict to develop during such actions. Technology can be a disruptive force at times in the workplace, and conflicts often arise when a new technology or software package is introduced. When an information service decides to shift to a new integrated library system, change is organization-wide and, if all goes well, the organization is revitalized. Organizational development techniques can assist with such challenges.

Fundamental, long-lasting change is the primary goal of organizational development. Another significant point is that the techniques are rooted in humanistic psychology (McKendall, 1993); as such, organizational development is often better left to the trained consultant rather than to a manager with only modest understanding of the methods.

STRESS AND THE ORGANIZATION

In 1936 Hans Selye introduced his concepts of General Adaptation Syndrome. He defined stress as a bodily reaction to any positive or negative stimuli. A more detailed definition by Charles Bunge is "a person's psychological and physiological response to the perception of a demand or challenge. The nature and intensity of this response depends upon the meaning one gives to that demand or challenge and on one's assessment of the resources that are available for meeting it" (Bunge, 1989: 93).

Excessive stress, personal or organizational, can diminish health and thereby adversely affect work productivity; however, "less agreement exists regarding the effects of stress on organizational effectiveness" (Zaccaro and Riley, 1987: 1). Some management researchers, such as James Quick (1992), suggest that organizational and staff stress is not necessarily bad. J. E. McGrath (1976) showed that in the workplace there is an inverted-U relationship between stress and performance. That is, when there is little or no stress, staff are in a state of boredom and performance/productivity is low as well. As stress increases, so does performance up to a point (after which it falls). Using a scale of 0 to 100 for the level of stress, somewhere near the midpoint in stress, performance begins to fall off and drop back to the low point, indicating boredom. The issue for management is to find the right level and type of stress to have maximum performance and not go beyond that point.

For many people, the response to too much stress is physiological, often taking the form of illness. Undoubtedly, stress contributes to mental illness, alcoholism, and drug and other substance abuse, as well as to other dysfunctional conditions that lead to poor job performance. It is also clear that stress is not just work-related. People can usually cope effectively when either personal or workplace stress is low, but problems develop when both are high. When coping strategies fail, burnout is often the result. Stress, distress, strain, and burnout are a continuum of:

- a condition wherein, on the whole, challenges are sources of happiness and productive responses
- a condition wherein perceived imbalances between demands and re- sources are painful, but coping strategies restore the balance and reduce the pain
- a condition where inappropriate coping strategies are out of control (i.e., are contributing to the problem); and the person's physical and mental resources are depleted (Bunge, 1990: 94)

Part of the challenge comes from the fact that what is stressful for one person may not be stressful for another. Thus, there is no way to list what will or will not be stressful in the workplace for everyone, nor is there a single "cure" that will resolve all stress. Some methods of coping can be taught, such as relaxation, meditation, and biofeedback. While these techniques are individualized and no organizational support is necessary, some large orga- nizations do offer training courses in these techniques to interested staff.

Stress is personal; it is difficult for a person or manager to discover whether a profession is significantly more stressful than another field. David Fisher claims, based on critical analysis of stress and burnout studies in the library profession published since 1980, that there is no empirical evidence that stress and burnout are any higher in library services than in similar professions (Fisher, 1990).

For Further Thought:

Managers need to know themselves. Can you identify any symptoms of stress that you have experienced? What action have you taken to overcome stress?

As one might expect, stress can be a significant factor in the change process and a major contributor to workplace burnout.

Check These Out:

Maria Vakola and Ioannis Nikolaou's excellent 2005 article "Attitudes Towards Organizational Change" (*Employee Relations* 27, no. 2: 160–174) addresses change, stress, and commitment. Karen Brown and Kate Marek's 2005 "Librarianship and Change" (*Library Administration & Management* 19, no. 2 [Spring]: 68–74) is a fine piece examining change and librarians.

INNOVATION AND INFORMATION SERVICES

What is the difference between creativity and innovation? The most straightforward answer is that creativity is the process of producing/generating new ideas while innovation is about implementing a new idea in an organization. Thus it is possible to be "innovative" through the introduction of a new idea for your organization even if the idea itself has existed for some time and or has been used in other organizations.

Based on literature review, Wang and Ahmed (2004) identified five areas of typical organizational innovativeness: product, market/service, process, behavioral, and strategic. In an academic library, an example of product innovation might be developing the concept of an electronic "institutional repository" for the parent institution. In terms of market/service innovation, it might be to offer faculty members office-delivery of documents (in-person or electronic). From a process point of view, ceasing to check in serials (we do know of one such case) might qualify as innovative. A behavioral example might be greeting everyone when they enter the library or archives and perhaps offering jelly beans or mints sponsored by a local company. A strategic innovation might be to shift from an institution-wide service focus to a tailored service focus—including staffing—aimed at a college, school, institute, etc.

Test Your Innovativeness:

Think of additional innovative ideas for an academic library you are familiar with. Pick another type of information service and try to come up with some ideas for each of the five areas.

Voelpel, Leibold, and Streb (2005: 57) correctly concluded that "recent academic and business evidence indicates that innovation is the key factor for companies' success and sustained fitness in a rapidly evolving, knowledge-networked economy." In their article they describe how one company, 3M, known for its innovations, fosters innovative thinking and actions. Although libraries and information services may not be able to set as clear a target for innovations as does 3M (30 percent of future sales should come from products that did not exist four years earlier), the principle is relevant to their situation—thinking about and acting innovatively. Statements such as 3M's make it very clear that senior management not only desires innovative ideas, but they expect and demand them. Senior managers in information services will demonstrate that they are either for or against innovation, even without thinking or knowing they are doing so. Top management values and beliefs are the key to whether an organization is innovative.

Check This Out:

An older but still very informative resource on innovation and information services is Carmel Maguire, Edward Kazlauskas, and Anthony Weir's 1994 *Information Services for Innovative Organizations* (San Diego, CA: Academic Press).

Anyone managing change must devote some thought to innovation as part of the change process. Does one want to be on the incremental end of the continuum—adopting ideas that are successfully and widely used in other libraries? Does one want to move toward the center, by using an idea that has a successful track record in other types of organizations, but has not yet been tried in a library? Or, does one want to be *the* innovator (on the radical end of the change continuum) by applying new knowledge to a library or information center product or service?

Assuming that you want to encourage original or at least new thinking on the part of the staff, what organizational and supervisory steps can you take? Research confirms what many individuals claimed and believed for a long time: an inflexible, tightly structured, and stratified organization (bureaucracy) frustrates innovation and encourages mediocrity. Encouraging original/new thinking about activities, processes, and issues confronting the organization can be very beneficial.

We suggested earlier that organizational culture plays a significant role in the success or failure of organizational change. Organizational culture influences creativity and innovation in at least two ways:

- Through shared values and norms, people make judgments and assumptions regarding the acceptability of creative/innovative behavior within the organization.
- Established forms of behavior and activity, especially as reflected in practices and procedures, lead people to develop perceptions about valued and nonvalued behaviors and activities (Martins and Terblanche, 2003: 68).

Other factors that encourage organizational innovation include:

- socialization regarding acceptable work behavior
- values related to acceptability of risk taking
- flexibility in actions and thinking
- freedom and encouragement to explore new ideas;
- cooperative, empowered work teams
- support from management
- treatment of mistakes as opportunities for learning rather than punishment
- tolerance of conflict as natural and useful in developing new ideas
- open and honest communication

Check This Out:

Charles O'Reilly and Michael Tushman produced an informative article in 2004, "The Ambidextrous Organization" (*Harvard Business Review* 82, no. 4 [April]: 74–81), on the subject of innovation and organizational culture.

What can the small organization do to encourage innovative thinking? The typical small public or school library is staffed by one professional, with perhaps a paraprofessional or volunteer to help. Sometimes the person is completely alone. Certainly such a situation can encourage stagnation, because the stimulation of working with professional peers is lacking. In such a situation, material about new ideas and their managerial applications is of utmost importance. It takes considerable mental stimulation to keep up with professional standards and to continue personal creative growth. At the least, one should keep up with the profession through journals and conferences to avoid settling into a dull, unimaginative routine. Outside hobbies broaden a person's scope and provide a wide source of ideas, and the interaction of two or more interests may spark a synthesis (idea linking) leading to an innovative idea.

Within the service (regardless of size), management will need to make special efforts to encourage innovation on the part of subordinates. In any unit of an organization, it is easy to overcontrol. Such an approach does provide the stable environment so often sought by senior management, yet the best method for generating new ideas is to encourage independent thinking and responsibility in subordinates. The more that subordinates feel a part of the unit's decisions and functions, the better the quality of their production (due to increased feelings of commitment and accomplishment). Because customer requirements shape library services and assist in maintaining programs that meet long-term user needs, customer input should be sought as well.

INNOVATION TECHNIQUES

Some techniques can assist an individual in generating new ideas/thoughts about ways of behaving or doing things. These operational techniques help people to overcome their fear of using their imaginations by enabling them to move back to the childhood pattern of asking "why," "what if," and "how." They then explore their environment to find the answers. Table 6.1 provides some suggestions for how to encourage staff to think in new ways. Table 6.2 outlines some of the basic "rules" for helping to ensure that the techniques are as successful as possible.

Table 6.1 **Some Techniques to Foster New Thinking**	
Logical/Problem-Solving Approach	• Start with a defined situation/activity. • Identify all elements of the situation/activity. • List all possible changes/options. • Consider each change/option against others. • Assess consequences.
Input-Output	• Identify desired outcome in broad terms. • List all possible changes/options that could lead to desired outcome. • Assess consequences.
Free Association/Brainstorming	• Provide a very general frame of reference for discussion (do *not* define the problem). • Encourage any and all thoughts even tangentially related to the topic under consideration. • Assess ideas after the flow of ideas/thoughts ceases.
These methods work best with small groups.	

Table 6.2
Basic "Rules" to Encourage New Thinking

- Treat group sessions as ongoing rather than one-time events. Staff members need time to adjust and realize that the purpose, value, and intent of management is serious.

- Keep group size small to encourage wide participation (five to seven people seems to work best).

- Provide serious, thoughtful, honest feedback to group about their ideas. Lack of such response tends to raise doubts about management's intent.

- Monitor early group discussions to ensure that no "judgments" are made during the idea generation phase of the process. Negative/judgmental reactions will kill the process.

Try These:

How free are you in your thinking? Here are two opportunities to review how structured your thinking may be.

1. How many squares is it possible to form by connecting the dots? Lines connecting the dots must stay within the grid.

```
•    •    •    •

•    •    •    •

•    •    •    •

•    •    •    •
```

2. List as many uses as you can for a brick. Do not take more than five minutes. See the last page of this chapter for the answers.

The successful management of innovation and change builds upon an understanding of how the service developed over time. We can only comprehend the present by examining the past. In addition, an awareness of the environment in which the service operates is necessary, together with data and information derived from a marketing program. The introduction of change and innovation depends on effective decision making, which will be considered in Chapter 7.

KEY POINTS TO REMEMBER:

- Change is enviable.
- Change is essential.
- Change is a managerial challenge.
- Change is either reactive or proactive.
- Change takes place along a continuum—incremental to radical.
- Change most often happens in terms of people, technology, structure, and/or strategy.
- Change will generate resistance.
- Change process models assist but do not completely solve organizational issues.
- Change management is an important managerial activity.
- Innovation may lead to uncertain outcomes, but those often are rewarding.
- Innovation and change are complex processes.
- Innovation is knowledge-intensive.
- Innovative/new ways of staff thinking can be developed.
- Innovation can be controversial (benefit or boondoggle).
- Innovation requires risk-taking.
- Innovation and effective change flourishes in flexible, open, learning-oriented, empowered organizations.

REFERENCES

Bamford, David, and Paul Forrester. 2003. "Managing Planned and Emergent Change Within an Operations Management Environment." *International Journal of Operations & Production Management* 23, no. 5/6: 546–564.

Beckhard, Richard. 1969. *Organization Development: Strategies and Models*. Reading, MA: Addison-Wesley.

Black, Janice A. 2000. "Fermenting Change." *Journal of Organizational Change Management* 13, no. 6: 520–525.

Brown, Karen, and Kate Marek. 2005. "Librarianship and Change: A Consideration of Weick's 'Drop Your Tools' Metaphor." *Library Administration & Management* 19, no. 2 (Spring): 68–74.

Bullock, R. J., and Donde Batten. 1985. "It's Just a Phase We're Going Through." *Group & Organizational Studies* 10, no. 4 (December): 383–412.

Bunge, Charles. 1989. "Stress in the Library Workplace." *Library Trends* 38, no. 1 (Summer): 93–102.

Burnes, Bernard. 2004. "Kurt Lewin and Complexity Theories." *Journal of Change Management* 4, no. 4 (December): 309–325.

————. 2004. *Managing Change*. 4th ed. New York: Prentice-Hall.

Curzon, Susan C. 2006. *Managing Change: A How-To-Do-It Manual for Librarians.* Rev. ed. New York: Neal-Schuman.

Fisher, David. 1990. "Are Librarians Burning Out?" *Journal of Librarianship* 22, no. 4 (October): 216–235.

Fitzgerald, Laurie A. 2002. "Chaos: The Lens that Transcends." *Journal of Organizational Change Management* 15, no. 4: 339–358.

Higgs, Malcom, and Deborah Rowland. 2000. "Building Change Capability." *Journal of Change Management* 1, no. 2 (June): 116–131.

————. 2005. "All Changes Great and Small." *Journal of Change Management* 5, no. 2 (June): 121–151.

Kegan, Robert, and Lisa Laskow Lahey. 2001. "The Real Reason People Won't Change." *Harvard Business Review* 79, no. 10 (October): 85–92.

Kotter, John. 1990. *A Force of Change: How Leadership Differs From Management.* New York: Simon & Schuster.

Kotter, John, and Leonard Schlesinger. 1979. "Choosing Strategies for Change." *Harvard Business Review* 57, no. 2 (February): 106–114.

Lewin, Kurt. 1951. *Field Theory in Social Sciences.* New York: Harper & Row.

Machiavelli, Niccolo. 1952. *The Prince.* New York: New American Library.

Maguire, Carmel, Edward Kazlauskas, and Anthony Weir. 1994. *Information Services for Innovative Organizations.* San Diego, CA: Academic Press.

Martins, E. C., and F. Terblanche. 2003. "Building Organizational Culture that Stimulates Creativity and Innovation." *European Journal of Innovation Management* 6, no. 1: 64–74.

McGrath, Joseph E. 1976. "Stress and Behavior in Organizations." In *Handbook of Industrial and Organizational Psychology,* edited by Marvin D. Dunnette. Chicago: Rand McNally.

McKendall, Marie. 1993. "The Tyranny of Change." *Journal of Business Ethics* 12, no. 2: 93–104.

McWilliam, Carol L., and Catherine Ward-Griffin. 2006. "Implementing Organizational Change in Health and Social Services." *Journal of Organizational Change Management* 19, no. 2: 119–135.

Moran, John, and Baird Brightman. 2001. "Leading Organizational Change." *Career Development International* 6, no. 2: 111–119.

O'Reilly, Charles, and Michael Tushman. 2004. "The Ambidextrous Organization." *Harvard Business Review* 82, no. 4 (April): 74–81.

Quick, James. 1992. *Stress and Well-Being in the Workplace.* Washington, DC: American Psychological Association.

Senior, Barbara. 2006. *Organizational Change.* 3rd ed. New York: Prentice-Hall.

Szamosi, Leslie, and Linda Duxbury. 2002. "Development of a Measure to Assess Organizational Change." *Journal of Organizational Change Management* 15, no. 2: 184–201.

Todnem, Rune. 2005. "Organizational Change Management." *Journal of Change Management* 5, no. 4: 369–380.

Vakola, Maria, and Ioannis Nikolaou. 2005. "Attitudes Towards Organizational Change." *Employee Relations* 27, no. 2: 160–174.

Voelpel, Sven C., Marius Leibold, and Christoph K. Streb. 2005. "The Innovation Meme: Managing Innovation Replicators for Organizational Fitness." *Journal of Change Management* 5, no. 1: 57–69.

Wang, Catherine, and Pervaiz Ahmed. 2004. "The Development and Validation of the Organizational Innovativeness Construct Using Confirmatory Factor Analysis." *European Journal of Innovation Management* 7, no. 4: 303–313.

Zaccaro, Stephen, and Ann Riley. 1987. "Stress, Coping, and Organizational Effectiveness." In *Occupational Stress and Organizational Effectiveness*, edited by Stephen Zaccaro and Ann Riley (1–18). New York: Praeger.

LAUNCHING PAD

Curzon, Susan Carol. 2006. *Managing Change.* Rev. ed. New York: Neal-Schuman.

Hatzakis, Tally, Mark Lycett, Robert D. Macredie, and Valerie A. Martin. 2005. "Toward the Development of a Social Capital Approach to Evaluating Change Management Interventions." *European Journal of Information Systems* 14, no. 1 (March): 60–74.

Jeal, Yvette. 2005. "Re-Engineering Customer Services: University of Salford Information Services Division." *New Library World* 106, nos. 7/8: 352–362.

Konings, Kees, and Ronald Dekker. 2005. "Strategy and Change Management in Delft University of Technology." *New Review of Information Networking* 11, no. 1 (May): 109–121.

Linstead, Stephen, Joanna Brewis, and Alison Linstead. 2005. "Gender in Change: Gendering Change." *Journal of Organizational Change Management* 18, no. 6: 542–560.

Schachter, Debbie. 2005. "Creative Chaos: Innovation in Special Libraries." *Information Outlook* 9, (12 December): 10–11.

Smith, Ian. 2006. "Continuing Professional Development and Workplace Learning 14: Communicating in Times of Change." *Library Management* 27, no. 1: 108–113.

ANSWERS TO EXERCISES

- The number of squares is 32. Think beyond the boundaries of the dots. Consider the diagonals.
- If you listed more than 25 uses for a brick, you did better than 90 percent of the people doing the exercise. If you listed one or more uses that reshaped the brick in some way, you did better than 98 percent. Most people do not think about reshaping the brick, and when they hear that someone else did so, they will say, "But you did not say we could change its shape." The response to that is, "You were not told you could not reshape it." Too often, we impose limits on ourselves when dealing with problems. Sometimes one must try to "break the brick."

7

Decision Making

"Even a correct decision is wrong when it was taken too late."
Lee Iacocca

"Risk comes from not knowing what you are doing."
Warren Buffet

INTRODUCTION

Napoleon is reputed to have said, "Nothing is more difficult and therefore more precious than the ability to decide." Whether he said this or not does not change the fact that the sentiment is accurate. A significant factor in your career is how well you handle problems, problem solving, and decision making. Related to those issues are the topics of Chapter 6, innovation and change.

Everyone makes decisions both on and off the job. We also develop a personal approach to both decision making and problem solving. An obvious difference between personal and workplace decision making is the number of people impacted by the quality of the decision(s).

Rogers and Blenko (2006: 52) wrote that "Decisions are the coin of the realm . . . Every success, every mishap; every opportunity seized or missed is the result of a decision someone made or failed to make." In a broad sense, decision making underlies all managerial action. Before one develops a plan, a decision takes place regarding the plan's goal(s). A unit does not hire someone until there is a decision regarding the required and desired skills and abilities of the successful candidate. Managers and supervisors monitor work performance based on decisions made about acceptable and unacceptable performance. The list could go on and on, but the point is clear that decision making is a part of daily work life. Management folklore aside, decision making occurs at all levels in an organization. Staff members, no matter at what level, do make some decisions.

Herbert Simon, in his classic studies of organizational behavior, stated that behavior involves both unconscious and conscious selections of actions (Simon, 1976). Furthermore, the conscious actions (such as those taken in planning) are decisions that one can, and should, analyze. Henry Mintzberg (1976: 55) described some of the complexities of decision making, and elaborated on what he meant by dynamic factors:

> Decision-making processes are stopped by interruptions, delayed and speeded up by timing factors, and forced to branch and cycle. These processes are, therefore, dynamic ones of importance. Yet it is the dynamic factors that the ordered sequential techniques of analysis (problem solving) are least able to handle. Thus, despite their important analysis, the dynamic factors go virtually without mention in the literature of management science.

DECISIONS AND ACCOUNTABILITY

Most decision-making situations consist of a number of variables that interact in unpredictable ways (dynamic factors as well as uncertainty). Thus, people will make the wrong decision occasionally. Some people do not like to make mistakes, so they try to avoid problematic decisions. Essentially they hope to avoid accountability for decisions that go wrong. From an organizational point of view, someone must be accountable. Accountability and committee/group decision making do not always go well together unless there is careful planning and understanding of the issues by all group members.

Accountability is a fact of life for any manager, and decision making normally calls for clear-cut accountability. Accountability is one reason that committee decision making may well be dangerous. Some years ago, for example, the *Los Angeles Times* published a news story that summarized the problem of committee decision making and accountability. The University of California is a large university system, and like many U.S. academic institutions it employs the committee format for many decision-making processes. At the time, there was concern about the English language entrance requirement for undergraduate admission to the University of California. The university established a system-wide committee to make a decision about which high school courses would meet the university's entrance requirements. Eventually, the university sent letters to California high schools announcing that journalism, speech, and drama courses would no longer satisfy the entrance requirement. Naturally, there were objections to the decision, especially from high school journalism teachers. In an attempt to learn when and how the decision came about, a *Los Angeles Times* reporter interviewed members of the committee that presumably made the decision as well as university officials, all of whom could not remember making such a decision. The reporter concluded the article by saying "the result: a circle of accused, bemused, and slightly embarrassed designated decision makers in search of an important decision that no one says he made. And yet a decision was made. Minutes of a June 3 committee meeting of the statewide Academic Senate say so!" (Speich, 1976: 34).

Problems such as the one described above occur in most organizations from time to time. Certainly, they occur most often when the organization makes extensive use of committees. However, one will also encounter situations in which the only decision maker involved remembers neither how, when, nor whether he or she made the decision. Unfortunately, the issue of ultimate accountability does not disappear.

Try This:

Think back to a major decision in your personal life. Do you consider that you made a good decision for yourself? For others involved? Do you feel that you are a good decision maker? Try to identify the reasons for your responses

---

DECISION-MAKING ENVIRONMENT

The unpredictability or uncertainty that surrounds most decision making, as well as the accountability factor (at least organizationally), means that a person has to assume some degree of risk with each decision. Throughout life we develop a "risk tolerance," which varies over time and according to risk-taking experiences. Buchanan and O'Connell (2006: 34) stated that "risk is an inescapable part of every decision. For most of the everyday choices people make, the risks are small. But on a corporate scale, the implications (both upside and downside) can be enormous."

Thinking about risk-taking, ambiguity, and conflict tolerance levels as a continuum helps one assess personal and staff levels of comfort with making decisions. (The continuum also helps in assessing such things as resistance to change, conflict management, and planning.) At one end of the scale is "flight," at the opposite end is "fight," with a midpoint of "flow."

Individuals at the flight end avoid risk, confrontation, and change as much as they can. Everyone, at times, faces a situation when flight is undoubtedly the best action to take. However, one should not become like

Linus in the *Peanuts* (1963) cartoon where he said, "This is a distinct philosophy of mine. No problem is so big or complicated that it can't be run away from." In the organizational setting, as far as decision making is concerned, a typical "flight" behavior is procrastination. How often have you heard, "We are still waiting for a decision," with regard to a problematic issue? Although it is not always the case, very often the "wait" is in fact decision avoidance in action. "Needing additional information" can also be an avoidance mechanism while not appearing so. Occasionally a decision-making situation will pass without the need to decide; however, such a situation is very rare in an organization. More often than not some decision is better than no decision.

Fight-inclined individuals see opportunities/challenges in change and decision making. They have confidence in their skills, accept occasional mistakes as unfortunate but natural outcomes of the processes, and are quick to move on when mistakes happen. Risk taking and ambiguity are not things they worry much about. Working for such people can be rewarding and exciting as well as frustrating and unsettling. At its most extreme ("gut" decisions), the results are spectacular—successes and failures both.

Most people and information services are somewhere in between the extremes of flight and fight, and they move toward one end or the other based on recent experiences. They also tend to shift along the continuum more frequently than do individuals at the extremes. Essentially they flow with events. They assess risk, have a concern about ambiguity, know mistakes will happen, and do their best to balance all the factors.

TYPES OF DECISIONS

One way to improve decision making is to think about two broad types of decisions—programmed and non-programmed. Programmed decisions are routine and occur on a regular basis (making a reference desk schedule, making choices for collection development, determining who prepares an annual report, and determining who may use or check out a particular item are examples). Such decisions are the stuff of daily decision making at all organizational levels in an information service. Rarely do people think of them as "decisions"; they are low risk, outcomes are highly predictable, and few people have trouble making them.

Non-programmed decisions are another matter. They are rarer, risks are high, outcomes uncertain, and the decision environment is often unstructured. They generally have wide implications for the organization. They are also relatively uncommon at lower levels of an organization (probably the most common situation for lower-level staff to confront a non-programmed decision is some type of emergency). Some examples of non-programmed information service decisions are decisions regarding remodeling or planning a new facility, purchasing a new automaton system, and selecting a new senior manager. On a personal/professional level, the decision whether to accept a new position or promotion is non-programmed.

Knowing who should make a decision is essential to keeping things flowing. "Even in companies respected for their decisiveness, however, there can be ambiguity over who is accountable for their decisions. As a result, the entire decision making process can stall" (Rogers and Blenko, 2006: 52). Assigning non-programmed decisions, as much as possible, to certain offices/positions will help avoid delays. The Rogers and Blenko article outlines how one can begin this process. One category of non-programmed decisions that must have careful thought is crisis/disaster management. (We touch on disaster planning in Chapter 18.)

Check This Out:

A good article addressing crisis decision making is Ken Naqlewski's 2006 "Are You Ready to Make Effective Decisions When Disaster Strikes?" (*Journal of Private Equity* 9, no. 2 [Spring]: 45–51).

STYLES OF DECISION MAKING

Various management writers have used a number of labels for different decision-making styles. As discussed earlier in this chapter, one major influence on a person's organizational decision-making style is risk tolerance. A second major factor is one's "value" orientation, that is, how much importance one places on task/technical issues vs. people/social issues. As with risk, there is a value continuum. It is possible to think of the two factors as axes on a grid similar to the "Managerial Grid" (in Chapter 13). One axis of the grid would represent tolerance of risk and the other axis would be task and people. The lower left corner of the grid would be low-risk/high-task (say 1.1), the lower right corner would be high-people/low-risk (5.1), the upper left corner would be high-risk/high-task (1.5), and the upper right corner would be high-risk/high-people (5.5).

Most individuals employ several styles of decision making, adjusting the style to the circumstances; however, they usually have a favored approach based on their past experiences. (Note: There is no one "best" style for every circumstance.)

A "directive style" would fall somewhere in the lower left quadrant of the grid. It is one with low risk tolerance and places a high value on tasks.

The style is practical/systematic in character. Another label for this approach is "reflective," although that label usually carries with it the implication of taking ample, sometimes seen as excessive, time to decide.

"Analytical" (upper left quadrant) style is another high task value approach but with a high risk tolerance. It can also be reflective in character, with a slightly greater speed in decision time.

The "behavioral style" falls in the lower right quadrant. Its high-people/low-risk orientation can lead to decisions that are less decisive than some might wish for. Occasionally, the people/social values lead to decisions that avoid conflict but do not solve the problem.

The fourth style is "conceptual" and it falls in the upper right quadrant. For some people, conceptual decisions lack a degree of practicality or seem hard to implement.

Realistically, most peoples' styles fall somewhere in the middle of the grid—some balancing of risk and tasks/people (perhaps 3.3). A label for this style would be "consistent."

Another "style" that received recent attention is what one might call reflexive or reactive. Other labels are "shooting from the hip," "gut decisions." These are labels for making a quick decision based on limited information and looking for few alternatives. Stewart Thomas (2006: 12) suggested that "the contest between rationality and gut instinct pervades the research on decision making." Eric Bonabeau (2003) indicated that while increasing numbers of decision makers are doing so, it is not a good idea to "trust one's gut" when making key decisions. He listed what he considers three major factors causing people to make the mistake of thinking/deciding based on instinct rather than on fact and assessment. First, as decisions become more complex, so do the number of alternatives that potentially can address the situation; developing and assessing more and more possibilities takes precious time. Second, as we all know, the volume of information grows faster than we are fully capable of handling. Finally and perhaps most significantly, the timeframe for making the decision keeps shrinking. While acknowledging that intuition has its place in the process, just as does one's conscience, he claims that thinking it can replace reason "is indulging in a risky delusion" (Bonabeau, 2003: 116).

Check These Out:

Meyer, David G. 2002. *Intuition: Its Powers and Perils*. New Haven, CT: Yale University Press.

Hayashi, Alden M. 2001. "When To Trust Your Gut." *Harvard Business Review* 79, no. 2 (February): 59–65.

Think About Your Decision Styles:

- How comfortable are you with uncertainty?
- How much "risk" do you usually take?
- Do you think and assess options or "just" decide?
- When there is a deadline, do you wait as long as possible or do you make the decision well in advance?
- When confronted with a people versus thing decision, which do you favor?
- When making a decision, do you seek advice whenever possible or only when necessary?
- How often do you regret a decision?

Rational Decision Making

Thomas's statement (2006) about the contest between rationality and gut instinct identifies what is the textbook approach to decision making—rationality. Hundreds of books and articles discuss various aspects and models of rational decision making. The concept has value and has its place in the decision process, but it does have limitations. Herbert Simon (1976) noted very early on that managers could never be 100 percent logically rational in their decision because of what he called "bounded rationality." Constraints (boundaries) on rational decision making are numerous; some of the obvious ones are time, money, information/data, conflicting goals/objectives, complexity, and even intellectual capability.

Rational decision making, as a concept, rests on at least three assumptions that are rarely fully valid in a given circumstance. The first assumption is that the decision is, or can be, made with complete information—thus there is no uncertainty/risk. The second assumption is that the decision maker will be without bias or emotion, and thus logical. No one is without biases and personal values; however, bias-free decisions are possible for many organizational decisions—most fall into the "thing" rather than the "people" category. When people issues are involved, the risk of bias or emotion becoming a factor increases. The third assumption is the decider knows the organization's future directions—thus the decision will be the "best" one possible. Predicting the future with any degree of accuracy is unlikely, thus making "best" best for today but not best for tomorrow.

Rational decision making, in spite of the above cautions, is a useful process. It is also a helpful tool when it comes to problem solving.

DECISION MAKING AND PROBLEM SOLVING

The common model of rational decision making consists of six steps. First, start by defining the situation requiring a decision (for example, a problem, opportunity, or challenge). Second, determine the objective(s) that the decision must address. Third, gather information about the issue and generate as many alternatives as possible—even those that might initially seem foolish. Fourth, evaluate each of the alternatives in terms of the decision objectives and consider what might be possible consequences or outcomes if the alternative is implemented. Fifth, carefully consider how the alternative would be implemented (for example, people, time, and resources). Sixth, implement and monitor the "best" alternative.

Something to Ponder:

Consider the following about what constitutes a "successful decision." In baseball, a batter is thought to be successful when making the right decision (getting a hit) between 30 and 40 percent of the time. The person becomes a superstar if, throughout a career, the right decision took place about 40 percent of the time. For a brain surgeon, anything less than 100 percent success is a major problem. The vast majority of organizational managers make success choices somewhere between the two extremes, but in reality they rarely get beyond 75 percent. Given the "bounded rationally" issues, that is an admirable level. Mistakes and wrong choices are a fact of managerial life; the goal is to limit them as much as possible.

Clearly, not every decision involves a problem, except under the broadest definition of problem. For example, selecting a method for providing selective dissemination of information to users is a problem only in the sense there may be several good alternatives. A decision about how to handle a specific complaint from a user, on the other hand, may indeed be a problem situation. Even a manager's values and beliefs influence the problem he or she chooses to work on. Guth and Tagiuri's research showed that managers primarily motivated by economic values prefer to make decisions about practical issues. Managers with a theoretical orientation prefer to work on long-term issues, such as planning and strategy. When the individuals have more political values, they tend to focus on competitive issues and those that will likely be career enhancing (Guth and Tagiuri, 1965).

Kepner and Tregoe (1965), among many writers on decision making, identified seven factors in analyzing (solving) problems. The following is a summary of their approach to problem analysis:

1. *Assume that a standard of performance exists against which one may compare real performance.* For most information services, this statement usually reads, "There should be a standard of performance against which one may compare real performance." A decision-making or problem-solving situation arises when there is a difference between the actual and desired results.

2. *Determine whether a deviation from the standards has occurred and determine the degree of deviation.* Once managers establish standards, it becomes possible to monitor if and how much deviation occurs. Without a standard, managers may only have a sense that deviation exists and staff members may or may not agree. Thus, standards save time and conflict.

3. *Locate the point of deviation in the sequence of activities or in the situation.* Frequently, it is more difficult to establish such a point than it might seem, especially when the deviation only appears in the finished product. The deviation may have entered the system at the very beginning, come into the system with the material itself, entered with a person somewhere during the processing sequence, or intruded into the presentation of the final product. The important thing is to correctly identify the source of deviation (a common problem with intuitive problem solving). Failure to identify the source correctly can create additional problems in terms of staff morale and trust.

4. *Ascertain what distinguishes the affected group from the unaffected group.* What constitutes the deviation? Once the manager carefully reviews what distinguishes the affected group from the unaffected group, the problem is almost solved.

5. *Look for a change in the system.* The change may be minor, or it may be in a related system; however, some type of change is causing the problem deviation. The only exception to this rule is when one is testing a new system.

6. *Analyze all possible causes that can be deduced from the relevant system changes.* First, identify all changes in the system. Then, examine each change to determine if it could be the cause of the problem, or if it is, in fact, the actual problem.

7. *Take the cause that most exactly explains the facts, correct that point in the system, and test the system to see whether deviation continues to occur.* If the deviation disappears, the proposed solution was correct; if not, continue to search for other potential causes. Managers ignore this step too often, which usually results in even more problems.

The seven steps described can be very useful in solving problems—both job-related and personal. Beginning information professionals should practice them on some simple problems until they become second nature.

Types of Solutions

Once a problem is identified, managers have options for how to solve it. Five of the more common solution methods are interim, adaptive, corrective, preventive, and contingency.

Interim solutions buy you time while you search for the cause of the problem. They will also buy time while implementing long-term solutions. All too often, interim solutions have a way of becoming permanent, or at least becoming long-term bandages.

Adaptive solutions do not really solve the problem, but they allow the organization to continue to function (or appear to function) somewhat normally. If an interim solution is a bandage, an adaptive solution is a plaster cast. It is often chosen in the hope that, with the application of a few cosmetic changes, the problem will take care of itself. Most job situations, unlike broken bones, do not heal themselves. More often than not, someone who glosses over a problem will find it coming back as a larger problem later.

Corrective solutions actually resolve the problem. Such solutions require time, effort, and careful analysis of the problem. Resolution is the ideal and, if a system is to be healthy, the corrective solution is the one to seek.

Preventive solutions go back to the Kepner and Tregoe idea of exploring decisions for adverse consequences. In this way, you solve not only the problem at hand, but also potential problems arising from the planned solution. This method takes even more time than a corrective solution, but it could repay its costs by allowing you more time in the future to devote to other management functions.

Contingency solutions simply involve the establishment of standby or emergency procedures to help offset the effects of a serious problem. Effective services typically have contingency plans for disasters, such as fires, earthquakes, and floods. Unfortunately, some managers do not make time to prepare such contingency plans. The issue is not *if* a disaster will strike, but only a question of *when*. While a disaster plan will not forestall a disaster, it will help keep the damage to a minimum.

INDIVIDUAL AND GROUP DECISION-MAKING PROCESSES

Managers must reflect on several categories of decision making—their own, that of those they work with on an individual level, and that of internal groups (committees and teams) and external groups (such as consortia and professional associations). Up to this point we have only addressed individual decision making. Although much of the foregoing discussion also applies to group decision making, there are some special group process issues. If anything, group decision making is even more complex than that of the individual.

You should not think of decision making as an "event." The vast majority of decisions develop over time. Yes, there is the moment of choice, but generally there is an elapse of time between knowing a decision is necessary and reaching the decision point. Even quick gut decisions usually draw upon some knowledge base. Research suggests that people who view decision making as a process rather than an event are more effective (Garvin and Roberto, 2001).

One important aspect of group decision making is how the group views the process—as searching for the best or as making the case. While this aspect affects individuals, it becomes critical in the group setting. When a group or team views it as advocacy or making the case, there is often a sense of competition to see if one's personal view can prevail. That type of atmosphere does not lend itself well to sound (or at least not rapid) decision making. Strong personal views and hidden agendas get in the way of meaningful and open exchanges, while limiting the number of alternatives that are developed and considered. (Note that for properly functioning teams this should not be an issue, as they will have addressed the problem during their formation/development process.)

Another issue is that vigorous debate about positions or alternatives can generate some degree of conflict. Here the fight, flight, and flow scale can come into play. In a group setting, it is likely that two, if not all three, of those behaviors will be present, and thus will impact the group process and the quality of the decision reached. Conflict, in and of itself, is not the problem. It can be beneficial when it is cognitive rather than emotional in character. The challenge is to achieve the highest possible level of cognitive conflict and the lowest level of emotional conflict. One way to meet the challenge is to carefully frame the decision goals for the group. Another technique is to monitor the group—when emotions are running high, call a "time-out" for the group.

Groups can easily fall into the trap of "groupthink." Two factors frequently play a role in groupthink. Perhaps the most common factor is the desire to get or keep things moving along. This desire often results in a too-quick decision, made without much effort and without assessing multiple options. The second common factor is the desire to be a "team player"; this desire, too, can reduce options and very likely can limit thoughtful critical assessment or idea generation.

Check This Out:

A good article that provides guidance on group decision making in an information service environment is H. Frank Cervone's 2005 "Managing Digital Libraries: The View from 30,000 Feet. Making Decisions, Methods for Digital Library Teams" (*OCLC Systems & Services* 21, no. 1: 30–35).

Information services increasingly face another form of group decision making—consortial. While all the elements and issues discussed above are in play in this context, some other issues complicate the matter further. First and foremost, unlike with internal group decisions, in consortial decision making there is rarely a single person "in charge" of the decision (in case of an impasse). Thus, accountability is very vague at best. Also, the choices for action, for a service that is concerned about a decision, are limited—accept and hope, pull out of the group, or fight to reverse the decision and, perhaps, risk breaking up the group.

Generally within consortia and similar groups, decisions become a situation where concessions and consensus are the keys to a resolution. Another C for such decision making is consideration—one may not always get what one would like—if the group is to succeed. A final C, often the most significant, is coalitions. In many ways, coalitions assist in moving matters forward, as they normally reduce the number of variables in play with a large group.

A major challenge for such groups is determining what is "best." The number of bests is substantially greater in a consortial environment than for a single service. There are the bests for each institution, the bests for coalitions, and, of course, the bests for the group as a whole.

Building trust is always a factor in group decision making, but it becomes more of a challenge for consortial members since they spend less time together than internal groups. Time is a key factor in creating trust, and it is limited in such situations. A related factor is that, more often than not, institutional representatives at such meetings are senior, if not the senior manager. Generally such people are not used to having their views openly challenged, which they may be in such a setting.

Time together, trust, concessions, and consensus are the key elements for successful consortial decision making.

Check This Out:

An outstanding article, if complex for those uncomfortable with qualitative methods, is Robert M. Hayes' 2003 "Cooperative Game: Theoretic Models for Decision-Making in the Context of Library Cooperation" (*Library Trends* 51, no. 3 [Winter]: 441–461).

DECISION AIDS

Many techniques exist to aid the decision maker in selecting the best alternative. Some of these techniques are quantitative in nature; other methods arc qualitative in nature. Quantitative methods are most useful in production areas.

Qualitative techniques are useful in assessing those elements in a decision-making situation that are value-oriented. Almost all decision making has some value elements, but those that relate to customer service and/or involve ethical situations can benefit from qualitative techniques.

Quantitative Techniques

Libraries and information services face ever-increasing pressure to be accountable. One very valuable tool to demonstrate accountability is hard data. Such hard data as increased usage, reference questions answered, and documents delivered are also useful in making decisions. Without question, decisions informed with hard data (evidence-based) carry greater creditability than those not so informed (anecdotal-based). An integrated library system (ILS) can provide a wealth of data, but without a plan for how to use the information, the data can be overwhelming. As Caroline Cummins (2006: 14) stated, "making sense of the data lurking in the ILS is crucial." Hiller and Self (2004: 129) defined data as "records of observations, facts, or information collected for reference or analysis." ILS are capable of providing an ocean of data; the good news is that most major vendors offer packages that make it possible to organize and analyze the data for the decision maker.

A somewhat new concept is data mining, sometimes labeled "biblio mining" in a library context (Nicholson, 2006). A short definition of data mining is the identification of new, useful patterns/trends in large quantities of data, through the use of statistical and mathematical techniques. (Computing power is what has made this a cost-effective technique even for small institutions.) A common use of the methodology is pattern recognition/description and prediction. Koontz and Jue (2004) describe a form of data mining (the Public Library Geographic Database). They identify several possible "questions" that one might address using the database, such as the relationship between collection usage and community demographics and the number/percentage of U.S. public libraries that serve areas with more than a 25 percent poverty level. (The article has some exercises for exploring the potential of the database and the concept of data mining.)

Another concept related to decision making and accountability is "evidence-based librarianship" (EBL), which is currently primarily employed in health sciences libraries in Canada, the United Kingdom and United States. Koufogiannakis and Crumly (2002: 112) defined EBL, in the health sciences context, as a means by which "a librarian helps health care professionals to formulate an answerable question, determine where they may best find the answer to that question, and use effective searching to find the evidence." Essentially EBL's goal is to make effective decisions about practical problems.

***

Check These Out:

A very good overview of EBL, along with an annotated bibliography on the concept, is Susan N. Lerdal's 2006 "Evidence-Based Librarianship: Opportunity for Law Librarians?" (*Law Library Journal* 98, no. 1 [Winter]: 33–60).

Mari Davis, Concepcion Wilson, and Anne Horn's 2205 "Informing Decision Making in Libraries: Information Research Input to LIS Education and Practice (*Australian Academic & Research Libraries* 36, no. 4 [December]: 195–213) is a thoughtful article that relates to decision making, data, accountability, and libraries.

***

While not the sole answer, quantitative aids are very useful. Some of the aids available are linear programming, matrix algebra, and linear mathematical equations—all forms of operational research techniques. In order to use linear programming, the circumstances must meet several conditions. First, there must be a definite objective, and the manager must be able to express the objective in a quantifiable way: money, time, or quantity. Second, the variables that will effect the outcome must have a linear relationship. Third, restrictions on variables must be present (otherwise, this approach would not be necessary). Linear programming is very mechanical; most library processes do not have a linear relationship. Even in the circulation of items in the collection—the most obvious place to apply the technique—there are enough variations in terms of work to make the application of quantifiable methods difficult.

Simulation model techniques attempt to carry out a solution in a controlled environment. The researcher or decision maker creates a model representing some aspects of the real-world situation and subjects the model to various changes, one at a time, to determine what *might* happen. Of course, all factors must be quantifiable. The simulation model attempts to trace changes in activities as variables come into play. It attempts to quantify the behavioral and nonlogical attributes of a situation.

The *Monte Carlo technique* is a simulation model in which the goal is to control chance. Random sampling helps to simulate natural events and to establish the probability of each of several outcomes. This type of simulation assists in answering a variety of questions: What are the chances of an event actually happening? Which of the alternative decisions appears to be best? What are the probabilities of a breakdown in a given unit or in a class of equipment? In the case of libraries, the use of this method can assist in decisions related to technology, new services, and changes in service.

Queuing theory deals with the length of time it takes to render a service or to process something. For instance, how long must staff, customers, and equipment remain idle because of an inefficient physical arrangement? Combining queuing theory and the Monte Carlo approach, a manager can determine expected arrival rates in a facility and the anticipated delay that arrival will generate. This approach could be quite valuable in a heavily used customer area (for example, an academic library's reserve room or a public library's reference room) in determining staffing patterns in a way that will meet demands most efficiently.

Another quantitative decision-making technique is the *game theory* developed by von Neumann and Morgenstern (1953). Since game theory deals basically with competitive situations, however, it is suited more for business adaptations than for information service use (the competition that does exist is not about increasing a "share" of the market at the expense of other services).

Two excellent, if older, books that provide useful quantitative applications to library decision making are *Book Availability and the Library User* (Buckland, 1975) and *Library Planning and Decision Making Systems* (Hamburg et al., 1974). Buckland considered collection development and customer needs and provided a number of useful models and suggestions. Using such approaches as Bradford's law of scatter, decision curves, probability analysis, chi-square, queuing theory, the Monte Carlo technique, and other quantitative methods, Buckland demonstrated a number of points:

1. Problems in library and information services tend to be worldwide, and solutions in one country often work in another. (Buckland collected his data in England; however, managers around the world have used some of his techniques.)
2. A wide variety of quantitative methods (rather than just one or two) can solve a complex problem (such as better user access to materials).
3. The material and ideas that come out of a quantitative approach are valuable, even to managers who are not mathematically inclined.

The book by Hamburg and associates attempted a much broader approach to library decision making. The authors focused on planning and decision making in large academic and public libraries. They too used a variety of quantitative methods. At one point, they discuss the value and limitations of this approach:

> Managerial decision making has become much more complex and difficult in both the private and public sectors as the American economic, political and social structures, and the corresponding business, governmental, and social organizational units, has grown larger and more complicated.... analytical decision models are being increasingly utilized. A model is simply a

representation of *some* aspects of the real world and is often mathematical in nature. The overall purpose of such models is to seek out the best combination of factors under the control of the decision maker to improve performance of the organization and make its goals more achievable. (Hamburg et al., 1974: 6–7).

A technique that any library or information services manager can use is a *decision tree*, which presents a graphical representation of different alternative decisions. It helps the manager understand the consequences of implementing different decisions. Successful use of decision trees depends upon the careful analysis of the situation and the examination of a variety of options.

An example of how a decision tree might apply to a library situation is the problem of how to increase access to a growing volume of serial publications in an environment of limited funding. A library might consider five broad options:

- subscribe to all the desired journals in hard copy
- expand traditional interinstitutional borrowing activities
- establish a cooperative subscription consortium to share the cost of subscribing to all the needed serials
- subscribe to electronic journals and electronic versions of paper-based journals
- subscribe to a document delivery service for access to necessary articles with customer direct ordering

Each option has consequences in terms of staffing, equipment, budget, customer satisfaction, and, perhaps, cost of services passed on to customers. By developing a decision tree and/or decision matrix (which incorporates the concept of probability of an event happening), the decision makers are provided with a picture of the outcomes, as shown in the following box:

Options	Outcomes
Add Subscription	increased processing support staff ($XX)
	decreased ILL staff ($XX)
Expand ILL	increased ILL staff ($XX)
	no change in processing staff ($0)
Create Consortium	professional staff to create/monitor
	new staff (courier) ($XX)
	decreased processing staff time ($XX)

(Continued)

Options	Outcomes	(Continued)
Subscribe Electronic	increased professional time to train customers ($XX)	
	decreased processing staff time ($XX)	
	decreased ILL staff ($XX)	
Subscribe Document	increased professional time (monitor costs)	
	decreased ILL staff ($XX)	
	decreased process staff ($XX)	

A knowledge of basic statistics is one of the manager's tools. If you do not feel that your knowledge is up to par, make sure that you study basic statistics. Not all textbooks present statistical topics in the same way. Find one that you feel comfortable with, and purchase a copy to keep close at hand in your office.

Qualitative Techniques

Because of the inability to validate ethical (value) judgments objectively, managers must ask a very basic question concerning the values employed. Whose standard of correctness should be employed? Another factor to be aware of is that decision making often appears to be an unconscious activity because it is one that goes on continuously in everyone's life. The steps that we outlined earlier can help bring this process to a more conscious level and perhaps improve the quality of the decisions being made.

Consider the decision (problem) of whether to charge "outside" customers a fee for library-provided access to remote databases. (We assume here that no law forbids such a practice.) An unlikely approach would be simply "to decide" to impose a fee. A more likely approach would be to attempt to use the quantitative methods previously outlined. Such an approach would help identify the major variables and assist in weighing the alternatives. But neither approach will resolve the ethical (value) conflicts that will arise; and ethical considerations often determine the final disposition of a matter. Thus, the hypothetical manager may have determined demands on the library's resources by "outsiders," the cost of providing the service, and an equitable fee (based on demand and cost). However, the basic question of deciding whether to charge a fee remains unanswered.

Some of the qualitative questions to answer are: Would creation of a fee service hurt the library's relations? Would it hurt the public relations of the institution of which the service is a part? Would continuing free service lead to greater industrial support of the institution and the library? Would a fee service be contrary to public welfare? To whom is the library obligated (if publicly supported) to provide free service, and under what circumstances? Every answer involves a value judgment.

Check This Out:

Decision aids often lead to the formulation of decision rules, such as how to allocate funds. Christopher D. Porter and Judi McLean Parks' 2004 "The Fairness of Decision Rules" (*Journal of Management* 30, no. 3 [June]: 329–349) is an interesting article that explores the value of such rules.

KEY POINTS TO REMEMBER:

- Careers are made or broken by the quality of decision taken.
- Decision making carries with it accountability.
- Decision outcomes are rarely completely certain or risk free.
- Decisions are either programmed or non-programmed.
- Programmed decision making takes place daily at all levels of the organization.
- Non-programmed decisions carry the greatest uncertainty and risk.
- Understanding decision-making and problem-solving processes is a managerial asset.
- Rational decision making, despite its limitations, is a useful tool.
- Rational decision making and problem solving are interrelated.
- Group/team decision making is more complex than individual decision making.
- Consortial decisions involve the three Cs: concessions, consensus, and coalitions.
- Decision aids are both quantitative and qualitative in character.

REFERENCES

Bonabeau, Eric. 2003. "Don't Trust Your Gut." *Harvard Business Review* 81, no. 5 (January): 116–123.

Buchanan, Leigh, and Andrew O'Connell. 2006. "A Brief History of Decision Making." *Harvard Business Review* 84, no. 1 (January): 32–41.

Buckland, Michael. 1975. *Book Availability and the Library User.* New York: Pergamon.

Cervone, H. Frank. 2005. "Managing Digital Libraries: The View from 30,000 Feet. Making Decisions, Methods for Digital Library Teams." *OCLC Systems & Services* 21, no. 1: 30–35.

Conlon, Donald E., Christopher O. Porter, and Judi McLean Parks. 2004. "The Fairness of Decision Rules." *Journal of Management* 30, no. 3 (June): 329–349.

Cummins, Caroline. 2006. "Below the Surface." *Library Journal* (Net Connect Supplement), Winter: 12–14.

Davis, Mari, Concepcion Wilson, and Anne Horn. 2005. "Informing Decision Making in Libraries: Information Research as Input to LIS Education and Practice." *Australian Academic & Research Libraries* 36, no. 4 (December): 195–213.

Garvin, David A., and Michael A. Roberto. 2001. "What You Don't Know About Making Decisions." *Harvard Business Review* 79, no. 8 (September): 108–116.

Guth, William, and Rento Tagiuri. 1965. "Personal Values and Corporate Strategy." *Harvard Business Review* 37 (September–October): 123–132.

Hamburg, Morris, et al. 1974. *Library Planning and Decision Making Systems.* Cambridge, MA: MIT Press.

Hayes, Robert M. 2003. "Cooperative Game: Theoretic Models for Decision-Making in the Context of Library Cooperation." *Library Trends* 51 no. 3 (Winter): 441–461.

Hiller, Steve, and James Self. 2004. "From Measurement to Management: Using Data Wisely for Planning and Decision Making." *Library Trends* 53, no. 1 (Summer): 129–155.

Kepner, Charles H., and Benjamin B. Tregoe. 1965. *The Rational Manager.* New York: McGraw-Hill.

Koontz, Christie, and Dean K. Jue. 2004. "Customer Data 24/7 Aids Library Planning and Decision Making." *Florida Libraries* 47, no. 1 (Spring): 17–19.

Koontz, Scott. 2003. "The Bibliomining Process: Data Warehousing and Data Mining for Library Decision Making." *Information Technology and Libraries* 22, no. 4 (December): 146–151.

Koufogiannakis, Densie, and Ellen Crumly. 2002. "Evidence-Based Librarianship." *Feliciter* 48, no. 3: 112–115.

Lerdal, Susan N. 2006. "Evidence-Based Librarianship: Opportunity for Law Librarians?" *Law Library Journal* 98, no. 1 (Winter): 33–60.

Mintzberg, Henry. 1976. "Planning on the Left Side and Managing on the Right." *Harvard Business Review* 54, no. 4 (July/August): 49–58.

Naglewski, Ken. 2006. "Are You Ready to Make Effective Decisions When Disaster Strikes?" *Journal of Private Equity* 9, no. 2 (Spring): 45–51.

Nicholson, Scott. 2006. "Proof in the Pattern." *Library Journal* 131, (Supplement January): 2–4, 6.

Peanuts. 1963. United Features Syndicate, Inc.

Rogers, Paul, and Marcia Blenko. 2006. "Who Has the D?" *Harvard Business Review* 84, no.1 (January): 52–61.

Simon, Herbert. 1976. *Administrative Behavior.* 3rd ed. New York: Free Press.

Speich, Daniel. 1976. "English Ruling, UC Decisions Sometimes Just Seem to Happen." *Los Angeles Times* (14 November, pt. 1): 34.

Thomas, Stewart. 2006. "Did You Ever Have to Make Up Your Mind?" *Harvard Business Review* 84, no. 1 (January): 12.

Von Neumann, John, and Oskar Morgenstern. 1953. *Theory of Games and Economic Behavior.* 2nd ed. New York: Wiley.

LAUNCHING PAD

Bazerman, Max H. 2001. *Judgment in Managerial Decision Making.* 5th ed. New York: Wiley.

Beghtol, Carol. 2005. "Ethical Decision-Making for Knowledge Representation and Organization Systems for Global Use." *Journal of the Society for Information Science and Technology* 56, no. 9 (July): 903–912.

Foudy, Gerri, and Alesia McManus. 2005. "Using a Decision Grid Process to Build Consensus in Electronic Resources Cancellation Decisions." *Journal of Academic Librarianship* 31, no. 6 (November): 533–538.

Lovallo, Dan, and Kahneman, Daniel. 2003. "Delusions of Success: How Optimism Undermines Executives' Decisions." *Harvard Business Review* 81, no. 7 (July): 56–63.

Mankins, Michael C., and Richard Steele. 2006. "Stop Making Plans: Start Making Decisions." *Harvard Business Review* 84, no. 1 (January): 76–84.

Paul, Souren, Carol Stoak Saunders, and William David Haseman. 2005. "A Question of Timing: The Impact of Information Acquisition on Group Decision Making." *Information Resources Management Journal* 18, no. 4 (October–December): 81–100.

Schachter, Debbie. 2006. "The Importance of Good Decision Making." *Information Outlook* 10, no. 4 (April): 12–13.

Welch, David A. 2001. *Decisions, Decisions: The Art of Effective Decision Making.* Amherst, NY: Prometheus Books.

8

The Planning Process

"It is a bad plan that admits of no modifications."
Publius Syrus

"The best way to predict the future is to create it."
Peter F. Drucker

INTRODUCTION

People in many cultures learn the word "plan" early in life. After an accident or problem, a parent, grandparent, or friend may say something like "Well, you didn't plan that very carefully, did you?" In later years at school, similar questions are common: "What courses do you plan to take?"; "How do you plan to handle the work load?"; and "What do you plan on doing after graduation?" The word comes up in casual conversation more often than we realize, until we think about it—travel plans, vacation plans, relocation plans, job plans, retirement plans, and so on. In spite of its widespread use, do we really understand the nature of planning?

How often have you felt that the fickle finger of fate has caused you problems? Most people can think of several such occasions, both in their personal life and work life. Individuals who can honestly claim that they experience few, if any, such occurrences are probably extraordinarily good planners rather than just "lucky."

As is true with personal decision making, personal planning, or lack of it, impacts only a few people. Planning in an organizational setting is a very different matter. Failure to plan can have devastating consequences for an organization. People who are uncomfortable with decision making are often equally uncomfortable with the planning process.

Organizational planning, and to some degree personal planning, allows you to check on progress toward a desired outcome. It assists in coordinating activities designed to achieve an outcome. Without a plan, the chances that random activity will achieve a desired organizational goal are extremely low. Planning is forward looking and forces you to consider the future. At its simplest, planning is nothing more than setting a direction. Plans indicate to people, both inside and outside the organization, where it expects to go.

Although most planning is voluntary, sometimes information services have no choice but to produce a plan. There may be a government requirement to create security plans. Perhaps one of the most common planning mandates is to generate a strategic plan. Such a mandate might come from the parent organization, which, in turn, must develop a systemwide strategic plan. In the United Kingdom, the Department of Culture, Media, and Sport requires public libraries to prepare a three-year library plan. In the United States, the Public Library Association has prepared a very detailed planning process to aid public librarians. The guide provides a structure for rethinking the library's role in the community, for the evaluation of choices and opportunities, and for developing appropriate service responses. A loose-leaf manual gives instructions on how each step in the process should be carried out (Himmell and Wilson, 1998). From 2000 onward, PLA published an important *PLA Results Series* to help public libraries plan.

Something to Ponder:

Think about the following statements and keep your answers in mind as you explore the remainder of this chapter.
- Usually when I start something I have a clear and detailed sense of what I want the outcome to be.
- In a work setting, when I give a task to someone, I only tell them what the objective/outcome should be, not how to accomplish the task.
- I set specific and measurable objectives for myself.
- Most of the objectives I set for myself and others are challenging but doable.
- Setting deadlines/schedules is easy for me, but keeping to them is difficult.
- I set both long-term and short-term goals for myself, with some short-term goals intended to help achieve the long-term goals.
- I tend to look at many options before I set a course of action.
- At work I stay to my plans for the day and avoid changing course, except in an emergency.
- I ask others for advice before setting goals and objectives.
- I follow all organizational policies, procedures, and rules.
- I devote some thought to "what if" actions and try to have some "contingency" actions in mind in case the unexpected happens.

Maurice Line (2004: 62–63) comments on long-term and short-term thinking and planning in library and information services: "There are very many examples of disastrous past failure to foresee effects ... [and] there are few who can predict longer-term effects of short-term measures. ... The ability of librarians to plan ahead is constrained by their parent body, and plans have to be made within more or less strict parameters."

PLANNING

Some people, including Henry Mintzberg (1994), argue that managers are too busy to plan. A review of their published statements shows that such theorists are apparently responding to a lack of written plans and to how some managers react to changing situations. Thus, a manager who has a goal in mind but not on paper, and who will change methods for achieving that goal, is a reactor and not a planner. We do not agree with this point of view. We believe that having a set goal is a plan, without having it on paper. The reality is that some managers do more planning than others (and some of them commit more of the plans to paper than others), but all managers plan to some degree. A key point is that effective planning takes time and careful thought.

A Point of Reflection:

Reflect about an organization in which you have worked. Was there any evidence of planning? If so, how was it made evident to you? Was the plan made available to all staff? Was the staff involved in developing the plan?

The Nature of Planning

According to Nohria and Stewart (2006), 21st-century managers must devote more time and thought to handling risk, uncertainty, and doubt. They make the point that planning is future-looking in nature, and a rapidly changing environment means ever more risk, uncertainty, and doubt. Further, they consider these three variables to be distinct yet interrelated.

Risk, with some amount of information, is something you can calculate ("I took a calculated risk"). On the other hand, uncertainty is incalculable (one simply cannot know). With risk and uncertainty, there is the underlying assumption that you know what you want, if not how to achieve it. "Doubt comes into play when there is no right outcome, when one must choose between two evils, or when good outcomes have bad side effects. ... How does one choose between valued objectives, for example, safety versus liberty, scientific discovery versus the sanctity of human life, individual versus group?" (Nohria and Stewart, 2006: 40). Although information services don't face making such weighty plans or choosing between such complex issues, they still have to consider risk, uncertainty, and, at times, doubt.

Some years ago Miles and Snow (1978) outlined four ways that organizations and people go about handling risk and uncertainty. There are the "defenders"—those who stay with what they do best and operate on the assumption that keeping to the narrow, well trodden path will minimize risk and uncertainty. Such behavior, in the past, often worked well, especially for long-established organizations, such as libraries and archives. Today, that style is undoubtedly a much higher risk strategy than its practitioners realize. "Analyzers" are inclined to take on a moderate amount of risk and uncertainty. Their approach is to watch and analyze what others are doing, and imitate what appears to be working ("Let's not be on the bleeding edge of the IT curve"). "Prospectors" see opportunities in risk taking and uncertainty. They want to be leading the way. Their plans devote little attention to "what if"—essentially they pay little attention to risk calculation or concern about uncertainty. As a consequence, they experience a higher rate of failed plans than do other types of organizations. When they succeed they create tremendous results, often forcing competitors out or causing major shifts in how all like organizations operate. Finally, there are the "reactors". These organizations or people are passive and only change direction when there is a crisis. Changing plans in a crisis is probably the riskiest of all options. As we noted earlier, effective planning requires time and careful thought—which are generally in short supply in a crisis.

Although there is no way to way to avoid risk, uncertainty, and doubt in the planning process, some techniques will make them less intimidating and problematic. The balance of this chapter will explore these techniques and planning processes.

Types of Plans

Most management scholars divide plans into three broad categories, each having an approximate time frame. *Strategic plans* are long-term (two to five years) and generally are the prerogative of senior or middle managers, at least in terms of starting the planning process. *Tactical plans* are mid-term in length (six months to two years) and are geared to moving the organization toward achieving its strategic plans. Middle managers and supervisors are the people who initiate work on tactical plans. *Operational plans* are short-term (one day to one year) and are intended to guide staff in their day-to-day activities; these plans obviously need to be clearly linked to the tactical and strategic plans. Such plans are generated by individuals, teams, supervisors, and middle managers. (Note: Effective organizational planning draws on input from all levels, not just those who generally start a planning process.) Tactical plans include marketing, goals, objectives, budgets, and policies, while common operational plans are programs, procedures, and rules. Two key elements in strategic plans are the mission and vision statements. Because, in the ideal world, all plans arise from and are linked to the organization's strategic plan, we begin with that planning process.

STRATEGIC PLANNING

Three important concepts need clarification to underscore their interrelated character as well as their differences: strategy, strategic planning, and strategic management. A strategy identifies and sets the overall direction of an organization. Strategic planning is the process of creating action steps designed to achieve the overall strategy. Strategic management involves all the staff in formulating and implementing activities intended to move toward the desired outcome of the strategy and strategic plan.

Think of the planning process structure (as shown in Figure 8.1) as starting with an environmental scan that provides the basic material for thinking about and formulating the overall strategy. The mission, vision, and value statements draw on both the environmental information and the organizational internal capabilities, resources, and parent body limitations. All these factors create the context for setting the strategy and designing a plan to move in the direction of the strategy. Once the strategic plan is set, work begins on identifying a set of goals and objectives. With the goals and objectives in place, it is relatively easy to determine what tasks are necessary to address the objectives.

Essentially a mission statement is the organization's very long-term strategy: What do we want to accomplish? Where do we want the organization to go? For a strategy and/or a plan to be useful, there must be congruity between the organization's capabilities and its operating environment.

Significantly, in many cases the strategic activities of libraries and other information services operate within a larger organization or system, which sets the parameters for thinking and planning. Maurice Line (2004: 63), quoted earlier in this chapter, also wrote:

> Few libraries operate on such a scale, and opportunities for long-term planning are limited. . . . Strategic planning was very popular in all types of library a few years ago, though I sense that its popularity has waned recently. . . . The best that can be done is to prepare a vision of what the library should aim to be like in the longer-term (ten years), a general strategy for moving towards that vision in the medium-term (five years say), and a one-year plan of action. Both vision and strategy should be revisited once a year.

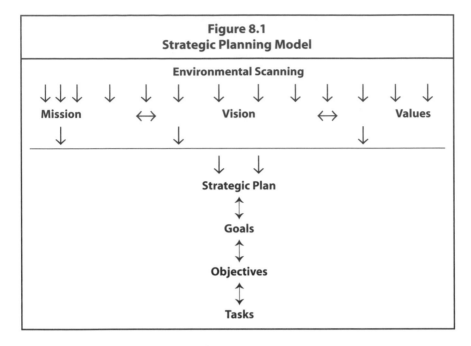

Figure 8.1
Strategic Planning Model

There is, or should be, a dynamic interaction between assessing the organizational environment and reviewing the mission and vision statements. Although the mission and vision statements should have a long-term perspective, you must revisit them periodically (in case of environmental or organizational changes). We addressed the basics of environmental scanning in Chapter 3. In the analysis and monitoring of the environment it is important to focus on the degree of congruence between the mission and vision statements and the environmental factors.

Most mission statements are relatively short and general in character, but not so general that they could apply to almost any other organization in the same field. Such statements vary in nature; some are only a few hundred words long while others may be several paragraphs in length. As you would expect, the longer statements contain greater detail. Striking the correct balance between conciseness and detail can be a challenge. V. Kasturi Rangan (2004) provides sound advice for achieving a good balance. He states, "Most non-profits have broad, inspiring mission statements—and they should. But they also need a systematic method that connects their callings to their programs" (Rangan, 2004: 112).

Fred David (1989) provided some insights into how to address the challenge of being short, general, and yet specific. He suggested thinking in terms of answering a series of questions. We modified the questions to better fit the information service context:

- What is our primary service community?
- What are our key programs and services?
- Who are our competitors within the service area?
- What are our key technologies?
- What are our basic values and aspirations, and what are the philosophical priorities of our activities?
- What is our fiscal operating base?
- What are our major strengths and weaknesses?
- What is our operating philosophy regarding staff?

A vision statement should likewise be concise, while providing clear guidance for the more detailed thinking and planning that must follow. A good vision statement is articulate, compelling, exciting, and challenging. It paints a broad picture of how the service will or should operate at some point in the future. It should be appealing to the staff, the service community, and all other interested parties. Burt Nanus drew up a list of questions to ask about a vision statement (1992, p. 28–29). His view is that for a statement to be useful the answer to all of the questions is "yes."

- Does the statement reflect the organization and its environment?
- Does it set forth a clear purpose?
- Is it forward-looking?
- Is it likely to inspire/motivate the staff?
- Is it challenging/ambitious but attainable?
- Will it require the staff to perform at high levels?
- Can it be easily understood?
- Does it communicate what is special about the services and programs that the organization hopes to achieve?

The following example is an actual mission and vision statement of a public library, although we deliberately omitted the name of the city.

Mission Statement

The mission of the City Public Library is to promote the development of independent, self-confident, literate citizens through the provision of open access to cultural, intellectual, and information resources.

Vision Statement

The City Public Library Board of Trustees envisions a future in which the library's collections, programs, and leadership help ensure:

- That every city resident has the opportunity to enjoy an intellectually and culturally rich life.
- That every child enters school with the requisite developmental skills.
- That every child experiences the pleasure of reading and the joy of learning.

- That our community celebrates and appreciates diversity.
- That those in need find assistance and information with ease.

Check These Out:

A Web search for library/records management mission and vision statements generates hundreds of valid hits. Some are good in terms of the above questions, some are fair, and few seem to lack something. Test some of the statements you find against the questions. Here are a few starting points:

Archives of Women in Science and Engineering
  (www.lib.iastate.edu/spcl/wise/miss.html)
National Press Club Archives (August 2006)
  (www.press.org/library/archives/index.cfm)
Congregation of Alexian Brothers Archives
  (www.alexianbrothers.org/english/archive/mission.html)
Brunel University Cult Film Archives
  (www.brunel.ac.uk/about/acad/sa/artresearch/smrc/cultfilm/)
National Archives of Scotland
  (www.nas.gov.uk/)
 Records Management Society of Great Britain
  (www.rms-gb.org.uk/about)
A sample of public library mission statements
  (http://midhudson.org/department/member_information/missions.htm)
Georgia Southwestern State University Library
  (www.gsw.edu/~library/Libmission.htm)

As we stated, both the mission and vision statements should draw on a detailed, thoughtful analysis of the environment. Abdul Karim (2004) listed four activities for an environmental scan:

- assessing trends and events in the external environment
- establishing relationships between them and the service
- making "sense" of the data
- extracting pertinent implications for the service in terms of strategy and decision making

There are several areas to consider when looking at the environment. One area is competition. Sample questions include: What are the relationships with other information services—local, regional, and national? Are there threats from "substitute" services? How good are the relationships with users—are they shifting to other resources? Are there concerns about the viability of suppliers/vendors—especially ICT?

With the scan information in mind, another activity to consider is what management writers refer to as SWOT (strengths, weaknesses, opportunities, and threats) analysis. This analysis can facilitate thinking through the implications of environmental data and the capabilities of your organization. Although the process does take time, especially when done as a group endeavor, it is usually well worth the effort. The process also feeds into the writing or revision of the mission and vision statements and of the strategic plan. In addition, it will help in thinking about what went right, went wrong, or changed since the last major planning effort. Two of the SWOT elements are outward-looking (opportunities and threats) and two are inward in character (strengths and weaknesses). Such factors as staff skills, competencies, programs, service-community relations, and fiscal base can be either a strength or weakness. When conducting a SWOT analysis, consider whether the factor will help or hinder the accomplishment of your strategy or plan. Likewise, opportunities and threats are anything that would hinder your plan.

Check This Out:

An example of a library SWOT analysis can be found at
    www.library.ubc.ca/home/swot-analysis.pdf (accessed August 2006).

For an information service, the preparation of a value statement can be a valuable exercise when done with the staff. (A value statement is a concise listing of operational priorities or values.) What might at first appear to be an unnecessary activity often leads to some rather surprising staff input regarding operational values (or at least their assumptions about what is "valued"). While there may be easy agreement that service to the user is a top priority, there are often strong differing views about how that goal translates into behavior and services. It is also likely that the discussion will raise ethical concerns. A value statement, while not essential for planning or for operational success, can be beneficial as long as the values are represented "on the floor and not just the wall."

GOALS

Mission and value statements and the strategic plan are all painted with broad brush strokes. By themselves they only provide a general sense of where and what the organization desires to do. They do not provide enough guidance to develop operational activities. Rather they are the pool of information from which you draw a series of goals that will lead to achieving the results put forth in the strategic plan.

A short definition of a strategic goal is an accomplishment that will aid in the achievement of a strategy. Most goals are mid-term to long-term in time frame. An information service might divide its goals into three broad categories, such as suggested by Heather Johnson (1994: 9): "service goals, resource management goals, and administrative/directional goals." It almost goes without saying that all the goals must align with the mission, vision, and strategy.

Useful goals are SMARTER goals—specific, measurable, acceptable, realistic, time-frame, extending, and rewarding. An example of a SMARTER goal for an archive might be "By 2010, 80 percent of archival electronic records will be accessioned within ten working days." The statement is specific and measurable. It also has two time frames. We don't know, on the face of it, if the goal is acceptable, realistic, extending, or rewarding. However, since it is an only slightly modified goal of an archive, we might well assume that there is some degree of staff acceptance of the goal as doable (realistic). It is unlikely that an organization would waste time formulating goals that do not, in some manner, stretch (extend) its capabilities. Just how rewarding its achievement may be is difficult to say; however, for information services the achievement of a goal that serves the parent body well often translates into greater support in the future.

OBJECTIVES

Objectives are the basis for achieving tactical and strategic plans. They underlie the daily activities in most organizations. Some management writers, such as Peter Drucker (1974), claim that the setting of objectives is the major factor in successful management.

Turning to an actual objective, we use an example from an educational information service, but again, we have made slight adjustments and have omitted the name of the institution. The institution took a slightly different approach, in that it started by establishing strategic goals and then subgoals and objectives. One strategic goal is to "prepare an information competent student." A subgoal is to "provide effective and sustainable instruction to 100 percent of a larger and more diverse student body and curricula by 2009." This particular subgoal has three objectives:

- Develop electronic tools, Web tutorials as alternatives to face-to-face instruction by creating two or more modules each year.
- Provide faculty and student mentors with tools and methods to integrate information competency into 60 percent of classes by 2009.

- Remodel and increase the capacity of the bibliographic instruction classroom by 2008. Remodeling will improve interaction by reconfiguring space and allowing instructors to control all workstations from the instructor's station. Capacity will be increased by 20–25 percent.

Again you can see the SMARTER elements in the objectives and how the objectives become the basis for effective action.

Once you establish the goals and objectives it becomes relatively easy to identify appropriate activities, programs, policies, procedures, and rules as well as the resources required to achieve the desired results.

Something to Think About:

Think of objectives for a public library, a university library, and an archive. Compare them to see if there are common objectives. Examine the language and style in which they are written. Are they written for the staff to read, or the users? Are they SMARTER?

POLICIES

Policies are statements that guide staff thinking in making decisions and handling work processes. Policies set limits within which to act. Policy implementation is something that almost all staff members take part in from time to time. A service may have a policy, for example, that access normally is granted to only certain categories of users, but that access may be granted to others under certain circumstances. The unit controlling access will probably generate unit-level rules that outline typical exceptions to the overall policy to ensure consistent staff interpretation.

There are several types of policies: originated, appealed, implied, and imposed. Information organizations must deal with all four types.

Originated policy is the ideal. Such a policy comes about from an organizational anticipation of the need for a policy. The more policies that come about in this way, the better it will be, because they originate from an understanding of the service's overall objectives. A danger for originated policy is structuring it so tightly that it becomes a rule, rather than the guide to thinking.

Appealed policy comes about from situations where there was no policy and one is necessary. Lacking a policy, staff will create their own when the need comes up—often unaware they are doing so. If several people do this, several somewhat different approaches probably exist. The most common way appealed policy arises is when a user becomes unhappy after experiencing the policy variations and brings to light the lack of consistency. Often the first-line staff appeal to someone in higher authority to sort out the differences. If that person finds the situation to be too nebulous or "important" to make a decision, then the problem moves around or up the hierarchy. When this happens, time passes, differences of opinion become entrenched in the absence of a resolution, and the likelihood of reaching a decision that pleases everyone decreases. There is little hope of completely stopping appealed policy making, but you do have options for keeping it to a minimum. One way to avoid appealed policy is to spend significant time and thought to developing originated policies that are clear enough to preclude the need for appeal and clarification.

Implied policy is the most dangerous type for user relations. Such policy arises from staff or user perception of what a policy actually intends. Senior managers usually assume that staff members understand and employ policies as intended. At the operational level, however, people may well be operating on the basis of what they believe is the intent of a policy. One way to reduce the risk of this happening is to provide new staff with some policy orientation sessions. It is also helpful to hold regular policy review sessions with all staff involved in policy implementation.

Imposed policy comes from outside agencies and groups with which the service must work. Some of this policy for information services comes from the parent organization (some examples are personnel, promotion, retirement, and budget policies). When the information service operates with one or more union or collective bargaining unit, policies covering such topics as work hours and conditions often are imposed through a contract. Such imposed policies may at times be in conflict with some of the parent body policies, so careful thought is usually required). National governments also can impose policy, especially if they are a primary source of funding (imposed policy might address public access or stipulate how funds are to be expended).

Something to Think About:

Review the four types of policies described above and give two examples of each taken from an information or library service known to you. If you feel that you don't have this depth of knowledge, try using an academic department in which you have studied.

PROCEDURES

Procedures are guides to action rather than to thought. They provide a chronological sequence of events that staff use to carry out the activities necessary to achieve a specific policy, objective, or outcome. Planning good procedures consists of a number of features, including keeping procedures to a minimum. Long lists of procedures that detail every action stifle initiative and individuality, and induce staff boredom. Failure to limit the number of procedures can lead to a morale problem, which often becomes a staffing problem. Because procedures are rather easy to generate, once you understand the process, some managers "procedure-ize" every activity they can. In the process, they create a deadly atmosphere for the people working for them. Having basic procedures in place, especially for complex activities, is essential, since they provide the framework for training new staff, as well as a baseline for evaluating unit outcomes. However, in those cases where it is possible to allow latitude, let the employees work out for themselves what is most effective. (Note: Allowing latitude does not mean "anything goes" in terms of performance. Instead, let the individual formulate how to achieve the standard.)

Procedures must serve a useful purpose. Information organizations often retain procedures that have outlived their usefulness simply because no one thinks to discard them. If a procedure reflects actual practice it may be a plan, but it also could be a carryover from activities involving objectives that no longer exist. A key question to ask is, "Did I *plan* the procedure or does it merely reflect existing practice?" Analyzing a procedure carefully (is it useful, is it still necessary, is it a plan) is the responsibility of every manager.

If the organization has clearly stated policies to guide (and promote) sound thinking and good procedures to guide actions (yet allow for individual initiative), then the work environment is usually more pleasant and effective. Striking the best balance is a challenge, but one that is easy to meet with some thought and staff input.

RULES

Rules are statements regarding specific actions one should or should not take in a given situation. Rules must be clear, easy to understand, fair, and not unnecessarily complex. As with other plans, periodic group discussions about operational rules help address enforcement as well as assess their ongoing utility. It should go without saying that new staff should receive proper orientation to any work rules. There should be no unwritten rules, as they can create only trouble and misunderstandings.

Some services inform a new employee of rules only after hiring the person rather than discussing rules during the recruitment and interview process. We believe prospective employees should be aware of any such rules prior to being offered the job.

Something to Think About:

At one time all new users of a library service were presented with a list of rules, which could be a formidable document. Does your public or university library have a list of rules? If it doesn't, how do customers find out what they are?

PROGRAMS

The term "program" is usually applied to a complex undertaking that involves several types of plans. George Terry defined a program as: "A comprehensive plan that includes future use of different resources in an integrated pattern and establishes a sequence of required actions and time schedules for each in order to achieve the stated objectives" (1972: 243).

Programs consist of policies, procedures, rules, job allocations, resource requirements, sources of resources, and other elements necessary to carry out a combination of objectives. Not every program includes all type of plans, but anything labeled as a program should outline actions to take (and when, where, and by whom). They should also indicate the purpose of those actions, and how the actions fit into the service's objectives. Also, programs need not be institution-wide; they can apply to a single department. (For example, consider the preservation program of an archive to increase microfilming or digitizing of materials already in the collection. Such a program would indicate how to select materials for treatment, how to handle them, what processes to employ, and who would do the work.)

When people think of policies, procedures, rules, and objectives as part of a system, they are better able to identity and isolate variables upon which the new program may have an impact. This is true because a sound program ties together a wide range of plans that the staff may view as being independent. Failing to consider the entire system and the interrelationships of the parts may well result in a problem at best and a disaster at worst.

BUDGETS

Budgets are plans of action expressed in terms of cost. The budget may express these costs in monetary terms, machine/person-hours, or a combination of these two. Budgets are simply estimates of what management thinks it will cost to carry out a plan of operation during a specified period of time. We explore budgets in Chapter 16.

WHO SHOULD PLAN?

Today's environment is such that effective planning, especially at the broad level, is rarely the work of just one or two individuals. Rather it is the result of highly collaborative efforts. Yes, probably only a few individuals do the majority of drafting and proposing; however, the final product reflects, or should reflect, the thoughts and input from the staff, the service community, and the governing and advisory bodies, as well as other interested parties.

An effective planning process, at any level, involves a fairly significant amount of time and effort. Much of the time and effort comes from the requisite give and take of ideas, feedback, and rethinking. Imposed plans may succeed, but success usually comes at a high organizational cost (for example, low morale, staff turnover, slow progress, or "unexpected" problems).

Check This Out:

Marianne Kotch's 2002 "Using the New Planning for Results Process to Create Local Standards of Library Service" (*Public Libraries* 41, no. 4: 216–219) is a good article that discusses both plan development and its nature.

VALUE OF PLANNING

Almost everyone agrees that planning is important, and that good plans are very useful at both the personal and the organizational level. That said, a growing body of literature raises serious questions about strategic and "long-range" planning and about whether there is difference between the two. There are also questions about what characterizes meaningful long-range planning.

Regarding planning versus strategic planning, J. Parker Ladwig (2005: 90) wrote:

> Strategic planning, is not the only organizational planning method. . . . A review of the library's history showed that the library had tried various corporate planning schemes in the past, for example zero-based budgeting, and total quality management (TQM). . . . We confirmed that strategic did seem the most comprehensive and that it had the most opportunity for our organization.

He went on to describe how some of the previous methods did not translate into the hoped-for outcomes and the planning group's hope for better results with strategic planning; only time will tell if the hopes were realized.

Kaplan and Norton (2006: 100) started their essay on implementing strategy by saying, "Strategic dreams often turn into nightmares if companies start engaging in extensive and distracting restructuring. It's far more effective to choose a design that works reasonably well, rather than develop a strategic system to tune the structure to the strategy." They also note that, due to changing circumstances, it is rare to achieve all the stated goals, and that adding restructuring to the plan creates more obstacles to that achievement.

Markins and Steele (2006: 76, 78, 81) were rather direct in their article;

> Is strategic planning completely useless? . . . In the fall of 2005, Markins Associates . . . surveyed senior executives from 156 large companies worldwide. . . . We asked these executives how their companies developed long-range plans and how effectively they thought their planning drove strategic decisions. The results [indicated] . . . that timing and structure of strategic planning are obstacles to good decision making. . . . No wonder only 11% of the executives are highly satisfied that strategic planning is worth the effort.

From an information service perspective, strategic or long-range planning is rather complex because so many services are part of a larger organization, and that body's concerns must drive the service's planning process. Sometimes the service faces a mandate to create a strategic plan; other times it may decide to develop a plan independently. When the former occurs, it is part of a systemwide activity in which "your plan will be incorporated into the broader plan." Although that may appear reasonable and logical, several factors all too often come into play. First, frequently you don't receive reasonably detailed systemwide planning assumptions (in some cases they do not exist). Without that information, you can find your efforts significantly modified in the final plan in order to "fit into the broad needs." A second issue is that, even with a set of systemwide assumptions, there can be significant differences between the solid trends in the information field and what are viewed as significant systemwide trends. This factor combined with a changing environment makes it clear why there often is disparity between envisioned results and the actual results.

If you explore some information service Web pages to look at mission and goals, you will probably notice that different services employ different terms for what appear to be similar concepts (strategic plan, long-range plan, and balanced score card are common labels). Posting a plan can generate some positive public relations as long as the plan is updated and there is progress toward the stated goals. The danger is that no one will modify the Web statement as the service actually makes adjustments to changing circumstances.

Ana Pacios (2004) undertook an analysis of some public and academic library plans posted on the Web, in an effort to determine if there was a difference between a "strategic plan" and a "long-range plan." The results were interesting. For example, for public libraries, regardless of the label, most of the plans contained mission statements, goals, and objectives; less than one-half but more than one-third contained a vision statement, environmental scan information, and action/tasks; less than 20 percent had a value statement or SWOT analysis. Her findings for academic libraries were that almost all statements were labeled as a strategic plan; mission, vision, and value statements, environmental scans, and goals and objectives were part of the overall plan—all appearing in one-third of the statements. Some of them—mission, for example—appeared in more than one-half of the plans. Again SWOT analysis was rarely mentioned in the plan. Pacios concluded that there was no significant difference between plans called strategic and those labeled long-range.

One of our favorite management writers, Henry Mintzberg, coauthored a book (Mintzberg, Ahlstrand, and Lampal, 1998) that provides a detailed assessment of strategic management. It provides insights into the strengths and weaknesses of various approaches to the process. The authors begin by likening strategy formulation to how blind people would describe an elephant when only grasping a part of the elephant. "Since no one has had the vision to see the entire beast, everyone has grabbed hold of some part or other and railed in utter ignorance about the rest" (Mintzberg et al., 1998: 3). The authors identified ten "schools" of strategy formulation. They suggest, "Pervasive strategic failure in many large corporations may well be attributed to the army of business school graduates who have been sent out with an incomplete tool kit" (Mintzberg et al., 1998: 20). Later, they indicate, "As we tried to point out in our critiques of the different schools, at times rather harsh, the greatest failings in strategic management have occurred when managers took one point of view too seriously" (Mintzberg et al., 1998: 368).

Like Mintzberg and his coauthors, we know that planning is essential for organizational success. However, you should never become too committed to the newest and greatest approach, be it management by objectives (MBO), TQM, scenario planning, or learning organization. Pick and choose thoughtfully, keeping local circumstances firmly in mind.

PROJECT MANAGEMENT

We end this chapter with a section on project management, since almost every information professional has to address "projects" many times in her or his career. No matter what label you use—assignment, task, or project—successfully handling the activity calls for very thoughtful planning.

Actually, although people often use the above terms interchangeably, they mean rather different things. Along with program, these terms form a continuum, with task at one end representing the smallest activity (such as loading a software update) and with program at the opposite end. A number of tasks make up a work assignment (maintaining all the online databases would be an example). Projects are single-purpose plans (installing a wireless network in public access areas, for example). A program is a combination of tasks, assignments, and projects (the service's ICT program, for example).

Projects have a four-stage life cycle—definition, planning, execution, and closing. Start by defining the "big picture" for the project: setting out specific goals, looking at how the project will impact other activities and programs, outlining the assumptions underlying the project, establishing a target completion date, and significantly developing a cost/resource estimate. Once you have the big picture well established, you can move on to creating plans that will achieve the project goals. During the execution stage you must monitor progress and often make rapid adjustments to stay on schedule. (Bringing in a project on time is wonderful; even better is doing so and being under budget. That only happens through consistent monitoring, thinking ahead, and trying to anticipate possible problems and potential solutions to those problems.) Closing is normally a short stage, with a focus on ensuring that the results are as expected, resolving "bugs," and assessing what did and didn't work in the project.

Teams and team building are almost always a part of project management. A key element in team functionality is how conducive the environment is for team work, and working to ensure such an environment is an important function for a project leader.

KEY POINTS TO REMEMBER:

- Planning aids in achieving goals by measuring progress, coordinating activities, addressing the future, and coping with uncertainty.
- Effective planning requires time and careful thought.
- Planning is forward-looking and entails elements of risk, uncertainty, and doubt.
- Planning takes on three time aspects: long-term (strategy), mid-term (tactical), and short-term (operational).
- Strategic plans build on several statements: mission, vision, and value.
- A mission statement sets overall organizational purpose (why we exist).
- A vision statement sets forth the long-term direction/goals.
- A value statement sets forth how the service expects to operate (service philosophy).
- Environmental scanning and SWOT analysis are key tools for effective long-term planning.
- Creating SMARTER goals and objectives is important to achieving the desired outcome(s) of any long-term plan.
- Plans come in several varieties: strategic, goals, objectives, policies, procedures, rules, programs, and budgets.
- Effective planning draws on input from all affected and interested parties.
- There are many models for long-term strategic planning.
- Successful project management requires careful and detailed planning.

REFERENCES

David, Fred R. 1989. "How Companies Define Their Mission." *Long Range Planning* 22, no. 1 (February): 90–97.

Drucker, Peter. 1974. *Management: Tasks, Responsibilities, and Practice.* New York: Harper.

Himmell, Ethel, and Bill Wilson. 1998. *Planning for Results: A Public Library Transformation Process.* Chicago: American Library Association

Johnson, Heather. 1994. "Strategic Planning for Modern Libraries." *Library Management* 15, no. 1: 7–18.

Kaplan, Robert S., and David P. Norton. 2006. "How to Implement a New Strategy Without Disrupting Your Organization." *Harvard Business Review* 84, no. 3 (March): 100–109.

Karim, Nor Shahriza Abdul. 2004. "The Link Between Environmental Scanning (ES) and Organizational Behavior." *Library Review* 53, no. 7: 356–362.

Kotch, Marianne. 2002. "Using the New Planning for Results Process to Create Local Standards of Library Service." *Public Libraries* 41, no. 4 (July/August): 216–219.

Ladwig, J. Parker. 2005. "Assess the State of Your Strategic Plan." *Library Administration & Management* 19, no. 2 (Spring): 90–93.

Line, Maurice. 2004. "Management Musings 15: Looking Ahead: How Far?" *Library Management* 25, nos. 1/2: 62–63.

Markins, Michael, and Richard Steele. 2006. "Stop Making Plans Start Making Decisions." *Harvard Business Review* 84, no. 1 (January): 76–84.

Miles, Raymond, and Charles C. Snow. 1978. *Organizational Strategy, Structure, and Process.* New York: McGraw-Hill.

Mintzberg, Henry. 1994. *The Rise and Fall of Strategic Planning.* New York: Prentice-Hall.

Mintzberg, Henry, Bruce Ahlstrand, and Joseph Lampal. 1998. *Strategic Safari: A Guided Tour Through the Wild of Strategic Management.* New York: Free Press.

Nanus, Burt. 1992. *Visionary Leadership.* San Francisco, CA: Jossey-Bass.

Nohria, Nitin, and Thomas A. Stewart. 2006. "Risk, Uncertainty, and Doubt." *Harvard Business Review* 84, no. 2 (February): 39–40.

Pacios, Ana R. 2004. "Strategic Plans and Long-Range Plans: Is There a Difference." *Library Management* 25, nos. 6/7: 259–269.

Rangan, V. Kasturi. 2004. "Lofty Missions, Down-to-Earth Plans." *Harvard Business Review* 82, no. 3 (March): 112–119.

Terry, George R. 1972. *Principles of Management.* 6th ed. Homewood, IL: Irwin.

LAUNCHING PAD

Bonn, Ingrid. 2005. "Improving Strategic Thinking." *Leadership & Organizational Development Journal* 26, no. 5: 336–354.

Bremer, Suzanne. 1994. *Long-Range Planning: A How-To-Do-It Manual for Public Librarians.* New York: Neal-Schuman.

Bryson, John. 1995. *Strategic Planning for Public and Nonprofit Organizations.* Rev. ed. San Francisco, CA: Jossey-Bass.

Gavetti, Giovanni, and Jan W. Rivkin. 2005. "How Strategists Really Think." *Harvard Business Review* 83, no. 9 (September): 152–153.

McClamroach, Jo, Jacqueline Byrd, and Steven Sowell. 2001. "Strategic Planning: Politics, Leadership, and Learning." *Journal of Academic Librarianship* 27, no. 5 (September): 372–378.

Nelson, Sandra. 2001. *The New Planning for Results: A Streamlined Approach.* Chicago: American Library Association.

9

Power, Authority, and Responsibility

"Champions take responsibility. When the ball is coming over the net, you can be sure I want the ball."

Billie Jean King

"To many leaders act as if the sheep... their people... are there for the benefit of the shepherd, not that the shepherd has responsibility for the sheep."

Ken Blanchard

INTRODUCTION

Planning is a major responsibility for managers in carrying their brief to ensure the service moves forward, and it is central to change management. They develop plans at both the macro and micro levels within the service. Although managers may personally implement some plans, many plans will become the responsibility of other people to implement.

In order to carry out a plan successfully, whether done by the manager or someone else, a person requires something more than people, money, and equipment to succeed. That something else is the authority as well as the responsibility to carry the activity through to a successful conclusion. Without this authority, it is doubtful whether a successful conclusion will be reached.

This chapter examines the concepts of power, authority, accountability, responsibility, and influence, and then considers the reality of organizational politics. Clearly the concepts have application beyond the implementation of plans. All managerial activities involve an element of power, authority, accountability, responsibility, and influence.

The terms "power," and "authority," and "influence," are often used interchangeably; however, they are very different concepts. *Power* is the ability to do something; *authority* is the right to do something; and *influence* is the ability to use examples or actions to cause others to change their behavior, something charismatic leaders often can do.

POWER

Power, like leadership, is easier to recognize than to define. It is generally invisible and it can be described as getting things done through other people.

The degree of power that people possess is evident in the sanctions available to them regardless of their position or office. Usually, managerial power sanctions include the ability to give, promise, and withdraw (or threaten to withdraw) rewards; inflict (or threaten to inflict) punishment; and fire (or threaten to fire) subordinates. These sanctions are common to all organizations and form the basis of power. In essence, they are penalties for failure to conform to, and accept, a supervisor's authority. From a positive point of view, power involves the giving of rewards for the acceptance of authority. Managers use power to realize the plans they have prepared in order to deliver the goals of their organization and service. However, managers are in turn influenced by the power exercised by the manager they report to, or their governing board.

The Expert:

"Organizational power derives from supplies of three 'basic commodities' that can be invested in action: *information* (data, technical knowledge, political intelligence, expertise); *resources* (funds, materials, space, staff, time); and *support* (endorsement, backing, approval, legitimacy)" (Kanter, 1983: 216).

One interesting feature common to most contemporary discussions of power is the negative reaction it invokes. Discussions often begin with the punishment (negative) aspects of power, which reflect the idea that power is harmful. This is generally not so.

A frequently overlooked aspect of power is its subjective nature. Opinions differ as to how much power a position or person should have. There is also a reciprocal aspect of power in that sanctions exist for both the supervisor and the supervised. Subordinates possess one very definite sanction for use against supervisors: their ability to control the quantity and quality of their output. For example, subordinates using this sanction can stage slow-downs or cause equipment breakdowns. Another tactic frequently employed by subordinates as a weapon against the indiscriminate use of power or authority by a supervisor is deliberate misinterpretation of instructions or orders. The weakness of such subordinate sanctions is that they require the cooperation of a large group of subordinates in order to be effective.

Another employee sanction is the process of striking, or organized insubordination. While many information services are agencies of a government unit and are therefore generally forbidden to strike, this sanction exists. In the United States, the legal basis against government employees' striking has been challenged, and strikes have occurred despite questions of legality.

Groups outside the organization also can contribute to the sanctions available to the subordinate. Unions, professional associations, and special-interest groups can bring pressure to bear on an institution and its administrators. One type of agency that can employ sanctions in many government-funded information organizations is the body that handles the employment process (for instance, the United States Civil Service). While sanctions can apply to both management and subordinates, subordinates are usually the ones requesting help. Referrals may be made to an independent body, such as a commission or industrial-relations tribunal: These groups are indeed powerful, as they can overrule a management decision regarding promotion, job security, and probation matters. Hearings are usually long and involved, with both winners and losers finding the process frustrating, stressful, and expensive. Because of the possibility of an independent body intervening and the potential visible and invisible costs to the organization, supervisors tend to avoid making decisions that are likely to cause an employee to request a hearing. The existence of independent bodies, therefore, acts as a strong sanction against blatantly prejudicial managerial actions.

To some degree, all sanctions act as psychological whips, because their very existence often generates the desired behavior in both employee and employer. Managers seldom issue ultimatums because everyone knows that existing sanctions will apply if undesirable behavior has not been eliminated. When it becomes necessary to apply sanctions, it is in a very real sense an admission of failure, because the undesirable behavior still exists. Negative power sanctions (punishments) are rarely as effective as positive sanctions (rewards) in maintaining desired behavior.

In 1965, Cartwright reviewed the literature on the nature of managerial power, providing one of the best brief conceptual summaries of the types of managerial power. Cartwright presented five categories of power:

1. Reward power arises from a subordinate's belief that the supervisor has the ability to grant rewards. (Example: raises or promotions.)

2. Coercive power arises from a subordinate's belief that the supervisor has the ability to impose punishments. (Example: transfers or demotions.)
3. Referent power arises from a subordinate's desire to be identified with the supervisor and that person's power.
4. Legitimate power arises from a subordinate's internalized belief that the supervisor has the right to direct that person's activities.
5. Expert power arises from the subordinate's belief that the supervisor has special knowledge and skills that make it reasonable that the supervisor directs the person's activities (Cartwright, 1965: 28–30).

These are potential sources of power.

Most managerial power is a combination of these categories, usually with one or two of them dominant. When a manager has strong expert and referent power, there is seldom a question about other styles. When expert power is weak, there is usually a significant question about legitimate power. How often have you heard (or made) the statement that "X shouldn't hold that job—he doesn't know anything about it"? When a person is appointed to a senior position, there always seems to be a testing period during which professionals wait to see how much "expert" knowledge the new manager possesses. Should the professionals find the manager lacking, a power struggle may result.

John Kotter identified six characteristics of managers who use power successfully for the good of the organization and its employees:

1. Effective managers are sensitive to the source of their power and are careful to keep their actions consistent with people's expectations.
2. Good managers understand—at least intuitively—the five bases of power and recognize which to draw on in different situations and with different people.
3. Effective managers recognize that all bases of power have merit in certain circumstances.
4. Successful managers have career goals that allow them to develop and use power.
5. Effective managers temper power with maturity and self-control.
6. Successful managers know that power is necessary to get things done (Kotter, 1977).

Kotter concentrated on the use of power; however, as noted earlier, included in the power mix is acceptance by subordinates and the reciprocal nature of power. David Mechanic identified several sources of informal power of subordinates. To him, a critical source of informal power is subordinate knowledge of, and information about, daily operations and activities.

Withholding such information can make supervisors look foolish and make bad decisions (Mechanic, 1962). Two other sources are the skills of the subordinate and how those skills impact on use of organizational resources. Power is an important issue in an organization. It is "good" or "bad" depending on whether it is used for the benefit of the organization or against the organization, or work unit. The goal should be to "use it, not abuse it" in furthering the organizational mission and goals.

Earlier we commented that power is generally invisible, and this can be seen in the discussion above. However, within some organizations, power may be perceived to be held by the managers who have the largest number of staff within their department or the largest slice of the organizational budget. But there are other factors that can endow a manager with power within an organization. They are the socialization of the staff within their department, and the networks the managers and their staff build within the wider organization and the user community. A small, well-organized department can hold and use power to its advantage within the organization. Information services are often small units within a much larger one, but use their influence to good effect.

> **Remember:**
>
> Power is latent; political behavior is the action.

AUTHORITY

Authority is a necessary part of organizational life. Fayol indicated that authority is the right to give orders and to exact obedience. Max Weber, in his *Theory of Social and Economic Organization*, suggested that there are three types of authority: (1) traditional, (2) charismatic, and (3) legal (Weber, 1947). Traditional authority is found in monarchies, and it gains a level of legitimacy through the concept of "divine right." This type of authority is inherited. Charismatic authority is moral authority gained through an individual's special abilities, visions, or sense of destiny. Gandhi, Mohammed, and Castro are examples of charismatic individuals. This type of authority seldom passes on to others; it ends with the death of the individual. Legal authority is a function of the position held by a person; it resides in the position or office rather than the person holding the office. Legal authority derives from laws established by legislative bodies to govern the ways in which a society agrees to function. It is legal authority that will be addressed in this chapter.

> **The Expert:**
>
> "Authority exists where one person has a formal right to command and another has a formal obligation to obey" (Wrong, 1979, cited in Drummond, 2001: 123).

All organizations, including information services, are concerned with the distribution of power and authority within the organization. Although Wrong's view of authority is widely held—the right to do something being associated with a position within an organization—this needs expansion when discussing managerial authority. R. V. Presthus provides a fuller definition in an excellent article on authority and organizational structure:

> Authority can be defined as the capacity to invoke compliance in others on the basis of formal position and any psychological rewards, inducements, or sanctions that may accompany formal position. The capacity to invoke compliance without relying on formal role or sanctions at its disposal may be called influence. A formal position is not necessarily involved but when extensive sanctions are available we are concerned with power.... Authority, power, and influence, are usually interlaced in operating situations. However, the definitions attempt to focus on the conception of organizing as a system in which interpersonal relations are structured in terms of the prescribed authority of the actors (Presthus, in Mailick and Van Ness, 1962: 123).

In an information service environment, a manager's authority consists of rights such as those related to making decisions, assigning work to subordinates, reviewing their work, and recommending their retention or release on the basis of performance. Occasionally, a manager has the formal right, but not the capability, to enforce actions, a difficulty that arises from the reciprocal and subjective nature of authority. Authority is reciprocal in that each person in the process uses the anticipated reactions of the other persons involved as the basis on which to act. The anticipated behavior may, or may not, materialize. Authority is subjective in that each person's estimate of how much authority others should or do have arises from that individual's moral and ethical values. In view of the reciprocal/subjective nature of authority, it is surprising that challenges to authority in an institution do not occur more frequently.

One reason for this lack of challenges is the legal basis of organizational authority. Authority is made legitimate by the process of socialization. One aspect of dealing with new employees is to integrate the person into the work group and organization. If the organization operates with certain individuals identified as having a degree of authority, and current employees accept this as being proper, new employees are likely to accept the situation as well. Because people are generally taught from birth to respect authority, the individual normally accepts institutional definitions and assignments of authority as a matter of course. Chester Barnard (1968) labeled this as the acceptance theory of authority.

While socialization is basic to the legitimization process, other factors are equally important for the acceptance of authority. There must be a constant validation process. A position may carry an accepted amount of authority, but the office holder must demonstrate an ability to retain that office and exercise its authority, usually through technical-professional skills and/or knowledge. Presthus (1962) calls this legitimation by expertise. Whenever subordinates begin to doubt a supervisor's ability or knowledge, that person loses authority and may resort to the use of sanctions. In so doing, the supervisor is partially admitting to a loss of authority by using whatever power is available. While the wielding of power may enforce conformity, that conformity will last only for a limited time.

Formal role and rank is another way to legitimate authority. For instance, if your position in the service is above mine, then you must have more authority than I do. In information services, especially in large archives and libraries, authority resides in small amounts in a number of positions, but each level in the structure must have some authority, resulting in a hierarchical pattern of authority; most bureaucratic organizations depend on this method of legitimating authority. As Presthus points out, however, both expertise and formal role methods of establishing the right to authority lead to conflict at the higher levels, where the office holder cannot be expert in all the fields in which authority has to be exercised.

Leadership that depends on personal qualities apart from technical expertise represents another method of legitimating authority. Presthus labeled this as legitimation by rapport, and it seems to have an element of Weber's ideas on charismatic authority. For many individuals, their real basis of authority lies not in position or professional skill, but in an ability to work with (and through) people. Some can hold a great deal of authority in an institution solely on the basis of being "a real person with a genuine interest in people." Individuals of this type hold their positions because of the affection and loyalty that subordinates and superiors have for them. They also have to demonstrate an understanding of the area managed or else they will not be able to hold authority for very long.

Authority is an active process, both subjective and reciprocal. It flows in two directions: downward, through an organizational structure of positions, and upward, from subordinates to individuals holding superior positions. The bases for validating authority are: traditional acceptance of authority, expertise, position, rank, and personal characteristics.

ACCOUNTABILITY

There is a direct relationship between accountability, power, and authority. The process of accountability includes three basic factors: legal, legislative, and administrative. Two of these (legal and legislative) are, for the most part, extra-institutional. Administrative accountability is basically internal in nature, although it can be external.

Legal accountability relates both to actions taken and actions not taken. Most frequently, the failures involve national laws or orders concerning such things as equal employment, affirmative action requirements, and access to services. Local and state statutes and regulations also have an impact on operations, since courts can and do impose financial or penal sanctions on managers and institutions found guilty of failing to act within the prescribed legal limits. At least one librarian was dismissed and fined for the way in which he handled book fines, even though he employed practices commonly used in libraries and acceptable to the library board. Those practices, though, were contrary to city ordinances, and when someone filed a complaint, legal action followed.

Legislative accountability bodies enforce accountability laws in two main ways: through the courts and through hearings. Because the cost of the judicial process mitigates frequent use, the legislative body can (and often does) call for hearings to determine whether the manager or agency carried out its wishes and/or orders. Investigative hearings, budgetary hearings, and new legislation hearings are some of the types frequently encountered. Lawmaking bodies also have the ability to reduce or increase an agency's authority and appropriations. Library and information services in the public sector have been especially vulnerable to the last-mentioned type of control, since in the past they did not build user-base support. Effective marketing programs are overcoming this problem.

The legislative control process operates within limits. No legislative body has the time to oversee all operational details of all agencies accountable to it. Since details are left to the agencies, interpretation of what a legislative order means and what can be done will vary. Usually, the legislative body visits an agency only during budget hearings, or when an agency makes a request, or when it receives a number of complaints about the agency. Although legislative values are imposed during the accountability process, the manager usually discovers that there is a wide range of activities not determined by legislative action; decisions or activities within such areas are not subject to legislative accountability.

Administrative accountability is common to all information agencies. For government agencies, including archives, record management, and library services, the matter is somewhat more complex than it is for private institutions. Political factors enter the picture. For instance, a government campaign to limit or reduce taxes may mean that services have to forgo requesting budget increases, even up to the existing legal limit, in order to support the government's position.

Check These Out:

Howell, Donna W. 2004. "The Politics of Public Library Boards." *Rural Libraries* 24, (1): 15–24.
Wade, Gordon S. 1991. *Working With Library Boards: A How-To-Do-It Manual for Librarians.* New York: Neal-Schuman.

Because many information services are accountable to the government, they must comply with government regulations on a wide range of activities, including those controlling accounting and purchasing. These regulations can cause a great deal of extra work for information agencies if they are followed faithfully, because they are seldom developed with the problems of purchasing information materials in mind; they also can take time to catch up with new publication formats. Securing an exception may involve a long, drawn-out legislative or bureaucratic process. In some jurisdictions, the funding authorities mistakenly want collection development funds to be used only for print materials. In order to purchase nonprint materials, it may be necessary either to spend time getting permission or "break the rules" by making nonprint orders look like print items.

Administrative accountability in government is complex, political, and often confusing, because different units may issue conflicting orders, each based on a legislative mandate. Frequently there are doubts as to where real accountability lies, especially when legislative and administrative units clash over an issue in which political gain seems to be the dominant factor.

RESPONSIBILITY

Although some people use the terms "accountability" and "responsibility" interchangeably, there is a significant distinction between them. In essence, responsibility is what one must do, whereas accountability is the being answerable for an action. Thus, accountability is important in the process of enforcing responsibility.

A manager is always completely accountable, and a manager can make someone else completely accountable, but responsibility has a dual character. Responsibility is always shared. An individual or unit has the responsibility or obligation to do something, but the individual or unit assigning that responsibility always retains a portion of responsibility. In a sense, delegating responsibility increases the responsibility of the delegator, because that person must then supervise the assigned responsibility.

When a person accepts a task, she/he also accepts responsibility without giving much thought to this concept. Someone who is unwilling to accept responsibility usually refuses the job. Everyone has worked at some time with an individual who did not accept responsibility for her or his work and performed just well enough to keep from being fired. No amount of talking or delegating responsibility will change such a person's attitude. Acceptance must come from within the individual. Responsibility is a person's obligation to himself or herself to perform given tasks.

Successful managers are those who are comfortable delegating responsibility and authority, and who also do not become unduly concerned about residual responsibility.

Try This:

Write down the differences between "accountability" and "responsibility," and give two examples of this in relation to a service of your choice.

Information Services: Power, Authority, and Accountability

There are differences in the source of power and authority between the public and the private sectors. Public and school libraries operating in the public sector derive their power and authority from a government jurisdiction. Academic libraries, together with special libraries, records management, and knowledge management services operating in the private sector, derive their power and authority from a parent organization, a governing board, or a corporate director. The nature of the parent organization determines the source of power and authority.

In general, information services that are part of larger organizations present their managers with interesting problems regarding power and authority. Certainly one of the first things that a new manager needs to do is gain a clear understanding of the power and authority associated with the position, as well as how it is tied to the next level. Many new professionals are surprised to learn that there are laws or regulations specifically relating to the way in which a service may operate. In the public sector, these laws are generally enacted by state, county, and municipal governments. In some countries, however, archives and libraries draw on national laws and regulations for their establishment.

In addition, national laws that do not specifically mention information services may have a surprisingly strong influence on what may or not be done in the way of service. An example is the U.S. Civil Rights Act of 1964. Since the purpose of the law was to assure equal treatment for all citizens, it would perhaps be expected that public information services not already providing equal service would be required to do so. Indeed, that is generally the case. However, the concept of equal service, from a legal point of view, is more complex than might be first expected. For example, in the mid-1970s, at least one library system in the United States ran into some problems with the local district attorney over the way in which the system funded its branch programs.

At that time, U.S. public libraries generally employed one of three basic methods for funding branches and their programs. One method was simply to divide the available branch services funds by the number of branches. This approach, however, did not take into account heavier work loads—and thus higher costs—for some locations. A second technique was to base funding on the level of use: home use of materials, reference questions answered, or some other measure of use. The most common practice (the third approach) was to combine these two methods, so that all branches received a minimum level of support with additional funding provided based on use. This was an attempt to ensure that heavily used (high-cost) branches could provide the level of service needed by their communities. At first glance, these methods, especially the third approach, seemed fair and not a violation of the Civil Rights Act. But this was not the case, since a local district attorney's office found several potential violations of both state and federal laws. Although the public library had no intention of creating unequal service, the system had in fact created that situation, and the outcome—not the intent—is what the courts examined.

What is not taken into account by funding based on level of use or dividing available funds is the changing composition of a community. Take the example of a library that has built a collection designed to meet the needs of the local community (say, a predominantly white middle-class group). Problems can arise when the community changes to, say, 60 percent Hispanic. The collection designed for the previous group probably would have less appeal to the new residents, and a slight drop in use would result in a slight decrease in funding. At this point, a cycle starts that is hard to break. Less money and increasing prices for materials will make it harder and harder to revamp a collection.

In an actual case, the City Attorney's report concluded: "As set forth above, the criterion of circulation, though neutral on its face, appears to function in a manner that is not racially neutral in fact, operation, effect, and consequences. As a result, existing disparities in the allocation of library resources between white and minority communities raises serious legal difficulties under applicable federal and state constitutional and statutory law" (*Report...*, 1975: 76).

Although the City Attorney took no legal action as a result of the report, it did stimulate the library, the library board, and others to review the situation completely. Over a period of years, increased funding and reallocation of resources has helped to improve the balance of service, and the system established a process to keep the situation from arising in the future.

This example demonstrates how easy it is to do something "by the book" and still find yourself facing potential trouble. Even with the best of intentions, people can run into problems for themselves and their services. If you have a question about the legality of a situation, ask for a legal opinion. However, you must remember that an opinion is just that: a best estimate of how the courts might construe the point of law in question. If you act on the basis of a legal opinion from a municipal or city attorney's office, you may still be found guilty of violating a law, although you probably will not pay a fine, because you acted in good faith (that is, you sought and followed legal advice). For libraries, such legal opinions can be very important. Consequently, the California State Library, to cite one example, has been publishing an annual list of the state attorney general's opinions regarding library and information service issues, as a guide for information professionals in the state.

Pause for Reflection:

Reflect on the terms "authority," "power," and "influence." Focus on the situation in your area, and, selecting a type of information service, identify the ways in which each impacts on the service.

INFLUENCE

The dividing line between "power" and "influence" at times can be blurred. Influence implies persuasion (Bierstedt, 1950), which can be exercised by using words, actions, or personality. Within an information service, people can be influential but not hold a position of power—or they may hold a position of power but have little influence.

Clearly the greater the influence you have, both within the service and the wider organization, the more likely it is that the service will benefit. But the emphasis is based on the ethical premise that influence is for the service's benefit rather than for personal gain. Managers who understand organizational politics can identify those who have influence within the service, the user community, the organization at large, and the profession.

Respect is a factor in gaining influence. You gain respect when you are straightforward: for example, knowing when to discuss an issue with a peer prior to raising it at an organization-wide meeting, or issuing an instruction within the information service. Over a period of time this ensures that you are seen as open and trustworthy. Developing good listening skills, understanding how to work effectively in committees, and thinking strategically all help you gain influence.

Status

Changes in authority or responsibility usually bring about changes in status; therefore, you should look at any proposed change in procedure or policy in terms of its impact on the existing delegation of authority and responsibility. What a manager may think of as a very minor change, subordinates may view as significant, so thoughtfully consider all changes and how they affect everyone.

The status that subordinates assign to an individual is not entirely the result of formal authority and rank. Most people dislike taking orders from those they consider equal to themselves unless they believe the individual has earned the right to do so based on work performance. For example, a clerk may take orders from a peer in areas where that peer has more experience or skill. In general, however, a person must hold an order-giving rank as a result of delegation by a superior if the peer group is to accept the orders. Clearly, the relationship between authority and status is very close.

The use of titles and other status symbols can be helpful, but can also be dangerous. Never attempt to use titles or status symbols as a substitute for real rewards for work performance, especially in place of promotions or salary increases. When using titles, be sure to use them for clearly defined activities and abilities. Many services make no clear distinction between the abilities, skills, and training required for top-grade clerical personnel and beginning-grade professionals. Some job descriptions are so confusing that you cannot readily determine whether the position requires, for example, the abilities of a clerk, paraprofessional, or professional. Confusion as to role, status, and authority results in poor workflow, communication, and morale. There should be a clear-cut distinction in titles, and the application of these titles should be consistent throughout the service.

Try This:

Check out the titles given to each member of staff in a service known to you. Are they made known to users, and if so, are they meaningful?

> **Tip:**
>
> Some services have badges for their staff that gives the first and family name of the individual, together with a job title. Getting a promotion can be an excuse for a staff get-together at which the new badge is presented. Users find it helpful to be able to distinguish between members of the staff—and to be able to put questions to the right person.

ROLE CONFUSION

Managers have a duty to keep the causes of stress as low as possible for the staff. One potential stress factor arises from how individuals perceive their roles. These have been identified as being role ambiguity, role conflict, or responsibility for others (Drummond, 2001: 209).

Role ambiguity can occur when staff members face situations in which the role requirements are unclear: for example, whom they report to or what is expected of them. Role conflict emerges if there are conflicting role requirements, such as following the rules set down by management versus the needs of users. Another form of conflict can revolve around duties about which staff members feel uncomfortable: perhaps having to deny a user access to a service, or perhaps meeting illegitimate role requirements that make demands outside their conditions of employment, such as a member of the support staff being asked to carry out duties that are deemed to be professional. Having to take responsibility for other people or for high-end resources, or having to make hard decisions can also be causes of stress.

There is another source of stress that centers on role confusion. This may arise if a staff member assumes a position of power within the information service as a result of influence on colleagues. A weak manager who fails to make clear the responsibilities and the limits of delegation held by every staff member is likely to suffer considerable stress. Who is the real "boss"?

TRUST AND DELEGATION

Trust and delegation go together; without trust, delegation will not be effective. Trust needs to be present between managers and their bosses, and between managers and their staff. It is an essential part of teamwork and is vital to knowledge management, where every person needs to share information fully and not hold back.

Organizational climate is one factor in trust. When things get tough people are less likely to share all their thoughts and ideas. In a sense, they start to "freeze." Delegating authority in these conditions presents a risk for managers, but Hurley (2006) has developed a model to predict whether a person will choose to trust another, in a given situation. He identifies ten factors that come into play during the decision-making process:

Decision-maker factors:
- the degree of risk tolerance of the truster
- the level of adjustment of the truster
- the amount of relative power held by the truster

Situational factors:
- the degree of security felt by the parties
- the number of similarities they have in common
- how well their interests are aligned
- the trustee demonstrates benevolent concern for their team
- the trustee is competent
- the trustee has demonstrated predictability and integrity
- the parties have good communication

Tip:

Creating an organizational climate in which team members can build and maintain trust with one another increases the effectiveness of the service; everyone benefits—the service, the community served, and the parent organization.

One of the signs of a poor organizational climate is the manipulation of situations in which people take action to ensure that they are the only beneficiary of the outcome. At its simplest level, this can be changing shift or leave rosters without concern for others. A more serious example would be the deliberate feeding of information to the manager that isn't quite accurate.

Building trust is a precursor to delegating responsibilities; as noted previously, delegation will not be effective without trust.

Delegating responsibilities is one of the challenges for a new manager. Learning how to delegate effectively comes with experience of working in a given situation. As emphasized, no two organizations operate in the same way, and it takes a little time to judge how the senior management views delegation. However, new managers quickly understand that they can't do everything—there are not enough hours in the day, nor do they necessarily have all of the skills and experience held by the people with whom they are working. Micromanaging is not a good idea.

There are some guidelines to help make the process more effective:

- Plan ahead and consider which tasks, responsibilities, or decisions can, and should be, delegated.
- Think about staff members—their strengths and weaknesses—and delegate to the person best suited, but don't play favorites.
- Delegate complete tasks so that the outcomes can be built into the appraisal process; it is part of building the learning organization.
- Building outcomes into the appraisal process is one incentive that can motivate the person to whom the work is delegated. Other incentives may be identified, such as training.
- Give clear instructions—verbally and perhaps backed up by an e-mail—so that clear parameters are set for the individual. An ambitious person may end up treading on colleagues' toes as a result of misplaced enthusiasm.
- Follow up on your instructions to ensure that there are no misunderstandings and that the work is in hand.
- Then let go. Don't micromanage—you have other tasks to do.
- Encourage staff members and wait for feedback when the work has been completed.
- Assess outcomes in a discussion with the person to whom the work was delegated—with their supervisor, if appropriate—and feed into the appraisal process.
- Consider whether benefit might be gained by additional training to extend the person's skills.

TEAMWORK

Teamwork is effective when trust and delegation are present and when the staff understands the concepts of authority and responsibility. Given the flatter hierarchies and extended service hours of most organizations in the information sector, teamwork is an effective way to organize staff. You can form teams to coordinate work across the service, to work on specific aspects of service, or as a facilitator to change management.

The team needs to have a mission: to know what is expected of it and whether there are "markers" that will measure progress and achievement. Clearly, "markers" can motivate a team. In addition to a mission, all team members have to understand the boundaries of the authority that it has been delegated as well as who has the responsibility to ensure that the team works effectively and efficiently.

Putting a team together presents a challenge for both the manager and the members of the team. Some training in working together—to learn trust, develop communication skills, and learn how best to use individual attributes, experience, and skills—will help get a team off to a good start. Team members should expect to encounter disagreements and perhaps conflict; they need to know how to handle these situations and use them as part of the learning process. Teams need to be in touch with the work of their other colleagues—it is easy for them to be focused only on their work to the exclusion of others. To this end, they need to have good communication both among team members, and with other colleagues.

Leading a team presents an opportunity for a person to develop leadership skills. Basic requirements are clearly those of having good communication and people skills in general. Bringing out the best in team members builds a group that creates respect for one another. The ability to build consensus and handle disagreements is required if the leader is to gain, and hold, the respect of the team. A basic attribute will be good time management skills and the experience of handling meetings efficiently and effectively.

Teamwork is one form of empowerment, but individuals may also be empowered to carry out tasks. Marlene Caroselli (2000: 107) identifies five levels of empowerment: inform, investigate, intend, initiate, and independence.

Check These Out:

Christopher, Connie. 2003. *Empowering Your Library: A Guide to Improving Service, Productivity, and Participation.* Chicago: American Library Association.
Manville, Brook, and Josiah Ober. 2003. "Beyond Empowerment: Building a Company of Citizens." *Harvard Business Review* 81, no. 1: 48–53.

Team Accountability

Tip:

"Team members frequently discuss the information that they are all aware of and fail to share unique information with one another" (Bazerman, Max, and Dolly Chugh. 2006. "Decisions without Blinders." *Business Review* 84, no. 1: 94).

As many information services have organized staff into teams, so questions of power, authority, responsibility and accountability become more important. It is a particular issue for knowledge managers and information services where a number of teams operate. In this situation, a sense of competition may emerge, and while this can be healthy, careful management is needed to ensure that it is not destructive of the service.

ETHICS AND SOCIAL RESPONSIBILITY

This is an appropriate point at which to consider ethics and social responsibility. Ethical behavior within business has been highlighted in recent years. Managerial interest in organizational social responsibility stems from H. R. Bowen's monograph *Social Responsibility of the Businessman* (1953). He believed that managers had an obligation to take into account societal values and objectives in addition to organizational needs when carrying out their managerial activities. In the information services area, many professionals strongly agree with that view. Carroll (1979, 1981) suggested that in for-profit organizations there are four areas of responsibility: economic, legal, discretionary, and ethical. Information services have responsibilities in all four areas. Social responsibility and ethics are probably two of the concepts that will differ from country to country. What follows draws heavily upon U.S. and Western European viewpoints.

Management ethics deal with right and wrong actions and activities. The difference between social responsibility and management ethics is the focus of the former on organizational action and activities and the latter on personal actions. While the definition appears clear-cut, it is seldom so in practice. A study published in the 1980s indicated that first-line supervisors (41 percent), middle managers (26 percent), and top managers (20 percent) all believed they had to compromise personal principles in order to conform to organizational expectations (Schmidt and Posner, 1982). A key to keeping ethical conflict to a minimum is for top management to behave in clearly ethical ways by setting a good example and to recognize that conflicts may exist in the minds of subordinates. A very simple example of how such a conflict could arise would be in a library with a policy that the collection should contain all points of view on subjects. Does the collection-development staff face a possible conflict between personal values and organizational expectations? The answer is often yes, depending upon the subject and an individual's religious, political, and other beliefs.

One of the ways to help reduce conflict is to have codes of ethics, both professional and organizational. Codes assist staff in thinking about ethical issues, as well as assisting top management to identify possible areas of conflict. Most national professional associations have such codes. However, in order to be effective, codes need to have some sanctions attached to violations of the code. Failure to include sanctions turns a code of ethics into a meaningless public-relations statements.

Check These Out:

Two examples of professional codes of ethics:
  The Society of American Archivists
  (www.archivists.org/governance/handbook/app_ethics.asp)
  The American Library Association
  (www.ala.org/ala/oif/statementspols/codeofethics/codeethics.htm)

The literature on managerial ethics suggest that five factors impact ethical decision making: laws, government regulations, ethical codes, social pressure, and the conflict between personal values and organizational needs. The basis for making the choices, from an academic point of view, comes from a branch of philosophy called normative ethics. Within this field, there are three groups of theories that provide the manager with some guidance in making a choice. The first are utilitarian theories, which hold that the outcomes of actions or decisions should be the basis for judgment as to the rightness or wrongness of a choice. John Stuart Mill is perhaps the most notable writer in this area. His idea that moral choices are those that produce the greatest good for the greatest number of people is nice, but determining the "good" is a complex and often impossible task. Perhaps it is easier to identify unethical choices; most would agree that a decision that enhanced only the position of the decision maker at the expense of others is unethical.

Moral rights theories hold that everyone has certain rights that should be respected in all decisions. Most management scholars believe all members of an organization have five fundamental rights: free consent, privacy, freedom of conscience, free speech, and due process. Human-rights criteria are somewhat easier to apply than are utilitarian criteria. It is easier for the decision maker to determine if the choice will violate one of the five rights.

For Further Thought:

Locate a copy of the code of ethics issued by your national professional association. (If one has not been issued, then look at the American Library Association's code.) Does the code provide *practical* guidance that can be acted upon by managers? What do you consider to be the most difficult ethical or moral dilemma that a manager is likely to encounter today?

Sometimes professionals find that a conflict may arise between a code developed by their professional association and an instruction issued by their manager. Questions of privacy can occur, or access to certain services or information. Divided views of ethical behavior are probably the greatest challenge that managers encounter.

THE VISIBLE ORGANIZATION

This term is used to describe the organization as it has been designed to operate; later discussion will cover the aspects of organizational life that are often not visible, such as organizational politics.

But first, consider the visible structure. Most organizations have a chart, which is a way of describing the governance of the organization. This is generally indicated in an hierarchical layout showing each tier of management and supervision and the place of departments and their staff in it. It becomes a visible indicator of accountability.

In order to assist the functioning of the organization, committees are often created, to operate at organizational, division, and department levels, and within departments.

Committees

Committees are important to an organization in a number of ways. They can serve in an advisory/informational capacity (gathering material and making recommendations), promote coordination and cooperation (especially among disparate areas), improve communication (which, unfortunately, can backfire), and make decisions. Although rhetoric about committees is often negative, everyone continues to use them. The reality is that committees, although occasionally ineffective, are frequently the best means of accomplishing a specific goal.

The structure of committees ranges from informal gatherings, such as a lunch group, to a formal standing committee that has a long list of responsibilities and powers. The manager who understands committees and knows how and when to best use them can be highly effective. Because the informal gathering differs from a committee meeting only in purpose, alert supervisors often encourage informal gatherings of committee people (or supervisors). Once gathered for social activities, coworkers find it is only natural to "talk shop," and perhaps more committee work will progress forward from there.

Permanent committees (standing committees) are useful at all levels of the organization. Their purpose is usually clearly related to important institutional activities. Large library and archives services have standing committees for a variety of purposes, such as the promotion committee (embodying the concept of peer evaluation), a system/database committee, and a materials selection committee. Although the membership of such committees should rotate, the committees themselves play a permanent, vital role in the service's operations and management.

The governing boards of information organizations operate much like committees, because they are just that, a committee. Top management uses committees to handle special problems or problems that cut across functional lines. Middle management can use them to coordinate existing operations, plan new programs and services, and evaluate work. For lower-level management, committees can be useful in handling special operational problems, unit decision making, and procedural change recommendations.

When setting up a committee, a manager needs to take time to formulate an accurate statement of what the committee is expected to do (its "charge"). A charge should clearly indicate which roles the committee should fill. Perhaps the greatest area of confusion—almost always due to a poorly prepared charge—is between an advisory and a decision-making role. It is not uncommon to read or hear about members of an advisory committee being angered when their advice is not taken. The time used to prepare a formal charge can ultimately save a lot of time and, not infrequently, emotional energy.

There are several advantages to using committees. Committees involve more people in decision making who can offer a variety of viewpoints, help coordinate work between departments, stimulate client interest in improving services, and help train managers and supervisors. Perhaps the most important of these advantages is that the committee allows a number of people, many of whom might otherwise have no voice but do have something to contribute, to enter the decision-making process. This allows staff to accept a decision that they, or their peers or users, helped formulate. (See Chapter 6, which presents methods of stimulating thinking in a group assembled to solve a problem.) Stimulating the interest of the user community is important: it helps to keep a service in touch with its community. One good way of obtaining that input is to have community members on committees that plan new services and programs.

A secondary aspect of a committee, regardless of its charge, is that it can involve staff from more than one department, as well as being helpful in training management/supervisory personnel. For instance, while a committee might have as its primary charge the coordination of work between two departments, this may produce a secondary benefit. Inexperienced personnel can serve with experienced members, which broadens their perspective about the service; they gain practice in working with peers and superiors on a common problem. This can be an invaluable staff development tool.

But there are several drawbacks of using committees: high cost, stalemate, inordinate delay, compromise, domination of the group by a single strong personality, and no true accountability. The high cost can be mitigated (in salary, time, and lost production) by closely monitoring the activities of committees. If they are proving wasteful and unproductive, they should be disbanded.

> **Tip:**
>
> Some businesses now hold meetings where staff members stand rather than sit down. Meetings are said to be shorter.

Another disadvantage involves the quality of the decisions reached by a committee. If all a committee can achieve is a compromise decision that would only worsen a situation if implemented, or a decision forced on the group by dedicated minority, then the committee has failed in its function. If an unworkable compromise forces a manager to create his or her own solution, then feelings may be hurt and future cooperation endangered. If the manager rejects a minority recommendation, then that minority will probably be especially vocal in opposing any proposed solutions.

Perhaps the greatest disadvantage of committee work is that, due to the shared responsibility of the committee, a manager cannot hold one person, not even the committee head, accountable for a poor decision. Even if an idea began with one person, the group's acceptance of it makes it their recommendation. Of course, a manager can disband committees that perform poorly, or appoint new members. It would be unfair to apply sanctions (such as withholding salary increases, promotions or demotions, or firing) against individual committee members for a committee's failures. In sum, if a manager needs to have accountability, he or she should probably not use a committee.

> **Tip:**
>
> Identifying all of the committees that exist in a service may not be easy. If you are working in an information service, try and list all of them. If you are not, try talking with a senior person who is and see how many committees he or she can identify.

THE INVISIBLE ORGANIZATION

In discussing power, authority, and responsibility, the focus up to this point has been on the visible and generally documented aspects of organizational life: for example, the formal work of committees. However, there are also less visible aspects which are derived from organizational politics and tacit influences on power and authority. Who has influence—and power—within the organization? Who influences the decisions that are made, and how is this achieved? This is where an understanding of the invisible structure of the organization is essential.

All organizations are political, and the game of politics is played out at every level, both within the organization and within the service. Some people have a liking for politics and are skilled at playing the game, but the majority of managers recognize that these skills must be developed with experience over time. Think about the game of chess—some people are natural players from an early age, but most develop skills after playing for some time.

Check This Out:

A useful guide to developing political skills can be found in Peter Block's 1987 *The Empowered Manager: Positive Political Skills at Work* (San Francisco: Jossey-Bass).

Politics enters into organizational life for a number of reasons. Even in the best of times there are never enough resources to be shared; disagreements can spring up between departments or teams down to the level of individuals; and there is often the question of self-interest. Managers feel that it is their duty to ensure that their domain has its "rightful share" of scarce resources.

Managers work to gain influence and control of major decisions and do this by building alliances and coalitions with other managers within the organization. This is where networking, building good working relationships, and being visible within the organization and the user community all play an important role. Managers develop public relations skills in order to be better advocates and lobbyists for their service. In our experience, the smaller the service, the more important it is for the manager to be a skilled advocate and lobbyist, both within the organization and the wider community. A manager has to ensure that the service is recognized as being essential and adds value to the organization and the community it serves. A high profile and positive image help to overcome any barriers.

Committees are the place where political skills are developed. Observing body language, listening to other members—what they say and the words they use, reading minutes and key reports are all indicators of where the real power and influence lies in a committee. It isn't always the person who says most or speaks longest who holds the power. Rather, it is the person who has done his or her homework before the meeting and talked with those who have influence over the decisions to be made. In universities, committee members who are on the faculty can be great supporters of the library if they are fully briefed about the strategic plans of the service and have a good working relationship with front-line staff members.

In very political organizations, some decisions may be made in informal meetings that take place before a formal committee meeting. On occasion, an issue may appear to be debated before a decision is made, but it may be an "agreed" decision. "Trading" can take place between individual members prior to a committee meeting—"you scratch my back, and I'll scratch yours." In large organizations, there is often a meeting of key members of a committee to examine the agenda before the full committee meets—this can exclude members of the committee external to the organization. The amount of information made available before the meeting and the order of items on an agenda may influence the views of the full committee. [Providing a great deal of written information and extensive documentation to committee members can be as frustrating as having information revealed at the meeting.]

Negotiation plays a role in committee work and in organizational politics. Information professionals develop good communication skills, including the art of listening—an important factor in negotiation.

Check This Out:

Ertel, Danny. 2004. "Getting Past Yes: Negotiating As If Implementation Mattered." *Harvard Business Review* 82, no. 11 (November): 60–68.

Effective negotiation requires:

- a carefully thought through strategy
- the ability to sort out what is important from the less important
- carefully considered tactics
- flexibility, developed by weighing up the costs
- a clear decision on your approach
- understanding your own strengths
- knowing the weaknesses of the other party(ies)
- a face-to-face meeting, if possible
- assertiveness but not aggressiveness
- not expecting to win every time, since losing sometimes brings benefits in the longer term

Coalitions and alliances play a role in organizational politics. Smaller departments can share their common interests in forming alliances within organizations when resources are allocated.

Coalitions become important in sharing access to resources among services. One example is the way that libraries set up cooperatives to purchase electronic resources or information systems. In such situations, it is important that there is a high degree of trust and respect between the parties involved.

Our experience in organizational politics indicates:

- Everyone needs time to develop political skills.
- Managers who are skilled at politics understand the organizational culture and climate and the tacit aspects of power and influence.
- Networking and visibility matter.
- It is essential to take care with what you say and to whom—the grapevine is powerful.
- Managers should know who owes the service favors and call them in when necessary.
- A willingness to compromise on small matters can increase influence and power.
- Behaving in an ethical manner is vital.
- It is beneficial to under-promise and over-deliver.
- The interests of users are paramount—without users the service would not exist.

Learning about organizational politics takes a little time. Again, it is important to remember that no two organizations play the game in exactly the same way.

KEY POINTS TO REMEMBER:

- Organizations are structured in different ways and there is a visible and an invisible structure.
- Whichever the structure, the amount of power, authority, and accountability that is allowed to each unit is the starting point. These concepts are reciprocal.
- Top management does not hold all the power, or even all the authority.
- Subordinates have the power and ability to withhold recognition of the skills and knowledge of their managers which effectively reduces that person's power and authority.
- Subordinates have the power to control the level and quality of their production, which places a control on the manager's actions.
- Managers should recognize that these concepts are reciprocal and act in a positive manner on that knowledge, so that the work environment has a strong element of mutual respect and, perhaps, understanding.
- All organizations are political, but political skills have to be learned before they are used.
- Always behave in an ethical manner.

REFERENCES

Barnard, Chester I. 1968. *The Functions of the Executive.* 30th anniversary ed. Cambridge, MA: Harvard University Press.

Bazerman, Max and Dolly Chugh. 2006. "Decisions Without Blinders." *Harvard Business Review* 84, no. 1 (January): 94.

Bierstedt, R. 1950. "An Analysis of Social Power." *American Sociological Review* 15, no. 6: 730–738.

Block, Peter. 1987. *The Empowered Manager: Positive Political Skills at Work.* San Francisco: Jossey-Bass.

Bowen, Howard Rothman. 1953. *Social Responsibility of a Businessman.* New York: Harper & Row.

Caroselli, Marlene. 2000. *Leadership Skills for Managers.* New York: McGraw-Hill.

Carroll, Archie B. 1979. "A Three-Dimensional Concept of Corporate Performance." *Academy of Management Review* 4 (October): 497–505.

Carroll, Archie B. 1981. *Business and Society.* Boston, MA: Little, Brown.

Cartwright, Dorwin. 1965. "Influence, Leadership and Control." In *The Handbook of Organizations,* edited by James G. March. Chicago: Rand McNally.

Drummond, Helga. 2001. *Introduction to Organizational Behavior.* New York: Oxford University Press.

Hurley, Robert F. (2006). "The Decision to Trust." *Harvard Business Review* 84, no. 9 (September): 55–62.

Kanter, Rosabeth Moss. 1983. *The Change Masters: Innovations for Productivity in the American Corporation.* New York: Simon and Schuster.

Kotter, John P. 1977. "Power, Dependence and Effective Management." *Harvard Business Review* 55, no. 4 (July–August): 135–136.

Mechanic, David. 1962. "Sources of Power of Lower Participants in Complex Organizations." *Administrative Science Quarterly* 7 (December): 349–364.

Presthus, R. V. 1962. "Authority in Organizations." In *Concepts and Issues in Administrative Behavior,* edited by S. Mailick and E. H. VanNess. Englewood Cliffs, NJ: Prentice-Hall.

Report on Legality of Branch Funding Disparities. 1975. Los Angeles: City Attorney of Los Angeles.

Schmidt, Warren H., and B. Posner. 1982. *Managerial Values and Expectations.* New York: American Management Association.

Weber, Max. 1947. *Theory of Social and Economic Organization.* Translated by A.M. Henderson and T. Parsons, T. Parsons editor. New York: Free Press.

Wrong, Dennis Hume. 1979. *Power, Its Forms, Bases and Uses.* Oxford: Basil Blackwell.

LAUNCHING PAD

Belanger, David. 1995. "Board Games: Examining the Trustee/Director Conflict." *Library Journal* 120, no. 19 (November 15): 38–45.

Butcher, David, and Martin Clarke. 2003. "Redefining Managerial Work: Smart Politics." *Management Decision* 41, no. 5: 477–487.

Gibelman, Margaret; Sheldon Gelman; and Daniel Pollack. 1997. "The Credibility of Nonprofit Boards." *Administration in Social Work* 21, no. 2: 21–40.

Gilmer, L. 2001. "Straddling Multiple Administrative Relationships." *Journal of Library Administration* 31, nos. 3/4: 219–224.

Golembiewski, Robert T. 1964. "Authority as a Problem in Overlays." *Administrative Science Quarterly* 9 (January): 23–49.

Grojean, M. W., C. J. Resick, M. W. Dickson, and D. B. Smith. 2005. "Leaders, Values and Organizational Climate: Examining Leadership Strategies for Establishing an Organizational Climate Regarding Ethics." *Journal of Business Ethics* 55, no. 3 (December II): 223–241.

Hannabuss, Stuart. 2000. "Being Negligent and Liable: A Challenge for Information Professionals." *Library Management* 21, nos. 6/7: 316–329.

Henington, David M. 1994. "Public Library Directors: Hierarchical Roles and Proximity to Power." *Library Trends* 43, no. 1 (Summer): 95–104.

Henry, Linda J. 1985. "Archival Advisory Committees: Why?" *The American Archivist* 48, no. 3 (Summer): 315–319.

Meijer, A. 2000. "Anticipating Accountability Processes." *Archives and Manuscripts* 28, no. 1: 52–63.

Miller, E. 2001. "Getting the Most from Your Boards and Advisory Councils." *Library Administration & Management* 15, no 4 (Autumn): 204–212.

Nonprofit Governance. 1997. Chicago: American Bar Association.

Synder, Herbert. 2005. "Management Basics: Life as a Library Board Member." *Indiana Libraries* 24, no.1: 52–53.

10

Delegation

"If a sufficient number of management layers are superimposed on top of each other, it can be assured that disaster is not left to chance."
Norman Augustine

"Delegating work is not the same as delegating responsibility."
Maurice Line

INTRODUCTION

Chester Barnard, as we mentioned earlier, defined an organization as two or more people consciously working together in a coordinated manner to achieve a common goal. What that means is that two people on a small boat working together to catch tuna fish (assuming they plan to sell the fish) are just as much an organization as the seafood company Chicken of the Sea International. The only difference is the size and scale of operations. The two fishermen would need little formal structure but would have to coordinate their activities and make sure that all essential activities were handled in a timely manner. Beyond a document formally recognizing their "partnership," they would likely just discuss who would handle what and trust one another to carry out the tasks. Chicken of the Sea, on the other hand, requires a complex formal structure to ensure that its worldwide operations are coordinated and performed. Both cases—and anything in between—reflect a process labeled delegation: making certain someone has the assignment to carry out all necessary tasks and that the tasks are coordinated.

Delegation is a means by which you can assess what tasks are required to achieve a goal/objective, allocating the tasks to members of the group, and structuring the working relationships in a way you believe will best assure the tasks will coordinate with one another. As the size of the organization increases, so does the complexity of the procedure and the need for formalization/recording of the structure.

For many people, the most tangible aspect of delegation is the organization chart. Such charts are a visual presentation of the organization's structure; their boxed labels and lines connecting the boxes describe an organization: what it does, how it goes about doing it, and who does it. Organization charts illustrate how the organization assigns formal authority and responsibility.

John Hamm had the following to say about the power and influence of the "org" chart:

> The organizational chart, because it represents individual power or influence, is an emotionally charged framework even during a company's most stable times. But when the corporate structure is changing, the org chart can truly become fearsome, particularly in companies where, because of the political culture, employees worry about risk to their personal status (Hamm, 2006: 117).

Although his focus was on the profit sector, his point applies equally well to information services. People do worry about their status in an organization, and the organizational chart is a clear picture for one and all to see where each colleague fits. How you analyze tasks, projects, and work assignments, and then go about structuring their relationship, determines how you draw the chart at the end of the delegation process.

Before discussing the process, the usage of "organization" in this chapter should be clarified. Previously the word "organization" was used in the Barnardian sense, meaning a social unit formed to achieve a specific objective. Here we will continue to use the term in that sense, but will also use it to refer to a method of arranging work units and resources to accomplish desired goals/objectives.

With regard to organizations, there are more variations than the two most people think of: profit and nonprofit. Within nonprofits, there are two major types—service-oriented and mutual benefit. Examples of benefit organizations are political parties, trade associations, professional associations, and unions. Service organizations have three subtypes: publicly funded organizations offering services to some people (University of Minnesota); privately funded institutions offering services to some people (Harvard University); and what are sometimes called commonweal organizations, which are publicly funded and offer services to anyone (Boston Public Library). What type of nonprofit or profit organization you work in can have an influence on the way you structure your information service.

DELEGATION PROCESS

You might think at first that delegation/structuring is something one does only once, when creating an organization. However, after a moment's thought, you realize that "restructuring" or "reorganizing" is something you hear/read about very often. You are likely to experience and implement a reorganization process a number of times in your information service career as services struggle to adapt to the twenty-first century environment.

As an environment becomes less stable and/or more complex, organizational flexibility becomes a key factor in long-term viability. For organizations, including information services, some of the environmental factors bringing pressure to be more flexible are:

- Consumer/user demand is less and less predictable.
- Technology is constantly and ever more rapidly changing.
- Competition for scarce resources is growing.
- Economic cycles are less and less predictable.
- Workforce expectations, especially those of younger workers, are changing quickly.
- Workforce lifestyles are changing.

Judy Hunter (2002: 13) rather concisely stated today's organizational needs:

> The factors that most affect the design of an organization can be categorized into two segments. The first segment consists of contextual elements that include strategy, environment, business size/life cycle, and culture. The second segment consists of structural elements that including reporting relationships, decision-making processes, communication processes, co ordination of work, forms of complexity and distinguishing characteristics. The responsibility of managers is to design organizations that fit these elements.

A 2006 issue of *The Economist* also addressed the idea that organizational structure must and is changing to meet the demands of a more complex world. The editors made the point that restructuring is especially necessary for "knowledge workers," who are playing a more and more dominant role in the workplace. They acknowledge that professional firms (knowledge workers) have existed for years—accounting, consulting, legal, etc.—and have successfully employed some form of partnership to structure their activities. However, they suggest that this does not work in large firms, and especially not in the nonprofit sector.

Traditional organizational structure came into being during an age when manufacturing/production was the major economic powerhouse and where the vast majority of people engaged in some form of physical labor. *The Economist* article noted, "'Alas,' writes Mr. Davenport, 'there is no Fredrick Taylor equivalent for knowledge work. As a result we lack measures, methods, and rules of thumb for improvement. Exactly how to improve knowledge work productivity...is one of the most important economic issues of our time'" (*Economist*: 10). One approach for a new structure is what the editors called "disaggregated." A disaggregated organization is one in which responsibility (and its necessary authority) is pushed down to front-line staff, more group processes, and many more leadership roles at lower levels. Interestingly, this is the type of restructuring that libraries and other information services have been undertaking for a number of years, as will become clear as you read this chapter.

Delegation of authority is the establishment of authority relationships that provide both horizontal and vertical coordination between working units in an institution. In the information services, its purpose is to help units work together to achieve the overall objectives of the service. Organizing/delegating brings together the necessary resources, personnel, and equipment in an arrangement that allows units and individuals to accomplish their activities as effectively as possible. Managers must clearly understand that the process of organizing combines both people and resources. George Terry's definition of organizing emphasizes this point:

> Organization is the establishing of effective behavioral relationships among persons so they may work together efficiently and gain personal satisfaction in doing selected tasks under given environmental conditions for the purpose of achieving some goal or objective (Terry, 1977: 298).

CREATING A STRUCTURE AND POTENTIAL CHALLENGES

There is a five-step cycle for organizing: (1) determining what activities need to be done; (2) creating logical groupings of the activities for an individual to perform (work assignments); (3) identifying combinations as work units (departmentation); (4) assuring that activities are connected to one another in a manner that promotes coordinated efforts (coordination and span of control); and, finally, (5) monitoring outcomes and reorganizing/adjusting the structure as necessary to achieve the desired outcomes (evaluation). Thus, proper organizing lets everyone know what their duties are and what to do. When duties are clear, performance improves and confusion/uncertainty should not exist (at least in terms of "who does what").

Lines of authority and responsibility also become clear, leaving no doubt as to who is responsible for what and who is accountable when accountability is necessary. Lines of communication (which normally follow those of authority and responsibility) become known, so that everyone knows where to send official communications and from whom to expect such communications.

Information service managers must keep several things in mind as they go about their organizing activities. First, *all* delegation means entrusting others to carry out some large or small part of the *delegator's responsibilities*. For first-time mangers, this can be a challenge. For some it is a matter of self-confidence/insecurity in a new role. Being responsible for reorganizing work patterns and telling people their new duties/activities can be daunting your first time, and even thereafter. How to gather useful information, how will the staff react, what if I don't get it "right"?—these are some of the issues that come up for everyone, not just first-timers. Getting it "right" is perhaps not the best way to think about the outcome because it implies there is one best answer. Given a rapidly changing environment, "right" will probably have a relatively short time span. Getting something that creates a positive improvement should be your goal, and recognizing that you will repeat the process again over time will help reduce fears of failure. As a first-timer, you will find that getting advice from more experienced people will also help.

Another challenge for some managers is their level of truly trusting others to do the job correctly. As a result, they attempt only to give task responsibility without the requisite authority. For the first-time manager, there is some reason for concern about staff performance, since there is no body of shared experience to draw upon. Only time will change that. However, it is usually not a good idea to keep too many tasks rather than delegating some, as that will only delay the learning/sharing process. Knowing what and when to delegate takes some time and experience.

Tip:

When you confront the need to think about delegating something ask yourself three questions to sort out important issues/concerns about when and when not to delegate.

- Because of my special knowledge/skill, do I need to be involved in this?
- Does this really fall within my sole responsibility and/or will it affect the entire unit or its budget?
- Is there a deadline and would it negatively impact unit performance if I don't do this myself?

When the answer is no to one or more of the questions delegation is probably a good option. Things like paperwork and other "routine" activities are always prime candidates for delegation. Clearly anything confidential and/or personnel matters should not be delegated. Often special projects and technical matters are most effectively handled on a shared basis.

Challenges also exist on the receiving side of delegation. One common issue is an unwillingness to accept the responsibility and authority. Sometimes this arises because those being asked to accept something new had bad experiences when they accepted a previous request from a particular manager. Occasionally one encounters an individual who simply does not want *any* responsibility. In that case, the manager should accept that fact and make certain the duties assigned to this person do not carry much responsibility (a job with low depth and scope; see below).

Another factor in reluctance is there may be little or no incentive for assuming an extra or new duty/activity. "We cannot do anything for you now, but we really appreciate your doing this. We will make this up to you later." Such managerial statements work only so long as the organization *does* do something positive for the person. Not only must there be delivery of the "make up"; the time frame for the delivery needs to be relatively short, certainly not more than a year.

In the broadest sense, you can think of delegation as a form of time management tool for both yourself and the organization. By developing clear reporting structures, assigning authority and responsibility, etc., you reduce the need for consultation as well as confusion about who does what and when. Making effective use of your time will make your work life less stressful. It is easy to slip into poor work habits that cost you valuable time, so by providing a structure for yourself and others you have a start on managing your time.

Check These Out:

Four very useful books on time management are:

David Allen's *Getting Things Done* (New York: Viking, 2001)

Stephen Covey's *Seven Habits of Highly Successful People* (New York: Simon & Schuster, 1989) and *First Things First* (New York: Simon & Schuster, 1994)

Patrick Lencioni's *Death by Meeting* (San Francisco: Jossey-Bass, 2004)

All organizations are social systems to a degree within which an informal organizational structure exists; in many ways, due to the nature of the work, information services are even more strongly impacted by informal groups. Job-related experiences give rise to informal groups, such as the "morning coffee regulars," "the bowling group," or "the lunch bunch." Whatever mutual factors brought the people together; all such work groups share a common, usually dominant, conversational theme: the job. News, complaints, rumors, and ideas are a normal part of their conversation. It is common that informal groups cut across departmental or unit lines; thus, information and rumors quickly spread through the entire service. If the staff views the formal communication lines (those established by the organizing process) as inadequate, the informal line of communication (grapevine), over which a manager has little or no control, soon takes over as the primary information source.

An able manager can use this informal structure to achieve organizational objectives. This is not to say that a manager should try to manipulate informal groups. Rather, the manager should observe the groups; it may well be possible to put together more productive work teams by grouping together like-minded people. A manager should apply that knowledge in a way that will increase everyone's satisfaction and productivity.

Some years ago, Harvey Sherman outlined the degrees of delegation with which a manager has to work. His scheme starts with the highest degree of delegation and progresses to the lowest.

- Take action—no further contact with me is needed.
- Take action—let me know what you did.
- Look into this problem—let me know what you intend to do, then do it, unless I say not to.
- Look into this problem—let me know what you intend to do; delay action until I give approval.
- Look into this problem—let me know alternative actions that are available with pros and cons and recommend one for my approval.
- Look into this problem—give me all the facts, I will decide what to do (Sherman, 1966: 83–84).

Something to Think About:

Reflect on an organization in which you have worked, and the person to whom you were responsible. Did they delegate tasks? If so, how did they ensure that the delegated tasks were completed satisfactorily? If the manager did not delegate, why do you think this was so? Was the manager's approach appropriate?

One point we cannot emphasize too strongly is that you can *never* delegate your accountability for the delegated task(s). (Accountability is essentially the responsibility for the work performance/project that remains with a manager/supervisor after she/he has delegated the work to others. You must justify—take the blame, if necessary—for poor work results. If there are performance issues, the manager/supervisor must take steps to correct the situation. Should the situation be beyond the person's skill/authority to correct, she/he must seek assistance from more senior staff.)

Another important factor to remember about information services and their relationship to their parent organization is that the most senior manager (director, dean, etc.), no matter how team-oriented or flat the organizational structure, is *always fully accountable for everything that does or does not take place in the service.* This is something many junior staff members sometimes fail to remember or perhaps even don't know. You can understand, with this in mind, why striking the best balance of responsibility, authority, and accountability across the service is a challenge.

Check This Out:

Phillip J. Jones provides a thoughtful assessment review of authority and accountability in the information service context in his 2000 "Individual Accountability and Individual Authority: The Missing Links" (*Library Administration & Management* 14, no. 3 [Summer]: 135–145).

ASSESSING WORK/JOB DESIGN

With the above discussion in mind you can understand the importance of carefully assessing what needs to be done and how to coordinate activities. You face several challenges when it comes to designing jobs. Almost every organization, and certainly most information services, have some tasks that are repetitive, boring, and/or tedious but which someone must carry out. At some time staff/volunteers want, expect, and more or less demand activities that are rewarding and/or challenging learning opportunities. They make that clear by "voting with their feet"—resigning and moving on to what they hope will be more satisfying opportunities. Your challenge is to find a way to get everything done and yet provide reasonably rewarding positions/jobs.

There are several aspects to job design: job depth, job scope, and work characteristics. *Job depth* is the degree to which the individual is able to control her/his work. A job that requires close adherence to standards, has detailed procedures for every step, or requires close supervision lacks depth. When there are established outcomes, but the means of achieving that outcome is in the hands of the individual, there is job depth. For a few people, low-depth jobs are what they want, as there is little responsibility beyond following what someone else has established as proper procedure. For others, only jobs with great depth are satisfactory.

Another challenge is to match people with jobs. When it comes to low-depth positions, it is best to spend the time to find a person who will be happy performing such job rather than taking a "really great person."

More often than not such individuals quickly become dissatisfied and ask for something better, in spite of what may have been said during the job interview about not being concerned about the nature of the work.

Job scope relates to how many different activities or operations the person performs and how often. As you might expect, a job with few activities and with a high rate of repetition has little scope; the reverse is true for wide-scope jobs. There is also a strong relationship between job scope and where the job appears on an organization chart. Low-scope jobs tend to be first line and near the lower part of the chart. As a person moves up the chart, so does job scope.

It is important to remember that a given position can contain jobs of varying depth and scope. For example, when an information service director prepares a proposal for a new service, there is high depth and scope; when she/he reviews monthly budget reports there is relatively low depth and scope.

Job characteristics, which we will explore in greater depth in Chapter 15, relate to what it will take to perform the job. These characteristics include which skills are necessary, knowledge needed, experience, independent judgment required, who the users are, and the importance of the job to the overall well-being of the service. Obviously there is an interconnection between job depth, scope, and characteristics; jobs of high depth and wide scope call for more knowledge, skill, and experience than do jobs with lower degrees of these factors. You should keep all three in mind as you engage in organizing.

Something to Think About:

Returning to the organization in which you have worked, and the job that you did, try and identify the job depth, job scope, and job characteristics. Were these made known to you? Were they picked up in the course of the employment? Had you consciously thought about them earlier?

Your primary task, then, is to assign people, or groups of people, to specific tasks in order to accomplish the service's objectives. To do this, you should consider the ideal as well as the current structure. The closer you come to the ideal, the better it is for the service. (Often there are facility limitations, lack of staff, equipment, or other resources that keep you from coming very close to the ideal.) Remember that a variety of possible structures exist; therefore, there should be a number of options to consider, not just one or two variations. The factors to consider when choosing a structure include: commonality, intimate association, frequency of use, managerial interest, competition, and policy control.

Keep in mind Joseph Boisse's point "that there is no 'best' way to organize a library" (Boisse, 1996: 77)—tall, flat, matrix, team-oriented, etc. Very often a mixed structure works well for handling the variety of activities that information services engage in within themselves. Another factor that is also important to concede and act upon, regardless of your own personal preferences or voices in the professional literature touting a particular structure, and that is, what are the expectations/requirements of the parent body? Such expectations/requirements can limit your effective options.

Check These Out:

To read about structural issues and the parent body's impact consult articles like Joanne Euster's 1990 "The New Hierarchy: Where's the Boss" (*Library Journal* 115 [May]: 41–44) and Thomas Shaughnessy's 1996 "Lessons From Restructuring" (*Journal of Academic Librarianship* 22, no. 4 [July]: 251–257).

Commonality may at first appear to be the simplest approach to implement, as it calls for grouping people who perform the same tasks into one unit or area. Determining the basis of commonality is not always as easy as it may seem. Consider word processing skills; commonality would suggest that a common pool of individuals to handle all the word processing and serving all units would be best for the service. Would increased production result from combining the workload from senior managers with the work of preparing order forms? In some cases it might; in others, probably not. The point to remember is that the application of commonality is more complex than it first appears.

A common approach in information services is *intimate association*. That is, all activities related to a particular set of goals and objectives are in one unit whose sole responsibility is the achievement of those goals and objectives. This normally results in most units having a variety of staff categories: clerical, paraprofessionals, and professionals. Some inefficiency can arise from this structure, as there are normally a large number of different activities; this means staff members may not be as proficient in any of the activities as they might if there were fewer activities to perform.

Frequency of use comes into play when one department accounts for the major share of the use of a function. For example, the responsibility for mounting and supporting electronic resources might well go to the public-service unit or staff that works most closely with end users. However, if two or more departments make equal use of a service, then a separate unit might well be considered (as in product/form departmentation—see below).

Strong managerial interest might lead to the assignment of an activity to a supervisor who is especially interested in the activity or function. There are two considerations to keep in mind when thinking about using this approach. First, the person who has the interest may not have the background to succeed. Second, the physical facility limitations may make it impossible to handle an assignment in this manner.

You might consider using *competition* when a unit is not achieving desired performance levels. One option is to create a second unit to perform some, or all, of the activities of the first unit, with the expectation that competitive spirit will develop between the two units and lead to higher performance. This is not an option many services can consider, due to limited resources; however, it might be possible to split the existing unit into two groups. Perhaps two teams of public service staff could enter into friendly competition in terms of quality service to users.

Finally, you can assign work on the basis of *policy control.* The assumption is that you can assign work and related policy that does not clearly belong to any one unit to whichever unit will most likely interpret the policy in the manner senior management expects. In a library setting, for instance, a manager can give the task of handling fines and other customer-fee assessment to any one of several units: circulation, document-delivery services, the reserve-materials unit (primarily in educational institutions), or perhaps even the reference unit. In an academic library, it is very possible that circulation and reserve might have very different views about assessing fines. Top management would probably assign the task of policy determination to the unit whose philosophy is closest to the desired interpretation.

The above clarifies our point that assigning work may not be as simple as you might expect. Creating a new unit to perform a task previously done by several units may appear to be a good idea on paper, but you should fully explore the ramifications of doing so before implementing the plan. Assigning work takes time and thought, and, when changing personnel, you must constantly reexamine assignments to ensure efficient work performance and a reasonable distribution of tasks among capable personnel.

Departmentation

Departmentation (step three of organizing) is the process of dividing work into semi-independent units. Each level in an organizational chart represents a unit of departmentation. You should organize the activities in terms of goal and objective accomplishment, not for your convenience or tradition.

There are five basic departmentation techniques in common use. Information services typically employ several, if not all, of the techniques, which are:

1. functional
2. territorial
3. product
4. user-services
5. equipment or process

Functional departmentation is the oldest method; the functions are: production, sales, and finance. In terms of information services, you need to broaden the definitions in order to understand how the traditional functions apply to the service. When *production* is defined as adding to the utility of goods or services, then you can understand how an archive adds value to the papers it acquires by processing, creating groupings of documents, and preparing finding aids. Defining *sales* as finding users who are willing to accept the goods or services at the price set by the service may help clarify how the public-access areas of an archive to fit into this category—limited handling of materials, only allowing pencil or laptop note taking, etc. Defining *finance* as securing and controlling the expenditure of funds, then the head of the archives engages in this function.

The functional method has a long and successful history. It has the advantage of being logical, it reflects the broad functions of any organization, and it ensures that staff members give proper attention to these basic functions. The major problem of using the functional method is that it is hard to employ in an institution having units in different (and sometimes distant) locations. The method can, on occasion, result in de-emphasizing institutional goals and objectives.

Traditionally, information services used the functional approach as the overall structure: technical (production), public (sales) services, and administration (finance). Since the early 1990s, information services, especially libraries, have moved away from this pattern as they adjust to a changing environment. You must keep in mind that organizing is an ongoing process, or should be as circumstances change.

A 2005 article (Higa et al.) describing the redesign of the University of Texas Southwestern Medical Center's library provides insight into the factors you need to consider when rethinking organizational structure. "The project's goals were as follows: Have the right people in the right number of jobs (allocated to the right tasks) to best support our current environment and the Library's stated vision for the future" (Higa et al., 2005: 42). The authors identified three major factors that lead to the undertaking:

- a growing gap between the staffing needs for new digital environment and adequate allocation of staff
- a problematic team approach that challenged traditional workloads
- the absence of a clear vision to unify staff efforts (Higa et al., 2005: 44)

The before and after organizational charts at the end of their article illustrates some of the ways you might go about departmentizing an information service. Also, their second factor highlights that just following the current trends in structuring does not automatically lead to success.

Territorial departmentation focuses on service points where distance is an issue. In theory, while all organizational functions (production, sales, and finance) can take place in each branch location, the result would be at best a loose federation rather than a single information service. Branches would probably be competing for a finite pool of resources to support their activities with little or no regard for the larger picture. Typically, information service branch operations only carry out a "sales" function, with a central unit handling all production and finance activities.

There are several situations in which you should not use the territorial approach. If there is a sense that there is a significant communication problem, dividing the organization into branches will do little to improve the perceived problem. Indeed, such an approach can make matters worse. The branches may become more isolated and begin to think of themselves as basically operating on their own.

Another reason not to use the territorial approach is if there are complaints about slow delivery of information to distant users. Delays usually are due to ineffective handling or routing services, not the service point location. Adding new service locations will only increase handling time.

The territorial approach is a *good* method for providing more personal service. Although service may be somewhat slower, the personal touch—usually because the user-to-staff ratio is better—results in increased client satisfaction. Having a large satisfied user base, especially if they are willing to speak out about the value received, can be a valuable asset when it comes time to ask for funding increases. Moreover, the existence of branches serves as a constant reminder to everyone of the system's existence. People are more prone to using convenient and familiar locations. Remember that today's users, especially those with Internet access, do not always have to use a service to secure desired information.

From management's viewpoint, there is another reason to use branch units. Since branch managers and supervisors are on their own very often when it comes to having to make quick decisions, they either develop or fail much more quickly than in a large centralized service. Branch supervisors become more confident in their decision-making ability as they get independent practice. Thus, branches can serve as a testing ground for individuals who may do well in even more responsible positions. Branches also provide more training opportunities than might exist with a central operation. That is, if there are 20 branch managers, it is cost-effective to bring in a trainer to conduct workshops on various management and professional matters; it would be harder to justify this training for five or six department heads in a large centralized operation.

As a means of organizing work for a high level of personalized service, the territorial method has much to offer. When used in the proper way, it can be an effective method of organizing that will assist in delivering quality service.

You can employ *product departmentation* to create little "institutions" out of larger ones. In libraries, this method sometimes carries the label *form division.* Under this approach, a unit takes on all the activities of the parent institution (generally with limited financial responsibilities), but for only one product (for example, serials, manuscripts, maps, government documents, media collections). When using the territorial method, staff members usually deal with all forms of materials but only one function (sales); in product departmentation, the staff specializes in the form and engages in all functions to some degree. This type of specialization allows staff to develop a high level of competence with all aspects of one format, gaining a depth of skills and knowledge that someone working with many formats has little opportunity to acquire. Another advantage is that the high knowledge level usually results in equally high quality of client service. User confidence increases, as does satisfaction with the materials and services received.

Clientele service departmentation is a useful approach in certain circumstances, the most obvious example being in public libraries that have a separate children's services unit. Other examples include young adult services, undergraduate libraries, services for the blind and shut-ins, and institutionalized services (for hospital wards, prisons, and nursing homes). In a corporate information service, it is not uncommon to have one service for the research and development staff and another for the rest of the staff. Normally, this structure focuses only on sales/service. In some cases, production activities are part of the unit; however, it is rare for the unit to have financial responsibility beyond managing the funds that the central unit assigns to the unit. Another feature of this departmentation method is that a wide variety of factors can come into play when designing such a unit: age, sex, income, health, educational level, subject interest, and how critical is the information need. Often, such units require special skills (such as storytelling or very sophisticated database searching) and special equipment (such as children's furniture, reading machines, or other equipment to assist the visually impaired). This approach can also produce a very high quality of service and a high level of user satisfaction. Client-oriented service also increases staff skills, because staff members develop in-depth expertise in one area.

Equipment/process departmentation is another method available to you for grouping work activities. Information services rarely employ this approach, except in areas such as photocopying, multimedia, and ICT applications. Proper use of this method depends upon two factors: money and space. For instance, it is generally too costly to provide photocopy equipment for each library unit, and few units would be able to provide the space even if the equipment were available. Therefore, it becomes cost-effective to set up a single central location with all the necessary equipment and have qualified staff available to support the needs of all units. One of the benefits that may get overlooked is that the rest of the staff does not need to devote much time to learning how the equipment works. That alone means better productivity: more of their time will be available for their primary responsibilities. All too often a service invests in the latest technology and hopes the existing staff will find the time and have the interest in learning how to use it. As services become more and more dependent on technology for delivering information, the less the "buy it and hope" approach is viable; it is better to invest in a little less technology and a little more in staff qualified in its use and maintenance.

Each form of departmentation has advantages and disadvantages. Only through careful analysis of a service's goals and the local environment can you determine which form(s) are the best match for the current environment. What works in one situation may not work in what appears to be an identical situation, even within the same library. Functional and product approaches are most common at the higher levels, while the lower levels normally use territorial, customer, and equipment methods to organize the work.

Something to Think About:

Reflect on departmentation in a service known to you. List the departments within the service and identify which departmentation technique has been used.

Before leaving the discussion of departmentation, we need to discuss other methods for organizing work groups: *matrix, team,* and *networked/virtual.*

A matrix approach combines functional and product departmentation. One major advantage of the matrix approach is its flexibility, especially in handling one-time projects. The simplest way to think of matrix organization is a grid that addresses multiple activities and reporting structures. Interest in matrix structuring peaked in the late 1970s and early 1980s, although many large international organizations adopt it for special projects. Thomas Sy and Laura Sue D'Annunzio (2005) provide an excellent overview of the concept and its current use.

Pure matrix is a semi-to-permanent arrangement of staff. Under this approach, staff work for several supervisors. Many years ago, the University of Nebraska Library attempted an ambitious matrix organization. While retaining the traditional department heads of acquisitions, cataloging, and reference, as well as a support staff in each department, other professional staff had duties in all three areas. Figure 10.1 provides a graphic which makes it easier to visualize the structure of a pure matrix organization. The time percentages are illustrative only; we are not recommending them in any manner. The chart shows that each librarian will be working in three areas on a regular basis. It may also mean that they are working for three different supervisors. Clearly, that is a violation of Fayol's dictum of "unity of command." Such an arrangement can create reporting problems. The Nebraska effort failed, not because of the problems attendant with trying to meet the expectations of three supervisors, but rather the individuals did not always have an equal interest in each area of responsibility and would tend to neglect or at least put off doing the less favored activities. The concept behind implementing this organizational structure was, in theory, sound; individuals could become better subject experts. Efforts were made to hire individuals with both a degree in librarianship and an advanced subject degree. They were then to work in that or a related subject area. By selecting, processing, and managing the collection they built, the idea was that they would provide more effective customer service. It was an interesting idea, but one that did not prove workable in that situation at that time.

Project matrix organizing has the advantage of bringing together existing staff with necessary skills to handle a special project; it helps you create a unit that emphasizes multiple organizational concerns. By combining the skills in a single unit, a task can be accomplished effectively, especially a task that is short-term in character. These units give you the flexibility to respond to changing situations. Their major disadvantage is the one we mentioned above—multiple supervisors.

Figure 10.1 **Percentage of Staff Time in a Matrix Organization**			
	Acquisitions Department	**Reference Department**	**Cataloging Department**
Librarian 1	10%	40%	50%
Librarian 2	40%	50%	10%
Librarian 3	50%	10%	40%
Librarian 4	10%	40%	50%

The Sy and D'Annunzio's (2005) article identified five areas of concern on the part of their respondents regarding the matrix structure. The most commonly mentioned concern should not come as a surprise—ambiguous authority. Two others—misaligned goals and unclear roles and responsibilities—are also issues that an organizing process is to resolve, not muddying the water as to who does what and when. The fourth concern—silo-focused employees—is a concern with almost any structure you might choose; in our view this is not a structural issue but rather training/team building with a focus on understanding the overall picture and needs. Their fifth concern is probably the key to the success or failure of the matrix form—a lack of a "matrix guardian," someone solely responsible for the matrix performance.

Team Structure

In the relatively recent past there has been a growing trend to design jobs for teams rather than individuals. To some degree, the use of work teams is an outcome of research and thinking about employee motivation, since teams are a form of job enrichment. Team building has been a major topic of discussion and implementation among information professionals for some years now. There is now enough history of team use to gain an understanding of its value and shortcomings.

There are two broad categories of teams: integrated and self-managed. Integrated teams receive task(s) from a manager and the team works out how and who will do what to achieve the desired outcome(s). Self-managed teams receive goals rather than tasks. They generally have a "contact" manager they may turn to for guidance and assistance but overall operate very independently. Needless to say, the issue of coordination between teams is a major concern for successful team operations. Another challenge for team-based organizations is performance evaluation and issues of accountability.

There were several reasons for the increased interest in and use of teams over the last few decades. One significant factor was the pressure to downsize or at the very least become much more efficient/productive without increasing staff size. Generally accomplishing such goals required giving all levels of staff greater responsibility and authority. Another factor was with achieving higher quality outputs and a greater "customer focus."

Also, as Lawler and Finegold (2000: 1) stated, "Today, many organizations are seeking to become 'the employer of choice' to attract and retain high quality employees. Twenty-five years ago many of these same firms were trying to improve the quality of work life and satisfaction of their employees. Although the language has changed, the core issue has stayed the same: how to design organizations and jobs that meet individual 'needs'." Self-managed work teams are one of the outcomes of trying to attract and retain top-flight employees.

Transitioning to teams requires everyone—managers and staff—to re-think roles and responsibilities. Ceasar Douglas (2002) noted that the transition period is critical to success and can take 24 months or more to complete satisfactorily. One of the first managerial shifts must be from a "command and control" mode of behavior to one of being an advisor, which is not always an easy transition for some people. Another issue for managers is their self-monitoring ability. (Self-monitoring is the ability to strategically adjust your "influencing behavior" to fit the situation.) For the staff, adapting team behavior and accepting those behaviors is critical. One behavior some people have difficulty with is group decision making and the time that takes. Related to group decision making is that conflict and its resolution is a part of the process; for some people conflict is something to avoid at almost any cost, including strongly held views. A few individuals have significant difficulty having their performance judged on the basis of group performance.

Some organizations use teams as the primary structure while others limit their use to selected areas. In either case, one fact you should keep in mind is, "Even a team that is autonomous in terms of its activities and decision making must still continually receive direction from higher levels of the organization" (Druskat and Wheeler, 2004: 65). Druskat and Wheeler go on to say, "To be sure, leading a team that needs to manage itself is, inherently, the role is highly ambiguous by nature (and, on the face of it, oxymoronic)" (2004: 66). Another fact to bear in mind is that the organization will hold the manager/leader/advisor responsible for the team(s) assigned to them.

Striking a balance between organizational and team needs raises the question of how do you handle teams. We will touch on four areas you can work on to develop team-oriented skills—interacting, anticipating, influencing, and empowering. To interact effectively you need to be socially and politically aware in terms of colleagues and the organization. Building successful teams calls for creating high levels of trust among team members, the team and yourself, and "your" team(s) and other teams. One characteristic of great managers, regardless of the presence or absence of teams, is the ability to look ahead and anticipate issues (a form of environmental scanning). Seeking information from others in the organization allows you to foresee upcoming events/issues/concerns. Watching team behavior can provide clues about what may become an issue requiring your involvement. Such anticipation provides you with lead time to consider courses of action. Being influential rather than "commanding" takes practice and a fair degree of patience, whether or not it is team-related. When it comes to empowering it is a matter of real delegation, being flexible (allow the team to try something different in spite of doubts you have), and coaching instead of directing.

Are teams yet another passing management fad? We don't have a definitive answer to that question, but we do believe that teams, in one form or another, will be an important element in information service operations for some time to come. Gibson, Tesone, and Blackwell (2003: 12) examined "five management fads that were very popular in the second half of the 1900s." The five fads they selected were MBO (Management By Objectives), sensitivity training, Quality Circles, TQM (Total Quality Management), and self-managed teams. The authors surveyed both managers and staff regarding the respondent's perception of the value of the concept today—2003. The only concept that all respondents thought was viable was self-managed teams. The other concepts were all rated highly by staff and many managers but only teams had 100 percent agreement on utility.

Try This:

Following are some questions to ponder regarding your approach to teams.
- When making decisions, do you consult with a few individuals whom you know and trust or with anyone who will be affected by the decisions?

  Rarely, Occasionally, Often.
- How often do you fall back on rules, procedures, and policies to achieve goals?

  Rarely, Occasionally, Often.
- How comfortable are you with group decision making?

  Rarely, Occasionally, Often.
- How comfortable are you being accountable for the performance of other people?

  Rarely, Occasionally, Often.
- How comfortable are you in work situations where you must trust people you don't have a long history with?

  Rarely, Occasionally, Often.

Networked/Virtual Structure

Although we may not be 100 percent confident about the long-term viability of self-managed teams, we are fully confident in saying there will be an ever increasing use of the networked/virtual structure. A networked/virtual structure is an organization in which there is a central core, with most of the workforce (both employees and consultants/contractors) linked to one another and the core through ICT connections. You can think of this approach as falling into three categories: single organization, single organization with e-outsourcing, and multiple organizations temporarily working as a group.

Teams and networked structure are becoming more and more intertwined. Piccoli, Powell, and Ives (2004: 359) wrote, "continuing development of information technologies (IT) have led to the creation of new organizational forms that are flexible and responsive. The virtual team represents an important example of these new organizational forms." Much of the original research focused on geographically separated teams. Today "virtual teams" research is shifting toward recognition they may be either remote or co-located. The issue is the use of technology to interact and work together with few, if any, face-to-face interactions, not dependent on the physical location of people.

Kirkman and Mathieu (2005: 702) employed a three-part definition of a virtual team:

(a) the extent to which team members use virtual tools to coordinate and execute team processes (including communication media such as e-mail and video conferencing and work tools such as group discussion support systems)
(b) the amount of informational value provided by such tools
(c) the synchronicity of team member virtual interaction

The authors suggest that today there is little difference between virtual and traditional teams. Further, those teams make choices about virtuality based on group structure, task(s), and how often they can meet face-to-face.

As Tricia Kelly suggested, there are some serious organizational challenges you need to consider in a networked/virtual environment. Building and sustaining the virtual team synergy, performance appraisal/monitoring, informal/social interaction, and professional isolation are some of the most significant concerns. Reading her article on this topic (Kelly, 2005) is a good way to learn about an information professional remote virtual team situation.

Although written communication is always important, it becomes critical in the virtual environment. As of today, the written message is the primary mode of communication in the virtual world, although visual capabilities are becoming more readily available at a reasonable cost. You must approach all virtual team messages with great care and thought. Too often we treat e-mail informally, giving it only brief thought while addressing the common expectation that a quick response is called for. How often have you realized you hit "send" too quickly? Often the result is at worst a slight embarrassment, but in a virtual team setting, such events can seriously damage trust, a vital element of the team's performance/success. Building team trust and knowledge of each team member's skills and abilities are dependent upon effective use of written language. Lacking the many visual clues you get in face-to-face communication, a "joke"/offhand remark may be lost in the virtual environment.

Most successful networked structures work best when there are at least some opportunities for face-to-face meetings, both formal and informal. The authors of this book have successfully collaborated on four book projects over the past seven years, with one in Wales and the other in Arizona. We have had four face-to-face meetings. We firmly believe that without such meetings we probably would not have collaborated for as long. We also agree with Kirkman and Mathieu (2005: 713) that there is a great need for managers to understand why teams select different degrees of virtuality and how those choices impact effectiveness.

Check This Out:

An excellent article describing the reorganization of a unit within an information service is Barbara Brattin's 2005 "Reorganizing Reference" (*Public Libraries* 44, no. 6 [November–December]: 340–346).

Optimal Size

You have several ways of thinking about how to achieve the necessary organizational interdependence of work groups—pooled, sequential, and reciprocal. You should base your selection of a structure in part on the requisite flow of information between units. The higher the flow, the stronger the coordination should be.

Pooled interdependence is most effective when the units do not directly depend on one another to carry out their day-to-day activities. One example of where this is appropriate is in branch libraries where each contributes to the overall success of the system but has little need to coordinate daily activities.

Sequential interdependence is where one unit must perform certain tasks before another unit can carry out some or most of its activities. An obvious information service example is that the acquisition of materials must come before processing them for users. The processing unit must complete its work before the customer-service unit has materials to offer customers.

Reciprocal interdependence is where there is a "give and take" on a daily basis. An example of this relationship is found between those who make decisions about what ought to be in the information collections and the unit that acquires the materials.

At some point in developing a structure, you must think about the question, "How many people or units can this position reasonably handle?" The issue was perhaps first brought out in a verse from the Bible regarding the number of persons that an individual can supervise. According to

Exodus 18: 17–18, Moses was told, "This thing is too heavy for thee. Thou are not able to perform it thyself all alone. Thou wilt surely wear away." Delegation is a *sharing* of responsibility and authority. No one is capable of making all the decisions required in our present complex social and institutional environment. Span of control denotes the degree of sharing.

A narrow span of control (few reports) results in a "tall" structure— multiple levels. A "flat" structure usually means a wide span of control. Use of teams flattens a structure when it is the sole method of structuring, but teams may add to the complexity when they supplement other structural forms.

The environmental rate of change is a factor in determining how many people/teams constitute a workable span of control. Quickly changing situations call for a narrow span of control. Information services have traditionally followed the classical rule of four to six full-time people as the best span of control.

There is a formula that can provide you with a sense of what adding another report does to a work load: $[N=n(2n-1)]$. Using that formula, there are 4,708 potential relationships when a person has 12 reports. (Note: The formula calculates the maximum number of relationships that *might* develop. Not all the possible relationships will develop, and those that do develop will not be of equal importance nor will they have equal frequencies.)

Another issue in determining the span of control is full-time versus part-time employees. Formulas deal with the number of positions, and most managers tend to think in terms of full-time equivalents (FTE). Although two half-time employees may equal one FTE, two people require more time than does one person. Both persons will have individual problems as well as common problems. The supervisor must address all the problems if the unit is to function efficiently. Some information services, especially those in educational institutions, depend upon student employees, almost all of whom work part-time. There is also the issue of volunteer staff, which adds yet another dimension to span of control. The result is that one task may be done by 15 to 20 persons. In such cases, good coordination is essential to keep everyone current on policies and procedures and to ensure proper work performance. Therefore, when thinking about the span of control and using formulas, it is important to think in terms of persons rather than full-time equivalents.

There are cost factors associated with span of control. First, as the span widens, the system costs more in terms of salaries, benefits, and equipment. A second cost is in terms of communication. As the span of control widens, communication becomes more complex and interaction time increases. Finally, coordination becomes more difficult as the number of supervisors increases; poor coordination carries with it a high performance cost.

There are arguments supporting wide spans of control. The primary argument maintains that subordinates assume more responsibility under a wide span of control because they have less supervision. There is a cost, however: management must select workers of better-than-average ability and motivation because they will be on their own more of the time. In conjunction with this is the idea that subordinates begin to develop their managerial skills as they exercise more independent judgments regarding their daily work activities. Moreover, people respond positively, maintain higher morale, and frequently perform better when they have less supervision.

Widening the span of control makes it essential that proper delegation of authority and responsibility takes place. Making it very clear who is responsible and has authority saves everyone time and reduces confusion. If you fail to provide complete work plans but still expect subordinates to know what to do, you will encounter confusion, delay, and extra cost.

Clearly defined, objective standards for judging work performance are necessary if one person is to supervise a large number of workers effectively. With objective standards in place, performance evaluation takes less time because the evaluation process does not involve prolonged discussions of subjective judgments. And, because workers know where they stand, morale is normally higher.

Judicious use of documents will also assist in broadening the span of control. Written policies leave less room for interpretation.

Through the careful use of personal contact, a supervisor can also expand her/his span of control. By creating an atmosphere of availability, the supervisor lets subordinates know that they can get help when necessary. Knowing that such support is available allows subordinates to work independently with the knowledge that help will be there when requested. Such situations tend to lead to high staff morale, but supervisors must maintain a balance between availability, personal concern, and socializing.

Finally, a personal factor enters into the question of the width of control. Even though some people try to expand the time available, there are only 24 hours in a day. Senior management should not allow any manager to let the job become a 24/7 affair. Failure to take action will, in the long run, cause the person, the work, and the staff to suffer. If a subordinate persists in overextending the workday, you should do as much as possible to reduce that individual's opportunities to work on such an extended basis.

Evaluation

The last step in organizing is to monitor the outcomes of the effort. As noted earlier, there is a tendency to think of organizing as a one-time activity rather than an ongoing process. Such thinking can lead to a stagnant organization, one that is still functional but not in the most cost-effective manner. While management needs to review the structure periodically, making frequent changes can be very costly to the service. It takes some time for staff to adjust to a new structure and make it work in the planned manner. Impatient managers can create problems as a result of quickly changing something they think may not be working out.

All organizations have a life cycle: creation, youth, middle age, and maturity. The general pattern for organizations as age increases is size increases. It becomes more mechanistic, specialized, decentralized, and bureaucratic. Information services tend to follow the same cycle, except size usually is slow-growing. Given that there is an organizational life cycle you should not be surprised that rethinking its structure is an ongoing process.

CENTRALIZATION/DECENTRALIZATION

When management writers discuss centralization/decentralization, they usually are addressing decision making, *not* physical location; that tradition is followed in this section. Beginning information professionals sometimes think that because a system has "branches," it is decentralized. They may be correct from an organizational theory point of view, if the branches have a high degree of decision-making autonomy. A system may be highly centralized in its decision making and yet have numerous branches. Some years ago, for example, a large metropolitan library system (63 branches) operated with the rule that a branch collection could only contain titles that were in the central library's collection. Branch librarians had to convince a collection development officer in "central" to order a title before a branch could do so. Thus, while having a widespread geographic distribution (physically highly decentralized), decision making regarding collection development was highly centralized.

Although decentralization has acquired something like hallowed status among employees by virtue of its association with phrases such as "more democratic" and "less authoritarian," it can lead to some very real problems. The following quotation from Ernest Dale (1952: 18), a major researcher in this area, indicates some of the problems:

> I find myself just a little annoyed at the tendency of all of us to adopt certain clichés about decentralization and then glibly announce that we're for it. I've been somewhat amused at some of my colleagues who have been vocal at expounding the virtues of decentralization and yet quite unconsciously are apt to be busily engaged in developing their own personal control over activities for which they are responsible.

Baker and France (1954: 37) echoed Dale's view when they wrote:

> An examination of the total activities of chief executives discloses that they continue to make most or all major decisions, either directly or through an

informal framework of strict rules, checks and balances, informal instructions and through mental compulsions on the part of subordinates to act as the boss would act.

The lip service given to the concept of decentralization often belies the reality of day-to-day operations. Given a little thought, it becomes clear that pure centralization *or* decentralization is impossible in almost any organizational setting. A one-person enterprise is an example of pure centralization. As soon as a second person joins the enterprise, there will be some degree of decentralization, however slight. Pure decentralization is anarchy and therefore, by definition, not an organization. Thus, in the real-work world of information service, it is a question of degree of decentralization rather than if there will be any.

Criteria for Decentralization

Ernest Dale developed four criteria for determining the degree of centralization within an organization. The criteria he developed arose from a management study he conducted for the American Management Association. They are as valid today as they were in 1952, when he carried out the research.

1. The greater the number of decisions made lower down in the management hierarchy, the greater the degree of decentralization.
2. The more important the decisions made lower down the management hierarchy (for example, the greater the sum of capital expenditure that can be approved by a plant manager without consulting anyone else), the greater the degree of decentralization.
3. More functions are affected by decisions made at the lower levels (thus, companies which permit only operational decisions to be made at separate branch plants are less decentralized than those which permit financial and personnel decisions to be made at branch plants).
4. The less checking required on the decision, the more decentralized the organization. Decentralization is greatest when no check at all is made, less when the supervisors have to consult before the decision is made. The fewer the people to be consulted and the lower they are in the management hierarchy, the greater the degree of decentralization (Dale, 1952: 105).

Although such criteria make the examination and analysis of an organization's structure more objective, they also involve several subjective elements. Appearances do not always reflect reality, and what someone says often differs sharply from what takes place.

For Further Thought:

Using our example of a large metropolitan library, consider if it was a decentralized service. Which factors affected the decision to operate a centralized or decentralized service?

Factors Affecting the Degree of Decentralization

Several factors affect the degree of decentralization within an organization: organizational philosophy, managerial interest, organizational strategy, environment, importance of the decision, size, organizational history, and staff abilities. As in other areas, there is no "right" degree of decentralization for an organization. You need to be flexible in this area, realizing that as circumstances change it may be necessary to adjust the level of decision making.

Many organizations, including information services, decentralize some areas and not others. In our earlier example, the large metropolitan library decided to decentralize the "sales" decisions and centralize the "financial" decisions. Such an arrangement reflects senior management's desire to closely monitor the financial transactions of the organization. Other managers might have a different philosophy, such as allowing lower-level managers to make financial decisions with the view that such responsibility assists junior managers in developing their managerial skills.

Managerial interest, and/or the personal need to be "in control," plays a significant role in how the service handles decision making. Some individuals are very uncomfortable delegating decision making to junior staff. In such cases, they will retain as much decision making as possible, frequently more than the person can effectively handle.

Organizational strategy does not often come into play in an information service setting but is a common issue in for-profit organizations. Single-product and single-service organizations tend to be more centralized than those that are multiple-product or multiple-service oriented.

As noted in Chapter 3, environment is always a factor in how an organization manages its affairs. Rapidly changing environments (turbulent) tend to generate decentralized decision making within an overall strategic plan. That is, lower-level managers have the power to make tactical decisions as long as they stay within the overall strategic plan. Placid environments tend to generate increasingly centralized decision making.

Another factor is the importance or cost of a decision. The correlation between the cost of a decision and how high up in the structure it is made is very positive: the more money involved, the higher the position of the person making the final decision. For instance, because most user fines and fees are small and involve or affect the service's long-term interests in minor ways, the decisions are in the hands of first-line staff. However, when it comes to determining who may use the service, instituting a new service, or planning a new facility, department heads or the director normally make these decisions. This is true, not because top-level administrators make fewer mistakes, but because one cannot fully delegate responsibility along with authority. Ultimately, the person accountable and responsible for a costly decision will most likely be the person to make it.

Uniformity of policy interpretation is also a type of cost factor. Because policies are guides to thinking, they are subject to varying interpretations; therefore, the variation in construing policies will increase as the number of persons interpreting them increases. Too much variation can cause substantial customer dissatisfaction. Consistency often requires moving decision making further up the organizational structure, thus reducing the number of decision makers.

Size is always a factor in establishing the degree of decentralization within a service. As an organization grows, it must become less and less centralized. Time is the controlling issue. If all decisions take place high in the organizational structure, enormous amounts of time are lost "waiting for person X to have time to review the matter." Too much waiting time will certainly result in more and more user dissatisfaction; thus, the tendency is to keep decision making as close to the users as possible in large organizations.

History also can play a significant role in determining the degree of decentralization, because there is a tendency in services to perpetuate the structure and procedures that characterized it in the past. Lacking a history of staff participation, a service will rarely adopt decentralized decision making in one step—even under new leadership. It takes time for the staff to become comfortable with the idea of making decisions. Thus, even new leadership should implement decentralization slowly.

Finally, staff abilities influence the degree of decentralization. Decentralization requires a staff that has the knowledge to make decisions. If those elements are lacking, the manager should either postpone decentralization until staff with the requisite abilities is available, or undertake staff development activities to improve skills.

LEARNING ORGANIZATIONS

Ever since Peter Senge's book *The Fifth Discipline* (1990) appeared there has been a high level of interest in his concept of a learning organization. Learning organizations attempt to generate/acquire and pass on information/knowledge within themselves with the goal of adjusting their activities based on "new" knowledge to create a more effective organization.

As a manager you have important roles to play in a learning organizational environment. You need to actively bring new ideas to the staff and wider organization; the discussion of new ideas also will assist you when you need to institute change. Actively removing barriers to sharing new ideas is also something you should do. The sharing process is one technique for reducing the "silo" effect that often afflicts units in large organizations. Another role is to assist staff in modifying their behavior in light of the new information.

KEY POINTS TO REMEMBER:

- Delegation is an important complex process.
- Organizational structure plays a key role in an organization's effectiveness.
- Knowing yourself in terms of "trusting" others is especially important when it comes to delegation.
- Do not delegate responsibility without providing the necessary authority.
- Assessing tasks and designing jobs is an essential step in creating an effective organizational structure.
- Successful restructuring requires detailed planning and thinking.
- Recognizing both the abilities and limitations of each staff member is basic to successful organizing.
- Teams and networked structures require special managerial skills.
- Width of span of control is dependent upon factors such as the speed of change and rate of growth.
- The concept of centralization/decentralization is more than an either/or issue; in most organizations both exist.
- Learning organizations tend to be more responsive to a changing environment because they value and act upon new ideas.

REFERENCES

Baker, Harold, and Richard France. 1954. *Centralization and Decentralization in Industrial Relations.* Princeton, NJ: Princeton University Press.

Boisse, Joseph A. 1996. "Adjusting the Horizontal Hold: Flattening the Organization." *Library Administration & Management* 10, no. 2 (Spring): 77–80.

Brattin, Barbara. 2005. "Reorganizing Reference." *Public Libraries* 44, no. 6 (November-December): 340–346.

Dale, Ernest. 1952. *Planning and Developing the Company Organization Structure Research Report 20.* New York: American Management Association.

Douglas, Ceasar. 2002. "The Effects of Managerial Influence Behavior on the Transition to Self-Managed Teams." *Journal of Managerial Psychology* 17, nos. 7/8: 628–635.

Druskat, Vanessa, and Jane V. Wheeler. 2004. "How to Lead Self-managing Teams." *MIT Sloan Management Review* 45, no. 4 (Summer): 65–71.

The Economist. 2006. "The New Organization." Special Supplement 378, no. 8461: 1–18.

Gibson, Jane Whitney, Dana V. Tesone, and Charles W. Blackwell. 2003. "Management Fads: Here Yesterday, Gone Today." *Advanced Management Journal* 68, no. 4 (Autumn): 2–17, 59.

Higa, Mori Lou, Brian Bunnett, Bill Maina, Jeff Perkins, Therona Ramos, Laurie Thompson, and Richard Wayne. 2005. "Redesigning a Library's Organizational Structure." *College & Research Libraries* 66, no. 1 (January): 41–58.

Hamm, John. 2006. "The Five Messages Leaders Must Manage." *Harvard Business Review* 84, no. 5 (May): 114–123.

Hunter, Judy. 2002. "Improving Organizational Performance Through the Use of Effective Organizational Structure." *Leadership in Health Services* 15, no. 3: 12–21.

Jones, Phillip J. 2000. "Individual Accountability and Individual Authority: The Missing Links." *Library Administration & Management* 14, no. 3 (Summer): 135–145.

Kelly, Tricia. 2005. "Where Is My Team? A Manager's Point of View Point on Working with a Remote Team of Information Specialists." *Quarterly Bulletin of the International Association of Agricultural Information Specialists* 50, no. 3/4: 119–124.

Kirkman, Bradley L., and John E. Mathieu. 2005. "The Dimensions and Antecedents of Team Virtuality." *Journal of Management* 31, no. 5 (October): 700–718.

Lawler, Edward E., and David Finegold. 2000. "Individualizing the Organization: Past, Present and Future." *Organizational Dynamics* 29, no. 1 (Summer): 1–15.

Piccoli, Gabriele, Anne Powell, and Blake Ives. 2004. "Virtual Teams: Team Control, Structure, Work Processes, and Team Effectiveness." *Information Technology & People* 17, no. 4: 359–379.

Senge, Peter. 1990. *The Fifth Discipline: The Art and Practice of the Learning Organization.* New York: Doubleday.

Sherman, Harvey. 1966. *It All Depends: A Pragmatic Approach to Organizations.* University, AL.: University of Alabama Press.

Sy, Thomas, and Laura Sue D'Annunzio. 2005. "Challenges and Strategies of the Matrix Organizations: Top-level and Mid-level Managers Perspectives." *Human Resource Planning* 28, no. 1: 39–48.

Terry, George R. 1977. *Principles of Management*, 7th ed. Homewood, IL: Richard Irwin.

LAUNCHING PAD

Adams, John T. 2002. "Constructive Change Comes from Within." *Association Management* 54, no. 9 (September): 48–51, 53, 55.

Bender, Laura. 1997. "Team Organization—Learning Organization: The University of Arizona Four Years into It." *Information Outlook* 1, no. 9 (September): 19–22.

Bernfeld, Betsy. 2004. "Developing a Team Management Structure in a Public Library." *Library Trends* 53, no. 1 (Summer): 112–128.

Christopher, Connie. 2003. *Empowering Your Library*. Chicago: American Library Association.

Hunter, Judy. 2002. "Improving Organizational Performance Through the Use of Effective Elements of Organizational Structure." *Leadership In Health Services* 15, no. 3: 12–21.

Lubans, John. 2003. "Teams in Libraries." *Library Administration & Management* 17, no. 3 (Summer): 144–145.

11

Performance, Quality, and Control

"Quality in a product or service is not what the supplier puts in. It is what the customer gets out and willing to pay for."

Peter F. Drucker

"Staff can be overworked and understretched at the same time."

Maurice Line

INTRODUCTION

Quality, value, assessment, and accountability: these concepts demand more and more attention on the part of managers. They reflect the expectations of those who fund and, most important, use information services.

This chapter focuses on performance in terms of the service as a whole and how to demonstrate quality and value to stakeholders—the policy makers, the funding bodies, the community served, and the staff. Only by analyzing the quantitative and qualitative data and information that you gather concerning the performance of the service staff can you see their achievements or take prompt action to correct identified problems.

WHY ANALYZE PERFORMANCE?

User Expectations

Since users are central to information services, let's first think about the performance factors that they view as important. People take a keen interest

> **Check This Out:**
>
> Cole, Bryan R., and John B. Harer. 2005. "The Importance of the Stakeholder in Performance Measurement: Critical Processes and Performance Measures for Assessing and Improving Academic Library Services and Programs." *College & Research Libraries* 66, no. 2 (March): 149–170.

in the level of service they receive from information services in both the private and public sectors. Generally, people have four criteria by which they judge services. They expect to get what they want, when they want it, at a cost that is acceptable to them, and delivered in a way that meets their expectations. Organizations that provide services work hard to ensure that the consumers' criteria are met, so as to retain user loyalty. This is as important for information services as it is for supermarkets. Most readers will have been at the receiving end of poor service at some time; they understand how this means that sometimes it is easy to walk away and become an ex-customer. User satisfaction is a paramount concern for all service providers.

> **Try This:**
>
> Think about an archive or library service that you use and consider how it matches up to the four criteria identified above. Are there other criteria that you would add?

Staff Expectations

In addition to the users, a second group has expectations. This is the staff of the service, whose level of performance in carrying out their tasks and responsibilities can make a difference to the user. Staff members expect to work in a high-performing service where they are valued by the stakeholders. Having the confidence to know that they are performing well enhances their job satisfaction. In turn, this creates and sustains an organizational climate in which a quality service is paramount. The better the service performs, the more likely the users are to return; conversely, staff who realize they are not achieving a high level of performance lose motivation, and service quality slides.

Accountability

The third group with expectations consists of those who fund the service and those to whom the service is accountable. In some cases they will be the same body, such as a law firm in the private sector. In other situations there can be two levels of accountability where there is a board that is accountable to a government department at the state or national level which oversees public expenditure drawn from tax revenues. The body providing the finance expects to receive value for the funding invested, together with positive feedback from the user community. The issue of accountability has become increasingly important in recent years. Long gone are the days when a director or chief of a service managed a service with little or no accountability. As the public, governments, and stockholders take a keen interest in how their dollars are spent, so the responsibility for managers to provide a cost-effective service increases.

Consider:

Accountability in the country or state in which you are living. Can you give four examples of accountability as they apply to any type of information service? We have suggested that greater emphasis is being placed on accountability. Does this agree with your experience?

Competition

At the same time as accountability increases, so managers face competition. Technology produces competition. Broadband access to the Internet in the home or at work provides easy access to online services providing alternative sources: consider Amazon.com, search engines such as Google, social networks, family history databases, and online books and journals. The perceived overall "cost" to a potential user of satisfying her/his information needs may be less when using an online service, rather than going to a records office or library. However, there are some services that are better experienced in person. Think of handling an historical document in an archive or experiencing the joy on a child's face during a story reading session at a public library.

Linked to the last point is that services are competing for people's time. People lead busy lives at home and at work and so have limited time when they use an information service. Services must ensure that they help users make effective use of their time. They do this by providing new users with basic information about the service delivered, either face-to-face or via a Web site, followed up with coaching and advice as needs change and become more sophisticated. Users gain considerable benefits when it is possible to request items online and have them available on arrival. Save the time of the user is the catchword.

> **Try This:** `
>
> Identify other forms of competition that challenge a service of your choice. How is it meeting these challenges?

Planning

Data and information relating to performance are vital inputs to the planning process. They are generated by systematic monitoring indicating what has happened in the past, what is happening now, and are used in the development of "what would happen if" scenarios. In addition to the ongoing planning process, you can use data and information when making the case to stakeholders for a change or improvement to a service. Without relevant and accurate data/information, planning is sterile.

Continuous Improvement

One of the outcomes of planning should be a process of continuous improvement. No organization should ever stand still—or worse, slide back. By examining data and information collected about performance and quality, managers and their teams are able to identify ways to increase the satisfaction of stakeholders. Senior management expects to "own" a high-performing service and receive value for the investment they make; users need to gain benefits from using the service; and staff members want to identify ways to increase job satisfaction. A program of continuous improvement creates a learning organization.

> **Check This Out:**
>
> The original text on learning organizations is well worth reading—Peter M. Senge's 1990 *The Fifth Discipline: The Art and Practice of the Learning Organization* (New York: Doubleday).

CAN YOU MEASURE "PERFORMANCE" AND "QUALITY"?

The questions of whether, and how to measure the performance and quality of services have been debated over the years. Some critics argue that "performance" and "quality" are elusive concepts that are difficult, or even impossible, to measure.

> **Check These Out:**
>
> Two seminal papers discussed the complexity of measurement and although they were written some years ago they still have value today.
>
> Gore, Daniel. 1978. "The Mischief in Measurement: A Caveat on the Hazards of Using Faulty Instruments to Measure Library Performance." *Library Journal* 103, no. 9 (May 1): 933–937.
>
> Orr, Richard. 1973. "Measuring the Goodness of Library Services: A General Framework For Considering Quantitative Measures." *Journal of Documentation* 29, no. 3: 315–332.

There is a temptation to measure anything that can be easily counted—for example, the number of fiction titles borrowed in a branch library or the number of documents consulted in a search room. Taking a library as an example, this would, however, tell us nothing about the number of books that are available to read. If a library's stock is small and someone has already read or consulted all of the titles in the genres that interest her/him, the user's borrowing rate will go down. Conversely, if there are more titles available, people may take out more books than they are likely to read, allowing them to make a further choice at home. The person borrowing the books may also pass them on to someone else to read. So it can be seen that there are several factors that lie beyond crude borrowing statistics. The impact of the reading of a book and degree of "value" or satisfaction to the reader may be greater for some readers than others, and "use" cannot be measured. The latter point about "use" becomes even more complex when electronic sources are accessed. Similar questions can be considered in relation to the use of documents and sources of information in other types of information services.

So in looking at data and information about performance and quality, key questions to ask are:

- What is being measured?
- What does it indicate?
- What is not being measured?

Dr. Evans has served on a number of accreditation "visiting teams" over the years, as the issues of accountability and measurement of quality have become more and more important. The types of questions the visiting teams ask have also changed to reflect the greater importance of proof of quality. This can be illustrated with the team questions for two areas of organizational management concern, and one for the library. The questions indicate how thinking about these issues has changed and also how much more evidence is necessary to prove quality and accountability.

Since planning is an essential part of successfully managing any organization, accrediting agencies take an interest in how educational institutions plan and the processes they employ to carry out an activity. Traditional ways of looking at planning revolved around resources, looking at inputs, processes, and outcomes. In that setting, the questions asked might be, "Does the institution have strategic and financial plans?" "Are the plans reasonably current, and do they involve all groups in the organization?" or "Do plans set clear goals and priorities?" But the questions changed to go beyond the resource level to require evidence of assessment and learning. The questions then became:

"Do plans draw upon institutional data?"
"In what ways do strategic and academic plans include learning goals and priorities?"
"What *ongoing* data collection (qualitative and quantitative) and analysis are used to assess the effectiveness of planning?"
"How does the planning process include the assessment of learning?"
"How is evidence of outcomes and effectiveness used in planning?"
"To what extent is learning an integral and embedded part of planning discussions?"

In terms of institutional effectiveness, the older resource questions might have been: "Does the institution have definitions of assessment?" "Is there an identified locus of responsibility for assessment?" or "How are assessment results disseminated and used?" Today's questions are more like the following: "In what ways does the institution engage in effective assessment activities?" "How are assessment results integrated into unit and institutional planning?" or "How is the institution moving toward a 'culture of evidence'?"

Try This:

Consider your experience of using a library or archive service.
What influences your view of the performance of the service?
List, in order of importance, the four factors most important to you.

Turning to some specific library or archives questions, it is possible to see more clearly the shift in thinking. Typical resource type questions used to be: "What is the size and currency of collections, budget, staff, and physical facilities?" "Does the service engage in periodic planning and program review processes?" or "Are the collections, and access to them, adequate?" The new questions are harder to answer from statistics alone. For example:

"How does the service collect and analyze data on its collections, staff, budget, etc.?"

"Does the service identify learning goals for itself, and are they linked to institutional learning goals?"

"Are satisfaction surveys *regularly* conducted and used?"

"How *does* the service assess the accomplishment of its learning goals?"

"How are assessment results *incorporated* into planning and improvements?"

"How are service learning goals *linked* with institutional learning goals?"

These are examples of the ever-growing importance of "proving one's worth" to the community served and the bodies that provide funding for information services.

Tip:

Managers can make users and staff aware of the achievements of their service by posting the outcomes of performance measures each month. For example: How many online searches were made? How many inquiries received?

TERMINOLOGY

The language of performance measurement draws on the fields of economics and management. Some common terms encountered are:

Benefit—whether a service gives value for money.

Control—results of past decisions.

Cost benefit analysis—determination and evaluation of the social costs and benefits of involvement, in order to decide whether or not a project should be undertaken.

Cost effectiveness—efficiency with which the service satisfies its objectives in terms of cost.

Effectiveness—performance of the right task, whether economical or not, or, "how well the service satisfies its objectives."

Efficiency—economical performance of a given task.

Evaluation—taking data or information collected in a systematic manner and comparing this with expected performance.

Impact measures—evidence of the value and impact of a service on users and the community at large: for example, improving the quality of life.

Outcomes assessment—derived by examining any benefit or change in behavior, knowledge, and skills on the part of those who have used the service.

Performance measurement—data to measure, or count, an aspect of service.

Planning—assessing the effects of alternative actions.

Quality—the degree of excellence

Quality assurance—refers to the processes associated with ensuring that given criteria in standards or guidelines are achieved.

Quality enhancement—focuses on the processes that are associated with improving quality.

Standard—a target for performance that should be capable of being measured.

Value—a level of benefit.

Check This Out:

Defining "need," "want," "demand," and "use" can be a brain teaser.
Maurice Line provided some thoughts in his 1974 "Draft Definitions" (*Aslib Proceedings* 26, no. 2: 87).

EVOLUTION OF MEASUREMENT METHODS

Earlier, attention was drawn to papers written in the 1970s that still contribute to discussions about performance, and work in the 1960s still has value today. Lancaster prepared two useful detailed reviews of the literature, which can be difficult to access in the digital age. The first review yielded theoretical constructs and definitions of terms which formed a foundation for later investigations; the second volume updated the review to the late 1980s (Lancaster, 1977, 1988).

Until the late 1960s, standards were developed by each sector and endorsed by governments or national associations; these became the principal measure of performance. Library standards covered such aspects of service as the number of books to be provided for the size of the community served, the numbers and levels of staff, size of buildings, etc., and measured inputs to the service. The organization holding accountability for the service was satisfied if the standards were met. Managers could use standards to good effect to lobby for increased resources if the service was shown to fall below the expected level. The accountable organization did not like to be seen to be "performing" at a lower level than similar services.

This approach worked reasonably well up to the middle of the 1960s—a time of affluence in the Western world. Then, as economic conditions tightened, a different approach emerged in the United States as public librarians became concerned that their vision of better libraries was beginning to fade. The American Library Association's Public Library Association commissioned a study which produced a strategy for public library change, indicating that standards be replaced by goals (Martin, 1972). This was followed by De Prospo, Altman, and Beasley's investigation (1973), which proposed four criteria for selecting "meaningful indicators" that retain their relevance today:

- Data collection must be amenable to the use of sampling techniques.
- The measurement criteria must differentiate between libraries.
- The measurement tests, while objectively based, should be constructed in a manner suitable for interpretation by practicing librarians.
- Data collected should provide administration with a tool for internal management and decision making.

It was recognized that quantitative measures might not be suitable in all situations. While they were appropriate to use in services where there was a high volume of transactions, such as urban public libraries, they were less applicable where services were provided for a scattered community, such as rural public libraries. In such circumstances, people believed that qualitative measures might provide more meaningful data for a small community service that was making an important contribution to the economy at large. That resulted in a further investment by the Public Library Association in the preparation of *A Planning Process for Public Libraries* by King Research, a consultancy that has made a number of major contributions to performance measurement. Their manual reflected the view that:

> Instead of standards to be applied nationally, this publication describes a planning process to be used by individual communities. Through the planning process outlined here, libraries will set up standards appropriate to local conditions and needs; design strategies to reach them; and inaugurate a planning cycle which involves continuous monitoring of progress and regular adjustment of objectives as community conditions and needs change (Palmour, Bellassai, and de Wath, 1980: xi).

Van House and others contributed to the publication of a series of volumes on output measures which included academic libraries (Van House, Weil, and McClure, 1990); public library service to children (Walter, 1992); public library effectiveness (Van House and Childers, 1993); and public library service for young adults (Walter, 1995). From the experience of this program of planning and measurement, a marketing approach was built into *The TELL IT! Manual*, described as being the complete program for evaluating library performance (Zweizig, Johnson, and Robbins, 1996).

A major influence from the mid 1980s has been the work of Parasuraman, Zeithaml, and Berry (1985) on service quality. This approach was adopted by the Association of Research Libraries and developed as LibQUAL™. A commercial service provides assessment tools and analyzes the data and information collected to benchmark services. This work is important as it focuses on outcomes and service quality. In the public library sector, *Hennen's Public Library Planner* (Hennen, 2004) is a tool that can be used for in-house assessment of quality. Over time attempts have been made to measure the value of public libraries, and Missingham (2005) describes the various approaches.

More recently, in the United Kingdom, the approach taken has been to assess the impact of publicly funded services. Early studies emerged in healthcare because the National Health Service absorbs a high level of public funding. Urquhart (2005) indicates that impact measurement examines "the three ways that information services usually make a difference—educationally (learning and skills for learning), socially (community cohesion, personal well-being) and ways of working (changing practice or decisions made)."

Check These Out:

Markless, Sharon and David Streatfield. 2006. *Evaluating the Impact of Your Library*. London: Facet Publishing.
Rubin, Rhea Joyce. 2005. *Demonstrating Results: Using Outcome Measurement in Your Library (PLA Results Series)*. Chicago: American Library Association.

As services moved into the hybrid era so e-metrics emerged to provide meaningful statistics for measuring the growing use of electronic services (Bertot and Davis, 2004). Bertot and McClure (2003), in discussing outcomes assessment in the networked environment, identify basic research questions to which managers need to have an answer today:

- What resources are required to support the services that a library provides?
- What services and/or resources is a library able to provide with its investments in library infrastructure (broadly defined as personnel, technology, collections, facilities, etc.)?
- Are the library's customers receiving value out of the community's investment in library services?
- What is the real and/or perceived quality of library services?
- What are the impacts of library services and resources on the community that the library serves?
- What level of effort is required by library staff to implement measurement activities?
- In what ways does the library contribute to the overall mission, goals and objectives of the community—or institutions within that community—that the library serves?

These questions could be broadened and put to any service in the information sector. New challenges arise in the networked environment given the levels of investment required.

Measurement research has encompassed a number of approaches—input, output, impact, value, and outcomes—but from the 1960s onward, there has been a parallel line of development which applies statistical techniques to internal operations. Trueswell, an industrial engineer, observed that Pareto's 80/20 rule could be applied to academic libraries with 80 percent of the number of transactions representing 20 percent of the stock (Trueswell, 1969). Empirical research was stimulated by the growth of information science, and Fairthorne, Bookstein and Brookes, among others, demonstrated that the laws of Zipf, Bradford and Lotka could be applied in bibliometrics. This has practical application in predicting, for example, the completeness of literature searches (Rousseau, 2005), and this line of enquiry is worth pursuing.

STANDARDS TODAY

We made the point that newer approaches to performance measurement emerged in the 1970s, but a different form of standard has value today in providing guidelines for best practice. One example is the information literacy instructional objectives for undergraduate music students prepared by the Bibliographic Instruction Subcommittee of the Music Library Association and based upon an ACRL standard (Cary and Sampsel, 2006).

Check These Out:

Coyle, Karen. 2005 "Libraries and Standards." *Journal of Academic Librarianship* 31, no. 4 (July): 373 376.
   Discusses the main U.S. organizations and the problems and issues involved in library standards.
Pember, Margaret. 2006. "Sorting Out the Standards: What Every Records and Information Professional Should Know." *Records Management Journal* 16, no. 1: 21–33.
   Considers the types of standards and how they are used in practice.

One field of international standardization that is vital for information services covers the technological issues that ensure that information and documents can be accessed, exchanged, and stored efficiently and effectively. Another is quality management, which may be adopted by the parent organization. *ISO 9000:2005* and *ISO: 9001: 2000* for quality management systems are published in a number of languages.

Check This Out:

The University of Malaya Library has adopted *ISO 9001: 2000*, and their experience of the planning, implementation, and maintenance of the quality management system is described in a 2006 article by Kiran Kaur, Mohamad Pauziaah, and George Sossamma ("Quality Management Service at the University of Malaya Library." *Library Management* 27, no. 4: 249–256).

The field of records management has been active in working with ISO to produce *ISO 15489-1* and *TR 15489-2* (2001) *Information and Documentation—Records Management.*

At a national level, the British Standards Institution has issued PAS *2001 and PD 7502: 2003* on knowledge management, which gives general guidance on knowledge management and how to measure the effectiveness, efficiency, and value of knowledge management within and between organizations. *BIP 0004: 2004* provides an introduction to knowledge management and *BS ISO 11620: 1998* focuses on library performance indicators. These are a few examples upon which to base practices that will optimize performance. The Web sites of national archives and libraries and the professional associations list relevant standards for their domain.

Check Out:

The Web site for your national professional body to identify relevant standards. If they are not listed, then try the U.S. sources www.loc.gov for libraries and www.archives.gov (both accessed August 2006) for archives and records management.

BASIC QUESTIONS BEFORE YOU START

Managers need to ask themselves some searching questions before studying performance. The following checklist has been adapted from one developed by Jean Bird following an examination of the use of a public library service (Redfern, 1976).

1. What do *you* mean by "performance," "quality," "effectiveness," "impact," or "outcomes"?

Can you define the term you have selected; how does it differ from other measures; have you defined "goals" and "needs" and "satisfaction"; can definitions be written down lucidly; do the definitions match your philosophy concerning the service?

2. Where does the demand for the measures originate?

From policy makers at government level; funding agency; parent organization; users, nonusers, or ex-users; the staff?

3. What is the purpose behind the request?

To continue or discontinue a service; improve practice or processes; to add or drop specific service strategies; to allocate resources among competing services; to accept or reject a service approach or theory; to justify existing activities; as a public relations exercise; to justify a new activity, etc?

4. What other information is needed to achieve your purpose?

Assessment of costs, efficiency, professional opinion, policymakers or users' opinions; comparison with standards, comparison with similar services, etc?

5. Before you measure.

Have you specified why you want to measure it, and what you are trying to measure? Have you designed the investigation; ascertained what sources to use; decided what method to use and designed a sample; decided how to analyze the data/information and present the findings? Have you costed this exercise in terms of visible and invisible costs (e.g., staff time, including your own)?

6. Who is to do the measuring?

Are you making the best use of available resources; would it be cost-efficient to bring in outside assistance; do you have the skills required; could there be a benefit in terms of staff development for the project? Have you discussed the exercise with stakeholders and obtained feedback?

7. After the exercise.

Have you collected all the data/information required; is it in a suitable form, reliable and valid for the purpose; sufficient to base decisions on? Is other data/information needed; in the course of collecting information/data has the problem area been altered; are your objectives still relevant and feasible? Have the outcomes been reviewed with the staff? What is their response?

8. What action is now required?

Returning to the purpose of the investigation, do you need to institute change, no change, deploy resources, communicate the outcomes and to whom; who should carry out this action; how and when should this be done; how will you assess the effect of the action taken?

By answering this set of questions the purpose of the exercise will be clarified, a cost/benefit analysis of the project undertaken, and consideration of the possible implications of the findings.

DIFFERENT APPROACHES FOR DIFFERENT SITUATIONS

Selecting which data collecting approach to adopt depends to a great extent on the reason for the exercise. Is it intended to:

- meet the requirements of an external body (e.g., government or accreditation);
- examine performance in a holistic way;
- examine the efficiency of service delivery;
- gather the users' views of the service?

External Agency Requirements

This will be a data/information gathering exercise conducted at regular intervals. The manager has to be well informed about the current objectives, policies, and procedures of the agency with an emphasis on *current*, as agencies frequently change their requirements. The data/information collected will form part of the internal management information system with responsibilities assigned to appropriate members of staff, and the outcomes being regularly examined with staff. Demonstrating to everyone the importance of the exercise increases motivation, and ensures that there isn't a rush to get information together to meet a deadline. If the exercise includes a visit by the external agency then staff must be fully briefed, a timetable set for the event—and a way to help everyone relax immediately after the visit. It can produce high stress levels for everyone so it's the day for a manager's treat—even if it is only donuts!

The trickiest situation to handle is when the outcome demonstrates that the service is underperforming and not meeting expectations. Should this happen the management team must speedily identify the reasons for the underperformance. Working with the supervisors, they must ensure that staff morale doesn't slide and that everyone works together to put matters right.

EXAMINING PERFORMANCE HOLISTICALLY

Quality Management

There is a large volume of writing about that elusive and indistinct concept of "quality." Imprecise adjectives are used, such as "goodness," "rightness," and "correctness," or words giving clues to its characteristics, such as "style," "label," "feel," and "elegance." Most definitions include both unarticulated and articulated aspects with the unarticulated aspect varying according to each person's perception and remaining largely undefined.

Defining quality in the information service setting is more difficult when the outcome isn't a physical product. How can "quality service" be defined? Can it be just "user satisfaction"? But that is a conundrum, as someone may be satisfied with information provided by an information professional, but not know that it is incomplete, or even inaccurate, or out-of-date. But if the user discovers the faults, then they judge that the information was less than satisfactory, which gives rise to the question of when to measure customer satisfaction?

Consider:

How do you judge the elusive concept of quality as a customer of any service—information or otherwise?
What is the most important factor to you?
How is quality demonstrated?

Most services, by their nature, are intangible, and Shaughnessy identified three points that help to explain "service intangibility."

First, services are often performances or processes rather than products, and unspecified (unarticulated) user expectations are the typical criteria by which a service is evaluated.

Second, most services are heterogeneous. Performance varies from producer to producer, from user to user, and from day to day. Most services are open long hours each day and every day of the week. Staffing varies because of the need to cover all the service hours, so uniform quality becomes more difficult to assure.

A third consideration is that frequently the production and consumption of many services are inseparable. Evaluations of quality are not based solely on the outcome of a service, but also involve evaluations of the process of service delivery, and a comparison of performance with consumer expectations (Shaughnessy, 1987). However customer expectations may vary over time, as well as not being unarticulated.

We referred earlier to research on service quality by Parasurman, Zeitaml, and Berry. They identified ten dimensions that, to a greater or lesser degree, determine the quality of a service:

1. reliability or consistency
2. responsiveness or timeliness

3. competence
4. access or approachability
5. courtesy
6. communication
7. credibility
8. security (including confidentiality)
9. understanding the customer needs
10. tangibles (such as physical facilities, appearance of personnel, and tools or equipment) (Parasuraman, Zeithaml, and Berry, 1985)

All of these elements apply in the information sector and can form a starting point for defining quality in a given environment.

Our experience indicates that a quality information service is one that is community-focused and places its emphasis on continuous, incremental improvements in its services by means of staff involvement (both professional and support) and operates some form of participative management. It requires the commitment of a top management that focuses on problem solving, rather than apportioning blame when a problem arises. An important factor is that every member of staff of the service has the responsibility for delivering quality to the user. Because information services by their nature are user focused so the typical result of implementing quality management is that it is less traumatic than in the case of a production/physical product organization.

Check This Out:

Look at some recent management journals. What is the very latest approach to quality management?

A number of approaches to quality management that take a holistic view have aspects that require careful consideration. First, the process is generally facilitated by a consultant, and should not be undertaken by an untrained and inexperienced person. Second, there will be visible costs— e.g., the hiring of a consultant—and invisible costs in terms of staff time. Third, the process will result in change, and this may give rise to staff concern; consider the climate of the service. The reasons for and against trying the process must be carefully considered.

Total Quality Management

Total Quality Management (TQM) originated in the for-profit production and service business sector in the 1980s, but has also been applied in the public sector. The major writers on quality management are W. Edward Deming (1986), Kaoru Ishikawa (1985), and Joseph M. Juran and A. Blanton Godfrey (1999).

An example of TQM developed by the Association of Research Libraries' Office of Management Services indicates what is involved. It uses a ten-step process that can be applied to almost any information setting (Barnard, 1993).

Phase One: *Initial Steps*
    Step One—Exploration
    Step Two—Decision to Implement (commitment)
Phase Two: *Organizing for Quality*
    Step Three—Leadership Planning
    • organizational assessment
    • understanding customers
    • vision and guiding principles
Phase Three: *Start-up*
    Step Four—Identifying Products, Services, and Customers
    Step Five—Assessment of Customer Expectations and Needs
    Step Six—Identifying and Measuring Critical Processes
    Step Seven—Initial Pilot Project Team(s)
    Step Eight—Team Member Skill Development
Phase Four: *Evaluation and Expansion*
    Step Nine—Creating a TQM Strategic Plan
    Step Ten—Divisional/Department Planning (Barnard, 1993)

Staff are likely to raise some concerns, typically:

- Because we implement TQM, does it imply that our current services and activities are *not* quality?
- Where do we find the time to do TQM and do our "real work"?
- If work teams become the focal point of providing service, what will happen to middle managers?

And perhaps of most concern to the staff:

- Is this a way to reduce staffing?

Any issues and staff concerns will need to be resolved before moving forward, but sound reasons for undertaking the process are:

- wanting to improve services
- assuring a high level of customer satisfaction
- building work teams which implement activities in new and more effective ways
- achieving a high level of staff commitment to the services provided
- having satisfied customers.

If political benefits result, so much the better, but that reason should not be the driving force.

Normally a senior manager is responsible for coordinating the various activities related to TQM implementation and ensuring that there is a link with the strategic plan or planning activities of the service.

An important element is understanding the customers/users. While most services have a solid understanding of what their services and products are, as well as what constitutes their primary customer base, what may not be fully understood is the customer base as defined by TQM (external and internal customers). Sirkin (1993) suggests that part of what indicates a "satisfied customer" is repeat use of services, referrals, and public praise/endorsement of the service.

Note: Although we generally used the term "user" rather than "customer," it is more appropriate to use the latter in discussing quality management for users behave in the same way as customers. In addition, "users" are increasingly having to pay a fee for all or elements of the service.

An element of the TQM customer concept is that there are two classes of customers to consider: the external customer, and the internal customer. The external customer is the person who is the ultimate owner of the product or service—the end user. The internal customer is the direct recipient of my work output. It is essential that both classes of customer be satisfied if TQM is to work properly.

The various types of work measurement which are an important element in the process will be reviewed later in this chapter. The first work measurement activity is to list all the significant processes the service carries out. The next question is, "What are the appropriate measures of quality for this process?" (Remember, internal customers are part of TQM, so the quality measurement may be in terms of a staff person or department.) Ultimately, the goal is continuous improvement, which requires an in-depth understanding of the processes derived from TQM. Lubans noted about data collection, "TQM tools, easily learned and used, are valuable methodology for uncovering a mess and defining the underlying problem" (Lubans, 1994).

There are a number of tools for TQM measurement, ranging from flow charts to scatter diagrams. Shewhart's approaches to continuous improvement use a four-step sequence: Plan, Do, Check, and Act (PDCA) (Shewhart, 1939).

The final step in the process is to act on the results of experiments and other data collection activities. Unsuccessful experiments need rethinking; successful results require planning for their implementation, which brings the organization back to the start of the cycle.

Teams and teamwork are distinctive elements of TQM. Staff involvement in problem solving, decision making, and quality improvement activities can be significant elements in staff motivation.

LibQUAL+™

This approach developed from TQM and now takes the form of an annual survey completed by subscribing libraries in a number of countries. The instrument measures user perceptions and expectations of library service quality in three dimensions: Affect of Service, Information Control, and Library as Place. Users are asked for their judgments on three scales for each question: the *desired* level of service they would like to receive, the *minimum* they are willing to accept, and the actual level of service they *perceive* to have been provided. Heath, Kyrillidou, and Askew (2004) describe how data collected using LibQUAL can be used for decision making.

Check This Out:

The Association of Research Libraries offers the service (www.libqual.org [accessed May 2006]).

Benchmarking

In common with LibQUAL+™, benchmarking provides information that demonstrates how one service can compare its performance with another service of similar size from the same sector that is a recognized leader, to bring about improvements to improve service quality. The process compares aspects of performance, identifies gaps, looks at ways to raise performance, introduces change, and monitors the outcomes. The emphasis is placed on a continuous process involving staff and users, and a sharing of information and outcomes with other services. It is a process of collaborative learning, and Griffin (2006) provides some practical guidelines to ensure a professional exchange and mutual benefit, which include:

- Always be totally honest and open.
- Clarify your areas of interest (to check that the partner can really help)
- Stress the benefits of a mutual exchange between professionals.
- Be prepared to provide more information about your activities than you are willing to receive in return.
- Know your situation in detail, including the performance measurements used.
- Clarify confidentiality and any restrictions (on either side).
- Identify sensitive areas (before you step on them).
- Benchmarking is only of benefit if the improvement actions are implemented.

- Remember that improvements are continuous and benchmarks go out of date quickly. Other services' performance will probably continue to improve in advance of your own.

When the first results emerge from benchmarking, there can be two reactions from those involved in the process. The first may be that of shock from reading the comparison—the service may be performing better than anticipated or perhaps less well. In either case, there is the motivation to draw on best practice adopted in similar services. By identifying differences and using these information and data to learn and consider change, improvements in operations will emerge as part of a learning culture. However, there is a caveat that copying another service slavishly needs careful consideration. Circumstances can quickly change, and doing things differently does not necessarily mean the other organization is doing things better.

In Europe, benchmarking has been adopted by governments and the European Commission as a way to learn from shared experiences in both the public and private sectors, and by small and large organizations. It can be used in conjunction with other improvement tools by exploiting the synergy between them. Dudden et al. have described the planning and implementation of the Medical Library Association Benchmarking Network (2006a) and the results of the 2002 survey which collected data from 344 hospital libraries (2006b). Charbonneau (2005) examined benchmarks for catalogers in U.S. academic libraries. Laeven and Smit (2003) describe the way that benchmarking is used in Dutch university libraries.

Check This Out:

The U.K. government adopted benchmarking as a key tool to improve performance in the public and private sectors, and a Web site gives a full and clear account of the process and how to adopt it (www.benchmarking.gov.uk [accessed August 2006]).

The next set of approaches is primarily concerned with measuring performance over time, but within the service.

Six Sigma

Based on the statistical tools and techniques of quality management developed by Joseph M. Juran, this approach was adopted by Motorola Inc. in the 1980s and has been implemented in some U.S. public libraries. It is both a philosophy and a technique designed to eliminate waste and improve performance. Using statistical analysis, it aims to bring down defects in processes and services to near zero. At the same time, it fosters a culture that focuses on creating value for the user and eliminating any redundant processes. Thomsett (2005) provides an introduction to the technique. Brett and Queen (2005) describe the application of Lean Six Sigma to streamline a records management service. Improving self-service using Six Sigma has been reported by Kumi and Morrow (2006).

Balanced Scorecard

The Balanced Scorecard was developed by Robert Kaplan and David Norton as an approach to strategic management based on a measurement system. It provides feedback on the internal operations and the external outcomes to assist organizations continuously improve strategic performance (Kaplan and Norton, 2006). The approach views the service from four perspectives for which metrics are developed, data are collected and analyzed. The perspectives are: the learning and growth perspective, the business process perspective, the customer perspective, and the financial perspective (www.balancedscorecard.org). Willis (2004) describes its use at the University of Virginia Library.

THE EFFICIENCY OF SERVICE DELIVERY

Users usually have less concern with what happens *within the service* and more concern about the level of the service provided to them at the *point of delivery*. You *must* monitor and control the quality and efficiency of the service operations. Control is integral to all the other functions of management, providing coordination of organizational activities and a means of assessing the success of those activities.

The control process has four components: establishing standards, measuring performance, comparing/evaluating performance against standards, and correcting deviations from the standards. Typical elements or issues relate quality, quantity, time, and cost.

A *standard* serves as a target for performance and should be measurable in some manner. Typical measures are quality, quantity, time, and cost. They are useful individually and often even more useful when combined. Some common combinations are cost/benefit, unit cost, and time/quantity. Standards assist in monitoring organizational performance. The key point is how they are established: historical, comparative, engineered, and subjective.

Historical data, or past performance, can assist in establishing a standard, if the component elements remain constant and serve as the initial standard until more scientific data is available. A problem is that there is no assurance that in the past the activity was done efficiently, effectively, or perhaps even very well. "We've always done it this way" does not always translate to being the best, or only, way. There may be implications for related activities that cause overall organizational performance to suffer. (Remember, part of the control/operations function is to coordinate activities and view the whole.)

Another source is *comparison* with the same activities in a number of like organizations, and benchmarking is one approach. Unless a systematic approach is taken and the information and data obtained from another service is robust, the outcomes may not be reliable. Also, no two institutions are totally identical, but the best use of comparative data is to establish standards.

Engineered standards are just a different label for "scientific management" and use hard data collected from work analysis.

There are times when subjective estimates and assessments of what is realistic as a standard must be used, for example: morale, public relations, image, and staff development. Such areas are almost impossible to directly measure in an objective manner. An attempt to measure some aspect of these issues can be made through questionnaires and surveys, but these are at best indirect and the questions asked would reflect subjective assessments about what is important. Having subjective standards is better than not having them, but recognize them for what they are.

By applying work-analysis techniques, managers can improve the climate of the work environment for everyone while establishing performance standards. Work analysis can also assist in solving layout problems in physical space, choosing a sequence for doing work, and finding ways of performing tasks more efficiently, so achieving coordination. The relationship between work analysis and budgeting becomes clear when it is recognized that most work-analysis techniques relate in one way or another to time or money. As a result, they provide much of the quality of the data needed for budgeting and planning.

Work sampling is a component of any work-analysis project requiring an understanding of basic statistics. A typical application would be in the acquisitions department, when establishing performance standards for the many tasks carried out in the unit. The process consists of two parts: establishing realistic workloads (standards) and comparing that to the staff's performance.

The current workload represents in statistical terms the study universe, or population. If you wanted to know with almost complete certainty what is being done within a unit, you would have to study *all* steps in the acquisitions unit for *one year*. Even then you could not be absolutely confident that some unusual characteristics made the year atypical. Fortunately, a reasonably small, properly selected sample of the work will provide results that will supply almost as much confidence as if you had studied the entire year's operation.

Sampling techniques and their use rest on certain assumptions regarding the nature of the phenomena under study. A basic assumption is that the form of a *distribution pattern* of natural phenomena (in this case, work activities) will resemble a *normal distribution* (bell-shaped curve). Normal distributions are ones in which the characteristics under study cluster around a central point. As you move away from the central point, there are fewer instances of those characteristics.

A *random sample* drawn from a normal population will probably display a pattern that is similar (although not identical) to the pattern displayed in the population from which it was drawn. Repeated samples from the same population would eventually duplicate the actual pattern.

Not all the work-analysis techniques relate directly to establishing standards. They may help improve the work flow so that standards can be set, or aid visualization of the interrelated nature of a set of activities to improve coordination, or establish that the present system is the best method, or control complex projects that may not be part of normal activities. All assist in controlling and monitoring organizational work activities.

The *block diagram* is the most elementary form of work analysis, providing a simple overview of the relationships among various units or activities within an organization, identifying possible problem areas.

The *flow diagram* introduces a finer level of analysis, as it gives a graphic view of both the work area and the movement of personnel or materials within that area—e.g., a scale drawing of the facility, with all activities clearly identified.

A *flow process chart* indicates the movement of an object of study, but does not relate the movement to a physical space. It answers questions such as "Is this the best sequence?" "What would happen if...?" or "Could we combine steps *x* and *y*?" It ensures that a step is not missed in the process.

The *decision flow chart*—typically used in systems analysis for computer applications—analyzes workflows in which numerous decisions occur.

Operations analysis studies the motions of the hands, eyes, and feet of an individual who is working on a particular activity in one location. This is the classic activity of Taylor's scientific management. It is most effective when used sparingly and on jobs that involve very high levels of repetition; this is where the classical time-and-motion study is very important. The goal is always the best, most effective arrangement.

Another useful type of analysis is *form analysis*. Paper, electronic forms, and files seem to multiply rapidly. Too often they remain in use because "we've always done it that way." The result is often unnecessary work for the department. An annual review should determine which still serve a function efficiently.

Man-Machine charts allow studies of the relationship between people and machines. When people or machines are idle for long periods, the organization's investment is not optimal.

Scheduling—the assignment of a specific time period for each component of work and for the total project—gives vitality and practical meaning to a plan, providing a way to compare actual progress against projected progress. *Gantt Charts* list departments or activities along the left-hand side of the form, together with the number of employees and their weekly capability. Each column represents one week (the numbers at the top of each column represent the ending day for that week). Whichever form of the Gantt chart is used, it will emphasize the importance of time values and people or things. When developing a complex schedule, a Gantt chart can help plan the workload in terms of overall objectives.

Other Useful Concepts

Many of the following techniques require a mathematical background. If necessary, take a course to refresh your understanding of how to gather and interpret the necessary data.

Linear programming can help determine the best use of scarce resources to achieve a specified goal by:

- improving the use of all organizational work resources
- keeping the costs of an operation or activity to a minimum
- determining volume-cost relationships
- selecting the optimum mix of customer services

Queuing theory deals with waiting lines and provides models for operations. You can apply the concept to people or things and is especially effective in determining the optimum number of service points. Users who have to wait too long become frustrated, angry, and, ultimately, ex-users. *Game theory* is useful when allocating resources between competing demands; *search theory* is for the optimization of locating information, while the *Monte Carlo method* addresses issues of chance occurrences. These are the most prominent techniques from among the many available. The appropriate application of these techniques enhances the image of a service that is effective and cost-conscious.

Tip:

If your understanding of statistics is rusty, it would be helpful to take a refresher course.
Numeracy is a basic skill for managers today.

> **Try This:**
>
> Now that you have read the section on work analysis, take each technique and give two additional examples of how it could be used in a library or archives setting.

COST ACCOUNTING

The preceding section made reference to costs and to work activities. One outcome of work analysis is, or can be, cost accounting—the process of comparing costs (expenses) with results (products or services). The purpose is to ascertain the actual cost of a single product or service (processing a document or answering a telephone inquiry, for example). When done properly, cost accounting is a powerful tool in preparing a budget, determining staffing needs, planning new services, or arranging new service locations. It is essential in making decisions about outsourcing. Only by having data on the unit costs for a process/activity can reasonable decisions be made about whether or not to use an outside agency.

A common way is to divide costs into three categories: labor, supplies, and overhead. Supplies such as pens, paper, and computer printer ink cartridges are easy to identify. But what about the computers, desks, and chairs, as well as the maintenance of these items? Supplies or overhead? Do you depreciate equipment cost over a fixed period and use only a given year's cost? Do you use the original purchase price or the cost of replacing the item? There are various methods and rationales used to decide these issues. If you overlook a cost, you will ignore the real organizational expenses.

Overhead (indirect) costs are those not directly attributable to the production of a particular product or service. Administrative salaries, building maintenance, utilities, travel expenses, and insurance are common overhead items. Because publicly funded activities usually take place in public buildings that are tax and rent free, some writers suggest that cost figures that do not take these factors into account are unrealistic. They suggest treating the building as a private one for accounting purposes, but this would require a great deal of time, effort, and money to establish realistic "rent" and tax figures. Would it be worth it? In today's culture of privatization, it may become necessary regardless of the time and effort required.

An expert should assist in establishing a proper cost accounting system. However, for "down and dirty" purposes, rough cost accounting is not that difficult. Use staff salaries, (not forgetting benefits, etc.) as labor costs, the annual supplies budget as supplies cost, and administrative salary as overhead. This provides the total cost to divide by the number of units of service or products produced in a year by a unit. The figure will probably be surprisingly high for unit costs.

SYSTEMS APPROACH

A system is any set of interacting variables. Each system is part of a larger system. For instance, a department's variables will include people, equipment, structure, and procedures. When changes occur in one variable, consequences may appear in the other variables. Further, changes in one department may affect an entire organization. Information services are usually part of a larger system, and that fact greatly influences internal changes.

System approaches consider the effects of any change on the entire process or organization rather than the effects of change on a single variable. It is a part of operations research and it may produce either flow diagrams or block diagrams that could lead to improvements.

Basic to understanding the systems approach and the design of management information systems (MIS) is the concept of information feedback, which explains the goal-seeking and self-correcting interplay that occurs between parts of a system. The feedback concept addresses the use of information as a means of control. A vital development for systems approaches was the notion of programming decisions by means of rules. One outcome was the automation of these activities. Machines then just follow the rules. The problem here, as always, is how to handle the unquantifiable or unexpected factors.

Without the computer, the vast amounts of quantitative data used to determine performance would not be readily available to managers. Nevertheless, it is only a tool. The human element is essential to examine the data, identify and interpret significant information, and take necessary action in any system comes before all else, even if it seems to lag behind technology at times.

GATHERING THE VIEWS OF USERS

Gathering views from the total community served presents challenges. In the case of clearly defined services such as a records management or an information services within one organization that has a discrete user community, opinions about the quality of the services delivered to them are relatively easy to gather from users, nonusers, and ex-users. In the case of services delivered to the public at large, an extensive community survey would then be required.

Gathering the opinions of users and ex-users is easier—the population can be defined from records held within the service. There are a number of approaches that can be used.

Two of the simplest methods are to gather feedback via a suggestion board near the entrance/exit of the service, or using the OPAC "comments" capability. The suggestion board provides a means for everyone to see what may be bugging users, and for staff to provide a speedy response. It acts as a "health barometer" for the service. There is a third method which is effective, where the staff uses a "No" log in which they record requests to which they have said "no." These are discussed, and ways are found to say "yes." MacMillan (2005) has described the use of this approach in a public library.

Surveys are a more complex method of gathering information in a variety of ways, generally employing some form of sampling. Questionnaires can be distributed by staff or sent by mail or e-mail. Interviews can yield more feedback and can be face-to-face, piggybacked on a national survey such as Gallup, or be administered by telephone.

Check This Out:

One way to gather feedback from the community served is to undertake a telephone survey.

Philip Calvert and Adam Pope's 2005 "Telephone Survey Research for Library Managers" (*Library Management* 26, no. 3: 139–151) indicates that the response rates are higher, data can be analyzed sooner, the cost is lower than alternative methods, and calls can be monitored for quality.

Focus groups are a popular means of gathering opinions. They consist of a relatively small number of people, more or less homogenous in character, who discuss a topic with the assistance of a trained leader who facilitates rather than directs the process.

To be effective the group must spend time discussing the topic, perhaps an hour or more, which requires a significant time commitment. Identifying willing people can be difficult, especially if the incentives to take part are limited. Finding inexpensive incentives that will appeal can be a challenge, but free online searches, refreshments, or gift certificates donated by a bookstore have been used. It is essential to get a cross-section of customers into the focus groups and gain their interest and active cooperation.

> **Check This Out:**
>
> Peter Z. McKay and Leticia Camacho prepared *Focus Groups & Libraries: A Selected Bibliography* in 2005, which is available at: www.ala.org/ala/rusa/rusaourassoc/rusasections/brass/brassprotools/brasspres/ miscellaneous/FocusGroupsBib.pdf (accessed May 2006).

Users are not always aware of all the services provided for them, and may have expectations for services that do not exist. Learning about what is, and what is not, known about the service is an important step in the assessment process.

Another technique involves unobtrusive methods, such as "mystery shoppers." This employs people not known to the staff who are briefed to ask a specific set of questions and note the answers received and how the enquiry was handled.

> **Check This Out:**
>
> Calvert, Philip. 2005. "It's a Mystery: Mystery Shopping in New Zealand's Public Libraries." *Library Review* 54, no. 1: 24–35.

All customers expect quality. Even if they do not complain, they may believe the quality of the service can be improved. It is likely that gathering feedback will identify more services and products than the service can provide given its current level of support. Having the customers' input can be the deciding factor in securing additional financial support, as budgeting authorities value the opinions of customers.

Quality and performance will grow in importance in both the private and public sectors. In the public sector, increasing attention is being paid to best value received in return for the expenditure of funds derived from taxation. The private sector is acutely aware of the requirement to maximize a return to stockholders. At the same time managers must know the level of performance of the service in order to plan and allocate resources. Staff members need to maximize their job satisfaction and take pride in the way they contribute to a high performing service.

KEY POINTS TO REMEMBER:

- Determining the effectiveness and efficiency of a service is of growing importance; there are a variety of approaches.
- Those who provide budgets for information services keep an eye on the bottom line and the extent to which the services satisfy the community served.
- Decision makers on governing boards are likely to be drawn from the business sector and expect to see familiar approaches to performance measurement.
- Managers need to have some basic mathematical and statistical skills, but also understand that data and information do not necessarily provide the sole answers about service efficiency and effectiveness—experience and judgment play a role.

REFERENCES

Barnard, Susan B. 1993. "Implementing Total Quality Management: A Model for Research Libraries." In *Integrating Total Quality Management in a Library Setting*, edited by Susan Jurow and Susan B. Barnard. New York: Haworth Press.

Bertot, John Carlo, and Charles R. McClure. 2003. "Outcomes Assessment in the Networked Environment: Research Questions, Issues, Considerations, and Moving Forward." *Library Trends* 51, no. 4 (Spring): 590–613.

Bertot, John Carlo, and Denise M. Davis. 2004. *Planning and Evaluating Library Networked Services and Resources*. Westport, CT: Libraries Unlimited.

Brett, Charles, and Patrick Queen. 2005. "Streamlining Enterprise Records Management with Lean Six Sigma." *Information Management Journal* 39, no. 6 (November-December): 58, 60–62.

British Standards Institution. 2004. *BIP 0004: 2004 An Introduction to Information Management*. London: British Standards Institution.

British Standards Institution. 1998. *BS ISO 11620:1998 Information and Documentation. Library Performance Indicators*. London: British Standards Institution.

British Standards Institution. 2001. *PAS 2001: 2001 Knowledge Management*. London: British Standards Institution.

British Standards Institution. 2003. *PD 7502: 2003 Guide to Measurements in Knowledge Management*. London: British Standards Institution.

Cary, Paul, and Laurie J. Sampsel. 2006. "Information literacy instructional objectives for undergraduate music students: a project of the Music Library Association, Bibliographic Instruction Subcommittee." *Notes* 62, no. 3 (March): 663–679.

Charbonneau, Mechael D. 2005. "Production Benchmarks for Catalogers in Academic Libraries." Are We There Yet?" *Libraries Resources & Technical Services* 49, 1 (January): 10–18.

Deming, W. Edward. 1986. *Out of Crisis.* Cambridge, MA: Massachusetts Institute of Technology Press.

De Prospo, Ernest R., Ellen Altman, and Kenneth E. Beasley. 1973. *Performance Measures for Public Libraries.* Chicago: American Library Association.

Dudden, Rosalind Farnam et al. 2006a. "The Medical Library Association Benchmarking Network: Development and Implementation." *Journal of the Medical Library Association* 94, no. 2 (April): 107–117.

Dudden, Rosalind Farnam et al. 2006b. "The Medical Library Association Benchmarking Network: Results" *Journal of the Medical Library Association* 94, no. 2 (April): 118–129.

Griffin, Peter. "Quality Network: Benchmarking." (October 2006) Available: www.quality.co.uk/benchadv.htm

Heath, Fred M., Martha Kyrillidou, and Consuella A. Askew. 2004. *Libraries Act on Their LibQual Findings: From Data to Action.* Binghamton NY: Haworth Information Press.

Hennen, Thomas. 2004. *Hennen's Public Library Planner: A Manual and Interactive CD-ROM.* New York: Neal-Schuman.

International Organization for Standardization. 2005. *ISO 9000: 2005 Quality Management Systems—Fundamentals and Vocabulary.* Geneva: International Organization for Standardization.

International Organization for Standardization. 2000. *ISO 9001: 2000 Quality Management Systems—Requirements.* Geneva: International Organization for Standardization.

International Organization for Standardization. 2001. *ISO 15489-1: 2001 and ISO/TR 15489-2. Information and Documentation—Records Management.* Geneva: International Organization for Standardization.

Ishikawa, Kaoru. 1985. *What is Total Quality.* Englewood Cliffs, NJ: Prentice-Hall.

Juran, Joseph M., and A. Blanton Godfrey. 1999. *Juran's Quality Handbook.* 5th ed. New York: McGraw-Hill.

Kaplan, Robert S., and David P. Norton. 2006. "The Balanced Scorecard: Measures That Drive Performance." *Harvard Business Review* 83, no. 7 (July–August): 172, 174–180.

Kaur, Kiran, Mohamad Pauziaah, and George Sossamma. 2006. "Quality Management Service at the University of Malaya Library." *Library Management* 27, no. 4: 249–256.

Kumi, Susan, and John Morrow. 2006. "Improving Self Service the Six Sigma Way at Newcastle University Library." *Program* 40, no. 2: 123–136.

Laeven, Hubert, and Anja Smit. 2003. "A Project to Benchmark University Libraries in The Netherlands." *Library Management* 24, nos. 6/7: 291–304.

Lancaster, F. Wilfred. 1988. *If You Want to Evaluate Your Library...* London: Library Association.

Lancaster, F. Wilfred. 1977. *The Measurement and Evaluation of Library Services.* Arlington, VA: Information Resources Press.

Lubans, John. 1994. "Sherlock's Dog, or Managers and Mess Finding." *Library Administration & Management* 8, no. 3 (Summer): 146.

MacMillan, Kathy. 2005. "Generating Goodwill: Turning No Into Yes." *American Libraries* 36, no. 10 (November): 48–49.

Martin, Allie-Beth. 1972. *A Strategy for Public Library Change: Proposed Public Library Goals-Feasibility Study*. Chicago: American Library Association.

Missingham, Roxanne. 2005. "Libraries and Economic Value: A Review of Recent Studies." *Performance Measurement and Metrics* 6, no. 3: 142–158.

Palmour, Vernon E., Marcia A. Bellassai, and Nancy de Wath. 1980. *A Planning Process for Public Libraries*. Chicago: American Library Association.

Parasuraman, A., Valaria A. Zeithaml, and Leonard L. Berry. 1985. "A Conceptual Model of Service Quality and its Implications for Future Research." *Journal of Marketing* 49 (Fall): 41–50.

Redfern, Margaret. ed. 1976. *The Effective Library: Report of the Hillingdon Project on Public Library Effectiveness*. London: Library Association.

Rousseau, Ronald. 2005. "Robert Fairthorne and the Empirical Power Laws." *Journal of Documentation* 61, no. 2: 194–202.

Senge, Peter. 1990. *The Fifth Discipline: The Art and Practice of the Learning Organization*. New York: Doubleday.

Shaughnessy, Thomas W. 1987. "Search for Quality." *Journal of Library Administration* 8, (1): 5–10.

Shewhart, Walter A. 1939. *Statistical Method from the Viewpoint of Quality Control*. Washington, DC: U.S. Department of Agriculture—Graduate School.

Sirkin, Arlene F. 1993. "Customer Service: Another Side of TQM." In *Integrating Total Quality Management in a Library Setting*, edited by Susan Jurow and Susan B. Barnard. New York: Haworth Press.

Thomsett, Michael C. 2005. *Getting Started in Six Sigma*. Hoboken, NJ: Wiley.

Trueswell, R.W. 1969. "User Circulation Satisfaction v. Size of Holdings at Three Academic Libraries." *College and Research Libraries* 30, no. 3: 204–214.

Urquhart, Christine. 2005. "Assessing Impact: Let Us Count the Ways?" *Library + Information Update* 4, no. 12 (December): 26–28.

Van House, Nancy, Beth T. Weil, and Charles R. McClure. 1990. *Measuring Academic Library Performance: A Practical Approach*. Chicago: American Library Association.

Van House, Nancy A., and Thomas A. Childers. 1993. *The Public Library Effectiveness Study: The Complete Report*. Chicago: American Library Association.

Walter, Virginia A. 1995. *Output Measures and More: Planning and Evaluating Public Library Services for Young Adults*. Chicago: American Library Association.

Walter, Virginia A. 1992. *Output Measures for Public Library Service to Children: A Manual of Standardized Procedures*. Chicago: American Library Association.

Willis, Alfred. 2004. "Using the Balanced Scorecard at the University of Virginia Library." *Library Administration and Management* 18, no. 2 (Spring): 64–67.

Zweizig, Douglas, Debra Wilcox Johnson, and Jane Robbins. 1996. *The TELL IT! Manual*. Chicago: American Library Association.

LAUNCHING PAD

Arnold, Julie, and Neal K. Kaske. 2005. "Evaluating the Quality of a Chat Service." *Portal: Libraries and the Academy* 5, no. 2 (April): 177–193

Calvert, Philip, Daniel G. Dorner, and G. E. Gorman. 2004. *Analysing What Your Users Need: A Guide for Librarians and Information Managers*. New York: Facet Publishing.

Crawford, John. 2006. *The Culture of Evaluation in Library and Information Services.* Oxford: Chandos.

Hendriks, Boyd, and Ian Wooler. 2006. "Establishing the Return on Investment for Information and Knowledge Services: A Practical Approach to Show Added Value for Information and Knowledge Centers, Corporate Libraries and Documentation Centers." *Business Information Review* 23, no. 1 (March): 13–25.

Hernon, Peter, and John R. Whitman. 2001. *Delivering Satisfaction and Quality: A Customer-Based Approach for Libraries.* Chicago: American Library Association.

Jankowska, Maria Anna, Karen Hertel, and Nancy J. Young. 2006. "Improving Library Service Quality to Graduate Students: LibQUAL+ Survey Results in a Practical Setting." *Portal: Libraries and the Academy* 6, no. 1 (January): 59–76.

Levy, Sarah, and Xi Shi. 2005. "A Theory-Guided Approach to Library Services Assessment." *College & Research Libraries* 66, no. 3 (May): 266–277.

Matthews, Joe. 2006. "The Library Balanced Scorecard: Is It In Your Future?" *Public Libraries* 46, no.6 (November–December): 64–71.

Reijers, Hajo A., and Wil M. P. van der Aalst. 2005. "The Effectiveness of Workflow Management Systems: Predictions and Lessons Learned." *International Journal of Information Management* 25, no. 5 (October): 458–472.

Rubin, Rhea Joyce. 2005. *Demonstrating Results: Using Outcome Measurement in Your Library.* Chicago: American Library Association.

"The High-Performance Organization." 2005. *Harvard Business Review* 83, no. 7 (July–August): 17–196.

Todaro, Julie, and Mark L. Smith. 2006. *Training Library Staff and Volunteers to Provide Extraordinary Customer Service.* New York: Neal-Schuman.

Varnet, Harvey, and Martha Rice Sanders. 2005. "Asking Better Questions: Small-Scale Assessment Measures That Inform Ongoing Work." *College and Research Libraries News* 66, no. 6 (June): 461–465.

Weightman, Alison L., and Jane Williamson. 2005. "The Value and Impact of Information Provided Through Library Services for Patient Care: A Systematic Review." *Health Information and Libraries Journal* 22, no. 1 (March): 4–25.

White, Andrew C., and Eric Djiva. 2006. *E-metrics for Library and Information Professionals: How to Use Data for Managing and Evaluating Electronic Resource Collections.* New York: Neal-Schuman.

Zeithaml, Valarie A., Leonard L. Berry, and A. Parasuraman. 1993. "The Nature and Determinants of Customer Expectations of Service." *Journal of the Academy of Marketing Science* 21, no. 1: 1–12.

12

Communication

"We cannot ignore tone of voice or attitudes. These may be just as important as the words used."

Maurice S. Trotter

"The most important thing in communication is hearing what is said."

Peter F. Drucker

INTRODUCTION

Society cannot function without communication, and good communication increases the effectiveness with which society, and hence organizations, operate. Good communication increases our comfort levels in relating to those around us. In the workplace, managers quickly understand that if they are to create a high-performing learning organization where the staff enjoys their work and users are motivated to use the service, then good communication policies and practices must be in place.

Communication skills are developed over time and are culture-dependent. They are influenced first by our upbringing within the culture we were born and lived. Then the experience of education, both formal and informal, develops these skills. As each new technology is introduced, so new skills come into play to adapt to the changing situation—think of texting and the cell phone.

This chapter generally reflects the social and cultural values of the authors, who have lived and worked in the United States, United Kingdom, the Nordic countries, and Australia. So readers may need to consider some of the concepts in terms of the particular cultural setting of their own information service. However, we work in societies that are increasingly diverse. Our information services are being staffed by people from a variety of cultural backgrounds and operate on a global basis, cooperating with colleagues and buying in services from overseas so everyone on the staff needs to be sensitive to differing communication styles.

Check This Out:

Neuro-linguistic programming studies the structure of how humans think and experience the world, developing models from which techniques emerge for changing thoughts, beliefs, and behaviors that limit a person. A good book to explore this topic is Joseph O'Connor and John Seymour's 1993 *Introducing Neuro-Linguistic Programming: Psychological Skills for Understanding and Influencing People* (London: Aquarian/Thorsons).

The success of managers and supervisors rests ultimately on their communication skills. Since management accomplishes goals working with people, and delivers services to people, it is essential that meaningful, understandable, clear communication—oral, written on paper, or sent electronically—takes place at all levels of the organization. Managers must work efficiently and effectively with their senior management, staff, and users.

Many of the complaints from the staff and senior management are caused by poor, ineffective, or nonexistent communication. Getting the right message upwards at the right time keeps senior management informed. Listening to staff and getting the right amount of messages to them—again, at the right time—helps them to feel part of the organization and work effectively. Users need to receive timely and appropriate messages as changes are introduced to services. What people often forget is that communication is both a complex pattern of personal behavior (influenced by each person's entire life experiences) and a two-way process (in which the receiver has as much responsibility as the sender). This second point about the responsibility of the receiver is often overlooked. True communication only takes place when a person receives the identical meaning and emotion meant and felt by the person sending the message. So both sender and receiver must make the effort to verify the intended

---

Tip:

Keep in mind that people from different cultures may have varying approaches to authority. Some may feel it is not appropriate to question a statement made by someone whom they perceive is in an "authority role."

---

meaning and how the message has been understood. The extra time spent verifying messages results in better performance and better relations, and, in the long run, saves the service time and money.

Complicating the process is the fact that communication consists of three elements. First, there are verbal, written-on-paper, and electronic communications—it takes practice to be equally effective in all three, especially in a managerial role. A second pair of elements is listening and reading—in many ways these two activities are even more difficult to master in the workplace. Third, there are the nonverbal aspects of communication—nonverbals can often completely change the intended and/or perceived meaning of a message. This chapter considers these elements.

Nearly 50 years ago it was estimated that more than 70 percent of the average person's time was spent in listening, speaking, reading, and writing (Berlo, 1960). Consider the messages that are occasionally sent and received solely by nonverbal means, and add in a person's nonverbal (observation) time, and the total time becomes 83 percent. Now this data was calculated before computers, the Internet, e-mail, and the cell phone were introduced. We have tried to find a figure to update the situation, without success—but it must be much higher. Clearly, communication is a pervasive phenomenon.

Try This:

Keep a diary for the next few days and jot down the time you spend in communicating and the method used. Separate out the time for study or work and other activities. See how study/work activities take place in "free time," and vice versa.

Despite the attention, energy, and time devoted to the communication process, sometimes it ends in failure rather than success—if success is defined as complete agreement on the intended and perceived meaning. Certainly, more often than not the general sense of a message gets through, but not always the precise meaning. Given all the potential problems in communicating, it is perhaps surprising that people are able to communicate and work together as well as they do.

Ralph Waldo Emerson supposedly said, "Communication is like a piece of driftwood in a sea of conflicting currents. Sometimes the shore will be littered with debris; sometimes it will be bare. The amount and direction of movement is neither aimless nor non-directional at all, but is a response to all the forces, winds and tides or current which come into play." In information services, where the staff must think about both internal and external communication, the currents and tides can become obstacles to effective communication.

> **Point of Reflection:**
>
> Reflect on the ways in which information is communicated within an organization. See how many you can list.

OBSTACLES TO UNDERSTANDING

In order to understand communication, it helps to have some knowledge of general semantics and semiotics.

Semantics is the study of the origins and effects of communication habits. If individuals understand the effects of their communication habits, then they may be able to control them. Certainly, all information professionals, whether or not they are managers or supervisors, should have some knowledge of semantics. The staff handling any level of enquiry is constantly involved in communicating, and, if they do not understand, the process will be less successful and not as effective and helpful as it could be.

> **Try This:**
>
> Drawing on your own experience, list four or five barriers to understanding in a university library.

Korzybski noted in *Science and Society* (1948) that all semantic work rests on three premises. First, words are not the things they represent. If they were we would have a universal language and no language-barriers. Second, words can never say everything about anything. Some factors must be left out otherwise we could never complete a sentence. Consider the sentence "The card is on the table." "Card" seems to be specific, but is it a playing card, a greeting card, a catalog card? What color? What size? What is the table—its physical description, its history? And just how did the card get there? Is that relevant? Because these factors are not present, total communication does not take place. Third, it is possible to use words about words about words to an infinite level of abstraction. The abstract and symbolic nature of words causes great difficulty in the communication process.

People are able to learn new labels for physical objects because there is a common reference point—for example, boghandel, libreria, siop lyfrau, librairie, bookstore. And usually, even when many of the characteristics of a physical object are left out of a message, we still have a general understanding of the meaning. Often, omitted critical elements can be identified and added to the message. Try this sentence: "The new 3 x 5 buff unit card that you could not find is stuck in the crack in the old wooden table in the corner of the staff lounge." The message is clearer than the earlier example because important elements that were not in the first sentence have been identified. These are physical characteristics, observable and identifiable.

However problems develop if there are no physical reference points when abstract feelings and concepts are to be conveyed. "You're a good friend," "You're not doing as well as I expected," "You did a good job," and especially "I love you" are all statements that are open to a wide range of interpretation (and misinterpretation). A librarian knows what an OPAC is, but do those outside the field know? How many new users know what to do when they are told to "check in the OPAC"? Here we have both professional jargon and an abstract concept clouding the communication process.

A psychological factor also can lead to communication problems. Biology researchers know that, upon first meeting, animals usually size one another up in order to establish dominant-submissive hierarchies. Maslow (1937) showed that people also attempt to establish similar relationships, usually after a brief initial exchange of seemingly neutral information. Again, this involves nonverbal as well as verbal behavior. When person A goes into person B's office to discuss a problem, but person B continues working as if no one is present, B is placing A in a subordinate position. When this happens, A is less likely to be receptive to ideas and suggestions. This factor can also be critical in staff-user interactions, because an enquiry can often take on the superior-subordinate character very quickly, which makes effective communication difficult. Consider enquiry staff sitting behind a desk or counter. The desk or counter and an associated monitor can be perceived to be a barrier by the user. This introduces the field of semiotics which adds to the richness in understanding communication, for it studies the messages generated by signs such as the barrier or body language and emotion.

Bartlett (1951) suggested that the mind constantly tries to link new materials into the existing mental patterns in order to make the new material meaningful. The relating of new information to old, unstated preconceptions and domination become three major psychological stumbling blocks to effective communication.

Try This:

Can you identify three experiences that have shaped your ideas and values?

We all constantly meet the problem of determining to what degree the "real" world agrees with the symbolic world, and the extent to which his or her conception of both agrees with anyone else's. As the similarity between individuals' worlds increases you find that the possibility that meaningful communication also increases. Consider the virtual reality of the Internet and Web. There are multiple user domains in which an individual takes on another persona and in some instances multiple personas. As virtual reality develops, so the distinction between real and virtual life(ves) blurs, adding to communication complexities (Turkle, 1995).

Another challenge in the communication process involves meaning. Words have more than one meaning, and meanings often change in relation to the context in which they occur. Certainly there are a great many more meanings than there are words. The *Random House Dictionary* (unabridged) lists 31 meanings for the word "fair." Some meanings are archaic or obsolete, illustrating the changing nature of word usage. One example is the term "classification," covering a variety of systems of arranging library materials. To say, "I classified 50 books yesterday" tells the listener nothing about the system used; it could have been UDC, LC, DDC, faceted, or any other system. If the listener is from a library that uses a system that differs from the one used in the speaker's library, then confusion would probably reign until it became apparent through further conversation (verification and clarification) that they were using different reference points. Given the differences in the classification systems and their ease of use, the statement may or may not be impressive. The listener cannot make that judgment until she/he knows the classification system involved.

Language structure also may create difficulties in communication. Most Indo-European languages employ a two-value orientation: good/bad, black/white. Yet other language families have different bases, such as the multivalue system of Chinese. A person who is only partially conversant in another language rather than truly bilingual (especially if the second language has a different value base) will probably miss a great deal of what is meant when someone speaks or writes in that second language.

If the staff and user community is multicultural and composed of several different generations, the manager should take extra care in drafting messages, memos, and instructions.

Syntax and morphology also contribute to problems in communication. It is naive to think that, if we are very careful, the "right" word will be found—the word that will solve all problems. (The "right" word would be one having identical meaning to sender and receiver, but this can happen only when they have the same background, knowledge, and experience.) A general transfer of meaning does take place, but not the "perfect understanding" so often sought. When staff members complain about lack of communication, the situation usually results from managers assuming that everything they said has been fully understood.

Remember:

The English language exists in very many different versions—what may be clear to a person in the United States may not be clear to colleagues in the United Kingdom or Australia.

If everyone in the service is careful to use job-related terms in a consistent manner, then true communication can take place. Without this consistency, the staff develops individualized meanings for words and things become hazy. One example is the difference between "policy" and "rule"; a supervisor needs to explain these terms to new employees making the differences clear. It is particularly important in matters of personnel action, salaries, and sick leave, where the difference between rule and policy is often critical. A newcomer may feel that policy is something that must occur rather than something that can occur.

Try This:

Archivists, librarians, and records managers have a technical vocabulary. List ten technical terms that might baffle the user.

The environment in which communication occurs influences listeners' interpretations of meaning. Physical factors, such as crowds or confined space, can significantly alter the interpretation that people place on words. Consider the difference between hearing the word "fire" in a restaurant with a large fireplace in the lounge and hearing it in an overcrowded lobby at a rock concert. In the first instance, the word might connote coziness, while in the second it could create panic. The emotional state of the individual is a factor as well. Workers who are anxious or worried about something can be extra-sensitive to what they perceive as a hidden meaning in a chance statement you might make. An effective communicator takes into consideration expectations and anxieties (especially if they are at a high level) when preparing any message.

The *way* in which you say something—emphasis, lack of emphasis, omissions, and order of presentation—also influences meaning. Only when you have had some experience working with the same people will the

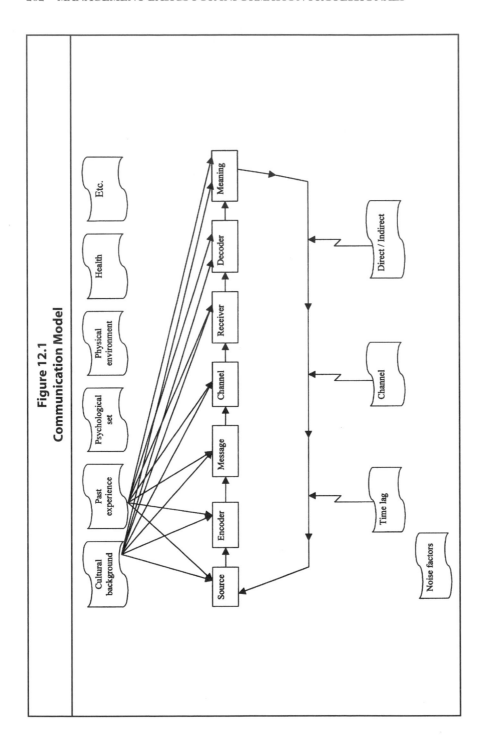

Figure 12.1
Communication Model

meanings of their word order, tone of voice, facial expressions, and other nonverbal characteristics be clear. This understanding is not always possible so it is best to remain constantly alert to these points, no matter how well the parties involved think they know one another. It is an essential factor to consider in teamwork.

Figure 12.1 represents an overview of the communication process, but it includes only a few of the "noise" factors that may alter a message. These factors are not physical sounds but psychological deterrents to understanding. In this sense, the factors discussed above are noise, and they all affect the communication process.

ORGANIZATIONAL BARRIERS TO COMMUNICATION

Up to this point, we focused on the individuals' problems in communicating, but the list of potential problems does not end there. The organizational structure of the service can influence the way in which staff interpret messages. A large archive or library service is a series of overlapping and interdependent units, each with its own immediate and long-range objectives. So each unit first interprets messages in light of their objectives; only after they finish that assessment do they take a broader view.

Work relationships, authority structure, and status also impact the communication process by influencing people's expectations regarding who should communicate with whom, about what, and in what way. We have found that varying interpretations of relationships within an organization also cause communication failures. These are then magnified by the continuous flux of personal as well as professional relationships within the service; you cannot even count on consistent misinterpretation.

Many information services operate over a number of sites, some of which may be located at a distance or overseas. Staff often work shifts over increasingly longer hours and some are likely to be teleworkers. Getting staff together at regular meetings can be a challenge but helps to overcome some of the barriers to communication. If people have the opportunity to meet their colleagues face to face, either in person or by teleconferencing, Webcam, or videophone, then they are better able to communicate and understand one another. In Western Australia—a large slice of the Australian continent—it is the policy of the State Library Service to fly managers out to visit the small branches across the state and for the staff to fly in for meetings and book exchanges. It is a vital part of the communication and training process.

Getting staff together, in person or using technology, ensures that the goals and activities of each unit, as well as those of the service as a whole, are subject to review and discussion. This is a form of direct feedback which can help resolve differences of opinion and priorities quickly. Social gatherings and "away-days" also bring benefits in improved communication.

GENERATIONAL BARRIERS TO COMMUNICATION

One of the aspects of working across the generations of members of staff and users of the service is that communication will be more effective if their preferences for mode and technology are taken into account. Hammill (2005) described generational differences in managing four generations; Table 12.1 draws on his observations concerning workplace communication. There is also a question of language. The "new" language that is used in texting can be confusing to the older generation.

Table 12.1 Workplace Communication across the Generations				
	Veterans (1922–1945)	**Baby Boomers (1946–1964)**	**Generation X (1965–1980)**	**Generation Y (1981–2000)**
Communication media	Rotary phones One-on-one Write a memo	Touch-tone phones Call me anytime	Cell phones Call me only at work	Internet Picture phones E-mail
Communications	Formal memo	In person	Direct Immediate	E-mail Voice mail

COMMUNICATION NEEDS

Both time and feedback are necessary for effective communication on the job. People need time to get to know one another and to start building a base of shared experiences and meanings. Staff needs to understand "the way we do it here." Different organizational cultures produce their own accepted practice. Knowing when a written message is expected by the receiver and whether it should be paper or electronic, or a phone message is sufficient, and the style all needs to be understood by newcomers to an organization. Each service has its practice that is often not explicitly described.

Providing sufficient time to assimilate messages is also an important factor in good communication and becomes increasingly challenging given the way that communication has speeded up in today's workplace.

Two forms of feedback are necessary. First, there must be direct and immediate feedback from the receiver about what the message means. If the message is not understood, or if the message appears to require making assumptions, it is the recipient's responsibility to request clarification. Without this feedback (questions or restatements of the message), the person sending the message will assume the recipient received and understood the message in the sense intended.

The second form of feedback consists of letting people who are communicating with you know exactly what you want, and need to know. A communication system can easily overload or can wither for a lack of information. Either process will be unsatisfactory. By knowing what people want and need to know, you can save everyone time and avoid frustration.

Occasionally, students question whether communication should be discussed in a management course—surely we all know about the process? Yes, that is true to a certain extent, but often our execution of it leaves much to be desired. One way to understand how complex communication in the workplace is, and how many flaws may exist in a system, is to review a list of "communication needs" that a library staff committee identified some years ago. Our experience leads us to believe that a list similar in length and content could be drawn up by such a committee in almost any large service.

The list is long, ranging from some very general items to some very specific problems and needs, and it indicates problems with communications. Managers and staff need more, not less, training in effective communication skills today.

PRINCIPLES OF EFFECTIVE COMMUNICATION

General points

Get information out before the fact, rather than during or after the fact.
Identify and communicate problem areas in order to provide guidance
  and assistance in resolving problems before they reach the crisis stage.
Define what is confidential.
Overcome "personality" blocks in communication.
Coach staff members in interpersonal communication.
Distribute information without creating a verbal electronic or paper overload.
Develop communication skills and techniques in all staff.
Select an appropriate method of communication and use technology
  more effectively.

Basic Organizational Communication Needs

Encourage all levels of staff to speak out without fear of rebuke or reprisal.

Provide a clear picture of each staff member's place in the organizational structure and clarify the chain of command.

Establish links with communication systems outside the organizational hierarchy.

Ensure that administrators are visible.

Maintain personal contact between administrators and staff.

Provide effective leadership and communication.

Supply administrative feedback to upward communication.

Keep open input and response channels in all directions, primarily upward.

Ensure that the system is interested in communicating with the individual.

Reduce communication barriers between groups of staff for example, between support and professional staff.

Overcome communication problems caused by geographic locations of units/flexiworking/teleworking/hours of shift, etc.

Define who needs to know what and when.

Establish a system-wide rapid communication mechanism for pressing matters.

Know the people with whom you interface in other units.

Maintain lateral communication between/among units/sections/teams/ staff performing similar functions.

Maintain lateral communication between/among units/sections/teams/ staff performing dissimilar functions.

Create a mechanism that will provide opportunity for ongoing consultation and understanding between units.

Specific Communication Needs of Staff

Tell the staff how and where they can obtain information.

Clarify the goals of the service.

Generate and encourage an interest in system and organizational goals at the beginning.

Ensure that supervisors, including unit heads, obtain training and orientation from those to whom they report.

Provide consistent orientation.

Provide procedure information and grievance policy.

Publicize staff development opportunities.

Provide a clear description of the criteria for the evaluation and promotion of all levels of staff.

Publicize salary schedules.

User Community

Identify the composition of the community served.

Identify and establish priorities for service to the public.

Provide and test appropriate communication channels to all the public(s).

Policy Dissemination

Provide information regarding planning, goals, policy, and budget at unit, service, and jurisdiction levels.
Publicize availability and disbursement of travel funds.
Ensure that policies are written down and made available in both hard copy and electronic formats.

Decision Making

Provide staff members with the opportunity to participate in decision-making processes that affect their work.
Keep the staff informed during a decision-making process.
Schedule adequate response time in a decision-making process.
Explain the rationale for determining who needs to be notified of individual decisions.
Inform staff members of budget and other resource decisions.

Individual Interest

Provide an opportunity for interested staff members to explore and develop service-related interests.
Obtain feedback from staff members who attend conferences and meetings.
Gather news from other services.
Keep staff current on local applications of changes in technology and information science.

Systemwide Consistency and Accountability

Provide consistent orientation.
Monitor morale in all units and teams.
Establish methods of monitoring communications management.
Make people accountable for their communications effectiveness, and aware of their deficiencies.
Maintain a consistent approach to the distribution of information in all units.
Equalize information delivery time to all units.
Ensure consistent and timely distribution of job postings.
Provide equal treatment and opportunity for all staff in receiving and providing information.
Observe and enforce deadlines throughout the system.
Standardize annual report procedures.
Standardize reporting procedures in general.
Ensure that policies are consistent and available in hard copy and electronic formats.

The list demonstrates how almost any management issue (budget, staffing, decision making, organization policy and procedures, customers, services, and so on) may generate a communication problem. It also illustrates the importance of communication to good management. This list came from working librarians, not academic researchers—people reporting their real frustrations and needs regarding on-the-job communication. The following sections explore some steps that can be taken to meet the needs identified above.

Try This:

Reflect on the communication needs of library users drawing on your experience of using a university library.
Note down six needs that are important to you.

COMMUNICATION ROLE OF SUPERVISORS

Supervisors are key communicators. In larger departmentalized services which have a supervisor for each unit, supervisors communicate up, down, and sideways as well as with users. Supervisors are responsible for orienting new employees to the service; this can include interviewing, introducing, instructing, discussing, suggesting, giving instructions, reporting, and sometimes disciplining. All these activities take place as the new employee meets coworkers, learns about the service's structure, learns about the job at hand, and tries to absorb a seemingly endless flow of new information that often seems confusing. If that person makes a mistake, much of the work will have to be done over—reinstructing, sustaining confidence, motivating—until performance becomes satisfactory. The entire communications process provides the opportunity for shared experiences and meaning, for learning how each person reacts and thinks, and what each person needs to know in order to work effectively with the others.

Conroy and Jones (1986) outlined the major purposes for managerial communication. It is a good list to keep in mind.

- To inform: convey both information and understanding.
- To gather information: collect input from others to help make decisions and solve problems.
- To motivate: change or reinforce behavior, prompt specific action.
- To instruct and/or train: enable another to carry out instructions, tasks, or procedures appropriately.

- To coach and/or discipline: encourage faster growth, prevent disciplinary action, help another learn how to do a specific task better, improve attitudes or behavior.
- To counsel: help someone with a personal problem that affects work productivity or morale.
- To mentor: help another succeed, usually by imparting better understanding of organizational policies, practices, or politics.
- To develop staff: guide staff progress and growth with performance appraisals and goal-setting sessions.
- To build teams: help work groups establish interpersonal rapport, build esprit de corps, and develop cohesion.

Graham and Valentine point out one of the important facts a supervisor must remember about the communication process:

> The communication problem is even more complex when the "established" or "official" channels are involved. These are in themselves seen as manipulative and therefore, received if at all, with considerable cynicism.

> But the fundamental problem is even more serious; the act of communicating at all is inherently manipulative. Attempts at communication are often evaluated in terms of observed change in behavior on the part of the receivers of the message (Graham and Valentine, 1973).

Since the staff may perceive a manipulative intent, you should always remain aware that a degree of hostility may be present, but that there are means to counteract hostility. First, try to establish authenticity by gaining rapport with the staff, engendering an atmosphere wherein staff realizes that they can freely discuss problems without fear of reprisal or rebuke. Also, by shortening the period of time between work activities and their evaluation, you can improve trust. Job evaluation is less threatening when it involves the immediate situation rather than a review of a person's annual performance. A third step that you can take is to involve the staff in all processes of the unit that are not sensitive or confidential in character, giving each person an opportunity to see that each job is important to the unit's success.

In addition, to establish "official" communication, all organizations must deal with formal and informal communication. Stevens (1983) developed the following division between formal and informal organizational communication which still holds today:

Formal communication:

- institutional publications (print and electronic)
- mission statements
- goals and objectives

- policies and procedures
- personnel files
- annual reports
- memos and other written materials
- staff newsletters
- schedules and hours

Informal communication:

- staff meetings
- one-on-one meetings
- training sessions
- staff association activities
- grapevine

WRITTEN AND ORAL COMMUNICATION

Deciding when to write or when to talk is a matter of fine judgment and an understanding of accepted organizational practices—some very formal, others rather informal. The decision extends to writing on paper or using an intranet, e-mail, or text message. Communication in the workplace is both informal and formal, and there are situations in which one may be more appropriate than another.

Information and communications technologies can either facilitate or act as barriers to communication unless policies and procedures are in place to overcome a growing problem. The computer, e-mail, voicemail, and cell phone are personalized to their user. The computer has a password; e-mails have unique addresses as do voicemail and cell phones. In the days when communication was written on paper and telephones lacked voicemail, then when someone was absent, a secretary or colleagues handled their mail or phone calls. Today this does not always happen—the communication system is personalized. It can be frustrating for someone wanting to make contact with the service who uses a specific phone extension or e-mail address and does not receive a prompt response. You need to ensure that there is a policy and procedure in place to overcome this potential problem. This can be a major challenge in a small service.

There is also the question of the work/life balance—where work communication can be carried over into personal time, and where personal messages are received in work time. Getting the balance right and getting an acceptable practice understood by staff needs sensitive handling and clear guidelines.

Written Communication

At times, it is best to provide written statements and then clarify them orally through question-and-answer exchanges. Policies should always be written down, and it certainly helps if instructions and procedures are clearly written. Generally, they are first made available in a draft form, distributed by e-mail. It is essential, however, that you follow up the distribution of the documents with an oral presentation that allows the staff to ask questions, or to use a staff e-group. When the document has been finalized it can be made available on the organization's Web site for those policies that affect users, and on the staff intranet for those that affect both staff and users.

Every letter and memo, whether electronic or paper, should be a "sales" letter of some kind, even if it attempts to sell a point of view on a minor matter. Persuasion results from fine directional hinting, not from overtly blunt or offensive statements. It is vital that memos are carefully worded; some managers spend as little time on memos as they do on casual oral presentations. Writing something down does not necessarily mean that it is clear.

In the memo in Figure 12.2, a manager employed the blunt approach and quickly received negative feedback both from superiors and subordinates.

Figure 12.2
Example of a Blunt Staff Memo

DATE: 1 May

TO: Reference Librarians

FROM: JKL

SUBJECT: Night Work

REMARKS: At present Circulation is minus aides so is Serials. Therefore it will be necessary for the Reference Librarians to be more active in the closing routine. If there is not an aide available and even if there is, please be helpful and place the current issues of the magazines on the slant shelves. Do not pile them up in the microfilm area. Do not put information file material in the microfilm area. Be responsible and do your part. You are lucky to be employed the way things are. Read and initial.

Tip:

When drafting any document, consider the context, the intended readership, and choose words carefully. If you have any doubts about grammar, check out Bill Walsh's 2004 book *The Elephants of Style* (New York: McGraw-Hill).

While the person made the sales point, even longtime staffers misread the attempted humor. Part of the problem arose from too much haste in writing as well as from the external employment situation for information professionals at the time—few jobs, many applicants.

Shared vocabulary is essential for any workplace communication. The important point to consider is the degree of abstraction of the material under consideration. Whenever possible, use simple sentences to communicate material. Restrict inspirational flights of prose to situations that are general in nature and concrete in subject matter. Jargon or shoptalk is all right if the reader understands it and if it does not actively interfere with or complicate the message's content.

Another staff memo (see Figure 12.3) may help to clarify the importance of thinking through a piece of written communication before sending it out in final form, and the importance of being clear.

In Figure 12.3, what is meant by good taste? Does that include sandals? For both men and women? What are the situations that require coat and tie? Where is the decision regarding this made? Will all supervisors define "appropriate" in the same way? Time and energy could have been easily saved if the director had written a specific memo about what was wanted. As it turned out, it took most of the summer to determine what "appropriate apparel" was.

The problem in the two illustrated memos lies in inadequate planning. Taking a few moments to review some of the following questions would improve these or any other written or oral communication.

- What am I trying to convey?
- With whom am I communicating?
- When is the best time to do this?
- Where is the best place?
- What is the best channel?
- Why am I communicating?
  —inform
  —persuade
  —publicize
  —resolve a problem
  —generate discussion
  —instruct
  —correct
  —report

The most important aspect of organizational communication is readability. The communication should include: a frame of reference (established at the beginning); a clear, well-thought-out statement of what is

---

Figure 12.3
Example of a Vague Staff Memo

BULLETIN 79-93

SUBJECT: Summer comfort

REMARKS:

1. Due to the necessity for energy conservation measures, temperatures must be maintained at somewhat higher levels during the summer months than has been the practice in the past. Accordingly, in the interest of good health and on-the-job effectiveness, employees should dress comfortably within the limits of good taste.

2. For male employees, neat looking, open neck short-sleeve dress shirts are appropriate. Of course, there will be occasions or situations when coats and neckties would be more suitable and should be worn. Similarly, female employees should feel free to wear neat, comfortable clothes.

3. This attention to added comfort does not diminish the responsibility of every employee to dress in a manner that is considerate of fellow employees and suitable for a government facility, nor does it modify existing requirements with respect to the wearing of uniforms.

4. Those employees who have questions concerning the appropriateness of clothing should discuss them with their immediate supervisors. Supervisors are responsible for assuring that employees dress appropriately and should not allow inappropriate attire in areas they supervise.

5. You are reminded that we can minimize the impact of higher summer temperatures by observing and controlling our work environment through measures [such] as:
   a. Closing blinds.
   b. Keeping corridor doors closed.
   c. Turning off lights in rooms with adequate natural light.
   d. Turning off lights in unoccupied areas.
   e. Turning off electrical equipment when it is not being used.

6. Authority: Director's letter II 10-6-93

---

meant or desired; and an explanation of how, when, and where the staff is to meet the expectations.

Electronic Communication

An intranet brings benefits to all members of staff by creating a more democratic working environment. The range of information that can be provided includes:

- policy documents needed for reference by staff
- replacements of hard-copy staff handbooks
- access to external databases
- training materials for staff development
- information about the parent organization
- contact details for cooperating services, suppliers, etc.
- news about the organization, of local interest, of people, or professional matters

The advantages of intranet communications are that:

- updating can be done speedily
- managers can be sure that staff members have access to the most recent information
- internal information can be broadcast quickly—e.g., dates, times, and agendas for meetings
- information can be quickly disseminated—e.g., the success of a member of staff
- internal discussion groups can be established
- the volume of paper circulated can be greatly reduced—and a few trees saved!
- the work of secretarial staff can be examined to produce a more interesting workload

Some points to remember in intranet communications:

- Every member of staff must have access—hardware, a password, and training.
- There is a real danger of information overload.
- One person must have responsibility for managing the intranet or else chaos may reign and information will not be updated systematically.

It is essential that one person is responsible for managing the intranet, to ensure that information is updated and out-of-date information deleted promptly. The design and layout of the intranet needs care and attention so that it is visually attractive and easy to navigate and locate information. You can add links to useful external information sources that can make the work of staff easier. For personnel staff, this may be links to relevant legislation available online. Managers will find checklists published by professional management bodies useful, and for specialist reference staff, the subject of focused databases and sources of information could be helpful. The aim of the intranet is to provide easy access to up-to-date information required by the service staff in their daily work. In a service where the staff work shifts, or where telework makes it difficult to get everyone together, an intranet will ensure that everyone has access to needed information. An intranet design does not last forever and needs periodic updating.

E-mail

Electronic communication is both a great blessing and a headache. One of the blessings is the quick and easy communication we now enjoy around the globe. One headache is the widespread expectation of a speedy response from the recipient.

In common with letters, e-mail can give time for the person receiving the communication to think before replying, if you wish to do so. Contrast this with a phone call, particularly on a cell phone. The humor that can pass between writer and receiver can lighten a heavy task. There are many benefits.

But recognize that it also brings problems, especially information overload. It can be difficult to keep up with e-mail. It is available to collect at home and on holiday, making it difficult to get away from the office. There can be a perceived sense of urgency about attending to e-mail, but sometimes the service goes down just when you expect to get a quick answer to a query. And even with the best filters, there is the constant issue of spam messages.

Guidelines and procedures for electronic communication are needed. First, for the use of e-mail: what are legitimate uses, particularly access to the Internet and, for example, sites such as e-Bay®? Second, for the management of electronic records: what is to be archived, by whom, where, and for how long? The guidelines will need to be clear to all members of staff within the organization. It is essential that a member of staff leaving the organization is not allowed to purge files without consultation and that his/her replacement has access to nonconfidential messages to enable work to flow smoothly. Paper records present fewer problems.

Check These Out:

Anandarajan, Murugan, and Claire Simmers, eds. 2004. *Personal Web Usage in the Workplace: A Guide to Effective Human Resource Management.* Hershey, PA: Information Science Publications.

Flynn, Nancy L., and Randolph Kahn. 2003. *E-mail Rules.* Lenexa, KS: ARMA International.

Ross, Catherine Sheldrick, and Patricia Dewdney. 1998. *Communicating Professionally.* 2nd ed. New York: Neal-Schuman.

Some basic points about using e-mail are:

- Make sure that you add your mailing address, phone, and fax number so that you can be identified and a reply sent in a different format if the recipient prefers this.
- Is your message really necessary or is it a form of "chat"? Never use it for gossip—you could be breaking a law.
- Make it short.
- Think before you write, and think before you send. It is easy to write in haste and have later regrets (perhaps over style, the content of the message itself, or words that reflected your emotions at the time).
- Indicate the subject, to allow the receiver to prioritize the opening of messages.
- Make sure the receiver will understand the content. Avoid using an abbreviation unless you know it will be understood.
- Do a spell check before sending.
- Remember legal constraints, since a message sent outside the library may be taken to represent the view of your employer. Do be careful, or you might find yourself in court.
- Observe the organizational policies and procedures for filing electronic mail.
- Select the discussion lists that you join carefully—they can be very time-consuming—and observe the same courtesies you would in joining a discussion around a table.

Tip:

Ensure that your service has guidelines for the use of e-mail, the Internet, and intranet that are revised regularly and communicated to all staff. They need to know what is expected of them.

For Further Thought:

Reflect on your use of e-mail and the Internet. Drawing on this experience, list six benefits and six potential problems for supervisors and managers.

Social Software

A few years ago, governments were anxious to increase access to official information and funded programs to place computers in public libraries, as in the United Kingdom. Handley (2005) discusses this in the discourse of empowerment and the broad context of government/citizen intermediation. But many changes have been taking place in social software that facilitates rapid exchanges of information and opinions, enabling anyone with Internet access to share information and provide feedback.

The blog provides feedback and news by a person in the form of an online diary, or a group of people may contribute to a blog on a specific topic. Blogs are the successor to the bulletin boards and e-mail lists of the 1980s emerging in the mid-1990s. They are a democratic and powerful way for people to make their views known.

You can employ an information service blog to communicate with users and among users. Knowledge management and children's services in a public library are examples of where blogs can bring benefits in facilitating communication and disseminating information.

Blogs have a downside, since they are a democratic means of communicating; an unpopular decision or action on the part of the service or a manager may give rise to unwelcome public attention. Conversely, a blog where the user community contributes may be of help if the service comes under threat. This has happened when public libraries have been facing closure. In this case, blogs became a tool to express public opinion.

If a manager is considering an official blog, then decisions about servers and software policies need to be made, covering the purpose of the blog, the nomination of a person to be the focal point for the blog, who can make a posting to the blog, and is the blog to be password protected. If in any doubt, then follow organizational guidelines. But guidelines are essential so that staff know and respect the purpose of the blog.

Wikis offer a more open means of communication, since they are a Web site that allows people to add, edit, or remove content, often without the need to register. Wikipedia is the largest example of a wiki acting as an online encyclopedia. The advantages of wikis are that they are usually up-to-date and can bring information and knowledge together on very specialized topics. The downside is that the information can be inaccurate and the updating facility is not always used by those best informed on the topic. Within an information service, they can be used for staff to exchange information.

Check These Out:

Stephens, Michael. *2006. Web 2.0 & Libraries: Best Practices for Social Software. Library Technology Reports.* Chicago: American Library Association.
Klobas, Jane, ed. 2006. *Wikis: Tools for Information Work and Collaboration.* Oxford: Chandos.

They are often very helpful for staff at reference or enquiry desks, in knowledge management, and for users to help other users with sources or services they have found helpful.

Oral Communication

While it is easy to understand that written communication requires well-developed skills, the possession of effective oral communication can be taken for granted, but it can be ineffective. Our experience suggests that managers and supervisors need to keep the following points in mind regarding oral communication.

- Do not take the supervisory/managerial position too seriously.
- Do let other people talk.
- Do listen carefully.
- Do not become overcommitted to an idea.
- Do try to keep the discussion from wandering aimlessly.
- Do keep it simple and straightforward.
- Do try to get to know the level of understanding of the person you are talking with.
- Do not argue.

A speaker's position within the organization naturally affects the way in which people respond and listen to that person. If someone holding a superior position acts in a superior manner, that person will have problems talking with subordinates. One danger for the new manager (as well as for the experienced manager) is becoming an instant expert on everything. An instant expert never hears anything that others say, unless it provides her/him with a springboard. Subordinates of such a person stop listening.

Total commitment to one idea—to the exclusion of entertaining a discussion of the idea's possible defects—is another way to lose an audience. When the manager believes that there is only one right way, and the workers know from experience that it is not working, the workers usually remain quiet until the system collapses.

Staying with the point of the conversation is essential from two points of view: internal and external. Provide only the details that are necessary for people to adequately get their jobs done within the service. And remember that users may not warm to someone who consistently gives more information than necessary (or information that has only slight relevance). Keep messages short and simple. This allows for greater clarity and it saves time.

Knowing the audience is essential for a speaker, as is selecting the appropriate level of presentation. Word choice and the manner of delivery are important in effective oral communication. Overly complicated messages cloud issues; likewise, simplistic approaches can insult an audience and/or reduce matters of complexity to clichés. If you spend a little time considering the level of understanding of an audience you'll achieve better communication.

Arguments seldom solve problems, and they do not lead to understanding, but the line between discussion and argument is often quite fine. To say emphatically "I disagree with that!" or "You are dead wrong!" is a very good way to turn a discussion into an argument. These statements should never be made by a supervisor. Supervisors who cut subordinates off (or down) in this way almost guarantee themselves serious personnel problems.

Although there are times when the direct approach is best, the indirect tack is usually the one to take when attempting to discuss personal feelings and behavior. This approach often uses third-party or hypothetical situations (based on actual knowledge of circumstances). However, if the indirect approach is not followed up by a more direct discussion, the entire point may well be lost or misunderstandings of a serious nature may occur. Always focus on the issue or situation, and not on the individual.

Consider:

Which is your preferred method of communication and why?
Do you need to brush up your skills in using any method?

Listening

A key factor in effective communication is listening. Listening is harder than most people realize. We hear about four times faster than most people speak; that leaves about three-quarters of our listening time free for the mind to wander. Consider how during a speech or lecture we have time to think about where we are going for lunch, errands to run, letters to write, something we want to say to someone in the audience or class, or a host of other matters unrelated to what the speaker is saying.

In addition to having substantial amounts of time available for the mind to wander while listening, we also "filter" what we do hear. Researchers on communication identify three major types of filtering: leveling, sharpening, and assimilation.

Leveling occurs when the recipient of a message omits certain elements of the original message and essentially changes its meaning. For example, assume a children's librarian is told a vacant position will not be filled until the level of usage of children's services increases. There has been a decline in the number of children getting library cards and attending story hours.

Further, the department head might develop a plan to increase the use of the services. The department head, in a leveling situation, might report to the department staff that the position was withdrawn because of a declining number of children. While part of the original content comes through the filtering process, the meaning has been changed through significant omissions.

Sharpening is a process in which a part of a message receives greater emphasis than in the original message. Assume during a staff development review a supervisor tells a staff member, "Your performance is excellent. If you continue at the present rate of development, you may be considered for a new position that we expect to have the next year or so." What the staff member tells others is, "I have been chosen for the new position the department will get next year." In essence, the person emphasizes what she/he wants to hear and plays down, or filters out, the qualifying elements.

Assimilation retains all of the original message and adds elements to it, so expanding the original meaning. Suppose a university president told the university librarian, "I am talking with a potential donor who is interested in making a major contribution to the new library building fund. I expect we will have an answer soon." The librarian reports to the staff that "the president is very supportive of a new library building—it is a priority. The president is working with a prospective donor at present and a new building will be started very soon, as soon as the donor makes the major contribution." All of the elements of the original message are present, but there are many added elements that essentially change the meaning.

Barriers to Effective Listening

Some of the most common problems in "hearing" a message are: The listener's assumption she/he knows the subject; the subject is uninteresting or of no concern to the listener, or the topic is unimportant. Operating with any of these ideas assures the message will be lost. Not only is the "extra" listening time wasted but also the one-quarter time needed to take in the message. The best way to overcome this problem is to make a conscious effort to suspend judgment. From the outset, keep an open mind; this may not be what you think it will be.

A related issue is the time spent assessing or criticizing the speaker's method of presentation. People who make presentations are particularly prone to criticizing others' presentations. When you do that, you cease listening to the content. How often do we hear, "Oh, it was a good talk, I think, but she/he had a horrible Power Point presentation, or there were too many pauses and asides"? The person making the comment had ceased to listen and transferred their attention to the delivery of the message. Keeping an open mind helps, but the real issue is to stop focusing on the "how" and switch to the "what" is being said. Think off and on during the presentation, "Am I thinking about the what, or the how of the message?" Failing to concentrate on the "what" erects barriers to effective communication.

Jumping to conclusions is something most people do, at least occasionally. Once you think, assume, or feel you know where the speaker is going with her/his talk, listening tends to fall off, if not cease. Again, suspending judgment until the message is complete is an effective way to keep communication open. Another technique that helps slow conclusion jumping is to consciously reflect on what is being said.

A less common but nonetheless significant barrier to effective listening is only wanting the "big picture," or general information. This barrier often takes the form of not wasting time spent on details—"spare me the details." Certainly the big picture/overview is essential, but often the details of how the speaker has arrived at the big picture are critical to understanding the message or situation. Thinking about how the details interconnect, and how the speaker is making the connections, helps to concentrate on the "what" of the message.

A related barrier is an overreaction to certain words or phrases. Each of us has a set of phrases and words we really do not like hearing. These phrases and words carry special meanings based on a past experience, when someone used them in a manner that caused us discomfort, harm, or emotional distress. Frequently these are relatively common words and phrases that have no special meaning for other people. In the workplace we must be cautious about overreacting to any message, especially when we hear words or phrases from our personal negative meaning set. One step to take is to spend time thinking about the words and phrases that tend to upset us. Thinking about what those are and why they cause us discomfort can help us control our reactions in the workplace. Another obvious step is to always wait before responding. An angry or confrontational response seldom leads to a discussion in which the people listen to one another. Rather, such a response, more often than not, leads to a situation of talking "at" one another. Thoughtful, nonemotional responses are much more likely to lead to real communication.

Some people appear too attentive when their minds are far, far away. The nonverbals suggest to the speaker that she/he has the attention of the listener. If there is no feedback when the speaker finishes, a normal assumption is that the message was understood, when in fact nothing came through. Body language and the signs we give, often unconsciously, can impede communication. Arms akimbo, running our hands through our hair, and other idiosyncrasies that we all possess can be very off-putting to someone who doesn't know us well.

Check This Out:

Lawton, Eunice. 2006. *Body Language and the First Line Manager.* Oxford: Chandos.

A related problem is conveying disagreement, either verbally or nonverbally, before the speaker has finished. Doing so effectively cuts off further communication. Essentially, such a response conveys to the speaker the sense the listener has reached a conclusion without hearing everything. Even when you disagree with what is said, not showing those feelings/thoughts until after the speaker finishes will improve the chances of having a meaningful discussion about the topic or issue.

Becoming overstimulated when questioning, or opposing, an idea also creates barriers to understanding. Overcoming this barrier requires practice and a substantial amount of self-awareness. In such situations, the natural pattern is to plan a response while the other person is still talking. Needless to say, little of what the person says is heard as your mind is focusing on the opportunity to respond. Something that is difficult to do without a considerable amount of practice is to listen for any elements where there is agreement. Using elements of agreement may improve listening to areas of disagreement and serve as starting points for resolving the disagreement.

Consider:

Are you a talker or a listener—have you got the balance right? Test this out with someone who knows you well.

When people withdraw attention, start daydreaming, or let boredom take over, effective communication begins to fall apart. Each of these processes insures the mind is elsewhere. At best, part of the mind is listening for the sound of voices to stop, serving as a signal that the meeting, the lecture, or presentation is over. A sign one is drifting toward one of these behaviors is when the person begins to "doodle," drawing pictures or designs. Another indication of an attention problem is starting to make mental or actual lists of things to do later. A commitment to listening must be developed, especially in the workplace. Part of that commitment is recognizing the signs that you are no longer listening. Another step is to prepare to provide accurate feedback as soon as the speaker finishes. Providing proper feedback requires that you listen to the content of the message.

There are two other barriers to mention. First, avoid the use of technical words or professional jargon in either sending messages or feedback, unless you are certain the other person(s) understands the jargon. Asking for feedback after delivering a message helps insure the intended and interpreted message meanings are sufficiently close to one another. Never be embarrassed to ask for clarification of a word, phrase, or the entire message—especially in work situations. Managers and supervisors should welcome such requests. Reacting in a negative manner will cut off essential feedback which in some circumstances leads to serious problems.

A second point is to make it clear if the listener has a problem with the physical aspect of hearing. If you have a hearing impairment, saying so allows speakers to adjust their presentation to help assure better communication. Likewise, if the speaker's voice does not carry well enough to hear, the speaker knows this. People frequently do this in formal presentation settings and neglect it in less formal situations. Failing to do so may result in important information being missed.

Try This:

Review your communication skills:
Which mode of communication are you most comfortable with?
Which mode of communication are you least comfortable with?
Now, thinking about communication in general:
What are your strengths?
What are your weaknesses?

Face-to-face communication entails more than what words are said and how they are said. Everyone in a conversation sends a variety of "messages" through their nonverbal actions. Earlier we touched on verbal quality (emphasis or lack of tone, speed, etc.), and these also are factors in the nonverbal communication process. Other elements in the process are facial expressions (frowns, smiles, eye contact, and the like); gestures (head nodding, hand movements, method of pointing, etc.); and body posture (arms and legs folded, angle of the body, space between interlcutors, and such). You may also send intended or unintended messages by the color of your clothes, the way you arrange your office furniture, and seating arrangements for meetings. Just to add to the complexity of the process, cultural background plays a major role in nonverbal communication.

Is it important to understand the nonverbal communication cues? In our opinion, absolutely! An estimated 60 percent of the real message comes from the nonverbal side of the communication process (Arthur,

1995). When working in a culturally diverse service, as so many of us do today, having a sound grasp of the nonverbal side of things is very important. Even in what may seem to be a homogenous group, there are likely to be some unexpected interpretations of what you might think of as unimportant actions or gestures.

Just two examples will illustrate the point. If you come from a Western European background, your "comfort zone" for conversation is at least three feet away from the others—in fact, a wider spacing is preferred. People from Latin America or Asia prefer to be much closer (one foot on average—and beware of the moving cigarette tip). Learning what is or is not the comfort range (interpersonal space) in a diverse group can take some time.

Eye contact is another area where culture matters. Most Western European background children learn early on to look at one's parents. A common phrase is, "look me in the eye when I'm talking to you." English-language novels are filled with nasty characters with "shifty eyes." For most Native American groups and most Asian peoples, on the other hand, direct eye contact is thought to be impolite at best and rude at worst, an attempt to gain control of another's spirit. Not understanding such differences can play havoc with work-related activities, from a job interview and throughout one's working life, all the way to retirement. Devoting a little time to learning about, and perhaps gaining some understanding of, the variations within your work group can pay dividends over time

---

Check These Out:

The following may give you a starting point for further exploring nonverbal communication:

Collett, Peter. 2004. "Show and Tell: Think You Can See When Someone is Lying?" *People Management* 10, no. 8: 34–35.

Page, Daniel. 2004. "The Importance of Nonverbal Communication in Information Service." *Library Mosaics* 15, no. 6: 11.

Underwood, Ruth. 2006. "How to Read a Face." *Newsweek* 148, no. 17: 65.

Whipple, Robert. 2006. "E-Body Language: Decoded." *T+D* 60, no. 2: 20–22.

Xu, Yu, and Ruth Davidhizar. "Intercultural Communication in Nursing Education." *Journal of Nursing Education* 44, no. 5: 209–215.

COMMUNICATING WITH THE DISSATISFIED USER

Because information services are user-oriented, and because there is no way that every user can be completely satisfied every time, inevitably there will be unhappy, dissatisfied, and, on occasion, angry users. To effectively handle these situations the staff must have well-developed communication abilities, especially careful, thoughtful listening skills.

Check This Out:

Melling, Maxine, and Joyce Little. 2002. *Building a Successful Customer Service Culture: A Guide for Library and Information Managers.* London: Facet Publishing.

Generally, there are three types of unhappy users that staff will encounter at some time: upset, angry, and disruptive.

The first level, and most common, is the confused and/or upset person. These are people who may not understand a policy or rule. With these users, and with those at other levels, attentive listening is the starting point. Asking for additional information is often helpful: "Tell me more," "What have you tried so far," "I do not quite understand, please tell me about..." By paraphrasing the person's comments, there is the indication that someone is listening to their problem; this allows for better communication. It is not a sound practice to make the response a personal choice ("I wish I could..."); it is better to respond in terms of the policy and practice of the service. The focus should be on determining what the situation is and finding a proper solution; keeping the person from becoming angry and ensuring that the issue/problem does not become a personal matter between the user and staff member.

Level two—the angry person—is more complex and also less common, or should be. Angry people can exhibit one of three categories of anger: controlled, expressed, and irrational. Occasionally the person who appears confused is really in a state of controlled anger. A sensible approach is to assume that anyone with a complaint/problem should be treated as if they are at some level of controlled anger. If you make this assumption and follow the appropriate steps, you should keep the situation under control. This applies to the first two of the following steps. Step three is only for people who are clearly in a controlled anger state.

The steps are to:

- rephrase/paraphrase the person's statement of concern
- always treat the person with respect and her/his concern as important
- clearly state the service's position on the concern, once the nature of the concern is fully understood

or

- present firmly and clearly the possible consequences of action contrary to the position of the service

When you rephrase the person's statement/concern, use your own words; do not "parrot" (repeat word for word) their comments. A key element in restating is not to talk down to, use professional jargon, or use words that are too elaborate. By paraphrasing, the user is given an opportunity to clarify any misunderstanding. It also indicates you are trying to understand the situation. In some cultures, parroting a person's comment is seen as a form of ridicule. Certainly, using phrases that equate the information service as the "authority" and the user as "subordinate" is almost certain to escalate the situation. Use of jargon and/or complex terms and words may also confuse and offend some customers.

By taking this action, a sense of personal respect for the person is conveyed. Another element in displaying respect for the person is to acknowledge the emotion(s) the person feels regarding the situation. This does not mean agreeing with the user regarding what the user wants; rather, it lets the person know there is respect for the individual and the goal is to find a satisfactory solution.

Explain the policy/issue from the perspective of the service and what the limits are on what can be done immediately. Keep the explanations in third-person terms; making it appear as if "I" can in fact do something, or am responsible for the problem, often leads to an even greater confrontation. Presenting the service's position clarifies the situation and establishes the issue(s) that need addressing in order to reach a solution.

An alternative approach, if the situation appears to be escalating, is to outline the possible consequences if the person persists. However, care must be taken not to threaten. Telling a person what may or will happen is very different from delivering an ultimatum. What this does is allow the person to make a decision about her/his behavior or position with full awareness of the possible outcomes. It demonstrates trust in the person's decision-making capability. While this step may make the person angrier than she/he already is, the demonstration of concern and respect for the person's rational decision-making capability more often than not leads to a successful resolution.

When the customer is openly angry, there are some slight differences in how to respond. Begin by acknowledging the person's anger. As with the controlled anger person, the goal is validation and understanding the anger and feelings. At the same time, be certain to identify the problem; rephrasing the concern allows the person to verify that there is or is not agreement concerning the nature of the problem.

Explain how the person's behavior affects you. By focusing on the behavior and its affect, the focus is kept off the person. Saying "this behavior..." rather than saying "you" usually makes the person much less defensive and consequently easier to handle. When doing this, it is better to avoid sweeping generalities about the behavior's impact. Personalizing the effects leaves little room for the angry person to argue, especially if it has already been acknowledged that the anger is a justifiable feeling.

Establishing the person's anger as valid, and then establishing how that anger affects the staff member, allows the conversation to focus on the nature of the problem and what solution(s) exist. Asking specific questions about the problem/issue and letting the individual fully respond usually narrows the scope of the problem and helps identify possible resolutions.

In level three, the disruptive individual is irrationally angry; the first step is to allow the person to vent her/his emotions. Although it is not enjoyable to listen to someone "rant and rave," there is a better chance of resolving the situation by first letting the person release their anger. A person who is irrationally angry will not be very likely to hear anything until she/he has "had their say." Being patient and listening for clues as to what is the issue is difficult but essential in such situations.

After the person finishes expressing the anger (one indication of this is when there are repetitive statements), the steps for expressed anger can be followed. There is little point in a long explanation or in apologizing unless it is clear there was an obvious error. All too often it is necessary in such situations to use direct confrontation. "Your behavior is disruptive to our work (and perhaps to other people here). If you do not stop, then we must . . . " (call the security office/police for example). Try to present the statement in a nonemotional manner. The statement sets clear limits and states what the consequences will be but leaves it to the angry person to decide what to do.

To summarize, when dealing with an upset user:

- Listen first, watching for nonverbal clues as to the emotional state of the person.
- Rephrase the person's concern in order to clarify the issue.
- Maintain a nonemotional state, if possible.
- Acknowledge the emotions and do not try to calm the person just in order to be comfortable. The goal is to find a solution.
- Being defensive usually does not help resolve the situation.
- State clearly the options and consequences in institutional rather than personal terms and, if possible, allow the user to decide which option to take.

We all know dealing with irate users is neither comfortable nor easy. It is something to work at and receive some training for. Having an opportunity to practice conflict-management skills in a workshop environment is very useful for front-line staff. Knowing and using conflict-management skills are two very different things. Staff members who work shifts that have limited or minimal staffing should be the first to receive training and practice in this area; they have fewer backup resources available should matters escalate.

> **Check This Out:**
>
> *Dealing with Difficult People: The Results-Driven Manager Series.* 2004. Boston, MA: Harvard Business School Press.

Pressures we experience on the job are enhanced if we are uncertain about our ability to handle various situations, especially those that are confrontational. Our users face stress and pressure of their own when interacting with our systems and services, and they expect staff to be as well trained in customer service excellence as is common in business today. It is as much our responsibility to deal with user conflicts as it is theirs. Conflict resolution can lead to problem resolution.

Sometimes an irate and dissatisfied user will take matters further and go outside the service and organization to the media. This happens occasionally, so every service needs to have a public relations policy that can be put in place to handle the situation quickly. Public relations activity is discussed in Chapter 5.

> **Check This Out:**
>
> Thenell, Jan. 2004. *Library's Crisis Communications Planner: A PR Guide for Handling Every Emergency.* Chicago: American Library Association. This book provides practical guidance for managing the situation if a complaint explodes beyond the service.

CHANNELS, DIRECTION, AND LEGITIMACY OF COMMUNICATION

Channels of communication run up, down, and across an organization. In cases of upward communication, tact and diplomacy are very important. Also, sensitive topics, such as disagreements with a supervisor's actions, probably should be discussed orally (with considerable supporting detail). Distinguish clearly between fact and opinion, being neither subservient nor truculent.

Communication with senior management and/or the governing board requires careful handling. Giving too many messages may present a picture of insecurity on the part of the manager. Giving too little infrequently means that they will not be fully informed about what is happening—they may start to feel insecure. If an unexpected crisis occurs, and they do sometimes, it is easier for the manager to handle if the senior management knows the manager well and can be comfortable in the knowledge that the situation will be handled skillfully. Seeing a disaster coming down the track and failing to inform senior management is a disaster waiting to happen. So, judge how much information should be passed upwards, how frequently this should be done, and using which channel. Discover how much communication should take place in social settings. There is a good Australian practice for senior managers within an organization to get together with their boss at the end of Friday afternoons for a sundowner. It is an opportunity to gather information from peers, discuss topics of common interest and concern in an informal setting. It oils the wheels of the organization and builds a strong support group amongst peers and their bosses. Problems and issues that might be bubbling up can be handled at an early stage. Two golden rules in upward communication—never be evasive and keep senior management informed.

In downward communication, diplomacy and tact are the keys to success. Avoid carelessness in communications, as it indicates a lack of respect for the person receiving the message. In union contract talks, careless speech has been known to lead to strikes. A manager must give explanations for actions rather than allow the workers' imaginations to fill the gap.

Superiors should always encourage subordinates to ask questions and to contribute ideas. Only in such ways can the manager know whether communication is effective and to what degree. If management encourages such behavior on all levels, the result is likely to be greater appreciation and loyalty throughout the library.

Although the classical function of the manager is to make decisions and to give orders, the reality is that it occupies only a small proportion of the time spent in communicating. In an information service, a vast amount of communicating takes place among peers in order to get tasks done. This type of communication in a collective enterprise involves not only the formal structure but also the informal structures of the service (status structure, friendship structure, prestige structure, etc.). All of these are in constant flux, belying the notion that all communication in an organization is downward and horizontal.

People communicate in order to achieve a goal, to satisfy a personal need, or to improve their immediate situation with respect to their personal desires. People need to communicate with those of higher status than themselves, which means that supervisors need to spend time with their subordinates. The effectiveness of this will depend on the individual relationships between supervisors and subordinates and the degree to which each subordinate's needs are satisfied by upward communication.

Be honest and friendly. This is as essential as allowing a person to speak in the first place. When communicating, do not worry about nervousness,

Everyone is nervous. Remain dignified yet informal, and respect the individual's right to courtesy, dignity, and the facts.

KEY POINTS TO REMEMBER:

- Effective and clear communication is vital in decision making, planning, delegation, and managing innovation and change. It depends on the active cooperation and effort of all parties. Staying passive means that little communication or understanding can ever really take place.
- Improved understanding leads to better working conditions, higher morale, and greater staff commitment. Supervisors have the responsibility to provide these benefits by ensuring that communications are as honest, clear, and open to discussion as possible.
- Ensure that there is not an information overload, particularly in electronic formats, which can present stress to staff members—and supervisors—and impede communication.
- Personality influences communication practices—for example, being outgoing or reserved.
- Develop a sense of humor and learn how to lighten situations when this will aid the communication process.
- Learn how to use the various channels efficiently and effectively, especially as new channels emerge
- Observing the strengths and weaknesses of staff identifies training needs. All staff members, at all levels, need to have excellent communication skills if quality service is to be provided.
- Five key points for clear and effective communication:
    1. Know what to communicate.
    2. Know who needs to know what.
    3. Know who should communicate with whom.
    4. Know how to time messages.
    5. Know how to listen and read.

REFERENCES

Arthur, Diane. 1995. "Importance of Body Language." *HRFocus* 72 (June): 22–23.

Bartlett, Frederic C. 1951. *The Mind at Work and Play.* London: Allen & Unwin.

Berlo, David K. 1960. *The Process of Communication.* New York: Holt.

Conroy, Barbara, and Barbara S. Jones. 1986. *Improving Communication in Libraries.* Phoenix, AZ: Oryx Press.

Graham, Roderick, and M. Valentine. 1973. "Management, Communication and the Destandardized Man." *Personnel Journal* 52 (November): 962–979.

Hammill, Greg. 2005. "Mixing and Managing Four Generations of Employees." *EduMagazine Online* (Winter/Spring). Available: www.fdu.edu/newspubs/magazine/05ws/generations.htm (accessed July 2006).

Handley, Martin. 2005. "The People's Network." *Information, Communication & Society* 8, no. 3 (September): 368–393.

Korzybski, Alfred. 1948. *Science and Society.* Lakeville, CT: International Non-Aristotelian Library.

Maslow, Abraham H. 1937. "Dominance-feeling, Behavior and Status." *Psychological Review* 44 (September): 404–429.

Stevens, Norman. 1983. *Communication Throughout Libraries.* Metuchen, NJ: Scarecrow Press.

Turkle, Sherry. 1995. *Life on the Screen.* New York: Simon & Schuster.

Withers, Rob. 2005. "Something Wiki This Way Comes: An Interactive Way of Posting, Updating and Tracking Changes in Information Used by Library Staff." *College & Research Libraries News* 66, no. 11 (December): 775–777.

LAUNCHING PAD

Andres, Hayward P. 2006. "The Impact of Communication Medium on Virtual Team Group Process." *Information Resources Management Journal* 19, no. 2 (April–June): 1–17.

Beranak, Peggy M. 2006. "Guidelines for Managing Dispersed Work Teams: Enhancing Communication and Productivity." *Handbook of Business Strategy* 7, no. 1: 359–362.

Chalmers, Mardi, Theresa Liedtka, and Carol Bednar. 2006. "A Library Communication Audit for the Twenty-First Century." *Portal: Libraries and the Academy* 6, no. 2 (April): 185–195.

Dromby, Frederick. 1995. "Organizational Communication Imperatives." *Organizational Studies* 16, (5): 908–1002.

Gordon, Rachel Singer, and Michael Stephens. 2006. "How and Why To Try a Blog for Staff Communication." *Computers in Libraries* 26, no. 2 (February): 50–51.

Gundry, Lisa, and Denise M. Rousseau. 1994. "Critical Incidents in Communicating Culture to Newcomers." *Human Relations* 47, no. 9 (September): 1063–1089.

Kuchi, Triveni. 2006. "Constant Change and the Strategic Role of Communication." *Library Management* 27, no. 4: 218–235.

Macaluso, Stephen J., and Barbara Whitney Petruzzelli. 2005. "The Library Liaison Toolkit: Learning to Bridge the Communication Gap." *Reference Librarian,* no. 89/90: 163–177.

Morley, Donald D., Pamela Shockley-Zalabak, and Ruggerio Cesaria. 1997. "Organizational Communication and Culture." *Journal of Business Communication* 34, no. 3 (July): 253–268.

Scammell, Alison. 2006. "Business Writing for Strategic Communications: The Marketing and Communications Mix. *Business Information Review* 23, no. 1 (March): 43–49.

Smith, Ken G., et al. 1994. "Top Management Team Demography and Process: The Role of Social Integration and Communication." *Administrative Science Quarterly* 39 (September): 412–439.

Tannen, Deborah. 2001. *Talking from 9 to 5: Women and Men at Work.* New York: Quill.
Yarwood, Dean L. 1995. "Humor and Administration: A Serious Inquiry into Unofficial Organizational Communication." *Public Journal Administration Review* 55, no. 1 (January): 81–91.
Zhang, Li. 2006. "Communication in Academic Libraries: An East Asian Perspective." *Reference Services Review* 34, no. 1: 164–176.

13

Motivation

"Only positive consequences encourage good future performance."
Kenneth Blanchard

"Your morale infects others whether you like it or not,"
Maurice Line

INTRODUCTION

Information services are in the business of linking users with the information or documents they need; so people are at the core of their operations. Ensuring that the staff is motivated to achieve and sustain a high level of service in terms of quality and productivity so that users are, in turn, motivated to use the service is a challenge for managers and supervisors. Ranganathan put it well when he described "the happy moment that epitomizes library service, when a librarian places a long-sought book in a reader's hand—resulting in a triple glow of satisfaction (the book glowing on its author's behalf)" (Vickery, 1970: 281). And the "triple glow" effect can be seen in any archive, information, or knowledge management service every day that has highly motivated staff and users.

Motivating people is a challenge for managers; their staff and users are individuals, each with her/his own internal state of mind that can produce either desirable or undesirable behavior. Experienced managers quickly discover that even if a prospective staff member's skills and experience are almost a perfect match for the position she/he would hold, there is *no* guarantee that high performance will result. You can never accurately predict a new hire's performance; even after the new hire has performed very well for several years in the position, there is *no* guarantee that this will continue.

In Chapter 1, we noted that the factors that cause people to perform well or poorly are complex and numerous: some relate to the way the work unit functions, while some will be external—for example, the economic climate or personal problems. Your challenge is to create the atmosphere and circumstances in which colleagues will give their best effort day in and day out. Expecting the best of staff, and demonstrating how to achieve this, is one step toward increasing motivation. Taking a negative view is the quickest way to lower motivation.

John Schermerhorn (1984) proposed a formula: ability × support × effort = performance. This indicates that performance is an interdependent outcome between supervisors and employees. In the formula, support is between ability and effort and is dependent on the supervisor and the organization. An employee with all the necessary abilities making the highest effort will not perform well if the supervisor and the organization fail to provide proper support. It is equally true that all the support in the world will not generate high performance if the employee lacks either the skill or willingness to make the effort. The idea of teamwork in the workplace is more than just an abstract concept; it is essential for successful performance.

Larger information services have been highly structured organizations that usually fit Weber's model of a bureaucratic institution, one characteristic of which is its dependence on a hierarchical organizational structure, procedures, and rules designed to maintain operational order. This type of work environment often leaves little room for innovation, flexibility, or independent action. Staff members often feel and think that they are "bottoms" and that management does not care what they think as long as productivity remains high. When this happens, morale drops and the quality of work suffers until management takes action. Users are often the first to notice the problem as they fail to receive the level of service they expect. However, in smaller services and knowledge management groups where there are close relationships among staff members, this problem is less likely to occur, and if identified, rapid action can then be more easily taken.

Over the past 50 years, management researchers have explored the factors that motivate and satisfy people in their work environment. There is still no single answer to the following question: How can employees be most effectively motivated, achieve high productivity and quality of work, without creating human-relations problems? However, there are a number of ideas, concepts, and theories that assist in motivating staff and understanding where sources of satisfaction and dissatisfaction may exist in the workplace.

We explore some of the main theories and concepts in the following pages. Much of the research was carried out in industrial settings where issues of productivity and quality were paramount before becoming an issue in the public sector. Some of the references may appear to be dated, but at the time there was more funding and a greater focus on behavioral research. Management theory is closely related to the social and economic conditions at a time at which it is formulated. Since these conditions are cyclic, they may well return; and being aware of the different theories will help to understand generational differences in the workplace. Some findings continue to influence management practices today. Having examined the theory we will turn to aspects of motivation as they affect the workplace today. A final section will consider motivating users.

MOTIVATION THEORIES

Motivation theories fall into three broad categories: content, process, and reinforcement.

- *Content* theories provide methods for profiling or analyzing staff in terms of "needs."
- *Process* theories provide insights into how people think about, and give meaning to, organizational "rewards."
- *Reinforcement* theories provide guidance about the way that people learn patterns of behavior when that behavior is the result of environmental (workplace) reinforcements.

Try This:

List three examples of the ways in which content, process, and reinforcement motivation theories can be used in an information service setting.

These theories and the research upon which the theories rest are complementary rather than contradictory. The various aspects of each can be drawn upon as circumstances require being aware that it is unlikely that another motivation theory will be contravened.

MOTIVATION AND BEHAVIOR

Motivation has its roots in the personal beliefs, attitudes, and experiences that induce a particular behavior pattern in a person. Motives arise partly from physiologically based needs (hunger, thirst, sleep, etc.) that cause a person to seek to satisfy these needs. In 1943, Abraham Maslow, a founder of content theory, published a paper on the hierarchy of needs (Maslow, 1943).

Human behavior is complex and not easy to predict. Beyond the basic survival behaviors—satisfying thirst, hunger, and the need for shelter—behavior results from learned or conditioned behavior, environmental circumstances, and life experiences. Even the methods for "acceptably" satisfying the basic needs result from social/cultural conditioning.

Culturally based conditioning can result in some values that are diametrically opposed to certain types of work environments (for example, competitive, team, or individual). Consider work teams having members from different cultures and generations: in a diverse society motives can, and will, differ. It follows that managers should not expect that all the staff members will share the same motives for performing their work. Morison, Erickson, and Dytchwald (2006) provide one example in drawing attention to the frustrations of mid-career employees, aged between 35 and 55, who are wrestling with middlescence, trying to balance work, family, and leisure while hoping to find new meaning in their jobs. Not everyone will move into the highest positions in today's flatter organizations, and the energy of this overlooked group needs to be refreshed through mentoring, new assignments, and training.

Point of Reflection:

Reflect on the cultural setting in which you are working or studying and identify four factors that shape the work or study environment.

Activity is the basic component of behavior—talking, eating, running, and reading, for example. You can choose to combine activities (eating while reading, for example) or to change from one activity to another, and people do so all the time. But why do individuals choose to engage in one activity over another? What causes them to change activities? Although the supervisor rarely has total control of employees' behavior, the ability to anticipate changes in behavior may provide a chance to guide them, and this can help to improve work performance.

Behavior is basically goal-oriented, even if the individual does not fully recognize the specific goal. The majority of the drives motivating distinctive individual behavior patterns are subconscious and not easily examined. Sigmund Freud studied subconscious motivation finding that people don't always know what they want, drawing an analogy between human consciousness and an iceberg: the greatest portion lies below the surface. Sometimes, an individual is not introspective. Someone else who observes that person may have a greater awareness of what motivates the individual than does the individual.

Motives and needs are internal; goals are external. Goals (incentives) are the rewards the individual expects to receive as a result of his/her activities. Many managers are successful in providing incentives to motivate their subordinates, but must avoid making an incentive(s) the focus of conflict. Incentives can be tangible (for example, pay increases, better working conditions, or new staff facilities) or intangible (for example, praise, empathy, or recognition of achievement in front of peers). Each employee will respond to combinations of incentives. The intangibles are probably more important—but also harder to identify.

In any particular situation, needs and motives will fluctuate in importance. An individual engages in a particular activity to satisfy some need. If it is impossible to satisfy a nonphysiological need in a given situation, people often suppress the need until they find a way to satisfy it. We can only exercise varying degrees of control over our physiological needs.

Most researchers classify behavior as either goal-directed or goal activity. *Goal-directed* behaviors assist in attaining a certain goal. (When a person is hungry, cooking a meal is a goal-directed activity.) *Goal activity* is engaging in the sought after goal. (In our hungry person example, eating the meal is the goal activity.) The *strength of need* increases during a period of goal-directed behavior and decreases during goal activity.

Two factors affecting the strength of a need are expectancy and availability. *Expectancy* affects motives and needs; *availability* affects the perception of goals and incentives. *Expectancy* arises from a person's experience and perceived probability of satisfying the need; *availability* is the person's assessment of how accessible certain goals and incentives actually are.

People act on their needs according to their perception of the world around them—in a sense, a personal worldview or a mental model. Supervisors should always remain aware that their mental model may differ substantially from that of their peers and subordinates. However, there are some factors that can help to determine what an employee's goals are and the types of activities and behaviors that person is likely to engage in. Some of these are:

- Cultural norms and values.
- Inherited biological capabilities, that is, physical or mental limitations.
- Generational cohort. Any experience in similar situations. (If positive, the person will be likely to repeat the type of behavior that created the reward. If unpleasant, the person may seek a new solution.)
- The individual's mobility, either physical or social. If a person cannot get away from an uncomfortable situation physically, he or she will respond accordingly, perhaps finding new employment in the area. (The availability of other jobs can affect employee behavior.)

These points suggest that similar actions do not necessarily reflect similar desires or wants. For example, an employee may agree to take responsibility for photo duplication services as an added duty. This employee may be motivated by the desire to control more activities; or may have a genuine interest in duplication processes and photography; or believe there is an opportunity to learn new skills or demonstrate existing skills that could lead to advancement in the organization; or a host of other reasons.

A corollary is that different actions may reflect similar desires. In the preceding example, someone interested in advancement might accept the new responsibility, but that same desire for advancement and recognition could lead someone else to turn down such a task in order to devote more attention to current responsibilities. (This would imply a belief that "shining" in one area will lead to advancement just as well as acquiring a "dull gloss" in several areas.)

Consequently, when managers see an employee carrying out a task, they should not assume they understand *why* the employee is engaging in a particular activity. All the actions should be carefully observed and conclusions should follow only after thoughtful analysis. The biggest mistake a supervisor can make is to project his or her needs on subordinates.

CONTENT THEORIES

Maslow's Theory of Motivation

Maslow's article "Theory of Human Motivation" (1943) became a basic source in almost all work in the field of employee motivation. The theory is based on three propositions about human behavior. First, humans are "wanting beings"; they always want, and those wants are unending. When a strong need is satisfied, that need's strength will diminish, but is immediately replaced with another need. The human condition tries to satisfy an endless series of needs. Second, a satisfied need is not a motivator of behavior. Unsatisfied needs are the only motivators. Third, human needs present themselves in a series of levels. When a person meets all the needs on one level, needs at the next highest level will demand attention and satisfaction.

Maslow's five levels of need illustrated in their hierarchical order appear in Figure 13.1:

1. physiological
2. security
3. social
4. esteem
5. self-actualization

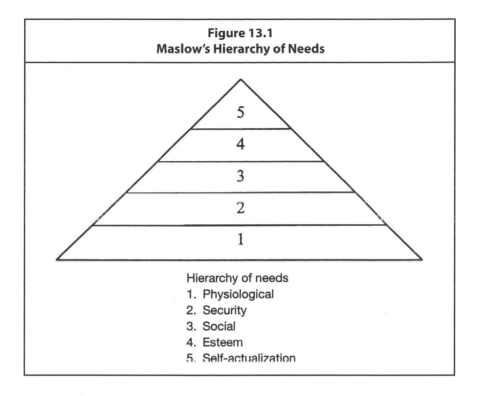

Figure 13.1
Maslow's Hierarchy of Needs

Hierarchy of needs
1. Physiological
2. Security
3. Social
4. Esteem
5. Self-actualization

Physiological needs, the most basic, tend to be relatively independent of one another (for example, hunger, thirst, and sleep). In an affluent society, physiological needs are not usually effective motivators of work behavior because a person can satisfy them in a variety of ways and with little effort. However, because levels of expectation rise in an affluent society, the definition of "satisfactory fulfillment" can vary. And there are always people who for some reason(s) have trouble fulfilling these needs to their satisfaction, no matter how affluent the society in which they live.

The second level relate to *security* or *safety* needs, reflecting a need for protection against danger and deprivation. This extends beyond self-preservation to some fundamental economic needs. Money is required for obtaining reasonable shelter and protection. A concern for safety is often manifest in the workplace in the preference for the familiar over the unfamiliar. Therefore the frequency with which changes are proposed and made also influences staff morale. Many people prefer an orderly, predictable work environment. A stable physical environment can be as important as knowing one's place in an organizational hierarchy. Knowing the limits of acceptable behavior falls into the area of safety needs. When you define unacceptable behavior and the associated penalties, employees know what to expect. Thus, even identifying penalties can represent a form of security. Without defined limits, a few people will test the limits of the manager's willingness to tolerate the behavior until they exceed the limits. Most factors relating to job security, promotions, and salary matters fall under safety needs.

Social needs include acceptance by coworkers, a friendly relationship with at least a few individuals, and the opportunity to associate with them and discuss problems. People are gregarious and want to belong to a group of "friends," so within every organization there is the informal organization that meets this need. However, meeting social needs also takes place outside of work, so you cannot always count on using social needs as a method for achieving or maintaining high-level work performance.

Satisfying *esteem needs* includes gaining both self-esteem, and the esteem of others. Self-confidence, achievement, self-respect, and independence are aspects of esteem needs which affects a person's reputation and need for recognition and appreciation. If work is not challenging, esteem satisfaction will be sought elsewhere. Another person may find the same job challenging and stay with it over several years, despite low pay, if that person receives satisfactory self-esteem. This needs level, as well as the last level, are very dependent upon personal considerations—much more so than with the first three levels. A competitive drive enters into satisfying esteem needs for some people: "I won" or "I was the best employee of the month" are examples of competition and esteem. Again, the desire to compete against others can be both within and without the organization. This desire does not hold for every culture, but it is certainly strong in U.S. society.

It is rare to completely satisfy self-esteem needs, partly because new goals for self-esteem emerge all the time. Esteem needs can be a useful incentive when attempting to motivate work behavior; if you can tie in tangible incentives, work performance often increases dramatically.

The highest level of need is *self-actualization* or self-fulfillment—the need for self-development, creativity, and job satisfaction. It assumes a person has a clear perception of her/his potential and limitations. People rarely satisfy this need mainly because they do not have a clear perception of their abilities. Even those who reach the highest positions seldom believe that they have achieved their potential, but perhaps they are simply unable to see that they achieved their own level of incompetence—remember the Peter Principle (Peter and Hull, 1969).

While the conceptualization of needs as a series of steps in a hierarchy is probably accurate, it is more useful to think of them as a series of waves. That is, as a wave rising to a peak, being satisfied, then tapering off, with yet another need-wave building behind the tapering wave. Figure 13.2 illustrates this approach, which resembles a biorhythm chart. Maslow believed that extended existence at any of the lower levels tends to deaden and eliminate

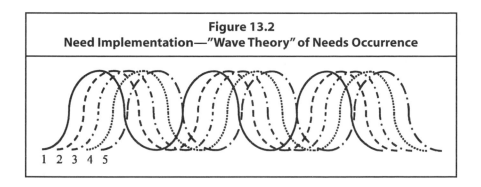

Figure 13.2
Need Implementation—"Wave Theory" of Needs Occurrence

1 2 3 4 5

any higher aspirations. People living at the physiological and security levels have very little need, if any, for self-esteem and self-actualization. They simply do not have the time and energy left after securing food and shelter to worry about higher level needs.

The belief that need stimulus automatically elicits a certain behavior is not completely accurate. Maslow suggested that an individual deprived of two needs normally tends to seek to fulfill the more basic one. However, enculturation factors or experimental experience can influence the choice, causing the person to select the option that fills the higher need. Finally, most human behavior is the result of a complex set of needs in which one need may happen to dominate another one, rather than from a single deep need.

Maslow's theory has been much discussed and, to some extent, accepted without supporting research evidence because it does not allow for research testing. For example, it is difficult to determine, on a conceptual level, where safety needs separate from physiological needs at the lower level, and from esteem needs at the higher level.

Many researchers, in particular Clayton Alderfer, have questioned the value of the theory. Alderfer, on the basis of one experiment in one organization, suggested that a modified form of the Maslow theory would provide a more promising approach to the study of human motivation and its application to the workplace. He retained the concepts of a need hierarchy without the requirement that "it be strictly ordered" (Alderfer, 1969: 154).

Alderfer's research supports what he called the ERG Theory: Existence, Relatedness, and Growth. His *existence needs* are similar to Maslow's physiological and safety needs. *Relatedness* draws on the needs that Maslow labeled "social and esteem needs," while Alderfer's *growth needs* are a combination of esteem and self-actualization. The primary difference between the two theories is that Alderfer does not assume a hierarchy in meeting the needs. There are no higher or lower levels, just needs. The concept of growth needs is especially useful in the workplace.

David McClelland and associates also developed a need theory drawing on Maslow's work to provide managers with better guidance when motivating employees, labeling their theory "acquired needs" (McClelland, 1961). The theory was derived from data collected using the Thematic Apperception Test methodology, which uses pictures with the person taking the test writing a short story about what they see in each picture. The stories were analyzed for themes representing three types of need:

- need for achievement (nAch)
- need for power (nPower)
- need for affiliation (nAff)

The concept behind the theory is that these needs are acquired as a result of life experiences; the amount acquired varies over time according to circumstances. As with other need-based theories, the notion is that needs motivate behavior. McClelland believed that managers can learn to recognize the three need profiles and then modify the work environment to encourage and promote better work performance. Some examples of how this theory can be applied are:

- High need for achievement = work in an area with high individual responsibility, with challenging but achievable goals—e.g., cataloging, appraising documents, and database or system management.
- High need for affiliation = work in an area where there is strong interpersonal interaction and communication—e.g., any of the public/customer service functions.
- High need for power = work in areas that entail directing the activities of others or controlling significant financial or equipment resources—e.g., collection development or Web-based catalogues.

Content theories examine how understanding human needs assists in predicting employee attitudes and behavior. Almost all assume that managers are responsible for determining and allocating work-related rewards, and should allocate the rewards so that all employees have the opportunity to realize some degree of work-related need satisfaction.

Try This:

Take the content theories of Maslow, Alderfer, and McClelland and draw up a table to compare the ways in which they are similar, and dissimilar.
Do you agree with their ideas?

PROCESS THEORIES

Process theories examine the way people think about work and which goals motivate them to perform to their maximum potential. Needs are just one of several factors that come together to generate certain types of work behavior. One aspect of process theories is the idea that people anticipate what is likely to occur given a particular behavior pattern (*expectancy*). One example is that while meeting deadlines is a normal part of the work environment, sometimes a manager must shorten the time frame for accomplishing an activity. Most employees would anticipate that, if they meet the changed deadline, the manager will at least praise them for a job well done, if not provide a more tangible reward. There may also be some expectancy on the part of the manager that comes into play, as we shall see in McGregor's theory (see below).

Another factor in process theories is *valence*. Valence is the strength of an employee's desire or preference for a particular outcome. The stronger the preference, when combined with a positive expectancy, the more likely it is that the individual will exceed established standards.

McGregor's Theory X and Theory Y

Douglas McGregor (1960) formulated the now classic Theory X and Theory Y. To some extent his theory can be placed into either process or reinforcement. However, because the theory addresses managers' expectations, this discussion is placed in the process section.

According to McGregor, the traditional organization (centralized decision making, superior subordinate pyramid, and external control of work) operates on a set of assumptions (expectations) about human nature and motivation. He proposed a continuum of assumptions with the end points, X and Y, representing opposite views of what motivates a worker.

Theory X assumes the following:

1. Work is inherently distasteful to most people and they will avoid it if they can.
2. As they dislike work most people are not ambitious, and have little desire for responsibility, preferring direction from above.
3. Most people have little capacity for creativity and for solving organizational problems.
4. Motivation occurs only at the physiological and security levels.
5. Most people must be closely controlled and often coerced to achieve organizational objectives.

On the other hand, Theory Y assumes:

1. The expenditure of physical and mental effort in work is as natural as play or rest. Depending upon controllable conditions, work can be a source of satisfaction (and will be voluntarily performed) or a source of punishment (and will be avoided, if possible).
2. External control and the threat of punishment are not the only ways to make people work. People exercise self-direction and self-control if they are committed to the objectives of the organization.
3. Commitment to objectives is a function of rewards associated with their achievement. The most significant of such rewards—the satisfaction of ego and self-actualization needs—can be direct products of effort directed toward organizational objectives.
4. The average human being learns, under proper conditions, not only to accept, but to seek responsibility. Avoiding responsibility, lacking ambition, and emphasizing security generally result from experience, not an inherent human characteristic.
5. The capacity to exercise a relatively high degree of creativity in the solution of organizational problems is widely, not narrowly, distributed in a population.
6. Under the conditions of modern industrial life, the intellectual potential of the average human being are only partially utilized (McGregor, 1960: 46–48).

Theory X assumes that employees' personal goals are totally incompatible with organizational objectives and that authority is the instrument of command and control. Theory Y asserts that people have much to offer an organization if they can fully accept its objectives. Managers using Theory Y believe the use of authority impedes the development of acceptance. The difference between the two theories is that Theory X precludes the use of motivational techniques (because of its assumptions regarding human nature), while Theory Y opens the door to their use. Managers who accept Theory X set up closely supervised rigid structures because they clearly feel that this is the appropriate method for handling unreliable, irresponsible, and immature people.

On the basis of his research McGregor questioned whether the Theory X view of human beings was correct. He concluded that it was generally inadequate and that management approaches developed on Theory X assumptions usually fail to motivate people whose basic needs are satisfied and who seek to fulfill their social, esteem, and self-actualization needs.

Managers operating under Theory Y do not usually try to structure the work environment too closely or supervise constantly. Instead, they try to help their staff develop by exposing them to progressively less external control, so allowing them to assume more and more self-control. Staff members receive the satisfaction of affiliation, esteem, and self-actualization in this kind of environment. Both the supervisor and supervised develop more positive attitudes and expectations toward one another. A manager who employs Theory X creates an environment that leads to low employee expectations and one that reinforces such expectations.

Figure 13.3
Example of Theory Y Misused in a Memo

INTERDEPARTMENTAL COMMUNICATION

DATE: 17 January 2007

TO: Division heads; branch librarians

FROM: Library Director

SUBJECT: Vacation

The budget situation for the remainder of the fiscal year is touch-and-go. We want to be sure we have a positive balance as of the end of June.

To this end, we want to reduce all possible expenditures without adversely affecting public service. One way we can save some money is by asking everyone to postpone vacations until July or later if this will not cause a hardship. This will not only save vacation pay, but will eliminate the need for additional part-time hours to cover vacation absences.

We are facing a year-end deficit. We cannot have a year-end deficit. This is one way a year-end deficit can be avoided.

Please explain this to the people in your division. If they have not made long-range plans, and if they can just as well take vacation after July 1, please urge them to do so. Review any vacation requests submitted to you, with postponement in mind.

GEE:ROL:dl

Footnote:

X-Y rating scale

X _____ Y

| 1 | 2 | 3 | 4 | 5 | 6 | 7 | 8 | 9 | 10 |

This is a Theory Y memo. It is based on the assumption that the staff will cooperate.

A work environment that fails to provide a reasonable level of satisfaction will usually have a high turnover rate as well as high absenteeism. However, before deciding that the application of Theory X is the cause of the problem, two factors must also be examined. First, consider the supervisory philosophy and supervisory methods of the manager; they may indicate a lack of understanding about the activities supervised and how the duties can most effectively be performed. Second, consider the supervisor as a person and assess whether that person has the basic skill sets and the desire to function as a supervisor. In other words, Theory X may be a factor, but it may be only part of the total problem. Figure 13.3 is an example of the misuse of a motivation concept.

McGregor believed that work is as natural, and often as satisfying, for people as is play. Since both are mental/physical activities, there appears to be no difference. However, according to Theory X, people make a distinction between the two on the basis of need satisfaction: an individual controls her/his play, while supervisors and management control work. Again, Theory X holds this assumption which actually causes people to think of work as a necessary evil, not as a source of personal challenge and potential source of satisfaction. Persons who feel their work is 'stifling' usually look, and find a reason, for spending more and more time away from work.

Information services, particularly those in the public sector, tend to lean more toward Theory Y, especially in term of the professional staff. Donald Sager's research in libraries documented the recognition that participative management and managers expecting and treating staff as if Theory Y were operative tended to have higher productivity than those that operated on the Theory X premise (Sager, 1979).

In the late 1950s and early 1960s, a number of people built on the work of Maslow, McGregor, and others. These include Chris Argyris, Frederick Herzberg, and Rensis Likert, who have been placed in the process category because their findings relate to how people develop according to the manager's expectations of employees.

Argyris' Immaturity/Maturity Theory

Argyris examined the effect of management practices on individual behavior and personal growth within an industrial work environment. He identified seven changes taking place in the personality of an individual as she or he develops into a mature person:

- An individual moves from a passive state as an infant to a state of increasing activity as an adult.
- An individual develops from a state of dependency to a state of related independence as an adult.
- An individual behaves in only a few ways as an infant but is capable of behaving in many ways as an adult.
- As an infant, the individual has erratic, casual, and shallow interests but develops deeper, stronger interests as an adult.
- The child's time perspective is very short, involving only the present, but with maturity, the time perspective involves both past and future.

- An infant is subordinate to everyone, but moves to an equal or a superior position as an adult.
- The child lacks self-awareness, but an adult is not only aware of the self but is also able to control this awareness (Argyris, 1965; 1973).

Argyris postulates that these changes exist as a continuum and that the healthy personality develops along the continuum from immaturity to maturity (see Table 13.1).

His primary interest focused on the effects of the workplace on an employee's maturation, specifically addressing the question of individual laziness and investigating whether the maturation level had an impact on work performance. He concluded that in terms of the workplace, an individual worker does not fully mature, because of the very management practices that supervisors employ in an effort to bring everyone to peak workplace efficiency. Employees may express their immaturity in a number of ways, including absenteeism, or not wanting to go to work. Often, managers are uncomfortable with a group of people who are able to think and act on their own.

According to Argyris, the formal organization has a built-in need to keep people in an immature state; he argues that the formal organization often reflects its founder's conception of how the institution should achieve its objectives. Managers first design the tasks, often based on scientific management concepts of task specialization, chain of command, unity of direction, and span of control. In these situations, management views employees as interchangeable elements in the organizational machine.

One of Argyris' consulting jobs involved a plant where top management was willing to allow employees to assemble the product in whatever way they thought best. They had to inspect the product, sign it, and handle any complaints. Initially, production dropped 70 percent and morale fell quickly.

Table 13.1 The Argyris Continuum	
Immaturity	**Maturity**
Passive	Increased activity
Dependence	Independence
Limited behavior patterns	Multiple behavior patterns
Erratic shallow interests	Deeper and stronger interests
Short time-perspective	Long time-perspective
Subordinate position	Equal or superordinate position
Lack of awareness of self	Awareness and control over self

Two months after its implementation, production rose. After four months, production was at an all-time high—all without supervisors having to inject their opinions about how to resolve production issues. Most impressive was a 94 percent decrease in waste and production errors, and a 96 percent drop in complaints. Clearly, employee control over how they performed their work improved product quality. The experiment was repeated in several other firms with consistent results. Several large corporations implemented variations of his method. The primary problem is that some managers cannot understand that large numbers of employees experience an increase in motivation when they receive proper incentives and responsibility.

Remember that Argyris' research took place in the 1950s and 1960s. Today there is more acceptance among top management that workers are dynamic and mature individuals capable of taking on responsibility.

The Herzberg Studies

Dr. Frederick Herzberg and his colleagues conducted a number of experiments in the late 1950s and early 1960s, concluding that the job itself was the most important motivator in the work environment. (Herzberg, 1959). They interviewed engineers and accountants concerning the good or bad points about their jobs. Their data showed that positive thoughts were highest when supervisors indicated to the employees they were doing a good job, or were considered to be an expert in their job or field. Fringe benefits did not produce positive feelings, as benefits generally produced negative thoughts when employees viewed them as inadequate. The same was true of salary. Negative thoughts and feelings resulted from the physiological and security aspects of the job; positive thoughts resulted from self-actualization, self-esteem, and social needs.

Job attitudes directly affect the quality of work. When people have a positive attitude toward their jobs, they use more creativity, are more careful, and try harder to achieve excellence. When they are unhappy, they are most likely to perform at the minimum acceptable level.

Donald Sager (1979) found that the opportunity to exercise creativity and initiative does not mean that every employee must have a say in all aspects of a library's operation. Nor does it mean that all employees will make use of the opportunities offered to them. What is critical is the understanding that using initiative and creativity is acceptable to management. The level of initiative might be as simple as being able to determine the sequence of daily activities. In essence, the understanding reduces frustration and demotivating factors.

Later work by Verrill and Wilkins (1986) noted that employees have difficulty remaining motivated when their supervisor does not exhibit highly motivated behavior. Certainly a supervisor's motivation may not instill similar motivation in subordinates, but the absence of motivation on a supervisor's part has a *very* negative influence on subordinates.

Herzberg proposed two sets of stimuli that produce job satisfaction or dissatisfaction: motivators and hygienic factors. *Motivators* produced improvement in performance and attitudes. *Hygienic factors* merely maintained morale and efficiency. For the interviewees, motivators were chances to become more expert and to handle more demanding assignments.

These conclusions are compatible with Maslow's hierarchy, in that the hygienic (environmental) factors and the motivators (the job itself) concern the various levels in the hierarchy. Esteem needs are more complex. Recognition is an earned personal quality, whereas status usually is a function of the job itself. Consequently, status is a self-esteem need, whereas recognition is a motivator.

Prior to Herzberg's work, managers placed an emphasis on the concept of job enlargement, that is, increasing the number of tasks an individual performs. Herzberg suggested that doing a little of this and a little of that was no way to motivate people since variety of this sort does not alleviate boredom. He proposed job *enrichment:* a deliberate upgrading of the scope, challenge, and responsibility of a person's work. Applying this concept in information services could prove useful as Herzberg identified (his critics notwithstanding) the key workplace motivator: *the job itself.* This may well explain why the emphasis on fringe benefits over the past 30 years, as well as "new" supervisory techniques, has done little to really motivate all employees, particularly support staff. Herzberg revisited his findings arguing the case for job enrichment:

> If you have employees on a job, use them. If you can't use them on the job, get rid of them, either via automation or by selecting someone with lesser ability. If you can't use them and you can't get rid of them, you will have a motivation problem(Herzberg, 2003: 96).

For Herzberg, the work motivation environment consists of two key elements: job content and job context. In Herzberg's studies, motivators/satisfiers are a function of *job content,* while hygiene/dissatisfiers relate to *job context.* One criticism of Herzberg's work is that the methodology, asking employees what they did or did not like, motivated them to misrepresent their true thoughts. Later work by numerous researchers, using different data-collecting techniques, demonstrated there were flaws in the concept (House and Wigdor, 1967). Then there is a third factor to consider, the job/work situation.

Most researchers divide the work situation into two categories: the immediate work environment and the organizational style or culture and climate as a whole. Factors such as the actions and attitudes of peers and supervisors, the atmosphere within the work unit, and interpersonal relationships have a significant impact on the *immediate work environment*. Many of the immediate factors are similar to factors identified with Maslow's self-esteem. *Organization-wide style* exists just as much as a style exists in the work unit. The organization-wide style sets the tone for how middle managers and supervisors handle their units, and although middle managers and supervisors may have a personal preferred style, they must also operate within the overall organizational tone.

Managers must remember that:

- Improvements in hygiene factors can prevent and/or help eliminate job dissatisfaction; they will not improve job satisfaction.
- Improvements in satisfier factors can increase job satisfaction; they will *not* prevent job dissatisfaction.

While management writers continue to debate the overall value of Herzberg's "two-factor" theory of motivation, none deny that it has practical value. One of the questions about the two-factor approach is, does a "satisfied" employee translate into a high performer?

In part, the answer to the question depends upon three alternative assumptions. These assumptions are:

- Satisfaction causes performance (S > P).
- Performance causes satisfaction (P > S).
- Rewards cause both performance and satisfaction (R > P, and R > S).

Each assumption has implications for managers. "Satisfaction causes performance" means that the focus should be on improving job satisfaction, but research does not indicate whether satisfaction is a good predictor of individual work performance. In the case of the second assumption, the manager should emphasize performance. The only way this can work is to have adequate rewards for high performance. Often the middle and lower-level managers have little power to change or increase rewards. The last assumption has two managerial implications. If the manager's concern is just about satisfaction, she/he should provide high rewards. If the concern is with both performance and satisfaction, the manager should provide high rewards for high performance and lower rewards for low performers. Most U.S. managers in both profit and nonprofit organizations operate on the basis of the last assumption. Table 13.2 reflects the consequences of high and low satisfaction drawing on materials in A. E. Locke's "Job Satisfaction and Job Performance" (1970).

The other point to remember is that those interviewed in the first study were semiprofessionals. Later experiments by Robert Ford with blue-collar workers and lower-level, white-collar workers at American Telephone and

Table 13.2		
Consequences of High and Low Satisfaction		
Job Facets	**High Satisfaction**	**Low Satisfaction**
Work itself	Come early; stay late; stay on the job	Seek transfer; be absent or late; quit
Supervision	Approach supervisors; accept advice; stay on the job	Avoid; complain and argue with; reject advice; quit
Co-workers	Approach; conform to peer values; socialize; stay on the job	Avoid; argue with; complain about; be absent; quit
Promotion	Increase effort; raise aspirations; suggest new ideas; stay on the job	Decrease effort; lower aspirations; less willing to contribute; quit
Pay	Increase effort; stay on the job	Complain; solicit competing offer; decrease effort; quit

Telegraph Company bore out Herzberg's findings in these situations as well (Ford, 1979). The work of Plate and Stone (1974) was an early effort to apply the Herzberg ideas in a library setting.

Likert's Management Systems

Rensis Likert (1958) indicated that managers fell into one of two categories of supervisor: production centered or employee centered. *Production-centered* supervisors advocate strict control of the work environment and view employees as instruments for getting the job done. They actively monitor the work at all stages, giving directions and correcting mistakes and are very hard drivers with the highest possible production as their primary goal. *Employee-centered* supervisors consider supervision rather than production to be their primary task providing information about production goals and general guidelines for doing the work. They then allow the employees to determine individual work patterns, as long as those patterns fit into the overall process, and to ask for assistance as necessary. Likert concluded that high-production groups had employee-centered supervisors, while low-production groups had production-centered supervisors. He then described a number of management styles in organizations that fall along a continuum, as shown in Table 13.3.

System 1 prevails when management has no confidence in subordinates and so does not involve them in decision making at any level. Fear, threats of punishment, and very occasional rewards characterize the motivation system supervisors employ. Top management retains most of the control,

Table 13.3
Likert Scale Leadership Process Used

Organizational Variable	System 1	System 2	System 3	System 4
Supervisors' confidence in subordinates	No confidence in subordinates	Condescending confidence such as master/servant	Substantial, but not complete confidence, controls decisions	Complete confidence
Motivational forces	Fear and threats	Some rewards but frequent punishment, little staff involvement in decisions	Rewards frequent, staff involvement in decisions	Many rewards, heavy staff involvement in decisions
Interaction with staff and its character	Little, and always with fear and distrust	Little, with condescension	Moderate	Extensive, and with full trust

and an informal organization usually develops that opposes the formal organization's goals.

System 2 is a moderately good "master-servant" relationship. Although there is more trust involved than in System 1, condescension usually characterizes top management. Major decisions and goal setting occur at the top, but middle and lower-level managers make many decisions. Punishment and reward make up the motivation system. Employees tend to be fearful of punishment and are seldom open with their supervisors. The informal organization resists the formal organizational goals but does not oppose them outright.

System 3 managers have substantial but not complete confidence in subordinates. Broad policy and general decisions take place at the top, but many decisions occur at all levels, because top management delegates responsibility. Communication flows up and down, and rewards are common. Superiors and subordinates interact, often with a strong degree of confidence. The informal organization may either support or partially resist the formal organization's goals.

System 4 exists when management has complete confidence in subordinates. Decision making exists throughout, and top management works to ensure integrated decision making occurs. Communication flows upward, downward, and laterally. Motivation takes place in part through participation in developing economic rewards, setting goals, improving methods, and appraising progress toward goals. Superiors and subordinates interact in a friendly, confident manner. The informal and formal organizations are the same, because the social forces support the organization's goals.

Information services tend to be either System 2 or System 3, although a very few are System 1 and some employ System 4. Size of service is a factor, and a collaborative working environment, such as knowledge management, will employ System 4. Larger services are moving toward System 4, as are individual supervisors in services that have no such formal policy. However, as discussion of participative management will indicate, this system also has challenges.

Later studies, particularly by Vroom and Mann (1960), contradicted Likert's conclusion that employee-centered supervisors are responsible for high production. One study found a higher production figure for a production-centered supervisor's group than for a group with an employee-centered supervisor. Another study concluded that the nature of the job determined the type of supervision that would work best. For instance, in situations that demand a high degree of worker confidence (when employees know the supervisor's goals for them), a firm, no-nonsense attitude on the part of the supervisor is most effective.

Try This:

Repeat the earlier exercise for the process theories of McGregor, Argyris, Herzberg, and Likert. Do you agree with their ideas?

REINFORCEMENT THEORIES

Perhaps the individual most associated with reinforcement theories as applied to human behavior is B. F. Skinner. These theories look at what the outcomes are of past actions when it comes to human behavior, rather than at motives or needs. The basic notion is that people learn from experiences and tend to want to repeat experiences that were good and avoid those that were bad. In the workplace, managerial behavior and actions serve as the stimulus for conditioning employee behavior and activities.

One of Skinner's terms is *operant conditioning*, which refers to the process of controlling or modifying behavior by manipulating the consequences of that behavior. In an organizational setting, the concept is better known as *organizational behavior modification*. There are four strategies associated with operant conditioning:

- Positive reinforcement results in increased frequency or strengthens behavior by providing a desirable (from the employee's point of view) consequence whenever the behavior occurs.

- Negative reinforcement results in increased frequency or strengthens behavior by providing an undesirable (from the employee's point of view) consequence whenever unwanted behavior occurs.
- Punishment results in decreased frequency or eliminates undesirable behavior by providing unpleasant consequences whenever such behavior occurs.
- Extinction results in decreased frequency or eliminates undesirable behavior by removing a desirable consequence whenever such behavior occurs.

Positive reinforcement calls for immediate reward when the desired behavior takes place. To use positive reinforcement successfully, the following essential steps are necessary. You must be certain:

- to identify desired behaviors for employees
- to maintain a variety of incentives/rewards
- to recognize employee differences in what is an incentive/reward
- that employees know what they must do to receive a reward/incentive
- to provide the reward/incentive immediately after the desired behavior is manifest

Negative reinforcement is most effective when used selectively—selectively in the sense that it is not the primary method of reinforcement. When using negative reinforcement, be certain:

- to tell the person what is wrong with what they did or are doing
- to tell the person how to correct what is wrong
- to implement the negative reinforcement in private
- to implement the negative reinforcement immediately after the the undesirable behavior occurs
- that the negative reinforcement is appropriate to the behavior

Managing by Results

Managing by results is a reinforcement method of employee motivation. When an employee behaves compatibly with organizational goals, that behavior usually results in the person receiving some form of reward (reinforcement). When the behavior is anti-organizational, the supervisor chooses from among three alternatives:

- Use negative reinforcement (punishment) to achieve goals (although other alternatives avoid some negative aspects of punishment).

- Reevaluate both the stimulus and the person, as a different approach might well be effective.
- Fire the person, which is a last resort and an indication of failure on both sides.

The supervisor establishes job content and performance standards for the subordinate, but the individual can vary the pattern as long as she/he achieves the required result. (The difference from Managing by Objectives [MBO] is that the supervisor sets goals and standards alone, rather than with the employee.) It requires initiative on the part of the employee, but that can only result as part of a gradual process; expecting overnight maturity is unrealistic as well as unfair.

This approach also demands that the employees know that performance evaluation will be in terms of production and know the method of evaluation. The ground rules for making any value judgment must be clear prior to when the supervisor makes a judgment.

Careful definition of the boundaries of acceptable employee behavior is always essential, and it is vital in this approach. The levels at which decisions may, and may not, be made must be clear. Yet freedom to act within those boundaries must also be present because the result is what matters, not the performance of activities leading to the result. The great temptation is to judge the activities, but this can do more harm than good in the working environment.

Both the supervisor and employee must realize that this system requires a great deal of interdependence. Moving in this direction is a risk for the supervisor, because ultimate responsibility remains with her/him. The supervisor must trust subordinates, and the workers must realize that both they and the supervisor are vulnerable. The organizational goal must be kept foremost in the minds of all concerned as they cooperate to achieve it.

Now Try This:

Repeat the earlier exercise and compare Skinner's approach with managing by results. Do you agree with these approaches?

THE MANAGERIAL GRID

In 1964, Robert Blake and Jan Mouton proposed a method of plotting different theories of management leadership styles graphically (see Figure 13.4). This involves a grid with two variables—concern for people and

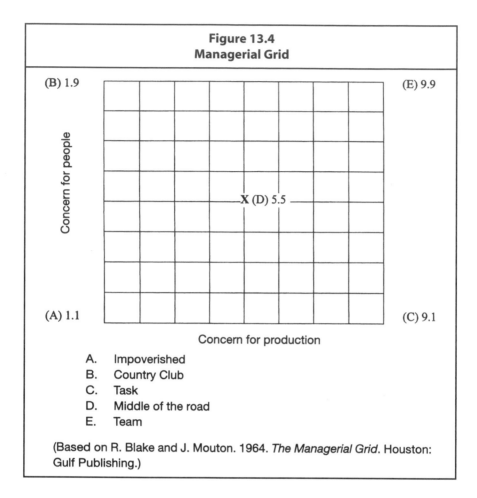

Figure 13.4
Managerial Grid

(B) 1.9

(E) 9.9

Concern for people

X (D) 5.5

(A) 1.1

(C) 9.1

Concern for production

A. Impoverished
B. Country Club
C. Task
D. Middle of the road
E. Team

(Based on R. Blake and J. Mouton. 1964. *The Managerial Grid*. Houston: Gulf Publishing.)

concern for production—and it is useful for summarizing all the preceding approaches.

Within the grid, the researchers placed five managerial styles. Concern for production is on the horizontal axis (scale 1–9) and concern for people on the vertical axis (scale 1–9). As either factor increases, its number becomes higher.

1. *Impoverished*: Managers use the least possible amount of energy to accomplish required work, and what effort they do exert is only enough to sustain organizational membership.
2. *Country club*: Managers give thoughtful attention to people's needs for interpersonal relationships, but the atmosphere is so friendly that production is poor.

3. *Task*: Operational efficiency results from arranging work so that human elements produce the least amount of interference.
4. *Middle of the road*: Managers achieve adequate performance by balancing the necessity for production with the maintenance of morale.
5. *Team*: Motivated persons producing for a common goal maintain both high production and high morale.

Style 1.1 on the grid (lower left) represents a laissez-faire style of supervision—minimal concern for both production and people (few rewards and no reinforcement). Style 1.9 (top left) represents maximum concern for people and minimum concern for production—the human-relations school (maximum positive and no negative reinforcement). The 9.1 style (lower right) shows maximum concern for production and minimal concern for people—authoritarian supervision (maximum negative and minimal positive reinforcement). And the 9.9 style (top right) demonstrates maximum concern for both production and people; a balance of positive and negative reinforcement. According to Blake and Mouton, the ideal leadership style is 9.9.

The 5.5 style (middle of the grid) is that of the middle-of-the-road supervisor who would rather suppress or compromise than bring conflict into the open and resolve it (primarily positive and limited negative reinforcement). The ideal style 9.9, on the other hand, develops committed employees who share common goals. Managers address conflicts squarely and resolve them in an atmosphere of openness and trust.

Naturally, every one of these styles has its drawbacks, including style 9.9—it is difficult to develop committed people, and a willingness to bring conflict into the open does not always have positive results. Even if a group becomes used to this type of approach, it is never certain how open conflict and competition resolution will be resolved.

PARTICIPATIVE MANAGEMENT

Participative management was a catchphrase among information professionals for many years (*Participative Management*, 1977). In fact, reading and listening to discussions might convince someone that this was the solution for all management problems, but participative management has not always produced the solution to management problems; in fact, it may have created some new ones.

The participative management concept is a style 4 on the Likert Scale, with ideas drawn from various researchers in the field of motivation. Figure 13.5 depicts the way in which all the motivation concepts in this chapter relate to one another and where participative management fits in the picture.

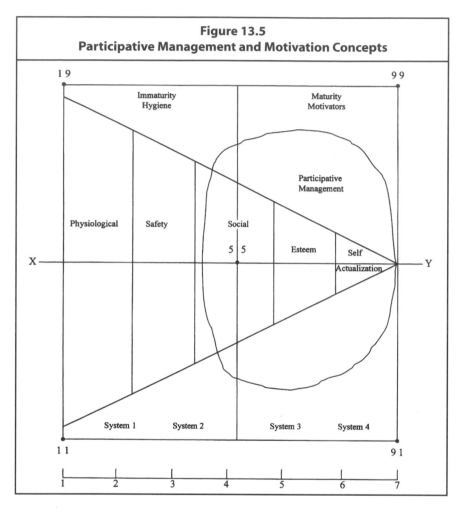

Figure 13.5
Participative Management and Motivation Concepts

As the term participative management implies, the entire staff should participate in the management of the organization. Also implied, but seldom practiced, is full participation by users. Ultimately, this whole process relies on group decision making, and in order to achieve this, there must be group discussions. In 1976, Maurice Marchant, author of *Participative Management in Academic Libraries*, wrote:

> Participative management requires group discussion, and each group should be small enough that all may take part. The group is concerned with issues of mutual concern. Thus, the director would not discuss cataloging changes without involving public services personnel. Nor would he allow the discussion to center on personalities but would hold it to resolution of the mutual problem (Marchant, 1976: 39).

One important factor stands out in this statement: people need to meet together in small groups; this quickly translates into costs of staff time. An alternative is to use e-mail, but when committee meetings are called, they can take up large quantities of time, especially if there is a need to reach a majority opinion or a consensus on an important issue. When there is a public-service requirement, time is a precious commodity, and hours spent in committee meetings do not serve the public well. One research library in the United States estimated that committee decisions on major issues cost approximately $5,000 per decision in staff salaries alone. Over time, extensive use of committees can also generate hostility.

One major difficulty is accountability. A committee simply is not accountable. How to handle accountability in a participative management environment is a problem that has rarely been addressed. Yet, decisions require accountability in precisely those areas in which the staff wants the most input. Given the authority relationships for agencies that receive government and public sector funding, accountability must be present. So, how can both accountability and staff input be achieved at the levels desired?

If a manager first determines staff views and then reserves the actual decision making for her/himself or a small group of staff members, this is not participative management. A better label for this approach is consultative management. Misuse of the label "participative management" by top management, when they really mean "consultative management," has probably caused more anger and frustration than people realize.

Managers may assume at first that they are involved in a textbook case (a service that is well run, has good staff relations, and excellent customer relations), making the implementation of participative management easy. However, the need for accountability quickly becomes clear, especially if the governing board of the service believes there have been a number of bad decisions. When this occurs, management begins to view committee deliberations as advisory rather than as binding decisions and staff begins to think they have been used. Distrust of management and poor motivation are the outcome.

All this presents a bleak picture of participative management. Currently, although you may philosophically support the concept, the ways in which you implement it requires careful thought and preparation. It should be made clear whether participation is advisory rather than executive (i.e., the consultative approach). Perhaps there could be greater use of delegation. If the structure is flattened, then individuals may have more accountability.

The original concept of participative management emerged in a decade of prosperity and a culture that supported it; however, a downturn in the economy or a change in political philosophy can make it necessary for a manager to make quick decisions that may be unpopular. Until managers can resolve such issues as serving users efficiently and effectively while attending the necessary meetings and also maintaining accountability, this approach should be handled with caution.

Rather than using participative management, managers should ask for advice and input from staff on decisions regarding them and the service's consultative management. Managers should make it clear that they will take staff views into account but that the decision will be made by the appropriate manager—the one with responsibility, authority, and accountability for the area affected. Using this approach, you can gain many of the benefits and avoid some of the problems.

Another Exercise:

Consider participative management and set down a table of pros and cons for its use, adding to the thoughts given in the text. Sum up the benefits for the manager and for the staff.

Recently Manville and Ober outlined an approach that recognizes that motivating in a knowledge economy rather than an industrial age is different. They suggest that people should be motivated by building organizations on an Athenian model, "underpinning all the achievements was a system of governance based on personal freedom, collective action, and an open democratic culture" (Manville and Ober, 2003: 50). "People with expertise came forward whenever their skills were needed, without becoming part of any standing bureaucracy" (2003: 51). This approach can be observed in small entrepreneurial organizations and in knowledge management.

PARTICIPATIVE MANAGEMENT IN PRACTICE

Increasing Motivation

There is sound theory on which to base good practice, but the motivators in terms of rewards differ between business and the non-for-profit and public sectors. People working for services operating in the private sectors may receive merit raises, stock allocation or bonuses when the firms are doing well. Some small entrepreneurial companies organize "fun-days," provide chill-out areas, or have a funky workplace that reflects the culture of the organization. In the public sector this flexibility, in terms of rewards and other motivators, is generally not possible. The motivators have to lie in the way staff members work together and the interaction they have with users to enhance what was termed job satisfaction, then became job commitment, and is now often referred to as job engagement.

Some basic guidelines to increase motivation are:

- Make sure everyone—from the most senior professional to the junior support staff—knows what is expected of them; check that they understand.
- Give staff discretion in dealing with users after training—it demonstrates confidence in them. Monitor progress.
- Give people the tools they need to do the job well—from the cleaners upward. Expect equipment and technology to consume an increasing proportion of the budget, since being well equipped for the job gives pride to individuals and makes their tasks easier.
- Provide opportunities for learning and extending skills, and let people shine.
- Remember praise is a good motivator, but be specific and notice how individuals are performing well.
- Listen to the staff—they need to believe that their ideas count and that you hear them.
- Make sure that staff members believe in the mission of the organization and the service. They need to take pride in their work and know it is important to the functioning of the organization.
- Encourage people to mix at work; colleagues can provide social support, especially if the going gets tough.

Problem Behavior

Changes in behavior patterns can happen for a number of reasons. People's behavior changes if they are stressed: personal problems are sometimes hard to leave at home; a person may be ill; or the service may be going through a period of change. This is likely to be first noticed by immediate work colleagues and then supervisors, but it is a managerial responsibility to enquire into unusual behavior patterns. Among the signs are: volatility, defensiveness, withdrawing, impulsiveness, approval dependence, and eccentricity. Not taking action affects not only the individual, but also their colleagues.

GENERATIONAL DIFFERENCES

With increasing numbers of volunteers and no age set for retirement, age variations among staff members can be wide, representing specific motivators of different generations.

Veterans (1929–1949) motivators:

- formality rather than informality
- communication face-to-face and phone, not e-mail or voicemail
- an explanation of the logic of actions
- traditional recognition—e.g., plaques, photos etc.

Baby Boomers (1950–1964) motivators:

- need to see clear steps toward defined goals
- want stated objectives and desired results in people-centered teams
- love pep talks
- prefer recognition with wide public profile—e.g., organization's newsletter

Gen X (1965–1979) motivators:

- tell them what needs to be done, but not how
- give multiple tasks, but allow them to set priorities
- avoid platitudes and buzzwords
- ask for their reactions and opinions
- allow time for fun
- no pep talks
- regular honest feedback and mentoring/coaching

Gen Y (1980–to date) motivators:

- provide opportunities for continuous learning and building skills
- need to know their goals and explain how they fit into the "big picture"
- emphasize the positive
- be more of a coach, less of a boss
- communicate informally through e-mail and hallway conversations (Stauffer, 2003)

MOTIVATING TEAMS

Although much of the research into motivation has been carried out in large industrial organizations, following on from the era of scientific management, some of the basic concepts of motivating teams are still relevant today, since many of the largest services still operate within a traditional hierarchical management structure.

But as organizations adopted a flatter hierarchy, technology was applied to routine administration and certain professional tasks, thus reducing staff size. Team working was introduced at a time when there was a change in the way that organizations view their staff.

Whether they are traditional employees or temps and contract workers, today's knowledge workers are not just labor—they are capital. And what differentiates outstanding companies is the productivity of their capital. . . . In a traditional workforce, the worker serves the system; in the knowledge sector, the system must serve the worker" (Drucker, 2002: 76–77).

That statement applies as much to the nonprofit sector as it does to the private sector. Most information services are part of a larger organization that has a governing board with membership drawn from the business sector. Business believes that retaining skilled staff is a sign of good management, since staff turnover adds to overheads such as training costs. There are other good reasons for the increase in teamwork: involving people who would be affected by decisions more readily achieves acceptance and implementation; as tasks becomes more complex expertise can be brought into the group; and when creating ideas or needing to retain information and experience, a group shares and retains that knowledge. So an emphasis is now placed on valuing a smaller staff working in teams, where self-motivation is important.

O'Connor (2006) reviewed the factors affecting individual performance in team environments and their implications for library management. He identified two categories of performance factors—extrinsic and intrinsic—which combine motivating factors, theoretical models, and practical evidence that attempt to measure an individual's input performance. The extrinsic factors are: *collective efficacy* or group buy-in; *social rewards and sanctions* or group acceptance or nonacceptance by the team of an individual member; *social dilemmas* or disagreements within a team; *social loafing* or freeloading, where a person is removed from individual accountability; *future interdependence* or the potential for future collaboration; and *social identity* or the need shared with other members of the in-group; but not with an out-group. The individual factors affecting performance in teams are: *individual identity, desire to achieve, member role differences, team size, status attainment,* and *member commitment.* The factors are not mutually exclusive but they help to understand how best to organize teams. O'Connor (2006) also identified three trends that demonstrated effective or ineffective management of teams. Outstanding was team composition and the importance of planning before implementing a team structure, followed by respect and communication within teams, and finally, the need for clearly defined and articulated goals.

Motivating teams to give optimum performance requires that they share enthusiasm, commitment, and values with their manager and have her/his trust. The manager should make a regular assessment of their output and way of working. In this working environment, the team can be empowered to take decisions to a prescribed level, having received initial training and continuing coaching to meet the goals set by the manager.

Virtual teams are increasingly part of the workplace, particularly in services that operate over extended hours, have staff working across the organization, work off-site or off-shore, and have flexible hours. They communicate by telephone or video conference, use Webcams or simple e-group or e-mails. Their challenges may be greater than a team working regular hours in one location, particularly if they do not have the opportunity to meet socially at regular intervals. To work effectively, the virtual team needs well-developed communication skills especially if they are working across cultures.

MOTIVATING USERS

Getting the message out to users and the wider community is the focus of Chapter 5, on marketing. However, in discussing motivation its easy to overlook the people who use or who could benefit from using information services. Outreach services heavily promoted by public libraries in the 1960s and 1970s were ways to motivate people to visit libraries in person. But that was in the pre-Internet era, before competition from the computer brought easy online access and before computer-based games became part of a child's life. School librarians know the challenges of getting students to read, lecturers are aware that students use Wikipedia rather than *Encyclopaedia Britannica*, and archivists know how much genealogical information is available through the Web. So there is a need to both market to and motivate users and others who could derive benefit by using the services offered.

Weller (2005) investigated information-seeking behavior, motivation and critical thinking in Gen Y students and found that only a very small percentage of the general population prefers to learn by reading. The community at large can find large archives and libraries intimidating if they have not been a frequent user and are not familiar with using computers to find and access information. They may be of a generation that has a fear of authority or a culture where a questioning of authority does not come easily. They may not understand the advice and information being offered, or may not want to appear to be ignorant, and perhaps not know what they want. Many users and potential users need reassurance in order to be motivated to use services. It has been interesting to watch the growth of interest in family history, particularly as it relates to the war service of parents and grandparents, among visitors to archives. Staff member can motivate less experienced and shy users by encouraging people to talk about their query, provide leaflets giving clear guidance, and mingle among them to ensure that they are finding what they want. Finding a box of microfilm, using a microfilm reader, and printing pages are all barriers for less experienced users who have a strong need for the information they are seeking. The theories of motivation outlined at the start of this chapter apply equally to users.

Keep in Mind:

The quality of the service provided to its clientele is dependent to a large degree upon the staff's willingness to perform appropriate tasks effectively and understand the needs of users.

Part of that willingness is a function of their personal motivation and management's ability to build and develop that motivation.

KEY POINTS TO REMEMBER:

- There are three types of motivation theories: content, process, and reinforcement.
- These theories should considered in relation to both staff and the user community.
- Motivation is inseparable from an individual's goals, values, psychic needs, and life experiences. What motivates one person may completely fail to strike a responsive chord in another.
- Most people modify their personal goals as they go through life. Some will set continually higher goals and challenges for themselves, whereas others restrict their ambitions and goals. A person who has lost motivation and self-confidence through a series of misfortunes may regain them if the opportunity to try again meets with success. Such a person would be fortunate to work for a supervisor who is sensitive and alert to the potential beneath the protective coat of caution and pessimism.
- Salary can be a powerful motivator. Supervisors should treat employees equitably and provide recognition and rewards for superior achievement.
- Keeping communication channels open can often resolve an issue before it becomes a problem.
- Flexibility is the key word in a good motivation system. No two people are alike, and human behavior is too complex for anyone to achieve long-term success as a manager if that person depends on rules, formulas, or a single system for handling every person and problem. In essence, good supervision requires situational thinking; that is, each case should be approached as though it were unique. In fact, most cases are unique to some degree.
- If managers treat staff members as they wish to be treated, there will be very few motivation or morale problems in the unit. We suggest that this formula is vital for a manager to remember and use.
- There are generation-specific motivators.
- A number of factors affect the performance of individuals working in a team environment.
- Motivating users encourages use of the service provided for them.

A highly motivated staff provides quality service, makes positive contributions to planning and decision making, and accepts change and delegation more readily. The ability to motivate colleagues is an attribute required in leadership which is discussed in the next chapter.

REFERENCES

Alderfer, Clayton P. 1969. "An Empirical Test of A New Theory of Human Needs." *Organizational Behavior and Human Performance* 4: 142–175.

Alemna, Anaba A. 1992. "Motivation and Productivity in Academic Libraries." *Journal of Library Administration* 16, no. 4: 45–56.

Argyris, Chris. 1965. *Integrating the Individual and the Organization.* New York: Wiley.

Argyris, Chris. 1973. "Personality and Organization Theory Revisited." *Administrative Science Quarterly* 18, no. 2: 747–767.

Bass, B., and G. Barret. 1987. "Motivation in a Third World Library." *International Library Review* 19, (July): 257.

Ford, Robert N. 1979. *Why Jobs Die and What to Do About It.* New York: AMACOM.

Drucker, Peter. 2002. "They're Not Employees, They're People." *Harvard Business Review* 80, no. 2 (February): 70–77.

Herzberg, Frederick. 1959. *Motivation to Work.* 2nd ed. New York: Wiley.

Herzberg, Frederick. 2003. "One More Time: How Do You Motivate Employees?" *Harvard Business Review* 81, no. 1 (January): 87–96.

House, Robert J., and Lawrence Wigdor. 1967. "Herzberg's Dual-Factor Theory of Job Satisfaction and Motivation." *Personnel Psychology* 20, no. 4 (Winter): 369–389.

Likert, Rensis. 1958. "Measuring Organizational Performance." *Harvard Business Review* 36: 41–50.

Likert, Rensis. 1967. *The Human Organization.* New York: McGraw-Hill.

Locke, Edwin A. 1970. "Job Satisfaction and Job Performance: A Theoretical Analysis." *Organizational Behavior and Human Performance* 5: 496.

Manville, Brook, and Josiah Ober. 2003. "Beyond Empowerment: Building a Company of Citizens." *Harvard Business Review* 81, no. 1 (January): 48–53

Marchant, Maurice P. 1976. *Participative Management in Academic Libraries.* Westport, CT: Greenwood.

Maslow, Abraham H. 1954. *Motivation and Personality.* New York: Harper.

Maslow, Abraham H. 1943. "A Preface to Motivational Theory." *Psychosomatic Medicine* 23: 85–99.

McClelland, David. 1961. *Achieving Society.* New York: Van Nostrand.

McGregor, Douglas. 1960. *The Human Side of Enterprise.* New York: McGraw-Hill.

Morison, Robert, Tamara Erickson, and Ken Dytchwald. 2006. "Managing Middlescence." *Harvard Business Review* 84, no. 3 (March 2006): 78–86.

O'Connor, Matthew. 2006. "A Review of Factors Affecting Individual Performance in Team Environments. Theories and Implications for Library Management." *Library Management* 27, no. 3: 135–143.

Participative Management, Quality of Worklife and Job Enrichment. 1997. Parkridge, NJ: Noyes Data Corporation.

Peter, Laurence, and Raymond Hull. 1969. *The Peter Principle.* New York: Morrow.

Plate, Kenneth P., and Elizabeth W. Stone. 1974. "Factors Affecting Librarians' Job Satisfaction: A Report of Two Studies." *Library Quarterly* 44, no. 2 (April): 97–110.

Sager, Donald J. 1979. "Leadership and Employee Motivation." In *Supervision of Employees in Libraries*, edited by R. E. Stevens. Urbana, IL: University of Illinois Graduate School of Library Science.

Schermerhorn, John R. 1984. *Management for Productivity*. New York: Wiley.

Stauffer, David. 2003. "Motivating Across Generations." *Harvard Management Update* (March).

Verrill, Phil, and Val Wilkins. 1986. "People Who Need People—Thoughts on Motivation." *Outlook on Research Libraries* 8 (October): 7–11.

Vickery, Brian. 1970. "The Triple Glow: Thoughts on Research in Librarianship." *Journal of Librarianship* 2, no. 4: 281–286.

Vroom, Victor H., and Floyd C. Mann. 1960. "Leader Authoritarianism and Employee Attitudes." *Personnel Psychology* 13, no. 2: 125–140.

Weller, Angela. 2005. "Information-seeking Behavior in Generation Y Students: Motivation, Critical Thinking, and Learning Theory." *Journal of Academic Librarianship* 31, no. 1 (January): 46–53.

LAUNCHING PAD

Alonzo, Vincent. 1997. "Poor Motivation A Top Factor in Unethical Behavior." *Incentive*, no. 171 (July): 14–16.

Badu, Edwin Ellis. 2005. "Employee Motivation in University Libraries in Ghana: A Comparative Analysis." *Information Development* 21, no. 1 (March): 38–46.

Haycock, Ken. 2005. "Collaborative Literature-Based Reading Programs with Motivation Components. *Teacher Librarian: The Journal for School Library Professionals* 33, no. 2 (December): 38.

Jatkevicius, James. 2005. "The Search for Meaning and Significance in Public Libraries. A View of Employee Expectations and Organizational Leadership." *Library Administration and Management* 19, no. 3 (Summer): 133–139.

Karp, Hank, Connie Fuller, and Danilo Sirias. 2002. *Bridging the Boomer Xer Gap: Creating Authentic Teams for High Performance at Work*. Palo Alto, CA: Davies-Black Publishing.

"Motivating People: How To Get the Best From Your Organization." 2003. *Harvard Business Review* 81, no. 1 (January): 41–136.

Performance Management: Measure and Improve the Effectiveness of Your Employees. 2006. Boston, MA: Harvard Business School Press.

Rowley, Jenny E. 1996. "Motivation of Staff in Libraries." *Library Management* 17, no. 5: 31–35.

Squire, Jan S. 1991. "Job Satisfaction and the Ethnic Minority Librarian." *Library Administration & Management* 5, no. 4 (Fall): 194–203.

University of Texas. Center for the Study of Work Teams. Available: www.workteams. unt.edu (July 2006).

Weiler, Angela. 2005. "Information-Seeking Behavior in Generation Y Students: Motivation, Critical Thinking, and Learning Theory." *Journal of Academic Librarianship* 31, no. 1 (January): 46.

14

Leadership

"Leadership is the capacity to translate vision into reality."
Warren Bennis

"Management is efficiency in climbing the ladder of success; leadership determines whether the ladder is leaning against the right wall."
Stephen R. Covey

INTRODUCTION

Leadership is a hot topic today around the world—in business, in politics, and not least, in the professions. Leaders must keep close to the members of the community they serve, listening to the messages people send to them. In turn, leaders must communicate a vision for the organization. Leaders have to make the right decisions at the right time, ensuring that all stakeholders are comfortable with these decisions. Leaders working with their team develop and implement strategies to move the organization forward, often in the face of constraints. Leaders find that meeting everyone's rising expectations makes the responsibilities that much more testing. Leaders have always faced challenges, but today's leaders know that they operate in a bright spotlight and their words and actions are subject to close scrutiny; and this can be uncomfortable at times. We live in an age of blogging, and the rapid changes that are taking place both within and beyond the information service increase these leadership challenges. And, taking the work/life balance into consideration, it may be more comfortable not to make a move into a designated leadership role.

However our experience indicates that leaders within an organization are not only found at the top level. Leaders emerge naturally at each level within an organizational structure. Supervisors and managers have always taken a leadership role, and they have been joined by team leaders as a result of the way services are organized today.

In a number of professions and business organizations, people voice concern that the top leadership positions are being filled by people from outside the field, an action that is felt to limit the career aspirations of professionals. People are concerned that a newcomer to the field does not possess the advantage of having the awareness, skills and knowledge, and network that is acquired over time in the field in which they are required to exercise leadership skills. Some consider that it could work to the disadvantage of a service. However, other people within the information professions are undertaking steps to prepare leaders by providing institutes and courses focusing on leadership development in professional schools.

Although you usually secure a designated leadership position later in a career, we introduce the concept to new professionals for three reasons. First, staff members are usually consulted about the selection of a new leader, and so need to have some understanding of the skills and attributes that are needed to be an effective leader. Second, some people move into a leadership role as a supervisor or team leader; they can be described as "hidden" leaders. In this group we include those who are nominated to take charge of a project becoming an "accidental leader." Others come forward in a crisis situation. Third, you acquire leadership skills over time, and starting early provides a head start to career development.

WHAT IS LEADERSHIP?

What do we mean by "leadership"? It isn't easy to define, and some writers have compared it with love, saying it is easier to recognize than to define.

Try This:

There are problems of defining "leadership."
Think of someone who you consider is a successful leader.
Now try and identify the qualities that make her or him a successful leader.

We developed a working definition of leadership as being a collaborative activity generating the opportunity for all members of an organization to engage in the visioning and motivation of one another to meet the challenges of a continually changing operating environment. The outcome is that the organization moves forward to achieve its goals fulfilling the information needs of the community it serves. Leaders require the characteristics and skills to make this happen. It's a long definition, but it contains some significant words: collaborative, opportunity, *all* members of an organization, visioning, motivating one another, challenges, continually changing environment, achieve, goals, characteristics, and skills. These terms are important for potential leaders. They indicate that leadership involves other people—followers who accept direction from the leader, which makes it possible for the leader to exercise leadership. A leader without followers leads nothing. Leadership involves the distribution of power between the leader and the members of her/his team. The authority of the leader guides the work of the team, and the leader uses influence to guide the team's work. But you could comment that some of these terms also appear in writings on management and wonder whether there really is a difference between leaders and managers.

The Differences Between Managing and Leading

Mintzberg (1973) identified a number of tasks common to the work of managers in any sector, and Bennis and Goldsmith provide a clear distinction between the two roles:

- The manager *administers*; the leader *innovates*.
- The manager is a *copy*; the leader is an *original*.
- The manager *maintains*; the leader *develops*.
- The manager accepts *reality*; the leader *investigates* it.
- The manager focuses on *systems and structure*; the leader focuses on *people*.
- The manager relies on *control*; the leader inspires *trust*.
- The manager has a *short range view*; the leader has a *long range perspective*.
- The manager asks *how and when*; the leader asks *what and why*.
- The manager has her eye on *the bottom line*; the leader has eyes on the *horizon*.
- The manager *imitates*; the leader *originates*.
- The manager *accepts the status quo*; the leader *challenges* it.
- The manager is the *classic good soldier*; the leader is her *own person*.
- The manager *does things right*; the leader *does the right thing* (Bennis and Goldsmith, 2003: 8–9)

Moving into a leadership role from a managerial or supervisory role tests any individual. Think about the descriptions of the two roles and you'll see that they are, in many ways, diametrically opposed. Yet it is from supervisors and managers that leaders emerge, so that this calls for a major shift of perspective. From having the responsibility for ensuring the smooth operation of part of an organization and focusing on the bottom line, leaders take a wider, forward-looking perspective.

The Expert:

"Management is mechanical—it's about resource allocation, efficiency, optimization...and there are processes you can follow up to help you manage effectively. Leadership is different—it's about vision and fire and winning people's hearts as well as their minds." Alan Thompson, Managing Director, Toshiba Computer Systems (quoted in Lucas, 2000).

APPROACHES TO LEADERSHIP

The literature of leadership in general is extensive and ranges from the research-based theory to the gurus—"how I did it," or "how I didn't make it to the top." All have value in understanding what it takes to become a leader.

The writings that form the theoretical base can be grouped into seven traditional approaches which draw from a number of disciplines, including psychology, management, sociology, and political science.

The *trait* approach was followed by most writers from the early 20th century until the late 1950s. It assumes that a person is either a born leader or a follower. However, as is the case with so many other personality trait studies (of the creative person, the successful writer, or the famous singer), the list of traits became very long, general in character, and sometimes contradictory. Hernon, Powell, and Young (2003) produced an interesting list as a result of their contemporary research into the "qualities" or traits of library directors.

The *behavioral* approach was influenced by a classic paper in which Lewin, Lippitt and White (1939) reported an experiment which examined three leadership styles: autocratic, democratic, and laissez-faire. Probably stimulated by world events in the 1940s researchers moved on to examine how people act when operating as a leader. One outcome was the development of a questionnaire at Ohio State University in the late 1950s that is still used today in leadership surveys—the Leadership Behavior Description Questionnaire (LBDQ). Originally it was a two-factor instrument measuring task-oriented and people-oriented behavior. Efforts to develop a more complex format have met with limited success.

Check This Out:

View the user documentation and try the Leader Behavior Description Questionnaire for yourself: www.cob.ohio-state.edu/offices/fiscal/lbdq (accessed September 2006).

In the 1960s, the focus shifted from personality traits to the environment in which leadership exists—the *situational* approach. Researchers began to study such factors as the interactions between the manager (leader) and the staff (followers), the organization's needs at any given time, the type of work that the organization performs, and/or the group's values, ethics, experiences, etc. Both experience and research studies indicate that the operating environment is an important factor in the success or failure of a leader, but is not the sole issue.

One of the best situational models is Fiedler's contingency theory (1978). Believing that there was no single best way to lead, his model contains three main variables: leader-member relationship, task structure, and leader's power position. Each variable has two subcomponents: good or bad relationships, structured or unstructured tasks, and strong or weak power position. Two other factors indicate whether the leader was/is relationship- or task-oriented. Research suggests that task-oriented leaders generally do better in situations that have good relationships, structured tasks, and either a weak or strong power position. When relationships are good, the task unstructured, and power position is strong they do equally well. The other situation in which task-oriented leaders perform well is in poor to moderate relationships, unstructured tasks, and a strong power position. Relationship-oriented leaders tend to do better in all the other situations.

In terms of information services, the leader's power position in relation to outside agencies may be low because the service is normally part of a larger organization. So when the service needs strong leadership in its relationship with other agencies and organizations, there may be a problem; the staff often fail to remember this constraint on their leader when assessing that person's success with outside groups. Within the service an individual has a clearly defined position of power resulting from the hierarchical structure that is typical of most services. Again, the more structured the work environment, the less room there is for maneuvering in order to obtain a desired result for the group.

Of the three factors identified by Fiedler's group, the one over which the leader has the most control is personal relations. By working on this aspect of leadership, an individual can achieve a certain degree of success, even if the other two factors are not as favorable as they might be.

The charismatic leaders are those who apparently have exceptional abilities to operate in difficult situations and, at the right time, inspire their followers to exceptional levels of effort and commitment. Think of Gandhi and Dr. Martin Luther King, Jr., or Lee Iacocca (Chrysler), or Rudolph Giuliani. Studies of charismatic leaders often take the form of biographies telling a success story. If one factor stands out from research and reading the biographies, it is that situation does matter. While a charismatic leader might succeed in one situation, he/she may fail in another.

Try This:

Think about history and identify three people who made their mark but failed to recognize that a situation had changed.

Check These Out:

Fiorina, Carly. 2006. *Tough Choices: A Memoir.* New York: Portfolio. Fiorina describes her downfall as CEO at Hewlett-Packard.
Giuliani, Rudolph W., with Ken Kurson. 2002. *Leadership.* New York: Little, Brown. Giuliani tells the story of his career and role as mayor of New York at the time of 9/11 attacks.

Transformational leadership emerged in the 1970s from the work of James McGregor Burns (1978), who blended the trait and behavioral concepts. A key element is influence, with both the leader and followers influencing one another. Burns distinguished two interrelated types of influence: transforming and transactional. Both charismatic and transformational leaders have vision, self-confidence, and the ability to arouse strong follower support, but transformational leaders posses two other factors—intellectual stimulation and individual consideration. *Transactional* leadership takes place when there is an exchange of valued "things" between leaders and followers such as economic rewards and support.

Check This Out:

Castiglione, James. 2006. "Organizational Learning and Transformational Leadership in the Library Environment." *Library Management* 27, nos. 4/5: 289–299.

One approach that has been adopted in a number of nonprofit information services is *servant-leadership*, introduced by Robert Greenleaf (1977). He considered that people who are viewed as great leaders first feel the need to serve, followed by a conscious choice to lead. Greenleaf felt that servant-leaders are more likely to be trusted, to use initiative, to be thoughtful listeners, to have an active imagination, to feel empathy, to be persuasive, to have foresight, and to become a builder of communities.

Check This Out:

The Greenleaf Center for Servant-Leadership (www.greenleaf.org [accessed June 2006]).

Thinking about today and what is likely to happen in the near future, adaptive leadership will be important for information services. Fulmer (2000), writing about adaptive organizations, describes the volatile and complex landscape in which organizations operate today, and information services form part of that landscape. There will be increasing need to anticipate the nature and speed of change that will take place in the social, political, economic, and technological systems within which services operate and to determine how they can best adapt to change. Melding the situational, transformational, and servant-leadership approaches could create adaptive leadership, but it will call for smart footwork.

The changes taking place in the public sector have prompted research into leadership in the library sector. Pors and Johannsen (2003) carried out a comprehensive survey into leadership and management in Danish libraries, one aspect of which focused on leadership roles. They analyzed the data in relation to the new public management and value-based management. The library leaders perceive their future roles as being oriented toward people and toward values. Mullins and Linehan carried out a wider investigation into leadership, examining the views of 30 top-level public librarians from Ireland, Britain, and the east coast of the United States. One finding explored senior library leaders' perceptions of leadership: whether they distinguished classic leadership from management and administrative practices, both conceptually and in their daily work. They found that in all three countries, leadership and management were confused, and that leadership is a scarce quality (Mullins and Linehan, 2006a). A second finding was that there was no universal behavior, even within national boundaries, for effective leadership, but two-thirds of the respondents prioritized the implementation of vision as being the most essential element of library leadership (Mullins and Linehan, 2006b). When questioned about their five-year vision, half of the respondents indicated it would include the maintenance and development of the current core services together with the introduction of innovation expansion of these services. Some 90 percent were optimistic that public libraries would survive into the middle of the century. One point that was stressed was that they are very different from managers in the private sector and other public sector areas. They believe they and their libraries are major catalysts of change in the social environments (Mullins and Linehan, 2006c). The respondents see the role played by followers as being the foundation of public library service. A partnership approach between leaders and followers is needed to develop and implement strategies and courses of action to meet organizational purpose and goals (Mullins and Linehan, 2005a). The perceptions of the senior public library leaders indicated that they supported the centrality of leadership for optimal strategic and operational practices in librarianship. However there is a challenge to identify and consider the leadership skills and personal attributes needed for success (Mullins and Linehan, 2005b.) Taken together, the findings of this transnational study appear to indicate that there is a need for leadership development programs to be provided for those at middle-management levels in the three countries, in order to ensure the health of public libraries at a time of major changes in their operating environments.

FOUR ASSUMPTIONS REGARDING LEADERSHIP

It was pointed out earlier that people sometimes find themselves thrust unexpectedly into a leadership role. In a crisis, an individual can emerge who possesses the traits that equip the person to take charge quickly and make effective decisions, perhaps as a result of an earlier life experience. At other times someone may be delegated to take charge of a project or team, becoming an "accidental" leader (Robbins and Finley, 2004). Leaders are not always the "boss" of the overall service. In these circumstances people assume a leadership role and quickly develop and demonstrate the necessary skills to operate effectively. However the majority of people recognized as being leaders head up a department or service in a designated leadership position.

Taking the last situation, four assumptions can be made. First, that the person has made a conscious decision to apply for a leadership position and has the responsibility for making that decision. Second, the position has been attained through an appointment process in which the staff participated but did not have the final decision. Systems of appointment vary from little or no staff input to staff voting on several candidates. In many cases, however, the actual hiring decision rests with an outside person or group. Therefore, in the minds of staff, the director or leader is to a greater or lesser degree appointed by decree of a higher authority. In addition the appointee's power position is not likely to differ from that of the former incumbent. All that is variable is the degree of informal influence the new leader can exert on higher positions, outside bodies and the user community.

A third assumption is that a person starts in the position with only the rank and authority assigned to the office. Initially, there is no leadership. Staff perform their duties because the supervisor is "boss," and because that is what they normally do. A leader will quickly move beyond this "do-it-because-I-told-you-to" approach and use their leadership skills rather than authority to accomplish things through people. Failure to move from strict reliance on authority almost always generates a tension-filled environment laced with distrust, suspicion, and hostility.

Ponder On This:

Return to the person you have identified as a leader—what has been the influence of the environment in which the person operates?

In professional or semiprofessional organizations, it is almost always a given that the professional staff shares, to some degree, most of the organizational goals and objectives (Krech et al., 1962). Support staff members are less likely to share the goals to the same extent. However, in an information service, it can be assumed that most full-time support staff members who have been there for more than three years share some of the organizational objectives. In particular, Presthus identified a close correlation between the values of professional and nonprofessional staff (1970). In practice this means that the supervisor's mode of operation strongly influences the quality of work performed.

Our fourth assumption is two-edged: no one is a born leader; you can learn the skills of leadership. To some degree, everyone has leadership potential in certain situations, which means that care should be taken in saying that someone does not have leadership potential. The specific situations that provoke the comment need clarification before doubt is cast on a person's leadership skills. Leadership is a complex process that depends on a combination of people and environmental factors.

Try This:

Examine the assumptions we have made about how a person becomes a leader. Drawing on your experience, do you agree or disagree with them? Are there any other assumptions you would want to add to the list?

FUNCTIONS OF LEADERSHIP

So what do leaders do? We tested our experience against a list of the functions of a leader prepared by Krech et al. (1962), and found that most functions were enduring. Over time the terminology changes, as in many aspects of management, but the concept remains the same.

Although some of the functions of a manager and leader appear to be the same, check back and look again at the differences identified by Bennis and Goldsmith (2003: 8–9). The leader takes a broader perspective, using an analytical approach, and develops people skills.

The most important function is to drive the service forward and manage change so the leader *develops the vision* for the service. The vision sets the direction for the service, enthusing and motivating staff. To achieve this, a leader is in close touch with top management and its thinking, the emerging needs of the community served, and what is happening in the outside world by *scanning the internal and external operating environment.*

Taking this information, the leader works with her/his team to anticipate changes, develop new ideas, and propose adjustments in the group's activities. The leader is a *planner,* working with the staff to turn the vision into reality and prepare concrete plans that can be implemented. These form the benchmarks or targets against which managers and supervisors monitor performance, feeding the resulting data and information back into the planning process.

One outcome of planning is that the leader, having oversight of all activities within the service, becomes responsible for *coordination,* reconciling personal service (the leader's own and the staff's) and organizational goals, being the ultimate *problem solver.*

A manager operates on authority receiving policy guidelines from above, but a leader derives the power as a *policy maker* both from above and from their subordinates as a result of gaining the trust of their subordinates in formulating policy with them. After consultation and taking advice, the leader has to be the ultimate *decision maker.*

A leader is more effective if he/she is an *expert in the field* in which the organization operates and the information sector in which the service is based. Being an expert facilitates communication, since a common language will be used with senior management and the team, and the leader is able to use the full capabilities of the parent organization and resources within the profession.

Tip:

Learning the technical vocabularies is important, especially within services serving specialized subject fields. Add to this the language of management and the professional sector. Being able to use these languages brings confidence to the leader, and to those with whom they come into daily contact.

A leader shares knowledge and skills willingly and in a manner suggesting *an equal relationship*, not a superior-subordinate relationship. This is the area that causes challenges for a leader recruited from outside the information sector.

Increasingly a leader has to be an *example setter*. In attitude and performance, the leader sets the tone and pace for the group, particularly in the field of ethical behavior. Sometimes a staff member emulates a leader's methods of working, attitudes, and, occasionally, even style of dress.

One important function is for the leader to be the *controller of internal relations*. In a service supervised by a leader, the formal and informal structures are usually very similar (a situation that is rare for the nonleader). The leader ensures that these structures are the hub around which all activities revolve. In this way the leader has responsibility for the organizational climate. In carrying out this function, the leader also functions as a *team builder*.

Although managers and supervisors share part of this function, the leader is the ultimate *arbitrator and mediator*. When the staff have respect and trust in their leader, they bring some of the tricky problems to that person for resolution.

Within any organization the leader makes the final decision about *rewards and reprimands*. This role is held both by a leader and a manager. Although neither one may personally administer rewards and reprimands, both approve or recommend such actions. The difference is that the manager often finds that staff may question rewards (as well as reprimands), but this does not generally happen in the case of a leader.

A leader will often tell a subordinate, "Go ahead and do X, and if there's any problem about it, I'll take the blame." The subordinate knows that this will be the case with a leader who accepts the role as a *substitute for individual responsibility*. Leaders do not force the subordinate to take the blame or, after saying that they will accept the responsibility, avoid it.

Because of their position, leaders set the tone of the service; people outside the service regard leaders as the *symbol of the group*. Within a service, a manager is always accountable for what takes place; however, for a leader the issue goes far beyond accountability.

A service expects its managers will be its spokespeople to outsiders. While other people may be capable of assuming this role, the staff "know" that the leader will not only present the service's position, but do everything possible to protect their interests. So the leader becomes the *representative to people external to the service*.

Leaders expect that sometimes they will receive the blame for actions over which they have no control. They know they can be a *scapegoat* and accept this as readily as they accept the *accountability* that accompanies their position.

So when a leader is being selected, these are some of the functions of an effective leader that prospective candidates must possess. Evidence of this experience should be found in a candidate's curriculum vitae and in a dialogue. A dialogue rather than simple questioning is likely to produce a better outcome for the service as there is also another factor to take in account when an external appointment is being considered. It is the issue of organizational culture. Has the prospective candidate had experience that would help her/him to adapt to a new setting quickly? How does this one compare with previous organizations? What was the size of the service and its staff and the parent organization? What stage of development was it at? How were the politics played? What responsibilities were delegated to the candidate, and what was the extent of the person's power and authority? We will expand on these points later in this chapter, but situations may not be transferable across organizations even if they are in the same sector of the information professions. A prospective new leader's success may be directly related to their current employer and may not be transferable.

But given the broad range of functions what should a person do to become a leader? Firstly check back to the list of functions of a leader. Consider whether you possess the attributes and skills and can achieve a healthy work/life balance and work—and then think about your motivation. Spreirer, Fontaine and Malloy (2006) draw attention to the damage that can be done by overachievers. Overachievers focus on tasks and goals, issue commands, and coerce and stifle their staff, which can damage the performance of an organization. Getting honest feedback from a mentor and colleagues help a prospective leader avoid this destructive behavior pattern.

The second step is to realize that there is a variety of leadership styles, just as there is a variety of managerial styles, but understand that leadership styles need to adapt to changing situations more frequently than managerial styles.

The third step is to develop leadership skills. To do this, an essential element is to aspire to be a leader who provides the vital incentive needed to learn. It is never too soon to start developing the essential knowledge and skills that are best acquired over a period of time, starting in the first professional post. There is no quick way to become an effective leader. Skills can be learned formally by taking a course in leadership organized by a university or professional association or informally through reading and short courses on specific aspects. But learning the theory has to be backed up by experience—working under supervision and putting theory into practice by taking the first steps as a supervisor or junior manager.

LEADERSHIP SKILLS AND UNDERSTANDING

Leaders never stop learning and reading provides the basics with leadership gurus such as Bennis (1998) and Ciampa and Watkins (1999) offering sound practical guidance. Compelling stories of people who emerged as leaders have been told by Giuliani (2002), focusing on the 9/11 attacks, and there is the experience of Shackleton, an Antarctic explorer who saved men stranded with him on an ice floe (Morrell and Capparell, 2001).

Check This Out:

Bennis, Warren, and Joan Goldsmith. 2003. *Learning to Lead: A Workbook on Becoming a Leader.* New York: Basic Books.

A systematic reading program delves deeper into wider aspects of information work, especially in related sectors with which collaboration becomes increasingly important. Leaders also keep up-to-date with changes in approaches to management and leadership issues, and of course, information and communications technologies. By maintaining currency in professional practice and issues leaders help staff with their informal learning. Reading has another benefit for it encourages *lateral thinking* which stimulates creativity building scenarios for the future. A mind can take apparently unconnected ideas and see interesting patterns, new opportunities, or possibilities.

Check This Out:

De Bono, Edward. 1971. *Lateral Thinking for Managers.* New York: American Management Association.

Lateral thinking feeds into *strategic planning.* Successful services and organizations know their purpose, have a sound sense of the future, and plan for the ways in which they will achieve their goals and handle future challenges. These are set down in a series of interrelated documents that are presented to stakeholders: the staff, the users, the community at large, and, not least, senior management. Often they are also circulated more widely within the profession press and via Web sites. Strategic planning argues for resources and then guides the allocation of those resources. Leaders work closely with their staff and users to ensure the stakeholders have a strong influence on the documents so that change can be anticipated. Leaders also ensure that while ensuring that the service is moving forward and anticipating change, the plans are realistic. Blue sky thinking is great at the start of a planning cycle, but reality with a touch of "it would be nice to have" is more likely to be achieved. The question of planning is explored in greater depth in Chapter 8, and managing change in Chapter 6.

Leadership is essentially a social process, and effective leaders have to connect with those around them. Two concepts have been described by Goleman—*emotional intelligence*, which creates awareness of our own feelings and those of others, and *social intelligence*, which explores our relationships with others (Goleman, 1995, 2006). Understanding these concepts is important to developing the behavior patterns essential for working effectively with staff, colleagues in the wider organization, the ultimate boss, and the community served.

Check These Out:

Daniel Goleman's 2004 seminal paper on emotional intelligence, "What Makes a Leader?" *Harvard Business Review* 82 (1 January): 82–91.

John F. Kihlstrom and Nancy Cantor's discussion of the development and definition of social intelligence in "Social Intelligence" (Available: http://socrates.berkeley.edu/~kihlstrm/social_intelligence.htm [accessed October 2006]).

Hernon, Peter and Nancy Rossiter. 2006. "Emotional Intelligence: Which Traits Are Most Prized?" *College & Research Libraries* 67, no. 3: 260–275.

Mills, John. 2006. "Affect, Emotional Intelligence and Librarian-User Interaction." *Library Review* 55, no. 9: 587–597.

Richer, Lisa. 2006. "Emotional Intelligence at Work: An Interview with Daniel Goleman." *Public Libraries* 45, no. 1: 24–28.

Another aspect of self-awareness to explore is the beliefs that we hold as individuals, which are shaped by the culture in which we were raised. Beliefs can influence the way in which *values, morals,* and *ethics* are approached. Some examples from the work environment include the way beliefs can influence the way in which issues such as diversity are viewed; *values* shape strategic plans, *morals* determine how people behave and react to situations, and *ethics* consider the ways in which moral questions are handled. The community of staff and users is now generally diverse, and moving from one cultural setting to another is challenging.

In terms of professional ethics professional bodies issue codes of conduct to guide their members in making ethical judgments. Examples are those prepared by the Society of American Archivists (2005) and the American Library Association (1995).

> **Try This:**
>
> We have provided examples of the way in which beliefs could influence the way that issues are handled in the workplace.
> Add to the list of examples.

In the information professions it is particularly important that leaders have well-developed *communication skills*, and these are reviewed in Chapter 12. Leaders have to communicate effectively with their staff, users, and senior management, and each group needs a different style and language appropriate for addressing them: senior management expects "management speak"; staff members use professional and technical terminology; and users may not appreciate either management or professional jargon. Leaders need to possess a good command of the language or languages used in the daily work of the organization; this can be challenging in bilingual communities. Skills in public speaking and in working with the media are essential. Writing skills become of greater importance, given the different styles needed—for example, in writing reports or e-mails.

Closely linked with the communication skills are the *political skills*. This is one group of skills that have to be experienced to be learned and they vary between one organization and another. All organizations and work teams revolve around politics—it's a fact of life. Leaders must become effective political players within the service, the parent organization, the community served, and the information professions. Internal politics play a part in resolving the disagreements and differences that emerge from any group having diverse needs. There are never enough resources to meet everyone's needs, and priorities have to be set even within the service. Organizational politics affect resource allocation, and political tactics are used to influence decisions and create coalitions, partnerships or alliances to ensure the continuing success of the service. Increasingly politics are involved in relationships with external agencies and professional groups. Many people start to develop these skills in community groups and at university, learning the reality of the cut and thrust and how to debate effectively. The best experience comes from winning some points and losing others.

Understanding the organizational culture and climate is a challenge for a leader who is new to an organization. Clues about the culture can be observed from the image that the organization presents on its Web site and in publications, from the interview process, the way people dress and talk, and the induction process and the way newcomers are introduced to their peers. The culture is based on history, the learning experience of the staff as the organization evolves and the beliefs, values, and assumptions brought in by new members of staff. It adds up to "the way we do it here." Sannwald (2000) notes that it has four functions: it gives members of an organization identity, it provides a collective commitment to the organization, it builds social stability, and it allows people to make sense of the organization. The organizational climate is more visible and changes more frequently as it reflects the ways in which the organization handles its environment and its people—for example, the decision-making process and managerial style. Within the information service a new leader will find that the climate was created by the previous leader. It is related to a leader's style of leadership, her/his attributes and skills, values, and actions. The climate within a service can be changed by a new leader, but the culture is deep-rooted and is created by others.

One factor that can affect a leader's effectiveness is the stage in the life cycle of the service and organization. When services or organizations are young, they need a leader with entrepreneurial skills at the stage of rapid growth. Many organizations then plateau for a time and reach a steady state needing stronger administrative skills. Then the service or organization may move into a period of rapid change as it adapts to changes in the operating environment. The factors that influence the cycle include economic conditions and major technological change. Getting the person with the right experience at the right time is essential—the leader with the wrong experience may not be successful.

At the center of politics is the way that the organization is governed and who holds the power. This is considered in greater depth in Chapter 9. It is vital to be able to distinguish between formal governance and who holds power and influences decisions, and most important, where the decisions are made that can benefit the service. This is another tricky area for a newcomer, who may not be able to get advice from the staff. Awareness of the way that decisions are made and who really holds the power comes from actively participating in the relevant committees and also the social functions that revolve around the organization. Observe and listen. By learning committee skills within the profession the experience can be carried over to boost performance in the organizational committee structure. Creating partnerships, alliances, and coalitions becomes important in working across the organization and with the information professions. Networking and visibility increase the prospect for success, principally for the information service but also for the leader. However in exercising political skills, leaders must have strong values and practice ethical behavior.

Writing about leadership skills makes a point about management that isn't always evident in textbooks. Like organizational culture, it is often assumed rather than stated. It is that management should be seamless and ideally needs to be presented as a hypertext. That is why we have returned to the people issues discussed earlier to examine *team-building skills*. This set of skills takes on greater importance as organizations continue to flatten, responding to changes brought about by information and communications technologies, by customer needs that may stretch over 24/7, teleworking, and the pressure to reduce overhead costs to focus on service and outcomes. Teams have always operated in information services—think of the traditional way in which services were organized around functions in the past. But now consider how services such as knowledge management emerged as a way for organizations to share information to create new products, or new ways to carry out their aims, and the global organizations in finance and the law. This requires teamworking.

Leaders help their staff to achieve the best possible performance; they depend on team members to work together, solve problems and provide a high level of service designed around the needs of users. Teams are gener ally in close daily contact with users, and so can pick up on changing needs and think about ways to adapt services. Instead of operating on a command-and-control basis, they call for consensus, and disagreements and conflict inevitably emerge. Leaders ensure that team members receive training and guidance to assist them in handling differences of opinion without stifling viewpoints. By empowering teams, the staff gains greater motivation to achieve the goals they have helped to set for the service. It is a set of people skills that is still evolving, as today there is less face-to-face working where the feelings of another person can be seen, and more contact by the less personal e-mail and telephone. With time, more services will link workstations with Webcams to personalize a conversation and use video conferencing to link team members operating from remote locations. A new set of skills focusing on *e-leadership* and virtual leadership in the technology mediated environment is required. Pulley and Sessa (2001) described five sets of paradoxes and complex challenges for e-organizations and their leaders: swift and mindful, individual and community, top down and grass roots, details and big picture, and flexible and steady.

One factor in the success of a team relates to the charge or purpose or primary task as assigned by the leader. Although it is not used by all organizations it can tell a team what parameters it has, its responsibilities and resources available. This can equally apply to a team set up for a special project, or reviewed at regular intervals with a more permanent team. It can help the team understand:

- what the problem (or task) is
- why it is important to the customers and organization at this time
- any boundaries or limitations, including time, money (and people)
- the beginning and end dates of a project, and key milestones for review
- the key measures related to the problem or process (or part of service) under study

- the scope of the team's authority—for example, to call in coworkers or outside experts, request normally inaccessible information, and make changes to the process
- who the core team members are and the amount of time allocated to the project or service (Scholtes, Joiner, and Striebel, 2003: 2–12).

It is very easy for a team to become overenthusiastic when self-managing a service or project, and the charge defines boundaries and responsibilities as well as reviews outcomes against anticipated performance.

Evered and Selman (1989) described a tool that can assist with achieving the vision, recognizing and accounting for all the relevant environmental and organizational factors and developing a coalition powerful enough to assure its successful implementation. This is the "acknowledge-create-empower" (A.C.E.) paradigm of leadership to use with staff to empower them and foster creativity. The fundamental belief of this paradigm is rethinking thoughts, commitment to accomplishment, collaborative involvement, mutual support, and individual growth, which in turn enables people in a group or team to produce results. Employees gain empowerment from the results they generate.

As individuals work toward their goals with the aid of the leader/manager, there is more acceptance of that person. Pelz (1966) suggests that in any situation, the more the leader helps other members to achieve their goals, the greater will be the members' acceptance of the leader. Acceptance of the leader helps productivity and relations within the organization. Employees will be reluctant to learn leadership responsibilities from someone whom they do not perceive as a leader. The manager/leader has to be perceived as an effective leader to achieve the best outcomes. But being effective doesn't mean that leaders are always right. There will be a wrong decision or action—and people will notice. Earlier we mentioned the mistakes that staff can make, and leaders are also not always right. However, if there is trust, the problem will be communicated to the leader. Everyone makes mistakes, and a leader who acknowledges the problem and sorts it out gains respect. It encourages staff to know that errors can be acknowledged, and it should be part of the ethos of a learning organization. Schoemaker and Gunther go a step forward and encourage deliberate mistakes. They consider that mistakes are necessary because we are overconfident, risk-averse, seek confirming evidence, and assume feedback is reliable. They suggest making intentional mistakes when:

- The potential gain outweighs the cost of the mistake.
- Decisions are made repeatedly.
- The environment has dramatically changed.
- The problem is complex and the solutions are numerous.

- Your organization's experience with a problem is limited (Schoemaker and Gunther, 2006: 112).

Taking a role model can help to identify the attributes of a leader, but following such a model slavishly will not necessarily lead to success. Far better is to have a mentor whom you respect and who can give friendly advice on developing leadership skills.

The learning process can be long and sometimes be a bumpy ride. But bumpy rides are essential. They demonstrate that the role is complex, and success depends on having a wide range of skills and attributes, and experience. We would add the need for time management skills, boundless energy, and a great sense of humor!

Point of Reflection:

Reflect on how you would want to develop your leadership style.
What would be the characteristics?
What strengths do you already have?
What do you feel you need to develop?

ORGANIZATIONAL STRUCTURES FOR EMPLOYEE-CENTERED LEADERSHIP

Employee centered strategies need organizational structures that are built on the way people work, rather than the tasks carried out in the service. Teamworking producing a greater employee input in decision-making activities, the challenging nature of work, and the decentralization of power has led to organizations that are less hierarchical. Also, the increased interdependence of the various units requires a greater emphasis on collaboration and a need for more communication and a better structure. With increased access to information at all levels through intranets and e-mails, organizational structures will continue to flatten, facilitating more participative management and leadership from within the service.

To ensure that the structure works effectively two factors need to be considered. The first is that it is important to recognize that individuals will be at varying levels of development and have different training needs. The effective leader helps each person to perform at their current level of development while at the same time increasing their skills and abilities. And, as the staff's skills and abilities develop, leaders gradually share more responsibility. But sometimes things do not go exactly as planned. When this happens, the leader takes time to study why, and recognizes that mistakes will sometimes be a natural outcome of work in an organization. The problems should be seen as an opportunity for the staff and leader to learn and develop their skills and abilities. This creates a learning organization. Secondly the structure needs to be made explicit to staff and users. Hierarchical structures had the advantage of being clear and responsibilities were clearly delineated. Everyone knew their place—and the users could easily identify "who did what." Teamworking is not so easy to set down in a diagram, but it is a good task to delegate to someone on the staff with a creative imagination and a sense of layout and color. And that may well be one of the younger members of staff.

Check This Out:

Farson, Richard E., and Ralph Keyes. 2002. "The Failure-Tolerant Leader." *Harvard Business Review* 80, no. 8 (August): 64–71.

Try This:

What are the disadvantages of employee-centered leadership that the senior manager has to be aware of? List them and put them in an order of importance. It may be helpful to do this exercise thinking of a specific organization.

GIVING ORDERS

Although giving orders or directions is a leadership skill, it is being considered separately, for it is one of the skills that can be very challenging. It is learned on the job, doesn't always come naturally, and can be daunting for a new graduate going into his/her first position as a junior supervisor or manager. But ultimately, if the person is to accomplish things through people with only an official grant of authority, he or she must give orders (directions). Without question, giving orders or directions has more to do with being a leader than any other activity. The managerial position already has inherent authority, but the authority of respect has to be developed to become a leader. Authority of respect is earned, and it is earned *slowly*. Respect is earned through shared experiences in which staff believes they have received fair treatment, proper recognition for work well done, sound advice and firm direction, recognition and fair treatment of poor performance, and a fair hearing for their interests, concerns, and grievances. If all this happens, the staff will give more than expected, and they will do so voluntarily. A climate of cooperation will exist, and the them-versus-us syndrome will cease to exist—at least to the degree in which it concerns the immediate supervisor.

From the leader's point of view, there are three broad categories of work climate: cooperation, compliance, and hostile compliance. (In merit systems—and very rarely in other systems—a fourth type exists: noncompliance. Noncompliance seldom lasts very long because someone will leave unless things change. Noncompliance usually occurs in places in which there is a high degree of job security.) Naturally, the preferred climate is cooperation, but this can only be achieved over a period of time because it requires mutual trust.

The typical climate is one of compliance. People do what they have to do to meet performance expectations, but they do no more or less. Enthusiasm is lacking, no initiative exists, mistakes are common, and mistakes often result from following the letter of an order even though it does not conform to previous practice ("Look, I did just what you told me to do. If there's a problem in the procedure, you correct it. That's what they pay you for!") This is a typical reaction when a procedure goes wrong in a compliance climate. If the supervisor allows the feelings to carry over to the next activity, more distrust develops. The situation can slide rather quickly from compliance to hostile compliance.

Hostile compliance can exist over a long period of time. Sides are taken, and each side does its best to catch the other side off guard. Civilities usually exist and work takes place—but at the absolute minimum level. Evidence is gathered to justify disciplinary action. The staff usually is well aware of this, but hopes to cause the supervisor difficulties by keeping production to the absolute minimum in quality and quantity (so that the boss will notice). They also wait for the order that, if carried out to the letter, will cause disaster for the supervisor.

Consider:

How comfortable are you with giving orders?
What tactics would you employ in situations of (a) hostile compliance or (b) noncompliance?

How can a climate of cooperation be developed? Start by delegating. Even within the smallest team, some delegation of tasks is usually possible. Give authority along with the delegation, so that the staff knows there is trust. This will also give the staff an opportunity to develop new skills. Because staff members usually welcome growth opportunities, a leader can enhance their positive feelings and encourage cooperation through delegation. Delegation also provides the leader with more time for planning and working on problems that establish a reputation for the leader as a planner and an expert—both of which are important for strong leadership.

Mistakes will occur whenever individuals take on new duties and attempt to perform new activities, as we have noted above. By treating these mistakes as learning and teaching experiences, a manager can enhance her/his reputation as an expert. By approaching the work in a positive manner, the manager fills the role of example setter—enthusiasm is contagious. Mistakes are normal, and if a peer relationship serves as the basis of teaching and correlation, rather than a superior-subordinate atmosphere, the experience can be positive for everyone.

Supervisors and managers must check on the progress of all delegated work. What is important is how the checking is done. Occasional checking lets the staff know there is an interest in their progress and the supervisor/manager is ready and willing to assist as necessary. At the beginning, a weekly or biweekly progress report is a good means of learning about progress and problems which will also dispel the image of someone hovering over employees' shoulders and worrying about what is happening.

When it comes to actually issuing an order or directive, there are two modes of presentation: a demand or a request. The factors discussed in Chapter 12 influence the way in which staff members perceive the directive—both its content and the intent behind it. Oral communication always contains nonverbal elements, and situational factors also enter into the process of interpreting a message.

People respond to requests more quickly than they do to demands in the cooperative and compliance environments. The mutual dependence between supervisor and staff is clear, and the recipient of the order feels the recognition of individual humanity. Requests are easier to modify than are demands, should that prove necessary.

Certain people do, however, require demands. Usually, this attitude is a result of past experience, and it takes time to overcome the past. Sometimes it cannot be changed. Of course, a few people are lazy and need incentives to keep them functioning above the minimum level. Others may simply be careless or indifferent, and may need the threat of a demand to put out a more effective work effort.

An order must be clear, and normally an explanation of the reason for it will gain goodwill. Unclear orders will produce poor staff effort and quickly undermine confidence in the supervisor. No order should leave any doubt in the person's mind as to what and how soon they must carry out the order. When managers fail to convey this information, they generate problems for themselves and their staff. On the other hand, when a manager conveys too much detail, the staff will wonder whether there is any respect for their ability. The best advice is be clear and strike a balance, telling everything that the employee needs to know but not so much as to confuse matters.

Nothing will destroy a supervisor's credibility more quickly than issuing unreasonable orders. Orders can be unreasonable in terms of time, volume of work, or the resources available to do the work. When pressured from above, it is easy to promise more than time permits. Managers should remember this and not give in, unless it is an emergency—and even then, be careful not to promise too much. Emergency or high-pressure situations will occur, but not too often in a well-managed organization. And, if staff and supervisor work well together, they can handle situations effectively. The occurrence of too many high pressure situations indicates a lack of planning and control by the manager; this will cause staff distrust, as well it should. Reasonable orders provide realistic goals and adequate time for accomplishment.

Starting off in a new supervisory position with these guidelines in mind, it is possible to move smoothly and in a reasonable period of time from having only the authority of position to having the authority of respect and trust. Individuals who move into a leadership mode of management will find their work easier than before, despite the many tasks involved, because there will be much greater staff support. In essence, one person fills the formal leadership role, while others in the group take on supporting leadership roles. In this way the unit moves to a collegial system without being aware of what is happening. Collegial management is about as close as one is likely to come to group leadership (as opposed to individual leadership) in a complex, highly structured organization such as an information service.

DO GENDER DIFFERENCES MATTER IN LEADERSHIP?

As women moved into higher-level managerial positions, the number of studies of the relationship between leadership and gender also increased. This is of interest to the information professions, since an increasing number of women occupy leadership positions, and change has taken place. At one time the literature of management indicated that decisions were said to be made in men's locker rooms, but given the rising numbers of women in senior positions, especially in the civil service and the public sector, more decisions are made today in the women's restrooms.

Is there a gender difference in leadership styles? The question has interested researchers. Valentine and Godkin (2000) explored the relationship between supervisor gender and perceived job design. They found that a supervisor's gender did influence a subordinate's perceptions of their job with the difference being attributed to different leadership styles. Those who had a woman supervisor perceived greater interpersonal aspects in their work, and those who were supervised by a man perceived greater structure in their work.

A review of the literature reported by Trinidad and Normore (2005) indicated that women adopt a democratic and participative leadership styles, with transformational leadership being the style most preferred by women. Manning (2002) argues that transformational leadership enables women to simultaneously carry out leadership and gender roles. The question of whether women's leadership styles are less effective than men's is derived from socialization (Appelbaum, Audet, and Miller, 2003). Women's styles are likely to be more effective in the context of team-based consensually driven organizational structures, but both men and women can learn from each other.

There is a lesson here for new leaders who are appointed to positions held by someone of the opposite gender, and for their staff. Knowing the style of the previous incumbent isn't immediately obvious to a newcomer. Having to make a mark—and at the same time tread carefully—isn't easy. It is a challenge for both the new leader and their staff, and can be difficult to meet. It isn't always easily recognized.

Leaders of the Future

Conger and Benjamin (1999: 250–251) consider that "workforce trends will demand that leaders of the future be all of the following:

- sensitive to the issues of diversity
- interpersonally competent
- skillful communicators and motivators
- community builders
- capable of building well-aligned organizational architectures
- developers of leaders"

This holds as much for information services as it does for other types of organization and we leave this chapter with words of an expert who sums the responsibilities of a leader.

> **The Expert:**
>
> "The first responsibility is to define reality. The last is to say thank you. In between the two, the leader must become a servant and a debtor. That sums up the progress of an artful leader." DePree, Max. 1989. *Leadership Is an Art*. New York: Dell Publishing.

KEY POINTS TO REMEMBER:

- Leaders can be found at every level in an information service.
- Leadership is difficult to define but easier to recognize.
- There are significant differences between managing and leading.
- Seven traditional approaches to leadership can be identified.
- Leadership functions are enduring.
- It is never too soon to start learning how to be a leader.
- Leaders need to have many different skills.
- Communication, political and team building skills are very important.
- Appropriate structures are needed for employee-centered services.
- Giving orders is a very challenging skill.

REFERENCES

American Library Association. 1995. *Code of Ethics.* Available: www.ala.org/ala/oif/statementpols/codeofethics/codeethics.htm (accessed June 2006).

Appelbaum, Steven H., Lynda Audet, and Joanne C. Miller. 2003. "Gender and Leadership? Leadership and Gender? A Journey Through the Landscape of Theories." *Leadership & Organizational Development* 24, no. 1: 43–51.

Bennis, Warren. 1998. *On Becoming a Leader.* London: Arrow Books.

Bennis, Warren, and Joan Goldsmith. 2003. *Learning to Lead: A Workbook on Becoming a Leader.* New York: Basic Books.

Burns, James McGregor. 1978. *Leadership.* New York: Harper Collins Publishers.

Ciampa, Dan, and Michael Watkins. 1999. *Right from the Start: Taking Charge in a New Leadership Role.* Boston, MA: Harvard Business School Press.

Conger, Jay A., and Beth Benjamin. 1999. *Building Leaders: How Successful Companies Develop the Next Generation.* San Francisco: Jossey-Bass.

Evered, Roger D., and James C. Selman. 1989. "Coaching and the Art of Management." *Organizational Dynamics* 18, no. 3 (Autumn): 18.

Fiedler, Fred E. 1978. "The Contingency Model and the Dynamics of the Leadership Process." In *Advances in Experimental Social Psychology,* ed. L. Berkowitz. New York: Academic Press, 60–112.

Fulmer, William E. 2000. *Shaping the Adaptive Organization: Landscapes, Learning, and Leadership in Volatile Times.* New York: AMACOM.

Giuliani, Rudolph, with Ken Kurson. 2002. *Leadership.* New York: Little, Brown.

Goleman, Daniel. 1995. *Emotional Intelligence.* New York: Bantam Books.

Goleman, Daniel. 2006. *Social Intelligence: The New Science of Human Relationships.* New York: Bantam Books.

Greenleaf, Robert K. 1977. *Servant Leadership: A Journey into the Nature of Legitimate Power and Greatness.* New York: Paulist Press.

Hernon, Peter; Ronald Powell; and Arthur Young. 2003. *The Next Library Leadership: Attributes of Academic and Public Library Directors.* Westport, CT: Libraries Unlimited.

Krech, David, et al. 1962. *Individual in Society.* New York: McGraw-Hill.

Lewin, Kurt, Ronald Lippitt, and Ralph White. 1939. "Patterns of Aggressive Behavior in Experimentally Created Social Climates." *Journal of Social Psychology* 10: 271–299.

Lucas, Ann F. 2000. *Leading Academic Change: Essential Roles for Department Chairs.* San Francisco: Jossey-Bass.

Manning, Tracey T. 2002. "Gender, Managerial Level, Transformational Leadership and Work Satisfaction." *Women in Management Review* 17, no. 5: 207–216.

Mintzberg, Henry. 1973. *The Nature of Managerial Work.* Englewood Cliffs, NJ: Prentice-Hall.

Morrell, Margot, and Stephanie Capparell. 2001. *Shackleton's Way: Leadership Lesson from the Great Antarctic Explorer.* London: Nicholas Brearley.

Mullins, John, and Margaret Linehan. 2005a. "Leadership and Followership in Public Services: Transnational Perspectives." *International Journal of Public Sector Management* 18, no. 7: 641–647.

Mullins, John, and Margaret Linehan. 2005b. "The Central Role of Leaders in Public Libraries." *Library Management* 26, nos. 6/7: 386–396.

Mullins, John, and Margaret Linehan. 2006a. "Are Public Libraries Led or Managed?" *Library Review* 55, no. 4: 237–248.

Mullins, John, and Margaret Linehan. 2006b. "Desired Qualities of Public Library Leaders." *Leadership & Organizational Development Journal* 27, no. 2: 133–143.

Mullins, John, and Margaret Linehan. 2006c. "Senior Public Librarians Looking to the Future." *New Library World* 107, nos. 3/4: 105–115.

Pelz, Donald C. 1966. *Scientists in Organizations: Productive Climates for Research and Development.* New York: Wiley.

Pors, Niels Ole, and Carl Gustav Johannsen. 2003. "Library Directors Under Cross-Pressure Between New Public Management and Value-Based Management." *Library Management* 24, nos. 1/2: 51–60

Presthus, Robert. 1970. *Technological Change and Occupational Response.* Washington, DC: Office of Education.

Pulley, Mary Lynn, and Valerie Sessa. 2001. "E-Leadership: Tackling Complex Challenges." *Industrial and Commercial Training* 33, no. 6: 225–230.

Robbins, Harvey, and Michael Finley. 2004. *The Accidental Leader: What to Do When You're Suddenly in Charge.* San Francisco: Jossey-Bass.

Sannwald, William. 2000. "Understanding Organizational Culture." *Library Administration & Management* 14, no. 1 (Winter): 8–14.

Schein, Edgar H. 2004. *Organizational Culture and Leadership.* 3rd ed. San Francisco: Jossey-Bass.

Scholtes, Peter R., Brian L. Joiner, and Barbara J. Striebel. 2003. *The Team Handbook.* 3rd ed. Madison, WI: Oriel.

Schoemaker, Paul J.H., and Robert E. Gunther. 2006. "The Wisdom of Deliberate Mistakes." *Harvard Business Review* 84, no. 6 (June): 109–115.

Society of American Archivists. 2005. *Code of Ethics.* Available: www.archivists.org/governance/handbook/app_ethics.asp (accessed June 2006).

Spreirer, Scott W., Mary H. Fontaine, and Ruth L. Malloy. 2006. "Leadership Run Amok: The Destructive Potential of Overachievers." *Harvard Business Review* 84, no. 6: 72–82.

Trinidad, Cristina, and Anthony H. Normore. 2005. "Leadership and Gender: A Dangerous Liaison?" *Leadership & Organization Development Journal* 26, no. 7: 574–590.

Valentine, Sean, and Godkin, Lynn. 2000. "Supervisor Gender, Leadership Style, and Perceived Job Design." *Women in Management Review* 15, no. 3: 117–129.

LAUNCHING PAD

Applegarth, Mike. 2006. *Leading Empowerment: A Practical Guide to Change.* Oxford: Chandos.

Cacioppe, Ron. 1997. "Leadership Moment by Moment!" *Leadership & Organization Development Journal* 18, no. 7: 335–345.

Dewey, Barbara I. 2005. "Leadership and University Libraries: Building to Scale at the Interface of Cultures." *Journal of Library Administration* 42, no. 1: 41–50.

"Inside the Mind of the Leader." *Harvard Business Review* 82, no. 1 (January): 6–109.

Dearstyne, Bruce W. ed. 2001. *Leadership and Administration of Successful Archival Programs.* Westport, CT: Libraries Unlimited.

Evans, G. Edward, and Patricia Layzell Ward. 2007. *Leadership Basics for Librarians and Information Professionals.* Lanham, MD: Scarecrow Press.

Kouzes, James M., and Posner, Barry Z. 2003. *The Leadership Challenge.* San Francisco: Jossey-Bass.

Mavrinac, Mary Ann. 2005. "Transformational Leadership: Peer Mentoring as a Values-Based Learning Process." *Portal: Libraries and the Academy* 5, no. 3 (July): 391–404.

Mosley, Pixie Anne. 2005. "Mentoring Gen X Managers: Tomorrow's Library Leadership is Already Here." *Library Administration & Management* 19, no. 4 (Fall): 185–192.

Mullins, John, and Margaret Linehan. 2005. "Leadership and Followership in Public Libraries: Transnational Perspectives." *International Journal of Public Sector Management* 18, no. 7: 641–647.

Politis, John. 2001. "The Relationship of Various Leadership Styles to Knowledge Management." *Leadership & Organization Development Journal* 22, no. 8: 354–364.

Winston, Mark. 2005. "Ethical Leadership: Professional Challenges and the Role of LIS Education." *New Library World* 106, nos. 5/6: 234–243.

Part III

Managing Resources

15

Managing People

"It is safest to employ honest men, even though they may not be the cleverest."
                                    Ekken Kaibara

"Good management consists in showing average people how to do the work of superior people."
                                    John D. Rockefeller

INTRODUCTION

January 1, 2006, was a significant date for many organizations, especially those in the United States. That was the day the first of the Boomer generation started turning 60, and thoughts of retirement became sharper. Why does this matter?

The answer is that Boomers make up the largest group in the workforce in the United States. Veterans comprise less than 10 percent, Generation X represents 34 percent, and Millennials only 12percent, the rest, 44 percent, are Boomers (Bridges and Johnson, 2006: 7). These numbers more or less mirror the population distribution which means the size of the workforce pool will be declining in the future. Not only will the workforce pool be smaller; as the last of the veterans and the Boomers begin to retire, organizations lose skills and knowledge, most of which took years to develop on the job rather than from classroom training sessions. Organizations are starting to recognize this as a serious issue and are taking steps to address it; in large part these steps are changes in personnel/retirement policies.

David Drickhamer opened his article with the following statement: "Many operations managers believe as a matter of faith that if they take care of their employees—offer continuous training, regularly assess their performance, and treat them with the same respect with which they would like to be treated—those employees will help deliver superior performance. Lo and behold, it's true" (Drickhamer, 2006: 42).

What makes for a great information service? Strong financial resources and a fine physical facility are important to success. Sound information resources geared to meeting the service community's requirements are also a major asset. However, in our view, the true key to having a great service is the quality and motivation of the people who make things happen. At the end of the day, the "people factor" is what makes or breaks a service. As older staff retire, they take with them essential knowledge and skills that need not be lost with a little foresight and planning. All the issues raised in the Drickhamer quotation are essential to having quality people who are motivated to provide the very best possible service. There are some other factors as well that we will address in this chapter.

With a sound human resource management (HRM) program, you can meet the challenges of poor facilities and/or inadequate funding. By actively planning for staffing needs and the careful selection and training of personnel, you can help to assure that the service program will be as effective as possible, given the available resources.

Staffing has never been simple, but in the past 25 years it has become increasingly complex. In many countries, increasing government regulations regarding employment practices (from recruitment to dismissal, resignation, and retirement) have created challenges for anyone involved in HRM.

Other factors complicating staffing are stagnant or diminishing budgets that often require staff adjustments, changing expectations of staff regarding the workplace, and employees' concerns about compensation and benefits. Recruitment and retention have become major concerns in most organizations, not just information services. Finding and keeping people with the requisite skill sets is a challenge that grows more problematic as people retire. Addressing the various issues requires attention to detail as well as changing labor legislation.

Probably 90 percent of a manager's time goes to handling "people issues" rather than technical problems. Most of the earlier chapters dealt with management activities first and people factors second. Here we look at how a service should go about attracting and retaining staff and retaining the best of them. As Keith Hammonds (2005: 92) noted, HRM is "about how you get the best and brightest people."

THE STAFFING PROCEDURE

Getting the best and brightest does not magically occur. You need to expend a significant amount of time on thoughtful planning. Effective HRM programs utilize a series of steps, all of which require a thorough understanding of the country's employment laws and regulations. Once that understanding exists, the staffing procedure normally consists of eight steps:

1. determining needs
2. job design
3. recruitment
4. selection
5. orientation and training
6. evaluation
7. coaching and discipline
8. resignation and termination

LEGAL CONCERNS IN HUMAN RESOURCE MANAGEMENT

Before exploring the eight HRM steps we will start by looking at legal issues that impact those steps. There are four primary areas where legal concerns come into play in HRM. Perhaps the most significant concerns are laws impacting recruitment and selection which lay out factors in assuring equal opportunities for employment. When it comes to retention, legislation exists that impacts what you can and can't do in terms of compensation/benefits as well as health and safety factors. Finally, for many public sector information services, there are issues about labor contracts and other aspects of labor relations.

Tip:

In the United States there are two useful Web sites for keeping current on HR legal issues: HRLegisState.com (state and federal employment law) and HRTools.com (compliance ideas for diversity, harassment, disability, and discipline/termination).

During the past 25 to 35 years, many countries passed legislation intended to assure equal employment opportunity for all citizens. The goal of U.S., U.K., and European Community legislation is to create an environment that protects employers, employees, and prospective employees while assuring that all citizens have equal access to employment opportunities.

Over the past 20 years, in the United States, it seems that every few months there is a new law, court decision, regulation, set of guidelines, or new court interpretation of some previous guideline or regulation that impacts on personnel matters. Monitoring the social, political, and legal dimensions of personnel or human resource management can be a full-time job.

Many of the legal issues in HRM in the United States trace their roots back to the U.S. Constitution and the right of equal opportunity. As is often the case, national legislation follows after state action has led the way. Thus, it was New York State that passed the first U.S. fair employment practices law. It was not until the 1964 Civil Rights Act that federal legislation addressed the issue.

In the United States, fair or *equal employment opportunity* (EEO) refers to an individual's right to employment and promotion without regard to race, color, religion, sex, age, health, or national origin. Any employer who does take such factors into consideration is practicing either *overt* or *covert discrimination*. Today, few employers purposefully fail to follow the various EEO laws. More often than not, the problem is covert—the outcome of procedures or processes that, while not intending to discriminate, have an outcome that is discriminatory (unlawful). (Note: The concept applies to all phases of employment—not just hiring, but promotion, training opportunities, etc.)

Many seemingly "fair" procedures, such as pre-employment tests, can be discriminatory if the test results in certain categories of applicants failing the test at a higher rate than the average for the test (covert discrimination). Testing, evaluation, and selection of new employees *must* be done in terms of real job-related criteria or *bona fide occupational qualifications* (BROQ), to use the U.S. legal phrase. Generally, race, color, religion, age, sex, ethnic background, disability, or marital status are not valid criteria. "Generally" is the term used, because there may be circumstances where one or more of the above may be legal requirements, for example, when selecting models for advertising or actors for a play/movie. However, in the case of information services, none of the authors are aware of a circumstance in which any of the above would be a BROQ for a service position.

Another HRM phrase used in the United States which is important to understand is *affirmative action*. Until very recently, affirmative action required employers to make an extra effort to hire and promote people in one of the "protected minorities." (Under U.S. federal law, using current terminology, the protected groups are: women, Latino/Latina, Asian and Pacific Islanders, African-Americans, and American Indians.) The goal of affirmative action is to counteract the effects of past discrimination, even though the current employer may not have had any role in creating past inequalities. In essence, the goal is to have the workforce more or less mirror the composition of the population in the local job market.

By the mid 1980s, affirmative action plans were legally complex, and some employers and nonprotected groups believed they were too complex.

A 1987 U.S. Supreme Court decision in *Johnson v. Transportation Agency, Santa Clara County*, started a process that has in some ways reduced the complexity from a legal point of view, but made it more confusing in practical terms.

For Further Thought:

The legislation concerning equal employment opportunity varies from country to country. Check on the relevant legislation for your country or state, and draw up two lists—one of its strengths and the other of its weaknesses.

Examples of Major Employment Legislation

	U.S.
1963	Equal Pay Act
1964	Civil Rights Act
1967	Age Discrimination Act
1970	Occupational Safety & Health Act
1974	Privacy Act
1978	Pregnancy Discrimination Act, Mandatory Retirement Act
1986	U.S. Supreme Court Ruling on Sexual Harassment
1986	Immigration and Control Act
1988	Worker Adjustment and Retraining Act
1990	Americans with Disabilities Act
1991	Civil Rights Act
1993	Family and Medical Leave Act

As noted earlier, employment legislation and regulation touches on all aspects of HRM, from recruitment to retirement. To conclude this section of the chapter, we will briefly outline some of the areas that a manager must keep in mind. Library managers *must* draw on the assistance of and depend upon their human resources/personnel offices to avoid making mistakes that could cost the organization large sums of money.

Legislation may set a national minimum wage, which is a factor for many services, such as public and academic libraries, that frequently depend on part-time student workers. Government regulations may also set the hours that an employee should work per day or pay period. Requiring someone to work beyond the legal amount requires paying a higher rate, such as "time and a half" or "double time." In some cases, the regulations may limit the options of either or both the employer and employee as to the form of extra compensation—time off or money.

EEO and affirmative action certainly play a role in where and how you recruit for a position. They influence the types of information and questions that you may and may not collect or ask during the recruitment/selection phase. It is common for services to use a "search committee" to select a new employee from a pool of applicants, especially for professional positions. Selection/search committees seldom consist of individuals well versed in employment law, and therefore they can unknowingly cause problems. Most HR offices send copies of interview guidelines to the person they understand will make the selection decision. It is up to that individual to share the information with committee members.

A potential problem area that is frequently overlooked is an implied promise/contract. Sometimes managers/supervisors have a very strong candidate that they hope to convince to accept the position. In attempting to "sell" the service and its parent organization, the manager may make a statement that can later be interpreted as an implied contract. A simple comment, such as "we always get an annual wage increase," may come back to haunt the speaker when there is no annual increase. If an applicant is given a summary of the major points in the personnel manual or benefits program, it is important to make it clear these are guidelines or reflect current practice and are not guaranteed in the future.

Workplace health and safety issues are frequently part of state or national employment laws and regulations. The Occupational Safety and Health Administration (OSHA) in the United States handles many of the issues such as workplace air quality, exposure and handling of materials that may pose a long-term health threat, and the required safety equipment. In the United States there are laws—local, state, or national—that relate to issues such as smoking and passive smoke in the workplace, AIDS in the workplace, and substance abuse. All of these issues involve dual rights or concerns; for example, the person who smokes and feels he/she has the right to smoke at work and the nonsmokers who think they have a right to a smoke-free workplace. These tend to be highly complex issues and a challenge to resolve.

For Further Thought:

List six aspects of information service work that could be affected by health and safety at work legislation. Then check the legislation for your country or state to see whether legislation or regulation covers them.

Most countries have legislation and regulations regarding unionization and/or collective bargaining. In the United States, one encounters a variety of situations where information services must work with unions or collective bargaining units. Many services have no such units, some only have staff unions, others have all nonsupervisory staff in a union or bargaining unit, and a small number have all but a very few of the top administrative staff in such groups. Regardless of what staff or how many staff are part of such groups, the contract or agreement adds another layer to HRM activities.

Finally, there are regulations that impact the benefits of the employees. These range from retirement program contributions to paid and unpaid leaves for maternity/paternity, or other family reasons.

DETERMINING STAFFING NEEDS

Assessing staffing needs involves several steps, starting with an assessment of existing staff. The purpose of the process is to help identify what type and how many staff you will need in the future. Doing an inventory of current staff in terms of years of experience (perhaps grouped into categories of 5, 10, 15 years of experience), skill sets (linguistic, technical, professional, customer relations), and potential for advancement helps start the process.

One of the authors uses the following method for calculating staffing needs:

Current staff

↓

Minus Losses

↓

Minus No Replacements

↓

Plus New Positions

ll

Staffing Needs

When it comes to estimating losses, you should consider four factors: retirements (relatively easy to project), promotions and/or transfers, terminations (voluntary and nonvoluntary), and deaths (a guess at best). One way to project a number for the last three factors is to assume past rates will probably continue at the same level in the future. Needless to say, you must be comfortable with such an assumption. If there is reason to believe opportunities for promotion will be better or worse than in the recent past, past history will be of little value in predicting needs. Today, more and more organizations are asking about retirement plans/timeframes (Fisher, 2006) to assist both in planning for needs as well as in thinking about how to address institutional memory loss.

Unfortunately for many services, estimating the number of positions lost (nonreplacement) is a significant issue. Budget cuts are a major factor in losing positions; all too often a "temporary hiring freeze" becomes a permanent reduction in staff. New technologies may result in the loss of one type of position but will add a new type. Changes in service emphasis may cause a reduction or phasing out of one type of position and an increase in another type. Reorganizations also result in changing skill set needs.

Estimating new positions must draw on reality, not wishful thinking. For most libraries, it is easier to secure additional funding for things than it is to get authorization to add new staff. Thus, estimates of changing types of staff for existing positions (usually referred to as full-time equivalents, or FTE) are usually more accurate than estimates of new FTEs. New programs, new buildings, and increased workloads are the normal basis for requesting additional FTEs. Unless you are very fortunate or have secured outside funding for a new position, it is uncommon to gain approval for an additional position with the first or even second request.

Conducting such a staffing-needs assessment every three or four years provides you with useful information and lead time for gaining the necessary approvals. It also ties long-term and strategic-planning activities to the staff-management process. It also helps the HR office provide better and timelier assistance in the recruitment and selection process, if the service shares the information with the office.

Assessment of Labor Availability

Assessing the "labor market" is something you should do. As Bridges and Johnson (2006) noted, there are core issues to learn about: "demographic trends, generational differences, continuous improvement opportunities, and experience and skill gaps are all areas that must be well understood.... The root causes of both the skilled staff shortage and aging workforce are related and include:

- demographic trends affecting the size of the available workforce
- demographic trends affecting the age of the available workforce
- attraction of both industry and position available
- hiring freezes and tenure based retention (Bridges and Johnson, 2006: 8).

We believe that the last two points are particularly important for information services.

Many countries have and do make periodic estimates of occupational supply and availability. Schools educating people for information work use such estimates to expand or contract their programs. Services use the estimates to project salary requirements; a person with a skill set in high demand and short supply will command a higher salary than when there is a greater supply. Increasing the level of compensation by a substantial amount for an FTE can be almost as difficult as securing an additional position. It can also create pay equity issues for other staff members.

Knowing how many FTEs to assign to a job type is part of the process of assessing staffing needs. Making this judgment calls for hard data. If the organization has some existing workload standards, the process is somewhat easier; often union or collective bargaining agreements address this issue. In the absence of standards or data, the process is more difficult. Almost any unit head would like to have additional staff and can give several sound reasons why such an addition is justifiable. Techniques that help measure work activities are of great value in making a judgment about when enough is enough (see Chapter 11). Lacking time to collect accurate in-house data, services can secure some measure of objectivity by making comparisons with units of similar size.

Hard data about past and present workloads and time to complete various tasks is important in deciding staffing levels in a particular unit. However, changes in technology and equipment must be factored in before making a final decision. As an example, one of the authors became the director of a library that was spending about $350,000 (U.S.) on materials for the collections. During the next two years, efforts to increase funding for collection building produced results. Naturally, the head of acquisitions requested additional staff to handle an increasing workload. At the time the unit was using a manual system. Comparisons with similar-size acquisition units did not suggest that additional staffing was essential, so, despite the protests, there was no increased staffing. In the third year, the library acquired an integrated automation system which included an acquisition module. Fifteen years later the acquisition budget was $2.8 million (U.S.) and the department handled the increase with a net decline of one FTE. Such an increase in funding for acquisitions could *not* have been handled without new technology.

Job Descriptions

We will use a model that U.S. Department of Labor suggests for developing job descriptions and deciding on the proper selection instruments. Figure 15.1 illustrates the model.

The analysis of staffing needs obviously must take organizational goals (OG) and long-term plans into consideration, just as decisions regarding staffing patterns. We emphasize this point, since it is a step that is overlooked in many services.

Figure 15.1
U.S. Department of Labor Model for Developing Job Descriptions

OG (Organizational Goals)
↓
JD (Job Design)
↓
JSC (Job Success Criterion)
↓
JS (Job Specifications)
||
SI (Selection Instruments)

Job Design

Job design (JD) asks the question, "What activities are necessary to accomplish organizational goals?" Answers to this apparently simple question are multiple and complex at times. The goal should be to have a comprehensive list of all tasks, not merely a few broad phrases. For example, a response for a reference service point should be more than "answer questions." It should cover all aspects of the work, such as providing answers to in-person questions, providing answers to telephone questions, handling e-mail queries, and providing users with assistance in finding information. Such detail is essential for developing sound job descriptions.

Once you have a list of tasks, it is possible to group them into logically related activities. To assist in the analysis, divide the activities into smaller units, called *elements*. An element is one action, such as opening incoming mail or reading e-mail messages. It is at this point that you may realize the person doing the action is either at a higher or lower level of skill set than is appropriate. Sometimes regrouping actions allows you to improve the unit's cost-effectiveness.

The grouping or regrouping of elements into related actions results in what HR officers refer to as *tasks*. The following would be a set of elements grouped into the task "sort e-mail reference questions":

- log in to e-mail account
- read e-mail questions
- decide who can best answer the question(s)
- forward question(s) to appropriate person
- log off

Your next step is to group related tasks into a *position*, a grouping of tasks performed by one person. As an example, an archivist and coordinator of records retention might constitute a position. Note: Everyone in the service occupies a position, and a position is not necessarily full-time.

A group of similar positions constitute a *job*, such as records manager. Only in the smallest organizations will there be a one-to-one relationship of positions and jobs. In most cases there will be several people in a job category. The elements, tasks, positions, and job become the basis for the job and position description used to recruit and select personnel.

For HR officers there is another step, that of developing a classification system. The purpose of a classification plan is to group together jobs that require the same skill sets and provide similar compensation to people in a given class. Because most services are part of larger organization, most likely there will be overlap between positions—with different position titles—that have the same basic skill set; some system should be in place to assure equal pay for equal work. An example might be an information service staff member who is also responsible for maintaining the networked server(s) that provide remote access. Such a person probably has a skill set similar to that of a person working in a computer center who is responsible for maintaining its servers. Note: Classification systems establish salary *ranges*, which means there can still be salary differences for individuals in the same classification category. (See Figure 15.2, which lists monthly salary ranges).

Job Success Criterion

Another step is establishing job success criteria (JSC). JSC are the key to selecting the right person for the right position. Establishing JSC is the most difficult and subjective of the steps in the model. While the goal of the process is simply to state, "what distinguishes successful from unsuccessful performance in the position," it is difficult to carry out. What constitutes

Figure 15.2 Title and Pay Classification—Occupational Subgroup			
Title Code	**Name**	**Range**	**Steps**
5007	Secretary II	$1,831–2,291	5
5008	Secretary I	$1,527–1,868	4
6456	Program Assistant II	$1,949–2,537	5
6457	Program Assistant I	$1,831–2,291	5
6759	Library Assistant IV	$2,087–2,305	5
6760	Library Assistant III	$1,949–2,537	5
6761	Library Assistant II	$1,831–2,291	5
6762	Library Assistant I	$1,527–1,868	4

success will vary from service to service, and from time to time in the same service. Many professionals would agree that the following items could/ should be on any list of JSC for a service position that handles user research questions:

- accurately determine the nature of questions
- provide accurate answers to questions

However, they might modify their view if any of the following were to occur:

- accurate, but is abrasive to user
- accurate, but is "talkative" with selected users and handles fewer questions
- accurate, quick, and pleasant with users, but abrasive with service staff

Before starting to interview candidates, you or the search committee should understand what JSCs are appropriate and sought for the open position. Also, it is essential that JSCs are the result of agreement among those currently performing the work, senior management, and the parent body HR office.

Job Specifications

Job specifications (JS) are the skills, traits, knowledge, and experience that should result in successful performance. JSs frequently appear in job descriptions and advertisements as educational background or degree required, years of experience, and a list of the specific skills sought. From a legal point of view, one should be certain that the items listed are in fact BFOQ (bona fide occupational qualifications). Merely saying that it is so will not satisfy a court; you must be able to prove it is true. Thus, in the United States, one should not say that a master's degree in library or information science is required unless one is ready to prove that the degree is necessarily a prerequisite for success in the position.

For Further Thought:

Look at four advertisements for posts in information and library services. What information is provided about (a) the organization advertising the post; (b) the post itself; and (c) the criteria for appointment? Compare the amount of information provided.

Selection Instruments

After completing the job/position description which draws on the JSC and JS, you should be able to identify the appropriate selection instruments (SI). During the 40-plus years of legislation regarding equal employment and affirmative action, there have been numerous U.S. court cases that in one way or another impact the selection process. Often the cases grew out of requirements that were not clearly associated with successful job performance or were vaguely stated. An example of an imprecise statement is "the successful applicant will have a lively personality." We don't know which would be more difficult to prove: (a) that a lively personality was *essential* for successful job performance, or (b) what factors are present in a "lively" personality. A better way of getting at what the writers of such statements were looking for would be to seek individuals with a "demonstrated ability to work effectively with customers and staff in a highly service-oriented environment." Although more "wordy," it is much clearer on what the service is seeking and less open to question. Another example would be instead of using the phrase "good speaking ability," use something like, "make oral presentations of technical material in such a manner as to be easily understood by a nontechnical audience."

Both of these suggested wordings could lead to appropriate selection instruments. For the first statement, evidence of demonstrated success could take the form of letters from previous supervisors and/or coworkers that specifically address the issue. Or, members of the search committee might ask the referees a question about the issue. Whichever method the selection committee or person decides upon, the applicant(s) should know there will be inquiries about the issue.

Making the Final Selection

There are several basic instruments to assist in making the final selection from a pool of applicants: application forms, letters or written statements of interest in the position, tests, reference checks, physical exams (often a requirement of the larger organization rather than the service), interviews, and oral presentations by the candidate. Whichever instruments you select, there must be a clear link from instrument to JSC and JS.

Written testing is usually done only in positions that have modest to low-level responsibilities, although some civil services have written tests for all positions—professional and nonprofessional. Oral presentations and/or the use of an interview question such as, "What would you do in the following situation...?" are a form of testing.

While it may appear self-evident that all applicants should go through an identical screening process, that is not always the case. (Asking slightly different questions or adding or omitting an activity to a candidate's interview would constitute a different screening process.) Today, in the United States and in many other countries, identical screening is essential if the process is to be legal.

RECRUITMENT

Once you know the position needs, the search begins for suitable applicants. Many large services conduct national searches for their professional positions while drawing the majority of their nonprofessionals from the local area. Immigration policies now make it more difficult to recruit people internationally.

Advertisements for openings should provide the basic job description information and indicate where and when a person should apply. Recruitment takes time; in the United States, a national search will probably require four to six months. That estimate covers the time from the development of the position description to the time the successful applicant begins work. In the United Kingdom, a number of special employment agencies provide a service that includes identification of possible candidates, initial screenings, and drawing up a short list.

The search often begins as an internal process; that is, an announcement of a vacancy goes to the service's staff. In some organizations, the policy is to interview any internal candidates before going outside. More often, the search is both internal and external—with the internal applicants having the advantage of knowing more about the organization's issues. Services in the United States also must place advertisements or recruit in places where persons in the "protected categories" (Civil Rights Acts) are likely to see position announcements.

Once there is a pool of applicants, the review or screening process begins. The process involves several elements: the application form, letters or statements of interest, the pre-employment test results (if required), a personal interview, and verification of qualifications and past work experience. Normally, a service selects only a few persons for in-person interviews. Thus the screening process relies on the applicant to supply the requisite information regarding her or his qualifications.

Application Forms

The application blank can provide a great deal of information about the person completing it, not only from the data provided but also from its presentation. It can reveal a good deal about the individual's motivation, writing skills, maturity, and ability to understand and follow directions. Such forms usually provide information about:

- the applicant's work history, including tenure in each position listed
- the applicant's educational background
- names of persons to contact regarding the applicant's suitability for the position (this should also provide an explanation of circumstances under which the person knows/knew the applicant)

There are certain questions you may not ask either on the application or during the interview. These questions are those that could lead to discriminatory selection practices. Obvious questions about the applicant's race, religion, and age are not acceptable in the United States. Some forms have a space to indicate sex, but often indicate this is "optional" information. There are times when the information about the applicant's sex would be useful. For example, not everyone's given name clearly identifies her/his gender. When writing to an applicant prior to meeting, a person with a gender neutral name should be addressed as "Dear Applicant."

When using the phrase "or equivalent" for a skill or background, you must be ready to clearly state what is and is not equivalent. Because the application form normally provides the basis for the initial screening of applicants to determine interview invitees, the form should provide space to list information regarding equivalent training and experience. Individuals not chosen for interviews and perhaps lacking a formal degree may claim there was discrimination, because they have an equivalent background but were not interviewed. Having a space on the form or requesting a written statement regarding any "or equivalents" will usually satisfy legal requirements.

National searches as opposed to local ones present several special problems. Two significant problems are costs and time. Few organizations have enough money to pay the travel and lodging expenses of every potential candidate. It is also unreasonable to expect candidates to pay their own way unless they have a very good chance of being selected. As noted, information services normally only conduct national searches for high-level positions. Professional association conventions and meetings are a partial means of reducing costs. Many national associations operate "placement" centers at their annual meetings, which allow prospective employees and employers to easily contact a large number of persons. A limiting factor is that setting up a meeting time can be a challenge, since both the interviewer and interviewee will probably have program interests and obligations. Also, when using a search committee, only one person from the service will be making a judgment about a person's potential for the position.

Letters/Statements of Interest

Institution-based application forms usually are very general; they seldom provide the applicant with an opportunity to demonstrate why she/he is suitable for the position. Requesting a cover letter stating the applicant's interest in the position and what special skills/experience she/he has helps bridge the gap between an institution-wide application blank and an in-person interview.

For such statements to be useful, the applicant should receive a full copy of the job description, not merely the text of an advertisement. Advertisements tend to be short due to cost concerns, and they seldom provide enough information for preparing meaningful statements. Posting the full description on the Web gives the applicant a better understanding of the job's duties and what her/his chances are for further consideration, as well as what to include in a statement. Most applicants and screeners believe such documents are very helpful, as they provide a fuller and fair picture of the applicant's qualifications.

Tests

When a vacant position calls for "testable" skills, it is very useful to have pre-interview tests. Testing has been criticized on several grounds: invalidity, invasion of privacy, or discrimination against certain classes of applicants. The only pre-employment tests that are legal in information service settings are those that assess a common skill: typing, alphabetizing, numerical computation, or similar measurable traits. A number of such tests exist, and they are valid. If a JSC is the requirement to type 70 words a minute error-free, there is no reason to interview a person who only manages to achieve 30 error-free words per minute. This, of course, assumes the 70 word error-free requirement is valid.

Skill tests are also useful during an interview, as the interviewer can discuss the test results with the applicant. Someone lacking the necessary skill for a particular position will usually recognize this fact when reviewing the test results. Such recognition may provide motivation to improve in certain skill areas in order to pass similar tests in the future. It also provides the applicant with an opportunity to give a satisfactory explanation why she/he had a problem in taking the test. If the interviewer believes there is merit in the explanation, the applicant can be given an opportunity to retest, using a different but equal version.

Interviews

The interview provides the opportunity to explore in-depth the applicant's background, experience, knowledge, and expertise, as well as oral and social skills. From the applicant's point of view, the interview provides an opportunity to assess the position, potential coworkers, and the institution. Interviews and how you handle them is a key component in hiring the best and brightest staff members. Careful planning of the interview process on your part will allow you to secure the most useful information in the time devoted to interviewing.

There are six aspects that ought to be part of any interview process. The first aspect is planning. Beyond the obvious—such as when to conduct the interview—some of the key planning issues are: where to interview, who should do the interview, what questions to ask, what the candidate ought to see, and how much time to build into the process for responding to candidate interests.

Check These Out:

Here are two excellent resources to assist you in understanding and planning interviews for job applicants:

Collins, Jim. 2001. *Good to Great*. New York: Harper Business Books.
Yate, Martin. 1987. *Hiring the Best*. Boston, MA: B. Adams.

The second, and perhaps the most critical, aspect of the interview process (especially in the United States) is the set of interview questions. This part is crucial for assuring that the service satisfies EEO requirements. Having a reasonably structured format is one of the best ways of assuring compliance. This helps ensure consistency and comparability of information about each candidate. It is also helpful in maintaining control of the interview and, at times, keeping an overly talkative candidate "on track." In the long run, the structure helps everyone (interviewers and candidate) get the most out of their time together.

Questions you ask *must* be job-related. You should be able to link each question to the job description. Lacking such a linkage, it would be best not to ask the question. At the same time you link questions to a job description, asking some open-ended questions can be beneficial. Open-ended questions give candidates an opportunity to respond more fully and demonstrate some of their skills. They also allow the interviewers to learn about oral skills and, at times, to assess the candidate's ability to respond to an unexpected situation.

Figure 15.3 provides a very brief guide to some of the topics covered by U.S. employment laws, with examples of legal and questionable questions.

Following are a few examples of legal open-ended questions that could apply to a variety of vacant positions.

- What would your (current or former) supervisor tell a friend about you?
- What special skills do you think you would bring to this job?

- Who and what has motivated you in the past?
- When did you last perform the duties of our vacant position?
- How would you handle the following situation? (Give some typical "problem" a person performing the job might face.)
- What did/do you most like and dislike about your prior/present position?
- What do you consider one of your major accomplishments in your present position?
- What goals did you set for yourself in your current/last position?
- What does the term "service" mean to you?
- How might you improve your job skills?
- Where do you see yourself a year from now? In three years? Five years? Ten years?
- What would you like to ask me/us about the job, the library, and/or the community?

Having a list of questions helps assure that the interview process both gathers *and* gives information; these form the third aspect of the complete interview process.

Figure 15.3
Brief Guide to Legal (U.S.) Interview Questions

Topic	Legal Questions	Discriminatory Questions
Family Status	Do you have any responsibilities that conflict with job attendance or travel requirements?	Are you married? What is your spouse's name? Do you have any children? Are you pregnant? What are your childcare arrangements?
Race, Physical Characteristics	None	What is your race? Are you of Asian extraction? To what race do you belong? You're from Mexico aren't you? Are you related to the Smith-Jones from Texas? (Any questions about parentage or relationships, national origins of parents or spouse.)
Religion	None (you may inquire about weekend availability.)	What is your religion? Which church do you attend? What are your religious holidays? Are you Catholic? What religious holidays will you take off if we hire you?

(cont'd.)

Figure 15.3
Brief Guide to Legal (U.S.) Interview Questions *(Continued)*

Topic	Legal Questions	Discriminatory Questions
Residence, Birthplace Nationality	What is your address? Where do you live? How long have you lived in _____?	Do you own or rent your home? Who resides with you? Where were you born? Where were parents born? May I see your birth certificate (or similar papers)? (You may ask if the candidate can supply such documentation if hired.) Are you a citizen? Where were you born? Does your visa allow you to work?
Sex, Living Arrangements	None	Are you married? How many children do you have? Any gender related questions.
Age	If hired, can you offer proof you are at least 18 years old?	How old are you? What is your birth date?
Arrests or Convictions of a Crime	Have you ever been convicted of crime? (You must state that a conviction will be considered only as it relates to fitness to perform the job sought.)	Have you ever been arrested?
Disability, Physical Abilities or Limitations	This job requires lifting and carrying; can you do that? Are you able to perform the essential physical functions of this job with or without reasonable accommodation? (Show the applicant the position description so she/he can give an informed answer.)	Do you have a physical disability? What is the nature of your disability or severity?
References	Statement that employment references will be checked.	Requirement for submission of "character" or religious references. ("Character" references are permitted for security or bonded positions.)
Notify in Case of Emergency	Name and address of *person* to be notified in case of accident or emergency.	Name and address of *relative* to be notified in case of accident or emergency.
Organizations	Are a member of _____? (It is permissible to ask about job related professional organizations.)	Are you a member of _____? (It is not permissible to ask about non-job related organizations.)

The fourth aspect of the process is the "personal impact" of both the candidate and the interviewers. Taking a few minutes at the start to create a friendly atmosphere helps candidates relax and be more effective during the formal interview. Things such as tone of voice, eye contact, personal appearance and grooming, posture, and gestures on the part of both candidate and interviewer influence both parties.

Related to impact is how the interviewer responds to the applicant (the fifth aspect). One trait interviewers must be careful to control is nonverbal behavior that may encourage or discourage an applicant in an inappropriate way. Another is to reflect interest in what the candidate is saying. Anyone with extensive experience with the interview process understands just how difficult controlling those two behaviors can be at times.

The sixth and final aspect is to process the information gathered fairly and equitably for all the interviewees. Some of the issues that can cause unfair processing are:

- overemphasis on negative information for one or two candidates
- stereotyping the "right" person for the position
- imprecise job information that leads to looking for irrelevant attributes in the candidates
- use of different weights for various attributes by different members of a search committee
- overuse of visual clues about the candidate that are not job-related
- placing too much emphasis on the candidate's similarity—such as sex, race, values—to interviewer
- not recognizing "contrast effects"—that is, when a strong candidate follows a very weak candidate, the contrast makes the stronger applicant look even stronger than she/he may be

Suggestions for Interviewees

- Research the service and parent organization ahead of time (go online).
- Develop a few questions to ask the interviewer(s) about the institution.
- Request a position description and develop a question or two about the position.
- Think about the answers you might give to questions that are likely to be part of the interview. (What interests you about this particular position? What do you consider your strengths and your weaknesses? What does the term "service" mean to you?)
- Dress appropriately.
- Be on time.

- Be certain to have the interviewer's/chairperson's name and learn the correct pronunciation.
- Remember that your "body language" also reflects your interest and attentiveness.
- Brief pauses before answering complex questions are appropriate—thinking before speaking is always a good idea.
- Respond to all parts of a multipart question; asking for clarification or for repetition of a part of such questions is appropriate.
- Asking how any personal or potentially illegal question(s) *relate to job performance* is appropriate; however, ask it in a nonconfrontational manner, as the question may be job-related.
- Thank the interviewer(s) for the opportunity to interview for the position.
- Ask about the anticipated time frame for deciding on who will be hired; this is appropriate.
- Make post-interview notes about some of the high and low points of the interview can be helpful in the future.

Verification and Evaluation

One of the more difficult and sensitive areas in any hiring procedure is verification of an applicant's education and work history. Letters of recommendation from former teachers and employers are often of questionable value due to the passage of time since the writer had direct contact with the applicant. It is not unheard of for a present employer to write and give glowing verbal recommendations for a person they wish would leave. Dismissing an employee may lead to legal action so some organizations "help" the person find employment elsewhere by giving less than full assessments.

Confidentiality issues may arise with references. Some public institutions in the United States state that candidates *may* see letters of recommendation. From the applicant's standpoint, it is unfortunate to keep using a person who is providing less than positive comments. On the other hand, it is almost impossible to secure an honest opinion in writing if the writer knows that the subject of a letter may see the recommendation. Some states (California and Colorado, for example) have open records laws that allow such examination, so use of letters may become even more of a rarity.

Another problem is fraudulent education or work history. One 1980s study in the United States found 17 percent of applicants misrepresented education, experience, or other job qualifications (*The Billings Gazette*, 1987). The researchers also noted that nine percent of people overstated their previous salaries. Only by checking can you determine whether or not the candidate has the skills and background claimed. An easy method for verifying a person's educational background is to require certified transcripts mailed directly to the service from each of the schools that the candidate lists. Likewise, any professional certification should be verified directly through the certifying agency. Photocopies and letters the candidate provides are not a satisfactory source of verification.

Final Decision

Once all the verification work is in, the final decision takes place. In most services, HR makes the call to the selected candidate to determine if the person is still available and interested in the position. HR is also usually the office that makes the decision on what salary and benefits to offer. Salary-level decisions are a mix of assessing the skills and background of the selectee, that person's prior salary history, and "equity" within the organization's and the work unit's salary structure. One of the most damaging events, in terms of morale, is to have a newcomer receive a higher salary than existing employees with similar skills, background, and experience.

When thinking about a salary offer, people, especially younger people, often only consider what is likely to appear on paychecks. (Even here, they often fail to think about the impact of taxes and other reductions on "take home" pay.) A more accurate way to think about the offer is the total compensation. Beginning and even some experienced managers think only of hourly, monthly, or annual pay rates, forgetting the benefits package and leave time. Both of these are part of the compensation package.

Good wages or pay have been powerful motivators to get people to work for an organization, and they still are in many countries. However, wages have lost some of their attraction and power in highly industrialized societies. When wages are more than enough to ensure survival or a decent standard of living, they begin to be less and less a motivating factor. This is *not* to say that money becomes unimportant. However, factors such as more challenging work, more meaningful activities, and time off play an equally important role.

Wages in industrialized societies become the "price" an organization pays to attract the types of talents and skills required to carry out its activities. In addition to wages, there can be all or some of the following "costs" in retaining employees:

- fully/partially paid health insurance
- fully/partially paid dental insurance
- fully/partially paid life insurance
- fully/partially paid disability insurance
- contribution to one or more retirement programs/pension schemes

- paid vacation and holidays
- paid sick leave
- paid family leave
- fully/partially paid educational expenses
- paid travel expenses for job-related training
- paid study leave
- subsidized mortgage
- relocation costs
- access to or provision of a maintained vehicle for travel between branches of the service
- bonus/awards for service or useful ideas

HR staffs know how to present the total compensation package so that a person may accept a position at a wage that is lower than the person originally thought was necessary. That office also works out a starting date for the new employee.

Check This Out:

Pat Tunstall's 2006 article "The Accidental Supervisor" (*Public Libraries* 45, no. 3: 50–57) is an excellent "case study" of the recruitment/selection process in a public library setting. The basics covered can apply to any information service that hires part-time support staff. The last three pages cover questions you might ask prospective part-time staff, a skill test for "pages," and an evaluation form.

THE NEW EMPLOYEE

A new employee's first few days on the job set the tone for what follows in terms of performance. "Glad to see you; go to work" is not the best method for getting a new person to become a productive employee. By planning a formal orientation process, you create a solid beginning for both the person and the service.

The first day for the new person should be a combination of orientation and some training in the job *and* time with HR to take care of all the new employee paperwork. Possible events for the first day might include:

- Start at the HR office to complete the hiring and payroll process.
- Escort new employee to the work area and reintroduce the person to her/his supervisor.

- Supervisor introduces person to other members of the department and the new employee is given a few minutes to put away personal items in desk/workstation.
- Supervisor provides a tour of the service and introduces new person to staff members and gives a short summary of what the person will be doing.
- Return to department for an overview of its activities.
- A demonstration of duties/activities the person is to perform.
- A period of supervised practice.
- Private practice time.
- A review session.

During this orientation/training time, which may last for some time when the tasks or duties are complex, the hiree should receive information about the significance of her/his duties. Earlier and frequent praise for work performed helps to develop a good working relationship.

New employees often find the first several days confusing and unsettling. Spreading orientation out over several days helps make the new information, people, and duties less overwhelming. The training also should be flexible in order to adapt to various learning speeds as well as the person's prior experience.

A new employee's past work experience may influence the way in which the person reacts to training. Experienced professional or supervisory personnel may require only an explanation of objectives, policies, practices, and potential problems. Beginning professionals should know the fundamentals of any starting position, though they will need to understand the local variations from standard practice. In any event, some monitoring will be necessary during the first month or two for beginners, as they will only know the basics.

Most clerical jobs demand careful, specific instruction, as do manual and unskilled jobs. Group training programs are very efficient for such positions, but turnover and the creation of new positions seldom allows for such training. Services that hire a large number of part-time workers are able to take advantage of group training as long as they plan the hiring process.

For Further Thought:

Review the events for the first day for a new employee. What information does a new employee need to be given on the first day? Try to list three points that would help to make a new employee feel welcome during the orientation process.

Tip:

Linking a new member of staff to someone at their level in the workgroup will provide a point of reference for any matters that require clarification—without the new employee feeling that she/he might be asking a supervisor a silly question. It helps the mentor by giving recognition and the motivation to check over those points that are often taken for granted.

DEVELOPING AND RETAINING STAFF

One concern for most of today's organizations is retention of their best people. Nora Spinks offered some interesting thoughts about generational difference and how that impacts retention: "If you were a child in the 50s (a Boomer), you saw that working hard was a strategy that led to success. Loyalty was rewarded with long-term employment through to retirement. However, if you were a child in the 70s or 80s (a Nexus), you saw adults working hard and getting laid off, downsized or reengineered out of a job anyway. Employment tenure was out of your control, employers offered you a job as long as they felt you were of value, then let you go" (Spinks, 2005: 11).

Check This Out:

Louis Uchitelle, a *New York Times* reporter, published an interesting book in 2006 about the loyalty question: *The Disposable American: Layoffs and Their Consequences* (New York: Knopf).

In many ways that approach by employers is coming back to haunt them. "Why should I have any loyalty to the organization if it has none for me?" is a question in the minds of most workers today. For many of them, all it takes is hint of staffing changes, real or imagined, or something else perceived as a threat to them, to get them started looking for some other work. They have experienced or heard of organizations that announce a staff reduction and actually say to the staff, "We don't need you but fully expect you to give a 100 percent work effort until the day you are terminated." The outcome was what you would expect; performance declined and people left as fast as possible.

With underlying "loyalty" weak at best, having programs that give ample opportunities to grow and develop is an important factor in long-term retention of the best and brightest people. You have two basic training/development areas to consider: specific job-related skills and career development competencies and opportunities.

Services today face a rapidly changing technological environment. Keeping staff current with the changes related to their activities is a major challenge, especially in times of "steady state" or declining budgets. Failure to maintain staff skills results in users receiving poorer service, which in turn leads to dissatisfaction. You face a dual technological challenge: acquiring and upgrading the necessary technology and finding funding for staff training. We will cover technology management in some detail in Chapter 18.

Beyond technological training, there are issues of providing training for individuals moving into supervisory/managerial positions as well as keeping staff current with changing professional standards. Other areas are training in handling "problem" users, disaster recovery, emergency procedures, security, and changing legal issues. All these areas fall into what HR officers call staff development.

Sometimes the HR office will offer institution-wide training that the service may find beneficial: basic supervision, improving writing skills, or communicating with customers. The only drawback to these programs is that, except for the very largest organizations, such programs seldom are given more than once a year and may not cover a topic any service staff need. In some countries, there are companies that offer similar types of programs. They come to a city and offer one-, two-, and sometimes three-day seminars or workshops. The major drawback of such programs is they are very general in character in order to draw enough participants to make the program profitable for the organizers, and they are seldom low-cost activities.

Professional associations are an excellent source of training opportunities. Such groups hold annual conventions and offer continuing education programs as part of the overall program. Unfortunately, there are very few such organizational opportunities for support staff. (The primary reason is that support staff have few opportunities for paid travel, and their salaries are substantially lower, making it almost impossible for them to pay for such programs on their own. Thus, staff associations have difficulty attracting enough people to a workshop to make the effort worthwhile.) As more educational institutions and professional bodies extend the range of distance education programs, training opportunities will increase—particularly with developments in computer and video conferencing.

In addition to funding concerns, you face the problem of limited staffing, at least in most services. With limited staff, it becomes difficult to have staff off at training programs for any length of time. Some jurisdictions are so shortsighted that they refuse to give time off to attend training programs even when the staff member is willing to pay for the program—shortsighted because in time the services become less and less effective.

PERFORMANCE APPRAISAL

Conventional management theory, at least in the United States, holds that performance appraisals are essential to the successful operation of any organization. In theory, it should help the worker to improve performance.
There is a substantial list of beliefs about the appraisal process:

- essential to good management
- natural, normal part of human activity
- assures at least minimum performance
- only valid method for granting or withholding economic benefits
- means of maintaining control of production/service
- essential for employee growth and development
- essential for motivating employees
- assesses quality/success of orientation and training programs
- means of objectively assessing an individual's work-related strengths and weaknesses
- reflects a continuous analysis of a person's daily work performance
- reflects an assessment of total performance, not just assigned duties
- reflects staff members' future and potential for advancement
- essential for planning library personnel needs
- key to successful counseling of staff members

This is an impressive list of objectives for a single process, but all writers on management and practitioners know the process has many land mines. They also know that only sometimes does the actual procedure match the ideal. In reality, the process has two goals that are seldom completely congruent. As you might guess from the above list, one goal is administrative in character and the other is behavioral. Administrative actions relate to the employee while the behavioral relate to actions the employee takes.

Aspects of the administrative goal are highly subjective in spite of the beliefs to the contrary. Thus, one aspect in the process becomes the basis for defending the decisions supervisors and managers make about salary increases, promotions, and dismissals. Another aspect is attempting to create "comparable data" from a series of subjective judgments by a number of supervisors/managers.

Confidential or secret aspects of the administrative process, where very few people know the results, are part of the need to have data to defend a judgment. Related to the preceding aspect is the fact that unless a person files a grievance, at least in the United States, the person seldom is *fully* informed about what and why certain judgments occurred. Finally, the appraisee becomes involved in the formal process only at the end.

Behavioral goals should help the individual identify areas where improvement is possible or necessary. These goals also identify areas where personal development might be desirable from the organization's point of view. Identifying exceptional performance is also to be part of the process. (Statisticians will tell anyone who will listen that the "bell-shaped" curve is the normal distribution of data; that is, the vast majority of cases will fall into the middle-average of the curve. On the other hand, anyone who reviews a significant number of appraisal forms knows that most organizations consist of primarily above-average or exceptional employees—mathematically impossible but managerially possible once a year.)

Saul Gellerman (1976) summarized the features of appraisal to achieve the "best" results:

Administrative Purposes	Behavioral Purposes
Secretive	Candid
Fixed	Flexible
Bureaucratic	Individualized

Attempting to achieve both sets of purposes in a single process is almost ludicrous. It would be better to utilize two separate systems, one for each set of purposes. (Many organizations claim they do this by calling the annual process an "annual development review" and asserting there is no connection between that process and any later salary adjustments; few employees believe this.)

To achieve the "comparable" data, organizations usually have an "appraisal form" that makes use of one of three format types: rating system, ranking system, and written performance criteria system. Ranking systems requires a supervisor to rank each subordinate from 1 to "n"—for example, a supervisor with seven subordinates would rank them from 1 to 7. Such systems require each person have an individual rank—no ties. Some supervisors who must use this system believe it can generate an environment in which teamwork becomes difficult, as there are no equals when it comes to performance assessment. The written system is the least comparable across the organization, even when there is a list of work-related factors the supervisor is to address for each subordinate.

Most rating systems use a five-level approach, with average in the middle and with two above and below average productivity. When it is time to conduct the appraisal process, there are some steps you can take to make it as positive as possible. One step is to make certain everyone has a shared understanding of the terms and categories used on the appraisal form.

To say, "you are a little below (or a little above) average, but not enough to warrant disciplinary action or to receive an award" will generate anger, arguments, tension, and frustration. The individuals receiving slightly below average are *not* likely to change their performance because they *know* the rater is wrong. For those slightly above but not rewarded, the most likely outcome is a *drop* in performance.

When you say to a person, "you did an average job this year," it usually results in the ratee thinking the rater cannot recognize excellence when it is sitting right in front of him/her. It generates anger and will not reinforce the person's good work habits.

The end result is a steady escalation of ratings until it appears as if all employees "walk on water" all year. That, in turn, leads to the organization imposing quotas that force supervisors to have a bell-curve result. One of the authors worked for one university that required every department to have one employee in the unacceptable category every year. Needless to say, this was difficult, unpleasant, and, in reality, inappropriate. One year the author dismissed a staff member and thought that would count for that year's "unacceptable" requirement, but received a surprise when told that did *not* count because the person was gone! The way the author circumvented the system was to get staff to agree that each person, including the supervisor, would each take a turn at being "unacceptable." A drawing of numbers set up the order. The result was an improvement in morale because everyone agreed it made the best of a bad situation.

Check These Out:

You can find an in-depth look at performance appraisal in general and in the context of information services in G. Edward Evans' 2004 book *Performance Management and Appraisal: A How-To-Do-It Manual* (New York: Neal-Schuman).

In 2006, Corey E. Miller and Carl Thornton explored the challenges of how to achieve reasonably accurate appraisals, in "How Accurate Are Your Performance Appraisals?" (*Public Personnel Management* 35, no. 2: 153–162).

A performance appraisal is not a universally accepted practice. W. Edward Deming (1993) listed evaluation by performance, merit rating, or annual review of performance as one of the seven deadly diseases of an organization . In many countries, the practice does not exist. For example, in 1982, Evans and Rugaas published an article that looked at variations in appraisal practices in various countries. In the United States there is a heavy emphasis on performance appraisals; in the United Kingdom, a moderate emphasis is placed on such appraisals; and in Nordic countries, there is no emphasis. In examining library performance in these countries, it was difficult to determine how the presence or absence of the practice influenced service. The situation may however change, since the U.K. government is pledged to policies based upon accountability in the public sector, which will extend to the individual worker.

Regardless of what you may think about the process, it does exist as a managerial fact of life in many countries. In such cases, you must learn to make the process as useful as possible. A key factor is that you must make certain there are no surprises for subordinates. Daily feedback—both immediate praise and correction—is the best way to assure good work performance. It will also provide some assurance there will be few, if any surprises at performance appraisal time.

For Further Thought:

Write down three reasons why you think that performance appraisal is important. List six points that you would wish to see covered in an appraisal interview?

Corrective Action

Naturally, you should discuss performance issues as they occur. The tendency to avoid any unpleasantness and to let the problem slide only hurts everyone in the long term. The employee may not even be aware there is something amiss until the annual review, when it is too late to take corrective action for the current review period. Further, other employees will observe the performance issues and may conclude you don't really care about performance. That in turn is likely to lead to their letting their work performance slide downhill. The result is a much more complex situation to resolve. Finally, the service also suffers, and in the end, so do the users.

Despite contentions of some human-relations school advocates, you should be willing to show displeasure when an individual performs in a grossly unacceptable manner—especially when it is a matter of willfulness or neglect. The idea that the superior-subordinate relationship is a delicate, fragile thing that can be easily destroyed by a hasty word or an ill-timed move on the part of the supervisor receives too much emphasis in the human-relations school.

A healthy system provides for a two-way exchange between supervisor and staff member. Each should be free to voice satisfaction or dissatisfaction. Attempts to avoid strains or other issues will bring great pressure on everyone and will solve nothing.

When it is necessary to take corrective action—for example, counseling sessions—there are some steps you can follow making the time as productive as possible. Start by stating the purpose of the session. Even if the situation has the potential for confrontation, speak quietly and plan on letting the employee talk as much as possible. *Listen* to the person; do not spend time planning a rebuttal. Periods of silence, even long ones, serve a good purpose—letting the parties think about what is taking place. Setting a time limit for the session often defeats the goal of the session as it may take a long time to get to the central issue(s). Expect the employee to be unhappy, probably argumentative, and occasionally, ready to initiate a "personal" attack. It is difficult but important not to take this behavior personally, or at least *not* respond in kind. Total resolution is not the only indication of a successful session. Sometimes it takes a series of sessions to reach a complete resolution. Try to end the session on a positive note and, if appropriate, schedule a follow-up session.

We subscribe to the "Five Rs" of performance counseling:

- right purpose
- right approach
- right time
- right technique
- right place

Some of the right purposes are to strengthen, maintain, or restore a working relationship; to motivate a person to greater productivity; to resolve personality conflicts; to discipline an employee; or to provide orientation or termination counseling. Right times are only when necessary, not when you are upset, during low activity times, and not too far in advance. In terms of place, it should be private—at a table not at a desk; do not allow telephone calls or other intrusions to interrupt the process. We touched on some of the approach factors in the preceding paragraph: little advance notice, start the session quickly and come to the point immediately, state the facts and do not accuse, and keep calm. After the initial statement, devote more time to listening rather than talking, and do not push the session. Finally, use one of two basic techniques, directive or nondirective. Directive sessions address issues such as rule or policy violations, correction of mistakes, and control of hostility. Nondirective meetings work best for concerns such as restoring a positive attitude or productivity, strengthening or restoring relationships, and motivating for greater teamwork.

For Further Thought:

Can you suggest four occasions when it might be necessary to take corrective action? What skills are needed to counsel a member of staff?

You ought to be as consistent as possible in your evaluations. Standards should not shift from one week to the next or alter from one employee to another. Remember that evaluating outcomes rather than the process (as long as the process does not cause trouble or problems) is the desirable goal.

Flexibility needs to be in concert with consistent evaluation. You should not hold a new employee as closely accountable for an error as an older, experienced person. This does *not* mean that you ignore the newcomer's problem. Naturally, a person lacking the skill to do a task needs additional training rather than criticism. If the training does not work, then other adjustments will be necessary.

Another step is to think about personal biases you have when it comes to judging people and their performance. Review prior appraisals, think about the next appraisal (keeping in mind any and all personal biases), and be ready to take further action if a person has a negative review for two years in succession.

In spite of your best efforts, there will be times when disciplinary action must occur. Needless to say, such action only follows after one or more counseling sessions have failed to resolve the issue. In the United States, HR units label the process "progressive discipline." What the process consists of is a series of steps that become progressively more severe and end with termination. Most of the time the process never reaches the termination stage as the parties resolve the issue earlier.

Effective supervisors/managers define "good discipline" as employee self-discipline that develops over time due to careful teaching, training, and guiding. Good discipline consists of six elements. It begins with training, mentoring, and teaching. After that there must be consistency, if one employee can or cannot behave/perform, you should begin a counseling process. Likewise, there is a need for consistency through time—not changing from day to day or with your mood. When you must take corrective steps, the action/step must be appropriate to the situation ("the punishment fit the crime"). The fourth element is to give credit whenever possible. Another element is remembering that the purpose is to correct not punish. Occasionally supervisors begin to think that their role is only to correct, and they forget to praise. Finally, *look* for opportunities to praise as often as watching for problems.

First-time supervisors often make the mistake of not addressing a problem early on. Frequently, it is because they know that in taking corrective action lies the potential for conflict, which they would rather avoid. Then, when they do take action, it is to "get tough," "crack down," and "show who is boss." More often than not, the result is a greater confrontation than would have occurred earlier because people are surprised by the abrupt change. The action taken is too severe and some or all of the trust that developed earlier generally disappears.

The authors have found the following dos and don'ts to be good guide
lines in handling corrective action or progressive discipline:

Policy

It is the policy that supervisory efforts should concentrate on developing
employees and on preventing serious personnel problems from occurring.
There will be times, however, when disciplinary action is appropriate.

Procedure

PROGRESSIVE DISCIPLINE

The service maintains a progressive discipline procedure to ensure a fair
method of disciplining employees. The progressive discipline system is
intended to give employees advance notice, whenever possible, of problems
with their conduct or performance in order to provide them an opportunity to correct any problems. Normally, progressive discipline involves oral
counseling and one or more written warnings before an employee is terminated. However, exceptions or deviations from the normal procedure may
occur whenever the service deems that circumstances warrant that one or
more steps in the process be skipped. Accordingly, circumstances may
sometimes warrant immediate termination. It should be remembered that
employment is at the mutual consent of the employee and the service.
Accordingly, either the employee or the service can terminate the employment relationship at will. If a problem arises which suggests that strong
action, such as a written warning, suspension or release from employment
be taken, the supervisor should immediately discuss the facts with his or
her supervisor and the director or assistant director of personnel services.

STANDARDS OF CONDUCT

Like all organizations, an information service requires order and discipline
to succeed and to promote efficiency, productivity, and cooperation among
employees. For this reason, it may be helpful to identify some examples of
types of conduct that are impermissible and that may lead to disciplinary
action, possibly including immediate discharge. Although it is not possible
to provide an exhaustive list of all types of impermissible conduct and
performance, the following are some examples.

1. Insubordination, including improper conduct toward a supervisor
   or refusal to perform tasks assigned by a supervisor in the appropriate manner.

2. Possession, distribution, sale, use, or being under the influence of alcoholic beverages or illegal drugs while on library property, while on duty, or while operating a vehicle or potentially dangerous equipment leased or owned by the service.
3. Release of confidential information about the service.
4. Theft or unauthorized removal or possession of property from the service, fellow employees, students, visitors or anyone on service property.
5. Altering or falsifying any time-keeping record, intentionally punching another employee's time card, allowing someone else to punch one's own time card, removing any time keeping record from the designated area without proper authorization or destroying such a record.
6. Absence for one or more consecutive workdays without notice to one's own supervisor or department head.
7. Falsifying or making a material omission on an employment application or any other service record.
8. Misusing, defacing, destroying, or damaging property of the service, a fellow employee, or a visitor.
9. Fighting on the property.
10. Bringing on the property dangerous or unauthorized materials, such as explosives, firearms, or other similar items.
11. Use of force or threat of force.
12. Misconduct.
13. Unsatisfactory performance.

A. What is progressive discipline?
1. It is a way of supervision that emphasizes prevention of serious personnel problems, not punishment of employees for misconduct.
   a. It helps determine the causes of unsatisfactory work or conduct.
   b. It helps improve employee performance.
   c. It ensures that employees have a fair chance to succeed on the job.
2. It is a procedure for taking thorough, corrective steps when it appears that an employee has failed to perform his or her work or conduct himself or herself in accordance with requirements.

B. Why do we have it?
1. We want effective employees: good work and good conduct.
   a. We work through others.
   b. Their success is our success.
2. We want to provide fairness and avoid having time-consuming personnel problems.

C. How does it work?

1. There are two main aspects of progressive discipline: being thorough and following a step-by-step procedure when a discipline problem arises.

   a. Being thorough means doing the following things when the employee appears to be at fault:

      i. Assess the situation—get the facts.

      ii. Weigh and determine the action to be taken, taking into consideration special circumstances, if any.

      iii. Act, being sure the action taken is appropriate to the offense.

      iv. Evaluate the action taken—did it work?

   b. Following a step-by-step procedure entails:

      i. oral warning

      ii. counseling

      iii. reprimand

      iv. suspension

      v. release

Corrective Action: What to Do

- consider the feelings of the individual
- keep "cool"
- analyze each situation
- show confidence in the individual's ability to make necessary changes
- *always* reprimand in private
- fully explain the problem and expected changes
- outline *specific* consequences of failure to change or future violations
- define objective of action(s) taken
- deal promptly with all rule violations

Corrective Action: What Not to Do

- sarcasm
- loss of temper
- humiliating an individual (using words that suggest a parent-child relationship)
- profanity and strong language
- public reprimands
- threats and/or bluffs
- showing favoritism
- delay tactics
- unduly harsh penalties
- inconsistent enforcement

Grievances

No matter how you try to work with and support staff, at some point in your career a situation will arise where a formal reprimand and/or dismissal are the only choices. When that happens, at least in the United States, you might anticipate the employee to file a grievance. (Note: Grievances can also arise out of a situation where there is a union contract for employees or when an employee believes she/he cannot get satisfaction from the supervisor.)

As with any step in the disciplinary/corrective process, it is important for you to maintain a solid paper record documenting what was done. Such a paper trail may include just a note on the desk calendar recording a discussion with Employee *X* about Situation *Y* that took place to memos to formal depositions.

Some writers liken a grievance to various stages of a river, where the goal is to stop the flow of water. At its source, it is a small trickle from a spring which is very easy to block. If not checked, it can become a small stream as additional issues accumulate and resolution becomes more complex, just as damming the stream is more difficult. As time passes without resolution, more and more baggage becomes attached to the original small issue. The grievance takes on a force of its own (a number of tributaries creating a river). Ultimately, it becomes a major river that is almost impossible to slow or stop.

The river analogy goes further in that a grievance takes many forms. It should follow existing channels—if present—or will cut its own in their absence. Its origin is difficult to determine from among multiple small sources. One can dam it up for a while (by not resolving the issue), but this only applies constant pressure on the dam and eventually will cause a weak point to collapse. Once the dam breaks, it is impossible to stop the flood; it must run its course. After the course is run, many things will have changed.

Providing a grievance procedure helps control "the river" by providing a channel for addressing the issue. Most large organizations have a procedure in place to handle such situations when they arise.

Whatever office or person receives the complaint, they must determine if the issue is "grievable." A grievable issue is work related and one that could be resolved through existing policies and procedures. Very often the first formal step, after determining the appropriateness of an issue, is for a person from HR or grievance committee/board to meet with the parties, including the supervisor's supervisor, to attempt to resolve the matter without further delay. Failure to resolve things at that time usually results in a formal "hearing" of the case by a group of individuals who have no association with the parties involved. Table 15.1 outlines a grievance procedure taken from a U.S. organization's HR manual and addressing a common type of grievance: "unfair disciplinary action."

Table 15.1
How the Staff Complaint/Grievance Committee Evaluates
Disciplinary Actions Taken

The process described in this outline is considered a reasonable test of "just cause," i.e., whether a supervisor has been fair and impartial in carrying out corrective action in a given case.

1) What evidence is available that the employee was aware of the rule s/he was punished for violating?
    a) Was this rule published in writing?
    b) Was it conspicuously and properly posted on department bulletin boards customarily used for announcements?
    c) Is the rule stated in clear, concise, easy-to-understand language?
    d) Did the organization make copies of this and other rules available to employees?
    e) How long has this rule been in effect?

2) Is the rule violated a reasonable one?
    a) Does it conform to acceptable organization and social practices?
    b) Does it appear to be justified for valid economic or safety reasons?
    c) Does it subject employees to any embarrassing social or personal indignities?
    d) Any indication that the rule is capricious, arbitrary, or punitive?

3) Did the supervisor investigate before taking action?
    a) Was the investigation thorough, fair, and objective?
    b) Did the supervisor have substantial evidence or proof?

4) What evidence is available that the rule has been consistently enforced against all employees in an impartial manner and without discrimination?
    a) Any evidence that this employee has been "singled out" for disciplinary purposes?
    b) Any evidence that other employees violated this rule without disciplinary action resulting?
    c) Are factual individual performance records available on all employees?
    d) If appropriate, did this employee receive adequate training compared with other employees?

5) What means were used to notify this employee that violation of this rule would place his or her job in jeopardy?
    a) What corrective action did the supervisor prior to disciplinary action take?
    b) What evidence is available that the employee received a formal warning prior to discharge?
    c) Does the organization's past practices show a consistent record for discharge following a "final warning"?

6) In this case, does the penalty meet the test of reasonableness?
    a) What is the employee's past record?
    b) Based on the employee's past record and his/her length of service, does the "punishment fit the crime"?
    c) What has been the organization's past practice on this type of rule violation?
    d) What actual damage resulted to the organization from this violation?

It is possible that another step could follow the committee/board action which would involve bringing in an arbitrator or mediator from outside the organization. Arbitrators/mediators will look for most of the same issues as the grievance committee.

Even the "objective outsider's" judgment may not be acceptable to the grieving party. In the United States, that situation is very likely to lead to a lawsuit. The following section lists some issues that can (and have) led to grievances and occasional lawsuits. The list is long and illustrates just how complex personnel management has become.

POTENTIAL LAWSUIT ISSUES

Sexual Harassment/Discrimination

- Nonrenewal of employment contract because of refusal to engage in romantic relationship with senior administrator.
- Claims that senior staff member(s) engage in sexual relationships/harassment of employees.
- Reverse discrimination suits by employees whose positions are terminated and filled by minority individuals.
- Resignation of staff because pervasive sexism created intolerable environment.
- Claims by female security officers of harassment by supervisors and fellow officers.

Downsizing/Reductions in Workforce

- Claims alleging layoffs of older long-service employees constituted age discrimination and/or sex discrimination.
- Claims that terminations violated employee handbook regarding implied contracts, notice, assurances regarding every reasonable effort to find comparable employment within institution.
- Suits alleging wrongful termination, breach of contract, emotional distress/defamation when terminations related to both financial crisis and poor performance.

Discrimination

- Suits by staff alleging failure to grant security of employment based on age, sex, and racial discrimination.
- Claims by handicapped employees alleging failure to provide reasonable accommodation.

Wrongful Termination

- Suits by employees alleging termination was in retaliation for grievances involving discrimination.

Breach of Commercial Contracts

- Suit by computer-software developer alleging institution interfered with and prevented successful completion of contract to install computer-network systems.
- Suit by food-service contractor alleging closure of food service center breached contract and resulted in substantial lost revenue and profit.
- Suit by corporation involving violation of patent rights in connection with research commercialization contracts.
- Suits by donors alleging institution improperly drafted or administered life income/annuity contracts involving sale of property or investment of gift proceeds.

Sexual Assault

- Suit by a visitor to the service who alleged a staff member raped her and the service was negligent its supervision of staff and its security of its facilities.

Accidental Injury/Vehicular Injury

- Suits by contractors and construction workers who have been seriously injured or killed as result of falls, electrocution and vehicle accidents; alleging failure to provide safe working conditions, violation of OSHA regulations, and negligent supervision.
- Suit by parents of a part-time worker who used personal car to run errand for the service and caused accident resulting in death of other driver.
- Claim involving service van driven by staff member that was involved in out-of-state accident resulting in death and serious injury to occupants of other car.
- Suit involving service "bookmobile" vehicle which struck and killed pedestrian.

AIDS

- Suit by custodian who is HIV-positive claiming infection caused by needle stick while cleaning service restrooms.

VOLUNTEERS

Why did we include this section in a basic management text? There are at least three answers. First, a very large number of information services are very dependent upon volunteer workers: archives, libraries, museums, and schools, for example. Second, volunteers and paid part-time staff are the most likely people a beginning information professional will be asked to supervise. Finally, there is some tendency to think of volunteers as beyond normal management practices, which is a serious mistake.

Volunteerism is a major source of assistance for all types of organizations. Some corporations encourage if not require that their employees engage in some type of volunteer work outside the workplace. Shin and Kleiner (2003: 63) noted that in 1999, U.S. volunteers contributed 19.9 billion hours of service. The value of the work, based on a $15.93 per hour rate, was estimated to be $225.9 billion. Certainly volunteer work has increased since 1999 and no matter what dollar value you place on such work many organizations would fail to achieve some of their goals without such contributions. There is some concern about being able to retain volunteers. Daniel Kadlec (2006: 76) reported there was a significant challenge for organizations dependent upon volunteers: "Nearly 38 million Americans who had volunteered in a nonprofit in the past didn't show up last year.... That is a waste of talent and desire". The "last year" in the quote was 2005. It will indeed be a waste of people power, if the trend continues, especially as the Boomer generation retires from full-time employment.

There is a vast pool of talented, energetic, and motivated volunteers to tap and retain. They also can become highly committed to a service's organizational goals, given the proper environment. Part of that environment is thinking about volunteers as just as important to quality service as any paid staff member. Creating the proper environment calls for careful thought and planning.

Planning the How and When of Volunteers

A good starting point for the thinking process for volunteers is to consider a few basic questions such as:

- Should we use volunteers? (a very key question to ponder)
- Where would we use volunteers?
- How would we use volunteers?
- Would the tasks be meaningful for volunteers?
- Who would supervise the volunteers?
- Do we have or can we create meaningful volunteer rewards?

Dale Freund (2005) explored the use of volunteers in libraries in terms of should you do it. On balance, he believed that, properly done and in the right circumstances, the answer is yes. Many information services can benefit from using volunteers but this should not be undertaken lightly; as Freund suggests, a volunteer program needs to be in the correct circumstances and properly designed.

Another important point to keep in mind during the early stages of your planning is there are three major volunteer categories, at least in the United States. One type is the "short-term" volunteer—someone who will work on special projects/events/activities but has little or no interest in a regular or ongoing commitment. Some examples are an annual book sale, disaster recovery efforts, or a capital fund-raising campaign. A second type is the "commitment volunteer." These volunteers have a strong personal interest in the subject/area they seek volunteer opportunities in and they expect to gain gratification, knowledge, useful skills as well as a sense of accomplishment from the work they perform. Gaining and retaining such volunteers is a goal of any long-term volunteer program; it is also a major challenge. The third variety of volunteer, in many ways, almost does not deserve the label volunteer. These are individuals who engage in the activity primarily because of outside pressure to do so. In the United States, there are two significant sources of such pressure: the workplace and schools. Many for-profit organizations, while not making volunteering mandatory, make it very clear they expect employees to engage in some form of volunteer work, although such organizations use a very broad definition of what constitutes "volunteer" activity. A few academic institutions have gone so far as to make some level of volunteer work a graduation requirement. Most do not do that but do put a fair amount of effort into encouraging students to do so—adding it to the student's official record, offering credit for the approved activities, and other benefits. The schools have been rather successful; in 2005, more than 3.3 million college students engaged in service to some nonprofit organization, averaging just under 100 hours per student (Pope, 2006: A1). With the right type of activities and recognition, these reluctant volunteers can become committed long-term workers. It almost goes without saying that all volunteers want meaningful work that they can see makes a difference.

Beyond these broad categories you must take into account the fact your recruiting efforts will not be the same as for paid staff. There are a number of pools to draw upon, each requiring a somewhat different approach both in message and where to place that message. Five of the pools are:

- retirees
- students
- homemakers

- employed people
- unemployed (most hoping to gain marketable skills or perhaps secure a paid position with the organization)

Reaching out to students, the employed, and the unemployed is relatively easy as you have organizations to contact which will assist in getting your message out. Retirees are somewhat more challenging; however, senior centers and other locations that offer senior programs are a good starting point. Homemakers are the biggest challenge; in this case school libraries have an inside track on getting great volunteers.

(Note: In this section our discussion focuses on unpaid volunteers engaged in information service work activities. In the next chapter, fiscal management, we will explore the concept of "Friends of the Library," who are also volunteers but with a different orientation.)

Once you have decided you can make effective use of volunteers for work activities you should employ most of the staffing concepts outlined earlier in this chapter. Rather too often services just decide some volunteers would be nice and think about what to have the person do after a volunteer agrees to come onboard. That approach works sometimes but is not recommended if you want a long-term committed volunteer. (Our guess is that many of the 38 million volunteers mentioned in Kadlec's articles experienced some variation of the "find then decide what" approach.)

Start with volunteer job descriptions for each type of activity just as you would for paid staff positions. Doing so provides a solid base for both parties regarding the what and how of the position. Surprises, such as "I don't want to make photocopies," are much less likely if the person reviewed a job description indicating photocopying was part of the expected job performance. As with paid positions, the job description should outline duties and experience/skills sought. (Note: After preparing the descriptions, it is wise to consult with the HR department to explore insurance issues, such as injury and liability coverage for volunteers.)

Unlike paid positions you rarely have a pool of volunteers to interview. That notwithstanding, the interview is just as important for both parties. This is the opportunity to assess skills, motivation, and the nature of the work.

Check This Out:

Rashelle Karp provides some excellent questions to consider asking a prospective volunteer in her 1993 book *Volunteers In Libraries* (Chicago: American Library Association).

If motivation is important for paid staff, it is critical for volunteers, if you expect to keep them. Some years ago William M. Marston (1979) suggested there are four basic personality types (the concept has taken on a number of labels over the years). For our purposes we will use Marston's original labels: dominance (D), influencing (I), steadiness (S), and conscientiousness (C). People of type D personality are action-oriented—get something done, seek quick results, solve the problem now. "I"s are people-oriented; they are verbal and enjoy interacting with people, and being liked is important to them. "S"s are dependable; they prefer to focus on one task at time and whenever possible they want a workplace where they can concentrate on the task at hand. "C"s are focused on standards/procedures as well as being detail-oriented. Think about yourself and your volunteers and recognize the importance of using different behaviors with each volunteer personality.

Possible Behaviors with Volunteers:

If you are a "D"
- Your usual style works well with other "D" volunteers.
- Be less formal than usual with "I" volunteers.
- Be more slow-going than usual with "S" volunteers.
- Be certain to present facts/evidence when working with "C."

If you are an "I"
- Avoid your usual "small talk" with "D" volunteers.
- Being yourself and reaching agreement works best with "I" volunteers.
- Be rather formal at first and stay focused on activities with "S" volunteers.
- Drop your normal approach and just deal with facts with "C" volunteers.

If you are an "S"
- Maintain your confidence how to do things when working with "D" volunteers.
- Be more open than usual when working with "I" volunteers.
- Be certain to give more your usual support/encouragement when working with "S" volunteers.
- Be confident about needs, even if no "standard" exists when working with "C" volunteers.

If you are a "C"
- Be less fact-oriented than usual, but hit the main/high points when working with "D" volunteers.
- Be as informal as possible, while conveying the facts, when working with "I" volunteers.
- Be patient, present facts/issues completely when working with "S" volunteers.
- Be yourself when working with another "C."

No matter what "style" you or the volunteer may be, providing lots of positive feedback is essential. This does not mean you shouldn't correct problems, but it must be done in as positive a manner as you can. Checking on volunteer job satisfaction is a key to keeping long-term volunteers—even with accurate job descriptions, the reality of the work, its location or colleagues, can make what appeared to be an attractive activity less than satisfying.

Volunteers probably require more training and development than do paid staff. This is particularly true when the volunteer has retired from a somewhat similar paid position elsewhere, such as a retired school librarian volunteering in an archive. Such people may have to unlearn years of past practices and/or modify beliefs about "how things should be done." Often the supervisor's assumption is that the person did this before and needs very little training, which sometimes also translates into limited orientation as well. Even when the volunteer has had a long association and interaction with the organization providing orientation that includes background on the organization's history, long-term strategies and goals, and so forth usually results in a more satisfying experience for both volunteer and volunteer supervisor(s).

There is little question but that volunteers provide wonderful assistance to thousands of information services; however, there are some areas where tension can arise between volunteers and paid staff. One obvious area is some fear/concern on the paid staff's part about their job security, especially where funding is tight or hiring freezes are in place. We are not aware of any documented case of paid staff losing positions because volunteers were available. However, we do know of instances where layoffs took place because of funding problems, with the organization later restarting a service based on volunteer help. Thus the concern is real and should be addressed openly and honestly.

Financial difficulties can also impact volunteer programs in at least two ways. When a budget situation becomes too tight, the volunteer coordinator may have less and less time to devote to the volunteer program as other duties take priority; few information services have the luxury of having a full-time position dedicated to a volunteer program. Rewards for volunteers are likely to become solely psychological in character; this will probably not matter to committed volunteers, but is likely to cause less committed people to leave.

A particular challenge is when volunteers and paid staff perform the same task(s). Whenever possible, you should avoid this situation. Performance assessment becomes a significant factor. Paid staff may resent the volunteer's apparent freedom to come and go with little or no notice. They may also think/observe the volunteers receiving encouragement or praise for work the staff believes is less than standard, or at least at a lower standard than they are expected to deliver. Your managerial creativity and ingenuity will face great challenges when you try to provide that extra level of encouragement to volunteers and retain their services, while not undermining paid staff morale.

Check These Out:

Connecticut State Library. *Guidelines for Using Volunteers In Libraries.* Available: www.cslib.org/volguide.htm (accessed October 30, 2006).

Driggers, Preston, and Eileen Duma. 2002. *Managing Library Volunteers.* Chicago: American Library Association.

Reed, Sally G. 1994. *Library Volunteers—Worth the Effort: A Program Manager's Guide.* Jefferson, NC: McFarland.

Volunteer Match. Available: www.volunteermatch.org (accessed October 30, 2006).

KEY POINTS TO REMEMBER:

- People—the staff—are *the* essential element in having a successful information service.
- Attracting and retaining the "best and brightest" is a complex undertaking.
- Legal aspects impact all personnel activities, from recruitment to retirement.
- Assessing staffing needs involves position reviews and looking at labor force demographics.
- Recruiting and selecting the best person requires care and thought, including and understanding of legal issues.
- Tools for the selection process must be chosen with an eye on legal concerns.
- Selecting and "landing" a candidate can be a complex activity involving the service staff and the parent body's HR office.
- Proper orientation of new staff (the first few days or weeks) are critical to good long term work performance.
- Performance appraisal is a process that few people like and one that can have as many negative as positive outcomes, unless handled thoughtfully.
- Discipline is a delicate activity that takes practice and skill in keeping personnel views at bay and objective data in the forefront.

REFERENCES

Bridges, Mark, and Heather Johnson. 2006. "The Aging Workforce: The Facts, the Fiction, the Future." *ASHRAE Journal* 48, no. 1 (January): 6–9.

Deming, W. Edward. 1993. *Out of Crisis*. Cambridge, MA: Massachusetts Institute of Technology Press.

Drickhamer, David. 2006. "Putting People First Pays Off." *Material Handing Management* 61, no.6 (June): 42, 44–45.

Evans, G. Edward, and Bendik Rugaas. 1982. "Another Look at Performance Appraisal in Libraries." *Journal of Library Administration* 3, (Summer): 61–69.

Fisher, Anne. 2006. "Retain Your Brains." *Fortune* 154, no. 2 (July 10): 49–50.

Freund, Dale. 2005. "Do Volunteers Belong in the Library?" *Rural Libraries* 25 no. 1: 19–41.

Gellerman, Saul. 1976. *Management of Human Resources*. New York: Holt, Rinehart.

Hammonds, Keith. 2005. "The Limits of People Power." *Wilson Quarterly* 29, no. 4 (Autumn): 91–92.

"Interview Questions Probe Integrity." 1987. *The Billings Gazette* (July 5): 4–5.

Kadlec, Daniel. 2006. "The Right Way to Volunteer." *Time* 168 no. 10 (September 4): 76.

Marston, William Moulton. 1979. *Emotions of Normal People*. Minneapolis: Persona Press.

Pope, Justin. 2006. "College Volunteers Skyrocket." *Arizona Daily Sun* (October 16, 2006): A1, A7.

Shin, Sunny, and Brian Kleiner. 2003. "How to Manage Unpaid Volunteers in Organizations." *Management Research News* 26 no. 2/3/4: 63–70.

Spinks, Nora. 2005. "Talking About My Generation." *Canadian Healthcare Manager* 12, no. 7 (November 1): 11–13.

LAUNCHING PAD

Butler, Timothy, and James Waldrop. 2004. "Understanding 'People' People." *Harvard Business Review* 82, no. 6 (June): 78–86.

Chon, John M., and Ann L. Kelsey. 2004. *Staffing the Modern Library: A How-To-Do-It Manual*. New York: Neal-Schuman.

Davenport, Thomas. 2005. *The Care and Feeding of Knowledge Worker*. Boston, MA: Harvard Business School Press.

Giesecke, Joan, and Beth McNeil. 2005. *Fundamentals of Library Supervision*. Chicago: American Library Association.

Montgomery, Jack, and Eleanor I. Cook. 2005. *Conflict Management for Libraries: Strategies for a Positive, Productive Workplace*. Chicago: American Library Association.

Whitmell, Vicki. 2005. "Workforce and Succession Planning in Special Libraries." *Feliciter* 51, no. 3: 135–137.

16

Managing Money

"Never ask of money spent
Where the spender thinks it went
Nobody was ever meant
To remember or invent
What he did with every cent."

Robert Frost

"The real needs of the present should not be sacrificed
to the hypothetical needs of the future."

Maurice Line

INTRODUCTION

With deep apologies to Mr. Frost we must report:

As we sigh and vent
Indeed you must account for
When and where each cent was spent.
Those who gave or lent
The funds you begged on knees bent
Expect you'll have a statement
True and fair of every cent.
Beware, should you fail expect a sad event
For off to jail you may be sent.

Poets we are not but the sentiments expressed are all too true and are explored in this chapter.

After having the best and brightest people, the second most important element in achieving a successful information service is securing adequate funding. Accomplishing that goal is challenging and calls upon all your managerial and political skills. You must realize that at times you'll not succeed through no fault of your own. Economic conditions may make it impossible for any service to receive funding at "normal" levels, and budget reductions may even occur. However, by preparing solid requests, having a track record of careful and thoughtful stewardship of funds granted, providing high-quality service to the user community, and having realistic but forward looking plans you will, more often than not, secure the maximum possible funding.

Fiscal management consists of three broad activities: identifying and securing funds, expending the funds, and accounting for and reporting on how you spent the funds. Kent Boese laid out some of the challenges you face in today's volatile economic environment in an editorial comment in *The Bottom Line.*

> Simply put, should inflation become a large problem in our economy, we will have weaker purchasing power with our money. Even if we are able to increase our budgets, we may be receiving fewer good and services for our buck in the future.... Having adequate funding is a subjective view... no matter what the funding level you are at, there is never room to spend money poorly.... If we become efficient financial organizations, but fail to provide the services expected of us, we can not consider ourselves successful (Boese, 2006).

Being a good/effective steward of funds is complex regardless of the size of service you look after. It begins by assessing what needs doing (especially user needs), the cost of the requisite activities, establishing priorities (with stakeholder input), creating a plan (the budget) reflecting the costs and priorities, and presenting the plan to the appropriate funding body(ies). We know of few, if any, cases where the cost of desired activities were/are below the realistic amount of money you are likely to receive. Thus setting priorities is a key element in fiscal planning/management.

To be a truly effective fiscal manager you should explore all possible (legal of course) sources of funding, not just the parent body. In the past, senior service people faced little pressure to secure "outside" funding; when they did, it was a nice plus for the service but not expected. Today's service leaders are often required to engage in fund raising, not just for "nice extras" but for basic operating funds.

No matter where you seek funding, you must have a well-crafted request/proposal. Preparing such documents takes time and effort and a fair amount of creativity as you will be in competition with a great many other services as well as, in some cases, other types of non-profit organizations for the available funds. Preparing grant requests and proposals to foundations and other agencies are topics for entire books but we will touch on the issues at the end of this chapter.

BUDGET AS A CONTROL DEVICE

A budget is a plan that serves three interrelated purposes: planning, coordinating, and control. It represents choices made about alternative possible expenditures. Further, it assists in coordinating work designed to achieving specific service goals. Funding authorities use the budget requests and expenditures as a means of comparing what the service proposed would happen against actual outcomes. It is one of the parent body's most powerful tools for holding service personnel accountable.

These purposes apply to all levels of the service; senior staff use budgets to monitor overall as well as departments' performance. Front-line budget managers use the budget to track day-to-day performance as well as over longer periods. (An example of the first-line use of the budget would be an acquisitions unit that develops plans on how much money needs to be expended each day to assure a reasonable work flow thoughout the fiscal year. Checking on actual performance against the planned expenditure provides useful information for control and coordination purposes.)

Profit-oriented organizations begin the budget process by estimating sales and income; information services start by projecting/estimating what income will be from the parent organization. They then turn to outside sources. Some are relatively predictable (user fees, endowment income, and other internally generated cash), while others are highly unpredictable (grant proposals and cooperative ventures/partnerships, for example). In point of fact, all budgeting is essentially forecasting—how much will you get and how much will it cost to operate over the budget cycle.

Overly optimistic predictions lead to problems when funding falls short and/or there unexpected costs. You rarely know much before the start of the budgetary period exactly how much you will receive. Often, the actual funding is an unknown until near the beginning of the fiscal year. (We know of cases where publicly funded services had to start a cycle without an approved budget because the politicians could not agree on how much to approve.) This can create some serious scrambling when there are shortfalls. There have a number of times when all agencies, except emergency departments had to close until the legislature or council reach a compromise. Sometimes unexpected external events will affect the budget during its cycle—for example, a change in currency exchange rates. The authors' experience has been that a conservative forecast is the safest and least disruptive to operations, and that having a contingency plan for times when the funders are quibbling over what and how much to fund also makes managerial life somewhat easier. Being in a service receiving public funding, is both a blessing and a curse. During stable economic and political times you can make reasonably accurate projections regarding upcoming appropriations. During other times predictability almost disappears and keeping the service operational is very stressful for everyone on the staff.

Budgets are not necessarily about money; you can and sometimes do employ nonmonetary units. Some organizations require information about physical units processed/produced or labor time as part of the "budget package." Labor units produced can also be a useful internal control mechanism. Such data is very useful when developing a new service/program and creating a realistic assessment of total costs and outcomes.

Because budgets are estimates, to be effective you must make expenditure adjustments as circumstances change. Budgets need to be flexible in order to meet rapid shifts in needs, but any major alteration requires careful thought and caution. Too many rapid changes can damage the integrity and stability of a budget as well as the organization. (Note: In most services there is only a limited authority to make budget adjustments; asking before doing is the best approach, especially for first-time budget managers.)

Financial planning and control consists of several basic steps:

1. Determine ongoing and desirable programs and establish priorities.
2. Estimate the costs of plans for each unit in monetary terms.
3. Combine all estimates into a well-balanced program. This will require investigation of each plan's financial feasibility and a comparison of the program with institutional goals.
4. Compare, for a given time, the estimates derived from Step 3 with the actual results, making corrections for any significant differences. (Use the budget as a standard for appraising the performance of the budget manager.)

A service's size does not materially affect the basic budgeting process, although in larger services, each step is more complex. As a service grows, it may come to employ separate budgets for departments, divisions, or work units. Because these units are somewhat independent, different performance standards may be appropriate for different units. A very large service may have dozens of internal budgets subsumed under its general budget.

The second step of budgetary control—combining and coordinating subsidiary budgets—can be exceedingly complicated. It certainly involves more than just totaling the small budgets. It must represent a total, feasible program that is consistent with the service's objectives. For this reason, very large services often have a person whose sole job it is to coordinate the budget.

In the final type of budgetary control, budget officers compare the actual performance (what has been accomplished, the volume of work, and so forth) against what was expected (budget). At the same time, supervisors and top management need to look at the existing circumstances in order to decide whether a major or a minor shift in budget allotments is necessary or desirable. By doing this every few months throughout the fiscal year, the service can help to control the unpredictability of the future. This step is most important because budgets are often prepared 12 to 18 months before they are approved and thus may represent predictions that are two years old at the time of review.

For Further Thought:

We have said that a budget is a plan and represents choices about alternative possible expenditures. Select an information service and list the possible areas of expenditure. Then select two areas and consider what factors might influence the decision to be made concerning choices in those areas.

RESPONSIBILITY CENTERS

Many organizations have taken to looking at budgets for its subunits in terms that reflect traditional accounting practice. They employ four categories of responsibility: expense center, revenue center, profit center, and investment center.

The control system (overall budget process) looks at an *expense center* in terms of monetary inputs rather than outputs. While expense centers do have outputs, top management or funding authorities do not believe it is useful to measure the outputs in monetary terms. In the past, the information service fell into this category in most organizations; today there may be an expectation the service will generate at least some income. Other units usually in the expense center category are human resources departments, research and development, legal, accounting, and public relations. Within the expense category, some organizations subdivide it into engineered and discretionary expense centers. Engineered centers are those where one can reasonably estimate the costs. An acquisitions budget would be an example where one can estimate cost increases for materials by using five-year averages and vendor estimates. Discretionary centers are often service areas where one cannot get reliable estimates, even with past averages; therefore, one uses the previous year's expense and plus or minus some percentage. Often the figure used for all "basic" increases is the previous year's consumer price index (CPI). For an information service, the budget for fee-based search services would most often be a discretionary expense center.

Revenue centers are units in which outputs are the focus of monetary interest but *not* compared directly with the center's input costs. Normally these are "sales" units. For an academic or special library, an example might be the budget for reprography services (photocopies, microform copies, or digitization) or other "chargeback" services. In a public library or archives, it could be the sale of postcards, prints, or other publications.

For Further Thought:

Draw up a list of six revenue centers that you might find in an information service.

The profit center and investment center categories do not apply except in the most unusual circumstances when it comes to information services. In a *profit center*, top management measures the center's performance on the basis of profit. The basic concept of a profit center is relatively self-sufficient and at least semiautonomous. One possible situation where this might apply is an information service in a profit organization where the organization places a "value/price" on the information it supplies other units of the organization. While the value/price is artificial, probably negotiated between the service and its client units, top managers see the negotiations as a means of making unit managers focus on their bottom line, thus improving the overall organizational performance.

Investment centers do not apply directly to information services. The method employed in this approach, measurement and evaluation, employs the ROI formula (return on investment).

$$\text{ROI} = \frac{\text{Sales} - \text{Expense}}{\text{Investment}}$$

The issue for profit-making organizations, especially those with investors, is the need to not only have sales that exceed expenses, but to have the ratio large enough to exceed the return on placing one's funds in a savings account. For information services, this type of return is not possible except perhaps in the case of an information broker (a for-profit operation.)

For Further Thought:

Consider an information service in the for-profit sector. How could top management measure the center's performance on the basis of profit? Try and identify two ways.

Information service budgets normally are of two types: operating and capital. *Operating budgets* identify amounts of money the service expects to expend on its activities (operating expense [OE]) over a specific time frame, usually a 12-month fiscal year [FY]. The fact that different organizations use different fiscal years (some examples are January 1 to December 31, June 1 to May 31, July 1 to June 30, and October 1 to September 30) as well as budget preparation cycles can cause surprising problems for information service consortiums attempting to fund cooperative projects.

Funding bodies can, and do, change their fiscal year which causes the service difficulty in maintaining journal and database subscriptions. The problem is not too great when the funding body shortens the FY by a month (at some point in time it will be necessary to address any funding shortfall). When the funders extend the FY by a month or more the problem may be acute due to lack of funds. The authors have worked in services where this has happened.

Capital budgets address planned expenditures on equipment (usually items designed to last more than two or perhaps three years). Expenditures for technology (hardware and infrastructure) usually fall into the capital expense category.

Preparation of capital budget requests may, or may not, follow the operating budget sequence. In some cases, the time period for the capital budget may be longer or shorter than the OE budget.

BUDGET CYCLE

There is some type of budget cycle, regardless of the time frame, and that cycle plays a role in the control aspect of budgeting. Good budget managers are normally dealing with at least four FYs. at any time. Those FYs are last year, this year, next year, and the year after that. Figure 16.1 is an example of a budget cycle. Let us assume the library's FY is July 1 to June 30 and look at the budget cycle and the reasons for the thinking about four different fiscal years simultaneously.

Figure 16.1								
Sample Budget Cycle								
Past fiscal year		Current fiscal year		Coming fiscal year		Future fiscal year		
July	Dec	July	Dec	July	Dec	July	Dec	July
X		***X***	+++∞∞	X		X		X
Key: ***, submit coming fiscal year budget. +++, defend coming fiscal budget. ∞∞, plan future fiscal year budget								

For the current year the manager must monitor expenditures, compare what has occurred against expectations, and make appropriate adjustments. A common practice requires senior managers to provide additional justifications to the funding body for the requested budget for the coming fiscal year. As part of that process, the person is likely to have to respond to questions about the expenditures in the past fiscal year. (Because budgets are estimates, funding bodies usually look at how well the requesting unit actually used its appropriated funds in prior years.) Senior management must be ready to defend past expenditures, explain how the service is doing with current funding, and justify why extra funds are necessary for the coming FY. In our experience, this process most often occurs sometime between July and December.

During the latter part of the fiscal year, April or May, many organizations ask for the initial request for the future fiscal year. In order to develop a realistic request, senior managers must think about how well they handled questions about past budgets, the status of the current budget, and make an educated guess as to what will be available in the coming year's budget. With that in mind, they then prepare the request for funding two years hence.

BUDGET PREPARATION

A natural question arises of who is responsible for the budget. Like so many questions, there is more than one answer. From a legal point of view, the service's senior manager is responsible, just as she/he is for everything that takes place within the service. From an operational perspective, there are a variety of possibilities. Only in the smallest service is the senior manger solely responsible for handling the operational budget. Almost every medium- and large-size service, with several units/departments, usually has delegated some discretionary spending power to some units. Very large services may even have a full-time budget officer usually reporting directly to the senior manager. Even when there is no budget officer, an effective senior manager whenever possible delegates some budgetary responsibility to unit heads. (Remember, however, that having delegated responsibility does not reduce the senior manager's overall accountability for budgetary performance.)

Such delegation accomplishes several things. First, it places the day-to-day budget decisions close to user service activities, making it easier to respond to changing needs. Second, it indicates to unit managers that the senior manager has a high level of trust in them and their abilities. Third, it provides middle managers with an opportunity to gain an understanding of budgeting. It also provides senior management with an opportunity to assess middle managers' potential for promotion to higher levels, which generally carry greater and greater budgetary responsibility. Finally, it gives the senior manager more time to maintain overall budgetary oversight.

For Further Thought:

Reflect on what must be considered when deciding who will be responsible for a library's budget and list three of the most important factors.

The initial budget preparation should begin with first-line supervisors providing their estimates of their funding needs on to their immediate supervisors and ultimately to senior management. Each successive management level combines and coordinates all subunit budgets and then passes its total on up. Finally, top management assesses all this information and formulates the overall budget.

Every service hopes to have a stable or, at best, a predictable fiscal environment. To some extent, the planning cycle (see the chapter on planning) assists in creating such an environment. One of the other elements involves the senior managers monitoring the economic and political environment both in terms of the service as well as its parent organization. By setting up a budget/financial planning committee, senior management accomplishes several things. First, it involves more people in the monitoring activities. Second, it involves others in thinking about future needs of the service. Third, it provides lower-level managers with solid budgetary planning and development experience. Finally, it can build commitment to the service as well generating some understanding of the limits of budgetary freedom the service has.

Even an economic recession can have an upside. Eileen Shanahan's "The Other Side of the Recession" (1991) points out several positive outcomes. One of her points is that a recession can reduce some of the bureaucratic aspects of budgeting and priority setting. One reflection of such changes, in the United States during the 1990s, was greater freedom for cities and counties to use state and federal funds in ways not previously allowed. Another change was "earmarking" revenues—that is, making a legal commitment that funds raised (a specific tax, for example) were tied to a specific purpose (library support, for example). Voters were more willing to vote for a tax or fee when they saw a direct result from the revenue. Another outcome was governments saw that variations in expenditures based on local needs resulted in greater acceptance of programs by the voters.

Strained relations with officials can develop when the difference between what the service needs are and the budgetary body's ability to fulfill those needs. Both sides can become very frustrated and suspicious of one another. That type of climate makes the process even more difficult. Several steps can be tried to ease such strained relations. One step is for the service staff to demonstrate their understanding of the tight circumstances by indicating actions they have taken to control and reduce expenses. Another step is to illustrate how providing a certain level of funding will address a larger/broader community issue. Funding authorities almost always prefer to receive suggestions for addressing a problem rather than having it simply put forth as a problem for them to solve. Yet another step is indicate there has been a concerted effort to seek out new revenue sources, such as grants, donor solicitation, or external fund raising.

Having a contingency plan for possible budget shortfalls is part of a stable environment. It will help avoid making hasty decisions that may be as harmful as the loss of funding. In cutting back, the people most affected, at least initially, are staff. Several studies have shown that cutting back adversely affects morale, job satisfaction, and staff retention; those in turn impact productivity at the time when it is most needed (Shaughnessy, 1989).

Some of the short-term tactics for dealing with fiscal distress include hiring freezes, staff reductions through attrition, across-the-board cuts, and deferred maintenance and equipment replacement. Unfortunately, fiscal distress for information services is not always a short-term problem. In the long term, Band-aid solutions will not work, and their use often severely damages support from both staff and users. An example is cutting funds for database access services.

Users are hurt in the long term and they may leave never to return if the cutbacks are too severe. (Cutting service hours is an easy choice for a manager but is usually a shortsighted solution.) Hiring freezes are less damaging, at least initially, to customers. The problem with a freeze is it can take time to achieve the needed savings, especially in the absence of staff turnover. Using a combination of cuts takes more time and effort, but, in the long run, is more likely to result in retained users and a more effective service. This is an example of where a thoughtfully developed contingency plan(s) demonstrates its value.

Glen Holt (2005) wrote an article about "getting beyond the pain," in which he begins with a depressing list of budgetary woes at the state/provincial and national levels in Canada, the United Kingdom, and the United States during the early years of the twenty-first century. He noted that the American Library Association estimated there had been $111 million cuts in public library funding between 2004 and when he wrote the article. Holt provides some ideas for addressing the situation: demonstrate the critical nature of the service (or some of its elements), demonstrate the service benefits, think broadly about possible funding sources, place greater emphasis on user/client focused service, and recognize that globalization does have an impact on the international marketplace for information. Spend some time thinking and pondering on the implications of those impacts. His concluding statement, "At the same time however, we must recognize the drastic changes that we will have to make to keep up with new ways of working and funding" (Holt, 2005: 189).

One of the probable "new ways" of funding is touched upon in a book by John Buschman (2003), in which he suggests that at least in North America the public (taxpayers) have decided that some public sector services, if not all, deserve less public support than in the past. Perhaps his view also applies to the United Kingdom (Ezard, 2004).

Check These Out:

L.S. Moyer published an article in 2005 outlining how one small public library responded to budget cuts: "Library Funding In a Budget-Cut World" (*Bottom Line* 18, no. 3: 112–115.)

For an academic library perspective read Samuel I. Huang's 2006 article "Where There's A Will, There's A Way" (*Bottom Line* 19, no. 3: 146–151).

In terms of a corporate environment, review Gitelle Seer's 2004 "No Pain, No Gain: Stretching the Library Dollar" (*Bottom Line* 17, no. 1: 10–14).

Gitelle Seer (2004: 10) made an important point: "Do not confuse short-term belt tightening with long-term financial strategies. It is sometimes hard to tell the difference, and your organization's management may give you few, if any, meaningful clues." Seer's advice, as is ours, is to monitor the internal and external environment like a hawk.

Every information service—regardless of the service community's size—faces four ongoing financial issues. The first involves trying to develop and maintain appropriate facilities and responsive users' services while remaining within budget. (Unfortunately few service budgets take the volume of work into account—or rather, few funding authorities do so.) It simply is a matter of trying to respond to changing needs while knowing there is little prospect of additional funding until the next fiscal period.

The second financial issue relates to the requirement of continually building and maintaining collections. Print collection growth requires space (= money) and time and staff effort (= money). Academic libraries often have this problem, whereas public libraries can alleviate it somewhat by withdrawing outdated and worn items. Archives grow in size and trust that technology will assist; most technology is costly. Records managers have perhaps the "easiest" time with this factor as many of their files have legally mandated retention time frames, and very often the files are stored off-site. Information services in corporate settings usually must maintain a fixed collection of current resources and depend on other services document delivery for older material.

The third financial issue relates to the second and revolves around the rapid growth of electronic resources. Database vendors are no less shy about increasing their prices each year at rates well above general inflation than were/are their print journal publishers. (Often these are one and the same, and you face a double hit for the same information or pay a premium for just one of the formats.)

Finally there are staffing concerns. Like serials, staffing is an ongoing commitment that escalates in cost with each year if staff members receive annual salary increases. Even when there are no salary increases, there will be an increase in benefit costs such as for health insurance. Even in an environment with modest budget increases, salaries and benefits can erode the funds for services and collections and the increasing need to invest in staff training and development to meet the challenges of continuous change.

DEFENDING THE REQUEST

Preparing a budget request is often easier than defending it. This stems from the fact that many agencies compete for the limited pool of funds, and each seeks to prove that its needs are the most urgent. Thus, the more care that you put into the preparation of a budget request and the reasons for requested increases, the more likely you are to secure the amount sought. Those agencies that do win the "battle of the budget" are usually the ones that recognize and act on the fact that budgeting is a very political process.

All U.S. information service managers ought to read the classic book by Aaron Wildavsky, *The Politics of the Budgetary Process* (1992). Some information professionals, especially students, have difficulty accepting Wildavsky's ideas, as the text deals with the U.S. government and, to a lesser extent, state governments. They see information services as cultural havens somehow removed from the "ugliness" of politics. Most graduates who read some or all of Wildavsky as students quickly see the connection when they take their first position.

Wildavsky's book contains many good ideas. We drew the following material from Wildavsky, but it is not a substitute for reading his entire book. Some readers have difficulty translating his emphasis on the U.S. federal government into an information service context. We suggest simply substituting the title of the service's parent body chief executive officer for the word president, and the title of the appropriate supervisory body for the word Congress. Doing so usually makes his ideas relevant to an information service.

Despite all the press given to such concepts as program and planning budgeting systems (PPBS) and zero-base budgeting (ZBB), most organizational budgets are basically line budgets (see next section). Organizations often find that when they do move to one of the "newer" budgeting modes, the end result is much the same—an incremental budget, because after an initial startup, people use the past year as their starting point. An incremental budget usually increases in size each passing year, if by nothing more than an inflation figure.

Exceptions to the incremental pattern do take place. If an agency is "under fire," depending on how serious the situation is, the funding body can use budget cuts to show displeasure. Also, taxpayers have come to demand reduced taxes; such cries result in real cuts for all governmental agencies. (In some cases, leading to nongovernment bodies taking over the provision of service as has happened in several U.S. cities in terms of their public libraries.) The largest cuts are usually in those deemed "nonessential" services (library, museum, schools, and other cultural activities). Police and fire protection (safety concerns) usually are the last to face reductions. This is clear evidence that government budgeting is a highly political process, reacting to voter concerns. What politician would want to explain to voters why she/he decided to close the local fire station rather than the library or the museum?

The incremental approach is present in most service budgets because of the long-term commitments (salaries, retirement programs, pension payments, and database and serial subscriptions). Also, if the user base increases, there will be pressure to hire additional staff. In jurisdictions with strong collective bargaining units, a workload agreement clause can cause a significant increase in staffing costs. Annual salary step and cost-of-living increases are difficult to control because the withholding of such increases is only temporary. Staff pressure will mount to make up for the losses they believe they suffered.

Like it or not "lobbying" is, or should, be part of the service's budget preparation and presentation. Perhaps a label that carries less negative connotation, at least in the United States, is advocacy. Both terms relate to the process of influencing people about the importance or value of an issue, cause, or service. Gloria Meraz (2002) describes three areas where information services can focus on in terms of lobbying—positioning oneself to be an effective lobbyist, achieving the most from lobbying sessions, and understanding the lobbying arena. One of her telling points is "decision makers tend to allocate funding to departments or agencies that are in trouble (crisis)...without showing some sort of crisis, libraries are not likely to receive large allocations of resources" (Meraz, 2002: 68). She notes that most services do not have to make up the crisis all they need to do is show the crisis.

One element in the advocacy/lobbying effort should draw on the user base which will be as vocal or as silent as the service leads them to believe they should be. A large user base is fine, but if they are silent during budget crunches, they are not politically useful. A little extra help extended to users—especially to politically influential groups—can go a long way at budget request time. There is nothing wrong with saying, "Look, we seem to be doing a good job for you, but with a little help and a little more money, we could really show you service!" People who are willing to speak for the service (whether or not they are actually called upon) at budget hearings can have a positive effect on funding agencies. (The "letter to your legislator" approach can be very useful, especially if it occurs year-round and can create a strong positive attitude in funders' minds before they begin thinking about budgets with the service in mind.)

Some years ago, Jennifer Cargill (1988) wrote a short but to the point article about "getting the budget message out." At that time, as it still remains today, one of the most difficult messages to convey to funding authorities, as well as to users, is the high rate of inflation of subscription prices (both electronic and paper). Finding a simple, accurate, and short way of explaining to non–information professionals why such price increase percentages are so large year after year is a challenge. As much you might like to find one, there is no "magic formula" explaining the situation.

Letters of support from users also influence the people of the finance office. Because they do the digging, provide reports, and make assessments and recommendations, their influence is significant. Developing a good working relationship with funding-authority staff members is an excellent idea, especially with the staff of the person who heads the committee that first hears the service's budget request. If your relationship is a year-round one, it will be easier to maintain and your chances of success improve further. Keeping in touch, finding out what will be needed for the hearings (well in advance), identifying possible areas of concern, and offering assistance within reasonable limits are all methods of developing a good working relationship. You must be careful to keep the relationship on a professional basis so there is no hint of personal favoritism. There is nothing wrong with inviting influential funding officers to attend special service functions (holiday parties, for example) at which a number of users and other influential persons will also be present. They may or may not attend, but they will have the service in mind as something other than a bottomless pit into which to throw money.

Study the mood of the people, and the funding authority with an eye on adjusting your approach as moods shift. During "hold the line on spending" periods, let your request demonstrate how well you are cooperating. Do not try to paint too rosy a picture—play it straight, and do not try to "put one over" on them. You may fool people once or twice because of all the other matters they have to consider, but eventually they will catch up to you. And when they do, you will lose any goodwill you developed over time and the service will probably suffer for a long time to come.

When presenting plans for new programs, be cautious in what you promise. Do not promise more than you know you can deliver, even when you think you can do much better. It is better to underpromise and over-deliver. As tempting as it may be to make promises in order to get money, resist! Funding officers' memories are long and detailed when necessary, and failure to deliver on past promises raises serious doubts about current promises.

Does all this sound too political for an information service? It should not, because it reflects the unwritten rules by which governments and other funding bodies play the budget politics game.

Check This Out:

A solid article that addresses most of the fiscal issues we covered above is Peter Clayton's 2001 "Managing the Acquisitions Budget: A Practical Perspective" (*Bottom Line* 14, no. 3: 145–151).

FORMS OF BUDGETS

Earlier, we noted there are two primary types of budget: operating expense (OE) and capital outlay/expense. For information services, the operating expense is the primary budget. There are several standard formats for presenting and managing the OE; line, performance, program, and zero-base. We also stated that the line budget is the predominate basic format used by nonprofits, at least in the United States. While the line format underlies almost all nonprofit budgets, more than two-thirds employ some "hybrid" or combination format. Therefore, we will address each of the standard formats. However, we will first cover the basic items that fall into the OE.

An *operating budget* addresses the projected relationships between income and expenses. Because the budgeting process usually begins with forecasts of income, one hopes that projected and actual national production and growth statistics will at least match. The OE defines the limits of the service's fiscal activities for a defined period of time. Within the total operating budget there is a series of budgets covering specific items of expenditure. These are generally interconnecting, and include a:

- materials budget
- labor budget

- distribution/expense budget
- administrative expense budget

A *materials budget* lists the types and quantities of raw materials, parts, and supplies required to carry out an activity. For information services, this takes the form of moneys for various types of collection building. It must take into account price increases (as fluctuations in the precarious currency market have proven so conclusively). For instance, projected changes in currency evaluation may warrant large-volume purchases early on in order to offset potential changes. Early purchase may help beat or reduce the impact of inflation.

A *labor budget* specifies the amount of direct labor needed to meet production schedules (usually in work hours). Multiplying this amount by the wage rate yields a total and per-unit labor cost. Among the points to consider is the difference that may exist between the costs of employing salaried as compared with hourly waged employees, and permanent as compared with contract staff, for the benefits may vary. Some institutions may require the involvement of the human resources office to ensure that you budget for the proper "type" of employee. The labor budget can also help in estimating costs when planning new programs or services.

The *distribution/expense budget* takes into account the estimated costs of services and record keeping. Distribution expenses are generally subdivided in terms of departmental responsibility: for example, public service and branch operations.

An *administrative expense budget*, as the name implies, details those expenses that result from performing general management functions. This might include senior and other administrative salaries, travel expenses, professional service fees, and office expenses. Like the other types of budgets, this type tends to reflect only one aspect of an operation.

What are the typical categories of expenditures included in an OE? In the case of services, the largest category is staff salaries (often representing as much as 60 to 65 percent of the total budget). This is one category of expense that most services cannot move or change during a given fiscal period. Usually the only way a manager gets to use salary moneys for some other purpose is by giving up an FTE or at least part of an FTE. Some services, in an effort to secure funds for technology, give up several FTEs. While the practice may secure needed funding, you must be certain the technology will, in fact, reduce labor costs over the long run. Many of the services that did this in the past now find that either there were substantially lower labor reductions or the support of the technology requires a new type of labor.

Collection building/maintaining funds (electronic and print) are the second-largest OE category. These funds may account for 25 to 30 percent of total budget. Like salaries, these funds tend to grow more quickly than most of the other categories.

Generally, there is less than 15 percent of the budget left for all other expense categories. Office supplies and equipment, especially technology, and maintenance contracts, are essential and take substantial portions of the remaining total. Telephone, postage, utilities (in some cases), facilities maintenance (in some cases), printing/promotional activities, membership fees, electronic service charges (such as OCLC), administrative and professional travel, bindery charges, and insurance are all categories that many services must consider. Is it any wonder that few services have much money left after covering the basic costs to pay for the increasing need for professional development activities and staff training and a host of other desirable categories that go unfunded by the authorities?

The following are subcategories of the above and indicate the range of activities that the remaining 15 percent of the service budget must cover: small equipment items, such as book trucks, step stools, office chairs, and desks—perhaps to meet changing health and safety standards; user and work area furniture related to technology usage; exhibit supplies; "security targets" for items in the collection; guidebooks and bibliographic instructional material; interlibrary loan/document delivery fees; and vehicle repair and licenses. The list could go on and on, but the above provides a clear sense of the budgetary challenges. One way to cover some of these expenses is to engage in fund raising (an activity we will cover later in this chapter). Generally, funds raised by the service are outside the OE and often the senior manager has substantial discretionary spending authority. In some cases, the funds are *restricted* to a single purpose.

Note: One often hears senior managers discussing restricted and unrestricted funds/accounts. Normally, the OE is unrestricted; that is, one may spend OE collection funds for any appropriate product. A restricted collection-development fund might require one only buy items on Middle Eastern archaeology. It is not uncommon for a donor to want to restrict the expenditure of her/his gift on areas in which she/he has a special interest. As experienced fund raisers know, securing an unrestricted gift is difficult, as "no one wants to give money for light bulbs or toilet paper."

For Further Thought:

Review the operating expense budget and its component parts, bearing in mind a specific information service known to you. Would you expect this service to have a materials budget, a labor budget, a distributive/expense budget, or an administrative budget? If not, why might there be a variation?

BUDGET TYPES

Before exploring the typical budget types we need to briefly mention two variations the information service professionals rarely encounter—lump sum and site budgets. A lump sum budget, as its name implies, is a single allocation and the funds are not tied to any category of expenditure. You have freedom to use the funds as needed, or at least only need your governing board deeming it appropriate. The freedom is wonderful until it comes to accountability when it becomes akin to wrestling a bear without a weapon.

Site budgets are allocations tied to a specific location (branch for example) in which almost all categories of expense are included. They can be a good method for giving more professionals early experience with managing an entire budget.

Another fund allocation method that may be employed with other budget types is the "formula," or mathematical model. You most commonly encounter a formula based budget in educational settings, where some form of student numbers are linked to a funding amount—more students translates into more money. Some public libraries may have something similar, with a per capita figure or percentage of taxes. More often than not the formula is starting point for the allocation process and other categories of funding also come into play.

Line-Item Budget Format

The line-item budget is the most common format. It has a long history of use and allows for easy comparison of expenditures from year to year. Figure 16.2 illustrates how the comparisons often appear in documents from funding authorities. The listing of requested and actual expenditures may cover as few as three years or as many as five or six.

We noted earlier that few U.S. funding authorities allow moving salary funds to any other line. All large organizations plan on some amount of "salary savings." That is, some FTE positions will be vacant for some time during a fiscal year. Beside unfilled positions, there is a high probability, in a large organization, of a few people taking some leave without pay or going on disability leave (a nonorganizational expense which in most cases is covered by insurance). All three of these possibilities mean some salary money will be unused—salary savings. Large organizations may expect that there will be an annual savings of 10 to 12 percent. They budget the full salaries but expect, and sometimes require, you achieve a certain level of salary savings by stating the targeted amount for the coming year. The result is a reluctance to allow unit managers to move funds out of the salary line.

Figure 16.2
Sample Line Item Budget

Account: 056739 Archives of Management

		Budget	Actual	Budget	Actual	Budget	Actual	Request
Code	Description	FY 06/7	FY 06/7	FY 07/8	FY 07/8	FY 08/9	FY 08/9	FY 09/10
422	Telephone	6,377	6,570	6,377	7,595	6,377	8,207	8,500
465	Travel	2,565	3,053	2,565	2,961	3,250	3,057	4,250
466	Postage	1,100	975	1,100	1,000	1,500	1,325	1,500
510	Office Supplies	4,217	4,198	4,275	4,279	4,500	4,482	5,200
511	Other Supplies	2,500	2,483	2,500	2,608	3,000	2,956	3,100

The authors have worked for organizations that required a written request and written approval before one could move funds from a line to another line. We have also worked in places where all that you needed to do was stay within the bottom line, excluding the salaries. Needless to say, we preferred the latter situation, since it allows one to respond more quickly to a changing situation. Each organization will have its rules on this matter, and the persons in charge of preparing the budgets and monitoring expenditures will need to know the operative rules.

Line-item budgets focus on classes of expenditures, with each class representing a "line" in the budget. Each major unit in a large organization, such as an archive, library, records unit, will have a budget number. In Figure 16.2, the budget number in the upper left corner identifies the library. That identifying number is permanent as long as the parent organization uses a particular fiscal management system. The budget number serves the same purpose as a customer identification number; it links a transaction to a specific unit.

Within each budget number there are lines representing the classes of expenditure the parent organization or funding authority wishes to track or monitor. Frequently, the lines also have a number associated with it. Figure 16.2 illustrates the labels that categorize expenditure as codes. Thus, in Figure 16.2, code 465 identifies expenses associated with travel. Whatever the label used for line items, the purpose is to allow for easy tracking of expenditures within a large organization. If the funding body wants to know how much the organization as a whole spent on office supplies, based on Figure 16.2, all it needs to do is add up all of the "510" lines in all of the active account numbers. With an automated accounting system, it is easy to generate such reports.

There is no "standard" number of expenditure classes for line-item budgets. That number varies from organization to organization; it may be dependent upon the particular characteristics of the automated accounting system in place as well as the personal preferences of the chief financial officer of the parent organization. Certainly, most of the classes we noted in the general section on OE are likely candidates for a line in the budget. It is in budgeting and human resource management where information managers most clearly feel the impact of their unit being part of a larger whole.

One special issue in service budgeting, regardless of format, is the purchase of materials for the collection—in particular, nonserial items. One never knows exactly how much the item will cost until it arrives. Experienced acquisitions staff can make good guesses as to discounts, any taxes, and shipping and handling charges, but they are only guesses. Representing roughly one-third of the total library budget, collection funds are important, and one needs a method to handle the "guesses." To that end, a library must use a system of *encumbrance* for collection purchases.

An encumbrance is a formal commitment to an expenditure. That is, one sets aside an amount of money equal to or slightly more than the expected price in advance of receiving the invoice. Figure 16.3 illustrates the manner in which one service automation system handles encumbrances.

Figure 16.3 Acquisitions					
Library Materials Funds **Books**					**University Library**
Department	**Appropriation**	**Expenditure**	**Encumbrance**	**Cash Balance**	**Free Balance**
Art/Art History	17,117.00	0	2,551.31	17,117.00	14,565.69
Bus. Admin.	21,000.00	1,181.43	5,682.03	19,818.57	14,136.54
Chem.	9,082.00	0	0	9,082.00	9,082.00
Etc.					
Etc.					
Etc.					
Total	686,081.00	4,501.92	24,474.01	681,579.08	657,105.07

The following is a very simple example of how the encumbrance process works:

Date	Budgeted	Encumbrance	Expended	Free Balance
7/1/09	100,000	0	0	100,000
7/2/09	100,000	100	0	99,900
8/2/09	100,000	0	95	99,905

At the start of the fiscal year there are 100,000 units to spend with nothing encumbered or expended. On day two you decide to order an item you think will cost 100 units, so you encumber that amount. The budgeted amount never changes, unless you transfer additional funds. The encumbrance is now 100, expended is zero, and free balance is 99,900. One month later, the item arrives and its invoice shows the actual price was 95 units. You now have zero encumbrance, 95 expended, and a free balance of 99,905. In the real world, it is not that simple. There are dozens of transactions each day, and data change in each of the other three right-hand categories.

The only two days of the year that the head of an acquisitions unit may know exactly how and where each penny was spent is the first and last day of the fiscal year. For the balance of the time, you can only approximate how much is available. Why is it an issue?

There are several reasons, but three of the most important are: budget control, spending the moneys allocated, and which of two accounting systems are in place—cash or accrual. The need for the first of these reasons should be clear without further comment.

Spending moneys allocated may seem an unusual reason; however, when acquiring materials for the collection, as experienced acquisitions staff knows, one cannot always count on receiving everything ordered and certainly not always in a timely manner. Items that are out of stock and promised by a certain date may never come back into stock or at least arrive much later than promised. Items dealers say are available in time turn out to not be available. Also, it takes vendors some time to deliver items. If one operates with a 12-month fiscal period and knows it takes an average of 45 days for delivery, does one stop placing orders six to seven weeks before the end of the fiscal period? Doing so leads to uneven workflow/loads and there is no assurance that all the outstanding orders will arrive on time. This concern leads to the third reason.

Most organizations employ either a cash or accrual accounting system. Unfortunately for most government-funded information services, the system is the cash basis. A cash system does *not* allow one to carry forward unexpended funds. Thus, any encumbered but not expended funds at the end of fiscal period revert to the funding authority. Clearly, with service funding problematic, losing even a small part of the yearly budget is unfortunate. Services operating under the cash system have only three options:

1. Spend early in the year and hope new desirable items released late in the year will be available when the new fiscal year begins.
2. Overencumber the appropriated amount about two months before the end of the fiscal year. This can be risky, as all the items might arrive and there would be no money to pay for them. Over time, acquisition staff can predict reasonably well the percentage of items that will not arrive and spend 98 to 99 percent of the available funds.
3. Ask vendors near the end of the fiscal year to *not* date their invoices. This allows the service and the vendor to date the invoices later so as to assure a steady work flow as well as expand the funds in a reasonable manner. Some of the invoices will be paid in the coming fiscal period and some from the current year.

Under the cash system, it is possible to carry the overencumbrances forward, but at a cost. Using our earlier encumbrance model, what would happen if the service decided to carry overencumbrances?

	Cash System			
Date	Budgeted	Encumbrance	Expended	Free Balance
Last Day/FY	100,000	10,000	90,000	0
First Day/FY	100,000	10,000	0	90,000

So one can see the result is that there are only 90,000 monetary units to spend over the next 12 months, a 10 percent reduction in funds available. One of the authors became the director of a special library operating on the cash system at the beginning of a new fiscal year and was told the acquisition librarian had encumbered all of coming year's collection-development funds! The choices were to not buy any new materials for the next 12 months or to cancel some of the encumbrances. Neither prospect was pleasant, but canceling old undelivered orders seemed the least damaging.

From a service point of view, the accrual system is the desirable system. This system allows one to carry over unexpended funds, or at least some percentage of the unused moneys. Again, our simplified example shows the difference between cash and accrual systems.

Here you have the full budgeted amount available plus the unexpended funds from the prior fiscal year. Sometimes it is possible to get the funding

		Accrual System		
Date	Budgeted	Encumbrance	Expended	Free Balance
Last Day/FY	100,000	10,000	90,000	0
First Day/FY	100,000	10,000	0	100,000

body to agree to allow the service to use the accrual system, at least for collection-development purposes. An information service professional can make a good case for the accrual system for collection-development purposes given the vagaries of the information producers industry. Sometimes the funding authorities may want to place an upper limit on the allowable amount you may carry forward. Given the cost of information resources and the size of most service budgets such a limitation may never be an issue.

Tables 16.1 and 16.2 illustrate other approaches to presenting a line budget showing revenue and expenses. Table 16.2 shows the relative position of a public library vis-à-vis other city departments; they serve as a reminder that government budgets are tied to the political process. Note: We modified the data slightly, but the relative funding levels reflect the actual situation.

Sometimes, as noted earlier line-item budgets use a formula to calculate some or all of the allocation. For a public library, this is quite frequently a per-capita figure based in part on a tax levy for library service. The local tax board sets the formula in a manner similar to setting school taxes and through elections requesting changes in the levy.

Academic libraries also use formulas which vary widely. A common formula is to set aside an arbitrary percentage of the total institutional budget for library service (5 percent has been suggested as an ideal figure). Another common method is to calculate a budget on a per-student FTE (the library receives a certain amount of money for each full-time-equivalent student attending the institution). Although this method is responsive in terms of student body size, it ignores unequal library use among students (undergraduate and graduate). And, when increases in enrollments are greater in the social sciences and humanities than in the "hard" sciences, library use may be much heavier. Also, two half-time students are likely to use the library service more than one-full time student, but will only count as one student.

Line budgets are probably the least complex to manage. A new budget request usually starts with last year's allocation as the base builds from there. More often than not you will have received some "guidelines" from the parent body about its overall plan for the budget. These will almost always indicate how much, if any, inflation you may add to which lines. You may be encouraged to shift monies from one line to another to better reflect

Table 16.1
Comparative Statement of Budget Appropriation

	2006–2007		2007–2008		Increase (Decrease) from 10/10/06 Revised Budget
	Budget	Estimated Expenditures	Department Request	Proposed Budget	Percent
Liberty Fund	16,831,136	17,532,393	30,321,411	17,751,250	6.7
Recreation and Parks Fund	29,858,515	29,890,956	35,483,681	30,800,380	5.7
City Employees Retirement Fund	60,969,748	60,754,315	59,374,474	59,374,474	1.9
Fire and Police Pension Fund	160,804,761	162,798,946	176,213,314	165,427,766	3.2
Other Funds	699,435,869	696,610,302	779,389,230	750,583,908	
Total–Departmental	967,900,029	976,586,912	1,070,782,110	1,023,937,778	6.9
Community Redevelopment	12,000	12,000	12,000	12,000	—
General City Purposes	10,561,604	8,618,978	10,214,403	10,183,729	2.7
Water and Electricity	20,630,000	21,529,000	22,040,256	24,940,000	20.9
Unappropriated Balance	23,513,387	10,000	82,050,000	82,050,000	260.4
Capital Improvement Expenditure Program	44,378,386	48,246,000	120,109,404	45,680,602	3.6
Community Development Trust	40,669,834	27,246,390	47,014,194	47,014,194	15.6
Library	14,716,351	10,504,938	21,227,418	21,227,418	44.6
Bicycle License	48,000	199,011	48,000	48,000	—
Public Facilities Trust	4,700,000	4,700,000	—	—	100.00
Enginering / Transportation Training–Travel	6,000	5,800	6,000	6,000	—
Special Parking Revenue Fund	3,075,848	2,345,160	4,078,307	2,620,000	14.8
Sewer Construction and Maintenance Fund	7,632,352	7,632,352	8,520,000	8,520,000	11.6
Special Purpose Funds	—	—	85,217	—	—
Bond Redemption & Interest	16,318,577	16,318,577	15,171,839	15,171,839	7.0
Total–Nondepartmental	186,262,339	147,453,423	330,541,821	257,872,781	39.3
Total	1,154,162,368	1,124,040,344	1,401,323,931	1,281,810,559	12.2

Table 16.2
Summary of a City Budget

Library Department

This department operates and maintains a central library having thirteen specialized reference and circulating book collections and reading rooms, four units in the civic center which offer specialized library service to City government, seven regional branches providing reference and circulating service in their respective regions of the City, fifty-five branches providing neighborhood service and five traveling branches; and controls its own funds.
Revenue

REVENUE

Receipts 2006–2007	Estimated Receipts 2007–2008		Budget 2008–2009
APPROPRIATIONS			
$ 8,870,399	$ 6,032,393	Mayor-Council Appropriation:	
--	--	Regular	$ 2,006,038
–	–	Reserved in Unappropriated Balance	500,000
		Property Tax and State Replacement of property Tax Revenue–One Percent Fund (Schedule 1)..	5,592,000
7,000,000	11,500,000	Local Assistance Trust Fund (Schedule 6)	11,500,000
$ 15,870,399	$ 17,532,393	Total Appropriations....................	$ 19,598,038
OTHER REVENUE			
$ 107,437	$ 53,684	Cash Balance, July 1	$ 159,900
553,060	610,000	Fines	671,000
159,794	182,000	Receipts from Water and Power Department...........	195,000
174,359	160,000	Other Receipts...	154,000
–	–	Fire Loss Reimbursement	72,000
$ 994,650	$ 1,005,684	Total Other Revenue....................	$ 1,251,900
$ 16,865,049	$ 18,538,077	Total Revenue..........................	$ 20,849,938

EXPENDITURES

Expenditures 1998-1999	Estimated Expenditures 1999-2000		Budget Appropriation 2000-2001
SALARIES			
$ 13,306,429	$ 14,148,987	General	$ 16,311,101
(346)	–	Overtime	–
$ 13,306,083	$ 14,148,987	Total Salaries..............................	$ 16,311,101
EXPENSE			
$ 6,736	$ 9,300	Office Equipment Expense...........................	$ 12,850
99,259	93,000	Printing and Binding	75,085
212	1,300	Traveling Expense	5,176
19,849	41,000	Contractual Expense	43,886
52,123	60,000	Transportation Expense	60,200
291,337	300,000	Library Book Repairs.................................	360,625
1,285	1,000	Uniforms	3,291
124,103	160,000	Office and Administrative Expense..................	225,532
33,771	40,000	Operating Supplies and Expense....................	71,203
$ 628,675	$ 705,600	Total Expense............................	$ 857,848

Expenditures 1998-1999	Estimated Expenditures 1999-2000		Budget Appropriation 2000-2001
EQUIPMENT			
$ 41,800	$ 246,000	Furniture, Office and Technical Equipment.................	$ 297,221
$ 41,800	$ 246,000	Total Equipment	$ 297,221
SPECIAL			
$ 2,373,337	$ 2,968,000	Library Materials	$ 3,382,768
600	--	Unappropriated Balance...............................	1000
$ 2,373,937	$ 2,968,000	Total Special	$ 3,383,768
$ 16,350,495	$ 18,068,587	Total Library............................	$ 20,849,938

your operating needs (an exception here is you rarely have freedom to shift salary monies). On the downside you may be instructed to reduce some or all lines by a certain amount. When it comes to reductions hope for being given a target amount and being allowed to find the necessary funds from lines you think will cause the least damage to user services.

Performance Budget

Earlier, we stated that experts do not think line-item budgets are as good as other budget formats from an efficiency and effectiveness point of view. Why is this so? One reason is that it is the easiest budget format for incremental increases taking place, or as critics say, "once a line always a line, and once a mistake always an ongoing mistake." Another issue is that the lines focus on categories of expense, not on how well, the unit expends its funds. There is no easy way of relating a line-item budget to a service's mission, goals, or objective. Thus, there is no identifiable relationship between expenditure and achievement. The other formats do link expenditure and achievements in various ways.

Some people view performance budgets as *the* tool for fiscal control. Performance budgets focus on what service staff members do (tasks) rather than on classes of expenditure. A performance budget is an expansion of a line-item budget, but gives managers and funding authorities a means to assess the unit's performance, at least in terms of quantity and establishing unit costs. The following example of a simplified performance budget shows the relationship between the line-item and performance formats:

Performance Budget				
	Acquisitions	**Cataloging**	**Reference**	**Circulation**	**Administration**
Salaries	$xx	$xx	$xx	$xx	$xx
Materials	$xx	$xx	$xx	$xx	$xx
Postage	$xx	$xx	$xx	$xx	$xx
Telephone	$xx	$xx	$xx	$xx	$xx
Office Supplies	$xx	$xx	$xx	$xx	$xx
etc.	$xx	$xx	$xx	$xx	$xx
etc.	$xx	$xx	$xx	$xx	$xx
Total	$xxx	$xxx	$xxx	$xxx	$xxx = Grand Total
%	xx%	xx%	xx%	xx%	xx% = 100%

Getting information about unit costs is easier with the performance budget. Such data is helpful in thinking about the cost-benefit of outsourcing a function. (Outsourcing is the practice of using a vendor to supply a service or function that the service traditionally did with its own staff.) While there is a substantial body of literature, at least in the United States, about this "new" idea of outsourcing, libraries have in fact been doing this in acquisitions for many years—especially in the area of acquiring serial publications.

Check These Out:

Good overviews of outsourcing can be found in:

Cunningham, Sharon. 2002. *Outsourcing*. London: Euromoney Institutional.

Pantry, Shelia, and Peter Griffiths. 2004. *Managing Outsourcing in Library and Information Services*. New York: Neal-Schuman.

Wilson, Karen A., and Marylou Colver. 1997. *Outsourcing Library Technical Services Operations*. Chicago: American Library Association.

The major drawback to the performance budget is that it is of little value in assessing quality. Thus, while a step closer to relating to the mission, goals, and objectives of the service, it still does not show a clear relationship between monies spent and service quality. One reason senior service managers might want to employ a performance budget internally is for staff development. In essence, you can give each functional department head her or his own line-item budget to manage. This approach provides a useful training tool for new information professionals, as well as raising the level of knowledge of the overall issues of managing the service budget on the part of all department heads. It also will usually result in more realistic budget requests from the department heads as they gain an understanding of budgetary issues.

Program Budgets

Program budgets relate the expenditures to the activities/programs the service provides and links monies spent on them to the service's mission, goals, and objectives. Needless to say, such budgets require substantially more time to prepare. The extra time requirement may account for the lower usage of this format. One example of how the program budget takes more time to prepare than a performance budget is in allocating staff time to various programs. While some staff may devote 100 percent of their time to a single program, others may have responsibilities in several programs.

The question for such individuals becomes how much time to attribute to program X and how much to program Y.

How a service defines its programs will depend upon how it defines its mission, goals, and objectives. (Later in this section, we give an example from a special library environment.) Whatever the case may be, implementing a program budget requires introducing three major operational concepts:

1. developing an analytical ability for examining in-depth service goals and objectives and the programs designed to meet them
2. creating a five-year programming process plan combined with a sophisticated management-information system
3. creating a budgeting mechanism that can take broad program decisions, translate them into refined budgetary decisions, and present the results for action

The following steps are necessary to accomplish the third task of identifying fiscally efficient operational programs that meet broad goals:

1. identify service objectives
2. relate broad objectives to specific service programs
3. relate programs to resource requirements
4. relate resource inputs to budget dollars
5. relate inputs to outputs

These steps not only provide a quick overview of how the program budget works, but they also indicate the interrelated nature of management activities. They also provide another indication of why program budgeting is time-consuming.

The next step in the formulation of a program budget is to determine appropriate work programs: groups of related activities that produce complete tasks and products. You then assign to each work program a cost which serves as the basis for the estimation of the work program's financial requirements.

Each work program has a unit justification, which states that program's general objectives and its scope of activities. Once you know the budget allocation, an allotment system helps assure that the manager may redirect funds if the work programs change.

You can assign to any activity within a service a time and cost factor. You then combine these factors in work measurements to determine how much time and money is necessary to do both the parts of a job as well as the whole job.

To determine staffing needs, you multiply the number of units of work programs by the time factor per work unit (usually, work hours) and then divide by the number of hours a person works per year. You determine the cost by dividing the work-hour cost of producing a measure of work by the annual number of work units; then multiplying that cost by the number of work units anticipated for the coming year.

This quantitative emphasis presents problems, though. First, how do you determine work-unit measurements? Is cataloging measured by titles or by volumes processed? It may not be both. Also, there is the problem of applying standards where they are amorphous, or nonexistent. A related problem is that measuring public service activities qualitatively is difficult at best (see Chapters 7 and 11). If unit production drops but quality of service increases, how do you measure that aspect? Can you measure the quality of the materials being used? What is the relative use of materials within the service, and how is that measured? These problems underline the necessity of clearly stated objectives at the outset of attempting to measure service.

The ultimate objective of program costing and work measurement is to develop a standard cost and performance for various functions, activities, and subactivities. The standard is simply an average based on past performance; you adjust it as new data become available. The following example is a program budget request prepared for a special service. It sets down the goals of the service, the tasks to be carried out, and the estimate of costs.

Table 16.3
Sample Program Budget Request—FY 2008

Goals:

I. To provide access to significant fish and wildlife research information developed under the Federal Aid in Fish and Wildlife Restoration, Anadromous Sport Fish Conservation, Endangered Species, and the Cooperative Fishery and Wildlife Research Unit programs for research staffs of contributing agencies.

II. To provide access to non-Federal aid, state-sponsored research for the staff of contributing agencies.

III To provide access to Federal aid and non-Federal aid research for the staff of non-contributing and private agencies.

In order to accomplish these goals the following objectives (services) have been determined:

A. Input (Indexing Services)

To acquire, evaluate, index and process research reports produced by the Federal Aid in Fish and Wildlife Restoration program, by the Anadromous Fish Conservation Act (sport fish only), the theses and dissertations produced by the Cooperative Research Unit programs, and the approved recovery plans required under the 1978 amendments to the Endangered Species Act, and non-Federal Aid state research. In addition, not to exceed 75 manuscripts submitted by the American Fisheries Society during 2008.   *(cont'd.)*

Table 16.3
Sample Program Budget Request—FY 2008 *(Continued)*

1. Acquisitions will be arranged by the U.S. Fish and Wildlife Service and coordinated by the Project Manager and Indexing Specialists. Five trips, one to each regional office of the Fish and Wildlife Service, will be planned for the purpose of promoting the acquisition of Federal Aid and non-Federal Aid reports. These trips will also serve to publicize the services and resources of the Reference Service. The project manager will attend the Federal Interagency Field Librarians Workshop and the Special Libraries Association Annual Conference.

* Personnel	$21,114.71
Travel	$ 4,800.00
Telephone	$ 432.00
Total:	$26,446.71

2. Evaluation of 1,200 reports for possible inclusion will be done, according to established selection criteria for the scope of the FWRS collection, by the Consultant (an experienced fish and wildlife biologist).

Consultant	$6,800.00

* Note: "Personnel," where shown, includes payroll, plus fringe benefits at 35%, cost of living salary escalation at 12%, and merit increases for 2008 at 2.5%.

3. Indexing of 650 reports will be done according to established selection criteria policies for bibliographic description and classification by subject content using the FWRS Fish and Wildlife Thesaurus by the Indexing Specialists. In addition, re-indexing needed to maintain consistency with the revised thesaurus will be done.

4. Processing entries for reports, including theses, for computerized storage, according to the most efficient mechanism, will be done by the indexing Specialists. Digital copies of all materials added to the data base will be prepared for archival purposes.

Personnel	$11,271.07
Data processing	$ 3,600.00
Digital copies	$ 500.00
Total	$15,371.07

B. Output

To provide customized retrospective literature searching to FWRS cooperators and clients.

1. Literature searching will be done according to established search strategy policy, using computer-stored information about the FWRS collection to produce web-based bibliographies (1,100 est.) by the reference staff.

(cont'd.)

Table 16.3
Sample Program Budget Request—FY 2008 *(Continued)*

Personnel	$ 12,484.87
Consultant	$ 520.00
Data processing	$ 2,762.00
Postage	$ 950.00
Telephone	$ 3,388.00
Total	$20,104.87

2. State indexes will be provided by the reference staff, when bibliographies are not appropriate to answer requests. Updated fish and wildlife indexes for each state will be produced and distributed once a year to each state fish and game headquarters.

Personnel	$6,326.07
Data processing	$ 600.00
Total	$6,926.07

3. Reproduction and dissemination of reports to fulfill requests will be done by photocopying original reports (est. 600,000 Pages) or digital copies (est. 4,000) by the Photocopy Clerk. The FWRS office will be open regular hours for users to examine and study reports first hand.

Personnel	$31,112.31
Digital copies	$ 2,200.00
Equipment rental	$19,087.10
Supplies	$ 5,400.00
Postage	$ 5,200.00
Printing	$ 6,445.50
Total	$ 69,744.91

C. Fish and Wildlife Reference Service Newsletter

To make known the services available from the FWRS to potential users in cooperating agencies and others, by mean of a quarterly *Newsletter*. This publication will provide information on new services, changes in activities, new literature added to the FWRS collection, and other information of interest to FWRS users. The *Newsletter* will be published quarterly and distributed without charge to 10,000 users and potential users.

Personnel	$28,563.26
Printing	$ 6,006.80
Postage	$ 2,000.00
Maintain mailing list	$ 2,000.00
Total	$38,570.06

(cont'd.)

Table 16.3
Sample Program Budget Request—FY 2008 *(Continued)*

D. Administration and Other Costs

This covers personnel time and other costs needed to administer the program of the agency. This includes training, supervision, representation at meetings, planning, budgeting, billing, space rental, miscellaneous office equipment and supplies, and part of the telephone and postage cost.

Personnel	$19,423.16
Other costs	$ 9,336.00
Total	$28,759.16

E. General and Administrative Expense, or Overhead

General and administrative expenses are calculated to cover certain expenses incurred by the city public library.

Expenses involved with activities of the personnel department, Payroll department, building maintenance and custodial care of facilities and equipment, accounting, printing and duplicating and security services, which are allocated to the Fish and Wildlife Reference Service.

In addition, a portion of the expenses of the City Librarian, the Director of Planning and Evaluation Services, and the Director of Technical Services are also included as a part of the expense allocation.

The expenses have been calculated to equal a rate of 17.0% of the operating budget and is a rate that is applicable to all contractual and grant funded services provided by the city public library to any state or federal agency.

F. Income

Charges are made to clients for all services and to cooperators for some duplication of materials. Estimated income is credited to the contract.

Summary of Program

Program	Amount	% of Total
A. Input	$ 48,617.71	19.53%
B. Output	$ 96,755.85	38.88%
C. FWRS *Newsletter*	$ 38,570.06	15.51%
D. Administration	$ 28,759.16	11.56%
E. General and Administrative Expense		
@ 17% of A through D	$ 36,162.87	14.53%
Grand Total Cost	$248,885.65	100%
F. Credits-Income	$ 35,000.00	
Net Cost	$213,885.65	

The primary weakness of the program budget lies in its emphasis on the quantification of service activities. Comparative evaluations will involve qualitative judgments, which are difficult to reflect in the quantitative elements in the budget.

In summary, program budgeting is not the following:

1. It is not revolutionary, except in its arrangement.
2. It is not a substitute for good judgment, opinion, experience, or knowledge.
3. It is not an attempt to computerize decision making.
4. It is not just another way to save money and cut expenses.
5. It is not the answer to every problem involving every financial issue.
6. Program budgeting is no more than a way to force budget managers to think very carefully about their mission, goals, objectives, services, priorities, and expenditure.

Zero-Base Budget

The budgeting wave of the future during the 1960s and early 1970s was thought to be program budgeting; however, problems in measuring service and the amount of time it took to gather information reduced the wave to a ripple. The next candidate for such a wave arrived in the form zero-base budgeting (ZBB) in the 1980s. It is currently little more than a ripple on a small pond. Supporters claimed ZBB was a possible replacement for the line, performance, and program formats. When taxpayers have major concerns about their tax burden, ZBB has rather widespread appeal, if not application. Thus, we may see ZBB resurfacing in the coming years.

Developed by Peter Phyrr as a means of achieving more effective planning and fiscal control, the basic concept of ZBB has become somewhat confused in the minds of the general public. The term zero-base comes from the first step in the process: the development of a hierarchy of functions based on the assumption that the unit or agency is starting operations for the first time (point zero). Thus, the focus of the planning and development of the ZBB is on the unit's purpose and on the function(s) it should perform in order to meet the reasons for its mission. In theory, a government or an organization that uses this budgeting system would become more cost-effective by continuously reviewing its purposes and attempting to remove unneeded activities. From a taxpayer's point of view, if governments would put ZBB theory into practice, the existing tax base would produce the maximum level of service at lowest cost. However, as was evidenced by former U.S. President Carter's administration's effort to impose ZBB on the federal government, theory and practice often are very far apart (Phyrr, 1970).

Several phases of ZBB are necessary in order to implement the system: construction, planning, budgeting, and control. The time-consuming part of the process, and the one that assures a more cost-effective use of the moneys available, is the construction phase. It is during the construction phase that the budget maker assumes that the unit is engaging in zero activity.

During the construction phase, the person who is responsible for an activity creates a series of function statements and function outcomes in terms of the basic purpose of the unit. For example, assume that you are the head of an archive. You might identify two functions (there probably would be more, but we will only illustrate two): "to ensure that users receive accurate assistance in their search for primary materials" and "to ensure that users receive proper instruction in the use of archival resources, especially publishing rights." The function outcome statement would be "accurate assistance" and "users instructed in the use of archival resources."

You then divide functional statements into a series of subfunctions, thereby creating a hierarchy of activities. Under the function "instructed . . . user," you might list a set of the subfunctions, such as: "to ensure the understanding of residual property rights" (outcome: identified skill), "to ensure that users who need assistance are identified" (outcome: users identified), and "to ensure that users learn archival research skills" (outcome: knowledgeable customer). One could go further and divide each subfunction. For example, the "identified skills" subfunction might have divisions such as "to ensure that users know how to differentiate between primary and secondary materials in an archival collection," and "to ensure that users know how to properly credit archival materials."

Our limited example illustrates just how time-consuming such a process would be for an information service. When you think about an entire organization in ZBB, it is not surprising that a very large percentage of the budget process is spent on "construction." No one disagrees that such a careful review of functions is valuable from time to time. But after their first "construction," very few individuals revisit their initial statement, which defeats a major purpose of ZBB.

"Decision packages" are the ultimate goal of the construction and planning phase of ZBB. As part of the construction process, you must establish a quantitative value and calculate the financial resources required to achieve each outcome statement. Normally, you calculate the quantitative figure and total cost on the basis of annual output rather than unit cost. These costing activities are very similar to those of program budgeting. The outcome statement with costs becomes a decision package (see Figure 16.4 for an example of a decision sheet).

During the next phase of ZBB, you study and question each "decision package" (functions, subfunctions, and subsubfunctions): "Do we need this output at this cost?" "Can we reduce the unit cost in any way (new equipment,

Figure 16.4
Sample Budget Decision Package

Program Name: Date: *May 21, 2007*

Building Renovation Program   Prepared by: *Lisa*

Description of Goals and Objectives:

To decorate the offices of all members of the law department.
To create a contemporary, pleasant, and business-like atmosphere for employees to work in
*   and customer to feel comfortable in.*

Feasibility Assessment:

1. Is the program legally required	_____ Yes	_X_ No
2. Technical feasibility	_X_ High	_____ Med. _____ Low
3. Operational feasibility	_X_ High	_____ Med. _____ Low
4. Economic benefits (describe below	_X_ High	_____ Med. _____ Low

Identifiable Benefits:	Potential	Probability of Occurrence	Probable Gross
Attraction of new customers	$ 5,000,000	.05	$250,000
Signing of major government * political contracts*	$ 8,000,000	.08	$640,000
Total Benefits	$13,000,000	.13	$890,000

Tangible Costs to Corporation:

Employment of outside decorating firm, *and lawyer time to consult with decorators* *about desired characteristics of the* *working environment*	$ 8,000,000	.10	$ 80,000
Total Costs	$ 8,000,000	.10	$ 80,000
Probable net benefits (cost)			$810,000

Intangible Benefits

Increased morale of workers.
"Contagious effect" of company's desire to improve working conditions and pride in image.
Public's and employees' recognition that company is competitive with majority of similar
*   corporations that have modern, well-coordinated offices.*

Economic Risks   _____ High   _____ Med.   _____ Low

Possible consequences of not acting:

Loss of potential significant business revenues and lowered employee enthusiasm.

more self-service)?" "If we increase our capability, how will that affect our unit cost?" From the questioning process, you develop several alternatives showing different levels of funding.

Typically, there is the minimum level of service package, the current-level package, and two other packages. One of the two others will be for a level somewhere between the minimum and current level and the second one for an increase over the current level. Frequently, there may be several packages with different increases proposed. This provides senior management with the opportunity to make informed decisions regarding the levels of service they wish to fund.

The last step in preparing the decision package(s) is to rank each option and package in terms of their decreasing benefit to the organization. Needless to say, a high percentage of the options suggesting increases rate higher than those with decreased support. In theory, the front-line manager has the opportunity to prioritize their activities.

Upon completion of prioritizing by the front-line manager, the packages go to that person's supervisor. Each higher level of manager repeats the ranking, because each higher level must balance more and more factors. Thus, the process that began in departments and units in the service continues until the senior manager reviews and perhaps reruns the packages. The funding body also reviews the ranking; it too may change the rankings. Thus, a final budget is established—one that should be more cost-effective and reflective of the purposes and services of all the agencies involved.

Clearly, the time necessary to prepare a comprehensive zero-base budget on an annual basis is enormous; few organizations that still employ some variation of ZBB revisit the construction annually. In addition, ZBB forces senior managers to review piles of paper. Most of the organizations that used ZBB decided the information overload at the most senior levels was too great. As a result, they terminated the ranking process one or two levels below the top.

Perhaps the largest negative for ZBB, other than time consumption, is its participative nature. Participation is important when using any budget format. Where the danger lies in ZBB is the ranking and reranking. If a first- or second-level manager experiences frequent rejections of her/his rankings, at best the person's commitment to ZBB will be in jeopardy; at worst, morale and commitment to the organization will fall, along with trust in the higher levels of management.

FUND ACCOUNTING

Because the majority of information services are part of nonprofit organizations, we include a brief section on fund accounting. This is a complex topic, and we can only provide some highlights.

Fund accounting is peculiar to nonprofits. Accountants developed the system as a result of the characteristics of nonprofits and of the users and uses of information. Four of the nonprofits' "special" characteristics are:

- the focus on social benefits
- the relative absence of profit-motivated behavior on the part of resource contributors (public and private)
- the special government- and constituent-imposed constraints on their activities
- the lack of generating a profit (this is not the same as generating income)

Users of fund accounting information are a diverse group, both internal and external to the organization.

There are similarities between fund accounting and profit-motivated accounting systems in terms of activities, terminology, and qualitative objectives. However, profit enterprises use a single-entry focus while fund accounting usually involves many fragmented financial reports. Such reports focus on separate individual funds and the flow of liquid assets rather than income.

The *general fund* exists to account for the unrestricted resources as well as resources not accounted for in any other group of accounts. (General-fund operating statements show revenues, expenditures, and encumbrances, as well as changes in fund balances.) *Debit service funds* track resources segregated for paying interest and principal on a general obligation debt. (Many information services have new facilities paid for in full, or in part, by bond issues—a general obligation debt.) *Capital project funds* control resources for the purpose of acquiring major fixed assets. (Reports on capital project funds seek to list sources, uses, and available resources for individual projects. Most service facilities projects are a combination of monies from public and private sources; such moneys would be part of the capital project fund.)

A *special-revenue fund* accounts for, and reports on, resources that come from special sources—for example, a foundation—or that carry restrictions on their use. (Many services, particularly national libraries, have endowment moneys which would fall into this category of fund.) Some municipalities, and some academic institutions, engage in some form of commercial activities. An example is the licensing of a patent developed at a university's engineering school. *Proprietor funds* are the means of accounting for such activities. There are two subtypes of proprietor funds: enterprise funds and internal service funds. *Enterprise funds* control activities that provide goods or services to the general public on user-charge basis. (Money from photocopy services in a service could be part of the enterprise fund, depending on the volume involved.) *Internal service funds* are similar, except the "customer" is part of the organization. (You may encounter "chargeback" situations in which one unit of an organization provides a service for another unit for a fee. Two common areas where chargebacks occur are computing and building maintenance.) The last type of fund is a *fiduciary fund*, which accounts for resources held by the agent or trustee for someone or a group. (This is not a type of fund most services would ever deal with.)

Long-term assets and obligations are not included in balance sheet reports on the above funds. However, control of such assets and liabilities must exist and somehow be recorded and disclosed. To that end, two types of groups of accounts serve this function: *general fixed-asset group* and *general long-term debit group.*

While service managers may have little direct involvement in fund accounting, they do have substantial indirect contact, whether they know it or not. Having some knowledge of fund accounting will assist in working more effectively with funding authorities.

Check This Out:

Smith, G. Stevenson. 2002. *Managerial Accounting for Libraries and Other Non-for-Profit Organizations.* 2nd ed. Chicago: American Library Association.

AUDITS AND AUDITORS

Accountability is a keystone in effective management. Without question, fiscal accountability is a concern to supporters and budget officials. Essentially, an audit is a post-action review by an independent appraiser. There are several types of audit, not all of which are financial in character; however, the majority of audits do have finances as the underlying concern.

External and internal audits are the two broad categories. In the United States, almost every for-profit and nonprofit must have an annual external audit conducted by an independent auditor. Normally, an independent auditor is a certified public accounting firm (CPA). There are two major purposes of the annual audit. The first is to assure that financial accounts and statements are accurate. Second, that the organization is following generally accepted accounting principles. Such audits, due to their legal implications, are very thorough. A service that is part of an organization that must have an annual external audit may expect occasional, if not annual, visits from the independent auditor. One never knows exactly what the auditor will want to review until she/he arrives; however, more often than not, it will be the collection-development fund accounts.

Internal audits, or operational audits, may or may not be fiscal in nature. Some of the typical audits are:

- financial records (accurate, proper, and in order)
- compliance (both internal and external policy and procedure)
- operational (evaluate effectiveness and/or efficiency of an operation)
- performance (purchasing, receiving, and payment records must follow proper fiscal and accounting regulations)
- fact finding (official job classifications and descriptions must accurately reflect the work being done)

More often than not parent body employees conduct the internal audit. These employees usually report to the chief operating officer of an organization in order to assure their independence of judgment. Compliance and operational audits may use outside consultants in order to have the depth of knowledge needed to make judgments about a particular area.

For Further Thought:

Reflect on the nature of the records that might be audited, and check the auditing requirements for services in your country and state.

The first time a unit manager/supervisor hears, "Auditors are arriving tomorrow," there is some degree of apprehension. Thoughts such as, "Did I do everything right?" "Can I remember why I signed the requisitions 11 months ago?" "Does the proper 'paper trail' exist?" or "Am I in some type of trouble?" are common. Auditors and audits generate a certain amount of anxiety, even in persons with experience in going through the process. Too often, the reaction to auditors is as if they are "snoopers" and "busybodies" who only create extra work. They do create extra work, but they provide an essential stamp of approval indicating sound accountability. Sound accountability is a major factor in receiving adequate funding for one's operation. Jennifer Cargill offered good advice some years ago in an article entitled, "Waiting for the Auditor" (1987). She ends her article with, "Following the Ps—Proper Prior Planning and Preparation—will make them Painless" (Cargill, 1987: 47). Doing so may not make it painless, but they will make it at least less painful.

INCOME GENERATION

Today, few services can expect to receive all the funds they need from their parent institutions or at least as not enough to operate the way they would like. James Walter made the point about public libraries in a 2005 editorial, "We are at such a crossroads in public libraries, as we seek funding from both public and private sources, we hone our political acumen to negotiate with city, county, state and federal officials to get the best financial resources for our readers. When those advocacy efforts don't work, we shift gears to marketing in new ways and identifying new resource sources." His comments could just as well apply to any type of information service, not just public libraries. New sources of revenue are surprisingly diverse, at least for those who think broadly.

We include the following in new sources: The traditional private individual donor; seeking grants and gifts from foundations; grants from various government agencies, both outright and for services provided to the agency; creating a "friends" group; and income generation from service activities and partnerships with various organizations, including profit-oriented groups. At best, we can only briefly touch on these topics and must refer readers to some of the sources devoted just to these topics.

Check These Out:

Two useful publications to read to get more in-depth information even though they may appear dated are *Becoming a Fundraiser*, by Victoria Steele and Stephen Edor, 1992 (Chicago: American Library Association); and "Ten Principles for Successful Fundraising," by Gary Hunt and Hwa-Wei Lee (*Bottom Line* 6 no. 3/4 [1993]: 111–121).

Developing and maintaining a special and positive image is important for all services—and it becomes essential for fund raising. There will be no opportunity for securing extra funds if the service's image is anything but positive. Having a positive image is not enough. You must communicate that image to users, the general public, as well as to prospective sources of new funding. Granting agencies are just as interested in the image of their grantees as are individual donors and private foundations.

This is an area where having a marketing plan linked to an active public relations program is essential in identifying special funding niches and opportunities. From an income-generation point of view, that niche may need modification or amplification to fully explain what it is your service does exceptionally well. We indicated earlier that finding sources of funding, other than the parent institution, for "light bulbs and toilet paper" is a challenge. Foundations, donors, and other grant-giving organizations are only interested in funding special projects that have a very high probability of success. Securing funding for this activity *may* free up general operating funds for important or special activities that are underfunded, if at all. Part of the niche aspect is using in-house expertise or doing something no other service in the area does or can do as well. There *will be* competition from other services and other organizations seeking extra funding, and it will require an investment of time and collaboration within the organization if it is to be successful.

Fund raising, while it may have to be a part-time activity, requires planning and leadership. It will not be effective if it is a matter of "I'll do it when I have time." Only the very large services have the luxury of a full-time fund raiser. Most must depend on the efforts of several people who devote some of their time to fund raising—a team approach. As with any team, there needs to be one person in charge to call meetings, set agendas, propose ideas, implement plans, push the initiative forward, and monitor outcomes. In essence, provide the leadership. Generally, that person is the senior or next-most senior manager of the service. One reason for this is because donors want to know they are working with the decision makers.

Regardless of source, income generation is largely a matter of "the right person asking the right source for the right amount for the right project at the right time and in the right way." As you might imagine, getting all those "rights" right takes planning, practice, preparation, and practical experience. Workshops help, but only real-world experience, and a few disappointments along the way, will translate theory and ideas into "money in the bank."

Funds are available from a variety of sources. Some are internally generated, assuming the funding authority allows the service to keep income it generates. One long-standing internal revenue source for libraries is the sale of duplicate or otherwise unwanted gifts/donations. "Gifts in kind" to libraries are very common; how they dispose of such items varies. Publicly supported libraries need to be aware of any regulations regarding the disposal of "public property" and just when an item gains such status. In some instances it becomes so once the item is donated and accepted; in other cases, it only becomes public property when added to the collection. In addition there may be tax implications for both the donor and recipient. Donors may benefit from a tax deduction for donations in cash or kind to charitable or public bodies.

Many services, especially libraries, impose fines for rule infractions, and lost or damaged items, all of which generate income. How the parent body treats such income can have an impact on your budget, since many U.S. jurisdictions require that all fines go into the general operating fund, not credited to the agency collecting the fine. As you might guess, not getting monies paid for a lost or damaged item can become a drain on your budget, particularly if you must repair or replace the item. That in turn puts more pressure on you to raise monies from somewhere. A similar situation may exist for fees charged for services, although it is much more common for the service to be able to retain all or most of that income.

Check This Out:

A good source for looking into the issue of internally generated income is Murry Martin and Betsy Park's 1998 *Charging and Collecting Fees and Fines* (New York: Neal-Schuman).

Another quasi internal source is through activities undertaken by non-staff people (support group) on behalf of the service—"Friends of Anywhere Service," "Service Associates," "Supporters of ———," or some other title. That group may be no more formal than some volunteers who handle an ongoing book sale or may be a formal legal entity (Foundation). In some situations, even governing board members may be expected to make an annual contribution to the service. There may be special types of "internal" funds such as endowments, wills, trusts, living trusts, etc. Such sources of funds are usually only found in larger or highly specialized services.

As information services generate an ever greater amount of its total budget from nonparent body sources, some have created a type of "foundation" to handle outside funds. In the United States, such foundations are legal entities and generally have a 501(c)(3) status with the IRS. Such status means they must not engage in any type of political activity. A major reason for having a foundation is to raise funds that are generally not taken into consideration by the service's parent body when setting the service's budget allocation. Another plus is the foundation may invest the funds raised to generate still additional income. Without doubt, such bodies can be very effective fund raisers as they are almost always composed of individuals who strongly support the service and its programs. Never underestimate the power of users voices when it comes to fund raising.

Check These Out:

Good sources that address establishing a foundation are:
   Edie, John A. 2002. *First Steps in Starting a Foundation*. 5th ed. Washington DC: Council on Foundations.
   Hopkins, Bruce. 2001. *Starting and Managing a Nonprofit Organization: A Legal Guide*. New York: Wiley.

We covered volunteers in the previous chapter and noted there that we would explore "friends groups" in this chapter. Our reasoning was that support groups, regardless of their name, almost always have a fund raising component to their activities, and the group as such seldom carries out routine service work—although there is often a high degree of crossover between the support group and service volunteers. The significant difference between a support group and a foundation, at least in the United States, is that few support groups have the IRS status 501(c)(3), which means they may engage in political activity and lobbying. Very often a service will have both a support group and a foundation. Even if they do not engage in political activities they have been a major local group, especially for public and school libraries, that raises supplemental funds for the service through such things as annual or ongoing book sales, bake sales, etc. Such groups have been raising a great deal of money for services over the years even though many of their events only raise a small sum the total is impressive.

Creating a relationship with Friends Groups is essential. Most will pay an annual subscription and expect to be approached for donations to special projects—perhaps the acquisition of an important archive or piece of equipment for a library. In return, the service may organize an annual dinner within the service in the case of prestigious collections, or at a local venue—for which a charge is levied. Invitations to the openings of exhibitions or displays of treasured items in the collection as well as a regular newsletter all help to encourage donations, especially if they can be tax-deductible. Networking in the community by the staff of the service helps to build links with potential members and recognition of members at other community events helps to strengthen relationships. The authors enjoy the relationships they have with a number of Friends Groups.

Check This Out:

For U.S. services, regardless of type, a group source of information about "friends" groups is the American Library Association's www.folusa.org.

There are also some rare and, in the past, overlooked opportunities to raise some substantial amounts of money locally—wills and trusts, "planned giving." Clearly bequests in a will only become a source of funds at death; however, today many nonprofit groups actively work with people to have the service be included in a will. (Based on one of the author's experiences, you must also continue to maintain and perhaps improve the service's relationship with individuals who have made a provision in their wills to benefit the service. You must not forget them.) Trusts, on the other hand, come in many shapes and sizes. Some may generate income for the service only during the donor's lifetime; others may generate income for both the donor and service during the donor's lifetime, while others only become effective on the donor's death. These are likely to increase in importance for information services over the coming years. As this chapter was being drafted one author received the following letter:

> Dear Charter Member,
> Enclosed is our *Legacy Circle* newsletter featuring an increasingly popular method of philanthropy—giving while living. As you will learn, making a charitable gift during your lifetime will support the National Museum of ———— and benefit you!

The rest of the material went on to describe the benefits of a trust agreement that would provide an income stream to both the donor and the Museum.

Check These Out:

One online source of information on planned giving is Charitable Donations Through Planned Giving (Available: www.paperglyphs.com/nporegulation/planned_giving.html [accessed November 29, 2006]).

A book to consult, regardless of service type, is Amy Sherman and Matthew Leher's 2000 *Legacies for Libraries: A Practical Guide to Planned Giving* (Chicago: American Library Association).

Partnerships with business are one of the newer fund-raising approaches for services, at least in the United States. Many services prefer to use the term "collaboration," as it seems less profit-oriented. Glen Holt (2006) listed several reasons for seeking "corporate partnerships." His last reason, in our opinion, is the most telling: "Co-funding through sponsorships can be a great way to build and share current and potential audiences between the public and private sector" (Holt, 2006: 35). What you need to do is think broadly/imaginatively to find sponsorship possibilities. We provide a case study with this book that illustrates an early example of an effective, if small-scale partnership between a branch library and a business. Partnerships with business can be extended to acquiring expertise that is not available within the service. Local radio and TV stations may provide airtime, local newspaper reporters can brief staff on how to write good copy, and public relations companies may well be prepared to offer their help to nonprofit services. Some national and state retail and banking organizations encourage their staff to work in the wider community. In London, staff from some of the major banks help children with their reading in local schools.

Grants and "gifts" from foundations and government agencies is our final "other funding" source category. The art of grantsmanship is something you can develop, but like any art it takes practice and then more practice before you have a consistent degree of success. Seeking grants is usually project-focused—seed money for a new program, partial support of a facilities project, funds for new or replacement equipment, etc. As such it requires carefully thought-out plans; in the case of facilities it may require the existence of working drawings for the project.

An important step, in fact a key step, is to be certain you know what a foundation's or agency's current funding priorities are. Although their broad interest seldom changes over time, their annual funding priorities within the broad area may in fact vary from year to year. Do your research before making a call or sending a letter of inquiry. Most granting agencies have Web sites where you can do a substantial amount of research about mission, priorities of the current funding cycle, what the funding cycle is, proposal guidelines, deadlines, and much more. Most grant-giving agencies are willing to talk by phone to explore projects. This can save the time of the agency and the service if the nature of the proposed project can be outlined, to see if it is within the scope of the agency. If it is, a valuable contact has been made.

Check These Out:

For Australia	www.fia.org.au
For the United Kingdom	www.fundraising,co.uk
	www.institute-of-funding.org.uk
For the United States	http://fdncenter.org/funders/grantmaker
	http://philanthropy.com

If you have no prior experience in grant/proposal preparation, taking a workshop or two is well worth the time and possible expense. Some grant-giving agencies organize workshops to outline their requirements. Also, when possible seek the assistance of an experienced grant writer. Be prepared to fail to get a grant on your first few efforts; keeping trying and you will succeed. The good news is that with many foundations, once you are successful, your chances of later grants go up—assuming you have delivered on the first grant.

> **Tip:**
>
> Many granting agencies look very favorably on collaborative proposals. A proposal that relate to several types of information services engaging in a cooperative effort appear to be very attractive to agencies. An example of this is in the 2007 LSTA grant guidelines in Arizona model: "the library and partnering organization(s) develop a strategy to share and promote resources."

Even if fund raising is a part-time activity there is an institutional cost. Time spent on fund raising is time not spent on service operations. The service's position as part of a larger whole usually means that it must get approval before undertaking fund-raising activities. Senior managers may not approve such activities if they believe funds raised would not outweigh the time and effort expended or to be in conflict with other "broader" fund-raising activities. One reason for this is to coordinate fund-raising activities and not have several units from the institution approaching a single source with different projects. Another reason is that one proposal may already be in front of the source and another proposal might cloud the issue. In addition, input will be required from the parent institution to ensure that it has been properly costed, and that the parent is fully aware of what the service plans to do. The authors have found that institutional accountants and lawyers provide excellent free advice.

Cultivating relationships is a key to successful fund raising. Major donations or modest ongoing gifts usually arise from long-term relationships based on respect and trust. For individual donors, this often means social contacts in a variety of settings, few of which relate directly to fund raising. For foundations and granting agencies, it means successful projects that delivered the promised outcomes.

Part of developing/cultivating prospects involves making sure the work is completed as planned and on time. Sending a funding agency a final report on the project, especially if that is not a requirement, reminds the agency of your service and what good "value" their funds generate. Even more effective are less formal contacts and communication; even just sending holiday greetings can help you keep in touch. The same idea applies to individual donors. Sending lists of items purchased for the collection using a donor's money or endowment income is a common practice in services. While donors for a new building or space in the service receive invitations to attend the grand opening, they are often forgotten until the next fund-raising effort takes place. Letting such donors know about favorable reactions of customers and the general public to the new space is a way to keep in touch without "putting on the touch."

> **For Further Thought:**
>
> Select an information service in the nonprofit sector and list six ways in which it might raise funds.

Some services are very successful at fund raising. The ways in which you do it are influenced by the organizational culture. One example is Los Angeles Public Library, which raised considerable funds to rebuild the library after a major fire. Whilst retaining important architectural features of the damaged building, some spectacular additions were built. And the donors have their names prominently displayed in the library.

An article by Yvette Tilson (1995) in *Bottom Line* provides a fine overview of library cost-recovery activities in the United Kingdom. The article reflects data she collected in a survey of academic, public, and special libraries in the United Kingdom. Her list of services for which some of these libraries now charge is a long one. A similar survey in other countries would probably produce very similar lists and perhaps add one or two additional items.

Excluding photocopying and fines, which she mentions in the article, her list included the following:

Audiovisual loans
Book loans
Book reservations
Interlibrary loans (appears to include all forms of document delivery)
Room letting (renting meeting rooms to public groups)
Entertainment (programs featuring speakers, films, etc.)
Library publications
Sale of withdrawn stock
Telecommunications
Reference access (fees charged to persons outside the primary service population)
Inquiries (fees for specialized in-depth information, also noted some discussion of charging for general reference questions taking more than ten minutes to answer)
Online services
CD-ROM access
Output from electronic sources
Consultancy (assistance in doing actual research/information-broker type activity)
Selective dissemination of information
Seminars
Publications (for example: postcards, local history booklets, etc.)

Perhaps her listing of photocopying—self and staff—covers all types of copying. If not, then one could add charging for paper copies from microforms and photographic copies of materials from an archive or special collection. To her list might be added consulting services and software/systems development. Although these are done by individual librarians and not the institution, publicly funded organizations usually require that a percentage of the royalties or fees earned are paid to them.

Seeking large-scale project funding is being encouraged by governments as they set up cross-sectoral or cross-national agencies to kick-start collaboration. For example the European Union offers a wide range of grants to encourage cross-European collaboration. Pors and Edwards (2001) described their experience of a project that linked Denmark, the United Kingdom, and Eastern European countries. Considerable benefits can be gained by the staffs of the services, and visibility is increased. They write of some of the frustrations that can be encountered, but also the value of the project.

Large-scale funding has an impact on the information service. Aside from staff time needed to oversee and manage the project, it will probably involve the recruitment of specialist and contract staff and the need for office space. Contract staff may work in a different way from regular staff— different hours of work, often into the small hours, may be less visible, and work under considerable pressure at different times during the project. They may be seen as having a glamorous role as they travel during the project, but the staff members of the service probably do not appreciate the time spent in airport lounges and away from home. It all needs careful management. Controlling budgets can be a headache if unexpected expenses arise. Yes, there are the downsides, but when these are overcome, considerable benefits can be gained by the service, and often the profession at large.

Experience with project funding indicates that the key to success is to consider the nature of the project—what is the benefit and the intended outcome? Income generation is essential today—but it must have an aim so good that it can be "sold" to a funding agency.

KEY POINTS TO REMEMBER:

- Fiscal management is about securing, expending, and accounting for the essential monies to operate the best possible information service.
- Budgeting is more than managing this year's allocation; it is thinking about what you will need in future as well how well you managed previous allocations.
- Budgeting is a political process which involves careful monitoring of your service's environment, if you hope to secure adequate funding.
- You seldom have a voice in the type of budget to use—line, performance, etc.—so your goal is to make the most effective use of what type is in place. This requires some study of the type's theory and methodology as well as assessing the organizational culture of the parent/funding body.
- Gaining an understanding of accounting and financial terminology will aid in developing sound relationships with those who devote their full-time attention to money matters in the parent organization.
- Securing funds from sources other than the parent body will become an increasingly important part of information services fiscal management activities.

REFERENCES

Baker, David. 1997. "Resource Management: the Context." In *Resource Management in Academic Libraries*, edited by David Baker. London: Library Association.

Boese, Kent. 2006. "Brother, Can You Spare Another $2.6 Billion?" Editorial. *Bottom Line* 19, no. 1.

Buschman, John. 2003. *Dismantling the Public Sphere*. Westport, CT: Libraries Unlimited.

Cargill, Jennifer. 1987. "Waiting for the Auditor: Some Interim Advice." *Wilson Library Bulletin* 67, (September): 45–47.

Cargill, Jennifer. 1988. "Financial Constraints: Explaining Your Position." *Wilson Library Bulletin* 68, (April): 32–34.

Ezard, John. 2004. "Libraries Hit by Fall In Book Borrowing." *The Guardian* (15 October). Available: www.guardian.co.uk/news/articles/0,1328082,00.html (accessed November 2006).

Holt, Glen. 2005. "Getting Beyond the Pain: Understanding and Dealing With Declining Library Funding." *Bottom Line* 18, no. 4: 185–190.

Holt, Glen. 2006. "Economics: Corporate Sponsorship." *Bottom Line* 19, no. 1: 35–39.

Hunt, Gary, and Hwa-Wei Lee. 1993. "Ten Principles for Successful Fundraising." *Bottom Line* 6, no. 3/4: 27–33.

Martin, Murry, and Betsy Park. 1998. *Charing Fees and Colleting Fines*. New York: Neal-Schuman.

Meraz, Gloria. 2002. "The Essentials of Financial Strength Through Sound Lobbying Fundamentals," *Bottom Line* 15, no. 2: 64–69.

Phyrr, Peter A. 1970. "Zero Base Budgeting." *Harvard Business Review* 48, no. 6 (November/December): 111–121.

Pors, Niels Ole, and Vilas Edwards. 2001. "International Co-operation: The West-East Relationship in EU Funded Projects." *Library Management* 22, no. 3: 124–130.

Seer, Gitelle. 2004. "No Pain, No Gain: Stretching the Library Dollar." *Bottom Line* 17, no. 1: 10–14.

Shanahan, Eileen. 1991. "The Other Side of the Recession." *Governing* 4 (March): 44.

Shaughnessy, Thomas. 1989. "Management Strategies for Financial Crisis." *Journal of Library Administration* 11, no. 1: 67.

Steele, Victoria, and Stephen Edor. 1992. *Becoming a Fundraiser: The Principles and Practices of Library Development.* Chicago: American Library Association.

Tilson, Yvette. 1995. "Income Generation and Pricing in Libraries." *Bottom Line* 8, no. 2: 23–36.

Wildavsky, Aaron. 1992. *The New Politics of the Budgetary Process,* 2nd ed. New York: HarperCollins.

LAUNCHING PAD

The Big Book of Library Grant Money 2007: Profiles of Private and Corporate Foundations and Direct Corporate Givers receptive to Library Grand Proposals. 2007. Chicago: American Library Association.

Guyer, Mark. 2002. *A Concise Guide to Getting Grants for Nonprofit Organizations.* New York: Kroshka Books.

Hallam, Arlita W., and Teresa R. Dalston. 2005. *Managing Budgets and Finances: A How-to-Do-It Manual for Librarians and Information Professionals.* New York: Neal-Schuman.

Hwang, Samuel. 2006. "Fund Raising: Where There Is a Will, There Is a Way." *Bottom Line* 19, no. 3: 146–151.

Library Trends. 2000. A special issue on development and fund raising. Vol. 48 no. 3.

Maxwell, D. Jackson. 2005. "Money, Money, Money: Taking the Pain Out of Grant Writing." *Teacher-Librarian* 32, no. 2 (February): 16–21.

McDermott, Irene E. 2006. "'Get Outta Here And Get Me Some Money Too': Web Resources for Public Library Fundraising." *Searcher* 14, no. 7 (July-August): 13–17.

Steele, Victoria, and Stephen Elder. 2000. *Becoming a Fundraiser: The Principles and Practices of Library Development.* 2nd ed. Chicago: American Library Association.

17

Managing Technology

> *"For a successful technology, reality must take precedence over public relations, for nature cannot be fooled."*
>
> Richard P. Feynman

> *"It is better to design systems around human beings than to redesign human beings to fit."*
>
> Maurice Line

INTRODUCTION

Managing technology presents interesting challenges. There is the challenge of maintaining currency with the pace of accelerating change and to also look at what is happening on the horizon. Technology generates some collaboration challenges, as it increases both the interdependency of the information service with the parent organization and with other information services. Information services are generally not self-sufficient, except for the very largest services and in some universities, but rather their needs form part of the overall provision of communications and information technology within an organization. Managers of information services collaborate with colleagues to arrive at the best solution that meets the needs of the organization as a whole.

Information services collaborate by working together as clients of specialist software vendors to discuss changing needs, which in turn drives the improvement of products. Negotiating contracts for the purchase of electronic resources is generally carried out through a consortium. This collaboration is essential if managers are to get the best outcome for their service at the most favorable cost; working together reduces the risk of making a poor investment.

The question of making a poor investment is important, since information and communications technology takes up an increasing percentage of the service's budget. Technology influences the layout and design of the physical service, and requires a rising level of investment of time and funding in staff training and user education.

Check This Out:

The American Library Association's TechSource Online (Available: www.techsource.ala.org [accessed October 2006]) is a good site for keeping in touch with developments in library technology.

ICT (information and communications technology) impacts every staff member and user. The administrative functions of front-line staff, such as user registration and staff rosters, are automated. Acquisitions and cataloguing are also online. Users access reference services remotely with documents and information being delivered in both print and digital formats. Middle and senior staff members within the service and the wider organization are able to access planning information online, creating more transparent decision making. The information service is at the hub of an organization and the community it serves. Having access to and using technology effectively and efficiently allows the service to anticipate and quickly adjust to changing circumstances to meet the emerging needs of its stakeholders.

COLLABORATION

Collaboration has always been part of the service ethic of information professionals. But many managers have stepped out of the information service to take on a wider technology role within the organization. Librarians have a long and successful record of developing large computer databases, collaborating with vendors, creating shared services, and handling frequent changes in technology. So perhaps it was not surprising that when information and communication technologies merged in the 1980s and universities developed student-centered learning that some people who were librarians stepped into positions as Chief Information Officers (CIOs) indicating they managed library, archives, records, learning support, and ICT services. They had a professional, technical, and, probably above all, user-centered approach to service, coupled with being decisive and good listeners. The critical and challenging role of the CIO when systems must deliver results is described by Broadbent (a former information professional now at Gartner Inc. and the Melbourne Business School) and Kitzis (2004).

The relationship between CIOs and academic research libraries has been examined by Snyder (2006). Hanson (2005) brought together papers describing convergence in the United Kingdom, and Wainwright (2005) discussed strategies for university academic information and delivery services in Australia.

There are signs of a growing trend in collaboration between independent software vendors in the information service sector, rather than the fierce competition that formerly existed. The aim is to lower the cost and technical barriers for services, making it easier to share data more easily.

The next developments in collaboration will bring together services across sectors, as government policies encourage linkages between archives, libraries, and museums. This will bring some exciting benefits for users crossing the boundaries—for example, between information and cultural services. It creates the need for e-leaders.

E-LEADERSHIP

A digital environment calls for a new paradigm for skills development and organizational learning in networked organizations, as management practices, leadership and ICT are integrated in ways not previously possible. At the same time there is pressure to reduce operating costs, and increase customer satisfaction. The e-leader has the challenge of thoughtfully integrating a service or organization using new technologies to closely link staff that can be physically dispersed, resulting in the isolation of individuals, yet ensuring that a social system remains.

The basics of leadership discussed in Chapter 14 remain valid, but with some changes in emphasis. In an e-environment there are paradoxes, greater ambiguity, and the need to understand behavioral complexity.

E-leaders need to take into account four considerations that should be built into the planning process:

1. the level of technology provided by the parent organization—few information services are free-standing
2. the need for good documentation since in a virtual environment there is less opportunity to turn to a colleague to clarify a detail in a policy or process
3. a regularly updated database of management information
4. the security of the ICT system.

The paradoxes of e-leadership are having the understanding to be, and be considered:

- swift and mindful
- individual and community
- top down and grass roots
- details and the big picture
- flexible and steady (Pulley and Sessa, 2001)

Try This:

Take the five paradoxes identified by Pulley and Sessa (2001) shown above and note down how they are evident in an information service known to you.

DELIVERING SERVICES

The process of service delivery continues to change in all types of information services. As the Internet provides a gateway to information services, so users can work from home, office, or classroom as well as in an archives search room or library. The degree of digitization varies, but at a minimum level, even the smallest service is striving for an online catalog. Some now do have the capability as small-scale software packages have become available. The largest academic libraries and information services in business, law, and healthcare access an increasing proportion of their sources in a digitized format and use the benefits of developments such as RSS to deliver a customized feed to their users.

The technological implications for service delivery are:

- the need for a robust infrastructure backed up by ready access to skilled technical support
- 24/7 access
- efficient information security policies
- excellent relationships with vendors and providers of outsourced services
- a realistic budget for maintenance, licenses, and upgrades
- an investment in staff and user training
- effective environmental scanning of potential impacts upon the service

But having the technologies is only part of the picture; it must be backed up by staff members who understand the needs of the user community, anticipate these needs, know the relevant sources, and deliver the required information in the preferred format at the right time. Information delivery still requires a human intervention.

Try This:

Select a type or specific example of information service.
Consider the implications of ICT for the service adding to the examples given above.

DATA FOR DECISION MAKING

The veterans among information professionals recall the days when management information was collected by counting records and maintaining statistics in paper records. One considerable benefit for managers is that technology now provides data to support planning and decision-making processes. Each level of management has different needs. Those handling day-to-day operations need data about units of work finished, and an inventory of supplies and forms. Middle managers require a combination of bottom and top information, such as current data about the performance of the units they oversee and historic data that demonstrates performance over time. In turn, they provide projections of future progress and needs to top management. Top management needs extend beyond the internal service data and draw on data prepared by the parent organization and its external environment. Such data enables senior management to develop and monitor strategic plans and overall long-term directions and goals.

Point of Reflection:

Consider a type of archive, library, or records management service and list all the ways that you can think of in which technology can be used to provide useful data for management.

Reflect on earlier chapters, particularly those on decision making, performance, quality, and control.

Some management gurus consider that technology is *the* driving force in the field today and should be the primary focus of interest, but since managers have a long history of operating without computers, they have developed a body of principles and practices which are technology-independent. Technology is a tool for managers, not an end in itself. If it provides more data, alternatives, and models more quickly to aid decision making or any other basic management function, that is welcome. However, managers must still understand how to assess the data and the decision-making process (or other function) in order to take effective action. Technology should not, and in most cases cannot, replace human judgment and assessment.

TECHNOLOGICAL CHANGE

If managers could see into the future, one area that they would like to be able to forecast would be technological change. What new technologies will emerge, and what will be rate of change? Just think about the way in which cell phones have changed during the past decade.

Information services have a long history in using computer technology. The Library of Congress developed work applications for the first generation systems (approximately 1951–1958) which moved into libraries in the early 1960s. Libraries are an example of a type of organization that shifted from dependence on manual systems to almost total dependence on technology. They employed most of the major computer systems starting in the 1960s with mainframes, shifting to minicomputers in the late 1970s, the client/server model in the 1980s, then moving to Web-based technology in the 1990s. Librarians demanded ever-growing functionality in the systems that they acquired so that by the mid 1980s, the terms "integrated library system" and "turnkey system" were filling the professional literature, and more holdings were acquired in a digital format.

This happened against a backdrop of a reduction in both the physical size of computers and the environmental requirements for housing the system, a substantial increase in system reliability, and reducing costs-per-million instructions.

Check Out:

The current cost-per-million instructions today compared to 1980. Could you draw a graph to illustrate the decline in costs?

Another important factor was a great increase in local data-storage capacity. Without such increased capacity, today's PC-based database applications would not be possible. Early minicomputers were "big" if they could handle half a gigabyte, while at the time of this writing even a home PC comes with several hundred gigabytes as standard—and upgrades are possible at nominal cost. While the cost per unit, such as instruction or storage, has dropped significantly, increased expectations and the need for improved capability still results in a substantial bill when replacing a system.

Looking to the future of integrated systems in archives, libraries, and museums, we expect more user-friendly developments. The design of integrated systems was based on the traditional catalogue, and although the systems handle print material well, they do not handle electronic content effectively. It must be capable of handling all the work within the service and deliver services to users working remotely via the Web. It must also be capable of interacting with other automation systems using appropriate standards and protocols. The tools to deliver e-content have fallen behind service needs (Breeding, 2006).

More archive and library services are likely to join consortia to acquire shared systems and hence share some costs. Users gain benefits from this approach. Georgia's public libraries are developing an open source integrated library system which could produce a challenge to commercial systems (www.open-ils.org).

Records management changed dramatically in a very short time span as word processing was introduced into offices followed by electronic mail. This produced challenges of capturing, storing, and retrieving electronic documents which may have legal standing, e.g., financial records required to be held for prescribed periods of time, audit trails for due processes, and personnel records. It involves questions of confidentiality and hence security and the capability to migrate to new systems, among others. E-mails are a challenge in all organizations, and procedures are required to ensure they are stored so that they can be retrieved at a later date.

Check These Out:

ARMA International. 2004. *Requirements for Managing Electronic Messages as Records*. Lenexa KS: ARMA International.
Findlay, Cassandra. 2002. "Future Proof: Ensuring the Long-Term Accessibility of Technology-Dependent Records." *Records Management Journal* 12 (3): 87–93.

Part of the technology manager's challenge is to deal with two issues. First is the integrated automation system used by the staff in the day-to-day performance of their work, and the second issue is user access to services and collections. Services have moved in the direction of being Web-based in order to circumvent, as much as possible, the variety of platforms and system capabilities that end-users employ.

One issue that is important in any network environment, but *critical* for their clients is server "up" time. With most services operating 24/7 for remote access, the need for reliable servers is an important issue. To achieve that goal, servers need to be "up" 99.9 percent of the time.

Four of the major benefits of operating some form of a client/server environment are:

- the capability of sharing files and interacting with other systems accessible through a local or wide area network
- the capability to move computing functions from a large central system to local servers and workstation/terminals
- the capability to reduce end-user training by providing graphical interfaces with point-and-click technology
- the capability to employ multiple applications from a single workstation/terminal

In addition, since services are usually part of a larger organization, the parent body may require going with a client/server environment.

Looking to the future in the library sector, OCLC continually expands services it provides to its members and so is at the cutting edge of developments and a reliable source for ICT forecasts. At the time of this writing, the latest environmental scan available is for 2003 (OCLC, 2003). OCLC suggests that the next period of change will be as great as the shift from the mainframe to the client/server. "Using sophisticated messaging, open-source solutions and new security protocols, data processing and information exchange will become tightly connected to business processes, facilitating new kinds of collaboration, partnering and connecting relationships." There are four aspects of the new "landscape that will impact information creation, dissemination and management: bringing structure to unstructured data; distributed component based software; a move to open-source software, and security, authentication and Digital Rights Management" (OCLC, 2003: 8–9). As OCLC's activities spread further around the world so a considerable amount of work is in progress to support access to materials written in scripts other than the Latin script as used for the English language.

Tip:

Keep abreast of technological change by following Lorcan Dempsey's Weblog on libraries, services, and networks (http://orweblog.oclc.org). Lorcan is Vice-President Research and OCLC's Chief Strategist.

The challenge to accurately predict the future direction of ICT, or the speed at which changes will occur, is a very good reason for scanning the computing and telecommunications media, talking with vendors, and attending professional briefings which provide a sense of what might happen.

Point of Reflection:

Reflect on the technology that an information service would like to have, but which doesn't exist at the present time.

PLANNING AND CONTROLLING COSTS

Migrating from one generation of equipment to another is a costly process. Unlike some other capital expenditures, the useful life span of digital technology has been dropping, so managers must view the financial investments in this area as being short term. The payoff comes in terms of the more efficient use of staff time and an enhanced service to users—for example, self-service issue systems in public and academic libraries. While managers at all levels understand that the useful life of equipment is getting shorter and shorter, funding officials in some organizations may not yet understand this fact. They often think, "If we provided X amount of money for technology equipment this year, we will not have to deal with this for four or five years." Managers face several challenges: planning for technology purchases, controlling costs, and ensuring that higher-funding authorities understand the nature of ICT costs and rates of change. Vaughan (2005) has described the challenges associated with maintaining the technology at a showcase academic research library, the Leid Library at Nevada University at Las Vegas. It provides a case study of the situation four years after opening.

Dugan (2002) identified three types of costs in the introduction of ICT—one-time/extraordinary costs, initial costs, and recurring costs—and described a model designed to identify and model costs. In order to minimize the risk of making a wrong purchasing decision Marshall University introduced a decision-making governance model by merging the Office of Computing with the University Libraries both administratively and financially. Their strategy took into account the expectations, the sales pitch, why the product was chosen, what went wrong, and what was learned (Prisk and Brooks, 2005).

Funding concerns underlie all aspects of managing information services. However, ICT can, if not properly controlled, use all of the available equipment moneys and still require additional funds. And a warning; anyone who has not experienced a system migration may well underestimate the overall cost of the project. In addition to the obvious hardware and new software costs, there are often reprogramming and/or reformatting expenses, and always staff and user training expenses.

Planning

A key factor in maintaining a successful ICT program is careful long-range planning. Accurately predicting future changes in technology direction and the time of those changes is almost impossible much beyond 18 to 24 months. Nevertheless, the best insurance for handling technology in as cost-effective a manner as possible is developing at least a five-year plan.

By treating the process as a rolling plan, the benefits of long-term planning can be gained while maintaining the flexibility to adjust the plan to address a changing environment. (A rolling plan is one that is reviewed and revised each year.) All of the elements discussed in Chapter 8 (Planning) apply in this context. What makes long-term technology planning somewhat different from other planning is the almost certain knowledge that the plan will probably never be carried out exactly the way presented—that each year will result in modifications as circumstances and technologies change.

Managers must think about and plan for ICT from at least four viewpoints. Most important are the strategic considerations: factors such as competitive differentiation, overall improvement in decision making, and improved operational processes. Thinking about technology both offensively and defensively are also useful exercises. From an offensive perspective, considering how to achieve or realize maximum benefit from the use of ICT is vital. Defensively, think in terms of controlled growth and what is happening in similar services. The fourth point of view that underlies most of the other aspects is cost-justification.

Critical success factors (CSFs) are mentioned in Chapter 8. In essence they are the five or six areas where "things *have* to go right" or "failure will hurt performance the most." CSFs are very useful in technology planning, and in many ways are easier to identify than organization-wide CSFs. From an information service point of view, one of the technology CSFs is network reliability—both local and connections to the Web. Another CSF is the reliability of the integrated automation system. One last example would be the integrity of the customer database. These examples are some of the CSFs for an information service. These factors become useful in planning the architecture and long-term needs of information service technology.

Try This:

Some examples of the critical success factors for information technology planning have been given. Can you add four more?

There are a number of models for technology planning; we favor Ember-ton's (1987) holistic approach. The first step is to gain agreement on, or verify, the current statement of the service's mission and goals reflecting the actual desires of top management and any other approving body. If that agreement exists, and the service has been conscientious about its planning activities relating function and activities to specific goals and objectives, the next step is to review those functions and activities in terms of which ones might benefit from some technology application.

One obvious advantage of starting with mission and goals is that they are both general in character, which means the uncertainty about future directions of technology is less of an issue. Using objectives which are much more specific and that reflect the purposes of current functions and activities allows the manager to plan this, and next years' technology requirements, in a realistic manner.

Another step is to examine each goal, objective, function, and activity and ask the question, "Could ICT assist in its performance or achievement?" Related questions are, "What type and how much technology would, or could, be appropriate?" or "What problem does the technology address?" One example of a goal: "To provide 24-hour access to its resources for its primary service population." By using a general statement assuming that the service decides technology is a factor in achieving or maintaining such a goal, managers can develop a long range plan with a long-term direction without too much concern about unexpected technological change. This approach does not necessarily lock the service into a particular technology solution for the long term. It also makes it easier for the decision makers to look at today's state-of-the-art technology and consider experts' opinions about future trends when deciding what do during the next 12 to 18 months.

Basic technical issues also play a key role in a successful planning process. It becomes important to have answers to questions such as:

- Are there any organizational policies that influence decision making?
- What types of data are required to reach an informed decision?
- Which technology offers the greatest payoff in relation to service goals and objectives?
- What are the functional advantages, if any, of the new technology?
- What are the technical prerequisites for using a specific technology?
- If different objectives require different technologies, what are the compatibility issues?
- Does the service have the infrastructure to support the new technology?
- Is the technology an "open system" or proprietary? If proprietary, how difficult would it be to migrate to another system in the future?
- What technical strategy will be most effective: network or standalone?
- How will staff and users be affected?

- What are the staffing and training requirements?
- What are user education requirements?
- What are the short- and long-term implications?

Beyond technical considerations, there are political and end-user issues to technology planning that take many forms. Some of the more typical are:

- What is the parent institution's attitude toward expenditures on technology? Is it a long-term or short-term view?
- Is there an organizational policy to centralize ICT services or are they decentralized?
- Will the expenditure and implementation of the technology create relationship problems with other units in the parent institution or collaborating services?
- What is the track record of the service with funding authorities when it comes to implementing technology?
- Will all end-users be able to access or benefit from the proposed technology?
- Is there an issue about differing end-user platforms or "average" users' system capability?
- Does the proposed technology relate/meet immediate and long-term needs of end-users?
- Does the proposed technology restrict or constrain end-user creativity in using technology?
- Is the system flexible enough to meet all end-user needs?
- Are there any end-users training implications?

The planning must involve functional, institutional, usage, risk, and staffing analysis as well as taking into account implementation and hardware assessment. Managers must remember technology planning is more than developing hardware and software systems; it requires understanding of the organization, its purpose(s), and its customers. What the managers' goal should be is to create an information environment appropriate for the service while meeting the parent organization's needs; not to add technology for technology's sake or to "prove" it is up-to-date. In essence, technology development follows a four-stage process: problem definition and data collecting, conceptual design, detailed design, and implementation.

Controlling Costs

Controlling technology costs are a manager's challenge and budget officer's nightmare. Taking the example of libraries, traditionally they have two categories of expense that are ongoing and always increasing in size:

salaries and journal subscription costs. Both present challenges for managers. Some techniques for controlling salary expenses are: not granting additional staff positions, limiting annual salary increases, imposing hiring freezes, and, occasionally, cutting existing positions. Options for controlling subscription price increases are generally fewer because they are outside the library manager's and parent institution manager's control. However many libraries have joined consortia to gain bargaining power with publishers in order to limit journal cancellations.

Technology costs are the third component in the ongoing, ever-increasing cost category for many services. They are also beyond the control of information service managers. Unlike journals, managers are not as able to decide to "cancel" technology but like journals, services may join consortia to gain better deals with vendors. Since services are very dependent on technology for carrying out daily activities they may be able to delay expenditure for a time; eventually money will need to be invested in upgrades. If vendors no longer support the technology, either newer hardware/software has to be acquired or the cost and frustration of attempting to maintain the existing technology has to be faced.

The two most effective tools for controlling technology costs are a rolling five-year plan and developing a clear picture to determine which functionality is absolutely essential to maintain and which would be "nice" to improve.

For the less experienced managers, the obvious costs are the hardware expenses, and perhaps some software. More experienced managers would add possible programming or reprogramming expenses—if the new equipment is from a different vendor. Staff training costs are always more than anticipated. One nightmare for managers is the prospect of the system vendor going out of business. In the early days of proprietary systems, libraries had to begin automating almost from square one—the entire investment in the old system was lost. With the introduction of "open systems" in the 1980s, the situation improved.

These factors are important cost concerns, but the one that makes ICT increasingly expensive is the demand for even greater functionality. Functionality requires development by the vendor, the cost of which is incorporated into the price of the new models. U.S. library managers who have been involved in several acquisitions of an automation system liken the process to buying a new automobile. It seems as if everything is an "option at an additional cost." Establishing set of system requirements prior to starting a search is very useful in controlling the costs.

Owning a home computer demonstrates the problem of the constant need to upgrade memory and storage capacity. Just when someone thinks her/his computer is up to standard and goes to buy a new software program, the package lists system requirements that exceed the computer's capability.

In an institutional setting, this scenario repeats itself over and over again with every employee who has a workstation. End-users request additional features and functionality, software producers create a new product meeting those desires, and system requirements escalate along with costs. Given this reality, we do not feel that services should attempt to be on the forward slope of the technology curve. Too often, significant problems exist in "leading edge" products, and some products never do mature. We suggest that the prudent manager should only aim to stay near the top of the curve, or just slightly behind. Someone else can work through the inevitable bugs. In most cases, securing equipment funding is difficult, and spending it on unproven products is risky. Working with staff to keep technology expectations at a reasonable level is essential in managing technology.

In addition to hardware and software costs there are also systems costs, which primarily revolve around the people costs. Gaining approval for additional staff is a challenge, and most services find that they need to devote more and more staff effort to administering the system. One aspect of that process for services in education or used by the public at large is creating and maintaining equal access to electronic services for all end-users who have a wide range of computing equipment.

Try This:

List six areas of expenditure on information and communications technology. Which do you expect to increase in the next five years, and which may decrease?

Personnel assigned to system administration are often not additional staff but reassigned existing staff. Technology may not reduce workloads— it assists staff to accomplish more work and often creates unexpected new opportunities and activities. Hence managers face the challenge of balancing traditional activities and newer systems administration responsibilities with few, if any, additional personnel. One positive element is that today's courses educating information professionals generally cover system administration activities.

A continuing trend in many organizations is to outsource services to control costs. Providers of specialist services are able to employ a wide range of expertise and amortize costs over a number of customers, perhaps moving some tasks offshore. ICT services can be considered for outsourcing, particularly in small organizations. It requires a clear understanding of expectations on the part of the customer and supplier, a consideration of what would happen if the supplier fails, a careful examination of internal costs and outsourcing, a legal contract, and close monitoring of the quality of service provided.

Check These Out:

Matthews, Joseph R. 2002. *Internet Outsourcing Using an Application Service Provider: A How-To-Do-It Manual for Librarians.* New York: Neal-Schuman.
Pantry, Sheila, and Peter Griffiths. 2004. *Managing Outsourcing in Library and Information Services.* New York: Neal-Schuman.

STAFF BACKGROUND AND TRAINING

One aspect of managing technology involves making certain staff at every level have the necessary background and training to handle the technology that is in place, as well as the technology it plans to acquire. Funding for staff development opportunities for the professional side of information work funding is usually limited. In the case of technology, such opportunities are *essential*. The challenge is to decide how to allocate the funding available.

Check This Out:

Jennings, Anna. 2005. "Determining and Meeting Personnel Training Needs." *Computers in Libraries* 25 (8 September): 13–15.

With new applications or a major upgrade, having staff do training on their own with a user manual is not good use of their time. Vendors of integrated systems offer training in the use of their system, and so it is easier to build training costs into the price of acquiring the system than to secure funds for training. Some software vendors offer training packages that are built into the application as a "tutoring" program, often accessed online, as a CD-ROM, or training video.

Managers plan for three types of training: entire staff for a new application or system, new or replacement staff, and end-users. With this in mind, it is evident why training costs must be a line item in the annual technology budget. One aspect of technology training is the need to demonstrate, not just tell, how something is done. Sometimes it is possible to use a mentor approach for service-wide training. One advantage is the mentor is better able to relate to the special needs of her/his coworker than is a general trainer. Training in groups is more cost-effective than the one-on-one approach—this is true for both staff and end-users.

Training in ICT is influenced by networking in general and the Internet in particular. Two widely used training technologies are multicasting and video-on-demand, which can be implemented on either local area networks, corporate wide area networks (intranet), or the Internet.

Multicasting permits large numbers of users to simultaneously receive the same video. This sharing of a single video stream promotes efficient use of network bandwidth while permitting organizations to provide informational video or new application training for large numbers of simultaneous users. For instance, if a new version of a database interface is implemented, an entire staff can be trained simultaneously while they remain seated at their own desktops. Moreover, since this technology can be implemented across the Internet and intranets, its distribution center can be centralized while the receiving nodes can be distributed across multiple sites (e.g., at branch libraries) or an entire WAN. One server sends the same single video file to a set or a range of IP addresses.

The primary advantage of multicasting is also one of its major liabilities. It forces individuals to work at a specific time and place. Video-on-demand, in some ways a mirror image of multicasting, addresses this lack of scheduling flexibility. Each user can access the same, or different, multimedia materials at any given moment, permitting hundreds of training lessons to be stored on a video server for ad hoc access by users.

While multicasting and video-on-demand have their individual strengths, in combination they provide a rich environment for delivering training. The ability to be implemented across networks makes them easy to manage, provides economies of scale, and permits personnel savings. Many services now create a physical space for training usage that is private and is equipped with necessary technology. Cell phones, RSS feeds and the iPod can be used to deliver instruction to individuals and are cost-effective ways of helping students to use services and resources with which they are not familiar.

Another training cost is the help desk function that the staff provides. With remote access, users will ask both information-related questions and questions about accessing the system. Staff members answering such calls need to understand ICT, especially if the user has her/his own PC and ISP for remote access. Bell and Shank (2004) have described the role of the "blended librarian." There is a need for specialists who can handle the traditional requests for information and also "walk through" the technical problems with the user. It requires subject knowledge, awareness of the many technical problems the user may encounter, and the communication skills of a call center operator. And the communication skills are paramount.

However, managers must establish clear guidelines for user expectations concerning the level of technical support that can be anticipated.

Today the education of the information professional provides a good background in the basic areas: database management, spreadsheets, word processing, online searching, presentation graphics, and developing Internet pages. Some will go on to gain a qualification in ICT. Support staff are less likely to have an educational background in ICT, so managers need to ensure that this is provided for them.

For Further Thought:

Reflect on the issues that a manager will encounter in developing a staff training program for information technology. Select the three most important issues.

In Chapter 6 (Change), change and resistance to change was discussed noting that a manager cannot always predict when, or if, resistance will occur. However, among the types of change that have a very high potential for resistance, technology rates high. Introducing new technology almost always generates some staff resistance; replacing a system or a major upgrade has less potential, but still is relatively high. In 1970, Dickson and Simmons identified nine areas of staff concern or reasons for resisting technology which still hold today. They also studied which were most likely to arise for four categories of staff: operating nonclerical, operating clerical, operating manager, and top management. The reasons are:

- threats to economic security
- threats to status or power
- increased job complexity
- uncertainty or unfamiliarity
- changed superior-subordinate relationships
- increased rigidity or time pressure
- role ambiguity
- feelings of insecurity

They found that operating nonclerical personnel were least likely to resist technology change. When they did, it was usually because of concerns about job complexity, lack of familiarity, and time pressure. Top management shared the first two concerns of the nonclerical staff but not the last, while also having concerns about role ambiguity and feeling insecure. The operating managers expressed all of these concerns, while operating clerical staff shared all these concerns except for job complexity (Dickson and Simmons, 1970). Some of the resistance can be overcome through training. However, communication is the key to success by those planning and implementing technology changes. Encouraging staff input concerning their technology needs and when the best time to make the changes is will also help overcome resistance.

There is one other technology-related staff issue for managers: "technostress." One element is physical, as staff members spend more and more time using a workstation looking at a display screen. Poor posture, equipment, lighting, and physical arrangement can lead to a variety of physical or health problems, ranging from mild headaches and eye strain to carpal tunnel syndrome. Managers must take ergonomic factors into account, and a number of countries, such as the United States, have legal requirements that must be met. Staff need information about posture and exercises to release tension and how to plan their work so that they do not spend long uninterrupted hours at a workstation. Getting away, even for a few minutes every hour, reduces technostress. Build into tasks a mix of technology- and nontechnology-based activities so that staff can take a break.

The second aspect of technostress is mental, which can be experienced by staff, managers, and end-users. Managers know that changes in technology will result in tension and/or stress, even if there is no resistance. Part of the tension/stress reduction process is having ample and adequate training for the changes; ample lead time and getting written information about the change and technology usage reduces stress when the change actually occurs. Providing ergonomic equipment/furniture reduces physical discomfort and reduces stress.

Working with vendors to produce user-friendly paper documentation and online manuals in the local language can reduce technostress. Vendors offer their products internationally and do not always make allowances for different forms of the English language. (Nothing builds stress more quickly than facing some deadline that requires the use of a new technology or software and not being able to make it work, even when every step in the vendor-supplied documentation has been followed.) Talking with managers currently using the product is always a good practice. Ask them "How good is the documentation?" and "How good is the vendor training or support?" This is a critical issue for information services in geographically remote areas, where

---

Check This Out:

Huwe, Terence K. 2005. "Running to Stand Still?" *Computers in Libraries* 25 (8 September): 34–36.

local support may be limited or nonexistent. Knowing what to expect allows managers to anticipate and prepare solutions before the problem arises. Some personal factors for managers to consider are:

- Is it really essential that I have the same technology and applications at home as in the office?
- Is it really essential that I do this work at home?
- Is it possible that I could make better use of office time so I do not have to take work home?
- Is it possible that this is a task that could just as effectively be delegated?
- Is it really essential that I check my office e-mail from home at night, on the weekend, at a conference, or even on vacation?
- Can I turn my cell phone off when I leave the office?
- Is it necessary that I become the "techie of techies" in my organization when that is not my area of responsibility?

Technostress may be a current buzzword, but technology job-related disabilities are a reality. It is not something managers can avoid for both staff and themselves, but it can be reduced or at least controlled.

Try This:

Thinking about a specific type of information service, list all the causes of technostress that you can think of. Then, in a second column, list ways of overcoming them.

ELECTRONIC RESOURCES

Information service managers have one task that few other technology managers have. Not only must they deal with hardware and software operational issues, they must manage the content that the hardware and software delivers to the end-users. This introduces issues of evaluation and selection of electronic resources which are appropriate for a particular service.

From a management perspective, there are legal questions as well as questions of ownership and permitted usage. In the past, when a collection basically consisted of printed materials and microforms, it was only a question of complying with copyright law. Not that copyright compliance was a minor matter or easy—it's just that it was the only significant legal issue related to the use of most collections.

Check These Out:

Lipinski, Tomas A. 2006. *The Complete Copyright Liability Handbook for Librarians and Educators.* New York: Neal-Schuman.
Padfield, Tim. 2004. *Copyright for Archivists.* 2nd ed. New York: Neal-Schuman

---

Today, services often have several format choices for the products they secure for their end-users—for example, print or Web-based versions. We use the word "secured" rather than "purchase" because there is a question of ownership with electronic materials. When subscribing to a print journal or purchasing a book, there is no question about ownership. Nor are there issues about who may use the material or how often it is used. If a journal has 12 issues on a shelf and 12 individuals want to read one of the issues all at the same time, there is nothing to keep them from doing so. Access to Web-based information products comes with a license that imposes a variety of limitations on library use.

Vendors of electronic products view licenses as a means of controlling use of their products and protecting their investment, as well as more likely assuring them a profit on that product. All too often libraries treat the "opening this seal is taken as accepting the licensing agreement" statement that usually accompanies a software product in the same way most people do the contract they sign when they rent a car at an airport—they accept it without reading the agreement. If the person renting a car read and understood the rental agreement, there would probably be very few vehicles rented. The same is true for licenses accompanying electronic information products.

License agreements are legal contracts. A legal contract, according to *Black's Law Dictionary* (1990: 322), is "a promise or set of promises constituting an agreement between the parties that gives each a legal duty to the other and has the right to seek a remedy for the reach of those duties. Its essentials are competent parties, subject matter a legal consideration, mutuality of agreement, and mutuality of obligations." Clearly a key element in that definition is a matter of *mutual* agreement. That implies the possibility, if not actuality, of discussions and negotiations between parties. Edward Warro (1993) points out that libraries can and should be proactive in the matter of reviewing and negotiating electronic licensing agreements.

The failure to read and modify such agreements could result in loss of, or limitations, on "rights" that exist for paper products—for example, fair use, interlibrary loan, and multiple copies for face-to-face educational use. The license can impose limits on who may use the material that are impossible for the library to control or monitor in any cost-effective manner. Very often the license contains a clause that would impose on the library the legal responsibility for controlling how the end-user uses the materials—clearly an impossible task. Occasionally there will be some limitations on the frequency of use or the number of simultaneous users. The authors are not aware of a vendor actually attempting to "seek a remedy" for a service failing to comply with the last item; however, that does not mean it will not happen.

A lawyer need not review every contract; however, what is necessary is a plan for dealing with electronic licensing that has input from the service's parent organization's legal counsel. That plan or document should outline what rights are essential for the service (to retain downloading, printing, and copying, for example) which are highly desirable for retention as well as those that are of little or no concern. Because of the growing importance of electronic measures to an organization, it is vital that the planning team include representatives of all the units that have a stake in having access to electronic resources.

Some of the important issues to consider in such a process are:

- institutional policy regarding contracts/licenses
- costs of the material, reviewing, negotiating individual licenses, and additional costs for retaining a "right"
- definitions of key issues, terms, and clauses
- implications for end-users—will it produce a digital divide?
- implications for library staff
- ownership and archiving issues
- indemnification issues

As stated above, a license may limit a right a service has with paper-based products under copyright laws. The goals of a service and its parent institution should be that end-users have as much freedom to access and use the material under the license agreement as they do under print copyright. If they do not, there is something wrong. In some cases, "user" carries a very limited meaning in the license when compared to the library's definition. Another problematic term is "lending"—most licenses tightly control, if not prohibit, lending. What remote access is possible? Any service supporting distance education, training, or other geographically widespread activity has a vested interest in remote access.

As a result of concern about scholarly communication being impeded by the cost of licenses, the Open Access Initiative emerged which has two systems for delivering research papers: OA repositories and OA journals (Yiotis, 2005). *Information Research* is an example of an OA journal (www.infr.net).

Try This:

Use your knowledge—and imagination—to predict the direction in which electronic products will move in the next five years.

SECURITY

Computers and related technology are capable of doing several things faster and more accurately than humans can; however, they are prone to certain faults that can cancel out their advantages. The saying "garbage in, garbage out" perhaps started with the first computer. Human input error is a problem, and given the invisible nature of electronic circuitry, an input error can cause serious problems before anyone notices the error. ("Fat fingers" play havoc in financial institutions and stock exchanges.) More rare, but still a reality and even harder to identify, are errors within the system—perhaps a programming conflict. Other types of difficulty arise when one or more individuals begin to manipulate the system for personal reasons—to change or cancel a change or gain access to information, for example. There is also the accidental or malicious destruction of a database, software, or entire system.

These and other reasons are why managers must have a concern for security. There are two aspects: system security and quality assurance. Broadly speaking, there are three types of control that will help ensure quality and security:

- information system controls
- procedural controls
- physical facility controls

Information system controls attempt to ensure accuracy, validity, and propriety of system activities. Many relate to input as well as output data. Some of the data entry controls are passwording (or codes) for different levels of staff, formatted data entry screens, and audible error signals. Another type of information system control is control logs, which preserve evidence of all system input.

Processing controls help assure that correctly entered data goes through processing properly. Some processing controls identify errors in arithmetic, calculations, or logical operations, or data not processed or data lost. These controls are for both hardware and software. For hardware, such controls include malfunction detection circuitry, circuitry for remote diagnostics, and redundant components. In terms of software, checks for internal file labels, "checkpoints" within a program assist in building an audit trail, and system security monitors are examples of processing control.

System output is another area of concern for procedural controls. One example is logging of output documents and reports and where those reports went. Control listings are a means of providing hard-copy evidence of all output produced. Distribution lists help control-personnel ensure that only authorized users receive output.

Storage control is also important. Someone must be responsible for maintaining and controlling access to databases. Access may be controlled through passwords/codes assigned to end-users, or through identification verification. The typical system has a three-level security procedure: user logon, user password, and unique file name. One essential security measure for storage is file backup of data and programs and storage of backup material in another location.

Physical facility controls involve a variety of security measures, from simply a locked room out of the public area to a high-security facility with elaborate environmental controls. In a distributed technology environment, physical security of equipment becomes more difficult and complex, but managers must attempt to provide some security if nothing more than equipment "lockdowns."

Another important security element in the Internet environment are "firewalls" that protect the network from unwanted access/intrusion by serving as a safe transfer point to and from other networks. Its function is to screen network activity and only allow authorized transmissions in or out. Unfortunately, firewalls are only able to deter, not completely prevent, unauthorized access. Problems of hacking will continue for the foreseeable future, and one security solution will be in the growing area of biometrics. Security systems using biometrics assess physical traits that make a person unique: voice verification, fingerprints, hand shape, keystroke analysis, and eye/retina scanning are some examples. A digitized biometrics profile is created for each user and special sensors then measure the person wanting access; and, if there is a match, then access is allowed.

Any service with public-access PCs can expect to deal with viruses or worms. Both can be a problem with staff machines; however, they are certainly problems for public machines. The difference between a virus and worms is that a worm is a distinct program that can run unaided, while a virus is a program code embedded into another program. Some are just a nuisance while others can destroy contents of memory and hard disks. They often migrate from one computer to another by means of the Internet, e-mail, or intranet. Having effective and up-to-date virus checking/cleaning software is important, as is using it on a regular basis. A virus-checking program that automatically scans any file downloaded from the Internet or an intranet is highly desirable.

Like the other aspects of managing technology maintaining security is a never ending but essential task.

Check This Out:

JISC is a U.K. body that advises higher education on information systems issues and has issued *JISC Senior Management Briefing Paper 13 Developing an Information Security Policy* (Available: www.jisc.ac.uk [accessed June 2006]).

KEY POINTS TO REMEMBER:

- Technology provides access to information for users and generates management information to aid decision making.
- Technology improves productivity, assists in data collection, analysis, and use.
- Staff time is freed up and it can make a service operate more cost effectively.
- Managers require enhanced skills.
- The proportion of the budget spent on the initial investment and associated recurrent costs will continue to increase and dominate annual expenditures.
- A major investment is needed to train staff to work effectively and efficiently.
- Users benefit from coaching that can help them to access information effectively.
- Rapid change will continue.
- Increasing attention is being paid to legal and security issues.
- Technology requires careful planning and control.

REFERENCES

Association of Research Libraries. 2002. "Strategic and Practical Consideration for Signing Electronic Information Delivery Agreement." Available: http://arl.licbooklet.html (accessed June 2006).

Bell, Steven J., and John Shank. 2004. "The Blended Librarian: A Blueprint for Redefining the Teaching and Learning Role of Academic Librarians." *College and Research Libraries News* 65, no. 7 (July–August): 372–375.

Black's Law Dictionary 1990. St. Paul, MN: West Publishing Co.

Breeding, Marshall. 2006. "Musing on the State of the ILS in 2006." *Computers in Libraries* 26, no. 3 (March): 26–28.

Broadbent, Marianne, and Ellen Kitzis. 2004. *The New CIO Leader: Setting the Agenda and Delivering Results.* Boston, MA: Harvard Business School Press.

Dickson, G. W., and J.K. Simmons. 1970. "The Behavioral Side of MIS." *Business Horizons* 13 (August): 63–71.

Dugan, R. E. 2002. "Information Technology Budget and Costs: Do You Know What Your Information Technology Costs Each Year?" *Journal of Academic Librarianship* 28, no. 4 (July): 238–243.

Emberton, John. 1987. "Effective Information System Planning and Implementation." *Information Age* 9 (July): 159–162.

Hanson, Terry, ed. 2005. *Managing Academic Support Services in Universities: The Convergence Experience.* London: Facet Publishing.

OCLC. 2003. *The 2003 OCLC Environmental Scan: Pattern Recognition. Executive Summary.* Available: www.oclc.org (accessed June 2006).

Prisk, Dennis P., and Monica G. Brooks. 2005. "Hip High-Tech Purchases Don't Always Turn Out as Planned." *Computers in Libraries* 25 (10 November–December): 10–12, 14, 16.

Pulley, Mary Lynn, and Valerie Sessa. 2001. "E-leadership: Tackling Complex Issues." *Industrial and Commercial Training* 33, no. 6: 225–230.

Snyder, Caroline. 2006. "CIOs and Academic Research Libraries." *Library Administration & Management* 20 (Spring): 72–74

Vaughan, Jason. 2005. "Lied Library @ Four Years: Technology Never Stands Still." *Library Hi Tech* 23, no. 1: 34–49.

Wainwright, Eric. 2005. "Strategies for University Academic Information and Service Delivery." *Library Management* 26, nos. 8/9: 439–456.

Warro, Edward. 1993. "What Have We Been Signing? A Look at Database Licensing Agreements." *Library Administration and Management* 8, no. 3: 173–177

Yiotis, Kristin. 2005. "The Open Access Initiative: A New Paradigm for Scholarly Communications." *Information Technology and Libraries* 24 (4 December): 157–162.

LAUNCHING PAD

Alcorn, Louise, and Maryellen Mott Allen. 2006. *Wireless Networking: A How-To-Do-It Manual for Librarians.* New York: Neal-Schuman.

Andrews, Judith, and Derek Law. 2004. *Digital Libraries: Policy, Planning, and Practice.* Burlington, VT: Ashgate.

Antelman, Kristin, Emily Lynema, and Andrew K. Pace. 2006. "Towards a Twenty-First Century Library Catalog." *Information Technology and Libraries* 24, no. 3 (September): 128–139.

Bielefield, Arlene, and Lawrence Cheeseman. 2006. *Technology and Copyright Law: A Guidebook for the Library, Research and Teaching Professions.* 2nd ed. New York: Neal-Schuman.

Bills, David B., et al. 2006. "The New Mobile Scholar and the Effective Use of Information and Communication Technology." *First Monday* 11, no. 4.

De Voe, Kristen. 2005. "When Can Subscriptions Become Electronic Only? Developing Guidelines for Decision Making." *Against the Grain* 17, no. 6 (December): 37–38, 40, 42.

Hein, Karen K. 2006. "Information Uncommon: Public Computing in the Life of Reference." *Reference Services Review* 34, no. 1: 33–42.

McLeod, Julie, and Catharine Hare. 2006. *Managing Electronic Records.* New York: Neal-Schuman.

Matthews, Joseph R. 2004. *Technology Planning: Preparing and Updating a Library Technology Plan.* New York: Neal-Schuman.

Schroeder, Alan T. 2006. "Digitizing a Real Estate Document Library." *Records Management Journal* 16, no. 1: 34–50.

Stanton, Jeffrey M., and Kathryn R. Stam. 2006. *The Visible Employee: Using Workplace Monitoring and Surveillance to Protect Information Assets—Without Compromising Employee Privacy or Trust.* Medford, NJ: Information Today.

Stevens, Norman D. 2006. "The Fully Electronic Library." *College & Research Libraries* 67, no. 1 (January): 5–14.

18

Managing and Planning Physical Facilities for Information Services

"All fine architectural values are human values, else not valuable."
Frank Lloyd Wright

"The job of buildings is to improve human relations; architecture must ease them, not make them worse."
Ralph Erskine

INTRODUCTION

Among the changing and challenging tasks of all managers in all organizations in the twenty-first century is that of managing facilities. For information services, the responsibility increases, for there are the staff members to consider as well as the people who visit the premises. Changes in the operating environment increase the responsibility and accountability which include:

- greater attention being given to environmental factors resulting from global warming and the need for buildings to be energy efficient
- concerns regarding the health and safety of staff and users
- the need for increased security of people, documents, and electronic data
- the impact of technology in the workplace, focusing attention on layout and design together with health and safety issues
- changing approaches to design

- the pressure to keep overhead costs down and the cost implications of poor management

The physical facility remains a central factor in planning and becomes more important as the use of services is subject to continual change. The premises influence communication, motivation, efficiency, and effectiveness on the part of staff members. It creates an atmosphere that can attract, confuse, or deter users. Often it is a showcase for the parent organization, bringing pride to those who fund its creation and prestige for the architect. All managerial skills are needed to manage an increasingly complex physical facility.

This chapter explores two basic issues: managing an existing facility and planning a new one. The aim is to provide a starting point and indicate resources that will provide further information.

MANAGING THE FACILITY

Managing the facility is a responsibility that all information professionals will do to some degree throughout their career. Service hours are generally longer than any one staff member's workday. Often service is provided seven days a week, and sometimes over 24 hours. Inevitably some problems will arise when few, if any, senior members of staff are on duty.

Housekeeping Matters

On a daily basis, housekeeping is an issue, as poor housekeeping can affect the health and safety of staff and users. It starts at ground level, with questions such as who picks up litter and empties wastebaskets and how often? How often are the public and staff restrooms cleaned and provisioned? Does custodial staff have responsibility to dust the books and shelves? If not, does anyone have the responsibility? It may seem like a small problem, but some health issues are involved—more for staff than users. Staff can become sick from extended exposure to "collection dust"—a fact certified by medical professionals. In extreme cases, the person may be unable to return to work.

Beyond the health issue, which is serious but not that common, there is the health of the collection to consider. Dust and dirt on the shelves act as a very fine abrasive on materials as users and staff pull them off and replace them. Over time, the small damage from one such cycle accumulates to the point that the item needs repair or replacement. Senior management has to balance and determine the average annual cost of such repair and replacement against the cost of having shelves dusted. Dust also plays havoc with computers, photocopiers, and other equipment.

There are other housekeeping issues: lights burn out, and there may be problems of temperature, sun control, and plumbing. What happens when a user reports that a water faucet in the restroom will not shut off and water is spilling over the floor late on a Saturday afternoon? What if a blind gets stuck? Is there someone or someplace to call? Will someone fix it before the start of the next shift? What does the staff do until the problem is resolved? Having plans and procedures in place assists in handling such issues, but developing them takes management time.

> **Tip:**
>
> Management by walkabout or showing the flag is one way to spot house-keeping problems. Take a notebook or PDA with you.

Although staff may not have formal responsibility delegated to them for housekeeping matters, all staff, from the most senior professional to the support staff, play a role in ensuring that the premises are maintained to the highest possible standard.

> **Check This Out:**
>
> Trotta, Carmine J., and Marcia Trotta. 2001. *The Librarian's Facility Management Handbook.* New York: Neal-Schuman.

Generally fixing matters related to housekeeping or the building are not the responsibility of the manager of the information service, but of the parent organization. A facilities manager arranges contracts and organizes the work of specialist maintenance staff such as plumbers and electricians. However the facilities management staff will not be on duty when all problems occur.

In some situations, custodial staff members are not part of the staff of the information service. If they are, there is a high probability they are unionized and have a contract clearly delineating the services provided. Anything not covered or going beyond contractual limits may be available, but only at an additional charge. With tight budgets, extra charges are difficult, if not impossible, to handle. One small example from experience: An ongoing discussion/issue with the custodial staff supervisor emerged from the vacuuming of carpets on stairways. While there was an agreement that custodians should vacuum floor carpets every day, the contract said nothing about the carpeted stairs *between floors.* The supervisor would vacuum the stairs but at an extra fee. Hence the issue would be part of the next contract negotiations. Although it is a minor matter, it takes time and generates occasional negative comments from users and staff. Who would have thought that becoming an information professional one would spend time determining who cleans the stairways?

Information service managers should work closely with facilities managers to ensure the specific needs of the information are discussed and taken into account when contracts are let or renewed. Conditions and needs change over time.

> **Try This:**
>
> Write down four reasons why housekeeping must be considered to be of high importance to the manager of an information service.

BUSINESS CONTINUITY MANAGEMENT

Business continuity management examines the external and internal risks that confront organizations hit by disasters, pandemics, and other unexpected happenings. With an increase in terrorism linked with organizations having a greater dependence on information and communications technologies, it becomes important to analyze and manage risks. As part of business continuity management many organizations have a crisis management team that operates at an organizational level.

Risk Management

Risk management firms help to determine how much insurance and what type should be purchased, as well as how much self-insurance (risk) it keeps. Organizations have to be aware of the risks they face in order to minimize the disruption to their operations in the event of a crisis, and insurers require regular risk assessments if adequate insurance cover is to be offered.

There are nine activities that contribute to a risk management program:

1. making information as accessible as possible
2. facilitating the sharing of information
3. reducing the duplication of data and information
4. setting up retention rules for data/information

5. ensuring legislative compliance
6. contributing to competitive intelligence
7. guiding people to reliable information
8. providing training
9. being at the forefront of technology

A risk management program will identify risks, analyze the situation, the potential costs involved, and how they can be effectively and efficiently managed. The crisis management team prepares scenarios, identifies the likely impact on the organization and ways to mitigate the crisis situation. In terms of costs in the event of a crisis they could be greater for a smaller organization than a larger one, for larger organizations are likely to have contracts to cover the replacement of the operations that are down. Crisis management recognizes that there is a "golden hour," the period during the earliest stages of managing a crisis when critical decisions are taken.

Health, Safety, and Security

Health, safety, and security are critical issues for management, staff, and users and so will be subject to a risk assessment. Many hazards can emerge in managing public facilities, and employers have a duty of care for staff and users. Laws enacted at either the national or local levels govern some points, and no insurance company will permit a policy holder to take unacceptable risks. If risk is taken a policy may become invalid.

Involving all members of staff in identifying risks is a good team exercise and makes people aware of potential hazards. They will also be able to offer good suggestions.

Check This Out:

Breighner, Mary, William Payton, and Jeanne Drewes. 2005. *Risk and Insurance Management Manual for Libraries.* Chicago: American Library Association.

An increasing challenge is maintaining a comfortable working environment as we experience the effects of global warming. One constant issue is controlling temperature and humidity levels. Probably every senior manager has wondered from time to time, "Why, if they can send people into outer space and not have them freeze or burn to death, can they not design a building heating, ventilating, and air conditioning (HVAC) system for earth that works?" One reason for the complaints is the variations in people's inner thermostats; some people need cool temperatures, others need warmer. In addition to individual preferences, over time systems break down, need to be taken out of service for maintenance, and simply wear out. As with custodial work, staff responsible for HVAC are rarely part of the information service staff. This makes issues of response time and level of service matters of discussion and complaints.

The greatest challenge is balancing concerns for people and the collections. Safety, in some cases, relates to the mission and goals of the service, and to the HVAC system. Safety is divided into three major areas: safety from physical harm, safety of belongings, and psychological safety. Managers must address all these areas and balance the needs of people, collections, and technology.

For services with significant preservation responsibilities, such as archives, research libraries, and national libraries, one balancing act is people, technology, and materials, all with climatological requirements. Both staff and customers generally prefer a working temperature at or near 72°F (22°C) with 50 to 60 percent humidity. Ideal storage conditions for collections are 60°F (15°C) and 50 percent or less humidity. This means compromise, usually in favor of people and technology, if the goal is to intermix people and materials. Separation may or may not be feasible or affordable, probably requiring two HVAC systems or modification of a single system into the equivalent of two systems.

To gain an overview of safety issues, conduct a security audit as part of the risk management program. One way is to create a security checklist drawing on the expert advice from the parent organization's facilities manager and then carry out the survey. If this expertise is not available from within the organization then the local police and/or fire department and the insurance company will usually provide professional advice for they have an interest in seeing that safe conditions exist, and generally welcome enquiries. These external bodies need to be aware of potential hazards before a crisis occurs.

A security audit covers all the safety areas noted above. Basics about existing fire protection equipment and emergency exits will be part of a survey. Unfortunately, people and "thing" safety can again come into conflict. In any service, except one-room facilities, there are likely to be one or more emergency exits located in areas not visible to the staff and users. (Emergency exits are usually mandated by fire protection and building codes. Their location is a function of distance between exit, the number of persons in an area, and the activities in the area.) While emergency exits provide for people's safety, they also provide a means by which people may leave, taking materials with them without following borrowing procedures.

Sometimes we read reports of cases where management decided that the safety of "things" was greater than that of people. The decision is to secure emergency exits in ways that in a real emergency usually result in a loss of life. One method of controlling the problem is at the initial design stage, placing staffed service points with visual control of all such exits. However, even in modest-sized buildings, this is almost impossible to accomplish. Another method is to install alarms so that opening the door sets off the alarm. Usually the best that happens is that staff are alerted to the unauthorized use of the exit, but by the time staff get to that door, the person is no longer in sight. Higher levels of security may be necessary, such as CCTV cameras or designated security staff, with the benefit being weighed against the installation and ongoing costs.

The question of who is permitted to use the service can be a security issue. Clearly a service provided in a corporate setting holding confidential information must ensure that there is no unauthorized use. Services open to the public generally require users to enroll on their first visit, and archives often ask users to sign in for each visit. There can be a difference in levels of access granted to certain categories of user, as in records management services and access to confidential documents. Some university libraries charge a fee for use by people not connected with the university, but this category of user may not have access to all databases due to licensing arrangements. Identification becomes more important, and passwords or a photo ID may be required. However the growing security problem comes from remote use and the "borrowing" of passwords to access databases. This can be a challenge to monitor.

Collection documents have a way of "growing legs" and walking out without being checked. (Dr. Evans maintains that a library can determine its core collection by knowing what is lost or missing.) Many services install a security system similar to that found in shops in the form of strips or "targets" attached to items in the collection and an exit control unit that sounds an alarm if the item has not been properly discharged. These systems are expensive to purchase, and the annual costs for targets can also be substantial. Is it worth the cost? The answer is, it depends on local circumstances. In making a decision about investing in a security system, managers should:

- collect data on thefts
  - user complaints about mutilated materials
  - number of items in "lost or missing" file
  - random sample of collection inventory
- collect data on "users forgetting" to check out items
- collect data on the amount of money spent annually on replacements
- collect data on the cost of security system to install, maintain, and estimate annual cost of targets

With these data in hand, a decision can be made about the cost-benefit of installing a collection security system.

ICT equipment presents a challenge, which is considered in Chapter 17.

Crime

We live in a society where crime seems to increase yearly. In the workplace and where there are members of the public are present organizations have had to increase security. The threats come from lower-level crimes such as thefts of personal belongings from staff and users, to acts of violence experienced in school libraries, rape in public libraries, and terrorist attacks on public libraries.

The security audit will identify areas with greater or lesser potential for trouble. User spaces in isolated or remote parts of the building are higher-risk areas than in large open areas which have many user spaces. Poorly lit and remote staircases are also high-risk areas. Information service managers have a number of options that range from:

- doing nothing (let the individual assume all risk)
- devoting some staff time to patrolling the building (which reduces time for productive work)
- hiring security staff or a firm to patrol the building (a costly but effective option)
- installing a variety of electronic surveillance equipment (costly and could carry unexpected legal consequences, e.g., questions of privacy)

But it is a question of taking action to protect both users and staff. Often at closing time there are only two or three staff members on duty to close down the facility. Some services may be sited in areas where the crime rate is high and/or geographically isolated, making the staff vulnerable, particularly during night shifts. Few, if any, staff decide to work in a library because they want to be a police officer. Management decisions are difficult at best; but, generally, some action is necessary and should be discussed with the board or senior management of the organization, staff and representatives of the user community.

Check These Out:

Cravey, Pamela. 2001. *Protecting Library Staff, Users, Collections, and Facilities: A How-To-Do-It Manual for Librarians.* New York: Neal-Schuman.
O'Neill, Robert. 1998. *Management of Library and Archival Security: From the Outside Looking In.* Binghamton, NY: Haworth Press.
Shuman, Bruce A. 1999. *Library Security and Safety Handbook.* Chicago: American Library Association.

These are some of the day-to-day facility management issues—enough to make the point that the physical facility requires managing and monitoring just as much as people and collections do.

DISASTER MANAGEMENT

During the course of a career, an information professional is likely to have to deal with one or more of the major facility disasters: fire, water problems, natural disasters, major vandalism, and terrorism.

One outcome of a security audit is a comprehensive security plan. Part of the plan addresses problems of a day-to-day nature that need resolution but require more funding than is currently available. Another part of the overall plan is a disaster preparedness document. Developing such a plan requires time and effort, but is essential. All the sections that form the service must participate in the plan's development since it affects everyone. A steering committee with a representative from each section is an effective method for developing and importantly, updating the plan.

Keys to developing a successful plan include:

- a realistic assessment of potential disasters
- a consideration of handling the differences between a service disaster and one that is part of a larger local or regional disaster
- a determination of collection salvage priorities
- a determination of insurance coverage and authority to commit funds for recovery
- procedures to activate when a disaster, or incident, occurs
- staff training to ensure that the procedures work, and that staff are aware of them
- a telephone tree for emergency telephone calls, starting with the person who will direct the recovery efforts
- a list with telephone numbers of recovery resource vendors and service providers
- preparing the schedule for a regular review of the operation of the plan and updating information.
- developing a partnership with a local service to which users can be directed when a disaster strikes.

The most common disaster is water damage, and not just from major storms or firefighting efforts. Water pipes and radiators break, and this may happen when the service is closed; a day may pass before anyone notices the problem. Even an unremarkable rainfall can cause damage if building maintenance has been deferred for too long. One way managers may try to save money is to decide not to have the roof redone or windows recaulked. Decisions to defer are relatively easy to make. Frequently, the work is not done until after a significant problem takes place, when the cost then is substantially higher than it would have been to correct the problem in the first place. This happens because to the basic repair costs is added costs associated with damage done to the building's contents—the damage to floor coverings, furniture, and equipment in addition to the contents. Most senior managers have had to handle the problem of deferred maintenance.

Reflect On:

The types of disasters that might occur in a service known to you.
List all the points that should be included in a disaster management program, taking into account the disasters you have identified.

Establishing a recovery plan for various natural disasters—earthquakes, hurricanes, tornadoes, and typhoons—vary with the type, expected frequency, and damage expected. Other factors are the age of the facility (newer structures are more likely to reflect higher building standards) and what, if any, disaster recovery plans may exist in the parent organization.

While the probability of a natural disaster occurring can be calculated, vandalism and terrorism are less predictable, and the results can be devastating. Nevertheless planning must consider acts of violence.

One of the areas where precautions must be taken is that of protecting computer systems. Although you can replace equipment, data may take time to recover or may be totally lost. Consider the problems a manager would face if all records were lost. Hence it is important that you have a regular backup schedule, at least once a day, and that copies are stored off-site to minimize the possibility that they will also be lost. In many services, it is assumed that this is done; reality does not always match intent. With a loss of power to the premises, then the Web site, intranet, and e-mail traffic will inevitably be affected.

One thing is certain about a major disaster: not everything will be salvageable. Some documents will be destroyed while most will have some damage, but there will not be time or money to save everything. Thus the value of setting priorities *before* the disaster strikes becomes apparent. What is irreplaceable (first priority); what is expensive and perhaps difficult to replace but is replaceable (second priority); and what is easy to replace (last priority)? Setting these priorities will prove more difficult than you might expect, as staff members will have differing views depending on their primary responsibilities. Checking with users and perhaps the parent institution, may indicate that staff and public views do not always agree. Information service managers may have to spend a substantial amount of time explaining and justifying the priorities and, eventually, reduce the size of the first and second priority categories.

A recovery plan must also address the financial aspects of the situation. Time is of the essence in the recovery of documents. Waiting 72 hours or more to process wet paper materials means that there is little point in trying to recover them. Waiting to get approval to commit moneys to handle recovery efforts until after disaster strikes will probably mean missing the window of opportunity to save paper-based materials. The senior information service managers will not have unlimited emergency spending authority, but having a reasonable upper-limit spending power is essential. This is why it is essential to know the level of insurance coverage, the average salvage costs for high-priority material and where to go for advice and assistance. They are important to manage the recovery process.

Establishing a disaster recovery team is essential. When the service designates a person responsible for preservation activities, that person should be a member of the team, if not the team leader. Whoever the team leader is, that person needs to be able to stay calm and think clearly in times of high stress. Managers, the team leader, and their team need to have cell phones with the number known to all staff. It helps to have a plan with procedures to implement, a trained staff who have practiced elements of the plan, and some disaster recovery supplies on hand. This assists the leader and team. Nevertheless, stress will be very high when it becomes time to implement the plan. Training programs can be good for team-building. For example, a basement can be filled with discarded documents and flooded and the staff supplied with boots, the staff can be given practical experience in handling wet documents.

A telephone tree provides name, landline telephone number, cell phone number, home e-mail address, and the order in which staff should receive calls regarding the disaster. If an event occurs during operational hours it is one matter, but another if it is happens after hours. Drawing on experience, the authors consider that, except when facility evacuation is necessary, the easiest time to handle such problems is after hours or times when the staffing is minimal. Even with a practiced plan, it takes some time to get it operational. Well-meaning staff, not part of the recovery team, can get in the way or create more problems than already exist. Being able to call in personnel when needed is much easier and effective than having people standing about wanting to do something. And remember that everyone wants to help when a disaster strikes.

Having a regular practice of fire drill, evacuation of the building and firefighting equipment creates awareness of procedures to be followed in an emergency and ensures that the premises can be speedily and safely evacuated. A fire drill can alert you to any minor problems that might ordinarily be overlooked such as hazards that temporarily block stairs or passages.

Another aspect of disaster management is dealing with the emotional impact that the staff and users will experience (Klasson, 2002). The feelings that are often generated need to be understood. It is sensible to be aware of counseling services that can be speedily contacted if required, since the full impact of the incident may not be immediately evident.

The Wider Picture:

The wider issues of disaster planning including communication with external agencies, coordination and preplanning are described in Thomas Drabek's 1995 *Disaster in Aisle 13 Revisited* (Available: www.library.ca.gov/CRB/96/05 over_4.html [accessed July 2006]).

Having a plan and failing to review it at regular intervals or not practicing its implementation is almost pointless. Practice will mean some time lost to information work, but will be well worth the investment. Also, copies of the plan must be in the hands of all key personnel, both at home and in the workplace—as well as appropriate insurance, police, fire, and security agencies.

Check These Out:

Alire, Camila. 2000. *Disaster Planning and Recovery Handbook*. New York: Neal-Schuman.

Halsted, Deborah; Richard Jasper; and Felicia Little. 2005. *Disaster Planning: A How-To-Do-It Manual with Planning Templates on CD-ROM*. New York: Neal-Schuman.

Jones, Virginia, and Kris E. Keyes. 2001. *Emergency Management of Records and Information Programs*. New York: ARMA International.

Kahn, Miriam. 2003. *Disaster Response and Planning for Libraries*. 2nd ed. Chicago: American Library Association.

Wellheiser, Johanna, Jude Scott, and John Barton. 2003. *An Ounce of Prevention: Integrated Disaster Planning of Archives, Libraries and Records Centers*. Lanham MD: Scarecrow Press and the Canadian Archives Foundation.

Professional journals provide graphic accounts of unexpected happenings, learning aids for managers and case studies for staff training sessions—for example, the aftermath of 9/11 or the 2005 floods in New Orleans.

CHANGES IN THE NATURE OF THE COLLECTION AND SERVICE PATTERNS

A further challenge for managers is the changing nature of collections and service patterns and the accelerating rate of change.

Many print and paper collections continue to grow in size, and managers must take one or more of the following actions: stop collection growth; find a way to store the collection more compactly; secure funding for an addition to the building; or secure funding for an entirely new facility. None of the options except the first are inexpensive. Generally the parent organization will not be willing to implement the first option and request the service to develop a plan to buy time.

One method is to deselect/relegate worn or outdated materials in the collection. The process is labor-intensive and does not buy much time if the materials are discarded. Storage in an off-site, lower-cost facility will buy more time, as there will be less concern by users and staff about discarding important items.

A common method of buying time is to use compact shelving/storage units. With most systems, extra capacity is gained because there are fewer aisles. Instead of one aisle between each row range of shelves, there may be one for every eight to ten ranges. Such systems increase storage capacity by at least 25 percent and often more, depending on how materials are arranged in the units. There are substantial investment costs.

But more documents are now born digital or parts of the paper-based collection are digitized. This reduces the volume of space required for storage and increases access for users who have remote access from their office, home, or dorm.

The changing publication formats and adapting space to changing user needs and services means that a radical remodelling may be necessary which would, for example, allow for the installation of a new technology. The way in which people access services change so a different configuration of space will be possible. Many universities and colleges have established an "information commons" providing onsite access to electronic resources. Approaches to learning mean that students now prefer to have work spaces

Check This Out:

Love Libraries is a campaign to make English libraries even better. To explore a new vision of a twenty-first century Reading Service showing how libraries were transformed in twelve weeks, see:
www.lovelibraries.co.uk/libraries_are_changing.php (accessed October 2006).

designed to enable them to work together as a team on group projects. The challenge is to design the layout of services in a logical, flexible and efficient manner way keeping remodeling costs to a minimum, while creating an environment that is comfortable and attractive for users and staff.

Middle and senior managers spend a surprising amount of time working on facility issues managing the current provision and anticipating change. How are the needs of users changing? How many require remote access? How many come to the service in person? How do their needs change? How are the formats changing? How are the policies concerning access versus holdings likely to change, and over what period of time? These are a few of the issues that raise questions. How to use the existing space in the best possible way? What will be the cost in staff time and effort versus renovation costs if we do or do not do *X*? All these factors will need to be taken into account. Having accurate scale drawings of the facility is essential and using scale drawings of the facility will save time, money, and frustration.

PLANNING FOR NEW SPACE

Only few information professionals will experience active involvement in planning a major addition or remodelling, or totally new facility. Many managers look forward such a project, but only a few look forward to doing it a second time around. Perhaps the major reason is for the less positive view is that almost all building projects become a series of compromises. This is especially true when attempting to plan a facility capable of handling growth for 20 years or more, and predicting the changes that may happen in that period of time. Perceived needs far exceed the funds available, resulting in a downsizing of the facility size or in the fit-out and equipment installed— sometimes all of them. The longer the time between funding the project and its completion, the greater will be the downsizing as costs generally escalate.

Tip:

Bringing users and staff together in focus groups provides helpful advice and gives them involvement in the project.

In an ideal situation, a new facility should be:

- flexible
- adaptable
- expandable

- accessible
- compact
- stable in climate control
- secure
- attractive
- economical to operate and maintain
- comfortable
- varied

Flexibility is essential since the use of the space changes, for example the volume of back office work is declining. Changes in the way enquiry staff work means that when formerly they sat at a desk, now they frequently stand at a higher smaller service desk (Warnement, 2003). A modular building with few, if any, internal weight-bearing walls is typical of a flexible design. Internal walls that are weight-bearing cannot be moved as needed without causing structural damage.

Adaptability may not be the same as flexibility. For example, public and special libraries and records management centers need to be located where their users gather naturally, but this can change over time as new shopping centers are built, or space reallocated in a commercial firm or government department. So the premises may need to be planned so that they can be adapted for other uses.

Given the inevitable growth of archives and libraries, having a facility that can be expanded is highly desirable. Funds for an addition or remodeling are easier to raise than for an entirely new building. The designer must consider where the future expansion space might be and how that relates to the existing structure. It is not uncommon for the area labeled "future expansion" on the original plans to turn out to be unsuitable, for various reasons, when the time comes to expand.

Libraries and archives also consider revenue raising space in new buildings such as bookstores, shops, cafés, or restaurants. Franchising these services brings in an income, attracts more visitors and provides additional services for users and staff.

The building will also need to take into account the needs of disabled users, and possibly those of parents with very young children.

Tip:

Professional journals such as *American Libraries* and *Library Journal* publish annual reviews of new and renovated archive and library premises which are sources of information about trends in design and architectural practices.

Ideally, the project consists of a primary planning team of five or more persons: architect, service representative, specialist space planning consultant, designer, representative of the parent institution, and, in some circumstances, a user. Larger teams are possible, but the larger the temporary group, the longer the process takes. Clearly many people will need to have input to the project at different stages, but everyone involved in every aspect of the project slows the planning activities.

Check This Out:

Ling, Edward. 1998. *Solid, Safe, Secure: Building Archives Repositories in Australia.* Canberra: National Archives of Australia.

The need for an architect is apparent. The service representative will be a senior manager, if not *the* senior manager, because decisions need to be taken reasonably quickly, especially in the later stages of the project. Parent institution representation is necessary if for no other reason than to monitor the cost of the project. There are other reasons, such as assuming the design will fit into any existing architectural master plan.

The space planning consultant must have specialist experience in the information sector (Boone, 2003). Planning any new building is a complex task with highly detailed data, down to the required nail and screw sizes. Archives and libraries are very complex building types, almost as complex as a hospital. Few managers will have had experience of such a project, and even fewer have that experience more than once. That also means that there are few projects, which, in turn, means that not many architects have this experience either. The consultant is usually the person on the planning team with the greatest experience in developing effective designs for information service operations. A consultant's role will be to ensure that the interior design will be functional with the appropriate level of detail required for the operation of the archive or library.

The input of a designer is important, for they will take the vision, image and ambiance that the service seeks to project and suggest ways in which this can be presented in finished space. The designer works closely with the architect and space consultant to ensure the most effective use of space emerges at the fit-out stage.

The building program is the key planning document. It is the outcome of joint effort between the service and the consultant, and provides the architect with the information needed to design the facility. Often it is also used to raise money for the project. To that end, it normally includes information about the existing services, collections, staff, and service population along with data about the parent organization. At the heart of the program, and essential for the architect, are data sheets for all the activities and units built in to the new facility. Data sheets cover not only the equipment and people that will occupy the space, but also the relationship of that space to other spaces in the facility (see Figure 18.1). For specialized spaces, such as for collections, there are standards for every sector which vary country by country.

There are several stages in the design phase of the project. The first yields conceptual drawings reflecting several different exterior designs and some blocks of interior space indicating work areas, collection space, etc. Selection of the exterior design and shape of the facility occurs at this point that can have major implications for the project. A plain square or rectangular building is the least costly. As the exterior walls become more complex (L-shaped, curved walls, or irregular in some way), the cost of the exterior rises, possibly leaving less money for the interior.

Very often, major archives and libraries holding national or university collections become symbols or monuments for the parent organization; these usually require dramatic architecture or an architectural statement. A cube or shoebox does not usually make much of a statement. Conflicts over exterior statements versus the requirement for adequate functional interior space emerge at the exterior design stage.

The second stage yields the schematic drawings reflecting the architect's interpretation of the building program. They start to reflect building and safety codes. Staff and user input is critical at this stage, as they will have to work in and use the space. The planning team should listen carefully to their comments and, whenever possible, incorporate them into the final design. It is at this stage that major adjustments in the location of this or that activity is the easiest to make since much of the detailed drafting will follow. An important consideration at this stage is the estimate of the running costs for the facility and how this has been minimized.

Final working drawings are the last design stage. Here the drawings are complete to the last detail—which way a door opens, how wide it is, what it is made of, what color it is, etc. They reflect all aspects of the building and the specification documents become the basis for the contractor to bid on and construct the building. There is a review and approval process by the "owners"—the service and its parent institution—that in essence states, "Yes, this is actually what we want built in all its detail." The reason this is important is because anything overlooked in the final drawing may be corrected or added, but for an additional charge. In the United States, such corrections are known as change orders; the more change orders the less money will be available for furniture and equipment. So a thorough review of the construction documents is critical to the level of funding available to finish the project as planned.

Figure 18.1
Sample Data Sheet

ADF 3502

UNIT: Archives and Special Collections
NAME OF AREA: Reception and Registration Area   **SQUARE FEET: 335**

ACTIVITIES:
This is the gateway where decisions are made about how to help patrons and visitors who come into the department. Researchers are interviewed, registered, and admitted to the reading room. Researchers use the online public terminal. Guests wait to see staff members. Researchers store personal items in lockers. The Reading Room supervisor is stationed here.
OCCUPANCY: *Public:*   3–4   *Staff:*   1   *Daily Uses:*   All day
    NOTES:

MAJOR DESIGN FEATUREĺ AND AMBIANCE OF AREA:
Entrance should be inviting to patrons. Should be made of some material (like glass) which suggests openness. (Possibly entire wall between exhibit and reception areas made of glass). Inside, the decor and finishings should suggest dignity, order, stability. The atmosphere should suggest the rarity, fragility, and importance of the collections. Staff members will have to supervise reading room as well as greet visitors. Desk should be positioned to have unobstructed view of both reading room and reception area. The piano, which is a collection item, and a small card catalog cabinet should be integrated into the room design. Doors lead to reading room, staff areas, and conference room. The only entry into the department is through the reception area.
Environment requirements: 76 degrees F +/– 5 degrees and 45% RH +/– 5%. Air should be filtered for gaseous and particulate pollution. Floor should be carpeted. Numerous electrical receptacles.
Security: alarmed door at entrance; panic button at reception desk; motion sensors; possibly electronic lock on door between reception and reading areas which may be activated by staff on duty.

PROXIMITY TO:
At entrance to department. Direct access to exhibit area. Direct access to reading room, but set off by physical and psychological barrier. Adjacent to conference room. Staff must supervise both reading room and reception areas.

---

1   Reception desk, designed in some clever way to enable staff person to supervise reception room and reading room at the same time, with:
　　1   Chair for staff
　　1   EWS
　　1   Telephone with general department number
　　1   Filing cabinet for forms, etc.
1   Small desk and chair where a researcher may sit and fill out registration form (This may be designed into the staff desk)
1   EIRAS (wheelchair access height)
2   Lounge chairs with a table for visitors
6   Lockers (half-height) for researcher personal belongings
1   Coat tree
1   Clock on wall
1   Small 3 foot by 3 foot exhibit case built into wall (specifications to follow)
1   Flat exhibit case for the display of very rare books that cannot be exhibited in a less secure area (7 feet wide x 3 feet high x 1.5 feet deep)
1   Small card catalog cabinet (18 inches x 33 inches)

Loyola Marymount University   11/30/07 Final Draft   Building Program
Miyawald Library   *Stockton Associates*   Appendix A: 47

(cont.)

Figure 18.1
Sample Data Sheet *(Continued)*

ADF 3502

UNIT: Archives and Special Collections
NAME OF AREA: Reception and Registration Area   **SQUARE FEET: 335**

SIGNAGE:
Sign at entrance indicating Archives and Special Collections; room number; registration and reception area sign.

COLLECTIONS:
  Books: 0   Non books: 0

PUBLIC SEATING:

  At Tables: 0   At Carrels: 0   Lounge: 0   Group Study: 0
                                     Other: 0
      Notes:

STAFF WORKSTATIONS: 1   **SERVICE POINTS: 1**

SPECIAL PURPOSE UNITS:
  Information Technology: *Other Electronic Equipment:*
    For the Public: *For the Public:*
    1 EIRAS   1 Wall clock

    For the Staff: *For the Staff:*
    1 EWS with printer   1 Telephone
                                             1 Special security system

NOTES:

INFORMATION PROVIDED BY: E. Stevens   **DATE FIRST ENTERED:** 6/11/07
                                                     DATE LAST REVISED: 11/16/07

Loyola Marymount University   11/30/07 Final Draft   Building Program
Miyawald Library   *Stockton Associates*   Appendix A: 48

> **Remember:**
>
> Spectacular buildings can present challenges for users. The Seattle Public Library opened in 2004 in a glass and metal-mesh structure with offset levels and spiraling rows of books. It won rave reviews from architects and librarians, but users and tourists kept getting lost. The designers intended to provide subtle hints that would guide people through the space, but the library had to employ a professional "wayfinder" to install signage.

There has been speculation that the number of visits made to academic libraries would decrease as remote use increased. Shill and Tonner (2003) surveyed over 300 U.S. academic libraries and described the types of recent building projects and the kinds of improvements made. A second paper examined the impact of changes on the use of the physical library finding that while there was decreased collection, reference and building usage in general, the majority of new and improved libraries had experienced sustained increases in the use of the physical facilities. Over a quarter reported an increase of over 100 percent (Shill and Tonner, 2004).

With the trend toward the development of joint-use services for example community libraries incorporating public and school libraries, or university and public libraries, the planning of facilities enters new possibilities. The needs of all users and staff must be taken into account—and there can be conflicting interests. But good communication, a positive approach to planning and goodwill can overcome difficulties and a cost effective solution emerge.

MOVING TO A NEW LOCATION

After completion, moving the collection into its new location becomes a staff challenge. Somehow, moving costs, probably because they are the last stage in the process, never seem to be adequate for the job at hand. Extras along the way have eaten into the project funds. So the staff have a dual challenge. The first is moving the materials from point X to point Y and maintaining the proper sequence for the materials—not as easy a planning task as it might seem. The second is to complete the first task with the funds available. The ideal solution is to employ professional movers who have experience of moving collections. Options beyond that are many, all the way up to trying to get enough volunteers to do the job for free (or at most, for the cost of food and drink for the day). Moving down the options in cost terms, it is vital to calculate increased staff costs in the supervision of putting things back in order after the move is complete. Munde (2003) reviews the after-costs for the Leid Library at the University of Nevada

Having completed the move a post-occupancy evaluation should be carried out, recording the outcomes for both the stakeholders, and colleagues planning new premises. Oder (2001) reported the challenges facing the San Francisco Public Library when its post-occupancy evaluation indicated dissatisfaction on the part of users and staff.

Planning a new facility is wonderful, a change of pace, and a source of frustration. A new facility brings a major change for staff and users alike. There will be high expectations for the new facility; most will be realized, a few will not. Change is stressful and sometimes some of the compromises required generate staff unhappiness. The staff actively involved in the planning process must make a major effort to communicate quickly, frequently, and accurately to the rest of the staff about progress, changes, and the reasons for change.

KEY POINTS TO REMEMBER:

- Housekeeping matters—for both stock and people.
- Business continuity is vital.
- Risks must be assessed for the purposes of safety and insurance.
- Health, safety, and security are of growing concern.
- Disasters happen.
- All information services need a disaster management plan that is regularly updated.
- The changing nature of collections and service patterns requires ongoing attention.
- Building and remodeling projects are complex and require professional assistance.
- Moving a collection is a staff challenge.
- A post-occupancy evaluation records outcomes for the stakeholders and professional colleagues.

REFERENCES

Boone, Michael. 2003. "Library Facility Planning—the Consultant's View: A Chat with Andrea Michaels." *Library Hi Tech* 21, no. 2: 246–252.

Klasson, M. 2002. "Rhetoric and Realism: Young User Reactions on the Linkoping Fire and its Consequences for Education and Democracy." *Library Review* 51, nos. 3/4: 171–180.

Munde, Gail. 2003. "After-Costs of Library Construction: A Case Study of Leid Library at the University of Nevada, Las Vegas." *Bottom Line* 16, no. 4: 143–150.

Oder, N. 2001. "SFPL Faces a Host of Challenges." *Library Journal* 126, no. 10 (1 June): 60–62.

Shill, Harold B., and Shawn Tonner. 2003. "Creating a Better Place: Physical Improvements in Academic Libraries, 1995–2002." *College and Research Libraries* 64, no. 6 (November): 431–466.

Shill, Harold B., and Shawn Tonner. 2004. "Does the Building Still Matter? Usage Patterns in New, Expanded, and Renovated Libraries, 1995–2002." *College and Research Libraries* 65, no. 2 (March): 123–150.

Warnement, Mary. 2003. "Size Matters: The Debate Over Reference Desk Height." *Portal: Libraries and the Academy* 3, no. 1 (January): 79–87.

LAUNCHING PAD

Bazillion, R. J. 2002. "Academic Library Construction: Managing the Design to Build Process." *Journal of Library Administration* 36, no. 4: 49–65.

Beagle, Donald Robert. 2006. *The Information Commons Handbook.* New York: Neal-Schuman.

Bisbrouck, Marie-Francoise. 2004. *Libraries as Places: Buildings for the 21st Century.* Munich, Germany: Saur.

Campbell, Jerry D. 2006. "Changing a Cultural Icon: The Academic Library as a Virtual Destination." *Educause Review* 41, no. 1 (January/February): 16–30.

Eden, Brad. 2005. "The UNLV Libraries: Four Years after the Construction of a New Main Library." *Library Hi Tech,* 23, no. 1: 5–7.

Gardner, Susan, and Susanna Eng. 2005. "What Students Want: Generation Y and the Changing Function of the Academic Library." *Portal: Libraries and the Academy* 5, no. 3 (July): 405–420.

Goetsch, Lori A., and Charles B. Lowry. 2001. "Creating a Culture of Security in the University of Maryland Libraries." *Portal: Libraries and the Academy* 1, no. 4: 455–464.

Ludwig, Logan, and Susan Starr. 2005. "Library as Place: Results of a Delphi Study." *Journal of the Medical Library Association* 93, no. 3 (July): 315–326.

Lushington, Nolan. 2002. *Libraries Designed for Users: A 21st Century Guide.* New York: Neal-Schuman.

Shepherd, F. 2002. "Diary of a Move." *Records Management Bulletin,* no. 109: 107–109.

Shuman, B. A. 2002. "Personal Safety in Library Buildings: Levels, Problems, and Solutions." *Reference Librarian,* nos. 75/76: 67–81.

Part IV

Career Development
and Your Future

19

Career Development

*"Success—it's a matter of having a positive attitude and apply-
ing motivational principles in a daily basis. . . . Motivation is
like a fire; unless you add fuel, it goes out."*

Jeff Keller

*"When good bosses go they leave behind them an organization
that can run without them."*

Maurice Line

INTRODUCTION

How you handle the transition between graduating from a professional
school to becoming a practitioner can have a considerable influence on
your career development. Actions and decisions can shape a rewarding and
enjoyable working life meeting the challenges and opportunities that will
be offered. Thinking about the future has never been as important as it is
today. The possibilities are enormous; information skills are transferable
skills, the work is challenging, and it offers great job satisfaction. There is
another factor, and that relates to the state of the labor market and the
shortages that result from the retirement of the boomer generations. All
professions and occupations are much aware that there will be a critical
shortage of staff and are looking for talent to fill vacancies. The prospects
haven't been better since the 1960s.

Everyone starts a new career with high hopes, expectations, and aspirations. We can dream about where we might be in the years ahead and how
our careers will develop. At one time it was a case of getting a foot on the
ladder in a sector of our choice, and moving upwards. Careers were often
based in a local large organization and, with hard work, people moved up

the ladder in a hierarchical structure. Today it is very different. The knowledge and skills gained are now transferable skills, valued more widely in the labor market. People now change jobs more frequently, they expect to get to the top faster and hence younger, and probably take a career break along the way. Continuing professional development is important and time and money is invested in gaining the skills essential in a rapidly changing information profession. They work in organizations that are less stable, often smaller and agile and having a flattened organizational structure. The community is more mobile. Technology enables teleworking. Family considerations enter into choices. There are challenges, but also more opportunities.

There is only one factor that can be accurately identified, which is that the work environment will change. Change is expected to occur more rapidly and be fundamental. Four issues will influence all our personal futures, grounded in economics, politics, social change and technological developments. How they will be manifest cannot be accurately foreseen, but some guesstimates can be made.

THE CHANGING LABOR MARKET

The labor markets are dynamic. Back in the 1970s, attempts were made to measure the size of the workforce, the number of posts available, and employers' forecasts of expansion, together with the numbers entering the professional schools. But several years experience indicated that there were major external forces affecting the forecasts. Now the individual is best placed to monitor change and the influence that it may exert on their future plans.

Economic change can produce a very good effect when economic conditions are booming. In the private sector expansion of activity calls for skills drawn from across the information professions. Increased economic activity and the drive to be competitive calls for people who can access, organize and retrieve information and areas such as knowledge management emerge. At one time a healthy economy resulted in an increase in government expenditure and favorable conditions for publicly funded services. However governments now tend to follow policies that dampen expenditure in the public sector, whether or not the economy is booming. A downturn in economic conditions usually results in a very different situation with a tightening of the labor market—fewer posts advertised and depressed salaries.

The U.S. Bureau of Labor Statistics expects the employment up to 2014 of archivists will increase as fast as the average for all occupations. The market will expand as both public and private organizations establish archives and organize records and information. Although the rate of turnover of archivists is low, the need to replace workers will create some additional job openings. For librarians, employment will grow more slowly than the average. But job opportunities are expected to be very good due to the number expected to retire in the coming decade as more than three in five librarians are aged 45 years or older. In addition the number of people entering librarianship has fallen in recent years, with more jobs than applicants in some cases (Bureau of Labor Statistics, 2006).

Political change often results in a change in policies at federal or state levels. For example, many governments consider the public library to be the natural place where the community at large can access the Internet. The raising of literacy and educational standards, in general, increases demand on public and school libraries. The pressure for enrollments to increase in publicly funded colleges and universities creates further demands upon academic libraries. Political change can also result in services being viewed less favorably; for example, school library services appear to be particularly vulnerable. External scrutiny of the operations of both government and the private sector now requires higher standards of record keeping, particularly as a result of growth in electronic records. Audit trails are important.

Social change alters the demand on publicly funded services; for example, cultural diversity, social exclusion, the graying of the population spring to mind. The community at large has an increasing need for up-to-date and accurate information in their daily life, and the public library is an important place for them to turn to. Parents wanting to encourage their children to read and learn see libraries as places where there is a range of learning materials. The graying of the community has seen a growth of interest in family history, resulting in increased demand being placed on local history collections and archives. Silver surfers often learn their basic IT skills in the public library.

The *impact of information and communications technologies* on information handling has resulted in a continual expansion in the range of specialist fields of practice, such as information management, knowledge management, Webmasters, records managers among others. As awareness grows about the value of accurate, relevant, up-to-date information in a range of organizations, so the Internet and intranets increase the demands for information handling skills. Within services there are fewer backroom jobs— cataloguing, for example—and more that interface with users, either in person, by phone or by e-mail, so that communication skills are more highly prized. The complexity of finding the information that a user experiences means that the professional takes on more of a coaching role. Cost questions are also taken into account more than in the past.

Finally there is the way in which approaches to management in general have changed, resulting in flatter organizational structures. So staying in one organization in one location may not be feasible—opportunities for advancement may well need to be sought elsewhere. Within information services change is also occurring as a result of outsourcing, as specialist posts may be lost. Collaborative working across the globe to provide, for example, 24/7 reference services may also bring about change. On the plus side the idea of a portfolio career might have been frowned upon in the past and moving between different professions was less easy. Now information professionals can draw on their transferable skills and create their own futures.

One thing is for sure: career development always takes place against a moving picture. Change influences career development, and remember that new or increased opportunities always emerge.

Career-oriented professionals monitor change closely. They read and watch the national and professional media, read the job advertisements, use the Web, and attend conferences and meetings, keeping in touch with changes in the world at large and the information field in particular. They make their own future.

Tip:

The U.S. Bureau of Labor Statistics Web site provides detailed information about specific occupations, including salaries in different sectors, and for librarians, state profiles (Available: www.bls.gov [accessed May 2006]).
Reflect on the labor market in your field of interest at a national and local level. Is it expanding or declining?
What local factors or decisions are influencing expansion or decline?

THE FIRST POST

Most students completing an initial professional program will have experienced the reality of work in an archives or library service before entering the course. One reason is that it is sensible to find out what professionals do and what it's like to work in an information service before making a commitment to the field. This experience is generally extended by working part-time or through a fieldwork program that is part of the course requirement. It provides not only an opportunity to gain additional work experience at a general level, but also a taste of a chosen field. Two benefits result. First, it provides a foundation from which to start making the links between theory and practice. Second, it is an ideal time to use eyes and ears and observe effective management practices, less effective practices, and those that are poor. Learning about good practice that can be adopted on becoming a manager is welcome, as is the experience that comes from being supervised by a person whose skills may need some development.

Though many managers will work by the textbook, having a boss who is an idiosyncratic manager can be challenging and rewarding.

Applying for a first post having completed the first professional qualification may well be influenced by the state of the job market and geographic or other constraints. It might be a compromise, but could be the sought-after opportunity. You can identify vacancies from a number of sources. Employers make recruiting visits to students, professional conferences hold placement fairs, advertisements are placed in newspapers, professional journals, or on the Web sites of professional bodies, and there is a growing number of specialist employment agencies. The employment agencies provide career advice on preparing a curriculum vitae (CV), match the candidate with a suitable post, and follow up to ensure that the employer and person placed are both satisfied with the outcomes. The agencies are well informed about the state of the job market in general, the specialist fields, and vacancies in different parts of the country. The fee is paid by the employer.

You could also approach an organization with a CV and cover letter to see if they have any suitable vacancies. It can pay off with larger information services. And even if they haven't been able to offer a post, they may come back to you later or remember your name if you apply for an advertised vacancy at a later date. It shows interest in and enthusiasm for the particular service.

MARKETING YOURSELF

Keep in mind that in applying for a post you are marketing yourself—you are looking for a buyer. The first step of selling yourself starts with preparing a CV or resume. The key factor to keep in mind is that it can perform two roles. First and foremost, it acts as a record of your milestones and achievements. It is all too easy to forget dates, and even events, that were important in your career as the years roll by. By keeping a record it forms the foundation for future applications for paid employment, voluntary work on professional and other committees, further study, travel scholarships, etc. Second, it is adapted for each application, selecting the information that is appropriate and relevant to that position.

Tip:

If you haven't started a CV, then start it today. The longer you put it off, the less easy it is to recall all relevant information.

Even at the start of a career there already is a substantial amount of information that needs to be gathered. To start there are the general details:

- Name, address, phone number, fax number, and e-mail address.
- Date, place of birth, nationality—if you are happy to provide this information.
- Education: high school, university—with marks, distinctions, and awards.
- Professional courses: university, title of program, any specialist papers taken, awards, and scholarships.
- Courses that develop additional skills such as IT, languages, communication etc.
- Work experience to date (including all that preceded entry to the professional course—and remember that any work with the public, even in supermarkets, for example, will have developed communication and team skills).
- Membership of relevant organizations, particularly professional bodies.
- Any attendance at professional conferences.
- A brief note of interests and hobbies—to provide a talking point at interviews.

As a career develops, then the record will include attendance at professional development courses, papers presented at conferences and other publications, professional awards, and, of course, posts held with achievements in these jobs. A mentor can provide good advice on what to include in a CV, and in turn will be better prepared to write references on your behalf.

In a competitive job market you could turn to a professional résumé writer. They are in touch with employers and know what the current approaches are and have skills in the design and layout of compelling documents. You can be sure that the finished product will not contain errors that a spell-checker can miss.

Check These Out:

Bolles, Richard Nelson. 2006. *What Color Is Your Parachute? A Practical Manual for Job Hunters and Career-Changers.* Berkeley, CA: Ten Speed Press.

Bolles, Richard Nelson. 2006. *What Color Is Your Parachute Workbook: How To Create a Picture of Your Ideal Job or Next Career.* Berkeley, CA: Ten Speed Press.

Dick Bolles also has a Web site (Available: www.jobhuntersbible.com [accessed May 2006]) with career and personality tests, articles, and practical advice.

Using the CV you can select the information that is relevant to each individual job application. Extract what is relevant to the position, what you want them to know, and the talents you can bring to the organization. Be honest and don't embellish your talents. The advice about length is generally to produce no more than two pages of information at this stage in a career. If it is longer, the prospective employer probably won't read it thoroughly and might even put it straight into a trash can. In some countries an unsuccessful applicant can challenge the employer using legal redress if they feel aggrieved. In this case great care needs to be taken when selecting the information to include. The final task in preparing the CV is to design this vital document. Keep the typeface and layout simple and uncluttered—so that you could put it through a reading test. Some applicants add a thumbnail photograph to help their identification at an interview.

Before making an application use research skills to find out information about a prospective employer and what the organization does. The organization's Web site will give clues about the organizational culture and climate that will help you decide whether you would be comfortable as an employee. The clues are subtle, but will be there—e.g., what its policy is on diversity.

Some employers require the completion of a form. Hopefully it will be available in an electronic format. An increasing number of employers are using sophisticated software to process applications by looking for keywords. Online forms often ask for a personal statement because they are looking for employees who can express themselves. A well-written answer can help to get an interview. Paper-based forms present a greater problem since it is not always easy to find a typewriter; not everyone has beautiful handwriting, and fitting information on forms may not be easy. Make several photocopies of the form and practice before completing the final application.

A covering letter or accompanying e-mail will be required, and if it is an e-mail, keep it formal. If the job specification indicates that specific knowledge or skills are required, or if there is a set of criteria for the appointment, then the attainments in respect of each should be set down clearly and concisely, using bulleted points. Some employers ask for the cover letter to be handwritten, which again can present a challenge for those who spend much of their time at a keyboard. Experimenting with different types of pens may increase legibility. For both the cover letter and the resume, the final product should be carefully proofread and set out on good quality paper. Taking care with the content and presentation can make the difference between making an application and securing an interview. Again, you are selling yourself—and it is likely to be a buyer's market.

Whatever the format of the form and cover letter, it will require very careful reading and checking; asking a third party to do this can be helpful. Often you read what you want to read, rather than what is on the screen or paper. And spell and grammar checkers are not always 100 percent correct. Keep a copy of all applications, and if they are in electronic format, back them up.

Try This:

List the factors that will influence your decision concerning job applications. Now put them in a priority order.

With any luck, the prospective employer will have been impressed with the application and offer an interview. Chapter 15 provides guidance about the interview process from the employer's perspective. Being interviewed is nerve-racking, whatever stage of career has been reached, but preparation reduces the stress factor, bringing confidence that you have prepared carefully and meet the job specification.

The offer of an interview is the start of the second stage of marketing. Although information is to hand about the prospective employer, now is the time to dig deeper. Use your professional skills to build up a profile of the organization using statistics, directory information, Web sites, annual reports, and information in professional journals. Collected together and arranged systematically, this forms your briefing document.

If the service is within traveling distance and open to the public, then an unobtrusive visit will add to the information gathered. What can you learn about it? Is information about the service freely available (i.e., does it market itself)? How long has it been established? What is its mission? What image does it present? Is it an appropriate for the community served today? Is there evidence of a good rapport between the staff and users? Ask some questions as a user. Is the staff helpful—from the custodial to the support staff to professionals? Is it housed in appropriate premises at the right location—and what is the dress code? Answers to the earlier questions in this list will add to the growing briefing document. The questions that come later in the list will help you to decide how to present yourself at interview. Even if you cannot visit the service in person, you should at least have a file of information in preparation for the vital interview. It takes time to gather all the information that's needed and it will probably happen at a busy time of the academic year, so ensure that course deadlines are met well ahead of time to allow time for job applications.

Part of the preparation focuses on how best to sell yourself to a prospective employer. Draw up a list of questions that may be asked, and prepare something interesting to say if the interview starts with "tell me something about yourself." Decide what is appropriate to say, and what not to say.

Sometimes minds go blank at the start of an interview, and it is easy to say the first thing that springs to mind. Do your homework about the questions that an employer shouldn't ask, and have ways to deflect them politely. Know the salary level you are seeking—and your bottom line. Carry out a mock interview with someone who knows you well so that they can offer constructive criticism to help adjust your presentation.

If in doubt about the dress code, be conservative. Traveling a distance can be a challenge, so allow sufficient time for everything to go wrong with your journey. Sometimes the interview process will last for a day, or even two, and involve a series of tests and interviews with different members of staff from the organization. So arrive prepared to stay for a while.

Get to the interview in good time and locate the place where you have to report to for the interview. Then take a short walk around to get some fresh air. In some situations you may meet up with other candidates. Talking with them in a friendly way can be the start of some good friendships that are renewed as your career progresses and you find yourself on the same short-lists. Before the interview process starts, take a couple of deep breaths, stand up straight, and then walk into the room. Someone will indicate where you are to sit, and if the courtesies of introductions include the shaking of hands, take time to put any papers or a bag down before shaking hands.

The chair of the interview committee will start the questioning, so smile and take another deep breath. As the questions are posed, remember the information that you have gathered—and the skills, strengths, and attributes that you could bring to the post. Make sure that you receive answers to the questions that you want answered. An interview is a two-way process and both sides of the table need to have reassurance that they are suited to each other. In larger organizations, the human resource management staff will generally be available to provide further information. If a tour of the information service is offered, then this will be a helpful way to learn more about the organization, even if you have already made your own tour.

Job offers are sometimes made at the interview, and while this is an enormous boost to morale, the sensible decision is respond that you are interested, but would like to take a short time to consider the offer. Employers realize that difficult decisions may need to be made if there is the question, for example, of relocation—especially if relocation involves a partner or family. A job offer should not be formally accepted until the terms and conditions have been made in writing and are acceptable.

SETTLING INTO A NEW POST

Moving into a new position is not easy. We are enthusiastic, making a fresh start, and want to demonstrate our skills and knowledge—all of these feelings are important as motivators. But they can produce problems for their supervisor. Yes, everyone wants to have a team member who is keen, talented, and committed. But sometimes new recruits can go over the top in attempting to prove themselves and believe that they can use their talents to updating local practices. It is best to remember that there are usually good reasons why the procedures are set the way they are, so look and listen and wait awhile before offering your advice as a newcomer. It may be that there are newer and better ways to carry out a task—a new graduate should be at the cutting edge of developments—but understand the reasons why things are being done in a certain way, before proposing a change.

Leaving study behind should also provide time to read more widely, particularly about the field in which you are working. Getting involved in professional matters through a professional association is an effective and enjoyable way to develop ideas and a network. (The authors of this text have all been deeply involved in professional activities at the national and international levels, and the collaboration for this book emerged from a professional conference in Vienna.) Becoming involved professionally provides the start of networking that can pay many dividends throughout a career. It cannot be predicted which of your peers at college will later become influential people.

Check This Out:

IFLA's New Professionals Discussion Group has a Web page (Available: www.ifla.org/VII/dg/npdg/ index.htm [accessed May 2006]).

Networking is essential within the service and its parent organization. Any large organization or information service operates like a series of tribes. Each department has its own technical jargon and local shorthand, ways of organizing itself, and socializing. Moving across these boundaries opens up new insights and adds to a deeper understanding of the organizational culture. Getting involved in staff associations and committees within the wider organization develops the awareness of who, and what, makes the organization tick.

MENTORS

Mentors and role models contribute to the process of career development. A mentor can be an asset at any stage in a career, providing advice and comment, when requested, on decisions that need to be made. They may be of the same sex, or of the opposite sex; the key factor is that they need to be able to understand the person they are mentoring and their goals. A mentor can offer realistic advice and provide a second opinion on a proposed course of action, but they cannot make decisions on behalf of the person mentored. They are not a crutch, but an informed sounding board. Their role is of adviser, counselor, friend, and supporter—and they need to be able to affirm decisions or provide alternative scenarios when requested to do so. In turn, the person being mentored needs to develop their listening skills, to be able to learn from the experience of others, and evaluate the advice that is offered.

Mentors need to be chosen with care, having demonstrated a rapport and interest in you as a new professional. They could be a member of the faculty in the professional school you attended or an experienced practitioner within the service. In making a choice, the authors believe that it is important that you have respect for the would-be mentor, a good rapport, and that both parties have a level of trust that enables advice to be offered and received in the spirit in which it is offered. The mentor may be asked to provide references and comment on strengths—and perhaps weaknesses. They should be able to offer advice about a post that might be considered and should have a view about its suitability. The mentor's networks may yield advance notice of a post not yet advertised. Some professional associations have established committees that match people willing to mentor with those seeking a mentor.

While a mentor can be of great benefit in career development, a role model can be helpful, but does not necessarily make a good mentor. A role model can demonstrate what can be achieved and, by observing their actions and style, appropriate strategies and tactics may become apparent to the less experienced professional.

For Further Thought:

Do you have a mentor?
List three attributes that you feel mentor needs to have.

APPRAISAL AND SELF-ASSESSMENT

The majority of organizations operate an appraisal system for their staff providing helpful feedback to the person being appraised. If it is a developmental process, rather than being an annual salary review, it offers an objective view of strengths and weaknesses as demonstrated by performance on the job.

Generally, the appraisal process has formal guidelines together with a list of questions to be posed. The person being appraised should study the documentation carefully and prepare for the interview. This is perhaps a statement of the obvious, but in a busy working situation it is not always easy to take time away to think about oneself. But it is particularly important to enable training needs to be discussed and for obtaining and providing accurate formal and informal feedback. Appraisal systems play a key role in career development. A third party may have observed talents that the person being appraised did not know they possessed.

Making a self-assessment is not easy, and a mentor should be able to provide input. The points to be considered include:

- level of qualifications held
- short courses attended
- any study in progress
- involvement in professional activities and committee work within the organization
- work experience to date
- level of job satisfaction
- preferred career direction
- preferred sector and specialization
- the areas that would not be welcomed at this stage
- personal strengths—what you do well
- personal weaknesses—what you do not do well
- level of commitment to working in the field—is the current type of service a long-term career goal or a shorter-term goal
- are there other factors that are important? Are there other activities outside work that are important which influence professional growth?

The last two factors are particularly important. Long-term intention to stay in the field may not be part of your career development, since information skills are transferable skills. Taking personal circumstances into account will result in better decisions. Carrying out a regular self-assessment assists career development at any point in a working life. A preferred move may require the acquisition of new skills or the honing of some that have been dormant.

Every time we take an exam or a course we heave a sigh of relief; it's easy to hope that it may be the last. But it is a case of lifelong learning and developing new skills. So education and training needs change over time. A first qualification in the information sector will be followed by a mix of courses in professional knowledge and skills, particularly in the technological aspects of professional practice. Some may take the option of pursuing a second-level master's degree in the information sector or the discipline of their undergraduate degree. Then there may be a shift to doctoral study to pursue research in a professional subject or academic discipline.

A recent development in the United States has been a post-qualification certificate program for public librarians, and we expect other sectors to introduce certification, following Australian and U.K. practice.

An increasing number of information and library schools now offer higher qualifications that link professional practice with management studies. A number of these programs are available in the distance-learning mode and, as a result, it is noticeable that prospective students are "shopping" around the world to identify the program that best meets their needs at the "right price." Students are skilled consumers, and the benefits of studying with a group of students from other countries include exposure to a wide range of practices and approaches to the delivery of information services, an expansion of a network, and can perhaps provide the impetus for travel. In addition to the "mixed" programs, studying for an MBA is an option for those who wish to extend their management knowledge and skills.

There is a wide range of options for continuing professional development, both within the profession and in the wider fields of management and IT. There are an increasing number of organizations offering courses. Some are associated with professional associations and state agencies, and others are in the private sector. The costs vary, and when looking for a course, get information on several, check out the speakers and their experience, try and identify someone who has taken the program, and examine the costs. Attending a national or international professional conference may give good value for money and provide good opportunities for networking and exchanging ideas over coffee.

> **Tip:**
>
> It is never too soon to start the process of self-assessment.
> Draw up a list of your strengths and weaknesses and revise it at the start of each year. It will assist in identifying training needs and thinking about the next career move

SETTING CAREER GOALS

The previous generation's view of a career was probably of a steady progression from the bottom to the top. Today's careers are more flexible, but the factors that contribute to the achievement of progress include having the appropriate qualifications, experience, attitude, and aptitude. Setting a career goal helps to sharpen the awareness of specific needs and how they can be met.

A point to make again is that not everyone graduating from an archives or library and information program will stay in a mainstream information post. Former graduates have become successful restaurant owners, asset managers, legal executives, financial executives, information entrepreneurs, newsreaders, publishers, writers, astrologists, songwriters, and yoga teachers—just in the experience of the authors. It is not a waste of a qualification to move in another career direction. Information skills are transferable skills and, when combined with another outside interest, can be used to change a career path. Managers within the profession who have developed their management skills often move into the broader field of management, becoming vice-chancellors or heads of departments in national or local government.

For Further Thought:

Reflect on your long-term career goals.
Chart a path to achieve these goals.
What do you need to do to get there?

One of the frustrations that many professionals face, in any field, is that the higher they move up the ladder, the greater the percentage of time spent on managing. Less time is devoted to using their professional knowledge and skills. The question of this balance needs to be considered at every point when a change of post is considered.

Moving within the profession will extend experience and skills, but this may not always be an upward move. A horizontal shift can also bring benefits in being able to extend skills, and sometimes a downward shift may be considered when wanting to move to a new field of specialization or sector. The nature of the move is the choice of the individual, who then needs to demonstrate to the prospective employer the talents they would bring to the post and the motivation for the shift.

There is also a focus on developing a portfolio of careers, using skills and talents in a number of fields to increase job mobility.

A final point to make about career goals is that they will change over time. Changes take place in one's personal life and in the profession, but having goals and knowing your personal values makes for better decisions when considering a change of post. Making job applications takes time—quite a considerable amount of time. It also involves an investment on the part of an employer.

Make sure any application is a serious one before investing your time and possibly wasting that of a potential employer.

Tip:

One of the joys of leaving a full-time post is that you have time to use your information skills in a direction that is solely of your choosing. Both writers have extended their skills in the archives field as volunteers working in collections in subject fields in which they have a passionate interest.

FLEXIBLE WAYS OF WORKING

To test the water before taking your career in a new direction, examine the range of flexible working practices available in many organizations. Since information services generally operate over extended hours, flexibility is often easier to arrange than in many other types of organization.

Part-time posts may be available. Job-shares can be organized with the benefit to the employer of having two people covering one post who have a degree of autonomy within which they arrange their responsibilities. A job-share is one way of using acquired professional expertise while moving into a new field. Flexible hours and annualized hours can be arranged in larger services. These arrangements can bring benefits to the employer by having a well-qualified and motivated staff member for some hours, rather than losing this employee altogether.

Check This Out:

Just as an organization is dependent on creating an effective job interview process for its hiring success, so is the person going for the interview dependent on careful job interview preparation for getting the sought-after position. A great source of ideas for being well prepared for what is practically always a stressful experience is Martin Yate's 2004 *Knock 'em Dead* (Avon, MA: Adams Media).

The growth of the Internet has introduced another flexible way of working, which is to telework or telecommute. Jassin and Moe (2005) discuss the ways in which information professionals can compete with offshore-based workers by developing their own telecommuting jobs. Working from home on a freelance basis can be effective for an increasing number of areas of professional practice. It has been common for indexers and abstractors to work in this way for many years, and the practice now extends to handling enquiries, marketing and public relations, information brokers, consultants, editors, etc. The range of work is expanding as services outsource more of their services. Working in this way requires good organization and communication skills, and close attention to customer care: the client. Professional associations are generally able to offer advice on the professional indemnity insurance that is essential when working independently in the information field.

Check These Out:

CILIP, the U.K. association for librarians and information professionals, provides advice on flexible working (Available: www.cilip.org.uk/jobscareers/career advice/flexibleworking? [accessed May 2006]) and about setting yourself up in business, which can be applied in any part of the world (Available: www.cilip.org.uk/jobscareers/careeradvice/ workingforyourself? [accessed May 2006]).

Another option is to take a temporary or contract post. Changes in the labor market have resulted in a greater number of people being employed on limited-term contracts. Contract working provides an opportunity to experience work with a range of employers, or in a variety of specialty posts. The employment agencies can assist an individual manage a career based on contract posts, particularly in the private sector. A number of writers in the management field have suggested that all professionals will develop portfolio careers in the future that involve greater flexibility and more switching between jobs. But there is one precaution to take if stepping back from a permanent or full-time post, and that is to consider the vital pension plan, and health and other insurances. This may not seem important in your 20s or 30s, but it can have an impact later in life. Take advice from a recommended financial counselor.

CAREER BREAKS

Career breaks benefit both the employee and the employer. In some occupations and countries, the need for a break is recognized in the conditions of employment. Academics may be granted study leave. The employer gains benefits, because the person who enjoys a break comes back refreshed and reinvigorated. Another benefit for the staff development program is that another member of staff can be offered the opportunity to demonstrate her/his skills in a different post. This assists the employer to assess her/his suitability for promotion.

For the person considering a break, there is a range of opportunities. Developmental internships or fellowships may be available for those designated as high flyers—for example, those organized by the Association of Research Libraries. In some universities, staff may be eligible for a sabbatical to pursue their personal research in order to maintain subject knowledge. Traveling overseas may be the choice at any stage in a career. Travel scholarships for short periods of time are offered by a number of organizations. Exchanges with professionals in other parts of the world can be set up with facilitators through exchange registers which list people seeking an exchange in all types of services and in a number of countries around the world. Most are for three or six months and often involve a swap of job, house, and car. Voluntary service overseas was, at one time, the province of the new graduate, but now as more people take early retirement, or a career break, their skills and experience can be of value in other countries.

Check This Out:

LIBEX offers a service to LIS workers from any non-U.K. country who wishes to exchange jobs with someone in the United Kingdom (Available: http://cilip. org.uk/jobscareers/libex [accessed May 2006]).

Breaks for family responsibilities, such as maternity or paternity leave, are becoming part of established employment policies and practices. This can help parents to enjoy, and more fully participate, in the early stages of their child's life. The length of time available, paid or unpaid, varies from one country to another.

At an interview that would precede a decision about the granting of leave, questions concerning the effect upon salary, conditions of service, and other employment benefits should be discussed, and a written agreement should be signed by both parties.

THE WORK/LIFE DEBATE

The general management literature demonstrates a continuing concern for the pressures that are being placed on managers and their staff as organizations strive to cut operating costs and as ICT changes the way in which work is done. Much has been written about the negative effects of stress that can affect anyone within an organization, regardless of age, gender, or job level. Progressing in a career can increase the susceptibility to stress. Learning a new job can mean taking work home, and acquiring new knowledge, qualifications, or skills. E-mail, the Internet, and intranets can add to the pressures of daily life, resulting in a situation where it is hard to break away from work, always needing to "catch-up." In its most serious manifestation, excessive eating, drinking, or smoking can be the individual's answer to the problem. But stress can damage physical and psychological health and reduce the effectiveness of a person's performance, which, in turn, impacts on the work of their colleagues. Recognizing the symptoms may be unpalatable to the employee and difficult for the employer. Organizations that provide in-house counseling, such as universities, may have a better way to help staff—and themselves.

The remedy lies with the individual, who should limit the amount of overtime worked, take all of a leave allowance, have a holiday, have a leisure-time interest, and enjoy time with family and friends for a full life.

MOVING FORWARD

Part of moving forward is making your talents known. Success is easier to achieve if others know about you, both within and outside the organization in which you are working. Looking for ways to do your job more effectively and presenting them to a supervisor—at the right time and in the right way—will show initiative, particularly if the thoughts have been developed as part of a team. Becoming known in the profession can come from joining committees, attending meetings, writing in the professional press, and making thoughtful contributions to discussion on the Internet. Developing the skills of listening helps a person to make her/his mark.

For Further Thought:

List four steps that you can take now to make others aware of your talents.

We have already made the point, but underline it again. The qualifications gained at the start of a career will need updating regularly, including subject knowledge, professional skills and knowledge, and management or technological expertise. The range of opportunities is wide: from a formal academic program to the institute or short course, from Web-based study to attending traditional distance learning in person. The choice means that geographic isolation or family and work commitments become less of a barrier.

> **Tip:**
>
> Never neglect your personal training and development needs at any stage of your career. Everyone needs to be a lifelong learner—and that applies as much to the boss as the junior.

Membership in a professional association pays dividends. Its journal, publications and Web site keep practitioners in touch with news and developments. But if you are serious about a management career, you need to add at least one other professional affiliation, in the field of management or computing or even both. Selecting appropriate discussion lists and contributing to discussion stimulates professional thinking and allows an exchange of viewpoints and experiences. Meetings provide an opportunity to exchange ideas, and make yourself known outside your library. Conferences provide exposure to a wide range of professional activities. Those who travel to the annual professional conference find that it is an exhilarating potpourri of meetings, exhibitors, and enthusiastic librarians and prospective employers.

Keeping in touch with change means that a range of sources will need to be consulted regularly, in both paper and electronic formats. First, reading a range of journals in the profession is essential. Clearly, the relevant national titles will be of primary importance, but there will also be international titles.

> **Tip:**
>
> Check the Web sites of your professional bodies and those in the field of management at the local, national, and international levels regularly.

Becoming a member of a professional committee develops the essential political skills needed in career development. Giving papers and talks enhances communication skills. Involvement in the activities of international associations extends a network and provides insight into professional practices overseas. No single country has a monopoly on good practice. And for the librarian who cannot travel and is geographically isolated, the Internet provides the means of taking part in debates around the globe without leaving your desk.

Increasingly recruitment to positions at the higher level is being out-sourced to headhunting agencies. Headhunters identify their targets through professional networks, tracking developments in the professions, and maintaining a database of exceptional people. Nazmi (2005) provides sound advice for people who are targeted by headhunters.

Sometimes you feel unhappy in a job and consider making a change. If so Seiss (2005) has a three-point plan to follow before making a final decision.

FACTORS THAT CONTRIBUTE TO SUCCESS

Here is the authors' list of factors that contribute to success in whatever direction a career takes.

- Know yourself, both the strengths and the weaknesses.
- Have high standards, both personal and professional, and demonstrate them in your daily work.
- Demonstrate commitment to whatever job you have.
- Cultivate clear thinking and maintain an objective viewpoint.
- Be reliable.
- Be adaptable.
- Cultivate and never lose your sense of humor.
- Understand the way that others think.
- Show a concern for others in your professional and personal life, but in unobtrusive ways.
- Keep at the cutting edge of change.
- Develop good communication and influencing skills.
- Acquire political skills.
- Extend managerial knowledge and know what is best practice in management thinking.
- Ensure that you are working effectively as a member of a team at all stages in a career.
- Know how to make decisions and change them if the situation demands.
- Delegate.
- Maintain control over your own time.
- Recognize mistakes that you have made and learn from them.
- Believe in yourself.
- Understand the career development requires an investment of time and money.
- Enjoy the job you are doing. If you don't enjoy the one you are in, find another.

FINAL THOUGHTS

Moving from a professional program to a first job is likely to produce culture shock, as the fundamental purpose of professional education is not to train students for a first job, but to prepare them for a professional career (Holley, 2003). It is important to understand that it is preparation for the longer term. The theory and principles learned support professionals throughout their career.

The direction a career may take will to an extent be conditioned by factors outside the control of the individual. These include economic, political, social, and technological change, and the state of the labor market. But there is a range of opportunities, and an individual has choice in selecting a direction in which to move. Career development depends on keeping well informed. Information-handling skills are transferable skills, and they can be used in many occupations outside the mainstream of the information professions.

The authors have enjoyed their careers in information and library work and in management, but couldn't have predicted the paths they would take when they first started. We have both had generally wonderful experiences as librarians and library educators; however, it is also true there have been one or two less than good experiences. So we'd like to pass on some advice: Monitor change and keep abreast of events, not only within librarianship and information work, but in what is happening in the wider world that might affect your career. For example, where will librarians fit into the growing market for knowledge managers? Continual self-appraisal and assessment will identify emerging education and training needs. The authors, though long in tooth and graying of hair, are still actively engaged in continual professional development.

A mentor who knows you well will provide objective advice on your strengths and weaknesses and whether you should apply for that post that caught your eye. And sometimes she/he will give reasons why you shouldn't.

Career goals are important, but flexibility is essential. Remember that realistic self-promotion will move a career forward. Finally, a key factor is the level of enjoyment and reward, both extrinsic and intrinsic, that the job is providing. Career development is a personal responsibility.

REFERENCES

Bureau of Labor Statistics, U.S. Department of Labor, *Occupational Outlook Handbook, 2002–07 Edition.* Available: www.bls.gov/ocos065htm [archivists] www.bls.gov ocos068.htm [librarians] (accessed May 2006).

Holley, Robert P. 2003. "The Ivory Tower as Preparation for the Trenches." *College and Research Libraries News* 64, no. 3 (March): 172–175.

Jassin, Marjorie, and Tricia Moe. 2005. "The Flat Track to New Career Options for Information Professionals." *Online* 29, no. 5 (September–October): 22–25.

Nazmi, Beverly. 2005. "How to Get the Best From a Headhunter: Responding to an Approach, Seeking Out Opportunities." *Business Information* Review 22, no. 4 (December): 227–233.

Seiss, Judith. 2005. "It's Your Career: What Are You Doing About It?" *One-Person Library* 22, no. 6 (October): 1–2.

Templeton, Mary Ellen. 1997. *Help! My Job Interview is Tomorrow!: How to Use the Library to Research an Employer*, 2nd ed. New York: Neal-Schuman.

Totta, Marcia. 2006. *Supervising Staff: A How-To-Do-It Manual.* New York: Neal-Schuman.

LAUNCHING PAD

"Managing Yourself." *Harvard Business Review* 83, no. 1 (January): 25–109.

Mason, Florence M., and Chris Dobson. 1998. *Information Brokering—How to Make Money Selling Information Services: A How-To-Do-It Manual.* New York: Neal-Schuman.

Newlen, Robert R. 2006. *Resume Writing and Interview Techniques That Work: A How-To-Do-It Manual for Librarians.* New York: Neal-Schuman.

Reyes, Veronica. 2006. "The Future Role of the Academic Librarians in Higher Education." *Portal: Libraries and the Academy* 6, no. 3 July: 301–309.

Tonkery, Dan. 2005. "Seven Helpful Steps To Get You To the Top." *Information Outlook* 9, no. 5 (June): 20–21.

Walster, Dian. 1993. *Managing Time: A How-To-Do-It Manual for School and Public Librarians.* New York: Neal-Schuman

Williamson, Jeanine M., Anne E. Pemberton, and John W. Lounsbury. 2005. "An Investigation of Career and Job Satisfaction in Relation to Personality Traits of Information Professionals." *Library Quarterly* 75, no. 2 (April): 122–141.

20

Looking Forward

"When it comes to the future, there are three kinds of people: those who let it happen, those who make it happen, and those who wondered what happened."
John M. Richardson, Jr.

"The real needs of the present must not be sacrificed to the temporary pressures of the present—and its likely needs of the future must not be sacrificed to the temporary pressures of the present."
Maurice Line

INTRODUCTION

In writing this text we focused on the management of information services as it is being practiced today and on trends for the immediate future. However, at various points we have indicated how vital it is to look ahead and think about potential changes that will impact on, and shape, services in the longer term. So we carried out an environmental scan, and the thoughts offered have been drawn from a range of sources and people. The critical factors center on two major resources available to managers: people and technology. That is, the quality of the people who will deliver the services, together with the shape of technology to come.

One forecast can be made with confidence. We firmly believe that management will continue to grow in importance. In addition, the challenges will increase, since life never appears to become simpler, but always grows in complexity as new situations emerge. Without having management theory and experience to reflect upon, no contemporary organization is able to perform effectively and efficiently and, most important, provide the level of service needed and expected by customers and users, while continually reducing, or at least controlling, costs. This applies to all organizations, including information services, as they adapt to growing expectations and as demands made upon them become more sophisticated.

In terms of technology, we expect rapid changes in capability and lower costs. Communications technology is just one example of change. In the space of 20 years, cell phones have moved from the size and weight of a brick capable of carrying voice messages to a small device capable of capturing moving images, accessing television and the Internet. How will technology develop in the next decade? And, more to the point, think about how this will change information services.

To meet these challenges, all professions, including the information professions, will have to identify and recruit people with leadership potential, and then ensure they receive the appropriate education, training, and experience to develop leadership skills. This will be happening at the same time that everyone investing time in a career will be looking for greater job satisfaction in a changing labor market. Taking into account predictions about demographics—lower birth rates and retirement of the Baby Boomers—the labor market is likely to be stable at best and a job seekers market. Young newcomers to the field may be less tolerant of situations/ positions if they do not believe they will be offered adequate growth and development opportunities. It means that organizations will have to increase opportunities and offer enhanced benefits in order to attract and retain quality staff. Demographic change also means that in addition to a reduction in the numbers of people entering the labor market, they are likely to be more mobile. This will affect all organizations at the same time as they will face increasing pressure to reduce overhead costs and make effective use of their staff. We see that one way to achieve both goals will be to organize staff into self-managing teams, which will increase job satisfaction and empower staff. For this to happen, strong leadership will be required, and we see that this, together with self-managing teams, will be a growth area.

Successful managers work in the present but must always consider what the future may hold, so that they can shape their planning, decision-making and resource needs accordingly.

CHANGES IN INFORMATION DELIVERY

Two major influences will shape the delivery of information. The first relates to people, of all ages, who need access to information and documents.

Societal change is an important influence. We have written about generational differences in attitudes to work, but this also affects information needs. Consider the generation of Baby Boomers now retiring, who will have more time at their disposal. Their information needs will change as they leave the workforce, and being highly educated achievers, they will expect a high level of service. A second factor relating to societal change is the time pressure felt by those in the workforce, particularly those with family responsibilities—men and women, younger and older. One example of change is the way that public libraries have adapted to provide service over seven days of the week, which helps those with children to make a library visit a family occasion. Offering story hours for the youngsters alongside coffee bars for the parents creates a library habit.

Think About:

Societal change, generational differences, and the likely impact on information services. We have given just two examples, but add to the list.

The second influence stems from information and communications technology, where increasing numbers of people access information and documents through the Internet or are remote users of information services.

One serious issue to consider, and which society must address at some point, is how to handle the changing costs of the digital information cycle: creation, distribution, storage and access. "Born digital" information has somewhat different cost factors, but basic issues remain on how to encourage people to create information and perhaps gain some income from the process. The economic models that work reasonably well for the print world are not working as well in the digital world. There are also changes in the way people use and interact with information and each other.

Consider the way in which academic libraries have become learning centers, allowing students, faculty, and administrators to log onto a range of services in addition to traditional library service. As increasing numbers of people study by distance learning, so the learning center becomes more important for remote users. Vendors of library software are developing more sophisticated portals using the concept of Library 2.0. This moves away from a simple Web catalog to create a "library" account for individuals within an institutional portal that provides news, information about the individual's account, new services, and how to make best use of the facilities available to them. One example of this increased facility is that by accessing a database such as Amazon, a user can see which libraries hold a title and whether it is available for loan (Miller, 2006).

The number of "born digital" documents is increasing exponentially in terms of journals, books, archives, and records, producing new challenges for their storage and particularly for their retrieval. In terms of storage, there is the question of capturing images, then selecting which items are to be stored and for what period of time. In terms of retrieval there are issues of privacy, copyright (who is allowed access), licensing—and of indexing. The process of digitization speeds up access, which heightens questions of copyright and access. And for all types of digital documents, there is the challenge of changing technology and storage media which can decay or be superseded. These are some of the challenging issues to which managers would like to have answers to inform decision making about the substantial investment required for the longer term. Concern about these questions can be swayed by the benefit to users of having easy online access to documents in their office or at home. Just consider the interest in genealogy that has resulted from people researching their family history online, which then prompts them to delve further into background research.

The changing ways in which information can be accessed and delivered mean that an information service will need to determine changing information needs in the user community together with management data concerning the penetration of the service, the impact that it makes, and the perceived value to users and the service's parent organization.

The response from information services will be to meet the challenges that we expect will come for dramatic new approaches to meeting competition and providing new end-user services.

Think Creatively:

Brainstorm new approaches to services to end-users and give a time frame when these will emerge in an information service of your choice.

Check These Out Regularly:

D-Lib Magazine (www.dlib.org)
Lorcan Dempsey's Weblog on libraries, services and networks (http://orweblog.oclc.org/)

ACCESS TO INFORMATION

We have given this a separate heading, for this is a topic where there is great current concern.

First there is the question of research and scholarly communication, which was once the sole province of universities and professional bodies in the academic disciplines which organized conferences and published scholarly journals. Some continue this practice, but many have passed this responsibility to the commercial sector. As a result, conferences have become more expensive, limiting attendance, and mergers in the publishing industry have resulted in a great deal of power being concentrated in a few commercial companies. Adding in the costs of publishing in an electronic format, publishers argued for high levels of subscription rates—and in many cases obtained them. Although libraries formed consortia to negotiate more favorable terms, subscription costs remain high. In addition, there is the issue of copyright and licensing, which limits access to journals. No longer can a retired academic walk into a university library and consult paper copies on a shelf; access to materials via electronic sources may not always be granted.

One powerful response has emerged from researchers in the academic sector, who have strong beliefs about open access to scholarly research. Thus a number of universities have, or are in the process of setting up, institutional repositories for information and knowledge sharing in the scholarly world (Walters, 2006).

There is a strong argument to be made for greater access to nonconfidential research that has been carried out with public funding. We feel that the shape of scholarly communication may well change in the near future.

A second question of access relates to information that should be deposited with archivists and records managers. In the days when records were kept on paper—for example, in the case of government or business—strict control was maintained over the deposit and storage of documents. With the introduction of electronic documents and e-mail, many records are regarded as being more personal and less easy to capture. Consider the volume of work that is often carried out from home. Ensuring that important documents are captured for storage is a challenge, but vital, as legal investigations have demonstrated the need for audit trails.

Archives are also feeling the pressure of the commercial market for items of literary or historical interest, as more are placed into the commercial market rather than being donated as gifts to collections.

PEOPLE MANAGEMENT

Working with self-managing teams will require that managers develop a changing skill set. This will include the enduring skills, such as communication, trust, and delegation, but increasingly managers will also require sound political skills. They will work within the service, alongside the team, but also out in the wider organization, marketing the service and keeping in contact with the user community. Collaboration across the range of information services will increase—working together will benefit users—and be welcomed by funding agencies. All of this requires that managers be able to apply effective political skills, both within the service with staff and users and in the external environment from which resources can be drawn.

Everyone in the information profession is likely to be more mobile, including the leaders. Organizations will change as a result of mergers, and new forms of information services will create new opportunities for staff. Within the information service this will require sound management and administration that allows the service to operate smoothly when staff members come and go. For the manager, it will require closer attention to how their teams organize information and records, so that a newcomer can quickly pick up the work of anyone, at any level, who leaves.

PLANNING

Planning and anticipating change in the operating environment will present opportunities and challenges. We have predicted that the pace of change will accelerate, particularly that of technology. The capabilities of computing and digitization will have a profound impact on access to, and delivery of, information—even greater than that of the Internet at the present time. As services such as Google and Yahoo become more sophisticated and develop better performance in terms of recall and precision, so users will have more information at their fingertips without necessarily feeling the need for an intermediary. However, the more sophisticated means of access will result in a greater multiplicity of access points, and users will benefit from coaching. So information services staff will change the allocation of their time to meet this emerging need and develop pedagogical skills.

The legal issues of copyright, intellectual property rights, and licensing will gradually be overcome as more partnerships emerge across services and national boundaries.

Technology has a major impact on planning, but we feel that there will also be major changes in economic, social, and political conditions as globalization increases and the balance of power and influence in the world changes. Exchange rates, diversity and migration, government and state policies, and the attitudes of the community toward taxation will be some of the issues that will occupy more of the manager and leader's thinking.

The funding of services will remain a major challenge, as user expectations increase and the possibilities of using technology grow. More activities within the service are likely to be outsourced. The direction in which the nonprofit sector has moved is more toward a business model, with governance in the hands of people drawn from industry and government. Their experience should ensure good governance, but they may not have the benevolence that services would like to see demonstrated, and this could conflict with the preferred style of the manager. The active support of the user community can be a powerful tool in the hands of a skilled advocate who has sound judgment and an ethical stance. Marketing the service and using public relations informs the user community and the governing board or committee.

THE USPS OF INFORMATION PROFESSIONALS

Information professionals have USPs (unique selling points) that rest on their ability to understand subject analysis; to recall, with relevance and precision; to know where to find information, how reliable it is, how it can be retrieved and packaged to satisfy user needs, and communicated effectively and efficiently. And as new challenges emerge, so many of the former ones will remain.

To be able to work effectively and efficiently information professionals will need to possess a sound subject knowledge of the service they are working for and to retain currency in addition to relevant and changing professional skills. Continuing professional development will increase in importance.

Information professionals will draw on the subject expertise of everyone working in the organization together with key members of the user community, using the skills of knowledge management; networking will become even more important.

A FINAL THOUGHT

Think globally will be the catchword, and U.S. librarians will be casting widely to learn from experience in other parts of the world. Younger countries can often leapfrog older countries when it comes to innovation; consider developments in China and Singapore with their vibrant public library services, and in archives and records management in Australia.

Check Out These Web Sites:

Shanghai Library (Available: www.library.sh.cn [accessed November 2006])
National Library Board of Singapore (Available: www.lib.gov.sg [accessed November 2006])
Australian Archives Gateway (Available: www.archivenet.gov.au [accessed November 2006])

REFERENCES

Miller, Paul. 2006. "Coming Together Around Library 2.0." *D-Lib Magazine* 12, no. 4 (April). Available: www.dlib.org/dlib/april06/miller/04miller.html (accessed November 2006).

Walters, Tyler O. 2006. "Strategies and Frameworks for Institutional Repositories and the New Support Infrastructure for Scholarly Communications." *D-Lib Magazine* 12, no. 10 (October). Available: www.dlib.org/dlib/October06/walters/10walters.html (accessed November 2006).

Name Index

Subject Index

About the Authors

G. EDWARD EVANS recently retired from his position as University Librarian at Loyola Marymount University. Finding retirement too boring, he now is librarian of the Harold S. Colton Memorial Library and Archives at the Museum of Northern Arizona. His career has included both practice and teaching, often during the same period of time. During his tenure at Loyola Marymount, he taught part-time at UCLA's Graduate School of Education and Information Studies and also taught courses in anthropology and archaeology at Loyola Marymount. As a Fulbright scholar, he taught at the University of Iceland and has offered courses in management at library schools in Norway, Denmark, Sweden, and Finland. He also served as an external examiner in management for the Department of Library Studies at the University of the West Indies. He holds two degrees in anthropology, an MLS, and a PhD.

PROFESSOR PATRICIA LAYZELL WARD is semi-retired; currently she is Hon. Archivist to the Festiniog Railway Company having worked in public and special libraries and enjoyed a long-time involvement in teaching and research. This included posts as Director of the Centre for Library and Information Management at Loughborough University and Chairs in Library and Information Studies at Curtin University, Perth, Western Australia, and the University of Wales Aberystwyth. She is Emeritus Editor of *Library Management*, author of conference papers and journal articles, examiner to a number of universities and has consulted in Europe, South America, South-East Asia, and Australia. She holds a Masters and Ph D from University College London, is a Fellow of CILIP and the Chartered Management Institute, an Associate of the Australian Library and Information Association, and a member of the American Library Association.

Beginning
JavaScript®

Third Edition

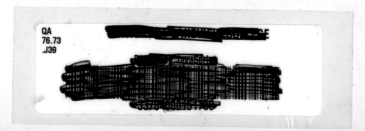

Beginning
JavaScript®

Third Edition

Paul Wilton

Jeremy McPeak

Wiley Publishing, Inc.

Beginning JavaScript® Third Edition

Published by
Wiley Publishing, Inc.
10475 Crosspoint Boulevard
Indianapolis, IN 46256
www.wiley.com

Copyright © 2007 by Wiley Publishing, Inc., Indianapolis, Indiana

Published simultaneously in Canada

ISBN: 978-0-470-05151-1

Manufactured in the United States of America

10 9 8 7 6 5 4 3 2 1

Library of Congress Cataloging-in-Publication Data:

Wilton, Paul, 1969–
 Beginning JavaScript / Paul Wilton, Jeremy McPeak.—3rd ed.
 p. cm.
 ISBN 978-0-470-05151-1 (paper/website)
 1. JavaScript (Computer program language) 2. World Wide Web. 3. Web servers. I. McPeak, Jeremy, 1979– II. Title.
 QA76.73.J39W55 2007
 005.13'3—dc22
                        2007008102

In memory of my mum, June Wilton, who in 2006 lost her brave battle against cancer. She was always very proud of me and my books and showed my books to anyone and everyone she happened to meet however briefly and whether they wanted to see them or not! She's very much missed.

—Paul Wilton

To my parents, Jerry and Judy, for their love and support.

—Jeremy McPeak

About the Authors

Paul Wilton started as a Visual Basic applications programmer at the Ministry of Defence in the UK, then found himself pulled into the Net. Having joined an Internet development company, he spent three years helping create Internet solutions. He's now running his own successful and rapidly growing company developing online holiday property reservation systems.

Jeremy McPeak began tinkering with web development as a hobby in 1998. Currently working in the IT department of a school district, Jeremy has experience developing web solutions with JavaScript, PHP, and C#. He has written several online articles covering topics such as XSLT, WebForms, and C#. He is also co-author of *Professional Ajax*. Jeremy can be reached through his web site at www.wdonline.com.

Acknowledgments

Firstly a big thank-you for her support to my partner Beci, who, now that the book's finished, will get to see me for more than 10 minutes a week.

I'd also like to say a very big thank you to Tom Dinse, who has been a great editor to work with and has done amazing work on the book.

Thanks also to Jim Minatel for making this book happen, and also his support in what has for me been yet another challenging and difficult year.

Many thanks to everyone who's supported and encouraged me over my many years of writing books. Your help will always be remembered.

Finally, pats and treats to my German shepherd Katie, who does an excellent job of warding off disturbances from door-to-door salespeople.

—Paul Wilton

Credits

Contents

Contents

Contents

Contents

Contents

Contents

Introduction

JavaScript is a scripting language that enables you to enhance static web applications by providing dynamic, personalized, and interactive content. This improves the experience of visitors to your site and makes it more likely that they will visit again. You must have seen the flashy drop-down menus, moving text, and changing content that are now widespread on web sites—they are enabled through JavaScript. Supported by all the major browsers, JavaScript is the language of choice on the Web. It can even be used outside web applications—to automate administrative tasks, for example.

This book aims to teach you all you need to know to start experimenting with JavaScript: what it is, how it works, and what you can do with it. Starting from the basic syntax, you'll move on to learn how to create powerful web applications. Don't worry if you've never programmed before—this book will teach you all you need to know, step by step. You'll find that JavaScript can be a great introduction to the world of programming: with the knowledge and understanding that you'll gain from this book, you'll be able to move on to learn newer and more advanced technologies in the world of computing.

Whom This Book Is For

In order to get the most out of this book, you'll need to have an understanding of HTML and how to create a static web page. You don't need to have any programming experience.

This book will also suit you if you have some programming experience already, and would like to turn your hand to web programming. You will know a fair amount about computing concepts, but maybe not as much about web technologies.

Alternatively, you may have a design background and know relatively little about the Web and computing concepts. For you, JavaScript will be a cheap and relatively easy introduction to the world of programming and web application development.

Whoever you are, we hope that this book lives up to your expectations.

What This Book Covers

You'll begin by looking at exactly what JavaScript is, and taking your first steps with the underlying language and syntax. You'll learn all the fundamental programming concepts, including data and data types, and structuring your code to make decisions in your programs or to loop over the same piece of code many times.

Once you're comfortable with the basics, you'll move on to one of the key ideas in JavaScript—the object. You'll learn how to take advantage of the objects that are native to the JavaScript language, such as dates and strings, and find out how these objects enable you to manage complex data and simplify your programs. Next, you'll see how you can use JavaScript to manipulate objects made available to you in the browser, such as forms, windows, and other controls. Using this knowledge, you can start to create truly professional-looking applications that enable you to interact with the user.

Long pieces of code are very hard to get right every time—even for the experienced programmer—and JavaScript code is no exception. You look at common syntax and logical errors, how you can spot them, and how to use the Microsoft Script Debugger to aid you with this task. Also, you need to examine how to handle the errors that slip through the net, and ensure that these do not detract from the experience of the end user of your application.

From here, you'll move on to more advanced topics, such as using cookies and jazzing up your web pages with dynamic HTML and XML. Finally, you'll be looking at a relatively new and exciting technology, remote scripting. This allows your JavaScript in a HTML page to communicate directly with a server, and useful for, say, looking up information on a database sitting on your server. If you have the Google toolbar you'll have seen something like this in action already. When you type a search word in the Google toolbar, it comes up with suggestions, which it gets via the Google search database.

All the new concepts introduced in this book will be illustrated with practical examples, which enable you to experiment with JavaScript and build on the theory that you have just learned. The appendix provides solutions to the exercises included at the end of most chapters throughout the book.

During the first half of the book, you'll also be building up a more complex sample application—an online trivia quiz—which will show you how JavaScript is used in action in a real-world situation.

What You Need to Use This Book

Because JavaScript is a text-based technology, all you really need to create documents containing JavaScript is Notepad (or your equivalent text editor).

Also, in order to try out the code in this book, you will need a web browser that supports a modern version of JavaScript. Ideally, this means Internet Explorer 6 or later and Firefox 1.5 or later. The book has been extensively tested with these two browsers. However, the code should work in most modern web browsers, although some of the code in later chapters, where you examine dynamic HTML and scripting the DOM, is specific to particular browsers; but the majority of the code presented is cross-browser. Where there are exceptions, they will be clearly noted.

Conventions

To help you get the most from the text and keep track of what's happening, we've used a number of conventions throughout the book.

Try It Out

The *Try It Out* is an exercise you should work through, following the text in the book.

1. They usually consist of a set of steps.
2. Each step has a number.
3. Follow the steps with your copy of the database.

How It Works

After each *Try It Out*, the code you've typed will be explained in detail.

> **Boxes like this one hold important, not-to-be forgotten information that is directly relevant to the surrounding text.**

Tips, hints, tricks, and asides to the current discussion are offset and placed in italics like this.

As for styles in the text:

- ❑ We *highlight in italic type* new terms and important words when we introduce them.
- ❑ We show keyboard strokes like this: Ctrl+A.
- ❑ We show file names, URLs, and code within the text like so: `persistence.properties`.
- ❑ We present code in two different ways:

```
In code examples we highlight new and important code with a gray background.
```

```
The gray highlighting is not used for code that's less important in the present
context, or that has been shown before.
```

Source Code

As you work through the examples in this book, you may choose either to type in all the code manually or to use the source-code files that accompany the book. All of the source code used in this book is available for download at `www.wrox.com`. Once at the site, simply locate the book's title (either by using the Search box or by using one of the title lists) and click the Download Code link on the book's detail page to obtain all the source code for the book.

Because many books have similar titles, you may find it easiest to search by ISBN; this book's ISBN is 978-0-470-05151-1.

Once you download the code, just decompress it with your favorite compression tool. Alternately, you can go to the main Wrox code download page at `www.wrox.com/dynamic/books/download.aspx` to see the code available for this book and all other Wrox books.

Errata

We make every effort to ensure that there are no errors in the text or in the code. However, no one is perfect, and mistakes do occur. If you find an error in one of our books, like a spelling mistake or faulty piece of code, we would be very grateful for your feedback. By sending in errata you may save another reader hours of frustration, and at the same time you will be helping us provide even higher-quality information.

To find the errata page for this book, go to www.wrox.com and locate the title using the Search box or one of the title lists. Then, on the book details page, click the Book Errata link. On this page you can view all errata that have been submitted for this book and posted by Wrox editors. A complete book list, including links to each book's errata, is also available at www.wrox.com/misc-pages/booklist.shtml.

If you don't spot "your" error on the Book Errata page, go to www.wrox.com/contact/techsupport .shtml and complete the form there to send us the error you have found. We'll check the information and, if appropriate, post a message to the book's errata page and fix the problem in subsequent editions of the book.

p2p.wrox.com

For author and peer discussion, join the P2P forums at p2p.wrox.com. The forums are a Web-based system on which you can post messages relating to Wrox books and related technologies and interact with other readers and technology users. The forums offer a subscription feature to e-mail you topics of interest of your choosing when new posts are made to the forums. Wrox authors, editors, other industry experts, and your fellow readers are present on these forums.

At http://p2p.wrox.com you will find a number of different forums that will help you not only as you read this book, but also as you develop your own applications. To join the forums, just follow these steps:

1. Go to p2p.wrox.com and click the Register link.

2. Read the terms of use and click Agree.

3. Complete the required information to join as well as any optional information you wish to provide, and click Submit.

4. You will receive an e-mail with information describing how to verify your account and complete the joining process.

   You can read messages in the forums without joining P2P, but in order to post your own messages, you must join.

Once you join, you can post new messages and respond to messages other users post. You can read messages at any time on the Web. If you would like to have new messages from a particular forum e-mailed to you, click the Subscribe to this Forum icon by the forum name in the forum listing.

For more information about how to use the Wrox P2P, be sure to read the P2P FAQs for answers to questions about how the forum software works, as well as many common questions specific to P2P and Wrox books. To read the FAQs, click the FAQ link on any P2P page.

Introduction to JavaScript and the Web

In this introductory chapter, you look at what JavaScript is, what it can do for you, and what you need in order to use it. With these foundations in place, you will see throughout the rest of the book how JavaScript can help you to create powerful web applications for your web site.

The easiest way to learn something is by actually doing it, so throughout the book you'll create a number of useful example programs using JavaScript. This process starts in this chapter, by the end of which you will have created your first piece of JavaScript code.

Additionally, over the course of the book you'll develop a complete JavaScript web application: an online trivia quiz. By seeing it develop, step by step, you'll get a good understanding of how to create your own web applications. At the end of this chapter, you'll look at the finished trivia quiz and consider the ideas behind its design.

Introduction to JavaScript

In this section you take a brief look at what JavaScript is, where it came from, how it works, and what sorts of useful things you can do with it.

What Is JavaScript?

Having bought this book, you are probably already well aware that JavaScript is some sort of *computer language*, but what is a computer language? Put simply, a computer language is a series of instructions that tell the computer to do something. That something can be one of a wide variety of things, including displaying text, moving an image, or asking the user for information. Normally the instructions, or what is termed *code*, are *processed* from the top line downward. This simply means that the computer looks at the code you've written, works out what action you want taken, and then takes that action. The actual act of processing the code is called *running* or *executing* it.

In natural English, here are instructions, or code, you might write to make a cup of instant coffee:

1. Put coffee crystals in cup.

2. Fill kettle with water.

3. Put kettle on to boil.

4. Has the kettle boiled? If so, then pour water into cup; otherwise, continue to wait.

5. Drink coffee.

You'd start running this code from the first line (instruction 1), and then continue to the next (instruction 2), then the next, and so on until you came to the end. This is pretty much how most computer languages work, JavaScript included. However, there are occasions when you might change the flow of execution, or even skip over some code, but you'll see more of this in Chapter 3.

JavaScript is an interpreted language, rather than a compiled language. What is meant by the terms *interpreted* and *compiled*?

Well, to let you in on a secret, your computer doesn't really understand JavaScript at all. It needs something to interpret the JavaScript code and convert it into something that it understands; hence it is an *interpreted language*. Computers understand only *machine code*, which is essentially a string of binary numbers (that is, a string of zeros and ones). As the browser goes through the JavaScript, it passes it to a special program called an *interpreter*, which converts the JavaScript to the machine code your computer understands. It's a bit like having a translator to translate English into Spanish, for example. The important point to note is that the conversion of the JavaScript happens at the time the code is run; it has to be repeated every time this happens. JavaScript is not the only interpreted language; there are others, including VBScript.

The alternative *compiled language* is one in which the program code is converted to machine code before it's actually run, and this conversion only has to be done once. The programmer uses a compiler to convert the code that he wrote to machine code, and it is this machine code that is run by the program's user. Compiled languages include Visual Basic and C++. Using a real-world analogy, it's like having someone translate your English document into Spanish. Unless you change the document, you can use it without retranslation as much as you like.

Perhaps this is a good point to dispel a widespread myth: JavaScript is not the script version of the Java language. In fact, although they share the same name, that's virtually all they do share. Particularly good news is that JavaScript is much, much easier to learn and use than Java. In fact, languages like JavaScript are the easiest of all languages to learn, but they are still surprisingly powerful.

JavaScript and the Web

For most of this book you'll look at JavaScript code that runs inside a web page loaded into a browser. All you need in order to create these web pages is a text editor — for example, Windows Notepad — and a web browser, such as Firefox or Internet Explorer, with which you can view your pages. These browsers come equipped with JavaScript interpreters.

In fact, the JavaScript language first became available in the web browser Netscape Navigator 2. Initially, it was called LiveScript. However, because Java was the hot technology of the time, Netscape decided that JavaScript sounded more exciting. When JavaScript really took off, Microsoft decided to add its own brand of JavaScript, called JScript, to Internet Explorer. Since then, Netscape, Microsoft, and others have released improved versions and included them in their latest browsers. Although these different brands and versions of JavaScript have much in common, there are enough differences to cause problems if you're not careful. Initially you'll be creating code that'll work with most browsers, whether Firefox, Internet Explorer, or Netscape. Later chapters look at features available only to Firefox 1.5 or later and Internet Explorer 6 and 7. You'll look into the problems with different browsers and versions of JavaScript later in this chapter, and see how to deal with them.

The majority of the web pages containing JavaScript that you create in this book can be stored on your hard drive and loaded directly into your browser from the hard drive itself, just as you'd load any normal file (such as a text file). However, this is not how web pages are loaded when you browse web sites on the Internet. The Internet is really just one great big network connecting computers. Access to web sites is a special service provided by particular computers on the Internet; the computers providing this service are known as *web servers*.

Basically the job of a web server is to hold lots of web pages on its hard drive. When a browser, usually on a different computer, requests a web page contained on that web server, the web server loads it from its own hard drive and then passes the page back to the requesting computer via a special communications protocol called *Hypertext Transfer Protocol (HTTP)*. The computer running the web browser that makes the request is known as the *client*. Think of the client/server relationship as a bit like a customer/shopkeeper relationship. The customer goes into a shop and says, "Give me one of those." The shopkeeper serves the customer by reaching for the item requested and passing it back to the customer. In a web situation, the client machine running the web browser is like the customer, and the web server providing the page requested is like the shopkeeper.

When you type an address into the web browser, how does it know which web server to get the page from? Well, just as shops have addresses, say, 45 Central Avenue, Sometownsville, so do web servers. Web servers don't have street names; instead they have *Internet protocol (IP) addresses*, which uniquely identify them on the Internet. These consist of four sets of numbers, separated by dots; for example, `127.0.0.1`.

If you've ever surfed the net, you're probably wondering what on earth I'm talking about. Surely web servers have nice `www.somewebsite.com` names, not IP addresses? In fact, the `www.somewebsite.com` name is the "friendly" name for the actual IP address; it's a whole lot easier for us humans to remember. On the Internet, the friendly name is converted to the actual IP address by computers called *domain name servers*, which your Internet service provider will have set up for you.

Toward the end of the book, you'll go through the process of setting up your own web server in a step-by-step guide. You'll see that web servers are not just dumb machines that pass pages back to clients, but in fact can do a bit of processing themselves using JavaScript. You'll look at this later in the book as well.

One last thing: Throughout this book we'll be referring to the Internet Explorer browser as IE.

Why Choose JavaScript?

JavaScript is not the only scripting language; there are others such as VBScript and Perl. So why choose JavaScript over the others?

The main reason for choosing JavaScript is its widespread use and availability. Both of the most commonly used browsers, IE and Firefox, support JavaScript, as do almost all of the less commonly used browsers. So you can assume that most people browsing your web site will have a version of JavaScript installed, though it is possible to use a browser's options to disable it.

Of the other scripting languages we mentioned, VBScript, which can be used for the same purposes as JavaScript, is supported only by Internet Explorer running on the Windows operating system, and Perl is not used at all in web browsers.

JavaScript is also very versatile and not just limited to use within a web page. For example, it can be used in Windows to automate computer-administration tasks and inside Adobe Acrobat .pdf files to control the display of the page just as in web pages, although Acrobat uses a more limited version of JavaScript. However, the question of which scripting language is the most powerful and useful has no real answer. Pretty much everything that can be done in JavaScript can be done in VBScript, and vice versa.

What Can JavaScript Do for Me?

The most common uses of JavaScript are interacting with users, getting information from them, and validating their actions. For example, say you want to put a drop-down menu on the page so that users can choose where they want to go to on your web site. The drop-down menu might be plain old HTML, but it needs JavaScript behind it to actually do something with the user's input. Other examples of using JavaScript for interactions are given by forms, which are used for getting information from the user. Again, these may be plain HTML, but you might want to check the validity of the information that the user is entering. For example, if you had a form taking a user's credit card details in preparation for the online purchase of goods, you'd want to make sure he had actually filled in those details before you sent the goods. You might also want to check that the data being entered are of the correct type, such as a number for his age rather than text.

JavaScript can also be used for various tricks. One example is switching an image in a page for a different one when the user rolls her mouse over it, something often seen in web page menus. Also, if you've ever seen scrolling messages in the browser's status bar (usually at the bottom of the browser window) or inside the page itself and wondered how that works, this is another JavaScript trick that you'll learn about later in the book. You'll also see how to create expanding menus that display a list of choices when a user rolls his or her mouse over them, another commonly seen JavaScript-driven trick.

Tricks are okay up to a point, but even more useful are small applications that provide a real service. For example, a mortgage seller's web site with a JavaScript-driven mortgage calculator, or a web site about financial planning that includes a calculator that works out your tax bill for you. With a little inventiveness, you'll be amazed at what can be achieved.

Tools Needed to Create JavaScript Web Applications

All that you need to get started with creating JavaScript code for web applications is a simple text editor, such as Windows Notepad, or one of the many slightly more advanced text editors that provide line numbering, search and replace, and so on. An alternative is a proper HTML editor; you'll need one that enables you to edit the HTML source code, because that's where you need to add your JavaScript. A number of very good tools specifically aimed at developing web-based applications, such as the excellent Dreamweaver 8 from Adobe, are also available. However, this book concentrates on JavaScript, rather than any specific development tool. When it comes to learning the basics, it's often best to write the code by hand rather than relying on a tool to do it for you. This helps you to understand the fundamentals of the language before you attempt the more advanced logic that is beyond a tool's capability. When you have a good understanding of the basics, you can use tools as timesavers so that you can spend more time on the more advanced and more interesting coding.

You'll also need a browser to view your web pages in. It's best to develop your JavaScript code on the sort of browsers you expect visitors to use to access your web site. You'll see later in the chapter that there are different versions of JavaScript, each supported by different versions of the web browsers. Each of these JavaScript versions, while having a common core, also contains various extensions to the language. All the examples that we give in this book have been tested on Firefox version 1.5, and IE versions 6 and 7. Wherever a piece of code does not work on any of these browsers, a note to this effect has been made in the text.

If you're running Windows, you'll almost certainly have IE installed. If not, a trip to www.microsoft .com/windows/ie/default.mspx will get you the latest version.

Firefox can be found at www.mozilla.com/firefox/all.html. When installing Firefox it's worth going for the custom setup. This will give you the option later on of choosing which bits to install. In particular it's worth selecting the Developer Tools component. While not essential, it's an extra that's nice to have.

Even if your browser supports JavaScript, it is possible to disable this functionality in the browser. So before you start on your first JavaScript examples in the next section, you should check to make sure JavaScript is enabled in your browser.

To do this in Firefox, choose Options from the Tools menu on the browser. In the window that appears, click the Content tab. From this tab make sure the Enable JavaScript check box is selected, as shown in Figure 1-1.

Figure 1-1

It is harder to turn off scripting in Internet Explorer. Choose Internet Options from the Tools menu on the browser, click the Security tab, and check whether the Internet or Local intranet options have custom security settings. If either of them does, click the Custom Level button and scroll down to the Scripting section. Check that Active Scripting is set to Enable.

A final point to note is how to open the code examples in your browser. For this book, you simply need to open the file on your hard drive in which an example is stored. You can do this in a number of ways. One way in IE6 is to choose Open from the File menu, and click the Browse button to browse to where you stored the code. Similarly, in Firefox choose Open File from the File menu, browse to the file you want, and click the Choose File button.

IE7, however, has a new menu structure and this doesn't include an Open File option. You can get around this by typing the drive letter of your hard drive followed by a colon in the address bar, for example, C: for your C drive. Alternatively you can switch back to the Classic menu of earlier versions of IE (see Figure 1-2). To do this you need to go to the Tools menu, select the Toolbars menu option, then ensure the Classic Menu option is selected.

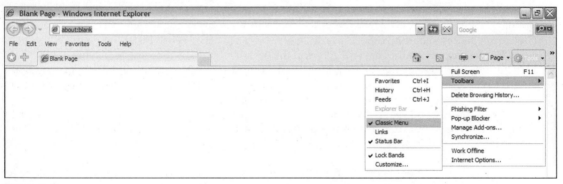

Figure 1-2

The <script> Tag and Your First Simple JavaScript Program

Enough talk about the subject of JavaScript; it's time to look at how to put it into your web page. In this section, you write your first piece of JavaScript code.

Inserting JavaScript into a web page is much like inserting any other HTML content; you use tags to mark the start and end of your script code. The tag used to do this is the <script> tag. This tells the browser that the following chunk of text, bounded by the closing </script> tag, is not HTML to be displayed, but rather script code to be processed. The chunk of code surrounded by the <script> and </script> tags is called a *script block*.

Basically, when the browser spots <script> tags, instead of trying to display the contained text to the user, it uses the browser's built-in JavaScript interpreter to run the code's instructions. Of course, the code might give instructions about changes to the way the page is displayed or what is shown in the page, but the text of the code itself is never shown to the user.

You can put the <script> tags inside the header (between the <head> and </head> tags), or inside the body (between the <body> and </body> tags) of the HTML page. However, although you can put them outside these areas — for example, before the <html> tag or after the </html> tag — this is not permitted in the web standards and so is considered bad practice.

The <script> tag has a number of attributes, but the most important one is the type attribute. As you saw earlier, JavaScript is not the only scripting language available, and different scripting languages need to be processed in different ways. You need to tell the browser which scripting language to expect so that it knows how to process that language. Your opening script tag will look like this:

```
<script type="text/javascript">
```

Including the type attribute is good practice, but within a web page it can be left off. Browsers such as IE and Firefox use JavaScript as their default script language. This means that if the browser encounters a <script> tag with no type attribute set, it assumes that the script block is written in JavaScript. However, use of the type attribute is specified as mandatory by W3C (the World Wide Web Consortium), which sets the standards for HTML.

Okay, let's take a look at the first page containing JavaScript code.

Try It Out   Painting the Document Red

This is a simple example of using JavaScript to change the background color of the browser. In your text editor (I'm using Windows Notepad), type the following:

```
<html>
<body BGCOLOR="WHITE">
<p>Paragraph 1</p>
<script type="text/javascript">
    document.bgColor = "RED";
</script>
</body>
</html>
```

Save the page as ch1_examp1.htm to a convenient place on your hard drive. Now load it into your web browser. You should see a red web page with the text Paragraph 1 in the top-left corner. But wait — didn't you set the <body> tag's BGCOLOR attribute to white? Okay, let's look at what's going on here.

How It Works

The page is contained within <html> and </html> tags. This block contains a <body> element. When you define the opening <body> tag, you use HTML to set the page's background color to white.

```
<BODY BGCOLOR="WHITE">
```

Then you let the browser know that your next lines of code are JavaScript code by using the <script> start tag.

```
<script type="text/javascript">
```

Everything from here until the close tag, `</script>`, is JavaScript and is treated as such by the browser. Within this script block, you use JavaScript to set the document's background color to red.

```
document.bgColor = "RED";
```

What you might call the *page* is known as the *document* for the purpose of scripting in a web page. The document has lots of properties, including its background color, `bgColor`. You can reference properties of the `document` by writing `document`, followed by a dot, followed by the property name. Don't worry about the use of `document` at the moment; you look at it in depth later in the book.

Note that the preceding line of code is an example of a JavaScript *statement*. Every line of code between the `<script>` and `</script>` tags is called a statement, although some statements may run on to more than one line.

You'll also see that there's a semicolon (;) at the end of the line. You use a semicolon in JavaScript to indicate the end of a statement. In practice, JavaScript is very relaxed about the need for semicolons, and when you start a new line, JavaScript will usually be able to work out whether you mean to start a new line of code. However, for good coding practice, you should use a semicolon at the end of statements of code, and a single JavaScript statement should fit onto one line rather than continue on to two or more lines. Moreover, you'll find there are times when you must include a semicolon, which you'll come to later in the book.

Finally, to tell the browser to stop interpreting your text as JavaScript and start interpreting it as HTML, you use the script close tag:

```
</script>
```

You've now looked at how the code works, but you haven't looked at the order in which it works. When the browser loads in the web page, the browser goes through it, rendering it tag by tag from top to bottom of the page. This process is called *parsing*. The web browser starts at the top of the page and works its way down to the bottom of the page. The browser comes to the `<body>` tag first and sets the document's background to white. Then it continues parsing the page. When it comes to the JavaScript code, it is instructed to change the document's background to red.

Try It Out   The Way Things Flow

Let's extend the previous example to demonstrate the parsing of a web page in action. Type the following into your text editor:

```
<html>
<body bgcolor="WHITE">
<p>Paragraph 1</p>
<script type="text/javascript">
   // Script block 1
   alert("First Script Block");
</script>
<p>Paragraph 2</p>
<script type="text/javascript">
   // Script block 2
```

```
        document.bgColor = "RED";
        alert("Second Script Block");
    </script>
    <p>Paragraph 3</p>
    </body>
    </html>
```

Save the file to your hard drive as ch1_examp2.htm and then load it into your browser. When you load the page you should see the first paragraph, Paragraph 1, followed by a message box displayed by the first script block. The browser halts its parsing until you click the OK button. As you can see in Figure 1-3, the page background is white, as set in the <body> tag, and only the first paragraph is currently displayed.

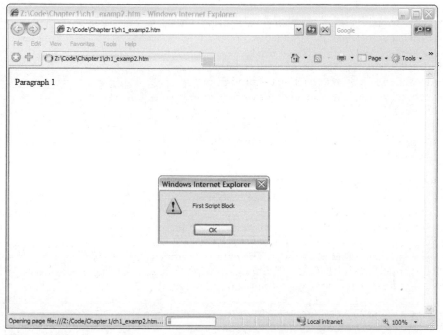

Figure 1-3

Click the OK button, and the parsing continues. The browser displays the second paragraph, and the second script block is reached, which changes the background color to red. Another message box is displayed by the second script block, as shown in Figure 1-4.

Click OK, and again the parsing continues, with the third paragraph, Paragraph 3, being displayed. The web page is complete, as shown in Figure 1-5.

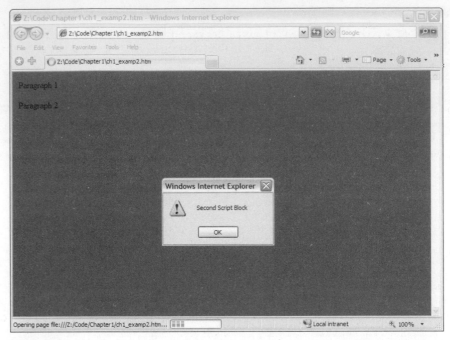

Figure 1-4

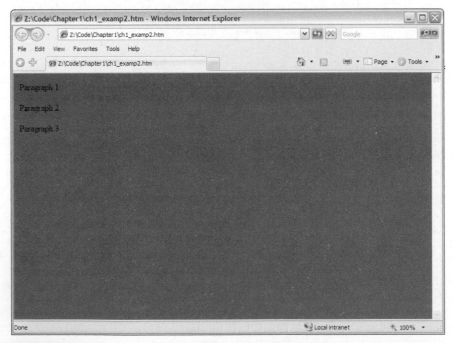

Figure 1-5

How It Works

The first part of the page is the same as in our earlier example. The background color for the page is set to white in the definition of the <body> tag, and then a paragraph is written to the page.

```
<html>
<body BGCOLOR="WHITE">
<p>Paragraph 1</p>
```

The first new section is contained in the first script block.

```
<script type="text/javascript">
    // Script block 1
    alert("First Script Block");
</script>
```

This script block contains two lines, both of which are new to you. The first line —

```
    // Script block 1
```

is just a *comment*, solely for your benefit. The browser recognizes anything on a line after a double forward slash (//) to be a comment and does not do anything with it. It is useful for you as a programmer because you can add explanations to your code that make it easier to remember what you were doing when you come back to your code later.

The alert() function in the second line of code is also new to you. Before learning what it does, you need to know what a *function* is.

Functions are defined more fully in Chapter 3, but for now you need only to think of them as pieces of JavaScript code that you can use to do certain tasks. If you have a background in math, you may already have some idea of what a function is: A function takes some information, processes it, and gives you a result. A function makes life easier for you as a programmer because you don't have to think about how the function does the task — you can just concentrate on when you want the task done.

In particular, the alert() function enables you to alert or inform the user about something by displaying a message box. The message to be given in the message box is specified inside the parentheses of the alert() function and is known as the function's *parameter*.

The message box displayed by the alert() function is *modal*. This is an important concept, which you'll come across again. It simply means that the message box won't go away until the user closes it by clicking the OK button. In fact, parsing of the page stops at the line where the alert() function is used and doesn't restart until the user closes the message box. This is quite useful for this example, because it enables you to demonstrate the results of what has been parsed so far: The page color has been set to white, and the first paragraph has been displayed.

When you click OK, the browser carries on parsing down the page through the following lines:

```
<p>Paragraph 2</p>
<script type="text/javascript">
    // Script block 2
    document.bgColor = "RED";
    alert("Second Script Block");
</script>
```

The second paragraph is displayed, and the second block of JavaScript is run. The first line of the script block code is another comment, so the browser ignores this. You saw the second line of the script code in the previous example—it changes the background color of the page to red. The third line of code is the `alert()` function, which displays the second message box. Parsing is brought to a halt until you close the message box by clicking OK.

When you close the message box, the browser moves on to the next lines of code in the page, displaying the third paragraph and finally ending the web page.

```
<p>Paragraph 3</p>
</body>
</html>
```

Another important point raised by this example is the difference between setting properties of the page, such as background color, via HTML and doing the same thing using JavaScript. The method of setting properties using HTML is *static*: A value can be set only once and never changed again by means of HTML. Setting properties using JavaScript enables you to dynamically change their values. By the term *dynamic*, we are referring to something that can be changed and whose value or appearance is not set in stone.

This example is just that, an example. In practice if you wanted the page's background to be red, you would set the `<body>` tag's BGCOLOR attribute to `"RED"`, and not use JavaScript at all. Where you would want to use JavaScript is where you want to add some sort of intelligence or logic to the page. For example, if the user's screen resolution is particularly low, you might want to change what's displayed on the page; with JavaScript, you can do this. Another reason for using JavaScript to change properties might be for special effects—for example, making a page fade in from white to its final color.

A Brief Look at Browsers and Compatibility Problems

You've seen in the preceding example that by using JavaScript you can change a web page's `document` background color using the `bgColor` property of the `document`. The example worked whether you used a Netscape or Microsoft browser, because both types of browsers support a `document` with a `bgColor` property. You can say that the example is *cross-browser compatible*. However, it's not always the case that the property or language feature available in one browser will be available in another browser. This is even sometimes the case between versions of the same browser.

> *The version numbers for Internet Explorer and Firefox browsers are usually written as a decimal number; for example, Firefox has a version 1.5. In this book we use the following terminology to refer to these versions. By version 1.x we mean all versions starting with the number 1. By version 1.0+ we mean all versions with a number greater than or equal to 1.*

One of the main headaches involved in creating web-based JavaScript is the differences between different web browsers, the level of HTML they support, and the functionality their JavaScript interpreters can handle. You'll find that in one browser you can move an image using just a couple of lines of code, but that in another it'll take a whole page of code, or even prove impossible. One version of JavaScript will contain a method to change text to uppercase, and another won't. Each new release of IE or Firefox browsers sees new and exciting features added to their HTML and JavaScript support. The good news is that to a much greater extent than ever before, browser creators are complying with standards set by organizations such as the W3C. Also, with a little ingenuity, you can write JavaScript that will work with both IE and Firefox browsers.

Which browsers you want to support really comes down to the browsers you think the majority of your web site's visitors, that is, your *user base*, will be using. This book is aimed at both IE6 and later and Firefox 1.5 and later.

If you want your web site to be professional, you need to somehow deal with older browsers. You could make sure your code is backward compatible — that is, it only uses features available in older browsers. However, you may decide that it's simply not worth limiting yourself to the features of older browsers. In this case you need to make sure your pages degrade gracefully. In other words, make sure that although your pages won't work in older browsers, they will fail in a way that means the user is either never aware of the failure or is alerted to the fact that certain features on the web site are not compatible with his or her browser. The alternative to degrading gracefully is for your code to raise lots of error messages, cause strange results to be displayed on the page, and generally make you look like an idiot who doesn't know what you're doing!

So how do you make your web pages degrade gracefully? You can do this by using JavaScript to determine which browser the web page is running in after it has been partially or completely loaded. You can use this information to determine what scripts to run or even to redirect the user to another page written to make best use of her particular browser. In later chapters, you see how to find out what features the browser supports and take appropriate action so that your pages work acceptably on as many browsers as possible.

Introducing the "Who Wants To Be A Billionaire" Trivia Quiz

Over the course of the first nine chapters of this book, you'll be developing a full web-based application, namely a trivia quiz. The trivia quiz works with both Firefox and IE6+ web browsers, making full use of their JavaScript capabilities.

Let's take a look at what the quiz will finally look like. The main starting screen is shown in Figure 1-6. Here the user can choose a time limit. Using a JavaScript-based timer, you keep track of how much time has elapsed.

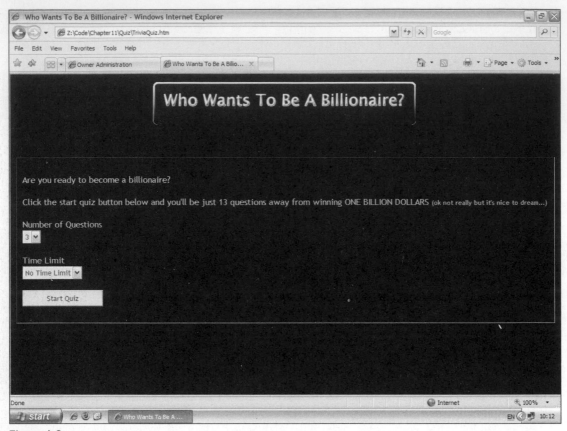

Figure 1-6

After clicking the Start Quiz button, the user is faced with a random choice of questions pulled from a database that you'll create to hold the trivia questions. There are two types of questions. The first, as shown in Figure 1-7, is the multiple-choice question. There is no limit to the number of answer options that you can specify for these types of questions: JavaScript handles them without the need for each question to be programmed differently.

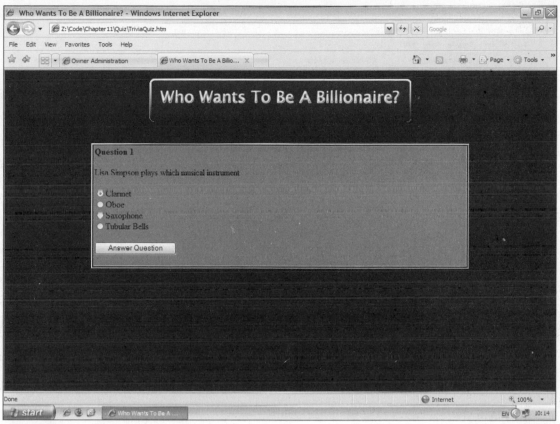

Figure 1-7

The second question style is a text-based one. The user types the answer into the text box provided, and then JavaScript does its best to intelligently interpret what the user has written. For example, for the question shown in Figure 1-8, Saxaphone is the correct answer. However, the JavaScript has been programmed to also accept the abbreviated form sax as a correct answer. You find out how to do this in Chapter 8.

15

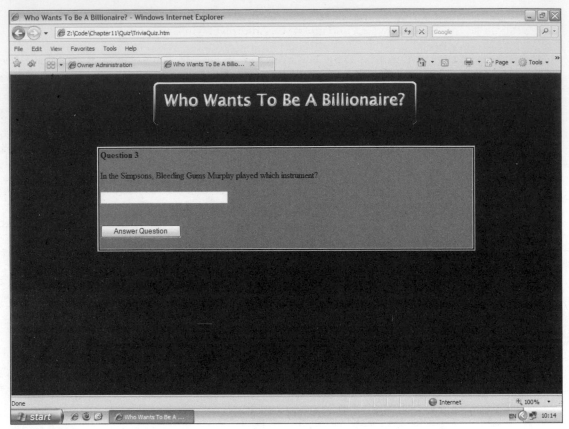

Figure 1-8

Finally, after the questions have all been answered, the final page of the quiz displays how much the user has won.

Ideas Behind the Coding of the Trivia Quiz

You've taken a brief look at the final version of the trivia quiz in action and will be looking at the actual code in later chapters, but it's worthwhile to consider the guiding principles behind its design and programming.

One of the most important ideas is code reuse. You save time and effort by making use of the same code again and again. Quite often in a web application you'll find that you need to do the same thing over and over again. For example, you'll need to make repeated use of the code that checks whether a question has been answered correctly. You could make as many copies of the code as you need, and add this code to your page wherever you need it. However, this makes maintaining the code difficult, because if you need to correct an error or add a new feature, you will need to make the change to the code in lots of different places. Once the code for a web application grows from a few lines in one page to many lines over a number of pages, it's quite difficult to actually keep track of the places where you have copied the code. So, with reuse in mind, the trivia quiz keeps in one place all the important code that will need to be used a number of times.

The same goes for any data you use. For example, in the trivia quiz you keep track of the number of questions that have been answered, and update this information in as few places as possible.

Sometimes you have no choice but to put important code in more than one place — for example, when you need information that can only be obtained in a particular circumstance. However, if you can keep it in one place, you'll find doing so makes coding more efficient.

In the trivia quiz, I've also tried to split the code into specific *functions*. You will be looking at JavaScript functions in detail in Chapter 3. In the trivia quiz, the function that provides a randomly selected question for your web page to display is in one place, regardless of whether this is a multiple-choice question or a purely text-based question. By doing this, you're not only writing code just once, you're also making life easier for yourself by keeping code that provides the same service or function in one place. As you'll see later in the book, the code for creating these different question types is very different, but at least putting it in the same logical place makes it easy to find.

When creating your own web-based applications, you might find it useful to break the larger concept, here a trivia quiz, into smaller ideas. Breaking it down makes writing the code a lot easier. Rather than sitting down with a blank screen and thinking, "Right, now I must write a trivia quiz," you can think, "Right, now I must write some code to create a question." We find this technique makes coding a lot less scary and easier to get started on. This method of splitting the requirements of a piece of code into smaller and more manageable parts is often referred to as "divide and conquer."

Let's use the trivia quiz as an example. The trivia quiz application needs to do the following things:

- Ask a question
- Retrieve and check the answer provided by the user to see if it's correct.
- Keep track of how many questions have been asked.
- Keep track of how many questions the user has answered correctly.
- If it's a timed quiz, keep track of the time remaining, and stop the quiz when the time is up.
- Show a final summary of the number of correct answers given out of the number answered.

These are the core ingredients for the trivia quiz. You may want to do other things, such as keep track of the number of user visits, but these are really external to the functionality of the trivia quiz.

After you've broken the whole concept into various logical areas, it's sometimes worth using the divide-and-conquer technique again to break the areas down into even smaller chunks, particularly if an area is quite complex or involved. As an example, let's take the first item from the preceding list.

Asking a question will involve the following:

- Retrieving the question data from where they're stored, for example from a database.
- Processing the data and converting them into a form that can be presented to the user. Here you need to create HTML to be displayed in a web page. How the data are processed depends on the question style: multiple choice or text based.
- Displaying the question for the user to answer.

As you build up the trivia quiz over the course of the book, you'll look at its design and some of the tricks and tactics that go into that design in more depth. You'll also break down each function as you come to it, to make it clear what needs to be done.

What Functionality to Add and Where?

How do you build up the functionality needed in the trivia quiz? The following list should give you an idea of what you add and in which chapter.

In Chapter 2, you start the quiz off by defining the multiple-choice questions that will be asked. You do this using something called an *array*, which is also introduced in that chapter.

In Chapter 3, where you learn about functions in more detail, you add a function to the code that will check to see whether the user has entered the correct answer.

After a couple of chapters of theory, in Chapter 6 you get the quiz into its first "usable" state. You display the questions to the user, and allow the user to answer those questions.

In Chapter 7, you enhance the quiz by turning it into what is called a *multi-frame application*. You add a button that the user can click to start the quiz, and specify that the quiz must finish after all the questions have been asked, repeating them indefinitely.

In Chapter 8, you add the text-based questions to the quiz. These must be treated slightly differently from multiple-choice questions, both in how they are displayed to the user and in how the user's answers are checked. As you saw earlier, the quiz will accept a number of different correct answers for these questions.

In Chapter 9, you allow the user to choose whether he or she wants to have a time limit for the quiz. If users choose to impose a time limit upon themselves, you count down the time in the status bar of the window and inform them when their time is up.

In Chapter 11, you complete the quiz by storing information about the user's previous results, using *cookies*, which are introduced in that chapter. This enables us to give the user a running average score at the end of the quiz.

Summary

At this point you should have a feel for what JavaScript is and what it can do. In particular, this brief introduction covered the following:

❑   You looked into the process the browser follows when interpreting your web page. It goes through the page element by element (parsing), and acts upon your HTML tags and JavaScript code as it comes to them.

❑   When you are developing for the web using JavaScript, you can choose to have your code executed in one of two places: server-side or client-side. Client-side is essentially the side on which the browser is running — the user's machine. Server-side refers to any processing or storage done on the web server itself.

❑ Unlike many programming languages, JavaScript requires just a text editor to start creating code. Something like Windows Notepad is fine for getting started, though more extensive tools will prove valuable once you get more experience.

❑ JavaScript code is embedded into the web page itself along with the HTML. Its existence is marked out by the use of `<script>` tags. As with HTML, script executes from the top of the page and works down to the bottom, interpreting and executing the code statement by statement.

❑ You were introduced to the online trivia quiz, which is the case study that you'll be building over the course of the book. You took a look at some of the design ideas behind the trivia quiz's coding, and learned how the functionality of the quiz will be built up over the course of the book.

Data Types and Variables

One of the main uses of computers is to process and display information. By processing, we mean that the information is modified, interpreted, or filtered in some way by the computer. For example, on an online banking web site, a customer may request details of all moneys paid out from his account in the last month. Here the computer would retrieve the information, filter out any information not related to payments made in the last month, and then display what's left in a web page. In some situations, information is processed without being displayed, and at other times, information is obtained directly without being processed. For example, in a banking environment, regular payments may be processed and transferred electronically without any human interaction or display.

In computing we refer to information as *data*. Data come in all sorts of forms, such as numbers, text, dates, and times, to mention just a few. In this chapter, you look specifically at how JavaScript handles data such as numbers and text. An understanding of how data are handled is fundamental to any programming language.

The chapter starts by looking at the various types of data JavaScript can process. Then you look at how you can store these data in the computer's memory so you can use them again and again in the code. Finally, you see how to use JavaScript to manipulate and process the data.

Types of Data in JavaScript

Data can come in many different forms, or *types*. You'll recognize some of the data types that JavaScript handles from the world outside programming — for example, numbers and text. Other data types are a little more abstract and are used to make programming easier; one example is the object data type, which you won't see in detail until Chapter 4.

Some programming languages are strongly typed languages. In these languages, whenever you use a piece of data, you need to explicitly state what sort of data you are dealing with, and use of those data must follow strict rules applicable to its type. For example, you can't add a number and a word together.

JavaScript, on the other hand, is a weakly typed language and a lot more forgiving about how you use different types of data. When you deal with data, you often don't need to specify type; JavaScript will work that out for itself. Furthermore, when you are using different types of data at the same time, JavaScript will work out behind the scenes what it is you're trying to do.

Given how easygoing JavaScript is about data, why talk about data types at all? Why not just cut to the chase and start using data without worrying about their type?

First of all, while JavaScript is very good at working out what data it's dealing with, there are occasions when it'll get things wrong, or at least not do what you want it to do. In these situations, you need to make it explicit to JavaScript what sort of data type you intended and how it should be used. To do that, you first need to know a little bit about data types.

A second reason is that data types enable you to use data effectively in your code. The things that can be done with data and the results you'll get depend on the type of data being used, even if you don't specify explicitly what type it is. For example, although trying to multiply two numbers together makes sense, doing the same thing with text doesn't. Also, the result of adding numbers is very different from the result of adding text. With numbers you get the sum, but with text you get one big piece of text consisting of the other pieces joined together.

Let's take a brief look at some of the more commonly used data types: numerical, text, and Boolean. You will see how to use them later in the chapter.

Numerical Data

Numerical data come in two forms:

❑ Whole numbers, such as 145, which are also known as *integers*. These numbers can be positive or negative and can span a very wide range in JavaScript: -2^{53} to 2^{53}.

❑ Fractional numbers, such as 1.234, which are also known as *floating-point* numbers. Like integers, they can be positive or negative, and they also have a massive range.

In simple terms, unless you're writing specialized scientific applications, you're not going to face problems with the size of numbers available in JavaScript. Also, although you can treat integers and floating-point numbers differently when it comes to storing them, JavaScript actually treats them both as floating-point numbers. It kindly hides the detail from you so you generally don't need to worry about it. One exception is when you want an integer but you have a floating-point number, in which case you'll round the number to make it an integer. You'll take a look at rounding numbers later in this chapter.

Text Data

Another term for one or more characters of text is a *string*. You tell JavaScript that text is to be treated as text and not as code simply by enclosing it inside quote marks ("). For example, "Hello World" and "A" are examples of strings that JavaScript will recognize. You can also use the single quote marks ('), so 'Hello World' and 'A' are also examples of strings that JavaScript will recognize. However, you must end the string with the same quote mark that you started it with. Therefore, "A' is not a valid JavaScript string, and neither is 'Hello World".

What if you want a string with a single quote mark in the middle, say a string like Peter O'Toole? If you enclose it in double quotes, you'll be fine, so "Peter O'Toole" is recognized by JavaScript. However, 'Peter O'Toole' will produce an error. This is because JavaScript thinks that your text string is Peter O (that is, it treats the middle single quote as marking the end of the string) and falls over wondering what the Toole' is.

Another way around this is to tell JavaScript that the middle ' is part of the text and is not indicating the end of the string. You do this by using the backslash character (\), which has special meaning in JavaScript and is referred to as an *escape character*. The backslash tells the browser that the next character is not the end of the string, but part of the text. So 'Peter O\'Toole' will work as planned.

What if you want to use a double quote inside a string enclosed in double quotes? Well, everything just said about the single quote still applies. So 'Hello "Paul"' works, but "Hello "Paul"" won't. However, "Hello \"Paul\"" will also work.

JavaScript has a lot of other special characters, which can't be typed in but can be represented using the escape character in conjunction with other characters to create *escape sequences*. These work much the same as in HTML. For example, more than one space in a row is ignored in HTML, so a space is represented by the term . Similarly, in JavaScript there are instances where you can't use a character directly but must use an escape sequence. The following table details some of the more useful escape sequences.

Escape Sequences	Character Represented
\b	Backspace
\f	Form feed
\n	New line
\r	Carriage return
\t	Tab
\'	Single quote
\"	Double quote
\\	Backslash
\xNN	NN is a hexadecimal number that identifies a character in the Latin-1 character set.

The least obvious of these is the last, which represents individual characters by their character number in the Latin-1 character set rather than by their normal appearance. Let's pick an example: Say you wanted to include the copyright symbol (©) in our string. What would your string need to look like? The answer is "\xA9 Paul Wilton".

Similarly, you can refer to characters using their Unicode escape sequence. These are written \uNNNN, where NNNN refers to the Unicode number for that particular character. For example, to refer to the copyright symbol using this method, you would use the string \u00A9.

Boolean Data

The use of yes or no, positive or negative, and true or false is commonplace in the physical world. The idea of true and false is also fundamental to digital computers; they don't understand maybes, only true and false. In fact, the concept of "yes or no" is so useful it has its own data type in JavaScript: the *Boolean* data type. The Boolean type has two possible values: `true` for yes and `false` for no.

The purpose of Boolean data in JavaScript is just the same as in the world outside programming: They enable us to answer questions and make decisions based on the answer. For example, if you are asked, "Is this book about JavaScript?" you would hopefully answer, "Yes it is," or you might also say, "That's true." Similarly you might say, "If it's false that the subject of the book is JavaScript, then put it down." Here you have a Boolean logic statement (named after its inventor George Boole), which asks a question and then does something based on whether the answer is true or false. In JavaScript, you can use the same sort of Boolean logic to give our programs decision-making abilities. You'll be taking a more detailed look at Boolean logic in the next chapter.

Variables — Storing Data in Memory

Data can be stored either permanently or temporarily.

You will want to keep important data, such as the details of a person's bank account, in a permanent store. For example, when Ms. Bloggs takes 10 dollars or pounds or euros out of her account, you want to deduct the money from her account and keep a permanent record of the new balance. Information like this might be stored in something called a *database*.

However, there are other cases where you don't want to permanently store data, but simply want to keep a temporary note of it. Let's look at an example. Say Ms. Bloggs has a loan from BigBadBank Inc., and she wants to find out how much is still outstanding on this loan. She goes to the online banking page for loans and clicks a link to find out how much she owes. This is data that will be stored permanently somewhere. However, suppose you also provide a facility for increasing loan repayments to pay off the loan early. If Ms. Bloggs enters an increased repayment amount into the text box on the web page, you might want to show how much sooner the loan will be paid. This will involve a few possibly complex calculations, so to make it easier, you want to write code that calculates the result in several stages, storing the result at each stage as you go along, before providing a final result. After you've done the calculation and displayed the results, there's no need to permanently store the results for each stage, so rather than use a database, you need to use something called a *variable*. Why is it called a variable? Well, perhaps because a variable can be used to store temporary data that can be altered, or varied.

Another bonus of variables is that unlike permanent storage, which might be saved to disk or magnetic tape, variables are held in the computer's memory. This means that it is much, much faster to store and retrieve the data.

So what makes variables good places for temporarily storing your data? Well, variables have a limited lifetime. When your visitors close the page or move to a new one, your variables are lost, unless you take some steps to save them somewhere.

Each variable is given a name so that you can refer to it elsewhere in your code. These names must follow certain rules.

As with much of JavaScript code, you'll find that variable names are case sensitive. For example, `myVariable` is not the same as `myvariable`. You'll find that this is a very easy way for errors to slip into your code, even when you become an expert at JavaScript.

Also, you can't use certain names and characters for your variable names. Names you can't use are called *reserved* words. Reserved words are words that JavaScript keeps for its own use, for example the word `var` or the word `with`. Certain characters are also forbidden in variable names; for example, the ampersand (`&`) and the percent sign (`%`). You are allowed to use numbers in your variable names, but the names must not begin with numbers. So `101myVariable` is not okay, but `myVariable101` is. Let's look at some more examples.

Invalid names include

- ❑   `with`
- ❑   `99variables`
- ❑   `my%Variable`
- ❑   `theGood&theBad`

Valid names include

- ❑   `myVariable99`
- ❑   `myPercent_Variable`
- ❑   `the_Good_and_the_Bad`

You may wish to use a naming convention for your variables; for example ,one that describes what sort of data you plan to hold in the variable. You can notate your variables in lots of different ways—none are right or wrong, but it's best to stick with one of them. One common method is *Hungarian notation*, where the beginning of each variable name is a three-letter identifier indicating the data type. For example, you may start integer variable names with `int`, floating-point variable names with `flt`, string variable names with `str`, and so on. However, as long as the names you use make sense and are used consistently, it really doesn't matter what convention you choose.

Declaring Variables and Giving Them Values

Before you can use a variable, you should declare its existence to the computer using the `var` keyword. This warns the computer that it needs to reserve some memory for your data to be stored in later. To declare a new variable called `myFirstVariable`, you would write the following:

```
var myFirstVariable;
```

Note that the semicolon at the end of the line is not part of the variable name, but instead is used to indicate to JavaScript the end of a statement. This line is an example of a JavaScript statement.

Once declared, a variable can be used to store any type of data. As we mentioned earlier, many other programming languages, called strongly typed languages, require you to declare not only the variable but also the type of data, such as numbers or text, that will be stored. However, JavaScript is a weakly typed language; you don't need to limit yourself to what type of data a variable can hold.

You put data into your variables, a process called *assigning values* to your variables, by using the equals sign (=). For example, if you want your variable named myFirstVariable to hold the number 101, you would write this:

```
myFirstVariable = 101;
```

The equals sign has a special name when used to assign values to a variable; it's called the *assignment operator*.

Try It Out   Declaring Variables

Let's look at an example in which a variable is declared, store some data in it, and finally access its contents. You'll also see that variables can hold any type of data, and that the type of data being held can be changed. For example, you can start by storing text and then change to storing numbers without JavaScript having any problems. Type the following code into your text editor and save it as ch2_examp1.htm:

```
<html>
<head>
</head>
<body>

<script language="JavaScript" type="text/javascript">

var myFirstVariable;

myFirstVariable = "Hello";
alert(myFirstVariable);

myFirstVariable = 54321;
alert(myFirstVariable);

</script>

</body>
</html>
```

As soon as you load this into your web browser, it should show an alert box with "Hello" in it, as shown in Figure 2-1. This is the content of the variable myFirstVariable at that point in the code.

Figure 2-1

Click OK and another alert box appears with 54321 in it, as shown in Figure 2-2. This is the new value you assigned to the variable myFirstVariable.

Figure 2-2

How It Works

Within the script block, you first declare your variable.

```
var myFirstVariable;
```

Currently, its value is the undefined value because you've declared only its existence to the computer, not any actual data. It may sound odd, but undefined is an actual primitive value in JavaScript, and it enables you to do comparisons. (For example, you can check to see if a variable contains an actual value or if it has not yet been given a value, that is, if it is undefined.) However, in the next line you assign myFirstVariable a string value, namely the value Hello.

```
myFirstVariable = "Hello";
```

Here you have assigned the variable a *literal* value, that is, a piece of actual data rather than data obtained by a calculation or from another variable. Almost anywhere that you can use a literal string or number, you can replace it with a variable containing number or string data. You see an example of this in the next line of code, where you use your variable myFirstVariable in the alert() function that you saw in the last chapter.

```
alert(myFirstVariable);
```

This causes the first alert box to appear. Next you store a new value in your variable, this time a number.

```
myFirstVariable = 54321;
```

The previous value of myFirstVariable is lost forever. The memory space used to store the value is freed up automatically by JavaScript in a process called *garbage collection*. Whenever JavaScript detects that the contents of a variable are no longer usable, such as when you allocate a new value, it performs the garbage collection process and makes the memory available. Without this automatic garbage collection process, more and more of the computer's memory would be consumed, until eventually the computer would run out and the system would grind to a halt. However, garbage collection is not always as efficient as it should be and may not occur until another page is loaded.

Just to prove that the new value has been stored, use the alert() function again to display the variable's new contents.

```
alert(myFirstVariable);
```

Assigning Variables with the Value of Other Variables

You've seen that you can assign a variable with a number or string, but can you assign a variable with the data stored inside another variable? The answer is yes, very easily, and in exactly the same way as giving a variable a literal value. For example, if you have declared the two variables myVariable and myOtherVariable, and have given the variable myOtherVariable the value 22, like this:

```
var myVariable;
var myOtherVariable;
myOtherVariable = 22;
```

then you can use the following line to assign myVariable the same value as myOtherVariable (that is, 22).

```
myVariable = myOtherVariable;
```

Try It Out   Assigning Variables the Values of Other Variables

Let's look at another example, this time assigning variables the values of other variables. Type the following code into your text editor and save it as ch2_examp2.htm:

```
<html>
<body>

<script language="JavaScript" type="text/javascript">

var string1 = "Hello";
var string2 = "Goodbye";

alert(string1);
alert(string2);

string2 = string1;

alert(string1);
alert(string2);

string1 = "Now for something different";

alert(string1);
alert(string2);

</script>

</body>
</html>
```

Load the page into your browser, and you'll see a series of six alert boxes appear. Click OK for each one to see the next. The first two show the values of string1 and string2 — Hello and Goodbye, respectively.

Then you assign `string2` the value that's in `string1`. The next two `alert` boxes show the contents of `string1` and `string2`; this time both are `Hello`.

Finally, you change the value of `string1`. Note that the value of `string2` remains unaffected. The final two `alert` boxes show the new value of `string1` (`Now for something different`) and the unchanged value of `string2` (`Hello`).

How It Works

The first thing you do in the script block is declare your two variables, `string1` and `string2`. However, notice that you have assigned them values at the same time that you have declared them. This is a shortcut, called *initializing*, that saves you typing too much code.

```
var string1 ="Hello";
var string2 = "Goodbye";
```

Note that you can use this shortcut with all data types, not just strings. The next two lines show the current value of each variable to the user using the `alert()` function.

```
alert(string1);
alert(string2);
```

Then you assign `string2` the value that's contained in `string1`. To prove that the assignment has really worked, you again show the user the contents of each variable using the `alert()` function.

```
string2 = string1;

alert(string1);
alert(string2);
```

Next, you set `string1` to a new value.

```
string1 = "Now for something different";
```

This leaves `string2` with its current value, demonstrating that `string2` has its own copy of the data assigned to it from `string1` in the previous step. You'll see in later chapters that this is not always the case. However, as a general rule, basic data types, such as text and numbers, are always copied when assigned, whereas more complex data types, like the objects you come across in Chapter 4, are actually shared and not copied. For example, if you have a variable with the string `Hello` and assign five other variables the value of this variable, you now have the original data and five independent copies of the data. However, if it was an object rather than a string and you did the same thing, you'd find you still have only one copy of the data, but that six variables share it. Changing the data using any of the six variable names would change them for all the variables.

Finally, the `alert()` function is used to show the current values of each variable.

```
alert(string1);
alert(string2);
```

Setting Up Your Browser for Errors

Although your code has been fairly simple so far, it is still possible to make errors when typing it in. As you start to look at more complex and detailed code, this will become more and more of a problem. So, before discuss how you can use the data stored in variables, this seems like a good point to discuss how to ensure that any errors that arise in your code are shown to you by the browser, so that you can go and correct them.

When you are surfing other people's web sites, you probably won't be interested in seeing when there are errors in their code. In this situation, it's tempting to find a way of switching off the display of error dialog boxes in the browser. However, as JavaScript programmers, we want to know all the gory details about errors in our own web pages; that way we can fix them before someone else spots them. It's important, therefore, to make sure the browsers we use to test our web sites are configured correctly to show errors and their details. In this section, this is exactly what we're going to do.

Displaying Errors in Firefox

Firefox keeps quiet about your errors, so if things go wrong you won't see any pop-up boxes warning you or alarm bells going off. However, one of its developer tools is the JavaScript Console, which contains details of any JavaScript problems on your page. It also reports other problems, such as invalid CSS.

To view this console from Firefox, go to the Tools menu and select JavaScript Console, as shown in Figure 2-3.

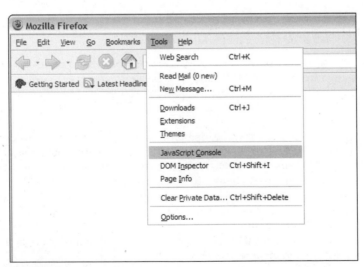

Figure 2-3

The JavaScript Console then pops open in its own separate window, as shown in Figure 2-4.

While you're developing your JavaScript code, it's as well to leave the JavaScript Console open. At the moment it is probably blank. Shortly you'll create a deliberate error and see what happens in the JavaScript Console.

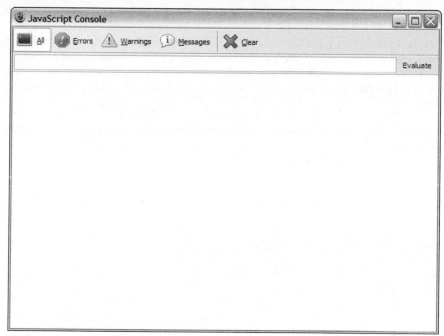

Figure 2-4

Displaying Errors in Internet Explorer

Normally, IE will by default display JavaScript errors using dialog boxes. However, it is possible to turn off the displaying of such errors, in which case you need to follow a few simple steps to re-enable error displaying. First open up Internet Explorer and select the Internet Options menu from the Tools menu, as shown in Figure 2-5.

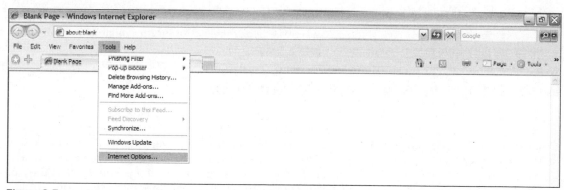

Figure 2-5

In the dialog box that appears, select the Advanced tab. Under Browsing, make sure the Disable script debugging (Other) check box is cleared and that the Display a notification about every script error check box is selected, as shown in Figure 2-6. Note that IE 4 doesn't have a Display notification about every script error check box, so you just need to clear the Disable script debugging check box. After you've done this, you can click OK to close the dialog box.

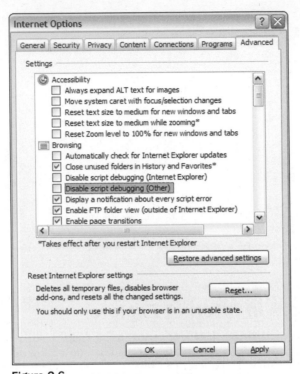

Figure 2-6

Okay, now that you have the display of error messages sorted out, you'll look at what happens when you have an error in your code. Note that as with Firefox there is a program available from Microsoft to help root out errors in your code; you'll see how to use it in Chapter 10.

What Happens When You Get an Error

As mentioned in the previous section, the use of a reserved word in a variable name will result in a JavaScript error in the browser. However, the error message displayed may not be instantly helpful since it may not indicate that you've used a reserved word in declaring your variables. Let's look at the sort of error messages you might see in this situation. Note that these error messages can also be produced by other mistakes not related to variable naming, which can get confusing at times. You'll look at these other mistakes later in the book—indeed, the whole of Chapter 10 is devoted to spotting and fixing errors.

Let's assume that you try to define a variable called with like this:

```
var with;
```

The word with is reserved in JavaScript. What errors will you see?

In Firefox you see nothing unless you open the JavaScript console, in which case you see something like what is shown in Figure 2-7.

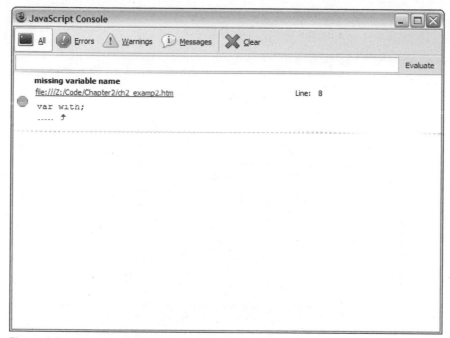

Figure 2-7

When you're developing code, it's probably easiest to leave the console open. You'll see a more sophisticated way of solving code problems in Chapter 10 when you look at Venkman, a program released by Mozilla, the creators of Firefox, to help with removing errors.

When you double-click the link to the file in the JavaScript Console, here file:///Z:/Code/ Chapter2/ch2_examp2.htm, it'll open up the source code of the file and take you to where the error occurred, as shown in Figure 2-8.

In Internet Explorer, as long as you have the display errors enabled, as discussed in the section above, the sort of message you can expect to see is shown in Figure 2-9.

If you have IE 6+ and didn't see either of the error messages in Figure 2-8 or Figure 2-9, don't panic. In the browser's status bar (usually at the bottom of the browser window), you'll notice a little yellow triangle with an exclamation mark inside it. Double-click the yellow triangle, and the error message dialog box appears. Make sure you check the Always display this message when a page error occurs check box.

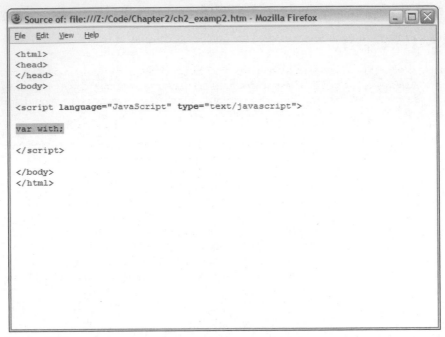

Figure 2-8

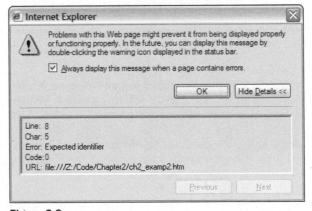

Figure 2-9

The rest of the book will show error messages for Firefox. Bear in mind, though, that it doesn't matter what your dialog box looks like, so long as you're getting an indication that an error has occurred and of what caused it.

Using Data — Calculations and Basic String Manipulation

Now that you've seen how to cope with errors, you can get back to the main subject of this chapter: data and how to use them. You've seen how to declare variables and how they can store information, but so far you haven't done anything really useful with this knowledge — so just why would you want to use variables at all?

What variables enable you to do is temporarily hold information that you can use for processing in mathematical calculations, in building up text messages, or in processing words that the user has entered. Variables are a little bit like the memory store button on the average pocket calculator. Say you were adding up your finances. You might first add up all the money you needed to spend, and then store it in temporary memory. After you had added up all your money coming in, you could deduct the amount stored in the memory to figure out how much would be left over. Variables can be used in a similar way: You can first gain the necessary user input and store it in variables, and then you can do your calculations using the values obtained.

In this section you'll see how you can put the values stored in variables to good use in both number-crunching and text-based operations.

Numerical Calculations

JavaScript has a range of basic mathematical capabilities, such as addition, subtraction, multiplication, and division. Each of the basic math functions is represented by a symbol: plus (+), minus (−), star (*), and forward slash (/), respectively. These symbols are called *operators* because they operate on the values you give them. In other words, they perform some calculation or operation and return a result to us. You can use the results of these calculations almost anywhere you'd use a number or a variable.

Imagine you were calculating the total value of items on a shopping list. You could write this calculation as follows:

Total cost of shopping = 10 + 5 + 5

or, if you actually calculate the sum, it's

Total cost of shopping = 20

Now let's see how to do this in JavaScript. In actual fact, it is very similar except that you need to use a variable to store the final total.

```
var TotalCostOfShopping;
TotalCostOfShopping = 10 + 5 + 5;
alert(TotalCostOfShopping);
```

First, you declare a variable, `TotalCostOfShopping`, to hold the total cost.

In the second line you have the code 10 + 5 + 5. This piece of code is known as an *expression*. When you assign the variable `TotalCostOfShopping` the value of this expression, JavaScript automatically calculates the value of the expression (20) and stores it in the variable. Notice that we've used the equals sign to tell JavaScript to store the results of the calculation in the `TotalCostOfShopping` variable. This is called *assigning* the value of the calculation to the variable, which is why the single equals sign (=) is called the *assignment operator*.

Finally, you display the value of the variable in an alert box.

The operators for subtraction and multiplication work in exactly the same way. Division is a little different.

Try It Out   **Calculations**

Let's take a look at an example using the division operator to see how it works. Enter the following code and save it as `ch2_examp3.htm`:

```html
<html>
<body>

<script language="JavaScript" type="text/javascript">
var firstNumber = 15;
var secondNumber = 10;
var answer;
answer = 15 / 10;
alert(answer);

alert(15 / 10);

answer = firstNumber / secondNumber;
alert(answer);

</script>

</body>
</html>
```

Load this into your web browser. You should see a succession of three `alert` boxes, each containing the value 1.5. These values are the results of three calculations.

How It Works

The first thing you do in the script block is declare your three variables and assign the first two of these variables values that you'll be using later.

```
var firstNumber = 15;
var secondNumber = 10;
var answer;
```

Next you set the `answer` variable to the results of the calculation of the expression 15/10. You show the value of this variable in an `alert` box.

```
answer = 15 / 10;
alert(answer);
```

This example demonstrates one way of doing the calculation, but in reality you'd almost never do it this way.

To demonstrate that you can use expressions in places you'd use numbers or variables, you show the results of the calculation of 15/10 directly by including it in the `alert()` function.

```
alert(15 / 10);
```

Finally you do the same calculation, but this time using the two variables `firstNumber`, which was set to 15, and `secondNumber`, which was set to 10. You have the expression `firstNumber / secondNumber`, the result of which you store in our `answer` variable. Then, to prove it has all worked, you show the value contained in `answer` by using your friend the `alert()` function.

```
answer = firstNumber / secondNumber;
alert(answer);
```

Most calculations will be done in the third way; that is, using variables, or numbers and variables, and storing the result in another variable. The reason for this is that if the calculation used literal values (actual values, such as 15 / 10), then you might as well program in the result of the calculation, rather than force JavaScript to calculate it for you. For example, rather than writing 15 / 10, you might as well just write 1.5. After all, the more calculations you force JavaScript to do, the slower it will be, though admittedly just one calculation won't tax it too much.

Another reason for using the result rather than the calculation is that it makes code more readable. Which would you prefer to read in code, 1.5 * 45 – 56 / 67 + 2.567 or 69.231? Still better, a variable named, for example, `PricePerKG`, makes code even easier to understand for someone not familiar with it.

Increment and Decrement Operators

A number of operations using the math operators are so commonly used that they have been given their own operators. The two you'll be looking at here are the *increment* and *decrement* operators, which are represented by two plus signs (++) and two minus signs (--), respectively. Basically, all they do is increase or decrease a variable's value by one. You could use the normal + and – operators to do this, for example:

```
myVariable = myVariable + 1;
myVariable = myVariable - 1;
```

(Note that you can assign a variable a new value that is the result of an expression involving its previous value.) However, using the increment and decrement operators shortens this to

```
myVariable++;
myVariable--;
```

The result is the same—the value of myVariable is increased or decreased by one—but the code is shorter. When you are familiar with the syntax, this becomes very clear and easy to read.

Right now, you may well be thinking that these operators sound as useful as a poke in the eye. However, in the next chapter when you look at how you can run the same code a number of times, you'll see that these operators are very useful and widely used. In fact, the ++ operator is so widely used it has a computer language named after it, C++. The joke here is that C++ is one up from C. (Well, that's programmer humor for you!)

As well as placing the ++ or -- after the variable, you can also place it before, like so:

```
++myVariable;
--myVariable;
```

When the ++ and -- are used on their own, as they usually are, it makes no difference where they are placed, but it is possible to use the ++ and -- operators in an expression along with other operators. For example:

```
myVar = myNumber++ - 20;
```

This code takes 20 away from myNumber and then increments the variable myNumber by one, before assigning the result to the variable myVar. If instead you place the ++ before, and prefix it like this:

```
myVar = ++myNumber - 20;
```

first myNumber is incremented by one, and then myNumber has 20 subtracted from it. It's a subtle difference but in some situations a very important one. Take the following code:

```
myNumber = 1;
myVar = (myNumber++ * 10 + 1);
```

What value will myVar contain? Well, because the ++ is postfixed (it's after the myNumber variable), it will be incremented afterwards. So the equation reads: Multiply myNumber by 10 plus 1 and then increment myNumber by one.

```
myVar = 1 * 10 + 1 = 11
```

Then add 1 to myNumber to get 12, but this is done after the value 11 has been assigned to myVar. Now take a look at the following code:

```
myNumber = 1;
myVar = (++myNumber * 10 + 1);
```

This time myNumber is incremented by one first, then times 10 and plus 1.

```
myVar = 2 * 10 + 1 = 21
```

As you can imagine, such subtlety can easily be overlooked and lead to bugs in code; therefore, it's usually best to avoid this syntax.

Before going on, this seems to be a good point to introduce another operator, +=. This operator can be used as a shortcut for increasing the value held by a variable by a set amount. For example,

```
myVar += 6;
```

does exactly the same thing as

```
myVar = myVar + 6;
```

You can also do the same thing for subtraction and multiplication, as shown here:

```
myVar -= 6;
myVar *= 6;
```

which is equivalent to

```
myVar = myVar - 6;
myVar = myVar * 6;
```

Operator Precedence

You saw that symbols that perform some function—like +, which adds two numbers together, and -, which subtracts one number from another—are called operators. Unlike people, not all operators are created equal; some have a higher *precedence*—that is, they get dealt with sooner. A quick look at a simple example will help demonstrate my point.

```
<html>
<body>

<script language="JavaScript" type="text/javascript">

var myVariable;

myVariable = 1 + 1 * 2;

alert(myVariable);

</script>

</body>
</html>
```

If you were to type this in, what result would you expect the alert box to show as the value of myVariable? You might expect that since 1 + 1 = 2 and 2 * 2 = 4, the answer is 4. Actually, you'll find that the alert box shows 3 as the value stored in myVariable as a result of the calculation. So what gives? Doesn't JavaScript add up right?

Well, you probably already know the reason from your understanding of mathematics. The way JavaScript does our calculation is to first calculate 1 * 2 = 2, and then use this result in the addition, so that JavaScript finishes off with 1 + 2 = 3.

Why? Because * has a higher precedence than +. The = symbol, also an operator (called the assignment operator), has the lowest precedence—it always gets left until last.

The + and – operators have an equal precedence, so which one gets done first? Well, JavaScript works from left to right, so if operators with equal precedence exist in a calculation, they get calculated in the order in which they appear when going from left to right. The same applies to * and /, which are also of equal precedence.

Try It Out   **Fahrenheit to Centigrade**

Take a look at a slightly more complex example—a Fahrenheit to centigrade converter. (Centigrade is another name for the Celsius temperature scale.) Type in this code and save it as ch2_examp4.htm:

```
<html>
<body>

<script language="JavaScript" type="text/javascript">
// Equation is °C = 5/9 (°F - 32).
var degFahren = prompt("Enter the degrees in Fahrenheit",50);
var degCent;

degCent = 5/9 * (degFahren - 32);

alert(degCent);

</script>

</body>
</html>
```

If you load the page into your browser, you should see a prompt box, like that shown in Figure 2-10, that asks you to enter the degrees in Fahrenheit to be converted. The value 50 is already filled in by default.

Explorer User Prompt	✕
Script Prompt:	OK
Enter the degrees in Fahrenheit	Cancel
50	

Figure 2-10

If you leave it at 50 and click OK, an `alert` box with the number 10 in it appears. This represents 50 degrees Fahrenheit converted to centigrade.

Reload the page and try changing the value in the prompt box to see what results you get. For example, change the value to 32 and reload the page. This time you should see 0 appear in the box.

As it's still a fairly simple example, there's no checking of data input so it'll let you enter abc as the degrees Fahrenheit. Later, in the "Data Type Conversion" section of this chapter, you'll see how to spot invalid characters posing as numeric data.

How It Works

The first line of the script block is a comment since it starts with two forward slashes (//). It contains the equation for converting Fahrenheit temperatures to centigrade and is in the example code solely for reference.

```
// Equation is °C = 5/9 (°F - 32).
```

Your task is to represent this equation in JavaScript code. You start by declaring your variables, degFahren and degCent.

```
var degFahren = prompt("Enter the degrees in Fahrenheit",50);
var degCent;
```

Instead of initializing the degFahren variable to a literal value, you get a value from the user using the prompt() function. The prompt() function works in a similar way to an alert() function, except that as well as displaying a message, it also contains a text box in which the user can enter a value. It is this value that will be stored inside the degFahren variable. The value returned is a text string but this will be implicitly converted by JavaScript to a number when you use it as a number, as discussed in the section on data type conversion later in this chapter.

You pass two pieces of information to the prompt() function:

- ❑ The text to be displayed — usually a question that prompts the user for input.
- ❑ The default value that is contained in the input box when the prompt dialog box first appears.

These two pieces of information must be specified in the given order and separated by a comma. If you don't want a default value to be contained in the input box when the prompt box opens, you should use an empty string (" ") for the second piece of information.

As you can see in the preceding code, the text is "Enter the degrees in Fahrenheit," and the default value in the input box is 50.

Next in the script block comes the equation represented in JavaScript. You store the result of the equation in the degCent variable. You can see that the JavaScript looks very much like the equation you have in the comment, except that you use degFahren instead of °F, and degCent rather than °C.

```
degCent = 5/9 * (degFahren - 32);
```

The calculation of the expression on the right-hand side of the equals sign raises a number of important points. First, just as in math, the JavaScript equation is read from left to right, at least for the basic math functions like +, –, and so on. Secondly, as you saw earlier, just as there is precedence in math, there is in JavaScript.

Starting from the left, first JavaScript works out 5/9 = .5556 (approximately). Then it comes to the multiplication, but wait . . . the last bit of our equation, degFahren – 32, is in parentheses. This raises the order of precedence and causes JavaScript to calculate the result of degFahren – 32 before doing the multiplication. For example, when degFahren is set to 50, (degFahren – 32) = (50 – 32) = 18. Now JavaScript does the multiplication, .5556 * 18, which is approximately 10.

What if you didn't use the parentheses? Then your code would be

```
degCent = 5/9 * degFahren - 32;
```

The calculation of 5/9 remains the same, but then JavaScript would have calculated the multiplication, 5/9 * degFahren. This is because the multiplication takes precedence over the subtraction. When degFahren is 50, this equates to 5/9 * 50 = 27.7778. Finally JavaScript would have subtracted the 32, leaving the result as –4.2221; not the answer you want!

Finally, in your script block, you display the answer using the alert() function.

```
alert(degCent);
```

That concludes a brief look at basic calculations with JavaScript. However, in Chapter 4 you'll be looking at the Math object, which enables you to do more complex calculations.

Basic String Operations

In an earlier section, you looked at the text or string data type, as well as numerical data. Just as numerical data have associated operators, strings have operators too. This section introduces some basic string manipulation techniques using such operators. Strings are covered in more depth in Chapter 4, and advanced string handling is covered in Chapter 8.

One thing you'll find yourself doing again and again in JavaScript is joining two strings together to make one string—a process that's termed *concatenation*. For example, you may want to concatenate the two strings "Hello " and "Paul" to make the string "Hello Paul". So how do you concatenate? Easy! Use the + operator. Recall that when applied to numbers, the + operator adds them up, but when used in the context of two strings, it joins them together.

```
var concatString = "Hello " + "Paul";
```

The string now stored in the variable concatString is "Hello Paul". Notice that the last character of the string "Hello " is a space—if you left this out, your concatenated string would be "HelloPaul".

Try It Out   Concatenating Strings

Let's look at an example using the + operator for string concatenation. Type the following code and save it as ch2_examp5.htm:

```
<html>
<body>

<script language="JavaScript" type="text/javascript">

var greetingString = "Hello";
```

```
    var myName = prompt("Please enter your name", "");
    var concatString;

    document.write(greetingString + " " + myName + "<br>");

    concatString = greetingString + " " + myName;

    document.write(concatString);

    </script>

    </body>
    </html>
```

If you load it into your web browser, you should see a prompt box asking for your name.

Enter your name and click OK. You should see a greeting and your name displayed twice on the web page.

How It Works

You start the script block by declaring three variables. You set the first variable, greetingString, to a string value. The second variable, myName, is assigned to whatever is entered by the user in the prompt box. You do not initialize the third variable, concatString, here. It will be used to store the result of the concatenation that you'll do later in the code.

```
var greetingString = "Hello";
var myName = prompt("Please enter your name", "");
var concatString;
```

In the last chapter, you saw how the web page was represented by the concept of a document and that it had a number of different properties, such as bgColor. You can also use document to write text and HTML directly into the page itself. You do this by using the word document, followed by a dot, and then write(). You then use document.write() much as you do the alert() function, in that you put the text that you want displayed in the web page inside the parentheses following the word write. Don't worry too much about this here, though, because it will all be explained in detail in Chapter 4. However, you now make use of document.write() in your code to write the result of an expression to the page.

```
document.write(greetingString + " " + myName + "<br>");
```

The expression written to the page is the concatenation of the value of the greetingString variable, a space (" "), the value of the myName variable, and the HTML <br> tag, which causes a line break. For example, if you enter Paul into the prompt box, the value of this expression will be as follows:

```
Hello Paul<br>
```

In the next line of code is a similar expression. This time it is just the concatenation of the value in the variable greetingString, a space, and the value in the variable myName. You store the result of this expression in the variable concatString. Finally, you write the contents of the variable concatString to the page using document.write().

```
concatString = greetingString + " " + myName;
document.write(concatString);
```

Mixing Numbers and Strings

What if you want to mix text and numbers in an expression? A prime example of this would be in the temperature converter you saw earlier. In the example, you just display the number without telling the user what it actually means. What you really want to do is display the number with descriptive text wrapped around it, such as "The value converted to degrees centigrade is 10."

Mixing numbers and text is actually very easy. You can simply join them together using the + operator. JavaScript is intelligent enough to know that when both a string and a number are involved, you're not trying to do numerical calculations, but rather that you want to treat the number as a string and join it to the text. For example, to join the text My age is and the number 101 together, you could simply do the following:

```
alert("My age is " + 101);
```

This would produce an `alert` box with "My age is 101" inside it.

Try It Out   Making the Temperature Converter User-Friendly

You can try out this technique of concatenating strings and numbers in our temperature-converter example. You'll output some explanatory text, along with the result of the conversion calculation. The changes that you need to make are very small, so load ch2_examp4.htm into your text editor and change the following line. Then save it as ch2_examp6.htm.

```
<html>
<body>

<script language="JavaScript" type="text/javascript">

// Equation is °C = 5/9 (°F - 32).

var degFahren = prompt("Enter the degrees in Fahrenheit",50);
var degCent;

degCent = 5/9 * (degFahren - 32);

alert(degFahren + "\xB0 Fahrenheit is " + degCent + "\xB0 centigrade");

</script>

</body>
</html>
```

Load the page into your web browser. Click OK in the prompt box to submit the value 50, and this time you should see the box shown in Figure 2-11.

Figure 2-11

How It Works

This example is identical to `ch2_examp4.htm`, except for one line:

```
alert(degFahren + "\xB0 Fahrenheit is " + degCent + "\xB0 centigrade");
```

so we will just look at this line here. You can see that the `alert()` function contains an expression. Let's look at that expression more closely.

First is the variable `degFahren`, which contains numerical data. You concatenate that to the string `"\xB0 Fahrenheit is "`. JavaScript realizes that because you are adding a number and a string, you want to join them together into one string rather than trying to take their sum, and so automatically converts the number contained in `degFahren` to a string. You next concatenate this string to the variable `degCent`, containing numerical data. Again JavaScript converts the value of this variable to a string. Finally you concatenate to the string `"\xB0 centigrade"`.

Note also the escape sequence used to insert the degree character into the strings. You'll remember from earlier in the chapter that `\xNN` can be used to insert special characters not available to type in directly. (*NN* is a hexadecimal number representing a character from the Latin-1 character table). So when JavaScript spots `\xB0` in a string, instead of showing those characters it does a lookup to see what character is represented by B0 and shows that instead.

Something to be aware of when using special characters is they are not necessarily cross-platform-compatible. Although you can use `\xNN` for a certain character on a Windows computer, you may find you need to use a different character on a Mac or a Unix machine.

You'll look at more string manipulation techniques in Chapter 4 — you'll see how to search strings and insert characters in the middle of them, and in Chapter 8 you'll see some very sophisticated string techniques.

Data Type Conversion

As you saw, if you add a string and a number together, JavaScript makes the sensible choice and converts the number to a string, then concatenates the two. Usually JavaScript has enough sense to make data type conversions like this whenever it needs to, but there are some situations in which you need to convert the type of a piece of data yourself. For example, you may be given a piece of string data that you want to think of as a number. This is especially likely if you are using forms to collect data from the user. Any values input by the user are treated as strings, even though they may contain numerical data, such as the user's age.

Why is changing the type of the data so important? Consider a situation in which you collect two numbers from the user using a form and want to calculate their sum. The two numbers are available to you as strings, for example "22" and "15". When you try to calculate the sum of these values using "22" + "15" you get the result "2215", because JavaScript thinks you are trying to concatenate two strings rather than trying to find the sum of two numbers.

In this section you'll look at two conversion functions that convert strings to numbers: parseInt() and parseFloat().

Let's take parseInt() first. This function takes a string and converts it to an integer. The name is a little confusing at first—why parseInt() rather than convertToInt()? The main reason for the name comes from the way that the function works. It actually goes through (that is, parses) each character of the string you ask it to convert and sees if it's a valid number. If it is valid, parseInt() uses it to build up the number; if it is not valid, the command simply stops converting and returns the number it has converted so far.

For example, if your code is parseInt("123"), JavaScript will convert the string "123" to the number 123. For the code parseInt("123abc"), JavaScript will also return the number 123. When the JavaScript interpreter gets to the letter a, it assumes the number has ended and gives 123 as the integer version of the string "123abc".

The parseFloat() function works in the same way as parseInt(), except that it returns floating-point numbers—fractional numbers—and that a decimal point in the string, which it is converting, is considered to be part of the allowable number.

Try It Out   Converting Strings to Numbers

Let's look at an example using parseInt() and parseFloat(). Enter the following code and save it as ch2_examp7.htm:

```
<html>
<body>

<script language="JavaScript" type="text/javascript">

var myString = "56.02 degrees centigrade";
var myInt;
var myFloat;

document.write("\"" + myString + "\" is " + parseInt(myString) +
    " as an integer" + "<BR>");

myInt = parseInt(myString);
document.write("\"" + myString + "\" when converted to an integer equals " +
    myInt + "<BR>");

myFloat = parseFloat(myString);
document.write("\"" + myString +
    "\" when converted to a floating point number equals " + myFloat);

</script>

</body>
</html>
```

Load it into your browser, and you'll see three lines written in the web page, as shown in Figure 2-12.

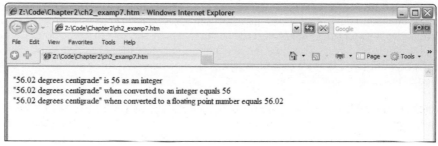

Figure 2-12

How It Works

Your first task in the script block is to declare some variables. The variable myString is declared and initialized to the string you want to convert. You could just as easily have used the string directly in this example rather than storing it in a variable, but in practice you'll find that you use variables more often than literal values. You also declare the variables myInt and myFloat, which will hold the converted numbers.

```
var myString = "56.02 degrees centigrade";
var myInt;
var myFloat;
```

Next, you write to the page the converted integer value of myString displayed inside a user-friendly sentence you build up using string concatenation. Notice that you use the escape sequence \" to display quotes (") around the string you are converting.

```
document.write("\"" + myString + "\" is " + parseInt(myString) +
    " as an integer" + "<BR>");
```

As you can see, you can use parseInt() and parseFloat() in the same places you would use a number itself or a variable containing a number. In fact, in this line the JavaScript interpreter is doing two conversions. First it converts myString to an integer, because that's what you asked for by using parseInt(). Then it automatically converts that integer number back to a string, so it can be concatenated with the other strings to make up your sentence. Also note that only the 56 part of the myString variable's value is considered a valid number when you're dealing with integers. Anything after the 6 is considered invalid and is ignored.

Next you do the same conversion of myString using parseInt(), but this time you store the result in the myInt variable. On the following line you use the result in some text you display to the user:

```
myInt = parseInt(myString);
document.write("\"" + myString + "\" when converted to an integer equals " +
    myInt + "<BR>");
```

Again, though `myInt` holds a number, the JavaScript interpreter knows that +, when a string and a number are involved, means you want the `myInt` value converted to a string and concatenated to the rest of the string so it can be displayed.

Finally, you use `parseFloat()` to convert the string in `myString` to a floating-point number, which you store in the variable `myFloat`. This time the decimal point is considered to be a valid part of the number, so it's anything after the 2 that is ignored. Again you use `document.write()` to write the result to the web page inside a user-friendly string.

```
myFloat = parseFloat(myString);
document.write("\"" + myString +
    "\" when converted to a floating point number equals " + myFloat);
```

Dealing with Strings That Won't Convert

Some strings simply are not convertible to numbers, such as strings that don't contain any numerical data. What happens if you try to convert these strings? As a little experiment, try changing the preceding example so that `myString` holds something that is not convertible. For example, change the line

```
var myString = "56.02 degrees centigrade";
```

to

```
var myString = "I'm a name not a number";
```

Now reload the page in your browser and you should see what's shown in Figure 2-13.

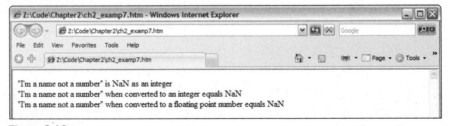

Figure 2-13

You can see that in the place of the numbers you got before, you get `NaN`. What sort of number is that? Well, it's *Not a Number* at all!

If you use `parseInt()` or `parseFloat()` with any string that is empty or does not start with at least one valid digit, you get `NaN`, meaning Not a Number.

`NaN` is actually a special value in JavaScript. It has its own function, `isNaN()`, which checks whether something is NaN or not. For example,

```
myVar1 = isNaN("Hello");
```

will store the value `true` in the variable `myVar1`, since `"Hello"` is not a number, whereas

```
myVar2 = isNaN("34");
```

will store the value `false` in the variable `myVar2`, since 34 can be converted successfully from a string to a number by the `isNaN()` function.

In the next chapter you'll see how you can use the `isNaN()` function to check the validity of strings as numbers, something that proves invaluable when dealing with user input, as you'll see in Chapter 6.

Arrays

Now we're going to look at a new concept—something called an *array*. An array is similar to a normal variable, in that you can use it to hold any type of data. However, it has one important difference, which you'll see below.

As you have already seen, a normal variable can only hold one piece of data at a time. For example, you can set `myVariable` to be equal to 25 like so:

```
myVariable = 25;
```

and then go and set it to something else, say 35:

```
myVariable = 35;
```

However, when you set the variable to 35, the first value of 25 is lost. The variable `myVariable` now holds just the number 35.

The following table illustrates the variable:

Variable name	Value
myVariable	35

The difference between such a normal variable and an array is that an array can hold *more than one* item of data at the same time. For example, you could use an array with the name `myArray` to store both the numbers 25 and 35. Each place where a piece of data can be stored in an array is called an *element*.

How do you distinguish between these two pieces of data in an array? You give each piece of data an *index* value. To refer to that piece of data you enclose its index value in square brackets after the name of the array. For example, an array called `myArray` containing the data 25 and 35 could be illustrated using the following table:

Element name	Value
myArray[0]	25
myArray[1]	35

Notice that the index values start at 0 and not 1. Why is this? Surely 1 makes more sense—after all, we humans tend to say the first item of data, followed by the second item, and so on. Unfortunately, computers start from 0, and think of the first item as the zero item, the second as the first item, and so on. Confusing, but you'll soon get used to this.

Arrays can be very useful since you can store as many (within the limits of the language, which specifies a maximum of two to the power of 32 elements) or as few items of data in an array as you want. Also, you don't have to say up front how many pieces of data you want to store in an array, though you can if you wish.

So how do you create an array? This is slightly different from declaring a normal variable. To create a new array, you need to declare a variable name and tell JavaScript that you want it to be a new array using the new keyword and the Array() function. For example, the array myArray could be defined like this:

```
var myArray = new Array();
```

Note that, as with everything in JavaScript, the code is case-sensitive, so if you type array() rather than Array(), the code won't work. This way of defining an array will be explained further in Chapter 4.

As with normal variables, you can also declare your variable first, and then tell JavaScript you want it to be an array. For example:

```
var myArray;
myArray = new Array();
```

Earlier you learned that you can say up front how many elements the array will hold if you want to, although this is not necessary. You do this by putting the number of elements you want to specify between the parentheses after Array. For example, to create an array that will hold six elements, you write the following:

```
var myArray = new Array(6);
```

You have seen how to declare a new array, but how do you store your pieces of data inside it? You can do this when you define your array by including your data inside the parentheses, with each piece of data separated by a comma. For example:

```
var myArray = new Array("Paul",345,"John",112,"Bob",99);
```

Here the first item of data, "Paul", will be put in the array with an index of 0. The next piece of data, 345, will be put in the array with an index of 1, and so on. This means that the element with the name myArray[0] contains the value "Paul", the element with the name myArray[1] contains the value 345, and so on.

Note that you can't use this method to declare an array containing just one piece of numerical data, such as 345, because JavaScript assumes that you are declaring an array that will hold 345 elements.

This leads to another way of declaring data in an array. You could write the preceding line like this:

```
var myArray = new Array();
myArray[0] = "Paul";
myArray[1] = 345;
myArray[2] = "John";
myArray[3] = 112;
myArray[4] = "Bob";
myArray[5] = 99;
```

You use each element name as you would a variable, assigning them with values. You'll learn this method of declaring the values of array elements in the following "Try It Out" section.

Obviously, in this example the first way of defining the data items is much easier. However, there will be situations in which you want to change the data stored in a particular element in an array after they have been declared. In that case you will have to use the latter method of defining the values of the array elements.

You'll also spot from the preceding example that you can store different data types in the same array. JavaScript is very flexible as to what you can put in an array and where you can put it.

Before going on to an example, note here that if, for example, you had defined your array called myArray as holding three elements like this:

```
var myArray = new Array(3);
```

and then defined a value in the element with index 130

```
myArray[130] = "Paul";
```

JavaScript would not complain and would happily assume that you had changed your mind and wanted an array that had (at least) 131 elements in it.

Try It Out | An Array

In the following example, you'll create an array to hold some names. You'll use the second method described in the preceding section to store these pieces of data in the array. You'll then display the data to the user. Type the code in and save it as ch2_examp8.htm.

```
<html>
<body>

<script language="JavaScript" type="text/javascript">

var myArray = new Array();
myArray[0] = "Bob";
myArray[1] = "Pete";
myArray[2] = "Paul";

document.write("myArray[0] = " + myArray[0] + "<BR>");
```

```
document.write("myArray[2] = " + myArray[2] + "<BR>");
document.write("myArray[1] = " + myArray[1] + "<BR>");

myArray[1] = "Mike";
document.write("myArray[1] changed to " + myArray[1]);

</script>

</body>
</html>
```

If you load this into your web browser, you should see a web page that looks something like the one shown in Figure 2-14.

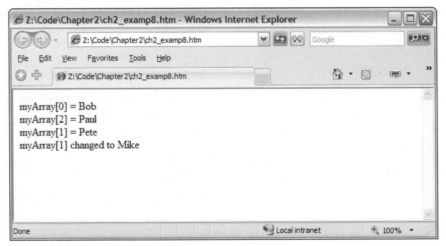

Figure 2-14

How It Works

The first task in the script block is to declare a variable and tell the JavaScript interpreter you want it to be a new array.

```
var myArray = new Array();
```

Now that you have your array defined, you can store some data in it. Each time you store an item of data with a new index, JavaScript automatically creates a new storage space for it. Remember that the first element will be at myArray[0].

Let's take each addition to the array in turn and see what's happening. Before you add anything, your array is empty. Then you add an array element with the following line:

```
myArray[0] = "Bob";
```

Your array now looks like this:

Index	Data Stored
0	Bob

Then you add another element to the array, this time with an index of 1.

```
myArray[1] = "Pete";
```

Index	Data Stored
0	Bob
1	Pete

Finally, you add another element to the array with an index of 2.

```
myArray[2] = "Paul";
```

Your array now looks like this:

Index	Data Stored
0	Bob
1	Pete
2	Paul

Next, you use a series of document.write() functions to insert the values that each element of the array contains into the web page. Here the array is out of order just to demonstrate that you can access it that way.

```
document.write("myArray[0] = " + myArray[0] + "<BR>");
document.write("myArray[2] = " + myArray[2] + "<BR>");
document.write("myArray[1] = " + myArray[1] + "<BR>");
```

You can treat each particular position in an array as if it's a standard variable. So you can use it to do calculations, transfer its value to another variable or array, and so on. However, if you try to access the data inside an array position before you have defined it, you'll get undefined as a value.

Finally, you change the value of the second array position to "Mike". You could have changed it to a number because, just as with normal variables, you can store any data type at any time in each individual data position in an array.

```
myArray[1] = "Mike";
```

Now your array's contents look like this:

Index	Data Stored
0	Bob
1	Mike
2	Paul

Just to show that the change you made has worked, you use `document.write()` to display the second element's value.

```
document.write("myArray[1] changed to " + myArray[1]);
```

A Multi-Dimensional Array

Suppose you want to store a company's personnel information in an array. You might have data such as names, ages, addresses, and so on. One way to create such an array would be to store the information sequentially — the first name in the first element of the array, then the corresponding age in the next element, the address in the third, the next name in the fourth element, and so on. Your array could look something like this:

Index	Data Stored
0	Name1
1	Age1
2	Address1
3	Name2
4	Age2
5	Address2
6	Name3
7	Age3
8	Address3

This would work, but there is a neater solution: using a *multi-dimensional array*. Up to now you have been using single-dimension arrays. In these arrays each element is specified by just one index — that is, one dimension. So, taking the preceding example, you can see `Name1` is at index `0`, `Age1` is at index `1`, and so on.

A multi-dimensional array is one with two or more indexes for each element. For example, this is how your personnel array could look as a two-dimensional array:

Index	0	1	2
0	Name1	Name2	Name3
1	Age1	Age2	Age3
2	Address1	Address2	Address3

You'll see how to create such multi-dimensional arrays in the following "Try It Out" section.

Try It Out   **A Two-Dimensional Array**

The following example illustrates how you can create such a multi-dimensional array in JavaScript code, and how you can access the elements of this array. Type in the code and save it as ch2_examp9.htm.

```
<html>
<body>

<script language="JavaScript" type="text/javascript">

var personnel = new Array();

personnel[0] = new Array();
personnel[0][0] = "Name0";
personnel[0][1] = "Age0";
personnel[0][2] = "Address0";

personnel[1] = new Array();
personnel[1][0] = "Name1";
personnel[1][1] = "Age1";
personnel[1][2] = "Address1";

personnel[2] = new Array();
personnel[2][0] = "Name2";
personnel[2][1] = "Age2";
personnel[2][2] = "Address2";

document.write("Name : " + personnel[1][0] + "<BR>");
document.write("Age : " + personnel[1][1] + "<BR>");
document.write("Address : " + personnel[1][2]);

</script>

</body>
</html>
```

If you load it into your web browser, you'll see three lines written into the page, which represent the name, age, and address of the person whose details are stored in the personnel[1] element of the array, as shown in Figure 2-15.

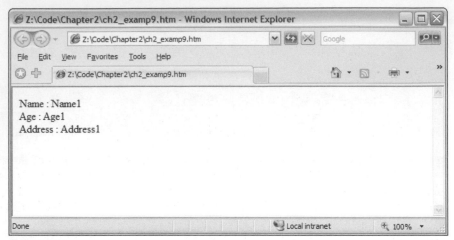

Figure 2-15

How It Works

The first thing to do in this script block is declare a variable, `personnel`, and tell JavaScript that you want it to be a new array.

```
var personnel = new Array();
```

Then you do something new; you tell JavaScript you want index 0 of the personnel array, that is, the element `personnel[0]`, to be another new array.

```
personnel[0] = new Array();
```

So what's going on? Well, the truth is that JavaScript doesn't actually support multi-dimensional arrays, only single ones. However, JavaScript enables us to fake multi-dimensional arrays by creating an array inside another array. So what the preceding line is doing is creating a new array inside the element with index 0 of our `personnel` array.

In the next three lines you put values into the newly created `personnel[0]` array. JavaScript makes it easy to do this: You just state the name of the array, `personnel[0]`, followed by another index in square brackets. The first index (0) belongs to the `personnel` array; the second index belongs to the `personnel[0]` array.

```
personnel[0][0] = "Name0";
personnel[0][1] = "Age0";
personnel[0][2] = "Address0";
```

After these lines of code, our array looks like this:

Index	0
0	Name0
1	Age0
2	Address0

The numbers at the top, at the moment just 0, refer to the personnel array. The numbers going down the side, 0, 1, and 2, are actually indices for the new personnel[0] array inside the personnel array.

For the second person's details, you repeat the process, but this time you are using the personnel array element with index 1.

```
personnel[1] = new Array();
personnel[1][0] = "Name1";
personnel[1][1] = "Age1";
personnel[1][2] = "Address1";
```

Now your array looks like this:

Index	0	1
0	Name0	Name1
1	Age0	Age1
2	Address0	Address1

You create a third person's details in the next few lines. You are now using the element with index 2 inside the personnel array to create a new array.

```
personnel[2] = new Array();
personnel[2][0] = "Name2";
personnel[2][1] = "Age2";
personnel[2][2] = "Address2";
```

The array now looks like this:

Index	0	1	2
0	Name0	Name1	Name2
1	Age0	Age1	Age2
2	Address0	Address1	Address2

You have now finished creating your multi-dimensional array. You end the script block by accessing the data for the second person (Name1, Age1, Address1) and displaying it in the page by using document.write(). As you can see, accessing the data is very much the same as storing them. You can use the multi-dimensional array anywhere you would use a normal variable or single-dimension array.

```
document.write("Name : " + personnel[1][0] + "<BR>");
document.write("Age : " + personnel[1][1] + "<BR>");
document.write("Address : " + personnel[1][2]);
```

Try changing the document.write() commands so that they display the first person's details. The code would look like this:

```
document.write("Name : " + personnel[0][0] + "<BR>");
document.write("Age : " + personnel[0][1] + "<BR>");
document.write("Address : " + personnel[0][2]);
```

It's possible to create multi-dimensional arrays of three, four, or even a hundred dimensions, but things can start to get very confusing, and you'll find that you rarely, if ever, need more than two dimensions. To give you an idea, here's how to declare and access a five-dimensional array:

```
var myArray = new Array();
myArray[0] = new Array();
myArray[0][0] = new Array();
myArray[0][0][0] = new Array();
myArray[0][0][0][0] = new Array();

myArray[0][0][0][0][0] = "This is getting out of hand"

document.write(myArray[0][0][0][0][0]);
```

That's it for arrays for now, but you'll return to them in Chapter 4 where you find out something shocking about them. You'll also learn about some of their more advanced features.

The "Who Wants To Be A Billionaire" Trivia Quiz — Storing the Questions Using Arrays

Okay, it's time to make your first steps in building the online trivia quiz. You're going to lay the foundations by defining the data that make up the questions and answers used in the quiz.

In this chapter you're just going to define multiple-choice questions, which have a single-letter answer. You'll be using arrays to store the questions and answers: a two-dimensional array for the questions and a single-dimensional one for the matching answers.

The format of each multiple-choice question will be the question followed by all the possible choices for answers. The correct answer to the question is specified using the letter corresponding to that answer.

For example, the question, "Who were the Beatles?" has options:

A. A sixties rock group from Liverpool

B. Four musically gifted insects

C. German cars

D. I don't know. Can I have the questions on baseball please?

And the answer in this case is A.

So how do you store this information in our arrays? Let's look at the array holding the questions first. You define the array something like this:

Index	0	1	2
0	Text for Question 0	Text for Question 1	Text for Question 2
1	Possible Answer A for Question 0	Possible Answer A for Question 1	Possible Answer A for Question 2
2	Possible Answer B for Question 0	Possible Answer B for Question 1	Possible Answer B for Question 2
3	Possible Answer C for Question 0	Possible Answer C for Question 1	Possible Answer C for Question 2
4	Possible Answer D for Question 0	Possible Answer D for Question 1	Possible Answer D for Question 2

Of course you can extend this array if you create further questions.

The answers array will then be defined something like this:

Index	Value
0	Correct answer to Question 0
1	Correct answer to Question 1
2	Correct answer to Question 2

Again, you can extend this array as you add more questions.

Now that you have an idea of how you are going to store the question data, let's have a look at the code. The name of the page to add the code to is `trivia_quiz.htm`. You start by creating the HTML tags at the top of the page.

```
<html>
<head>
<title>Wrox Online Trivia Quiz</title>
</head>
<body>
```

Then, in the body of the page, you start a JavaScript block in which you declare two variables, questions and answers, and define them as new arrays. The purpose of these variables should be pretty self-explanatory! However, as in the rest of the code, you add comments so that it is easy to work out what you are doing.

```
<script language="JavaScript" type="text/javascript">

// questions and answers arrays will holds questions and answers
var questions = new Array();
var answers = new Array();
```

Next you move straight on to define our first question. Since the questions will be in a two-dimensional array, your first task is to set questions[0] to a new array. You assign the first element in this array, questions[0][0], to the text of the question, and the following elements to the possible answers.

```
// define question 1
questions[0] = new Array();

// the question
questions[0][0] = "The Beatles were";

// first choice
questions[0][1] = "A sixties rock group from Liverpool";

// second choice
questions[0][2] = "Four musically gifted insects";

// third choice
questions[0][3] = "German cars";

// fourth choice
questions[0][4] = "I don't know. Can I have the questions on baseball please?";
```

Having defined the first question, let's set the first answer. For multiple-choice questions you need only to set the element with the corresponding index in the answers array to the character representing the correct choice. In the previous question the correct answer is "A sixties rock group from Liverpool". As this is the first choice, its letter is A.

```
// assign answer for question 1
answers[0] = "A";
```

Let's define two more questions for the quiz. They both take the same format as the first question.

```
// define question 2
questions[1] = new Array();
questions[1][0] = "Homer Simpson's favorite food is";
questions[1][1] = "Fresh salad";
questions[1][2] = "Doughnuts";
questions[1][3] = "Bread and water";
questions[1][4] = "Apples";

// assign answer for question 2
```

```
answers[1] = "B";

// define question 3
questions[2] = new Array();
questions[2][0] = "Lisa Simpson plays which musical instrument?";
questions[2][1] = "Clarinet";
questions[2][2] = "Oboe";
questions[2][3] = "Saxophone";
questions[2][4] = "Tubular bells";

// assign answer for question 3
answers[2] = "C";
```

You end the script block by creating an alert box that tells you that the array has been initialized.

```
alert("Array Initialized");

</script>
</body>
</html>
```

Save the page as `trivia_quiz.htm`. That completes the definition of your quiz's questions and answers. In the next chapter you can move on to writing code that checks the correct answers to the questions against the answers supplied by the user.

Summary

In this chapter you have built up knowledge of the fundamentals of JavaScript's data types and variables, and how to use them in operations. In particular, you saw that

❑ JavaScript supports a number of types of data, such as numbers, text, and Booleans.

❑ Text is represented by strings of characters and is surrounded by quotes. You must match the quotes surrounding strings. Escape characters enable you to include characters in your string that cannot be typed.

❑ Variables are JavaScript's means of storing data, such as numbers and text, in memory so that they can be used again and again in your code.

❑ Variable names must not include certain illegal characters, like the percent sign (%) and the ampersand (&), or be a reserved word, like `with`.

❑ Before you can give a value to a variable, you must declare its existence to the JavaScript interpreter.

❑ JavaScript has the four basic math operators, represented by the symbols plus (+), minus (−), star (*), and forward slash (/). To assign values of a calculation to a variable, you use the equals sign (=), termed the assignment operator.

❑ Operators have different levels of precedence, so multiplication and division will be calculated before addition and subtraction.

❑   Strings can be joined together, or concatenated, to produce one big string by means of the + operator. When numbers and strings are concatenated with the + operator, JavaScript automatically converts the number into a string.

❑   Although JavaScript's automatic data conversion suits us most of the time, there are occasions when you need to force the conversion of data. You saw how parseInt() and parseFloat() can be used to convert strings to numbers. Attempting to convert strings that won't convert will result in NaN (Not a Number) being returned.

❑   Arrays are a special type of variable that can hold more than one piece of data. The data are inserted and accessed by means of a unique index number.

Exercise Questions

Suggested solutions to these questions can be found in Appendix A.

Question 1

Write a JavaScript program to convert degrees centigrade into degrees Fahrenheit, and to write the result to the page in a descriptive sentence. The JavaScript equation for Fahrenheit to centigrade is as follows:

```
degFahren = 9 / 5 * degCent + 32
```

Question 2

The following code uses the prompt() function to get two numbers from the user. It then adds those two numbers together and writes the result to the page:

```
<html>
<body>
<script language="JavaScript" type="text/javascript">

var firstNumber = prompt("Enter the first number","");
var secondNumber = prompt("Enter the second number","");
var theTotal = firstNumber + secondNumber;
document.write(firstNumber + " added to " + secondNumber + " equals " +
   theTotal);

</script>
</body>
</html>
```

However, if you try the code out, you'll discover that it doesn't work. Why not?

Change the code so that it does work.

Decisions, Loops, and Functions

So far, you've seen how to use JavaScript to get user input, perform calculations and tasks with that input, and write the results to a web page. However, a pocket calculator can do all this, so what is it that makes computers different? That is to say, what gives computers the appearance of having intelligence? The answer is the capability to make decisions based on information gathered.

How will decision-making help you in creating web sites? In the last chapter you wrote some code that converted temperature in degrees Fahrenheit to centigrade. You obtained the degrees Fahrenheit from the user using the `prompt()` function. This worked fine if the user entered a valid number, such as 50. If, however, the user entered something invalid for the Fahrenheit temperature, such as the string aaa, you would find that your code no longer works as expected. Now, if you had some decision-making capabilities in your program, you could check to see if what the user has entered is valid. If it is, you can do the calculation, and if it isn't, you can tell the user why and ask him to enter a valid number.

Validation of user input is probably one of the most common uses of decision making in JavaScript, but it's far from being the only use. The trivia quiz also needs some decision-making capabilities so that you can check if the answer given by the user is right or wrong. If it's right, you need to take certain steps, such as telling the user that she is right and increasing her score. If the answer is wrong, a different set of code needs to be executed to tell her that she's wrong.

In this chapter you'll look at how decision making is implemented in JavaScript and how you can use it to make your code smarter.

Decision Making — The if and switch Statements

All programming languages enable you to make decisions — that is, they enable the program to follow a certain course of action depending on whether a particular *condition* is met. This is what gives programming languages their intelligence.

For example, in a situation in which you use JavaScript code that is compatible only with version 4 or later browsers, the condition could be that the user is using a version 4 or later browser. If you discover that this condition is not met, you could direct him to a set of pages that are compatible with earlier browsers.

Conditions are comparisons between variables and data, such as the following:

❑   Is *A* bigger than *B*?

❑   Is *X* equal to *Y*?

❑   Is *M* not equal to *N*?

For example, if the variable `browserVersion` held the version of the browser that the user was using, the condition would be this:

❑   Is `browserVersion` greater than or equal to 4?

You'll notice that all of these questions have a yes or no answer — that is, they are Boolean based and can only evaluate to `true` or `false`. How do you use this to create decision-making capabilities in your code? You get the browser to test for whether the condition is `true`. If (and only if) it is `true`, you execute a particular section of code.

Look at another example. Recall from Chapter 1 the natural English instructions used to demonstrate how code flows. One of these instructions for making a cup of coffee is:

❑   Has the kettle boiled? If so, then pour water into cup; otherwise, continue to wait.

This is an example of making a decision. The condition in this instruction is "Has the kettle boiled?" It has a `true` or `false` answer. If the answer is `true`, you pour the water into the cup. If it isn't `true`, you continue to wait.

In JavaScript, you can change the flow of the code's execution depending on whether a condition is `true` or `false`, using an `if` statement or a `switch` statement. You will look at these shortly, but first we need to introduce some new operators that are essential for the definition of conditions — *comparison operators*.

Comparison Operators

In the last chapter you saw how mathematical functions, such as addition and division, were represented by symbols, such as plus (+) and forward slash (/), called operators. You also saw that if you want to give a variable a value, you can assign to it a value or the result of a calculation using the equals sign (=), termed the assignment operator.

Decision making also has its own operators, which enable you to test conditions. Comparison operators, just like the mathematical operators you saw in the last chapter, have a left-hand side (LHS) and a right-hand side (RHS), and the comparison is made between the two. The technical terms for these are the *left operand* and the *right operand*. For example, the less-than operator, with the symbol <, is a comparison operator. You could write 23 < 45, which translates as "Is 23 less than 45?" Here, the answer would be true (see Figure 3-1).

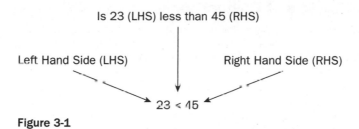

Figure 3-1

There are other comparison operators, the more useful of which are summarized in the following table:

Operator Symbol	Purpose
==	Tests if LHS is equal to RHS
<	Tests If LHS is less than RHS
>	Tests if LHS is greater than RHS
<=	Tests if LHS is less than or equal to RHS
>=	Tests if LHS is greater than or equal to RHS
!=	Tests if LHS is not equal to RHS

You'll see these comparison operators in use in the next section when you look at the if statement.

Precedence

Recall from Chapter 2 that operators have an order of precedence. This applies also to the comparison operators. The == and != comparison operators have the lowest order of precedence, and the rest of the comparison operators, <, >, <=, and >=, have an equal precedence.

All of these comparison operators have a precedence that is below operators, such as +, -, *, and /. This means that if you make a comparison such as 3 * 5 > 2 * 5, the multiplication calculations are worked out first, before their results are compared. However, in these circumstances, it's both safer and clearer if you wrap the calculations on either side inside parentheses, for example, (3 * 5) > (2 * 5). As a general rule, it's a good idea to use parentheses to ensure that the precedence is clear, or you may find yourself surprised by the outcome.

Assignment versus Comparison

One very important point to mention is the ease with which the assignment operator (=) and the comparison operator (==) can be mixed up. Remember that the = operator assigns a value to a variable and that the == operator compares the value of two variables. Even when you have this idea clear, it's amazingly easy to put one equals sign where you meant to put two.

Assigning the Results of Comparisons

You can store the results of a comparison in a variable, as shown in the following example:

```
var age = prompt("Enter age:", "");
var isOverSixty = parseInt(age) > 60;
  document.write("Older than 60: " + isOverSixty);
```

Here you obtain the user's age using the prompt() function. This returns, as a string, whatever value the user enters. You then convert that to a number using the parseInt() function you saw in the previous chapter and use the greater-than operator to see if it's greater than 60. The result (either true or false) of the comparison will be stored in the variable isOverSixty.

If the user enters 35, the document.write() on the final line will write this to the page:

```
Older than 60: false
```

If the user entered 61, this will be displayed:

```
Older than 60: true
```

The if Statement

The if statement is one you'll find yourself using in almost every program that is more than a couple of lines long. It works very much as it does in the English language. For example, you might say in English, "If the room temperature is more than 80 degrees Fahrenheit, then I'll turn the air conditioning on." In JavaScript, this would translate into something like this:

```
if (roomTemperature > 80)
{
    roomTemperature = roomTemperature - 10;
}
```

How does this work? See Figure 3-2.

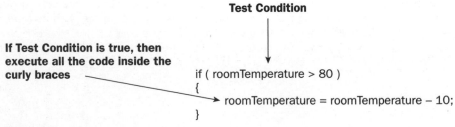

Figure 3-2

Notice that the test condition is placed in parentheses and follows the `if` keyword. Also, note that there is no semicolon at the end of this line. The code to be executed if the condition is `true` is placed in curly braces on the line after the condition, and each of these lines of code does end with a semicolon.

The curly braces, `{}`, have a special purpose in JavaScript: They mark out a *block* of code. Marking out lines of code as belonging to a single block means that JavaScript will treat them all as one piece of code. If the condition of an `if` statement is `true`, JavaScript executes the next line or block of code following the `if` statement. In the preceding example, the block of code has only one statement, so we could equally as well have written this:

```
if (roomTemperature > 80)
    roomTemperature = roomTemperature - 10;
```

However, if you have a number of lines of code that you want to execute, you need the braces to mark them out as a single block of code. For example, a modified version of the example with three lines of code would have to include the braces.

```
if (roomTemperature > 80)
{
    roomTemperature = roomTemperature - 10;
    alert("It's getting hot in here");
    alert("Air conditioning switched on");
}
```

A particularly easy mistake to make is to forget the braces when marking out a block of code to be executed. Instead of the code in the block being executed when the condition is true, you'll find that *only the first line* after the `if` statement is executed. However, the other lines will always be executed regardless of the outcome of the test condition. To avoid mistakes like these, it's a good idea to always use braces, even where there is only one statement. If you get into this habit, you'll be less likely to leave them out when they are actually needed.

Try It Out   The if Statement

Let's return to our temperature converter example from Chapter 2 and add some decision-making functionality. Enter the following code and save it as `ch3_examp1.htm`:

```
<html>
<body>

<script language="JavaScript" type="text/javascript">

var degFahren = Number(prompt("Enter the degrees Fahrenheit",32));
var degCent;

degCent = 5/9 * (degFahren - 32);

document.write(degFahren + "\xB0 Fahrenheit is " + degCent +
    "\xB0 centigrade<BR>");

if (degCent < 0)
{
```

```
      document.write("That's below the freezing point of water");
}

if (degCent == 100)
    document.write("That's the boiling point of water");

</script>

</body>
</html>
```

Load the page into your browser and enter 32 into the prompt box for the Fahrenheit value to be converted. With a value of 32, neither of the if statement's conditions will be true, so the only line written in the page will be that shown in Figure 3-3.

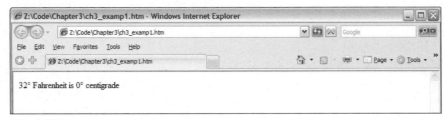

Figure 3-3

Now reload the page and enter 31 for the Fahrenheit value. This time you'll see two lines in the page, as shown in Figure 3-4.

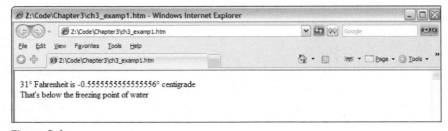

Figure 3-4

Finally, reload the page again, but this time, enter 212 in the prompt box. The two lines shown in Figure 3-5 will appear in the page.

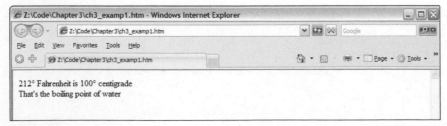

Figure 3-5

How It Works

The first part of the script block in this page is taken from the example `ch2_examp4.htm` in Chapter 2. You declare two variables, `degFahren` and `degCent`. The variable `degFahren` is given an initial value obtained from the user with the `prompt()` function. Note the `prompt()` function returns a string value, which you then explicitly convert to a numeric value using the `Number()` function. The variable `degCent` is then set to the result of the calculation `5/9 * (degFahren - 32)`, which is the Fahrenheit-to-centigrade conversion calculation.

```
var degFahren = Number(prompt("Enter the degrees Fahrenheit",32));
var degCent;

degCent = 5/9 * (degFahren - 32);
```

Then you write the result of your calculation to the page.

```
document.write(degFahren + "\xB0 Fahrenheit is " + degCent +
   "\xB0 centigrade<BR>");
```

Now comes the new code; the first of two `if` statements.

```
if (degCent < 0)
{
   document.write("That's below the freezing point of water");
}
```

This `if` statement has the condition that asks, "Is the value of the variable `degCent` less than zero?" If the answer is yes (`true`), the code inside the curly braces executes. In this case, you write a sentence to the page using `document.write()`. If the answer is no (`false`), the processing moves on to the next line after the closing brace. Also worth noting is the fact that the code inside the `if` statement's opening brace is indented. This is not necessary, but it is a good practice to get into because it makes your code much easier to read.

When trying out the example, you started by entering 32, so that `degFahren` will be initialized to 32. In this case the calculation `degCent = 5/9 * (degFahren - 32)` will set `degCent` to 0. So the answer to the question "Is `degCent` less than zero?" is `false`, because `degCent` is equal to zero, not less than zero. The code inside the curly braces will be skipped and never executed. In this case, the next line to be executed will be the second `if` statement's condition, which we'll discuss shortly.

When you entered 31 in the prompt box, `degFahren` was set to 31, so the variable `degCent` will be -0.55555555556. So how does your `if` statement look now? It evaluates to "Is -0.55555555556 less than zero?" The answer this time is `true`, and the code inside the braces, here just a `document.write()` statement, executes.

Finally, when you entered 212, how did this alter the `if` statement? The variable `degCent` is set to 100 by the calculation, so the `if` statement now asks the question, "Is 100 less than zero?" The answer is `false`, and the code inside the braces will be skipped over.

In the second `if` statement, you evaluate the condition "Is the value of variable `degCent` equal to 100?"

```
if (degCent == 100)
   document.write("That's the boiling point of water");
```

There are no braces here, so if the condition is true, the only code to execute is the first line below the if statement. When you want to execute multiple lines in the case of the condition being true, then braces are required.

You saw that when degFahren is 32, degCent will be 0. So your if statement will be "Is 0 equal to 100?" The answer is clearly false, and the code won't execute. Again, when you set degFahren to 31, degCent will be calculated to be -0.55555555556; "Is –0.55555555556 equal to 100?" is also false, and the code won't execute.

Finally, when degFahren is set to 212, degCent will be 100. This time the if statement is "Is 100 equal to 100?" and the answer is true, so the document.write() statement executes.

As you have seen already, one of the most common errors in JavaScript, even for experts, is using one equals sign for evaluating, rather than the necessary two. Take a look at the following code extract:

```
if (degCent = 100)
    document.write("That's the boiling point of water");
```

This condition will always evaluate to true, and the code below the if statement will always execute. Worse still, your variable degCent will be set to 100. Why? Because a single equals sign assigns values to a variable; only a double equals sign compares values. The reason an assignment always evaluates to true is that the result of the assignment expression is the value of the right-hand side expression and this is the number 100, which is then implicitly converted to a Boolean and any number besides 0 and NaN converts to true.

Logical Operators

You should have a general idea of how to use conditions in if statements now, but how do you use a condition such as "Is degFahren greater than zero, but less than 100?" There are two conditions to test here. You need to test whether degFahren is greater than zero *and* whether degFahren is less than 100.

JavaScript enables you to use such multiple conditions. To do this you need to learn about three more operators, the logical operators AND, OR, and NOT. The symbols for these are listed in the following table.

Operator	Symbol
AND	&&
OR	||
NOT	!

Notice that the AND and OR operators are *two* symbols repeated: && and ||. If you type just one symbol, & or |, strange things will happen because these are special operators called *bitwise operators* used in binary operations — for logical operations you must always use two.

After you've learned about the three logical operators, you'll take a look at how to use them in if statements, with plenty of practical examples. So if it seems a bit confusing on first read, don't panic. All will become clear. Let's look at how each of these works, starting with the AND operator.

AND

Recall that we talked about the left-hand side (LHS) and the right-hand side (RHS) of the operator. The same is true with the AND operator. However, now the LHS and RHS of the condition are Boolean values (usually the result of a condition).

The AND operator works very much as it does in English. For example, you might say, "If I feel cold *and* I have a coat, then I'll put my coat on." Here, the left-hand side of the "and" word is "Do I feel cold?" and this can be evaluated as `true` or `false`. The right-hand side is "Do I have a coat?" which again is evaluated to either `true` or `false`. If the left-hand side is true (I am cold) *and* the right-hand side is true (I do have a coat), then you put your coat on.

This is very similar to how the AND operator works in JavaScript. The AND operator actually produces a result, just as adding two numbers together produces a result. However, the AND operator takes two Boolean values (on its LHS and RHS) and results in another Boolean value. If the LHS and RHS conditions evaluate to `true`, the result will be `true`. In any other circumstance, the result will be `false`.

Following is a *truth table* of possible evaluations of left-hand sides and right-hand sides and the result when AND is used.

Left-Hand Side	Right-Hand Side	Result
true	true	true
false	true	false
true	false	false
false	false	false

Although the table is, strictly speaking, true, it's worth noting that JavaScript doesn't like doing unnecessary work. Well, who does! If the left-hand side is `false`, then even if the right-hand side does evaluate to `true` it won't make any difference to the final result—it'll still be `false`. So to avoid wasting time, if the left-hand side is `false`, JavaScript doesn't even bother checking the right-hand side and just returns a result of `false`.

OR

Just like AND, OR also works much as it does in English. For example, you might say that if it is raining *or* if it is snowing, then you'll take an umbrella. If either of the conditions "it is raining" or "it is snowing" is true, then you will take an umbrella.

Again, just like AND, the OR operator acts on two Boolean values (one from its left-hand side and one from its right-hand side) and returns another Boolean value. If the left-hand side evaluates to `true` or the right-hand side evaluates to `true`, the result returned is `true`. Otherwise, the result is `false`. The following table shows the possible results.

Left-Hand Side	Right-Hand Side	Result
true	true	true
false	true	true
true	false	true
false	false	false

As with the AND operator, JavaScript likes to avoid doing things that make no difference to the final result. If the left-hand side is `true`, then whether the right-hand side is `true` or `false` makes no difference to the final result—it'll still be `true`. So, to avoid work, if the left-hand side is `true`, the right-hand side is not evaluated, and JavaScript simply returns `true`. The end result is the same—the only difference is in how JavaScript arrives at the conclusion. However, it does mean you should not rely on the right-hand side of the OR operator to be executed.

NOT

In English, we might say, "If I'm *not* hot, then I'll eat soup." The condition being evaluated is whether we're hot. The result is true or false, but in this example we act (eat soup) if the result is false.

However, JavaScript is used to executing code only if a condition is `true`. So if you want a `false` condition to cause code to execute, you need to switch that `false` value to `true` (and any `true` value to `false`). That way you can trick JavaScript into executing code after a `false` condition.

You do this using the NOT operator. This operator reverses the logic of a result; it takes one Boolean value and changes it to the other Boolean value. So it changes `true` to `false` and `false` to `true`. This is sometimes called *negation*.

To use the NOT operator, you put the condition you want reversed in parentheses and put the `!` symbol in front of the parentheses. For example:

```
if (!(degCent < 100))
{
    // Some code
}
```

Any code within the braces will be executed only if the condition `degCent < 100` is `false`.

The following table details the possible results when using NOT.

Right-Hand Side	Result
true	false
false	true

Multiple Conditions Inside an if Statement

The previous section started by asking how you could use the condition "Is degFahren greater than zero, but less than 100?" One way of doing this would be to use two if statements, one nested inside another. *Nested* simply means that there is an outer if statement, and inside this an inner if statement. If the condition for the outer if statement is true, then (and only then) the nested inner if statement's condition will be tested.

Using nested if statements, your code would be:

```
if (degCent < 100)
{
    if (degCent > 0)
    {
        document.write("degCent is between 0 and 100");
    }
}
```

This would work, but it's a little verbose and can be quite confusing. JavaScript offers a better alternative — using multiple conditions inside the condition part of the if statement. The multiple conditions are strung together with the logical operators you just looked at. So the preceding code could be rewritten like this:

```
if (degCent > 0 && degCent < 100)
{
    document.write("degCent is between 0 and 100");
}
```

The if statement's condition first evaluates whether degCent is greater than zero. If that is true, the code goes on to evaluate whether degCent is less than 100. Only if both of these conditions are true will the document.write() code line execute.

Try It Out   Multiple Conditions

This example demonstrates multi-condition if statements using the AND, OR, and NOT operators. Type in the following code, and save it as ch3_examp2.htm:

```
<html>
<body>

<script language="JavaScript" type="text/javascript">

var myAge = Number(prompt("Enter your age",30));

if (myAge >= 0 && myAge <= 10)
{
    document.write("myAge is between 0 and 10<br>");
}

if ( !(myAge >= 0 && myAge <= 10) )
{
```

```
        document.write("myAge is NOT between 0 and 10<br>");
   }

   if ( myAge >= 80 || myAge <= 10 )
   {
        document.write("myAge is 80 or above OR 10 or below<br>");
   }

   if ( (myAge >= 30 && myAge <= 39) || (myAge >= 80 && myAge <= 89) )
   {
        document.write("myAge is between 30 and 39 or myAge is between 80 and 89");
   }

   </script>

   </body>
   </html>
```

When you load it into your browser, you should see a prompt box appear. Enter the value 30, then press Return, and the lines shown in Figure 3-6 are written to the web page.

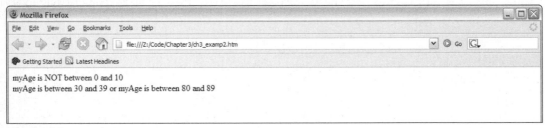

Figure 3-6

How It Works

The script block starts by defining the variable myAge and initializing it to the value entered by the user in the prompt box and converted to a number.

```
   var myAge = Number(prompt("Enter your age",30));
```

After this are four if statements, each using multiple conditions. You'll look at each in detail in turn.

The easiest way to work out what multiple conditions are doing is to split them up into smaller pieces and then evaluate the combined result. In this example you have entered the value 30, which has been stored in the variable myAge. You'll substitute this value into the conditions to see how they work.

Here's the first if statement:

```
   if (myAge >= 0 && myAge <= 10)
   {
        document.write("myAge is between 0 and 10<BR>");
   }
```

The first `if` statement is asking the question "Is `myAge` between 0 and 10?" You'll take the LHS of the condition first, substituting your particular value for `myAge`. The LHS asks "Is 30 greater than or equal to 0?" The answer is `true`. The question posed by the RHS condition is "Is 30 less than or equal to 10?" The answer is `false`. These two halves of the condition are joined using `&&`, which indicates the AND operator. Using the AND results table shown earlier, you can see that if LHS is `true` and RHS is `false`, you have an overall result of `false`. So the end result of the condition for the `if` statement is `false`, and the code inside the braces won't execute.

Let's move on to the second `if` statement.

```
if ( !(myAge >= 0 && myAge <= 10) )
{
    document.write("myAge is NOT between 0 and 10<BR>");
}
```

The second `if` statement is posing the question "Is `myAge` not between 0 and 10?" Its condition is similar to that of the first `if` statement, but with one small difference: You have enclosed the condition inside parentheses and put the NOT operator (`!`) in front.

The part of the condition inside the parentheses is evaluated and, as before, produces the same result — `false`. However, the NOT operator reverses the result and makes it `true`. Because the `if` statement's condition is `true`, the code inside the braces *will* execute this time, causing a `document.write()` to write a response to the page.

What about the third `if` statement?

```
if ( myAge >= 80 || myAge <= 10 )
{
    document.write("myAge is either 80 and above OR 10 or below<BR>");
}
```

The third `if` statement asks, "Is `myAge` greater than or equal to 80, or less than or equal to 10?" Taking the LHS condition first — "Is 30 greater than or equal to 80?" — the answer is `false`. The answer to the RHS condition — "Is 30 less than or equal to 10?" — is again `false`. These two halves of the condition are combined using `||`, which indicates the OR operator. Looking at the OR result table earlier in this section, you see that `false` OR `false` produces a result of `false`. So again the `if` statement's condition evaluates to `false`, and the code within the curly braces does not execute.

The final `if` statement is a little more complex.

```
if ( (myAge >= 30 && myAge <= 39) || (myAge >= 80 && myAge <= 89) )
{
    document.write("myAge is between 30 and 39 " +
                "or myAge is between 80 and 89<BR>");
}
```

It asks the question, "Is `myAge` between 30 and 39 or between 80 and 89?" Let's break the condition down into its component parts. There is a left-hand-side and a right-hand-side condition, combined by means of an OR operator. However, the LHS and RHS themselves have an LHS and RHS each, which are combined using AND operators. Notice how parentheses are used to tell JavaScript which parts of the condition to evaluate first, just as you would do with numbers in a mathematical calculation.

Let's look at the LHS of the condition first, namely `(myAge >= 30 && myAge <= 39)`. By putting the condition into parentheses, you ensure that it's treated as a single condition; no matter how many conditions are inside the parentheses, it only produces a single result, either `true` or `false`. Breaking down the conditions in the parentheses, you have "Is 30 greater than or equal to 30?" with a result of `true`, and "Is 30 less than or equal to 39?" again with a result of `true`. From the AND table, you know `true` AND `true` produces a result of `true`.

Now let's look at the RHS of the condition, namely `(myAge >= 80 && myAge <= 89)`. Again breaking the condition down, you see that the LHS asks, "Is 30 greater than or equal to 80?" which gives a `false` result, and the RHS asks, "Is 30 less than or equal to 89?" which gives a `true` result. You know that `false` AND `true` gives a `false` result.

Now you can think of your `if` statement's condition as looking like `(true || false)`. Looking at the OR results table, you can see that `true` OR `false` gives a result of `true`, so the code within the braces following the `if` statement will execute, and a line will be written to the page.

However, remember that JavaScript does not evaluate conditions where they won't affect the final result, and the preceding condition is one of those situations. The LHS of the condition evaluated to `true`. After that, it does not matter if the RHS of the condition is `true` or `false` because only one of the conditions in an OR operation needs to be `true` for a result of `true`. Thus JavaScript does not actually evaluate the RHS of the condition. We did so simply for demonstration purposes.

As you have seen, the easiest way to approach understanding or creating multiple conditions is to break them down into the smallest logical chunks. You'll find that with experience, you will do this almost without thinking, unless you have a particularly tricky condition to evaluate.

Although using multiple conditions is often better than using multiple `if` statements, there are times when it makes your code harder to read and therefore harder to understand and debug. It's possible to have 10, 20, or more than 100 conditions inside your `if` statement, but can you imagine trying to read an `if` statement with even 10 conditions? If you feel that your multiple conditions are getting too complex, break them down into smaller logical chunks.

For example, imagine you want to execute some code if `myAge` is in the ranges 30–39, 80–89, or 100–115, using different code in each case. You could write the statement like so:

```
if ( (myAge >= 30 && myAge <= 39) || (myAge >= 80 && myAge <= 89) ||
     (myAge >= 100 && myAge <= 115) )
{
   document.write("myAge is between 30 and 39 " +
                  "or myAge is between 80 " +
                  "and 89 or myAge is between 100 and 115");
}
```

There's nothing wrong with this, but it is starting to get a little long and difficult to read. Instead you could create another `if` statement for the code executed for the 100–115 range.

else and else if

Imagine a situation where you want some code to execute if a certain condition is true, and some other code to execute if it is false. You can achieve this by having two `if` statements, as shown in the following example:

```
if (myAge >= 0 && myAge <= 10)
{
    document.write("myAge is between 0 and 10");
}

if ( !(myAge >= 0 && myAge <= 10) )
{
    document.write("myAge is NOT between 0 and 10");
}
```

The first `if` statement tests whether `myAge` is between 0 and 10, and the second for the situation where `myAge` is not between 0 and 10. However, JavaScript provides an easier way of achieving this: with an `else` statement. Again, the use of the word `else` is similar to its use in the English language. You might say, "If it is raining, I will take an umbrella; otherwise I will take a sun hat." In JavaScript you can say `if` the condition is `true`, then execute one block of code; `else` execute an alternative block. Rewriting the preceding code using this technique, you would have the following:

```
if (myAge >= 0 && myAge <= 10)
{
    document.write("myAge is between 0 and 10");
}
else
{
    document.write("myAge is NOT between 0 and 10");
}
```

Writing the code like this makes it simpler and therefore easier to read. Plus it also saves JavaScript from testing a condition to which you already know the answer.

You could also include another `if` statement with the `else` statement. For example

```
if (myAge >= 0 && myAge <= 10)
{
    document.write("myAge is between 0 and 10");
}
else if ( (myAge >= 30 && myAge <= 39) || (myAge >= 80 && myAge <= 89) )
{
    document.write("myAge is between 30 and 39 " +
                   "or myAge is between 80 and 89");
}
else
{
    document.write("myAge is NOT between 0 and 10, " +
                   "nor is it between 30 and 39, nor is it between 80 and 89");
}
```

The first if statement checks whether myAge is between 0 and 10 and executes some code if that's true. If it's false, an else if statement checks if myAge is between 30 and 39 or 80 and 89, and executes some other code if either of those conditions is true. Failing that, you have a final else statement, which catches the situation in which the value of myAge did not trigger true in any of the earlier if conditions.

When using if and else if, you need to be extra careful with your curly braces to ensure that the if and else if statements start and stop where you expect, and you don't end up with an else that doesn't belong to the right if. This is quite tricky to describe with words — it's easier to see what we mean with an example.

```
if (myAge >= 0 && myAge <= 10)
{
document.write("myAge is between 0 and 10");
if (myAge == 5)
{
document.write("You're 5 years old");
}
else
{
document.write("myAge is NOT between 0 and 10");
}
```

Notice that we haven't indented the code. Although this does not matter to JavaScript, it does make the code more difficult for humans to read and hides the missing curly brace that should be before the final else statement.

Correctly formatted and with the missing bracket inserted, the code looks like this:

```
if (myAge >= 0 && myAge <= 10)
{
    document.write("myAge is between 0 and 10<br>");
    if (myAge == 5)
    {
        document.write("You're 5 years old");
    }
}
else
{
    document.write("myAge is NOT between 0 and 10");
}
```

As you can see, the code is working now; it is also a lot easier to see which code is part of which if block.

Comparing Strings

Up to this point you have been looking exclusively at using comparison operators with numbers. However, they work just as well with strings. All that's been said and done with numbers applies to strings, but with one important difference. You are now comparing data alphabetically rather than numerically, so there are a few traps to watch out for.

In the following code, you compare the variable myName, which contains the string "Paul", with the string literal "Paul".

```
var myName ="Paul";
if (myName == "Paul")
{
    alert("myName is Paul");
}
```

How does JavaScript deal with this? Well, it goes through each letter in turn on the LHS and checks it with the letter in the same position on the RHS to see if it's actually the same. If at any point it finds a difference, it stops, and the result is `false`. If, after having checked each letter in turn all the way to the end, it confirms that they are all the same, it returns `true`. The condition in the preceding `if` statement will return `true`, and so you'll see an `alert` box.

However, string comparison in JavaScript is case sensitive. So `"P"` is not the same as `"p"`. Taking the preceding example, but changing the variable `myName` to `"paul"`, you find that the condition is `false` and the code inside the `if` statement does not execute.

```
var myName ="paul";
if (myName == "Paul")
{
    alert("myName is Paul");
}
```

The `>=`, `>`, `<=`, and `<` operators work with strings as well as with numbers, but again it is an alphabetical comparison. So `"A" < "B"` is `true`, because A comes before B in the alphabet. However, JavaScript's case sensitivity comes into play again. `"A" < "B"` is `true`, but `"a" < "B"` is `false`. Why? Because uppercase letters are treated as always coming *before* lowercase letters. Why is this? Each letter has a code number in the ASCII and Unicode character sets, and the code numbers for uppercase letters are lower than the code numbers for lowercase letters. This is something to watch out for when writing your own code.

The simplest way to avoid confusion with different cases is to convert both strings to either uppercase or lowercase before you compare them. You can do this easily using the `toUpperCase()` or `toLowerCase()` functions, which you'll learn about in the next chapter.

The switch Statement

You saw earlier how the `if` and `else if` statements could be used for checking various conditions; if the first condition is not valid, then another is checked, and another, and so on. However, when you want to check the value of a particular variable for a large number of possible values, there is a more efficient alternative, namely the `switch` statement. The structure of the `switch` statement is given in Figure 3-7.

The best way to think of the `switch` statement is "Switch to the code where the case matches." The `switch` statement has four important elements:

- ❑ The test expression
- ❑ The `case` statements
- ❑ The `break` statements
- ❑ The `default` statement

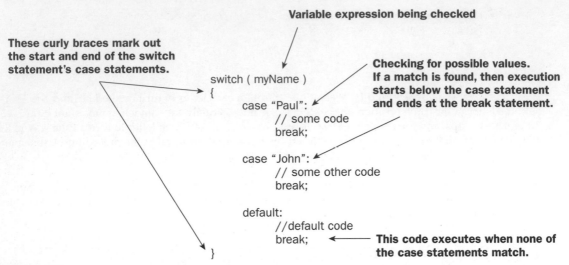

Variable expression being checked

These curly braces mark out the start and end of the switch statement's case statements.

```
switch ( myName )
{
    case "Paul":
        // some code
        break;

    case "John":
        // some other code
        break;

    default:
        //default code
        break;
}
```

Checking for possible values. If a match is found, then execution starts below the case statement and ends at the break statement.

This code executes when none of the case statements match.

Figure 3-7

The test expression is given in the parentheses following the switch keyword. In the previous example you are testing using the variable myName. Inside the parentheses, however, you could have any valid expression.

Next come the case statements. It's the case statements that do the condition checking. To indicate which case statements belong to your switch statement, you must put them inside the curly braces following the test expression. Each case statement specifies a value, for example "Paul". The case statement then acts like if (myName == "Paul"). If the variable myName did contain the value "Paul", execution would commence from the code starting below the case: "Paul" statement and would continue to the end of the switch statement. This example has only two case statements, but you can have as many as you like.

In most cases, you want only the block of code directly underneath the relevant case statement to execute, and not *all* the code below the relevant case statement, including any other case statements. To achieve this, you put a break statement at the end of the code that you want executed. This tells JavaScript to stop executing at that point and leave the switch statement.

Finally you have the default case, which (as the name suggests) is the code that will execute when none of the other case statements match. The default statement is optional; if you have no default code that you want to execute, you can leave it out, but remember that in this case no code will execute if no case statements match. It is a good idea to include a default case, unless you are absolutely sure that you have all your options covered.

Try It Out   Using the switch Statement

Let's take a look at the switch statement in action. The following example illustrates a simple guessing game. Type in the code and save it as ch3_examp3.htm.

```
<html>
<body>

<script language="JavaScript" type="text/javascript">
```

```
var secretNumber = prompt("Pick a number between 1 and 5:", "");
secretNumber = parseInt(secretNumber);

switch (secretNumber)
{
case 1:
   document.write("Too low!");
   break;

case 2:
   document.write("Too low!");
   break;

case 3:
   document.write("You guessed the secret number!");
   break;

case 4:
   document.write("Too high!");
   break;

case 5:
   document.write("Too high!");
   break;

default:
   document.write("You did not enter a number between 1 and 5.");
   break;
}
document.write("<BR>Execution continues here");

</script>

</body>
</html>
```

Load this into your browser and enter, for example, the value 1 in the prompt box. You should then see something like what is shown in Figure 3-8.

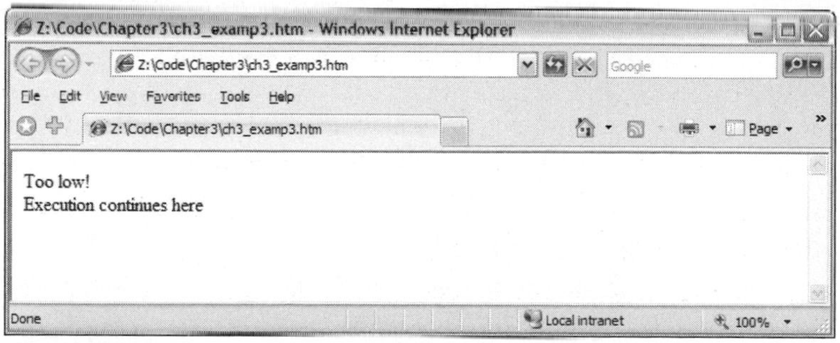

Figure 3-8

If, on the other hand, you enter the value 3, you should see a friendly message letting you know that you guessed the secret number correctly, as shown in Figure 3-9.

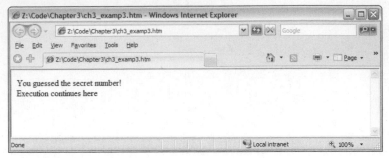

Figure 3-9

How It Works

First you declare the variable secretNumber and set it to the value entered by the user via the prompt box. Note that you use the parseInt() function to convert the string that is returned from prompt() to an integer value.

```
var secretNumber = prompt("Pick a number between 1 and 5:", "");
secretNumber = parseInt(secretNumber);
```

Next you create the start of the switch statement.

```
switch (secretNumber)
{
```

The expression in parentheses is simply the variable secretNumber, and it's this number that the case statements will be compared against.

You specify the block of code encompassing the case statements using curly braces. Each case statement checks one of the numbers between 1 and 5, because this is what you have specified to the user that she should enter. The first simply outputs a message that the number she has entered is too low.

```
case 1:
    document.write("Too low!");
    break;
```

The second case statement, for the value 2, has the same message, so the code is not repeated here. The third case statement lets the user know that she has guessed correctly.

```
case 3:
    document.write("You guessed the secret number!");
    break;
```

Finally, the fourth and fifth case statements output a message that the number the user has entered is too high.

```
case 4:
   document.write("Too high!");
   break;
```

You do need to add a `default` case in this example, since the user might very well (despite the instructions) enter a number that is not between 1 and 5, or even perhaps a letter. In this case you add a message to let the user know that there is a problem.

```
default:
   document.write("You did not enter a number between 1 and 5.");
   break;
```

A default statement is also very useful for picking up bugs — if you have coded some of the case statements incorrectly, you will pick that up very quickly if you see the `default` code being run when it shouldn't be.

You finally have added the closing brace indicating the end of the `switch` statement. After this you output a line to indicate where the execution continues.

```
}
document.write("<BR>Execution continues here");
```

Note that each `case` statement ends with a `break` statement. This is important to ensure that execution of the code moves to the line after the end of the `switch` statement. If you forget to include this, you could end up executing the code for each `case` following the `case` that matches.

Executing the Same Code for Different Cases

You may have spotted a problem with the `switch` statement in this example — you want to execute the same code if the user enters a 1 or a 2, and the same code for a 4 or a 5. However, in order to achieve this, you have had to repeat the code in each case. What you want is an easier way of getting JavaScript to execute the same code for different cases. Well, that's easy! Simply change the code so that it looks like this:

```
switch (secretNumber)
{
case 1:
case 2:
   document.write("Too low!");
   break;

case 3:
   document.write("You guessed the secret number!");
   break;

case 4:
case 5:
   document.write("Too high!");
   break;

default:
   document.write("You did not enter a number between 1 and 5.");
   break;
}
```

If you load this into your browser and experiment with entering some different numbers, you should see that it behaves exactly like the previous code.

Here, you are making use of the fact that if there is no break statement underneath the code for a certain case statement, execution will continue through each following case statement until a break statement or the end of the switch is reached. Think of it as a sort of free fall through the switch statement until you hit the break statement.

If the case statement for the value 1 is matched, execution simply continues until the break statement under case 2, so effectively you can execute the same code for both cases. The same technique is used for the case statements with values 4 and 5.

Looping — The for and while Statements

Looping means repeating a block of code when a condition is true. This is achieved in JavaScript with the use of two statements, the while statement and the for statement. You'll be looking at these shortly, but why would you want to repeat blocks of code anyway?

Well, take the situation where you have a series of results, say the average temperature for each month in a year, and you want to plot these on a graph. The code needed for plotting each point will most likely be the same. So, rather than write out the code 12 times (once for each point), it's much easier to execute the same code 12 times by using the next item of data in the series. This is where the for statement would come in handy, because you know how many times you want the code to execute.

In another situation, you might want to repeat the same piece of code when a certain condition is true, for example, while the user keeps clicking a Start Again button. In this situation, the while statement would be very useful.

The for Loop

The for statement enables you to repeat a block of code a certain number of times. The syntax is illustrated in Figure 3-10.

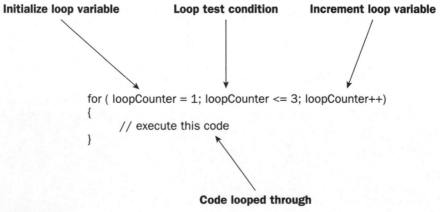

Figure 3-10

Let's look at the makeup of a `for` statement. You can see from Figure 3-10 that, just like the `if` and `switch` statements, the `for` statement also has its logic inside parentheses. However, this time that logic split into three parts, each part separated by a semicolon. For example, in Figure 3-10 you have the following:

```
(var loopCounter = 1; loopCounter <= 3; loopCounter++)
```

The first part of the `for` statement's logic is the *initialization* part of the `for` statement. To keep track of how many times you have looped through the code, you need a variable to keep count. It's in the initialization part that you initialize variables. In the example you have declared `loopCounter` and set it to the value of 1. This part is only executed once during the execution of the loops, unlike the other parts. You don't need to declare the variable if it was declared earlier in the code.

```
var loopCounter;
for (loopCounter = 1; loopCounter <= 3; loopCounter++)
```

Following the semicolon, you have the *test condition* part of the `for` statement. The code inside the `for` statement will keep executing for as long as this test condition evaluates to `true`. After the code is looped through each time, this condition is tested. In Figure 3-10, you execute for as long as `loopCounter` is less than or equal to 3. The number of times a loop is performed is often called the number of *iterations*.

Finally, you have the *increment* part of the `for` loop, where variables in our loop's test condition have their values incremented. Here you can see that `loopCounter` is incremented by one by means of the `++` operator you saw in Chapter 2. Again, this part of the `for` statement is repeated with every loop of the code. Although we call it the increment part, it can actually be used to decrease or *decrement* the value — for example, if you wanted to count down from the top element in an array to the first.

After the `for` statement comes the block of code that will be executed repeatedly, as long as the test condition is `true`. This block of code is contained within curly braces. If the condition is never `true`, even at the first test of the loop condition, then the code inside the `for` loop will be skipped over and never executed.

Putting all this together, how does the `for` loop work?

1. Execute initialization part of the `for` statement.
2. Check the test condition. If `true`, continue; if not, exit the `for` statement.
3. Execute code in the block after the `for` statement.
4. Execute the increment part of the `for` statement.
5. Repeat steps 2 through 4 until the test condition is `false`.

Try It Out   Converting a Series of Fahrenheit Values

Let's change the temperature converter so that it converts a series of values, stored in an array, from Fahrenheit to centigrade. You will be using the `for` statement to go through each element of the array. Type in the code and save it as `ch3_examp4.htm`.

```html
<html>
<body>

<script language="JavaScript" type="text/javascript">
```

```
var degFahren = new Array(212, 32, -459.15);
var degCent = new Array();
var loopCounter;

for (loopCounter = 0; loopCounter <= 2; loopCounter++)
{
   degCent[loopCounter] = 5/9 * (degFahren[loopCounter] - 32);
}

for (loopCounter = 2; loopCounter >= 0; loopCounter--)
{
   document.write("Value " + loopCounter + " was " + degFahren[loopCounter] +
               " degrees Fahrenheit");
   document.write(" which is " + degCent[loopCounter] +
               " degrees centigrade<BR>");
}

</script>

</body>
</html>
```

On loading this into your browser, you'll see a series of three lines in the page, containing the results of converting our array of Fahrenheit values into centigrade (as shown in Figure 3-11).

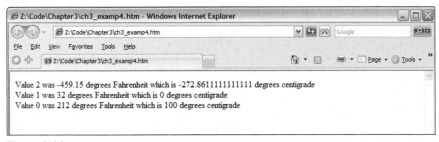

Figure 3-11

How It Works

The first task is to declare the variables you are going to use. First, you declare and initialize degFahren to contain an array of three values: 212, 32, and -459.15. Next, degCent is declared as an empty array. Finally, loopCounter is declared and will be used to keep track of which array index you are accessing during your looping.

```
var degFahren = new Array(212, 32, -459.15);
var degCent = new Array();
var loopCounter;
```

Following this comes our first for loop.

```
for (loopCounter = 0; loopCounter <= 2; loopCounter++)
{
    degCent[loopCounter] = 5/9 * (degFahren[loopCounter] - 32);
}
```

In the first line, you start by initializing the `loopCounter` to 0. Then the `for` loop's test condition, `loopCounter <= 2`, is checked. If this condition is `true`, the loop executes for the first time. After the code inside the curly braces has executed, the incrementing part of the `for` loop, `loopCounter++`, will be executed, and then the test condition will be re-evaluated. If it's still `true`, another execution of the loop code is performed. This continues until the `for` loop's test condition evaluates to `false`, at which point looping will end, and the first statement after the closing curly brace will be executed.

The code inside the curly braces is the equation you saw in earlier examples, only this time you are placing its result into the `degCent` array, with the index being the value of `loopCounter`.

In the second `for` loop, you write the results contained in the `degCent` array to the screen.

```
for (loopCounter = 2; loopCounter >= 0; loopCounter--)
{
    document.write("Value " + loopCounter + " was " + degFahren[loopCounter] +
                   " degrees Fahrenheit");
    document.write(" which is " + degCent[loopCounter] +
                   " degrees centigrade<BR>");
}
```

This time you're counting *down* from 2 to 0. The variable `loopCounter` is initialized to 2, and the loop condition remains `true` until `loopCounter` is less than 0. This time `loopCounter` is actually decremented each time rather than incremented, by means of `loopCounter--`. Again, `loopCounter` is serving a dual purpose: It keeps count of how many loops you have done and also provides the index position in the array.

Note that in these examples, you've used whole numbers in your loops. However, there is no reason why you can't use fractional numbers, although it's much less common to do so.

The for...in Loop

This loop works primarily with arrays, and as you'll see in the next chapter, it also works with something called objects. It enables you to loop through each element in the array without having to know how many elements the array actually contains. In plain English, what this loop says is "For each element in the array, execute some code." Rather than your having to work out the index number of each element, the `for...in` loop does it for you and automatically moves to the next index with each iteration (loop through).

Its syntax for use with arrays is:

```
for (index in arrayName)
{
    //some code
}
```

In this code extract, index is a variable you declare prior to the loop, which will automatically be populated with the next index value in the array. arrayName is the name of the variable holding the array you want to loop through.

Let's look at an example to make things clearer. You'll define an array and initialize it with three values.

```
var myArray = new Array("Paul","Paula","Pauline");
```

To access each element using a conventional for loop, you'd write this:

```
var loopCounter;
for (loopCounter = 0; loopCounter < 3; loopCounter++)
{
    document.write(myArray[loopCounter]);
}
```

To do exactly the same thing with the for...in loop, you write this:

```
var elementIndex;
for (elementIndex in myArray)
{
    document.write(myArray[elementIndex]);
}
```

As you can see, the code in the second example is a little clearer, as well as being shorter. Both methods work equally well and will iterate three times. However, if you increase the size of the array, for example by adding the element myArray[3] = "Philip", the first method will still loop only through the first three elements in the array, whereas the second method will loop through all four elements.

The while Loop

Whereas the for loop is used for looping a certain number of times, the while loop enables you to test a condition and keep on looping while it's true. The for loop is useful when you know how many times you need to loop, for example when you are looping through an array that you know has a certain number of elements. The while loop is more useful when you don't know how many times you'll need to loop. For example, if you are looping through an array of temperature values and want to continue looping when the temperature value contained in the array element is less than 100, you will need to use the while statement.

Let's take a look at the structure of the while statement, as illustrated in Figure 3-12.

You can see that the while loop has fewer parts to it than the for loop. The while loop consists of a condition which, if it evaluates to true, causes the block of code inside the curly braces to execute once; then the condition is re-evaluated. If it's still true, the code is executed again, the condition is re-evaluated again, and so on until the condition evaluates to false.

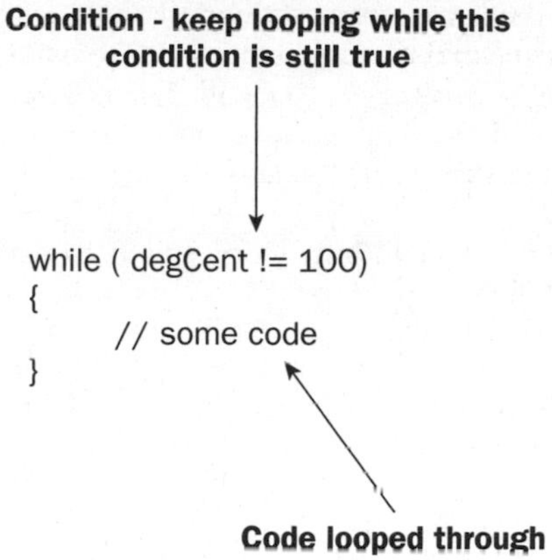

**Condition - keep looping while this
condition is still true**

```
while ( degCent != 100)
{
        // some code
}
```

Code looped through

Figure 3-12

One thing to watch out for is that if the condition is `false` to start with, the `while` loop never executes. For example:

```
degCent = 100;

while (degCent != 100)
{
        // some code
}
```

Here, the loop will run if `degCent` does not equal `100`. However, since `degCent` is `100`, the condition is `false`, and the code never executes.

In practice you would normally expect the loop to execute once; whether it executes again will depend on what the code inside the loop has done to variables involved in the loop condition. For example:

```
degCent = new Array();
degFahren = new Array(34, 123, 212);
var loopCounter = 0;
while (loopCounter < 3)
{
    degCent[loopCounter] = 5/9 * (degFahren[loopCounter] - 32);
    loopCounter++;
}
```

The loop will execute so long as `loopCounter` is less than `3`. It's the code inside the loop (`loopCounter++;`) that increments `loopCounter` and will eventually cause `loopCounter < 3` to be `false` so that the loop stops. Execution will then continue on the first line after the closing brace of the `while` statement.

Something to watch out for is the *infinite loop*—a loop that will never end. Suppose you forgot to include the `loopCounter++;` line in the code. Leaving this line out would mean that `loopCounter` will remain at 0, so the condition (`loopCounter < 3`) will always be `true`, and the loop will continue until the user gets bored and cross, and shuts down her browser. However, it is an easy mistake to make and one JavaScript won't warn you about.

It's not just missing lines that can cause infinite loops, but also mistakes inside the loop's code. For example:

```
var testVariable = 0;
while (testVariable <= 10)
{
    alert("Test Variable is " + testVariable);
    testVariable++;
    if (testVariable = 10)
    {
        alert("The last loop");
    }
}
```

See if you can spot the deliberate mistake that leads to an infinite loop—yes, it's the `if` statement that will cause this code to go on forever. Instead of using `==` as the comparison operator in the condition of the `if` statement, you put `=`, so `testVariable` is set to 10 again in each loop, despite the line `testVariable++`. This means that at the start of each loop, the test condition always evaluates to `true`, since 10 is less than or equal to 10. Put the extra `=` in to make `if (testVariable == 10)`, and everything is fine.

The do...while loop

With the `while` loop, you saw that the code inside the loop only executes if the condition is `true`; if it's `false`, the code never executes, and execution instead moves to the first line after the `while` loop. However, there may be times when you want the code in the `while` loop to execute at least once, regardless of whether the condition in the `while` statement evaluates to `true`. It might even be that some code inside the `while` loop needs to be executed before you can test the `while` statement's condition. It's situations like this for which the `do...while` loop is ideal.

Look at an example in which you want to get the user's age via a prompt box. You want to show the prompt box but also make sure that what the user has entered is a number.

```
var userAge;
do
{
    userAge = prompt("Please enter your age","")
}
while (isNaN(userAge) == true);
```

The code line within the loop—

```
userAge = prompt("Please enter your age","")
```

—will be executed regardless of the `while` statement's condition. This is because the condition is not checked *until* one loop has been executed. If the condition is `true`, the code is looped through again. If it's `false`, then looping stops.

Note that within the while statement's condition, you are using the isNaN() function that you saw in Chapter 2. This checks whether the userAge variable's value is NaN (not a number). If it is not a number, the condition returns a value of true; otherwise it returns false. As you can see from the example, it enables you to test the user input to ensure the right data has been entered. The user might lie about his age, but at least you know he entered a number!

The do...while loop is fairly rare; there's not much you can't do without it, so it's best avoided unless really necessary.

The break and continue Statements

You met the break statement earlier when you looked at the switch statement. Its function inside a switch statement is to stop code execution and move execution to the next line of code after the closing curly brace of the switch statement. However, the break statement can also be used as part of the for and while loops when you want to exit the loop prematurely. For example, suppose you're looping through an array, as you did in the temperature conversion example, and you hit an invalid value. In this situation, you might want to stop the code in its tracks, notify the user that the data is invalid, and leave the loop. This is one situation where the break statement comes in handy.

Let's see how you could change the example where you converted a series of Fahrenheit values (ch3_examp4.htm) so that if you hit a value that's not a number you stop the loop and let the user know about the invalid data.

```
<script language="JavaScript" type="text/javascript">
var degFahren = new Array(212, "string data", -459.67);
var degCent = new Array();
var loopCounter;

for (loopCounter = 0; loopCounter <= 2; loopCounter++)
{
    if (isNaN(degFahren[loopCounter]))
        {
            alert("Data '" + degFahren[loopCounter] + "' at array index " +
                loopCounter + " is invalid");
            break;
        }

    degCent[loopCounter] = 5/9 * (degFahren[loopCounter] - 32);
}
```

You have changed the initialization of the degFahren array so that it now contains some invalid data. Then, inside the for loop, an if statement is added to check whether the data in the degFahren array is not a number. This is done by means of the isNaN() function; it returns true if the value passed to it in the parentheses, here degFahren[loopCounter], is not a number. If the value is not a number, you tell the user where in the array you have the invalid data. Then you break out of the for loop altogether, using the break statement, and code execution continues on the first line after the end of the for statement.

That's the break statement, but what about continue? The continue statement is similar to break in that it stops the execution of a loop at the point where it is found, but instead of leaving the loop, it starts execution at the next iteration, starting with the for or while statement's condition being re-evaluated, just as if the last line of the loop's code had been reached.

In the break example, it was all or nothing — if even one piece of data was invalid, you broke out of the loop. It might be better if you tried to convert all the values in degFahren, but if you hit an invalid item of data in the array, you notify the user and continue with the next item, rather than giving up as our break statement example does.

```
if (isNaN(degFahren[loopCounter]))
    {
        alert("Data '" + degFahren[loopCounter] + "' at array index " +
            loopCounter + " is invalid");
        continue;
    }
```

Just change the break statement to a continue. You will still get a message about the invalid data, but the third value will also be converted.

Functions

A function is something that performs a particular task. Take a pocket calculator as an example. It performs lots of basic calculations, such as addition and subtraction. However, many also have function keys that perform more complex operations. For example, some calculators have a button for calculating the square root of a number, and others even provide statistical functions, such as the calculation of an average. Most of these functions could be done with the basic mathematical operations of add, subtract, multiply, and divide, but that might take a lot of steps — it's much simpler for the user if she only needs to press one button. All she needs to do is provide the data — numbers in this case — and the function key does the rest.

Functions in JavaScript work a little like the function buttons on a pocket calculator: They encapsulate a block of code that performs a certain task. Over the course of the book so far, you have come across a number of handy built-in functions that perform a certain task, such as the parseInt() and parseFloat() functions, which convert strings to numbers, and the isNaN() function, which tells you whether a particular value can be converted to a number. Some of these functions return data, such as parseInt(), which returns an integer number; others simply perform an action, but return no data. You'll also notice that some functions can be passed data, whereas others cannot. For example, the isNaN() function needs to be passed some data, which it checks to see if it is NaN. The data that a function requires to be passed are known as its *parameter(s)*.

As you work your way through the book, you'll be coming across many more useful built-in functions, but wouldn't it be great to be able to write your own functions? After you've worked out, written, and debugged a block of code to perform a certain task, it would be nice to be able to call it again and again when you need it. JavaScript gives us the ability to do just that, and this is what you'll be concentrating on in this section.

Creating Your Own Functions

Creating and using your own functions is very simple. Figure 3-13 shows an example of a function.

You've probably already realized what this function does and how the code works. Yes, it's the infamous Fahrenheit-to-centigrade conversion code again.

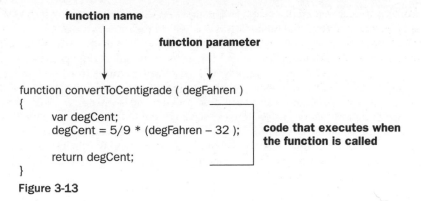

function name

function parameter

```
function convertToCentigrade ( degFahren )
{
        var degCent;
        degCent = 5/9 * (degFahren – 32 );

        return degCent;
}
```

code that executes when the function is called

Figure 3-13

Each function you define in JavaScript must be given a unique name for that particular page. The name comes immediately after the `function` keyword. To make life easier for yourself, try using meaningful names so that when you see it being used later in your code, you'll know exactly what it does. For example, a function that takes as its parameters someone's birthday and today's date and returns the person's age could be called `getAge()`. However, the names you can use are limited, much as variable names are. For example, you can't use words reserved by JavaScript, so you can't call your function `with()` or `while()`.

The parameters for the function are given in parentheses after the function's name. A parameter is just an item of data that the function needs to be given in order to do its job. Usually, not passing the required parameters will result in an error. A function can have zero or more parameters, though even if it has no parameters you must still put the open and close parentheses after its name. For example, the top of your function definition must look like the following:

```
function myNoParamFunction()
```

You then write the code, which the function will execute when called on to do so. All the function code must be put in a block with a pair of curly braces.

Functions also give you the ability to return a value from a function to the code that called it. You use the `return` statement to return a value. In the example function given earlier, you return the value of the variable `degCent`, which you have just calculated. You don't have to return a value if you don't want to, but you should always include a `return` statement at the end of your function, although JavaScript is a very forgiving language and won't have a problem if you don't use a `return` statement at all.

When JavaScript comes across a `return` statement in a function, it treats it a bit like a `break` statement in a `for` loop — it exits the function, returning any value specified after the `return` keyword.

You'll probably find it useful to build up a "library" of functions that you use frequently in JavaScript code, which you can cut and paste into your page whenever you need them.

Having created your functions, how do you use them? Unlike the code you've seen so far, which executes when JavaScript reaches that line, functions only execute if you ask them to, which is termed *calling* or *invoking* the function. You call a function by writing its name at the point where you want it to be called and making sure that you pass any parameters it needs, separated by commas. For example:

```
myTemp = convertToCentigrade(212);
```

This line calls the `convertToCentigrade()` function you saw earlier, passing `212` as the parameter and storing the `return` value from the function (that is, `100`) in the `myTemp` variable.

Have a go at creating your own functions now, taking a closer look at how parameters are passed. Parameter passing can be a bit confusing, so you'll first create a simple function that takes just one parameter (the user's name) and writes it to the page in a friendly welcome string. First, you need to think of a name for your function. A short but descriptive name is `writeUserWelcome()`. Now you need to define what parameters the function expects to be passed. There's only one parameter — the user name. Defining parameters is a little like defining variables — you need to stick to the same rules for naming, so that means no spaces, special characters, or reserved words. Let's call your parameter `userName`. You need to add it inside parentheses to the end of the function name (note that you don't put a semicolon at the end of the line).

```
function writeUserWelcome(userName)
```

Okay, now you have defined your function name and its parameters; all that's left is to create the function body — that is, the code that will be executed when the function is called. You mark out this part of the function by wrapping it in curly braces.

```
function writeUserWelcome(userName)
{
    document.write("Welcome to my website " + userName + "<br>");
    document.write("Hope you enjoy it!");
}
```

The code is simple enough; you write out a message to the web page using `document.write()`. You can see that `userName` is used just as you'd use any normal variable; in fact, it's best to think of parameters as normal variables. The value that the parameter has will be that specified by the JavaScript code where the function was called.

Let's see how you would call this function.

```
writeUserWelcome("Paul");
```

Simple, really — just write the name of the function you want to call, and then in parentheses add the data to be passed to each of the parameters, here just one piece. When the code in the function is executed, the variable `userName`, used in the body of the function code, will contain the text `"Paul"`.

Suppose you wanted to pass two parameters to your function — what would you need to change? Well, first you'd have to alter the function definition. Imagine that the second parameter will hold the user's age — you could call it `userAge` since that makes it pretty clear what the parameter's data represents. Here is the new code:

```
function writeUserWelcome(userName, userAge)
{
    document.write("Welcome to my website" + userName + "<br>");
    document.write("Hope you enjoy it<br>");
    document.write("Your age is " + userAge);
}
```

You've added a line to the body of the function that uses the parameter you have added. To call the function, you'd write the following:

```
writeUserWelcome("Paul",31);
```

The second parameter is a number, so there is no need for quotes around it. Here the userName parameter will be Paul, and the second parameter, userAge, will be 31.

Try It Out   Fahrenheit to Centigrade Function

Let's rewrite the temperature converter page using functions. You can cut and paste most of this code from ch3_examp4.htm—the parts that have changed have been highlighted. When you've finished, save it as ch3_examp5.htm.

```
<html>
<body>

<script language="JavaScript" type="text/javascript">

function convertToCentigrade(degFahren)
{
   var degCent;
   degCent = 5/9 * (degFahren - 32);

   return degCent;
}

var degFahren = new Array(212, 32, -459.15);
var degCent = new Array();
var loopCounter;

for (loopCounter = 0; loopCounter <= 2; loopCounter++)
{
   degCent[loopCounter] = convertToCentigrade(degFahren[loopCounter]);
}

for (loopCounter = 2; loopCounter >= 0; loopCounter--)
{
   document.write("Value " + loopCounter + " was " + degFahren[loopCounter] +
               " degrees Fahrenheit");
   document.write(" which is " + degCent[loopCounter] +
               " degrees centigrade<br>");
}

</script>

</body>
</html>
```

When you load this page into your browser, you should see exactly the same results that you had with ch3_examp4.htm.

How It Works

At the top of the script block you declare your `convertToCentigrade()` function. You saw this function earlier:

```
function convertToCentigrade(degFahren)
{
   var degCent;
   degCent = 5/9 * (degFahren - 32);

   return degCent;
}
```

If you're using a number of separate `script` blocks in a page, it's very important that the function be defined before any script calls it. If you have a number of functions, you may want to put them all in their own script block at the top of the page — between the `<head>` and `</head>` tags is good. That way you know where to find all your functions, and you can be sure that they have been declared before they have been used.

You should be pretty familiar with how the code in the function works. You declare a variable `degCent`, do your calculation, store its result in `degCent`, and then return `degCent` back to the calling code. The function's parameter is `degFahren`, which provides the information the calculation needs.

Following the function declaration is the code that executes when the page loads. First you define the variables you need, and then you have the two loops that calculate and then output the results. This is mostly the same as before, apart from the first `for` loop.

```
for (loopCounter = 0; loopCounter <= 2; loopCounter++)
{
   degCent[loopCounter] = convertToCentigrade(degFahren[loopCounter]);
}
```

The code inside the first `for` loop puts the value returned by the function `convertToCentigrade()` into the `degCent` array.

There is a subtle point to the code in this example. Notice that you declare the variable `degCent` within your function `convertToCentigrade()`, and you also declare it as an array after the function definition.

Surely this isn't allowed?

Well, this leads neatly to the next topic of this chapter — variable scope.

Variable Scope and Lifetime

What is meant by *scope*? Well, put simply, it's the scope or extent of a variable's availability — which parts of your code can access a variable and the data it contains. Any variables declared in a web page outside of a function will be available to all script on the page, whether that script is inside a function or otherwise — we term this a *global* or *page-level scope*. However, variables declared inside a function are visible *only* inside that function — no code outside the function can access them. So, for example, you could declare a variable degCent in every function you have on a page *and* once on the page outside any function. However, you can't declare the variable *more* than once inside any one function or *more* than once on the page outside the functions. Note that reusing a variable name throughout a page in this way, although not illegal, is not standard good practice — it can make the code very confusing to read.

Function parameters are similar to variables: They can't be seen outside the function, and although you can declare a variable in a function with the same name as one of its parameters, it would cause a lot of confusion and might easily lead to subtle bugs being overlooked. It's therefore bad coding practice and best avoided, if only for the sake of your sanity when it comes to debugging!

So what happens when the code inside a function ends and execution returns to the point at which the code was called? Do the variables defined within the function retain their value when you call the function the next time?

The answer is no: Variables not only have the scope property — where they are visible — but they also have a *lifetime*. When the function finishes executing, the variables in that function die and their values are lost, unless you return one of them to the calling code. Every so often JavaScript performs garbage collection (which we talked about in Chapter 2), whereby it scans through the code and sees if any variables are no longer in use; if so, the data they hold are freed from memory to make way for the data of other variables.

Given that global variables can be used anywhere, why not make all of them global? Global variables are great when you need to keep track of data on a global basis. However, because they are available for modification anywhere in your code, it does mean that if they are changed incorrectly due to a bug, that bug could be anywhere within the code, making debugging difficult. It's best, therefore, to keep global variable use to a minimum, though sometimes they are a necessary evil — for example, when you need to share data among different functions.

The Trivia Quiz — Building One of the Basic Functions

In the previous chapter you declared the arrays that hold the questions and answers for your trivia quiz. You also populated these arrays with the first three questions. At that point you didn't have enough knowledge to actually make use of the data, but with what you've learned in this chapter, you can create a function that uses the information in the arrays to check whether an answer is correct.

Load trivia_quiz.htm and alter it as shown here:

```html
<html>
<head>
<title>Wrox Online Trivia Quiz</title>

<script language="JavaScript" type="text/javascript">

function answerCorrect(questionNumber, answer)
{
```

```
    // declare a variable to hold return value
    var correct = false;

    // if answer provided is same as correct answer then correct variable is true
    if (answer == answers[questionNumber])
        correct = true;

    // return whether the answer was correct (true or false)
    return correct;
}
```

```
// Questions variable will holds questions
var questions = new Array();
var answers = new Array();

// define question 1
questions[0] = new Array();

// the question
questions[0][0] = "The Beatles were";

// first choice
questions[0][1] = "A sixties rock group from Liverpool";

// second choice
questions[0][2] = "Four musically gifted insects";

// third choice
questions[0][3] = "German cars";

// fourth choice
questions[0][4] = "I don't know. Can I have the questions on baseball please?";

// assign answer for question 1
answers[0] = "A";

// define question 2
questions[1] = new Array();
questions[1][0] = "Homer Simpson's favorite food is";
questions[1][1] = "Fresh salad";
questions[1][2] = "Doughnuts";
questions[1][3] = "Bread and water";
questions[1][4] = "Apples";

// assign answer for question 2
answers[1] = "B";

// define question 3
questions[2] = new Array();
questions[2][0] = "Lisa Simpson plays which musical instrument?";
questions[2][1] = "Clarinet";
```

```
    questions[2][2] = "Oboe";
    questions[2][3] = "Saxophone";
    questions[2][4] = "Tubular bells";

    // assign answer for question 3
    answers[2] = "C";
    </script>
    </head>

    <body>

    </body>
    </html>
```

The only changes here are that you've removed the alert() function, which told the user that the array was initialized, and added a function, answerCorrect(), which checks whether a trivia question has been answered correctly. This function has been added inside the script block in the head of the page. The answerCorrect() function takes two parameters: the question index from the arrays in the parameter questionNumber and the answer the user has given in the parameter answer. It then checks whether the user's answer is in fact correct—if it is, the function returns true, otherwise it returns false.

Currently the code checks the answer given by the user by checking to see whether the element of the answers array with an index of questionNumber is equal to the answer parameter. Given how simple this function is, couldn't you have just included the code wherever it's needed? Why go to the bother of creating a function? The answer to this query is that we have plans for that function. Currently, its role is simply to check whether the multiple-choice response, a single letter given by the user, is the same as the letter stored in the answers array. However, later we'll expand the trivia quiz to handle text-based questions such as, "Which President was involved in the Watergate scandal?" and we want the answer to be considered correct whether the user enters Richard Nixon, Nixon, R Nixon, and so on. This involves more than a simple comparison, so at some point we'll expand the answerCorrect() function to incorporate this extra intelligence. By including it in just one function, you need to change your code in only one place and can do so without breaking other parts of your program. Code using your function expects only a true or false result—how this function comes by this result is irrelevant.

To test your new answerCorrect() function, let's write some code that goes through each of the questions in the questions array and uses the answerCorrect() function to work out which answer is correct. Insert the following lines into the body of the page, inside the script block after the questions and answers array have been defined. After you've finished testing, you can delete this code because it does not form part of the final trivia quiz.

```
    // define question 3
    questions[2] = new Array();
    questions[2][0] = "Lisa Simpson plays which musical instrument";
    questions[2][1] = "Clarinet";
    questions[2][2] = "Oboe";
    questions[2][3] = "Saxophone";
    questions[2][4] = "Tubular Bells";

    // assign answer for question 3
    answers[2] = "C";

    </script>
```

```
</head>
<body>
```

```
<script language="javascript" type="text/javascript">
document.write("The Answer to Question 1 is " + answers[0] + "<br>");
document.write("The Answer to Question 2 is " + answers[1] + "<br>");
document.write("The Answer to Question 3 is " + answers[2]);
</script>
</body>
</html>
```

The code writes all the answers to the page by accessing the answer array and getting the letter in there that corresponds to the correct answer for each question.

If you load trivia_quiz.htm into your browser, you should see what is shown in Figure 3-14.

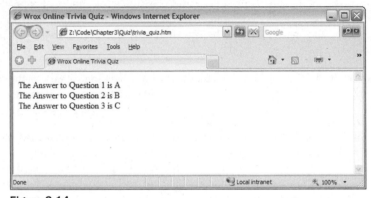

Figure 3-14

Note that the questions and answers arrays holding the question and answer data have global scope within the page, something that we warned you about in the previous section. However, here it is necessary because the arrays need to be accessed by both the function and the JavaScript code within the page.

Summary

In this chapter you have concluded your look at the core of the JavaScript language and its syntax. Everything from now on builds on these foundations, and with the less interesting syntax under your belt, you can move on to more interesting things in the remainder of the book.

The chapter looked at the following:

❑ **Decision making with the** if **and** switch **statements.** The ability to make decisions is essentially what gives the code its "intelligence." Based on whether a condition is true or false, you can decide on a course of action to follow.

❑ **Comparison operators.** The comparison operators compare the value on the left of the operator (left-hand side, LHS) with the value on the right of the operator (right-hand side, RHS) and return a Boolean value. Here is a lost of the main comparison operators:

  ❑ == is the LHS equal to the RHS?

  ❑ != is the LHS not equal to the RHS?

  ❑ <= is the LHS less than or equal to the RHS?

  ❑ >= is the LHS greater than or equal to the RHS?

  ❑ < is the LHS less than the RHS?

  ❑ > is the LHS greater than the RHS?

❑ **The if statement.** Using the if statement, you can choose to execute a block of code (defined by being in curly braces) when a condition is true. The if statement has a test condition, specified in parentheses. If this condition evaluates to true, the code after the if statement will execute.

❑ **The else statement.** If you want code to execute when the if statement is false, you can use the else statement that appears after the if statement.

❑ **Logical operators.** To combine conditions, you can use the three logical operators: AND, OR, and NOT, represented by &&, ||, and !, respectively.

  ❑ The AND operator returns true only if both sides of the expression are true.

  ❑ The OR operator returns true when either one or both sides of an expression are true.

  ❑ The NOT operator reverses the logic of an expression.

❑ **The switch statement.** This compares the result of an expression with a series of possible cases, and is similar in effect to a multiple if statement.

❑ **Looping with for, for...in, while, and do...while.** It's often necessary to repeat a block of code a number of times, something JavaScript enables by looping.

  ❑ **The for loop.** Useful for looping through code a certain number of times, the for loop consists of three parts: the initialization, test condition, and increment parts. Looping continues while the test condition is true. Each loop executes the block of code and then executes the increment part of the for loop before re-evaluating the test condition to see if the results of incrementing have changed it.

  ❑ **The for...in loop.** This is useful when you want to loop through an array without knowing the number of elements in the array. JavaScript works this out for you so that no elements are missed.

  ❑ **The while loop.** This is useful for looping through some code for as long as a test condition remains true. It consists of a test condition and the block of code that's executed only if the condition is true. If the condition is never true, then the code never executes.

  ❑ **The do...while loop.** This is similar to a while loop, except that it executes the code once and then keeps executing the code as long as the test condition remains true.

❑ break **and** continue **statements.** Sometimes you have a good reason to break out of a loop prematurely, in which case you need to use the break statement. On hitting a break statement, code execution stops for the block of code marked out by the curly braces and starts immediately after the closing brace. The continue statement is similar to break, except that when code execution stops at that point in the loop, the loop is not broken out of, but instead continues as if the end of that reiteration had been reached.

❑ **Functions are reusable bits of code.** JavaScript has a lot of built-in functions that provide programmers services, such as converting a string to a number. However, JavaScript also enables you to define and use your own functions using the function keyword. Functions can have zero or more parameters passed to them and can return a value if you so wish.

❑ **Variable scope and lifetime.** Variables declared outside a function are available globally — that is, anywhere in the page. Any variables defined inside a function are private to that function and can't be accessed outside of it. Variables have a lifetime, the length of which depends on where the variable was declared. If it's a global variable, its lifetime is that of the page — while the page is loaded in the browser, the variable remains alive. For variables defined in a function, the lifetime is limited to the execution of that function. When the function has finished being executed, the variables die, and their values are lost. If the function is called again later in the code, the variables will be empty.

Exercise Questions

Suggested solutions to these questions can be found in Appendix A.

Question 1

A junior programmer comes to you with some code that appears not to work. Can you spot where he went wrong? Give him a hand and correct the mistakes.

```
var userAge = prompt("Please enter your age");

if (userAge = 0);
{
    alert("So you're a baby!");
}
else if ( userAge < 0 | userAge > 200)
    alert("I think you may be lying about your age");
else
{
    alert("That's a good age");
}
```

Question 2

Using document.write(), write code that displays the results of the 12 times table. Its output should be the results of the calculations.

```
12 * 1 = 12
12 * 2 = 24
12 * 3 = 36
.....
12 * 11 = 132
12 * 12 = 144
```

Question 3

Change the code of Question 2 so that it's a function that takes as parameters the times table required and the values at which it should start and end. For example, you might try the four times table displayed starting with 4 * 4 and ending at 4 * 9.

Question 4

Modify the code of Question 3 to request the times table to be displayed from the user; the code should continue to request and display times tables until the user enters -1. Additionally, do a check to make sure that the user is entering a valid number; if the number is not valid, ask her to re-enter it.

JavaScript — An Object-Based Language

In this chapter, you look at a concept that is central to JavaScript, namely *objects*. But what are objects, and why are they useful?

First, we have to break it to you: You have been using objects throughout this book (for example, an array is an object). JavaScript is an object-based language, and therefore much of what you do involves manipulating objects. You'll see that when you make full use of these objects, the range of things you can do with JavaScript expands immensely.

We'll start this chapter by taking a look at the idea of what objects are and why they are important. We'll move on to what kinds of objects are used in JavaScript, how to create them and use them, and how they simplify many programming tasks for you. Finally, you'll see in more detail some of the most useful objects that JavaScript provides and how to use these in practical situations.

Not only does JavaScript itself consist of a number of these things called objects (which are also called *native JavaScript objects*), but also the browser itself is modeled as a collection of objects available for your use. You'll learn about these objects in particular in the next chapter.

Object-Based Programming

Object-based programming is a slightly scarier way of saying "programming using objects." But what are these objects that you will be programming with? Where are they, and how and why would you want to program with them? In this section, you'll look at the answers to these questions, both in general programming terms and more specifically within JavaScript.

A Brief Introduction to Objects

To start the introduction to objects, let's think about what is meant by an object in the "real world" outside computing. The world is composed of things, or objects, such as tables, chairs, and cars (to name just a few!). Let's take a car as an example, to explore what an object really is.

How would you define our car? You might say it's a blue car with four-wheel drive. You might specify the speed at which it's traveling. When you do this, you are specifying *properties* of the object. For example, the car has a color property, which in this instance has the value blue.

How do you use our car? You turn the ignition key, press the gas pedal, beep the horn, change the gear (that is, choose between 1, 2, 3, 4, and reverse on a manual car, or drive and reverse on an automatic), and so on. When you do this, you are using *methods* of the object.

You can think of methods as being a bit like functions. Sometimes, you may need to use some information with the method, or pass it a parameter, to get it to work. For example, when you use the changing gears method, you need to say which gear you want to change to. Other methods may pass information back to the owner. For example, the dipstick method will tell the owner how much oil is left in the car.

Sometimes using one or more of the methods may change one or more of the object's properties. For example, using the accelerator method will probably change the car's speed property. Other properties can't be changed: for example, the body-shape property of the car (unless you hit a brick wall with the speed property at 100 miles per hour!).

You could say that the car is defined by its collection of methods and properties. In object-based programming, the idea is to model real-world situations by objects, which are defined by their methods and properties.

Objects in JavaScript

You should now have a basic idea of what an object is—a "thing" with methods and properties. But how do you use this concept in JavaScript?

In the previous chapters you have (for the most part) been dealing with *primitive* data. These are *actual* data, such as strings and numbers. This type of data is not too complex and is fairly easy to deal with. However, not all information is as simple as primitive data. Let's look at an example to clarify things a little.

Suppose you had written a web application that displayed timetable information for buses or trains. Once the user has selected a journey, you might want to let him know how long that journey will take. To do that, you need to subtract the arrival time from the departure time.

However, that's not quite as simple as it may appear at first glance. For example, consider a departure time of 14:53 (for 2:53 p.m.) and an arrival time of 15:10 (for 3:10 p.m.). If you tell JavaScript to evaluate the expression 15.10–14.53, you get the result 0.57, which is 57 minutes. However, you know that the real difference in time is 17 minutes. Using the normal mathematical operators on times doesn't work!

What would you need to do to calculate the difference between these two times? You would first need to separate the hours from the minutes in each time. Then, to get the difference in minutes between the two times, you would need to check whether the minutes of the arrival time were greater than the minutes of the departure. If so, you can simply subtract the departure time minutes from the arrival time minutes. If not, you need to add 60 to the arrival time minutes and subtract one from the arrival time hours to compensate, before taking the departure time minutes from the arrival time minutes. You then need to subtract the departure time hours from the arrival time hours, before putting the minutes and hours that you have arrived at back together.

This would work okay so long as the two times were in the same day. It wouldn't work, for example, with the times 23:45 and 04:32.

This way of working out the time difference obviously has its problems, but it also seems very complex. Is there an easier way to deal with more complex data such as times and dates?

This is where objects come in. You can define your departure and arrival times as Date objects. Because they are Date objects, they come with a variety of properties and methods that you can use when you need to manipulate or calculate times. For example, you can use the getTime() method to get the number of milliseconds between the time in the Date object and January 1, 1970, 00:00:00. Once you have these millisecond values for the arrival and departure times, you can simply subtract one from the other and store the result in another Date object. To retrieve the hours and minutes of this time, you simply use the getHours() and getMinutes() methods of the Date object. You'll see more examples of this later in the chapter.

The Date object is not the only object that JavaScript has to offer. Another object was introduced in Chapter 2, but to keep things simple, we didn't tell you it was an object at the time. That object was the Array object. Recall that an array is a way of holding a number of pieces of data at the same time.

Array objects have a property called length that tells you how many pieces of data, or rather how many elements, the array holds. You actually used this property in the trivia quiz in Chapter 3 to work out how many times you needed to loop through the array.

Array objects also have a number of methods. One example is the sort() method, which can be used to sort the elements within the array into alphabetical order.

You should now have an idea why objects are useful in JavaScript. You have seen the Date and Array objects, but there are many other objects that JavaScript makes available so that you can achieve more with your code. These include the Math and String objects, which we will talk more about later in the chapter.

Using JavaScript Objects

Now that you have seen the *why* of JavaScript objects, you need to look at the *what* and the *how*.

Each of the JavaScript objects has a collection of related properties and methods that can be used to manipulate a certain kind of data. For example, the Array object consists of methods to manipulate arrays and properties to find out information from them. In most cases, to make use of these methods and properties, you need to define your data as one of these objects. In other words, you need to create an object.

In this section, you'll look at how to go about creating an object and, having done that, how you use its properties and methods.

Creating an Object

You have already seen an example of an Array object being created. To create an Array object, you used the following JavaScript statement:

```
var myArray = new Array();
```

So how is this statement made up?

The first half of the statement is familiar to you. You use the `var` keyword to define a variable called `myArray`. This variable is initialized, using the equals sign assignment operator (=), to the right-hand side of the statement.

The right-hand side of the statement consists of two parts. First you have the operator `new`. This tells JavaScript that you want to create a new object. Next you have `Array()`. This is the *constructor* for an `Array` object. It tells JavaScript what type of object you want to create. Most objects have constructors like this. For example, the `Date` object has the `Date()` constructor. The only exception you see in this book is the `Math` object, and this will be explained in a later part of the chapter.

You also saw in Chapter 2 that you can pass parameters to the constructor `Array()` to add data to your object. For example, to create an `Array` object that has three elements containing the data `"Paul"`, `"Paula"`, and `"Pauline"`, you use

```
var myArray = new Array("Paul", "Paula", "Pauline");
```

Let's see some more examples, this time using the `Date` object. The simplest way to create a `Date` object is like this:

```
var myDate = new Date();
```

This will create a `Date` object containing the date and time that it was created. However,

```
var myDate = new Date("1 Jan 2010");
```

will create a `Date` object containing the date 1 January 2010.

How object data are stored in variables differs from how primitive data, such as text and numbers, are stored. (Primitive data are the most basic data possible in JavaScript.) With primitive data, the variable holds the data's actual value. For example,

```
var myNumber = 23;
```

means that the variable `myNumber` will hold the data `23`. However, variables assigned to objects don't hold the actual data, but rather a *reference* to the memory address where the data can be found. This doesn't mean you can get hold of the memory address — this is something only JavaScript has details of and keeps to itself in the background. All you need to remember is that when you say that a variable references an object, you mean it references a memory address. This is shown in the following example:

```
var myArrayRef = new Array(0, 1, 2);
var mySecondArrayRef = myArrayRef;
myArrayRef[0] = 100;
alert(mySecondArrayRef[0]);
```

First you set variable `myArrayRef` reference to the new array object, and then you set `mySecondArrayRef` to the same reference — for example, now `mySecondArrayRef` is set to reference the same array object. So when you set the first element of the array to `100`, as shown here:

```
myArrayRef [0] = 100;
```

and display the contents of the first element of the array referenced in `mySecondArrayRef` as follows:

```
alert(mySecondArrayRef[0]);
```

you'll see it has also magically changed to 100! However, as you now know, it's not magic; it's because both variables referenced the same array object, because when it comes to objects, it's a reference to the object and not the object itself that is stored in a variable. When you did the assignment, it didn't make a copy of the array object, it simply copied the reference. Contrast that with the following:

```
var myVariable = "ABC";
var mySecondVariable = myVariable;
myVariable = "DEF";
alert(mySecondVariable);
```

In this case you're dealing with a string, which is primitive data type, as are numbers. This time it's the actual data that are stored in the variable, so when you do this:

```
var mySecondVariable = myVariable;
```

`mySecondVariable` gets its own separate copy of the data in `myVariable`. So the alert at the end will still show `mySecondVariable` as holding `"ABC"`.

To summarize this section, you create a JavaScript object using the following basic syntax:

```
var myVariable = new ObjectName(optional parameters);
```

Using an Object's Properties

Accessing the values contained in an object's properties is very simple. You write the name of the variable containing (or referencing) your object, followed by a dot, and then the name of the object's property.

For example, if you defined an `Array` object contained in the variable `myArray`, you could access its `length` property like this:

```
myArray.length
```

But what can you do with this property now that you have it? You can use it as you would any other piece of data and store it in a variable.

```
var myVariable = myArray.length;
```

Or you can show it to the user:

```
alert(myArray.length);
```

In some cases, you can even change the value of the property, like this:

```
myArray.length = 12;
```

However, unlike variables, some properties are read-only—you can get information from them, but you can't *change* information inside them.

Calling an Object's Methods

Methods are very much like functions in that they can be used to perform useful tasks, such as getting the hours from a particular date or generating a random number. Again like functions, some methods return a value, such as the Date object's getHours() method, while others perform a task, but return no data, such as the Array object's sort() method.

Using the methods of an object is very similar to using properties, in that you put the object's variable name first, then a dot, and then the name of the method. For example, to sort the elements of an Array in the variable myArray, you may use the following code:

```
myArray.sort();
```

Just as with functions, you can pass parameters to some methods by placing the parameters between the parentheses following the method's name. However, whether or not a method takes parameters, you must still put parentheses after the method's name, just as you did with functions. As a general rule, anywhere you can use a function, you can use a method of an object.

Primitives and Objects

You should now have a good idea about the difference between primitive data, such as numbers and strings, and object data, such as Dates and Arrays. However, we mentioned earlier that there is also a String object. Where does this fit in?

In fact there are String, Number, and Boolean objects corresponding to the string, number, and Boolean primitive data types. For example, to create a String object containing the text "I'm a String object" you can use the following code:

```
var myString = new String("I'm a String object");
```

The String object has the length property just as the Array object does. This returns the number of characters in the String object. For example,

```
var lengthOfString = myString.length;
```

would store the data 19 in the variable lengthOfString (remember that spaces are referred to as characters too).

But what if you had declared a primitive string called mySecondString holding the text "I'm a primitive string" like this:

```
var mySecondString = "I'm a primitive string";
```

and wanted to know how many characters could be found in this primitive string?

This is where JavaScript helps you out. Recall from previous chapters that JavaScript can handle the conversion of one data type to another automatically. For example, if you tried to add a string primitive to a number primitive, like this,

```
theResult = "23" + 23;
```

JavaScript would assume that you want to treat the number as a string and concatenate the two together, the number being converted to text automatically. The variable theResult would contain "2323"—the concatenation of 23 and 23, and not the sum of 23 and 23, which would be 46.

The same applies to objects. If you declare a primitive string and then treat it as an object, such as by trying to access one of its methods or properties, JavaScript will know that the operation you're trying to do won't work. The operation will only work with an object; for example, it would be valid with a String object. In this case, JavaScript converts the plain-text string into a temporary String object, just for that operation.

So, for your primitive string mySecondString, you can use the length property of the String object to find out the number of characters it contains. For example:

```
var lengthOfSecondString = mySecondString.length;
```

This would store the data 22 in the variable lengthOfSecondString.

The same ideas expressed here are also true for number and Boolean primitives and their corresponding Number and Boolean objects. However, these objects are not used very often, so we will not be discussing them further in this book.

The JavaScript Native Objects

So far you have just been looking at what objects are, how to create them, and how to use them. Now take a look at some of the more useful objects that are native to JavaScript—that is, those that JavaScript makes available for you to use.

You won't be looking at all of the native JavaScript objects, just some of the more commonly used ones, namely the String object, the Math object, the Array object, and the Date object. Later in the book, a whole chapter is devoted to each of the more complex objects, such as the String object (Chapter 8) and the Date object (Chapter 9).

String Objects

Like most objects, String objects need to be created before they can be used. To create a String object, you can write this:

```
var string1 = new String("Hello");
var string2 = new String(123);
var string3 = new String(123.456);
```

However, as you have seen, you can also declare a string primitive and use it as if it were a String object, letting JavaScript do the conversion to an object for you behind the scenes. For example:

```
var string1 = "Hello";
```

Using this technique is preferable so long as it's clear to JavaScript what object you expect to have created in the background. If the primitive data type is a string, this won't be a problem and JavaScript will work it out. The advantages to doing it this way are that there is no need to create a String object itself and you avoid the troubles with comparing string objects. When you try to compare string objects with primitive string values, the actual values are compared; but with String objects, it's the object references that are compared.

The String object has a vast number of methods and properties. In this section, you'll be looking only at some of the less complex and more commonly used methods. However, in Chapter 8 you'll look at some of the trickier, but very powerful, methods associated with strings and the regular expression object (RegExp). Regular expressions provide a very powerful means of searching strings for patterns of characters. For example, if you want to find "Paul" where it exists as a whole word in the string "Pauline, Paul, Paula", you need to use regular expressions. However, they can be a little tricky to use, so we won't discuss them further in this chapter — we want to save some fun for later!

With most of the String object's methods, it helps to remember that a string is just a series of individual characters and that, as with arrays, each character has a position, or index. Also as with arrays, the first position, or index, is labeled 0 and not 1. So, for example, the string "Hello World" has the character positions shown in the following table:

Character Index	0	1	2	3	4	5	6	7	8	9	10
Character	H	e	l	l	o		W	o	r	l	d

The length Property

The length property simply returns the number of characters in the string. For example,

```
var myName = new String("Paul");
document.write(myName.length);
```

will write the length of the string "Paul" (that is, 4) to the page.

The charAt() and charCodeAt() Methods — Selecting a Single Character from a String

If you want to find out information about a single character within a string, you need the charAt() and charCodeAt() methods. These methods can be very useful for checking the validity of user input, something you'll see more of in Chapter 6 when you look at HTML forms.

The charAt() method takes one parameter: the index position of the character you want in the string. It then returns that character. charAt() treats the positions of the string characters as starting at 0, so the first character is at index 0, the second at index 1, and so on.

For example, to find the last character in a string, you could use this code:

```
var myString = prompt("Enter some text","Hello World!");
var theLastChar = myString.charAt(myString.length - 1);
document.write("The last character is " + theLastChar);
```

In the first line you prompt the user for a string, with the default of "Hello World!", and store this string in the variable myString.

In the next line, you use the charAt() method to retrieve the last character in the string. You use the index position of (myString.length - 1). Why? Let's take the string "Hello World!" as an example. The length of this string is 12, but the last character position is 11 because the indexing starts at 0. Therefore, you need to subtract one from the length of the string to get the last character's position.

In the final line, you write the last character in the string to the page.

The charCodeAt() method is similar in use to the charAt() method, but instead of returning the character itself, it returns a number that represents the decimal character code for that character in the Unicode character set. Recall that computers only understand numbers—to the computer, all your strings are just numeric data. When you request text rather than numbers, the computer does a conversion based on its internal understanding of each number and provides the respective character.

For example, to find the character code of the first character in a string, you could write this:

```
var myString = prompt("Enter some text","Hello World!");
var theFirstCharCode = myString.charCodeAt(0);
document.write("The first character code is " + theFirstCharCode);
```

This will get the character code for the character at index position 0 in the string given by the user, and write it out to the page.

Character codes go in order, so, for example, the letter A has the code 65, B 66, and so on. Lowercase letters start at 97 (a is 97, b is 98, and so on). Digits go from 48 (for the number 0) to 57 (for the number 9). You can use this information for various purposes, as you'll see in the next example.

Try It Out   Checking a Character's Case

The following is an example that detects the type of the character at the start of a given string—that is, whether the character is uppercase, lowercase, numeric, or other.

```
<html>
<head>
<script language="JavaScript" type="text/javascript">
function checkCharType(charToCheck)
{
    var returnValue = "O";
    var charCode = charToCheck.charCodeAt(0);

    if (charCode >= "A".charCodeAt(0) && charCode <= "Z".charCodeAt(0))
    {
        returnValue = "U";
    }
    else if (charCode >= "a".charCodeAt(0) && charCode <= "z".charCodeAt(0))
    {
        returnValue = "L";
    }
    else if (charCode >= "0".charCodeAt(0) && charCode <= "9".charCodeAt(0))
    {
        returnValue = "N";
    }
```

```
        return returnValue;
}
</script>
<head>

<body>
<script language="JavaScript" type="text/javascript">

var myString = prompt("Enter some text","Hello World!");
switch (checkCharType(myString))
{
    case "U":
        document.write("First character was upper case");
        break;
    case "L":
        document.write("First character was lower case");
        break;
    case "N":
        document.write("First character was a number");
        break;
    default:
        document.write("First character was not a character or a number");
}
</script>
</body>
</html>
```

Type in the code and save it as ch4_examp1.htm.

When you load the page into your browser, you will be prompted for a string. A message will then be written to the page informing you of the type of the first character that you entered — whether it is uppercase, lowercase, a number, or something else, such as a punctuation mark.

How It Works

To start with, you define a function checkCharType(), which is used in the body of the page. You start this function by declaring the variable returnValue and initializing it to the character "O" to indicate it's some other character than a lowercase letter, uppercase letter, or numerical character.

```
function checkCharType(charToCheck)
{
    var returnValue = "O";
```

You use this variable as the value to be returned at the end of the function, indicating the type of character. It will take the values U for uppercase, L for lowercase, N for number, and O for other.

The next line in the function uses the charCodeAt() method to get the character code of the first character in the string stored in charToCheck, which is the function's only parameter. The character code is stored in the variable charCode.

```
    var charCode = charToCheck.charCodeAt(0);
```

In the following lines you have a series of if statements, which check within what range of values the character code falls. You know that if it falls between the character codes for A and Z, it's uppercase, and so you assign the variable returnValue the value U. If the character code falls between the character codes for a and z, it's lowercase, and so you assign the value L to the variable returnValue. If the character code falls between the character codes for 0 and 9, it's a number, and you assign the value N to the variable returnValue. If the value falls into none of these ranges, then the variable retains its initialization value of O for other, and you don't have to do anything.

```
if (charCode >= "A".charCodeAt(0) && charCode <= "Z".charCodeAt(0))
{
    returnValue = "U";
}
else if (charCode >= "a".charCodeAt(0) && charCode <= "z".charCodeAt(0))
{
    returnValue = "L";
}
else if (charCode >= "0".charCodeAt(0) && charCode <= "9".charCodeAt(0))
{
    returnValue = "N";
}
```

This probably seems a bit weird at first, so let's see what JavaScript is doing with your code. When you write

```
"A".charCodeAt(0)
```

it appears that you are trying to use a method of the String object on a string literal, which is the same as a primitive string in that it's just characters and not an object. However, JavaScript realizes what you are doing and does the necessary conversion of literal character "A" into a temporary String object containing "A". Then, and only then, does JavaScript perform the charCodeAt() method on the String object it has created in the background. When it has finished, the String object is disposed of. Basically, this is a shorthand way of writing the following:

```
var myChar = new String("A");
myChar.charCodeAt(0);
```

In either case the first (and in this string the only) character's code is returned to you. For example, "A".charCodeAt(0) will return the number 65.

Finally you come to the end of the function and return the returnValue variable to where the function was called.

```
    return returnValue;
}
```

You might wonder why you bother using the variable returnValue at all, instead of just returning its value. For example, you could write the code as follows:

```
if (charCode >= "A".charCodeAt(0) && charCode <= "Z".charCodeAt(0))
{
    return "U";
```

```
    }
    else if (charCode >= "a".charCodeAt(0) && charCode <= "z".charCodeAt(0))
    {
        return "L";
    }
    else if (charCode >= "0".charCodeAt(0) && charCode <= "9".charCodeAt(0))
    {
        return "N";
    }
    return "O";
```

This would work fine, so why not do it this way? The disadvantage of this way is that it's difficult to follow the flow of execution of the function, which is not that bad in a small function like this, but can get tricky in bigger functions. With the original code you always know exactly where the function execution stops: It stops at the end with the only return statement. The version of the function just shown finishes when any of the return statements is reached, so there are four possible places where the function might end.

In the body of your page, you have some test code to check that the function works. You first use the variable myString, initialized to "Hello World!" or whatever the user enters into the prompt box, as your test string.

```
    var myString = prompt("Enter some text","Hello World!");
```

Next, the switch statement uses the checkCharType() function that you defined earlier in its comparison expression. Depending on what is returned by the function, one of the case statements will execute and let the user know what the character type was.

```
    switch (checkCharType(myString))
    {
        case "U":
            document.write("First character was upper case");
            break;
        case "L":
            document.write("First character was lower case");
            break;
        case "N":
            document.write("First character was a number");
            break;
        default:
            document.write("First character was not a character or a number");
    }
```

That completes the example, but before we move on, it's worth noting that this example is just that — an example of using charCodeAt(). In practice, it would be much easier to just write

```
    if (char >= "A" && char <= "Z")
```

rather than

```
    if (charCode >= "A".charCodeAt(0) && charCode <= "Z".charCodeAt(0))
```

which you have used here.

The fromCharCode() Method—Converting Character Codes to a String

The method `fromCharCode()` can be thought of as the opposite of `charCodeAt()`, in that you pass it a series of comma-separated numbers representing character codes, and it converts them to a single string.

However, the `fromCharCode()` method is unusual in that it's a *static* method—you don't need to have created a `String` object to use it with, it's always available to you.

For example, the following lines put the string `"ABC"` into the variable `myString`:

```
var myString;
myString = String.fromCharCode(65,66,67);
```

The `fromCharCode()` method can be very useful when used with variables. For example, to build up a string consisting of all the uppercase letters of the alphabet, you could use the following code:

```
var myString = "";
var charCode;

for (charCode = 65; charCode <= 90; charCode++)
{
    myString = myString + String.fromCharCode(charCode);
}

document.write(myString);
```

You use the `for` loop to select each character from A to Z in turn and concatenate this to `myString`. Note that while this is fine as an example, it is more efficient and less memory-hungry to simply write this instead:

```
var myString = "ABCDEFGHIJKLMNOPQRSTUVWXYZ";
```

The indexOf() and lastIndexOf() Methods—Finding a String Inside Another String

The methods `indexOf()` and `lastIndexOf()` are used for searching for the occurrence of one string inside another. A string contained inside another is usually termed a *substring*. They are useful when you have a string of information, but only want a small part of it. For example, in the trivia quiz, when someone enters a text answer, you want to check if certain keywords are present within the string.

Both `indexOf()` and `lastIndexOf()` take two parameters:

❑   The string you want to find

❑   The character position you want to start searching from (optional)

As with the `charAt()` method, character positions start at 0. If you don't include the second parameter, searching starts from the beginning of the string.

The return value of `indexOf()` and `lastIndexOf()` is the character position in the string at which the substring was found. Again, it's zero-based, so if the substring is found at the start of the string, then 0 is returned. If there is no match, then the value –1 is returned.

For example, to search for the substring `"Paul"` in the string `"Hello paul. How are you Paul"`, you may use the code

```
<script language="JavaScript" type="text/javascript">

var myString = "Hello paul. How are you Paul";
var foundAtPosition;

foundAtPosition = myString.indexOf("Paul");
alert(foundAtPosition);

</script>
```

This code should result in a message box containing the number 24, which is the character position of `"Paul"`. You might be wondering why it's 24, which clearly refers to the second `"Paul"` in the string, rather than 6 for the first `"paul"`. Well, this is due to case sensitivity again. It's laboring the point a bit, but JavaScript takes case sensitivity very seriously, both in its syntax and when making comparisons. If you type `IndexOf()` instead of `indexOf()`, JavaScript will complain. Similarly, `"paul"` is not the same as `"Paul"`. Mistakes with case are so easy to make, even for experts, that it's best to be very aware of case when programming.

You've seen `indexOf()` in action, but how does `lastIndexOf()` differ? Well, whereas `indexOf()` starts searching from the beginning of the string, or the position you specified in the second parameter, and works towards the end, `lastIndexOf()` starts at the end of the string, or the position you specified, and works towards the beginning of the string.

> In the current example you first search using `indexOf()`, which finds the first `"Paul"` (changed to the correct case from the last example). The alert box displays this result, which is character position 6. Then you search using `lastIndexOf()`. This starts searching at the end of the string, and so the first `"Paul"` it comes to is the last one in the string at character position 24. Therefore, the second alert box displays the result 24.

```
<script language="JavaScript" type="text/javascript">

var myString = "Hello Paul. How are you Paul";
var foundAtPosition;

foundAtPosition = myString.indexOf("Paul");
alert(foundAtPosition);

foundAtPosition = myString.lastIndexOf("Paul");
alert(foundAtPosition);

</script>
```

Try it Out   Counting Occurrences of Substrings

In this example, you look at how to use the "start character position" parameter of indexOf(). Here you will count how many times the word Wrox appears in the string.

```
<html>
<body>
<script language="JavaScript" type="text/javascript">
var myString = "Welcome to Wrox books. ";
myString = myString + "The Wrox website is www.wrox.com. ";
myString = myString + "Visit the Wrox website today. Thanks for buying Wrox";

var foundAtPosition = 0;
var wroxCount = 0;

while ( foundAtPosition != -1)
{
   foundAtPosition = myString.indexOf("Wrox",foundAtPosition);
   if (foundAtPosition != -1)
   {
      wroxCount++;
      foundAtPosition++;
   }
}

document.write("There are " + wroxCount + " occurrences of the word Wrox");

</script>
</body>
</html>
```

Save this example as ch4_examp2.htm. When you load the page into your browser, you should see the following sentence: There are 4 occurrences of the word Wrox.

How It Works

At the top of the script block, you built up a string inside the variable myString, which you then want to search for the occurrence of the word Wrox. You also define two variables: wroxCount will contain the number of times Wrox is found in the string, and foundAtPosition will contain the position in the string of the current occurrence of the substring Wrox.

You then used a while loop, which continues looping all the while you are finding the word Wrox in the string—that is, while the variable foundAtPosition is not equal to -1. Inside the while loop, you have this line:

```
foundAtPosition = myString.indexOf("Wrox",foundAtPosition);
```

Here you search for the next occurrence of the substring Wrox in the string myString. How do you make sure that you get the next occurrence? You use the variable foundAtPosition to give you the starting position of your search, because this contains the index after the index position of the last occurrence of the substring Wrox. You assign the variable foundAtPosition to the result of your search, the index position of the next occurrence of the substring Wrox.

Each time `Wrox` is found (that is, each time `foundAtPosition` is not -1) you increase the variable `wroxCount`, which counts how many times you have found the substring, and you increase `foundAtPosition` so that you continue the search at the next position in the string.

```
if (foundAtPosition != -1)
{
    wroxCount++;
    foundAtPosition++;
}
```

Finally, you `document.write()` the value of the variable `wroxCount` to the page.

In the Chapter 3, we talked about the danger of infinite loops, and you can see that there is a danger of one here. If `foundAtPosition++` were removed, you'd keep searching from the same starting point and never move to find the next occurrence of the word `Wrox`.

The `indexOf()` and `lastIndexOf()` methods are more useful when coupled with the `substr()` and `substring()` methods, which you'll be looking at in the next section. Using a combination of these methods enables you to cut substrings out of a string.

The substr() and substring() Methods — Copying Part of a String

If you wanted to cut out part of a string and assign that cut-out part to another variable or use it in an expression, you would use the `substr()` and `substring()` methods. Both methods provide the same end result — that is, a part of a string — but they differ in the parameters they require.

The method `substring()` takes two parameters: the character start position and the character end position of the part of the string you want. The second parameter is optional; if you don't include it, all characters from the start position to the end of the string are included.

For example, if your string is `"JavaScript"` and you want just the text `"Java"`, you could call the method like so:

```
var myString = "JavaScript";
var mySubString = myString.substring(0,4);
alert(mySubString);
```

As with all the methods of the `String` object so far, the character positions start at 0. However, you might be wondering why you specified the end character as 4. This method is a little confusing because the end character is the end marker; it's not included in the substring that is cut out. You can think of the parameters as specifying the *length* of the string being returned: the parameters 0 and 4 will return (4 - 0) characters starting at and including the character at position 0. Depicted graphically it looks like this:

Character Position	0	1	2	3	4	5	6	7	8	9
Character	J	a	v	a	S	c	r	i	p	t

Like substring(), the method substr() again takes two parameters, the first being the start position of the first character you want included in your substring. However, this time the second parameter specifies the length of the string of characters that you want to cut out of the longer string. For example, you could rewrite the preceding code like this:

```
var myString = "JavaScript";
var mySubString = myString.substr(0,4);
alert(mySubString);
```

As with the substring() method, the second parameter is optional. If you don't include it, all the characters from the start position onward will be included.

The main reason for using one method rather than the other is that the substring() method is supported by IE 3+ and by NN 2+ browsers. However, the substr() method only works with version 4 (and later) browsers.

Let's look at the use of the substr() and lastIndexOf() methods together. In the next chapter, you'll see how you can retrieve the file path and name of the currently loaded web page. However, there is no way of retrieving the file name alone. So if, for example, your file is http://mywebsite/temp/myfile.htm, you may need to extract the myfile.htm part. This is where substr() and lastIndexOf() are useful.

```
var fileName = window.location.href;
fileName = fileName.substr(fileName.lastIndexOf("/") + 1);
document.write("The file name of this page is " + fileName);
```

The first line sets the variable fileName to the current file path and name, such as /mywebsite/temp/myfile.htm. Don't worry about understanding this line; you'll be looking at it in the next chapter.

The second line is where the interesting action is. You can see that this code uses the return value of the lastIndexOf() method as a parameter for another method, something that's perfectly correct and very useful. The goal in using fileName.lastIndexOf("/") is to find the position of the final forward slash (/), which will be the last character before the name of the file. You add one to this value, because you don't want to include that character, and then pass this new value to the substr() method. There's no second parameter here (the length), because you don't know it. As a result, substr() will return all the characters right to the end of the string, which is what you want.

> This example retrieves the name of the page on the local machine, because you're not accessing the page from a web server. However, don't let this mislead you into thinking that accessing files on a local hard drive from a web page is something you'll be able to do with JavaScript alone. To protect users from malicious hackers, JavaScript's access to the user's system, such as access to files, is very limited. You'll learn more about this later in the book.

The toLowerCase() and toUpperCase() Methods — Changing the Case of a String

If you want to change the case of a string, for example to remove case sensitivity when comparing strings, you need the toLowerCase() and toUpperCase() methods. It's not hard to guess what these two methods do. Both of them return a string that is the value of the string in the String object, but with its case converted to either upper or lower depending on the method invoked. Any non-alphabetical characters remain unchanged by these functions.

In the following example, you can see that by changing the case of both strings you can compare them without case sensitivity being an issue.

```
var myString = "I Don't Care About Case"

if (myString.toLowerCase() == "i don't care about case")
{
    alert("Who cares about case?");
}
```

Even though `toLowerCase()` and `toUpperCase()` don't take any parameters, you must remember to put the two empty parentheses — that is, `()` — at the end, if you want to call a method.

The Math Object

The `Math` object provides a number of useful mathematical functions and number manipulation methods. You'll be taking a look at some of them here, but you'll find the rest described in detail at the W3C site: www.w3schools.com/jsref/default.asp.

The `Math` object is a little unusual in that JavaScript automatically creates it for you. There's no need to declare a variable as a `Math` object or define a new `Math` object before being able to use it, making it a little bit easier to use.

The properties of the `Math` object include some useful math constants, such as the `PI` property (giving the value 3.14159 and so on). You access these properties, as usual, by placing a dot after the object name (`Math`) and then writing the property name. For example, to calculate the area of a circle, you may use the following code:

```
var radius = prompt("Give the radius of the circle", "");
var area = (Math.PI)*radius*radius;
document.write("The area is " + area);
```

The methods of the `Math` object include some operations that are impossible, or complex, to perform using the standard mathematical operators (+, −, *, and /). For example, the `cos()` method returns the cosine of the value passed as a parameter. You'll look at a few of these methods now.

The abs() Method

The `abs()` method returns the absolute value of the number passed as its parameter. Essentially, this means that it returns the positive value of the number. So −1 is returned as 1, −4 as 4, and so on. However, 1 would be returned as 1 because it's already positive.

For example, the following code would write the number 101 to the page.

```
var myNumber = -101;
document.write(Math.abs(myNumber));
```

The ceil() Method

The ceil() method always rounds a number up to the next largest whole number or integer. So 10.01 becomes 11, and –9.99 becomes –9 (because –9 is greater than –10). The ceil() method has just one parameter, namely the number you want rounded up.

Using ceil() is different from using the parseInt() function you saw in Chapter 2, because parseInt() simply chops off any numbers after the decimal point to leave a whole number, whereas ceil() rounds the number up.

For example, the following code writes two lines in the page, the first containing the number 102 and the second containing the number 101:

```
var myNumber = 101.01;
document.write(Math.ceil(myNumber) + "<BR>");
document.write(parseInt(myNumber));
```

The floor() Method

Like the ceil() method, the floor() method removes any numbers after the decimal point, and returns a whole number or integer. The difference is that floor() always rounds the number down. So if you pass 10.01 you will be returned 10, and if you pass –9.99 you will see –10 returned.

The round() Method

The round() method is very similar to ceil() and floor(), except that instead of always rounding up or always rounding down, it rounds up only if the decimal part is .5 or greater, and rounds down otherwise.

For example:

```
var myNumber = 44.5;
document.write(Math.round(myNumber) + "<BR>");

myNumber = 44.49;
document.write(Math.round(myNumber));
```

This code would write the numbers 45 and 44 to the page.

Summary of Rounding Methods

As you have seen, the ceil(), floor(), and round() methods all remove the numbers after a decimal point and return just a whole number. However, which whole number they return depends on the method used: floor() returns the lowest, ceil() the highest, and round() the nearest equivalent integer. This can be a little confusing, so the following is a table of values and what whole number would be returned if these values were passed to the parseInt() function, and ceil(), floor(), and round() methods.

Parameter	parseInt() returns	ceil() returns	floor() returns	round() returns
10.25	10	11	10	10
10.75	10	11	10	11
10.5	10	11	10	11
−10.25	−10	−10	−11	−10
−10.75	−10	−10	−11	−11
−10.5	−10	−10	−11	−10

Remember that parseInt() *is a native JavaScript function and not a method of the* Math *object, like the other methods presented in this table.*

Try It Out   **JavaScript's Rounding Functions Results Calculator**

If you're still not sure about rounding numbers, the following example should help. Here, you'll look at a calculator that gets a number from the user, then writes out what the result would be when you pass that number to parseInt(), ceil(), floor(), and round().

```
<html>
<body>
<script language="JavaScript" type="text/javascript">

var myNumber = prompt("Enter the number to be rounded","");

document.write("<h3>The number you entered was " + myNumber + "</h3><br>");
document.write("<p>The rounding results for this number are</p>");
document.write("<table width=150 border=1>");
document.write("<tr><th>Method</th><th>Result</th></tr>");
document.write("<tr><td>parseInt()</td><td>"+ parseInt(myNumber) +"</td></tr>");
document.write("<tr><td>ceil()</td><td>" + Math.ceil(myNumber) + "</td></tr>");
document.write("<tr><td>floor()</td><td>"+ Math.floor(myNumber) + "</td></tr>");
document.write("<tr><td>round()</td><td>" + Math.round(myNumber) +"</td></tr>");
document.write("</table>")

</script>
</body>
</html>
```

Save this as ch4_examp3.htm and load it into a web browser. In the prompt box, enter a number, for example 12.354, and click OK. The results of this number being passed to parseInt(), ceil(), floor(), and round() will be displayed in the page formatted inside a table, as shown in Figure 4-1.

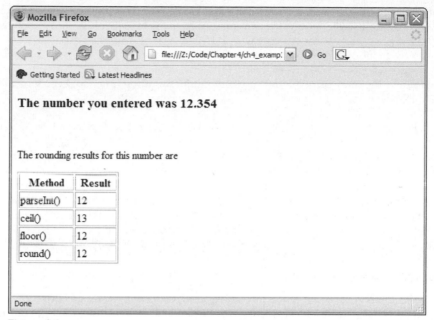

Figure 4-1

How It Works

The first task is to get the number to be rounded from the user:

```
var myNumber = prompt("Enter the number to be rounded","");
```

Then you write out the number and some descriptive text.

```
document.write("<h3>The number you entered was " + myNumber + "</h3><br>");
document.write("<p>The rounding results for this number are</p>");
```

Notice how this time some HTML tags for formatting have been included — the main header being in
<h3> tags, and the description of what the table means being inside a paragraph <p> tag.

Next you create the table of results.

```
document.write("<table width=150 border=1>");
document.write("<tr><th>Method</th><th>Result</th></tr>");
document.write("<tr><td>parseInt()</td><td>"+ parseInt(myNumber) +"</td></tr>");
document.write("<tr><td>ceil()</td><td>" + Math.ceil(myNumber) + "</td></tr>");
document.write("<tr><td>floor()</td><td>"+ Math.floor(myNumber) + "</td></tr>");
document.write("<tr><td>round()</td><td>" + Math.round(myNumber) +"</td></tr>");
document.write("</table>")
```

You create the table header first before actually displaying the results of each rounding function on a separate row. You can see how easy it is to dynamically create HTML inside the web page using just JavaScript. The principles are the same as with HTML in a page: You must make sure your tag's syntax is valid or otherwise things will appear strange or not appear at all.

Each row follows the same principle, but uses a different rounding function. Let's look at the first row, which displays the results of parseInt().

```
document.write("<tr><td>parseInt()</td><td>"+ parseInt(myNumber) +"</td></tr>");
```

Inside the string to be written out to the page, you start by creating the table row with the <tr> tag. Then you create a table cell with a <td> tag and insert the name of the method from which the results are being displayed on this row. Then you close the cell with </td> and open a new one with <td>. Inside this next cell you are placing the actual results of the parseInt() function. Although a number is returned by parseInt(), because you are concatenating it to a string, JavaScript automatically converts the number returned by parseInt() into a string before concatenating. All this happens in the background without you needing to do a thing. Finally, you close the cell and the row with </td></tr>.

The random() Method

The random() method returns a random floating-point number in the range between 0 and 1, where 0 is included and 1 is not. This can be very useful for displaying random banner images or for writing a JavaScript game.

Let's look at how you would mimic the roll of a single die. In the following page, 10 random numbers are written to the page. Click the browser's Refresh button to get another set of random numbers.

```
<html>
<body>
<script language="JavaScript" type="text/javascript">
var throwCount;
var diceThrow;
for (throwCount = 0; throwCount < 10; throwCount++)
{
    diceThrow = (Math.floor(Math.random() * 6) + 1);
    document.write(diceThrow + "<br>");
}

</script>
</body>
</html>
```

You want diceThrow to be between 1 and 6. The random() function returns a floating-point number between 0 and just under 1. By multiplying this number by 6, you get a number between 0 and just under 6. Then by adding 1, you get a number between 1 and just under 7. By using floor() to always round it down to the next lowest whole number, you can ensure that you'll end up with a number between 1 and 6.

If you wanted a random number between 1 and 100, you would just change the code so that Math.random() is multiplied by 100 rather than 6.

The pow() Method

The pow() method raises a number to a specified power. It takes two parameters, the first being the number you want raised to a power, and the second being the power itself. For example, to raise 2 to the power of 8 (that is, to calculate 2 * 2 * 2 * 2 * 2 * 2 * 2 * 2), you would write Math.pow(2,8) — the result being 256. Unlike some of the other mathematical methods, like sin(), cos(), and acos(), which are not commonly used in web programming unless it's a scientific application you're writing, the pow() method can often prove very useful.

Try It Out   **Using pow()**

In the following example, you write a function using pow(), which fixes the number of decimal places in a number — a function that's missing from earlier versions of JavaScript, though it has now been added to JScript 5.5 and JavaScript 1.5, as you'll see later in this chapter. This helps demonstrate that even when a function is missing from JavaScript, you can usually use existing functions to create what you want.

```
<html>
<head>
<script language="JavaScript" type="text/javascript">

function fix(fixNumber, decimalPlaces)
{
    var div = Math.pow(10,decimalPlaces);
    fixNumber = Math.round(fixNumber * div) / div;
    return fixNumber;
}
</script>
</head>
<body>
<script language="JavaScript" type="text/javascript">

var number1 = prompt("Enter the number with decimal places you want to fix","");
var number2 = prompt("How many decimal places do you want?","");

document.write(number1 + " fixed to " + number2 + " decimal places is: ");
document.write(fix(number1,number2));

</script>
</body>
</html>
```

Save the page as ch4_examp4.htm. When you load the page into your browser, you will be presented with two prompt boxes. In the first, enter the number for which you want to fix the number of decimal places, for example 2.2345. In the second, enter the number of decimal places you want fixed, for example 2. Then the result of fixing the number you have entered to the number of decimal places you have chosen will be written to the page, as shown in Figure 4-2. For the example numbers, this will be 2.23.

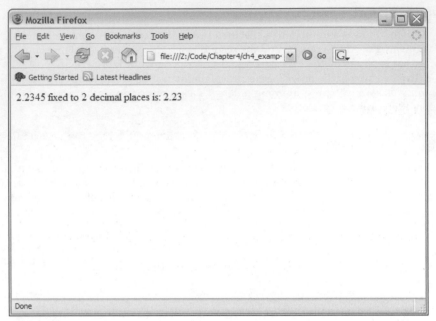

Figure 4-2

How It Works

In the head of the page you define the function `fix()`. This function will fix its `fixNumber` parameter to a maximum of its `decimalPlaces` parameter's number of digits after the decimal place. For example, fixing `34.76459` to a maximum of three decimal places will return `34.765`.

The first line of code in the function sets the variable `div` to the number `10` raised to the power of the number of decimal places you want.

```
function fix(fixNumber, decimalPlaces)
{
    var div = Math.pow(10,decimalPlaces);
```

Then, in the next line, you calculate the new number.

```
    fixNumber = Math.round(fixNumber * div) / div;
```

What the code `Math.round(fixNumber * div)` does is move the decimal point in the number that you are converting to after the point in the number that you want to keep. So for `2.2345`, if you want to keep two decimal places, you convert it to `223.45`. The `Math.round()` method rounds this number to the nearest integer (in this case `223`) and so removes any undesired decimal part.

You then convert this number back into the fraction it should be, but of course only the fractional part you want is left. You do this by dividing by the same number (`div`) that you multiplied by. In this example, you divide `223` by `100`, which leaves `2.23`. This is `2.2345` fixed to two decimal places. This value is returned to the calling code in the line

```
        return fixNumber;
}
```

In the body of the page you use two prompt boxes to get numbers from the user. You then display the results of using these numbers in your `fix()` function to the user using `document.write()`.

Number Object

As with the `String` object, `Number` objects need to be created before they can be used. To create a `Number` object, you can write the following:

```
var firstNumber = new Number(123);
var secondNumber = new Number('123');
```

However, as you have seen, you can also declare a number as primitive and use it as if it were a `Number` object, letting JavaScript do the conversion to an object for you behind the scenes. For example:

```
var myNumber = 123.765;
```

As with the `String` object, this technique is preferable so long as it's clear to JavaScript what object you expect to have created in the background. So, for example,

```
var myNumber = "123.567";
```

will lead JavaScript to assume, quite rightly, that it's a string, and any attempts to use the `Number` object's methods will fail.

You'll look at just the `toFixed()` method of the `Number` object because that's the most useful method for everyday use.

The toFixed() Method

The `toFixed()` method is new to JavaScript 1.5 and JScript 5.5—so basically it's available in Netscape 6+ and IE 5.5+ only. The method cuts a number off after a certain point. Let's say you want to display a price after sales tax. If your price is $9.99 and sales tax is 7.5 percent, that means the after-tax cost will be $10.73925. Well, this is rather an odd amount for a money transaction—what you really want to do is fix the number to no more than two decimal places. Let's create an example.

```
var itemCost = 9.99;
var itemCostAfterTax = 9.99 * 1.075;
document.write("Item cost is $" + itemCostAfterTax + "<br>");
itemCostAfterTax = itemCostAfterTax.toFixed(2);
document.write("Item cost fixed to 2 decimal places is " + itemCostAfterTax);
```

The first `document.write()` will output the following to the page:

```
Item cost is 10.73925
```

However, this is not the format you want; instead you want two decimal places, so on the next line enter this:

```
itemCostAfterTax = itemCostAfterTax.toFixed(2);
```

You use the `toFixed()` method of the `Number` object to fix the number variable that `itemCost AfterTax` holds to two decimal places. The method's only parameter is the number of decimal places you want your number fixed to. This line means that the next `document.write` displays this:

```
Item cost fixed to 2 decimal places is 10.74
```

The first thing you might wonder is why 10.74 and not 10.73? Well, the `toFixed()` method doesn't just chop off the digits not required; it also rounds up or down. In this case, the number was 10.739, which rounds up to 10.74. If it'd been 10.732, it would have been rounded down to 10.73.

Note that you can only fix a number from 0 to 20 decimal places.

Because this method is only supported on newer browsers, it's a good idea to check first to see if the browser supports it, like so:

```
var varNumber = 22.234;
if (varNumber.toFixed)
{
    // Browser supports toFixed() method
    varNumber = varNumber.toFixed(2)
}
else
{
    // Browser doesn't support toFixed() method so use some other code
    var div = Math.pow(10,2);
    varNumber = Math.round(varNumber * div) / div;
}
```

Array Objects

You saw how to create and use arrays in Chapter 2, and earlier in this chapter we mentioned that they are actually objects.

As well as storing data, `Array` objects also provide a number of useful properties and methods you can use to manipulate the data in the array and find out information such as the size of the array.

Again, this is not an exhaustive look at every property and method of `Array` objects, but rather just some of the more useful ones.

The length Property—Finding Out How Many Elements Are in an Array

The `length` property gives you the number of elements within an array. You have already seen this in the trivia quiz in Chapter 3. Sometimes you know exactly how long the array is, but there are situations where you may have been adding new elements to an array with no easy way of keeping track of how many have been added.

The `length` property can be used to find the index of the last element in the array. This is illustrated in the following example:

```
var names = new Array();

names[0] = "Paul";
names[1] = "Catherine";
names[11] = "Steve";

document.write("The last name is " + names[names.length - 1]);
```

Note that you have inserted data in the elements with index positions 0, 1, and 11. The array index starts at 0, so the last element is at index length - 1, which is 11, rather than the value of the length property, which is 12.

Another situation in which the length property proves useful is where a JavaScript method returns an array it has built itself. For example, in Chapter 8 on advanced string handling, you'll see that the String object has the split() method, which splits text into pieces and passes back the result as an Array object. Because JavaScript created the array, there is no way for you to know, without the length property, what the index is of the last element in the array.

The concat() Method — Joining Arrays Together

If you want to take two separate arrays and join them together into one big array, you can use the Array object's concat() method. The concat() method returns a new array, which is the combination of the two arrays: the elements of the first array, then the elements of the second array. To do this, you use the method on your first array and pass the name of the second array as its parameter.

For example, say you have two arrays, names and ages, and separately they look like this:

names array			
Element Index	0	1	2
Value	Paul	Catherine	Steve

ages array			
Element Index	0	1	2
Value	31	29	34

If you combine them using names.concat(ages), you will get an array like this:

Element Index	0	1	2	3	4	5
Value	Paul	Catherine	Steve	31	29	34

In the following code, this is exactly what you are doing:

```
var names = new Array("Paul","Catherine","Steve");
var ages = new Array(31,29,34);

var concatArray;

concatArray = names.concat(ages);
```

It's also possible to combine two arrays into one, but assign the new array to the name of the existing first array, using `names = names.concat(ages)`.

If you were to use `ages.concat(names)`, what would be the difference? Well, as you can see in the following table, the difference is that now the `ages` array elements are first, and the elements from the `names` array are concatenated on the end.

Element Index	0	1	2	3	4	5
Value	31	29	34	Paul	Catherine	Steve

The slice() Method—Copying Part of an Array

When you just want to copy a portion of an array, you can use the `slice()` method. Using the `slice()` method, you can slice out a portion of the array and assign that to a new variable name. The `slice()` method has two parameters:

❑   The index of the first element you want copied

❑   The index of the element marking the end of the portion you are slicing out (optional)

Just as with string copying with `substr()` and `substring()`, the start point is included in the copy, but the end point is not. Again, if you don't include the second parameter, all elements from the start index onward are copied.

Suppose you have the array `names` shown in the following table.

Index	0	1	2	3	4
Value	Paul	Sarah	Louise	Adam	Bob

If you want to create a new array with elements 1, `Sarah`, and 2, `Louise`, you would specify a start index of 1 and an end index of 3. The code would look something like this:

```
var names = new Array("Paul","Sarah","Louise","Adam","Bob");
var slicedArray = names.slice(1,3);
```

Note that when JavaScript copies the array, it copies the new elements to an array in which they have indexes 0 and 1, and not their old indexes of 1 and 2. After slicing, the slicedArray looks like this:

Index	0	1
Value	Sarah	Louise

The first array, names, is unaffected by the slicing.

The join() Method — Converting an Array into a Single String

The join() method concatenates all the elements in an array and returns them as a string. It also enables you to specify any characters you want to insert *between* elements as they are joined together. The method has only one parameter, and that's the string you want between elements.

An example will help explaining things. Imagine that you have your weekly shopping list stored in an array, which looks something like this:

Index	0	1	2	3	4
Value	Eggs	Milk	Potatoes	Cereal	Banana

Now you want to write out your shopping list to the page using document.write(). You want each item to be on a different line, so this means you need to use the <br> tag between each element. First, you need to declare your array.

```
var myShopping = new Array("Eggs","Milk","Potatoes","Cereal","Banana");
```

Now, convert the array into one string with the join() method.

```
var myShoppingList = myShopping.join("<br>");
```

Now the variable myShoppingList will hold the following text:

```
"Eggs<br>Milk<br>Potatoes<br>Cereal<br>Banana"
```

which you can write out to the page with document.write().

```
document.write(myShoppingList);
```

The shopping list will appear in the page with each item on a new line, as shown in Figure 4-3.

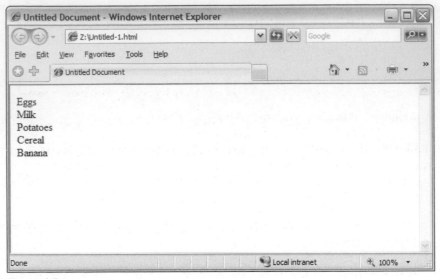

Figure 4-3

The sort() Method — Putting Your Array in Order

If you have an array that contains similar data, such as a list of names or a list of ages, you may want to put them in alphabetical or numerical order. This is something that the sort() method makes very easy. In the following code, you define your array and then put it in ascending alphabetical order using names.sort(). Finally, you output it so that you can see that it's in order.

```
var names = new Array("Paul","Sarah","Louise","Adam","Bob");
var elementIndex;

names.sort();
document.write("Now the names again in order" + "<BR>");

for (elementIndex = 0; elementIndex < names.length; elementIndex++)
{
    document.write(names[elementIndex] + "<BR>");
}
```

Don't forget that the sorting is case sensitive, so Paul will come before paul. Remember that JavaScript stores letters encoded in their equivalent Unicode number, and that sorting is done based on Unicode numbers rather than actual letters. It just happens that Unicode numbers match the order in the alphabet. However, lowercase letters are given a different sequence of numbers, which come after the uppercase letters. So the array with elements Adam, adam, Zoë, zoë, will be sorted to the order Adam, Zoë, adam, zoë.

Note that in your `for` statement you've used the `Array` object's `length` property in the condition statement, rather than inserting the length of the array (5), like this:

```
for (elementIndex = 0; elementIndex < 5; elementIndex++)
```

Why do this? After all, you know in advance that there are five elements in the array. Well, what would happen if you altered the number of elements in our array by adding two more names?

```
var names = new Array("Paul","Sarah","Louise","Adam","Bob","Karen","Steve");
```

If you had inserted 5 rather than `names.length`, your loop code wouldn't work as you want it to. It wouldn't display the last two elements unless you changed the condition part of the `for` loop to 7. By using the `length` property, you've made life easier, because now there is no need to change code elsewhere if you add array elements.

Okay, you've put things in ascending order, but what if you wanted descending order? That is where the `reverse()` method comes in.

The reverse() Method — Putting Your Array into Reverse Order

The final method you'll look at for the `Array` object is the `reverse()` method, which — no prizes for guessing — reverses the order of the array so that the elements at the back are moved to the front. Let's take the shopping list again as an example.

Index	0	1	2	3	4
Value	Eggs	Milk	Potatoes	Cereal	Banana

If you use the `reverse()` method

```
var myShopping = new Array("Eggs","Milk","Potatoes","Cereal","Banana");
myShopping.reverse();
```

you end up with the array elements in this order:

Index	0	1	2	3	4
Value	Banana	Cereal	Potatoes	Milk	Eggs

To prove this you could write it to the page with the `join()` method you saw earlier.

```
var myShoppingList = myShopping.join("<br>")
document.write(myShoppingList);
```

Try It Out   Sorting an Array

When used in conjunction with the `sort()` method, the `reverse()` method can be used to sort an array so that its elements appear in reverse alphabetical or numerical order. This is shown in the following example:

```
<html>
<body>
<script language="JavaScript" type="text/javascript">

var myShopping = new Array("Eggs","Milk","Potatoes","Cereal","Banana");

var ord = prompt("Enter 1 for alphabetical order, and -1 for reverse order", 1);

if (ord == 1)
{
   myShopping.sort();
   document.write(myShopping.join("<br>"));
}
else if (ord == -1)
{
   myShopping.sort();
   myShopping.reverse();
   document.write(myShopping.join("<br>"));
}
else
{
document.write("That is not a valid input");
}
</script>
</body>
</html>
```

Save the example as `ch4_examp5.htm`. When you load this into your browser, you will be asked to enter some input depending on whether you want the array to be ordered in forward or backward order. If you enter 1, the array will be displayed in forward order. If you enter –1, the array will be displayed in reverse order. If you enter neither of these values, you will be told that your input was invalid.

How It Works

At the top of the script block you define the array containing your shopping list. Next you define the variable `ord` to be the value entered by the user in a prompt box.

```
var ord = prompt("Enter 1 for alphabetical order, and -1 for reverse order", 1);
```

This value is used in the conditions of the `if` statements that follow. The first `if` checks whether the value of `ord` is 1 — that is, whether the user wants the array in alphabetical order. If so, the following code is executed:

```
myShopping.sort();
document.write(myShopping.join("<br>"));
```

The array is sorted and then displayed to the user on separate lines using the `join()` method. Next, in the `else if` statement, you check whether the value of `ord` is `-1` — that is, whether the user wants the array in reverse alphabetical order. If so, the following code is executed:

```
myShopping.sort();
myShopping.reverse();
document.write(myShopping.join("<br>"));
```

Here, you sort the array before reversing its order. Again the array is displayed to the user by means of the `join()` method.

Finally, if `ord` has neither the value `1` nor the value `-1`, you tell the user that his input was invalid.

```
document.write("That is not a valid input");
```

Date Objects

The `Date` object handles everything to do with date and time in JavaScript. Using it, you can find out the date and time now, store your own dates and times, do calculations with these dates, and convert the dates into strings.

The `Date` object has a lot of methods and can be a little tricky to use, which is why Chapter 9 is dedicated to the date, time, and timers in JavaScript. You'll also see in Chapter 11 how you can use dates to determine if there's been anything new added to the web site since the user last visited it. However, in this section you'll focus on how to create a `Date` object and some of its more commonly used methods.

Creating a Date Object

You can declare and initialize a `Date` object in four ways. In the first method, you simply declare a new `Date` object without initializing its value. In this case, the date and time value will be set to the current date and time on the PC on which the script is run.

```
var theDate1 = new Date();
```

Secondly, you can define a `Date` object by passing the number of milliseconds since January 1, 1970, at 00:00:00 GMT. In the following example, the date is 31 January 2000 00:20:00 GMT (that is, 20 minutes past midnight).

```
var theDate2 = new Date(949278000000);
```

It's unlikely that you'll be using this way of defining a `Date` object very often, but this is how JavaScript actually stores the dates. The other formats for giving a date are simply for our convenience.

Next, you can pass a string representing a date, or a date and time. In the following example, you have `"31 January 2010"`.

```
var theDate3 = new Date("31 January 2010");
```

However, you could have written 31 Jan 2010, Jan 31 2010, 01-31-2010, or any of a number of valid variations you'd commonly expect when writing down a date normally — if in doubt, try it out. Note that Firefox and Netscape browsers don't support the string `"01-31-2010"` as a valid date format. If you are writing your web pages for an international audience outside the United States, you need to be aware of the different ways of specifying dates. In the United Kingdom and many other places, the standard is day, month, year, whereas in the United States the standard is month, day, year. This can cause problems if you specify only numbers — JavaScript may think you're referring to a day when you mean a month. The easiest way to avoid such headaches is to, where possible, always use the name of the month. That way there can be no confusion.

In the fourth and final way of defining a `Date` object, you initialize it by passing the following parameters separated by commas: year, month, day, hours, minutes, seconds, and milliseconds. For example:

```
var theDate4 = new Date(2010,0,31,15,35,20,20);
```

This date is actually 31 January 2010 at 15:35:20 and 20 milliseconds. You can specify just the date part if you wish and ignore the time.

Something to be aware of is that in this instance January is month 0, not month 1, as you'd expect, and December is month 11. It's very easy to make a mistake when specifying a month.

Getting Date Values

It's all very nice having stored a date, but how do you get the information out again? Well, you just use the `get` methods. These are summarized in the following table.

Method	Returns
getDate()	The day of the month
getDay() and so on	The day of the week as an integer, with Sunday as 0, Monday as 1,
getMonth()	The month as an integer, with January as 0, February as 1, and so on
getFullYear()	The year as a four-digit number
toDateString()	Returns the full date based on the current time zone as a human-readable string. For example "Wed 31 Dec 2003".

For example, if you want to get the month in `ourDateObj`, you can simply write the following:

```
theMonth = myDateObject.getMonth();
```

All the methods work in a very similar way, and all values returned are based on local time, meaning time local to the machine the code is running on. It's also possible to use Universal Time, previously known as GMT, which we'll discuss in Chapter 9.

Try It Out   Using the Date Object to Retrieve the Current Date

In this example, you use the `get date type` methods you have been looking at to write the current day, month, and year to a web page.

```html
<html>
<body>

<script language="JavaScript" type="text/javascript">

var months = new Array("January","February","March","April","May","June","July",
                       "August","September","October","November","December");
var dateNow = new Date();
var yearNow = dateNow.getFullYear();
var monthNow = months[dateNow.getMonth()];
var dayNow = dateNow.getDate();
var daySuffix;

switch (dayNow)
{
case 1:
case 21:
case 31:
   daySuffix = "st";
   break;
case 2:
case 22:
   daySuffix = "nd";
   break;
case 3:
case 23:
   daySuffix = "rd";
   break;
default:
   daySuffix = "th";
   break;
}

document.write("It is the " + dayNow + daySuffix + " day ");
document.write("in the month of " + monthNow);
document.write(" in the year " + yearNow);

</script>
</body>
</html>
```

Save the code as `ch4_examp6.htm`. If you load up the page, you should see a correctly formatted sentence telling you what the current date is.

How It Works

The first thing you do in the code is declare an array and populate it with the months of a year. Why do this? Well, there is no method of the `Date` object that'll give you the month by name instead of as a number. However, this poses no problem; you just declare an array of months and use the month number as the array index to select the correct month name.

```javascript
var months = new Array("January","February","March","April","May","June","July",
                       "August","September","October","November","December");
```

Next you create a new `Date` object and by not initializing it with your own value, you allow it to initialize itself to the current date and time.

```
var dateNow = new Date();
```

Following this you set the `yearNow` variable to the current year, as returned by the `getFullYear()` method.

```
var yearNow = dateNow.getFullYear();
```

Note that `getFullYear()` only became available with version 4 browsers, such as IE 4 and NN 4.06 and above. Prior to this, there was only the `getYear()` method, which on some browsers returned only a two-digit year.

You then populate your `monthNow` variable with the value contained in the array element with an index of the number returned by `getMonth()`. Remember that `getMonth()` returns the month as an integer value, starting with 0 for January—this is a bonus because arrays also start at 0, so no adjustment is needed to find the correct array element.

```
var monthNow = months[dateNow.getMonth()];
```

Finally, the current day of the month is put into variable `dayNow`.

```
var dayNow = dateNow.getDate();
```

Next you use a `switch` statement, which you learned about in the last chapter. This is a useful technique for adding the correct suffix to the date that you already have. After all, your application will look more professional if you can say `"it is the 1st day"`, rather than `"it is the 1 day"`. This is a little tricky, however, because the suffix you want to add depends on the number that precedes it. So, for the first, twenty-first, and thirty-first days of the month, you have this:

```
switch (dayNow)
{
case 1:
case 21:
case 31:
   daySuffix = "st";
   break;
```

For the second and twenty-second days, you have this:

```
case 2:
case 22:
   daySuffix = "nd";
   break;
```

and for the third and twenty-third days, you have this:

```
case 3:
case 23:
   daySuffix = "rd";
   break;
```

Finally, you need the `default` case for everything else. As you will have guessed by now, this is simply `"th"`.

```
default:
    daySuffix = "th";
    break;
}
```

In the final lines you simply write the information to the HTML page, using `document.write()`.

Setting Date Values

To change part of the date in a `Date` object, you have a group of `set` functions, which pretty much replicate the `get` functions described earlier, except that you are setting, not getting, the values. These functions are summarized in the following table.

Method	Description
`setDate()`	The date of the month is passed in as the parameter to set the date
`setMonth()`	The month of the year is passed in as an integer parameter, where 0 is January, 1 is February, and so on
`setFullYear()`	This sets the year to the four-digit integer number passed in as a parameter

Note that for security reasons, there is no way for web-based JavaScript to change the current date and time on a user's computer.

So, to change the year to 2009, the code would be as follows:

```
myDateObject.setFullYear(2009);
```

Setting the date and month to the twenty-seventh of February looks like this:

```
myDateObject.setDate(27);
myDateObject.setMonth(1);
```

One minor point to note here is that there is no direct equivalent of the `getDay()` method. After the year, date, and month have been defined, the day is automatically set for you.

Calculations and Dates

Take a look at the following code:

```
var myDate = new Date("1 Jan 2010");
myDate.setDate(32);
document.write(myDate);
```

Surely there is some error—since when has January had 32 days? The answer is that of course it doesn't, and JavaScript knows that. Instead JavaScript sets the date to 32 days from the first of January—that is, it sets it to the first of February.

The same also applies to the setMonth() method. If you set it to a value greater than 11, the date automatically rolls over to the next year. So if you use setMonth(12), that will set the date to January of the next year, and similarly setMonth(13) is February of the next year.

How can you use this feature of setDate() and setMonth() to your advantage? Well, let's say you want to find out what date it will be 28 days from now. Given that different months have different numbers of days and that you could roll over to a different year, it's not as simple a task as it might first seem. Or at least that would be the case if it were not for setDate(). The code to achieve this task is as follows:

```
var nowDate = new Date();
var currentDay = nowDate.getDate();
nowDate.setDate(currentDay + 28);
```

First you get the current system date by setting the nowDate variable to a new Date object with no initialization value. In the next line you put the current day of the month into a variable called currentDay. Why? Well, when you use setDate() and pass it a value outside of the maximum number of days for that month, it starts from the first of the month and counts that many days forward. So, if today's date is the January 15 and you use setDate(28), it's not 28 days from the fifteenth of January, but 28 days from the first of January. What you want is 28 days from the current date, so you need to add the current date to the number of days ahead you want. So you want setDate(15 + 28). In the third line you set the date to the current date, plus 28 days. You stored the current day of the month in currentDay, so now you just add 28 to that to move 28 days ahead.

If you want the date 28 days prior to the current date, you just pass the current date minus 28. Note that this will most often be a negative number. You need to change only one line, and that's the third one, which you change to

```
nowDate.setDate(currentDay - 28);
```

You can use exactly the same principles for setMonth() as you have used for setDate().

Getting Time Values

The methods you use to retrieve the individual pieces of time data work much like the get methods for date values. The methods you use here are:

- ❏ getHours()
- ❏ getMinutes()
- ❏ getSeconds()
- ❏ getMilliseconds()
- ❏ toTimeString()

These methods return respectively the hours, minutes, seconds, milliseconds, and full time of the specified Date object, where the time is based on the 24-hour clock: 0 for midnight and 23 for 11 p.m. The last method is similar to the toDateString() method in that it returns an easily readable string, except that in this case it contains the time (for example, "13:03:51 UTC").

Note that the getMilliseconds() method is available only in IE 4+ and NN 4.06+ browsers.

Try It Out   **Writing the Current Time into a Web Page**

Let's look at an example that writes out the current time to the page.

```
<html>
<body>
<script language="JavaScript" type="text/javascript">

var greeting;

var nowDate = new Date();
var nowHour = nowDate.getHours();
var nowMinute = nowDate.getMinutes();
var nowSecond = nowDate.getSeconds();

if (nowMinute < 10)
{
   nowMinute = "0" + nowMinute;
}

if (nowSecond < 10)
{
   nowSecond = "0" + nowSecond;
}

if (nowHour < 12)
{
   greeting = "Good Morning";
}
else if (nowHour < 17)
{
   greeting = "Good Afternoon";
}
else
{
   greeting = "Good Evening";
}

document.write("<h4>" + greeting + " and welcome to my website</h4>");
document.write("According to your clock the time is ");
document.write(nowHour + ":" + nowMinute + ":" + nowSecond);

</script>
</body>
</html>
```

Save this page as ch4_examp7.htm. When you load it into a web browser, it writes a greeting based on the time of day as well as the current time, as shown in Figure 4-4.

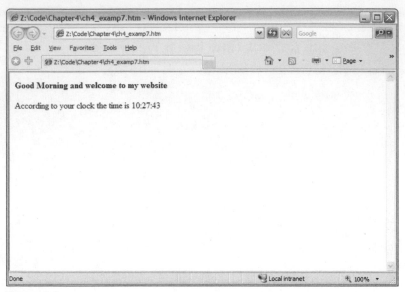

Figure 4-4

How It Works

The first two lines of code declare two variables — `greeting` and `nowDate`.

```
var greeting;
var nowDate = new Date();
```

The `greeting` variable will be used shortly to store the welcome message on the web site, whether this is `"Good Morning"`, `"Good Afternoon"`, or `"Good Evening"`. The `nowDate` variable is initialized to a new `Date` object. Note that the constructor for the `Date` object is empty, so JavaScript will store the current date and time in it.

Next, you get the information on the current time from `nowDate` and store it in various variables. You can see that getting time data is very similar to getting date data, just using different methods.

```
var nowHour = nowDate.getHours();
var nowMinute = nowDate.getMinutes();
var nowSecond = nowDate.getSeconds();
```

You may wonder why the following lines are included in the example:

```
if (nowMinute < 10)
{
    nowMinute = "0" + nowMinute;
}

if (nowSecond < 10)
{
    nowSecond = "0" + nowSecond;
}
```

These lines are there just for formatting reasons. If the time is nine minutes past 10, then you expect to see something like 10:09. You don't expect 10:9, which is what you would get if you used the getMinutes() method without adding the extra zero. The same goes for seconds. If you're just using the data in calculations, you don't need to worry about formatting issues — you do here because you're inserting the time the code executed into the web page.

Next, in a series of if statements, you decide (based on the time of day) which greeting to create for displaying to the user.

```
if (nowHour < 12)
{
    greeting = "Good Morning";
}
else if (nowHour < 17)
{
    greeting = "Good Afternoon";
}
else
{
    greeting = "Good Evening";
}
```

Finally, you write out the greeting and the current time to the page.

```
document.write("<h4>" + greeting + " and welcome to my website</h4>");
document.write("According to your clock the time is ");
document.write(nowHour + ":" + nowMinute + ":" + nowSecond);
```

You'll see in Chapter 9 on dates, times, and timers how you can write a continuously updating time to the web page, making it look like a clock.

Setting Time Values

When you want to set the time in your Date objects, you have a series of methods similar to those used for getting the time:

❑   setHours()

❑   setMinutes()

❑   setSeconds()

❑   setMilliseconds()

These work much like the methods you use to set the date, in that if you set any of the time parameters to an illegal value, JavaScript assumes you mean the next or previous time boundary. If it's 9:57 and you set minutes to 64, the time will be set to 10:04 — that is, 64 minutes from 9:00.

This is demonstrated in the following code:

```
var nowDate = new Date();
nowDate.setHours(9);
nowDate.setMinutes(57);
```

```
alert(nowDate);

nowDate.setMinutes(64);
alert(nowDate);
```

First you declare the nowDate variable and assign it to a new Date object, which will contain the current date and time. In the following two lines you set the hours to 9 and the minutes to 57. You show the date and time using an alert box, which should show a time of 9:57. The minutes are then set to 64 and again an alert box is used to show the date and time to the user. Now the minutes have rolled over the hour so the time shown should be 10:04.

If the hours were set to 23 instead of 9, setting the minutes to 64 would not just move the time to another hour but also cause the day to change to the next date.

JavaScript Classes

In this section you'll be looking at some quite tricky and advanced stuff. It's not essential stuff, so you may want to move on and come back to it later.

You've seen that JavaScript provides a number of objects built into the language and ready for us to use. It's a bit like a house that's built already and you can just move on in. However, what if you want to create your own house, to design it for your own specific needs? In that case you'll use an architect to create technical drawings and plans that provide the template for the new house — the builders use the plans to tell them how to create the house.

So what does any of this have to do with JavaScript and objects? Well, JavaScript enables you to be an architect and create the templates for your own objects to your own specification, to fill your specific needs. Let's say, for example, you were creating a cinema booking system. JavaScript doesn't come with any built-in cinema booking objects, so you'd have to design your own. What you need to do is create objects modeled around the real world. So for a simple cinema booking system, you might have an object representing customers' booking details and an object for the cinema where the bookings have been made. As well as being able to store information, you can create your own methods for an object. So for a booking system, you might want an "add new booking" method or a method that gets the details of all the bookings currently made.

Where you have no need to store data but simply want functionality, such as the fix() function you saw before, it's generally easier just to have a code library rather than to create a special object.

Just as a builder of a house needs an architect's plans to know what to build and how it should be laid out, you need to provide blueprints telling JavaScript how your object should look. For example, you need to define its methods and provide the code for those methods. The key to this is JavaScript's support for the definition of classes. Classes are essentially templates for an object, as the architect's drawings are the template used to build a house. Before you can use your new object type, you need to define its class, methods, and properties. The important distinction is that when you define your class, no object based on that class is created. It's only when you create an instance of your class using the new keyword that an object of that class type, based on your class blueprint or prototype, is created.

A class consists of three things:

- ❑   A constructor
- ❑   Method definitions
- ❑   Properties

A constructor is a method that is called every time one of your objects based on this class is created. It's useful when you want to initialize properties or the object in some way. You need to create a constructor even if you don't pass any parameters to it or it contains no code. (In that case it'd just be an empty definition.) As with functions, a constructor can have zero or more parameters.

You used methods when you used JavaScript's built-in objects; now you get the chance to use classes to define your own methods performing specific tasks. Your class will specify what methods you have and the code that they execute. Again, you have used properties of built-in objects before and now get to define your own. You don't need to declare your class's properties. You can simply go ahead and use properties in your class without letting JavaScript know in advance.

Let's create a simple class based on the real-world example of a cinema booking system.

Defining a Class

Let's start by creating a class for a customer's booking. This class will be called the CustomerBooking class. The first thing you need to do is create the class constructor.

The constructor for your class is shown here:

```
function CustomerBooking (bookingId, customerName, film, showDate)
{
  this.customerName = customerName;
  this.bookingId = bookingId;
  this.showDate = showDate;
  this.film = film;
}
```

Your first thought might be that what you have here is simply a function, and you'd be right. It's not until you start defining the CustomerBooking class properties and methods that it becomes a class. This is in contrast to some programming languages, which have a more formal way of defining classes.

When you look at the code, the important thing to note is that the constructor function's name must match that of the class you are defining — in this case the CustomerBooking class. That way, when a new instance of your class as an object (termed an *object instance*) is created, this function will be called automatically. Note that you have four parameters for your constructor function, and that these are used inside the class itself. However, note that you use the this keyword. For example:

```
this.customerName = customerName;
```

Inside a constructor function or within a class method, the this keyword will refer to that object instance of your class. Here you refer to the customerName property of this class object, and you set it to equal the `customerName` parameter. If you have used other object-oriented programming languages, you might wonder where you defined this `customerName` property. The answer is that you didn't; simply by assigning a property a value, JavaScript creates it for you. There is no check that the property exists; JavaScript creates it as it needs to. The same is true if you use the object with a property never mentioned in your class definition. All this free property creation might sound great, but it has drawbacks, the main one being that JavaScript won't tell you if you accidentally misspell a property name; it'll just create a new property with the misspelled name, something that can make it difficult to track bugs. One way around this problem is to create methods that get a property's value and enable you to set a property's value. Now this may sound like hard work, but it can reduce bugs or at least make them easier to spot. Let's create a few property `get`/`set` methods for the `CustomerBooking` class.

```
CustomerBooking.prototype.getCustomerName = function()
{
 return this.customerName;
}


CustomerBooking.prototype.setCustomerName = function(customerName)
{
 this.customerName = customerName;
}


CustomerBooking.prototype.getShowDate = function()
{
 return this.showDate;
}


CustomerBooking.prototype.setShowDate = function(showDate)
{
 this.showDate = showDate;
}


CustomerBooking.prototype.getFilm = function()
{
 return this.film;
}


CustomerBooking.prototype.setFilm = function(film)
{
 this.film = film;
}


CustomerBooking.prototype.getBookingId = function()
{
 return this.bookingId;
}


CustomerBooking.prototype.setBookingId = function(bookingId)
{
 this.bookingId = bookingId;
}
```

Now you have defined a set and get method for each of your class's four properties: bookingId, film, customerName, and showDate. Let's look at how you created one of the methods, the getCustomerName() method.

```
CustomerBooking.prototype.getCustomerName = function()
{
  return this.customerName;
}
```

The first thing you notice is that this is a very odd way of defining a function. On the left you set the class's prototype property's getCustomerName to equal a function, which you then define immediately afterwards. In fact, JavaScript supplies most objects with a prototype property, which allows new properties and methods to be created. So whenever you want to create a method for your class, you simply write the following:

```
className.prototype.methodName = function(method parameter list)
{
    // method code
}
```

You've created your class, but how do you now create new objects based on that class? Well, you look at this in the next section.

Creating and Using Class Object Instances

You create instances of your classes in the same way you created instances of built-in JavaScript classes: using the new keyword. So to create a new instance of your CustomerBooking class, you'd write this:

```
var firstBooking = new
  CustomerBooking(1234, "Robert Smith","Raging Bull", "25 July 2004 18:20");

var secondBooking = new
  CustomerBooking(1244, "Arnold Palmer","Toy Story", "27 July 2004 20:15");
```

Here, as with a String object, you have created two new objects and stored them in variables, firstBooking and secondBooking, but this time it's a new object based on your class.

Let's call the getCustomerName() method of each of the two objects and write the results to the page.

```
document.write("1st booking person's name is " +
               firstBooking.getCustomerName() + "<br>");
document.write("2nd booking person's name is " +
               secondBooking.getCustomerName());
```

And you'll see the following written into the page from information contained in your class objects:

```
1st booking person's name is Robert Smith
2nd booking person's name is Arnold Palmer
```

Now let's put this together in a page.

```
<html>
<body>

<script language="JavaScript" type="text/javascript">

// CustomerBooking class

function CustomerBooking(bookingId, customerName, film, showDate)
{
  this.customerName = customerName;
  this.bookingId = bookingId;
  this.showDate = showDate;
  this.film = film;
}

CustomerBooking.prototype.getCustomerName = function()
{
 return this.customerName;
}

CustomerBooking.prototype.setCustomerName = function(customerName)
{
 this.customerName = customerName;
}

CustomerBooking.prototype.getShowDate = function()
{
 return this.showDate;
}

CustomerBooking.prototype.setShowDate = function(showDate)
{
 this.showDate = showDate;
}

CustomerBooking.prototype.getFilm = function()
{
 return this.film;
}

CustomerBooking.prototype.setFilm = function(film)
{
 this.film = film;
}

CustomerBooking.prototype.getBookingId = function()
{
 return this.bookingId;
}

CustomerBooking.prototype.setBookingId = function(bookingId)
{
```

```
    this.bookingId = bookingId;
}


var firstBooking = new CustomerBooking(1234,
                        "Robert Smith","Raging Bull", "25 July 2004 18:20");
var secondBooking = new CustomerBooking(1244,
                        "Arnold Palmer","Toy Story", "27 July 2004 20:15");
document.write("1st booking persons name is " +
                firstBooking.getCustomerName() + "<br>");
document.write("2nd booking persons name is " +
                secondBooking.getCustomerName());

</script>

</body>
</html>
```

At the top of the page is your <script> tag, inside of which is the code that defines your class. You must include class definition code in every page that uses your class to create objects. For convenience, you may therefore decide to put your class definitions in a separate file and import that file into each page that uses the class. You can do this using the <script> tag, but instead of putting the code inside the open and close tags, you'll use the script tag's src attribute to point to the file containing the JavaScript. For example, if you create a file called MyCinemaBookingClasses.js and put your class code in there, you can import it into a page as shown here:

```
<script language="JavaScript" src="MyCinemaBookingClasses.js"></script>
```

The src attribute points to the URL of your class, which in this case assumes that the class's .js file is in the same directory as your page.

An Array of Items

So far you have a class for items that you can put a single booking into, but no class representing all the bookings taken by a cinema. So how can you create a cinema class that supports the storage of zero or more items? The answer is using an array, which we discuss in Chapter 3.

Let's start by defining your class, which you'll call the cinema class, and add to the script block with your CustomerBooking class.

```
// cinema class

function cinema()
{
    this.bookings = new Array();
}
```

Here you define the constructor. Inside the constructor, you initialize the bookings property that will hold all the CustomerBooking class objects.

Next you need to add a way of making bookings for the cinema; for this you create the `addBooking()` method.

```
cinema.prototype.addBooking = function(bookingId, customerName, film, showDate)
{
    this.bookings[bookingId] = new CustomerBooking(bookingId,
                                        customerName, film, showDate);

}
```

The method takes four parameters, the details needed to create a new booking. Then, inside the method, you create a new object of type `CustomerBooking`. A reference to this object is stored inside your `bookings` array, using the unique `bookingId` to associate the place in which the new object is stored.

Let's look at how you can access the items in the array. In the following method, called `getBookingsTable()`, you go through each booking in the cinema and create the HTML necessary to display all the bookings in a table.

```
cinema.prototype.getBookingsTable = function()
{
  var booking;
    var bookingsTableHTML = "<table border=1>";

    for (booking in this.bookings)
    {
      bookingsTableHTML += "<tr><td>";
    bookingsTableHTML += this.bookings[booking].getBookingId();
    bookingsTableHTML += "</td>";

    bookingsTableHTML += "<td>";
    bookingsTableHTML += this.bookings[booking].getCustomerName();
    bookingsTableHTML += "</td>";

    bookingsTableHTML += "<td>";
    bookingsTableHTML += this.bookings[booking].getFilm();
    bookingsTableHTML += "</td>";

        bookingsTableHTML += "<td>";
    bookingsTableHTML += this.bookings[booking].getShowDate();
    bookingsTableHTML += "</td>";
      bookingsTableHTML += "</tr>";
    }
      bookingsTableHTML += "</table>";
    return bookingsTableHTML;
}
```

You can access each booking by its unique `bookingId`, but what you want to do is simply loop through all the bookings for the cinema, so you use a `for...in` loop, which will loop through each item in the `items` array. Each time the loop executes, `booking` will be set by JavaScript to contain the `bookingId` of the next booking; it doesn't contain the item itself but its associated keyword.

Since you have the associated keyword, you can access the item objects in the array like this:

```
this.bookings[booking]
```

Remember that this refers to the object instance of your class. You then use the `CustomerBooking` object's `get` methods to obtain the details for each booking. Finally, on the last line, you return the HTML — with your summary of all the bookings — to the calling code.

Let's put this all together in a page and save the page as `ch4_examp8.htm`.

```html
<html>
<body>

<h2>Summary of bookings</h2>

<script language="JavaScript" type="text/javascript">

// CustomerBooking class

function CustomerBooking(bookingId, customerName, film, showDate)
{
  this.customerName = customerName;
  this.bookingId = bookingId;
  this.showDate = showDate;
  this.film = film;
}

CustomerBooking.prototype.getCustomerName = function()
{
 return this.customerName;
}

CustomerBooking.prototype.setCustomerName = function(customerName)
{
 this.customerName = customerName;
}

CustomerBooking.prototype.getShowDate = function()
{
 return this.showDate;
}

CustomerBooking.prototype.setShowDate = function(showDate)
{
  this.showDate = showDate;
}

CustomerBooking.prototype.getFilm = function()
{
 return this.film;
}

CustomerBooking.prototype.setFilm = function(film)
{
  this.film = film;
}

CustomerBooking.prototype.getBookingId = function()
{
```

```
   return this.bookingId;
}

CustomerBooking.prototype.setBookingId = function(bookingId)
{
 this.bookingId = bookingId;
}

// cinema class

function cinema()
{
   this.bookings = new Array();
}

cinema.prototype.addBooking = function(bookingId, customerName, film, showDate)
{
   this.bookings[bookingId] = new CustomerBooking(bookingId,
                                         customerName, film, showDate);
}


cinema.prototype.getBookingsTable = function()
{
  var booking;
    var bookingsTableHTML = "<table border=1>";

    for (booking in this.bookings)
    {
      bookingsTableHTML += "<tr><td>";
    bookingsTableHTML += this.bookings[booking].getBookingId();
    bookingsTableHTML += "</td>";

    bookingsTableHTML += "<td>";
    bookingsTableHTML += this.bookings[booking].getCustomerName();
    bookingsTableHTML += "</td>";

    bookingsTableHTML += "<td>";
    bookingsTableHTML += this.bookings[booking].getFilm();
    bookingsTableHTML += "</td>";

         bookingsTableHTML += "<td>";
    bookingsTableHTML += this.bookings[booking].getShowDate();
    bookingsTableHTML += "</td>";
      bookingsTableHTML += "</tr>";
     }
      bookingsTableHTML += "</table>";
     return bookingsTableHTML;
}
```

```
var londonOdeon = new cinema();
londonOdeon.addBooking(342, "Arnold Palmer","Toy Story", "15 July 2009 20:15");
londonOdeon.addBooking(335, "Louise Anderson","The Shawshank Redemption", "27 July
2009 11:25");
londonOdeon.addBooking(566, "Catherine Hughes",
```

```
                              "Never Say Never", "27 July 2009 17:55");
londonOdeon.addBooking(324, "Beci Smith",
                              "Shrek", "29 July 2009 20:15");


document.write(londonOdeon.getBookingsTable());

</script>
```

```
</body>
</html>
```

Your new code is the lines

```
var londonOdeon = new cinema();
londonOdeon.addBooking(342, "Arnold Palmer","Toy Story", "15 July 2009 20:15");
londonOdeon.addBooking(335, "Louise Anderson",
                              "The Shawshank Redemption", "27 July 2009 11:25");
londonOdeon.addBooking(566, "Catherine Hughes",
                              "Never Say Never", "27 July 2009 17:55");
londonOdeon.addBooking(324, "Beci Smith","Shrek", "29 July 2009 20:15");


document.write(londonOdeon.getBookingsTable());
```

These create a new cinema object and store a reference to it in the variable londonOdeon. You then create four new bookings using the cinema class's addBooking() method. On the final line, you write the HTML returned by the getBookingsTable() method to the page.

Your page should now look like that shown in Figure 4-5.

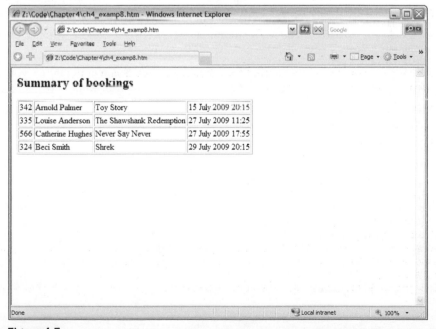

Figure 4-5

The cinema booking system you have created is very basic to say the least! However, it gives you an idea of how JavaScript classes can be used to help make code more maintainable and how they can be used to model real-world problems and situations.

Summary

In this chapter you've taken a look at the concept of objects and seen how vital they are to an understanding of JavaScript, which represents virtually everything with objects. You also looked at some of the various native objects that the JavaScript language provides to add to its functionality.

You saw that:

- ❑ JavaScript is object-based — it represents things, such as strings, dates, and arrays, using the concept of objects.

- ❑ Objects have properties and methods. For example, an `Array` object has the `length` property and the `sort()` method.

- ❑ To create a new object, you simply write `new ObjectType()`. You can choose to initialize an object when you create it.

- ❑ To set an object's property's value or get that value, you simply write `ObjectName.ObjectProperty`.

- ❑ Calling the methods of an object is similar to calling functions. Parameters may be passed, and return values may be passed back. Accessing the methods of an object is identical to accessing a property, except that you must remember to add parentheses at the end, even when there are no parameters. For example, you would write `ObjectName.ObjectMethod()`.

- ❑ The `String` object provides lots of handy functionality for text and gives you ways of finding out how long the text is, searching for text inside the string, and selecting parts of the text.

- ❑ The `Math` object is created automatically and provides a number of mathematical properties and methods. For example, to obtain a random number between 0 and 1, you use the method `Math.random()`.

- ❑ The `Array` object provides ways of manipulating arrays. Some of the things you can do are find the length of an array, sort its elements, and join two arrays together.

- ❑ The `Date` object provides a way of storing, calculating with, and later accessing dates and times.

- ❑ JavaScript enables you to create your own type of objects using classes. These can be used to model real-world situations and for making code easier to create and more maintainable, though they do require extra effort at the start.

In the next chapter, you'll turn your attention to the web browser itself and, particularly, the various objects that it makes available for your JavaScript programming. You'll see that the use of browser objects is key to creating powerful web pages.

Exercise Questions

Suggested solutions to these questions can be found in Appendix A.

Question 1

Using the Date object, calculate the date 12 months from now and write this into a web page.

Question 2

Obtain a list of names from the user, storing each name entered in an array. Keep getting another name until the user enters nothing. Sort the names in ascending order and then write them out to the page, with each name on its own line.

Question 3

You saw earlier in the chapter when looking at the pow() method how you could use it inventively to fix a number to a certain number of decimal places. However, there is a flaw in the function you created. A proper fix() function should return 2.1 fixed to three decimal places as

    2.100

However, your fix() function instead returns it as

    2.1

Change the fix() function so that the additional zeros are added where necessary.

Programming the Browser

Over the past three chapters, you've examined the core JavaScript language. You've seen how to work with variables and data, perform operations on those data, make decisions in your code, loop repeatedly over the same section of code, and even how to write your own functions. In the preceding chapter you moved on to learn how JavaScript is an object-based language, and you saw how to work with the native JavaScript objects. However, you are not interested only in the language itself—you want to find out how to write script for the web browser. Using this ability, you can start to create more impressive web pages.

Not only is JavaScript object-based, but the browser is also made up of objects. When JavaScript is running in the browser, you can access the browser's objects in exactly the same way that you used JavaScript's native objects in the last chapter. But what kinds of objects does the browser provide?

The browser makes available a remarkable number of objects. For example, there is a window object corresponding to the window of the browser. You have already been using two methods of this object, namely the alert() and prompt() methods. For simplicity, we previously referred to these as functions, but they are in fact methods of the browser's window object.

Another object made available by the browser is the page itself, represented by the document object. Again, you have already used methods and properties of this object. Recall from Chapter 1 that you used the document object's bgColor property to change the background color of the page. You have also been using the write() method of the document object to write information to the page.

A variety of other objects exist, representing a lot of the HTML that you write in the page. For example, there is an img object for each <img> tag that you use to insert an image into your document.

The collection of objects that the browser makes available to you for use with JavaScript is generally called the *Browser Object Model (BOM)*.

> *You will often see this termed the Document Object Model (DOM). However, throughout this book, we'll use the term DOM to refer to the W3C's standard Document Object Model, which is discussed in Chapter 13.*

All this added functionality of JavaScript comes with a potential downside. Which collections of objects are made available to you is highly dependent on the brand and version of the browser that you are using. Some objects are made available in some browsers and not in others, whereas other objects have different properties and methods in different browsers. The good news is that browsers are following the W3C's guidelines much more than they used to. This means that if you follow the W3C guidelines, your code is more likely to work with different browsers. Note, however, some browser writers have interpreted the W3C standards in a different way. You will see much more about the differences between the BOMs of IE and Firefox browsers in Chapter 12.

However, in this chapter you will concentrate on the core functionality of the BOM, the objects that are common to all browsers. You can achieve a lot in JavaScript by just sticking to such objects. You can find more information on them online at `http://www.w3schools.com/dhtml/dhtml_domreference.asp` and `http://msdn.microsoft.com/library/default.asp?url=/workshop/author/dhtml/dhtml_node_entry.asp`.

Introduction to the Browser Objects

In this section, we introduce the objects of the BOM that are common to all browsers.

In Chapter 4, you saw that JavaScript has a number of native objects that you have access to and can make use of. Most of the objects are those that you need to create yourself, such as the `String` and `Date` objects. Others, such as the `Math` object, exist without you needing to create them and are ready for use immediately when the page starts loading.

When JavaScript is running in a web page, it has access to a large number of other objects made available by the web browser. Rather like the `Math` object, these are created for you rather than your needing to create them explicitly. As mentioned, the objects, their methods, properties, and events are all mapped out in the BOM.

The BOM is very large and potentially overwhelming at first. However, you'll find that initially you won't be using more than 10 percent of the available objects, methods, and properties in the BOM. You'll start in this chapter by looking at the more commonly used parts of the BOM, shown in Figure 5-1. These parts of the BOM are, to a certain extent, common across all browsers. Later chapters will build on this so that by the end of the book you'll be able to really make the BOM work for you.

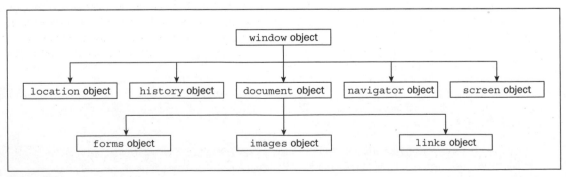

Figure 5-1

The BOM has a hierarchy. At the very top of this hierarchy is the window object. You can think of this as representing the frame of the browser and everything associated with it, such as the scrollbars, navigator bar icons, and so on.

Contained inside our window frame is the page. The page is represented in the BOM by the document object. You can see these two objects represented in Figure 5-2.

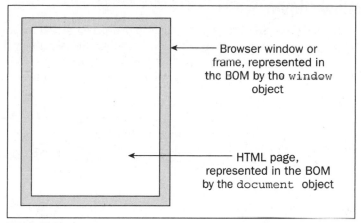

Browser window or frame, represented in the BOM by the window object

HTML page, represented in the BOM by the document object

Figure 5-2

Now let's look at each of these objects in more detail.

The window Object — Our Window onto the Page

The window object represents the browser's frame or window, in which your web page is contained. To some extent, it also represents the browser itself and includes a number of properties that are there simply because they don't fit anywhere else. For example, via the properties of the window object, you can find out what browser is running, the pages the user has visited, the size of the browser window, the size of the user's screen, and much more. You can also use the window object to access and change the text in the browser's status bar, change the page that is loaded, and even open new windows.

The window object is a *global object*, which means you don't need to use its name to access its properties and methods. In fact, the global functions and variables (the ones accessible to script anywhere in a page) are all created as properties of the global object. For example, the alert() function you have been using since the beginning of the book is, in fact, the alert() method of the window object. Although you have been using this simply as

```
alert("Hello!");
```

you could write

```
window.alert("Hello!");
```

However, since the window object is the global object, it is perfectly correct to use the first version.

Some of the properties of the `window` object are themselves objects. Those common to both IE and NN include the `document`, `navigator`, `history`, `screen`, and `location` objects. The `document` object represents your page, the `history` object contains the history of pages visited by the user, the `navigator` object holds information about the browser, the `screen` object contains information about the display capabilities of the client, and the `location` object contains details on the current page's location. You'll look at these important objects individually later in the chapter.

Using the window Object

Let's start with a nice, simple example in which you change the default text shown in the browser's status bar. The status bar (usually in the bottom left of the browser window) is usually used by the browser to show the status of any document loading into the browser. For example, on IE and Firefox, after a document has loaded, you'll normally see `Done` in the status bar. Let's change that so it says `Hello and Welcome`.

To change the default message in the window's status bar, you need to use the `window` object's `defaultStatus` property. To do this you can write the following:

```
window.defaultStatus = "Hello and Welcome";
```

Or, because the `window` is the global object, you can just write this:

```
defaultStatus = "Hello and Welcome";
```

Either way works, and both are valid; however, writing `window` in front makes it clear exactly where the `defaultStatus` property came from. Otherwise it might appear that `defaultStatus` is a variable name. This is particularly true for less common properties and methods, such as `defaultStatus`. You'll find yourself becoming so familiar with more common ones, such as `document` and `alert()`, that you don't need to put `window` in front to remind you of their context.

Let's put the code in a page.

```
<html>
<head>
<script language="JavaScript" type="text/javaScript">
window.defaultStatus = "Hello and Welcome";
</script>
</head>
</html>
```

Save the page as `ch5_examp1.htm` and load it into your browser. You should see the specified message in the status bar.

At this point, it's worth highlighting the point that within a web page you shouldn't use names for your functions or variables that conflict with names of BOM objects or their properties and methods. If you do, you may not get an error, but instead get unexpected results. For example, in the following code you declare a variable named `defaultStatus`. You then try to set the `defaultStatus` property of the `window` object to `Welcome to my website`. However, this won't change the default message in the status bar; instead the value in the `defaultStatus` variable will be changed.

```
var defaultStatus;
defaultStatus = "Welcome to my website";
```

In this situation you need to use a different variable name.

As with all the BOM objects, you can look at lots of properties and methods for the window object. However, in this chapter you'll concentrate on the history, location, navigator, screen, and document properties. All five of these properties contain objects (the history, location, navigator, screen, and document objects), each with its own properties and methods. In the next few pages, you'll look at each of these objects in turn and find out how they can help you make full use of the BOM.

The history Object

The history object keeps track of each page that the user visits. This list of pages is commonly called the *history stack* for the browser. It enables the user to click the browser's Back and Forward buttons to revisit pages. You have access to this object via the window object's history property.

Like the native JavaScript Array object, the history object has a length property. You can use this to find out how many pages are in the history stack.

As you might expect, the history object has the back() and forward() methods. When they are called, the location of the page currently loaded in the browser is changed to the previous or next page that the user has visited.

The history object also has the go() method. This takes one parameter that specifies how far forward or backward in the history stack you want to go. For example, if you wanted to return the user to the page before the previous page, you'd write this:

```
history.go(-2);
```

To go forward three pages, you'd write this:

```
history.go(3);.
```

Note that go(-1) and back() are equivalent, as are go(1) and forward().

The location Object

The location object contains lots of potentially useful information about the current page's location. Not only does it contain the URL (Uniform Resource Locator) for the page, but also the server hosting the page, the port number of the server connection, and the protocol used. This information is made available through the location object's href, hostname, port, and protocol properties. However, many of these values are only really relevant when you are loading the page from a server and not, as you are doing in the present examples, loading the page directly from a local hard drive.

In addition to retrieving the current page's location, you can also use the methods of the location object to change the location and refresh the current page.

You can navigate to another page in two ways. You can either set the location object's href property to point to another page, or you can use the location object's replace() method. The effect of the two is the same; the page changes location. However, they differ in that the replace() method removes the current page from the history stack and replaces it with the new page you are moving to, whereas using the href property simply adds the new page to the top of the history stack. This means that if the replace() method has been used and the user clicks the Back button in the browser, the user can't go back to the original page loaded. If the href property has been used, the user can use the Back button as normal.

For example, to replace the current page with a new page called myPage.htm, you'd use the replace() method and write the following:

```
window.location.replace("myPage.htm");
```

This will load myPage.htm and replace any occurrence of the current page in the history stack with myPage.htm.

To load the same page and to add it to the history of pages navigated to, you use the href property:

```
window.location.href = "myPage.htm";
```

and the page currently loaded is added to the history. In both of the preceding cases, window is in front of the expression, but as the window object is global throughout the page, you could have written the following:

```
location.replace("myPage.htm");
```

or

```
location.href = "myPage.htm";
```

The navigator Object

The navigator object is another object that is a property of the window object and is available in both IE and Firefox browsers. Its name is more historical than descriptive. Perhaps a better name would be the "browser object," because the navigator object contains lots of information about the browser and the operating system in which it's running.

Probably the most common use of the navigator object is for handling browser differences. Using its properties, you can find out which browser, version, and operating system the user has. You can then act on that information and make sure the user is directed to pages that will work with his browser. The last section in this chapter is dedicated to this important subject, so we will not discuss it further here.

The screen Object

The screen object property of the window object contains a lot of information about the display capabilities of the client machine. Its properties include the height and width properties, which indicate the vertical and horizontal range of the screen, respectively, in pixels.

Another property of the screen object, which you will be using in an example later, is the colorDepth property. This tells you the number of bits used for colors on the client's screen.

The document Object — The Page Itself

Along with the `window` object, the `document` object is probably one of the most important and commonly used objects in the BOM. Via this object you can gain access to the properties and methods of some of the objects defined by HTML tags inside your page.

Unfortunately, it's here that the BOMs of different browsers can differ greatly. In this chapter you will concentrate on those properties and methods of the `document` object that are common to all browsers. More advanced manipulation of the browser document object will appear in Chapters 12 and 13.

The `document` object has a number of properties associated with it, which are also arrays. The main ones are the `forms`, `images`, and `links` arrays. IE supports a number of other array properties, such as the `all` array property, which is an array of all the tags represented by objects in the page. However, you'll be concentrating on using objects that have cross-browser support, so that you are not limiting your web pages to just one browser.

You'll be looking at the `images` and `links` arrays shortly. A third array, the `forms[]` array, will be one of the topics of the next chapter when you look at forms in web browsers. First, though, you'll look at a nice, simple example of how to use the `document` object's methods and properties.

Using the document Object

You've already come across some of the `document` object's properties and methods, for example the `write()` method and the `bgColor` property.

Try It Out   Setting Colors According to the User's Screen Color Depth

In this example you set the background color of the page according to how many colors the user's screen supports. This is termed *screen color depth*. If the user has a display that supports just two colors (black and white), there's no point in you setting the background color to bright red. You accommodate different depths by using JavaScript to set a color the user can actually see.

```
<html>
<body>
<script language="JavaScript" type="text/javaScript">
switch (window.screen.colorDepth)
{
   case 1:
   case 4:
      document.bgColor = "white";
      break;
   case 8:
   case 15:
   case 16:
      document.bgColor = "blue";
      break;
   case 24:
   case 32:
      document.bgColor = "skyblue";
      break;
   default:
      document.bgColor = "white";
```

```
}
    document.write("Your screen supports " + window.screen.colorDepth +
                "bit color");
</script>
</body>
</html>
```

Save the page as ch5_examp2.htm. When you load it into your browser, the background color of the page will be determined by your current screen color depth. Also, a message in the page will tell you what the color depth currently is.

You can test that the code is working properly by changing the colors supported by your screen. On Windows, you can do this by right-clicking on the desktop and choosing the Properties option. Under the Settings tab, there is a section called "Color quality" in which you can change the number of colors supported. By refreshing the browser, you can see what difference this makes to the color of the page.

On Netscape and Firefox browsers, it's necessary to shut down and restart the browser to observe any effect.

How It Works

As you saw earlier, the window object has the screen object property. One of the properties of this object is the colorDepth property, which returns a value of 1, 4, 8, 15, 16, 24, or 32. This represents the number of bits assigned to each pixel on your screen. (A pixel is just one of the many dots that your screen is made up of.) To work out how many colors you have, you just calculate the value of 2 to the power of the colorDepth property. For example, a colorDepth of 1 means that there are two colors available, a colorDepth of 8 means that there are 256 colors available, and so on. Currently, most people have a screen color depth of at least 8, but usually of 16 or 24, with 32 increasingly common.

The first task of your script block is to set the color of the background of the page based on the number of colors the user can actually see. You do this in a big switch statement. The condition that is checked for in the switch statement is the value of window.screen.colorDepth.

```
    switch (window.screen.colorDepth)
```

You don't need to set a different color for each colorDepth possible, because many of them are similar when it comes to general web use. Instead, you set the same background color for different, but similar, colorDepth values. For a colorDepth of 1 or 4, you set the background to white. You do this by declaring the case 1: statement, but you don't give it any code. If the colorDepth matches this case statement, it will fall through to the case 4: statement below, where you do set the background color to white. You then call a break statement, so that the case matching will not fall any further through the switch statement.

```
    {
        case 1:
        case 4:
            document.bgColor = "white";
            break;
```

You do the same with `colorDepth` values of 8, 15, and 16, setting the background color to blue as follows:

```
case 8:
case 15:
case 16:
   document.bgColor = "blue";
   break;
```

Finally, you do the same for `colorDepth` values of 24 and 32, setting the background color to sky blue.

```
case 24:
case 32:
   document.bgColor = "skyblue";
   break;
```

You end the `switch` statement with a `default` case, just in case the other `case` statements did not match. In this `default` case, you again set the background color to white.

```
default:
   document.bgColor = "white";
}
```

In the next bit of script, you use the `document` object's `write()` method, something you've been using in these examples for a while now. You use it to write to the document — that is, the page — the number of bits the color depth is currently set at, as follows:

```
document.write("Your screen supports " + window.screen.colorDepth +
               "bit color")
```

You've already been using the `document` object in the examples throughout the book so far. You used its `bgColor` property in Chapter 1 to change the background color of the page, and you've also made good use of its `write()` method in the examples to write HTML and text out to the page.

Now let's look at some of the slightly more complex properties of the `document` object. These properties have in common the fact that they all contain arrays. The first one you look at is an array containing an object for each image in the page.

The images Array

As you know, you can insert an image into an HTML page using the following tag:

```
<img alt="USA" name=myImage src="usa.gif">
```

The browser makes this image available for you to script in JavaScript by creating an `img` object for it with the name `myImage`. In fact, each image on your page has an `img` object created for it.

Each of the `img` objects in a page is stored in the `images[]` array. This array is a property of the document object. The first image on the page is found in the element `document.images[0]`, the second in `document.images[1]`, and so on.

If you want to, you can assign a variable to reference an img object in the images[] array. It can make code easier to read. For example, if you write

```
var myImage2 = document.images[1];
```

the myImage2 variable will contain a reference to the img object inside the images[] array at index position 1. Now you can write myImage2 instead of document.images[1] in your code, with exactly the same effect.

You can also access img objects in the images array by name. For example, the img object created by the <img> tag, which has the name myImage, can be accessed in the document object's images array property like this:

```
document.images["myImage"]
```

Because the document.images property is an array, it has the properties of the native JavaScript Array object, such as the length property. For example, if you want to know how many images there are on the page, the code document.images.length will tell you.

Try It Out   Image Selection

The img object itself has a number of useful properties. The most important of these is its src property. By changing this you can change the image that's loaded. The next example demonstrates this.

```
<html>
<body>
<img name=img1 src="" border=0 width=200 height=150>
<script language="JavaScript" type="text/javaScript">
    var myImages = new Array("usa.gif","canada.gif","jamaica.gif","mexico.gif");
    var imgIndex = prompt("Enter a number from 0 to 3","");
    document.images["img1"].src = myImages[imgIndex];
</script>
</body>
</html>
```

Save this as ch5_examp3.htm. You will also need four image files, called usa.gif, canada.gif, jamaica.gif, and mexico.gif. You can create these yourself or obtain the ones provided with the code download for the book.

When this page is loaded into the browser, a prompt box asks you to enter a number from 0 to 3. A different image will be displayed depending on the number you enter.

How It Works

At the top of the page you have your HTML <img> tag. Notice that the src attribute is left empty and is given the name value img1.

```
<img name=img1 src="" border=0 width=200 height=150>
```

Next you come to the script block where the image to be displayed is decided. On the first line you define an array containing a list of image sources. In this example, the images are in the same directory as the HTML file, so a path is not specified. If yours are not, make sure you enter the full path (for example, `C:\myImages\mexico.gif`).

Then you ask the user for a number from 0 to 3, which will be used as the array index to access the image source in the `myImages` array.

```
var imgIndex = prompt("Enter a number from 0 to 3","");
```

Finally you set the `src` property of the `img` object to the source text inside the `myImages` array element with the index number provided by the user.

```
document.images["img1"].src = myImages[imgIndex];
```

Don't forget that when you write `document.images["img1"]`, you are accessing the `img` object stored in the `images` array. You've used the image's name, as defined in the `name` attribute of the `<img>` tag, but you could have used `document.images[0]`. It's an index position of 0, because it's the first (and only) image on this page.

The links Array

For each hyperlink tag `<A>` defined with an `href` attribute, the browser creates an A object. The most important property of the A object is the `href` property, corresponding to the `href` attribute of the tag. Using this, you can find out where the link points to, and you can change this, even after the page has loaded.

The collection of all A objects in a page is contained within the `links[]` array, much as the `img` objects are contained in the `images[]` array, as you saw earlier.

Connecting Code to Web Page Events

Chapter 4 introduces objects that are defined by their methods and properties. However, objects also have events associated with them. We did not mention this before, because native JavaScript objects do not have these events, but the objects of the BOM do.

So what are these events?

Events occur when something in particular happens. For example, the user clicking on the page, clicking on a hyperlink, or moving his mouse pointer over some text all cause events to occur. Another example, which is used quite frequently, is the load event for the page.

Why are you interested in events?

Take as an example the situation in which you want to make a menu pop up when the user clicks anywhere in your web page. Assuming that you can write a function that will make the pop-up menu appear, how do you know *when* to make it appear, or in other words, *when* to call the function? You somehow need to intercept the event of the user clicking in the document, and make sure your function is called when that event occurs.

To do this, you need to use something called an *event handler*. You associate this with the code that you want to execute when the event occurs. This provides you with a way of intercepting events and making your code execute when they have occurred. You will find that adding an event handler to your code is often known as "connecting your code to the event." It's a bit like setting an alarm clock — you set the clock to make a ringing noise when a certain event happens. With alarm clocks, the event is when a certain time is reached.

Event handlers are made up of the word on and the event that they will handle. For example, the click event has the onclick event handler, and the load event has the onload event handler.

A number of ways exist to connect your code to an event using event handlers. In this chapter you'll look at a two of the easiest ways of adding events, ways that have been around since Netscape 2 and so are supported even by older browsers, as well as by current ones. In Chapter 12 you're going to look at newer and standards-friendly ways of adding events.

Event Handlers as Attributes

The first and most common method is to add the event handler's name and the code you want to execute to the HTML tag's attributes.

Let's create a simple HTML page with a single hyperlink, given by the element <A>. Associated to this element is the A object. One of the events the A object has is the click event. The click event fires, not surprisingly, when the user clicks the hyperlink.

```
<html>
<body>
<A href="somepage.htm" name="linkSomePage">
    Click Me
</A>
</body>
</html>
```

As it stands, this page does nothing a normal hyperlink doesn't do. You click it, and it navigates the window to another page, called somepage.htm, which would need to be created. There's been no event handler added to the link — yet!

As mentioned earlier, one very common and easy way of connecting the event to your code is to add it directly to the tag of the object whose event you are capturing. In this case, it's the click event of the A object, as defined by the <A> tag. On clicking the link, you want to capture the event and connect it to your code. You need to add the event handler, in this case onclick, as an attribute to your <A> tag. You set the value of the attribute to the code you want to have executed when the event occurs.

Let's rewrite the <A> tag to do this as follows:

```
<A href="somepage.htm" name="linkSomePage" onclick="alert('You Clicked?')">
    Click Me
</A>
```

You can see that you have added onclick="alert('You Clicked?')" to the definition of the <A> tag. Now, when the link is clicked, you see an alert box. After this, the hyperlink does its usual stuff and takes you to the page defined in the href attribute.

This is fine if you have only one line of code to connect to the event handler, but what if you want a number of lines to execute when the link is clicked?

Well, all you need to do is define the function you want to execute and call it in the onclick code. Let's do that now.

```
<html>
<body>
<script language="JavaScript">
function linkSomePage_onclick()
{
    alert('You Clicked?');
    return true;
}
</script>
<A href="somepage.htm" name="linkSomePage"
    onclick="return linkSomePage_onclick()">
        Click Me
</A>
</body>
</html>
```

Within the script block you have created a function, just a standard function, and given it a descriptive name to help you when reading the code. Here we're using ObjectName_event() as the function name. That way you can instantly see what object on the page this relates to and which event is being connected to. So, in the preceding example, the function is called linkSomePage_onclick(), because you are referring to the onclick event handler for the A object with name linkSomePage. Note that this naming convention is simply something created by the author; it's not compulsory, and you can use whatever convention you prefer as long as you are consistent.

The onclick attribute is now connected to some code that calls the function linkSomePage_onclick(). Therefore, when the user clicks the hyperlink, this function will be executed.

You'll also see that the function returns a value, true in this case. Also, where you define your onclick attribute, you return the return value of the function by using the return statement before the function name. Why do this?

The value returned by onclick="return linkSomePage_onclick()" is used by JavaScript to decide whether the normal action of the link — that is, going to a new page — should occur. If you return true, the action continues, and you go to somepage.htm. If you return false, the normal chain of events (that is, going to somepage.htm) does not happen. You say that the action associated with the event is canceled. Try changing the function to this:

```
function linkSomePage_onclick()
{
    alert('This link is going nowhere');
    return false;
}
```

Now you'll find that you just get a message, and no attempt is made to go to somepage.htm.

Not all objects and their events make use of the return value, so sometimes it's redundant. Also, it's not always the case that returning false cancels the action. For reasons of browser history rather than logic, it's sometimes true that cancels the action. Generally speaking, it's best to return true and deal with the exceptions as you find them.

Some events are not directly linked with the user's actions as such. For example, the window object has the load event, which fires when a page is loaded, and the unload event, which fires when the page is unloaded (that is, when the user either closes the browser or moves to another page).

Event handlers for the window object actually go inside the <body> tag. For example, to add an event handler for the load and unload events, you'd write the following:

```
<body language="JavaScript" onload="myOnLoadfunction()"
      onunload="myOnUnloadFunction()">
```

Notice that you have specified the language attribute of the <body> tag as JavaScript. This is because the <body> tag is not contained within a JavaScript script block defined with the <script> tag. As usual, since JavaScript is the default scripting language, this can be left off.

Event Handlers as Properties

Now let's look at the second way to connect to events.

With this method, you first need to define the function that will be executed when the event occurs. Then you need to set that object's event handler property to the function you defined.

This is illustrated in the following example:

```
<html>
<body>
<script language="JavaScript" type="text/javascript">
function linkSomePage_onclick()
{
    alert('This link is going nowhere');
    return false;
}
</script>
<A href="somepage.htm" name="linkSomePage">
   Click Me
</A>
<script language="JavaScript" type="text/javaScript">
   window.document.links[0].onclick = linkSomePage_onclick;
</script>
</body>
</html>
```

Save this as ch5_examp4.htm.

You define the function linkSomePage_onclick(), much as you did before. As before, you can return a value indicating whether you want the normal action of that object to happen.

Next you have the `<A>` tag, whose object's event you are connecting to. You'll notice there is no mention of the event handler or the function within the attributes of the tag.

The connection is made between the object's event and our function on the final lines of script, as shown in the following code:

```
<script language="JavaScript" type="text/javaScript">
    document.links[0].onclick = linkSomePage_onclick;
</script>
```

As you saw before, `document.links[0]` returns the A object corresponding to the first link in your web page, which is your `linkSomePage` hyperlink. You set this object's `onclick` property to reference your function — this makes the connection between the object's event handler and your function. Note that no parentheses are added after the function name. Now whenever you click the link, your function gets executed.

The first method of connecting code to events is easier, so why would you ever want to use the second?

Perhaps the most common situation in which you would want to do this is one in which you want to capture an event for which there is no HTML tag to write your event handler as an attribute. It is also useful if you want the code attached to an event handler to be changed dynamically.

Try It Out   Displaying a Random Image when the Page Loads

Let's look at another example in which you connect to a hyperlink's click event to randomly change the image loaded in a page.

```
<html>
<head>
<script language="JavaScript" type="text/javascript">
var myImages = new Array("usa.gif","canada.gif","jamaica.gif","mexico.gif");

function changeImg(imgNumber)
{
    var imgClicked = document.images[imgNumber];
    var newImgNumber = Math.round(Math.random() * 3);
    while (imgClicked.src.indexOf(myImages[newImgNumber]) != -1)
    {
        newImgNumber = Math.round(Math.random() * 3);
    }
    imgClicked.src = myImages[newImgNumber];
    return false;
}

</script>
</head>
<body>
 <img name="img0" src="usa.gif" border="0" onclick="return changeImg(0)">
 <img name="img1" src="mexico.gif" border="0" onclick="return changeImg(1)">
</body>
</html>
```

Save the page as ch5_examp5.htm. Again, you will need four image files for the example, which you can create or retrieve from the code download available with this book.

Load the page into your browser. You should see a page like that shown in Figure 5-3.

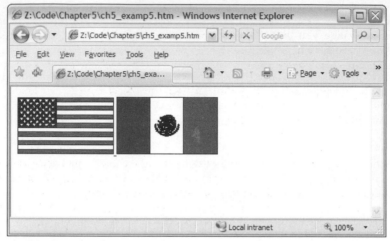

Figure 5-3

If you click an image, you'll see it change to a different image, which is selected randomly.

How It Works

The first line in the script block at the top of the page defines a variable with page-level scope. This is an array that contains your list of image sources.

```
var myImages = new Array("usa.gif","canada.gif","jamaica.gif","mexico.gif");
```

Next you have the changeImg() function, which will be connected to the onclick event handler of an <IMG> tag surrounding each of your images. You are using the same function for both images' onclick event handlers and indeed can connect one function to as many event handlers as you like. You pass this function one parameter—the index in the images array of the img object related to that click event—so that you know which image you need to act on.

In the first line of the function, you use the passed parameter to declare a new variable that points to the img object in the images[] array corresponding to the image that was clicked, as follows:

```
function changeImg(imgNumber)
{
    var imgClicked = document.images[imgNumber];
```

Following this, you set the newImgNumber variable to a random integer between 0 and 3. The Math.random() method provides a random number between 0 and 1, and you multiply that by three to get a number between 0 and 3. This number is converted to an integer (0, 1, 2, or 3) by means of

`Math.round()`. This integer will provide the index for the image `src` that you will select from the `myImages` array.

```
var newImgNumber = Math.round(Math.random() * 3);
```

The next lines are a `while` loop, the purpose of which is to ensure that you don't select the same image as the current one. If the string contained in `myImages[newImgNumber]` is found inside the `src` property of the current image, you know it's the same and that you need to get another random number. You keep looping until you get a new image, at which point `myImages[newImgNumber]` will not be found in the existing `src` and `-1` will be returned by the `indexOf()` method, breaking out of the loop.

```
while (imgClicked.src.indexOf(myImages[newImgNumber]) != -1)
{
    newImgNumber = Math.round(Math.random() * 3);
}
```

Finally, you set the `src` property of the `img` object to the new value contained in your `myImages` array. You return `false` to stop the link from trying to navigate to another page; remember that the HTML link is only there to provide a means of capturing an `onclick` event handler.

```
imgClicked.src = myImages[newImgNumber];
return false;
}
```

Next you connect the `onclick` event of the first `<IMG>` tag to the `changeImg()` function:

```
<img name=img0 src="usa.gif" border="0" onclick="return changeImg(0)">
```

And now to the second `<IMG>` tag:

```
<img name="img1" src="mexico.gif" border="0" onclick="return changeImg(1)">
```

Passing 1 in the `changeImg()` function lets the function know that image 1, the second image in the page, needs to be changed.

Browser Version Checking Examples

Many browsers, versions of those browsers, and operating systems are out there on the Internet, each with its own version of the BOM and its own particular quirks. It's therefore important that you make sure your pages will work correctly on all browsers, or at least *degrade gracefully*, such as by displaying a message suggesting that the user upgrade her browser.

Although you can go a long way with cross-browser-compatible code, there may come a time when you want to add extra features that only one browser supports. The solution is to write script that checks the browser name, version, and, if necessary, operating system, and executes script that is compatible with these variants.

You can check for browser details in two main ways. The first is to see if the object and property you use in your code are actually available in the user's browser. Let's say for example that our code relies on the document object's `all` property, which is available to browsers like IE version 4+, but not to any Firefox or Netscape browsers. If you write

```
If (document.all)
{
 // our code using the document.all property
}
```

the `if` statement's condition will evaluate to `true` if the property returns a valid value; if the property is not supported, its value will be `undefined`, and the `if` statement will evaluate to `false`. To check whether a particular method is supported, you can do this:

```
if (document.getElementById)
{
// code
}
else
{
        // Alternative code
}
```

You've "tested" the existence of the method as you did with properties. Just remember not to include the opening or closing brackets after the method even if it normally has a number of parameters. The `getElementById` method, for example, has one parameter.

The next example shows how to use object checking to ensure that you execute the right code for the right browser; this technique is not foolproof but can be very useful.

Try It Out   Checking for Supported Browser Properties

```
<html>
<body>

<script language="JavaScript" type="text/javascript">
var browser = "Unknown";
var version = "0";

// NN4+
if (document.layers)
{
 browser = "NN";
 version = "4.0";

 if (navigator.securityPolicy)
 {
        version = "4.7+";
 }
}
else if (document.all)
{
 browser = "IE"
 version = "4"
```

```
    }

    // IE5+
    if (window.clipboardData)
    {
     browser = "IE"
     version = "5+"
    }
    // Firefox/NN6+
    else if (window.sidebar)
    {
     browser = "Firefox";
     version = "1+";
    }
    document.write(browser + " " + version);

    </script>

    </body>
    </html>
```

Save this example as ch5_examp6.htm.

How It Works

The page looks at which BOM and JavaScript properties the browser supports and, based on that, makes a rough guess as to the browser type. So on the first lines you check to see if the browser's document object has the layers property.

```
    if (document.layers)
    {
     browser = "NN";
     version = "4.0";

     if (navigator.securityPolicy)
     {
             version = "4.7+";
     }
    }
```

Because only NN 4 supports the layers property, you can assume this is an NN 4 browser or at least a browser that supports the NN 4 layers feature. The inner if statement looks to see if the navigator object supports the securityPolicy property; this property is supported by only Netscape Navigator version 4 and in particular only by sub-version 4.7 and later. However, the slight danger here is that a rare browser not from Netscape or Microsoft might support the securityPolicy property but not other features of NN 4.7+ browsers. It's wise to test with as many varieties of browser as you expect to have visit the web site and see what happens. If one fails, you can see which property it fails on and write code to check for it.

Next you have a test for the document object's all property, a property supported by IE 4+ and Opera 7+.

```
else if (document.all)
{
 browser = "IE"
 version = "4"
}
```

To see if the browser is an IE 5+ browser, check the `window` object's `clipboardData` property, which is currently supported only by IE 5+.

```
// IE5+
if (window.clipboardData)
{
 browser = "IE"
 version = "5+"
}
```

The final bit of checking is for the `sidebar` property supported by Firefox, which deals with the sidebar tool.

```
// Firefox/NN6+
else if (window.sidebar)
{
browser = "Firefox";
 version = "1+";
}
```

On the last line you write out the results of the BOM property checking.

```
document.write(browser + " " + version);
```

Hopefully, this example demonstrates how to use object checking to see if a particular feature is supported by a browser. In the example, you haven't actually used the various features; it's simply a way of demonstrating how to check for browser-specific objects. When writing your own code, be sure to double-check whether a particular feature you're using is supported by all the browsers you expect to visit your web site. If some of the browsers you expect to visit don't support a particular feature, then test for the feature and write alternative code for the browsers that don't support it.

You'll be seeing much more advanced object checking in Chapter 12.

No Script at All

Sometimes people switch off JavaScript in their browsers, or use a browser that doesn't support JavaScript, though that's quite rare these days. To cover this situation, you can use the `<noscript>` tag. Any HTML inside the `<noscript>` tag will be displayed only to browsers that don't support JavaScript or on which JavaScript has been disabled:

```
<html>
<body>
<noscript>
This website requires JavaScript to be enabled.
</noscript>
</body>
<html>
```

Browser Checking Using the Navigator Object

The second method of checking browser details is using the `navigator` object property of the `window` object. In particular, you use the `appName` and `userAgent` properties of the `navigator` object. The main problem with this method is that a less common browser may well declare itself to be a particular version of Internet Explorer or Firefox but not actually support all the JavaScript or BOM objects, properties, or methods of that browser. Therefore this method of "browser sniffing" has fallen out of favor and is not the recommended way of checking for compatibility. It's really a last resort when all other methods have failed, such as when two different browsers support the same object and property but implement them so that they work in two different ways. Object checking wouldn't help you in that circumstance, so you'd have to fall back on using the `navigator` object.

The `appName` property returns the model of the browser, such as Microsoft Internet Explorer or Netscape.

The `userAgent` property returns a string containing various bits of information, such as the browser version, operating system, and browser model. However, the value returned by this property varies from browser to browser, so you have to be very, very careful when using it. For example, you can't assume that it starts with the browser version. It does under NN, but under IE the browser version is embedded in the middle of the string.

Try It Out   **Checking for and Dealing with Different Browsers**

In this example, you create a page that uses the aforementioned properties to discover the client's browser and browser version. The page can then take action based upon the client's specifications.

```html
<html>
<head>
<script language="JavaScript" type="text/javaScript">

function getBrowserName()
{
    var lsBrowser = navigator.userAgent;
    if (lsBrowser.indexOf("MSIE") >= 0)
    {
        lsBrowser = "MSIE";
    }
    else if (lsBrowser.indexOf("Netscape") >= 0)
    {
        lsBrowser = "Netscape";
    }
    else if (lsBrowser.indexOf("Firefox") >= 0)
    {
        lsBrowser = "Firefox";
    }
    else if (lsBrowser.indexOf("Safari") >= 0)
    {
        lsBrowser = "Safari";
    }
    else if (lsBrowser.indexOf("Opera") >= 0)
    {
        lsBrowser = "Opera";
    }
    else
```

```
        {
            lsBrowser = "UNKNOWN";
        }
        return lsBrowser;
    }


function getBrowserVersion()
{
    var findIndex;
    var browserVersion = 0;
    var browser = getBrowserName();

    browserVersion = navigator.userAgent;
    findIndex = browserVersion.indexOf(browser) + browser.length + 1;
    browserVersion = parseFloat(browserVersion.substring(findIndex,findIndex + 3));
    return browserVersion;
}

</script>
</head>
<body>
<script language="JavaScript" type="text/javaScript">

var browserName = getBrowserName();
var browserVersion = getBrowserVersion();

if (browserName == "MSIE")
{
    if (browserVersion < 5.5)
    {
        document.write("Your version of Internet Explorer is too old");
    }
    else
    {
        document.write("Your version of Internet Explorer is fully supported");
    }

}
else if (browserName == 'Firefox')
{
    document.write("Firefox is fully supported");
}
else if (browserName == 'Netscape')
{
 if (browserVersion < 6)
 {
        document.write("Your version of Netscape is too old");
 }
 else
 {
        document.write("Your version of Netscape is fully supported");
 }
}
```

```
else
{
    document.write("<h2>Sorry this browser version is not supported</h2>");
}

</script>
<noscript>
    <h2>This website requires a browser supporting scripting</h2>
</noscript>
</body>
</html>
```

Save this script as `ch5_examp7.htm`.

If the browser is Firefox, Internet Explorer 5.5+, or Netscape Navigator 6+, a message appears telling the user that the browser is supported. If it's an earlier version of IE or Navigator, the user will see a message telling him his version of that browser is not supported.

If it's not one of those browsers, he'll see a message saying his browser is unsupported. This is not particularly friendly, so in practice you could have available a plain and simple version of the page without scripting — something with as much functionality as possible without JavaScript.

If the browser doesn't support JavaScript or the user has turned off support, then he'll see a message telling him the web site needs JavaScript to work.

How It Works

The script block in the head of the page defines two important functions. The `getBrowserName()` function finds out the name of the browser and the `getBrowserVersion()` function finds out the browser version.

The key to the browser checking code is the value returned by the `navigator.userAgent` property. Here are a few example user agent strings from current browsers:

1. Mozilla/4.0 (compatible; MSIE 6.0; Windows NT 5.1; SV1; .NET CLR 1.1.4322; .NET CLR 2.0.40607)

2. Mozilla/4.0 (compatible; MSIE 7.0; Windows NT 5.1; .NET CLR 2.0.40607)

3. Mozilla/5.0 (Windows; U; Windows NT 5.1; en-GB; rv:1.8.0.4) Gecko/20060508 Firefox/1.5.0.4

4. Mozilla/5.0 (Windows; U; Windows NT 5.1; en-US; rv:1.7.5) Gecko/20060127 Netscape/8.1

5. Opera/9.00 (Windows NT 5.0; U; en)

Here each line of the `userAgent` string has been numbered. Looking closely at each line it's not hard to guess which browser each agent string relates to. In order:

1. Microsoft Internet Explorer 6

2. Microsoft Internet Explorer 7 (beta 3)

3. Firefox 1.5

4. Netscape 8.1

5. Opera 9.0

181

Using this information, let's start on the first function, getBrowserName(). First you get the name of the browser, as found in navigator.userAgent, and store it in the variable lsBrowser. This will also be used as the variable to store the return value for the function.

```
function getBrowserName()
{
    var lsBrowser = navigator.userAgent;
```

The string returned by this property tends to be quite long and does vary slightly sometimes. However, by checking for the existence of certain keywords, such as MSIE or Netscape, you can determine the browser name. Start with the following lines:

```
if (lsBrowser.indexOf("MSIE") >= 0)
{
    lsBrowser = "MSIE";
}
```

These lines search the lsBrowser string for Microsoft. If the indexOf value of this substring is 0 or greater, you know you have found it, and so you set the return value to MSIE.

The following else if statement does the same, except that it is modified for Netscape.

```
else if (lsBrowser.indexOf("Netscape") >= 0)
{
    lsBrowser = "Netscape";
}
```

This principle carries on for another three if statements, in which you also check for Firefox, Safari, and Opera. If you have a browser you want to check for, this is the place to add its if statement. Just view the string it returns in navigator.userAgent and look for its name or something that uniquely identifies it.

If none of the if statements match, you return UNKNOWN as the browser name.

```
else
{
    lsBrowser = "UNKNOWN";
}
```

The value of lsBrowser is then returned to the calling code.

```
    return lsBrowser;
}
```

You now turn to the final function, getBrowserVersion().

The browser version details often appear in the userAgent string right after the name of the browser. For these reasons, your first task in the function is to find out which browser you are dealing with. You declare and initialize the browser variable to the name of the browser, using the getBrowserName() function you just wrote.

```
function getBrowserVersion()
{
   var findIndex;
   var browserVersion = 0;
   var browser = getBrowserName();
```

If the browser is MSIE (Internet Explorer), you need to use the userAgent property again. Under IE, the userAgent property always contains MSIE followed by the browser version. So what you need to do is search for MSIE, then get the number following that.

You set findIndex to the character position of the browser name plus the length of the name, plus one. Doing this ensures you to get the character after the name and after the following space or / character that follows the name and is just before the version number. browserVersion is set to the floating-point value of that number, which you obtain using the substring() method. This selects the character starting at findIndex, your number, and whose end is one before findIndex, plus three. This ensures that you just select three characters for the version number.

```
browserVersion = navigator.userAgent;
findIndex = browserVersion.indexOf(browser) + browser.length + 1;
browserVersion = parseFloat(browserVersion.substring(findIndex, findIndex + 3));
```

If you look back to the userAgent strings, you see that IE7's is as follows:

```
Mozilla/4.0 (compatible; MSIE 7.0; Windows NT 5.1; .NET CLR 2.0.40607)
```

So findIndex will be set to the character index of the number 7 following the browser name. browserVersion will be set to three characters from and including the 7, giving the version number as 7.0.

At the end of the function you return browserVersion to the calling code, as shown here:

```
   return browserVersion;
}
```

You've seen the supporting functions, but how do you make use of them? Well, in the following code, which executes as the page is loaded, you obtain two bits of information — browser name and version — and use these to filter which browser the user is running.

```
var browserName = getBrowserName();
var browserVersion = getBrowserVersion();

if (browserName == "MSIE")
{
   if (browserVersion < 5.5)
   {
      document.write("Your version of Internet Explorer is too old");
   }
   else
   {
      document.write("Your version of Internet Explorer is fully supported");
   }
}
```

The first of the `if` statements is shown in the preceding code and checks to see if the user has IE. If she does, it then checks to see if the version is one earlier, less, than version 5.5. If it is, she is told the IE she has is too old. If it is IE5.5+, she is told it's fully supported.

You do this again for Firefox and Netscape. The Firefox version isn't checked in this example, but you can check it if you want to:

```
else if (browserName == 'Firefox')
{
   document.write("Firefox is fully supported");
}
else if (browserName == 'Netscape')
{
 if (browserVersion < 6)
 {
        document.write("Your version of Netscape is too old");
 }
 else
 {
        document.write("Your version of Netscape is fully supported");
 }
}
else
{
   document.write("<h2>Sorry this browser version is not supported</h2>")
}
```

On the final part of the `if` statements is the `else` statement that covers all other browsers and tells the user the browser is not supported.

Finally, there are some `<noscript>` tags for early browsers and for users who have chosen to disable JavaScript. These will display a message informing the user that she needs a JavaScript-enabled browser.

```
<noscript>
   <h2>This website requires a browser supporting scripting</h2>
</noscript>
```

As mentioned earlier, although this script will work fine at the moment, it's possible that browsers will change their `userAgent` strings and you'll need to update the function to keep track of this. Also, some browsers pretend to be other browsers even if they don't function 100 percent the same, which can leave your code showing errors.

For these reasons, stick to the object checking method, which was detailed earlier in the chapter and will be covered more fully in Chapter 12.

Summary

You've covered a lot in this chapter, but now you have all the grounding you need to move on to more useful things, such as forms and user input, and later to more advanced areas of text and date manipulation.

❏ You turned your attention to the browser, the environment in which JavaScript exists. Just as JavaScript has native objects, so do web browsers. The objects within the web browser, and the hierarchy they are organized in, are described by something called the Browser Object Model (BOM). This is essentially a map of a browser's objects. Using it, you can navigate your way around each of the objects made available by the browser, together with their properties, methods, and events.

❏ The first of the main objects you looked at was the window object. This sits at the very top of the BOM's hierarchy. The window object contains a number of important sub-objects, including the location object, the navigator object, the history object, the screen object, and the document object.

❏ The location object contains information about the current page's location, such as its file name, the server hosting the page, and the protocol used. Each of these is a property of the location object. Some properties are read-only, but others, such as the href property, not only enable us to find the location of the page, but also can be changed so that we can navigate the page to a new location.

❏ The history object is a record of all the pages the user has visited since opening his or her browser. Sometimes pages are not noted (for example, when the location object's replace() method is used for navigation). You can move the browser forward and backward in the history stack and discover what pages the user has visited.

❏ The navigator object represents the browser itself and contains useful details of what type of browser, version, and operating system the user has. These details enable you to write pages dealing with various types of browsers, even where they may be incompatible.

❏ The screen object contains information about the display capabilities of the user's computer.

❏ The document object is one of the most important objects. It's an object representation of our page and contains all the elements, also represented by objects, within that page. The differences between Netscape and Microsoft browsers are particularly prominent here. If you want cross-browser-compatible pages, you will find you are quite limited as to which elements you can access.

❏ The document object contains three properties that are actually arrays. These are the links[], images[], and forms[] arrays. Each contains all the objects created by the <A>, <img>, and <form> tags on the page, and it's our way of accessing those tags.

❏ The images[] array contains an img object for each <img> element on the page. You found that even after the page has loaded, you can change the properties of images. For example, you can make the image change when clicked. The same principles for using the images[] array apply to the links[] array.

❏ You next saw that BOM objects have events as well as methods and properties. You handle these events in JavaScript by using event handlers, which you connect to code that you want to have executed when the event occurs. The events available for use depend on the object you are dealing with.

❑ Connecting a function that you have written to an event handler is simply a matter of adding an attribute to the element corresponding to the particular object you are interested in. The attribute has the name of the event handler you want to capture and the value of the function you want to connect to it.

❑ In some instances, such as for the document object, a second way of connecting event handlers to code is necessary. Setting the object's property with the name of the event handler to our function produces the same effect as if you did it using the event handler as an attribute.

❑ In some instances, returning values from event functions enables you to cancel the action associated with the event. For example, to stop a clicked link from navigating to a page, you return false from the event handler's code.

❑ Finally, you looked at how you can check what type of browser the user has so that you can make sure the user sees only those pages or parts of a page that his browser is compatible with. The navigator object provides you with the details you need, in particular the appName and userAgent properties. You can also check specific BOM properties to see if they are supported before using them. If a browser doesn't support a specific property needed for your code to work, you can either write alternative code or let the user know he needs to upgrade his browser.

That's it for this chapter. In the next chapter you move on to more exciting form scripting, where you can add various controls to your page to help you gather information from the user.

Exercise Questions

Suggested solutions to these questions can be found in Appendix A.

Question 1

Create a page with a number of links. Then write code that fires on the window onload event, displaying the href of each of the links on the page.

Question 2

Create two pages, one called IEOnly.htm and the other called FFOnly.htm. Each page should have a heading telling you what page is loaded, for example

```
<H2>Welcome to the Internet Explorer only page</H2>
```

Using the functions for checking browser type, connect to the window object's onload event handler and detect what browser the user has. Then, if it's the wrong page for that browser, redirect to the other page.

Question 3

Insert an image in the page with the <img> tag. When the mouse pointer rolls over the image, it should switch to a different image. When the mouse pointer rolls out (leaves the image), it should swap back again.

6

HTML Forms — Interacting with the User

Web pages would be very boring if you could not interact with or obtain information from the user, such as text, numbers, or dates. Luckily, with JavaScript this is possible. You can use this information within the web page, or it can be posted to the web server where you can manipulate it and store it in a database if you wish. In this chapter you'll concentrate on using the information within the web browser, which is called *client-side processing.* In Chapters 14 and 15 you'll see how to send this information to a web server and store it in a database, which is called *server-side processing.*

You're quite accustomed to various user interface elements. For example, the Windows operating system has a number of standard elements, such as buttons you can click; lists, drop-down list boxes, and radio buttons you can select from; and boxes you can check. The same applies with any graphical user interface (GUI) operating system, whether it's a Mac, Unix, or Linux system. These elements are the means by which we now interface with applications. The good news is that you can include many of these types of elements in your web page — and even better, it's very easy to do so. When you have such an element — say, a button — inside your page, you can then tie code to its events. For example, when the button is clicked, you can fire off a JavaScript function you've created.

It's important to note at this point that the elements we discuss in this chapter are the common elements made available by HTML, and not ActiveX elements, Java Applets, or plug-ins. You'll look at some of these in Chapter 15.

All of the HTML elements used for interaction should be placed inside an HTML form. In Netscape 4+, it's compulsory for the elements to be inside a form; otherwise they won't be displayed. It's also compulsory if you submit the form to a server. Let's start by taking a look at HTML forms and how you interact with them in JavaScript.

HTML Forms

Forms provide you with a way of grouping together HTML interaction elements with a common purpose. For example, a form may contain elements that enable the input of a user's data for registering on a web site. Another form may contain elements that enable the user to ask for a car insurance quote. It's possible to have a number of separate forms in a single page. You don't need to worry about pages containing multiple forms until you have to submit information to a web server — then you need to be aware that the information from only one of the forms on a page can be submitted to the server at one time.

To create a form, you use the `<form>` and `</form>` tags to declare where it starts and where it ends. The `<form>` tag has a number of attributes, such as the `action` attribute, which determines where the form is submitted to; the `method` attribute, which determines how the information is submitted; and the `target` attribute, which determines the frame to which the response to the form is loaded.

Generally speaking, for client-side scripting where you have no intention of submitting information to a server, these attributes are not necessary. They will come into play in a later chapter when you look at programming server pages. For now the only attribute you need to set in the `<form>` tag is the `name` attribute, so that you can reference the form.

So, to create a blank form, the tags required would look something like this:

```
<form name="myForm">
</form>
```

You won't be surprised to hear that these tags create a `Form` object, which you can use to access the form. You can access this object in two ways.

First, you can access the object directly using its name — in this case `document.myForm`. Alternatively, you can access the object through the `document` object's `forms[]` array property. Remember that the last chapter included a discussion of the `document` object's `images[]` array and how you can manipulate it like any other array. The same applies to the `forms[]` array, except that instead of each element in the array holding an `IMG` object, it now holds a `Form` object. For example, if our `Form` is the first `Form` in the page, you reference it using `document.forms[0]`.

Many of the attributes of the `<form>` tag can be accessed as properties of the `Form` object. In particular, the `name` property of the `Form` object mirrors the `name` attribute of the `<form>` tag.

Try It Out | The forms Array

Let's have a look at an example that uses the `forms` array. Here you have a page with three forms on it. Using the `forms[]` array, you access each `Form` object in turn and show the value of its `name` property in a message box.

```
<html>
<head>
<script language="JavaScript" type="text/javascript">
function window_onload()
{
    var numberForms = document.forms.length;
```

```
    var formIndex;
    for (formIndex = 0; formIndex < numberForms; formIndex++)
    {
        alert(document.forms[formIndex].name);
    }
}
</script>
</head>
<body language=JavaScript type="text/javascript" onload="window_onload()">
<form name="form1">
<p>This is inside form1</p>
</form>
<form name="form2">
<p>This is inside form2</p>
</form>
<form name="form3">
<p>This is inside form3</p>
</form>
</body>
</html>
```

Save this as ch6_examp1.htm. When you load it into your browser, you should see three alert boxes, each of which shows the name of a form.

How It Works

Within the body of the page you define three forms. Each form is given a name and contains a paragraph of text.

Within the definition of the <body> tag, the window_onload() function is connected to the window object's onload event handler

```
<body language=JavaScript onload="return window_onload()">
```

This means that when the page is loaded, your window_onload() function will be called.

The window_onload() function is defined in a script block in the head of the page. Within this function you loop through the forms[] array. Just like any other JavaScript array, the forms[] array has a length property, which you can use to determine how many times you need to loop. Actually, because you know how many forms there are, you can just write the number in. However, this example uses the length property, since that makes it easier to add to the array without having to change the function. Generalizing your code like this is a good practice to get into.

The function starts by getting the number of Form objects within the forms array and storing that number in the variable numberForms.

```
function window_onload()
{
    var numberForms = document.forms.length;
```

Next you define a variable, formIndex, to be used in your for loop. After this comes the for loop itself.

```
var formIndex;
for (formIndex = 0; formIndex < numberForms; formIndex++)
{
    alert(document.forms[formIndex].name);
}
```

Remember that because the indexes for arrays start at 0, your loop needs to go from an index of 0 to an index of numberForms – 1. You enable this by initializing the formIndex variable to 0, and setting the condition of the for loop to formIndex < numberForms.

Within the for loop's code, you pass the index of the form you want (that is, formIndex) to document .forms[], which gives you the Form object at that array index in the forms array. To access the Form object's name property, you put a dot at the end of the name of the property, name.

Other Form Object Properties and Methods

The HTML form controls commonly found in forms, which you will look at in more detail shortly, also have corresponding objects. One way to access these is through the elements[] property of the Form object. This is an array just like the forms[] array property of the document object that you saw earlier. The elements[] array contains all the objects corresponding to the HTML interaction elements within the form, with the exception of the little-used <input type=image> element. As you'll see later, this property is very useful for looping through each of the elements in a form. For example, you can loop through each element to check that it contains valid data prior to submitting a form.

Being an array, the elements[] property of the Form object has the length property, which tells you how many elements are in the form. The Form object also has the length property, which also gives you the number of elements in the form. Which of these you use is up to you because both do the same job, although writing document.myForm.length is shorter, and therefore quicker to type and less lengthy to look at in code, than document.myForm.elements.length.

When you submit data from a form to a server, you normally use the Submit button, which you will come to shortly. However, the Form object also has the submit() method, which does nearly the same thing. It differs in that it does not call the onsubmit event handler for the submit event of the Form object.

Recall that in the last chapter you saw how return values passed back from an event handler's code can affect whether the normal course of events continues or is canceled. You saw, for example, that returning false from a hyperlink's onclick event handler causes the link's navigation to be canceled. Well, the same principle applies to the Form object's onsubmit event handler, which fires when the user submits the form. If you return true to this event handler, the form submission goes ahead; if you return false, the submission is canceled. This makes the onsubmit event handler's code a great place to do form validation — that is, to check that what the user has entered into the form is valid. For example, if you ask for the user's age and she enters mind your own business, you can spot that this is text rather than a valid number and stop her from continuing.

In addition to there being a Reset button, which we'll discuss later in the chapter, the Form object has the reset() method, which clears the form, or restores default values if these exist.

Creating blank forms is not exactly exciting or useful, so now let's turn our attention to the HTML elements that provide interaction functionality inside our forms.

HTML Elements in Forms

About ten elements are commonly found within `<form>` elements. The most useful are shown in Figures 6-1, 6-2, 6-3, and 6-4, ordered into general types. We give each its name and, in parentheses, the HTML needed to create it, though note this is not the full HTML but only a portion.

Text Input Elements

Text Box
(`<INPUT type="text">`)

some text I typed

Password Box
(`<INPUT type="Password">`)

••••••••••••••••

TextArea
(`<TEXTAREA></TEXTAREA>`)

Here is some text I typed in to this control

Figure 6-1

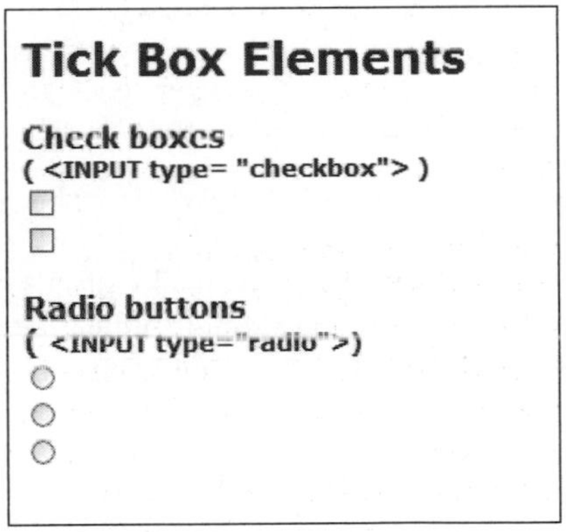

Tick Box Elements

Check boxes
(`<INPUT type="checkbox">`)
☐
☐

Radio buttons
(`<INPUT type="radio">`)
○
○
○

Figure 6-2

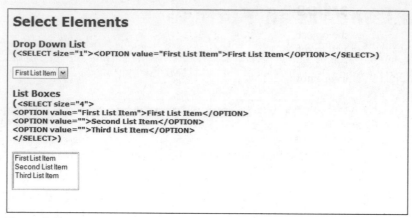

Figure 6-3

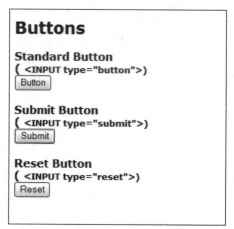

Figure 6-4

As you can see, most of the `<form>` elements are created by means of the `<input>` tag. One of the `<input>` tag's attributes is the `type` attribute. It's this attribute that decides which of the HTML elements this tag will be. Examples of values for this attribute include `button` (to create a button) and `text` (to create a text box).

Each form element inside the web page is made available to you as — yes, you guessed it — an object. As with all the other objects you have seen, each element's object has its own set of distinctive properties, methods, and events. You'll be taking a look at each form element in turn and how to use its particular properties, methods, and events, but before you do that, let's look at properties and methods that the objects of the form elements have in common.

Common Properties and Methods

One property that all the objects of the form elements have in common is the name property. You can use the value of this property to reference that particular element in your script. Also, if you are sending the information in the form to a server, the element's name property is sent along with any value of the form element, so that the server knows what the value relates to.

Most form element objects also have the value property, which returns the value of the element. For example, for a text box, the value property returns the text that the user has entered in the text box. Also, setting the value of the value property enables you to put text inside the text box. However, the use of the value property is specific to each element, so you'll look at what it means as you look at each individual element.

All form element objects also have the form property, which returns the Form object in which the element is contained. This can be useful in cases where you have a generic routine that checks the validity of data in a form. For example, when the user clicks a Submit button, you can pass the Form object referenced by the form property to your data checker, which can use it to loop through each element on the form in turn, checking that the data in the element are valid. This is handy if you have more than one form defined on the page or where you have a generic data checker that you cut and paste to different pages — this way you don't need to know the form's name in advance.

Sometimes it's useful to know what type of element you're dealing with, particularly where you're looping through the elements in a form using the elements[] array property of the Form object. This information can be retrieved by means of the type property, which each element's object has. This property returns the type of the element (for example, button or text).

All form element objects also have the focus() and blur() methods. *Focus* is a concept you might not have come across yet. If an element is the center of the focus, any key presses made by the user will be passed directly to that element. For example, if a text box has focus, pressing keys will enter values into the text box. Also, if a button has the focus, pressing the Enter key will cause the button's onclick event handler code to fire, just as if a user had clicked the button with his mouse.

The user can set which element currently has the focus by clicking on it or by using the Tab key to select it. However, you as the programmer can also decide which element has the focus by using the form element's object's focus() method. For example, if you have a text box for the user to enter his age and he enters an invalid value, such as a letter rather than a number, you can tell him that his input is invalid and send him back to that text box to correct his mistake.

Blur, which perhaps could be better called "lost focus," is the opposite of focus. If you want to remove a form element from being the focus of the user's attention, you can use the blur() method. When used with a form element, the blur() method usually results in the focus shifting to the page containing the form.

In addition to the focus() and blur() methods, all the form element's objects have the onfocus and onblur event handlers. These are fired, as you'd expect, when an element gets or loses the focus, respectively, due to user action or the focus() and blur() methods. The onblur event handler can be a good place to check the validity of data in the element that has just lost the focus. If the data are invalid, you can set the focus back to the element and let the user know why the data he entered are wrong.

One thing to be careful of is using the `focus()` and `blur()` methods in the `onfocus` or `onblur` event handler code. There is the danger of an infinite loop occurring. For example, consider two elements, each of whose `onfocus` events passes the focus to the other element. Then, if one element gets the focus, its `onfocus` event will pass the focus to the second element, whose `onfocus` event will pass the focus back to the first element, and so on until the only way out is to close the browser down. This is not likely to please your users!

Also be very wary of using the `focus()` and `blur()` methods to put focus back in a problem field if that field or others depend on some of the user's input. For example, say you have two text boxes, one in which you want the user to enter her city and the other in which you want her to enter her state. Also say that the input into the state text box is checked to make sure that the specified city is in that state. If the state does not contain the city, you put the focus back on the state text box so that the user can change the name of the state. However, if the user actually input the wrong city name and the right state name, she may not be able to go back to the city text box to rectify the problem.

Button Form Elements

We're starting our look at form elements with the standard button element because it's probably the most commonly used and is fairly simple. The HTML tag to create a button is the `<input>` tag. For example, to create a button called `myButton`, which has the words "Click Me" on its face, the `<input>` tag would need to be as follows:

```
<input type="button" name="myButton" value="Click Me">
```

The `type` attribute is set to `button`, and the `value` attribute is set to the text you want to appear on the face of the button. You can leave the `value` attribute off, but you'll end up with a blank button, which will leave your users guessing as to its purpose.

This element creates an associated `Button` object; in this example it is called `myButton`. This object has all the common properties and methods described earlier, including the `value` property. This property enables you to change the text on the button face using JavaScript, though this is probably not something you'll need to do very often. What the button is really all about is the `click` event.

You connect to the button's `onclick` event handler just as you did with the `onclick` events of other HTML tags such as the `<A>` tag. All you need to do is define a function that you want to have executed when the button is clicked (say, `button_onclick()`) and then add the `onclick` event handler as an attribute of the `<input>` tag as follows:

```
<input type="button" onclick="button_onclick()">
```

Try It Out   Counting Button Clicks

In the following example you use the methods described previously to record how often a button has been clicked.

```
<html>
<head>
<script language="JavaScript" type="text/javascript">
var numberOfClicks = 0;
```

```
function myButton_onclick()
{
    numberOfClicks++;
    window.document.form1.myButton.value = 'Button clicked ' + numberOfClicks +
    ' times';
}
</script>
</head>
<body>
<form name=form1>
    <input type='button' name='myButton' value='Button clicked 0 times'
    onclick="myButton_onclick()">
</form>
</body>
</html>
```

Save this page as ch6_examp2.htm. If you load this page into your browser, you will see a button with "Button clicked 0 times" on it. If you repeatedly press this button, you will see the number of button clicks recorded on the text of the button.

How It Works

You start the script block in the head of the page by defining a global variable, accessible anywhere inside your page, called numberOfClicks. You record the number of times the button has been clicked in this variable, and use this information to update the button's text.

The other piece of code in the script block is the definition of the function myButton_onclick(). This function is connected to the onclick event handler in the <input> tag in the body of the page. This tag is for a button element called myButton and is contained within a form called form1.

```
<form name=form1>
    <input type='button' name='myButton' value='Button clicked 0 times'
    onclick="myButton_onclick()">
</form>
```

Let's look at the myButton_onclick() function a little more closely. First, the function increments the value of the variable numberOfClicks by one.

```
function myButton_onclick()
{
    numberOfClicks++;
```

Next, you update the text on the button face using the Button object's value property.

```
    window.document.form1.myButton.value = 'Button clicked ' + numberOfClicks +
    ' times';
}
```

The function in this example is specific to this form and button, rather than a generic function you'll be using in other situations. Therefore the code in this example refers to the form and button directly using window.document.form1.myButton. Remember that the window object has a property containing the document object, which itself holds all the elements in a page, including the <form> element, and that the button is embedded inside your form.

Try It Out   onmouseup and onmousedown

Two less commonly used events supported by the `Button` object are the `onmousedown` and `onmouseup` events. You can see these two events in action in the next example.

```
<html>
<head>
<script language="JavaScript" type="text/javascript">
function myButton_onmouseup()
{
    document.form1.myButton.value = "Mouse Goes Up"
}
function myButton_onmousedown()
{
    document.form1.myButton.value = "Mouse Goes Down"
}
</script>
</head>
<body>
<form name=form1>
    <input type='button' name='myButton' value=' Mouse Goes Up '
    onmouseup="myButton_onmouseup()"
    onmousedown="myButton_onmousedown()">
</form>
</body>
</html>
```

Save this page as `ch6_examp3.htm` and load it into your browser. If you click the button with your left mouse button and keep it held down, you'll see the text on the button change to "Mouse Goes Down." As soon as you release the button, the text changes to "Mouse Goes Up."

How It Works

In the body of the page you define a button called `myButton` within a form called `form1`. Within the attributes of the `<input>` tag you attach the function `myButton_onmouseup()` to the `onmouseup` event handler, and the function `myButton_onmousedown()` to the `onmousedown` event handler.

```
<form name=form1>
    <input type='button' name='myButton' value=' Mouse Goes Up '
    onmouseup="myButton_onmouseup()"
    onmousedown="myButton_onmousedown()">
</form>
```

The `myButton_onmouseup()` and `myButton_onmousedown()` functions are defined in a script block in the head of the page. Each function consists of just a single line of code, in which you use the `value` property of the `Button` object to change the text that is displayed on the button's face.

An important point to note is that events like `onmouseup` and `onmousedown` are triggered only when the mouse pointer is actually over the element in question. For example, if you click and hold down the mouse button over your button, then move the mouse away from the button before releasing the mouse button, you'll find that the `onmouseup` event does not fire and the text on the button's face does not change. In this instance it would be the `document` object's `onmouseup` event handler code that would fire, if you'd connected any code to it.

Don't forget that, like all form element objects, the Button object also has the onfocus and onblur events, though they are rarely used in the context of buttons.

The Submit and Reset Buttons

Two additional button types are the Submit and Reset buttons. You define these buttons just as you do a standard button, except that the type attribute of the <input> tag is set to submit or reset rather than to button. For example, the Submit and Reset buttons in Figure 6-4 were created using the following code:

```
<input type="submit" value="Submit" name="submit1">
<input type="reset" value="Reset" name="reset1">
```

These buttons have special purposes, which are not related to script.

When the Submit button is clicked, the form data from the form that the button is inside gets sent to the server automatically, without the need for any script.

When the Reset button is clicked, all the elements in a form are cleared and returned to their default values (the values they had when the page was first loaded).

The Submit and Reset buttons have corresponding objects called Submit and Reset, which have exactly the same properties, methods, and events as a standard Button object.

Text Elements

The standard text element enables users to enter a single line of text. This information can then be used in JavaScript code or submitted to a server for server-side processing.

A text box is created by means of the <input> tag, much as your button was, but with the type attribute set to text. Again, you can choose not to include the value attribute, but if you do include it this value will appear inside the text box when the page is loaded.

In the following example the <input> tag has two additional attributes, size and maxlength. The size attribute determines how many characters wide the text box is, and maxlength determines the maximum number of characters the user can enter in the box. Both attributes are optional and use defaults determined by the browser.

For example, to create a text box 10 characters wide, with a maximum character length of 15, and initially containing the words Hello World, your <input> tag would be as follows:

```
<input type="text" name="myTextBox" size=10 maxlength=15 value="Hello World">
```

The Text object that this element creates has a value property, which you can use in your scripting to set or read the text contained inside the text box. In addition to the common properties and methods we discussed earlier, the Text object also has the select() method, which selects or highlights all the text inside the text box. This may be used if the user has entered an invalid value, and you can set the focus to the text box and select the text inside it. This then puts the user's cursor in the right place to correct the data and makes it very clear to the user where the invalid data is. The value property of Text objects always returns a string data type, even if number characters are being entered. If you use the value as a number, JavaScript normally does a conversion from a string data type to a number data type for you, but this is not always the case. For example, JavaScript won't do the conversion if the operation you're doing is valid for a string. If you have a form with two text boxes and you add the values returned from these, JavaScript concatenates rather than adds the two values, so 1 plus 1 will be 11 and not 2. To fix this, you need to convert all the values involved to a numerical data type, for example by using parseInt() or parseFloat() or Number(). However, if you subtract the two values, an operation only valid for numbers, JavaScript says "Aha, this can only be done with numbers, so I'll convert the values to a number data type." Therefore, 1 minus 1 will be returned as 0 without your having to use parseInt() or parseFloat(). This is a tricky bug to spot, so it's best to get into the habit of converting explicitly to avoid problems later.

In addition to the common event handlers, such as onfocus and onblur, the Text object has the onchange, onselect, onkeydown, onkeypress, and onkeyup event handlers.

The onselect event fires when the user selects some text in the text box.

More useful is the onchange event, which fires when the element loses focus if (and only if) the value inside the text box is different from the value it had when it got the focus. This enables you to do things like validity checks that occur only if something has changed.

As mentioned before, the onfocus and onblur events can be used for validating user input. However, they also have another purpose, and that's to make a text box read-only. In IE 4.0+ and NN 6 you can use the READONLY attribute of the <input> tag or the readOnly property of the Text object to prevent the contents from being changed. However, these techniques won't work in NN 4.x. You can get around this using the blur() method. All you need to do is add an onfocus event handler to the <input> tag defining the text box and connect it to some code that blurs the focus from the text box with the blur() method.

```
<input type="text" name=txtReadonly value="Look but don't change"
    onfocus="window.document.form1.txtReadonly.blur()"
    READONLY=true>
```

The onkeypress, onkeydown, and onkeyup events fire, as their names suggest, when the user presses a key, when the user presses a key down, and when a key pressed down is let back up respectively.

Try It Out   A Simple Form with Validation

Let's put all the information on text boxes and buttons together into an example. In this example you have a simple form consisting of two text boxes and a button. The top text box is for the user's name, and the second is for her age. You do various validity checks. You check the validity of the age text box when it loses focus. However, the name and age text boxes are only checked to see if they are empty when the button is clicked.

```
<html>
<head>
<script language="JavaScript" type="text/javascript">
function butCheckForm_onclick()
{
    var myForm = document.form1;
    if (myForm.txtAge.value == "" || myForm.txtName.value == "")
```

```
        {
            alert("Please complete all the form");
            if (myForm.txtName.value == "")
            {
                myForm.txtName.focus();
            }
            else
            {
                myForm.txtAge.focus();
            }
        }
        else
        {
            alert("Thanks for completing the form " + myForm.txtName.value);
        }
    }
    function txtAge_onblur()
    {
        var txtAge = document.form1.txtAge;
        if (isNaN(txtAge.value) == true)
        {
            alert("Please enter a valid age");
            txtAge.focus();
            txtAge.select();
        }
    }
    function txtName_onchange()
    {
        window.status = "Hi " + document.form1.txtName.value;
    }
    </script>
    </head>
    <body>
    <form name=form1>
        Please enter the following details:
        <p>
        Name:
        <br>
        <input type="text" name=txtName onchange="txtName_onchange()">
        <br>
        Age:
        <br>
        <input type="text" name=txtAge onblur="txtAge_onblur()" size=3 maxlength=3>
        <br>
        <input type="button" value="Check Details" name=butCheckForm
            onclick="butCheckForm_onclick()">
    </form>
    </body>
    </html>
```

After you've entered the text, save the file as ch6_examp4.htm and load it into your web browser.

In the text box shown in Figure 6-5, type your name. When you leave the text box you'll see Hi yourname appear in the status bar at the bottom of the window.

Enter an invalid value into the age text box, such as aaaa, and when you try to leave the box, it'll tell you of the error and send you back to correct it.

Finally, click the Check Details button and both text boxes will be checked to see that you have completed them. If either is empty, you'll get a message telling you to complete the whole form, and it'll send you back to the box that's empty.

If everything is filled in correctly, you'll get a message thanking you, as shown in Figure 6-5.

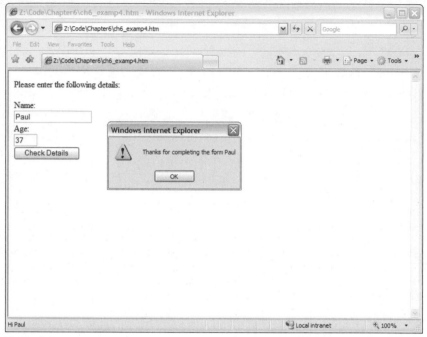

Figure 6-5

Note that this example does not work properly on Firefox or Netscape browsers; we'll discuss why shortly.

How It Works

Within the body of the page, you create the HTML tags that define your form. Inside your form, which is called `form1`, you create three form elements with the names `txtName`, `txtAge`, and `butCheckForm`.

```
<form name=form1>
   Please enter the following details:
   <p>
   Name:
   <br>
   <input type="text" name=txtName onchange="txtName_onchange()">
   <br>
   Age:
```

```
      <br>
      <input type="text" name=txtAge onblur="txtAge_onblur()" size=3 maxlength=3>
      <br>
      <input type="button" value="Check Details" name=butCheckForm
         onclick="butCheckForm_onclick()">
   </form>
```

You'll see that for the second text box (the `txtAge` text box), you have included the `size` and `maxlength` attributes inside the `<input>` tag. Setting the `size` attribute to 3 gives the user an idea of how much text you are expecting, and setting the `maxlength` attribute to 3 helps ensure that you don't get overly large numbers entered for the age value!

The first text box's onchange event handler is connected to the function `txtName_onchange()`, the second text box's onblur event handler is connected to the function `txtAge_onblur()`, and the button's `onclick` event handler is connected to the function `butCheckForm_onclick()`. These functions are defined in a script block in the head of the page. You will look at each of them in turn, starting with `butCheckForm_onclick()`.

The first thing you do is define a variable, `myForm`, and set it to reference the Form object created by your `<form>` tag later in the page.

```
function butCheckForm_onclick()
{
   var myForm = document.form1;
```

Doing this reduces the size of your code each time you want to use the `form1` object. Instead of `document.form1` you can just type `myForm`. It makes your code a bit more readable and therefore easier to debug, and it saves typing. When you set a variable to be equal to an existing object, you don't (in this case) actually create a new `form1` object; instead you just point your variable to the existing `form1` object. So when you type `myForm.name`, JavaScript checks your variable, finds it's actually storing the location in memory of the object `form1`, and uses that object instead. All this goes on behind the scenes so you don't need to worry about it and can just use `myForm` as if it were `document.form1`.

After getting your reference to the Form object, you then use it in an `if` statement to check whether the value in the text box named `txtAge` or the text box named `txtName` actually contains any text.

```
if (myForm.txtAge.value == "" || myForm.txtName.value == "")
{
   alert("Please complete all the form");
   if (myForm.txtName.value == "")
   {
      myForm.txtName.focus();
   }
   else
   {
      myForm.txtAge.focus();
   }
}
```

If you do find an incomplete form, you alert the user. Then in an inner `if` statement, you check which text box was not filled in. You set the focus to the offending text box, so that the user can start filling it in straightaway without having to move the focus to it herself. It also lets the user know which text box our program requires her to fill in. To avoid annoying your users, make sure that text in the page tells them which fields are required.

If the original outer `if` statement finds that the form is complete, it lets the user know with a thank-you message.

```
    else
    {
        alert("Thanks for completing the form " + myForm.txtName.value);
    }
}
```

In this sort of situation, it's probably more likely to submit the form to the server than to let the user know with a thank-you message. You can do this using the `Form` object's `submit()` method, or with a normal Submit button.

The next of your three functions is `txtAge_onblur()`, which is connected to the `onblur` event of your `txtAge` text box. The purpose of this function is to check that the string value the user entered into the age box actually consists of number characters.

```
function txtAge_onblur()
{
    var txtAge = document.form1.txtAge;
```

Again at the start of the function, you declare a variable and set it to reference an object; this time it's the `Text` object created for the `txtAge` text box that you define further down the page. Now, instead of having to type `document.form1.txtAge` every time, you just type `txtAge`, and it does the same thing. It certainly helps save those typing fingers, especially since it's a big function with multiple use of the `txtAge` object.

The following `if` statement checks to see whether what has been entered in the `txtAge` text box can be converted to a number. You use the `isNaN()` function to do this for you. If the value in the `txtAge` text box is not a number, it's time to tell the user and set the focus back to the offending element with the `focus()` method of the corresponding `Text` object. Additionally, this time you highlight the text by using the `Text` object's `select()` method. This makes it even clearer to the user what he has to fix, and he can rectify the problem without needing to delete text first.

```
    if (isNaN(txtAge.value) == true)
    {
        alert("Please enter a valid age");
        txtAge.focus();
        txtAge.select();
    }
}
```

You could go further and check that the number inside the text box is actually a valid age — for example, 191 is not a valid age, nor is 255 likely to be. You just need to add another `if` statement to check for these possibilities.

This function is connected to the onblur event handler of the txtAge text box, but why didn't you use the onchange event handler, with its advantage that it only rechecks the value when the value has actually been changed? The onchange event would not fire if the box was empty both before focus was passed to it and after focus was passed away from it. However, leaving the checking of the form completion until just before the form is submitted is probably best because some users prefer to fill in information out of order and come back to some form elements later.

The final function is for the txtName text box's onchange event. Its use here is a little flippant and intended primarily as an example of the onchange event.

```
function txtName_onchange()
{
    window.status = "Hi " + document.form1.txtName.value)
}
```

When the onchange event fires (when focus is passed away from the name text box and its contents have changed), you take the value of the txtName box and put it into the window's status bar at the bottom of the window. It simply says Hi yourname. You access the status bar using the window object's status property, although you could just enter the following:

```
status = "Hi " + document.form1.txtName.value;
```

Here window is in front just to make it clear what you are actually accessing. It would be very easy when reading the code to mistake status for a variable, so in this situation, although it isn't strictly necessary, putting window in front does make the code easier to read, understand, and therefore debug.

Problems with Firefox, Netscape, and the blur Event

The previous example will fail with Firefox and Netscape if you enter a name in the name text box and then an invalid age into the age box (for example, if you enter abc and then click the Check Form button). With IE the blur event fires and displays an alert box if the age is invalid, but the button's click event doesn't fire. However, in FF/NN, both events fire with the result that the invalid age alert is hidden by the "form completed successfully" alert box.

In addition, if you enter an invalid age for both IE and Firefox/Netscape browsers and then switch to a different program altogether, the "invalid age" alert box appears, which is annoying for the user. It could be that the user was opening up another program to check the details.

Although this is a fine example, it is not great for the real world. A better option would be to check the form when it's finally submitted and not while the user is entering data. Or, alternatively, you can check the data as they are entered but not use an alert box to display errors. Instead you could write out a warning in red next to the erroneous input control, informing the user of the invalid data, and then also get your code to check the form when it's submitted. In the dynamic HTML chapters you'll see how to write to the page after it's been loaded.

The Password Text Box

The only real purpose of the password box is to enable users to type in a password on a page and to have the password characters hidden, so that no one can look over the user's shoulder and discover his or her password. However, when sent to the server, the text in the password is sent as plain text — there is no encryption or any attempt at hiding the text — so it's not a secure way of passing information.

Defining a password box is identical to defining a text box, except that the type attribute is password.

```
<input name="password1" type="password">
```

This form element creates an associated Password object, which is identical to the Text object in its properties, methods, and events.

The Hidden Text Box

The hidden text box can hold text and numbers just like a normal text box, with the difference being that it's not visible to the user. A hidden element? It may sound as useful as an invisible painting, but in fact it proves to be very useful.

To define a hidden text box, you have the following HTML:

```
<input type="hidden" name=myHiddenElement>
```

The hidden text box creates a Hidden object. This is available in the elements array property of the Form object and can be manipulated in JavaScript like any other object, although you can actually set its value only through its HTML definition or through JavaScript. As with a normal text box, its value is submitted to the server when the user submits the form.

So why are hidden text boxes useful? Imagine you have a lot of information that you need to obtain from the user, but to avoid having a page stuffed full of elements and looking like the control panel of the space shuttle, you decide to obtain the information over more than one page. The problem is, how do you keep a record of what was entered in previous pages? Easy — you use hidden text boxes and put the values in there. Then, in the final page, all the information is submitted to the server — it's just that some of it is hidden. Anyway, you'll see more about this in Chapter 16.

textarea Element

The textarea element allows multi-line input of text. Other than this, it acts very much like the text box element.

However, unlike the text box, the textarea element has its own tag, the <textarea> tag. It also has two additional attributes: COLS and ROWS. The COLS attribute defines how many characters wide the text area will be, and the ROWS attribute defines how many character rows there will be. You set the text inside the element by putting it between the start and close tags, rather than by using the value attribute. So if you want a textarea element 40 characters wide by 20 rows deep with initial text Hello World on the first line and Line 2 on the second line, you define it as follows:

```
<textarea name=myTextArea cols=40 rows=20>Hello World
Line 2
</textarea>
```

Another attribute of the <textarea> tag is the wrap attribute, which determines what happens when the user types to the end of a line. The default value for this is soft, so the user does not have to press Return at the end of a line, though this can vary from browser to browser. To turn wrapping on, you can use one of two values: soft (this includes just the wrap attribute on its own) and hard. As far as client-side processing goes, both do the same thing: they switch wrapping on. However, when you come to server-side processing, they do make a difference in terms of which information is sent to the server when the form is posted.

If you set the wrap attribute on by setting it to soft, wrapping will occur on the client side, but the carriage returns won't be posted to the server, just the text. If the wrap attribute is set to hard, any carriage returns caused by wrapping will be converted to hard returns — it will be as if the user had pressed the Enter key, and these returns will be sent to the server. Also, you need to be aware that the carriage-return character is determined by the operating system that the browser is running on — for example, in Windows a carriage return is \r\n, whereas on a Macintosh the carriage return is \r and on Unix a carriage return is \n. To turn off wrapping client-side, set wrap to off.

The Textarea object created by the <textarea> tag has the same properties, methods, and events as the Text object you saw previously, except that the text area doesn't have the maxlength attribute. Note that there is a value property even though the <textarea> tag does not have a value attribute. The value property simply returns the text between the <textarea> and </textarea> tags. The events supported by the Textarea object include the onkeydown, onkeypress, onkeyup, and onchange event handlers.

Try It Out   Event Watching

To help demonstrate how the keydown, keypress, keyup, and change events work (in particular, the order in which they fire), you'll create an example that tells you what events are firing.

```
<html>
<head>
<script language="JavaScript" type="text/javascript">

function DisplayEvent(eventName)
{
    var myMessage = window.document.form1.textarea2.value;
    myMessage = myMessage + eventName;
    window.document.form1.textarea2.value = myMessage;
}
</script>
</head>

<body>
<form name=form1>
    <textarea rows=15 cols=40 name=textarea1
        onchange="DisplayEvent('onchange\n');"
        onkeydown="DisplayEvent('onkeydown\n');"
        onkeypress="DisplayEvent('onkeypress\n');"
        onkeyup="DisplayEvent('onkeyup\n\n');"></textarea>
    <textarea rows=15 cols=40 name=textarea2></textarea>
    <br><br>
    <input type="button" value="Clear Event TextArea"
        name=button1 onclick="window.document.form1.textarea2.value=''">
</form>
</body>
</html>
```

Save this page as `ch6_examp5.htm`. Load the page into your browser and see what happens when you type any letter into the first text area box. You should see the events being fired listed in the second text area box (onkeydown, onkeypress, and onkeyup), as shown in Figure 6-6. When you click outside the first text area box, you'll see the onchange event fire.

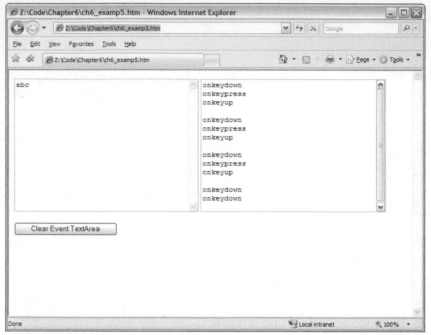

Figure 6-6

Experiment with the example to see what events fire and when.

How It Works

Within a form called `form1` in the body of the page, you define two text areas and a button. The first text area is the one whose events you are going to monitor. You attach code that calls the `DisplayEvent()` function to each of the onchange, onkeydown, onkeypress, and onkeyup event handlers. The value passed to the function reflects the name of the event firing.

```
<textarea rows=15 cols=40 name=textarea1
    onchange="DisplayEvent('onchange\n');"
    onkeydown="DisplayEvent('onkeydown\n');"
    onkeypress="DisplayEvent('onkeypress\n');"
    onkeyup="DisplayEvent('onkeyup\n\n');"></textarea>
```

Next you have an empty text area the same size as the first.

```
<textarea rows=15 cols=40 name=textarea2></textarea>
```

Finally you have your button element.

```
<input type="button" value="Clear Event TextArea"
    NAME=button1 onclick="window.document.form1.textarea2.value=''">
```

Notice that the `onclick` event handler for the button is not calling a function, but just executing a line of JavaScript. Although you normally call functions, it's not compulsory; if you have just one line of code to execute, it's easier just to insert it rather than create a function and call it. In this case, the `onclick` event handler is connected to some code that sets the contents of the second text area to empty (`' '`).

Now let's look at the `DisplayEvent()` function. This is defined in a script block in the head of the page. It adds the name of the event handler that has been passed as a parameter to the text already contained in the second text area.

```
function DisplayEvent(eventName)
{
    var myMessage = window.document.form1.textarea2.value;
    myMessage = myMessage + eventName;
    window.document.form1.textarea2.value = myMessage;
}
```

Check Boxes and Radio Buttons

The discussions of check boxes and radio buttons are together because their objects have identical properties, methods, and events. A check box enables the user to check and uncheck it. It is similar to the paper surveys you may get where you are asked to "check the boxes that apply to you." Radio buttons are basically a group of check boxes, with the property that only one can be checked at once. Of course, they also look different, and their group nature means that they are treated differently.

Creating check boxes and radio buttons requires our old friend the `<input>` tag. Its `type` attribute is set to `"checkbox"` or `"radio"` to determine which box or button is created. To set a check box or a radio button to be checked when the page is loaded, you simply insert the keyword `checked` into the `<input>` tag. This is handy if you want to set a default option like, for example, those "Check this box if you want our junk mail" forms you often see on the Net, which are usually checked by default, forcing you to uncheck them. So to create a check box that is already checked, your `<input>` tag will be the following:

```
<input type="checkbox" name=chkDVD checked value="DVD">
```

To create a checked radio button, the `<input>` tag would be as follows:

```
<input type="radio" name=radCPUSpeed checked value="1 GHz">
```

As previously mentioned, radio buttons are group elements. In fact, there is little point in putting just one on a page, because the user won't be able to choose between any alternative boxes.

To create a group of radio buttons, you simply give each radio button the same `name`. This creates an array of radio buttons going by that name that you can access, as you would with any array, using its index.

For example, to create a group of three radio buttons, your HTML would be as follows:

```
<input type="radio" name=radCPUSpeed checked value="800 MHz">
<input type="radio" name=radCPUSpeed value="1 GHz">
<input type="radio" name=radCPUSpeed value="1.5 GHz">
```

You can put as many groups of radio buttons in a form as you want, by just giving each group its own unique name. Note that you have only used one CHECKED attribute, since only one of the radio buttons in the group can be checked. If you had used the CHECKED attribute in more than one of the radio buttons, only the last of these would have actually been checked.

Using the value attribute of the check box and radio button elements is not the same as with previous elements you've looked at. First, it tells you nothing about the user's interaction with an element, because it's predefined in your HTML or by your JavaScript. Whether a check box or radio button is checked or not, it still returns the same value. Second, when a form is posted to a server, only the values of the checked check boxes and radio buttons are sent. So, if you have a form with 10 check boxes and the user submits the form with none of these checked, then nothing is sent to the server except a blank form. You'll learn more about this when you look at server-side scripting in Chapter 16.

Each check box has an associated Checkbox object, and each radio button in a group has a separate Radio object. As mentioned earlier, with radio buttons of the same name you can access each Radio object in a group by treating the group of radio buttons as an array, with the name of the array being the name of the radio buttons in the group. As with any array, you have the length property, which will tell you how many radio buttons are in the group.

For determining whether a user has actually checked or unchecked a check box, you need to use the checked property of the Checkbox object. This property returns true if the check box is currently checked and false if not.

Radio buttons are slightly different. Because radio buttons with the same name are grouped together, you need to test each Radio object in the group in turn to see if it has been checked. Only one of the radio buttons in a group can be checked, so if you check another one in the group, the previously checked one will become unchecked, and the new one will be checked in its place.

Both Checkbox and Radio have the event handlers onclick, onfocus, and onblur, and these operate as you saw for the other elements, although they can also be used to cancel the default action, such as clicking the check box or radio button.

Try It Out   Check Boxes and Radio Buttons

Let's look at an example that makes use of all the properties, methods, and events we have just discussed. The example is a simple form that enables a user to build a computer system. Perhaps it could be used in an e-commerce situation, to sell computers with the exact specifications determined by the customer.

```
<html>
<head>
<script language="JavaScript" type="text/javascript">

var radCpuSpeedIndex = 0;

function radCPUSpeed_onclick(radIndex)
```

```
{
   var returnValue = true;
   if (radIndex == 1)
   {
      returnValue = false;
      alert("Sorry that processor speed is currently unavailable");
      // Next line works around a bug in IE that doesn't cancel the
      // Default action properly
      document.form1.radCPUSpeed[radCpuSpeedIndex].checked = true;
   }
   else
   {
      radCpuSpeedIndex = radIndex;
   }
   return returnValue;
}
function butCheck_onclick()
{
   var controlIndex;
   var element;
   var numberOfControls = document.form1.length;
   var compSpec = "Your chosen processor speed is ";
   compSpec = compSpec + document.form1.radCPUSpeed[radCpuSpeedIndex].value;
   compSpec = compSpec + "\nWith the following additional components\n";
   for (controlIndex = 0; controlIndex < numberOfControls; controlIndex++)
   {
      element = document.form1[controlIndex];
      if (element.type == "checkbox")
      {
         if (element.checked == true)
         {
            compSpec = compSpec + element.value + "\n";
         }
      }
   }
   alert(compSpec);
}
</script>
</head>
<body>
<form name=form1>
 <p> Tick all of the components you want included on your computer <br><br>
<table> <tr>
   <td>DVD-ROM</td>
   <td><input type="checkbox" name="chkDVD" value="DVD-ROM"></td>
</tr> <tr>
   <td>CD-ROM</td>
   <td><input type="checkbox" name="chkCD" value="CD-ROM"></td>
</tr> <tr>
   <td>Zip Drive</td>

   <td><input type="checkbox" name="chkZip" value="ZIP Drive"></td>
</tr>
</table>
<p>
```

```
Select the processor speed you require <table>
<tr>
   <td><input type="radio" name="radCPUSpeed" checked
      onclick="return radCPUSpeed_onclick(0)" value="3.8 GHz"></td>
   <td>3.8 GHz</td>    <td><input type="radio" name="radCPUSpeed"
      onclick="return radCPUSpeed_onclick(1)" value="4.8 GHz"></td>
   <td>4.8 GHz</td>
   <td><input type="radio" name="radCPUSpeed"
      onclick="return radCPUSpeed_onclick(2)" value="6 Ghz"></td>
   <td>6 GHz</td> </tr>
</table>
</p> <input type="button" value="Check Form" name="butCheck"
   onclick="return butCheck_onclick()">
</form>
</body>
</html>
```

Save the page as ch6_examp6.htm and load it into your web browser. You should see a form like the one shown in Figure 6-7.

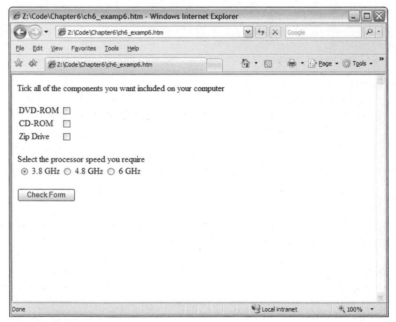

Figure 6-7

Check some of the check boxes, change the processor speed, and click the Check Form button. A message box will appear, listing the components and processor speed you selected. For example, if you select a DVD-ROM and a Zip drive and a 6 GHz processor speed, you will see something like what is shown in Figure 6-8.

Figure 6-8

Note that the 4.8 GHz processor is out of stock, so if you choose that, a message box will appear telling you that it's out of stock, and the 4.8 GHz processor speed radio button won't be selected. The previous setting will be restored when the user dismisses the message box.

How It Works

Let's first look at the body of the page, where you define the check boxes and radio buttons and a standard button inside a form called `form1`. You start with the check boxes. They are put into a table simply for formatting purposes. No functions are called, and no events are linked to.

```
<table>
<tr>
   <td>DVD-ROM</td>
   <td><input type="checkbox" name=chkDVD value="DVD-ROM"></td>
</tr>
<tr>
   <td>CD-ROM</td>
   <td><input type="checkbox" name=chkCD value="CD-ROM"></td>
</tr>
<tr>
   <td>Zip Drive</td>
   <td><input type="checkbox" name=chkZip value="ZIP Drive"></td>
</tr>
</table>
```

Next come the radio buttons for selecting the required CPU speed, and these are a little more complex. Again they are put into a table for formatting purposes.

```
<table>
<tr>
   <td><input type="radio" name=radCPUSpeed checked
      onclick="return radCPUSpeed_onclick(0)" value="3.8 GHz"></td>
   <td>3.8 Ghz</td>
   <td><input type="radio" name=radCPUSpeed
      onclick="return radCPUSpeed_onclick(1)" value="4.8 GHz"></td>
   <td>4.8 GHz</td>
   <td><input type="radio" name=radCPUSpeed
      onclick="return radCPUSpeed_onclick(2)" value="6 GHz"></td>
   <td>6 GHz</td>
</tr>
</table>
```

The radio button group name is radCPUSpeed. Here the first one is set to be checked by default by the inclusion of the word CHECKED inside the <input> tag's definition. It's a good idea to ensure that you have one radio button checked by default, because if you do not and the user doesn't select a button, the form will be submitted with no value for that radio group.

You're making use of the onclick event of each Radio object. For each button you're connecting to the same function, radCPUSpeed_onclick(), but for each radio button, you are passing a value — the index of that particular button in the radCPUSpeed radio button group array. This makes it easy to determine which radio button was selected. You'll look at this function a little later, but first let's look at the standard button that completes your form.

```
<input type="button" value="Check Form" name=butCheck
    onclick="return butCheck_onclick()">
```

This button's onclick event handler is connected to the butCheck_onclick() function and is for the user to click when she has completed the form.

So you have two functions, radCPUSpeed_onclick() and butCheck_onclick(). These are both defined in the script block in the head of the page. Let's look at this script block now. It starts by declaring a variable radCpuSpeedIndex. This will be used to store the currently selected index of the radCPUSpeed radio button group.

```
var radCpuSpeedIndex = 0;
```

Next you have the radCPUSpeed_onclick() function, which is called by the onclick event handler in each radio button. Your function has one parameter, namely the index position in the radCPUSpeed[] array of the radio object selected.

```
function radCPUSpeed_onclick(radIndex)
{
    var returnValue = true;
```

The first thing you do in the function is declare the returnValue variable and set it to true. You'll be returning this as your return value from the function. In this case the return value is important because it decides whether the radio button remains checked as a result of the user clicking it. If you return false, that cancels the user's action, and the radio button remains unchecked. In fact no radio button becomes checked, which is why you keep track of the index of the checked radio button so you can track which button was the previously checked one. To allow the user's action to proceed, you return true.

As an example of this in action, you have an if statement on the next line. If the radio button's index value passed is 1 (that is, if the user checked the box for a 4.8 GHz processor), you tell the user that it's out of stock and cancel the clicking action by setting returnValue to false.

```
if (radIndex == 1)
{
    returnValue = false;
    alert("Sorry that processor speed is currently unavailable");
    document.form1.radCPUSpeed[radCpuSpeedIndex].checked = true;
}
```

As previously mentioned, canceling the clicking action results in no radio buttons being checked. To rectify this, you set the previously checked box to be checked again in the following line:

```
document.form1.radCPUSpeed[radCpuSpeedIndex].checked = true;
```

What you are doing here is using the `Array` object for the `radCpuSpeed` radio group. Each array element actually contains an object, namely each of your three `Radio` objects. You use the `radCpuSpeedIndex` variable as the index of the `Radio` object that was last checked, since this is what it holds.

Finally, in the `else` statement you set `radCpuSpeedIndex` to the new checked radio button's index value.

```
else
{
    radCpuSpeedIndex = radIndex;
}
```

In the last line of the function, the value of `returnValue` is returned to where the function was called and will either cancel or allow the clicking action.

```
    return returnValue;
}
```

Your second function, `butCheck_onclick()`, is the one connected to the button's `onclick` event. In a real e-commerce situation, this button would be the place where you'd check your form and then submit it to the server for processing. Here you use the form to show a message box confirming which boxes you have checked, as if you didn't already know!

At the top you declare the four local variables, which will be used in the function. The variable `numberOfControls` is set to the form's `length` property, which is the number of elements on the form. The variable `compSpec` is used to build up the string that you'll display in a message box.

```
function butCheck_onclick()
{
    var controlIndex;
    var element;
    var numberOfControls = document.form1.length;
    var compSpec = "Your chosen processor speed is ";
    compSpec = compSpec + document.form1.radCPUSpeed[radCpuSpeedIndex].value;
    compSpec = compSpec + "\nWith the following additional components\n";
```

In the following line you add the value of the radio button the user has selected to your message string:

```
compSpec = compSpec + document.form1.radCPUSpeed[radCpuSpeedIndex].value;
```

The global variable `radCpuSpeedIndex`, which was set by the radio button group's `onclick` event, contains the array index of the selected radio button.

An alternative way of finding out which radio button was clicked would be to loop through the radio button group's array and test each radio button in turn to see if it was checked. The code would look something like this:

```
var radIndex;
for (radIndex = 0; radIndex < document.form1.radCPUSpeed.length; radIndex++)
{
    if (document.form1.radCPUSpeed[radIndex].checked == true)
    {
        radCpuSpeedIndex = radIndex;
        break;
    }
}
```

But to get back to the actual code, you'll notice a few new-line (\n) characters thrown into the message string for formatting reasons.

Next you have your big `for` statement.

```
for (controlIndex = 0; controlIndex < numberOfControls; controlIndex++)
    {
        element = document.form1[controlIndex];
        if (element.type == "checkbox")
        {
            if (element.checked == true)
            {
                compSpec = compSpec + element.value + "\n";
            }
        }
    }
    alert(compSpec);
}
```

It's here that you loop through each element on the form using `document.form1[controlIndex]`, which returns a reference to the element object stored at the `controlIndex` index position.

You'll see that in this example the `element` variable is set to reference the object stored in the `form1[]` array at the index position stored in variable `controlIndex`. Again, this is for convenient shorthand purposes; now to use that particular object's properties or methods, you just type `element`, a period, and then the method or property name, making your code easier to read and debug, which also saves on typing.

You only want to see which check boxes have been checked, so you use the `type` property, which every HTML element object has, to see what element type you are dealing with. If the `type` is `checkbox`, you go ahead and see if it's a checked check box. If so, you append its value to the message string in `compSpec`. If it is not a check box, it can be safely ignored.

Finally, you use the `alert()` method to display the contents of your message string.

The select Elements

Although they look quite different, the drop-down list and the list boxes are actually both elements created with the <select> tag, and strictly speaking they are both select elements. The select element has one or more options in a list that you can select from; each of these options is defined by means of the <option> tag. Your list of <option> tags goes in between the <select> and </select> tags.

The size attribute of the <select> tag is used to specify how many of the options are visible to the user.

For example, to create a list box five rows deep and populate it with seven options, your <select> tag would look like this:

```
<select name=theDay size=5>
<option value=0 selected>Monday
<option value=1>Tuesday
<option value=2>Wednesday
<option value=3>Thursday
<option value=4>Friday
<option value=5>Saturday
<option value=6>Sunday
</select>
```

Notice that the Monday <option> tag also contains the word selected; this will make this option the default selected one when the page is loaded. The values of the options have been defined as numbers, but text would be equally valid.

If you want this to be a drop-down list, you just need to change the size attribute in the <select> tag to 1, and presto, it's a drop-down list.

If you want to let the user choose more than one item from a list at once, you simply need to add the multiple attribute to the <select> definition.

The **<select>** tag creates a Select object. This object has an options[] array property, and this array is made up of Option objects, one for each <option> element inside the <select> element associated with the Select object. For instance, in the preceding example, if the <select> element was contained in a form called theForm with the following:

```
document.theForm.theDay.options[0]
```

you would access the option created for Monday.

How can you tell which option has been selected by the user? Easy: You use the Select object's selectedIndex property. You can use the index value returned by this property to access the selected option using the options[] array.

The Option object also has index, text, and value properties. The index property returns the index position of that option in the options[] array. The text property is what's displayed in the list, and the value property is the value defined for the option, which would be posted to the server if the form were submitted.

If you want to find out how many options there are in a select element, you can use the length property of either the Select object itself or of its options[] array property.

Let's see how you could loop through the options[] array for the preceding select box:

```
var theDayElement = window.document.form1.theDay;
document.write("There are " + theDayElement.length + "options<br>");
var optionCounter;
for (optionCounter = 0; optionCounter < theDayElement.length; optionCounter++)
{
    document.write("Option text is " + theDayElement.options[optionCounter].text)
    document.write(" and its value is ");
    document.write(theDayElement.options[optionCounter].value);
    document.write("<br>")
}
```

First you set the variable theDayElement to reference the Select object. Then you write the number of options to the page, in this case 7.

Next you use a for loop to loop through the options[] array, displaying the text of each option, such as Monday, Tuesday, and so on, and its value, such as 0, 1, and so on. If you create a page based on this code, it must be placed after the <select> tag has been defined.

It's also possible to add options to a select element after the page has finished loading. You'll look at how this is done next.

Adding New Options

To add a new option to a select element, you simply create a new Option object using the new operator and then insert it into the options[] array of the Select object at an empty index position.

When you create a new Option object, there are two parameters to pass — the first is the text you want to appear in the list, and the second the value to be assigned to the option.

```
var myNewOption = new Option("TheText","TheValue");
```

You then simply assign this Option object to an empty array element, for example:

```
document.theForm.theSelectObject.options[0] = myNewOption;
```

If you want to remove an option, you simply set that part of the options[] array to null. For example, to remove the element you just inserted, you need the following:

```
document.theForm.theSelectObject.options[0] = null;
```

When you remove an Option object from the options[] array, the array is reordered so that the array index value of each of the options above the removed one has its index value decremented by one.

When you insert a new option at a certain index position, be aware that it will overwrite any Option object that is already there.

Try It Out   **Adding and Removing List Options**

Use the list-of-days example you saw previously to demonstrate adding and removing list options.

```
<html>
<head>
<script language="JavaScript" type="text/javascript">
function butRemoveWed_onclick()
{
   if (document.form1.theDay.options[2].text == "Wednesday")
   {
      document.form1.theDay.options[2] = null;
   }
   else
   {
      alert('There is no Wednesday here!');
   }
}
function butAddWed_onclick()
{
   if (document.form1.theDay.options[2].text != "Wednesday")
   {
      var indexCounter;
      var days = document.form1.theDay;
      var lastoption = new Option();
      days.options[6] = lastoption;
      for (indexCounter = 6;indexCounter > 2; indexCounter--)
      {
      days.options[indexCounter].text = days.options[indexCounter - 1].text;
      days.options[indexCounter].value = days.options[indexCounter - 1].value;
      }
      var option = new Option("Wednesday",2);
      days.options[2] = option;
   }
   else
   {
      alert('Do you want to have TWO Wednesdays?????');
   }
}
</script>
</head>
<body>
<form name=form1>
<select name=theDay size=5>
   <option value=0 selected>Monday
   <option value=1>Tuesday
   <option value=2>Wednesday
   <option value=3>Thursday
   <option value=4>Friday
   <option value=5>Saturday
   <option value=6>Sunday
</select>
<BR>
<input type="button" value="Remove Wednesday" name=butRemoveWed
```

```
        onclick="butRemoveWed_onclick()">
<input type="button" value="Add Wednesday" name=butAddWed
    onclick="butAddWed_onclick()">
<BR>
</form>
</body>
</html>
```

Save this as ch6_examp7.htm. If you type the page in and load it into your browser, you should see the form shown in Figure 6-9. Click the Remove Wednesday button, and you'll see Wednesday disappear from the list. Add it back by clicking the Add Wednesday button. If you try to add a second Wednesday or remove a nonexistent Wednesday, you'll get a polite warning telling you that you can't do that.

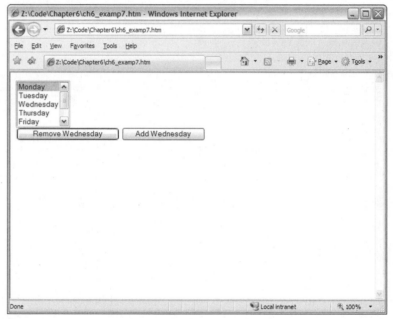

Figure 6-9

How It Works

Within the body of the page, you define a form with the name form1. This contains the select element, which includes day-of-the-week options that you have seen previously. The form also contains two buttons, as shown here:

```
<input type="button" value="Remove Wednesday" name=butRemoveWed
    onclick="butRemoveWed_onclick()">
<input type="button" value="Add Wednesday" name=butAddWed
    onclick="butAddWed_onclick()">
```

Each of these buttons has its onclick event handler connected to some code that calls one of two functions: butRemoveWed_onclick() and butAddWed_onclick(). These functions are defined in a script block in the head of the page. You'll take a look at each of them in turn.

218

At the top of the page you have your first function, butRemoveWed_onclick(), which removes the Wednesday option.

```
function butRemoveWed_onclick()
{
   if (document.form1.theDay.options[2].text == "Wednesday")
   {
      document.form1.theDay.options[2] = null;
   }
   else
   {
      alert('There is no Wednesday here!');
   }
}
```

The first thing you do in the function is a sanity check: You must try to remove the Wednesday option only if it's there in the first place! You make sure of this by seeing if the third option in the array (with index 2 because arrays start at index 0) has the text "Wednesday". If it does, you can remove the Wednesday option by setting that particular option to null. If the third option in the array is not Wednesday, you alert the user to the fact that there is no Wednesday to remove. Although this code uses the text property in the if statement's condition, you could just as easily have used the value property; it makes no difference.

Next you come to the butAddWed_onclick() function, which, as the name suggests, adds the Wednesday option. This is slightly more complex than the code required to remove an option. First you use an if statement to check that there is not already a Wednesday option.

```
function butAddWed_onclick()
{
   if (document.form1.theDay.options[2].text != "Wednesday")
   {
      var indexCounter;
      var days = document.form1.theDay;
      var lastoption = new Option();
      days.options[6] = lastoption;
      for (indexCounter = 6;indexCounter > 2; indexCounter--)
      {
      days.options[indexCounter].text = days.options[indexCounter - 1].text;
      days.options[indexCounter].value = days.options[indexCounter - 1].value;
      }
```

If there is no Wednesday option, you then need to make space for the new Wednesday option to be inserted.

Before you do this, you define two variables, indexCounter and days (which refers to theDay select element and is a shorthand reference for your convenience). Next you create a new option with the variable name lastoption and assign this new option to the element at index position 6 in your options array, which previously had no contents. You next assign the text and value properties of each of the Option objects from Thursday to Sunday to the Option at an index value higher by one in the options array, leaving a space in the options array at position 2 to put Wednesday in. This is the task for the for loop within the if statement.

Next, you create a new `Option` object by passing the text `"Wednesday"` and the value 2 to the `Option` constructor. The `Option` object is then inserted into the `options[]` array at position 2, and presto, it appears in your select box.

```
        var option = new Option("Wednesday",2);
        days.options[2] = option;
    }
```

You end the function by alerting the user to the fact that there is already a Wednesday option in the list, if the condition in the `if` statement is `false`.

```
    else
    {
        alert('Do you want to have TWO Wednesdays?????');
    }
}
```

Adding New Options with Internet Explorer

In IE, additional properties, methods, and events are associated with the select options. In particular, the `options[]` array you are interested in has the additional `add()` and `remove()` methods, which add and remove options. These make life a little simpler.

Before you add an option, you need to create it. You do this just as before, using the `new` operator.

The `add()` method enables you to insert an `Option` object that you have created and takes two parameters. You pass the option that you want to add as the first parameter. The optional second parameter enables you to specify which index position you want to add the option in. This parameter won't overwrite any `Option` object already at that position, but instead will simply move the `Option` objects up the array to make space. This is basically the same as what you had to code into the `butAddWed_onclick()` function using your `for` loop.

Using the `add()` method, you can rewrite the `butAddWed_onclick()` function in your `ch6_examp7.htm` example to look like this:

```
function butAddWed_onclick()
{
    if (document.form1.theDay.options[2].text != "Wednesday")
    {
        var option = new Option("Wednesday",2);
        document.form1.theDay.options.add(option,2);
    }
    else
    {
        alert('Do you want to have TWO Wednesdays?????');
    }
}
```

The `remove()` method takes just one parameter, namely the index of the option you want removed. When an option is removed, the options at higher index positions are moved down the array to fill the gap.

Using the `remove()` method, you can rewrite the `butRemoveWed_onclick()` function in your `ch6_examp7.htm` example to look like this:

```
function butRemoveWed_onclick()
{
    if (document.form1.theDay.options[2].text == "Wednesday")
    {
            document.form1.theDay.options.remove(2);
    }
    else
    {
        alert('There is no Wednesday here!');
    }
}
```

Modify the previous example and save it as `ch6_examp8_IE.htm` before loading it into IE. You'll see that it works just as the previous version did.

Select Element Events

Select elements have three event handlers, `onblur`, `onfocus`, and `onchange`. You've seen all these events before. You saw the `onchange` event with the text box element, where it fired when focus was moved away from the text box *and* the value in the text box had changed. Here it fires when the user changes which option in the list is selected.

| Try It Out | Using the Select Element for Date Difference Calculations |

Let's take a look at an example that uses the `onchange` event and makes good use of the select element in its drop-down list form. Its purpose is to calculate the difference, in days, between two dates set by the user via drop-down list boxes.

```
<html>
<head>
<script language="JavaScript" type="text/javascript">
function writeOptions(startNumber, endNumber)
{
  var optionCounter;
  for (optionCounter = startNumber; optionCounter <= endNumber; optionCounter++)
  {
      document.write('<option value=' + optionCounter + '>' + optionCounter);
  }
}
function writeMonthOptions()
{
    var theMonth;
    var monthCounter;
    var theDate = new Date(1);
    for (monthCounter = 0; monthCounter < 12; monthCounter++)
    {
        theDate.setMonth(monthCounter);
        theMonth = theDate.toString();
        theMonth = theMonth.substr(4,3);
        document.write('<option value=' + theMonth + '>' + theMonth);
```

```
      }
   }
   function recalcDateDiff()
   {
     var myForm = document.form1;
      var firstDay = myForm.firstDay.options[myForm.firstDay.selectedIndex].value;
      var secondDay =
         myForm.secondDay.options[myForm.secondDay.selectedIndex].value;
      var firstMonth =
         myForm.firstMonth.options[myForm.firstMonth.selectedIndex].value;
      var secondMonth =
         myForm.secondMonth.options[myForm.secondMonth.selectedIndex].value;
      var firstYear =
         myForm.firstYear.options[myForm.firstYear.selectedIndex].value;
      var secondYear =
         myForm.secondYear.options[myForm.secondYear.selectedIndex].value;
      var firstDate = new Date(firstDay + " " + firstMonth + " " + firstYear);
      var secondDate = new Date(secondDay + " " + secondMonth + " " + secondYear);
      var daysDiff = (secondDate.valueOf() - firstDate.valueOf());
      daysDiff = Math.floor(Math.abs((((daysDiff  / 1000) / 60) / 60) / 24));
      myForm.txtDays.value = daysDiff;
      return true;
   }
   function window_onload()
   {
      var theForm = document.form1;
      var nowDate = new Date();
      theForm.firstDay.options[nowDate.getDate() - 1].selected = true;
      theForm.secondDay.options[nowDate.getDate() - 1].selected = true;
      theForm.firstMonth.options[nowDate.getMonth()].selected = true;
      theForm.secondMonth.options[nowDate.getMonth()].selected = true;
      theForm.firstYear.options[nowDate.getFullYear()- 1970].selected = true;
      theForm.secondYear.options[nowDate.getFullYear() - 1970].selected = true;
   }
</script>
</head>
<body language=JavaScript onload="return window_onload()">
<form name=form1>
<p>
First Date<br>
<select name=firstDay size=1 onchange="return recalcDateDiff()">
<script language=JavaScript>
   writeOptions(1,31);
</script>
</select>
<select name=firstMonth size=1 onchange="return recalcDateDiff()">
<script language=JavaScript>
   writeMonthOptions();
</script>
</select>
<select name=firstYear size=1 onchange="return recalcDateDiff()">
<script language=JavaScript>
   writeOptions(1970,2020);
</script>
</select>
```

```
</p>
<p>
Second Date<br>
<select name=secondDay size=1 onchange="return recalcDateDiff()">
<script language=JavaScript>
   writeOptions(1,31);
</script>
</select>
<select name=secondMonth size=1 onchange="return recalcDateDiff()">
<script language=JavaScript>
   writeMonthOptions();
</script>
</select>
<select name=secondYear size=1 onchange="return recalcDateDiff()">
<script language=JavaScript>
   writeOptions(1970,2020);
</script>
</select>
</p>
Total difference in days
<input type="text" name=txtDays value=0 readonly>
<br>
</form>
</body>
</html>
```

Call the example ch6_examp9.htm and load it into your web browser. You should see the form shown in Figure 6-10, but with both date boxes set to the current date.

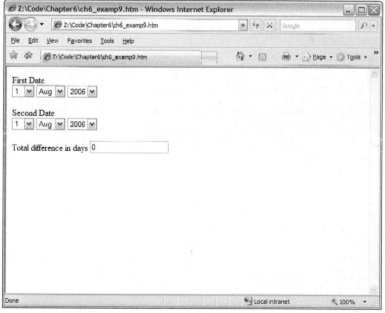

Figure 6-10

If you change any of the select boxes, the difference between the days will be recalculated and shown in the text box.

How It Works

In the body of the page, the form in the web page is built up with six drop-down list boxes and one text box. Let's look at an example of one of these select elements: take the first `<select>` tag, the one that allows the user to choose the day part of the first date.

```
<select name=firstDay size=1 onchange="return recalcDateDiff()">
<script language=JavaScript>
   writeOptions(1,31);
</script>
</select>
```

The `size` attribute has been set to 1 so that you have a drop-down list box rather than a list box, though strictly speaking 1 is the default, so you don't have to specify it. The `onchange` event handler has been connected to the `recalcDateDiff()` function that you'll be looking at shortly.

However, no `<option>` tags are defined within the `<select>` element. The drop-down list boxes need to be populated with too many options for you to enter them manually. Instead you populate the options using the functions, which make use of the `document.write()` method.

The date and year options are populated using the `writeOptions()` function declared in the head of the page. The function is passed two values: the start number and the end number of the options that you want the select element to be populated with. Let's look at the `writeOptions()` function.

```
function writeOptions(startNumber, endNumber)
{
  var optionCounter;
  for (optionCounter = startNumber; optionCounter <= endNumber; optionCounter++)
  {
      document.write('<option value=' + optionCounter + '>' + optionCounter);
  }
}
```

The function is actually quite simple, consisting of a `for` loop that loops from the first number (`startNumber`) through to the last (`endNumber`) using the variable `optionCounter`, and writes out the HTML necessary for each `<option>` tag. The text for the option and the `value` attribute of the `<option>` tag are specified to be the value of the variable `optionCounter`. It's certainly a lot quicker than typing out the 31 `<option>` tags necessary for the dates in a month.

For the year select box, the same function can be reused. You just pass 1970 and 2020 as parameters to the `writeOptions()` function to populate the year select box.

```
<select name=firstYear size=1 onchange="return recalcDateDiff()">
<script language=JavaScript>
   writeOptions(1970,2020);
</script>
</select>
```

To populate the month select box with the names of each month, you will need a different function. However, the principle behind populating the `<select>` element remains the same: You do it using `document.write()`. The function in this case is `writeMonthOptions()`, as you can see from the following month select element:

```
<select name=firstMonth size=1 onchange="return recalcDateDiff()">
<script language=JavaScript>
   writeMonthOptions();
</script>
</select>
```

The new function, `writeMonthOptions()`, is defined in the head of the page. Let's take a look at it now. You start the function by defining three variables and initializing the variable, `theDate`, to the first day of the current month.

```
function writeMonthOptions()
{
   var theMonth;
   var monthCounter;
   var theDate = new Date(1);
```

You use the `Date` object you have stored to get the months as text (`Jan`, `Feb`...`Dec`). You get these months by setting the month in the `theDate` variable from `0` up to `11` using the `setMonth()` method in a `for` loop. Although the `Date` object does not provide a method for returning the date as anything other than a number, it does have the `toString()` method, which returns the value, as a string, of the date stored in the variable. It returns the date in the format of day of the week, month, day of the month, time, and finally year, for example, `Sat Feb 19 19:04:34 2000`. You just need the month part. Since you always know where it will be in the string and that its length is always 3, you can easily use the `String` object's `substr()` method to extract the month.

```
for (monthCounter = 0; monthCounter < 12; monthCounter++)
{
   theDate.setMonth(monthCounter);
   theMonth = theDate.toString();
   theMonth = theMonth.substr(4,3);
   document.write('<option value=' + theMonth + '>' + theMonth);
}
}
```

Now that you have your month as a string of three characters, you can create the `<option>` tag and populate its text and value with the month.

For user convenience, it would be nice during the loading of the page to set both of the dates in the select elements to today's date. This is what you do in the `window_onload()` function, which is connected to the window's `onload` event by means of the `<body>` tag.

```
<body language="JavaScript" onload="return window_onload()">
```

The `window_onload()` function is defined in the head of the page. You start the function by setting the `theForm` variable to reference your `Form` object, because it shortens the reference needed in your code. Next you create a variable to hold a `Date` object to store today's date.

```
function window_onload()
{
    var theForm = document.form1;
    var nowDate = new Date();
```

Setting each of the `<select>` box's initial values is easy; the value returned by the `Date` object `nowDate` can be modified to provide the required index of the `options[]` array. For the day, the correct index is simply the day of the month minus one — remember that arrays start at 0, so day 1 is actually at index 0. The `selected` property is set to `true` to make that day the currently selected option in the list.

```
    theForm.firstDay.options[nowDate.getDate() - 1].selected = true;
    theForm.secondDay.options[nowDate.getDate() - 1].selected = true;
```

The month is even easier because the `getMonth()` function returns a value from 0 to 11 for the month, which exactly matches the necessary index value for our `options[]` array.

```
    theForm.firstMonth.options[nowDate.getMonth()].selected = true;
    theForm.secondMonth.options[nowDate.getMonth()].selected = true;
```

For the year, because you are starting with 1970 as your first year, you need to take 1970 from the current year to get the correct index value.

```
    theForm.firstYear.options[nowDate.getFullYear() - 1970].selected = true;
    theForm.secondYear.options[nowDate.getFullYear() - 1970].selected = true;
}
```

The final part of your code that you need to look at is the function connected to the `onchange` event of each select element, namely the `recalcDateDiff()` function. Your first task with this function is to build up the two dates the user has selected using the drop-down lists.

```
function recalcDateDiff()
{
  var myForm = document.form1;
  var firstDay = myForm.firstDay.options[myForm.firstDay.selectedIndex].value;
  var secondDay =
      myForm.secondDay.options[myForm.secondDay.selectedIndex].value;
  var firstMonth =
      myForm.firstMonth.options[myForm.firstMonth.selectedIndex].value;
  var secondMonth =
      myForm.secondMonth.options[myForm.secondMonth.selectedIndex].value;
  var firstYear =
      myForm.firstYear.options[myForm.firstYear.selectedIndex].value;
  var secondYear =
      myForm.secondYear.options[myForm.secondYear.selectedIndex].value;
```

You go through each select element and retrieve the value of the selected `Option` object. The `selectedIndex` property of the `Select` object provides the index you need to reference the selected `Option` object in the `options[]` array. For example, in the following line the index is provided by `myForm.firstDay.selectedIndex`:

```
var firstDay = myForm.firstDay.options[myForm.firstDay.selectedIndex].value;
```

You then use that value inside the square brackets as the index value for the options[] array of the firstDay select element. This provides the reference to the selected Option object, whose value property you store in the variable firstDay.

You use this technique for all the remaining select elements.

You can then create new Date objects based on the values obtained from the select elements and store them in the variables firstDate and secondDate.

```
var firstDate = new Date(firstDay + " " + firstMonth + " " + firstYear);
var secondDate = new Date(secondDay + " " + secondMonth + " " + secondYear);
```

Finally, you need to calculate the difference in days between the two dates.

```
var daysDiff = (secondDate.valueOf() - firstDate.valueOf());
daysDiff = Math.floor(Math.abs((((daysDiff  / 1000) / 60) / 60) / 24));
```

The Date object has a method, valueOf(), which returns the number of milliseconds from the first of January, 1970, to the date stored in the Date object. You subtract the value of the valueOf property of firstDate from the value of the valueOf property of secondDate and store this in the variable daysDiff. At this point, it holds the difference between the two dates in milliseconds, so you convert this value to days in the following line. By dividing by 1,000 you make the value seconds, dividing the resulting number by 60 makes it minutes, by 60 again makes it hours, and finally you divide by 24 to convert to your final figure of difference in days. The Math object's abs() method makes negative numbers positive. The user may have set the first date to a later date than the second, and since you want to find only the difference between the two, not which is earlier, you make any negative results positive. The Math.floor() method removes the fractional part of any result and returns just the integer part rounded down to the nearest whole number.

Finally you write the difference in days to the txtDays text box in the page.

```
myForm.txtDays.value = daysDiff;
return true;
}
```

That completes our look at the more useful form elements available in web pages. The next section returns to the trivia quiz, where you can put your newfound knowledge to good use and actually create a working quiz page.

The Trivia Quiz

It's time to return to the trivia quiz as you left it in Chapter 3. So far you have defined the questions and answers in arrays, and defined a function to check whether the user's answer is correct. Now that you know how to create HTML forms and elements, you can start using them in the quiz to provide the user input. By the end of this section the question form will look like Figure 6-11.

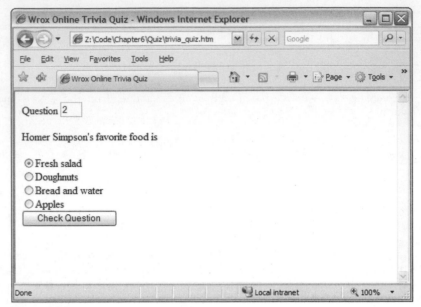

Figure 6-11

At present our questions are multiple-choice; you represent the multiple-choice options by a radio button group.

You create the form elements dynamically using our old friend document.write() and the information contained in the questions array. When the user has selected the radio button representing the answer, she then clicks the Check Question button, which calls your checkAnswer() function. This tells the user if she got the question right and lets her know. You then move on to the next question.

Let's start by creating the form elements.

Creating the Form

The first thing you need to do is add a form to your page in which the radio buttons will be written. Load trivia_quiz.htm and change the bottom of the page, below which the questions and answers arrays are defined, as follows:

```
// assign answer for question 3
answers[2] = "C";

</script>
</head>
<body>

<form name="QuestionForm">
Question
<input type="text" name=txtQNumber size=1>
<script language="JavaScript" type="text/javascript">
```

```
    document.write(getQuestion());
  </script>
  <input type="button" value="Check Question" name="buttonCheckQ"
    onclick="return buttonCheckQ_onclick()">
  </form>
  </body>
</html>
```

You're inserting the new form, named QuestionForm, inside the body of the page.

The elements on the form are a text box, defined by the following line:

```
<input type="text" name=txtQNumber size=1>
```

This will hold the current question number, and a button named buttonCheckQ.

```
<input type="button" value="Check Question" name="buttonCheckQ"
    onclick="return buttonCheckQ_onclick()">
```

When clicked, this will check the answer supplied by the user and let her know if she got it correct or not. The button has its onclick event connected to a function, buttonCheckQ_onclick(), which you'll create in a moment.

Where are the radio buttons you can see in Figure 6-11? Well, you'll be using the document.write() method again to dynamically insert the questions as the page is loaded. That way you can pick a random question each time from your question array. The following code inserts the question using the second function you need to add, getQuestion():

```
<script language="JavaScript" type="text/javascript">
    document.write(getQuestion());
</script>
```

Creating the Answer Radio Buttons

You saw in the code that the radio buttons required will be inserted by the getQuestion() function, and that the buttonCheckQ_onclick() function is connected to the button's onclick event handler. You'll now add these functions to the top of the page in the same script block as the answerCorrect() function that you defined in Chapter 3.

Add the following lines to the top of the trivia_quiz.htm page:

```
<html>
<head>
<title>Wrox Online Trivia Quiz</title>
<script language="JavaScript" type="text/javascript">
var questionNumber;
function answerCorrect(questionNumber, answer)
{
    // declare a variable to hold return value
    var correct = false;
    // if answer provided is same as answer then correct answer is true
```

```
        if (answer == answers[questionNumber])
            correct = true;
        // return whether the answer was correct (true or false)
        return correct;
}
```

```
function getQuestion()
{
    questionNumber = Math.floor(Math.random() * (questions.length));
    var questionHTML = "<p>" + questions[questionNumber][0] + "</p>";
    var questionLength = questions[questionNumber].length;
    var questionChoice;
    for (questionChoice = 1;questionChoice < questionLength;questionChoice++)
    {
        questionHTML = questionHTML + "<input type=radio name=radQuestionChoice"
        if (questionChoice == 1)
        {
            questionHTML = questionHTML + " checked";
        }
        questionHTML = questionHTML + ">";
        questionHTML = questionHTML + questions[questionNumber][questionChoice];
        questionHTML = questionHTML + "<br>";
    }
    document.QuestionForm.txtQNumber.value = questionNumber + 1;
    return questionHTML;
}
function buttonCheckQ_onclick()
{
    var answer = 0;
    while (document.QuestionForm.radQuestionChoice[answer].checked != true)
    {
        answer++;
    }
    answer = String.fromCharCode(65 + answer);
    if (answerCorrect(questionNumber,answer) == true)
    {
        alert("You got it right");
    }
    else
    {
        alert("You got it wrong");
    }
    window.location.reload();
}
```

```
// questions and answers arrays will hold questions and answers
```

You will discuss the getQuestion() function first, which is used to build up the HTML needed to display the question to the user. You first want to select a random question from your questions array, so you need to generate a random number, which will provide the index for the question. You store this number in the global variable questionNumber that you declared at the top of the script block.

```
function getQuestion()
{
    questionNumber = Math.floor(Math.random() * (questions.length));
```

You generate a random number between 0 and 1 using the `Math.random()` method, and then multiply that by the number of questions in the `questions` array. This number is converted to an integer using the `Math` object's `floor()` method, which returns the lowest integer part of a floating-point number. This is exactly what you want here: a randomly selected number from 0 to `questions.length` minus one. Don't forget that arrays start at an index of 0.

Your next task is to create the radio buttons, which allow the user to answer the question. You do this by building up the HTML that needs to be written to the page inside the variable `questionHTML`. You can then display the question using just one `document.write()`, which writes the whole question out in one go.

You start this process by declaring the `questionHTML` variable and setting it to the HTML needed to write the actual question to the page. This information is stored in the first index position of the second dimension of your `questions` array — that is, `questions[questionNumber][0]`, where `questionNumber` is the random index you generated before.

```
var questionHTML = "<p>" + questions[questionNumber][0] + "</p>";
var questionLength = questions[questionNumber].length;
var questionChoice;
```

To create the possible answers for the user to select from, you need to know how many radio buttons are required, information that's stored in the `length` property of the second dimension of your `questions` array. Remember that the second dimension is really just an `Array` object stored in a particular position of your `questions` array and that `Array` objects have a `length` property. You use the variable `questionLength` to store the length of the array and also to declare another variable, `questionChoice`, which you will use to loop through your array.

Now you can start looping through the question options and build up the radio button group. You do this in the next `for` loop. If it's the first radio button that you are creating the HTML for, you add the `checked` word to the `<input>` tag. You do this to ensure that one of the radio buttons is checked, just in case the user tries to press the Check Answer button without actually providing one first.

```
for (questionChoice = 1;questionChoice < questionLength;questionChoice++)
{
    questionHTML = questionHTML + "<input type=radio name=radQuestionChoice"
    if (questionChoice == 1)
    {
        questionHTML = questionHTML + " checked";
    }
    questionHTML = questionHTML + ">";
    questionHTML = questionHTML + questions[questionNumber][questionChoice];
    questionHTML = questionHTML + "<br>";
}
```

For example, on one loop of the `for` loop, the HTML built up in `questionHTML` may be the following:

```
<input type=radio name=radQuestionChoice checked> A sixties rock group from
Liverpool<br>
```

With the looping finished and `questionHTML` containing the complete HTML needed to display one question, all that remains to do is to display the question number for the current question in the text box in the form, and then return the `questionHTML` string to the calling code. You use `questionNumber + 1` as the question number purely for user friendliness. Even though it might be a question at index 0, most people think of starting at question 1 not question 0.

```
    document.QuestionForm.txtQNumber.value = questionNumber + 1;
    return questionHTML;
}
```

That completes the `getQuestion()` function. The final new code you need to look at is the `buttonCheckQ_onclick()` function that fires when the button is clicked. You saw this added to your code earlier.

You start the function by declaring the variable `answer` and initializing it to 0. You'll be using this as the index when looping through the radio button group and also to hold the actual answer.

```
function buttonCheckQ_onclick()
{
    var answer = 0;
```

You then use a `while` statement to loop through each of the radio buttons, incrementing the `answer` variable until it hits upon a radio button that is checked. At this point the loop ends and you now know which radio button the user chose as his answer, namely the one at the index stored in the `answer` variable.

```
    while (document.QuestionForm.radQuestionChoice[answer].checked != true)

    {
        answer++;
    }
```

Since your answers array holds the answers as A, B, C, D, and so on, you need to convert the radio button index contained in `answer` into a character. You do this in the next line.

```
    answer = String.fromCharCode(65 + answer);
```

This makes use of the fact that the character code for A is 65, so that if the user chooses the first radio button — the one with an index of 0 — you just need to add 65 and the index number contained in `answer` to get the answer's character code. This code is converted to a character by means of the `String` object's `fromCharCode()` method. Remember that some methods of the `String` object, called *static methods*, can be used without having to actually create a `String` object; you can use the native `String` object, which is always present.

The `answerCorrect()` function you created in Chapter 3 is then used as part of an `if` statement. You pass the question number and the answer character to the function, and it returns `true` if the answer is correct. If it does return `true`, you show a message box telling the user that he got the question right; otherwise the `else` statement lets him know that he got it wrong.

```
    if (answerCorrect(questionNumber,answer) == true)
    {
        alert("You got it right");
    }
```

```
    else
    {
       alert("You got it wrong");
    }
```

Finally, you reload the page to select another random question.

```
    window.location.reload();
}
```

In the next chapter you'll be making the Trivia Quiz a more sophisticated multi-frame-based application, also adding necessary features like one to make sure that the user doesn't get the same question twice.

Summary

In this chapter you looked at how to add a user interface onto your JavaScript so that you can interact with your users and acquire information from them. Let's look at some of the things we discussed in this chapter.

❑ The HTML form is where you place elements making up the interface in a page.

❑ Each HTML form groups together a set of HTML elements. When a form is submitted to a server for processing, all the data in that form are sent to the server. You can have multiple forms on a page, but only the information in one form can be sent to the server.

❑ A form is created with the opening tag `<form>` and ends with the close tag `</form>`. All the elements you want included in that form are placed in between the open and close `<form>` tags. The `<form>` tag has various attributes — for client-side scripting, the name attribute is the important one. You can access forms with either their name attribute or their ID attribute.

❑ Each `<form>` element creates a `Form` object, which is contained within the `document` object. To access a form named `myForm`, you write `document.myForm`. The `document` object also has a `forms[]` property, which is an array containing every form inside the document. The first form in the page is `document.forms[0]`, the second is `document.forms[1]`, and so on. Using the `length` property of an `Array` object, `document.forms.length` tells you how many forms are on the page.

❑ Having discussed forms, we then went on to look at the different types of HTML elements that can be placed inside forms, how to create them, and how they are used in JavaScript.

❑ The objects associated with the form elements have a number of properties, methods, and events that are common to them all. They all have the `name` property, which you can use to reference them in your JavaScript. They also all have the `form` property, which provides a reference to the `Form` object in which that element is contained. The `type` property returns a text string telling you what type of element this is; types include `text`, `button`, and `radio`.

❑ You also saw that the methods `focus()` and `blur()`, and the events `onfocus` and `onblur`, are available to every form element object. Such an element is said to receive the focus when it becomes the active element in the form, either because the user has selected that element or because you used the `focus()` method. However an element got the focus, its `onfocus` event will fire. When another element is set as the currently active element, the previous element is said to lose its focus, or to blur. Again, loss of focus can be the result of the user selecting another element or the use of the blur() method; either way, when it happens the onblur event fires. You saw that the firing of onfocus and onblur can, if used carefully, be a good place to check things like the validity of data entered by a user into an element.

❑ All elements return a value, which is the string data assigned to that element. The meaning of the value depends on the element; for a text box, it is the value inside the text box, and for a button, it's the text displayed on its face.

❑ Having discussed the common features of elements, we then looked at each of the more commonly used elements in turn, starting with the button element.

❑ The button element's purpose in life is to be clicked by the user, where that clicking fires some script you have written. You can capture the clicking by connecting to the button's onclick event. A button is created by means of the <input> tag with the type attribute set to button. The value attribute determines what text appears on the button's face. Two variations on a button are the submit and reset buttons. In addition to acting as buttons, they also provide a special service not linked to code. The submit button will automatically submit the form to the server; the reset button clears the form back to its default state when loaded in the page.

❑ The text element allows the user to enter a single line of plain text. A text box is created by means of the <input> tag with the type attribute set to text. You can set how many characters the user can enter and how wide the text box is with the maxlength and size attributes, respectively, of the <input> tag. The text box has an associated object called Text, which has the additional events onselect and onchange. The onselect event fires when the user selects text in the box, and the more useful onchange event fires when the element loses focus and its contents have changed since the element gained the focus. The firing of the onchange event is a good place to do validation of what the user has just entered. If she entered illegal values, such as letters when you wanted numbers, you can let the user know and send her back to correct her mistake. A variation on the text box is the password box, which is almost identical to the text box except that the values typed into it are hidden and shown as an asterisk. Additionally, the text box also has the onkeydown, onkeypress, and onkeyup events.

❑ The next element you looked at was the text area, which is similar to the text box except that it allows multiple lines of text to be entered. This element is created with the open tag <textarea> and closed with the </textarea> tag, the width and height in characters of the text box being determined by the COLS and ROWS attributes respectively. The wrap attribute determines whether the text area wraps text that reaches the end of a line and whether that wrapping is sent when the contents are posted to the server. If this attribute is left out, or set to off, no wrapping occurs; if set to soft, it causes wrapping client-side, but is not sent to the server when the form is sent; if set to hard, it causes wrapping client-side and is sent to the server. The associated Textarea object has virtually the same properties, methods, and events as a Text object.

❑ You then looked at the check box and radio button elements together. Essentially they are the same type of element, except that the radio button is a grouped element, meaning that only one in a group can be checked at once. Checking another one causes the previously checked button to be unchecked. Both elements are created with the <input> tag, the type attribute being checkbox or radio. If checked is put inside the <input> tag, that element will be checked when the page is loaded. Creating radio buttons with the same name creates a radio button group. The name of a radio button actually refers to an array, and each element within that array is a radio button defined on the form to be within that group. These elements have associated objects called Checkbox and Radio. Using the checked property of these objects, you can find out whether a check box or radio button is currently checked. Both objects also have the onclick event in addition to the common events onfocus and onblur.

❑ Next in your look at elements were the drop-down list and list boxes. Both in fact are actually the same select element, with the size attribute determining whether it's a drop-down or list box. The <select> tag creates these elements, the size attribute determining how many list items are visible at once. If a size of 1 is given, a drop-down box rather than a list box is created. Each item in a select element is defined by the <option> tag, or added to later by means of the Select object's options[] array property, which is an array containing each Option object for that element. However, adding options after the page is loaded is different for Firefox and Microsoft browsers. The Select object's selectedIndex property tells you which option is selected; you can then use that value to access the appropriate option in the options[] array and use the Option object's value property. The Option object also has the text and index properties, text being the displayed text in the list and index being its position in the Select object's options[] array property. You can loop through the options[] array, finding out its length from the Select object's length property. The Select object has the onchange event, which fires when the user selects another item from the list.

❑ Finally, you added a basic user interface to the trivia quiz. Now questions are created dynamically with the document.write() method and the user can select his answer from a group of radio buttons.

In the next chapter you'll look at how, once you have created a frameset in a page, you can access code and variables between frames. You'll also look at how to open new windows using JavaScript, and methods of manipulating them when they are open. You'll see the trivia quiz become a frame-based application.

Exercises

Suggested solutions to these questions can be found in Appendix A.

Question 1

Using the code from the temperature converter example you saw in Chapter 2, create a user interface for it and connect it to the existing code so that the user can enter a value in degrees Fahrenheit and convert it to centigrade.

Question2

Create a user interface that allows the user to pick the computer system of her dreams, similar in principle to the e-commerce sites selling computers over the Internet. For example, she could be given a choice of processor type, speed, memory, and hard drive size, and the option to add additional components like a DVD-ROM drive, a sound card, and so on. As the user changes her selections, the price of the system should update automatically and notify her of the cost of the system as she has specified it, either by using an alert box or by updating the contents of a text box.

Windows and Frames

Until now, the pages you have been looking at have just been single pages. However, many web applications make use of frames to split up the browser's window, much as panes of glass split up a real window. It's quite possible that you'll want to build web sites that make use of such frames. The good news is that JavaScript enables the manipulation of frames and allows functions and variables you create in one frame to be used from another frame. One advantage of this is that you can keep common variables and functions in one place but use them from many places. You start this chapter by looking at how you can script across such frames.

But a number of other good reasons exist for wanting to access variables and functions in another frame. Two important reasons are to make your code *modular* and to gain the ability to maintain information between pages.

What do we mean by *modular*? In other programming languages, like Visual Basic, you can create a module—an area to hold general functions and variables—and reuse it from different places in your program. Well, when using frames you can put all of your general functions and variables into one area, such as the top frame, which you can think of as your code module. Then you can call the functions repeatedly from different pages and different frames.

If you put the general functions and variables in a page that defines the frames that it contains (that is, a frameset-defining page), then if you need to make changes to the pages inside the frames, any variables defined in the frameset page will retain their value. This provides a very useful means of holding information even when the user is navigating your web site. A further advantage is that any functions defined in the frameset-defining page can be called by subsequent pages and have to be loaded into the browser only once, making your page's loading faster.

The second subject of this chapter is how you can open up and manipulate new browser windows. There are plenty of good uses for new windows. For example, you may wish to open up an "external" web site in a new window from your web site, but still leave your web site open for the user. *External* here means a web site created and maintained by another person or company. Let's say you have a web site about cars—well, you may wish to have a link to external sites, such as manufacturing web sites (for example, that of Ford or General Motors). Perhaps even more useful is using small windows as dialog boxes, which you can use to obtain information from the user. Just as you can script between frames, you can do similar things between certain windows. You find out how later in the chapter, but let's start by looking at scripting between frames.

Frames and the window Object

Frames are a means of splitting up the browser window into various panes, into which you can then load different HTML documents. The frames are defined in a frameset-defining page by the `<frameset>` and `<frame>` tags. The `<frameset>` tag is used to contain the `<frame>` tags and specifies how the frames should look on the page. The `<frame>` tags are then used to specify each frame and to include the required documents in the page.

You saw in Chapter 5 that the `window` object represents the browser's frame on your page or document. If you have a page with no frames, there will be just one `window` object. However, if you have more than one frame, there will be one `window` object for each frame. Except for the very top-level window of a frameset, each `window` object is contained inside another.

The easiest way to demonstrate this is through an example in which you create three frames, a top frame with two frames inside it.

Try It Out   Multiple Frames

For this multi-frame example, you'll need to create three HTML files. The first is the frameset-defining page.

```
<html>
<frameset rows="50%,*" ID="TopWindow">
<frame name="UpperWindow" src="UpperWindow.htm">
<frame name="LowerWindow" src="LowerWindow.htm">
</frameset>
</html>
```

Save this as `TopWindow.htm`. Note that the `src` attributes for the two `<frame>` tags in this page are `UpperWindow.htm` and `LowerWindow.htm`. You will create these next.

```
<html>
<head>
<script language="JavaScript" type="text/javascript">
function window_onload()
{
alert("The name of the upper frame's window object is " + window.name);
alert("The location of UpperWindow's parent is " +
window.parent.location.href);
}
</script>
</head>
<body onload="return window_onload()">
<p>Upper Frame</p>
</body>
</html>
```

The preceding page is the source page for the top frame with the name `UpperWindow` and needs to be saved as `UpperWindow.htm`. The final page is very similar to it:

```
<html>
<head>
<script language="JavaScript" type="text/javascript">
function window_onload()
{
alert("The name of the lower frame's window object is " + window.name);
alert("The location of LowerWindow's parent is " +
window.parent.location.href);
}
</script>
</head>
<body onload="return window_onload()">
<p>Lower Frame</p>
</body>
</html>
```

This is the source page for the lower frame; save it as `LowerWindow.htm`.

These three pages fit together so that `UpperWindow.htm` and `LowerWindow.htm` are contained within the `TopWindow.htm` page.

When you load them into the browser, you have three `window` objects. One is the *parent* `window` object and contains the file `TopWindow.htm`, and two are *child* `window` objects, containing the files `UpperWindow.htm` and `LowerWindow.htm`. The two child `window` objects are contained within the parent `window`, as shown in Figure 7-1.

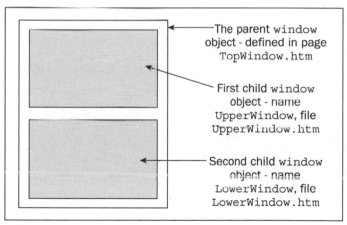

Figure 7-1

If any of the frames had frames contained inside them, these would have `window` objects that were children of the `window` object of that frame.

When you load `TopWindow.htm` into your browser, you'll see a series of four message boxes, as shown in Figures 7-2 through 7-5. These are making use of the `window` object's properties to gain information and demonstrate the `window` object's place in the hierarchy.

Figure 7-2

Figure 7-3

Figure 7-4

Figure 7-5

How It Works

Look at the frameset-defining page, starting with TopWindow.htm, as shown in the following snippet:

```
<html>
<frameset rows="50%,*" ID=TopWindow>
<frame name="UpperWindow" src="UpperWindow.htm">
<frame name="LowerWindow" src="LowerWindow.htm">
</frameset>
</html>
```

The frameset is defined with the <frameset> tag. You use two attributes: rows and ID. The rows attribute takes the value "50%,*" meaning that the first frame should take up half of the length of the window, and the second frame should take up the rest of the room. The ID attribute is used to give a name that you can use to reference the page.

The two child windows are created using <frame> tags. In each of the <frame> tags, you specify a name by which the window objects will be known and the src attribute of the page that will be loaded into the newly created windows and will form the basis of the document object that each window object contains.

Let's take a look at the UpperWindow.htm file next. In the <body> tag of the page, you attach a function, window_onload(), to the window object's onload event handler. This event handler is called when the browser has finished loading the window, the document inside the window, and all the objects within the document. It's a very useful place to put initialization code or code that needs to change things after the page has loaded but before control passes back to the user.

```
<body onload="return window_onload()">
```

This function is defined in a script block in the head of the page as follows:

```
function window_onload()
{
alert("The name of the upper frame's window object is " + window.name);
alert("The location of UpperWindow's parent is " +
window.parent.location.href);
}
```

The window_onload() function makes use of two properties of the window object for the frame that the page is loaded in: its name and parent properties. The name property is self-explanatory — it's the name you defined in the frameset page. In this case, the name is UpperWindow.

The second property, the parent property, is very useful. It gives you access to the window object of the frame's parent. This means you can access all of the parent window object's properties and methods. Through these, you can access the document within the parent window as well as any other frames defined by the parent. Here, you display a message box giving details of the parent frame's file name or URL by using the href property of the location object (which itself is a property of the window object).

The code for LowerWindow.htm is identical to the code for UpperWindow.htm, but with different results because you are accessing a different window object. The name of the window object this time is LowerWindow. However, it shares the same parent window as UpperWindow, and so when you access the parent property of the window object, you get a reference to the same window object as in UpperWindow. The message box demonstrates this by displaying the file name/URL or href property, and this matches the file name of the page displayed in the UpperWindow frame.

Please note that the order of display of messages may vary among different types of browsers and even different operating systems. This may not be important here, but there will be times when the order in which events fire is important and affects the working of your code. It's an incompatibility that's worth noting and watching out for in your own programs.

Coding Between Frames

You've seen that each frame exists as a different window and gets its own window object. In addition, you saw that you can access the window object of a frameset-defining page from any of the frame pages it specifies, by using the window object's parent property. When you have a reference to the parent window's window object, you can access its properties and methods in the same way that you access the window object of the current page. In addition, you have access to all the JavaScript variables and functions defined in that page.

Try It Out   **Using the Frameset Page as a Module**

Let's look at a more complex example, wherein you use the top frame to keep track of pages as the user navigates the web site. You're creating five pages in this example, but don't panic; four of them are almost identical. The first page that needs to be created is the frameset-defining page.

```html
<html>
<head>
<title>The Unchanging frameset page</title>
<script Language="JavaScript" type="text/javascript">
var pagesVisited = new Array();
function returnPagesVisited()
{
var returnValue = "So far you have visited the following pages\n";
var pageVisitedIndex;
var numberOfPagesVisited = pagesVisited.length;
for (pageVisitedIndex = 0; pageVisitedIndex < numberOfPagesVisited;
pageVisitedIndex++)
    {
returnValue = returnValue + pagesVisited[pageVisitedIndex] + "\n";
    }
return returnValue;
}
function addPage(fileName)
{
var fileNameStart = fileName.lastIndexOf("/") + 1;
fileName = fileName.substr (fileNameStart);
pagesVisited[pagesVisited.length] = fileName;
return true;
}
</script>
</head>
<frameset cols="50%,*">
<frame name=fraLeft src="page_a.htm">
<frame name=fraRight src="page_b.htm">
</frameset>
</html>
```

Save this page as `frameset_page.htm`.

Notice that the two frames have the `src` attributes initialized as `page_a.htm` and `page_b.htm`. However, you also need to create `page_c.htm` and `page_d.htm` because you will be allowing the user to choose the page loaded into each frame from these four pages. You'll create the `page_a.htm` page first, as shown in the following:

```html
<html>
<head>
<script language="JavaScript" type="text/javascript">
function butShowVisited_onclick()
{
document.form1.txtaPagesVisited.value = window.parent.returnPagesVisited();
}
</script>
</head>
```

```
<body onload="window.parent.addPage(window.location.href);">
<center>
<font size=6 color=MidnightBlue face=verdana>
This is Page A
</font>
</center>
<p>
<A href="page_a.htm">Page A</A>
<A href="page_b.htm">Page B</A>
<A href="page_c.htm">Page C</A>
<A href="page_d.htm">Page D</A>
</p>
<form name=form1>
<textarea rows=10 cols=35 name=txtaPagesVisited wrap=hard>
</textarea>
<br>
<input type="button" value="List Pages Visited" name=butShowVisited
onclick="butShowVisited_onclick()">
</form>
</body>
</html>
```

Save this page as page_a.htm.

The other three pages are identical to page_a.htm, except for one line, so you can just cut and paste the text from page_a.htm. Change the HTML that displays the name of the page loaded to the following:

```
<center>
<font size=6 color=MidnightBlue face=verdana>
This is Page B
</font>
</center>
```

Then save this as page_b.htm.

Do the same again, to create the third page (page C):

```
<center>
<font size=6 color=MidnightBlue face=verdana>
This is Page C
</font>
</center>
```

Save this as page_c.htm.

The final page is again a copy of page_a.htm except for the following lines:

```
<center>
<font size=6 color=MidnightBlue face=verdana>
This is Page D
</font>
</center>
```

Save this as page_d.htm.

Load `FramesetPage.htm` into your browser and navigate to various pages by clicking the links. Then click the List Pages Visited button in the left-hand frame, and you should see a screen similar to the one shown in Figure 7-6.

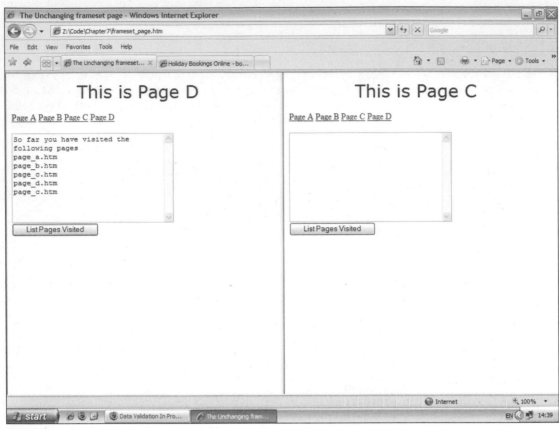

Figure 7-6

Click the links in either frame to navigate to a new location. For example, click the Page C link in the right frame, then the Page D link in the left frame. Click the left frame's List Pages Visited button and you'll see that `page_c.htm` and `page_d.htm` have been added to the list.

Normally when a new page is loaded, any variables and their values in the previous page are lost, but with framesets it does not matter which page is loaded into each frame — the top frame remains loaded and its variables keep their values. What you are seeing in this example is that, regardless of which page is loaded in each frame, some global variable in the top frame is keeping track of the pages that have been viewed and the top frame's variables and functions can be accessed by any page loaded into either frame.

> You'll see later that there are restrictions when the pages you load into the frames are from external sources — more on this later in the chapter.

How It Works

Let's first look at the JavaScript in frameset_page.htm, which is the frameset-defining page. The head of the page contains a script block. The first thing you do in this script block is declare the variable pagesVisited and set it to reference a new Array object. In the array, you'll be storing the file name of each page visited as the user navigates the site.

```
var pagesVisited = new Array();
```

You then have two functions. The first of the two functions, returnPagesVisited(), does what its name suggests — it returns a string containing a message and a list of each of the pages visited. It does this by looping through the pagesVisited array, building up the message string inside the variable returnValue, which is then returned to the calling function.

```
function returnPagesVisited()
{
var returnValue = "So far you have visited the following pages\n";
var pageVisitedIndex;
var numberOfPagesVisited = pagesVisited.length;
for (pageVisitedIndex = 0; pageVisitedIndex < numberOfPagesVisited;
pageVisitedIndex++)
    {
returnValue = returnValue + pagesVisited[pageVisitedIndex] + "\n";
    }
return returnValue;
}
```

The second function, addPage(), adds the name of a page to the pagesVisited array.

```
function addPage(fileName)
{
var fileNameStart = fileName.lastIndexOf("/") + 1;
fileName = fileName.substr(fileNameStart);
pagesVisited[pagesVisited.length] = fileName;
return true;
}
```

The fileName parameter passed to this function is the full file name and path of the visited page, so you need to strip out the path to get just the file name. The format of the string will be something like file:///D:/myDirectory/page_b.htm, and you need just the bit after the last / character. So in the first line of code, you find the position of that character and add one to it because you want to start at the next character.

Then, using the substr() method of the String object in the following line, you extract everything from character position fileNameStart right up to the end of the string. Remember that the substr() method takes two parameters, namely the starting character you want and the length of the string you want to extract, but if the second parameter is missing, all characters from the start position to the end are extracted.

You then add the file name into the array, the length property of the array providing the next free index position.

You'll now turn to look collectively at the frame pages, namely page_a.htm, page_b.htm, page_c.htm, and page_d.htm. In each of these pages, you create a form called form1.

```
<form name=form1>
<textarea rows=10 cols=35 name=txtaPagesVisited wrap=hard>
</textarea>
<br>
<input type="button" value="List Pages Visited" name=butShowVisited
onclick="butShowVisited_onclick()">
</form>
```

This contains the textarea control that will display the list of pages visited, and a button the user can click to populate the textarea.

When one of these pages is loaded, its name is put into the pagesVisited array defined in frameset_page.htm by the window object's onload event handler's being connected to the addPage() function that you also created in frameset_page.htm. You connect the code to the event handler in the <body> tag of the page as follows:

```
<body onload="window.parent.addPage(window.location.href);">
```

Recall that all the functions you declare in a page are contained, like everything else in a page, inside the window object for that page, but that because the window object is the global object, you don't need to prefix the name of your variables or functions with window.

However, this time the function is not in the current page, but in the frameset_page.htm page. The window containing this page is the parent window to the window containing the current page. You need, therefore, to refer to the parent frame's window object using the window object's parent property. The code window.parent gives you a reference to the window object of frameset_page.htm. With this reference, you can now access the variables and functions contained in frameset_page.htm. Having stated which window object you are referencing, you just add the name of the function you are calling, in this instance the addPage() function. You pass this function the location.href string, which contains the full path and file name of the page, as the value for its one parameter.

As you saw earlier, the button on the page has its onclick event handler connected to a function called butShowVisited_onclick(). This is defined in the head of the page.

```
function butShowVisited_onclick()
{
document.form1.txtaPagesVisited.value = window.parent.returnPagesVisited();
}
```

In this function you call the parent window object's returnPagesVisited() function, which, as you saw earlier, returns a string containing a list of pages visited. The value property of the textarea object is set to this text.

That completes your look at the code in the frame pages, and as you can see, there's not much of it because you have placed all the general functions in the frameset page. Not only does this code reuse make for less typing, but it also means that all your functions are in one place. If there is a bug in a function, fixing the bug for one page also fixes it for all other pages that use the function. Of course, it only makes sense to put general functions in one place; functions that are specific to a page and are never used again outside it are best kept in that page.

Code Access Between Frames

You've just seen how a child window can access its parent window's variables and functions, but how can frames inside a frameset access each other?

You saw a simple example earlier in this chapter, so this time let's look at a much more complex example. When created, your page will look like the one shown in Figure 7-7.

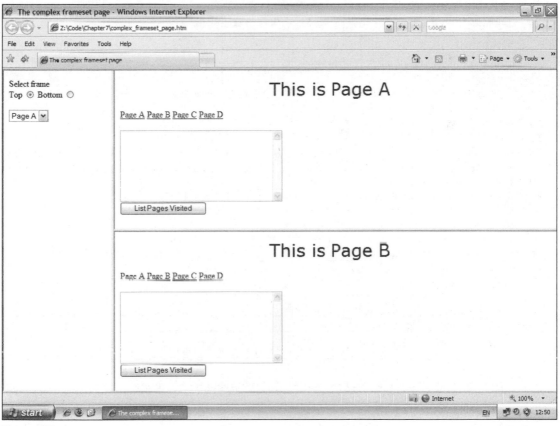

Figure 7-7

A diagram of the frame layout is shown in Figure 7-8. The text labels indicate the names that each frame has been given in the `<frameset>` and `<frame>` tags, with the exception of the top frame, which is simply the window at the top of the frameset hierarchy.

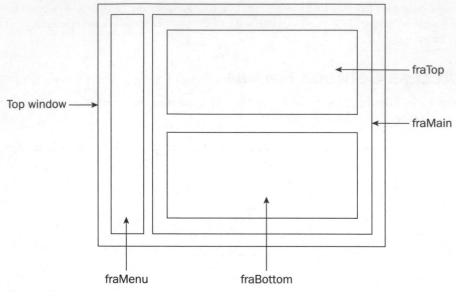

Figure 7-8

The easiest way to think of the hierarchy of such a frames-based web page is in terms of familial relationships, which can be shown in a family tree. If you represent your frameset like that, it looks something like the diagram in Figure 7-9.

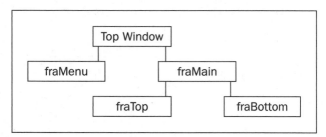

Figure 7-9

From the diagram you can see that `fraBottom`, the right-hand frame's bottom frame, has a parent frame called `fraMain`, which itself has a parent, the top window. Therefore, if you wanted to access a function in the top window from the `fraBottom` window, you would need to access `fraBottom`'s parent's parent's `window` object. You know that the `window` object has the `parent` property, which is a reference to the parent window of that `window` object. So let's use that and create the code to access a function, for example, called `myFunction()`, in the top window.

```
window.parent.parent.myFunction();
```

Let's break this down. The following code gets you a reference to the parent `window` object of the window in which the code is running.

```
window.parent
```

The code is in `fraBottom`, so `window.parent` will be `fraMain`. However, you want the top window, which is `fraMain`'s parent, so you add to the preceding code to make this:

```
window.parent.parent
```

Now you have a reference to the top window. Finally, you call `myFunction()` by adding that to the end of the expression.

```
window.parent.parent.myFunction();
```

What if you want to access the `window` object of `fraMenu` from code in `fraBottom`? Well, you have most of the code you need already. You saw that `window.parent.parent` gives you the top window, so now you want that window's child `window` object called `fraMenu`. You can get it in three ways, all with identical results.

You can use its index in the `frames[]` array property of the `window` object as follows:

```
window.parent.parent.frames[0]
```

Alternatively, you can use its name in the `frames[]` array like this:

```
window.parent.parent.frames["fraMenu"]
```

Finally, you can reference it directly by using its name as you can with any `window` object:

```
window.parent.parent.fraMenu
```

The third method is the easiest unless you don't know the name of a frame and need to access it by its index value in the `frames[]` array, or are looping through each child frame in turn.

Since `window.parent.parent.fraMenu` gets you a reference to the `window` object associated with `fraMenu`, to access a function `myFunction()` or variable `myVariable`, you would just type one of these lines:

```
window.parent.parent.fraMenu.myFunction
```

or

```
window.parent.parent.fraMenu.myVariable
```

What if you want to access not a function or variable in a page within a frame, but a control on a form or even the links on that page? Well, let's imagine you want to access, from the `fraBottom` page, a control named `myControl`, on a form called `myForm` in the `fraMenu` page.

You found that `window.parent.parent.fraMenu` gives you the reference to `fraMenu`'s `window` object from `fraBottom`, but how do you reference a form there?

Basically, it's the same as how you access a form from the inside of the same page as the script, except that you need to reference not the `window` object of that page but the `window` object of `fraMenu`, the page you're interested in.

Normally you write `document.myForm.myControl.value`, with `window` being assumed since it is the global object. Strictly speaking, it's `window.document.myForm.myControl.value`.

Now that you're accessing another window, you just reference the window you want and then use the same code. So you need this code if you want to access the `value` property of `myControl` from `fraBottom`:

```
window.parent.parent.fraMenu.document.myForm.myControl.value
```

As you can see, references to other frames can get pretty long, and in this situation it's a very good idea to store the reference in a variable. For example, if you are accessing `myForm` a number of times, you could write this:

```
var myFormRef = window.parent.parent.fraMenu.document.myForm;
```

Having done that, you can now write

```
myFormRef.myControl.value;
```

rather than

```
window.parent.parent.fraMenu.document.myForm.myControl.value;
```

The top Property

Using the `parent` property can get a little tedious when you want to access the very top window from a frame quite low down in the hierarchy of frames and `window` objects. An alternative is the `window` object's `top` property. This returns a reference to the `window` object of the very top window in a frame hierarchy. In the current example, this is top window.

For instance, in the example you just saw, this code:

```
window.parent.parent.fraMenu.document.myForm.myControl.value;
```

could be written like this:

```
window.top.fraMenu.document.myForm.myControl.value;
```

Although, because the `window` is a global object, you could shorten that to just this:

```
top.fraMenu.document.myForm.myControl.value;
```

So when should you use `top` rather than `parent`, or vice versa?

Both properties have advantages and disadvantages. The `parent` property enables you to specify `window` objects relative to the current window. The window above this window is `window.parent`, its parent is `window.parent.parent`, and so on. The `top` property is much more generic; `top` is always the very top window regardless of the frameset layout being used. There will always be a `top`, but there's not necessarily going to always be a `parent.parent`. If you put all your global functions and variables that you want accessible from any page in the frameset in the very top window, `window.top` will always be valid regardless of changes to framesets beneath it, whereas the `parent` property is dependent on the frameset structure above it. However, if someone else loads your web site inside a frameset page of his own, then suddenly the `top` window is not yours but his, and `window.top` is no longer valid. You can't win, or can you?

One trick is to check to see whether the `top` window contains your page; if it doesn't, reload the `top` page again and specify that your `top` page is the one to be loaded. For example, check to see that the file name of the `top` page actually matches the name you expect. The `window.top.location.href` will give you the name and path—if they don't match what you want, use `window.top.location` `.replace("myPagename.htm")` to load the correct `top` page. However, as you'll see later, this will cause problems if someone else is loading your page into a frameset she has created—this is where something called the *same-origin policy* applies. More on this later in the chapter.

Try It Out   Scripting Frames

Let's put all you've learned about frames and scripting into an example based on the frameset you've been looking at. You're going to be reusing a lot of the pages and code from the previous example in this chapter.

The first page you're creating is the top window page.

```html
<html>
<head>
<title>The complex frameset page</title>
<script language="JavaScript" type="text/javascript">
var pagesVisited = new Array();
function returnPagesVisited()
{
var returnValue = "So far you have visited the following pages\n";
var pageVisitedIndex;
var numberOfPagesVisited = pagesVisited.length;
for (pageVisitedIndex = 0; pageVisitedIndex < numberOfPagesVisited;
pageVisitedIndex++)
    {
returnValue = returnValue + pagesVisited[pageVisitedIndex] + "\n";
    }
return returnValue;
}
function addPage(fileName)
{
var fileNameStart = fileName.lastIndexOf("/") + 1;
fileName = fileName.substr(fileNameStart);
pagesVisited[pagesVisited.length] = fileName;
return true;
}
</script>
</head>
<frameset cols="200,*">
<frame name=fraMenu src="menu_page.htm">
<frame name=fraMain src="main_page.htm">
</frameset>
</html>
```

As you can see, you've reused a lot of the code from `frameset_page.htm`, so you can cut and paste the script block from there. Only the different code lines are highlighted. Save this page as `complex_frameset_page.htm`.

Next, create the page that will be loaded into `fraMenu`, namely `menu_page.htm`.

```html
<html>
<head>
<script language="JavaScript" type="text/javascript">
function choosePage_onchange()
{
var choosePage = document.form1.choosePage;
var windowobject;
if (document.form1.radFrame[0].checked == true)
    {
windowobject = window.parent.fraMain.fraTop;
    }
else
    {
windowobject = window.parent.fraMain.fraBottom;
    }
windowobject.location.href =
choosePage.options[choosePage.selectedIndex].value;
return true;
}
</script>
</head>
<body>
<form name=form1>
Select frame<br>
Top <input name="radFrame" checked type=radio>
Bottom <input name="radFrame" type=radio>
<br><br>
<select name=choosePage language="JavaScript" type="text/javascript"
onchange="choosePage_onchange()">
<option value=page_a.htm>Page A
<option value=page_b.htm>Page B
<option value=page_c.htm>Page C
<option value=page_d.htm>Page D
</select>
</form>
</body>
</html>
```

Save this as `menu_page.htm`.

The `fraMain` frame contains a page that is simply a frameset for the `fraTop` and `fraBottom` pages.

```html
<html>
<frameset rows="50%,*">
<frame name=fraTop src="page_a.htm">
<frame name=fraBottom src="page_b.htm">
</frameset>
</html>
```

Save this as `main_page.htm`.

For the next four pages you reuse the four pages — `page_a.htm`, `page_b.htm`, `page_c.htm`, and `page_d.htm` — from the first example. You'll need to make a few changes, as shown in the following code. (Again, all the pages are identical except for the text shown in the page, so only `page_a.htm` is shown. Amend the rest in a similar way.)

```
<html>
<head>
<script language="JavaScript" type="text/javascript">
function butShowVisited_onclick()
{
document.form1.txtaPagesVisited.value = window.top.returnPagesVisited();
}
function setFrameAndPageControls(linkIndex)
{
var formobject = window.parent.parent.fraMenu.document.form1;
formobject.choosePage.selectedIndex = linkIndex;
if (window.parent.fraTop == window.self)
    {
formobject.radFrame[0].checked = true;
    }
else
    {
formobject.radFrame[1].checked = true;
    }
return true;
}
</script>
</head>
<body
onload="return window.top.addPage(window.location.href);">
<center>
<font size=6 color=MidnightBlue face=verdana>
This is Page A
</font>
</center>
<p>
<A href="page_a.htm" name="pageALink"
onclick="return setFrameAndPageControls(0)">Page A</A>
<A href="page_b.htm" name="pageBLink"
onclick="return setFrameAndPageControls(1)">Page B</A>
<A href="page_c.htm" name="pageCLink"
onclick="return setFrameAndPageControls(2)">Page C</A>
<A href="page_d.htm" name="pageDLink"
onclick="return setFrameAndPageControls(3)">Page D</A>
</p>
<form name=form1>
<textarea rows=8 cols=35 name=txtaPagesVisited>
</textarea>
<br>
<input type="button" value="List Pages Visited" name=butShowVisited
onclick="butShowVisited_onclick()">
</form>
</body>
</html>
```

Resave the pages under their old names.

Load `complex_frameset_page.htm` into your browser, and you'll see a screen similar to the one shown in Figure 7-7.

The radio buttons allow the user to determine which frame he wants to navigate to a new page. When he changes the currently selected page in the drop-down list, that page is loaded into the frame selected by the radio buttons.

If you navigate using the links in the pages inside the `fraTop` and `fraBottom` frames, you'll notice that the selected frame radio buttons and the drop-down list in `fraMenu` on the left will be automatically updated to the page and frame just navigated to. Note that as the example stands, if the user loads `page_a.htm` into a frame the select list doesn't allow it to load the same page in the other frame. You could improve on this example by adding a button that loads the currently selected page into the chosen frame.

The List Pages Visited buttons display a list of visited pages, as they did in the previous example.

How It Works

You've already seen how the code defining the top window in `complex_frameset_page.htm` works, as it is very similar to the previous example. However, you'll just look quickly at the `<frameset>` tags where, as you can see, the names of the windows are defined in the names of the `<frame>` tags.

```
<frameset cols="200,*">
<frame name=fraMenu src="menu_page.htm">
<frame name=fraMain src="main_page.htm">
</frameset>
```

Notice also that the `cols` attribute of the `<frameset>` tag is set to `"200,*"`. This means that the first frame will occupy a column 200 pixels wide, and the other frame will occupy a column taking up the remaining space.

Let's look in more detail at the `fraMenu` frame containing `menu_page.htm`. At the top of the page, you have your main script block. This contains the function `choosePage_onchange()`, which is connected to the `onchange` event handler of the select box lower down on the page. The select box has `options` containing the various page URLs.

The function starts by defining two variables. One of these, `choosePage`, is a shortcut reference to the `choosePage Select` object further down the page.

```
function choosePage_onchange()
{
var choosePage = document.form1.choosePage;
var windowobject;
```

The `if...else` statement then sets your variable `windowobject` to reference the `window` object of whichever frame the user has chosen in the `radFrame` radio button group.

```
if (document.form1.radFrame[0].checked == true)
    {
windowobject = window.parent.fraMain.fraTop;
```

```
    }
else
    {
windowobject = window.parent.fraMain.fraBottom;
    }
```

As you saw earlier, it's just a matter of following through the references, so window.parent gets you a reference to the parent window object. In this case, window.top would have done the same thing. Then window.parent.fraMain gets you a reference to the window object of the fraMain frame. Finally, depending on which frame you want to navigate in, you reference the fraTop or fraBottom window objects contained within fraMain, using window.parent.fraMain.fraTop or window.parent.fraMain.fraBottom.

Now that you have a reference to the window object of the frame in which you want to navigate, you can go ahead and change its location.href property to the value of the selected drop-down list item, causing the frame to load that page.

```
windowobject.location.href =
choosePage.options[choosePage.selectedIndex].value;
return true;
}
```

As you saw before, main_page.htm is simply a frameset-defining page for fraTop and fraBottom. Let's now look at the pages you're actually loading into fraTop and fraBottom. Because they are all the same, you'll look only at page_a.htm.

Let's start by looking at the top script block. This contains two functions, butShowVisited_onclick() and setFrameAndPageControls(). You saw the function butShowVisited_onclick() in the previous example.

```
function butShowVisited_onclick()
{
document.form1.txtaPagesVisited.value = window.top.returnPagesVisited();
}
```

However, because the frameset layout has changed, you do need to change the code. Whereas previously the returnPagesVisited() function was in the parent window, it's now moved to the top window. As you can see, all you need to do is change the reference from window.parent.returnPagesVisited(); to window.top.returnPagesVisited();.

As it happens, in the previous example the parent window was also the top window, so if you had written your code in this way in the first place, there would have been no need for changes here. It's often quite a good idea to keep all your general functions in the top frameset page. That way all your references can be window.top, even if the frameset layout is later changed.

The new function in this page is setFrameAndPageControls(), which is connected to the onclick event handler of the links defined lower down on the page. This function's purpose is to make sure that if the user navigates to a different page using the links rather than the controls in the fraMenu window, those controls will be updated to reflect what the user has done.

The first thing you do is set the `formobject` variable to reference the `form1` in the `fraMenu` page, as follows:

```
function setFrameAndPageControls(linkIndex)
{
var formobject = window.parent.parent.fraMenu.document.form1;
```

Let's break this down.

```
window.parent
```

gets you a reference to the `fraMain` window object. Moving up the hierarchy, you use the following code to get a reference to the `window` object of the top window:

```
window.parent.parent
```

Yes, you're right. You could have used `window.top` instead, and this would have been a better way to do it. We're doing it the long way here just to demonstrate how the hierarchy works.

Now you move down the hierarchy, but on the other side of your tree diagram, to reference the `fraMenu`'s `window` object.

```
window.parent.parent.fraMenu
```

Finally, you are interested only in the form and its controls, so you reference that object like this:

```
window.parent.parent.fraMenu.document.form1
```

Now that you have a reference to the form, you can use it just as you would if this were code in `fraMenu` itself.

The function's parameter `linkIndex` tells you which of the four links was clicked, and you use this value in the next line of the function's code to set which of the options is selected in the drop-down list box on `fraMenu`'s form.

```
formobject.choosePage.selectedIndex = linkIndex;
```

The `if...else` statement is where you set the `fraMenu`'s radio button group `radFrame` to the frame the user just clicked on, but how can you tell which frame this is?

```
if (window.parent.fraTop == window.self)
    {
formobject.radFrame[0].checked = true
    }
else
    {
formobject.radFrame[1].checked = true
    }
```

You check to see whether the current `window` object is the same as the `window` object for `fraTop`. You do this using the `self` property of the `window` object, which returns a reference to the current `window` object, and `window.parent.fraTop`, which returns a reference to `fraTop`'s `window` object. If one is equal to the other, you know that they are the same thing and that the current window is `fraTop`. If that's the case, the `radFrame` radio group in the `fraMenu` frame has its first radio button checked. Otherwise, you check the other radio button for `fraBottom`.

The last thing you do in the function is return `true`. Remember that this function is connected to an A object, so returning `false` cancels the link's action, and `true` allows it to continue, which is what you want.

```
return true;
}
```

Opening New Windows

So far in this chapter, you have been looking at frames and scripting between them. In this section, you'll change direction slightly and look at how you can open up additional browser windows.

Why would you want to bother opening up new windows? Well, they can be useful in all sorts of different situations, such as the following:

❑   You might want a page of links to web sites, in which clicking a link opens up a new window with that web site in it.

❑   Additional windows can be useful for displaying information. For example, if you had a page with products on it, the user could click a product image to bring up a new small window listing the details of that product. This can be less intrusive than navigating the existing window to a new page with product details, and then requiring the user to click Back to return to the list of products. You'll be creating an example demonstrating this later in this chapter.

❑   Dialog windows can be very useful for obtaining information from users, although overuse may annoy them.

Something you do need to be aware of is that some users have programs installed to block pop-up windows, and the latest versions of Firefox and Internet Explorer also enable the user to switch off the ability to open new windows. By default, new windows created automatically when a page loads are usually blocked. However, windows that open only when the user must perform an action, for example clicking a link or button, are not normally blocked by default, but the user may change the browser settings to block them.

Opening a New Browser Window

The `window` object has an `open()` method, which opens up a new window. It takes three parameters, although the third is optional, and it returns a reference to the `window` object of the new browser window.

The first parameter of the `open()` method is the URL of the page that you want to have opened in the new window. However, if you want, you can pass an empty string for this parameter and get a blank page, and then use the `document.write()` method to insert HTML into the new window dynamically. You'll see an example of this later in the chapter.

The second parameter is the name you want to allocate to the new window. This is not the name you use for scripting, but instead is used for the `target` attribute of things such as hyperlinks and forms. For example, if you set this parameter to `myWindow` and set a hyperlink on the original page to

```
<A href="test3.htm" TARGET=myWindow>Test3.htm</A>
```

then clicking that hyperlink will cause the hyperlink to act on the new window opened. This means that `test3.htm` will be loaded into the new window and not the current window. The same applies to the `<form>` tag's `target` attribute, which you'll be looking at in the chapters on server-side JavaScript. In this case, if a form is submitted from the original window, the response from the server can be made to appear in the new window.

When a new window is opened, it is opened (by default) with a certain set of properties, such as `width` and `height`, and with the normal browser-window features. Browser-window features include things such as a location entry field and a menu bar with navigation buttons.

The third parameter of the `open()` method can be used to specify values for the `height` and `width` properties. Also, because by default most of the browser window's features are switched off, you can switch them back on using the third parameter of the `open()` method. You'll look at browser features in more detail shortly.

Let's first look at an example of the code you need to open a basic window. You'll name this window `myWindow` and give it a `width` and `height` of 250 pixels. You want the new window to open with the `test2.htm` page inside.

```
var newWindow;
newWindow = window.open("test2.htm","myWindow","width=250,height=250");
```

You can see that `test2.htm` has been passed as the first parameter; that is the URL of the page you want to open. You've named the window `myWindow` in the second parameter. In the third parameter, you've set the `width` and `height` properties to `250`.

You'll also notice that you've set the variable `newWindow` to the return value returned by the `open()` method, which is a reference to the `window` object of the new window just opened. You can now use `newWindow` to manipulate the new window and gain access to the `document` contained inside it using the `window.document` property. You can do everything with this reference that you did when dealing with frames and their `window` objects. For example, if you wanted to change the background color of the `document` contained inside the new window, you would type this:

```
newWindow.document.bgColor = "RED";
```

How would you close the window you just opened? Easy, you just use the `window` object's `close()` method like this:

```
newWindow.close();
```

Try It Out   Opening Up New Windows

Let's look at the example mentioned earlier of a products page in which clicking a product brings up a window listing the details of that product. In a shameless plug, you'll be using a couple of Wrox books as examples — though with just two products on your page, it's not exactly the world's most extensive online catalog.

```html
<html>
<head>
<title>Online Books</title>
<script language="JavaScript" type="text/javascript">
var detailsWindow;
function showDetails(bookURL)
{
detailsWindow = window.open(bookURL,"bookDetails","width=400,height=350");
detailsWindow.focus();
return false;
}
</script>
</head>
<body>
<h2 align=center>Online Book Buyer</h2>

<p>
Click any of the images below for more details
</p>
<strong>Professional Active Server Pages .Net</strong>
<br>
<img src="pro_asp.jpg" border="0" onclick="return
showDetails('pro_asp_details.htm')">
<br><br>
<strong>Beginning Dreamweaver MX 2004</strong>
<br>
<img src="beg_dreamweaver.jpg" border="0" onclick="return
showDetails('beg_dreamweaver_details.htm')">
</body>
</html>
```

Save this page as online_books.htm. You'll also need to create two images and name them pro_asp.jpg and beg_dreamweaver.jpg. Alternatively, you can find these files in the code download. Note that if the user has disabled JavaScript, the window won't be opened. You can get around this by adding the page details to the href attribute as follows:

```html
<a href="pro_asp_details.htm"
onclick="return showDetails(this.href);"><img ...></a>
```

You now need to create the two details pages, both plain HTML.

```html
<html>
<head>
<title>Professional ASP.NET 2.0</title>
</head>
<body>
<strong>Professional ASP.NET 2.0</strong>
<br>
Subjects
<br>
ASP
```

```
<br>
Internet
<br>
<HR color=#cc3333>
<p><strong>Book overview</strong> </p>
<p>This comprehensive compendium provides a broad and thorough
investigation of all aspects of programming with ASP.NET. Entirely revised
and updated for the 2.0 Release of .NET, this book will give you the information
you need to master ASP.NET and build dynamic, successful, enterprise Web
applications.
</p>
</body>
</html>
```

Save this as pro_asp_details.htm.

```
<html>
<head>
<title>Beginning Dreamweaver MX 2004</title>
</head>
<body>
<strong>Beginning Dreamweaver MX 2004</strong>
<br>
<strong>Subjects</strong>
Dreamweaver<br>
Internet<br>
Web Design<br>
XML and Scripting<br>
<HR color=#cc3333>
<p><strong>Book overview<strong></p>
<p>With this book you'll quickly be creating powerful,
dynamic web sites with Dreamweaver MX 2004 - Macromedia's powerful, integrated web
development and editing tool.
You'll learn how to use the tools and features of
Dreamweaver to construct three complete sites using
HTML, JavaScript, Active Server Pages (ASP), and databases.
</p>
</body>
</html>
```

Save the final page as beg_dreamweaver_details.htm.

Load online_books.htm into your browser and click either of the two images. A new window containing the book's details should appear above the existing browser window. Click the other book image, and the window will be replaced by one containing the details of that book.

How It Works

The files pro_asp_details.htm and beg_dreamweaver_details.htm are both plain HTML files, so you won't look at them. However, in online_books.htm you find some scripting action, which you *will* look at here.

In the script block at the top of the page, you first define the variable detailsWindow.

```
var detailsWindow;
```

You then have the function that actually opens the new windows.

```
function showDetails(bookURL)
{
detailsWindow = window.open(bookURL,"bookDetails","width=400,height=350");
detailsWindow.focus();
return false;
}
```

This function is connected to the onclick event handlers of book images that appear later in the page. The parameter bookURL is passed by the code in the onclick event handler and will be either beg_asp3_details.htm or prof_js_details.htm.

You create the new window with the window.open() method. You pass the bookURL parameter as the URL to be opened. You pass bookDetails as the name you want applied to the new window. If the window already exists, another new window won't be opened, and the existing one will be navigated to the URL that you pass. This only occurs because you are using the same name (bookDetails) when opening the window for each book. If you had used a different name, a new window would be opened.

By storing the reference to the window object just created in the variable detailsWindow, you can access its methods and properties. On the next line, you'll see that you use the window object, referenced by detailsWindow, to set the focus to the new window — otherwise it will appear behind the existing window if you click the same image in the main window more than once.

Although you are using the same function for each of the image's onclick event handlers, you pass a different parameter for each, namely the URL of the details page for the book in question.

```
<strong>Professional Active Server Pages .Net</strong>
<br>
<img src="pro_asp.jpg" border="0"
onclick="return showDetails('pro_asp_details.htm')">
<br><br>
<strong>Beginning Dreamweaver MX 2004</strong>
<br>
<img src="beg_dreamweaver.jpg" border="0"
onclick="return showDetails('beg_dreamweaver_details.htm')">
</A>
```

Adding HTML to a New Window

You learned earlier that you can pass an empty string as the first parameter of the window object's open() method and then write to the page using HTML. Let's see how you would do that.

First, you need to open a blank window by passing an empty value to the first parameter that specifies the file name to load.

```
var newWindow = window.open("","myNewWindow","width=150,height=150");
```

Now you can open the window's document to receive your HTML.

```
newWindow.document.open();
```

This is not essential when a new window is opened, because the page is blank; but with a document that already contains HTML, it has the effect of clearing out all existing HTML and blanking the page, making it ready for writing.

Now you can write out any valid HTML using the document.write() method.

```
newWindow.document.write("<h4>Hello</h4>");
newWindow.document.write("<p>Welcome to my new little window</p>");
```

Each time you use the write() method, the text is added to what's already there until you use the document.close() method.

```
newWindow.document.close();
```

If you then use the document.write() method again, the text passed will replace existing HTML rather than adding to it.

Adding Features to Your Windows

As you have seen, the window.open() method takes three parameters, and it's the third of these parameters that you'll be looking at in this section. Using this third parameter, you can control things such as the size of the new window created, its start position on the screen, whether the user can resize it, whether it has a toolbar, and so on.

Features such as menu bar, status bar, and toolbar can be switched on or off with yes or 1 for on and no or 0 for off. You can also switch these features on by including their names without specifying a value.

The list of possible options shown in the following table is not complete, and not all of them work with both IE and Firefox browsers.

Window Feature	Possible Values	Description
copyHistory	yes, no	Copy the history of the window doing the opening to the new window
directories	yes, no	Show directory buttons
height	integer	Height of new window in pixels
left	integer	Window's left starting position in pixels
location	yes, no	Show location text field
menubar	yes, no	Show menu bar
resizable	yes, no	Enable the user to resize the window after it has been opened

Window Feature	Possible Values	Description
scrollbars	yes, no	Show scrollbars if the page is too large to fit in the window
status	yes, no	Show status bar
toolbar	yes, no	Show toolbar
top	integer	Window's top starting position in pixels
width	integer	Width of new window in pixels

As mentioned earlier, this third parameter is optional. If you don't include it, all the window features default to yes, except the window's size and position properties, which default to preset values. For example, if you try the following code, you'll see a window something like the one shown in Figure 7-10:

```
<html>
<head>
<script language="JavaScript" type="text/javascript">
var newWindow;
newWindow = window.open("","myWindow");
</script>
</head>
</html>
```

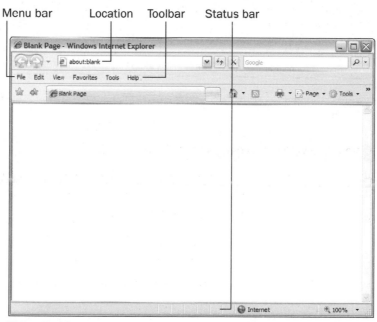

Figure 7- 10

However, if you specify even one of the features, all the others (except size and position properties) are set to no by default. For example, although you have defined its size, the following code produces a window with no features, as shown in Figure 7-11:

```
var newWindow;
newWindow = window.open("","myWindow","width=200,height=120")
```

The larger window is the original page, and the smaller one on top (shown in Figure 7-11) is the pop-up window.

Figure 7-11

Let's see another example. The following creates a resizable 250-by-250-pixel window, with a location field and menu bar:

```
var newWindow;
newWindow =
window.open("","myWindow","width=250,height=250,location,menubar,resizable")
```

A word of warning, however: Never include spaces inside the features string; otherwise some browsers will consider the string invalid and ignore your settings.

Scripting Between Windows

You've taken a brief look at how you can manipulate the new window's properties and methods, and access its document object using the return value from the window.open() method. Now you're going to look at how the newly opened window can access the window that opened it and, just as with frames, how it can use functions there.

The key to accessing the window object of the window that opened the current window is the window object's opener property. This returns a reference to the window object of the window that opened the current window. So the following code will change the background color of the opener window to red:

```
window.opener.document.bgColor = "RED"
```

You can use the reference pretty much as you used the window.parent and window.top properties when using frames.

Try It Out   **Inter-Window Scripting**

Let's look at an example wherein you open a new window and access a form on the opener window from the new window.

```html
<html>
<head>
<script language="JavaScript" type="text/javascript">
var newWindow;
function butOpenWin_onclick()
{
var winTop = (screen.height / 2) - 125;
var winLeft = (screen.width / 2) - 125;
var windowFeatures = "width=250,height=250,";
windowFeatures = windowFeatures + "left=" + winLeft + ",";
windowFeatures = windowFeatures + "top=" + winTop;
newWindow = window.open("newWindow.htm","myWindow",windowFeatures);
}
function butGetText_onclick()
{
if (typeof(newWindow) == "undefined" || newWindow.closed == true)
    {
alert("No window is open");
    }
else
    {
document.form1.text1.value = newWindow.document.form1.text1.value;
    }
}

function window_onunload()
{
if (typeof(newWindow) != "undefined" && newWindow.closed == false)
    {
newWindow.close();
    }
}

</script>
</head>
<body onunload="window_onunload()">
<form name=form1> <input type="button" value="Open newWindow" name=butOpenWin
onclick="butOpenWin_onclick()"> <br><br> NewWindow's Text <br>
<input type="text" name=text1>
<br> <input type="button" value="Get Text" name=butGetText
onclick="return butGetText_onclick()">
</form>
</body>
</html>
```

This is the code for your original window. Save it as openerwindow.htm. Now you'll look at the page that will be loaded by the opener window.

```
<html>
<head>
<script language="JavaScript" type="text/javascript">
function butGetText_onclick()
{
document.form1.text1.value = window.opener.document.form1.text1.value;
}
</script>
</head>
<body>
<form name=form1>
Opener window's text<BR>
<input type="text" name=text1>
<br>
<input type="button" value="Get Text" name=butGetText language="JavaScript"
type="text/javascript"
onclick="butGetText_onclick()">
</form>
</body>
</html>
```

Save this as newWindow.htm.

Open openerwindow.htm in your browser, and you'll see a page with the simple form shown in Figure 7-12.

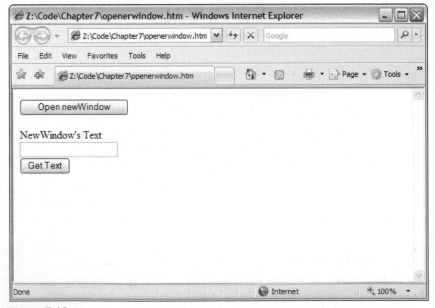

Figure 7-12

Click the `Open newWindow` button, and you'll see the window shown in Figure 7-13 open above the original page.

Figure 7-13

Type something into the text box of the new window. Then return to the original opener window, click the Get Text button, and you'll see what you just typed into `newWindow` appear in the text box on the opener window's form.

Change the text in the opener window's text box and then return to the `newWindow` and click the Get Text button. The text you typed into the opener window's text box will appear in `newWindow`'s text box.

How It Works

Let's look at the opener window first. In the head of the page is a script block in which a variable and three functions are defined. At the top you have declared a new variable, `newWindow`, which will hold the `window` object reference returned by the `window.open()` method you'll use later. Being outside any function gives this variable a global scope, so you can access it from any function on the page.

```
var newWindow;
```

Then you have the first of the three functions in this page, `butOpenWin_onclick()`, which is connected further down the page to the Open newWindow button's `onclick` event handler. Its purpose is simply to open the new window.

Rather than have the new window open up anywhere on the page, you use the built-in `screen` object, which is a property of the `window` object, to find out the resolution of the user's display and place the window in the middle of the screen. The `screen` object has a number of read-only properties, but you're interested here in the `width` and `height` properties. You initialize the `winTop` variable to the vertical position onscreen at which you want the top edge of the popup window to appear. The `winLeft` variable is set to the horizontal position onscreen at which you want the left edge of the pop-up window to appear. In this case, you want the position to be in the middle of the screen both horizontally and vertically.

```
function butOpenWin_onclick()
{
var winTop = (screen.height / 2) - 125;
var winLeft = (screen.width / 2) - 125;
```

You build up a string for the window features and store it in the windowFeatures variable. You set the width and height to 250 and then use the winLeft and winTop variables you just populated to create the initial start positions of the window.

```
var windowFeatures = "width=250,height=250,";
windowFeatures = windowFeatures + "left=" + winLeft + ",";
windowFeatures = windowFeatures + "top=" + winTop;
```

Finally, you open the new window, making sure you put the return value from window.open() into global variable newWindow so you can manipulate it later.

```
newWindow = window.open("newWindow.htm","myWindow",windowFeatures);
}
```

The next function is used to obtain the text from the text box on the form in newWindow.

In this function you use an if statement to check two things. First, you check that newWindow is defined and second, that the window is actually open. You check because you don't want to try to access a nonexistent window, for example if no window has been opened or a window has been closed by the user. The typeof operator returns the type of information held in a variable, for example number, string, Boolean, object, and undefined. It returns undefined if the variable has never been given a value, as newWindow won't have been if no new window has been opened.

Having confirmed that a window has been opened at some point, you now need to check whether it's still open, and the window object's closed property does just that. If it returns true, the window is closed, and if it returns false, it's still open. (Do not confuse this closed property with the close() method you saw previously.)

In the if statement you'll see that checking if newWindow is defined comes first, and this is no accident. If newWindow really were undefined, newWindow.closed would cause an error, because there are no data inside newWindow. However, you are taking advantage of the fact that if an if statement's condition will be true or false at a certain point regardless of the remainder of the condition, the remainder of the condition is not checked.

```
function butGetText_onclick()
{
if (typeof(newWindow) == "undefined" || newWindow.closed == true)
    {
alert("No window is open");
    }
```

If newWindow exists and is open, the else statement's code will execute. Remember that newWindow will contain a reference to the window object of the window opened. This means you can access the form in newWindow, just as you'd access a form on the page the script's running in, by using the document object inside the newWindow window object.

```
else
    {
document.form1.text1.value = newWindow.document.form1.text1.value;
    }
}
```

The last of the three functions is window_onunload(), which is connected to the onunload event of this page and fires when either the browser window is closed or the user navigates to another page. In the window_onunload() function, you check to see if newWindow is valid and open in much the same way that you just did. You must check to see if the newWindow variable is defined first. With the && operator, JavaScript checks the second part of the operation only if the first part evaluates to true. If newWindow is defined, and does therefore hold a window object (even though it's possibly a closed window), you can check the closed property of the window. However, if newWindow is undefined, the check for its closed property won't happen, and no errors will occur. If you check the closed property first and newWindow is undefined, an error will occur, because an undefined variable has no closed property.

```
function window_onunload()
{
if (typeof(newWindow) != "undefined" && newWindow.closed == false)
    {
newWindow.close();
    }
}
```

If newWindow is defined and open, you close it. This prevents the newWindow's Get Text button from being clicked when there is no opener window in existence to get text from (since this function fires when the opener window is closed).

Let's now look at the code for the page that will be loaded in your newWindow, namely newWindow.htm. This page contains one function, butGetText_onclick(). This is connected to the onclick event handler of the Get Text button in the page and is used to retrieve the text from the opener window's text box.

```
function butGetText_onclick()
{
document.form1.text1.value = window.opener.document.form1.text1.value;
}
```

In this function, you use the window.opener property to get a reference to the window object of the window that opened this one, and then use that reference to get the value out of the text box in the form in that window. This value is placed inside the text box in the current page.

Moving and Resizing Windows

Before leaving the subject of windows, let's look at the methods available to you for resizing and moving existing windows.

After you have opened a window, you can change its onscreen position and its size using the window object's resizeTo() and moveTo() methods, both of which take two arguments in pixels.

Imagine that, having just opened a new window, like this:

```
var newWindow = window.open(myURL,"myWindow","width=125,height=150,resizable");
```

you want to make it 350 pixels wide by 200 pixels high and move it to a position 100 pixels from the left of the screen and 400 pixels from the top. What code would you need?

```
newWindow.resizeTo(350,200);
newWindow.moveTo(100,400);
```

You can see that you can resize your window to 350 pixels wide by 200 pixels high using `resizeTo()`. Then you move it so it's 100 pixels from the left of the screen and 400 pixels from the top of the screen using `moveTo()`.

The `window` object also has `resizeBy()` and `moveBy()` methods. These each take two parameters, in pixels. For example:

```
newWindow.resizeBy(100,200);
```

This code will increase the size of `newWindow` by 100 pixels horizontally and 200 pixels vertically. Similarly,

```
newWindow.moveBy(20,50);
```

will move the `newWindow` by 20 pixels horizontally and 50 pixels vertically.

When using these methods, you must bear in mind that users can manually resize these windows if they so wish. In addition, the size of the client's screen in pixels will vary between users.

Security

Browsers, such as Firefox and Internet Explorer, put certain restrictions on what information scripts can access between frames and windows.

If all the pages in these frames and windows are based on the same server, or on the same computer when you're loading them into the browser locally, as you are in these examples, you have a reasonably free rein over what your scripts can access and do. However, some restrictions do exist. For example, if you try to use the `window.close()` method in a script page loaded into a browser window that the user opened, as opposed to a window opened by your script, a message box will appear giving the user the option of canceling your `close()` method and keeping the window open.

When a page in one window or frame hosted on one server tries to access the properties of a window or frame that contains a page from a different server, the same-origin policy comes into play, and you'll find yourself very restricted as to what your scripts can do.

Imagine you have a page hosted on a web server whose URL is `http://www.myserver.com`. Inside the page is the following script:

```
var myWindow =
window.open("http://www.anotherserver.com/anotherpage.htm","myWindow");
```

Now you have two windows, one that is hosted at www.myserver.com and another that is hosted on a different server, www.anotherserver.com. Although this code does work, the same-origin policy prevents any access to the `document` object of one page from another. For example, the following code in the opener page will cause a security problem and will be prevented by the browser:

```
var myVariable = myWindow.document.form1.text1.value;
```

Although you do have access to the `window` object of the page on the other server, you have access to a limited subset of its properties and methods.

The same-origin restriction applies to frames and windows equally. The idea behind it is very sound: It is there to prevent hackers from putting your pages inside their own and extracting information by using code inside their pages. However, the restrictions are fairly severe, perhaps too severe, and mean that you should avoid scripting across frames or windows if the pages are hosted on different servers.

Trivia Quiz

As you left it in the previous chapter, the trivia quiz was simply a single page that asked a single randomly selected question. Your task for the trivia quiz in this chapter is to convert it from a single-page application to a multi-frame-based application containing six pages. This is not a small change and will require a lot of work. The enhancements in this chapter will transform the quiz into something resembling a proper application. When the application is first loaded, the user will be presented with the screen shown in Figure 7-14.

As you can see, this is quite a change from the way the quiz looked in Chapter 6! Next you'll look at the strategy for creating this application.

On some browsers, for example some versions of Internet Explorer 6, you may see a warning bar when you load the quiz. This only occurs when you load the page from your local computer; it won't occur if the page is loaded from a web site. When it asks if you want to run the active content, click Yes.

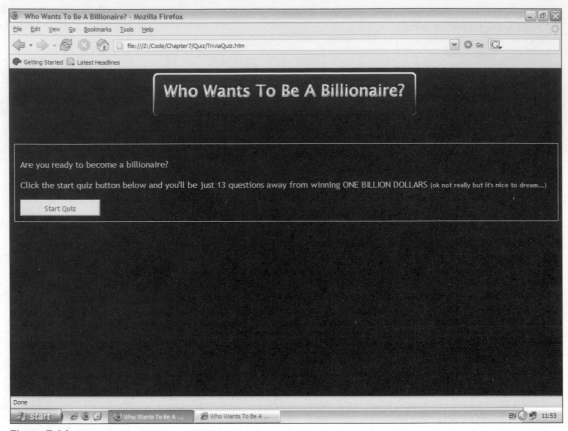

Figure 7-14

Creating the New Trivia Quiz

The idea behind using frames is that there will be a page called globalfunctions.htm to hold all the global functions that you use again and again. This page will be loaded into a frame called fraGlobalFunctions.

There will also be a page that simply displays the banner, Who Wants To Be A Billionaire, shown in Figure 7-14. This page is called menubar.htm and will be loaded into a frame called fraMenubar.

The third and fourth pages are where all the action takes place as far as the user is concerned. The QuizPage.htm is where the quiz is started — it displays the welcome message and Start Quiz button that you can see in Figure 7-14. The AskQuestion.htm page is where the questions are displayed and answered, and finally, when the quiz is finished, where the results are listed. These will be loaded into the frame called fraQuizPage.

The two other pages are called TriviaQuiz.htm and TopFrame.htm, whose job is solely to define the framesets for the frames containing the other pages. These frameset pages will be contained in the frames called Top window and fraTopFrame.

The frame structure of the application is shown in Figure 7-15, along with the name of each frame. Note that although the fraGlobalFunctions frame is shown, it's actually invisible to the user, so they won't be able to easily see the code and cheat by reading the answers.

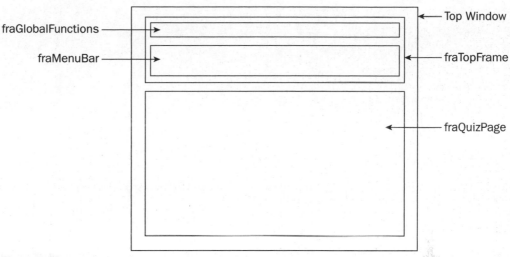

Figure 7-15

In terms of a tree diagram, the frames look like those shown in Figure 7-16.

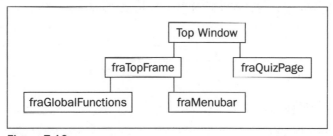

Figure 7-16

You'll now look at each frame in turn and give the code for the page or pages that will be loaded into it.

Top Window

Figure 7-17 shows the frame structure, with the top window frame highlighted.

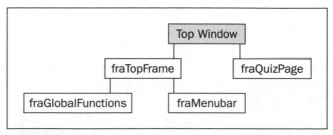

Figure 7-17

Create the frameset page that defines the top and bottom frames that you can see.

```
<!DOCTYPE HTML PUBLIC "-//W3C//DTD HTML 4.01 Frameset//EN"
"http://www.w3.org/TR/html4/frameset.dtd">
<html>
<head>
<meta http-equiv="Content-Type" content="text/html; charset=iso-8859-1">
<title>Wrox Online Trivia Quiz</title>
</head>
<frameset rows="120,*" border="0">
<frame src="TopFrame.htm" name="fraTopFrame">
<frame src="QuizPage.htm" name="fraQuizPage">
</frameset>
</html>
```

Save this as `TriviaQuiz.htm`.

This is the page the user loads into his browser. It defines the frames `fraTopFrame` and `fraQuizPage` and specifies the pages that will be loaded into them.

fraQuizPage

The next frame you're looking at is `fraQuizPage`, whose position in the frames hierarchy is shown in Figure 7-18. This frame will have two pages loaded into it in turn: `QuizPage.htm` and `AskQuestion.htm`.

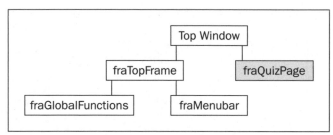

Figure 7-18

QuizPage.htm

In the previous screenshot you saw what the trivia quiz looks like before the quiz has started. You simply have a start page with a bit of text and a button to click that starts the quiz. When the quiz is finished, this page is loaded again if the user asks to restart the quiz.

Let's create that start page. When you've finished typing the code, save the page as `QuizPage.htm`.

```
<!DOCTYPE HTML PUBLIC "-//W3C//DTD HTML 4.01 Transitional//EN"
"http://www.w3.org/TR/html4/loose.dtd">
<html>
<head>
<meta http-equiv="Content-Type" content="text/html; charset=iso-8859-1">
<title>Quiz Page</title>
<script language="JavaScript" type="text/javascript">
function cmdStartQuiz_onclick()
```

```
{
window.top.fraTopFrame.fraGlobalFunctions.resetQuiz();
window.location.href = "AskQuestion.htm";
}
</script>
<style type="text/css">
<!--
body {
 background-color: #000033;
}
body,td,th {
 font-family: Trebuchet MS, helvetica, sans-serif;
 color: #CCCCCC;
}

input, select {

 font-family: "Trebuchet MS", "Lucida Sans", Georgia, "Times New Roman", Times,
serif;
 font-size: 13px;
 color: #333333;
 padding: 1px;
 background: #EEE;

}
.SmallText {font-size: 12px}

div#MainBodyDIV
{
 border:1px;
 border-color:#CCCCCC;
 border-style:groove;
 padding:10px;
 margin-top:20px;
}
-->
</style>
</head>
<body>

<div id="MainBodyDIV">
<p>Are you ready to become a billionaire?</p>
<p>Click the Start Quiz button below and you'll be just 13 questions away from
winning ONE BILLION DOLLARS.
<span class="SmallText">(ok not really but it's nice to dream...)</span> </p>
<form name="frmQuiz">
<input name="cmdStartQuiz" type=button value="Start Quiz"
onclick="return cmdStartQuiz_onclick()" style="width:150px; height:30px;">
</p>
</form>
</div>

</p>
</body>
</html>
```

AskQuestion.htm

After the Start Quiz button has been clicked, the next page loaded into the `fraQuizPage` frame is `AskQuestion.htm`, as shown in Figure 7-19 (the questions are randomly selected, so you may have a different start question).

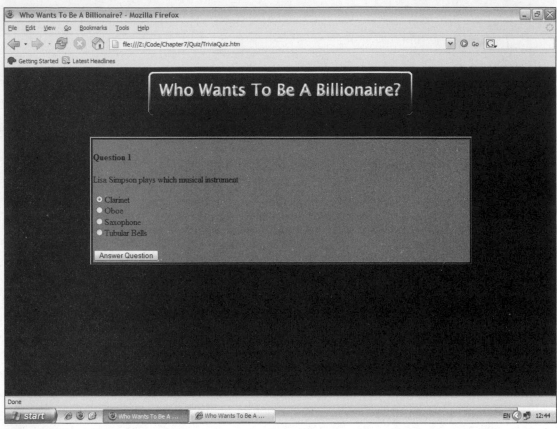

Figure 7-19

When the Answer Question button is clicked, the user's answer is checked, and this page is reloaded. If there are more questions to ask, then another, different, randomly selected question is shown. If you've come to the end of the quiz, a results page like the one shown in Figure 7-20 is displayed. Actually, the results page and question-asking pages are the same HTML page, but they're created dynamically depending on whether the quiz has ended.

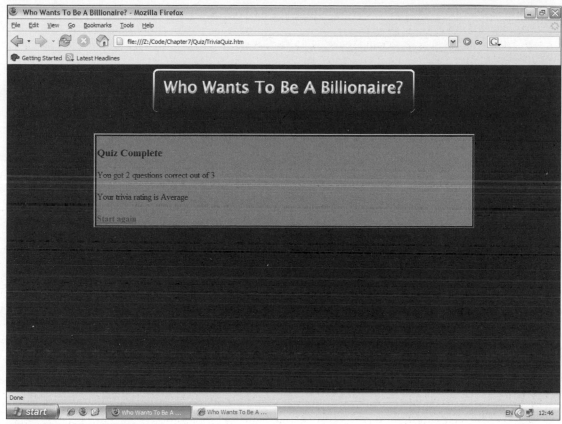

Figure 7-20

You'll now create that page, which should be saved as AskQuestion.htm.

```
<!DOCTYPE HTML PUBLIC "-//W3C//DTD HTML 4.01 Transitional//EN"
"http://www.w3.org/TR/html4/loose.dtd">
<html>
<head>
<meta http-equiv="Content-Type" content="text/html; charset=iso-8859-1">
<title>Ask Questions</title>
<script language="JavaScript" type="text/javascript">
var globalFunctions;
globalFunctions = window.top.fraTopFrame.fraGlobalFunctions;
function getAnswer()
{
var answer = 0;
while (document.QuestionForm.radQuestionChoice[answer].checked != true)
    {
answer++;
    }
```

```
return String.fromCharCode(65 + answer);
}
function buttonCheckQ_onclick()
{
var questionNumber = globalFunctions.currentQNumber;
if (globalFunctions.answerCorrect(questionNumber,getAnswer()) == true)
    {
alert("You got it right");
    }
else
    {
alert("You got it wrong");
    }
window.location.reload();
}
</script>
</head>
<body style="background-color: #000033;">
<table align=center border="2" width="70%">
<tr>
<td bgcolor=RoyalBlue>
<form name="QuestionForm">
<script language="JavaScript" type="text/javascript">
document.write(globalFunctions.getQuestion());
</script>
</form>
</td>
</tr>
</table>
</body>
</html>
```

fraTopFrame

The next frame you're looking at is `fraTopFrame`, whose position in the frames hierarchy is shown in Figure 7-21.

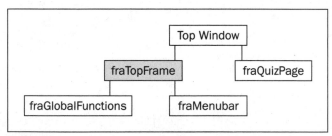

Figure 7-21

This other frame defined in `Topwindow` is, in fact, another frameset-defining page. It defines one visible frame, the one containing the page heading, and a second frame, which is not visible and which contains your global functions, but no HTML. Let's create that frameset-defining page next.

```
<!DOCTYPE HTML PUBLIC "-//W3C//DTD HTML 4.01 Frameset//EN"
"http://www.w3.org/TR/html4/frameset.dtd">
<html>
<head>
<meta http-equiv="Content-Type" content="text/html; charset=iso-8859-1">
<title>Top Frame</title>
</head>
<frameset rows="0,*" border="0">
<frame src="GlobalFunctions.htm" name="fraGlobalFunctions">
<frame src="Menubar.htm" name="fraMenubar">
</frameset>
</html>
```

Save this page as TopFrame.htm.

You can see that it defines the two frames called fraGlobalFunctions and fraMenubar, which you will look at next.

fraMenubar

You'll next create the page for the fraMenubar frame, whose position in the frames hierarchy is shown in Figure 7-22.

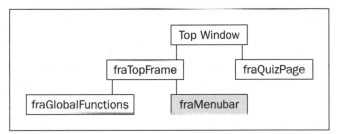

Figure 7-22

```
<!DOCTYPE HTML PUBLIC "-//W3C//DTD HTML 4.01 Transitional//EN"
"http://www.w3.org/TR/html4/loose.dtd">
<html>
<head>
<title>Menu Bar</title>
<meta http-equiv="Content-Type" content="text/html; charset=iso-8859-1">
</head>
<body style="background-color:#000033">
<div style="text-align:center;">
 <img src="images/MainLogo.gif" width="489" height="81" id="MainLogoImg">
</div>
</body>
</html>
```

Save this as menubar.htm.

This page just defines the heading that can be seen throughout the trivia quiz. It also uses an image called MainLogo.gif, which you will need to create or retrieve from the code download.

fraGlobalFunctions

In Figure 7-23, you can see where `fraGlobalFunctions` fits into your frames hierarchy.

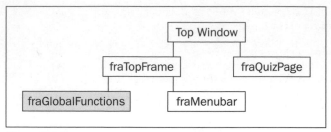

Figure 7-23

Now turn your attention to the final new page, namely `globalfunctions.htm`, which serves as a module containing all your general JavaScript functions. It is contained in the frame `fraGlobalFunctions`. You may recognize some of the code from the `trivia_quiz.htm` page that constituted the trivia quiz you created in Chapter 6.

```
<!DOCTYPE HTML PUBLIC "-//W3C//DTD HTML 4.01 Transitional//EN"
"http://www.w3.org/TR/html4/loose.dtd">
<html>
<head>
<meta http-equiv="Content-Type" content="text/html; charset=iso-8859-1">
<title>Global functions</title>
<script language="JavaScript" type="text/javascript">
// questions and answers variables will holds questions and answers
var questions = new Array();
var answers = new Array();
var questionsAsked;
var numberOfQuestionsAsked = 0;
var numberOfQuestionsCorrect = 0;
var currentQNumber = -1;
// define question 1
questions[0] = new Array();
questions[0][0] = "The Beatles were";
questions[0][1] = "A sixties rock group from Liverpool";
questions[0][2] = "Four musically gifted insects";
questions[0][3] = "I don't know - can I have the questions on baseball please";
// assign answer for question 1
answers[0] = "A";
// define question 2
questions[1] = new Array();
questions[1][0] = "Homer Simpson's favorite food is";
questions[1][1] = "Fresh salad";
questions[1][2] = "Doughnuts";
questions[1][3] = "Bread and water";
questions[1][4] = "Apples";
// assign answer for question 2
answers[1] = "B";
```

```
// define question 3
questions[2] = new Array();
questions[2][0] = "Lisa Simpson plays which musical instrument";
questions[2][1] = "Clarinet";
questions[2][2] = "Oboe";
questions[2][3] = "Saxophone";
questions[2][4] = "Tubular Bells";
// assign answer for question 3
answers[2] = "C";
function resetQuiz()
{
var indexCounter;
currentQNumber = -1;
questionsAsked = new Array();
for (indexCounter = 0; indexCounter < questions.length;indexCounter++)
    {
questionsAsked[indexCounter] = false;
    }
numberOfQuestionsAsked = 0;
numberOfQuestionsCorrect = 0;
}
function answerCorrect(questionNumber, answer)
{
// declare a variable to hold return value
var correct = false;
// if answer provided is same as answer then correct answer is true
if (answer == answers[questionNumber])
    {
numberOfQuestionsCorrect++;
correct = true;
    }
// return whether the answer was correct (true or false)
return correct;
}
function getQuestion()
{
if (questions.length != numberOfQuestionsAsked)
    {
var questionNumber = Math.floor(Math.random() * questions.length)
while (questionsAsked[questionNumber] == true)
        {
questionNumber = Math.floor(Math.random() * questions.length);
        }
var questionLength = questions[questionNumber].length;
var questionChoice;
numberOfQuestionsAsked++;
var questionHTML = "<h4>Question " + numberOfQuestionsAsked +  "</h4>";
questionHTML = questionHTML + "<p>" + questions[questionNumber][0];
questionHTML = questionHTML + "</p>";
for (questionChoice = 1;questionChoice < questionLength;questionChoice++)
     {
questionHTML = questionHTML + "<input type=radio "
questionHTML = questionHTML + "name=radQuestionChoice"
```

```
if (questionChoice == 1)
        {
questionHTML = questionHTML + " checked";
        }
questionHTML = questionHTML + ">" +
questions[questionNumber][questionChoice];
questionHTML = questionHTML + "<br>"
    }
questionHTML = questionHTML + "<br><input type='button' "
questionHTML = questionHTML + " value='Answer Question'";
questionHTML = questionHTML + "name=buttonNextQ ";
questionHTML = questionHTML + "onclick='return buttonCheckQ_onclick()'>";
currentQNumber = questionNumber;
questionsAsked[questionNumber] = true;
    }
else
    {
var questionHTML = "<h3>Quiz Complete</h3>";
questionHTML = questionHTML + "You got " + numberOfQuestionsCorrect;
questionHTML = questionHTML + " questions correct out of "
questionHTML = questionHTML + numberOfQuestionsAsked;
questionHTML = questionHTML + "<br><br>Your trivia rating is "
switch(Math.round(((numberOfQuestionsCorrect / numberOfQuestionsAsked) * 10)))
        {
case 0:
case 1:
case 2:
case 3:
questionHTML = questionHTML + "Beyond embarrassing";
break;
case 4:
case 5:
case 6:
case 7:
questionHTML = questionHTML + "Average";
break;
default:
questionHTML = questionHTML + "Excellent"
        }
questionHTML = questionHTML + "<br><br><A "
questionHTML = questionHTML + "href='quizpage.htm'><strong>"
questionHTML = questionHTML + "Start again</strong></A>"
    }
return questionHTML;
}
</script>
</head>
<body>
</body>
</html>
```

Save this page as GlobalFunctions.htm. That completes all the pages, so now it's time to load the new trivia quiz and find out how it works.

How It Works

Load `TriviaQuiz.htm` into your browser to start the quiz and try it out.

Although there does appear to be a lot of new code, much of it is identical to that in the previous version of the trivia quiz.

You will take a closer look at the pages `QuizPage.htm` and `AskQuestion.htm`, which are loaded into the `fraQuizPage` frame, and `GlobalFunctions.htm`, which is loaded into the `fraGlobalFunction` frame.

Of the other pages, `TriviaQuiz.htm` and `TopFrame.htm` are simply frameset-defining pages, and `menubar.htm` simply defines the heading for the page.

QuizPage.htm

This is a simple page. You define a function, `cmdStartQuiz_onclick()`, which is connected to the `onclick` event handler of the Start Quiz button further down the page.

```
function cmdStartQuiz_onclick()
{
window.top.fraTopFrame.fraGlobalFunctions.resetQuiz();
window.location.href = "AskQuestion.htm";
}
```

In this function, you reset the quiz by calling the `resetQuiz()` function, which is in your `fraGlobal Functions` frame. You'll be looking at this shortly. To get a reference to the `window` object of `fraGlobalFunctions`, you need to get a reference to the `fraTopFrame` that is under the top window.

On the second line of the function, you navigate the frame to `AskQuestion.htm`, the page where the questions are asked. Let's look at that next.

AskQuestion.htm

In this page, you'll access the functions in the `fraGlobalFunctions` frame a number of times, so you declare a page-level variable and set it to reference the `window` object of `fraGlobalFunctions`. This saves on typing and makes your code more readable.

```
var globalFunctions;
globalFunctions = window.top.fraTopFrame.fraGlobalFunctions;
```

You then come to the `getAnswer()` function, which retrieves from the form lower in the page the option the user chose as her answer. It does this by looping through each option in the form, incrementing the variable `answer` until it finds the option that has been checked by the user. Remember that the answers are stored as A, B, C, and so on, so you convert the index number to the correct character using the `fromCharCode()` method of the `String` object. This is identical to the action of the first half of the `buttonCheckQ_onclick()` function that you saw in the previous incarnation of the trivia quiz.

```
function getAnswer()
{
var answer = 0;
while (document.QuestionForm.radQuestionChoice[answer].checked != true)
  {
```

```
        answer++;
        }
    return String.fromCharCode(65 + answer);
    }
```

The second function, butCheckQ_onclick(), will be connected to the Check Answer button's onclick event. It is similar to the second half of the function with the same name in the previous version of the quiz. However, now it refers to the answerCorrect() function in the fraGlobalFunctions frame rather than the current page, and uses the getAnswer() function rather than the variable answer.

```
function buttonCheckQ_onclick()
{
var questionNumber = globalFunctions.currentQNumber;
if (globalFunctions.answerCorrect(questionNumber,getAnswer()) == true)
    {
alert("You got it right");
    }
else
    {
alert("You got it wrong");
    }
window.location.reload();
}
```

As in Chapter 6, the form that displays the question to the user is populated dynamically, by means of document.write(). However, this time the function, getQuestion(), is located in the GlobalFunctions.htm page.

GlobalFunctions.htm

Much of this page is taken from the trivia_quiz.htm page that you created in Chapter 6. At the top of the page you add four more page-level variables.

```
var questions = new Array();
var answers = new Array();
var questionsAsked;
var numberOfQuestionsAsked = 0;
var numberOfQuestionsCorrect = 0;
var currentQNumber = -1;
```

You then define the questions and answers arrays exactly as you did previously. The first new function, resetQuiz(), is shown here:

```
function resetQuiz()
{
var indexCounter;
currentQNumber = -1;
questionsAsked = new Array();
for (indexCounter = 0; indexCounter < questions.length;indexCounter++)
    {
questionsAsked[indexCounter] = false;
```

```
    }
numberOfQuestionsAsked = 0;
numberOfQuestionsCorrect = 0;
}
```

When the quiz is started or restarted, this function is called to reset all the global quiz variables back to a default state. For example, the questionsAsked variable is reinitialized to a new array, the length of which will match the length of the questions array, with each element being set to a default value of false, indicating that the corresponding question has not yet been asked.

You then have the answerCorrect() function, which is the same as in the previous chapter. The rest of the page is made up of the getQuestion() function, which has undergone major changes since the previous version.

Previously, you asked questions randomly and kept going until the user got bored. Now you're going to keep track of which questions have been asked and how many questions have been asked. The questionsAsked array will store which questions have already been asked, so you can avoid repeating questions. The variable numberOfQuestionsAsked keeps track of how many have been asked so far, so you can stop when you've used up your question database. The variable numberOfQuestionsCorrect will be used to record the number of right answers given. These variables were defined in the head of the page.

Turning to getQuestion(), you can see that the very first thing the function does is use an if statement to see if you have asked as many questions as there are questions in the database. The length property of your questions array tells you how many elements there are in your array, and numberOfQuestionsAsked tells you how many have been asked so far. If you have asked all the questions, then later on you'll see that the function writes out an end page with details of how many the user got correct and rates her trivia knowledge.

```
function getQuestion()
{
if (questions.length != numberOfQuestionsAsked)
    {
var questionNumber = Math.floor(Math.random() * questions.length)
while (questionsAsked[questionNumber] == true)
    {
questionNumber = Math.floor(Math.random() * questions.length);
    }
```

You can see from the preceding code that the selection of the question is random, as it was in the Chapter 6 version of the quiz. However, you have added a while loop that makes use of the questionsAsked array you declared earlier. Each time a question is asked, you set the value of the element in the questionsAsked array at the same position as its question number to true. By checking to see if a particular array position is true, you can tell if the question has already been asked, in which case the while loop keeps going until it hits a false value — that is, an unasked question.

Now that you know which question you want to ask, you just need to go ahead and ask it, which is the purpose of the next lines of code.

```
var questionLength = questions[questionNumber].length;
var questionChoice;
numberOfQuestionsAsked++;
var questionHTML = "<h4>Question " + numberOfQuestionsAsked +  "</h4>";
questionHTML = questionHTML + "<p>" + questions[questionNumber][0];
questionHTML = questionHTML + "</p>";
for (questionChoice = 1;questionChoice < questionLength;questionChoice++)
        {
questionHTML = questionHTML + "<input type=radio "
questionHTML = questionHTML + "name=radQuestionChoice"
if (questionChoice == 1)
            {
questionHTML = questionHTML + " checked";
            }
questionHTML = questionHTML + ">" +
questions[questionNumber][questionChoice];
questionHTML = questionHTML + "<br>"
        }
questionHTML = questionHTML + "<br><input type='button' "
questionHTML = questionHTML + " value='Answer Question'";
questionHTML = questionHTML + "name=buttonNextQ ";
questionHTML = questionHTML + "onclick='return buttonCheckQ_onclick()'>";
```

This code is almost identical to its previous form in Chapter 6, except that you now create the button as well as the answer options dynamically. Why? At the beginning of the function you saw that an `if` statement checked whether you had reached the end of the quiz. If not, you created another question, as you are doing here. If the quiz has come to an end, you don't want to create an array of answers. Instead you want to create an end-of-quiz form. The only way to avoid having the Answer Question button there is to make it part of the dynamic question creation.

Finally, you see that the `questionsAsked` array is updated—that is, the question just asked is stored in the array as follows:

```
currentQNumber = questionNumber;
questionsAsked[questionNumber] = true;
    }
```

The `else` part of the `if` statement from the top of the function is shown next. Its purpose is to create the "quiz completed" message. You build up the HTML necessary, storing it in the `questionHTML` variable. You not only specify how many questions the user got right out of how many were asked, but you also rate his knowledge.

```
else
    {
questionHTML = "<h3>Quiz Complete</h3>";
questionHTML = questionHTML + "You got " + numberOfQuestionsCorrect;
questionHTML = questionHTML + " questions correct out of "
questionHTML = questionHTML + numberOfQuestionsAsked;
questionHTML = questionHTML + "<br><br>Your trivia rating is "
```

The rating is done with the `switch` statement, where the statement is based on questions answered correctly divided by the number of questions asked, which for simplicity you multiply by 10 and round to the nearest integer. Then you use the `case` statements to create the correct rating. Remember that code execution starts at the first `case` statement that matches and continues until either the `switch` statement ends or a `break` statement is reached. So if your rating calculation

```
Math.round(((numberOfQuestionsCorrect / numberOfQuestionsAsked) * 10
```

were 1, the code would start executing from the `case 1:` statement and continue until the `break` statement in `case 3`. Essentially this means that a rating of 0–3 will be described as `Beyond embarrassing`, 4–7 as `Average`, and anything else, that is, the default case, as `Excellent`.

```
switch(Math.round(((numberOfQuestionsCorrect / numberOfQuestionsAsked) * 10)))
    {
case 0:
case 1:
case 2:
case 3:
questionHTML = questionHTML + "Beyond embarrassing";
break;
case 4:
case 5:
case 6:
case 7:
questionHTML = questionHTML + "Average";
break;
default:
questionHTML = questionHTML + "Excellent"
    }
```

Finally, you add a link to allow the user to restart the quiz.

```
questionHTML = questionHTML + "<br><br><A "
questionHTML = questionHTML + "href='quizpage.htm'><strong>"
questionHTML = questionHTML + "Start again</strong></A>"
    }
```

At the end of the function, you return the HTML to be written into the page: either a new question or the end-of-quiz results.

```
return questionHTML;
}
```

That completes the discussion of the trivia quiz for this chapter. In the next chapter you'll use advanced string manipulation to pose questions requiring a text-based, rather than option-based, answer.

Summary

For various reasons, having a frame-based web site can prove very useful. Therefore, you need to be able to create JavaScript that can interact with frames and with the documents and code within those frames.

❑ You saw that an advantage of frames is that, by putting all of your general functions in a single frame, you can create a JavaScript code module that all of your web site can use.

❑ You saw that the key to coding with frames is getting a reference to the window objects of other frames. You saw two ways of accessing frames higher in the hierarchy, using the window object's parent property and its top property.

❑ The parent property returns the window object that contains the current window object, which will be the page containing the frameset that created the window. The top property returns the window object of the window containing all the other frames.

❑ Each frame in a frameset can be accessed through three methods. One is to use the name of the frame. The second is to use the frames[] array and specify the index of the frame. The third way is to access the frame by its name in the frames array — for example, parent.frames.frameName. This the safest way, because it avoids any collision with global variables.

❑ If the frame you want to access is defined in another window, you need the parent or top property to get a reference to the window object defining that frame, and then you must specify the name or position in the frames[] array.

You then looked at how you can open new, additional browser windows using script.

❑ Using the window object's open() method, you can open new windows. The URL of the page you want to open is passed as the first parameter; the name of the new window is passed as the second parameter; the optional third parameter enables you to define what features the new window will have.

❑ The window.open() method returns a value, which is a reference to the window object of the new window. Using this reference, you can access the document, script, and methods of that window, much as you do with frames. You need to make sure that the reference is stored inside a variable if you want to do this.

❑ To close a window, you simply use the window.close() method. To check if a window is closed, you use the closed property of the window object, which returns true if it's closed and false if it's still open.

❑ For a newly opened window object to access the window that opened it, you need to use the window.opener property. Like window.parent for frames, this gives a reference to the window object that opened the new one and enables you to access the window object and its properties for that window.

❑ After a window is opened, you can resize it using resizeTo(x,y) and resizeBy(x,y), and move it using moveTo(x,y) and moveBy(x,y).

You also looked briefly at security restrictions for windows and frames that are not of the same origin. By "not of the same origin," you're referring to a situation in which the document in one frame is hosted on one server and the document in the other is hosted on a different server. In this situation, very severe restrictions apply, which limit the extent of scripting between frames or windows.

In the next chapter you look at advanced string manipulation and how you can use it to add different types of questions to your trivia quiz.

Exercise Questions

Suggested solutions to these questions can be found in Appendix A.

Question 1

In the previous chapter's exercise questions, you created a form that allowed the user to pick a computer system. He could view the details of his system and its total cost by clicking a button that wrote the details to a `textarea`. Change the example so it's a frames-based web page; instead of writing to a text area, the user should write the details to another frame.

Question 2

The first example in this chapter was a page with images of books, in which clicking on a book's image brought up information about that book in a pop-up window. Amend this so that the pop-up window also has a button or link that, when clicked, adds the item to the user's shopping basket. Also, on the main page, give the user some way of opening up a shopping basket window with details of all the items he has purchased so far, and give him a way of deleting items from this basket.

String Manipulation

In Chapter 4 you looked at the String object, which is one of the native objects that JavaScript makes available to you. You saw a number of its properties and methods, including the following:

- ❑ length — The length of the string in characters

- ❑ charAt() and charCodeAt() — The methods for returning the character or character code at a certain position in the string

- ❑ indexOf() and lastIndexOf() — The methods that allow you to search a string for the existence of another string and that return the character position of the string if found

- ❑ substr() and substring() — The methods that return just a portion of a string

- ❑ toUpperCase() and toLowerCase() — The methods that return a string converted to upper- or lowercase

In this chapter you'll look at four new methods of the String object, namely split(), match(), replace(), and search(). The last three, in particular, give you some very powerful text-manipulation functionality. However, to make full use of this functionality, you need to learn about a slightly more complex subject.

The methods split(), match(), replace(), and search() can all make use of *regular expressions*, something JavaScript wraps up in an object called the RegExp object. Regular expressions enable you to define a pattern of characters, which can be used for text searching or replacement. Say, for example, that you have a string in which you want to replace all single quotes enclosing text with double quotes. This may seem easy — just search the string for ' and replace it with " — but what if the string is Bob O'Hara said "Hello"? You would not want to replace the single-quote character in O'Hara. You can perform this text replacement without regular expressions, but it would take more than the two lines of code needed if you do use regular expressions.

Although split(), match(), replace(), and search() are at their most powerful with regular expressions, they can also be used with just plain text. You'll take a look at how they work in this simpler context first, to become familiar with the methods.

Additional String Methods

In this section you will take a look at the `split()`, `replace()`, `search()`, and `match()` methods, and see how they work without regular expressions.

The split() Method

The `String` object's `split()` method splits a single string into an array of substrings. Where the string is split is determined by the separation parameter that you pass to the method. This parameter is simply a character or text string.

For example, to split the string `"A,B,C"` so that you have an array populated with the letters between the commas, the code would be as follows:

```
var myString = "A,B,C";
var myTextArray = myString.split(',');
```

JavaScript creates an array with three elements. In the first element it puts everything from the start of the string `myString` up to the first comma. In the second element it puts everything from after the first comma to before the second comma. Finally, in the third element it puts everything from after the second comma to the end of the string. So, your array `myTextArray` will look like this:

A		B	C

If, however, your string were `"A,B,C,"` JavaScript would split it into four elements, the last element containing everything from the last comma to the end of the string; in other words, the last string would be an empty string.

A		B	C

This is something that can catch you off guard if you're not aware of it.

Try It Out   **Reversing the Order of Text**

Let's create a short example using the `split()` method, in which you reverse the lines written in a `<textarea>` element.

```
<!DOCTYPE HTML PUBLIC "-//W3C//DTD HTML 4.01 Transitional//EN"
"http://www.w3.org/TR/html4/loose.dtd">
<html>
<head>
<meta http-equiv="Content-Type" content="text/html; charset=iso-8859-1">
<title>Example 1</title>
<script language="JavaScript" type="text/JavaScript">
function splitAndReverseText(textAreaControl)
{

    var textToSplit = textAreaControl.value;
    var textArray = textToSplit.split('\n');
    var numberOfParts = 0;
```

```
        numberOfParts = textArray.length;
        var reversedString = "";
        var indexCount;
        for (indexCount = numberOfParts - 1; indexCount >= 0; indexCount--)
        {
            reversedString = reversedString + textArray[indexCount];
            if (indexCount > 0)
            {
                reversedString = reversedString + "\n";
            }
        }

        textAreaControl.value = reversedString;
}
</script>
</head>
<body>
<form name=form1>
<textarea rows="20" cols="40" name="textarea1" wrap-"soft">Line 1
Line 2
Line 3
Line 4</textarea>
<br>
<input type="button" value="Reverse Line Order" name="buttonSplit"
    onclick="splitAndReverseText(document.form1.textarea1)">
</form>
</body>
</html>
```

Save this as ch8_examp1.htm and load it into your browser. You should see the screen shown in Figure 8-1.

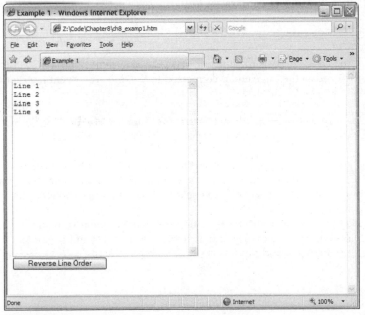

Figure 8-1

293

Clicking the Reverse Line Order button reverses the order of the lines, as shown in Figure 8-2.

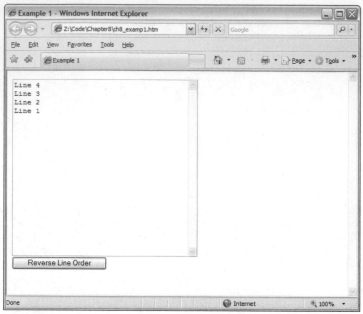

Figure 8-2

Try changing the lines within the text area to test it further.

> *Although this example works on Internet Explorer as it is, an extra line gets inserted. If this troubles you, you can fix it by replacing each instance of* \n *with* \r\n *for Internet Explorer.*

How It Works

The key to how this code works is the function `splitAndReverseText()`. This function is defined in the script block in the head of the page and is connected to the `onclick` event handler of the button further down the page.

```
<input type="button" value="Reverse Line Order" name=buttonSplit
    onclick="splitAndReverseText(document.form1.textarea1)">
```

As you can see, you pass a reference of the text area that you want to reverse as a parameter to the function. By doing it this way, rather than just using a reference to the element itself inside the function, you make the function more generic, so you can use it with any `textarea` element.

Now, on with the function. You start by assigning the value of the text inside the `textarea` element to the `textToSplit` variable. You then split that string into an array of lines of text using the `split()` method of the `String` object and put the resulting array inside the `textArray` variable.

```
function splitAndReverseText(textAreaControl)
{
   var textToSplit = textAreaControl.value;
   var textArray = textToSplit.split('\n');
```

So what do you use as the separator to pass as a parameter for the split() method? Recall from Chapter 2 that the escape character \n is used for a new line. Another point to add to the confusion is that Internet Explorer seems to need \r\n rather than \n.

You next define and initialize three more variables.

```
   var numberOfParts = 0;
   numberOfParts = textArray.length;
   var reversedString = "";
   var indexCount;
```

Now that you have your array of strings, you next want to reverse them. You do this by building up a new string, adding each string from the array, starting with the last and working toward the first. You do this in the for loop, where instead of starting at 0 and working up as you usually do, you start at a number greater than 0 and decrement until you reach 0, at which point you stop looping.

```
   for (indexCount = numberOfParts - 1; indexCount >= 0; indexCount--)
   {
      reversedString = reversedString + textArray[indexCount];
      if (indexCount > 0)
      {
         reversedString = reversedString + "\n";
      }
   }
```

When you split the string, all your line formatting is removed. So in the if statement you add a linefeed (\n) onto the end of each string, except for the last string; that is, when the indexCount variable is 0.

Finally you assign the text in the textarea element to the new string you've built.

```
   textAreaControl.value = reversedString;
}
```

After you've looked at regular expressions, you'll revisit the split() method.

The replace() Method

The replace() method searches a string for occurrences of a substring. Where it finds a match for this substring, it replaces the substring with a third string that you specify.

Let's look at an example. Say you have a string with the word May in it, as shown in the following:

```
   var myString = "The event will be in May, the 21st of June";
```

Now, say you want to replace May with June. You can use the replace() method like so:

```
myCleanedUpString = myString.replace("May","June");
```

The value of myString will not be changed. Instead, the replace() method returns the value of myString but with May replaced with June. You assign this returned string to the variable myCleanedUpString, which will contain the corrected text.

```
"The event will be in June, the 21st of June"
```

The search() Method

The search() method enables you to search a string for a particular piece of text. If the text is found, the character position at which it was found is returned; otherwise -1 is returned. The method takes only one parameter, namely the text you want to search for.

When used with plain text, the search() method provides no real benefit over methods like indexOf(), which you've already seen. However, you'll see later that it's when you use regular expressions that the power of this method becomes apparent.

In the following example, you want to find out if the word Java is contained within the string called myString.

```
var myString = "Beginning JavaScript, Beginning Java, Professional JavaScript";
alert(myString.search("Java"));
```

The alert box that occurs will show the value 10, which is the character position of the J in the first occurrence of Java, as part of the word JavaScript.

The match() Method

The match() method is very similar to the search() method, except that instead of returning the position at which a match was found, it returns an array. Each element of the array contains the text of each match that is found.

Although you can use plain text with the match() method, it would be completely pointless to do so. For example, take a look at the following:

```
var myString = "1997, 1998, 1999, 2000, 2000, 2001, 2002";
myMatchArray = myString.match("2000");
alert(myMatchArray.length);
```

This code results in myMatchArray holding an element containing the value 2000. Given that you already know your search string is 2000, you can see it's been a pretty pointless exercise.

However, the match() method makes a lot more sense when we use it with regular expressions. Then you might search for all years in the twenty-first century — that is, those beginning with 2. In this case, your array would contain the values 2000, 2000, 2001, and 2002, which is much more useful information!

Regular Expressions

Before you look at the `split()`, `match()`, `search()`, and `replace()` methods of the `String` object again, you need to look at regular expressions and the `RegExp` object. Regular expressions provide a means of defining a pattern of characters, which you can then use to split, search for, or replace characters in a string when they fit the defined pattern.

JavaScript's regular expression syntax borrows heavily from the regular expression syntax of Perl, another scripting language. The latest versions of languages, such as VBScript, have also incorporated regular expressions, as do lots of applications, such as Microsoft Word, in which the Find facility allows regular expressions to be used. The same is true for Dreamweaver. You'll find your regular expression knowledge will prove useful even outside JavaScript.

Regular expressions in JavaScript are used through the `RegExp` object, which is a native JavaScript object, as are `String`, `Array`, and so on. There are two ways of creating a new `RegExp` object. The easier is with a regular expression literal, such as the following:

```
var myRegExp = /\b'|'\b/;
```

The forward slashes (`/`) mark the start and end of the regular expression. This is a special syntax that tells JavaScript that the code is a regular expression, much as quote marks define a string's start and end. Don't worry about the actual expression's syntax yet (the `\b'|'\b`) — that will be explained in detail shortly.

Alternatively, you could use the `RegExp` object's constructor function `RegExp()` and type the following:

```
var myRegExp = new RegExp("\\b'|'\\b");
```

Either way of specifying a regular expression is fine, though the former method is a shorter, more efficient one for JavaScript to use, and therefore generally preferred. For much of the remainder of the chapter, you'll use the first method. The main reason for using the second method is that it allows the regular expression to be determined at runtime (as the code is executing and not when you are writing the code). This is useful if, for example, you want to base the regular expression on user input.

Once you get familiar with regular expressions, you will come back to the second way of defining them, using the `RegExp()` constructor. As you can see, the syntax of regular expressions is slightly different with the second method, so we'll return to this subject later.

Although you'll be concentrating on the use of the `RegExp` object as a parameter for the `String` object's `split()`, `replace()`, `match()`, and `search()` methods, the `RegExp` object does have its own methods and properties. For example, the `test()` method enables you to test to see if the string passed to it as a parameter contains a pattern matching the one defined in the `RegExp` object. You'll see the `test()` method in use in an example shortly.

Simple Regular Expressions

Defining patterns of characters using regular expression syntax can get fairly complex. In this section you'll explore just the basics of regular expression patterns. The best way to do this is through examples.

Let's start by looking at an example in which you want to do a simple text replacement using the `replace()` method and a regular expression. Imagine you have the following string:

```
var myString = "Paul, Paula, Pauline, paul, Paul";
```

and you want to replace any occurrence of the name "Paul" with "Ringo."

Well, the pattern of text you need to look for is simply `Paul`. Representing this as a regular expression, you just have this:

```
var myRegExp = /Paul/;
```

As you saw earlier, the forward-slash characters mark the start and end of the regular expression. Now let's use this expression with the `replace()` method.

```
myString = myString.replace(myRegExp, "Ringo");
```

You can see that the `replace()` method takes two parameters: the `RegExp` object that defines the pattern to be searched and replaced, and the replacement text.

If you put this all together in an example, you have the following:

```
<!DOCTYPE HTML PUBLIC "-//W3C//DTD HTML 4.01 Transitional//EN"
"http://www.w3.org/TR/html4/loose.dtd">
<html>
<body>
<script language="JavaScript" type="text/JavaScript">
  var myString = "Paul, Paula, Pauline, paul, Paul";
  var myRegExp = /Paul/;
  myString = myString.replace(myRegExp, "Ringo");
  alert(myString);
</script>
</body>
</html>
```

If you load this code into a browser, you will see the screen shown in Figure 8-3.

Figure 8-3

You can see that this has replaced the first occurrence of `Paul` in your string. But what if you wanted all the occurrences of `Paul` in the string to be replaced? The two at the far end of the string are still there, so what happened?

Well, by default the RegExp object looks only for the first matching pattern, in this case the first Paul, and then stops. This is a common and important behavior for RegExp objects. Regular expressions tend to start at one end of a string and look through the characters until the first complete match is found, then stop.

What you want is a global match, which is a search for all possible matches to be made and replaced. To help you out, the RegExp object has three attributes you can define. You can see these listed in the following table.

Attribute Character	Description
g	Global match. This looks for all matches of the pattern rather than stopping after the first match is found.
i	Pattern is case-insensitive. For example, Paul and paul are considered the same pattern of characters.
m	Multi-line flag. Only available in IE 5.5+ and NN 6+, this specifies that the special characters ^ and $ can match the beginning and the end of lines as well as the beginning and end of the string. You'll learn about these characters later in the chapter.

If you change our RegExp object in the code to the following, a global case-insensitive match will be made.

```
var myRegExp = /Paul/gi;
```

Running the code now produces the result shown in Figure 8-4.

Figure 8-4

This looks as if it has all gone horribly wrong. The regular expression has matched the Paul substrings at the start and the end of the string, and the penultimate paul, just as you wanted. However, the Paul substrings inside Pauline and Paula have also been replaced.

The RegExp object has done its job correctly. You asked for all patterns of the characters Paul to be replaced and that's what you got. What you actually meant was for all occurrences of Paul, when it's a single word and not part of another word, such as Paula, to be replaced. The key to making regular expressions work is to define exactly the pattern of characters you mean, so that only that pattern can match and no other. So let's do that.

1. You want paul or Paul to be replaced.

2. You don't want it replaced when it's actually part of another word, as in Pauline.

How do you specify this second condition? How do you know when the word is joined to other characters, rather than just joined to spaces or punctuation or the start or end of the string?

To see how you can achieve the desired result with regular expressions, you need to enlist the help of regular expression special characters. You'll look at these in the next section, by the end of which you should be able to solve the problem.

Regular Expressions: Special Characters

You will be looking at three types of special characters in this section.

Text, Numbers, and Punctuation

The first group of special characters you'll look at contains the character class's special characters. *Character class* means digits, letters, and whitespace characters. The special characters are displayed in the following table.

Character Class	Characters It Matches	Example
\d	Any digit from 0 to 9	\d\d matches 72, but not aa or 7a
\D	Any character that is not a digit	\D\D\D matches abc, but not 123 or 8ef
\w	Any word character; that is, A–Z, a–z, 0–9, and the underscore character (_)	\w\w\w\w matches Ab_2, but not £$%* or Ab_@
\W	Any non-word character	\W matches @, but not a
\s	Any whitespace character, including tab, newline, carriage return, formfeed, and vertical tab	\s matches *tab*
\S	Any non-whitespace character	\S matches A, but not the tab character
.	Any single character other than the newline character (\n)	. matches a or 4 or @
[. . .]	Any one of the characters between the brackets	[abc] will match a or b or c, but nothing else [a-z] will match any character in the range a to z
[^ . . .]	Any one character, but not one of those inside the brackets	[^abc] will match any character except a or b or c [^a-z] will match any character that is not in the range a to z

Note that uppercase and lowercase characters mean very different things, so you need to be extra careful with case when using regular expressions.

Let's look at an example. To match a telephone number in the format 1-800-888-5474, the regular expression would be as follows:

```
\d-\d\d\d-\d\d\d-\d\d\d\d
```

You can see that there's a lot of repetition of characters here, which makes the expression quite unwieldy. To make this simpler, regular expressions have a way of defining repetition. You'll see this a little later in the chapter, but first let's look at another example.

Try It Out   ## Checking a Passphrase for Alphanumeric Characters

You'll use what you've learned so far about regular expressions in a full example in which you check that a passphrase contains only letters and numbers — that is, alphanumeric characters, and not punctuation or symbols like @, %, and so on.

```
<!DOCTYPE HTML PUBLIC "-//W3C//DTD HTML 4.01 Transitional//EN"
"http://www.w3.org/TR/html4/loose.dtd">
<html>
<head>
<title>Example</title>
<meta http-equiv="Content-Type" content="text/html; charset=iso-8859-1">
</head>
<body>
<script language="JavaScript" type="text/JavaScript">
function regExpIs_valid(text)
{
   var myRegExp = /[^a-z\d ]/i;
   return !(myRegExp.test(text));
}
function butCheckValid_onclick()
{
   if (regExpIs_valid(document.form1.txtPhrase.value) == true)
   {
      alert("Your passphrase contains only valid characters");
   }
   else
   {
      alert("Your passphrase contains one or more invalid characters");
   }
}
</script>
<form name=form1>
Enter your passphrase:
<br>
<input type="text" name=txtPhrase>
<br>
<input type="button" value="Check Character Validity" name=butCheckValid
   onclick="butCheckValid_onclick()">
</form>
</body>
</html>
```

Save the page as ch8_examp2.htm, and then load it into your browser. Type just letters, numbers, and spaces into the text box; click the Check Character Validity button; and you'll be told that the phrase contains valid characters. Try putting punctuation or special characters like @, ^, $, and so on into the text box, and you'll be informed that your passphrase is invalid.

How It Works

Let's start by looking at the regExpIs_valid() function defined at the top of the script block in the head of the page. That does the validity checking of our passphrase using regular expressions.

```
function regExpIs_valid(text)
{
   var myRegExp = /[^a-z\d ]/i;
   return !(myRegExp.test(text));
}
```

The function takes just one parameter: the text you want to check for validity. You then declare a variable, myRegExp, and set it to a new regular expression, which implicitly creates a new RegExp object.

The regular expression itself is fairly simple, but first let's think about what pattern you are looking for. What you want to find out is whether your passphrase string contains any characters that are not letters between A and Z or between a and z, numbers between 0 and 9, or spaces. Let's see how this translates into a regular expression.

First you use square brackets with the ^ symbol.

```
[^]
```

This means you want to match any character that is not one of the characters specified inside the square brackets. Next you add a-z, which specifies any character in the range a through z.

```
[^a-z]
```

So far your regular expression matches any character that is not between a and z. Note that, because you added the i to the end of the expression definition, you've made the pattern case-insensitive. So our regular expression actually matches any character not between A and Z or a and z.

Next you add \d to indicate any digit character, or any character between 0 and 9.

```
[^a-z\d]
```

So your expression matches any character that is not between a and z, A and Z, or 0 and 9. Finally, you decide that a space is valid, so you add that inside the square brackets.

```
[^a-z\d ]
```

Putting this all together, you have a regular expression that will match any character that is not a letter, a digit, or a space.

On the second and final line of the function you use the RegExp object's test() method to return a value.

```
return !(myRegExp.test(text));
```

The test() method of the RegExp object checks the string passed as its parameter to see if the characters specified by the regular expression syntax match anything inside the string. If they do, true is returned; if not, false is returned. Your regular expression will match the first invalid character found, so if you get a result of true, you have an invalid passphrase. However, it's a bit illogical for an is_valid function to return true when it's invalid, so you reverse the result returned by adding the NOT operator (!).

Previously you saw the two-line validity checker function using regular expressions. Just to show how much more coding is required to do the same thing without regular expressions, here is a second function that does the same thing as regExpIs_valid() but without regular expressions.

```
function is_valid(text)
{
    var isValid = true;
    var validChars = "abcdefghijklmnopqrstuvwxyz1234567890 ";
    var charIndex;
    for (charIndex = 0; charIndex < text.length;charIndex++)
    {
        if ( validChars.indexOf(text.charAt(charIndex).toLowerCase()) < 0)
        {
            isValid = false;
            break;
        }
    }
    return isValid;
}
```

This is probably as small as the non-regular expression version can be, and yet it's still 15 lines long. That's six times the amount of code for the regular expression version.

The principle of this function is similar to that of the regular expression version. You have a variable, validChars, which contains all the characters you consider to be valid. You then use the charAt() method in a for loop to get each character in the passphrase string and check whether it exists in your validChars string. If it doesn't, you know you have an invalid character.

In this example, the non-regular expression version of the function is 15 lines, but with a more complex problem you could find it takes 20 or 30 lines to do the same thing a regular expression can do in just a few.

Back to your actual code: The other function defined in the head of the page is butCheckValid_onclick(). As the name suggests, this is called when the butCheckValid button defined in the body of the page is clicked.

This function calls your regExpis_valid() function in an if statement to check whether the passphrase entered by the user in the txtPhrase text box is valid. If it is, an alert box is used to inform the user.

```
function butCheckValid_onclick()
{
    if (regExpIs_valid(document.form1.txtPhrase.value) == true)
    {
        alert("Your passphrase contains valid characters");
    }
```

If it isn't, another alert box is used to let the user know that his text was invalid.

```
else
{
    alert("Your passphrase contains one or more invalid characters");
}
}
```

Repetition Characters

Regular expressions include something called repetition characters, which are a means of specifying how many of the last item or character you want to match. This proves very useful, for example, if you want to specify a phone number that repeats a character a specific number of times. The following table lists some of the most common repetition characters and what they do.

Special Character	Meaning	Example
{n}	Match n of the previous item	x{2} matches xx
{n,}	Match n or more of the previous item	x{2,} matches xx, xxx, xxxx, xxxxx, and so on
{n,m}	Match at least n and at most m of the previous item	x{2,4} matches xx, xxx, and xxxx
?	Match the previous item zero or one time	x? matches nothing or x
+	Match the previous item one or more times	x+ matches x, xx, xxx, xxxx, xxxxx, and so on
*	Match the previous item zero or more times	x* matches nothing, or x, xx, xxx, xxxx, and so on

You saw earlier that to match a telephone number in the format 1-800-888-5474, the regular expression would be \d-\d\d\d-\d\d\d-\d\d\d\d. Let's see how this would be simplified with the use of the repetition characters.

The pattern you're looking for starts with one digit followed by a dash, so you need the following:

```
\d-
```

Next are three digits followed by a dash. This time you can use the repetition special characters — \d{3} will match exactly three \d, which is the any-digit character.

```
\d-\d{3}-
```

Next there are three digits followed by a dash again, so now your regular expression looks like this:

```
\d-\d{3}-\d{3}-
```

Finally, the last part of the expression is four digits, which is \d{4}.

```
\d-\d{3}-\d{3}-\d{4}
```

You'd declare this regular expression like this:

```
var myRegExp = /\d-\d{3}-\d{3}-\d{4}/
```

Remember that the first / and last / tell JavaScript that what is in between those characters is a regular expression. JavaScript creates a RegExp object based on this regular expression.

As another example, what if you have the string Paul Paula Pauline, and you want to replace Paul and Paula with George? To do this, you would need a regular expression that matches both Paul and Paula.

Let's break this down. You know you want the characters Paul, so your regular expression starts as

```
Paul
```

Now you also want to match Paula, but if you make your expression Paula, this will exclude a match on Paul. This is where the special character ? comes in. It enables you to specify that the previous character is optional—it must appear zero (not at all) or one time. So, the solution is

```
Paula?
```

which you'd declare as

```
var myRegExp = /Paula?/
```

Position Characters

The third group of special characters you'll look at are those that enable you to specify either where the match should start or end or what will be on either side of the character pattern. For example, you might want your pattern to exist at the start or end of a string or line, or you might want it to be between two words. The following table lists some of the most common position characters and what they do.

Position Character	Description
^	The pattern must be at the start of the string, or if it's a multi-line string, then at the beginning of a line. For multi-line text (a string that contains carriage returns), you need to set the multi-line flag when defining the regular expression using /myreg ex/m. Note that this is only applicable to IE 5.5 and later and NN 6 and later.
$	The pattern must be at the end of the string, or if it's a multi-line string, then at the end of a line. For multi-line text (a string that contains carriage returns), you need to set the multi-line flag when defining the regular expression using /myreg ex/m. Note that this is only applicable to IE 5.5 and later and NN 6 and later.
\b	This matches a word boundary, which is essentially the point between a word character and a non-word character.
\B	This matches a position that's not a word boundary.

For example, if you wanted to make sure your pattern was at the start of a line, you would type the following:

```
^myPattern
```

This would match an occurrence of `myPattern` if it was at the beginning of a line.

To match the same pattern, but at the end of a line, you would type the following:

```
myPattern$
```

The word-boundary special characters \b and \B can cause confusion, because they do not match characters but the positions between characters.

Imagine you had the string `"Hello world!, let's look at boundaries said 007."` defined in the code as follows:

```
var myString = "Hello world!, let's look at boundaries said 007.";
```

To make the word boundaries (that is, the boundaries between the words) of this string stand out, let's convert them to the | character.

```
var myRegExp = /\b/g;
myString = myString.replace(myRegExp, "|");
alert(myString);
```

You've replaced all the word boundaries, \b, with a |, and your message box looks like the one in Figure 8-5.

Figure 8-5

You can see that the position between any word character (letters, numbers, or the underscore character) and any non-word character is a word boundary. You'll also notice that the boundary between the start or end of the string and a word character is considered to be a word boundary. The end of this string is a full stop. So the boundary between the full stop and the end of the string is a non-word boundary, and therefore no | has been inserted.

If you change the regular expression in the example, so that it replaces non-word boundaries as follows:

```
var myRegExp = /\B/g;
```

you get the result shown in Figure 8-6.

Figure 8-6

Now the position between a letter, number, or underscore and another letter, number, or underscore is considered a non-word boundary and is replaced by an | in our example. However, what is slightly confusing is that the boundary between two non-word characters, such as an exclamation mark and a comma, is also considered a non-word boundary. If you think about it, it actually does make sense, but it's easy to forget when creating regular expressions.

You'll remember this example from when we started looking at regular expressions:

```
<html>
<body>
<script language="JavaScript" type="text/JavaScript">
  var myString = "Paul, Paula, Pauline, paul, Paul";
  var myRegExp = /Paul/gi;
  myString = myString.replace(myRegExp, "Ringo");
  alert(myString);
</script>
</body>
</html>
```

We used this code to convert all instances of `Paul` or `paul` to `Ringo`.

However, we found that this code actually converts all instances of `Paul` to `Ringo`, even when the word `Paul` is inside another word.

One way to solve this problem would be to replace the string `Paul` only where it is followed by a non-word character. The special character for non-word characters is `\W`, so you need to alter our regular expression to the following:

```
var myRegExp = /Paul\W/gi;
```

This gives the result shown in Figure 8-7.

Figure 8-7

It's getting better, but it's still not what you want. Notice that the commas after the second and third `Paul` substrings have also been replaced because they matched the `\W` character. Also, you're still not replacing `Paul` at the very end of the string. That's because there is no character after the letter `l` in the last `Paul`. What is after the `l` in the last `Paul`? Nothing, just the boundary between a word character and a non-word character, and therein lies the answer. What you want as your regular expression is `Paul` followed by a word boundary. Let's alter the regular expression to cope with that by entering the following:

```
var myRegExp = /Paul\b/gi;
```

Now you get the result you want, as shown in Figure 8-8.

Figure 8-8

At last you've got it right, and this example is finished.

Covering All Eventualities

Perhaps the trickiest thing about a regular expression is making sure it covers all eventualities. In the previous example your regular expression works with the string as defined, but does it work with the following?

```
var myString = "Paul, Paula, Pauline, paul, Paul, JeanPaul";
```

Here the `Paul` substring in `JeanPaul` will be changed to `Ringo`. You really only want to convert the substring `Paul` where it is on its own, with a word boundary on either side. If you change your regular expression code to

```
var myRegExp = /\bPaul\b/gi;
```

you have your final answer and can be sure only `Paul` or `paul` will ever be matched.

Grouping Regular Expressions

The final topic under regular expressions, before we look at examples using the `match()`, `replace()`, and `search()` methods, is how you can group expressions. In fact it's quite easy. If you want a number of expressions to be treated as a single group, you just enclose them in parentheses, for example `/(\d\d)/`. Parentheses in regular expressions are special characters that group together character patterns and are not themselves part of the characters to be matched.

The question is, Why would you want to do this? Well, by grouping characters into patterns, you can use the special repetition characters to apply to the whole group of characters, rather than just one.

Let's take the following string defined in `myString` as an example:

```
var myString = "JavaScript, VBScript and Perl";
```

How could you match both `JavaScript` and `VBScript` using the same regular expression? The only thing they have in common is that they are whole words and they both end in `Script`. Well, an easy way would be to use parentheses to group the patterns `Java` and `VB`. Then you can use the `?` special character to apply to each of these groups of characters to make the pattern match any word having zero or one instances of the characters `Java` or `VB`, and ending in `Script`.

```
var myRegExp = /\b(VB)?(Java)?Script\b/gi;
```

Breaking this expression down, you can see the pattern it requires is as follows:

1. A word boundary: `\b`
2. Zero or one instance of VB: `(VB)?`
3. Zero or one instance of Java: `(Java)?`
4. The characters `Script`: `Script`
5. A word boundary: `\b`

Putting these together, you get this:

```
var myString = "JavaScript, VBScript and Perl";
var myRegExp = /\b(VB)?(Java)?Script\b/gi;
myString = myString.replace(myRegExp, "xxxx");
alert(myString);
```

The output of this code is shown in Figure 8-9

Figure 8-9

If you look back at the special repetition characters table, you'll see that they apply to the item preceding them. This can be a character, or, where they have been grouped by means of parentheses, the previous group of characters.

However, there is a potential problem with the regular expression you just defined. As well as matching VBScript and JavaScript, it also matches VBJavaScript. This is clearly not exactly what you meant.

To get around this you need to make use of both grouping and the special character `|`, which is the alternation character. It has an or-like meaning, similar to `||` in `if` statements, and will match the characters on either side of itself.

Let's think about the problem again. You want the pattern to match VBScript or JavaScript. Clearly they have the Script part in common. So what you want is a new word starting with Java or starting with VB; either way it must end in Script.

First, you know that the word must start with a word boundary.

```
\b
```

Next you know that you want either VB or Java to be at the start of the word. You've just seen that in regular expressions | provides the "or" you need, so in regular expression syntax you want the following:

```
\b(VB|Java)
```

This matches the pattern VB or Java. Now you can just add the Script part.

```
\b(VB|Java)Script\b
```

Your final code looks like this:

```
var myString = "JavaScript, VBScript and Perl";
var myRegExp = /\b(VB|Java)Script\b/gi;
myString = myString.replace(myRegExp, "xxxx");
alert(myString);
```

Reusing Groups of Characters

You can reuse the pattern specified by a group of characters later on in our regular expression. To refer to a previous group of characters, you just type \ and a number indicating the order of the group. For example, the first group can be referred to as \1, the second as \2, and so on.

Let's look at an example. Say you have a list of numbers in a string, with each number separated by a comma. For whatever reason, you are not allowed to have two instances of the same number in a row, so although

```
009,007,001,002,004,003
```

would be okay, the following:

```
007,007,001,002,002,003
```

would not be valid, because you have 007 and 002 repeated after themselves.

How can you find instances of repeated digits and replace them with the word ERROR? You need to use the ability to refer to groups in regular expressions.

First let's define the string as follows:

```
var myString  = "007,007,001,002,002,003,002,004";
```

Now you know you need to search for a series of one or more number characters. In regular expressions the \d specifies any digit character, and + means one or more of the previous character. So far, that gives you this regular expression:

```
\d+
```

You want to match a series of digits followed by a comma, so you just add the comma.

```
\d+,
```

This will match any series of digits followed by a comma, but how do you search for any series of digits followed by a comma, then followed again by the same series of digits? As the digits could be any digits, you can't add them directly into our expression like so:

```
\d+,007
```

This would not work with the 002 repeat. What you need to do is put the first series of digits in a group; then you can specify that you want to match that group of digits again. This can be done with \1, which says, "Match the characters found in the first group defined using parentheses." Put all this together, and you have the following:

```
(\d+),\1
```

This defines a group whose pattern of characters is one or more digit characters. This group must be followed by a comma and then by the same pattern of characters as in the first group. Put this into some JavaScript, and you have the following:

```
var myString  = "007,007,001,002,002,003,002,004";
var myRegExp = /(\d+),\1/g;
myString = myString.replace(myRegExp, "ERROR");
alert(myString);
```

The alert box will show this message:

```
ERROR,1,ERROR,003,002,004
```

That completes your brief look at regular expression syntax. Because regular expressions can get a little complex, it's often a good idea to start simple and build them up slowly, as we have done here. In fact, most regular expressions are just too hard to get right in one step — at least for us mere mortals without a brain the size of a planet.

If it's still looking a bit strange and confusing, don't panic. In the next sections, you'll be looking at the String object's split(), replace(), search(), and match() methods with plenty more examples of regular expression syntax.

The String Object — split(), replace(), search(), and match() Methods

The main functions making use of regular expressions are the String object's split(), replace(), search(), and match() methods. You've already seen their syntax, so you'll concentrate on their use with regular expressions and at the same time learn more about regular expression syntax and usage.

The split() Method

You've seen that the split() method enables us to split a string into various pieces, with the split being made at the character or characters specified as a parameter. The result of this method is an array with each element containing one of the split pieces. For example, the following string:

```
var myListString = "apple, banana, peach, orange"
```

could be split into an array in which each element contains a different fruit, like this:

```
var myFruitArray = myListString.split(", ");
```

How about if your string is this instead?

```
var myListString = "apple, 0.99, banana, 0.50, peach, 0.25, orange, 0.75";
```

The string could, for example, contain both the names and prices of the fruit. How could you split the string, but retrieve only the names of the fruit and not the prices? You could do it without regular expressions, but it would take many lines of code. With regular expressions you can use the same code, and just amend the split() method's parameter.

Try It Out   Splitting the Fruit String

Let's create an example that solves the problem just described — it must split your string, but include only the fruit names, not the prices.

```
<!DOCTYPE HTML PUBLIC "-//W3C//DTD HTML 4.01 Transitional//EN"
"http://www.w3.org/TR/html4/loose.dtd">
<html>
<body>
<script language="JavaScript" type="text/JavaScript">
var myListString = "apple, 0.99, banana, 0.50, peach, 0.25, orange, 0.75";
var theRegExp = /[^a-z]+/i;
var myFruitArray = myListString.split(theRegExp);
document.write(myFruitArray.join("<br>"));
</script>
</body>
</html>
```

Save the file as ch8_examp3.htm and load it in your browser. You should see the four fruits from your string written out to the page, with each fruit on a separate line.

How It Works

Within the script block, first you have your string with fruit names and prices.

```
var myListString = "apple, 0.99, banana, 0.50, peach, 0.25, orange, 0.75";
```

How do you split it in such a way that only the fruit names are included? Your first thought might be to use the comma as the `split()` method's parameter, but of course that means you end up with the prices. What you have to ask is, "What is it that's between the items I want?" Or in other words, what is between the fruit names that you can use to define your split? The answer is that various characters are between the names of the fruit, such as a comma, a space, numbers, a full stop, more numbers, and finally another comma. What is it that these things have in common and makes them different from the fruit names that you want? What they have in common is that none of them are letters from a through z. If you say "Split the string at the point where there is a group of characters that are not between a and z," then you get the result you want. Now you know what you need to create your regular expression.

You know that what you want is not the letters a through z, so you start with this:

```
[^a-z]
```

The ^ says "Match any character that does not match those specified inside the square brackets." In this case you've specified a range of characters not to be matched—all the characters between a and z. As specified, this expression will match only one character, whereas you want to split wherever there is a single group of one or more characters that are not between a and z. To do this you need to add the + special repetition character, which says "Match one or more of the preceding character or group specified."

```
[^a-z]+
```

The final result is this:

```
var theRegExp = /[^a-z]+/i
```

The / and / characters mark the start and end of the regular expression whose `RegExp` object is stored as a reference in the variable `theRegExp`. You add the `i` on the end to make the match case-insensitive.

Don't panic if creating regular expressions seems like a frustrating and less-than-obvious process. At first, it takes a lot of trial and error to get it right, but as you get more experienced, you'll find creating them becomes much easier and will enable you to do things that without regular expressions would be either very awkward or virtually impossible.

In the next line of script you pass the `RegExp` object to the `split()` method, which uses it to decide where to split the string.

```
var myFruitArray = myListString.split(theRegExp);
```

After the split, the variable `myFruitArray` will contain an `Array` with each element containing the fruit name, as shown here:

Array Element Index	0	1	2	3
Element value	apple	banana	peach	orange

You then join the string together again using the `Array` object's `join()` methods, which you saw in Chapter 4.

```
document.write(myFruitArray.join("<BR>"))
```

The replace() Method

You've already looked at the syntax and usage of the `replace()` method. However, something unique to the `replace()` method is its ability to replace text based on the groups matched in the regular expression. You do this using the $ sign and the group's number. Each group in a regular expression is given a number from 1 to 99; any groups greater than 99 are not accessible. Note that in earlier browsers, groups could only go from 1 to 9 (for example, in IE 5 or earlier or Netscape 4 and earlier). To refer to a group, you write $ followed by the group's position. For example, if you had the following:

```
var myRegExp = /(\d)(\W)/g;
```

then $1 refers to the group (\d), and $2 refers to the group (\W). You've also set the global flag g to ensure that all matching patterns are replaced — not just the first one.

You can see this more clearly in the next example. Say you have the following string:

```
var myString = "1999, 2000, 2001";
```

If you wanted to change this to `"the year 1999, the year 2000, the year 2001"`, how could you do it with regular expressions?

First you need to work out the pattern as a regular expression, in this case four digits.

```
var myRegExp = /\d{4}/g;
```

But given that the year is different every time, how can you substitute the year value into the replaced string?

Well, you change your regular expression so that it's inside a group, as follows:

```
var myRegExp = /(\d{4})/g;
```

Now you can use the group, which has group number 1, inside the replacement string like this:

```
myString = myString.replace(myRegExp, "the year $1");
```

The variable `myString` now contains the required string `"the year 1999, the year 2000, the year 2001"`.

Let's look at another example in which you want to convert single quotes in text to double quotes. Your test string is this:

```
'Hello World' said Mr. O'Connerly.
He then said 'My Name is O'Connerly, yes that's right, O'Connerly'.
```

One problem that the test string makes clear is that you want to replace the single-quote mark with a double only where it is used in pairs around speech, not when it is acting as an apostrophe, such as in the word that's, or when it's part of someone's name, such as in O'Connerly.

Let's start by defining the regular expression. First you know that it must include a single quote, as shown in the following code:

```
var myRegExp = /'/;
```

However, as it is this would replace every single quote, which is not what you want.

Looking at the text, you should also notice that quotes are always at the start or end of a word — that is, at a boundary. On first glance it might be easy to assume that it would be a word boundary. However, don't forget that the ' is a non-word character, so the boundary will be between it and another non-word character, such as a space. So the boundary will be a non-word boundary, or in other words, \B.

Therefore, the character pattern you are looking for is either a non-word boundary followed by a single quote, or a single quote followed by a non-word boundary. The key is the "or," for which you use | in regular expressions. This leaves your regular expression as the following:

```
var myRegExp = /\B'|'\B/g;
```

This will match the pattern on the left of the | or the character pattern on the right. You want to replace all the single quotes with double quotes, so the g has been added at the end, indicating that a global match should take place.

Try It Out   Replacing Single Quotes with Double Quotes

Let's look at an example using the regular expression just defined.

```
<!DOCTYPE HTML PUBLIC "-//W3C//DTD HTML 4.01 Transitional//EN"
"http://www.w3.org/TR/html4/loose.dtd">
<html>
<head>
<title>example</title>
<meta http-equiv="Content-Type" content="text/html; charset=iso-8859-1">
<script language="JavaScript" type="text/JavaScript">
function replaceQuote(textAreaControl)
{
   var myText = textAreaControl.value;
   var myRegExp = /\B'|'\B/g;
   myText = myText.replace(myRegExp,'"');
   textAreaControl.value = myText;
}
</script>
</head>
```

```
<body>
<form name="form1">
<textarea rows="20" cols="40" name="textarea1">
'Hello World' said Mr O'Connerly.
He then said 'My Name is O'Connerly, yes that's right, O'Connerly'.
</textarea>
<br>
<input type="button" VALUE="Replace Single Quotes" name="buttonSplit"
    onclick="replaceQuote(document.form1.textarea1)">
</form>
</body>
</html>
```

Save the page as ch8_examp4.htm. Load the page into your browser and you should see what is shown in Figure 8-10.

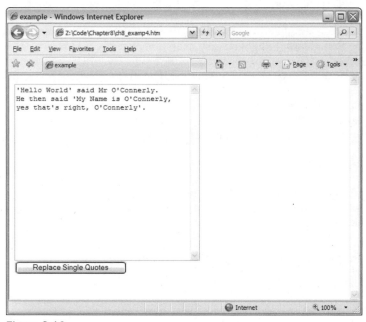

Figure 8-10

Click the Replace Single Quotes button to see the single quotes in the text area replaced as in Figure 8-11.

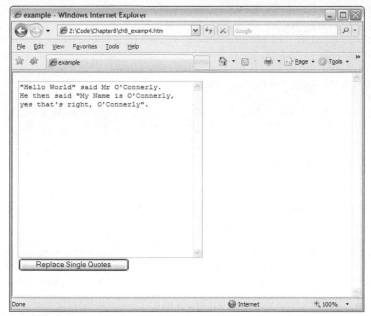

Figure 8-11

Try entering your own text with single quotes into the text area and check the results.

How It Works

You can see that by using regular expressions, you have completed a task in a couple of lines of simple code. Without regular expressions, it would probably take four or five times that amount.

Let's look first at the `replaceQuote()` function in the head of the page where all the action is.

```
function replaceQuote(textAreaControl)
{
    var myText = textAreaControl.value;
    var myRegExp = /\B'|'\B/g;
    myText = myText.replace(myRegExp,'"');
    textAreaControl.value = myText;
}
```

The function's parameter is the `textarea` object defined further down the page — this is the text area in which you want to replace the single quotes. You can see how the `textarea` object was passed in the button's tag definition.

```
<input type="button" value="Replace Single Quotes" name="buttonSplit"
    onclick="replaceQuote(document.form1.textarea1)">
```

In the `onclick` event handler, you call `replaceQuote()` and pass `document.form1.textarea1` as the parameter — that is the `textarea` object.

Returning to the function, you get the value of the `textarea` on the first line and place it in the variable `myText`. Then you define your regular expression (as discussed previously), which matches any non-word boundary followed by a single quote or any single quote followed by a non-word boundary. For example, `'H` will match, as will `H'`, but `O'R` won't because the quote is between two word boundaries. Don't forget that a word boundary is the position between the start or end of a word and a non-word character, such as a space or punctuation mark.

In the function's final two lines, you first use the `replace()` method to do the character pattern search and replace, and finally you set the `textarea` object's value to the changed string.

The search() Method

The `search()` method enables you to search a string for a pattern of characters. If the pattern is found, the character position at which it was found is returned, otherwise `-1` is returned. The method takes only one parameter, the `RegExp` object you have created.

Although for basic searches the `indexOf()` method is fine, if you want more complex searches, such as a search for a pattern of any digits or one in which a word must be in between a certain boundary, then `search()` provides a much more powerful and flexible, but sometimes more complex, approach.

In the following example, you want to find out if the word `Java` is contained within the string. However, you want to look just for `Java` as a whole word, not part of another word such as `JavaScript`.

```
var myString = "Beginning JavaScript, Beginning Java 2, Professional JavaScript";
var myRegExp = /\bJava\b/i;
alert(myString.search(myRegExp));
```

First you have defined your string, and then you've created your regular expression. You want to find the character pattern `Java` when it's on its own between two word boundaries. You've made your search case-insensitive by adding the `i` after the regular expression. Note that with the `search()` method, the `g` for global is not relevant, and its use has no effect.

On the final line you output the position at which the search has located the pattern, in this case `32`.

The match() Method

The `match()` method is very similar to the `search()` method, except that instead of returning the position at which a match was found, it returns an array. Each element of the array contains the text of a match made.

For example, if you had the string

```
var myString = "The years were 1999, 2000 and 2001";
```

and wanted to extract the years from this string, you could do so using the `match()` method. To match each year, you are looking for four digits in between word boundaries. This requirement translates to the following regular expression:

```
var myRegExp = /\b\d{4}\b/g;
```

You want to match all the years so the g has been added to the end for a global search.

To do the match and store the results, you use the match() method and store the Array object it returns in a variable.

```
var resultsArray = myString.match(myRegExp);
```

To prove it has worked, let's use some code to output each item in the array. You've added an if statement to double-check that the results array actually contains an array. If no matches were made, the results array will contain null — doing if (resultsArray) will return true if the variable has a value and not null.

```
if (resultsArray)
{
  var indexCounter;
  for (indexCounter = 0; indexCounter < resultsArray.length; indexCounter++)
  {
    alert(resultsArray[indexCounter]);
  }
}
```

This would result in three alert boxes containing the numbers 1999, 2000, and 2001.

Try It Out   Splitting HTML

In the next example, you want to take a string of HTML and split it into its component parts. For example, you want the HTML <P>Hello</P> to become an array, with the elements having the following contents:

<P>	Hello	</P>

```
<!DOCTYPE HTML PUBLIC "-//W3C//DTD HTML 4.01 Transitional//EN"
"http://www.w3.org/TR/html4/loose.dtd">
<html>
<head>
<title>example</title>
<meta http-equiv="Content-Type" content="text/html; charset=iso-8859-1">
<script language="JavaScript" type="text/JavaScript">
function button1_onclick()
{
    var myString = "<table align=center><tr><td>";
    myString = myString + "Hello World</td></tr></table>";
    myString = myString +"<br><h2>Heading</h2>";
    var myRegExp = /<[^>\r\n]+>|[^<>\r\n]+/g;
    var resultsArray = myString.match(myRegExp);
    document.form1.textarea1.value = "";
    document.form1.textarea1.value = resultsArray.join ("\r\n");
}
</script>
</head>
<body>
```

```
<form name="form1">
    <textarea rows="20" cols="40" name="textarea1"></textarea>
    <input type="button" value="Split HTML" name="button1"
        onclick="return button1_onclick();">
</form>
</body>
</html>
```

Save this file as `ch8_examp5.htm`. When you load the page into your browser and click the Split HTML button, a string of HTML is split, and each tag is placed on a separate line in the text area, as shown in Figure 8-12.

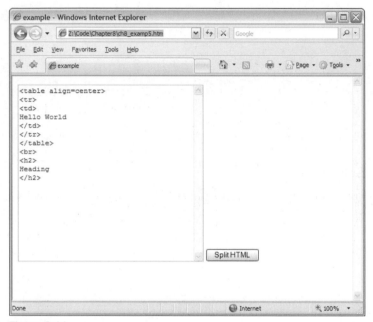

Figure 8-12

How It Works

The function `button1_onclick()` defined at the top of the page fires when the Split HTML button is clicked. At the top, the following lines define the string of HTML that you want to split:

```
function button1_onclick()
{
    var myString = "<table align=center><tr><td>";
    myString = myString + "Hello World</td></tr></table>";
    myString = myString +"<br><h2>Heading</h2>";
```

Next you create your `RegExp` object and initialize it to your regular expression.

```
var myRegExp = /<[^>]\r\n]+>|[^<>]\r\n]+/g;
```

Let's break it down to see what pattern you're trying to match. First note that the pattern is broken up by an alternation symbol: |. This means that you want the pattern on the left or the right of this symbol. You'll look at these patterns separately. On the left you have the following:

❑   The pattern must start with a <.

❑   In [^>\r\n]+, you specify that you want one or more of any character except the > or a \r (carriage return) or a \n (linefeed).

❑   > specifies that the pattern must end with a >.

On the right, you have only the following:

❑   [^<>\r\n]+ specifies that the pattern is one or more of any character, so long as that character is not a <, >, \r, or \n. This will match plain text.

After the regular expression definition you have a g, which specifies that this is a global match.

So the <[^>\r\n]+> regular expression will match any start or close tags, such as <p> or </p>. The alternative pattern is [^<>\r\n]+, which will match any character pattern that is not an opening or closing tag.

In the following line you assign the resultsArray variable to the Array object returned by the match() method:

```
var resultsArray = myString.match(myRegExp);
```

The remainder of the code deals with populating the text area with the split HTML. You use the Array object's join() method to join all the array's elements into one string with each element separated by a \r\n character, so that each tag or piece of text goes on a separate line, as shown in the following:

```
document.form1.textarea1.value = "";
document.form1.textarea1.value = resultsArray.join("\r\n");
}
```

Using the RegExp Object's Constructor

So far you've been creating RegExp objects using the / and / characters to define the start and end of the regular expression, as shown in the following example:

```
var myRegExp = /[a-z]/;
```

Although this is the generally preferred method, it was briefly mentioned that a RegExp object can also be created by means of the RegExp() constructor. You might use the first way most of the time. However, there are occasions, as you'll see in the trivia quiz shortly, when the second way of creating a RegExp object is necessary (for example, when a regular expression is to be constructed from user input).

As an example, the preceding regular expression could equally well be defined as

```
var myRegExp = new RegExp("[a-z]");
```

Here you pass the regular expression as a string parameter to the `RegExp()` constructor function.

A very important difference when you are using this method is in how you use special regular expression characters, such as \b, that have a backward slash in front of them. The problem is that the backward slash indicates an escape character in JavaScript strings — for example, you may use \b, which means a backspace. To differentiate between \b meaning a backspace in a string and the \b special character in a regular expression, you have to put another backward slash in front of the regular expression special character. So \b becomes \\b when you mean the regular expression \b that matches a word boundary, rather than a backspace character.

For example, say you have defined your `RegExp` object using the following:

```
var myRegExp = /\b/;
```

To declare it using the `RegExp()` constructor, you would need to write this:

```
var myRegExp = new RegExp("\\b");
```

and not this:

```
var myRegExp = new RegExp("\b");
```

All special regular expression characters, such as \w, \b, \d, and so on, must have an extra \ in front when you create them using `RegExp()`.

When you defined regular expressions with the / and / method, you could add after the final / the special flags m, g, and i to indicate that the pattern matching should be multi-line, global, or case-insensitive, respectively. When using the `RegExp()` constructor, how can you do the same thing?

Easy. The optional second parameter of the `RegExp()` constructor takes the flags that specify a global or case-insensitive match. For example, this will do a global case-insensitive pattern match:

```
var myRegExp = new RegExp("hello\\b","gi");
```

You can specify just one of the flags if you wish — such as the following:

```
var myRegExp = new RegExp("hello\\b","i");
```

or

```
var myRegExp = new RegExp("hello\\b","g");
```

The Trivia Quiz

The goal for the trivia quiz in this chapter is to enable it to set questions with answers that have to be typed in by the user, in addition to the multiple-choice questions you already have. To do this you'll be making use of your newfound knowledge of regular expressions to search the reply that the user types in for a match with the correct answer.

The problem you face with text answers is that a number of possible answers may be correct and you don't want to annoy the user by insisting on only *one* specific version. For example, the answer to the question "Which president was involved in the Watergate scandal?" is Richard Milhous Nixon. However, most people will type Nixon, or maybe Richard Nixon or even R Nixon. Each of these variations is valid, and using regular expressions you can easily check for all of them (or at least many plausible alternatives) in just a few lines of code.

What will you need to change to add this extra functionality? In fact changes are needed in only two pages: the GlobalFunctions.htm page and the AskQuestion.htm page.

In the GlobalFunctions.htm page, you need to define your new questions and answers, change the getQuestion() function, which builds up the HTML to display the question to the user, and change the answerCorrect() function, which checks whether the user's answer is correct.

In the AskQuestion.htm page, you need to change the function getAnswer(), which retrieves the user's answer from the page's form.

You'll start by making the changes to GlobalFunctions.htm that you created in the last chapter, so open this up in your HTML editor.

All the existing multiple-choice questions that you define near the top of the page can remain in exactly the same format, so there's no need for any changes there. How can this be if you're using regular expressions?

Previously you checked to see that the answer the user selected, such as A, B, C, and so on, was equal to the character in the answers array. Well, you can do the same thing here, but using a very simple regular expression that matches the character supplied by the user with the character in the answers array. If they match, you know the answer is correct.

Now you'll add the first new text-based question and answer directly underneath the last multiple-choice question in the GlobalFunctions.htm file.

```
// define question 4
questions[3] = "In the Simpsons, Bleeding Gums Murphy played which instrument?";
// assign answer for question 4
answers[3] = "\\bsax(ophone)?\\b";
```

The question definition is much simpler for text-based questions than for the multiple-choice questions: it's just the question text itself.

The answer definition is a regular expression. Note that you use \\b rather than \b, since you'll be creating your regular expressions using new RegExp() rather than using the / and / method. The valid answers to this question are sax and saxophone, so you need to define your regular expression to match either of those. You'll see later that the case flag will be set so that even SaxoPhone is valid, though dubious, English! Let's break it down stage by stage as shown in the following table.

Expression	Description
\\b	The \\b indicates that the answer must start with a word boundary; in other words, it must be a whole word and not contained inside another word. You do this just in case the user for some reason puts characters before his answer, such as My answer is saxophone.
Sax	The user's answer must start with the characters sax.
(ophone)?	You've grouped the pattern ophone by putting it in parentheses. By putting the ? just after it, you are saying that that pattern can appear zero or one time. If the user types sax, it appears zero times, and if the user types saxophone, it appears once — either way you make a match.
\\b	Finally you want the word to end at a word boundary.

The second question you'll create is

```
"Which American president was involved in the Watergate scandal?"
```

The possible correct answers for this are quite numerous and include the following:

```
Richard Milhous Nixon
Richard Nixon
Richard M. Nixon
Richard M Nixon
R Milhous Nixon
R. Milhous Nixon
R. M. Nixon
R M Nixon
R.M. Nixon
RM Nixon
R Nixon
R. Nixon
Nixon
```

This is a fairly exhaustive list of possible correct answers. You could perhaps accept only Nixon and Richard Nixon, but the longer list makes for a more challenging regular expression.

```
// define question 5
questions[4] = "Which American president was involved in the Watergate scandal?";
// assign answer for question 5
answers[4] = "\\b((Richard |R\\.? ?)(Milhous |M\\.? )?)?Nixon\\b";
```

Add the question-and-answer code under the other questions and answers in the GlobalFunctions.htm file.

Let's analyze this regular expression now.

Expression	Description
`\\b`	This indicates that the answer must start with a word boundary, so the answer must be a whole word and not contained inside another word. You do this just in case the user for some reason puts characters before his answer, such as `My answer is President Nixon`.
`((Richard |R\\.? ?)`	This part of the expression is grouped together with the next part, `(Milhous |M\\.? )?)`. The first parenthesis creates the outer group. Inside this is an inner group, which can be one of two patterns. Before the `|` is the pattern `Richard`, and after it is the pattern `R` followed by an optional dot (`.`) followed by an optional space. So either `Richard` or `R` will match. Since the `.` is a special character in regular expressions, you have to tell JavaScript you mean a literal dot and not a special-character dot. You do this by placing the `\` in front. However, because you are defining this regular expression using the `RegExp()` constructor, you need to place an additional `\` in front.
`(Milhous |M\\.? )?)?`	This is the second subgroup within the outer group. It works in a similar way to the first subgroup, but it's `Milhous` rather than `Richard` and `M` rather than `R` that you are matching. Also, the space after the initial is not optional, since you don't want `RMNixon`. The second `?` outside this inner group indicates that the middle name/initial is optional. The final parenthesis indicates the end of the outer group. The final `?` indicates that the outer group pattern is optional—this is to allow the answer `Nixon` alone to be valid.
`Nixon\\b`	Finally the pattern `Nixon` must be matched, and followed by a word boundary.

That completes the two additional text-based questions. Now you need to alter the question creation function, `getQuestion()`, again inside the file `GlobalFunctions.htm`, as follows:

```
function getQuestion()
{
    if (questions.length != numberOfQuestionsAsked)
    {
        var questionNumber = Math.floor(Math.random() * questions.length);
        while (questionsAsked[questionNumber] == true)
        {
            questionNumber = Math.floor(Math.random() * questions.length);
        }
        var questionLength = questions[questionNumber].length;
        var questionChoice;
        numberOfQuestionsAsked++;
        var questionHTML = "<h4>Question " + numberOfQuestionsAsked +  "</h4>";
        // Check if array or string
        if (typeof questions[questionNumber] == "string")
        {
            questionHTML = questionHTML + "<p>" + questions[questionNumber] + "</p>";
```

```
            questionHTML = questionHTML + "<p><input type=text name=txtAnswer ";
            questionHTML = questionHTML + " maxlength=100 size=35></p>";
            questionHTML = questionHTML + '<script type="text/javascript">';
                         + 'document.QuestionForm.txtAnswer.value = "";<\/script>';
      }
      else
      {
      questionHTML = questionHTML + "<p>" + questions[questionNumber][0];
      questionHTML = questionHTML + "</p>";
      for (questionChoice = 1;questionChoice < questionLength;questionChoice++)
      {
          questionHTML = questionHTML + "<input type=radio ";
          questionHTML = questionHTML + "name=radQuestionChoice";
          if (questionChoice == 1)
          {
             questionHTML = questionHTML + " checked";
          }
          questionHTML = questionHTML + ">" +
             questions[questionNumber][questionChoice];
          questionHTML = questionHTML + "<br>"
      }
      }
      questionHTML = questionHTML + "<br><input type='button' "
      questionHTML = questionHTML + "value='Answer Question'";
      questionHTML = questionHTML + "name=buttonNextQ ";
      questionHTML = questionHTML + "onclick='return buttonCheckQ_onclick()'>";
      currentQNumber = questionNumber;
      questionsAsked[questionNumber] = true;
   }
   else
   {
      questionHTML = "<h3>Quiz Complete</h3>";
      questionHTML = questionHTML + "You got " + numberOfQuestionsCorrect;
      questionHTML = questionHTML + " questions correct out of ";
      questionHTML = questionHTML + numberOfQuestionsAsked;
      questionHTML = questionHTML + "<br><br>Your trivia rating is ";
      switch(Math.round(((numberOfQuestionsCorrect / numberOfQuestionsAsked) * 10)))
      {
          case 0:
          case 1:
          case 2:
          case 3:
             questionHTML = questionHTML + "Beyond embarrassing";
             break;
          case 4:
          case 5:
          case 6:
          case 7:
             questionHTML = questionHTML + "Average";
             break;
          default:
             questionHTML = questionHTML + "Excellent"
      }
      questionHTML = questionHTML + "<br><br><A href='quizpage.htm'><strong>";
```

```
        questionHTML = questionHTML + "Start again</strong></A>";
    }
    return questionHTML;
}
```

You can see that the `getQuestion()` function is mostly unchanged by your need to ask text-based questions. The only code lines that have changed are the following:

```
if (typeof questions[questionNumber] == "string")
{
    questionHTML = questionHTML + "<p>" + questions[questionNumber] + "</p>";
    questionHTML = questionHTML + "<p><input type=text name=txtAnswer ";
    questionHTML = questionHTML + " maxlength=100 size=35></P>";
    // Next line necessary due to bugs in Netscape 7.x
    questionHTML = questionHTML + '<script type="text/javascript">'
                        + 'document.QuestionForm.txtAnswer.value = "";<\/script>';
}
else
{
```

The reason for this change is that the questions for multiple-choice and text-based questions are displayed differently. Having obtained your question number, you then need to check to see if this is a text question or a multiple-choice question. For text-based questions, you store the string containing the text inside the `questions[]` array; for multiple-choice questions, you store an array inside the `questions[]` array, which contains the question and options. You can check to see whether the type of data stored in the `questions[]` array at the index for that particular question is a string type. If it's a string type, you know you have a text-based question; otherwise you can assume it's a multiple-choice question. Note that Netscape 7.x has a habit of keeping previously entered data in text fields. This means that when the second text-based question is asked, the answer given for the previous text question is automatically pre-entered.

You use the `typeof` operator as part of the condition in your `if` statement in the following line:

```
if (typeof questions[questionNumber] == "string")
```

If the condition is `true`, you then create the HTML for the text-based question; otherwise the HTML for a multiple-choice question is created.

The second function inside `GlobalFunctions.htm` that needs to be changed is the `answerCorrect()` function, which actually checks the answer given by the user.

```
function answerCorrect(questionNumber, answer)
{
    // declare a variable to hold return value
    var correct = false;
    // if answer provided is same as answer then correct answer is true
    var answerRegExp = new RegExp(answers[questionNumber],"i");
    if (answer.search(answerRegExp) != -1)
    {
        numberOfQuestionsCorrect++;
        correct = true;
    }
```

```
      // return whether the answer was correct (true or false)
      return correct;
}
```

Instead of doing a simple comparison of the user's answer to the value in the answers[] array, you're now using regular expressions.

First you create a new RegExp object called answerRegExp and initialize it to the regular expression stored as a string inside your answers[] array. You want to do a case-insensitive match, so you pass the string i as the second parameter.

In your if statement, you search for the regular-expression answer pattern in the answer given by the user. This answer will be a string for a text-based question or a single character for a multiple-choice question. If a match is found, you'll get the character match position. If no match is found, -1 is returned. Therefore, if the match value is not -1, you know that the user's answer is correct, and the if statement's code executes. This increments the value of the variable numberOfQuestionsCorrect, and sets the correct variable to the value true.

That completes the changes to GlobalFunctions.htm. Remember to save the file before you close it.

Finally, you have just one more function you need to alter before your changes are complete. This time the function is in the file AskQuestion.htm. The function is getAnswer(), which is used to retrieve the user's answer from the form on the page. The changes are shown in the following code:

```
function getAnswer()
{
    var answer = 0;
    if (document.QuestionForm.elements[0].type == "radio")
    {
        while (document.QuestionForm.radQuestionChoice[answer].checked != true)
            answer++;
        answer =  String.fromCharCode(65 + answer);
    }
    else
    {
        answer = document.QuestionForm.txtAnswer.value;
    }
    return answer;
}
```

The user's answer can now be given via one of two means: an option being chosen in an option group, or text being entered in a text box. You determine which way was used for this question by using the type property of the first control in the form. If the first control is a radio button, you know this is a multiple-choice question; otherwise you assume it's a text-based question.

If it is a multiple-choice question, you obtain the answer, a character, as you did before you added text questions. If it's a text-based question, it's simply a matter of getting the text value from the text control written into the form dynamically by the getQuestion() function in the GlobalFunctions.htm page.

Save the changes to the page. You're now ready to give your updated trivia quiz a test run. Load TriviaQuiz.htm to start the quiz. You should now see the text questions you've created (see Figure 8-13).

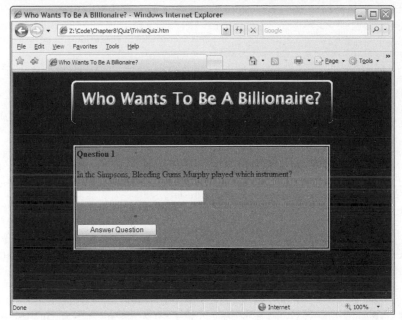

Figure 8-13

Although you've learned a bit more about regular expressions while altering the trivia quiz, perhaps the most important lesson has been that using general functions, and where possible placing them inside common code modules, makes later changes quite simple. In less than 20 lines, mostly in one file, you have made a significant addition to the quiz.

Summary

In this chapter you've looked at some more advanced methods of the String object and how you can optimize their use with regular expressions.

To recap, the chapter covered the following points:

- ❑ The split() method splits a single string into an array of strings. You pass a string or a regular expression to the method that determines where the split occurs.

- ❑ The replace() method enables you to replace a pattern of characters with another pattern that you specify as a second parameter.

- ❑ The search() method returns the character position of the first pattern matching the one given as a parameter.

- ❑ The match() method matches patterns, returning the text of the matches in an array.

- ❑ Regular expressions enable you to define a pattern of characters that you want to match. Using this pattern, you can perform splits, searches, text replacement, and matches on strings.

❑ In JavaScript the regular expressions are in the form of a RegExp object. You can create a RegExp object using either myRegExp = /myRegularExpression/ or myRegExp = new RegExp("myRegularExpression"). The second form requires that certain special characters that normally have a single \ in front now have two.

❑ The g and i characters at the end of a regular expression (as in, for example, myRegExp = /Pattern/gi;) ensure that a global and case-insensitive match is made.

❑ As well as specifying actual characters, regular expressions have certain groups of special characters, which allow any of certain groups of characters, such as digits, words, or non-word characters, to be matched.

❑ Special characters can also be used to specify pattern or character repetition. Additionally, you can specify what the pattern boundaries must be, for example at the beginning or end of the string, or next to a word or non-word boundary.

❑ Finally, you can define groups of characters that can be used later in the regular expression or in the results of using the expression with the replace() method.

❑ You also updated the trivia quiz in this chapter to allow questions to be set that require a text-based response from the user, in addition to the multiple-choice questions you have already seen.

In the next chapter you'll take a look at using and manipulating dates and times using JavaScript, and time conversion between different world time zones. Also covered is how to create a timer that executes code at regular intervals after the page is loaded. You'll be adapting the trivia quiz so that the user can select a time within which it must be completed — enabling him to specify, for example, that five questions must be answered in one minute.

Exercise Questions

Suggested solutions to these questions can be found in Appendix A.

Question 1

What problem does the code below solve?

```
var myString = "This sentence has has a fault and and we need to fix it."
var myRegExp = /(\b\w+\b) \1/g;
myString = myString.replace(myRegExp,"$1");
```

Now imagine that you change that code, so that you create the RegExp object like this:

```
var myRegExp = new RegExp("(\b\w+\b) \1");
```

Why would this not work, and how could you rectify the problem?

Question 2

Write a regular expression that finds all of the occurrences of the word "a" in the following sentence and replaces them with "the":

"a dog walked in off a street and ordered a finest beer"

The sentence should become:

"the dog walked in off the street and ordered the finest beer"

Question 3

Imagine you have a web site with a message board. Write a regular expression that would remove barred words. (I'll let you make up your own words!)

Date, Time, and Timers

In Chapter 4 we discuss that the concepts of date and time are embodied in JavaScript through the Date object. You looked at some of the properties and methods of the Date object, including the following:

- ❏ The methods getDate(), getDay(), getMonth(), and getFullYear() enable you to retrieve date values from inside a Date object.

- ❏ The setDate(), setMonth(), and setFullYear() methods enable you to set the date values of an existing Date object.

- ❏ The getHours(), getMinutes(), getSeconds(), and getMilliseconds() methods retrieve the time values in a Date object.

- ❏ The setHours(), setMinutes(), setSeconds(), and setMilliseconds() methods enable you to set the time values of an existing Date object.

One thing not covered in that chapter was the idea that the time depends on your location around the world. In this chapter you'll be correcting that omission by looking at date and time in relation to *world time*.

For example, imagine you have a chat room on your web site and want to organize a chat for a certain date and time. Simply stating 15:30 is not good enough if your web site attracts international visitors. The time 15:30 could be Eastern Standard Time, Pacific Standard Time, the time in the United Kingdom, or even the time in Kuala Lumpur. You could of course say 15:30 EST and let your visitors work out what that means, but even that isn't foolproof. There is an EST in Australia as well as in the United States. Wouldn't it be great if you could automatically convert the time to the user's time zone? In this chapter you'll see how.

As well as looking at world time, you'll also be looking at how to create a *timer* in a web page. You'll see that by using the timer you can trigger code, either at regular intervals or just once (for example, five seconds after the page has loaded). You'll see how you can use timers to add a real-time clock to a web page and how to create scrolling text in the status bar. Timers can also be useful for creating animations or special effects in your web applications. Finally, you'll be using the timer to enable the users of your trivia quiz to give themselves a time limit for answering the questions.

World Time

The concept of *now* means the same point in time everywhere in the world. However, when that point in time is represented by numbers, those numbers differ depending on where you are. What is needed is a standard number to represent that moment in time. This is achieved through Coordinated Universal Time (UTC), which is an international basis of civil and scientific time and was implemented in 1964. It was previously known as GMT (Greenwich Mean Time), and, indeed, at 0:00 UTC it is midnight in Greenwich, London.

The following table shows local times around the world at 0:00 UTC time.

San Francisco	New York (EST)	Greenwich, London	Berlin, Germany	Tokyo, Japan
4:00 pm	7:00 pm	0:00 (midnight)	1:00 am	9:00 am

Note that the times given are winter times—no daylight saving hours are taken into account.

The support for UTC in JavaScript comes from a number of methods of the Date object that are similar to those you have already seen. For each of the set-date- and get-date–type methods you've seen so far, there is a UTC equivalent. For example, whereas setHours() sets the local hour in a Date object, setUTCHours() does the same thing for UTC time. You'll be looking at these methods in more detail in the next section.

In addition, three more methods of the Date object involve world time.

You have the methods toUTCString() and toLocaleString(), which return the date and time stored in the Date object as a string based on either UTC or local time. Most modern browsers also have these additional methods: toLocaleTimeString(), toTimeString(), toLocaleDateString(), and toDateString().

If you simply want to find out the difference in minutes between the current locale's time and UTC, you can use the getTimezoneOffset() method. If the time zone is behind UTC, such as in the United States, it will return a positive number. If the time zone is ahead, such as in Australia or Japan, it will return a negative number.

Try It Out   The World Time Method of the Date Object

In the following code you use the toLocaleString(), toUTCString(), getTimezoneOffset(), toLocaleTimeString(), toTimeString(), toLocaleDateString(), and toDateString() methods and write their values out to the page.

```
<!DOCTYPE HTML PUBLIC "-//W3C//DTD HTML 4.01 Transitional//EN"
"http://www.w3.org/TR/html4/loose.dtd">
<html>
<head>
<title>example</title>
<script language="JavaScript" type="text/javascript">
   var localTime = new Date();
</script>
</head>
```

```
<body>
<h4>
   UTC Time is
   <script language="JavaScript" type="text/javascript">

      document.write(localTime.toUTCString());
   </script>
</h4>
<h4>
   Local Time is
   <script language="JavaScript" type="text/javascript">
      document.write(localTime.toLocaleString());
   </script>
</h4>
<h4>
   Time Zone Offset is
   <script language="JavaScript" type="text/javascript">
      document.write(localTime.getTimezoneOffset());
</script>
</h4>


<h4>
Using toLocalTimeString() gives:
<script language="JavaScript" type="text/javascript">
if (localTime.toLocaleTimeString)
{
   document.write(localTime.toLocaleTimeString())
}
</script>
</h4>


<h4>
Using toTimeString() gives:
<script language="JavaScript" type="text/javascript">
if (localTime.toTimeString)
{
   document.write(localTime.toTimeString() )
}
</script>
</h4>


<h4>
Using toLocaleDateString() gives:
<script language="JavaScript" type="text/javascript">
if (localTime.toLocaleDateString)
{
   document.write(localTime.toLocaleDateString())
}
</script>
</h4>

<h4>
Using toDateString() gives:
```

```
<script language="JavaScript" type="text/javascript">
if (localTime.toDateString)
{
  document.write(localTime.toDateString())
}
</script>
</h4>


</body>
</html>
```

Save this as `timetest.htm` and load it into your browser. What you see, of course, depends on which time zone your computer is set to, but your browser should show something similar to Figure 9-1.

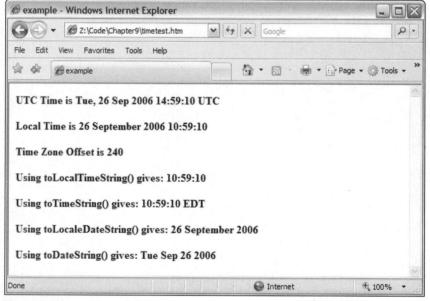

Figure 9-1

Here the computer's time is set to 10:59:10 a.m. on September 26, 2006, in America's Eastern Standard Time (for example, New York).

How It Works

So how does this work? In the script block at the top of the page, you have just this one line:

```
var localTime = new Date();
```

This creates a new Date object and initializes it to the current date and time based on the client computer's clock. (Note that in fact the Date object simply stores the number of milliseconds between the date and time on your computer's clock and midnight UTC on January 1, 1970.)

Within the body of the page you have seven more script blocks that use the three world time methods you looked at earlier. Note that some of them are enclosed in an if statement, for example this one:

```
if (localTime.toLocaleTimeString)
{
  document.write(localTime.toLocaleTimeString())
}
```

The if statement checks to see if the browser supports the method and only makes use of it if so. Older browsers don't support all of the date/time methods so doing this prevents ugly errors.

In the following line you write the string returned by the toUTCString() method to the page:

```
document.write(localTime.toUTCString());
```

This converts the date and time stored inside the localTime Date object to the equivalent UTC date and time.

Then the following line returns a string with the local date and time value:

```
document.write(localTime.toLocaleString());
```

Since this time is just based on the user's computer's clock, the string returned by this method also adjusts for Daylight Saving Time (as long as the clock adjusts for it).

Next, this code writes out the difference, in minutes, between the local time zone's time and that of UTC.

```
document.write(localTime.getTimezoneOffset());
```

You may notice in Figure 9-1 that the difference between New York time and UTC time is written to be 240 minutes, or 4 hours. Yet in the previous table, you saw that New York time is 5 hours behind UTC. So what is happening?

Well, in New York on September 26, daylight saving hours are in use. While in the summer it's 8:00 p.m. in New York when it's 0:00 UTC, in the winter it's 7:00 p.m. in New York when it's 0:00 UTC. Therefore, in the summer the getTimezoneOffset() method returns 240, whereas in the winter the getTimezoneOffset() method returns 300.

To illustrate this, compare Figure 9-1 to Figure 9-2, where the date on the computer's clock has been advanced by two months.

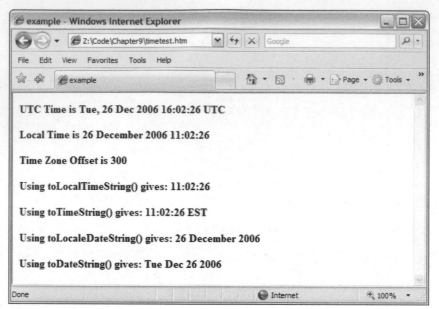

Figure 9-2

The next two methods are `toLocaleTimeString()` and `toTimeString()`, as follows:

```
<h4>
Using toLocalTimeString() gives:
<script language="JavaScript" type="text/javascript">
document.write(localTime.toLocaleTimeString())
</script>
</h4>


<h4>
Using toTimeString() gives:
<script language="JavaScript" type="text/javascript">
 document.write(localTime.toTimeString() )
</script>
</h4>
```

These methods display just the time part of the date and time held in the `Date` object. The `toLocaleTimeString()` method displays the time as specified by the user on his computer. The second method displays the time but also gives an indication of the time zone (in the example, EST for Eastern Standard Time in America).

The final two methods display the date part of the date and time. The `toLocaleDateString()` displays the date in the format the user has specified on his computer. On Windows operating systems, this is set in the regional settings of the PC's Control Panel. However, because it relies on the user's PC setup, the look of the date varies from computer to computer. The `toDateString()` method displays the current date contained in the PC date in a standard format.

Of course, this example relies on the fact that the user's computer's clock is set correctly, not something you can be 100 percent sure of — it's amazing how many users have their local time zone settings set completely wrong.

Setting and Getting a Date Object's UTC Date and Time

When you create a new `Date` object, you can either initialize it with a value or let JavaScript set it to the current date and time. Either way, JavaScript assumes you are setting the *local* time values. If you want to specify UTC time, you need to use the `setUTC` type methods, such as `setUTCHours()`.

The following are the seven methods for setting UTC date and time:

- ❏   `setUTCDate()`

- ❏   `setUTCFullYear()`

- ❏   `setUTCHours()`

- ❏   `setUTCMilliseconds()`

- ❏   `setUTCMinutes()`

- ❏   `setUTCMonth()`

- ❏   `setUTCSeconds()`

The names pretty much give away exactly what each of the methods does, so let's launch straight into a simple example, which sets the UTC time.

```
<!DOCTYPE HTML PUBLIC "-//W3C//DTD HTML 4.01 Transitional//EN"
"http://www.w3.org/TR/html4/loose.dtd">
<html>
<body>
<script language= "JavaScript" type="text/javascript">
var myDate = new Date();
myDate.setUTCHours(12);
myDate.setUTCMinutes(0);
myDate.setUTCSeconds(0);
document.write("<h3>" + myDate.toUTCString() + "</h3>")
document.write("<h3>" + myDate.toLocaleString() + "</h3>")
</script>
</body>
</html>
```

Save this as `settimetest.htm`. When you load it in your browser, you should see something like that shown in Figure 9-3 in your web page, although the actual date will depend on the current date and where you are in the world.

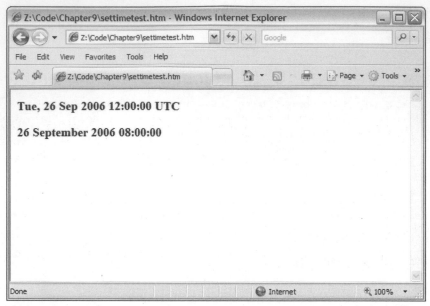

Figure 9-3

You might want to change your computer's time zone and time of year to see how it varies in different regions and with daylight saving changes. For example, although I'm in the United Kingdom, I have changed the settings on my computer for this example to Eastern Standard Time in the U.S. In Windows you can make the changes by opening the Control Panel and then double-clicking the Date/Time icon.

So how does this example work? You declare a variable, myDate, and set it to a new Date object. Because you haven't initialized the Date object to any value, it contains the local current date and time.

Then, using the setUTC methods, you set the hours, minutes, and seconds so that the time is 12:00:00 UTC (midday, not midnight).

Now, when you write out the value of myDate as a UTC string, you get 12:00:00 and today's date. When you write out the value of the Date object as a local string, you get today's date and a time that is the UTC time 12:00:00 converted to the equivalent local time. The local values you'll see, of course, depend on your time zone. For example, New Yorkers will see 08:00:00 during the summer and 07:00:00 during the winter because of daylight savings. In the United Kingdom, in the winter you'll see 12:00:00, but in the summer you'll see 13:00:00.

For getting UTC dates and times, you have the same functions you would use for setting UTC dates and times, except that this time, for example, it's getUTCHours() and not setUTCHours().

❑   getUTCDate()

❑   getUTCDay()

❑   getUTCFullYear()

- ❑ getUTCHours()

- ❑ getUTCMilliseconds()

- ❑ getUTCMinutes()

- ❑ getUTCMonth()

- ❑ getUTCSeconds()

Notice that this time there is an additional method, getUTCDay(). This works in the same way as the getDay() method and returns the day of the week as a number, from 0 for Sunday to 6 for Saturday. Because the day of the week is decided by the day of the month, the month, and the year, there is no setUTCDay() method.

Before moving on to look at timers, let's use your newly gained knowledge of the Date object and world time to create a world time converter. Later in this chapter, when you've learned how to use timers, you'll update the example to produce a world time clock.

Try It Out   World Time Converter (Part I)

The world time converter consists of two pages. The first is a frameset page, and the second is the page where the time conversion form exists. Let's start by creating the frameset page.

```
<!DOCTYPE HTML PUBLIC "-//W3C//DTD HTML 4.01 Frameset//EN"
"http://www.w3.org/TR/html4/frameset.dtd">
<html>
<head>
</head>
<frameset cols="250,*" frameborder="0">
    <frame src="worldtimeconverter.htm" name=formFrame>
    <frame src="about:blank" name=resultsFrame>
</frameset>
</html>
```

This simply divides the page into two frames. However, by setting the border between the frames to 0, you can make it look like just a single page. Save this frameset page as WorldTimeConverterFrameset.htm.

The left frame will contain the form in which the user can select the city whose time she wants, and the right frame will show the results of the conversion. The right frame will be written using code, so there is no page to create for that.

Next, create the left frame's page.

```
<html>
<head>
<script language="javascript" type="text/javascript">
var timeDiff;
var selectedCity;
var daylightSavingAdjust = 0;
function updateTimeZone()
{
```

```
      var lstCity = document.form1.lstCity;
      timeDiff = lstCity.options[lstCity.selectedIndex].value;
      selectedCity = lstCity.options[lstCity.selectedIndex].text;
      updateTime();
}
function getTimeString(dateObject)
{
   var timeString;
   var hours = dateObject.getHours();
   if (hours < 10)
      hours = "0" + hours;
   var minutes = dateObject.getMinutes();
   if (minutes < 10)
      minutes = "0" + minutes;
   var seconds = dateObject.getSeconds()
   if (seconds < 10)
      seconds = "0" + seconds;
   timeString = hours + ":" + minutes + ":" + seconds;
   return timeString;
}
function updateTime()
{
   var nowTime = new Date();
   var resultsFrame = window.top.resultsFrame.document;
   resultsFrame.open()
   resultsFrame.write("Local Time is " + getTimeString(nowTime) + "<br>");
   nowTime.setMinutes(nowTime.getMinutes() + nowTime.getTimezoneOffset() +
      parseInt(timeDiff) + daylightSavingAdjust);
   resultsFrame.write(selectedCity + " time is " + getTimeString(nowTime));
   resultsFrame.close();
}
function chkDaylightSaving_onclick()
{
   if (document.form1.chkDaylightSaving.checked)
   {
      daylightSavingAdjust = 60;
   }
   else
   {
      daylightSavingAdjust = 0;
   }
   updateTime();
}
</script>
</head>
<body onload="updateTimeZone()">
<form name=form1>
<select size=5 name=lstCity language=JavaScript onchange="updateTimeZone();">
<option value=60 selected>Berlin
<option value=330>Bombay
<option value=0>London
<option value=180>Moscow
<option value=-300>New York (EST)
<option value=60>Paris
<option value=-480>San Francisco (PST)
```

```
<option value=600>Sydney
</select>
<p>
It's summertime in the selected city
and its country adjusts for summertime daylight saving
<input type="checkbox" name=chkDaylightSaving language=JavaScript
    onclick="return chkDaylightSaving_onclick()">
</p>
</form>
</body>
</html>
```

Save this page as `WorldTimeConverter.htm`. Then load the `WorldTimeConverterFrameset.htm` page into your browser.

The form layout looks something like that shown in Figure 9-4. Whenever the user clicks a city in the list, her local time and the equivalent time in the selected city are shown. In the example shown in Figure 9-4, the local region is set to Eastern Standard Time in the U.S. (for a city such as New York), and the selected city is Berlin, with the daylight saving box checked.

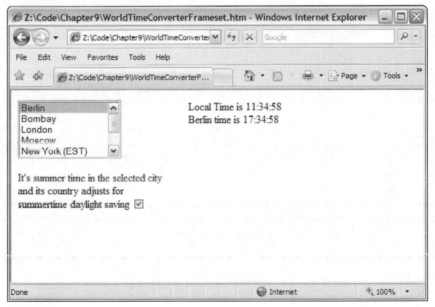

Figure 9-4

It's worth pointing out that this is an example and not a totally foolproof one, because of the problems presented by daylight saving. Some countries don't have it, others do at fixed times of year, and yet others do but at varying times of the year. This makes it difficult to predict accurately when a country will have its daylight saving period. You have tried to solve this problem by adding a check box for the user to click if the city she chooses from the list is using daylight saving hours (which you assume will put the time in the city forward by one hour).

In addition, don't forget that some users may not even have their regional settings set correctly — there's no easy way around this problem.

How It Works

Before you look at `WorldTimeConverter.htm`, let's just pick up on one point in the frameset-defining page `WorldTimeConverterFrameset.htm`.

```
<frame src="about:blank" name=resultsFrame>
```

Notice how you have set the `src` attribute of the right-hand frame to `"about:blank"`. This is necessary for some browsers, mainly Netscape — without it, `document.write()` will sometimes fail because there is no page loaded to write to. Note that as it stands, this example doesn't work with Opera 7. To make it work you simply need to create a blank HTML page and load that into the results frame.

Now you'll turn to the page `WorldTimeConverter.htm`, where most of the action is. In the body of the page is a form in which you've defined a list box using a `<select>` element.

```
<select size=5 name=lstCity language=JavaScript onchange="updateTimeZone();">
<option value=60 selected>Berlin
<option value=330>Bombay
<option value=0>London
<option value=180>Moscow
<option value=-300>New York (EST)
<option value=60>Paris
<option value=-480>San Francisco (PST)
<option value=600>Sydney
</select>
```

Each of the options displays the city's name in the list box and has its value set to the difference in minutes between that city's time zone (in winter) and UTC. So London, which uses UTC, has a value of 0. Paris, which is an hour ahead of UTC, has a value of 60 (that is, 60 minutes). New York, which is five hours behind UTC, has a value of -300.

You'll see that you have captured the `change` event of the `<select>` element and connected it to the function `updateTimeZone()` defined in a script block in the head of the page. This function involves three global variables defined at the top of the script block.

```
var timeDiff;
var selectedCity;
var daylightSavingAdjust = 0;
```

The function `updateTimeZone()` updates two of these, setting the variable `timeDiff` to the value of the list's selected option (that is, the time difference between the selected city and UTC time) and the variable `selectedCity` to the text shown for the selected option (that is, the selected city).

```
function updateTimeZone()
{
   var lstCity = document.form1.lstCity;
   timeDiff = lstCity.options[lstCity.selectedIndex].value;
   selectedCity = lstCity.options[lstCity.selectedIndex].text;
```

In the final part of the function `updateTimeZone()`, the function `updateTime()` is called, as shown in the following:

```
    updateTime();
}
```

Before you go on to look at this function, you return to the final part of the form on the page. This is a check box, which the user clicks if the city she has chosen from the select list is in the summertime of a country that uses daylight saving hours.

```
<input type="checkbox" name=chkDaylightSaving language=JavaScript
    onclick="return chkDaylightSaving_onclick()">
```

As you can see, this check box's `click` event is connected to another function, `chkDaylightSaving_onclick()`.

```
function chkDaylightSaving_onclick()
{
    if (document.form1.chkDaylightSaving.checked)
    {
        daylightSavingAdjust = 60;
    }
    else
    {
        daylightSavingAdjust = 0;
    }
```

Inside the `if` statement, the code accesses the check box's `checked` property, which returns `true` if it is checked and `false` otherwise. If it has been checked, you set the global variable `daylightSavingAdjust` to 60 for summertime daylight saving; otherwise it's set to 0.

```
    updateTime();
}
```

At the end of this function (as at the end of the function `updateTimeZone()` you saw earlier), the `updateTime()` function is called. You'll look at that next.

In the function `updateTime()`, you write the current local time and the equivalent time in the selected city to the right-hand frame, named `resultsFrame`, which you defined in the frameset page.

You start at the top of the function by creating a new `Date` object, which is stored in the variable `nowTime`. The `Date` object will be initialized to the current local time.

```
function updateTime()
{
    var nowTime = new Date();
```

Next, to make your code more compact and easier to understand, you define a variable, `resultsFrame`, which will reference the `document` object contained in the `resultsFrame` window.

```
    var resultsFrame = window.top.resultsFrame.document;
```

With your reference to the `resultsFrame` document, you then open the document to write to it. Doing this will clear anything currently in the document and provide a nice blank document to write your HTML into. The first thing you write is the local time based on the new `Date` object you just created. However, you want the time to be nicely formatted as *hours:minutes:seconds*, so you've written another function, `getTimeString()`, which does this for you. You'll look at that shortly.

```
resultsFrame.open()
resultsFrame.write("Local Time is " + getTimeString(nowTime) + "<br>");
```

Having written the current time to your `resultsFrame`, you now need to calculate what the time would be in the selected city before also writing that to the `resultsFrame`.

You saw in Chapter 4 that if you set the value of a `Date` object's individual parts (such as hours, minutes, and seconds) to a value beyond their normal range, JavaScript assumes you want to adjust the date, hours, or minutes to take this into account. For example, if you set the hours to `36`, JavaScript simply changes the hours to `12` and adds one day to the date stored inside the `Date` object. You use this to your benefit in the following line:

```
nowTime.setMinutes(nowTime.getMinutes() + nowTime.getTimezoneOffset() +
    parseInt(timeDiff) + daylightSavingAdjust);
```

Let's break this line down to see how it works. Suppose that you're in New York, with the local summer time of 5:11, and you want to know what time it is in Berlin. How does your line of code calculate this?

First you get the minutes of the current local time; it's 5:11, so `nowTime.getMinutes()` returns `11`.

Then you get the difference, in minutes, between the user's local time and UTC using `nowTime.getTimezoneOffset()`. If you are in New York, which is different from UTC by 4 hours during the summer, this is 240 minutes.

Then you get the integer value of the time difference between the standard winter time in the selected city and UTC time, which is stored in the variable `timeDiff`. You've used `parseInt()` here because it's one of the few situations where JavaScript gets confused and assumes you want to join two strings together rather than treat the values as numbers and add them together. Remember that you got `timeDiff` from an HTML element's value, and that an HTML element's values are strings, even when they hold characters that are digits. Since you want the time in Berlin, which is 60 minutes different from UTC time, this value will be `60`.

Finally, you add the value of `daylightSavingsAdjust`. This variable is set in the function `chkdaylightsaving_onclick()`, which we discussed earlier. Since it's summer where you are and Berlin uses daylight saving hours, this value is `60`.

So you have the following:

```
11 + 240 + 60 + 60 = 371
```

Therefore `nowTime.setMinutes()` is setting the minutes to `371`. Clearly, there's no such thing as 371 minutes past the hour, so instead JavaScript assumes you mean 6 hours and 11 minutes after 5:00, that being 11:11 — the time in Berlin that you wanted.

Finally, the `updateTime()` function writes the results to the `resultsFrame`, and then closes off the document writing.

```
    resultsFrame.write(selectedCity + " time is " + getTimeString(nowTime));
    resultsFrame.close();
}
```

In the `updateTime()` function, you saw that it uses the function `getTimeString()` to format the time string. Let's look at that function now. This function is passed a `Date` object as a parameter and uses it to create a string with the format *hours:minutes:seconds*.

```
function getTimeString(dateObject)
{
    var timeString;
    var hours = dateObject.getHours();
    if (hours < 10)
        hours = "0" + hours;
    var minutes = dateObject.getMinutes();
    if (minutes < 10)
        minutes = "0" + minutes;
    var seconds = dateObject.getSeconds()
    if (seconds < 10)
        seconds = "0" + seconds;
    timeString = hours + ":" + minutes + ":" + seconds;
    return timeString;
}
```

Why do you need this function? Well, you can't just use this:

```
getHours() + ":" + getMinutes() + ":" + getSeconds()
```

That won't take care of those times when any of the three results of these functions is less than 10. For example, 1 minute past noon would look like 12:1:00 rather than 12:01:00.

The function therefore gets the values for hours, minutes, and seconds and checks each to see if it is below 10. If it is, a zero is added to the front of the string. When all the values have been retrieved, they are concatenated in the variable `timeString` before being returned to the calling function.

In the next section you're going to look at how, by adding a timer, you can make the displayed time update every second like a clock.

Timers in a Web Page

You can create two types of timers, one-shot timers and continually firing timers. The *one-shot timer* triggers just once after a certain period of time, and the second type of timer continually triggers at set intervals. You will investigate each of these types of timers in the next two sections.

Within reasonable limits you can have as many timers as you want and can set them going at any point in your code, such as at the window `onload` event or at the click of a button. Common uses for timers include advertisement banner pictures that change at regular intervals or display the changing time in a web page. Also all sorts of animations done with DHTML need `setTimeout()` or `setInterval()` — you'll be looking at DHTML later on in the book.

One-Shot Timer

Setting a one-shot timer is very easy: you just use the `window` object's `setTimeout()` method.

```
window.setTimeout("your JavaScript code", milliseconds_delay)
```

The method `setTimeout()` takes two parameters. The first is the JavaScript code you want executed, and the second is the delay, in milliseconds (thousandths of a second), until the code is executed.

The method returns a value (an integer), which is the timer's unique ID. If you decide later that you want to stop the timer firing, you use this ID to tell JavaScript which timer you are referring to.

For example, to set a timer that fires three seconds after the page has loaded, you could use the following code:

```
<!DOCTYPE HTML PUBLIC "-//W3C//DTD HTML 4.01 Transitional//EN"
"http://www.w3.org/TR/html4/loose.dtd">
<html>
<head>
<script language="JavaScript" type="text/javascript">
var timerID;
function window_onload()
{
    timerID = setTimeout("alert('Times Up!')",3000);
    alert("Timer Set");
}
</script>
</head>
<body language = JavaScript onload="window_onload()">
</body>
</html>
```

Save this file as `timertest.htm`, and load it into your browser. In this page a message box appears 3,000 milliseconds (that is, 3 seconds) after the `onload` event of the window has fired.

Although `setTimeout()` is a method of the `window` object, you'll remember that because the `window` object is at the top of the hierarchy, you don't need to use its name when referring to its properties and methods. Hence, you can use `setTimeout()` instead of `window.setTimeout()`.

It's important to note that setting a timer does not stop the script from continuing to execute. The timer runs in the background and fires when its time is up. In the meantime the page runs as usual, and any script after you start the timer's countdown will run immediately. So, in this example, the alert box telling you that the timer has been set appears immediately after the code setting the timer has been executed.

What if you decided that you wanted to stop the timer before it fired?

To clear a timer you use the window object's clearTimeout() method. This takes just one parameter, the unique timer ID that the setTimeout() method returns.

Let's alter the preceding example and provide a button that you can click to stop the timer.

```
<!DOCTYPE HTML PUBLIC "-//W3C//DTD HTML 4.01 Transitional//EN"
"http://www.w3.org/TR/html4/loose.dtd">
<html>
<head>
<script language-JavaScript type-"text/javascript">
var timerID;
function window_onload()
{
    timerID = setTimeout("alert('Times Up!')",3000);
    alert("Timer Set");
}
function butStopTimer_onclick()
{
    clearTimeout(timerID);
    alert("Timer has been cleared");
}
</script>
</head>
<body onload="window_onload()">
<form name=form1>
<input type="button" value="Stop Timer" name=butStopTimer language-JavaScript
    onclick="return butStopTimer_onclick()">
</form>
</body>
</html>
```

Save this as timertest2.htm and load it into your browser. Now if you click the Stop Timer button before the three seconds are up, the timer will be cleared. This is because the button is connected to the butStopTimer_onclick() function, which uses the timer's ID timerID with the clearTimeout() method of the window object.

Try It Out — Updating a Banner Advertisement

You'll now look at a bigger example using the setTimeout() method. The following example creates a web page with an image banner advertisement that changes every few seconds.

```
<!DOCTYPE HTML PUBLIC "-//W3C//DTD HTML 4.01 Transitional//EN"
"http://www.w3.org/TR/html4/loose.dtd">
<html>
<head>
<script language=JavaScript type="text/javascript">
var currentImgNumber = 1;
var numberOfImages = 3;
function window_onload()
{
    setTimeout("switchImage()",3000);
}
function switchImage()
```

```
    {
        currentImgNumber++;
        document.imgAdvert.src = "AdvertImage" + currentImgNumber + ".jpg";
        if (currentImgNumber < numberOfImages)
        {
            setTimeout("switchImage()",3000);    }
        }
</script>
</head>
<body onload="window_onload()">
<img src="AdvertImage1.jpg" name="imgAdvert">
</body>
</html>
```

After you've typed in the code, save the page as Adverts.htm. You'll also need to create three images named AdvertImage1.jpg, AdvertImage2.jpg, and AdvertImage3.jpg (alternatively, the three images are supplied with the downloadable code for the book).

When the page is loaded, you start with a view of AdvertImage1.jpg, as shown in Figure 9-5.

Figure 9-5

In three seconds this changes to the second image, shown in Figure 9-6.

Figure 9-6

Finally, three seconds later, a third and final image loads, shown in Figure 9-7.

Figure 9-7

How It Works

When the page loads, the `<img>` tag has its `src` attribute set to the first image.

```
<img src="AdvertImage1.jpg" name="imgAdvert">
```

Within the `<body>` tag, you connect the `window` object's `onload` event handler to the function `window_onload()`.

```
function window_onload()
{
    setTimeout("switchImage()",3000)
}
```

In this function you use the `setTimeout()` method to start a timer running that will call the function `switchImage()` in three seconds. Since you don't have to clear the timer, you haven't bothered to save the timer ID returned by the `setTimeout()` method.

The `switchImage()` function changes the value of the `src` property of the `img` object corresponding to the `<img>` tag in your page.

```
function switchImage()
{
    currentImgNumber++;
    document.imgAdvert.src = "AdvertImage" + currentImgNumber + ".jpg";
```

Your advertisement images are numbered from one to three: `AdvertImage1.jpg`, `AdvertImage2.jpg`, and `AdvertImage3.jpg`. You keep track of the number of the advertisement image that is currently loaded in the page in the global variable `currentImgNumber`, which you defined at the top of the script block and initialized to `1`. To get the next image you simply increment that variable by one, and then update the image loaded by setting the `src` property of the `img` object, using the variable `currentImgNumber` to build up its full name.

```
    if (currentImgNumber < numberOfImages)
    {
        setTimeout("switchImage()",3000);
    }
}
```

You have three advertisement images you want to show. In the `if` statement you check to see whether `currentImgNumber`, which is the number of the current image, is less than three. If it is, it means there are more images to show, and so you set another timer going, identical to the one you set in the `window` object's `onload` event handler. This timer will call this function again in three seconds.

In earlier browsers, this was the only method of creating a timer that fired continually at regular intervals. However, in version 4 and later browsers, you'll see next that there's an easier way.

Setting a Timer that Fires at Regular Intervals

Modern browsers saw new methods added to the `window` object for setting timers, namely the `setInterval()` and `clearInterval()` methods. These work in a very similar way to `setTimeout()` and `clearTimeout()`, except that the timer fires continually at regular intervals rather than just once.

The method set.Interval() takes the same parameters as setTimeout(), except that the second parameter now specifies the interval, in milliseconds, between each firing of the timer, rather than just the length of time before the timer fires.

For example, to set a timer that fires the function myFunction() every five seconds, the code would be as follows:

```
var myTimerID = setInterval("myFunction()",5000);
```

As with setTimeout(), the setInterval() method returns a unique timer ID that you'll need if you want to clear the timer with clearInterval(), which works identically to clearTimeout(). So to stop the timer started in the preceding code, you would use the following:

```
clearInterval(myTimerID);
```

Try It Out   World Time Converter (Part 2)

Let's change the world time example that you saw earlier, so that it displays local time and selected city time as a continually updating clock.

You'll be making changes to the WorldTimeConverter.htm file, so open that in your text editor. Add the following function before the functions that are already defined:

```
var daylightSavingAdjust = 0;
function window_onload()
{
   updateTimeZone();
   window.setInterval("updateTime()",1000);
}
function updateTimeZone()
{
```

Next edit the <body> tag so it looks like this:

```
<body onload="return window_onload()">
```

Resave the file, and then load WorldTimeConverterFrameset.htm into your browser. The page should look the same as the previous version of the time converter, except that the time is updated every second.

How It Works

The changes were short and simple. In the function window_onload(), you have added a timer that will call the updateTime() function every 1,000 milliseconds — that is, every second. It'll keep doing this until you leave the page. Previously your updateTime() function was called only when the user clicked either a different city in the list box or the summertime check box.

The window_onload() function is connected to the window object's onload event in the <body> tag, so after the page has loaded your clock starts running.

That completes your look at this example and also your introduction to timers. Next you're going to use this knowledge to alter the trivia quiz so that it is a time-limit-based quiz.

The Trivia Quiz

In this chapter you'll be making two changes to the trivia quiz. You'll allow the user to select first how long she has to complete the quiz and second how many questions she wants to answer.

Converting the quiz to a timer-based one requires only that you change two pages, namely `QuizPage.htm` and `GlobalFunctions.htm`.

Your first change in `QuizPage.htm` will be to the form at the start of the quiz, because you need to allow the user to select her time limit and number of questions. Then you'll change the `cmdStartQuiz_onclick()` function so that when it calls the `resetQuiz()` function in the `GlobalFunctions.htm` page, it also passes (as parameters) the time limit and number of questions that the user has selected.

Now you go on to the `GlobalFunctions.htm` page itself, where you need to alter the `resetQuiz()` function so that, if necessary, it starts a timer based on the time limit selected. Then new functions dealing with the time limit need to be created: one puts a message in the scroll bar notifying the user how much time she has left; the other deals with the situation when the time limit is up.

You'll start by making the changes to `QuizPage.htm`, so open this in your text editor.

The first change you'll make is to the form, which currently contains just a button.

```
<form name="frmQuiz">
<p>
Number of Questions <br>
<select name="cboNoQuestions" size="1">
   <option value="3">3
   <option value="5">5
</select>
</p>
<p>
Time Limit <br>
<select name="cboTimeLimit" size="1">
   <option value="-1">No Time Limit
   <option value="60">1 Minute
   <option value="180">3 Minutes
   <option value="300">5 Minutes
</select>
</p>
<input name=cmdStartQuiz type=button value="Start Quiz"
   onclick="return cmdStartQuiz_onclick()">
</form>
```

You've added two new controls; both are drop-down list boxes created using the `<select>` tag. In the first list box you enable the user to choose how many questions she wants to answer, and in the second the time limit within which she must answer the questions.

Next you need to alter the `cmdStartQuiz_onclick()` function defined at the top of the page.

```
<script language=JavaScript>
function cmdStartQuiz_onclick()
```

```
    {
        var cboNoQuestions = document.frmQuiz.cboNoQuestions;
        var noQuestions = cboNoQuestions.options[cboNoQuestions.selectedIndex].value;
        var cboTimeLimit = document.frmQuiz.cboTimeLimit;
        var timeLimit = cboTimeLimit.options[cboTimeLimit.selectedIndex].value;
        window.top.fraTopFrame.fraGlobalFunctions.resetQuiz(noQuestions,timeLimit);
        window.location.href = "AskQuestion.htm";
    }
</script>
```

This function is connected to the `cmdStartQuiz` button's `onclick` event handler and is how the user kicks off the quiz. Previously you just called the `resetQuiz()` function in the global module and then loaded the `AskQuestion.htm` page. Now you need to get the values the user has selected in the select elements for the number of questions and time limit. As you'll see in a minute, the `resetQuiz()` function has been changed and now takes two parameters, namely the number of questions to be answered and a time limit.

At the start of the `cmdStartQuiz_onclick()` function, you first set a variable `cboNoQuestions` to reference the `cboNoQuestions` control in the form (where the user chooses how many questions she wants to answer). You can then use that reference instead of the more long-winded full reference via the document and form. The benefit of doing this is that it keeps the lines shorter and more readable.

On the second line you get the value of the selected option in the select control for the number of questions and store this value in the `noQuestions` variable.

In the following two lines you do the same thing again, except that this time it's the time limit control and value that you need to deal with.

Finally, in the last new line of the function, you reset the quiz, this time passing the number of questions to be answered (`noQuestions`) and time limit (`timeLimit`).

That completes all the changes for the page `QuizPage.htm`, so you can resave the page in your text editor and close it.

Now turn your attention to the `GlobalFunctions.htm` page and start by looking at the changes you need to make to the `resetQuiz()` function, as shown in the following:

```
function resetQuiz(numberOfQuestions, SelectedTimeLimit)
{
    timeLeft = SelectedTimeLimit;
    totalQuestionsToAsk = numberOfQuestions;
    var indexCounter;
    currentQNumber = -1;
    questionsAsked = new Array();
    for (indexCounter = 0; indexCounter < questions.length;indexCounter++)
    {
        questionsAsked[indexCounter] = false;
    }
    numberOfQuestionsAsked = 0;
    numberOfQuestionsCorrect = 0;
    if (timeLeft == -1)
    {
```

```
      window.status = "No Time Limit";
   }
   else
   {
      quizTimerId = window.setInterval("updateTimeLeft()",1000);
   }
}
```

The first change is to your function's definition. Previously it took no parameters, now it takes two: the number of questions to be answered and the time limit within which the quiz must be completed.

Your next change is to set two new global variables, timeLeft and totalQuestionsToAsk, to the values passed to the function. You'll see later that these global variables are used elsewhere to determine if enough questions have been asked and to check to see if the time limit has been reached.

The final change to this function is the setting of the timer that will monitor how much time is left. One of the options open to the user is no time limit at all, which is represented by the value -1. If the time limit is -1, you just put a message in the status bar of the browser window using the window object's status property. Note that on Netscape browsers the No Time Limit text in the status bar gets overwritten by Document:Done when the frames change. If, however, the time limit is not -1, you start a timer, using setInterval(), which will call the function updateTimeLeft() every second.

The updateTimeLeft() function is a new function, so let's create that now. Add it to the script block underneath all the other function definitions.

```
function updateTimeLeft()
{
   timeLeft--;
   if (timeLeft == 0)
   {
      alert("Time's Up");
      numberOfQuestionsAsked = totalQuestionsToAsk;
      window.top.fraQuizPage.location.href = "AskQuestion.htm";
   }
   else
   {
      var minutes = Math.floor(timeLeft / 60);
      var seconds = timeLeft - (60 * minutes);
      if (minutes < 10)
         minutes = "0" + minutes;
      if (seconds < 10)
         seconds = "0" + seconds;
      window.status = "Time left is " + minutes + ":" + seconds;
   }
}
```

This function does three things: It decrements the time left, it stops the quiz if the time left has reached 0, and finally it notifies the user of the time remaining by putting a message in the browser's status bar.

As you saw earlier, when the quiz is reset with the `resetQuiz()` function, the global variable `timeLeft` is set to the amount of time, in seconds, that the user has to complete the quiz. The `updateTimeLeft()` function is called every second, and in the first line you decrement the number of seconds left by one.

```
timeLeft--;
```

In the following `if` statement you check to see if `timeLeft` is 0. If it is, that means no seconds are left, and you end the quiz by setting the global variable `numberOfQuestionsAsked` to the same value as the number of questions the user wanted to answer, which is stored in global variable `totalQuestionsToAsk`. Then, when you navigate the page to `AskQuestion.htm`, that page will think that all the questions to be asked have been asked and will end the quiz rather than ask another question.

If there is still time left, the `else` part of the `if` statement executes and updates the status bar with the number of minutes and seconds left.

You need to split `timeLeft`, which is in seconds, into minutes and seconds. First you get the number of minutes using the following line:

```
var minutes = Math.floor(timeLeft / 60);
```

This returns just the whole-number part of the seconds when divided by 60, which is the number of minutes you need. You get the seconds in the following line:

```
var seconds = timeLeft - (60 * minutes);
```

This is just `timeLeft` (the total seconds) minus the number of seconds represented by the `minutes` value. So if `timeLeft` is 61, you have this:

```
minutes = 61 / 60 = 1.01667
```

The result is 1 as a whole number, followed by this:

```
seconds = 61 - (60 * 1) = 1
```

You want to display this as a string in the status bar in the format *minutes:seconds*, which is 01:01 in this case. However, just concatenating minutes and seconds will leave you with something like 1:1 when the value of either is less than 10. Currently minutes can't go above 5, so you could just add the 0 anyway, but by using an `if` statement, you are future-proofing it for the situation where you allow the user a time limit over nine minutes.

To fix this problem you add an extra 0 when the values are less than 10.

```
if (minutes < 10)
    minutes = "0" + minutes;
if (seconds < 10)
    seconds = "0" + seconds;
```

Finally, you change the value displayed in the window's status bar.

```
window.status = "Time left is " + minutes + ":" + seconds;
```

In the two preceding functions, you used some new globally defined variables you have not yet defined, so let's do that now.

```
var timeLeft =-1;
var totalQuestionsToAsk = 0;
var quizTimerId = 0;
```

Place these at the top of the script block.

Finally you've got just two small changes to make to the function `getQuestion()`, and that completes the trivia quiz for this chapter.

The first change is to the `if` statement at the top of the function.

```
if (totalQuestionsToAsk != numberOfQuestionsAsked)
{
    var questionNumber = Math.floor(Math.random() * questions.length);
```

Previously you asked another question as long as you had not used up all the questions available. Now you ask another question as long as the `totalQuestionsToAsk` variable does not equal the number of questions actually asked. The global variable `totalQuestionsToAsk` had its value determined by the user when she selected the number of questions she wanted to answer from the drop-down list. You passed this value to the `resetQuiz()` function, which did the actual setting of the variable's value.

The second change is to code in the `else` statement when the quiz is actually ended and you write out the summary of how the user did. Remember that you set a timer to keep track of how much time is left before the quiz must end. Well, now that the quiz has ended you need to stop that timer, which you do by using the `clearInterval()` method, passing the timer ID that you stored in the global variable `quizTimerId`, which you set when the timer was started. However, you mustn't try to stop the timer if no timer was set because the user did not select a time limit.

```
        currentQNumber = questionNumber;
        questionsAsked[questionNumber] = true;
    }
    else
    {
        if (timeLeft != -1)
        {
            clearInterval(quizTimerId);
        }
        questionHTML = "<h3>Quiz Complete</h3>";
        questionHTML = questionHTML + "You got " + numberOfQuestionsCorrect;
```

Well, that's all the changes made, so resave `GlobalFunctions.htm`. You can start the quiz by loading `TriviaQuiz.htm` into your browser.

Hopefully you should see a page like that shown in Figure 9-8.

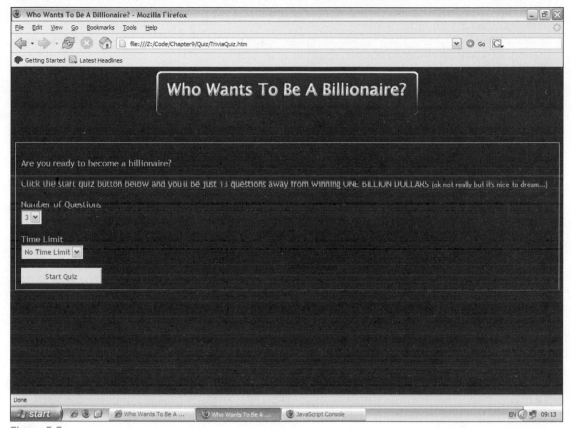

Figure 9-8

If you choose a time limit and then click the Start Quiz button, you'll be presented with the first question (randomly selected), and the timer, which is displayed in the status bar at the bottom of the page, will start counting down.

> In Firefox and IE 7 browsers the ability of JavaScript to change the status bar text is disabled by default. To enable it in Firefox you'll need to go to Tools ⇨ Options and select the Content tab. Then, to enable JavaScript, click the Advanced Options button. Select the check box Change Status Bar Text. In IE7 you'll need to go to Tools ⇨ Internet Options. Then select the Security tab. Click Internet, then click custom level, and scroll down to the Allow status bar updates via script check box and select it.

That completes all the changes to the trivia quiz for this chapter. You'll be returning to the trivia quiz in Chapter 11 to see how you can store information on the user's computer so that you can provide a table of previous results.

Summary

You started the chapter by looking at Coordinated Universal Time (UTC), which is an international standard time. You then looked at how to create timers in web pages.

The particular points we covered were the following:

❑ The Date object enables you to set and get UTC time in a way similar to setting a Date object's local time by using methods (such as setUTCHours() and getUTCHours()) for setting and getting UTC hours with similar methods for months, years, minutes, seconds, and so on.

❑ A useful tool in international time conversion is the getTimezoneOffset() method, which returns the difference, in minutes, between the user's local time and UTC. One pitfall of this is that you are assuming the user has correctly set his time zone on his computer. If not, getTimezoneOffset() is rendered useless, as will be any local date and time methods if the user's clock is incorrectly set.

❑ Using the setTimeout() method, you found you could start a timer going that would fire just once after a certain number of milliseconds. setTimeout() takes two parameters: the first is the code you want executed, and the second is the delay before that code is executed. It returns a value, the unique timer ID that you can use if you later want to reference the timer; for example, to stop it before it fires, you use the clearTimeout() method.

❑ To create a timer that fires at regular intervals, you used the setInterval() method, which works in the same way as setTimeout(), except that it keeps firing unless the user leaves the page or you call the clearInterval() method.

❑ Finally, using your new knowledge of timers, you changed the trivia quiz so that the user can determine how many questions she wants to answer and within what time limit the quiz must be completed.

In the next chapter you'll be looking at the top seven mistakes of all time, ones every programmer makes at some point regardless of how much of an expert he or she may claim to be. You'll also be looking at a script debugger for IE and how it can be used to step through live code, line by line. Finally, you'll be looking at how to avoid errors and how to deal with errors when you get them.

Exercise Questions

Suggested solutions to these questions can be found in Appendix A.

Question 1

Create a web page with an advertisement image at the top. When the page loads, select a random image for that advertisement. Every four seconds, make the image change to a different one, making sure a different advertisement is selected until all the advertisement images have been seen.

Question 2

Create a form that gets the user's date of birth. Then, using that information, tell her on what day of the week she was born.

Common Mistakes, Debugging, and Error Handling

Even a JavaScript guru makes mistakes, even if they are just annoying typos. In particular, when code expands to hundreds of lines, the chance of something going wrong becomes much greater. In proportion, the difficulty in finding these mistakes, or bugs, also increases. In this chapter you will look at various techniques that will help you minimize the problems that arise from this situation.

You'll start by taking a look at the top seven JavaScript coding mistakes. After you know what they are, you'll be able to look out for them when writing code. Hopefully, so that you won't make them so often!

Then you'll look at the Microsoft script debugger, which can be used with Internet Explorer. You'll see how you can use it to step through your code and check the contents of variables while the code is running, a process that enables us to hunt for difficult bugs. You'll also take a briefer look at the debugging tools available for Firefox.

Finally, you'll look at how you can cope with errors when they do happen, so that you prevent users from seeing your coding mistakes.

I Can't Believe I Just Did That: Some Common Mistakes

It's time to do a rundown of seven common mistakes. Some of these you'll learn to avoid as you become more experienced, but others may haunt you forever!

You'll find it very useful in this chapter if your browser is set up to show errors. You did this in Chapter 2 in the section "Setting Up Your Browser for Errors." So if you don't already have error display set up, now would be a good time to do so.

1: Undefined Variables

JavaScript is actually very easygoing when it comes to defining your variables before assigning values to them. For example, the following will implicitly create the new variable abc and assign it to the value 23.

```
abc = 23;
```

Although strictly speaking, you should define the variable explicitly.

```
var abc = 23;
```

(Actually, whether you use the var keyword has a consequence on the scope that the variable has, so in fact it is always best to use the var keyword.)

However, if a variable is actually used before it has been defined, an error will arise. For example, the following code will cause the error shown in Figure 10-1 if the variable abc has not been previously defined (explicitly or implicitly).

```
alert(abc);
```

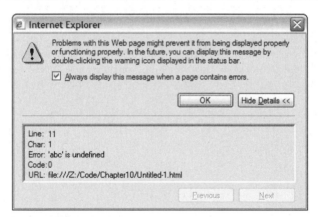

Figure 10-1

In Firefox you'll need to look in the JavaScript console, which you can view by choosing Tools ➪ JavaScript Console.

In addition, you must remember that function definitions also have parameters, which if not declared correctly can lead to the same type of error.

Take a look at the following code:

```
function resetQuiz(numberOfQustions, timeLimit)
{
    timeLeft = timeLimit;
    totalQuestionsToAsk = numberOfQuestions;
    currentQNumber = -1;
    questionsAsked = new Array();
```

```
    numberOfQuestionsAsked = 0;
    numberOfQuestionsCorrect = 0;
}
```

If you call this function, you get an error message similar to the one shown in Figure 10-2.

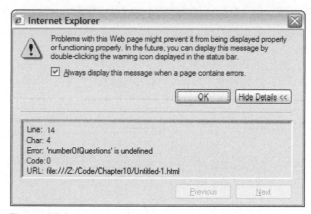

Figure 10-2

The error here is actually a simple typo in the function definition. The first parameter has the typo: it should read `numberOfQuestions`, not `numberOfQustions`. What can be confusing with this type of error is that although the browser tells us the error is on one line, in fact the source of the error is on some other line.

2: Case Sensitivity

This is a major source of errors, particularly because it can be difficult to spot at times.

For example, spot the three case errors in the following code:

```
var myName = "Paul";
If (myName == "paul")
    alert(myName.toUppercase());
```

The first error is that you have typed `If` rather than `if`. However, JavaScript won't tell us that the error is an incorrect use of case, but instead IE will tell us `Object expected` and Firefox will tell us that `If is not defined`. Although error messages give us some idea of what's gone wrong, they often do so in an oblique way. In this case IE thinks you are trying to use an object called an `If` object and Firefox thinks you are trying to use an undefined variable called `If`.

Okay, with that error cleared up, you come to the next error, not one of JavaScript syntax, but a logic error. Remember that `Paul` does not equal `paul` in JavaScript, so `myName == "paul"` is `false`, even though it's quite likely that you didn't care whether the word is `paul` or `Paul`. This type of error will result in no error message at all, just the code not executing as you'd planned.

The third fault is with the `toUpperCase()` method of the `String` object contained in `myName`. You've written `toUppercase`, with the `c` in lowercase. IE will give us the message `Object doesn't support`

363

this property or method and Firefox will report that myName.toUppercase is not a function. On first glance it would be easy to miss such a small mistake and start checking your JavaScript reference guide for that method. You might wonder why it's there, but your code is not working. Again, you always need to be aware of case, something that even experts get wrong from time to time.

3: Incorrect Number of Closing Braces

In the following code you define a function and then call it. However, there's a deliberate mistake. See if you can spot where it is.

```
function myFunction()
{
x = 1;
y = 2;
if (x <= y)
{
if (x == y)
{
alert("x equals y");
}
}
myFunction();
```

If you properly format the code you'll have a much easier time spotting the error.

```
function myFunction()
{
    x = 1;
    y = 2;
    if (x <= y)
    {
        if (x == y)
        {
            alert("x equals y");
        }
    }
myFunction();
```

Now you can see that you've forgotten to mark the end of the function with a closing curly brace. When there are a lot of if, for, or do while statements, it's easy to have too many or too few closing braces. With proper formatting, this problem is much easier to spot.

4: Missing Plus Signs During Concatenation

In the following code, there's a deliberate concatenation mistake.

```
var myName = "Paul";
var myString = "Hello";
var myOtherString = "World";
myString = myName + " said " + myString + " " myOtherString;
alert(myString);
```

There should be a + operator between " " and myOtherString in the fourth line of code.

Although easy to spot in just a few lines, this kind of mistake can be harder to spot in large chunks of code. Also, the error message that a mistake like this causes can be misleading. Load this code into a browser and you'll be told Error : Expected by IE and Missing ; before statement by Firefox. It's surprising how often this error crops up.

5: Equals Rather than Is Equal To

Take a look at the following code:

```
var myNumber = 99;
if (myNumber = 101)
{
    alert("myNumber is 101");
}
else
{
    alert("myNumber is " + myNumber);
}
```

You'd expect, at first glance, that the alert() method in the else part of the if statement would execute, telling us that the number in myNumber is 99, but it won't. You've made the classic "one equals sign instead of two equals signs" mistake. Hence, instead of comparing myNumber with 101, you have set myNumber to equal 101. If, like me, you program in languages, such as Visual Basic, that use only one equals sign for both comparison and assignment, you'll find that every so often this mistake crops up. It's just so easy to make.

What makes things even trickier is that no error message will be raised; it is just your data and logic that will suffer. Assigning a variable a value in an if statement may be perverse, but it's perfectly legal so there will be no complaints from JavaScript. When embedded in a large chunk of code, a mistake like this is easily overlooked. Just remember, next time your program's logic seems crazy, that it's worth checking for this error.

6: Incorrect Number of Closing Parentheses

Take a look at the following code:

```
if (myVariable + 12) / myOtherVariable < myString.length)
```

Spot the mistake?

The problem is that you've missed a parenthesis at the beginning. You want myVariable + 12 to be calculated before the division by myOtherVariable is calculated, so quite rightly you know you need to put it in parentheses.

```
(myVariable + 12) / myOtherVariable
```

However, the `if` statement's condition must also be in parentheses. Not only is the initial parenthesis missing, but also you have one more closing parenthesis than you have opening parentheses; the numbers must match. For each parenthesis opened, there must be a corresponding closing parenthesis. Your code should be as follows:

```
if ((myVariable + 12) / myOtherVariable < myString.length)
```

When you have lots of opening and closing parentheses, it's very easy to miss one or have one too many.

7: *Using a Method as a Property and Vice Versa*

The final common error is where either you forget to put parentheses after a method with no parameters, or you use a property and do put parentheses after it.

When calling a method you must always have parentheses following its name; otherwise JavaScript thinks that it must be a property. For example, examine the following code:

```
var nowDate = new Date;
alert(nowDate.getMonth);
```

In the first line you have used the `Date` constructor, which is simply a method of the `Date` object, with no parentheses.

On the second line, you call the `getMonth()` method of the `Date` object, except that you've forgotten the parentheses here also.

This is how lines should be:

```
var nowDate = new Date();
alert(nowDate.getMonth());
```

Just as you should always have parentheses after a method, you should never have parentheses after a property, otherwise JavaScript thinks you are trying to use a method of that object:

```
var myString = new String("Hello");
alert(myString.length());
```

In the second line you have used parentheses after the `length` property, making JavaScript think it is a method. You should have written it like this:

```
var myString = new String("Hello");
alert(myString.length);
```

This mistake may seem like an obvious one in two lines, but it's easy to slip up when you're pounding out lots and lots of code.

Now that you've seen these top seven mistakes, you'll take a look at one way to make remedying them easier. This is through the use of the Microsoft script debugger.

Microsoft Script Debugger

The Microsoft script debugger for use with IE is a very useful tool for discovering what's gone wrong and why. Using it, you can halt the execution of your script and then step through code line by line to see exactly what is happening.

You can also find out which data are being held in variables and execute statements on the fly. Without the script debugger, the best you can do is use the `alert()` method in your code to show the state of variables at various points.

The script debugger works with IE 5+.

Obtaining the Script Debugger

You can currently download the script debugger from the following URL:

`www.microsoft.com/downloads/details.aspx?FamilyID=2f465be0-94fd-4569-b3c4-dffdf19ccd99&displaylang=en`

If the URL changes, a search for "script debugger" on the Microsoft web site, `www.microsoft.com`, ought to find its new home.

Other programs, such as Microsoft Visual Studio, also come with a built-in script debugger so there's no need to install this one.

In addition, Windows 2000 automatically comes with the script debugger, although it may not be set up on your system. To install it, open the Control Panel and choose Add/Remove Programs. Click the Add/Remove Windows Components button, and in the window that opens, scroll down the list to the script debugger. If it is not checked, then check it and click Next to install it.

To see if the script debugger is already installed, launch Internet Explorer and select the View menu. If one of the menu options is Script Debugger, as shown in Figure 10-3, the debugger is installed. If you do not find this menu option, it is still possible that the script debugger is already installed, but disabled. See the end of the next section to learn how to enable the script debugger, and then check for the menu option again.

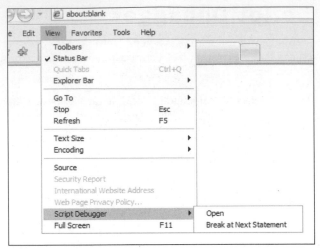

Figure 10-3

Installing the Script Debugger

After downloading the script debugger, you need to install it. First, you need to run the file you have just downloaded, for example from the Windows Start bar's Run menu option. You should then see the dialog box shown in Figure 10-4, asking whether you want to install the debugger: Click the Yes button.

Figure 10-4

Next the license screen appears, as shown in Figure 10-5. Check the license, and then click the Yes button to agree to the conditions and install the debugger.

Figure 10-5

Next you get to choose where you want to install the debugger (see Figure 10-6). Anywhere on your local machine is fine.

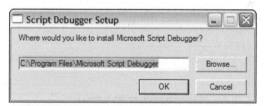

Figure 10-6

Click OK, and if a screen appears asking whether you want to create the directory, just click Yes.

The script debugger will now install. When it's complete, you see the message shown in Figure 10-7.

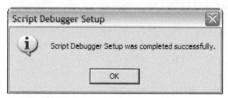

Figure 10-7

Click OK and if asked whether you want to restart the computer, click Yes.

After the computer has restarted, open Internet Explorer. If you go to the View menu, you should see the Script Debugger option. If not, the script debugger may be disabled. To enable it in IE 5 and later, go to Tools ⇨ Internet Options. Then select the Advanced tab to see a screen similar to that shown in Figure 10-8.

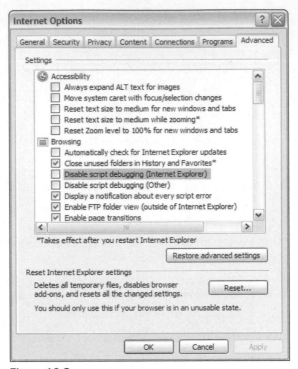

Figure 10-8

Make sure that the Disable script debugging (Internet Explorer) check box is cleared, as shown in Figure 10-8. Click OK, and then close the browser. When you reopen the browser you should see the Script Debugger option in the View menu.

Using the Script Debugger

It's important to point out that there are actually two versions of the script debugger: the basic version that you installed in the previous section and a more sophisticated version that comes with programs like Microsoft Visual Studio .Net. The more sophisticated version does everything that the basic version does, but the screen layout and look will vary slightly, as will some of the keys and icons. You'll be looking at just the basic version here, so all screenshots are applicable to that.

Opening a Page in the Debugger

You can open a page in the script debugger in a number of ways, but here you'll just look at the three that are most useful. However, before you start let's create a page you can debug. Note the deliberate typo in line 14. Be sure to include this typo if creating the page from scratch.

```
<!DOCTYPE HTML PUBLIC "-//W3C//DTD HTML 4.01 Transitional//EN"
"http://www.w3.org/TR/html4/loose.dtd">
<html>
<head>
<script language="JavaScript" type="text/javascript">
function writeTimesTable(timesTable)
{
   var counter;
   var writeString;
   for (counter = 1; counter < 12; counter++)
   {
      writeString = counter + " * " + timesTable + " = ";
      writeString = writeString + (timesTable * counter);
      writeString = writeString + "<br>";
      documents.write(writeString);
   }
}
</script>
</head>
<body>
<div><script language=JavaScript type="text/javascript">
   writeTimesTable(2)
</script>
</div>
</body>
</html>
```

Save this page as `debug_timestable.htm`.

When you load this page into Internet Explorer, you'll discover the first way of activating the script debugger: It is activated automatically when there is an error in your code.

You should see a message box, similar to that shown in Figure 10-9, asking whether you wish to debug. Click Yes.

Figure 10-9

Having said that you want to debug, you should see the screen shown in Figure 10-10. The debugger has opened and stopped on the line where the error is and highlighted it in yellow, although this may not be obvious from the black-and-white screenshots in this chapter. The deliberate mistake is that you've written `documents.write` rather than `document.write`. The view is read-only so you can't edit it here; you need to return to your text editor to correct it. Let's do that, and then reload the page.

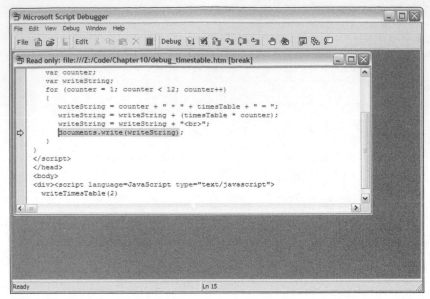

Figure 10-10

Having corrected the mistake and reloaded the page, you should see the two times table in your web page, as shown in Figure 10-11.

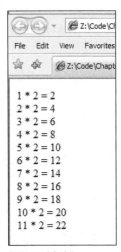

Figure 10-11

The second method you're going to use to open the debugger begins with loading the page you want to debug into your browser; then you use the Break at Next Statement menu option under Script Debugger on the Internet Explorer View menu, as shown in Figure 10-12.

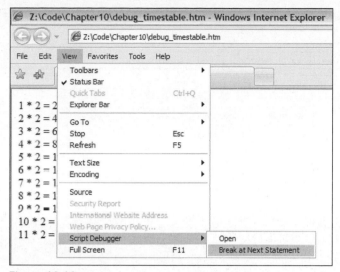

Figure 10-12

You've already got `debug_timestable.htm` loaded, so select View ⇨ Script Debugger ⇨ Break at Next Statement. Not much appears to happen, but reload the page by clicking the refresh icon or pressing F5, and the debugger will open at the next JavaScript statement executed.

Where the next JavaScript statement occurs in your page depends on your code. If you have code in the page other than a function or code connected to an event handler, the first line the browser executes will be the next JavaScript statement. In your case, this is the code calling the following function:

```
<script>writeTimesTable(2)</script>
```

If there is no code in the page except code inside event handlers or functions, the next statement executed will be that fired in an event handler, such as the `window` object's `onload` event handler or a button's `onclick` event handler.

Note that with some setups of the script debugger, the browser brings up a dialog box saying that an exception of type "Runtime Error" was not handled. This does not mean that there is an error in the code, but is simply the way Break at Next Statement works.

As you can see from Figure 10-13, the next statement executed in your example occurs when the browser reaches the script embedded in your web page that calls the `writeTimesTable()` function. Again, this script is highlighted in yellow by the debugger.

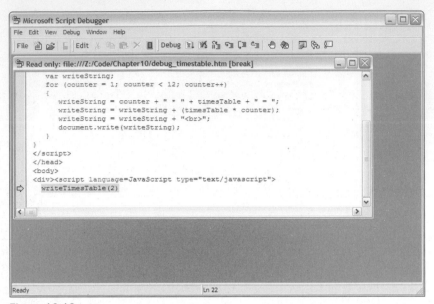

Figure 10-13

You're now going to use the Step Into icon, illustrated here, which can be found on the top toolbar.

Click this icon and the debugger will execute the current line of code and move to the next line, in this case your function. (You'll look more fully at stepping through code and examining the contents of variables shortly.) You can also press the F8 key to step into the code, which is often easier than clicking the icon.

Finally, let's look at a third way of opening the debugger, which is probably the easiest and most useful.

Imagine you want to stop your code's execution and open the debugger just before the `for` loop is executed. You can do this by simply adding the keyword `debugger` to your script, which will stop the execution at that point and open the debugger. Let's do that now.

You need to close the debugger, return to your text editor, and add the following code to `debug_timestable.htm`:

```
function writeTimesTable(timesTable)
{
    var counter;
    var writeString;
    debugger
    for (counter = 1; counter < 12; counter++)
    {
        writeString = counter + " * " + timesTable + " = ";
```

```
        writeString = writeString + (timesTable * counter);
        writeString = writeString + "<br>";
        document.write(writeString);
    }
}
```

Now refresh the page in Internet Explorer, and you'll find that the debugger opens, with code execution paused on the line with the `debugger` keyword in it (see Figure 10-14).

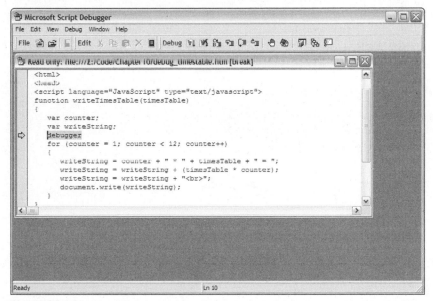

Figure 10-14

Again you can click the Step Into icon you used previously, and watch the code execute statement by statement.

Stepping Through Code

There are three important ways of stepping through code, each involving one of the icons from the top toolbar of the script debugger.

You've seen that one way is to step into the code. This simply means that every line of code is executed on a line-by-line basis. If a function is called, you step into that function and start executing the code inside the function statement by statement, before stepping out again at the end and returning to the calling line. To do this you use the Step Into icon.

You may find that having stepped into a function you get halfway through and decide the function is not the source of the bug, and that you want to execute the remaining lines of code in the function, then continue step by step from the point at which the function was called. This is called stepping out of the function, and to do it you use the Step Out icon.

Instead of the icon you can press Ctrl+Shift+F8.

There may also be times when you have some code with a bug in it that calls a number of functions. If you know that some of the functions are bug-free, then you may want to just execute those functions instead of stepping into them and seeing them executed line by line. For this the debugger has the Step Over icon, which executes the code within a function but without your having to go through it line by line.

Or you can press Shift+F8.

Let's alter your times-table code in `debug_timestable.htm` and demonstrate the three kinds of stepping action. Note that the `debugger` keyword has been removed from the `writeTimesTable()` function and is now in the second script block.

```
<html>
<head>
<script language=JavaScript type="text/javascript">
function writeTimesTable(timesTable)
{
   var counter;
   var writeString;
   for (counter = 1; counter < 12; counter++)
   {
     writeString = counter + " * " + timesTable + " = ";
     writeString = writeString + (timesTable * counter);
     writeString = writeString + "<BR>";
     document.write(writeString);
   }
}
</script>
</head>
<body>
<div><script language=JavaScript type="text/javascript">
var timesTable;
debugger
for (timesTable = 1; timesTable <= 12; timesTable++)
{
   document.write("<P>")
   writeTimesTable(timesTable)
   document.write("</P>")
}
</script></div>
</body>
</html>
```

Save this as `debug_timestable2.htm`. When you load it into your browser, the script debugger will be opened by the `debugger` statement, as shown in Figure 10-15.

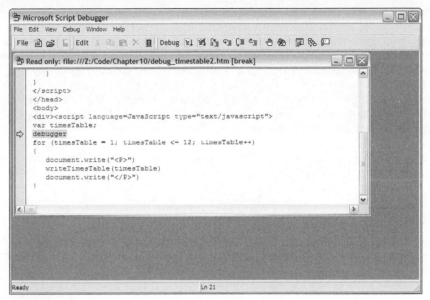

Figure 10-15

Click the Step Into icon and code execution will move to the next statement. In this case, the next statement is the first statement in the `for` loop in which you initialized the variable `timesTable` to the value of 1, as shown in Figure 10-16.

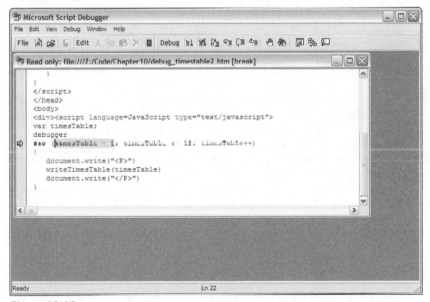

Figure 10-16

When you click the Step Into icon again, the `timesTable = 1` statement is executed and you step to the next statement due to be executed, which is the condition part of the `for` loop. With `timesTable` set to 1, you know that the condition `timesTable <= 12` is going to be `true`. Click the Step Into icon and the condition executes and indeed you find you're right, the condition is `true`. Now the first statement inside the `for` loop, `document.write("<P>")`, is up for execution.

When you click the Step Into icon again it will take you to the first calling of your `writeTimesTable()` function. You want to see what's happening inside that function, so click Step Into again and you'll step into the function. Your screen should look like the one shown in Figure 10-17.

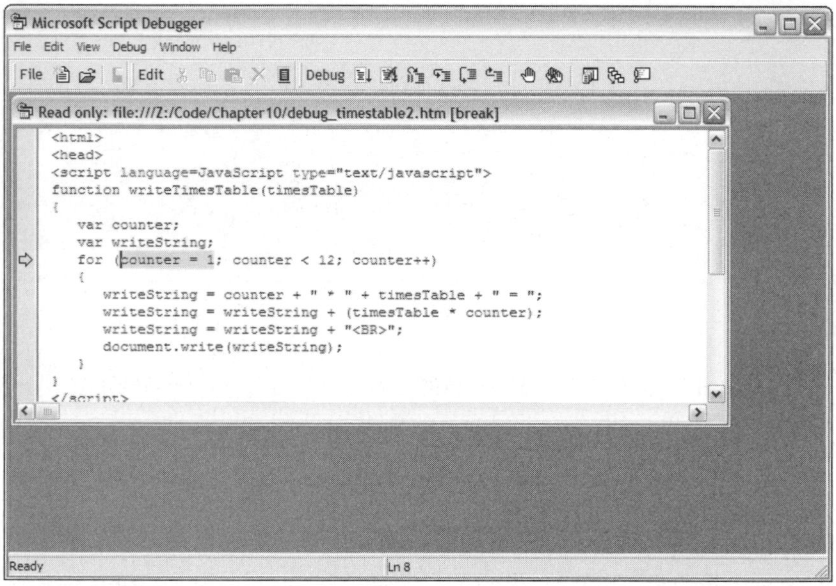

Figure 10-17

The next statement to be executed is not the `var counter;` or `var writeString;` line, but instead the `for` loop's initialization condition. The first two lines have been executed, but the script debugger does not enable us to step through variable declarations line by line.

Click the Step Into icon a few times to get the gist of the flow of execution of the function. In fact, stepping through code line by line can get a little tedious. So let's imagine you're happy with this function and want to run the rest of it. Start single-stepping from the next line after the function was called. To do this, click the Step Out icon.

Now the function has been fully executed, and you're back out of it and at the next line, `document.write("</P>")`, as you can see from Figure 10-18.

Figure 10-18

Click the Step Into icon to see that the `document.write()` line will be executed, and the next statement in the flow of execution is the increment part of your `for` loop. Click Step Into again and execution will continue to the condition part of the `for` loop. Clicking Step Into twice more brings you back to the calling of the `writeTimesTable()` function. You've already seen this in action, so really you want to step over it and go to the next line. Well, no prizes for guessing that the Step Over icon is what you need to click to do this.

Click the Step Over icon and the function will be executed, but without your having to step through it statement by statement. You should find yourself back at the `document.write("</P>")` line.

If you've finished debugging, you can run the rest of the code without stepping through each line by clicking the Run icon on the toolbar, shown after this paragraph. Let's do that; then you can return to the browser and see the results of the code you have executed. You should see a page of times tables from `1*1=1` to `11*12=132` in the browser.

Instead of clicking the icon you can also press the F5 key.

Breakpoints

Breakpoints are markers you can set in the debugger that force code execution to stop at that point and start single-stepping through the code.

Load your `debug_timestable2.htm` page into the browser. This will open the debugger and stop execution at the line with your `debugger` statement. Now imagine that you want to stop in your `writeTimesTable()` function on the line that writes the results of the times table to the page, namely `document.write(writeString)`, as shown in Figure 10-19. This is the last statement in the `for` loop. However, we're busy people and don't want to manually step through every line before that. What you can do is set a breakpoint on that line and then click the Run icon, which will restart the code execution in the normal fashion (that is, without single-stepping). Then, when the breakpoint is reached, code execution will stop and you can start single-stepping if you want.

To set the breakpoint, you need to scroll up the code window in the debugger until you can see the line on which you want to put the breakpoint. Click that line; then click the Toggle Breakpoint icon on the toolbar, shown here.

Any line with a breakpoint on it is indicated by the reddish-brown dot on the left of the code window and by the line itself being set to a reddish brown, although the line may not always be colored. You can set as many or as few breakpoints at one time as you wish, so if you want to break on other lines you can add breakpoints there too.

To unset a breakpoint you just click the relevant line of code and click the Toggle Breakpoint icon again, and that toggles it off. To clear all breakpoints at once you can click the Clear All Breakpoints icon shown here (see Figure 10-19).

Okay, now let's start the code running again by clicking the Run icon in the toolbar.

You'll find that the code resumes executing without single-stepping until it reaches your breakpoint, at which point it stops. You can either single-step using the Step Into icon or click the Run icon again, in which case execution continues unless another breakpoint is reached.

Leave the debugger open with code execution halted on your breakpoint; you'll be using it in a moment.

Figure 10-19

The Command Window

While you're stepping through code and checking its flow of execution, what would be really useful is the ability to check the values contained inside variables, to evaluate conditions, and even to change things on the fly. You can do all of these things using the debugger's command window.

Hopefully you still have the debugger open with execution halted at the breakpoint you set previously. The line stopped on in Figure 10-19 is repeated here:

```
document.write(writeString);
```

Let's see how you can find out the value currently contained in the variable `writeString`.

First you need to open the command window from within the debugger. You do this by clicking the Command Window icon, illustrated here, or by selecting Command Window from the View menu.

In the command window, type the name of the variable you want to examine, in this case `writeString`; then click Enter. This will cause the value contained in the variable to be printed below your command in the command window, as shown in Figure 10-20.

381

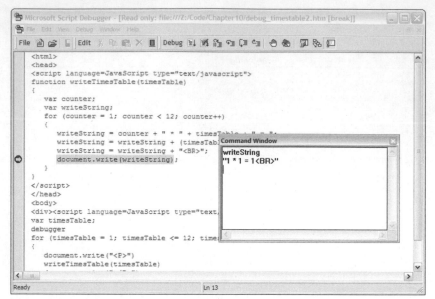

Figure 10-20

If you want to change a variable, you can write a line of JavaScript into the command window and press Enter. Try it with the following code:

```
writeString = "Changed on the Fly<BR>"
```

Now remove the breakpoint (see the previous section for instructions) and click the Run icon. If you switch to the browser, you see the results of your actions: Where the 1*1 times table result should be, the text you changed on the fly has been inserted. Note that this alteration does not change your actual HTML source file, just the page currently loaded in the browser.

The command window can also evaluate conditions. Refresh the browser to reset the debugger and leave execution stopped at your `debugger` statement. Click the Step Into icon twice and execution will stop on the condition in the `for` statement.

Type the following into the command window and press Enter:

```
timesTable <= 12
```

Because this is the first time the loop has been run, as shown in Figure 10-21, `timesTable` is equal to 1 and so the condition `timesTable <= 12` evaluates to `true`. Note that the debugger sometimes represents `true` by the value –1 and `false` by the value 0, so you may see the value –1 instead of `true`.

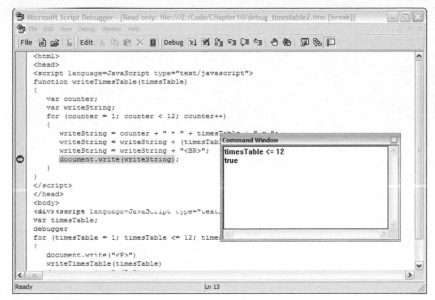

Figure 10-21

You can also use the command window to access properties of the browser's Browser Object Model (BOM). For example, if you type `window.location.href` into the command window and press Enter, it will tell you where the current page is stored.

In fact, the command window can execute any single line of JavaScript including functions.

Call Stack Window

When you are single-stepping through the code, the call stack window keeps a running list of which functions have been called to get to the current point of execution in the code.

Let's create an example web page that demonstrates the call stack very nicely.

```
<!DOCTYPE HTML PUBLIC "-//W3C//DTD HTML 4.01 Transitional//EN"
"http://www.w3.org/TR/html4/loose.dtd">
<html>
<head>
<script language=JavaScript type="text/javascript">
function firstCall()
{
    secondCall();
}
function secondCall()
{
    thirdCall();
}
function thirdCall()
{
```

```
    //
}
function button1_onclick()
{
    debugger
    firstCall();
}
</script>
</head>
<body>
<input type="button" value="Button" name=button1
    onclick="return button1_onclick()">
</body>
</html>
```

Save this page as `debug_callstack.htm`, and then load it into IE. After you've done this, all you'll see is a blank web page with a button. Click the button and the debugger will be opened at the `debugger` statement in the `button1_onclick()` function, which is connected to the button's `onclick` event handler.

To open the call stack window, click the Call Stack icon in the toolbar, shown here, or choose Call Stack from the View menu.

Your debugger now looks like what is shown in Figure 10-22.

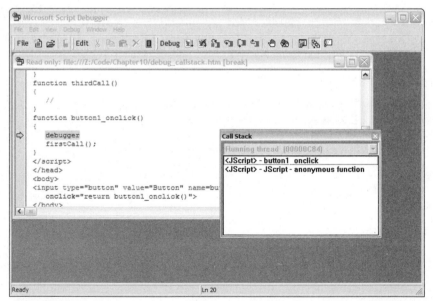

Figure 10-22

Every time a function is called, the debugger adds the function to the top of the call stack. You can already see that the first function called was actually the code attached to the onclick event handler of your button. The anonymous function is the event handler code that calls your onclick function. Next, added to the call stack is the function called by the onclick event handler, which is the function button1_onclick() shown at the top of the call stack.

If you want to see where each function was first entered, you need only double-click the function name in the call stack window. Double-click <Jscript> - Jscript - anonymous function and the calling line — that is, the code connected to the onclick attribute of the <input> tag — will be shown. Now double-click the top line — <Jscript> - button1_onclick — and that will take you back to the current execution point.

Now single-step twice, using the Step Into icon. The first step is to the line that calls the firstCall() function. The second step takes you into that function itself. The function is immediately added to the call stack, as shown in Figure 10-23.

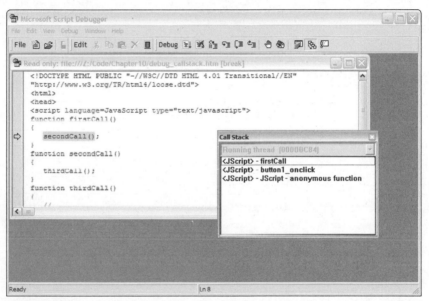

Figure 10-23

Click the Step Into icon again and you'll step into the second function, secondCall(). Again this is added to the call stack. One more click takes you into the third function, thirdCall(), again with its name being added to the top of the call stack.

Now click Step Into again and as you leave the function thirdCall() you will see that its name is removed from the top of the call stack. Another click takes you out of the second function secondCall(), whose name is also now removed from the stack. Each additional click takes you out of a function, and removes its name from the call stack, until eventually all the code has been executed and you're back to the browser again.

Your demo page was very simple to follow, but with complex pages, especially multi-frame pages, the call stack can prove very useful for tracking where you are, where you have been, and how you got there.

Running Documents Window

The final window you'll look at is the running documents window. This window lists each instance of Internet Explorer running and shows you which pages, or documents, are currently loaded in that instance.

Let's create some example pages demonstrating the use of the running documents window.

The running documents window proves most useful with frame-based pages, so let's create a page with two frames inside it.

```
<!DOCTYPE HTML PUBLIC "-//W3C//DTD HTML 4.01 Frameset//EN"
"http://www.w3.org/TR/html4/frameset.dtd">
<html>
<frameset rows="50%,*">
    <frame name="topFrame" src="debug_topFrame.htm">
    <frame name="bottomFrame" src="debug_bottomFrame.htm">
</frameset>
</html>
```

This first page defines the frameset. Save it as debug_frameset.htm.

Next is the page for the top window.

```
<!DOCTYPE HTML PUBLIC "-//W3C//DTD HTML 4.01 Transitional//EN"
"http://www.w3.org/TR/html4/loose.dtd">
<html>
<head>
<title>example</title>
<script language=JavaScript type="text/javascript">
function button1_onclick()
{
    var x;
    x = 1 + 1;
    alert(x)
}
</script>
</head>
<body>
<h2>Top Frame</h2>
<input type="button" value="Button" name="button1"  onclick="return
button1_onclick()">
</body>
</html>
```

Save this page as debug_topFrame.htm.

Finally, enter the third page.

```
<!DOCTYPE HTML PUBLIC "-//W3C//DTD HTML 4.01 Transitional//EN"
"http://www.w3.org/TR/html4/loose.dtd">
<html>
<head>
<script language=JavaScript type="text/javascript">
function button1_onclick()
{
    var x;
    x = 2 * 2;
    alert(x);
}
</script>
</head>
<body>
<h2>Bottom Frame</h2>
<input type="button" value="Button" name="button1"
    onclick="return button1_onclick()">
</body>
</html>
```

Save this page as debug_bottomFrame.htm.

Now load debug_frameset.htm into the browser. You will see two frames, each containing a button.

You can view all the pages currently loaded in the frames by first opening the debugger by choosing Script debugger ⇨ Open from the View menu. Now with the debugger open you need to view the running documents window by clicking the Running Documents icon in the toolbar, shown here, or selecting Running Documents from the View menu.

This will initially show each instance of Internet Explorer running on the machine. Click the plus sign to open a window that shows which pages are currently loaded, or running, in that instance of Internet Explorer. When pages are in framesets, as ours are, then pages contained within the window frameset page are included, indented underneath the frameset page (see Figure 10-24). You'll need to click the plus sign again to open them.

The easiest way to debug the code within the top frame is to right-click debug_topFrame.htm in the Running Documents window and select Break at Next Statement. Then click the button in the top frame and the debugger will open, with execution stopped at the first statement due to be executed (onclick="return button1_onclick()").

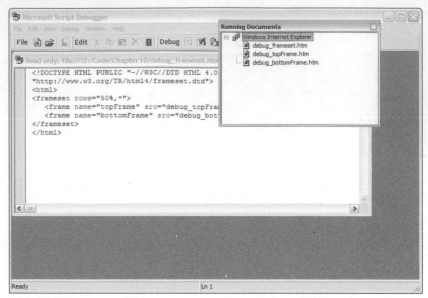

Figure 10-24

That concludes your brief tour of the Microsoft script debugger. This debugger is excellent for debugging pages so that they will work in IE. However, it won't help us spot errors caused by cross-browser incompatibility. For example, what works in Firefox might throw an error in IE, and a page that you've debugged successfully in IE could easily throw an error in Firefox. Aside from this problem, the debugger is a great help for spotting logic errors in your code.

Firefox Debugging with Venkman

Like IE, Firefox has a debugger of its own, called Venkman. It provides all the features and debugging power of the IE debugger: For example, you can step into, over, and out of your code, work with breakpoints, and access a call stack window.

You can download Venkman from

```
https://addons.mozilla.org/firefox/216/
```

> *Unfortunately, at the time of this writing, September 2006, Venkman and Firefox have bugs that make their use together difficult. After the initial install Venkman works, but later attempts to open it fail. Firefox must be restarted for Venkman to work again. Hopefully by the time you read this Venkman will be working again!*

To install Venkman, open Firefox and go to the `mozilla.org` URL mentioned earlier; then follow the instructions. After Venkman is installed you'll need to close down and restart Firefox. A brief guide to Venkman can be found at:

```
www.hacksrus.com/~ginda/venkman/
```

When Firefox is reopened you can launch the debugger. If you now look under the Tools ⇨ JavaScript Debugger menu you will see that an extra menu option has appeared (see Figure 10-25).

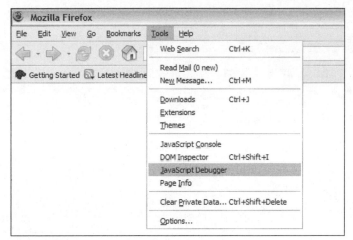

Figure 10-25

Choosing JavaScript Debugger opens Venkman, as shown in Figure 10-26.

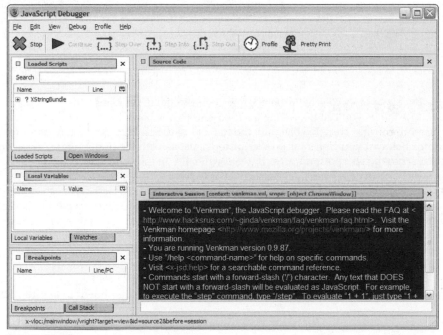

Figure 10-26

The important first step is to launch Venkman. Then you can load the page or frameset that you wish to debug into Firefox. Leave Venkman open, switch to Firefox, and load the `debug_timestable2.htm` file you created earlier. As soon as it's loaded the page runs and comes to a stop on the debugger command and highlights where it has stopped, just as in the IE debugger (see Figure 10-27).

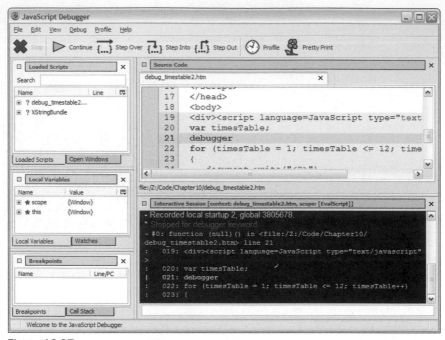

Figure 10-27

Although the layout and icons are different from those in the IE debugger, the concepts are the same, as are the sorts of things you can do. As Figure 10-27 shows, the black background of the interactive window at the bottom-right corner is basically the same as in the IE debugger's command window. In the long text box below it you can enter JavaScript code, just as with the IE debugger. If you enter `timesTable` into the text box and press Enter, it will tell you the value contained in the `timesTable` variable, which, because it hasn't yet been given, is currently void.

Click the Step Into icon on the debugger's toolbar and the code goes to the next line. The step over, step into, and step out commands work here very much as they do in the IE debugger, but there are some differences. For example, the `for` loop head is just one step with Venkman, whereas the MS debugger steps to the initialization first and then to the condition. Also, while the MS debugger runs over variable declarations, Venkman doesn't.

Keep stepping until you are in the `writeTimesTable()` function, as shown in Figure 10-28.

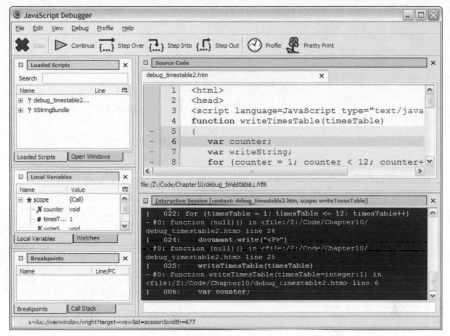

Figure 10-28

Notice that the window in the middle on the left-hand side, named Local Variables, has changed. It now shows under the heading scope the variables within the scope of this function. In this function these are the counter, timesTable, and writeString variables. The current values of each variable are also shown, void in the case of variables yet to be assigned a value.

In the bottom left-hand corner are the Breakpoints and Call Stack windows. Currently you see only the Breakpoints window, but by clicking the Call Stack tab under the window you can switch to that window. (You can switch back with the Breakpoints tab.) Click the Call Stack tab to show the current state of the call stack, as shown in Figure 10-29.

As Figure 10-29 shows, there are two items in the call stack: the writeTimesTable() function call and the code that called it.

To set a breakpoint, you click the gray area in the source code window on the line where you want to set a breakpoint (see Figure 10-30).

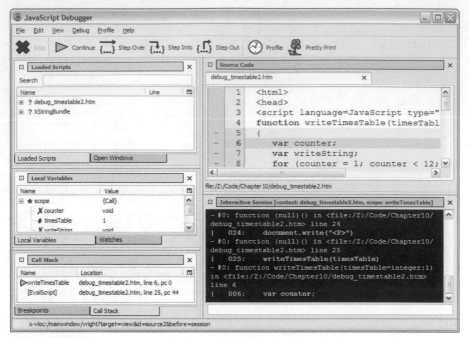

Figure 10-29

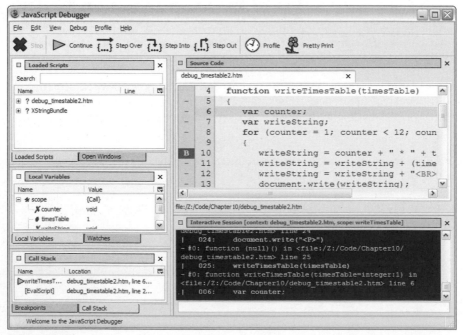

Figure 10-30

In Figure 10-30, we clicked the gray area on the `writeString = counter...` line, and the gray area has turned red and been marked with the letter B to show it's a breakpoint. If you click the breakpoint again it will turn orange and be marked with the letter F to indicate that this is a future breakpoint. Clicking a third time removes the breakpoint. Alternatively, you could right-click the breakpoint listed in the breakpoint window and clear it there—or, indeed, clear all breakpoints. Note that a future breakpoint is a breakpoint that is not set for this execution of the code but that will be set next time the page is executed, for example if you reload the page.

The final window is the Loaded Scripts window, situated in Figure 10-30 in the top left-hand corner. This shows currently loaded files. In your case there is just one document, but there can be more than one if, for example, a frameset is loaded. This is the equivalent of the IE debugger's Running Documents window.

The Venkman debugger is a little more sophisticated than the basic IE debugger, and it's worth reading the full and quite extensive documentation on the Venkman home page for details.

Error Handling

When writing your programs, you want to be informed of every error. However, when you've finally deployed the code to a web server for the whole world to access, the last thing you want the user to see is a lot of error message dialog boxes. Of course, writing bug-free code would be a good start, but keep the following points in mind:

❑ Occasions arise when conditions beyond your control lead to errors. A good example of this is when you are relying on something, such as a Java applet, that isn't on the user's computer and that you have no way of checking for.

❑ Murphy's Law states that anything that can go wrong will go wrong!

Preventing Errors

The best way to handle errors is to stop them from occurring in the first place. That seems like stating the obvious, but there are a number of things you should do if you want error-free pages.

1. Check pages thoroughly on as many different platforms and browsers as possible. Of course this is easier said than done, given the number of possible variations, and it's easier with a professional web site created by a team of people with the hardware, software, and time to check platform and browser compatibility. The alternative is for you to decide which browsers and platforms are supported and state your requirements on your first web page. Then verify that your page works with the specified combinations. Use the browser- and platform-checking code you saw earlier in the book to send unsupported users to a nice, safe, and probably boring web page with reduced functionality, or maybe just supply them with a message that their browser/platform is not supported.

2. Validate your data. If there is a way for users to enter dud data that will cause your program to fall over, then they will. If your code will fall over if a text box is empty, you must check that it has something in it. If you need a whole number, you must check that that's what the user has entered. Is the date the user just entered valid? Is the e-mail address `mind your own business` the user just entered likely to be valid? No, so you must check that it is in the format `something@something.something`.

Okay, so let's say you've carefully checked your pages and there is not a syntax or logic error in sight. You've added data validation that confirms that everything the user enters is in a valid format. Things can still go wrong, and problems may arise that you can do nothing about. Here's a real-world example of something that can still go wrong.

Yours truly, Paul, created an online message board that used something called remote scripting, a Microsoft technology that enables us to transfer data from a server to a web page. It relies on a small Java applet to enable the transfer of data. Paul checked the code and everything was fine. After launching the board, it worked just fine, except that in about 5 percent of cases the Java applet initialized, but then caused an error. To cut a long story short, remote scripting worked fine, except in a small number of cases where the user was behind a particular type of firewall (a firewall is a means of stopping hackers from getting into a local computer network). Now, there is no way of determining whether a user is behind a certain type of firewall, so there is nothing that can be done in that sort of exceptional circumstance. Or is there?

In fact IE 5+ and Firefox include something called the `try...catch` statement. It's also part of the ECMAScript 3 standard. This enables you to try to run your code; if it fails, the error is caught by the `catch` clause and can be dealt with as you wish. For the message board, Paul used a `try...catch` clause to catch the Java applet's failure and redirected the user to a more basic page that still displayed messages, but without using the applet.

Let's now look at the `try...catch` statements.

The try...catch Statements

The `try...catch` statements work as a pair; you can't have one without the other.

You use the `try` statement to define a block of code that you want to try to execute.

You use the `catch` statement to define a block of code that will execute if an exception to the normal running of the code occurs in the block of code defined by the `try` statement. The term *exception* is key here: It means a circumstance that is extraordinary and unpredictable. Compare that with an *error*, which is something in the code that has been written incorrectly. If no exception occurs, the code inside the `catch` statement is never executed. The `catch` statement also enables you to get the contents of the exception message that would have been shown to the user had you not caught it first.

Let's create a simple example of a `try...catch` clause.

```
<!DOCTYPE HTML PUBLIC "-//W3C//DTD HTML 4.01 Transitional//EN"
"http://www.w3.org/TR/html4/loose.dtd">
<html>
<body>
<script language="JavaScript" type="text/javascript">
try
{
    alert('This is code inside the try clause');
    alert('No Errors so catch code will not execute');
}
catch(exception)
{
```

```
      if (exception.description == null)
      {
         alert("Firefox says the error is " + exception.message)
      }
      else
      {
         alert("Internet Explorer says the error is " + exception.description);
      }
   }
</script>
</body>
</html>
```

Save this as `TryCatch.htm`.

First you define the `try` statement; you mark out which block of code is within the `try` statement by enclosing it in curly braces.

Next comes the `catch` statement. You've included `exception` in parentheses right after the `catch` statement. This `exception` is simply a variable name. It will store an `Exception` object containing information about any exception thrown during execution of code inside the `try` code block. Although you've used `exception`, you could use any valid variable name. For example, `catch(exceptionObject)` would be fine and certainly more descriptive.

The `Exception` object contains two properties that provide information about the exception that occurred. The bad news is that while both IE and Firefox support the `Exception` object and both have two properties, the names of these properties differ.

The IE version of the `Exception` object has the `number` and `description` properties. The `number` property is a unique number for that error type. The `description` property is the error message the user would normally see.

With Firefox, the properties of the `Exception` object are `name` and `message`. The `name` property is a unique name for that type of error and the `message` property is much like the IE `description` property in that it gives a more detailed explanation of what went wrong. These properties are also part of the ECMAScript 3 standard and IE and Opera 6+ support them.

Within the curly braces after the `catch` statement is the code block that will execute if and only if an error occurs. In this case, the code within the `try` code block is fine, and so the `alert()` method inside the `catch` block won't execute.

Insert a deliberate error.

```
try
{
   alert('This is code inside the try clause');
   ablert ('Exception will be thrown by this code');
}
catch(exception)
{
   if (exception.description == null)
```

```
    {
        alert("Firefox says the error is " + exception.message)
    }
    else
    {
        alert("Internet Explorer says the error is " + exception.description);
    }
}
```

Now when you load the page, the first `alert()` method, the `try` block of code, will execute fine and the alert box will be displayed to the user. However, the second `ablert()` statement will cause an error and code execution will start at the first statement in the `catch` block.

Because the IE and Firefox `Exception` objects support different properties, you need different code for each. How do you tell whether the browser is IE or Firefox?

By checking to see whether the `exception.description` property is `null`, you can tell whether the `description` property is supported, and therefore whether the browser is one of those supporting the property, such as IE. If the property is equal to `null`, it is not supported by the browser, so you need to display the `message` property of the `Exception` object instead. If the property is not `null`, it has a value and therefore does exist and can be used.

If you're using Internet Explorer, the error description displayed will be `Object expected`. If you're using Firefox, the same error is interpreted differently and reported as `ablert is not defined`.

If you change the code again, so it has a different error, you'll see something important.

```
try
{
    alert('This is code inside the try clause');
    alert('This code won't work');
}
catch(exception)
{
    if (exception.description == null)
    {
        alert("Firefox says the error is " + exception.message)
    }
    else
    {
        alert("Internet Explorer says the error is " + exception.description);
    }
}
```

If you load this code into an IE or Firefox browser, instead of the error being handled by your `catch` clause, you get the normal browser error message telling you `Expected ')'`.

The reason for this is that this code contains a syntax error: The functions and methods are valid, but you have an invalid character. The single quote in the word `won't` has ended the string parameter being passed to the `alert()` method. At that point JavaScript syntax, or language rules, specifies that a closing parenthesis should appear, which is not the case here. Before executing any code, JavaScript goes through all the code and checks for syntax errors, or code that breaches JavaScript's rules. If a syntax error is found, the browser deals with it as usual; your `try` clause never runs and therefore cannot handle syntax errors.

Throwing Errors

The `throw` statement can be used within a `try` block of code to create your own run-time errors. Why create a statement to generate errors, when a bit of bad coding will do the same?

Throwing errors can be very useful for indicating problems such as invalid user input. Rather than using lots of `if...else` statements, you can check the validity of user input, then use `throw` to stop code execution in its tracks and cause the error-catching code in the `catch` block of code to take over. In the `catch` clause, you can determine whether the error is based on user input, in which case you can notify the user what went wrong and how to correct it. Alternatively, if it's an unexpected error, you can handle it more gracefully than with lots of JavaScript errors.

To use `throw`, you type `throw` and include the error message after it.

```
throw "This is my error message";
```

Remember that when you catch the `Exception` object in the `catch` statement, you can get hold of the error message that you have thrown. Although there's a string in this example `throw` statement, you can actually throw any type of data, including numbers and objects.

Try It Out   **try...catch and Throwing Errors**

In this example you'll be creating a simple factorial calculator. The important parts of this example are the `try...catch` clause and the `throw` statements. It's a frameset page to enable us to demonstrate that things can go wrong that you can't do anything about. In this case, the page relies on a function defined within a frameset page, so if the page is loaded on its own, a problem will occur.

First let's create the page that will define the frameset and that also contains an important function.

```
<!DOCTYPE HTML PUBLIC "-//W3C//DTD HTML 4.01 Transitional//EN"
"http://www.w3.org/TR/html4/loose.dtd">
<html>
<head>
<title>Example</title>
<script language="JavaScript" type="text/javascript">
function calcFactorial(factorialNumber)
{
   var factorialResult = 1;
   for (; factorialNumber > 0; factorialNumber--)
   {
       factorialResult = factorialResult * factorialNumber;
   }
return factorialResult;
}
</script>
</head>
<frameset COLS="100%,*">
    <frame name="fraCalcFactorial" src="CalcFactorial.htm">
</frameset>
</html>
```

Save this page as `CalcFactorialTopFrame.htm`.

```html
<!DOCTYPE HTML PUBLIC "-//W3C//DTD HTML 4.01 Transitional//EN"
"http://www.w3.org/TR/html4/loose.dtd">
<html>
<head>
<title>Example</title>
<script language="JavaScript" type="text/javascript">
function butCalculate_onclick()
{
    try
    {
        if (window.top.calcFactorial == null)
            throw "This page is not loaded within the correct frameset";
        if (document.form1.txtNum1.value == "")
            throw "!Please enter a value before you calculate its factorial";
        if (isNaN(document.form1.txtNum1.value))
            throw "!Please enter a valid number";
        if (document.form1.txtNum1.value < 0)
            throw "!Please enter a positive number";
        document.form1.txtResult.value =
            window.parent.calcFactorial(document.form1.txtNum1.value);
    }
    catch(exception)
    {
        if (typeof(exception) == "string")
        {
            if (exception.charAt(0) == "!")
            {
                alert(exception.substr(1));
                document.form1.txtNum1.focus();
                document.form1.txtNum1.select();
            }
            else
            {
                alert(exception);
            }
        }
        else
        {
            if (exception.description == null)
            {
alert("The following error occurred " + exception.message)
            }
            else
            {
                alert("The following error occurred " + exception.description);
            }
        }
    }
}
</script>
</head>
<body>
```

```
<form name="form1">
   <input type="text" name=txtNum1 size=3> factorial is
   <input type="text" name=txtResult size=25><br>
   <input type="button" value="Calculate Factorial"
      name=butCalculate onclick="butCalculate_onclick()">
</form>
</body>
</html>
```

Save this page as `CalcFactorial.htm`. Then load the first page, `CalcFactorialTopFrame.htm`, into your browser.

The page consists of a simple form with two text boxes and a button. Enter the number 4 into the first box and click the Calculate Factorial button. The factorial of 4, which is 24, will be calculated and put in the second text box. (See Figure 10-31.)

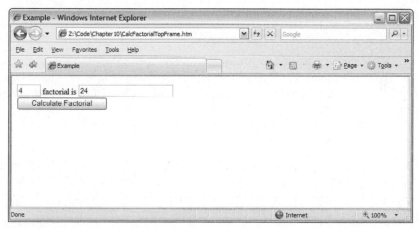

Figure 10-31

The factorial of a number is the product of all the positive integers less than or equal to that number. For example, the factorial of 4 (written 4!) is 1 * 2 * 3 * 4 = 24. Factorials are used in various branches of mathematics, including statistics. Here, you want only to create a function that does something complex enough to be worthy of a function, but not so complex as to distract you from the main purpose of this example: the `try...catch` and `throw` statements.

If you clear the first text box and click Calculate Factorial, you'll be told that a value needs to be entered. If you enter an invalid non-numeric value into the first text box, you'll be told to enter a valid value. If you enter a negative value, you'll be told to enter a positive value.

Also, if you try loading the page `CalcFactorial.htm` into your browser and enter a value in the text box and click Calculate Factorial, you'll be told that the page is not loaded into the correct frameset.

As you'll see, all of these error messages are created using the `try...catch` and `throw` statements.

How It Works

Because this example is all about `try...catch` and `throw`, you'll concentrate just on the `CalcFactorial.htm` page, in particular the `butCalculate_onclick()` function, which is connected to the `onclick` event handler of the form's only button.

You'll start by looking at the `try` clause and the code inside it. The code consists of four `if` statements and another line of code that puts the calculated factorial into the second text box. Each of the `if` statements is checking for a condition that, if true, would cause problems for your code.

The first `if` statement checks that the `calcFactorial()` function, in the top frameset window, actually exists. If not, it throws an error, which will be caught by the `catch` block. If the user loads the `CalcFactorial.htm` page rather than the frameset page `CalcFactorialTopFrame.htm`, then without this `throw` statement your code will fail.

```
try
{
    if (window.top.calcFactorial == null)
        throw "This page is not loaded within the correct frameset";
```

The next three `if` statements check the validity of the data entered into the text box by the user. First you check that something has actually been entered in the box, then that what has been entered is a number, and then finally you check that the value is not negative. Again if any of the `if` conditions is true, you throw an error, which will be caught by the `catch` block. Each of the error messages you define starts with an exclamation mark, the purpose of which is to mark the error as a user input error, rather than an error such as not being in a frameset.

```
    if (document.form1.txtNum1.value == "")
        throw "!Please enter a value before you calculate its factorial";
    if (isNaN(document.form1.txtNum1.value))
        throw "!Please enter a valid number";
    if (document.form1.txtNum1.value < 0)
        throw "!Please enter a positive number";
```

If everything is fine, the `calcFactorial()` function will be executed and the results text box will be filled with the factorial of the number entered by the user.

```
    document.form1.txtResult.value =
        window.parent.calcFactorial(document.form1.txtNum1.value);
}
```

Finally, turn your attention to the `catch` part of the `try...catch` statement. First, any message thrown by the `try` code will be caught by the `exception` variable.

```
catch(exception)
{
```

The type of data contained in `exception` will depend on how the error was thrown. If it was thrown by the browser and not by your code, `exception` will be an object, the `Exception` object. If it's thrown by your code, then in this instance you've thrown only primitive strings. So the first thing you need to do is decide what type of data `exception` contains. If it's a string, you know it was thrown by your code and can deal with it accordingly. If it's an object, and given that you know none of your code throws objects, you assume it must be the browser that has generated this exception and that `exception` is an `Exception` object.

```
if (typeof(exception) == "string")
{
```

If it was code that generated the exception using a `throw` (and so `exception` is a string), you now need to determine whether the error is a user input error, such as the text box not containing a value to calculate, or whether it was another type of error, such as the page not being loaded in your frameset. All the user input exception messages had an exclamation mark at the beginning, so you use an `if` statement to check the first character. If it is a `!`, you notify the user of the error and then return focus to your control. If it's not, you just display an error message.

```
if (exception.charAt(0) == "!")
{
   alert(exception.substr(1));
   document.form1.txtNum1.focus();
   document.form1.txtNum1.select();
}
else
{
   alert(exception);
}
}
```

If `exception` was not a string, you know you have an `exception` object and need to display either the `message` property if it's Firefox or the `description` property if it's IE. You use `if e.description == null` check to see which property is supported.

```
else
{
   if (exception.description == null)
   {
      alert("The following error occurred " + exception.message)
   }
   else
   {
      alert("The following error occurred " + exception.description);
   }
}
}
```

Nested try...catch Statements

So far you've been using just one `try...catch` statement, but it's possible to include a `try...catch` statement inside another `try` statement. Indeed, you can go further and have a `try...catch` inside the `try` statement of this inner `try...catch`, or even another inside that, the limit being what it's actually sensible to do.

So why would you use nested `try...catch` statements? Well, you can deal with certain errors inside the inner `try...catch` statement. If, however, you're dealing with a more serious error, the inner `catch` clause could pass that error to the outer `catch` clause by throwing the error to it.

Here's an example.

```
try
{
   try
   {
      ablurt ("This code has an error");
   }
   catch(exception)
   {
      var eMessage
      if (exception.description == null)
      {
         eMessage = exception.name;
      }
      else
      {
         eMessage = exception.description;
      }
      if (eMessage == "Object expected" || eMessage == "ReferenceError")
      {
         alert("Inner try...catch can deal with this error");
      }
      else
      {
         throw exception;
      }
   }
}
catch(exception)
{
   alert("Error the inner try...catch could not handle occurred");
}
```

In this code you have two try...catch pairs, one nested inside the other.

The inner try statement contains a line of code that contains an error. The catch statement of the inner try...catch checks the value of the error message caused by this error. If the exception message is either Object expected or ReferenceError, the inner try...catch deals with it by way of an alert box.

In fact, both the exception messages checked for are the same thing, but reported differently by IE and Firefox. Note that these examples use the Firefox Exception object's name property rather than the message for comparison, because name is a much shorter one-word description of the exception than message, which is a sentence describing the exception.

However, if the error caught by the inner catch statement is any other type of error, it is thrown up in the air again for the catch statement of the outer try...catch to deal with.

Let's change the butCalculate_onclick() function from the previous example, CalcFactorial.htm, so that it has both an inner and an outer try...catch.

```
function butCalculate_onclick()
{
    try
    {
        try
        {
            if (window.top.calcFactorial == null)
                throw ("This page is not loaded within the correct frameset");
            if (document.form1.txtNum1.value == "")
                throw("!Please enter a value before you calculate its factorial");
            if (isNaN(document.form1.txtNum1.value))
                throw("!Please enter a valid number");
            if (document.form1.txtNum1.value < 0)
                throw("!Please enter a positive number");
            document.form1.txtResult.value =
                window.parent.calcFactorial(document.form1.txtNum1.value);
        }
        catch (exception)
        {
            if (typeof(exception) == "string" && exception.charAt(0) == "!")
            {
                alert(exception.substr(1));
                document.form1.txtNum1.focus();
                document.form1.txtNum1.select();
            }
            else
            {
                throw exception;
            }
        }
    }
    catch(exception)
    {
        switch (exception)
        {
        case "This page is not loaded within the correct frameset":
            alert(exception);
            break;
        default :
            alert("The following critical error has occurred \n" + exception);
        }
    }
}
```

The inner try. . .catch deals with user input errors. However, if the error is not a user input error thrown by us, it is thrown for the outer catch statement to deal with. The outer catch statement has a switch statement that checks the value of the error message thrown. If it's the error message thrown by us because the calcFactorialTopFrame.htm is not loaded, the switch statement deals with it in the first case statement. Any other error is dealt with in the default statement. However, there may well be occasions when there are lots of different errors you want to deal with in case statements.

finally Clauses

The `try...catch` statement has a `finally` clause that defines a block of script that will execute whether or not an exception was thrown. The `finally` clause can't appear on its own; it must be after a `try` block, which the following code demonstrates.

```
try
{
    ablurt("An exception will occur");
}
catch(exception)
{
    alert("Exception occurred");
}
finally
{
    alert("Whatever happens this line will execute");
}
```

The `finally` part is a good place to put any cleanup code that needs to be executed regardless of any errors that occurred previously.

Summary

In this chapter you looked at the less exciting part of coding, namely bugs. In an ideal world you'd get things right the first time, every time, but in reality any code more than a few lines long is likely to suffer from bugs.

❑ You first looked at some of the more common errors, those made not just by JavaScript beginners, but also by experts with lots of experience.

❑ You installed the script debugger, which works with Internet Explorer. Without the script debugger any errors throw up messages, but nothing else. With the script debugger you get to see exactly where the error might have been and to examine the current state of variables when the error occurred. Also, you can use the script debugger to analyze code as it's being run, which enables you to see its flow step by step, and to check variables and conditions.

❑ You looked at Venkman, the script debugger for Firefox. You saw that it works much like the IE debugger and in some ways is superior to it. Although these debuggers have different interfaces, their principles are the same.

❑ Some errors are not necessarily bugs in your code, but in fact exceptions to the normal circumstances that cause your code to fail. (For example, a Java applet might fail because a user is behind a firewall.) You saw that the `try...catch` statements are good for dealing with this sort of error, and that you can use the `catch` clause with the `throw` statement to deal with likely errors, such as those caused by user input. Finally, you saw that if you want a block of code to execute regardless of any error, you can use the `finally` clause.

In the next chapter you'll be looking at a way to store information on the user's computer using something called a *cookie*. Although they may not be powerful enough to hold a user's life history, they are certainly powerful enough for you to keep track of a user's visits to your web site and of what pages he views when he visits. With that information you can provide a more customized experience for the user.

Exercise Questions

Suggested solutions to these questions can be found in Appendix A.

Question 1

The example `debug_timestable2.htm` has a deliberate bug. For each times table it creates only multipliers with values from 1 to 11.

Use the script debugger to work out why this is happening, and then correct the bug.

Question 2

The following code contains a number of common errors. See if you can spot them:

```
<html>
<head>
</head>
<body>
<script language=JavaScript>
function checkForm(theForm)
{
    var formValid = true;
    var elementCount  = 0;
    while(elementCount =< theForm.length)
    {
        if (theForm.elements[elementcount].type == "text")
        {
            if (theForm.elements[elementCount].value() = "")
                alert("Please complete all form elements")
                theForm.elements[elementCount].focus;
                formValid = false;
                break;
        }
    }
    return formValid;
}
</script>
<form name=form1 onsubmit="return checkForm(document.form1)">
    <input type="text" ID=text1 name=text1>
    <br>
    CheckBox 1<input type="checkbox" ID=checkbox1 name=checkbox1>
    <br>
    CheckBox 2<input type="checkbox" ID=checkbox2 name=checkbox2>
    <br>
    <input type="text" ID=text2 name=text2>
    <p>
    <input type="submit" value="Submit" ID=submit1 name=submit1>
    </p>
</form>
</body>
</html>
```

Storing Information: Cookies

Our goal as web site programmers should be to make the web site experience as easy and pleasant for the user as possible. Clearly, well-designed pages with easily navigable layouts are central to this, but they're not the whole story. You can go one step further by learning about your users and using information gained about them to personalize the web site.

For example, imagine a user, whose name you asked on the first visit, returns to your web site. You could welcome her back to the web site by greeting her by name. Another good example is given by a web site, such as Amazon's, that incorporates the one-click purchasing system. By already knowing the user's purchasing details, such as credit-card number and delivery address, you can allow the user to go from viewing a book to buying it in just one click, making the likelihood of the user purchasing it that much greater. Also, based on information, such as the previous purchases and browsing patterns of the user, it's possible to make book suggestions.

Such personalization requires that information about users be stored somewhere in between their visits to the web site. Previous chapters have mentioned that accessing the user's local file system from a web application is pretty much off limits because of security restrictions included in browsers. However, you, as a web site developer, can store small amounts of information in a special place on the user's local disk, using what is called a *cookie*. There may be a logical reason why they are named cookies, but it also provides authors with the opportunity to make a lot of second-rate, food-related jokes!

Baking Your First Cookie

The key to cookies is the document object's cookie property. Using this property, you can create and retrieve cookie data from within your JavaScript code.

You can set a cookie by setting document.cookie to a *cookie string*. You'll be looking in detail at how this cookie string is made up later in the chapter, but let's first create a simple example of a cookie and see where the information is stored on the user's computer.

A Fresh-Baked Cookie

The following code will set a cookie with the UserName set as Paul, and an expiration date of 28 December, 2020.

```
<html>
<head>
<script language="JavaScript" type="text/javascript">
    document.cookie = "UserName=Paul;expires=Tue, 28 Dec 2020 00:00:00;";
</script>
</head>
<body>
<p>This page just created a cookie</p>
</body>
</html>
```

Save the page as FreshBakedCookie.htm. You'll see how the code works as you learn the parts of a cookie string, but first let's see what happens when a cookie is created.

How you view cookies without using code varies with the browser you are using. You'll see how to do it first in IE, and then in Firefox.

Viewing Cookies in IE

In this section you'll see how to look at the cookies that are already stored by IE on your computer. You'll then load the cookie-creating page you just created with the preceding code to see what effect this has.

First you need to open IE. The examples in this chapter use IE 7, so if you're using IE 6 you may find the screenshots and menus in slightly different places.

Before you view the cookies, you'll first clear the temporary Internet file folder for the browser, because this will make it easier to view the cookies that your browser has stored. In IE, select Internet Options from the Tools menu, which is shown in Figure 11-1.

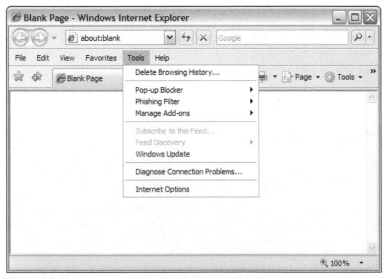

Figure 11-1

408

Having selected this option, you'll be presented with the Internet Options dialog box shown in Figure 11-2.

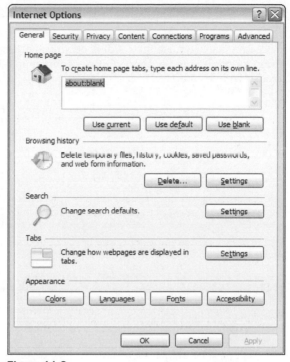

Figure 11-2

Click the Delete button under Browsing History. Another dialog box appears, as shown in Figure 11-3.

Figure 11-3

Click the Delete files button next to Temporary Internet Files, and select Yes when it asks if you're sure.

You now have a nice clean cache, which makes it easy to see when you create a cookie. You can now close the dialog box and return to the main Internet Options dialog box.

Let's have a look at the cookies you have currently residing on your machine. From the Internet Options dialog box, click the Settings button next to the Delete button grouped under Browsing History. You should see the dialog box shown in Figure 11-4.

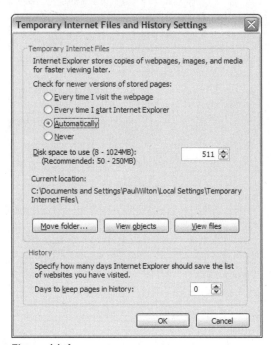

Figure 11-4

Now click the View Files button, and a list of all the temporary pages and cookie files on your computer will be displayed. If you followed the previous instructions and deleted all temporary Internet files, there should be nothing listed except any cookies from web sites you've visited, as shown in Figure 11-5.

The actual cookies, their names, and their values, may look slightly different depending on your computer's operating system.

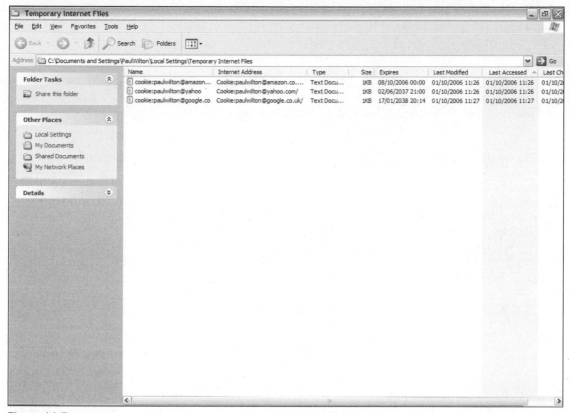

Figure 11-5

You can examine the contents of the cookies by double-clicking them. Note that you may get a warning about the potential security risk of opening a text file, although you are fairly safe with cookies because they are simply text files. In Figure 11-6 you can see the contents of the cookie file named google set by the search engine Google.

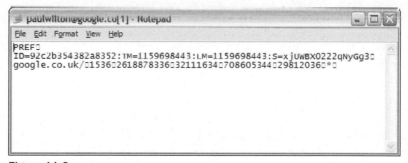

Figure 11-6

As you can see, a cookie is just a plain old text file. Each web site, or *domain name*, has its own text file where all the cookies for that web site are stored. In this case there's just one cookie currently stored for `google.co.uk`. Domains like `amazon.com` will almost certainly have many cookies set.

In Figure 11-6, you can see the cookie's details. Here, the name of the cookie is `PREF`; its value is a series of characters, which although indecipherable to you make sense to the Google web site. It was set by the domain `google.co.uk`, and it relates to the root directory `/`. The contents probably look like a mess of characters, but don't worry: When you learn how to program cookies, you'll see that you don't need to worry about setting the details in this format.

After you have finished, close the cookie and click OK on the dialog boxes to return to the browser.

Now let's load the `FreshBakedCookie.htm` page into your IE browser. This will set a cookie. Let's see how it has changed things by returning to the Internet Options dialog box (by choosing Internet Options from the Tools menu). Click the Settings button, and then click View Files. Your computer now shows something like the information in Figure 11-7.

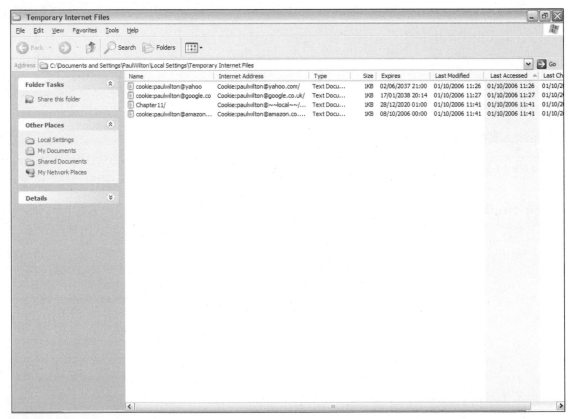

Figure 11-7

Because you are creating a cookie from a web page that is stored on the local hard drive rather than a server, its domain name has been set to the name of the directory the web page is stored in. Obviously, this is a little artificial. In reality, people will be loading your web pages from your web site on the Internet and not off your local hard drive. The Internet address is based on the directory the FreshBakedCookie.htm file was in. You can also see that it expires on December 28, 2020, as you specified when you created the cookie. Double-click the cookie to view its contents, which look like those in Figure 11-8.

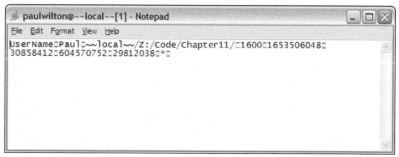

Figure 11-8

You can see the name you gave to the cookie at the left, UserName, its value, Paul, and also the directory it's applicable to. The expiration date is there as well; it's just not in an easily recognizable form. Note that you may sometimes need to close the browser and reopen it before you see the cookie file.

Viewing Cookies In Firefox

There is no sharing of cookies between browsers, so the cookies stored when you visited web sites using an IE browser won't be available to Firefox and vice versa.

FF keeps its cookies in a totally different place from IE, and the contents are viewed by a different means. To view cookies in Firefox 1.5, choose Options from the Tools menu. Then select the Privacy tab and finally select the Cookies tab and you should see the dialog box shown in Figure 11-9.

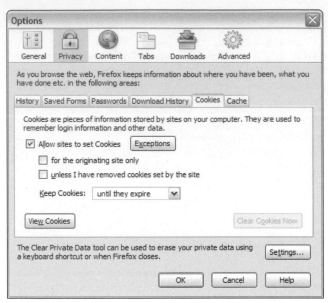

Figure 11-9

Click View Cookies and his will open another dialog box listing all the cookies currently stored on your PC. It should look something like what is shown in Figure 11-10.

Figure 11-10

Click OK to get back to the browser, and load `FreshBakedCookie.htm`. Then repeat the process you followed previously to get to the Cookie Manager, and you should find that the `UserName` cookie has been added to the box. Because it's loaded from a file on your PC and not the Internet, the cookie has a blank web address. The expanded cookie details are shown in Figure 11-11.

Figure 11-11

Note that buttons are provided at the bottom of the Cookie Manager to remove the cookie selected or all of the cookies that are stored.

Now that you've seen how to view cookies manually, let's look at how you create them and read them using code. You'll start by looking at each of the parts making up a cookie string.

> *Note that cookie management has changed in Firefox 2.0. You'll still find it under the Tools ⇨ Options menu but now there's no Cookie tab. Instead there is a Show Cookies button. Clicking the Show Cookies button will open a new dialog box that lets you view and delete cookies.*

The Cookie String

When you are creating a cookie there are six parts you can set: `name`, `value`, `expires`, `path`, `domain`, and `secure`, although the latter four of these are optional. You'll now look at each of these in turn.

name and value

The first part of the cookie string consists of the name and value of the cookie. The name is used so that you can reference the cookie later, and the value is the information part of the cookie.

This name/value part of the cookie string is compulsory; it sort of defeats the point of the cookie if you don't store a name or value, because storing information is what cookies are all about. You should make sure that this part comes first in the cookie string.

The value for the cookie is a primitive string, although of course the string can hold number characters if it is numerical data that you want to store. If you are storing text, certain characters, such as semicolons, cannot be used inside the value, unless you use a special encoding, which you'll see later. In the case of semicolons, this is because they are used to separate the different parts of the cookie within the cookie string.

In the following line of code, you set a cookie with the name `UserName` and the value `Paul`.

```
document.cookie = "UserName=Paul;";
```

This cookie has a very limited *lifespan*, which is the length of time the information will continue to exist. If you don't set an expiration date, a cookie will expire when the user closes the browser. The next time the user opens the browser the cookie will be gone. This is fine if you just want to store information for the life of a user *session*, which is a single visit by the user to your web site. However, if you want to ensure that your cookie is available for longer, you must set its expiration date, which you'll look at next.

expires

If you want a cookie to exist for longer than just a single user session, you need to set an expiration date using the second part of the cookie string, `expires`, as follows:

```
document.cookie = "UserName=Paul;expires=Tue, 28 Dec 2020 00:00:00 GMT; ";
```

The cookie set by the previous line of code will remain available for future use right up until December 28, 2020. Note that the format of the expiration date is very important, especially for IE browsers. It should be the same format the cookie is given by the `toGMTString()` method. This method is similar to the `toUTCString()` method that you saw in Chapter 9.

In practice, you'll probably use the `Date` object to get the current date, and then set a cookie to expire three or six months after this date. Otherwise, you're going to need to rewrite your pages on December 28, 2020.

For example, you could write the following:

```
var expireDate = new Date();
expireDate.setMonth(expireDate.getMonth() + 6);
document.cookie = "UserName=Paul;expires=" + expireDate.toGMTString() + ";";
```

This will create a new cookie called `UserName` with the value of `Paul`, which will expire six months from the current date. Note that other factors can cause a cookie to expire before its expiration date, such as the user deleting the cookie or the upper cookie limit being reached.

path

You'll find that 99 percent of the time you will only need to set the `name`, `value`, and `expires` parts of a cookie. However, at times the other three parts, such as the `path` part that you are looking at in this section, need to be set. The final two parts, `domain` and `secure`, are for advanced use beyond the scope of a beginners' book, but you'll look at them briefly just for completeness.

You're probably used to the idea of there being directories on your hard drive. Rather than storing everything on your computer in one place on the hard drive, you divide it into these directories. For example, you might keep your word-processing files in `My Documents`, your image files in `My Images`, and so on. You probably also subdivide your directories, so under `My Images` you might have subdirectories called `My Family` and `My Holiday`.

Well, web servers use the same principle. Rather than putting the whole web site into one web directory, it's common and indeed sensible to divide it into various different directories. For example, if you visit the Wrox web site at www.wrox.com, and then click one of the book categories, you'll find that the path to the page navigated to is now www.wrox.com/Books/.

This is all very interesting, but why is it relevant to cookies?

The problem is that cookies are specific not only to a particular web domain, such as www.wrox.com, but also to a particular path on that domain. For example, if a page in www.wrox.com/Books/ sets a cookie, then only pages in that directory or its subdirectories will be able to read and change the cookie. If a page in www.wrox.com/academic/ tried to read the cookie, it would fail. Why are cookies restricted like this?

Take the common example of free web space. A lot of companies on the Web enable you to sign up for free web space. Usually everyone who signs up for this web space has a site at the same domain. For example, Bob's web site might be at www.freespace.com/members/bob/. Belinda might have hers at www.freespace.com/members/belinda. If cookies could be retrieved and changed regardless of the path, then any cookies set on Bob's web site could be viewed by Belinda and vice versa. This is clearly something neither of them would be happy about. Not only is there a security problem, but if, unknown to each other, they both have a cookie named MyHotCookie, there would be problems with each of them setting and retrieving the same cookie. When you think how many users a free web space provider often has, you can see that there is potential for chaos.

Okay, so now you know that cookies are specific to a certain path, but what if you want to view your cookies from two different paths on your server? Say for example you have an online store at www.mywebsite.com/mystore/ but you subdivide the store into subdirectories, such as /Books and /Games. Now let's imagine that your checkout is in the directory www.mywebsite.com/mystore/Checkout. Any cookies set in the /Books and /Games directories won't be visible to each other or pages in the /Checkout directory. To get around this you can either set cookies only in the /mystore directory, since these can be read by that directory and any of its subdirectories, or you can use the path part of the cookie string to specify that the path of the cookie is /mystore even if it's being set in the /Games or /Books or /Checkout subdirectories.

For example, you could do this like so:

```
document.cookie = "UserName=Paul;expires=Tue, 28 Dec 2020 00:00:00" +
";path=/mystore;";
```

Now, even if the cookie is set by a page in the directory /Books, it will still be accessible to files in the /mystore directory and its subdirectories, such as /Checkout and /Games.

If you want to specify that the cookie is available to all subdirectories of the domain it is set in, you can specify a path of the root directory using the / character.

```
document.cookie = "UserName=Paul;expires=Tue, 28 Dec 2020 00:00:00;path=/;";
```

Now, the cookie will be available to all directories on the domain it is set from. If the web site is just one of many at that domain, it's best not to do this because everyone else will also have access to your cookie information.

It's important to note that although Windows computers don't have case-sensitive directory names, many other operating systems do. For example, if your web site is on a Unix- or Linux-based server, the path property will be case-sensitive.

domain

The fourth part of the cookie string is the `domain`. An example of a domain is `wrox.com` or `pawilton.com`. Like the `path` part of the cookie string, the `domain` part is optional and it's unlikely that you'll find yourself using it very often.

By default, cookies are available only to pages in the domain they were set in. For example, if you have your first web site running on a server with the domain `MyPersonalWebSite.MyDomain.Com` and you have a second web site running under `MyBusinessWebSite.MyDomain.Com`, a cookie set in one web site will not be available to pages accessed under the other domain name, and vice versa. Most of the time this is exactly what you want, but if it is not, you can use the `domain` part of the cookie string to specify that a cookie is available to all subdomains of the specified domain. For example, the following sets a cookie that can be shared across both subdomains:

```
document.cookie = "UserName=Paul;expires=Tue, 28 Dec 2020 00:00:00;path=/" +
";domain=MyDomain.Com;";
```

Note that the domain must be the same: You can't share `www.SomeoneElsesDomain.com` with `www.MyDomain.com`.

secure

The final part of the cookie string is the `secure` part. This is simply a Boolean value; if it's set to `true` the cookie will be sent only to a web sever that tries to retrieve it using a secure channel. The default value, which is `false`, means the cookie will always be sent, regardless of the security. This is only applicable where you have set up a server with SSL (Secure Sockets Layer).

Creating a Cookie

To make life easier for yourself, you'll write a function that enables you to create a new cookie and set certain of its attributes with more ease. You'll look at the code first and create an example using it shortly.

```
function setCookie(cookieName, cookieValue, cookiePath, cookieExpires)
{
    cookieValue = escape(cookieValue);
    if (cookieExpires == "")
    {
        var nowDate = new Date();
        nowDate.setMonth(nowDate.getMonth() + 6);
        cookieExpires = nowDate.toGMTString();
    }
    if (cookiePath != "")
    {
        cookiePath = ";Path=" + cookiePath;
    }
    document.cookie = cookieName + "=" + cookieValue +
        ";expires=" + cookieExpires + cookiePath;
}
```

The `secure` and `domain` parts of the cookie string are unlikely to be needed, so you allow just the `name`, `value`, `expires`, and `path` parts of a cookie to be set by the function. If you don't want to set a path or expiration date, you just pass empty strings for those parameters. If no path is specified, the current directory and its subdirectories will be the path. If no expiration date is set, you just assume a date six months from now.

The first line of the function introduces the `escape()` function, which you've not seen before.

```
cookieValue = escape(cookieValue);
```

When we talked about setting the value of a cookie, we mentioned that certain characters cannot be used directly, such as a semicolon. (This also applies to the name of the cookie.) To get around this problem, you can use the built-in `escape()` and `unescape()` functions. The `escape()` function converts characters that are not text or numbers into the hexadecimal equivalent of their character in the Latin-1 character set, preceded by a `%` character.

For example, a space has the hexadecimal value `20`, and the semicolon the value `3B`. So the following code produces the output shown in Figure 11-12:

```
alert(escape("2001 a space odyssey;"));
```

Figure 11-12

You can see that each space has been converted to `%20`, the `%` indicating that it represents an escape or special character rather than an actual character, and that `20` is the ASCII value of the actual character. The semicolon has been converted to `%3B`, as you'd expect.

As you'll see later, when retrieving cookie values you can use the `unescape()` function to convert from the encoded version to plain text.

Back to your function; next you have an `if` statement.

```
if (cookieExpires == "")
{
    var nowDate = new Date();
    nowDate.setMonth(nowDate.getMonth() + 6);
    cookieExpires = nowDate.toGMTString();
}
```

This deals with the situation in which an empty string (`""`) has been passed for the `cookieExpires` parameter of the function. Because most of the time you want a cookie to last longer than the session it's created in, you set a default value for `expires` that is six months after the current date.

Next, if a value other than an empty string (" ") has been passed to the function for the cookiePath parameter, you need to add that value when you create the cookie. You simply put "path=" in front of any value that has been passed in the cookiePath parameter.

```
if (cookiePath != "")
{
    cookiePath = ";Path=" + cookiePath;
}
```

Finally, on the last line you actually create the cookie, putting together the cookieName, cookieValue, cookieExpires, and cookiePath parts of the string.

```
document.cookie = cookieName + "=" + cookieValue +
    ";expires=" + cookieExpires + cookiePath;
```

You'll be using the setCookie() function whenever you want to create a new cookie because it makes setting a cookie slightly easier than having to remember all the parts you want to set. More importantly, it can be used to set the expiration date to a date six months ahead of the current date.

For example, to use the function and set a cookie with default values for expires and path, you just type the following:

```
setCookie("cookieName","cookieValue","","")
```

Try It Out   **Using setCookie()**

You'll now put all this together in a simple example in which you use your setCookie() function to set three cookies named Name, Age, and FirstVisit. You then display what is in the document.cookie property to see how it has been affected.

```
<!DOCTYPE HTML PUBLIC "-//W3C//DTD HTML 4.01 Transitional//EN"
"http://www.w3.org/TR/html14/loose.dtd">
<html>
<head>
<script language="JavaScript" type="text/JavaScript">
function setCookie (cookieName, cookieValue, cookiePath, cookieExpires)
{
    cookieValue = escape(cookieValue);
    if (cookieExpires == "")
    {
        var nowDate = new Date();
        nowDate.setMonth(nowDate.getMonth() + 6);
        cookieExpires = nowDate.toGMTString();
    }
    if (cookiePath != "")
    {
        cookiePath = ";Path=" + cookiePath;
    }
    document.cookie = cookieName + "=" + cookieValue +
        ";expires=" + cookieExpires + cookiePath;
}
setCookie("Name","Bob","","");
```

```
setCookie("Age","101","","");
setCookie("FirstVisit","10 May 2007","","");
alert(document.cookie);
</script>
</head>
<body>
</body>
</html>
```

Save the example as CreateCookie.htm and load it into a web browser.

You'll see the alert box shown in Figure 11-13. Note that all three cookies are displayed as name/value pairs separated from the others by semicolons, and also that the expiration date is not displayed. If you had set the path parameter, this also would not have been displayed. The UserName cookie from a previous example is also displayed.

Figure 11-13

How It Works

You've already seen how the setCookie() function works, so let's look at the three lines that use the function to create three new cookies.

```
setCookie("Name","Bob","","");
setCookie("Age","101","","");
setCookie("FirstVisit","10 May 2007","","");
```

It is all fairly simple. The first parameter is the name that you'll give the cookie. (You'll see shortly how you can retrieve a value of a cookie based on the name you gave it.) It's important that the names you use be only alphanumeric characters, with no spaces, punctuation, or special characters. Although you can use cookie names with these characters, doing so is more complex and best avoided. Next you have the value you want to give the cookie. The third parameter is the path, and the fourth parameter is the date you want the cookie to expire on.

For example, take the first line where you use the setCookie() function. Here you are setting a cookie that will be named Name and have the value Bob. You don't want to set the path or expires parts, so you just pass an empty string (""). Note that you must pass the empty string. You can't pass nothing at all.

The remaining two lines in the previous code snippet set the cookies named Age and FirstVisit and set their values to 101 and 10 May 2007, respectively.

If you did want to set the path and the expiration date, how might you change your code?

Well, imagine that you want the path to be /MyStore and the expiration date to be one year in the future. Then you can use the setCookie() function in the following way:

```
var expireDate = new Date();
expireDate.setMonth(expireDate.getMonth() + 12);
setCookie("Name","Bob","/MyStore",expireDate.toGMTString());
```

First you create a new Date object, and by passing no parameter to its constructor, you let it initialize itself to the current date. In the next line, you add 12 months to that date. When setting the cookie using setCookie() you pass "/MyStore" as the path and expireDate.toGMTString() as the expires parameter.

What about the situation in which you've created your cookie, say one named Name with a value of Bob, and you want to change its value? To do this you can simply set the same cookie again, but with the new value. To change the cookie named Name from a value of Bob to a value of Bobby you'd need the following code:

```
setCookie("Name","Bobby","","");
```

What if you want to delete an existing cookie? Well that's easy. Just make it expire by changing its value and setting its expiration date to a date in the past, as in the following example:

```
setCookie("Name","","","Mon, 1 Jan 1990 00:00:00");
```

Getting a Cookie's Value

In the preceding example you used document.cookie to retrieve a string containing information about the cookies that have been set. However, this string has two limitations.

First, the cookies are retrieved in name/value pairs, with each individual cookie separated by a semicolon. The expires, path, domain, and secure parts of the cookie are not available to you and cannot be retrieved.

Second, the cookie property enables you to retrieve only *all* the cookies set for a particular path and, when they are hosted on a web server, that web server. So, for example, there's no simple way of just getting the value of a cookie with the name Age. To do this you'll have to use the string manipulation techniques you learned in previous chapters to cut the information you want out of the returned string.

A lot of different ways exist to get the value of an individual cookie, but the way you'll use has the advantage of working with all cookie-enabled browsers. You use the following function:

```
function getCookieValue(cookieName)
{
   var cookieValue = document.cookie;
   var cookieStartsAt = cookieValue.indexOf(" " + cookieName + "=");
   if (cookieStartsAt == -1)
   {
      cookieStartsAt = cookieValue.indexOf(cookieName + "=");
   }
```

```
        if (cookieStartsAt == -1)
        {
            cookieValue = null;
        }
        else
        {
            cookieStartsAt = cookieValue.indexOf("=", cookieStartsAt) + 1;
            var cookieEndsAt = cookieValue.indexOf(";", cookieStartsAt);
            if (cookieEndsAt == -1)
            {
                cookieEndsAt = cookieValue.length;
            }
            cookieValue = unescape(cookieValue.substring(cookieStartsAt,
                cookieEndsAt));
        }
        return cookieValue;
    }
```

The first task of the function is to get the `document.cookie` string and store it in the variable `cookieValue`.

```
    var cookieValue = document.cookie;
```

Next you need to find out where the cookie with the name passed as a parameter to the function is within the `cookieValue` string. You use the `indexOf()` method of the `String` object to find this information, as shown in the following line:

```
    var cookieStartsAt = cookieValue.indexOf(" " + cookieName + "=");
```

The method will return either the character position where the individual cookie is found or `-1` if no such name, and therefore no such cookie, exists. You search on " " + cookieName + "=" so that you don't inadvertently find cookie names or values containing the name that you require. For example, if you have xFoo, Foo, and yFoo as cookie names, a search for Foo without a space in front would match xFoo first, which is not what you want!

If `cookieStartsAt` is `-1`, the cookie either does not exist or it's at the very beginning of the cookie string so there is no space in front of its name. To see which of these is true, you do another search, this time with no space.

```
    if (cookieStartsAt == -1)
    {
        cookieStartsAt = cookieValue.indexOf(cookieName + "=");
    }
```

In the next `if` statement you check to see whether the cookie has been found. If it hasn't, you set the `cookieValue` variable to `null`.

```
    if (cookieStartsAt == -1)
    {
        cookieValue = null;
    }
```

If the cookie has been found, you get the value of the cookie you want from the document.cookie string in an else statement. You do this by finding the start and the end of the value part of that cookie. The start will be immediately after the equals sign following the name. So in the following line, you find the equals sign following the name of the cookie in the string by starting the indexOf() search for an equals sign from the character at which the cookie name/value pair starts.

```
else
{
    cookieStartsAt = cookieValue.indexOf("=", cookieStartsAt) + 1;
```

You then add one to this value to move past the equals sign.

The end of the cookie value will either be at the next semicolon or at the end of the string, whichever comes first. You do a search for a semicolon, starting from the cookieStartsAt index, in the next line.

```
var cookieEndsAt = cookieValue.indexOf(";", cookieStartsAt);
```

If the cookie you are after is the last one in the string, there will be no semicolon and the cookieEndsAt variable will be -1 for no match. In this case you know the end of the cookie value must be the end of the string, so you set the variable cookieEndsAt to the length of the string.

```
if (cookieEndsAt == -1)
{
    cookieEndsAt = cookieValue.length;
}
```

You then get the cookie's value using the substring() method to cut the value that you want out of the main string. Because you have encoded the string with the escape() function, you need to unescape it to get the real value, hence the use of the unescape() function.

```
cookieValue = unescape(cookieValue.substring(cookieStartsAt,
    cookieEndsAt));
}
```

Finally you return the value of the cookie to the calling function.

```
return cookieValue;
```

Try It Out   What's New?

Now you know how to create and retrieve cookies. Let's use this knowledge in an example in which you check to see if any changes have been made to a web site since the user last visited it.

You'll be creating two pages for this example. The first is the main page for a web site; the second is the page with details of new additions and changes to the web site. A link to the second page will appear on the first page only if the user has visited the page before (that is, if a cookie exists) but has not visited since the page was last updated.

Let's create the first page.

```
<!DOCTYPE html PUBLIC "-//W3C//DTD html 4.01 Transitional//EN">
<html>
<head>
<title>Cookie Example</title>
<script language="JavaScript" type="text/javascript">
var lastUpdated = new Date("Tue, 28 Dec 2020");
function getCookieValue(cookieName)
{
   var cookieValue = document.cookie;
   var cookieStartsAt = cookieValue.indexOf(" " + cookieName + "=");
   if (cookieStartsAt == -1)
   {
      cookieStartsAt = cookieValue.indexOf(cookieName + "=");
   }
   if (cookieStartsAt == -1)
   {
      cookieValue = null;
   }
   else
   {
      cookieStartsAt = cookieValue.indexOf("=", cookieStartsAt) + 1;
      var cookieEndsAt = cookieValue.indexOf(";", cookieStartsAt);
      if (cookieEndsAt == -1)
      {
         cookieEndsAt = cookieValue.length;
      }
      cookieValue = unescape(cookieValue.substring(cookieStartsAt,
         cookieEndsAt));
   }
   return cookieValue;
}
function setCookie(cookieName, cookieValue, cookiePath, cookieExpires)
{
   cookieValue = escape(cookieValue);
   if (cookieExpires == "")
   {
      var nowDate = new Date();
      nowDate.setMonth(nowDate.getMonth() + 6);
      cookieExpires = nowDate.toGMTString();
   }
   if (cookiePath != "")
   {
      cookiePath = ";Path=" + cookiePath;
   }
   document.cookie = cookieName + "=" + cookieValue +
      ";expires=" + cookieExpires + cookiePath;
}
</script>
</head>
<body>
<h2 align=center>Welcome to my website</h2>
<br><br>
<center>
```

```
<script>
var lastVisit = getCookieValue("LastVisit");
if (lastVisit != null)
{
   lastVisit = new Date(lastVisit);
   if (lastVisit < lastUpdated)
   {
      document.write("<A href=\"WhatsNew.htm\">");
      document.write("<img src=\"WhatsNew.gif\" border=0></A>");
   }
}
var nowDate = new Date();
setCookie("LastVisit", nowDate.toGMTString(),"","")
</script>
</center>
</body>
</html>
```

This page needs to be saved as MainPage.htm. Note that it contains the two functions, setCookie() and getCookieValue(), that you created earlier. Also note that the image WhatsNew.gif is referenced by this page; either create such an image, or retrieve the image from the code download.

Next, you'll just create a simple page to link to for the What's New details.

```
<html>
<body>
<h2 align=center>Here's what's new on this website</h2>
</body>
</html>
```

Save this page as WhatsNew.htm.

Load MainPage.htm into a browser. The first time you go to the main page, there will be nothing but a heading saying Welcome to my website. Obviously, if this were a real web site, it would have a bit more than that, but it suffices for this example. However, refresh the page and suddenly you'll see the page shown in Figure 11-14.

If you click the image you're taken to the WhatsNew.htm page detailing all the things added to the web site since you last visited. Obviously nothing has actually changed in your example web site between you loading the page and then refreshing it. You got around this for testing purposes by setting the date when the web site last changed, stored in variable lastUpdated, to a date in the future (here, December 28, 2020).

Figure 11-14

How It Works

The WhatsNew.htm page is just a simple HTML page with no script, so you will confine your attention to MainPage.htm. In the head of the page in the first script block, you declare the variable lastUpdated.

```
var lastUpdated = new Date("Tue, 28 Dec 2020");
```

Whenever you make a change to the web site, this variable needs to be changed. It's currently set to Tue, 28 Dec 2020, just to make sure you see a What's New image when you refresh the page. A better alternative for live pages would be the document.lastModified property, which returns the date on which the page was last changed.

The rest of the first script block contains the two functions getCookieValue() and setCookie() that you looked at earlier. These haven't changed, so we won't discuss them in detail here.

The interesting material is in the second script block within the body of the page. First you get the date of the user's last visit from the LastVisit cookie using the getCookieValue() function.

```
var lastVisit = getCookieValue("LastVisit");
```

If it's null, the user has either never been here before, or it has been six or more months since the last visit and the cookie has expired. Either way, you won't put a What's New image up because everything is new if the user is a first-time visitor, and a lot has probably changed in the last six months — more than what your What's New page will detail.

If `lastVisit` is not `null`, you need to check whether the user visited the site before it was last updated, and if so to direct the user to a page that shows what is new. You do this within the `if` statement.

```
if (lastVisit != null)
{
   lastVisit = new Date(lastVisit);
   if (lastVisit < lastUpdated)
   {
       document.write("<A href=\"WhatsNew.htm\">");
       document.write("<img src=\"WhatsNew.gif\" border=0></A>");
   }
}
```

You first create a new `Date` object based on the value of `lastVisit` and store that back into the `lastVisit` variable. Then, in the condition of the inner `if` statement, you compare the date of the user's last visit with the date on which you last updated the web site. If things have changed since the user's last visit, you write the What's New image to the page, so the user can click it and find out what's new. Note that you use the escape character `\"` for the double-quote characters inside the strings that are written to the page; otherwise, JavaScript will think they indicate the end of the string.

Finally, at the end of the script block, you reset the `LastVisit` cookie to today's date and time using the `setCookie()` function.

```
var nowDate = new Date();
setCookie("LastVisit", nowDate.toGMTString(),"","")
```

Cookie Limitations

You should be aware of a number of limitations when using cookies.

The first is that although all modern browsers support cookies, the user may have disabled them. In Firefox you can do this by selecting the Options menu, followed by the privacy tab and the cookies tab. In IE you select Internet Options on the Tools menu. Select the Privacy tab and you can change the level with the scroll control. Most users have session cookies enabled by default. Session cookies are cookies that last for as long as the user is browsing your web site. After he's closed the browser the cookie will be cleared. More permanent cookies are also normally enabled by default. However, third-party cookies, those from a third-party site, are usually disabled. These are the cookies used for tracking people from site to site and hence the ones that raise the most privacy concerns.

Both the functions that you've made for creating and getting cookies will cause no errors when cookies are disabled, but of course the value of any cookie set will be `null` and you need to make sure your code can cope with this.

You could set a default action for when cookies are disabled. In the previous example, if cookies are disabled, the What's New image will never appear.

Alternatively, you can let the user know that your web site needs cookies to function by putting a message to that effect in the web page.

Another tactic is to actively check to see whether cookies are enabled and, if not, to take some action to cope with this, such as by directing the user to a page with less functionality that does not need cookies. How do you check to see if cookies are enabled?

In the following script you set a test cookie and then read back its value. If the value is null, you know cookies are disabled.

```
setCookie("TestCookie","Yes","","");
if (getCookieValue("TestCookie") == null)
    {
        alert("This website requires cookies to function");
    }
```

A second limitation is on the number of cookies you can set on the user's computer for your web site and how much information can be stored in each. For each domain you can store up to 20 cookies, and each *cookie pair* — that is, the name and value of the cookie combined — must not be more than 4,096 characters in size. It's also important to be aware that all browsers do set some upper limit for the number of cookies stored. When that limit is reached, older cookies, regardless of expiration date, are often deleted. Modern browsers have a 300-cookie limit, though this may vary between browsers.

To get around the 20-cookie limit, you can store more than one piece of information per cookie. This example uses multiple cookies:

```
setCookie("Name","Karen","","")
setCookie("Age","44","","")
setCookie("LastVisit","10 Jan 2001","","")
```

You could combine this information into one cookie, with each detail separated by a semicolon.

```
setCookie("UserDetails","Karen;44;10 Jan 2001","","")
```

Because the setCookie() function escapes the value of the cookie, there is no confusion between the semicolons separating pieces of data in the value of the cookie, and the semicolons separating the parts of the cookie. When you get the cookie value back using getCookieValue(), you just split it into its constituent parts; however, you must remember the order you stored it in.

```
var cookieValues = getCookieValue("UserDetails");
cookieValues = cookieValues.split(";")
alert("Name = " + cookieValues[0]);
alert("Age = " + cookieValues[1]);
alert("Last Visit = " + cookieValues[2]);
```

Now you have acquired three pieces of information and still have 19 cookies left in the jar.

Cookie Security and IE6 and IE7

IE6 has introduced a new security policy for cookies based on the P3P recommendations made by the World Wide Web Consortium (W3C), a web standards body that deals with not only cookies but HTML, XML, and various other browser standards. (You'll learn more about W3C in Chapter 13. Its web site is at www.w3.org and contains a host of information, though it's far from being an easy read.) The general aim of P3P is to reassure users who are worried that cookies are being used to obtain personal information about their browsing habits. In IE 6 and 7 you can select Tools ⇨ Internet Options and click the Privacy tab to see where you can set the level of privacy with regards to cookies (see Figure 11-15). You have to strike a balance between setting it so high that no web site will work and so low that your browsing habits and potentially personal data may be recorded.

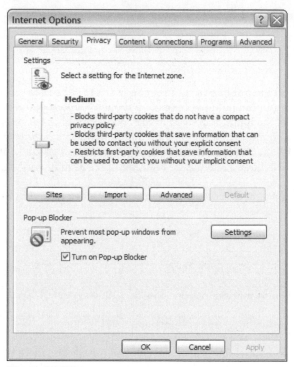

Figure 11-15

Generally, by default session cookies — cookies that last for only as long as the user is browsing your web site — are allowed. As soon as the user closes the browser, the session ends. However, if you want cookies to outlast the user's visit to your web site, you need to create a privacy policy in line with the P3P recommendations. This sounds a little complex, and certainly the fine details of the policy can be. However, IBM has created software that makes creating the XML for the policy fairly easy. It's not cheap, but there is a 90-day free trial. It can be downloaded from www.alphaworks.ibm.com/tech/p3peditor.

Plenty of other policy creation software is available; this just happens to be quite easy to use. P3PEdit is available for much lower cost from http://policyeditor.com/.

Try It Out   Storing Previous Quiz Results

Let's return to the trivia quiz one last time and, using your knowledge of cookies, add the functionality to keep track of previous quiz results. You're going to calculate the user's average score for all the completed quizzes. You'll also allow the user to reset the statistics.

You need to alter only one page of the trivia quiz: the GlobalFunctions.htm page. First you need to add the two cookie functions, getCookieValue() and setCookie(), that you introduced earlier in the chapter. You can add these anywhere within the script block—here they've been added after all the other functions.

```
function getCookieValue(cookieName)
{
    var cookieValue = document.cookie;
    var cookieStartsAt = cookieValue.indexOf(" " + cookieName + "=");
    if (cookieStartsAt == -1)
    {
        cookieStartsAt = cookieValue.indexOf(cookieName + "=");
    }
    if (cookieStartsAt == -1)
    {
        cookieValue = null;
    }
    else
    {
        cookieStartsAt = cookieValue.indexOf("=", cookieStartsAt) + 1;
        var cookieEndsAt = cookieValue.indexOf(";", cookieStartsAt);
        if (cookieEndsAt == -1)
        {
            cookieEndsAt = cookieValue.length;
        }
        cookieValue = unescape(cookieValue.substring(cookieStartsAt,
            cookieEndsAt));
    }
    return cookieValue;
}
function setCookie(cookieName, cookieValue, cookiePath, cookieExpires)
{
    cookieValue = escape(cookieValue);
    if (cookieExpires == "")
    {
        var nowDate = new Date();
        nowDate.setMonth(nowDate.getMonth() + 6);
        cookieExpires = nowDate.toGMTString();
    }
    if (cookiePath != "")
    {
        cookiePath = ";Path=" + cookiePath;
    }
    document.cookie = cookieName + "=" + cookieValue +
        ";expires=" + cookieExpires + cookiePath;
}
```

The final change you need to make is to the getQuestion() function. It's in this function that either a new question is written to the page or, if all the questions have been asked, the final results are displayed. Currently you just write the number of questions that the user got right and rate the result. Now you're going to keep a running average of previous results and display this information as well. The addition is toward the end of the function, after the script that writes a rating to the page.

```
        default:
            questionHTML = questionHTML + "Excellent"
    }
    var previousNoCorrect = Math.floor(getCookieValue("previousNoCorrect"));
    var previousNoAsked = Math.floor(getCookieValue("previousNoAsked"));
    var currentAvgScore = Math.round(numberOfQuestionsCorrect /
        numberOfQuestionsAsked * 100);
    questionHTML = questionHTML + "<br>The percentage you've " +
        " answered correctly in this quiz is " + currentAvgScore + "%";
    if (previousNoAsked == 0)
    {
        previousNoCorrect = 0;
    }

    previousNoCorrect = previousNoCorrect + numberOfQuestionsCorrect;
    previousNoAsked = previousNoAsked + numberOfQuestionsAsked;

    currentAvgScore = Math.round(previousNoCorrect / previousNoAsked * 100);
    setCookie("previousNoAsked", previousNoAsked,"","");
    setCookie("previousNoCorrect", previousNoCorrect,"","");
    questionHTML = questionHTML + "<br>This brings your average todate to " +
        currentAvgScore + "%"
    questionHTML = questionHTML + "<p><input type=button " +
        "value='Reset Stats' " +
        "onclick=\"window.top.fraTopFrame.fraGlobalFunctions.setCookie" +
        "('previousNoAsked', 0,'','1 Jan 1970')\" " +
        "name=buttonReset>"
    questionHTML = questionHTML + "<p><input type=button " +
        "value='Restart Quiz' " +
        "onclick=\"window.location.replace('quizpage.htm')\" " +
        "name=buttonRestart>"
}
return questionHTML;
}
```

How It Works

So how does this new code work?

First you use cookies to retrieve the number of questions previously answered correctly and the number of questions previously asked in total.

```
var previousNoCorrect = Math.floor(getCookieValue("previousNoCorrect"));
var previousNoAsked = Math.floor(getCookieValue("previousNoAsked"));
```

Note that if no cookie is set, CookieValue() will return null, which Math.floor() converts to 0.

You then work out the average of the current score, which is simply the number of questions the user got correct in this quiz divided by the number the user answered and multiplied by 100.

```
var currentAvgScore = Math.round(numberOfQuestionsCorrect /
    numberOfQuestionsAsked * 100);
```

You then add the average result to questionHTML, the string of HTML you'll be writing to the page.

```
questionHTML = questionHTML + "<br>The percentage you've " +
    " answered correctly in this quiz is " + currentAvgScore + "%";
```

Next you check to see if the number of questions asked was previously 0. If it was, the user has reset the stats, or this is the first time she has taken the quiz. You reset the number correct to 0, because it would hardly make sense if out of no questions answered your user got 10 right!

```
if (previousNoAsked == 0)
{
    previousNoCorrect = 0;
}
```

Then you update the number of questions that the user previously answered correctly and the total number of previously answered questions, before using this information to calculate the running average of all the quizzes the user has taken since playing your quiz or resetting the stats.

```
previousNoCorrect = previousNoCorrect + numberOfQuestionsCorrect;
previousNoAsked = previousNoAsked + numberOfQuestionsAsked;

currentAvgScore = Math.round(previousNoCorrect / previousNoAsked * 100);
```

You update your cookies with the new values in the next lines, using the setCookie() function you created earlier.

```
setCookie("previousNoAsked", previousNoAsked,"","");
setCookie("previousNoCorrect", previousNoCorrect,"","");
```

In the final new lines, you complete the construction of the results string, adding the running average and then creating two buttons. The first button will reset the number of questions asked by setting the previousNoAsked variable to 0, and the second is a replacement for the link that restarts the quiz.

```
questionHTML = questionHTML + "<br>This brings your average todate to " +
    currentAvgScore + "%"
questionHTML = questionHTML + "<p><input type=button " +
    "value='Reset Stats' " +
    "onclick=\"window.top.fraTopFrame.fraGlobalFunctions.setCookie" +
    "('previousNoAsked', 0,'','1 Jan 1970')\" " +
    "name=buttonReset>"
questionHTML = questionHTML + "<p><input type=button " +
    "value='Restart Quiz' " +
    "onclick=\"window.location.replace('quizpage.htm')\" " +
    "name=buttonRestart>"
```

On the button creation lines, you need to include single quotes inside double quotes inside more double quotes. This will confuse JavaScript because it'll think the string has ended before it actually has. This is the reason that you use the special escape character \", which indicates that the double quotes are not delimiting a string, but are part of the string itself.

Save the page and load TriviaQuiz.htm.

Now when you complete the quiz, you'll see a summary something like the one in Figure 11-16.

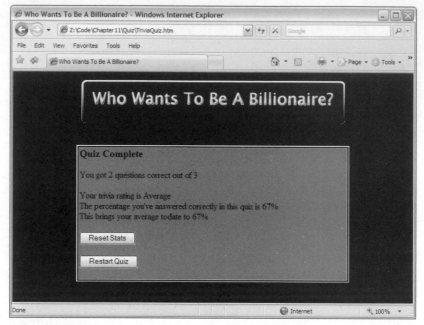

Figure 11-16

That completes the changes to the trivia quiz for this chapter.

Summary

In this chapter, you looked at how you can store information on the user's computer and use this information to personalize the web site. In particular you found the following:

❑ The key to cookies is the `document` object's `cookie` property.

❑ Creating a cookie simply involves setting the `document.cookie` property. Cookies have six different parts you can set. These are the name, the value, when it expires, the path it is available on, the domain it's available on, and finally whether it should be sent only over secure connections.

❑ Although setting a new cookie is fairly easy, you found that retrieving its value actually gets all the cookies for that domain and path, and that you need to split up the cookie name/value pairs to get a specific cookie using `String` object methods.

❑ Cookies have a number of limitations. First, the user can set the browser to disable cookies, and second, you are limited to 20 cookies per domain and a maximum of 4,096 characters per cookie name/value pair.

❑ Finally, you added the display of a running average for the trivia quiz.

Exercise Questions

Suggested solutions to these questions can be found in Appendix A.

Question 1

Create a page that keeps track of how many times the page has been visited by the user in the last month.

Question 2

Use cookies to load a different advertisement every time a user visits a web page.

Introduction to Dynamic HTML

Dynamic HTML (DHTML) is a term with various meanings, but it can boiled down to one basic concept: dynamically changing a web page after it is loaded into the browser. For example, it can be used to change the color and style of text when the mouse pointer moves over it. It is also widely used to enhance the experience a visitor has when visiting a web page, making the page more interactive.

Before the advent of DHTML, web pages were static. That is, when an HTML document was downloaded and displayed in the user's browser, no changes could be made to the page's content or appearance. With DHTML, however, you can change the appearance of the existing content and even move content around on the screen. Want to change that heading color to red? No problemo. Want to make text scroll across the screen? You got it.

JavaScript provides you with a means of writing DHTML pages. You've already seen this in action with the example in Chapter 5 in which you enabled the user to change an image loaded into the page with the click of a button. Today's browsers go beyond this, and you can change virtually anything in a web page.

In this chapter, you'll take an introductory look at DHTML. You'll look at how you can change things and move things around on the page. At the end of the chapter, you'll build a scrolling marquee to display whatever text you desire.

Cross-Browser Issues

In mid-1997, Netscape released the fourth version of its Navigator browser. Not only was this an iteration from Navigator 3, but it was the first browser to support DHTML. This support, however, was rudimentary at best. Netscape chose to implement its own proprietary version of DHTML. This implementation, while unique, extremely limited what users could accomplish with the browser.

Later that year, Microsoft released Internet Explorer 4 (IE4), and it, too, supported DHTML. Microsoft's offering, however, far exceeded that of Netscape's. It was still far from perfect, but DHTML in IE4 enabled you to do so much more than Netscape allowed. The entrance of this browser quickly ushered DHTML to the forefront and IE4 became the browser of choice for developers.

Despite the favor IE4 held at the time, it was advantageous for developers to build DHTML scripts that worked in both browsers, as Netscape still held a good portion of the browser market. Some called this obligation to code for both browsers "DHTML hell," and rightly so. The amount of JavaScript needed for one DHTML script could easily double due to *code branching* (writing code specifically for a particular browser by using browser detection) and getting said script to work correctly (especially in Netscape) was very time-consuming.

Fast-forward to today, and the number of browsers has doubled: We now have Internet Explorer 7, Firefox 1.5, Safari 2, and Opera 9. However, the DHTML hell of the late '90s is nothing more than a bad memory. Today's modern browsers are far more consistent in their support for DHTML, thankfully. But a few gotchas still exist — the most prominent being event handling.

Events

Events are an important part of DHTML. Most of the time, DHTML code reacts to something that the user did: the content's color changed when he moved his mouse over certain content, a hidden element showed itself when he clicked a specific link, or a list of words popped up that match the keystrokes the user made.

In Chapter 5, you learned about events and how to connect code to them, and every example you saw and worked through works in every browser. However, as you move on to more advanced event handling concepts, you'll start to notice differences between browsers. These browsers can easily be divided into two groups: Internet Explorer (IE) and the other modern-day browsers (non-IE).

Event Handlers as Attributes (Revisited)

You learned in Chapter 5 that the most common way to add an event is to add the event handler's name and the code you want to execute to the HTML tag's attributes. This is an easy way to add an event handler to a specific HTML tag:

```
<html>
<body>
    <a href="somepage.htm" name="linkSomePage" onmouseover="alert('You Moved?')"
        onclick="alert('You Clicked?')">
        Click Me
    </a>
</body>
</html>
```

This HTML page contains one link. When you move your mouse pointer over it, an alert box displays the text You Moved?; it also displays the message You Clicked? when you click it. Simple, right? This works in all the major browsers. So what's the problem with it?

What if you wanted to do this on several links within a page? Sure, you could copy and paste the event attributes as many times as you want, but if you ever wanted to change the messages in the alert boxes, you'd have to edit every one that you used. Also, what if you wanted to use only one function to handle both the `onmouseover` and `onclick` events and display the appropriate message according to which event was fired?

This is where things get a little complicated, and you have to adjust your code to accommodate the differences between IE and the other browsers.

Events in Internet Explorer

When an event fires in IE, the browser populates a global object called `event` with the data associated with the fired event. You can access this object through the `window` object like this:

```
var myEvent = window.event;
```

`event` has a variety of properties, each containing a specific piece of information that you can use. The first you'll cover is the `type` property, which you can use to retrieve the type of event that fired.

The Event Type

The `type` property returns a string containing the name of the event without the `on` prefix. So the `onclick` event is returned as `click`, and the `onmouseover` event is returned as `mouseover`.

Try It Out   **Using the type Property**

Let's look at how you can use this useful property in an example.

```
<!DOCTYPE html PUBLIC "-//W3C//DTD XHTML 1.0 Transitional//EN"
    "http://www.w3.org/TR/xhtml1/DTD/xhtml1-transitional.dtd">

<html xmlns="http://www.w3.org/1999/xhtml" >
<head>
    <title>Using the type Property</title>

    <script type="text/javascript">
    function paragraph_eventHandler() {
        if (window.event.type == "click") { //The click event was fired.
            alert("You Clicked Me!");
        } else if (window.event.type == "mouseover") { //The mouseover event.
            alert("You Tickled Me!");
        }
    }
    </script>
</head>
<body>
    <p onmouseover="paragraph_eventHandler()">
        Move your mouse over me.
    </p>
    <p onclick="paragraph_eventHandler()">
        Click me!
    </p>
</body>
</html>
```

Save this as `IE_type_property.htm`. When you load this page into IE, you'll see some plain, ordinary text in two paragraphs. When you move your mouse over the first paragraph, you're greeted with an alert box stating `You Tickled Me!` (see Figure 12-1).

Figure 12-1

If you click the text in the second paragraph, you'll see an alert box saying `You Clicked Me!`, as shown in Figure 12-2.

Figure 12-2

How It Works

The body of the page contains two <p/> elements, both of which contain text. The first paragraph assigns the paragraph_eventHandler() function to handle the mouseover event. So when this paragraph is clicked, the browser knows to call the event handler.

```
<p onmouseover="paragraph_eventHandler()">
    Move your mouse over me.
</p>
```

The second paragraph follows the same concept. However, instead of handling the mouseover event, paragraph_eventHandler() handles the click event.

```
<p onclick="paragraph_eventHandler()">
    Click me!
</p>
```

A script block resides in the head of the page. The JavaScript in this code block consists of only one function, called `paragraph_eventHandler()`, which handles the `click` and `mouseover` events of the two paragraphs created earlier.

```
function paragraph_eventHandler() {
    //more code here
}
```

The function determines the type of event by using the `window.event.type` property:

```
function paragraph_eventHandler() {
    if (window.event.type == "click") { //The click event was fired.
        //more code here
    } else if (window.event.type == "mouseover") { //The mouseover event.
        //more code here
    }
}
```

To determine the event, compare the `type` property to the event name. Unlike the names of event handlers, the names of events do not have the `on` prefix. Therefore, the desired events for this example are `click` and `mouseover`. Then, based upon the event, the function uses the `alert()` method to display the appropriate message to the user like this:

```
function paragraph_eventHandler() {
    if (window.event.type == "click") { //The click event was fired.
        alert("You Clicked Me!");
    } else if (window.event.type == "mouseover") { //The mouseover event.
        alert("You Tickled Me!");
    }
}
```

Now when the user causes these events to fire by moving or clicking her mouse, an alert box displays a message corresponding to the event that was fired.

The `type` property is supported by Internet Explorer, Firefox, Safari, and Opera. The only difference is in how you access it, which is discussed later.

The srcElement Property

Another valuable piece of information offered by the `event` object is the `srcElement` property. This property retrieves the HTML element that receives the event. For example, consider the following HTML:

```
<a href="somePage.htm" onclick="alert('Hello! You clicked me!')">Click Me</a>
```

When you click this link, an alert box displays the message Hello! You clicked me! That's obvious, right? What may not be so obvious is what actually receives the click event: the <a/> element. If you were to check the srcElement property during this event, it would point to this particular <a/> element. This information is particularly useful when you need to manipulate the element that received the event.

Try It Out   **The srcElement Property**

The following code demonstrates an image rollover:

```
<!DOCTYPE html PUBLIC "-//W3C//DTD XHTML 1.0 Transitional//EN"
    "http://www.w3.org/TR/xhtml1/DTD/xhtml1-transitional.dtd">

<html xmlns="http://www.w3.org/1999/xhtml" >
<head>
    <title>Using the srcElement Property</title>

    <script type="text/javascript">
    function image_eventHandler() {
        var sourceElement = window.event.srcElement; //Get the element.
        var eventType = window.event.type; //Get the type of event.

        if (eventType == "mouseover") { //The mouse rolled over the image.
            sourceElement.src - "o.gif"; //So change the image's src property.
        }

        if (eventType == "mouseout") { //The mouse moved out.
            sourceElement.src = "x.gif"; //So change it back to the original.
        }
    }
    </script>
</head>
<body>
    <img src="x.gif" onmouseover="image_eventHandler()"
        onmouseout="image_eventHandler()" />
</body>
</html>
```

Save this file as IE_srcElement_property.htm. Figure 12-3 shows what the page looks like when loaded into IE.

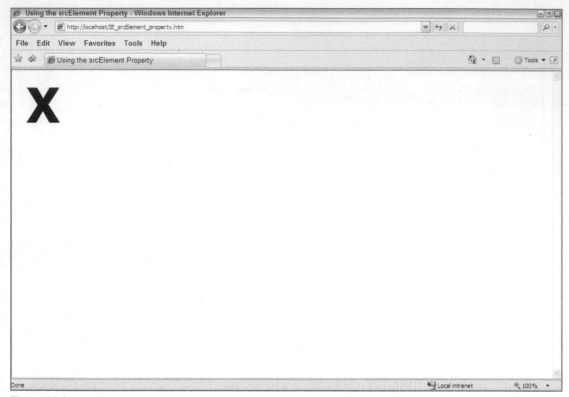

Figure 12-3

Move your mouse over the picture and it will change from an X to an O (see Figure 12-4). Moving the mouse pointer off the image makes it revert back to X.

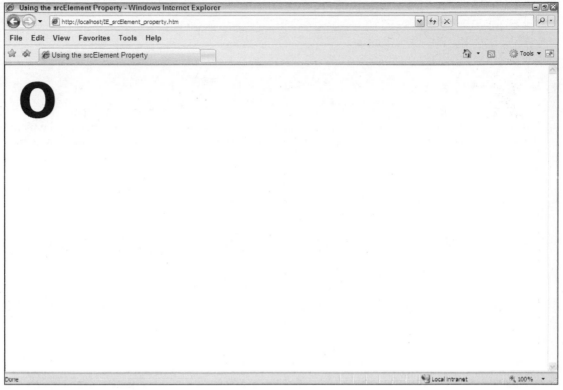

Figure 12-4

How It Works

The script block contains one function, called `image_EventHandler()`, which handles the `mouseover` and `mouseout` events for the `<img/>` element in the page's body. The first two lines of this function retrieve `window.event.srcElement` and `window.event.type`. These values are assigned to the `sourceElement` and `eventType` variables respectively.

```
function image_eventHandler() {
    var sourceElement = window.event.srcElement;
    var eventType = window.event.type;

    //more code here
}
```

Next, check the event's type to see if it was the `mouseover` event. To do this, compare `eventType` to the string `mouseover`.

```
function image_eventHandler() {
    var sourceElement = window.event.srcElement;
```

```
        var eventType = window.event.type;

        if (eventType == "mouseover") { //The mouse rolled over the image
            sourceElement.src = "o.gif"; //So change the image's src property.
        }

        //more code here
    }
```

If it is the mouseover event, then change the image's src property to o.gif. This changes the picture displayed by the <img/> element to show an O. Now check for the mouseout event and change the image's src property back to x.gif.

```
function image_eventHandler() {
    var sourceElement = window.event.srcElement;
    var eventType = window.event.type;

    if (eventType == "mouseover") { //The mouse rolled over the image
        sourceElement.src = "o.gif"; //So change the image's src property.
    }

    if (eventType == "mouseout") { //The mouse moved out.
        sourceElement.src = "x.gif"; //So change it back to the original.
    }
}
```

Because you did this, the image now displays an X again, and it will stay that way until the mouse pointer moves over it again.

Events in Other Browsers

Even though the implementation between the IE and the non-IE browsers differs, the basic principles are the same. Unlike IE, however, non-IE browsers do not have a global event object that keeps track of the events. Instead, it is in the hands of developers (meaning you) to access the events. Consider the following HTML:

```
<p onmouseover="paragraph_eventHandler(event)">
    Move your mouse over me.
</p>
<p onclick="paragraph_eventHandler(event)">
    Click me!
</p>
```

This HTML may look familiar. In fact, it was used in the Try It Out section for the window.event.type property. But there's a small change: The event, represented by event, is explicitly passed to paragraph_eventHandler(). The strange thing about this variable is that it is not defined anywhere; instead, it is an argument used only with event handlers connected through HTML attributes. It contains a reference to the current event object.

It is important not to confuse this event object with IE's event object. They may share the same name, but the similarities almost end there. Non-IE browsers do not have a global event object like window.event; their event object is a predefined attribute that is passed to the event handlers when the event fires.

Because the event object is now being passed to the `paragraph_eventHandler()` function, the function definition must accommodate this functionality.

```
function paragraph_eventHandler(evt) {

}
```

This code simply adds an argument, called `evt`, to the function, which gives you easy access to the event object passed to the function.

Try It Out   The type Property for the Other Browsers

Although the non-IE event object differs from the IE event object, they both expose a few of the same properties. One such property is the `type` property, which performs the same function in IE and non-IE browsers alike. This example shows how to use it.

```
<!DOCTYPE html PUBLIC "-//W3C//DTD XHTML 1.0 Transitional//EN"
    "http://www.w3.org/TR/xhtml1/DTD/xhtml1-transitional.dtd">

<html xmlns="http://www.w3.org/1999/xhtml" >
<head>
    <title>Using the type Property in Other Browsers</title>

    <script type="text/javascript">
    function paragraph_eventHandler(evt) {
        if (evt.type == "click") { //The click event was fired.
            alert("You Clicked Me!");
        } else if (evt.type == "mouseover") { //The mouseover event was fired.
            alert("You Tickled Me!");
        }
    }
    </script>
</head>
<body>
    <p onmouseover="paragraph_eventHandler(event)">
        Move your mouse over me.
    </p>
    <p onclick="paragraph_eventHandler(event)">
        Click me!
    </p>
</body>
</html>
```

Save this as `OB_type_property.htm` (OB means "other browsers"). Load this page into Firefox, Safari, or Opera, and you'll see two paragraphs that contain text. Move the mouse pointer over the first paragraph, and an alert box displays the text `You Tickled Me!`. Clicking on the second paragraph shows another alert box displaying the text `You Clicked Me!`

How It Works

Two paragraphs are defined in the body of the page (déjà vu!). The first paragraph handles the `mouseover` event by assigning the `onmouseover` attribute to `paragraph_eventHandler()` and passing the event object to the function. The second paragraph's `onclick` attribute is set to the same function, and handles the `click` event.

447

> The event object passed to the event handlers must be named `event`; otherwise, the code will not work.

In the script block, the `paragraph_eventHandler()` function is defined, and it accepts one argument, called `evt`. This argument provides easy access to the event object.

```
function paragraph_eventHandler(evt) {
    //more code here
}
```

Next, the code checks to see which event called the event handler. It does this by using the `type` property and comparing it to the event names (again, without the `on` prefix).

```
function paragraph_eventHandler(evt) {
    if (evt.type == "click") { //The click event was fired.
        alert("You Clicked Me!");
    } else if (evt.type == "mouseover") { //The mouseover event was fired.
        alert("You Tickled Me!");
    }
}
```

Not many differences separate this code from the code in the IE-specific example. The only difference is in how the `type` property is accessed. IE uses the `window.event` object, and the non-IE browsers use the implicit event object, which is passed to the event handler.

The target Property

When an event fires, it is useful to know what element it fired on. IE grants developers access to this information with the `srcElement` property. The other browsers' event object does not support this specific property, but it does have the `target` property. This property retrieves the HTML element that received the event.

Try It Out   The target Property

Use of the `target` property closely resembles that of IE's `srcElement` property. The main difference is in how you access the property, and this example shows you how.

```
<!DOCTYPE html PUBLIC "-//W3C//DTD XHTML 1.0 Transitional//EN"
    "http://www.w3.org/TR/xhtml1/DTD/xhtml1-transitional.dtd">

<html xmlns="http://www.w3.org/1999/xhtml" >
<head>
    <title>Using the target Property</title>

    <script type="text/javascript">
    function image_eventHandler(evt) {
        var eventTarget = evt.target;  //Get the element.
        var eventType = evt.type;   //Get the type of event.

        if (eventType == "mouseover") { //The mouse rolled over the image.
```

```
                eventTarget.src - "o.gif"; //So change the image's src property.
        }

        if (eventType == "mouseout") { //The mouse moved out.
            eventTarget.src = "x.gif"; //So change it back to the original picture.
        }
    }
    </script>
</head>
<body>
    <img src="x.gif" onmouseover="image_eventHandler(event)"
        onmouseout="image_eventHandler(event)" />
</body>
</html>
```

Save this file as `OB_target_property.htm`. When it's loaded into Firefox, Safari, or Opera, you'll see a picture of an X. When the mouse pointer moves over the `<img/>` element, the picture changes to an O. The picture reverts back to an X when the mouse pointer exits the `<img/>` element.

How It Works

The only JavaScript code in the script block is one function: `image_eventHandler()`, which handles the `mouseover` and `mouseout` events of the `<img/>` element in the page's body. It accepts one argument, called `evt`, which provides access to the event object. Following is the function definition.

```
function image_eventHandler(evt) {
    //more code here
}
```

In order for the rollover to work, the function needs two pieces of information: the event type, and the HTML element where the event fired.

```
function image_eventHandler(evt) {
    var eventTarget = evt.target;  //Get the element.
    var eventType = evt.type;  //Get the type of event.

    //more code here
}
```

The first line of this code creates a variable called `eventTarget`, which contains the value of the `target` property of the event object (the HTML element that received the event). Next, create the `eventType` variable and assign it the value of the fired event type.

Now use this information to check the type of event that called the function. Do this by comparing `eventType` to that of the names of event types. The following code checks to see if the `mouseover` event fired:

```
function image_eventHandler(evt) {
    var eventTarget = evt.target;  //Get the element.
```

449

```
        var eventType = evt.type;  //Get the type of event.

        if (eventType == "mouseover") { //The mouse rolled over the image.
            eventTarget.src = "o.gif"; //So change the image's src property.
        }

        //more code here
    }
```

If so, change the target's `src` property (the target is the `<img/>` element). The next step is to check to see if the event is `mouseout`. Follow the same step for the `mouseover` event, but this time compare `eventType` to the string `mouseout`.

```
    function image_eventHandler(evt) {
        var eventTarget = evt.target;  //Get the element.
        var eventType = evt.type;  //Get the type of event.

        if (eventType == "mouseover") { //The mouse rolled over the image.
            eventTarget.src = "o.gif"; //So change the image's src property.
        }

        if (eventType == "mouseout") { //The mouse moved out.
            eventTarget.src = "x.gif"; //So change it back to the original picture.
        }
    }
```

This code changes the image's picture back to `x.gif`, thereby reverting it to its original state.

Now Play Together, Kids

The challenge DHTML developers face is getting their code to work in every major browser. In the DHTML hell of yesteryear, getting code to work in the major browsers was a headache at best. Times change, thankfully, and getting DHTML code to play nicely with today's major browsers is quite simple. In fact, this is one of the easiest cross-browser problems developers face.

The first problem to tackle is how to get the browsers to retrieve the event object similarly. As a quick recap, IE has a global object called `event` (or `window.event`). Non-IE browsers require an event object, also called `event`, to be passed to the event handler. The two objects are similarly named, so use that to your advantage. Essentially, when you're assigning the events with the HTML attributes, use the method for non-IE browsers like this:

```
    <img src="x.gif" onmouseover="image_eventHandler(event)"
        onmouseout="image_eventHandler(event)" />
```

This HTML does two things. First, it allows non-IE browsers to handle the events; this is the same HTML used in the `target` property example. The event object is passed to `image_eventHandler()`. Second, and this is only for IE, the HTML passes the global `event` object to `image_eventHandler()`. Even though the `event` object is global, it is possible to pass it to other functions. Therefore, no matter if the user is viewing the web page in IE, Firefox, Safari, or Opera, the appropriate event object is passed to `image_eventHandler()`.

The second problem is how to handle the event. The image rollover DHTML script must retrieve the element that the event fired upon. In IE, this element is retrieved with the `srcElement` property. In non-IE browsers, the `target` property is the desired property. Thankfully, this problem has a straightforward solution: branch the code according to which browser is displaying the page. In Chapter 5 you learned how to use object detection to determine which browser the user is using. Do the same thing here. Consider the following code:

```
var elementTarget; //contains either the srcElement or the target property

if (evt.srcElement) { //The browser is IE
    elementTarget = evt.srcElement;
}

//more code here
```

The first line of this code creates a variable called `elementTarget`, which stores either the `srcElement` or `target` property, depending upon the browser that loaded the page. The next line uses object detection to determine the browser. In this case, the `srcElement` is checked. If it exists, then the browser is IE, and you can safely use the property.

Next, write code for the other browsers. If the `srcElement` property doesn't exist, the browser obviously isn't IE, and you can use the `target` property.

```
var elementTarget; //contains either the srcElement or the target property

if (evt.srcElement) { //The browser is IE
    elementTarget = evt.srcElement;
} else { //The browser is non-IE
    elementTarget = evt.target;
}
```

Now you can use the `elementTarget` variable to access the HTML element that the event was fired upon. The following example shows the only time the code branches to accommodate the differing browsers.

Try It Out   Cross-Browser Image Rollover

This example modifies the image rollover you previously wrote to work in all modern browsers.

```
<!DOCTYPE html PUBLIC "-//W3C//DTD XHTML 1.0 Transitional//EN"
    "http://www.w3.org/TR/xhtml1/DTD/xhtml1-transitional.dtd">

<html xmlns="http://www.w3.org/1999/xhtml" >
<head>
    <title>Cross-browser Image Rollover</title>

    <script type="text/javascript">
    function image_eventHandler(evt) {
        var elementTarget;

        if (evt.srcElement) { //The browser is IE
            elementTarget = evt.srcElement;
```

```
        } else { //The browser is non-IE
            elementTarget = evt.target;
        }

        if (evt.type == "mouseover") { //The mouse rolled over the image.
            elementTarget.src = "o.gif"; //So change the image's src property.
        }

        if (evt.type == "mouseout") { //The mouse moved out.
            elementTarget.src = "x.gif"; //So change it back to the original.
        }
    }
    </script>
</head>
<body>
    <img src="x.gif" onmouseover="image_eventHandler(event)"
        onmouseout="image_eventHandler(event)" />
</body>
</html>
```

Save this file as `CB_image_rollover.htm` (CB means cross-browser). Open this page with any modern browser (IE, Firefox, Opera, or Safari), and you'll see something similar to Figure 12-5.

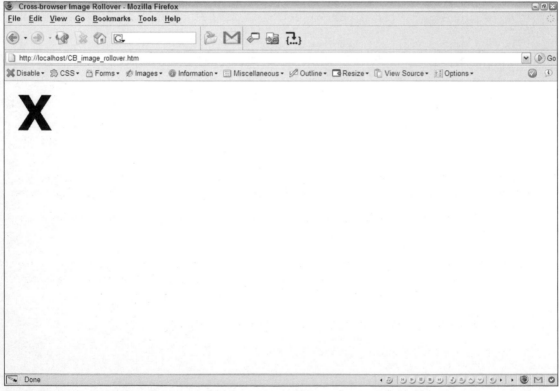

Figure 12-5

Move the mouse pointer over the image, and it changes to an O (see Figure 12-6).

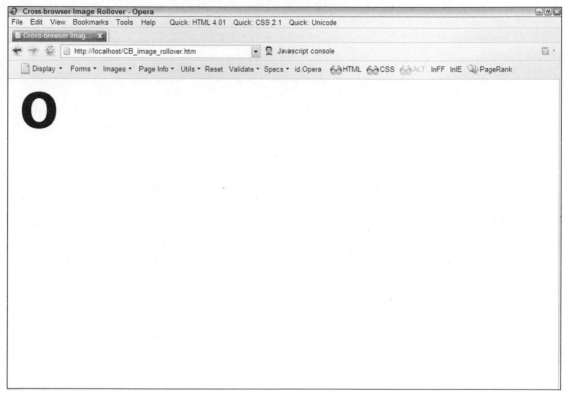

Figure 12-6

How It Works

A single `<img/>` element resides in the page's body. The `src` attribute is set to `x.gif`. Also, `onmouseover` and `onmouseout` event handlers are set to the value of `image_eventHandler(event)`.

```
<img src="x.gif" onmouseover="image_eventHandler(event)"
    onmouseout="image_eventHandler(event)" />
```

This not only suits the needs of non-IE browsers, but also passes the IE-specific global `event` object to the `image_eventHandler()` function. This enables the function to use both event objects, depending on which browser displays the web page.

In the script block, the `image_eventHandler()` function is defined.

```
function image_eventHandler(evt) {
    var elementTarget;

    //more code here
}
```

It accepts an event object as an argument, and the first line creates a variable called `elementTarget`. Next, the code branches to accommodate the different browsers:

```
function image_eventHandler(evt) {
    var elementTarget;

    if (evt.srcElement) { //The browser is IE
        elementTarget = evt.srcElement;
    } else { //The browser is non-IE
        elementTarget = evt.target;
    }

    //more code here
}
```

This code consolidates the differing event object implementations into one usable variable: `elementTarget`. To do this, use object detection to determine the browser and assign the appropriate property to the `elementTarget` variable.

Since this function handles two events, it needs to determine which event called the function. As you already know, the `type` property contains this information. First check to see if the event was caused by the mouse pointer moving over the image element:

```
function image_eventHandler(evt) {
    var elementTarget;

    if (evt.srcElement) { //The browser is IE
        elementTarget = evt.srcElement;
    } else { //The browser is non-IE
        elementTarget = evt.target;
    }

    if (evt.type == "mouseover") { //The mouse rolled over the image.
        elementTarget.src = "o.gif"; //So change the image's src property.
    }

    //more code here
}
```

If this is the case, change the `src` property of the `<img/>` element to `o.gif`, which changes the picture that is displayed to the user. Notice that this is where the `elementTarget` variable is used.

Next, check to see if the event was caused by the user moving the mouse pointer off of the image:

```
function image_eventHandler(evt) {
    var elementTarget;

    if (evt.srcElement) { //The browser is IE
        elementTarget = evt.srcElement;
    } else { //The browser is non-IE
        elementTarget = evt.target;
    }

    if (evt.type == "mouseover") { //The mouse rolled over the image.
```

```
        elementTarget.src = "o.gif"; //So change the image's src property.
    }

    if (evt.type == "mouseout") { //The mouse moved out.
        elementTarget.src = "x.gif"; //So change it back to the original.
    }
}
```

This code compares the type property to the string mouseout and changes the image's src property back to x.gif if this event was fired. And with these final few lines of code, your first cross-browser DHTML script is complete!

These examples have focused on using the event handler attributes of HTML elements. The next section focuses on using event handlers that are assigned through JavaScript.

Event Handlers as Properties Revisited

There is one glaring difference between assigning event handlers with HTML attributes and assigning them with JavaScript. With the HTML attributes, you were able to pass arguments to the function handling the event (for example, the event object). When using properties, though, you cannot pass any arguments to the function when assigning the event handler:

```
document.images[0].onmouseover - image_eventHandler(event); //This is wrong!

document.images[0].onmouseover = image_eventHandler; //This is correct.
```

This isn't really a problem for IE, as the event object is a part of the window object, which is global. For non-IE browsers, the browser automatically passes the event object to the event handler when the event fires. So handling events in this fashion is *almost* identical to handling them as you did in the previous section.

Try It Out   **Image Rollover with Property Event Handlers**

The following HTML is yet another implementation of the image rollover script:

```
<!DOCTYPE html PUBLIC "-//W3C//DTD XHTML 1.0 Transitional//EN"
    "http://www.w3.org/TR/xhtml1/DTD/xhtml1-transitional.dtd">

<html xmlns="http://www.w3.org/1999/xhtml" >
<head>
    <title>Cross-browser Image Rollover</title>
</head>
<body>
    <img src="x.gif" />

    <script type="text/javascript">
    function image_eventHandler(evt) {
        var elementTarget;
        var eventType;

        if (window.event) { //The browser is IE
            elementTarget = window.event.srcElement;
            eventType = window.event.type;
        } else { //The browser is non-IE
```

```
            elementTarget = evt.target;
            eventType = evt.type;
        }

        if (eventType == "mouseover") { //The mouse rolled over the image.
            elementTarget.src = "o.gif"; //So change the image's src property.
        }

        if (eventType == "mouseout") { //The mouse moved out.
            elementTarget.src = "x.gif"; //So change it back to the original.
        }
    }


    document.images[0].onmouseover = image_eventHandler;
    document.images[0].onmouseout = image_eventHandler;
    </script>
</body>
</html>
```

Save this file as CB_image_rollover_property_events.htm. When loaded into a browser, a picture of an X is visible.

How It Works

In the body of the page, a single <img/> element is defined. This is a simple element: Only the src attribute is used.

```
<img src="x.gif" />
```

Here's where things start to change. Instead of putting the <script/> element in the head of the page, you put it in the body. This is done for one reason: The image needs to be loaded into the document before it can be accessed with JavaScript. Attempting to access an HTML element before it's loaded into the document results in an error.

You can't access an HTML element in JavaScript if it hasn't been loaded by the browser.

The first thing in the script block is the image_eventHandler() function. It is essentially the same as in the prior sections, but this iteration contains a few changes. The first is the addition of the eventType variable. This variable will contain the value of the type property of the event object.

```
function image_eventHandler(evt) {
    var elementTarget;
    var eventType;

    //more code here
}
```

You do this because the function now has to handle two different event objects. The evt parameter is used only in non-IE browsers; the following line generates an error if you run it in IE:

```
alert(evt.type); //throws an error in IE
```

This happens because IE does not pass a value to event handlers when the event fires. So when branching the code to assign elementTarget, you must also assign the eventType variable its value, like this:

```
function image_eventHandler(evt) {
    var elementTarget;
    var eventType;

    if (window.event) { //The browser is IE
        elementTarget = window.event.srcElement;
        eventType = window.event.type;
    }

    //more code here
}
```

This code uses the global window.event object to retrieve the event's type and assign it to eventType.

Next, get the same information for the non-IE browsers:

```
function image_eventHandler(evt) {
    var elementTarget;
    var eventType;

    if (window.event) { //The browser is IE
        elementTarget = window.event.srcElement;
        eventType = window.event.type;
    } else { //The browser is non-IE
        elementTarget = evt.target;
        eventType = evt.type;
    }

    //more code here
}
```

This code uses the evt parameter to retrieve the target and type properties. At this point you have the information you need; now it's time to use it in changing the image element's src property.

```
function image_eventHandler(evt) {
    var elementTarget;
    var eventType;

    if (window.event) { //The browser is IE
        elementTarget = window.event.srcElement;
        eventType = window.event.type;
    } else { //The browser is non-IE
        elementTarget = evt.target;
        eventType = evt.type;
    }

    if (eventType == "mouseover") { //The mouse rolled over the image.
        elementTarget.src = "o.gif"; //So change the image's src property.
    }
```

```
    if (eventType == "mouseout") { //The mouse moved out.
        elementTarget.src = "x.gif"; //So change it back to the original.
    }
}
```

This code hasn't changed from the previous examples: It determines what event called the function and changes the src property accordingly. Now all that is left is to wire up the events. Do so by using the onmouseover and onmouseout properties of the image element.

```
document.images[0].onmouseover = image_eventHandler;
document.images[0].onmouseout = image_eventHandler;
```

This code retrieves the image element by using the images collection. There is only one image in the document. Therefore, the index of 0 is used to retrieve the element.

These sections have walked you through many rollover examples. The next section departs from JavaScript and introduces you to Cascading Style Sheets.

CSS: A Primer

Cascading style sheets (CSS) is an important technology that developers use to build many DHTML scripts. Cascading Style Sheets is a language that enables you to apply a set of styles to various HTML tags. For example, you may want all <h1/> elements in the web page to be colored blue and underlined. Before CSS you would do this with various formatting tags, such as <font> and <u>. This approach worked; however, it caused a few problems.

The first problem with this approach is that you need to wrap the content with these formatting tags, and styling different pieces of content the same way requires repeated tag use. This results in extra work for web page authors. Also, changing an existing style (say blue underlined text) to a new style (red boldface text), requires the change of every <font> and <u> tag throughout the document.

To add to this problem, you may want to set a very specific size for the text of the <h1> tags. The sizes offered by the font are very limited, and those few sizes enable you to specify only whether the font should be larger or smaller than normal. The font sizes are relative to the font size the user has set in her browser. This makes it possible for text to be rendered in an unreadable size.

HTML also does not give you control over where elements appear in the page. The browser displays HTML elements according to where the tags appear in the source code. Therefore, the following HTML will always display Hello on the first line and World on the second line:

```
<p>Hello</p>
<p>World</p>
```

This is what is referred to as the *document flow* — how the browser naturally displays the web page. Without CSS, it is not possible to change the document flow. You can use formatting tags for different types of positioning (like lists or tables), but you can't specify an exact position.

CSS solves each of these problems. It enables you to specify certain styles that can be used throughout the entire web page easily and efficiently. It also gives you more control over how the web page looks, thereby giving you more power to make the page look the way you first envisioned it.

Adding Some Style to HTML

You can add style to an HTML page by creating style sheets within the `<style>` tag or by specifying `style` attributes in an element's opening tag. There are a number of ways to define style, but this primer covers only three of them:

❏ Defining a style for certain HTML elements, for example a style for all paragraph elements.

❏ Creating a style class. You then specify in the class attribute of a tag the name of the style class to be applied.

❏ Specifying style for just one element.

The `<style>` Tag

You can use the first two ways of adding style mentioned in the previous list — defining a style for a type of tag and defining a style class — by creating a `<style/>` element inside the `<head/>` element.

To define the style for a particular element, use the following format:

```
elementName {
    style-property-name: style property value;
    another-style-property: another value;
}
```

This CSS code is referred to as a CSS *rule*. A rule consists first of a *selector*. A selector selects the HTML element to which the style rule will be applied. In the previous example, `elementName` is the selector. Any HTML element name can be used as a selector; just remember to take out the angle brackets (< and >). For example, to define a selector for all `<p>` tags, you would use an `elementName` of p.

After the selector comes a set of *style declarations* inside the curly braces. A declaration consists of a property name, a colon (instead of an equals sign), and then the property's value. Style declarations are separated by semicolons. For example, let's say you want all `<p>` tags to be blue, in the Arial font, and 10 points in size. First create a rule to select the `<p>` tags. Then add the declarations by specifying the `font-family`, `font-size`, and `color` properties. The following code does this:

```
<html>
<head>
    <style>
        p {
            font-family: arial;
            font-size: 10pt;
            color: blue;
        }
    </style>
</head>
```

```
<body>
    <p>Some blue arial 10 point text</p>
    <p>Also blue arial 10 point text</p>
</body>
</html>
```

The first property specified is `font-family`, which is assigned the value `arial`. This is followed by a semicolon to mark the end of that style declaration. Next the `font-size` property is defined and its value set to `10pt`. Finally you specify the `color` property and its value of `blue`. Both the paragraphs defined in the page will have the same font, font size, and color.

If you want to define similar properties for the `<td>` tags, add a rule inside the `<style>` tag.

```
<style>
    p {
        font-family: arial;
        font-size: 10pt;
        color: blue;
    }

    td {
        font-family: arial;
        font-size: 12pt;
        color: red;
    }
</style>
```

This CSS sets the `<td>` tags to have the same font family as the `<p>` tags, but their font's size is larger and their text is rendered in red. This is the basic behavior of CSS, but it doesn't help if you want some paragraphs in a larger font while others remain in the 10-point font.

CSS is not limited to this basic functionality, however. You can define what are called *classes*: CSS rules that can be applied to a variety of elements. In fact, with CSS classes, you can make any element emulate almost any other.

A class's selector is a custom name that you define. Classes are distinguished by a dot in front of their names. The following code defines a class called `heading1`:

```
<style>
    p {
        font-family: arial;
        font-size: 10pt;
        color: blue;
    }

    .heading1 {
        font-size: 24pt;
        color: orange;
    }
</style>
```

The `heading1` class's style declarations specify that the `font-size` should be `24pt` and that the `color` should be `orange`. Applying this class to an HTML element requires the use of the `class` attribute. All elements within the `<body/>` element can be classed. The following code modifies the previous HTML example. The first of the two paragraphs is classed as `heading1`.

```
<html>
<head>
    <style>
        p {
            font-family: arial;
            font-size: 10pt;
            color: blue;
        }

        .heading1 {
            font-size: 24pt;
            color: orange;
        }
    </style>
</head>
<body>
    <p class="heading1">A Heading in orange arial 24 point text</p>
    <p>Some blue arial 10 point text</p>
</body>
</html>
```

Now the first paragraph has the `heading1` class of style applied. Therefore, it is rendered as orange 24-point text in the Arial font. The `heading1` class does not declare a font face property; it inherits the font face from the p rule. The style defined in the p rule is applied to all `<p/>` elements. So the first `<p/>` element has both the p rule and the `heading1` rule applied to it. If the same style declarations are defined in both rules, the declarations in the class rule take precedence. Therefore the first paragraph has the Arial font applied from the `<p/>` definition, but the `size` and `color` style declarations of the `heading1` class override those defined in the p rule.

The style Attribute

The third way of defining styles uses the `style` attribute, which most HTML elements support. For example, if you wanted just one paragraph to be in green italics you could change the HTML tag definition like this:

```
<p style="font-style: italic; color: green">
    Some green arial 10 point text
</p>
```

Define the style declarations inside the `style` attribute of the tag, just as you did previously when it was inside the `<style>` tag. First set the `font-style` attribute to `italic`; then, after a semicolon, set the `color` to `green`. As before, the setting of the `color` property here overrides the setting in the style sheet definition for all `<p/>` elements. However, the paragraph will still use the `font-family` and `font-size` properties set in the `<style/>` tag.

Cascading Style Sheets

The style declarations defined for one element may cascade down to the elements contained within that element; hence the name Cascading Style Sheets. In other words, some style declarations of a parent element cascade down to the child elements inside. For example, in the following code no rules are defined for the two paragraph elements. Instead a rule for <div/> elements is created, and one such element contains a sole <p/> element. The paragraph outside the <div/> has no style applied to it, yet the <p/> inside the <div/> inherits the style set for the <div/> tag.

```
<html>
<head>
    <style>
        div {
            font-family: arial;
            font-size: 10pt;
            color: blue;
        }
    </style>
</head>
<body>
    <p>This text has no style.</p>
    <div>
        <p>This text inherits style from its parent div element.</p>
    </div>
</body>
</html>
```

Styling Properties

In the previous sections you learned how to select elements in the HTML page to apply styles to, but you didn't cover much in the way of actual style properties. After all, what use is a style sheet where hardly any style is declared?

Properties are essentially broken up into distinct groups. Although it is outside the scope of this primer to cover all properties, there are quite a few to discuss.

Colors and Background

Probably the simplest styles you can apply to a web page are colors. You can change the color of text (foreground color), as well as the color of the background. You are not limited to using a color for your background; you may also choose to use an image.

Foreground Color

Changing the foreground color is quite simple, and you have seen examples of it in this chapter. The CSS property that controls this color is the color property, and you have a variety of ways to assign its value. This little section will show you the many ways you can assign the color red to your text.

The first method of assigning color is the use of a color keyword.

```
color: red;
```

Using this approach ensures that your CSS is quite readable; however, you are limiting yourself when using keywords. The CSS specification defines 17 color keywords that every browser should implement: aqua, black, blue, fuchsia, gray, green, lime, maroon, navy, olive, orange, purple, red, silver, teal, white, and yellow. Some browsers implement many more colors, while others do not. You can easily avoid any problems caused by this discrepancy by using either the previously listed names or one of the other color values.

The second approach enables you to assign the specific red, green, and blue values of a color by using rgb() notation. This notation allows two types of values: integer values that range form 0–255, and percentage values from 0%–100%. You assign a value for red, green, and blue.

```
color: rgb(255, 0, 0);
color: rgb(100%, 0%, 0%);
```

Whether you use plain integers or percentages, the result of the preceding CSS will be the same.

Lastly, you can use hexadecimal values to assign colors. In order to do this, you must prepend the hexadecimal number with a pound sign (#). Hexadecimal numbers in CSS typically consist of three pairs of numbers.

```
color: #FF0000;
```

The first pair is red (FF), the second is green (00), and the third is blue (00). You can also use three digits, like this:

```
color: #f00;
```

When the browser finds three-digit hexadecimal values, it converts them to a six-digit form and replicates the digits. So the previous three-digit value becomes the six-digit value you just looked at.

The concept of using colors does not end with foreground color. These same principles are used in background color (and anywhere you can use color) as well.

Backgrounds and Color

In order to assign a color to an element's background, you must use the background-color property:

```
background-color: gray;
color: red;
```

The first line sets the background color of the element to gray, and the text assumes the color red. As mentioned earlier, the preceding color principles apply to background colors as well. You can use color names, hexadecimal numbers, or rgb() notation to assign a background color.

Sometimes all you want is a little color, but other times you want to spruce up your web site with more — like an image. Through CSS, it's possible to enable an element to display an image in its background. To do this, you use the background-image property:

```
background-image: url(myImage.gif);
```

The first thing you may notice is the use of the `url()` notation. This specific example shows the use of a relative URI, meaning that `myImage.gif` is located in the same directory as this style sheet. You can also use an absolute URI like the following:

```
background-image: url(http://www.yoursite.com/myImage.gif);
```

Both ways are correct. Remember that you can use both `background-color` and `background-image`; you're not limited to using just one or the other.

It is also possible to use single quotes (') or double quotes(") in `url()` notation like this:
`background-image: url("myImage.gif");`. *However, this does not work in some Mac browsers. For compatibility reasons, it is best to leave quotes out.*

Fonts and Text

Text is the most important aspect of any web site. Ninety-nine percent of the time, a visitor comes to read what you have to say. Therefore, it's important to learn how to style your text. You've already learned how to set the color of text; now take a look at how you can set the type of font, as well as its size, weight, and decoration.

The `font-family` property, as its name suggests, sets the font for the text. You have a variety of fonts installed on your computer at your disposal; you can also use generic fonts in the event that a viewer's computer lacks the font (or fonts) you specify:

```
font-family: arial, verdana, sans-serif;
```

In this CSS, the `font-family` property is set to three values: `arial`, `verdana`, and `sans-serif`. If the viewer's computer does not have the Arial font installed, the browser attempts to use Verdana. If neither Arial nor Verdana is installed, the browser uses the generic sans-serif font. Using a generic font, even if it is the "last resort" font, is encouraged, as it tells the browser what type of font to use if none of your preferred fonts are available. Following is the list of generic fonts:

- ❏ serif
- ❏ sans-serif
- ❏ cursive
- ❏ fantasy
- ❏ monospace

There's no limit to the amount of fonts you can assign to the `font-family` property. Just know that the browser will attempt to use each font in the order you specify.

Now that you've set a font family, you should also set a size. The CSS property you use to do this is aptly named `font-size`. This property accepts a variety of units for values, and you've already seen the use of points as a measurement. Another popular unit for font size is pixels. When you specify a font size in pixels, the browser renders the text using pixels as the font measurement. For example, see the following CSS:

```
font-size: 12px;
```

When the browser renders text with this style, the font is set to 12 pixels in height. There is also no limit to the size you can use; however, you'll want to use something that is easy to read.

When you want to emphasize a certain part of the text, you have several options. First, you can bold your text with the font-weight property:

```
font-weight: bold;
```

This will make the text bold and allow the user to see that it is important in some way. You can also italicize your text by using the font-style property:

```
font-style: italic;
```

This italicizes the text. To make life a bit easier, the CSS specification gives you a quick way to set your font preferences by assigning these values to the font property. The font property's syntax looks like this:

```
font: font-style font-weight font-size font-family;
```

For example, if you wanted to set the font contained in an element to be 12-point bold text and to use the Verdana font face, your CSS would look like this:

```
font: bold 12pt verdana;
```

You don't have to specify each value of each property, only the ones you desire. However, it is important to keep them in the order listed earlier. Take the following example:

```
font: bold italic verdana 12pt; /* Wrong Format */
```

This CSS is not in the correct format, because font-style should come before font-weight, and font-size should come before font-family. Some browsers may display the text with the desired style; however, other browsers may not—so it is best to keep to the standard order.

Lastly, you can underline text by using the text-decoration property:

```
text-decoration: underline;
```

This property is not related to the font properties discussed earlier. Therefore, you cannot add underline to the font property.

Links, by default, are underlined. You can change this by setting text-decoration *to* none.

The presentation of your text plays an important role in the way users perceive your web site. Make sure that it is easy to read: the proper size, color, and emphasis will make your visitors happy.

Showing and Hiding Elements

All elements are shown by default; however, you may wish to hide (or show) content based upon an action the user takes. For example, you can show an element that contains information on a specific link when the user moves her mouse over the link, or you can cause an element to pop up in order to display information about a certain form element that the user is currently typing in.

But how do you show and hide elements? With the `visibility` property:

```
visibility: hidden;
```

Setting this property to `hidden` hides the element. Using this property, however, has a side effect. Hiding an element does not remove it from the document's flow; instead you see the area in which the element is located, yet the element's contents are hidden. In other words, you end up with a blank area when an element is hidden.

To show a hidden element, set the `visibility` property to `visible`:

```
visibility: visible;
```

The element's contents (and the element itself) are visible once again to the user when you use this value.

Hiding an element with the `visibility` property causes a blank space to appear where the element used to be seen. This can sometimes cause an undesired result. To solve this issue, CSS also provides another way of hiding an element. By using the `display` property, you can remove an element completely from the document's flow, showing no evidence that the element was there. To do this, set the `display` property to `none`, like this:

```
display: none;
```

The `display` property can accept other values, which cause the element to be displayed again. For simplicity's sake, we'll cover two here. The first is the value `block`. Setting the `display` property to `block` tells the browser to render the element as a block, much as it displays paragraphs.

```
display: block;
```

The second value is `inline`. This property displays the element not as a block, but as a line. Many elements have an inline display by default, like `<span/>` elements and `<a/>` elements.

```
display: inline;
```

It is important to note that the visibility and display properties are two different properties and should be treated as such. The `display` property has the ability to remove an element visually from the HTML page, and the `visibility` property simply hides or shows an element.

It's All About Position

HTML content normally flows from the top to the bottom of a page, the position of the output being based on where the tag is defined in the page. Consider the following HTML:

```
<P>Paragraph 1</P>
<P>Paragraph 2</P>
```

When the browser renders this HTML, the paragraphs appear one after the other.

```
Paragraph 1
Paragraph 2
```

However, it is possible to position content with style sheets. You can do it in many ways, but this primer only covers two. With *absolute positioning* the positioned element is removed from the document's flow and can be placed anywhere in the browser's viewport. With *relative positioning* the element is calculated according to the normal flow, but it can be shifted relative to its original position. You can specify whether an element is positioned relatively or absolutely by using the `position` style attribute, which takes the values `relative` and `absolute`.

The keys to positioning an element are the CSS properties `left` and `top`. You can use a number of different units for these values, but for simplicity's sake we'll stick here with those most commonly used: pixels and percentages. Let's start with pixels.

When you set your computer screen's display resolution, you can choose values like 800 * 600 or 1024 * 768, and so on. These values are actually pixels, so 800 * 600 means that your screen will be treated as being 800 pixels wide by 600 pixels high. These values are independent of your actual physical monitor size; they determine the maximum sizes of the browser window. If the user has an 800-by-600 screen and you set a `<div/>` element to appear 1,000 pixels from the top, the element will be offscreen. You need to also keep in mind that the user can resize the browser window and that screen resolution is a theoretical maximum. Also, the browser toolbars and frame take up some space.

As far as absolute positioning is concerned, the top left-hand corner of the browser window is 0,0 and the bottom right-hand corner will be at the upper limit of the values that determine screen resolution. So for 800 * 600 resolutions, the bottom right-hand corner is at the coordinates 800,600, whereas for 1024 * 768 resolutions, it's 1024,768, as shown in Figure 12-7.

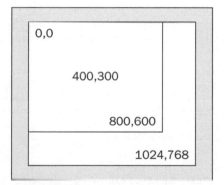

Figure 12-7

If you specified that a `<div/>` element's `left` style attribute be set to 400 pixels and its `top` style attribute to 300 pixels, the element's top left-hand corner would be near the middle of a browser window on an 800 * 600 resolution display. If the display were set to 1024 * 768, the top left-hand corner would be about two-fifths across the browser window by about two-fifths down. This position has been marked approximately on the diagram in Figure 12-7.

Let's look at an example. Imagine you have an absolutely positioned `<div/>` element at a position `left` of 200 and `top` of 100, and with other style attributes specifying it should be 200 pixels wide by 200 pixels deep and have a background color of `blue`. Your browser window would look something like what is shown in Figure 12-8.

Figure 12-8

Now how can you position a paragraph contained within the `<div/>` element relative to that `<div/>` element? If you think of the `<div/>` element as a sort of screen within a screen, in this case a screen of resolution 200 * 200, relative positioning is easier to understand.

If you think of the `<div/>` element as a browser window itself, the top left-hand corner of the `<div/>` element is 0,0 and the bottom right-hand corner is 200,200 — that is, the `<div/>` element's width and height — in this case. If you then specify that the `<p/>` element should be at the relative position `left` of 100 and `top` of 100, that would leave the top left-hand corner of the `<p/>` element in exactly the middle of the `<div/>` element in which it is contained.

What if you relatively position a tag that is not inside another tag? Well, in that case it'll be relative to the `<body/>` element, which is the whole page itself. Essentially this is the same as absolute positioning if the whole page fills the screen.

Let's see the HTML for a page with the `<div/>` and `<p/>` elements at the positions we're discussing.

```
<html>
<head>
    <style>
        .divStyle1 {
            background-color: blue;
            position : absolute;
            width: 200px; height: 200px;
        }

        .pStyle1 {
            color: white;
            position : relative;
        }
    </style>
</head>
<body>
    <div style="left: 200px; top: 200px" class="divStyle1">
        <p class="pStyle1" style="left: 100px; top: 100px">My Paragraph</p>
    </div>
</body>
</html>
```

Type this into a text editor and save it as `relativepos.htm`.

In the `<style/>` element, you create two style classes: `divStyle1` and `pStyle1`. Within these, you specify the style declarations previously discussed. In `divStyle1` you specify a blue background, that the positioning should be absolute, and the width and height in pixels. `pStyle1` specifies only the color of the text and that it should be positioned relatively.

Then, in the `<div/>` element, the CSS class `divStyle1` is assigned by using the `class` attribute, and the `style` attribute specifies the `left` and `top` positions of the tag. Because the `divStyle1` class's specified positioning should be absolute, the values `200` and `200` will be absolute screen values.

In the `<p/>` element, you apply the `pStyle1` class and then specify the position of the element as `100px` and `100px`. This time the element is placed relative to its position in the document flow, with `0,0` as the top left-hand corner of the `<div/>` and `200,200` as the bottom right-hand corner.

> *Most modern browsers require you to specify the measuring unit when assigning values for* `top`, `left`, `height`, *and* `width`. *As with the* `font-size` *property we looked at earlier, you simply add* `px` *to the end of the numerical value.*

On a screen with a resolution of `800 * 600` and the browser window maximized, the example should look like what is shown in Figure 12-9.

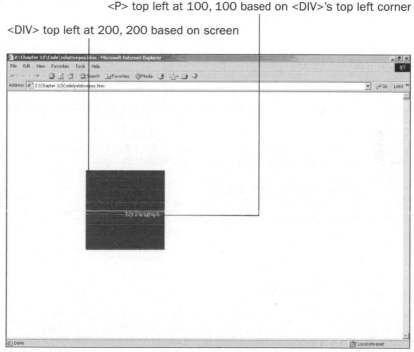

Figure 12-9

Remember that the `left` and `top` style properties apply to the left and top of the element, respectively, putting the top left of the letter M at position `100, 100` within the `<div/>` element.

In addition to specifying position properties as pixels, you can use percentages. To do this you simply put % at the end of the value instead of px. For example, to position the <div/> and <p/> elements so that the top left of the <div/> appears in the middle of the browser window and the top left of the <p/> element appears in the middle of the <div/>, regardless of screen resolution, you'd write the following code:

```
<div style="left: 50%; top: 50%" class="divStyle1">
    <p class="pStyle1" style="left: 50%;top: 50%">My Paragraph</p>
</div>
```

Dynamic HTML

You might be wondering why you have this introduction to style sheets in a book about JavaScript. Remember, DHTML is the manipulation of an HTML document after it is loaded into the browser, and the most common way to manipulate the document is by changing the way HTML elements look. In order to do this, you need to go over a few topics. First, you'll take a look at how to find an element in the document. Second, you'll look at how you can change an element's style programmatically.

Accessing Elements

The Document Object Model (DOM) holds the ability you need to find and access HTML elements; the DOM is a hierarchical tree, and you can certainly climb it, inspect every branch and leaf, and find what you're looking for. However, the DOM provides a much easier way to find specific elements.

The DOM exposes a method called getElementById(), which is used to find, in a web page, specific HTML elements whose id attributes match that of the argument passed to the method. Consider the following HTML as an example:

```
<div id="divAdvert">Here is an advertisement</div>
```

This HTML creates a <div/> element, and the id attribute is assigned divAdvert. With this information, you can easily retrieve this element by using getElementById().

```
var divAdvert = document.getElementById("divAdvert");
```

This JavaScript code retrieves the <div/> element created earlier, and you can use the divAdvert variable to programmatically manipulate it. There are a variety of ways to change HTML elements; the most common, though, are changing the way an element looks and changing an element's position.

Changing Appearances

Probably the most common use for DHTML is to change the way an element looks. Such a change can create an interactive experience for visitors to your web site, and can even be used to alert them to important information or that an action is required by them. Changing the way an element looks consists almost exclusively of changing CSS properties for an HTML element. You can do this two ways through JavaScript: You can change each CSS property, or you can change the value of the element's class attribute.

Using the style Property

In order to change specific CSS properties, you must look, once again, to the DOM. All modern browsers implement the `style` object, which maps directly to the element's `style` attribute. This object contains CSS properties, and by using it you can change any CSS property that the browser supports. Use the style property like this:

```
oHtmlElement.style.cssProperty = value;
```

The CSS property names generally match those used in a CSS file; therefore, changing the text color of an element requires the use of the `color` property, like this:

```
var divAdvert = document.getElementById("divAdvert");  //Get the desired element

divAdvert.style.color = "blue";  //Change the text color to blue
```

There are some cases, however, in which the property name is a little different from the one seen in a CSS file. CSS properties that contain a hyphen (-) are a perfect example of this exception. In the case of these properties, you remove the hyphen and capitalize the first letter of the word that follows the hyphen. The following code shows the incorrect and correct ways to do this:

```
divAdvert.style.background-color = "gray";  //Wrong

divAdvert.style.backgroundColor = "gray";  //Correct
```

You can also use the `style` object to retrieve styles that have previously been declared. However, if the `style` property you try to retrieve has not been set with the `style` attribute (inline styles) or with the `style` object, you will not retrieve the property's value. Consider the following style sheet which sets the style for the element with `divAdvert` as its `id`:

```
<style>
    #divAdvert {
        background-color: gray;
    }
</style>
```

First, a new concept is present in this CSS. Look at the selector, and how it is preceded by a pound sign (#). In CSS, this symbol is an ID selector, and it selects an HTML element whose ID attribute matches the selector name (without the pound sign). Therefore, this style rule is applied to the `<div/>` element defined earlier in the section. In this CSS, you set the element to have a background color of gray. Also, the HTML element has changed to include the use of the `style` attribute:

```
<div id="divAdvert" style="color: green">I am an advertisement.</div>
```

When the browser renders this element, it will have green text on a gray background. If you had used the `style` object to retrieve the value of both the `background-color` and `color` properties, you'd get mixed results:

```
var divAdvert = document.getElementById("divAdvert");  //Get the desired element

alert(divAdvert.style.backgroundColor);  //Alerts an empty string

alert(divAdvert.style.color);  //Alerts green
```

You get these results because the `style` object accesses the `style` attribute of the element. If the style declaration is set in the `<style/>` block, you cannot retrieve that property's value with the `style` object.

Try It Out   Using the style Object

Let's look at a simple example of changing the appearance of some text by using the `style` object.

```
<!DOCTYPE html PUBLIC "-//W3C//DTD XHTML 1.0 Transitional//EN"
    "http://www.w3.org/TR/xhtml1/DTD/xhtml1-transitional.dtd">

<html xmlns="http://www.w3.org/1999/xhtml" >
<head>
    <title>Using the style Object</title>
    <style type="text/css">
        #divAdvert {
            font: 12pt arial;
        }
    </style>
    <script type="text/javascript">
    function divAdvert_onMouseOver() {
        //Get the element
        var divAdvert = document.getElementById("divAdvert");

        //Italicize the text
        divAdvert.style.fontStyle = "italic";

        //Underline the text
        divAdvert.style.textDecoration = "underline";
    }

    function divAdvert_onMouseOut() {
        //Get the element
        var divAdvert = document.getElementById("divAdvert");

        //Set the font-style to normal
        divAdvert.style.fontStyle = "normal";

        //Remove the underline
        divAdvert.style.textDecoration = "none";
    }
    </script>
</head>
<body>
    <div id="divAdvert" onmouseover="divAdvert_onMouseOver()"
        onmouseout="divAdvert_onMouseOut()">Here is an advertisement.</div>
</body>
</html>
```

Save this as `style_object.htm`. When you run this in your browser you should see a single line of text, as shown in Figure 12-10.

Figure 12-10

Roll your mouse over the text, and you'll see it become italicized and underlined (see Figure 12-11).

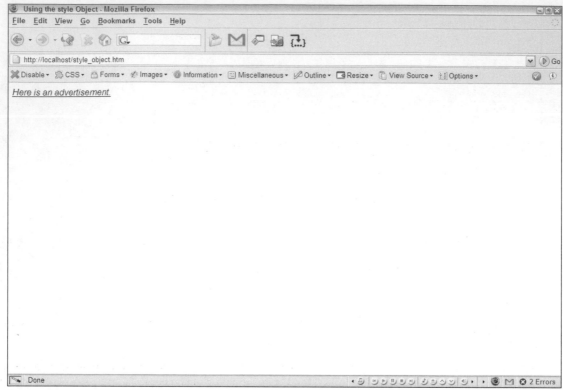

Figure 12-11

And when you move your mouse off of the text, it returns back to normal.

How It Works

In the page's body, a `<div/>` element is created and has an `id` of `divAdvert`. Hook up the `mouseover` and `mouseout` events to the `divAdvert_onMouseOver()` and `divAdvert_onMouseOut()` functions, respectively, which are defined in the `<script/>` block in the head of the page.

When the mouse pointer enters the `<div/>` element, the `divAdvert_onMouseOver()` function is called. The following shows the function declaration and the first line:

```
function divAdvert_onMouseOver() {
    //Get the element
    var divAdvert = document.getElementById("divAdvert");

    //more code here
}
```

Before you can do anything to the `<div/>` element, you must first retrieve it. You do this simply by using the `getElementById()` method. Now that you have the element, you can manipulate its style. First, make the text italic with the `fontStyle` property:

```
function divAdvert_onMouseOver() {
    //Get the element
    var divAdvert = document.getElementById("divAdvert");

    //Italicize the text
    divAdvert.style.fontStyle = "italic";

    //more code here
}
```

Next, underline the text by using the textDecoration property:

```
function divAdvert_onMouseOver() {
    //Get the element
    var divAdvert = document.getElementById("divAdvert");

    //Italicize the text
    divAdvert.style.fontStyle = "italic";

    //Underline the text
    divAdvert.style.textDecoration = "underline";
}
```

Because you set the textDecoration property to underline, the text displayed in the <div/> element becomes underlined.

Naturally, you do not want to keep the text italicized and underlined; so use the mouseout event to change the text back to its original state. When this event fires, the divAdvert_onMouseOut() function is called.

```
function divAdvert_onMouseOut() {
    //Get the element
    var divAdvert = document.getElementById("divAdvert");

    //Set the font-style to normal
    divAdvert.style.fontStyle = "normal";

    //Remove the underline
    divAdvert.style.textDecoration = "none";
}
```

The code for this function somewhat resembles that for the divAdvert_onMouseOver() function. First, you retrieve the divAdvert element; next, set the fontStyle property to normal, thus removing the italics. Lastly, set the textDecoration to none, which removes the underline from the text.

Changing the class Attribute

As you learned earlier, you can assign a CSS class to elements by using the element's class attribute. This attribute is exposed in the DOM by the className property and can be changed through JavaScript to associate a different style rule with the element.

```
oHtmlElement.className = sNewClassName;
```

Using the `className` property to change an element's style is advantageous in two ways. First, it reduces the amount of JavaScript you have to write, which no one is likely to complain about. Second, it keeps style information out of the JavaScript file and puts it into the CSS file where it belongs. Making any type of changes to the style rules is easier because you do not have to have several files open in order to change them.

Try It Out   **Using the className Property**

Let's revisit the code from `style_object.htm` from the previous section, but with a few revisions.

```
<!DOCTYPE html PUBLIC "-//W3C//DTD XHTML 1.0 Transitional//EN"
    "http://www.w3.org/TR/xhtml1/DTD/xhtml1-transitional.dtd">

<html xmlns="http://www.w3.org/1999/xhtml" >
<head>
    <title>Using the className Property</title>
    <style type="text/css">
        .defaultStyle {
            font: normal 12pt arial;
            text-decoration: none;
        }

        .newStyle {
            font: italic 12pt arial;
            text-decoration: underline;
        }
    </style>
    <script type="text/javascript">
    function divAdvert_onMouseOver() {
        //Get the element
        var divAdvert = document.getElementById("divAdvert");

        //Change the className
        divAdvert.className = "newStyle";
    }

    function divAdvert_onMouseOut() {
        //Get the element
        var divAdvert = document.getElementById("divAdvert");

        //Change the className
        divAdvert.className = "defaultStyle";
    }
    </script>
</head>
<body>
    <div id="divAdvert" class="defaultStyle" onmouseover="divAdvert_onMouseOver()"
        onmouseout="divAdvert_onMouseOut()">Here is an advertisement.</div>
</body>
</html>
```

Save this file as `className_property.htm`. This page behaves in the exact same manner as `style_object.htm`. When you place your mouse pointer over the text, the text becomes italicized and underlined; when you move your pointer off of the text, it changes back to normal.

How It Works

There are a few key differences between this HTML page and the one created using the `style` object. For starters, the `#divAdvert` style rule is removed and replaced with two CSS classes:

```
.defaultStyle {
    font: normal 12pt arial;
    text-decoration: none;
}

.newStyle {
    font: italic 12pt arial;
    text-decoration: underline;
}
```

The first class, called `defaultStyle`, is the rule first applied to the `<div/>` element. It declares a normal 12-point Arial font with no underlining. Next, another class called `newStyle` is created. This new rule contains style declarations to specify 12-point italic Arial that is underlined. With these changes, the `<div/>` element definition is changed to use the `defaultStyle` CSS class:

```
<div id="divAdvert" class="defaultStyle" onmouseover="divAdvert_onMouseOver()"
    onmouseout="divAdvert_onMouseOut()">Here is an advertisement.</div>
```

Notice that the `id` attribute is the same: JavaScript still needs to access the element in order to change its `className` property. The `onmouseover` and `onmouseout` event handlers remain the same, as you need the same functionality that `style_object.htm` has.

The last change is in the JavaScript itself. When the `mouseover` event fires on the element, the associated `divAdvert_onMouseOver()` function is called. This function consists of two lines of code as opposed to the three lines you used for the `style` object.

```
function divAdvert_onMouseOver() {
    //Get the element
    var divAdvert = document.getElementById("divAdvert");

    //Change the className
    divAdvert.className = "newStyle";
}
```

The first statement retrieves the `<div/>` element by using the `getElementById()` method. The function goes on to change the `className` property to the value `newStyle`. With this line, the `divAdvert` element takes on a new style rule and the browser changes the way it looks.

When you move your mouse pointer off of the text, the `mouseout` event fires and `divAdvert_onMouseOut()` executes. This function is almost identical to `divAdvert_onMouseOver()`, except that the `className` is set back to its original value:

```
function divAdvert_onMouseOut() {
    //Get the element
    var divAdvert = document.getElementById("divAdvert");

    //Change the className
    divAdvert.className = "defaultStyle";
}
```

By setting `className` back to `defaultStyle`, the browser displays the `<div/>` element as it previously did, with no italics or underlining.

Positioning and Moving Content

Changing the appearance of an element is an important pattern in DHTML, and it finds its place in many DHTML scripts. However, there is more to DHTML than just changing the way content appears on the page; you can also change the position of an element with JavaScript.

Earlier in the chapter you learned about the `position` CSS property, where you can specify an element to be absolutely or relatively positioned. You also learned about the `top` and `left` properties, which enable you to position the elements where you desire. You can do the same thing with JavaScript by changing the values of these properties.

Just Move It Over There

Moving content with JavaScript is just as easy as using the `style` object. You use the `position` property to change the type of position desired, and by using the `left` and `top` properties, you can position the element.

```
var divAdvert = document.getElementById("divAdvert");

divAdvert.style.left = "100px"; //Set the left position
divAdvert.style.top = "100px";  //Set the right position
```

This code first retrieves the `divAdvert` element. Then it sets the element 100 pixels from the left and top edges. Notice the addition of `px` to the value assigned to the positions. Many browsers require you to specify a unit when assigning a positional value; otherwise, the browser will not position the element.

Try It Out   Moving an Element Around

Moving an element around on the page, as you've seen, is quite similar to changing other styles with the style object. However, the ability to move an element on the page is one that is used quite often, and you will definitely see it later in the chapter. Therefore, you are going to build a page that enables you to specify the location of an element through form fields.

```
<!DOCTYPE html PUBLIC "-//W3C//DTD XHTML 1.0 Transitional//EN"
    "http://www.w3.org/TR/xhtml1/DTD/xhtml1-transitional.dtd">

<html xmlns="http://www.w3.org/1999/xhtml">
<head>
    <title>Positioning</title>
    <style type="text/css">
        #divBox {
            position: absolute;
            background-color: silver;
            width: 150px;
            height: 150px;
        }

        input {
            width: 100px;
        }
    </style>
    <script type="text/javascript">
    function moveBox() {
        var divBox = document.getElementById("divBox");
        var inputLeft = document.getElementById("inputLeft");
        var inputTop = document.getElementById("inputTop");

        divBox.style.left = parseInt(inputLeft.value) + "px";
        divBox.style.top = parseInt(inputTop.value) + "px";
    }
    </script>
</head>
<body>
    <div id="divBox">
        <form id="formBoxController" onsubmit="moveBox(); return false;">
            <p>Left: <input type="text" id="inputLeft" /></p>
            <p>Top: <input type="text" id="inputTop" /></p>
            <p><input type="submit" value="Move The Box" /></p>
        </form>
    </div>
</body>
</html>
```

Save this file as positioning.htm. When you load the page into your browser, you should see a silver box in the upper left-hand corner of the viewport. Inside this box you'll see a form with two fields and a button, as shown in Figure 12-12.

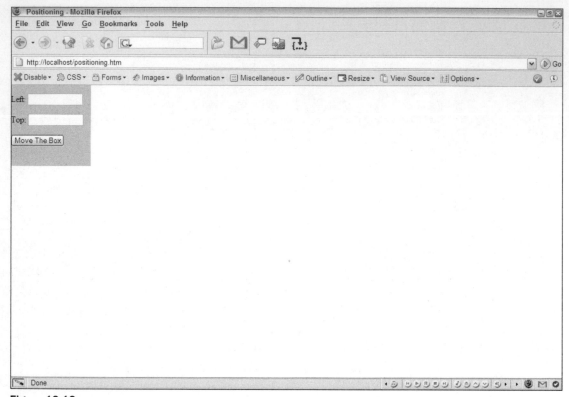

Figure 12-12

When you enter numerical values in the text fields and press the button, the box will move to the coordinates you specified. Figure 12-13 shows the box moved to 100,100.

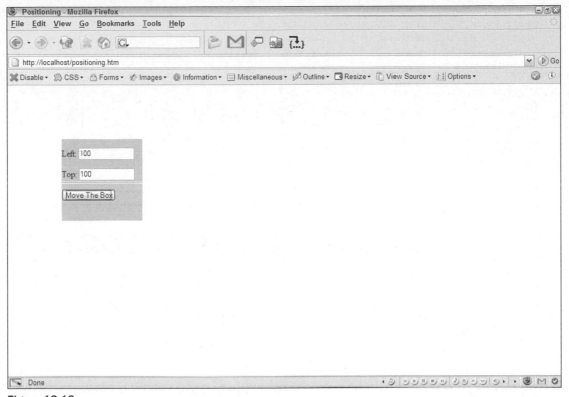

Figure 12-13

How It Works

In the body of the page, you define a `<div/>` tag with an `id` of `divBox`:

```
<div id="divBox"></div>
```

Inside this element is a form consisting of three `<input/>` elements. Two of these are text boxes in which you can input the `left` and `top` positions to move the `<div/>` to, and these have `ids` of `inputLeft` and `inputTop`, respectively. The third `<input/>` is a Submit button.

```
<div id="divBox">
    <form id="formBoxController">
        <p>Left: <input type="text" value="0" id="inputLeft" /></p>
        <p>Top: <input type="text" value="0" id="inputTop" /></p>
        <p><input type="submit" value="Move The Box" /></p>
    </form>
</div>
```

When you click the Submit button, the browser fires the submit event for the form. When a submit button is pressed, the browser attempts to send data to the web server. This attempt at communication causes the browser to reload the page, making any change you made through DHTML reset itself. Therefore, you must force the browser to not reload the page. You do this by setting the submit event to return a value of false.

```
<div id="divBox">
    <form id="formBoxController" onsubmit="return false;">
        <p>Left: <input type="text" value="0" id="inputLeft" /></p>
        <p>Top: <input type="text" value="0" id="inputTop" /></p>
        <p><input type="submit" value="Move The Box" /></p>
    </form>
</div>
```

Now, when you click the Submit button, it appears that nothing happens. This is the desired result.

In order for the <div/> element to be moved around on the page, it needs to be positioned. This example positions the element absolutely, although it would be possible to position it relatively as well.

```
#divBox {
    position: absolute;
    background-color: silver;
    width: 150px;
    height: 150px;
}
```

Aside from the position, you also specify the box to have a background color of silver, and set the height and width to be 150 pixels each, to make it a square. At this size, however, the text boxes in the form actually extend past the box's borders. In order to fix this, set a rule for the <input/> tags as well.

```
input {
    width: 100px;
}
```

By setting the <input/> tags to be 100 pixels wide, you can fit everything nicely into the box. So at this point, the HTML is primarily finished and it's styled. All that remains is to write the JavaScript to retrieve the values from the form fields and move the box to the coordinates provided by the form.

The function responsible for this is called moveBox(), and it is the only function on this page.

```
function moveBox() {
    var divBox = document.getElementById("divBox");  //Get the box
    var inputLeft = document.getElementById("inputLeft");  //Get one form field
    var inputTop = document.getElementById("inputTop");  //Get the other one

    //more code here
}
```

The function starts by retrieving the HTML elements needed to move the box. First it gets the <div/> element itself, followed by the text boxes for the left and top positions, and stores them in the inputLeft and inputTop variables, respectively. With the needed elements selected, you can now move the box.

```
function moveBox() {
    var divBox = document.getElementById("divBox");
    var inputLeft = document.getElementById("inputLeft");
    var inputTop = document.getElementById("inputTop");

    divBox.style.left = parseInt(inputLeft.value) + "px";
    divBox.style.top = parseInt(inputTop.value) + "px";
}
```

These two new lines to moveBox() do just that. In the first new line, you use the value property to retrieve the value of the text box for the left position. You pass that value to the parseInt() function because you want to make sure that value is an integer. Then append px to the number, making sure that all browsers will position the box correctly. Next, do the same thing for positioning the top: Get the value from the inputTop text box, pass it to parseInt(), and append px to it.

One last thing: Currently, nothing happens when you click the submit button. You're using the form's submit event to suppress the page from attempting to send data to the server. Add in a call to moveBox() there, too. You need only to separate the statements with a semicolon.

```
<div id="divBox">
    <form id="formBoxController" onsubmit="moveBox(); return false;">
        <p>Left: <input type="text" value="0" id="inputLeft" /></p>
        <p>Top: <input type="text" value="0" id="inputTop" /></p>
        <p><input type="submit" value="Move The Box" /></p>
    </form>
</div>
```

And with that addition, the box moves to the location specified by the numbers input by the user.

Example: Animated Advertisement

Changing the appearance and position of an element are important patterns in DHTML, and they find their places in many DHTML scripts. Perhaps the most creative use of DHTML is in animating content on the page. You can perform a variety of animations with DHTML. You can fade text elements or images in and out, give them a swipe animation (making it look like as if they are wiped onto the page), and animate them to move around on the page.

Animation can give important information the flair it needs to be easily recognized by your reader, as well as adding a "that's cool" factor. Performing animation with DHTML follows the same principles of any other type of animation: You make seemingly insignificant changes one at a time in a sequential order until you reach the end of the animation. Essentially, with any animation you have the following requisites:

1. The starting state
2. The movement towards the final goal
3. The end state; stopping the animation

Moving an absolutely positioned element, as we're going to do in this section, is no different. First, with CSS, position the element at the start location. Then perform the animation up until you reach the end point, which signals the end of the animation.

In this section you'll learn how to animate content to bounce back and forth between two points. To do this you need one important piece of information: the content's current location.

Are We There Yet?

The DOM in modern browsers exposes the `offsetTop` and `offsetLeft` properties of an HTML element object. These two properties return the calculated position relative to the element's parent element: `offsetTop` tells you the `top` location, and `offsetLeft` tells you the `left` position. The values returned by these properties are numerical values, so you can easily check to see where your element currently is in the animation. For example:

```
var endPointX = 394;

if (oElement.offsetLeft < endPointX) {
    //Continue animation
}
```

The preceding code specifies the end point — in this case, `394` — and assigns it to the `endPointX` variable. You can then check to see if the element's `offsetLeft` value is currently less than that of the end point. If it is, you can continue the animation. This example brings us to the next topic in content movement: performing the animation.

Get 'Er Done

In order to perform an animation, you need to modify the `top` and `left` properties of the `style` object incrementally and quickly. In DHTML, you do this with periodic function execution until it's time to end the animation. To do this, use one of two methods of the `window` object: `setTimeout()` or `setInterval()`. This example uses the `setInterval()` method to periodically move an element.

Try It Out   Animating Content

The following HTML page moves an element across the page from right to left:

```
<!DOCTYPE html PUBLIC "-//W3C//DTD XHTML 1.0 Transitional//EN"
    "http://www.w3.org/TR/xhtml1/DTD/xhtml1-transitional.dtd">

<html xmlns="http://www.w3.org/1999/xhtml" >
<head>
    <title>Moving Content</title>
    <style type="text/css">
        #divAdvert {
            position: absolute;
            font: 12px Arial;
            top: 4px;
            left: 0px;
        }
    </style>
    <script type="text/javascript">
    var switchDirection = false;  //To keep track of which way we're going

    function doAnimation() {
        var divAdvert = document.getElementById("divAdvert");  //Get the element
        var currentLeft = divAdvert.offsetLeft; //Get the current left position
```

```
            var newLocation; //Will store the new location

        if (switchDirection == false) {
            newLocation = currentLeft + 2; //Move the text 2 pixels to the right

            if (currentLeft >= 400) { //We've reached our destination
                switchDirection = true; //So let's turn around
            }
        } else {
            newLocation = currentLeft - 2; //Move the text 2 pixels to the left

            if (currentLeft <= 0) { //We've reached our destination
                switchDirection = false; //So let's turn around
            }
        }

        divAdvert.style.left = newLocation + "px"; //Change the left position
    }
    </script>
</head>
<body onload="setInterval(doAnimation, 10)">
    <div id="divAdvert">Here is an advertisement.</div>
</body>
</html>
```

Save this page as moving_content.htm and load it into your browser. When you load the page into the browser, the content should start moving from left to right, starting at the left edge of the viewport. When the content reaches a left position of 400 pixels, the content switches directions and begins to move back toward the left edge. This animation is continuous, so it should bounce between the two points (0 and 400) perpetually.

How It Works

Inside the body of the page is a <div/> element. This element has an id of divAdvert so that you can retrieve it with JavaScript, as this is the tag you want to animate.

```
<div id="divAdvert">Here is an advertisement.</div>
```

There are no style attributes in this tag, as all the style information is inside the style sheet. In the style sheet, you define a starting point for this <div/>. You want the animation to go first from left to right, and you want it to start at the left edge of the browser.

```
#divAdvert {
    position: absolute;
    font: 12pt arial;
    top: 4px;
    left: 0px;
}
```

The first style declaration positions the element absolutely. Next, specify the font as 12-point Arial. The next declaration positions the element four pixels from the top of the browser's viewport. Setting the top position away from the topmost edge makes the text a little easier to read. Finally, position the divAdvert along the left edge of the viewport with the left property.

Within the script block is a global variable called switchDirection.

```
var switchDirection = false;  //To keep track of which way we're going
```

This variable keeps track of the direction in which the content is currently going. If switchDirection is false, then the content is moving from left to right, which is the default. If switchDirection is true, then the content is moving from right to left.

Next in the script block you find the doAnimation() function, which performs the animation.

```
function doAnimation() {
    var divAdvert = document.getElementById("divAdvert");  //Get the element
    var currentLeft = divAdvert.offsetLeft; //Get the current left position
    var newLocation; //Will store the new location

    // more code here
}
```

First you retrieve the divAdvert element with the getElementById() method; you also retrieve the offsetLeft property and assign its value to the currentLeft variable. You use this variable to check the content's current position. Next you create a variable called newLocation. This variable will contain the new left position, but before you assign its value you need to know the direction in which the content is moving.

```
function doAnimation() {
    var divAdvert = document.getElementById("divAdvert");  //Get the element
    var currentLeft = divAdvert.offsetLeft; //Get the current left position
    var newLocation; //Will store the new location

    if (switchDirection == false) {
        newLocation = currentLeft + 2; //Move the text 2 pixels to the right

        if (currentLeft >= 400) { //We've reached our destination
            switchDirection = true; //So let's turn around
        }
    }

    //more code here
}
```

First check the direction by checking the switchDirection variable. Remember, if it is false, the animation is moving from left to right; so assign newLocation to contain the content's current position and add 2, thus moving the content 2 pixels to the right.

You then need to check if the content has reached the left position of 400 pixels. If it has, then you need to switch the direction of the animation, and you do this by changing switchDirection to true. So the next time doAnimation() runs, it will begin to move the content from right to left.

The code for this new direction is similar to the previous code, except for a few key differences.

```
function doAnimation() {
    var divAdvert = document.getElementById("divAdvert");  //Get the element
    var currentLeft = divAdvert.offsetLeft; //Get the current left position
```

```
    var newLocation; //Will store the new location

    if (switchDirection == false) {
        newLocation = currentLeft + 2; //Move the text 2 pixels to the right

        if (currentLeft >= 400) { //We've reached our destination
            switchDirection = true; //So let's turn around
        }
    }

    else {
        newLocation = currentLeft - 2; //Move the text 2 pixels to the left

        if (currentLeft <= 0) { //We've reached our destination
            switchDirection = false; //So let's turn around
        }
    }

    //more code here
}
```

The first difference is the value assigned to newLocation; instead of adding 2 to the current location, you subtract 2, thus moving the content 2 pixels to the left. Next, check if currentLeft is less than or equal to 0. If it is, you know you've reached the ending point of the right-to-left movement and need to switch directions again by assigning switchDirection to be false.

Finally, set the new position of the content.

```
function doAnimation() {
    var divAdvert = document.getElementById("divAdvert");  //Get the element
    var currentLeft = divAdvert.offsetLeft; //Get the current left position
    var newLocation; //Will store the new location

    if (switchDirection == false) {
        newLocation = currentLeft + 2; //Move the text 2 pixels to the right

        if (currentLeft >= 400) { //We've reached our destination
            switchDirection = true; //So let's turn around
        }
    }

    else {
        newLocation = currentLeft - 2; //Move the text 2 pixels to the left

        if (currentLeft <= 0) { //We've reached our destination
            switchDirection = false; //So let's turn around
        }
    }

    divAdvert.style.left = newLocation + "px"; //Change the left position
}
```

This final line completes the doAnimation() function, and it sets the element's left position to the value contained in the newLocation variable.

To run the animation, use the `onload` event handler in the `<body/>` element, and use the `window.setInterval()` method to continuously execute `doAnimation()`. The following code runs `doAnimation()` every 10 milliseconds:

```
<body onload="setInterval(doAnimation, 10)">
```

At this speed, the content moves at a pace that is easily seen by those viewing the page.

Summary

DHTML is a large topic, and we've touched on some of its fundamentals in this chapter. With this knowledge, you can explore other avenues of DHTML and create more complex user interface tricks.

The main points this chapter covered were as follows:

❑ Despite leaps and bounds by browser makers, some discrepancies still exist. You learned how to cope with two different event objects by branching your code to consolidate two different APIs into one.

❑ Style sheets can be used to set the style for various types of tags, or for individual tags. You can also define classes that you can apply to certain tags using the `class` attribute. Styles include the font, color, and position of a tag.

❑ DHTML enables you to change a page after it is loaded into the browser, and you can perform a variety of user interface tricks to add some flair to your page.

❑ You learned how to change a tag's style by using the `style` and `className` properties.

❑ You also learned the basics of animation in DHTML, and made text bounce back and fourth between two points.

Exercise Questions

Suggested solutions to these questions can be found in Appendix A.

Question 1

Create a web page that contains two links. The first link should say Show First Box and the second Show Second Box. Then add two `<div/>` elements and set their id attributes to boxOne and boxTwo. Give them a height, width, background color, and position, and then hide them. Next, set up the links so that when you click the first one, only the first box shows, and when you click the second one, only the second box shows.

Question 2

Create a `<div/>` element that floats around the page. Use the edges of the browser's viewport as a boundary.

Dynamic HTML in Modern Browsers

In the last chapter you were introduced to DHTML, getting a small glimpse of what it can do with a scrolling text animation. You also saw that web developers need to use different code for different browsers to achieve the same results, which makes their lives difficult. In this chapter you'll be concentrating on writing code according to the web standards set by the W3C. In general, you can write code that will work with IE 6+, Firefox, Opera, and Safari without having to make big changes.

One of the most misunderstood sections in the W3C Web standards is the Document Object Model, or DOM for short. The DOM gives developers a way of representing everything on a web page so that it is accessible via a common set of properties and methods in JavaScript, or any other object-based programming language. By everything, we mean *everything*. You can change the graphics, tables, forms, and even text itself by altering a relevant DOM property with JavaScript.

The DOM should not be confused with the Browser Object Model (BOM) that was introduced in Chapter 5. You'll see the differences between the two in detail shortly. For now, though, think of the BOM as a browser-dependent representation of every feature of the browser, from the browser buttons, URL address line, and title bar to the browser window controls, as well as parts of the web page, too. The DOM, however, deals only with the contents of the browser window or web page — in other words, the HTML document. It makes the document available in such a way that any browser can use exactly the same code to access and manipulate the content of the document. To summarize, the BOM gives you access to the browser and some of the document, whereas the DOM gives you access to all of the document, but *only* the document.

The great thing about the DOM is that it is browser- and platform-independent. This means that developers can finally consider the possibility of writing a piece of JavaScript code that dynamically updates the page, as you saw in the last chapter, and that will work on any DOM-compliant browser without any tweaking. You should not need to code for different browsers or take excessive care when coding.

The DOM achieves this independence by representing the contents of the page as a generic tree structure. Whereas in the BOM you might expect to access something by looking up a property relevant to that part of the browser and adjusting it, the DOM requires navigation through its representation of the page through nodes and properties that are not specific to the browser. You'll explore this structure a little later.

However, to use the DOM standard, ultimately developers require browsers that completely implement the standard, something that no browser does 100 percent efficiently. Unfortunately, IE 5.5 didn't support many aspects of the standard. IE 6 and 7 have greatly improved standards support, but still fall short of full implementation. Even Firefox, which at least aims to support the standard, still falls short in some ways.

This makes the DOM sound like an impossible ideal, yet it doesn't exist purely as a standard. Features of the DOM standard have been implemented in browsers as far back as Netscape 2. However, in Netscape versions 2, 3, and 4, many HTML page elements and their properties were not scriptable at all — whereas, as you have seen, IE made nearly all page elements and their properties scriptable. Unfortunately, the way in which Netscape 4 provided scripting access to some elements was often incompatible with the way in which IE made those elements available. Thus a Document Object Model standard was developed. The latest versions of IE, Mozilla, Opera, and Safari support many features outlined in the standard.

To provide a true perspective on how the DOM fits in, we need to take a brief look at its relationship with some of the other currently existing web standards. We should also talk about why there is more than one version of the DOM standard, and why there are different sections within the standard itself. (Microsoft, in particular, added a number of extensions to the W3C DOM.) After understanding the relationships, you can look at using JavaScript to navigate the DOM and to dynamically change content on web pages in more than one browser, in a way that used to be impossible with pure DHTML. The following items are on your agenda:

❑ The HTML, ECMAScript, XML, and XHTML web standards

❑ The DOM standards

❑ The DOM tree structure

❑ Writing cross-browser DHTML

Remember that the examples within this chapter are targeted only at the DOM and therefore will be supported only by IE 6+, Firefox 1+, Opera, and Safari.

Why Do We Need Web Standards?

When Tim Berners-Lee created HTML in 1991, he probably had little idea that this technology for marking up scientific papers via a set of tags for his own global hypertext project, known as the World Wide Web, would within a matter of years become a battleground between the two giants of the software business of the mid-1990s. HTML was a simple derivation from the meta-language Standard Generalized Markup Language (SGML) that had been kicking around academic institutions for decades. Its purpose was to preserve the structure of the documents created with it. HTML depends on a protocol, HyperText Transfer Protocol (HTTP), to transmit documents back and forth between the resource and the viewer (for example, the server and the client computer). These two technologies formed the foundation of the Web, and it quickly became obvious in the early 1990s that there needed to be some sort of policing of both specifications to ensure a common implementation of HTML and HTTP so that communications could be conducted worldwide.

In 1994, Tim founded the World Wide Web Consortium (W3C), a body that set out to oversee the technical evolution of the Web. It has three main aims:

❑ To provide universal access, so that anybody can use the Web

❑ To develop a software environment to allow users to make use of the Web

❑ To guide the development of the Web, taking into consideration the legal, social, and commercial issues that arise

Each new version of a specification of a web technology has to be carefully vetted by W3C before it can become a standard. The HTML and HTTP specifications are subject to this process, and each new set of updates to these specifications yields a new version of the standard. Each standard has to go through a working draft, a candidate recommendation, and a proposed recommendation stage before it can be considered a fully operational standard. At each stage of the process, members of the W3C consortium vote on which amendments to make, or even on whether to cancel the standard completely and send it back to square one.

It sounds like a very painful and laborious method of creating a standard format, and not something you'd think of as spearheading the cutting edge of technical revolution. Indeed, the software companies of the mid-1990s found the processes involved too slow, so they set the tone by implementing new innovations themselves and then submitting them to the standards body for approval. Netscape started by introducing new elements in its browser, such as the `<font>` element, to add presentational content to the web pages. This proved popular, so Netscape added a whole raft of elements that enabled users to alter aspects of presentation and style on web pages. Indeed, JavaScript itself was such an innovation from Netscape.

When Microsoft entered the fray, it was playing catchup for the first two iterations of its Internet Explorer browser. However, with Internet Explorer 3 in 1996, they established a roughly equal set of features to compete with Netscape and so were able to add their own browser-specific elements. Very quickly, the Web polarized between these two browsers, and pages viewable on one browser quite often wouldn't appear on another. One problem was that Microsoft had used its much stronger position in the market to give away its browser for free, whereas Netscape still needed to sell its own browser because it couldn't afford to freely distribute its flagship product. To maintain a competitive position, Netscape needed to offer new features to make the user want to purchase its browser rather than use the free Microsoft browser.

Things came to a head with both companies' version 4 browsers, which introduced dynamic page functionality. Unfortunately, Netscape did this by the means of a `<layer>` element, whereas Microsoft chose to implement it via scripting language properties and methods. The W3C needed to take a firm stand here, because one of its three principal aims had been compromised: that of universal access. How could access be universal if users needed a specific vendor's browser to view a particular set of pages? They decided on a solution that used existing standard HTML elements and Cascading Style Sheets, both of which had been adopted as part of the Microsoft solution. As a result, Microsoft gained a dominant position in the browser war. It hasn't relinquished this position; the Netscape Navigator browser never had a counter to Internet Explorer's constant updates, and its replacement, Firefox, has been slow to expand its user base. Current usage statistics hover between 70 versus 30 percent and 90 versus 10 percent in Microsoft's favor.

With a relatively stable version of the HTML standard in place with version 4.01, which boasts a set of features that will take any browser manufacturer a long time to implement completely, attention was turned to other areas of the Web. A new set of standards was introduced in the late 1990s to govern the means of presenting HTML (style sheets) and the representation of the HTML document in script (the Document Object Model or DOM). Other standards emerged, such as Extensible Markup Language (XML), which offers a common format for representing data in a way that preserves its structure. You'll take a look now at the main standards that have been created, and learn a bit about what each of the technologies does.

The Web Standards

The W3C web site (www.w3.org) has a huge number of standards in varying stages of creation. Not all of these standards concern us, and not all of the ones that concern us can be found at this web site. However, the vast majority of standards that do concern us can be found there.

You're going to take a brief look now at the technologies and standards that have an impact on JavaScript and find out a little background information about each. Some of the technologies may be unfamiliar, but you need to be aware of their existence at the very least.

HTML

The HTML standard is maintained by W3C. This standard might seem fairly straightforward, given that each version should have introduced just a few new elements, but in reality the life of the standards body was vastly complicated by the browser wars. The versions 1.0 and 2.0 of HTML were simple, small documents, but when W3C came to debate HTML version 3.0, they found that much of the new functionality it was discussing had already been superceded by new additions, such as the `<applet/>` and `<style/>` elements, to the version 3.0 browser's `appletstyle`. Version 3.0 was discarded, and a new version, 3.2, became the standard.

However, a lot of the features that went into HTML 3.2 had been introduced at the behest of the browser manufacturers and ran contrary to the spirit of HTML, which was intended solely to define structure. The new features, stemming from the `<font>` element, just confused the issue and added unnecessary presentational features to HTML. These features really became redundant with the introduction of style sheets. So suddenly, in the version 3 browsers, there were three distinct ways to define the style of an item of text. Which was the correct way? And if all three ways were used, which style did the text ultimately assume? Version 4.0 of the HTML standard was left with the job of unmuddling this chaotic mess and designated a lot of elements for deprecation (removal) in the next version of the standards. It was the largest version of the standard so far and included features that linked it to style sheets and the Document Object Model, and also added facilities for the visually impaired and other unfairly neglected minority interest areas. The current version of the HTML standard is 4.01.

ECMAScript

JavaScript itself followed a trajectory similar to that of HTML. It was first used in Netscape Navigator and then added to Internet Explorer. The Internet Explorer version of JavaScript was christened Jscript and wasn't far removed from the version of JavaScript found in Netscape Navigator. However, once again there were differences between the two implementations and a lot of care had to be taken in writing script for both browsers.

Oddly enough, it was left to the European Computer Manufacturers Association (ECMA) to propose a standard specification for JavaScript. This didn't appear until a few versions of JavaScript had already been released. Unlike HTML, which had been developed from the start with the W3C consortium, JavaScript was a proprietary creation. This is the reason that it is governed by a different standards body. Microsoft and Netscape both agreed to use ECMA as the standards vehicle/debating forum, because of its reputation for fast-tracking standards and perhaps also because of its perceived neutrality. The name ECMAScript was chosen so as not to be biased toward either vendor's creation and also because the "Java" part of JavaScript was a trademark of Sun licensed to Netscape. The standard, named ECMA-262, laid down a specification that was roughly equivalent to the JavaScript 1.1 specification.

That said, the ECMAScript standard covers only core JavaScript features, such as the primitive data types of numbers, strings, and Booleans, native objects like the `Date`, `Array`, and `Math` objects, and the procedural statements like `for` and `while` loops, and `if` and `else` conditionals. It makes no reference to client-side objects or collections, such as `window`, `document`, `forms`, `links`, and `images`. So, although the standard helps to make core programming tasks compatible when both JavaScript and JScript comply with it, it is of no use in making the scripting of client-side objects compatible between the main browsers. Some incompatibilities remain.

All current implementations of JavaScript are expected to conform to the current ECMAScript standard, which is ECMAScript edition 3, published in December 1999. As of November 2006, ECMAScript edition 4 is under development.

Although in the version 3 browsers there were quite a few irregularities between the Microsoft and Netscape dialects of JavaScript, they're now similar enough to be considered the same language. The Opera and Safari browsers also support and offer the same kind of support for the standard. This is a good example of how standards have provided a uniform language across browser implementations, although a feature war similar to the one that took place over HTML still rages to a lesser degree over JavaScript.

XML

Extensible Markup Language, or XML, is a standard for creating markup languages (such as HTML). XML itself has been designed to look as much like HTML as possible, but that's where the similarities end.

HTML is actually an application of the meta-language SGML, which is also a standard for generating markup languages. SGML has been used to create many markup languages, but HTML is the only one that enjoys universal familiarity and popularity. XML, on the other hand, is a direct subset of SGML. SGML is generally considered to be too complex for people to be able to accurately represent it on a computer, so XML is a simplified subset of SGML. XML is also much easier to read than SGML.

XML's main use is for the creation of customized markup languages that are very similar in look and structure to HTML. One main use of XML is in the representation of data. Whereas a normal database can store information, databases don't allow individual stored items to contain information about their structure. XML can use the element structure of markup languages to represent any kind of data in which information contained in the structure might otherwise be lost, from mathematical and chemical notations to the entire works of Shakespeare. For instance, an XML document could be used to record that Mark Anthony doesn't appear until Scene II Act I of Shakespeare's play *Julius Caesar*, whereas a relational database would struggle to do this without a lot of extra fields, as the following example shows:

```
<play>
   <act1>
      <scene1>
         ...
      </scene1>
      <scene2>
         <mark_anthony>
            Caesar, my lord?
         </mark_anthony>
      </scene2>
      <scene3>
         ...
      </scene3>
   </act1>
   <act2>
      ...
   </act2>
   <act3>
      ...
   </act3>
   <act4>
      ...
   </act4>
   <act5>
      ...
   </act5>
</play>
```

XML is also completely cross-platform, because it contains just text. This means that an application on Windows can package up the data in this format, and a completely different application on Unix should be able to unravel and read those data.

XML is more complex than HTML. Whereas a browser will take HTML code, interpret the relevant details, and display the corresponding web page without any intervention, interpreting XML requires several extra steps.

Because you're creating the markup language yourself, you need first to create a set of rules through which the language will be run. You can do this in one of two ways, either with an *XML schema* or with a *Document Type Definition* (DTD). Both of these are used to draw up rules, such as which elements you can use in your markup language, which attributes these elements take, and what kind of data these attributes are expecting.

Secondly, when you've written your XML document in your new language, it must be checked against both the syntax rules laid down for XML documents and the rules in the schema or the DTD to see if the code conforms. You'll be taking an in-depth look at XML in the next chapter.

XHTML

XHTML 1.0 is where the XML and HTML standards meet. XHTML is just a respecification of the HTML 4.01 standard as an XML application. The advantages of this allow XHTML to get around some of the problems caused by a browser's particular interpretation of HTML, and more importantly to provide a specification that allows the Web to be used by clients other than browsers, such as those provided on handheld computers, mobile phones, or any software device that might be connected to the Internet (perhaps even your refrigerator!).

XHTML also offers a common method for specifying your own elements, instead of just adding them randomly. You can specify new elements via a common method using an XML DTD and an XML *namespace*. (A namespace is a means of identifying one set of elements uniquely from any other set of elements.) This is particularly useful for the new markup languages, such as Wireless Markup Language (WML), which are geared toward mobile technology and require a different set of elements to be able to display on the reduced interfaces.

That said, anyone familiar with HTML should be able to look at an XHTML page and understand what's going on. There are differences, but not ones that add new elements or attributes.

The following is a list of the main differences between XHTML and HTML:

❑   XHTML recommends an XML declaration to be placed at the top of the file in the following form: `<?xml-version='1.0'?>`.

❑   You also have to provide a DTD declaration at the top of the file, referencing the version of the DTD standard you are using.

❑   You have to include a reference to the XML namespace within the HTML element.

❑   You need to supply all XHTML element names in lowercase, because XML is case-sensitive.

❑   The `<head/>` and `<body/>` elements must always be included in an XHTML document.

❑   Tags must always be closed and nested correctly. When only one tag is required, such as with line breaks, the tag is closed with a slash (for example, `<br/>`).

❑   Attribute values must always be denoted by quotation marks.

This set of rules makes it possible to keep a strict hierarchical structure to the elements, which in turn makes it possible for the Document Object Model to work correctly. This is the route that HTML is currently taking, and all future HTML standards will be XHTML standards. This also makes it possible to standardize markup languages across all device types, so that the next version of WML (the markup language of mobile devices) will also be compliant with the XHTML standard. You should now be creating your HTML documents according to the previously specified rules. If you do so, you will find it much, much easier to write JavaScript that manipulates the page via the DOM and works in the way it was intended.

It's now time for you to consider the Document Object Model itself.

The Document Object Model

The Document Object Model (DOM) is, as previously mentioned, a way of representing the document independent of browser type. It allows a user to access the document via a common set of objects, properties, methods, and events, and to alter the contents of the web page dynamically using scripts.

Several types of script languages, such as JavaScript and VBScript, are available. Each requires a slightly different syntax and therefore a different approach when you're programming. Even when you're using a language common to all browsers, such as JavaScript, you should be aware that some small variations are usually added to the language by the vendor. So, to guarantee that you don't fall afoul of a particular implementation, the W3C has provided a generic set of objects, properties, and methods that should be available in all scripting languages, in the form of the DOM standard.

The DOM Standard

We haven't talked about the DOM standard so far, and for a particular reason: It's not the easiest standard to follow. Supporting a generic set of properties and methods has proved to be a very complex task, and the DOM standard has been broken down into separate levels and sections to deal with the different areas. The different levels of the standard are all at differing stages of completion.

Level 0

Level 0 is a bit of a misnomer, as there wasn't really a level 0 of the standard. This term in fact refers to the "old way" of doing things—the methods implemented by the browser vendors before the DOM standard. Someone mentioning level 0 properties is referring to a more linear notation of accessing properties and methods. For example, typically you'd reference items on a form with the following code:

```
document.forms[0].elements[1].value = "button1";
```

We're not going to cover such properties and methods in this chapter, because they have been superceded by newer methods.

Level 1

Level 1 is the first version of the standard. It is split into two sections: one is defined as core (objects, properties, and methods that can apply to both XML and HTML) and the other as HTML (HTML-specific objects, properties, and methods). The first section deals with how to go about navigating and manipulating the structure of the document. The objects, properties, and methods in this section are very abstract. The second section deals with HTML only and offers a set of objects corresponding to all the HTML elements. This chapter mainly deals with the second section—level 1 of the standard.

In 2000, level 1 was revamped and corrected, though it only made it to a working draft and not to a full W3C recommendation.

Level 2

Level 2 is complete and many of the properties, methods, and events have been implemented by modern browsers. It has sections that add specifications for events and style sheets to the specifications for core and HTML-specific properties and events. (It also provides sections on views and traversal ranges, neither of which will be covered in this book; you can find more information at www.w3.org/TR/2000/PR-DOM-Level-2-Views-20000927/ and www.w3.org/TR/2000/PR-DOM-Level-2-Traversal-Range-20000927/.) You will be making use of some of the features of the event and style sections of this level of the DOM later in this chapter because they have been implemented in the latest versions of both browsers.

Level 3

Level 3 is still under development. It is intended to resolve a lot of the complications that still exist in the event model in level 2 of the standard, and adds support for XML features, such as contents models and being able to save the DOM as an XML document.

Browser Compliance with the Standards

Almost no browser has 100 percent compliance with *any* standard, although some, such as Firefox and Opera, come pretty close with the DOM. Therefore, there is no guarantee that all the objects, properties, and methods of the DOM standard will be available in a given version of a browser, although a few level 1 and level 2 objects, properties, and methods have been available in all the browsers for some time. However, IE6++ and Firefox offer by far the closest compliance, with Opera and Safari catching up.

Much of the material in the DOM standards has only recently been clarified, and a lot of DOM features and support have been added to only the latest browser versions. For this reason, examples in this chapter will be guaranteed to work on only the latest versions of IE, Firefox, Opera, and Safari. Although cross-browser scripting is a realistic goal, backwards support isn't at all.

Although the standards might still not be fully implemented, they do give you an idea as to how a particular property or method should be implemented, and provide a guideline for all browser manufacturers to agree to work toward in later versions of their browsers. The DOM doesn't introduce any new HTML elements or style sheet properties to achieve its ends. The idea of the DOM is to make use of the existing technologies, and quite often the existing properties and methods of one or other of the browsers.

Differences Between the DOM and the BOM

As mentioned earlier, there are two main differences between the Document Object Model and the Browser Object Model. However, complicating the issue is the fact that a BOM is sometimes referred to under the name DOM. Look out for this in any literature on the subject.

First, the DOM covers only the document of the web page, whereas the BOM offers scripting access to all areas of the browsers, from the buttons to the title bar, including some parts of the page.

Second, the BOM is unique to a particular browser. This makes sense if you think about it: You can't expect to standardize browsers, because they have to offer competitive features. Therefore, you need a different set of properties and methods and even objects to be able to manipulate them with JavaScript.

Representing the HTML Document as a Tree Structure

Because HTML is standardized so that web pages can contain only the standard features supported in the language, such as forms, tables, images, and the like, a common method of accessing these features is needed. This is where the DOM comes in. It provides a uniform representation of the HTML document, and it does this by representing the entire HTML document/web page as a *tree structure*.

Only the more recent browser versions allow access to all parts of the web page via such a tree structure. Previous versions would only partially represent web pages in this tree structure, and leave bits, such as the text, beyond reach and inaccessible to script.

In fact, it is possible to represent any HTML document (in fact, any XML document) as a tree structure. The only precondition is that the HTML document should be well formed. You've already learned why this is such a desirable attribute, but it doesn't hurt to emphasize it again. Different browsers might be tolerant, to a greater or lesser extent, of quirks such as unclosed tags, or HTML form controls not being enclosed within a <form> element; however, for the structure of the HTML document to be accurately depicted, you need to be able to always predict the structure of the document. Abuses of the structure, such as unclosed tags, stop you from depicting the structure as a true hierarchy, and therefore cannot be allowed. The ability to access elements via the DOM depends on the ability to represent the page as a hierarchy.

What Is a Tree Structure?

If you're not familiar with the concept of trees, don't worry. They're just a diagrammatic means of representing a hierarchical structure.

Let's consider the example of a book with several chapters. If instructed to, you could find the third line on page 543 after a little searching. If an updated edition of the book were printed with extra chapters, more likely than not you'd fail to find the same text if you followed those same instructions. However, if the instructions were changed to, say, "Find the chapter on still-life painting, the section on using watercolors, and the paragraph on positioning light sources," you'd be able to find that even in a reprinted edition with extra pages and chapters, albeit with perhaps a little more effort than the first request required.

Books aren't particularly dynamic examples, but given something like a web page, where the information could be changed daily, or even hourly, can you see why it would be of more use to give the second set of directions than the first? The same principle applies with the DOM. Navigating the DOM in a hierarchical fashion, rather than in a strictly linear way, makes much more sense. When you treat the DOM as a tree, it becomes easy to navigate the page in this fashion. Consider how you locate files on Windows using Windows Explorer, which creates a tree view of folders through which you can drill down. Instead of looking for a file alphabetically, you locate it by going into a particular folder.

The rules for creating trees are simple. You start at the top of the tree with the document and the element that contains all other elements in the page. The document is the *root node*. A *node* is just a point on the tree representing a particular element or attribute of an element, or even the text that an element contains. The root node contains all other nodes, such as the DTD declaration, the XML declaration, and the root element (the HTML or XML element that contains all other elements). The root element should always be the <html> element in an HTML document. Underneath the root element are the HTML elements that the root element contains. Typically an HTML page will have <head> and <body> elements inside the <html> element. These elements are represented as nodes underneath the root element's node, which itself is underneath the root node at the top of the tree (see Figure 13-1).

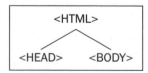

Figure 13-1

The two nodes representing the <head> and <body/> elements are examples of *child nodes*, and the <html/> element's node above them is a *parent node*. Since the <head/> and <body/> elements are both child nodes of the <html/> element, they both go on the same level underneath the parent node <html/> element. The <head/> and <body/> elements in turn contain other child nodes/HTML elements, which will appear at a level underneath their nodes. So child nodes can also be parent nodes. Each time you encounter a set of HTML elements within another element, they each form a separate node at the same level on the tree. The easiest way of explaining this clearly is with an example.

An Example HTML Page

Let's consider a basic HTML page such as this:

```
<!DOCTYPE html PUBLIC " //W3C//DTD XHTML 1.0 Transitional//EN"
"http://www.w3.org/TR/xhtml1/DTD/xhtml1-transitional.dtd">

<html xmlns="http://www.w3.org/1999/xhtml" ><head>
</head>
<body>
    <h1>My Heading</h1>
    <p>This is some text in a paragraph</p>
</body>
</html>
```

The <html/> element contains <head/> and <body/> elements. Only the <body/> element actually contains anything. It contains an <h1/> element and a <p/> element. The <h1/> element contains the text My Heading. When you reach an item, such as text, an image, or an element, that contains no others, the tree structure will terminate at that node. Such a node is termed a *leaf node*. You then continue to the <p/> node, which contains some text, which is also a node in the document. You can depict this with the tree structure shown in Figure 13-2.

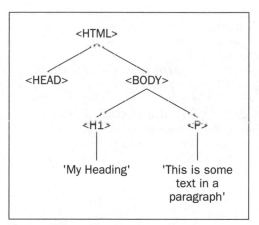

Figure 13-2

Simple, eh? This example is almost too straightforward, so let's move on to a slightly more complex one that involves a table as well.

```
<!DOCTYPE html PUBLIC "-//W3C//DTD XHTML 1.0 Transitional//EN"
"http://www.w3.org/TR/xhtml1/DTD/xhtml1-transitional.dtd">

<html xmlns="http://www.w3.org/1999/xhtml" >
<head>
    <title>This is a test page</title>
</head>
<body>
    <span>Below is a table...</span>
    <table border="1">
        <tr>
            <td>Row 1 Cell 1</td>
            <td>Row 1 Cell 2</td>
        </tr>
        <tr>
            <td>Row 2 Cell 1</td>
            <td>Row 2 Cell 2</td>
        </tr>
    </table>
</body>
</html>
```

There is nothing out of the ordinary here. The document just contains a table with two rows, and two cells in each row. You can once again represent the hierarchical structure of your page (for example, the fact that the <html/> element contains a <head/> and a <body/> element, and that the <head/> element contains a <title/> element, and so on) using your tree structure, as shown in Figure 13-3.

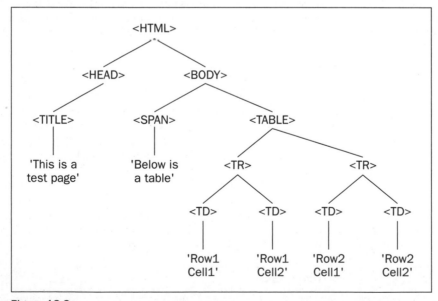

Figure 13-3

The top level of the tree is simple enough; the <html/> element contains <head/> and <body/> elements. The <head/> element in turn contains a <title/> element and the <title/> element contains some text. This text node is a child node that terminates the branch (a leaf node). You can then go back to the next node, the <body/> element node, and go down that branch. Here you have two elements contained within the <body/> element, the <span/> and <table/> elements. Although the <span/> element contains only text and terminates there, the <table/> element contains two rows <tr/>, and the two <tr/> elements contain two table cell <td/> elements. Only then do you get to the bottom of the tree with the text contained in each table cell. Your tree is now a complete representation of your HTML code.

The DOM Objects

What you have seen so far has been highly theoretical, so let's get a little more practical now.

The DOM provides you with a concrete set of objects, properties, and methods that you can access through JavaScript to navigate the tree structure of the DOM. Let's start with the set of objects, within the DOM, that is used to represent the nodes (elements, attributes, or text) on your tree.

Base DOM Objects

Three objects, shown in the following table, are known as the base DOM objects.

Object	Description
Node	Each node in the document has its own Node object
NodeList	This is a list of Node objects
NamedNodeMap	This provides access by name rather than by index to all the Node objects

This is where the DOM differs from the BOM quite extensively. The BOM objects have names that relate to a specific part of the browser, such as the window object, or the forms and images arrays. As mentioned earlier, to be able to navigate in the web page as though it were a tree, you have to do it abstractly. You can have no prior knowledge of the structure of the page; everything ultimately is just a node. To move around from HTML element to HTML element, or element to attribute, you have to go from node to node. This also means you can add, replace, or remove parts of your web page without affecting the structure as a whole, as you're just changing nodes. This is why you have three rather obscure-sounding objects that represent your tree structure.

I've already mentioned that the top of your tree structure is the root node, and that the root node contains the XML declaration, the DTD, and the root element. Therefore you need more than just these three objects to represent your document. In fact there are different objects to represent the different types of nodes on the tree.

High-Level DOM Objects

As you have seen, nodes come in a variety of types. Is the node an element, an attribute, or just plain text? The Node object has different objects to represent each possible type of node. The following is a complete list of all the different node type objects that can be accessed via the DOM. A lot of them won't concern you in this book because they pertain only to XML documents and not HTML documents, but you should notice that your three main types of nodes, namely element, attribute, and text, are all covered.

Object	Description
Document	The root node of the document
DocumentType	The DTD or schema type of the XML document
DocumentFragment	A temporary storage space for parts of the document
EntityReference	A reference to an entity in the XML document
Element	An element in the document
Attr	An attribute of an element in the document
ProcessingInstruction	A processing instruction
Comment	A comment in an XML document or HTML document
Text	Text that must form a child node of an element
CDATASection	A CDATA section within the XML document
Entity	An unparsed entity in the DTD
Notation	A notation declared within a DTD

We won't go over most of these objects in this chapter, but if you need to navigate the DOM of an XML document, you will have to use them.

Each of these objects inherits all the properties and methods of the Node object, but also has some properties and methods of its own. You will be looking at some examples in the next section.

DOM Properties and Methods

If you tried to look at the properties and methods of all the objects in the DOM, it would take up half the book. Instead you're going to actively consider only three of the objects, namely the node object, the element object, and the document object. This is all you'll need to be able to create, amend, and navigate your tree structure. Also, you're not going to spend ages trawling through each of the properties and methods of these objects, but rather look only at some of the most useful properties and methods and use them to achieve specific ends. You'll start with two of the most useful methods of the document object itself.

Methods of the document Object: Returning an Element or Elements

Let's begin at the most basic level. You have your HTML web page, so how do you go about getting back a particular element on the page in script? The two cross-browser ways of doing this are in the following table.

Methods of the document Object	Description
getElementById(idvalue)	Returns a reference (a node) to an element, when supplied with the value of the id attribute of that element
getElementsByTagName(tagname)	Returns a reference (a node list) to a set of elements that have the same tag as the one supplied in the argument

The first of the two methods, getElementById(), requires you to ensure that every element you want to access in the page uses an id attribute, otherwise a null value (a word indicating a missing or unknown value) will be returned by your method. Let's go back to your first example and add some id attributes to your elements.

```
<!DOCTYPE html PUBLIC "-//W3C//DTD XHTML 1.0 Transitional//EN"
"http://www.w3.org/TR/xhtml1/DTD/xhtml1-transitional.dtd">

<html xmlns="http://www.w3.org/1999/xhtml"><head>
    <title>example</title>
</head>
<body>
    <h1 id="Heading1">My Heading</h1>
    <p id="Paragraph1">This is some text in a paragraph</p>
</body>
</html>
```

Now you can use the getElementById() method to return a reference to any of the HTML elements with id attributes on your page. For example, if you add the following code, you can reference the <h1/> element:

```
<!DOCTYPE html PUBLIC "-//W3C//DTD XHTML 1.0 Transitional//EN"
"http://www.w3.org/TR/xhtml1/DTD/xhtml1-transitional.dtd">

<html xmlns="http://www.w3.org/1999/xhtml">
    <title>example</title>
</head>
<body>
    <h1 id="Heading1">My Heading</h1>
    <p id="Paragraph1">This is some text in a paragraph</p>
    <script type="text/javascript">
        alert(document.getElementById("Heading1"));
    </script>
</body>
</html>
```

This will display the page shown in Figure 13-4.

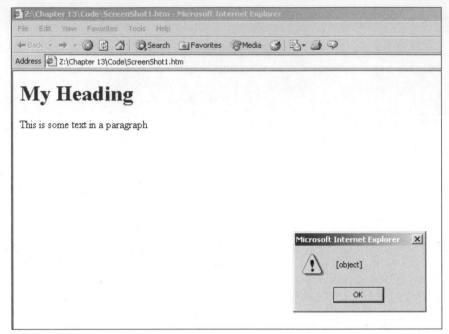

Figure 13-4

You might have been expecting it to return something along the lines of `<h1/>` or `<h1 id="Heading1">`, but all it's actually returning is a reference to the `<h1/>` element. This reference to the `<h1/>` element is more useful though, as you can use it to alter attributes of the element, such as by changing the color or size. You can do this via the `style` object.

```
<!DOCTYPE html PUBLIC "-//W3C//DTD XHTML 1.0 Transitional//EN"
"http://www.w3.org/TR/xhtml1/DTD/xhtml1-transitional.dtd">

<html xmlns="http://www.w3.org/1999/xhtml">
<head>
    <title>example</title>
</head>
<body>
    <h1 id="Heading1">My Heading</h1>
    <p id="Paragraph1">This is some text in a paragraph</p>
    <script type="text/javascript">
        var H1Element = document.getElementById("Heading1");
        H1Element.style.fontFamily = "Arial";
    </script>
</body>
</html>
```

If you display this in the browser, you see that you can directly influence the attributes of the `<h1/>` element in script, as you have done here by changing its font type to Arial (see Figure 13-5).

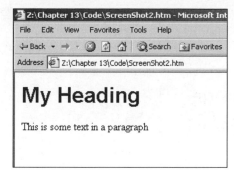

Figure 13-5

The second of the two methods, `getElementsByTagName()`, works in the same way, but, as its name implies, it can return more than one element. If you were to go back to the second example with the table and use this method to return the table cells (`<td/>`) in your code, you would get a total of four table cells returned to your object. You'd still have only one object returned, but this object would be a collection of elements. To reference a particular element in the collection, you would have to be more precise. You need to specify an index number, which you do using the `item()` method.

```
<!DOCTYPE html PUBLIC "-//W3C//DTD XHTML 1.0 Transitional//EN"
"http://www.w3.org/TR/xhtml1/DTD/xhtml1-transitional.dtd">

<html xmlns="http://www.w3.org/1999/xhtml">
<head>
    <title>This is a test page</title>
</head>
<body>
    <span>Below is a table...   </span>
    <table border="1">
        <tr>
            <td>Row 1 Cell 1</td>
            <td>Row 1 Cell 2</td>
        </tr>
        <tr>
            <td>Row 2 Cell 1</td>
            <td>Row 2 Cell 2</td>
        </tr>
    </table>
    <script type="text/javascript">
        var TDElement = document.getElementsByTagName("td").item(0);
        TDElement.style.fontFamily = "arial";
    </script>
</body>
</html>
```

Like arrays, collections are zero-based, and so the first element in the table would correspond to the index number 0. If you ran this example, once again using the `style` object, it would alter the style of the contents of the first table cell only in the table, as shown in Figure 13-6.

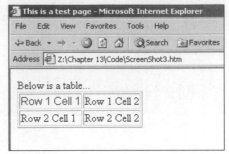

Figure 13-6

Once again, all the attributes of each element are available to the DOM. You can use these to alter any aspect of the element, from presentation to the actual links contained. If you wanted to reference all the cells in this way, you would have to mention each one explicitly in the code, and assign a new variable for each element as follows:

```
<script type="text/javascript">
    var TDElement0 = document.getElementsByTagName("td").item(0);
    var TDElement1 = document.getElementsByTagName("td").item(1);
    var TDElement2 = document.getElementsByTagName("td").item(2);
    var TDElement3 = document.getElementsByTagName("td").item(3);
    TDElement0.style.fontFamily = "arial";
    TDElement1.style.fontFamily = "arial";
    TDElement2.style.fontFamily = "arial";
    TDElement3.style.fontFamily = "arial";
</script>
```

One thing to note about the `getElementsByTagName()` method is that it takes the element names within quotation marks and without the angle brackets <> that normally surround tags.

Where the DOM and BOM Overlap

One quick point to consider here is that in the previous set of examples you've used a feature that you introduced in the previous chapter under the heading of the Browser Object Model to access the style properties of an element, namely the `style` object. However, you're still using part of the DOM. This is a common point of confusion, because although the DOM is concerned only with the contents of the browser window, the BOM concerns itself with some features inside the browser window as well as the different parts of the actual browser. This overlap inside the browser window, where both object models can be used, is where things aren't quite so clear. It happened because browsers had object models for the contents of the document long before there were standards outlining them. Style is one major area in which browsers have supported scripting properties and methods, which is definitely part of the document, but currently still browser-dependent.

Given this information, the `style` object (discussed in Chapter 12) might appear to be part of the Browser Object Model and not the Document Object Model because it is browser-dependent. However, although the `style` object isn't addressed in level 1 of the DOM, it isn't because the `style` object is non-standard. The `style` object isn't covered in the standard because the first version of the standard left styles to the second level. They're not totally resolved there either, and it will probably be the third version in which they get properly sorted. Though it is browser-dependent, the `style` object actually works well in both browsers and supplies a very similar set of properties, which is why we're using it for this example. You could also use the DOM method `setAttribute()` (which you will look at shortly) to set the `style` attributes, but this is a lot messier and currently works only in Firefox.

Properties of the document Object: Returning a Reference to the Topmost Element

You've now got a reference to individual elements on the page, but what about the tree structure mentioned earlier? The tree structure encompasses all the elements and nodes on the page and gives them a hierarchical structure. If you want to reference that structure, you need a particular property of the `document` object that returns the outermost element of your document. In HTML, this should always be the `<html/>` element. The property that returns this element is `documentElement`, as shown in the following table.

Property of the document Object	Description
documentElement	Returns a reference to the outermost element of the document (the root element, for example `<html/>`)

You can use `documentElement` as follows. If you go back to the previous example code, you can transfer your entire DOM into one variable like this:

```
<!DOCTYPE html PUBLIC "-//W3C//DTD XHTML 1.0 Transitional//EN"
"http://www.w3.org/TR/xhtml1/DTD/xhtml1-transitional.dtd">

<html xmlns="http://www.w3.org/1999/xhtml">
<head>
    <title>example</title>
</head>
<body>
    <h1 id="Heading1">My Heading</h1>
    <p id="Paragraph1">This is some text in a paragraph</p>
    <script type="text/javascript">
        var Container = document.documentElement;
    </script>
</body>
</html>
```

The variable `Container` now contains the root element, which is `<html/>`. The `documentElement` property has returned a reference to this element in the form of an object, an `Element` object to be precise. The `Element` object has its own set of properties and methods. If you want to use them, you can refer to them by using the variable name, followed by the method or property name.

```
Container.elementObjectProperty
```

Fortunately, the `Element` object has only one property.

Property of the Element Object

The property of the `Element` object is a reference to the tag name of the element, as shown in the following table.

Property of the Element Object	Description
tagName	Can return the element tag name

In the previous example the variable `Container` contained the `<html/>` element, but using this property you can demonstrate that property. Add the following highlighted line, which makes use of the `tagName` property.

```
<!DOCTYPE html PUBLIC "-//W3C//DTD XHTML 1.0 Transitional//EN"
"http://www.w3.org/TR/xhtml1/DTD/xhtml1-transitional.dtd">

<html xmlns="http://www.w3.org/1999/xhtml">
<head>
    <title>example</title>
</head>
<body>
    <h1 id="Heading1">My Heading</h1>
    <p id="Paragraph1">This is some text in a paragraph</p>
    <script type="text/javascript">
        var Container = document.documentElement;
        alert(Container.tagName);
    </script>
</body>
</html>
```

This code will now return proof that your variable `Container` holds the outermost element, and by implication all other elements within (see Figure 13-7).

Now that you can return any individual element, and the root element, you can look at how you can start navigating your tree structure.

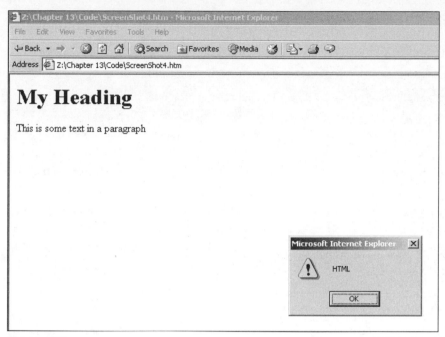

Figure 13-7

Properties of the Node Object: Navigating the Document

You now have your element or elements from the web page, but what happens if you want to move through your page systematically, from element to element, or from attribute to attribute? This is where you need to step back to a higher level. To move among elements, attributes, and text, you have to move among nodes in your tree structure. It doesn't matter what is contained within the node, or rather, what sort of node it is. This is why you need to go back to one of the objects you called base objects. Your whole tree structure is made up of these base-level Node objects.

Following is a list of some common properties of the Node object that provide information about the node—whether it is an element, attribute, or text—and enable you to move from one node to another.

Properties of the Node Object	Description of Property
firstChild	Returns the first child node of an element
lastChild	Returns the last child node of an element
previousSibling	Returns the previous child node of an element at the same level as the current child node
nextSibling	Returns the next child node of an element at the same level as the current child node
ownerDocument	Returns the root node of the document that contains the node (note this is not available in IE 5 or 5.5)
parentNode	Returns the element that contains the current node in the tree structure
nodeName	Returns the name of the node
nodeType	Returns the type of the node as a number
nodeValue	Sets the value of the node in plain text format

Let's take a quick look at how some of these properties work. Consider once more the first example.

```
<!DOCTYPE html PUBLIC "-//W3C//DTD XHTML 1.0 Transitional//EN"
"http://www.w3.org/TR/xhtml1/DTD/xhtml1-transitional.dtd">

<html xmlns="http://www.w3.org/1999/xhtml">
<head>
    <title>example</title>
</head>
<body>
    <h1 id="Heading1">My Heading</h1>
    <p id="Paragraph1">This is some text in a paragraph</p>
    <script type="text/javascript">
        var H1Element = document.getElementById("Heading1");
        H1Element.style.fontFamily = "Arial";
    </script>
</body>
</html>
```

You can now use H1Element to navigate your tree structure, access the contents of the text, and change it. Note that Firefox, Opera, and Safari count all instances of whitespace as child nodes; therefore, this example won't work in them. If you add the following lines, you are setting the reference in the variable PElement to the next element in the tree structure on the same level.

```
<!DOCTYPE html PUBLIC "-//W3C//DTD XHTML 1.0 Transitional//EN"
"http://www.w3.org/TR/xhtml1/DTD/xhtml1-transitional.dtd">

<html xmlns="http://www.w3.org/1999/xhtml">
<head>
    <title>example</title>
```

```
</head>
<body>
    <h1 id="Heading1">My Heading</h1>
    <p id="Paragraph1">This is some text in a paragraph</p>
    <script type="text/javascript">
        var H1Element = document.getElementById("Heading1");
        H1Element.style.fontFamily = "Arial";
        var PElement = H1Element.nextSibling;
        PElement.style.fontFamily = "Arial";
    </script>
</body>
</html>
```

In effect, you are navigating through the tree structure as shown in Figure 13-8.

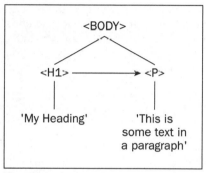

Figure 13-8

The same principles also work in reverse. You can go back and add yet more code that navigates back to the previous node and changes the text of your previous element to your example.

```
<!DOCTYPE html PUBLIC "-//W3C//DTD XHTML 1.0 Transitional//EN"
"http://www.w3.org/TR/xhtml1/DTD/xhtml1-transitional.dtd">

<html xmlns="http://www.w3.org/1999/xhtml">
<head>
</head>
<body>
    <h1 id="Heading1">My Heading</h1>
    <p id="Paragraph1">This is some text in a paragraph</p>
    <script type="text/javascript">
        var H1Element = document.getElementById("Heading1");
        H1Element.style.fontFamily = "Arial";
        var PElement = H1Element.nextSibling;
        PElement.style.fontFamily = "Arial";
        H1Element = PElement.previousSibling;
        H1Element.style.fontFamily = "Courier";
    </script>
</body>
</html>
```

What you're doing here is setting the first <h1/> element to the font Arial; you're then navigating across to the next sibling, which is the next child node of your <body/> element. The first child is the <h1/> element; the second one is the <p/> element. Note that with Firefox, Opera, and Safari things are different; there are lots of whitespace text nodes as child nodes in the body between the element nodes.

You set the font to Arial here as well. Your new two lines of code then use the previousSibling property to jump back to your <h1/> element, and then you again change the fontFamily style, but this time you change it to Courier. So the sum effect of your program is to change the <h1/> element to Courier, and the <p/> element to Arial.

Try It Out   **Navigating Your HTML Document Using the DOM**

Up until now you've been cheating, because you haven't truly navigated your HTML document. You've just used document.getElementById() to return an element and navigated to different nodes from there. Now let's use the documentElement property of the document object and do this properly. You'll start at the top of your tree and move down through the child nodes to get at those elements; then you'll navigate through your child nodes and change the properties in the same way as before.

Type the following into your text editor:

```
<!DOCTYPE html PUBLIC "-//W3C//DTD XHTML 1.0 Transitional//EN"
"http://www.w3.org/TR/xhtml1/DTD/xhtml1-transitional.dtd">

<html xmlns="http://www.w3.org/1999/xhtml">
<head>
    <title>NavLast</title>
</head>
<body>
    <h1 id="Heading1">My Heading</h1>
    <p id="Paragraph1">This is some text in a paragraph</p>

    <script type="text/javascript">
    var htmlElement;       // htmlElement stores reference to <html>
    var headingElement;    // headingElement stores reference to <head>
    var bodyElement;       // bodyElement stores reference to <body>
    var h1Element;         // h1Element stores reference to <h1>
    var pElement;          // pElement stores reference to <p>

    htmlElement = document.documentElement;
    headingElement = htmlElement.firstChild;

    alert(headingElement.tagName);

    if (headingElement.nextSibling.nodeType == 3)
    {
    bodyElement = headingElement.nextSibling.nextSibling;
    }
    else
    {
    bodyElement = headingElement.nextSibling;
    }
```

```
alert(bodyElement.tagName);

if (bodyElement.firstChild.nodeType == 3)
{
h1Element = bodyElement.firstChild.nextSibling;
}
else
{
h1Element = bodyElement.firstChild;
}

alert(h1Element.tagName);
h1Element.style.fontFamily = "Arial";

if (h1Element.nextSibling.nodeType -- 3)
{
pElement = h1Element.nextSibling.nextSibling;
}
else
{
pElement = h1Element.nextSibling;
}

alert(pElement.tagName);
pElement.style.fontFamily = "Arial";

if (pElement.previousSibling.nodeType==3)
{
h1Element = pElement.previousSibling.previousSibling
}
else
{
h1Element = pElement.previousSibling
}

h1Element.style.fontFamily = "Courier"
</script>

</body>
</html>
```

Save this as `navlast.htm`. Then open the page in your browser (this example works in IE, Firefox, Opera, and Safari), clicking OK in each of the message boxes until you see the page shown in Figure 13-9.

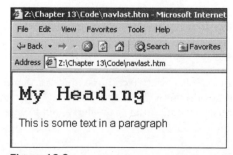

Figure 13-9

How It Works

You've hopefully made this example very transparent by adding several alerts to demonstrate where you are along each section of the tree. You've also named the variables with their various elements, to give a clearer idea of what is stored in each variable. (You could just as easily have named them a, b, c, d, and e, so don't think you need to be bound by this naming convention.)

You start at the top of the script block by retrieving the whole document using the documentElement property.

```
var htmlElement = document.documentElement;
```

The root element is the <html/> element, hence the name of your first variable. Now if you refer to your tree, you'll see that the HTML element must have two child nodes: one containing the <head/> element and the other containing the <body/> element. You start by moving to the <head/> element. You get there using the firstChild property of your Node object, which contains your <html/> element. You use your first alert to demonstrate that this is true.

```
alert(headingElement.tagName);
```

Your <body/> element is your next sibling across from the <head/> element, so you navigate across by creating a variable that is the next sibling from the <head/> element.

```
if (headingElement.nextSibling.nodeType == 3)
    {
    bodyElement = headingElement.nextSibling.nextSibling;
    }
    else
    {
    bodyElement = headingElement.nextSibling;
    }

    alert(bodyElement.tagName);
```

Here you check to see what the nodeType of the nextSibling of headingElement is. If it returns 3, you set bodyElement to be the nextSibling of the nextSibling of headingElement; otherwise you just set it to be the nextSibling of headingElement. Why do you do this? The answer lies with the implementation of the DOM in Firefox, Opera, and Safari. You would think that the next sibling of the <head/> element in the tree would be the <body/> element, and indeed it is in IE 6+. However, Firefox, Opera, and Safari count all instances of whitespace as nodes in the document. To navigate through the tree in a way that works in both browsers, you check to see whether the next sibling has a nodeType of 3. If it does, it is a text node, and you need to move along the next node.

You use an alert to prove that you are now at the <body/> element.

```
alert(bodyElement.tagName);
```

The <body/> element in this page also has two children, the <h1/> and <p/> elements. Using the firstChild property, you move down to the <h1/> element. Again you check whether the child node is whitespace for Firefox, Opera, and Safari. You use an alert again to show that you have arrived at <h1/>.

```
if (bodyElement.firstChild.nodeType == 3)
{
    h1Element = bodyElement.firstChild.nextSibling;
}
else
{
    h1Element = bodyElement.firstChild;
}

alert(h1Element.tagName);
```

After the third alert, the style will be altered on your first element, changing the font to Arial.

```
h1Element.style.fontFamily = "Arial";
```

You then navigate across to the <p/> element using the nextSibling property, again checking for whitespace.

```
if (h1Element.nextSibling.nodeType == 3)
{
    pElement = h1Element.nextSibling.nextSibling;
}
else
{
    pElement = h1Element.nextSibling;
}

alert(pElement.tagName);
```

You change the <p/> element's font to Arial also.

```
pElement.style.fontFamily = "Arial";
```

Finally, you use the previousSibling property to move back in your tree to the <h1/> element and this time change the font to Courier.

```
if (pElement.previousSibling.nodeType==3)
{
    h1Element = pElement.previousSibling.previousSibling
}
else
{
    h1Element = pElement.previousSibling
}

h1Element.style.fontFamily = "Courier";
```

This is a fairly easy example to follow because you're using the same tree structure you created with diagrams, but it does show how the DOM effectively creates this hierarchy and that you can move around within it using script.

Methods of the Node Object: Adding and Removing Elements from the Document

You can now move through your tree structure and alter the contents of elements as you go, but you still can't fundamentally alter the structure of your HTML document. Help is at hand, though, because the Node object's methods let you do this.

Following is a list of methods that enable you to alter the structure of an HTML document by creating new nodes and adding them to your tree.

Methods of the Node Objects	Description
appendChild(newNode)	Adds a new node object to the end of the list of child nodes. This method returns the appended node.
cloneNode(cloneChildren)	Returns a duplicate of the current node. It accepts a Boolean value. If the value is true, then the method clones the current node and all child nodes. If the value is false, only the current node is cloned and child nodes are left out of the clone.
hasChildNodes()	Returns true if a node has any child nodes.
insertBefore(newNode, referenceNode)	Inserts a new node object into the list of child nodes before the node stipulated by referenceNode. Returns the inserted node.
removeChild(childNode)	Removes a child node from a list of child nodes of the node object. Returns the removed node.
replaceChild(newChild, oldChild)	Replaces the old child node object with a new child node object. Returns the replaced node.

You'll look at how they work shortly.

Methods of the document Object: Adding and Removing Elements from the Document

In addition to the methods of the Node object listed previously, the document object itself boasts some methods for creating elements, attributes, and text, shown in the following table.

Methods of the document Object	Description
createElement(elementName)	Creates an element node with a specified name. Returns the created element.
createTextNode(text)	Creates and returns a text node with the specified text.
createAttribute(attributeName)	Creates an attribute node with a specified name. Returns the created attribute node.

The best way to demonstrate both sets of methods for the Node object and the document object at one time is with an example.

Try It Out   Create HTML Elements and Text with DOM JavaScript

You'll create a web page with just paragraph `<p/>` and heading `<h1/>` elements, but instead of HTML you'll use the DOM properties and methods to place these elements on the web page. Figure 13-10 shows IE. However, you don't have to make any changes for the example to work equally well in Firefox. Now start up your preferred text editor and type in the following:

```
<!DOCTYPE html PUBLIC "-//W3C//DTD XHTML 1.0 Transitional//EN"
"http://www.w3.org/TR/xhtml1/DTD/xhtml1-transitional.dtd">

<html xmlns="http://www.w3.org/1999/xhtml">
<head>
    <title>Creating Nodes</title>
</head>
<body>
    <script type="text/javascript">
    var newText = document.createTextNode("My Heading");
    var newElem = document.createElement("h1");

    newElem.appendChild(newText);
    document.body.appendChild(newElem);

    newText = document.createTextNode("This is some text in a paragraph");
    newElem = document.createElement("p");

    newElem.appendChild(newText);
    document.body.appendChild(newElem);
    </script>
</body>
</html>
```

Save this page as `create.htm` and open it in a browser.

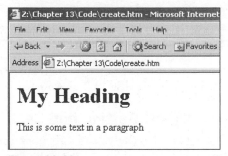

Figure 13-10

How It Works

It all looks a bit dull and ordinary, doesn't it? And yes, you could have done this much more simply with HTML. That isn't the point, though. The idea is that you use DOM properties and methods, accessed with JavaScript, to insert these features. The first two lines of the script block are used to define the variables in your script, which are initialized to hold the text you want to insert into the page and the HTML element you wish to insert.

```
var newText = document.createTextNode("My Heading");
var newElem = document.createElement("h1");
```

You start at the bottom of your tree first, by creating a text node with the `createTextNode()` method. Then use the `createElement()` method to create an HTML heading.

At this point the two variables are entirely separate from each other. You have a text node, and you have an <h1/> element, but they're not connected. The next line enables you to attach the text node to your HTML element. You reference the HTML element you have created with the variable name `newElem`, use the `appendChild()` method of your node, and supply the contents of the `newText` variable you created earlier as a parameter.

```
newElem.appendChild(newText);
```

Let's recap. You created a text node and stored it in the `newText` variable. You created an <h1/> element and stored it in the `newElem` variable. Then you appended the text node as a child node to the <h1/> element. That still leaves you with a problem: You've created an element with a value, but the element isn't part of your document. You need to attach the entirety of what you've created so far to the document body. Again, you can do this with the `appendChild()` method, but this time supply it to the `document.body` object.

```
document.body.appendChild(newElem);
```

This completes the first part of your code. Now all you have to do is repeat the process for the <p/> element.

```
newText = document.createTextNode("This is some text in a paragraph");
newElem = document.createElement("p");

newElem.appendChild(newText);
document.body.appendChild(newElem);
```

You create a text node first; then you create an element. You attach the text to the element, and finally you attach the element and text to the body of the document. This completes the creation of parts of the HTML document in script.

You've now created elements and changed text, but you've left out one of the important parts of the web page, namely attributes. You'll look at how to use attributes now.

Methods of the Element Object: Getting and Setting Attributes

Although it is still acceptable to set the `style` attributes through the `style` object, if you want to set any other element attributes, you should use the DOM-specific methods of the `Element` object.

The three methods you can use to return and alter the contents of an HTML element's attributes are `getAttribute()`, `setAttribute()`, and `removeAttribute()`, as shown in the following table.

Methods of the Element Object	Description
getAttribute(attributeName)	Returns the value of an attribute
setAttribute(attributeName, value)	Sets the value of an attribute
removeAttribute(attributeName)	Removes the value of an attribute and replaces it with the default value

Let's take a quick look at how these methods work now. In the previous example, createElement() and createTextNode() were used to add HTML elements and text to your page, but you didn't actually make use of createAttribute(). That's because there's a much easier method of creating attributes: using the setAttribute() and getAttribute() methods.

Try It Out   Creating Attributes

You're now going to take your previous example and add some attributes to it that will affect the presentation and layout of your text. You must be sure to replicate the case of these lines when you type them because incorrect case will prevent the example from working correctly.

Open create.htm in a text editor and add the following highlighted lines:

```
<!DOCTYPE html PUBLIC "-//W3C//DTD XHTML 1.0 Transitional//EN"
"http://www.w3.org/TR/xhtml1/DTD/xhtml1-transitional.dtd">

<html xmlns="http://www.w3.org/1999/xhtml">
<head>
    <title>Creating Attributes</title>
</head>
<body>

    <script type="text/javascript">
    var newText = document.createTextNode("My Heading");
    var newElem = newElem = document.createElement("h1");

    newElem.setAttribute("align", "center");
    newElem.appendChild(newText);
    document.body.appendChild(newElem);

    newText = document.createTextNode("This is some text in a paragraph");
    newElem = document.createElement("p");

    alert(newElem.getAttribute("align"));
    newElem.setAttribute("align", "right");
    alert(newElem.getAttribute("align"));

    newElem.appendChild(newText);
    document.body.appendChild(newElem);
    </script>
</body>
</html>
```

Save this as attribute.htm and open it in a browser. Your page will look like what is shown in Figure 13-11.

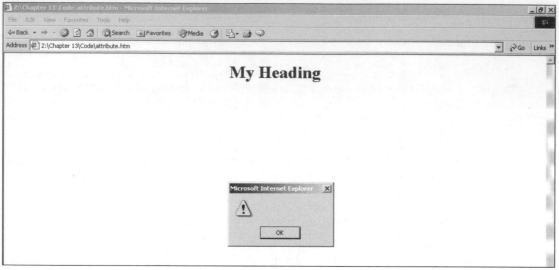

Figure 13-11

Click OK on the alert, and the second time it should display correctly (see Figure 13-12).

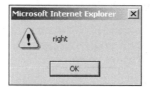

Figure 13-12

Click OK again to reach the screen shown in Figure 13-13.

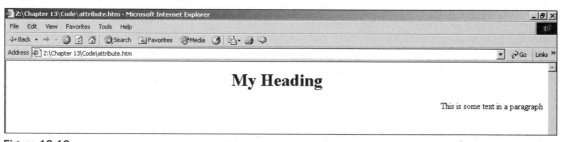

Figure 13-13

How It Works

You've added four lines of code here to augment your existing document structure. The first takes your `<h1/>` element and adds an `align` attribute to it.

```
var newText = document.createTextNode("My Heading");
var newElem = newElem = document.createElement("h1");
```

```
newElem.setAttribute("align", "center");
```

Note that in the setAttribute() method, align is in lowercase per the XHTML standards recommended earlier in this chapter. If it were in uppercase, as follows, the example would fail in some browsers (such as IE):

```
newElem.setAttribute("ALIGN","center");
```

The setAttribute() method takes align, an existing attribute (meaning that it is specified for that particular element in the HTML specifications), and supplies it with the value center. The result positions your text in the center of the page.

> *Strictly speaking, the align attribute is deprecated under XHTML, but you have used it because it works and because it has one of the most easily demonstrable visual effects on a web page.*

So setAttribute() takes the name of the attribute first and the value second. If you set the attribute name to be a nonexistent attribute, it will have no effect on the page. You can also set the attribute to a nonexistent value, which is perfectly legal, but once again there will be no effect on the page.

The second part of the code is very similar to the first.

```
newText = document.createTextNode("This is some text in a paragraph");
newElem = document.createElement("p");
```

```
alert(newElem.getAttribute("align"));
newElem.setAttribute("align", "right");
alert(newElem.getAttribute("align"));
```

After you've created the <p/> element and the accompanying text, you use getAttribute() to return the value of the align attribute. Because align hasn't been set yet, it returns no value, not even the default. You then use the setAttribute() method to set the align attribute to right, and use getAttribute() to return the value. This time it returns right. This is then reflected in the final display of the web page.

What have you seen so far? You started with a nearly empty DOM hierarchy. You then returned the HTML document to a variable, navigated through the different parts of it via DOM objects outside the hierarchy itself (the Node objects), and changed the contents of objects, thus altering the content of the web page. Then you inserted DOM objects into the hierarchy, thus inserting new elements into the page. This leaves just one area of the DOM to cover: the event model.

The DOM Event Model

The DOM event model is introduced in level 2 of the DOM standard. It's a way of handling events and providing information about these events to the script. It provides guidelines for a standard way of determining what generated an event, what type of event it was, and when and where the event occurred.

All of this was, of course, trackable in earlier versions of IE, and to a lesser extent in Netscape, through the event object as you saw in the last chapter. However, the main problem was that the ways of accessing this object and the names of its properties were completely different between the two browsers.

The DOM event model doesn't look complete in some ways, and might yet be tweaked in level 3 of the standard, but what it does do is introduce a basic set of objects, properties, and methods. It also makes some important distinctions.

First there is an event object, which provides information about the element that has generated an event and enables you to retrieve it in script. If you want to make it available in script, it must be passed as a parameter to the function connected to the event handler, as you saw in the previous chapter. It is not globally available, as the IE event object is.

The standard outlines several properties and methods of the event object that have long since been a source of dispute between IE and other browsers. You will be using only the properties, so here you will be considering them alone.

Properties of the event Object	Description
bubbles	Indicates whether an event can bubble (pass control from one element to another)
cancelable	Indicates whether an event can have its default action canceled
currentTarget	Indicates which event is currently being processed
eventPhase	Indicates which phase of the event flow an event is in
target (DOM browsers only)	Indicates which element caused the event; in the DOM event model, text nodes are the possible target of an event
timeStamp (Firefox only)	Indicates at what time the event occurred
type	Indicates the name of the event

Secondly, the DOM introduces a MouseEvent object, which deals with events generated specifically by the mouse. This is useful because you might need more specific information about the event, such as the position in pixels of the cursor, or the element the mouse has come from.

Properties of the mouse Event Object	Description
altKey	Indicates whether the Alt key was pressed when the event was generated.
button	Indicates which button on the mouse was pressed.
clientX	Indicates where in the browser window, in horizontal coordinates, the mouse pointer was when the event was generated.

Properties of the mouse Event Object	Description
clientY	Indicates where in the browser window, in vertical coordinates, the mouse pointer was when the event was generated.
ctrlKey	Indicates whether the Ctrl key was pressed when the event was generated.
metaKey	Indicates whether the meta key was pressed when the event was generated.
relatedTarget (DOM browsers only)	In the DOM event model text nodes are the (possible) target of the mouseover event. This object is similar to IE's event.toElement and event.fromElement.
screenX	Indicates where in the browser window, in horizontal coordinates relative to the origin in the screen coordinates, the mouse pointer was when the event was generated.
screenY	Indicates where in the browser window, in vertical coordinates relative to the origin in the screen coordinates, the mouse pointer was when the event was generated.
shiftKey	Indicates whether the Shift key was pressed when the event was generated.

Although any event might create an event object, only a select set of events can generate a MouseEvent object. On the occurrence of a MouseEvent event, you'd be able to access properties from the event object and the MouseEvent object. With a non-mouse event, none of the mouse object properties in the preceding table would be available. The following mouse events can create a mouse event object:

❑ click occurs when a mouse button is clicked (pressed and released) with the pointer over an element or text

❑ mousedown occurs when a mouse button is pressed with the pointer over an element or text

❑ mouseup occurs when a mouse button is released with the pointer over an element or text

❑ mouseover occurs when a mouse button is moved onto an element or text

❑ mousemove occurs when a mouse button is moved and it is already on top of an element or text

❑ mouseout occurs when a mouse button is moved out and away from an element or text

To get at an event using the DOM, all you have to do is query the event object created by the individual element that raised the event. For example, in the following code the <p/> element will raise a dblclick event:

```
<p ondblclick="handle(event)">Paragraph</p>

<script type="text/javascript">
function handle(e)
```

```
    {
        alert(e.type);
    }
    </script>
```

You have to pass the `event` object created by the `<p/>` element as an argument in the function call to be able to use it within the function. You can then use the parameter passed as the `event` object and use its general properties made available through the DOM.

However, this is where the browsers get shaky. IE 6 and 7 do not support many of the DOM properties mentioned in the table. Instead, IE has its own set of IE-specific properties, which we won't be discussing here.

If you ran the previous example, it would just tell you what kind of event raised your event-handling function. This might seem self-evident in the preceding example, but if you had included the following extra lines of code, any one of three elements could have raised the function:

```
<p ondblclick="handle(event)">Paragraph</p>
<h1 onclick="handle(event)">Heading 1</h1>
<span onmouseover="handle(event)">Special Text</span>

<script type="text/javascript">
function handle(e)
{
    alert(e.type);
}
</script>
```

This makes the code much more useful. In general you will use relatively few event handlers to deal with any number of events, and you can use the event properties as a filter to determine what type of event happened and what HTML element triggered it, so that you can treat each event differently.

In the following example, you see that you can take different courses of action depending on what type of event is returned:

```
<p ondblclick="handle(event)">Paragraph</p>
<h1 onclick="handle(event)">Heading 1</h1>
<span onmouseover="handle(event)">Special Text</span>
...
<script type="text/javascript">
function handle(e)
{
    if (e.type == "mouseover")
    {
        alert("You moved over the Special Text");
    }
}
</script>
```

Try It Out   Using the DOM Event Model

Let's take a quick look at an example that creates a mouse event object when the user clicks anywhere on the screen and returns to the user the x and y coordinates of the position of the mouse pointer when the mouse button was clicked (see Figure 13-14). This example will work in IE 5+ and Firefox.

Open a text editor and type in the following:

```
<!DOCTYPE html PUBLIC "-//W3C//DTD XHTML 1.0 Transitional//EN"
"http://www.w3.org/TR/xhtml1/DTD/xhtml1-transitional.dtd">

<html xmlns="http://www.w3.org/1999/xhtml">
<head>
</head>
<body onclick="handleClick(event)">
    Click anywhere on the screen if you're using Firefox.
    Click on this text if you're using IE, Opera, or Safari.

    <script language="JavaScript">
    function handleClick(e)
    {
        alert("You clicked on the screen at X" + e.clientX +" and Y" + e.clientY);
    }
    </script>
</body>
</html>
```

Save this as mouseevent.htm and run it in your browser.

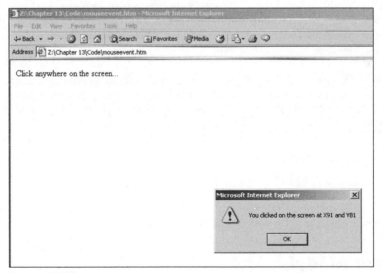

Figure 13-14

Now click OK, move the pointer in the browser window, and click again. A different result appears.

How It Works

This example is consistent with the event-handling behavior: The browser waits for an event, and every time that event occurs it raises the corresponding function. It will continue to wait for the event until you exit the browser or that particular web page. In this example, you use the <body/> element to raise a click event.

```
<body onclick="handleClick(event)">
```

Whenever that function is encountered, the handleClick() function is raised and a new MouseEvent object is generated. Remember that MouseEvent objects give you access to event object properties as well as MouseEvent object properties, even though you don't use them in this example.

The function takes the mouse event object and assigns it the reference e.

```
function handleClick(e)
{
    alert("You clicked on the screen at X" + e.clientX +" and Y" + e.clientY);
}
```

Inside the function you use the alert() statement to display the contents of the clientX and clientY properties of the mouse event object on the screen. This MouseEvent object is overwritten and re-created every time you generate an event, so the next time you click the mouse pointer it returns new coordinates for the x and y positions.

As described earlier, one problem that precludes greater discussion of the DOM event model is the fact that not all browsers support it in any detail. Specifically, IE, the most popular browser by far, doesn't fully support it. You will see in a later example that you are still in a position of having to code for both browsers when it comes to returning information about events via properties, but this should provide a little taste of how they work, and how they will work in future browsers. We won't go into any further detail here about events, but you will be returning to the DOM event object model later in the chapter in an example that discusses how to cross-code.

Despite advances in standards compliance, there are still differences among the major browsers that require you to use browser-specific code. In the following sections you'll walk through the creation of a DHTML toolbar for Internet Explorer. You'll then adapt that script for Firefox, and finally you'll make it cross-browser.

DHTML Example: Internet Explorer 5+

We've spent a few pages on the DOM event model, and although this chapter is primarily focused on the web standards, we should briefly cover the IE event model.

The IE Event Model

DHTML under IE provides the event object, which we briefly discussed in the previous chapter. This object is a property of the window object, and one such object exists for each open browser window. It provides you with lots of very useful information about the most recent event to fire, such as details regarding the event that was fired, which element caused the event to fire, information about where the user's mouse pointer is, which buttons or keys were pressed, and much, much more.

The event object has a lot of properties and methods, but you are going to concentrate on only a few of the more useful ones. You'll take a look at these in the following sections.

Why Did the Event Fire?

The event object enables you to find information about what the user did to cause the event to fire. For example, you can check to see where the mouse pointer is, which mouse buttons have been clicked, and which keys have been pressed.

The properties screenX and screenY of the event object provide you with the coordinates of the user's mouse pointer at the time of the event. Because the event object is already created for you, you simply use it by typing its name followed by the property or method you're interested in.

```
event.screenX
```

The preceding entry gets you a reference to the horizontal position, in pixels, of the user's mouse pointer.

Contrast this with the following code:

```
event.screenY
```

This gets you a reference to the vertical position, in pixels, of the mouse pointer. Remember that screen coordinates start at 0, 0 in the top left-hand corner of the screen.

The button property of the event object tells you which mouse button, if any, the user has pressed. It returns a number, between 0 and 7 (inclusive), indicating the following:

- ❏ 0: No button is pressed.
- ❏ 1: Left button is pressed.
- ❏ 2: Right button is pressed.
- ❏ 3: Left and right buttons are both pressed.
- ❏ 4: Middle button is pressed.
- ❏ 5: Left and middle buttons are both pressed.
- ❏ 6: Right and middle buttons are both pressed.
- ❏ 7: All three buttons (left, right, and middle) are pressed.

Finally, you can find out whether a key has been pressed and, if so, which key it was by using the keyCode property of the event object. This returns a number that indicates the Unicode character code corresponding to the key pressed. If no key was pressed, the number returned will be 0.

Finding Out Which Elements Are Involved in the Event

The event object has three properties: fromElement, srcElement, and toElement. These properties provide a reference to the objects of the elements involved in the event. For example, in a mouseover event the following conditions apply:

❑ The fromElement property will refer to the object of whichever element the user's mouse pointer was on before moving over the element that fired the onmouseover event.

❑ The srcElement property will be the object of the element that caused the event to fire. For example, if the mouse pointer just rolled over an image, the srcElement will be that <img/> element's object.

❑ The toElement property is the object of the element that the user's mouse pointer is about to move to, for example in an mouseout event. How does the browser know where the mouse is going? Well, it raises the events for a particular user action after they have actually happened, although the delay is only microseconds. It's rather like a live TV broadcast that is actually transmitted with a short delay so that swear words can be bleeped out.

Each of these properties provides the actual object of the element, which you can use and manipulate as if you had referenced the element directly. This ability can be particularly useful when you're writing generic code that is placed in the event of a higher object, such as document.

Building a DHTML Toolbar

The DHTML script you'll write in this section will be a toolbar, a UI element that is used often in applications. The Back, Forward, Stop, and Home buttons in your web browser are good examples. The toolbar you're going to build will consists only of icons (so no text), and clicking a button will either run JavaScript code or take the user to another web page.

You'll generate the HTML dynamically using DOM methods. So before you get too deep into the code, let's look at what your generated HTML will look like.

The HTML Structure

The toolbar itself is nothing more than a <div/> element, and it will contain any number of buttons.

```
<div class="toolbar">
    <span href="go_someplace" class="toolbar-button">
        <img src="icon_location" class="toolbar-icon" />
    </span>
</div>
```

The buttons, too, are <span/> elements. Buttons have a CSS class of toolbar-button, and each contain an href attribute. The <span/> element does not have this attribute in the HTML specification, so the browser will ignore the attribute and its value when it displays the HTML. You can, however, access it with JavaScript and program the desired functionality by using the click event. When the user moves her mouse over a button, you'll change the CSS class name to toolbar-button-hover. This will enable you to easily change the style of the button. So to clarify, you'll need to handle the mouseover, mouseout, and click events.

Inside each button is an `<img/>` element, which serves as your icon. These have a CSS class of `toolbar-icon`, and you'll constrain the size of the image through CSS. Speaking of which, you should go over how you want to style your toolbar.

Adding Style

You want this toolbar to resemble the UI constructs people are accustomed to seeing. This is important because you want the user to know how to use the toolbar without any instruction. If she recognizes the toolbar, she'll know what to do.

Styling the Toolbar

Your toolbar will have a grayish background color.

```
.toolbar
{
    background-color: #E4E2D5;
    padding: 2px;
}
```

You'll also add some padding around the edges. It's obvious that the buttons are contained inside the toolbar; however, adding some padding will emphasize that fact, and give the toolbar a clean look.

Styling the Buttons

As stated earlier, the buttons are `<span/>` elements, and they have two states: a default state, and a state when the mouse pointer hovers over the button. Therefore, you'll need at least two rules, each with their own properties and values.

The first rule is the default state of the button; in other words, this is what it looks like before a mouse pointer hovers over the button.

```
.toolbar-button
{
    display: inline-block;
    height: 24px;
    width: 24px;
    padding: 3px;
}
```

This rule sets the button to be displayed as an `inline-block` element. That may seem like a contradiction, but it is an actual value for this property. This value allows the inside of an element to be formatted as a block level element, but the element itself is formatted as an inline element. Next, the button is set to be 24 pixels in height and width. Lastly, three pixels of padding are added to the button. This padding is added for the same reasons padding was added to the `toolbar` class.

Now, add the style rule for the button's second state: when the mouse hovers over the button.

```
.toolbar-button-hover
{
    display: inline-block;
    height: 24px;
```

```
        width: 24px;
        border: 1px solid #316AC5;
        background-color: #C1D2EE;
        padding: 2px;
        cursor: pointer;
    }
```

You've already seen the first three properties; they were used in the `toolbar-button` class. Next, a blue border one pixel in width is added to the element, and the background color is changed to a light blue. The padding is decreased to two pixels. You do this because padding and borders add extra height and width to the HTML element. Take a look at Figure 13-15, which illustrates this concept.

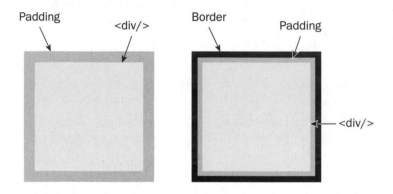

Both elements 30 pixels
in height and width

Figure 13-15

This is a side-by-side comparison of the `toolbar-button` and `toolbar-button-hover` classes. The `toolbar-button` class is 24 pixels in height and width plus three pixels of padding per side. That makes `toolbar-button` 30 pixels in height and width.

The `toolbar-button-hover` class starts with the same 24 pixels in height and width. You then add a one-pixel border, which adds two pixels to the height and width. Then you add two pixels of padding on each side, which makes `toolbar-button-hover` 30 pixels in height and width, just like `toolbar-button`. If you used three pixels of padding instead of two in `toolbar-button-hover`, the button would grow in size when the mouse pointer hovered over it, as Figure 13-16 shows.

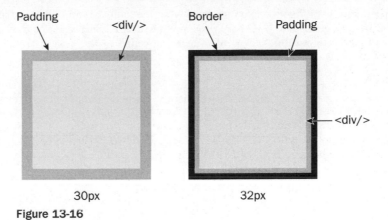

Figure 13-16

Let's take a second and look at these two rules. Notice that each has three properties with the same values (display, height, and width). You can take these properties out and write a new rule for all <span/> elements inside the toolbar.

```
.toolbar span
{
    display: inline-block;
    height: 24px;
    width: 24px;
}
```

You can now slim down the toolbar-button and toolbar-button-hover classes:

```
.toolbar-button
{
    padding: 3px;
}

.toolbar-button-hover
{
    border: 1px solid #316AC5;
    background-color: #C1D2EE;
    padding: 2px;
    cursor: pointer;
}
```

By making this change, you can easily add style that is shared by both states.

The last property we'll discuss for the button is the cursor property. The mouse cursor (or pointer) is an important user interface component. It can tell the user when something is going on in the background or let him know when he can highlight text. It also changes to a hand when he moves the cursor over a link, letting him know that something will happen when he clicks it.

As stated earlier, you want the user to understand what the toolbar is and what it does. By using the `cursor` property and setting it to `pointer`, you show the user a hand when he moves his mouse over a button. This offers the suggestion "Hey you! You can click me!"

Styling the Icons

The last style rule you need to write is one for the icons. These are simple `<img/>` elements with a CSS class name of `toolbar-icon`.

```css
.toolbar-icon
{
    height: 24px;
    width: 24px;
}
```

By assigning `height` and `width`, you can constrain the image to a certain size. This will make sure that the icons look uniform.

Storing Button Information

You need some way to store the button information. In this script, you'll use a multi-dimensional array to contain information for specific buttons. Let's start with the first array. Let's call it `myToolbar`.

```javascript
var myToolbar = new Array();
```

Each element in this array, `myToolbar[x]`, will also be declared as an array. Each of these inner arrays will hold information for a particular button.

You start this process with the array element of index 0.

```javascript
myToolbar[0] = new Array();
```

Now you can use the elements of this array, namely `myToolbar[0][0]` and `myToolbar[0][1]`, to hold information about the first button. That information will be the image location for the icon and the page (or JavaScript code) to load when the button is clicked. So you see that the following code holds the location of the icon:

```javascript
myToolbar[0][0] = "img/green.gif";
```

The next line holds the web location, or JavaScript code, to load.

```javascript
myToolbar[0][1] = "javascript: alert('You Clicked the Green Button!')";
```

Each button follows this pattern of defining a new `Array` object and inserting it in the first dimension. Then you make the second dimension of the array hold the icon information and the link or JavaScript code to load.

```javascript
myToolbar[0]    = new Array();
myToolbar[0][0] = "img/green.gif";
myToolbar[0][1] = "javascript: alert('You Clicked the Green Button!')";

myToolbar[1]    = new Array();
```

```
myToolbar[1][0] = "img/blue.c
myToolbar[1][1] = "javascri

myToolbar[2]    = new Arr
myToolbar[2][0] = "img/r
myToolbar[2][1] = "htt
```

Building the Toolbar

You need a function to b
createToolbar() tha
of your toolbar, and t
know how the HTM

The first step is t

```
function createToo
{
    var toolbar = documen
    toolbar.id = sName;
    toolbar.className = "toolba

    //more code here

    document.body.appendChild(toolbar);
}
```

In this code you create the <div/> element with the createElement()
name, specified by the first argument, as its id attribute. You then assign its
append it to the document with the appendChild() method.

You now have an empty toolbar, so you need to use the myToolbar array to populate it w
You'll do this with a for loop.

```
function createToolbar(sName, aButtons)
{
    var toolbar = document.createElement("div");
    toolbar.id = sName;
    toolbar.className = "toolbar";

    for (var i = 0; i < aButtons.length; i++)
    {
        var thisButton = aButtons[i];

        var button = document.createElement("span");
        var icon = document.createElement("img");

        //more code here
    }

    document.body.appendChild(toolbar);
}
```

Inside the loop, you get the element of the
thisButton. This enables you to easily a
<span/> and <img/> elements. The but
able references the <img/> element.

Next, add the href attribute to bu
contained in the thisButton[1]

```
function createToolbar
{
    var toolbar = do
    toolbar.id = s
    toolbar.classN

    for (var i
    {
        var
```

rray that corresponds to this button and assign it to
ccess the button's information. Then you create the required
ton variable references the `<span/>` element, and the icon vari-

ton with the `setAttribute()` method. The value of this attribute is
element of the `thisButton` array. Also set the CSS class.

```
sName, aButtons)

cument.createElement("div");
Name;
ame = "toolbar";

= 0; i < aButtons.length; i++)

nisButton = aButtons [i];

button = document.createElement("div");
ar icon = document.createElement("img");

button.setAttribute("href", thisButton[1]);
button.className = "toolbar-button";

icon.src = thisButton[0];
icon.className = "toolbar-icon";

button.appendChild(icon);
toolbar.appendChild(button);
}

document.body.appendChild(toolbar);
}
```

This code also sets the `src` and `className` properties for the icon. You then append `icon` to `button` and add the button to the toolbar.

With this code, the toolbar is created and populated with buttons, but it currently has no functionality. Remember, you want hover effects, and you want something to happen when a button is clicked.

Handling User Interaction

User interaction is an important part of DHTML; you usually want your HTML to react to something a user does, and the toolbar is no exception. As already mentioned, there are three areas of user interaction you want to handle:

❑   When the user moves her mouse pointer over a button

❑   When the user moves her mouse pointer off a button

❑   When the user clicks a button

You'll write one function to handle these events: `button_mouseHandler()`.

The button_mouseHandler() Function

Using one function to handle the three mouse events is a time- and code-saving measure, especially in the case of this DHTML script. The function begins with its definition and two variables:

```
function button_mouseHandler()
{
    var eType = event.type;
    var eSrc = event.srcElement;

    //more code here
}
```

This DHTML script is quite similar to the image rollover scripts you wrote in the previous chapter. Here, you're concerned only with the element that the event was fired upon (the source element) and the event type that called the event handler. The next step is to write the code for the mouseover event.

```
function button_mouseHandler()
{
    var eType = event.type;
    var eSrc = event.srcElement;

    if (eType == "mouseover")
    {
        eSrc.className = "toolbar-button-hover";
    }

    //more code here
}
```

This code checks to see if the event type is a mouseover event, and, if so, it changes the source element's className property to toolbar-button-hover.

Now it's time to handle the mouseout event. When the mouse pointer leaves the button, the desired effect is to return the previously highlighted button to its original state. Therefore, the following code changes the className property of the source element (of the mouseout event) back to toolbar-button.

```
function button_mouseHandler()
{
    var eType = event.type;
    var eSrc = event.srcElement;

    if (eType == "mouseover")
    {
        eSrc.className = "toolbar-button-hover";
    }
    else if (eType == "mouseout")
    {
        eSrc.className = "toolbar-button";
    }

    //more code here
}
```

Now things are beginning to take shape. When the mouse pointer moves over the button, its style changes to give a highlight effect, and the mouse pointer leaving the button returns it to its original state. Now you need to write the code to handle the `click` event, and the following code does this:

```
function button_mouseHandler()
{
    var eType = event.type;
    var eSrc = event.srcElement;

    //more code here

    if (eType == "mouseover")
    {
        eSrc.className = "toolbar-button-hover";
    }
    else if (eType == "mouseout")
    {
        eSrc.className = "toolbar-button";
    }
    else if (eType == "click")
    {
        eSrc.className = "toolbar-button";
        window.location.href = eSrc.getAttribute("href");
    }
}
```

The code handling the `click` event does two things. First, it returns the clicked button's `className` property back to `toolbar-button`, and second, it navigates to the desired web page, or executes JavaScript code.

But alas, all is not well. If you were to run this code, you would notice a few weird things happening. Buttons would highlight and unhighlight at strange times, the icons would grow to the size of the buttons, and you'd see some very strange results if you clicked on a button when the mouse pointer was over an icon (the browser would navigate to the URL specified in the `<img/>` element's `src` property). These behaviors may seem weird, but they are normal. As the mouse pointer moves over the `<img/>` element, it is no longer over the `<span/>` element (the button). Therefore, the `mouseout` event fires as the mouse leaves the `<span/>` and enters the `<img/>`.

A simple solution to this problem is to check the source element's `tagName` property, and, if it's `IMG`, to access the image's parent node: the `<span/>` element that represents the button.

```
function button_mouseHandler()
{
    var eType = event.type;
    var eSrc = event.srcElement;

    if (eSrc.tagName == "IMG")
    {
        eSrc = eSrc.parentNode;
    }

    if (eType == "mouseover")
```

```
        {
            eSrc.className = "toolbar-button-hover";
        }
        else if (eType == "mouseout")
        {
            eSrc.className = "toolbar-button";
        }
        else if (eType == "click")
        {
            eSrc.className = "toolbar-button";
            window.location.href = eSrc.getAttribute("href");
        }
    }
```

Now the eSrc variable will always reference the <span/> element, making the button behave as you would expect it to.

Finishing createToolbar()

With the mouse event handler written, you can assign it to handle the appropriate events. Do this in createToolbar().

```
function createToolbar(sName, aButtons)
{
    var toolbar = document.createElement("div");
    toolbar.id   = sName;
    toolbar.className = "toolbar";


    for (var i = 0; i < aButtons.length; i++)
    {
        var thisButton = aButtons[i];

        var button = document.createElement("span");
        var icon = document.createElement("img");

        button.setAttribute("href", thisButton[1]);
        button.className = "toolbar-button";

        button.onclick = button_mouseHandler;
        button.onmouseover = button_mouseHandler;
        button.onmouseout = button_mouseHandler;

        icon.src = thisButton[0];
        icon.className = "toolbar-icon";

        button.appendChild(icon);
        toolbar.appendChild(button);
    }

    document.body.appendChild(toolbar);
}
```

Now the code for the toolbar is complete. You have the toolbar, you populated it with buttons, and you added interactivity for those buttons. Now you need only to call createToolbar().

Finishing Up

Creating a toolbar is easy; however, there is one caveat you must consider. Since you generate the HTML elements dynamically and append them to document.body, you must create the toolbar while the document is loading, or after the document is loaded. If you attempt to load the toolbar at any other time, you'll get errors in your page.

In this exercise, you'll use the onload event handler to create the toolbar after the document is loaded. Following is the complete source code for the toolbar DHTML script. Open the text editor of your choice and type the following:

```
<!DOCTYPE html PUBLIC "-//W3C//DTD XHTML 1.0 Transitional//EN"
"http://www.w3.org/TR/xhtml1/DTD/xhtml1-transitional.dtd">

<html xmlns="http://www.w3.org/1999/xhtml">
<head>
    <title>IE Toolbar</title>
    <style type="text/css">
    .toolbar
    {
        background-color: #E4E2D5;
        padding: 2px;
    }

    .toolbar span
    {
        display: inline-block;
        height: 24px;
        width: 24px;
    }

    .toolbar-button
    {
        padding: 3px;
    }

    .toolbar-button-hover
    {
        border: 1px solid #316AC5;
        background-color: #C1D2EE;
        padding: 2px;
        cursor: pointer;
    }

    .toolbar-icon
    {
        height: 24px;
        width: 24px;
    }
    </style>
    <script type="text/javascript">
    function button_mouseHandler()
    {
        var eType = event.type;
```

```
        var eSrc = event.srcElement;

        if (eSrc.tagName == "IMG")
        {
            eSrc = eSrc.parentNode;
        }

        if (eType == "mouseover")
        {
            eSrc.className = "toolbar-button-hover";
        }
        else if (eType == "mouseout")
        {
            eSrc.className = "toolbar-button";
        }
        else if (eType == "click")
        {
            eSrc.className = "toolbar-button";
            window.location.href = eSrc.getAttribute("href");
        }
    }

    function createToolbar(sName, aButtons) {
        var toolbar = document.createElement("div");
        toolbar.id  = sName;
        toolbar.className = "toolbar";

        for (var i = 0; i < aButtons.length; i++)
        {
            var thisButton = aButtons[i];

            var button = document.createElement("span");
            var icon = document.createElement("img");

            button.setAttribute("href", thisButton[1]);
            button.className = "toolbar-button";

            button.onclick = button_mouseHandler;
            button.onmouseover = button_mouseHandler;
            button.onmouseout = button_mouseHandler;

            icon.src = thisButton[0];
            icon.className = "toolbar-icon";

            button.appendChild(icon);
            toolbar.appendChild(button);
        }

        document.body.appendChild(toolbar);
    }

    var myToolbar = new Array();

    myToolbar[0]    = new Array();
    myToolbar[0][0] = "img/green.gif";
```

```
      myToolbar[0][1] = "javascript: alert('You Clicked the Green Button!')";

      myToolbar[1]    = new Array();
      myToolbar[1][0] = "img/blue.gif";
      myToolbar[1][1] = "javascript: alert('You Clicked the Blue Button!')";

      myToolbar[2]    = new Array();
      myToolbar[2][0] = "img/red.gif";
      myToolbar[2][1] = "http://www.wrox.com";
      </script>
   </head>
   <body onload="createToolbar('myToolbar', myToolbar);">

   </body>
   </html>
```

Save this file as `toolbar_ie.htm`. When you load it into Internet Explorer, you should see something like what is shown in Figure 13-17.

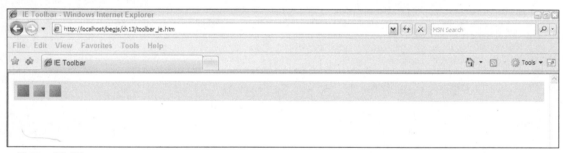

Figure 13-17

Move your mouse pointer over the buttons, and you'll see them become highlighted. When you move your mouse over another button, the previous button un-highlights itself. Click any of the buttons. The green and blue buttons will display an alert box, and the red button will take you to www.wrox.com.

DHTML Example: The Toolbar in Firefox and Opera

Writing the toolbar script for Firefox is surprisingly easy, as most of the code can be reused. As you've already learned, IE and Firefox share many similarities, but they greatly differ in their event models.

The toolbar script follows this same pattern. You'll have to make a change in the CSS and change the event handlers to work with the DOM event model, but other than that your code will remain unchanged.

Try It Out   The Toolbar in Firefox and Opera

Open your text editor of choice and type the following:

```
<!DOCTYPE html PUBLIC "-//W3C//DTD XHTML 1.0 Transitional//EN"
"http://www.w3.org/TR/xhtml1/DTD/xhtml1-transitional.dtd">

<html xmlns="http://www.w3.org/1999/xhtml">
<head>
    <title>Firefox, Opera, and Safari Toolbar</title>
    <style type="text/css">
    .toolbar
    {
        background-color: #E4E2D5;
        padding: 2px;
    }

    .toolbar span
    {
        display: -moz-inline-stack;
        display: inline-block;
        height: 24px;
        width: 24px;
    }

    .toolbar button
    {
        padding: 3px;
    }

    .toolbar-button-hover
    {
        border: 1px solid #316AC5;
        background-color: #C1D2EE;
        padding: 2px;
        cursor: pointer;
    }

    .toolbar-icon
    {
        height: 24px;
        width: 24px;
    }
    </style>
    <script type="text/javascript">
    function button_mouseHandler(e)
    {
        var eType = e.type;
        var eSrc = e.target;

        if (eSrc.tagName == "IMG")
        {
            eSrc = eSrc.parentNode;
```

```
        }

        if (eType == "mouseover")
        {
            eSrc.className = "toolbar-button-hover";
        }
        else if (eType == "mouseout")
        {
            eSrc.className = "toolbar-button";
        }
        else if (eType == "click")
        {
            eSrc.className = "toolbar-button";
            window.location.href = eSrc.getAttribute("href");
        }
    }

    function createToolbar(sName, aButtons)
    {
        var toolbar = document.createElement("div");
        toolbar.id  = sName;
        toolbar.className = "toolbar";

        for (var i = 0; i < aButtons.length; i++)
        {
            var thisButton = aButtons[i];

            var button = document.createElement("span");
            var icon = document.createElement("img");

            button.setAttribute("href", thisButton[1]);
            button.className = "toolbar-button";

            button.onclick = button_mouseHandler;
            button.onmouseover = button_mouseHandler;
            button.onmouseout = button_mouseHandler;

            icon.src = thisButton[0];
            icon.className = "toolbar-icon";

            button.appendChild(icon);
            toolbar.appendChild(button);
        }

        document.body.appendChild(toolbar);
    }

    var myToolbar = new Array();

    myToolbar[0]    = new Array();
    myToolbar[0][0] = "img/green.gif";
    myToolbar[0][1] = "javascript: alert('You Clicked the Green Button!')";

    myToolbar[1]    = new Array();
```

```
        myToolbar[1][0] = "img/blue.gif";
        myToolbar[1][1] = "javascript: alert('You Clicked the Blue Button!')";

        myToolbar[2]    = new Array();
        myToolbar[2][0] = "img/red.gif";
        myToolbar[2][1] = "http://www.wrox.com";
    </script>
  </head>
  <body onload="createToolbar('myToolbar', myToolbar)">

  </body>
</html>
```

Save this file as `toolbar_ff.htm`. Open it in Firefox, Opera, or Safari, and you should see something like what is shown in Figure 13-18.

Figure 13-18

How It Works

This code remains largely the same as in the IE example. The changes, few as they may be, begin with the CSS. In the IE example you styled the buttons to be displayed inline-block, forcing the buttons to sit side by side while adding block-style options. In this second example you had to do something different.

```
.toolbar span
{
    display: -moz-inline-stack;
    display: inline-block;
    height: 24px;
    width: 24px;
}
```

Firefox does not support the `inline-block` value, but it does have a vendor-specific equivalent called `-moz-inline-stack`. Directly under it is another `display` style declaration, which is for Opera. Firefox will ignore this second `display` declaration, as it does not recognize `inline-block` as a valid value for the `display` property.

Now let's jump to the mouse event handler. The primary changes made to the function are the values of the `eType` and `eSrc` variables, as well as an added parameter.

```
function button_mouseHandler(e)
{
    var eType = e.type;
    var eSrc = e.target;

    if (eSrc.tagName == "IMG")
    {
        eSrc = eSrc.parentNode;
    }

    if (eType == "mouseover")
    {
        eSrc.className = "toolbar-button-hover";
    }
    else if (eType == "mouseout")
    {
        eSrc.className = "toolbar-button";
    }
    else if (eType == "click")
    {
        eSrc.className = "toolbar-button";
        window.location.href = eSrc.getAttribute("href");
    }
}
```

Since you're now dealing with the DOM event model, you need to add a parameter to the function for the event object. Then you use the target property to retrieve the element where the event fired. The remainder of the function remains untouched: You make sure that eSrc is a button and change the element's className property according to the event.

Creating Cross-Browser DHTML

By now you've written one DHTML script and adapted it to work in both IE and Firefox. In this section, you'll combine the two versions into one cross-browser version. You probably already have an idea of what code you'll change, as you've already changed it once. However, here you'll employ a few tricks as well to ensure that the script works in both browsers.

Try It Out   **The Cross-Browser Toolbar**

Open your text editor and type the following:

```
<!DOCTYPE html PUBLIC "-//W3C//DTD XHTML 1.0 Transitional//EN"
"http://www.w3.org/TR/xhtml1/DTD/xhtml1-transitional.dtd">

<html xmlns="http://www.w3.org/1999/xhtml">
<head>
    <title>Cross-Browser Toolbar</title>
    <style type="text/css">
    .toolbar
    {
        background-color: #E4E2D5;
```

```
    padding: 2px;
}

.toolbar span
{
    display: -moz-inline-stack;
    display: inline-block;
    height: 24px;
    width: 24px;
}

.toolbar-button
{
    padding: 3px;
}

.toolbar-button-hover
{
    border: 1px solid #316AC5;
    background-color: #C1D2EE;
    padding: 2px;
    cursor: pointer;
}

.toolbar-icon
{
    height: 24px;
    width: 24px;
}
</style>
<script type="text/javascript">
function button_mouseHandler(e)
{
    var eType;
    var eSrc;

    if (window.event)
    {
        eType = event.type;
        eSrc = event.srcElement;
    }
    else
    {
        eType = e.type;
        eSrc = e.target;
    }

    if (eSrc.tagName == "IMG")
    {
        eSrc = eSrc.parentNode;
    }

    if (eType == "mouseover")
    {
        eSrc.className = "toolbar-button-hover";
```

```
        }
        else if (eType == "mouseout")
        {
            eSrc.className = "toolbar-button";
        }
        else if (eType == "click")
        {
            eSrc.className = "toolbar-button";
            window.location.href = eSrc.getAttribute("href");
        }
    }

    function createToolbar(sName, aButtons)
    {
        var toolbar = document.createElement("div");
        toolbar.id  = sName;
        toolbar.className = "toolbar";

        for (var i = 0; i < aButtons.length; i++)
        {
            var thisButton = aButtons[i];

            var button = document.createElement("span");
            var icon = document.createElement("img");

            button.setAttribute("href", thisButton[1]);
            button.className = "toolbar-button";

            button.onclick = button_mouseHandler;
            button.onmouseover = button_mouseHandler;
            button.onmouseout = button_mouseHandler;

            icon.src = thisButton[0];
            icon.className = "toolbar-icon";

            button.appendChild(icon);
            toolbar.appendChild(button);
        }

        document.body.appendChild(toolbar);
    }

var myToolbar = new Array();

myToolbar[0]    = new Array();
myToolbar[0][0] = "img/green.gif";
myToolbar[0][1] = "javascript: alert('You Clicked the Green Button!')";

myToolbar[1]    = new Array();
myToolbar[1][0] = "img/blue.gif";
myToolbar[1][1] = "javascript: alert('You Clicked the Blue Button!')";

myToolbar[2]    = new Array();
myToolbar[2][0] = "img/red.gif";
myToolbar[2][1] = "http://www.wrox.com";
```

```
    </script>
</head>
<body onload="createToolbar('myToolbar', myToolbar)">

</body>
</html>
```

Save this file as `toolbar_xb.htm`. Open it in IE, Firefox, and/or Opera. You should see the same thing you saw in the previous two examples.

How It Works

As in the Firefox and Opera example, we'll look only at the changes made to this version; those changes are confined to the `button_mouseHandler()` function. Because this is a cross-browser example, the code must cater to both the IE and DOM event models.

```
function button_mouseHandler(e)
{
    var eType;
    var eSrc;

    if (window.event)
    {
        eType = event.type;
        eSrc = event.srcElement;
    }
    else
    {
        eType = e.type;
        eSrc = e.target;
    }

    if (eSrc.tagName == "IMG")
    {
        eSrc = eSrc.parentNode;
    }

    if (eType == "mouseover")
    {
        eSrc.className = "toolbar-button-hover";
    }
    else if (eType == "mouseout")
    {
        eSrc.className = "toolbar-button";
    }
    else if (eType == "click")
    {
        eSrc.className = "toolbar-button";
        window.location.href = eSrc.getAttribute("href");
    }
}
```

This new code uses object detection to assign `eType` and `eSrc` their proper values. When this process is complete, the function behaves as it did in the previous examples.

This example hasn't been very large, or overly complex. However, the concepts and problems reflect a difficulty DHTML authors face all the time: working with two different event models and using CSS workarounds to ensure that the DHTML displays correctly in both types of browser. If you're aware of this difficulty, dealing with it really isn't too hard.

Summary

This chapter has featured quite a few diversions and digressions, but these were necessary to demonstrate the position and importance of the Document Object Model in JavaScript.

This chapter covered the following points:

❑   You started by outlining four of the main standards — HTML, ECMAScript, XML, and XHTML — and examined the relationships among them. You saw that a common aim emerging from these standards was to provide guidelines for coding HTML web pages. Those guidelines in turn benefited the Document Object Model, making it possible to access and manipulate any item on the web page using script if web pages were coded according to these guidelines.

❑   You examined the Document Object Model and saw that it offered a browser- and language-independent means of accessing the items on a web page, and that it resolved some of the problems that dogged older browsers. You saw how the DOM represents the HTML document as a tree structure and how it is possible for you to navigate through the tree to different elements and use the properties and methods it exposes in order to access the different parts of the web page.

❑   Although sticking to the standards provides the best method for manipulating the contents of the web page, none of the main browsers yet implements it in its entirety. You looked at the most up-to-date examples and saw how they provided a strong basis for the creation of dynamic, interoperable web pages because of their support of the DOM.

Exercise Questions

Suggested solutions to these questions can be found in Appendix A.

Question 1

Here's some HTML code that creates a web page. Re-create this page, using JavaScript to generate the HTML using only DOM objects, properties, and methods. Test your code in IE, Firefox, Opera, and Safari (if you have it) to make sure it works in them.

Hint: Comment each line as you write it to keep track of where you are in the tree structure, and create a new variable for every element on the page (for example, not just one for each of the TD cells, but nine variables).

```html
<html>
<head>
</head>
<body>
    <table>
        <thead>
            <tr>
                <td>Car</td>
                <td>Top Speed</td>
                <td>Price</td>
            </tr>
        </thead>
        <tbody>
            <tr>
                <td>Chevrolet</td>
                <td>120mph</td>
                <td>$10,000</td>
            </tr>
            <tr>
                <td>Pontiac</td>
                <td>140mph</td>
                <td>$20,000</td>
            </tr>
        </tbody>
    </table>
</body>
</html>
```

Question 2

Augment your DOM web page so that the table has a border and only the headings of the table (that is, not the column headings) are center-aligned. Again, test your code in IE, Firefox, Opera, and Safari (if you have it).

Hint: Add any extra code to the end of the script code you have already written.

JavaScript and XML

In the previous chapter you took a brief look at Extensible Markup Language (XML). Like HTML, it consists of elements. You saw that its purpose was to describe data rather than to actually display information in any particular format, which is the purpose of HTML. There is nothing special about XML. It is just plain text with the addition of some XML tags enclosed in angle brackets. You can use any software that can handle plain text to create and edit XML.

In this chapter you'll be covering the fundamentals of XML. It's a huge topic and deserves a whole book to do it justice, so this'll be a taster to get you started. Before you get down to coding, let's look at what XML can be used for.

What Can XML Do for Me?

Developers like XML for a variety of reasons. It makes many web development tasks much simpler than they would be with HTML, it also makes possible many tasks that HTML simply cannot do. It is a powerful language with the ability to mold to your specific needs.

XML is a data-centric language. It not only contains data, but it describes those data by using semantic element names. The document's structure also plays a part in the description. Unlike HTML, XML is not a formatting language; in fact, a properly structured XML document is devoid of any formatting elements. This concept is often referred to as the "separation of content and style," and is part of XML's success, as it makes the language simple and easy to use.

For example, you can use XML as a data store like a database. In fact, XML is well suited for large and complex documents because the data are structured; you design the structure and implement it using your own elements to describe the data enclosed in the element. The ability to define the structure and elements used in an XML document is what makes XML a *self-describing* language. That is, the elements describe the data they contain, and the structure describes how data are related to each other.

Another method in which XML has become useful is in retrieving data from remote servers. Probably the most widely known applications of this method are the RSS and Atom formats for web syndication. These XML documents, and others like them, contain information readily available to anyone. Web sites or programs can connect to the remote server, download a copy of the XML document, and use the information however needed.

A third, and extremely helpful, application of XML, is the ability to transfer data between incompatible systems. An XML document is a plain text document; therefore, all operating systems can read and write to XML files. The only major requirement is an application that understands the XML language and the document structure. For example, Microsoft recently released details on Microsoft Office Open XML, the file format used in Microsoft Office 2007. The files themselves are actually Zip files. However, any program written to read the XML files contained in the Zip file can display the data with no problem; it doesn't matter whether they were written under Windows XP, Mac OS X, any flavor of Linux, or any other operating system.

The Basics of XML

The advantage of XML over other document formats is that it specifies a protocol by which a document can describe itself. For example, a document might describe itself as a particular chapter in a book, containing the chapter's title, the sections, and the text, which is broken into different paragraphs. In order to write XML documents, you need to have a firm grasp on the fundamentals of the language.

Understanding XML Syntax

XML is a simple language with simple syntax and rules. By following the guidelines in this section, you'll create XML documents with little trouble.

XML Is a Well-Formed Language

Well-formed documents are those that comply with the rules of XML syntax. The requirements include, but are not limited to, the following:

❑   All elements must have an opening and closing tag, or a closing slash in the empty element.

❑   Elements must be nested correctly within the root element.

It is important to make well-formed XML documents because every XML parser is built according to the XML specification. It is an unforgiving language, meaning that any XML parser that follows the standard specification will never display documents that are not well formed.

Close the Tags!

The XML specification requires that all elements must have an opening tag and a closing tag. This is one way in which XML is unlike HTML, in which several elements have no closing tag (like <img> and <br>). So when you open a tag, you need to close it when it contains the data that you want it to.

```
<?xml version="1.0" encoding="iso-8859-1"?>

<myElement>Some data go here</myElement>
```

This example shows a simple XML document. The first line contains the XML declaration. This tells the application that is going to use this XML document which version of the specification the document uses. Right now there is only version 1.0 (version 1.1 is coming soon). Note that the line starts with <? and ends with ?>. These are the delimiters that indicate there is an XML declaration instruction between them. In this case, the instruction tells which version of XML the document uses. The declaration also states the character encoding used in the document. In this case the document conforms to the 1.0 specification of XML and uses the ISO-8859-1 (Latin-1/West European) character set.

XML declarations have no closing tag.

After the declaration, you see a couple of tags enclosing some text. The first tag is the opening tag for the myElement element, and the second is the closing tag for the same element. XML is a case-sensitive language; therefore, make sure the closing tag exactly matches the opening tag.

A well-formed element does not need to have any data between the opening and closing tags. Take the following line as an example:

```
<myElement></myElement>
```

This, too, is a well-formed XML element, even though it contains no data. This is referred to as an *empty element*. In elements such as these, use a shorthand version of closing the tag.

```
<myElement />
```

This line of code, as far as an XML parser is concerned, is identical to the previous line of code. So when you have empty elements, you can use the shorthand way of closing them.

There is no rule in XML that states an element must contain data.

Correctly Nest Elements

For years, browser makers have built their Web browsers to render and display pages that are not well formed. Not that it's a problem, as the Web has grown by leaps and bounds because of the everyman/-woman. However, if you loaded these HTML documents into an XML parser, it would throw error after error. The largest culprit would most likely be incorrectly nested elements.

XML requires properly nested elements, they cannot overlap as they can in HTML. For example, the following XML document is not well formed:

```
<?xml version="1.0" encoding="iso-8859-1"?>

<myDogs>
    <name>Morgan</name>
    <name>Molly
</myDogs></name>
```

This XML is almost well formed; however, the second <name/> element's closing tag comes after the <myDogs/> closing tag. This is an example of overlapping elements and will make any XML document invalid. Close an open element before you close its parent element.

If you follow these two rules, you'll have an easy time when writing XML documents. And speaking of which, let's delve more into XML's syntax.

Document Structure

XML was designed to provide a means of storing data in a structured way. All XML documents must have at least one element. The first element in the document is called the *root element* or the *document element*. No matter which name you use, both terms mean the same thing. All XML documents must have a root element, and they cannot have more than one.

Think of an operating system's directory structure. Everything begins with the root directory (C:). This main directory can have many subdirectories, and those subdirectories can have many more subdirectories, and so on.

An XML document is very similar. You start with the root element and build the document from there. For example, look at the following XML document:

```
<?xml version="1.0" encoding="iso-8859-1"?>

<myDogs>
    <name>Morgan</name>
    <name>Molly</name>
</myDogs>
```

The first element, `<myDogs/>`, is the root element of the document. From here, two elements called `<name/>` are added. You could even go farther and add more data (and elements) until you're satisfied with the document. There is no limit to the amount of elements you can use in a document; just remember that there can be only one root element, and that the document builds off of that element.

XML Elements

XML uses elements to describe the data enclosed in the document. So when you create your own XML documents, make sure that the elements properly describe the data enclosed in them. Let's expand upon the dogs document.

```
<?xml version="1.0" encoding="iso-8859-1"?>

<myDogs>
    <dog breed="Labrador Retriever">
        <name>Morgan</name>
    </dog>
    <dog breed="Labrador Retriever">
        <name>Molly</name>
    </dog>
</myDogs>
```

This document has some new information, and the document structure has changed as a result. Despite the changes, the document is still well formed, as each opening tag has a corresponding closing tag, and the elements are nested correctly.

The very first line of an XML document contains the XML declaration. In this case the document conforms to the 1.0 specification of XML and uses the ISO-8859-1 (Latin-1/West European) character set.

The next line describes the start tag of the root element of the document. In this example, it's saying "This document contains information on my dogs."

```
<myDogs>
```

The next line opens the <dog/> element, a child of the root element. This element contains information regarding one of the dogs.

```
<dog breed="Labrador Retriever">
    <name>Morgan</name>
</dog>
```

Obviously, this information has changed from the simpler XML document in the previous section. Adding the <dog/> element enables you to add as much information as you want for each dog.

Also added to the <dog/> element is the breed attribute, which contains the particular breed of the dog. Elements can have attributes, which are values passed to the application (in this case the Internet browser such as IE or Netscape) but are not part of the element content. Attributes are contained in the opening tag of the element and their values must be enclosed with quotes. Some people use attributes in place of creating a child node.

Lastly, the <dog/> element contains one child element called name, which holds the name of the dog.

The next <dog/> element contains the same type of data:

```
<dog breed="Labrador Retriever">
    <name>Molly</name>
</dog>
```

And finally, the last line defines the end of the root element.

```
</myDogs>
```

The elements (and attributes) in this document properly describe the data they enclose. You can look at this document and have no problem deciphering what the data are, and how they relate to the elements.

Character Data

Character data may be any legal (Unicode) character with the exception of <. The < character is reserved for the start of an opening or closing tag.

XML also provides a few useful entity references to clarify whether you are specifying character data or markup. Specifically, XML provides the following entity references:

Actual Character	Entity Reference
>	&gt;
<	&lt;
&	&amp;
'	&apos;

Obviously, the `&lt;` entity reference is useful for character data. The other entity references can be used within markup where there could be confusion, such as the following:

```
<statement value = "She said, "Don't go there!"" />
```

This line should be written as follows:

```
<statement value = "She said, &quot;Don&apos;t go there!&quot;" />
```

CDATA

A pretty good rule of thumb is to consider anything outside of an element's tags to be character data and anything inside the tags to be markup. But, unfortunately, in one case this is not true. In the special case of CDATA blocks, all element tags and entity references are ignored by an XML processor, which treats them just like any old character data.

CDATA blocks have been provided as a convenience measure when you want to include large blocks of special characters as character data but do not want to have to use entity references. What if you wanted to write about an XML document in XML? Consider the following example:

```
<example>
    &lt;document&gt;
        &lt;name&gt;mrs smith&lt;/name&gt;
        &lt;email&gt;mrssmith@herdomain.com&lt;/email&gt;
    &lt;/document&gt;
</example>
```

As this code demonstrates, such a task requires the use of entity references for all opening and closing tags, which looks messy and makes the code tricky to read.

To avoid this inconvenience, use a CDATA block to specify that all character data should be considered character data whether or not they "look like" an opening/closing tag or entity reference, like this:

```
<example>
    <![CDATA[
        <document>
            <name>mrs smith</name>
            <email>mrssmith@herdomain.com</email>
        </document>
    ]]>
</example>
```

Comments

Not only will you sometimes want to include elements that you want the XML processor to ignore (that is, display as character data) in XML documents, but sometimes you will want to put into the document character data that you want the XML processor to ignore (that is, not display at all). This is where comments come in.

Note that comments will be displayed when you use the default style sheet. This type of text is called comment text.

XML comments are similar to HTML comments. In HTML, comments are specified with the `<!--` and `-->` syntax. In XML, comments are created in just the same way! So the following would be a valid XML comment:

```
<!--List Audioslave -->
<name>Chris Cornell</name>
<name>Tom Morello</name>
<name>Timmy C</name>
<name>Brad Wilk</name>
<!-- End the names -->
```

Keep a few rules in mind when using comments in XML documents. First, never have a hyphen or a double hyphen (- or --) within the text of the comment; these might be confusing to the XML processor. Second, never place a comment within an opening or closing tag. Thus, the following code would be poorly formed XML:

```
<name <!--The name --> >Tom Morello</name>
```

Likewise, never place a comment inside an entity declaration and never place a comment before the XML declaration.

XML declarations must always be the first line in any XML document.

Use comments to comment out groups of elements, if necessary. Thus, in the following case, all the names will be ignored except for `Brad Wilk`:

```
<!-- don't show these names
<name>Chris Cornell </name>
<name>Tom Morello </name>
<name>Timmy C</name>
-->
<name>Brad Wilk</name>
```

When commenting groups of elements, make sure that the remaining XML is well formed.

Creating an XML Document

It's time to put all this theory into practice. XML is all about data, so data are needed for the example, and you'll use information about my dogs. Here are some data fields to include:

❑   Name

❑   Age

❑   Breed

❑   Full blood

❑   Coat color

Using these data fields, it's possible to create the document's structure.

```
<?xml version="1.0" encoding="iso-8859-1"?>

<myDogs>
    <dog breed="">
        <name></name>
        <age>
            <years></years>
            <months></months>
        </age>
        <fullBlood></fullBlood>
        <color></color>
    </dog>
</myDogs>
```

What's listed here is the basic document structure; the data will be added later. Let's discuss the elements listed here.

Remember, elements should be descriptive of the data they will contain. Also keep in mind that XML is case-sensitive. An element's closing tag should exactly match its corresponding opening tag.

```
<?xml version="1.0" encoding="iso-8859-1"?>
```

As you already know, the first line is the XML declaration, telling the XML parser that you're using version 1.0 and the ISO-8859-1 (Latin-1/West European) character set. Next comes the root element, `<myDogs/>`.

```
<myDogs>
</myDogs>
```

This element is descriptive of the document; therefore, anyone who sees this document can easily infer that the data contained in it relate to my dogs. And since this is the root element, all other tags are contained within it.

```
<myDogs>
    <dog breed="">
    </dog>
</myDogs>
```

The `<dog/>` element is a direct child to `<myDogs/>`, and it contains data specific to an individual dog. It has one attribute, called `breed`, whose value matches that of the specific breed of this dog. The next elements, children of `<dog/>`, contain information that is even more specific:

```
<myDogs>
    <dog breed="">
        <name></name>
        <age>
            <years></years>
            <months></months>
        </age>
        <fullBlood></fullBlood>
        <color></color>
    </dog>
</myDogs>
```

The `<name/>` element contains the dog's name, and the `<age/>` element expresses the dog's age. Because ages typically are counted in months and years, `<age/>` contains two child elements, `<years/>` and `<months/>`. Next, the `<fullBlood/>` element contains one of two Boolean values: yes or no. Naturally, if the dog is a purebreed, the value contained in this element is yes. And last, the `<color/>` element will contain the color of the dog's coat.

What you have here is a well-formed XML document structure, but let's take it a step further and see how you can make it valid.

Document Type Definition

If you make a layout mistake in building your XML file, the browser will tell you where things don't match up; it will not inform you if the mistake is related to the actual data. We are all human and prone to mistakes (not often, but they do happen!).

This section introduces a new term: *valid*. XML documents can be well formed or they can be valid, or they can be both. Valid documents are well-formed documents that also conform to a Document Type Definition (DTD). A DTD provides the structure for an XML document. Look at an e-mail; it has structure. The e-mail has a To: field, a Subject: field, and a body. There are even optional CC: and BCC: fields. The e-mail program fills in the From: field, and the date and time sent, for us, but they are there. The structure is so familiar you don't really notice it, unless it gets messed up in the transmission! This structure makes e-mail easy to read. If a program attempts to process this e-mail (which is data, when you get down to it), it must know the e-mail's structure in order to parse it. Knowing the structure means being able to parse it correctly each and every time, time after time.

DTDs lay out the way an XML file is to be marked up. Anyone following this DTD can process an XML file from others who have also built their XML files to the same DTD. Following a DTD also enables you to trap errors if a file that is not well formed or that has the wrong data is passed to the application.

Enough about what a DTD can do. Let's build one and see.

Creating the First DTD File

The purposes of a DTD are as follows:

❑   Declare what the markup is

❑   Declare what the markup means

But how do you build one? There is an entire specification on how to write DTDs. This section only touches on some of the items that can be used in a DTD.

Open any text editor (Notepad in Windows works just fine) and start a new file, name it `mydogs.dtd`, and follow along. Here is what the DTD for the `myDogs` document will look like:

```
<!-- The myDogs DTD -->
<!ELEMENT myDogs (dog+)>

<!-- The <dog/> section -->
```

```
<!ELEMENT dog (name, age, fullBlood, color)>
   <!ATTLIST dog breed CDATA #REQUIRED>
   <!ELEMENT name (#PCDATA)>
   <!ELEMENT age (years, months)>
       <!-- The <age/> section-->
       <!ELEMENT months (#PCDATA)>
       <!ELEMENT years (#PCDATA)>
       <!-- END age section-->
   <!ELEMENT fullBlood (#PCDATA)>
   <!ELEMENT color (#PCDATA)>
   <!-- END <dog/> section -->
<!-- END of myDogs DTD-->
```

The first line, which follows, is a comment. Anything between the `<!--` and `-->` will be ignored.

```
<!-- The myDogs DTD -->
```

It's always good to comment your code. All element declarations follow the following format:

<!ELEMENT elementName (content)>

This declaration is used to declare the elements used in the document. To define the root element, use myDogs as the element name. Under myDogs are multiple `<dog/>` elements, thus the + symbol.

```
<!ELEMENT myDogs (dog+)>
```

Next is another comment to indicate that what follows is the definition for the `<dog/>` element.

```
<!-- The <dog/> section -->
```

If you refer back to the desired XML structure, you'll see that the `<dog/>` element has an attribute called breed and contains the following elements: name, age, fullBlood, and color.

```
<!ELEMENT dog (name, age, fullBlood, color)>
```

The commas between each child name and the next indicate that `<dog/>` has strict ordering. If any element is out of order, the XML document is not valid. Because age has sub-elements, they will be defined later. Next, define the breed attribute.

```
<!ATTLIST dog breed CDATA #REQUIRED>
```

Defining attributes are similar to elements, and follow the following pattern:

<!ATTLIST elementName attributeName attributeType defaultValue>

There are several attribute types, but the most common is CDATA. For the default value, #REQUIRED is used to tell the XML parser that the breed attribute must be used in every `<dog/>` element. There are also other possible default values to use, but #REQUIRED best fits the document's needs. (After all, you want to know what type of dog you have, don't you?)

Use # in #REQUIRED (and in the following code, in #PCDATA) to prevent these words from being interpreted as element names.

Here is the start of the actual element type definitions. These follow the same rules we just went over.

```
<!ELEMENT name (#PCDATA)>
<!ELEMENT age (months, years)>
    <!-- The <age/> section-->
    <!ELEMENT years (#PCDATA)>
    <!ELEMENT months (#PCDATA)>
    <!-- END age section-->
<!ELEMENT fullBlood (#PCDATA)>
<!ELEMENT color (#PCDATA)>
    <!-- END <dog/> section -->
<!-- END of myDogs DTD-->
```

That's it, and this is the simplest way to write the DTD. When you write the XML document, you'll reference this DTD by using the `<!DOCTYPE>` declaration in the XML document.

Bring on the Data

You now have the means to make a well-formed XML document valid. Let's add some actual data to it. The following table shows the data to use:

Data Fields	Dog 1	Dog 2	Dog 3
Name	Morgan	Molly	Casey
Age	10 months	8 years	6 years
Breed	Labrador Retriever	Labrador Retriever	Pomeranian
Full Blood	Yes	Yes	Yes
Color	Chocolate	Yellow	Brown

Once again, open any plain-text editor, and create this XML document:

```
<?xml version="1.0" encoding="iso-8859-1"?>

<!DOCTYPE myDogs SYSTEM "myDogs.dtd">

<myDogs>
    <dog breed="Labrador Retriever">
        <name>Morgan</name>
        <age>
            <years>0</years>
            <months>10</months>
        </age>
        <fullBlood>yes</fullBlood>
        <color>chocolate</color>
    </dog>
```

```
    <dog breed="Labrador Retriever">
        <name>Molly</name>
        <age>
            <years>8</years>
            <months>11</months>
        </age>
        <fullBlood>yes</fullBlood>
        <color>yellow</color>
    </dog>
    <dog breed="Pomeranian">
        <name>Casey</name>
        <age>
            <years>6</years>
            <months>2</months>
        </age>
        <fullBlood>yes</fullBlood>
        <color>brown</color>
    </dog>
</myDogs>
```

Save this file as `mydogs.xml`. There's not much of anything new in this XML document. The document structure matches that of the design made earlier in the section — but, of course, data now populate the `<dog/>` elements. There is, however, the addition of the DTD file you created earlier.

```
<!DOCTYPE myDogs SYSTEM "myDogs.dtd">
```

`!DOCTYPE` tells the XML parser that you are specifying a document to use as part of this file. Immediately following is `myDogs`, the name of the root element. `SYSTEM` lets the parser know that the document uses external DTD, a DTD found outside of the XML file. Finally, `"myDogs.dtd"` is the location of the DTD. If the DTD were on a web server, the URI would be a path like `http://myserver/myxmlstuff/myfile.dtd`. If the DTD and the XML file reside in the same folder, only the name of the DTD file needs referencing.

If you did not want an external DTD but instead wished to include the DTD within the XML file, this is what a portion of it would look like:

```
<?xml version="1.0" encoding="iso-8859-1"?>
```

```
<!DOCTYPE myDogs [
<!-- The myDogs DTD-->
<!ELEMENT myDogs (dog+)>
<!-- The dog section -->
<!ELEMENT dog (name, age, fullBlood, color)>
 <!ATTLIST dog breed CDATA #REQUIRED>
.........(rows removed for demonstration).........
<!-- END of myDogs DTD-->
]>
<myDogs>
```

Either way you go, an XML parser that can validate XML documents will consider this file to be valid.

Go ahead and load `mydogs.xml` into your browser. In IE 7, you should see a page like what is shown in Figure 14-1.

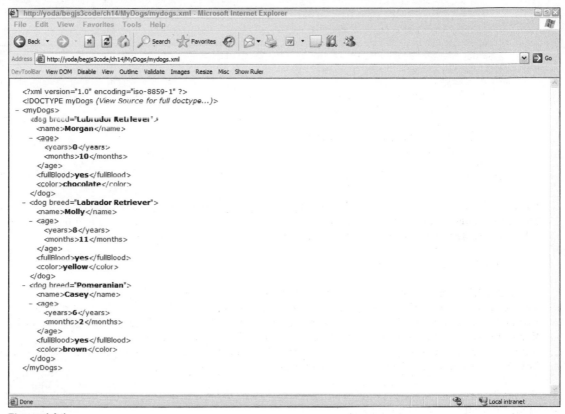

Figure 14-1

And in Firefox, the document should look like what is shown in Figure 14-2.

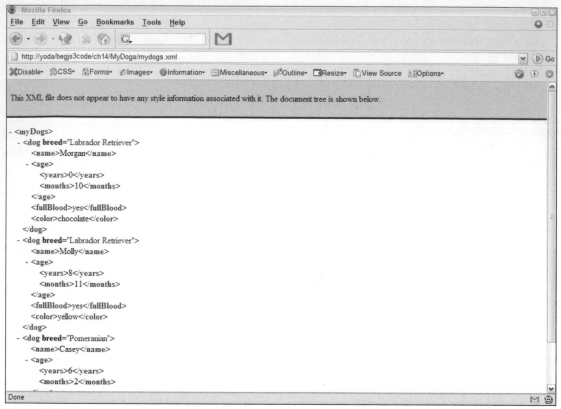

Figure 14-2

If a mistake is made in the XML documents, even a small one, the browser displays an error message like those in Figure 14-3 and Figure 14-4.

The deliberate mistake made here was the changing of the closing tag of `</myDogs>` to `</mydogs>`.

Because the browser can display XML, it checks the document to make sure it is well formed. Note that you may see a different look depending on which browser you use. Both IE and Firefox use XSLT, which formats the document to look as it does (you'll learn more about XSLT later in the chapter). Other browsers, however, do not.

> **Firefox cannot validate XML documents. IE doesn't validate documents by default, but you can download a tool to do so. It is called Internet Explorer Tools for Validating XML and Viewing XSLT Output and can be found at** www.
> `microsoft.com/downloads/details.`
> `aspx?FamilyID=d23c1d2c-1571-4d61-bda8-adf9f6849df9&DisplayLang=en.`

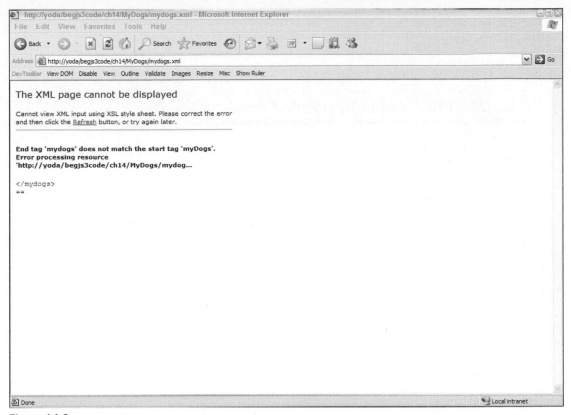

Figure 14-3

Here is something else: Look at the XML file in the browser (see Figure 14-1), and you'll see several red dashes next to some opening tags. Clicking these dashes closes the corresponding part of the document hierarchy. You can expand and collapse elements/nodes that have children. Therefore, it's possible to collapse an entire <dog/> element, or the whole document.

The reason you can display this XML file in IE5+ and Firefox and have it be colored and collapsible is that those browsers have a default style sheet built in for those XML files that don't reference a style sheet of their own. The use of a style sheet with XML is termed Extensible Stylesheet Language (XSL). (More on this later.)

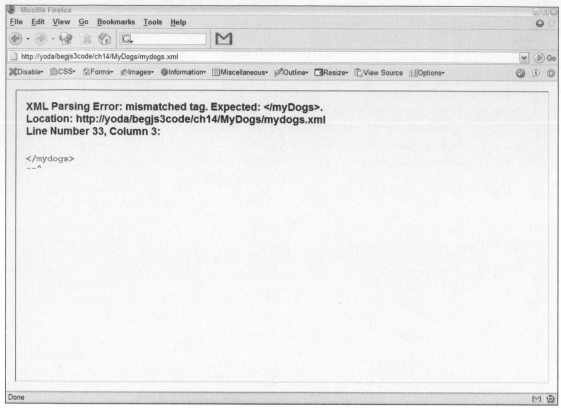

Figure 14-4

Altering the Look of XML

So far you have defined data and have seen those data displayed in a browser, but will your users like reading raw information? Nope, and this section shows you how to display and format it. This section doesn't teach Cascading Style Sheets (CSS); you saw the basics of CSS in Chapter 12. Instead, it covers only how to use them with XML.

Style Sheets and XML

Using CSS serves several purposes:

❑ It improves the clarity of the document when the document is displayed

❑ You can write once, use often

❑ One change can be reflected in many places

❑ You can present the same data in different ways for different purposes

With a style sheet, all the display rules are kept in one file that is linked to the source document. So you need to define what your display rules will be and associate them with your XML tags.

Create a new file called `mydogs.css` and type the following:

```
dog
{
 margin: 15px;
 display: block;
}


name
{
 display: block;
 font: bold 18pt Arial;
}

age
{
 display: block;
 color: red;
}

fullBlood
{
 display: none;
}

color
{
 display: block;
 font-style: italic;
}
```

Here some style rules are defined to match the elements that have data: dog, name, age, fullBlood, and color. Each one of these defined elements in the XML document contains data to be displayed. Just like you learned in Chapter 12, element names can be used in CSS to apply a style to that element.

What makes a style rule work are the properties, which are between the curly braces ({ }). Action is taken against the matched element. Starting with your dog element there are two properties: margin and display. The margin property is new. It's basically an edge that surrounds an element. If margin is 0px, then the edge around the element is zero pixels. If it is 15px, then there is a 15-pixel buffer around the element. In this case, the margin property emphasizes where a dog's data begins and ends.

The remainder of the elements, with the exception of fullBlood, are set to be placed on their own line with display: block (fullBlood is set to not be shown at all). The name element's text is bolded 18 point Arial. age's text is colored red, and the color element is italicized.

There are now two files: mydogs.xml and mydogs.css, but the XML file needs to reference the CSS file. Open mydogs.xml and add the following line after the XML declaration. Save the file as mydogs_css.xml.

```
<?xml-stylesheet href="mydogs.css" type="text/css"?>
```

When you open your XML file in IE, you should see the screen shown in Figure 14-5.

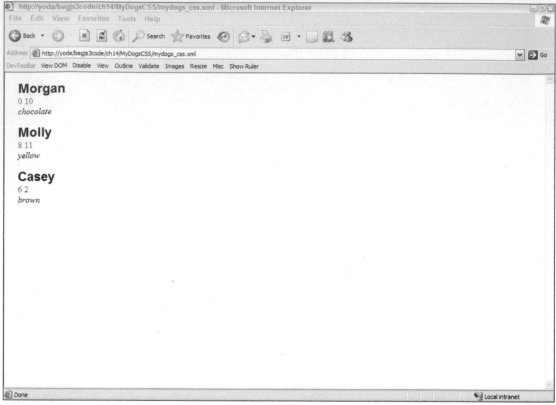

Figure 14-5

Figure 14-6 shows how the file looks in Firefox.

One thing you may notice is that the data are displayed, yet there's nothing really to describe what they're about. You, of course, know exactly what these data are, because you wrote it. CSS can make data look pretty, but what if you want more? It's a good thing you asked.

Extensible Stylesheet Language

The following sections show you how to use XSL to format XML documents using XSLT transformations.

What Is an XSLT Transformation?

XSLT is a template-based programming language that enables you to restructure your content to create the look you require. XSLT transformations can allow different kinds of software applications to exchange data. They can also be used to generate multiple views of the same source document to enable a web site's content to be displayed on myriad devices.

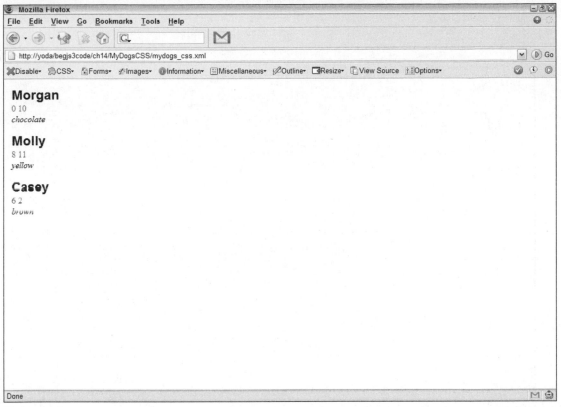

Figure 14-6

XSLT's elements and attributes provide a declarative programming language for processing XML data. You can use XSLT's vocabulary to grab content from other documents, create new elements and attributes, or, more commonly, some combination of the two.

An XSLT 1.0 transformation requires two starting documents (an XML source document and an XSLT style sheet) to produce a single result document (the upcoming XSLT 2.0 won't require this). The process begins when an XSLT style sheet is applied to an XML document to generate a result tree that is usually saved as an XML or HTML document (see Figure 14-7).

> *XSLT is a powerful language capable of turning XML into virtually any other text-based language or format.*

Like CSS, XSLT has a construct called a rule, and it is responsible for selecting elements to which to apply the transformation.

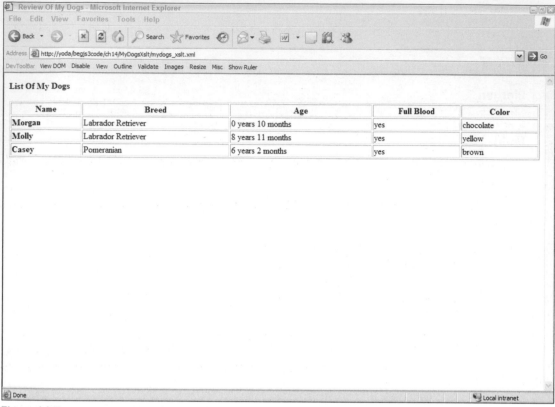

Figure 14-7

What Is a Template Rule?

An XSLT style sheet contains template rules that define the following:

❑ The criteria for selecting elements from the source tree

❑ Instructions for restructuring the selected content to create the result tree

Template rules are the key building blocks of XSLT transformations. A template rule has two parts: a pattern and a template. The pattern (usually an element name) is then matched against elements in the source tree to determine which nodes to select for processing. The template provides instructions for processing the selected content.

Each template rule constructs a result tree fragment of markup and content. An XSLT transformation's result tree is created when all the result tree fragments are combined in the order specified to form a completed whole.

Now let's go through an example style sheet and get into more detail about XSLT's template rules.

Example Template

The XSLT style sheet document needs to include an XML version declaration (just like any other XML document).

```
<?xml version="1.0" encoding="iso-8859-1"?>
```

Next, declare XSLT's namespace prefix. XSLT's namespace-prefixed elements enable an XSLT processor to distinguish them from other kinds of markup in the style sheet, such as the HTML elements contained within a template rule.

XSLT's namespace prefix is declared within the style sheet's root element, which is allowed to be either `xsl:stylesheet` or `xsl:transform`.

An XSLT version attribute should be included between the root element and the `xsl` namespace-prefix declaration.

The XSLT namespace is identified by its unique URI value (`http://www.w3.org/1999/XSL/Transform`), not by the `xsl` prefix.

```
<?xml version="1.0" encoding="ISO-8859-1"?>
<xsl:stylesheet version="1.0" xmlns:xsl="http://www.w3.org/1999/XSL/Transform">
```

Now that the namespace prefix is declared, you can go about creating some template rules that will transform the source glossary document into an HTML table. Much like an old-fashioned mail merge, the HTML markup fragments in the following template provide the XSLT processor with a model for restructuring the source content.

The `xsl:template` element is used to encapsulate template rules. The value of its `match` attribute contains an XPath statement that is used as a pattern to select source elements for processing. A document's first template almost always has a `match` value of `/`, which means the document root.

```
<?xml version="1.0" encoding="utf-8"?>

<xsl:stylesheet version="1.0"
    xmlns:xsl="http://www.w3.org/1999/XSL/Transform">

<xsl:template match="/">
    <html>
        <head>
            <title>Review Of My Dogs</title>
        </head>
        <body>
            <h4>List Of My Dogs</h4>
            <table width="100%" border="1">
                <thead>
                    <tr>
                        <th>Name</th>
                        <th>Breed</th>
                        <th>Age</th>
                        <th>Full Blood</th>
                        <th>Color</th>
```

```
                    </tr>
                </thead>
                <tbody>
                    <xsl:apply-templates/>
                </tbody>
            </table>
        </body>
    </html>
</xsl:template>
```

The `apply-templates` element signals an XSLT processor to look for other template rules and apply them at that point in the style sheet's structure. The results of each rule combine to form the result tree of the completed transformation.

The following template matches each <dog/> element in the XML document, and creates table rows until it runs out of <dog/> elements to process.

```
<xsl:template match="dog">
    <tr>
        <td>
            <strong>
                <xsl:value-of select="name" />
            </strong>
        </td>
        <td>
            <xsl:value-of select="@breed" />
        </td>
        <td>
            <xsl:apply-templates select="age" />
        </td>
        <td>
            <xsl:value-of select="fullBlood" />
        </td>
        <td>
            <xsl:value-of select="color" />
        </td>
    </tr>
</xsl:template>
```

Notice how the `value-of` element also uses a `select` attribute to choose the content from the source document you wish to use to create the result document. This code also uses the `<xsl:apply-templates />` directive; its `select` attribute contains `"age"`, so the XML parser knows to look for another template that selects the <age/> element.

```
<xsl:template match="age">
    <xsl:value-of select="years"/> years
    <xsl:value-of select="months"/> months
</xsl:template>
</xsl:stylesheet>
```

This template selects <age/> elements and retrieves the value of their children: <years/> and <months/>. To give these values meaning, this code adds the words years and months after the elements' values. This way anyone viewing this information will have no problem deciphering what these values represent.

The finished XSL file looks like this:

```
<?xml version="1.0" encoding="utf-8"?>

<xsl:stylesheet version="1.0"
    xmlns:xsl="http://www.w3.org/1999/XSL/Transform">

<xsl:template match="/">
    <html>
        <head>
            <title>Review Of My Dogs</title>
        </head>
        <body>
            <h4>List Of My Dogs</h4>
            <table width="100%" border="1">
                <thead>
                    <tr>
                        <th>Name</th>
                        <th>Breed</th>
                        <th>Age</th>
                        <th>Full Blood</th>
                        <th>Color</th>
                    </tr>
                </thead>
                <tbody>
                    <xsl:apply-templates/>
                </tbody>
            </table>
        </body>
    </html>
</xsl:template>

<xsl:template match="dog">
    <tr>
        <td>
            <strong>
                <xsl:value-of select="name" />
            </strong>
        </td>
        <td>
            <xsl:value-of select="@breed" />
        </td>
        <td>
            <xsl:apply-templates select="age" />
        </td>
```

```
            <td>
                <xsl:value-of select="fullBlood" />
            </td>
            <td>
                <xsl:value-of select="color" />
            </td>
        </tr>
</xsl:template>

<xsl:template match="age">
    <xsl:value-of select="years"/> years
    <xsl:value-of select="months"/> months
</xsl:template>

</xsl:stylesheet>
```

Be sure to save it as `mydogs.xsl`.

Linking an XML Document to Its XSL Style Sheet

Much as in the CSS example earlier in the chapter, associating an XSL style sheet to an XML document requires the use of an XML processing instruction. In fact, the syntax used is identical except for the value of the `type` attribute, which will be either `text/css` or `text/xsl`, depending on which flavor of style sheet is used.

Following are the two variations side by side, to illustrate the different values of the `type` attribute.

```
<?xml-stylesheet type="text/xsl" href="mydogs.xsl"?>
<?xml-stylesheet type="text/css" href="mydogs.css"?>
```

The correct placement of the style sheet declaration is within a document's prologue (after the XML declaration and before the root element).

Now alter the `mydogs_css.xml` file and tell it to refer to the `mydogs.xsl` file. Open up `mydogs_css.xml` and alter the top part as shown here:

```
<?xml version="1.0" encoding="iso-8859-1"?>

<?xml-stylesheet type="text/xsl" href="mydogs.xsl"?>

<!DOCTYPE myDogs SYSTEM "mydogs.dtd">

<myDogs>
```

```
<dog>
...
....
```

Apart from deleting the reference to your mydogs.css file and adding a reference to the mydogs.xsl file, you leave the file the same. Save it as mydogs_xslt.xml and load it into IE, and you'll see the page shown in Figure 14-8.

Figure 14-9 shows what it looks like in Firefox.

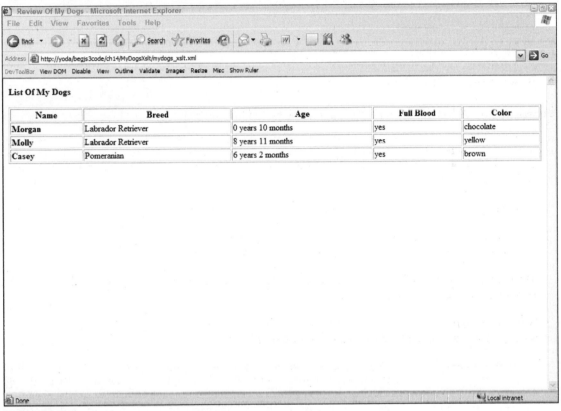

Figure 14-8

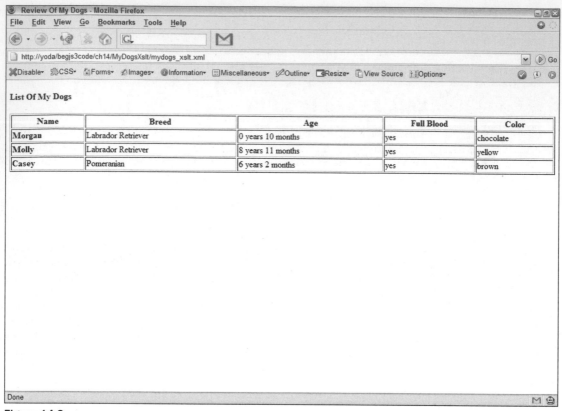

Figure 14-9

Manipulating XML with JavaScript

The good news is that you learned most of what you need to manipulate XML in a web browser from the previous chapter, when you learned about manipulating the DOM. The bad news is that although browser support for XML JavaScript is getting better and better with each new browser release, it's still far from perfect and a lot of cross-browser issues still exist. Because of this, this section will concentrate on script cross-compatible with IE5.5+ (on Windows; the Mac version of IE doesn't support XML), Firefox, and Opera, because these browsers have much improved XML JavaScript support.

The first task is to read the XML document. This is where the most cross-browser problems are located because IE and the other browsers have different ways of reading documents, Firefox and Opera being the more standards-compliant and IE being the easier to use and more comprehensive. The good news is that once the XML document is loaded, the differences between IE, Firefox, and Opera are smaller, although Microsoft has added a lot of useful (but nonstandard) extensions to its implementation.

> Safari 2 does have some XML support, but its implementation for loading XML documents is much different from that of IE, Firefox, and Opera, and requires the use of the XMLHttpRequest object covered in Chapter 16.

Retrieving an XML File in IE

Internet Explorer relies upon the ActiveXObject() object and the MSXML library to fetch and open XML documents. A variety of ActiveX objects are available for scripting; to create an ActiveX object, simply call the ActiveXObject() constructor and pass a string containing the version of the ActiveX object you wish to create.

```
var xmlDoc = new ActiveXObject("Microsoft.XMLDOM");
xmlDoc.load("myfile.xml");
```

This code creates an XML DOM object that enables you to load and manipulate XML documents by using the version string "Microsoft.XMLDOM". When the XML DOM object is created, load an XML document by using the load() method. This code loads a fictitious file called myfile.xml.

There are multiple versions of the Microsoft MSXML library, with each newer version offering more features and better performance than the one before. However, the user's computer must have these versions installed before you can use them, and the version selection code can become complex. Thankfully, Microsoft recommends checking for only two versions of MSXML. Their version strings are as follows:

❑   Msxml2.DOMDocument.6.0

❑   Msxml2.DOMDocument.3.0

You want to use the latest version possible when creating an XML DOM, and the following function does this:

```
function createDocument()
{
    //Temporary DOM object.
    var xmlDoc;

    //Create the DOM object for IE
    if (window.ActiveXObject)
    {
        var versions =
        [
            "Msxml2.DOMDocument.6.0",
            "Msxml2.DOMDocument.3.0"
        ];

        for (var i = 0; i < versions.length; i++)
        {
```

```
            try
            {
                xmlDoc = new ActiveXObject(versions[i]);
                return xmlDoc;
            }
            catch (error)
            {
                //do nothing here
            }
        }
    }
    //no version was found; return null
    return null;
}
```

This code defines the createDocument() function. Its first line creates the xmlDoc variable. This is a temporary variable used in the creation of an XML DOM. The next line of code is an if statement, and it checks to see if the browser is IE by seeing if window.ActiveXObject exists. If the condition is true, then an array called versions is created, and the two MSXML versions are added as elements to the array.

```
var versions =
[
    "Msxml2.DOMDocument.6.0",
    "Msxml2.DOMDocument.3.0"
];
```

The order in which they're added is important; you want to always check for the latest version first, so the version strings are added with the newest at index 0.

Next is a for loop to loop through the elements of the versions array. Inside the loop is a try...catch statement.

```
for (var i = 0; i < versions.length; i++)
{
    try
    {
        xmlDoc = new ActiveXObject(versions[i]);
        return xmlDoc;
    }
    catch (error)
    {
        //do nothing here
    }
}
```

If the ActiveXObject object creation fails in the try block, then code execution drops to the catch block. Nothing happens at this point: The loop iterates to the next index in versions and attempts to create another ActiveXObject object with the other MSXML version strings. If every attempt fails, then the loop exits and returns null. Use the createDocument() function like this:

```
var xmlDoc = createDocument();
```

By using this function, you can create the latest MSXML XML DOM object easily.

Determining When the XML File Has Loaded

Before you actually attempt to manipulate the XML file, first make sure it has completely loaded into the client's browser cache. Otherwise, you're rolling the dice each time the page is viewed and running the risk of a JavaScript error being thrown whenever the execution of your script precedes the complete downloading of the XML file in question. Fortunately, there are ways to detect the current download state of an XML file.

The async property denotes whether the browser should wait for the specified XML file to fully load before proceeding with the download of the rest of the page. This property, whose name stands for *asynchronous*, is set by default to true, meaning the browser will not wait on the XML file before rendering everything else that follows. Setting this property to false instructs the browser to load the file first and then, and only then, to load the rest of the page.

```
var xmlDoc = createDocument();
xmlDoc.async = false; //Download XML file first, then load rest of page.
xmlDoc.load("myfile.xml");
```

The simplicity of the async property is not without its flaw. When you set this property to false, IE will stall the page until it makes contact and has fully received the specified XML file. When the browser is having trouble connecting and/or downloading the file, the page is left hanging like a monkey on a branch. This is where the onreadystatechange event handler and readyState property can help (as long as the async property is true).

The readyState property of IE exists for XML objects and many HTML objects, and returns the current loading status of the object. The following table shows the four possible return values.

Return Values for the readyState Property	Description
1	The object is initializing, but no data are being read (loading).
2	Data are being loaded into the object and parsed (loaded).
3	Parts of the object's data have been read and parsed, so the object model is available. However, the complete object data are not yet ready (interactive).
4	The object has been loaded, its content parsed (completed).

The value you're interested in here is the last one, 4, which indicates the object has fully loaded. To use the readyState property, assign a function to handle the readystatechange event, which fires every time the readyState changes.

```
//The function to handle the onreadystatechange event.
function xmlDoc_readyStateChange()
{
    //Check for the readyState. If it's 4, it's loaded!
    if (xmlDoc.readyState == 4)
    {
        alert("XML file loaded!");
    }
}

var xmlDoc = createDocument();
xmlDoc.onreadystatechange = xmlDoc_readyStateChange;

xmlDoc.load("myfile.xml");
```

This code first creates a function called xmlDoc_readyStateChange(). Use this function to handle the readystatechange event. Inside the function, check the readyState property to see if its value is equal to 4. If it is, then the XML file is completely loaded and the alert text "XML file loaded!" is displayed. Next, create the XML DOM object and assign the xmlDoc_readyStateChange() function to the onreadystatechange event handler. The last line of code initiates the loading of myfile.xml.

Retrieving an XML File in Firefox and Opera

Loading an XML document in Firefox and Opera is a little different from doing the same thing in IE, as these browsers use a more standards-centric approach. Creating an XML DOM doesn't require the use of an add-on as it does in IE; the DOM is a part of the browser and JavaScript implementation.

```
var xmlDoc = document.implementation.createDocument("","",null);
xmlDoc.load("myfile.xml");
```

This code creates an empty DOM by using the createDocument() method of the document.implementation object. After the DOM object is created, use the load() method to load an XML document; it is supported by Firefox and Opera as well.

Determining When the File is Loaded

Much like IE, Firefox and Opera support the async property, which allows the file to be loaded asynchronously or synchronously. The behavior of loading synchronously is the same in these browsers as in IE. However, things change when you want to load a file asynchronously.

Not surprisingly, Firefox and Opera use a different implementation from IE when it comes to checking the load status of an XML file. In fact, these two browsers do not enable you to check the status with something like the readyState property. Instead, Firefox and Opera expose an onload event handler that executes when the file is loaded and the DOM object is ready to use.

```
//Handles the onload event
function xmlDoc_load()
{
    alert("XML is loaded!");
}

var xmlDoc = document.implementation.createDocument("","",null);
xmlDoc.onload = xmlDoc_load;
xmlDoc.load("myfile.xml");
```

This code loads the fictitious file myfile.xml in asynchronous mode. When the load process completes, the load event fires and calls xmlDoc_load(), which then shows the text XML is loaded! to the user.

Cross-Browser XML File Retrieval

As you can see, the different ways of creating XML DOM objects require you to seek a cross-browser solution. You can easily do this with object detection to determine which browser is in use. In fact, you can easily edit the createDocument() function to include Firefox and Opera support. Look at the following code:

```
function createDocument()
{
    //Temporary DOM object.
    var xmlDoc;

    //Create the DOM object for IE
    if (window.ActiveXObject)
    {
        var versions =
        [
            "Msxml2.DOMDocument.6.0",
            "Msxml2.DOMDocument.3.0"
        ];

        for (var i = 0; i < versions.length; i++)
        {
            try
            {
                xmlDoc = new ActiveXObject(versions[i]);
                return xmlDoc;
            }
            catch (error)
            {
                //do nothing here
            }
        }
    }
    //Create the DOM for Firefox and Opera
    else if (document.implementation && document.implementation.createDocument)
    {
        xmlDoc = document.implementation.createDocument("","",null);
        return xmlDoc;
    }
```

```
        //no version was found; return null
        return null;
}
```

The code highlighted in gray is the only new code added to the function, and it creates an XML DOM for Firefox and Opera with `document.implementation.createDocument()` and returns the DOM object to the caller. Using the function is exactly as you saw earlier: Now it works across browsers.

```
var xmlDoc = createDocument();
xmlDoc.async = false;
xmlDoc.load("myfile.xml");
```

Displaying a Daily Message

Now that you know how to load XML documents, let's jump right into building your first XML-enabled JavaScript application, a message-of-the-day display.

To begin, use the following simple XML file. You'll retrieve and display the daily message using DHTML. Save it as `motd.xml`.

```xml
<?xml version="1.0"?>

<messages>
    <daily>Today is Sunday.</daily>
    <daily>Today is Monday.</daily>
    <daily>Today is Tuesday.</daily>
    <daily>Today is Wednesday.</daily>
    <daily>Today is Thursday.</daily>
    <daily>Today is Friday.</daily>
    <daily>Today is Saturday.</daily>
</messages>
```

As you can see, this basic XML file is populated with a different message for each day of the week. First add the `createDocument()` function to the page.

```html
<html>
<head>
    <title>Message of the Day</title>
    <script type="text/javascript">
    function createDocument()
    {
        //Temporary DOM object.
        var xmlDoc;

        //Create the DOM object for IE
        if (window.ActiveXObject)
        {
            var versions =
            [
                "Msxml2.DOMDocument.6.0",
                "Msxml2.DOMDocument.3.0"
```

```
            ];

            for (var i = 0; i < versions.length; i++)
            {
                try
                {
                    xmlDoc = new ActiveXObject(versions[i]);
                    return xmlDoc;
                }
                catch (error)
                {
                    //do nothing here
                }
            }
        }
        //Create the DOM for Firefox and Opera
        else if (document.implementation && document.implementation.createDocument)
        {
            xmlDoc = document.implementation.createDocument("","",null);
            return xmlDoc;
        }
        //no version was found; return null
        return null;
    }


    //More code to come
    </script>
</head>
```

Before you dig into the body of the page, there's one more function you need to add to the head of the page. This function is called getDailyMessage(), which retrieves and returns the message of the day.

```
<html>
<head>
    <title>Message of the Day</title>
    <script type="text/javascript">
    function createDocument()
    {
        //Temporary DOM object.
        var xmlDoc;

        //Create the DOM object for IE
        if (window.ActiveXObject)
        {
            var versions =
            [
                "Msxml2.DOMDocument.6.0",
                "Msxml2.DOMDocument.3.0"
            ];

            for (var i - 0; i < versions.length; i++)
            {
                try
                {
```

```
                    xmlDoc = new ActiveXObject(versions[i]);
                    return xmlDoc;
            }
            catch (error)
            {
                //do nothing here
            }
        }
    }
    //Create the DOM for Firefox and Opera
    else if (document.implementation && document.implementation.createDocument)
    {
        xmlDoc = document.implementation.createDocument("","",null);
        return xmlDoc;
    }
    //no version was found; return null
    return null;
}
```

```
//Gets the message from the XML file
function getDailyMessage()
{
    //Get the node list of <daily/> elements.
    var messages = xmlDoc.getElementsByTagName("daily");
    //Create a date object.
    var dateobj = new Date();
    //And get today's day.
    var today = dateobj.getDay();

    //Return the message.
    return messages[today].firstChild.nodeValue;
}
</script>

</head>
```

First use the `getElementsByTagName()` method to retrieve the `<daily/>` elements. As you already know, this will return a node list of all the `<daily/>` elements. The next task is to find a numerical representation of the day of the week. Do this by first creating a `Date` object and using its `getDay()` method. This gives you a digit between 0 and 6 with 0 being Sunday, 1 being Monday, and so on; the digit is assigned to the `today` variable. Finally, use that variable as an index of the `messages` node list to select the correct `<daily/>` element and retrieve its text.

You may have noticed that `xmlDoc` in `getDailyMessage()` isn't declared anywhere in the head of the HTML document. It is used in `createDocument()`, but that variable is declared within the context of the function. You actually declare the global `xmlDoc` in the body of the HTML page.

```
<body>
<div id="messageContainer"></div>

<script type="text/javascript">
    //Create the DOM object
    var xmlDoc = createDocument();
```

```
        //We'll load it in synchronous mode.
        xmlDoc.async = false;
        //Load the XML file
        xmlDoc.load("motd.xml");

        document.getElementById("messageContainer").innerHTML = getDailyMessage();
    </script>
    </body>
    </html>
```

The first HTML element found in the body is a <div/> element with an id of messageContainer. Use this <div/> to display the message of the day.

Following the <div/> is the last <script/> element in the page. In this code block, you create a DOM document and assign it to the global xmlDoc variable. Then load the motd.xml file synchronously and set the message container's innerHTML to the message of the day by calling getDailyMessage().

Try It Out   **Tabulating the Dogs**

Write up a web page that uses a modified version of the dogs XML file. Save the following as mydogs_js.htm.

```
<html>
<head>
    <title>My Dogs Final</title>
    <script type="text/javascript">
    function createDocument()
    {
        //Temporary DOM object.
        var xmlDoc;

        //Create the DOM object for IE
        if (window.ActiveXObject)
        {
            var versions =
            [
                "Msxml2.DOMDocument.6.0",
                "Msxml2.DOMDocument.3.0"
            ];

            for (var i = 0; i < versions.length; i++)
            {
                try
                {
                    xmlDoc = new ActiveXObject(versions[i]);
                    return xmlDoc;
                }
                catch (error)
                {
                    //do nothing here
                }
            }
```

```
        }
        //Create the DOM for Firefox and Opera
        else if (document.implementation && document.implementation.createDocument)
        {
            xmlDoc = document.implementation.createDocument("","",null);
            return xmlDoc;
        }
        //no version was found; return null
        return null;
}


var xmlDocument = createDocument();
xmlDocument.load("mydogs_js.xml");

function displayDogs()
{
    //Get the <dog/> elements.
    var dogNodes = xmlDocument.getElementsByTagName("dog");
    //Create a <table/> element.
    var table = document.createElement("table");
    table.setAttribute("cellPadding",5); //Give the table some cell padding.
    table.setAttribute("width", "100%");
    table.setAttribute("border", "1");

    /*** Begin <thead/> Element. ***/
    var tableHeader = document.createElement("thead");
    //Create a <tr/> element.
    var tableRow = document.createElement("tr");

    //Loop through the child nodes of a <dog/> element.
    for (var i = 0; i < dogNodes[0].childNodes.length; i++)
    {
        var currentNode = dogNodes[0].childNodes[i];
        //Check to see if the child node is an element.
        if (currentNode.nodeType == 1)
        {
            //Create a <th/> element.
            var tableHeaderCell = document.createElement("th");
            //Create a text node with currentNode's nodeName.
            var textData = document.createTextNode(currentNode.nodeName);

            //Append the text node to the heading.
            tableHeaderCell.appendChild(textData);
            //Append heading to the row.
            tableRow.appendChild(tableHeaderCell);
        }
    }
    //Append the row with the column headers to the <thead/>
    tableHeader.appendChild(tableRow);
    //Append the <thead/> to the table.
    table.appendChild(tableHeader);
    /*** End <thead/> Element. ***/

    /*** Begin <tbody/> Element. ***/
    var tableBody = document.createElement("tbody");
```

```
                    //Loop through the <dog/> elements.
                    for (var i = 0; i < dogNodes.length; i++)
                    {
                        //Create a new <tr/> element.
                        var tableRow = document.createElement("tr");

                        //Now loop through this <dog/>'s child nodes.
                        for (var j = 0; j < dogNodes[i].childNodes.length; j++)
                        {
                            //Store the current node for easier access.
                            var currentNode = dogNodes[i].childNodes[j];
                            //Check the node to see if it's an element.
                            if (currentNode.nodeType == 1)
                            {
                                //Create a data cell.
                                var tableDataCell = document.createElement("td");
                                //Create a text node with currentNode's nodeName.
                                var textData = document.createTextNode
                                (
                                    currentNode.firstChild.nodeValue
                                );

                                //Append the text node to the data cell.
                                tableDataCell.appendChild(textData);

                                //Append the data cell to the row.
                                tableRow.appendChild(tableDataCell);
                            }
                        }
                        //Append the row to the <tbody/>.
                        tableBody.appendChild(tableRow);
                    }

                    //Append the tbody to the table
                    table.appendChild(tableBody);

                    /*** End <tbody/> Element. ***/

                    document.body.appendChild(table);
                }
            </script>
    </head>
    <body>
        <a href="javascript: displayDogs();">Display Dogs</a>
    </body>
</html>
```

Open up `mydogs.xml`, and modify it to look like this. Save the modified version as `mydogs_js.xml`.

```
<myDogs>
    <dog>
        <name>Morgan</name>
        <breed>Labrador Retriever</breed>
        <age>0 years, 10 months</age>
```

```
                <fullBlood>yes</fullBlood>
                <color>chocolate</color>
        </dog>
        <dog>
                <name>Molly</name>
                <breed>Labrador Retriever</breed>
                <age>8 years, 11 months</age>
                <fullBlood>yes</fullBlood>
                <color>yellow</color>
        </dog>
        <dog>
                <name>Casey</name>
                <breed>Pomeranian</breed>
                <age>6 years, 2 months</age>
                <fullBlood>yes</fullBlood>
                <color>brown</color>
        </dog>
    </myDogs>
```

When you open this page in your browser, you'll see a web page with only a link visible. When you click the link, you should see something like what is shown in Figure 14-10.

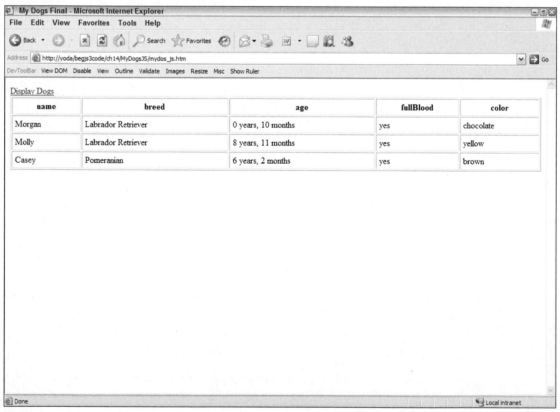

Figure 14-10

How It Works

The first thing you do is create a DOM object and load an XML document into it.

```
function createDocument()
{
    //Temporary DOM object.
    var xmlDoc;

    //Create the DOM object for IE
    if (window.ActiveXObject)
    {
        var versions =
        [
            "Msxml2.DOMDocument.6.0",
            "Msxml2.DOMDocument.3.0"
        ];

        for (var i = 0; i < versions.length; i++)
        {
            try
            {
                xmlDoc = new ActiveXObject(versions[i]);
                return xmlDoc;
            }
            catch (error)
            {
                //do nothing here
            }
        }
    }
    //Create the DOM for Firefox and Opera
    else if (document.implementation && document.implementation.createDocument)
    {
        xmlDoc = document.implementation.createDocument("","",null);
        return xmlDoc;
    }
    //no version was found; return null
    return null;
}

var xmlDocument = createDocument();
xmlDocument.load("mydogs_final.xml");
```

The workhorse of this page is the next function, displayDogs(). Its job is to build a table and populate it with the information from the XML file.

```
function displayDogs()
{
        //Get the <dog/> elements.
        var dogNodes = xmlDocument.getElementsByTagName("dog");
        //Create a <table/> element.
        var table = document.createElement("table");
        table.setAttribute("cellPadding",5); //Give the table some cell padding.
```

```
table.setAttribute("width", "100%");
table.setAttribute("border", "1");
```

The first thing you do is use the `getElementsByTagName()` method to retrieve the `<dog/>` elements and assign the resulting array to `dogNodes`. Next, create a `<table/>` element by using the `document.createElement()` method, and set its `cellPadding`, `width`, and `border` attributes.

Next, create the table header and heading cells. For the column headers, use the tag names of the `<dog/>` element's children (name, breed, age, and so on).

```
/*** Begin <thead/> Element. ***/
var tableHeader = document.createElement("thead");
//Create a <tr/> element.
var tableRow = document.createElement("tr");

//Loop through the child nodes of a <dog/> element.
for (var i = 0; i < dogNodes[0].childNodes.length; i++)
{
    var currentNode = dogNodes[0].childNodes[i];

    //More code here.
}
//Append the row with the column headers to the <thead/>
tableHeader.appendChild(tableRow);
//Append the <thead/> to the table.
table.appendChild(tableHeader);
```

The first few lines of this code create `<thead/>` and `<tr/>` elements. Then the code loops through the first `<dog/>` element's child nodes (more on this later). After the loop, append the `<tr/>` element to the table header and add the header to the table. Now let's look at the loop.

```
/*** Begin <thead/> Element. ***/
var tableHeader = document.createElement("thead");
//Create a <tr/> element.
var tableRow = document.createElement("tr");

//Loop through the child nodes of a <dog/> element.
for (var i = 0; i < dogNodes[0].childNodes.length; i++)
{
    var currentNode = dogNodes[0].childNodes[i];
    //Check to see if the child node is an element.
    if (currentNode.nodeType == 1)
    {
        //Create a <th/> element.
        var tableHeaderCell = document.createElement("th");
        //Create a text node with currentNode's nodeName.
        var textData = document.createTextNode(currentNode.nodeName);

        //Append the text node to the heading.
        tableHeaderCell.appendChild(textData);
        //Append heading to the row.
        tableRow.appendChild(tableHeaderCell);
    }
```

```
}
//Append the row with the column headers to the <thead/>
tableHeader.appendChild(tableRow);
//Append the <thead/> to the table.
table.appendChild(tableHeader);
```

The goal is to use the element names as headers for the column. However, you're looping through every child node of a <dog/> element, so any instance of whitespace between elements is counted as a child node in Firefox and Opera. To solve this problem, check the current node's type with the nodeType property. If it's equal to 1, then the child node is an element. Next create a <th/> element, and a text node containing the current node's nodeName, which you append to the header cell. And finally, append the <th/> element to the row.

The second part of displayDogs() builds the body of the table and populates it with data. It is similar in look and function to the header generation code.

```
/*** Begin <tbody/> Element. ***/
var tableBody = document.createElement("tbody");

//Loop through the <dog/> elements.
for (var i = 0; i < dogNodes.length; i++)
{
    //Create a new <tr/> element.
    var tableRow = document.createElement("tr");

    //More code here

    //Append the row to the <tbody/>.
    tableBody.appendChild(tableRow);
}

//Append the tbody to the table.
table.appendChild(tableBody);

/*** End <tbody/> Element. ***/
```

First create the <tbody/> element. Next, loop through the dogNodes array, cycling through the <dog/> elements. Inside this loop, create a <tr/> element and append it to the table's body. When the loop exits, append the <tbody/> element to the table. Now add data cells to the row:

```
/*** Begin <tbody/> Element. ***/
var tableBody = document.createElement("tbody");

//Loop through the <dog/> elements.
for (var i = 0; i < dogNodes.length; i++)
{
    //Create a new <tr/> element.
    var tableRow = document.createElement("tr");

    //Now loop through this <dog/>'s child nodes.
    for (var j = 0; j < dogNodes[i].childNodes.length; j++)
    {
        //Store the current node for easier access.
```

```
                    var currentNode = dogNodes[i].childNodes[j];
                    //Check the node to see if it's an element.
                    if (currentNode.nodeType == 1)
                    {
                        //Create a data cell.
                        var tableDataCell = document.createElement("td");
                        //Create a text node with currentNode's nodeName.
                        var textData = document.createTextNode(
                            currentNode.firstChild.nodeValue
                        );

                        //Append the text node to the data cell.
                        tableDataCell.appendChild(textData);

                        //Append the data cell to the row.
                        tableRow.appendChild(tableDataCell);
                    }
                }
                //Append the row to the <tbody/>.
                tableBody.appendChild(tableRow);
            }

            //Append the tbody to the table.
            table.appendChild(tableBody);

            /*** End <tbody/> Element. ***/
```

This inner loop cycles through the child elements of `<dog/>`. First assign the `currentNode` variable to reference the current node. This will enable you to access this node a little more easily (much less typing!). Next, check the node's type. Again, some browsers count whitespace as child nodes, so you need to make sure the current node is an element. When it's confirmed that the current node is an element, create a `<td/>` element and a text node containing the text of `currentNode`. Append the text node to the data cell, and append the data cell to the table row created in the outer `for` loop.

At this point the table is completed, so add it to the HTML page. You do this with the following:

```
        document.body.appendChild(table);
    }
```

Now all you have to do is invoke the `displayDogs()` function. To do this, you place a hyperlink in the page's body to call the function when clicked.

```
    <a href="javascript: displayDogs();">Display Dogs</a>
```

Summary

In this chapter you've taken a very brief look at XML, created your first XML document (a DTD), and then formatted the XML document using CSS and XSL. You looked at the following:

❑ What XML is used for

❑ How to create a well-formed and valid XML document

❑ The rules of XML syntax

❑ The XML data elements

❑ XSLT (Extensible Stylesheet Language Transformations)

❑ How XSLT can be used instead of CSS to display XML, and how it goes much further and enables HTML formatting to be created on the fly with XSLT

❑ Manipulating XML documents with JavaScript

❑ How to load an XML file and then manipulate its document with JavaScript

Exercise Questions

Suggested solutions to these questions can be found in Appendix A.

Question 1

Create an XML document that logically orders the following data for a school:

❑ Child's name

❑ Child's age

❑ Class the child is in

Use the following data:

Bibby Jones	13	1B
Beci Smith	12	1B
Jack Wilson	14	2C

Question 2

Using JavaScript, load the information from the XML file into a page and display it when the user clicks a link.

Using ActiveX and Plug-Ins with JavaScript

Today's browsers provide a lot of built-in functionality; however, there are many things they cannot do unaided, such as playing video or sound. Functionality of this sort has become quite common on the Internet, and it is thanks to plug-ins and their ability to extend browser functionality.

Plug-ins are applications that are downloaded and, as their name suggests, "plugged into" the browser. Many different plug-ins exist today; the more common ones include Adobe Flash Player, which plays Flash movies, and RealNetworks' Real Audio and video player, which plays real audio and media files.

Essentially, plug-ins are objects that encapsulate all the functionality they need to perform their tasks, such as playing audio files, in a way that hides the complexity from the programmer. They are usually written in languages such as C++ and Java.

Plug-ins usually, but not always, have some sort of user interface. For example, the Real Audio plug-in has a user interface that displays buttons to play, pause, and stop the playing of an audio file (see Figure 15-1).

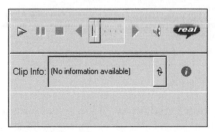

Figure 15-1

Some plug-ins make objects with various methods and properties available to you. You can access these through JavaScript, much as you access the methods and properties of the `window` object or the `Math` object. For example, the RealOne player plug-in makes available the `DoPlay()` method that you can use to play a sound clip.

Plug-ins have been around for quite some time; in fact, Netscape supported them back in version 3. You probably won't be shocked to find out that Microsoft does things differently from the other browser makers. IE does not support plug-ins, but IE 4.0+ running on Windows does support ActiveX controls, which provide the same functionality.

Fortunately, as you'll see, using ActiveX controls is similar to using Firefox plug-ins, and with a few tweaks can be done with almost the same code. The main difference is actually making sure that the plug-in or ActiveX control is available for use and ready to run in the user's browser in the first place. We'll cover this problem in more detail for Firefox and IE before going on to discuss using the plug-ins and ActiveX controls.

Checking for and Embedding Plug-ins in Firefox

It's nice to create a script to use a WizzoUltra3D plug-in for the web page experience of a lifetime, but unless the visitor to your web page also has the WizzoUltra3D plug-in installed on his computer, his experience of the web page is going to be one full of bugs and error messages. It is therefore important that you not only correctly add the HTML required to use the plug-in in your page, but also use JavaScript to check to see if the user's browser has the plug-in installed that your page makes use of. You look at both these topics in this section.

Even though this section focuses on Firefox, the same principles can be applied to Apple Safari and Opera.

Adding a Plug-in to the Page

To make use of a plug-in that is installed in the user's browser, you need to use HTML to tell the browser where and when in your page you want to use it. This process is called *embedding* the plug-in.

In Firefox, the key to embedding plug-ins is the non-standard `<embed/>` element. This inserts the visible interface, if any, of the plug-in at that point in the page. The `<embed/>` element supports a number of general attributes applicable to all plug-ins, such as `height`, `width`, `pluginspage`, `src`, and `type`. You'll look at the last two of these attributes, `src` and `type`, in more detail here. You will also look at the `pluginspage` attribute in the next section.

Most plug-ins display content that is stored on a web server. For example, a plug-in for sound, such as Real Audio, will play music from a file with the `.ra` extension, and the Flash plug-in will play Flash movies, that is, files with the `.swf` extension. The `<embed/>` element's `src` attribute enables you to specify the initial file for the plug-in to load and play. This will be a URL pointing to the file, usually hosted on the same web server as the HTML page. It's from this file that the browser determines what sort of plug-in is required. For example, if the `src` is `http://www.myserver.com/myflashmovie.swf`, then by checking the type of the file, the browser can see that a Flash player plug-in needs to be used.

However, not all plug-ins require data from an external source and therefore a value for the `src` attribute. In such situations, how can the browser tell what plug-in to load? Well, that's where the `<embed/>` element's `type` attribute comes in. The actual value for the `type` attribute will be specific to the plug-in. You can find out this information by typing `about:plugins` in the location bar. The plug-in information loads into the browser, as shown in Figure 15-2.

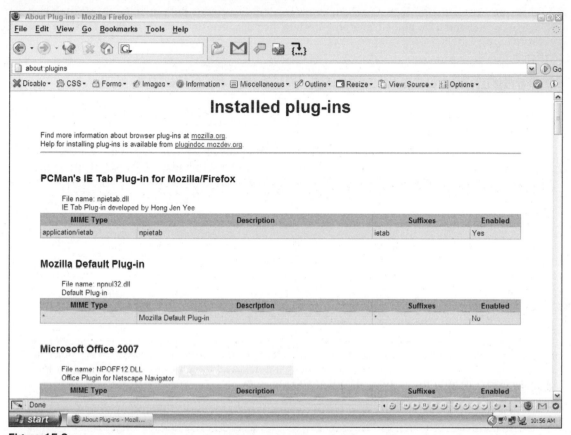

Figure 15-2

You'll see a list of all the plug-ins installed on your browser. The value required for the `type` attribute is listed as the Multipurpose Internet Mail Extensions (MIME) type, which specifies a type of content such as a web page, an image, or a Flash file. For example, the MIME type for Flash is `application/x-shockwave-flash`.

In addition to a number of attributes common to all plug-ins, you can also use the `<embed/>` element to specify properties specific to a particular plug-in. For example, the Flash plug-in supports the `quality` attribute, which determines the image quality of the Flash movie. To set this attribute in the `<embed/>` element, you just add it to the list of attributes set, as shown in the following example:

```
<embed id="FlashPlugIn1"
    src="topmenu.swf"
    border=0
```

```
        height=100
        width=500
        quality=high
        type="application/x-shockwave-flash"
</embed>
```

Although Firefox supports the <embed/> element, it also supports the use of the HTML standard <object/> element for embedding plug-ins into the page, in a similar way to IE, which you will see shortly.

Checking for and Installing Plug-ins in Firefox

After you decide what type of plug-in you want to embed into the page, what happens if the browser finds that this particular plug-in does not exist on the user's computer?

To solve this problem you can set the pluginspage attribute of <embed/> to point to a URL on the plug-in creator's page. If the plug-in is not on the user's computer, a link to the URL specified in the pluginspage attribute will be displayed within the web page. The user can click the link and load the plug-in so that your web page will function properly.

For example, with Flash the pluginspage attribute needed is this:

```
PLUGINSPAGE="http://www.adobe.com/shockwave/download/index.cgi?P1_Prod_Version=
ShockwaveFlash">
```

However, if the user doesn't have the plug-in installed, you might prefer to send her to a version of your web site that doesn't rely on that plug-in. How do you know whether a plug-in is installed?

The navigator object, introduced in Chapter 5, has a property called plugins, which is an array of Plugin objects, one for each plug-in installed on that browser. You can access a Plugin object in the plugins array either by using an index value that indexes all the plug-ins installed on the user's browser, or by using the name of the plug-in application.

> Internet Explorer has a navigator.plugins **array, but it is always empty.**

Each Plugin object has four properties: description, filename, length, and name. You can find these values by viewing the plug-ins information page that you saw earlier.

Let's use Flash as an example. Type **about:plugins** in the location bar and press enter. Figure 15-3 shows the Installed plug-ins page in Netscape, but this page remains largely the same in Firefox 2. You can see that Flash has Shockwave Flash as its name property. The filename and description properties have obvious meanings. The length property gives the number of MIME types supported by the plug-in.

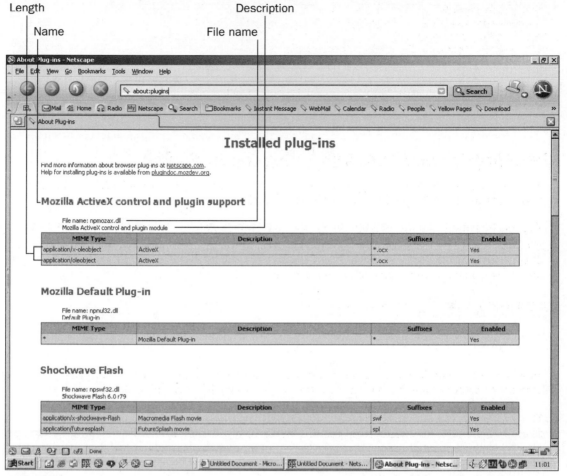

Figure 15-3

As mentioned earlier, the `name` property can be used to reference the `Plugin` object in the `plugins` array. So, the following code will set the variable `shockWavePlugin` to the `Plugin` object for Flash, if it's installed:

```
var shockWavePlugin = navigator.plugins["Shockwave Flash"];
```

If it's not, `navigator.plugins["Shockwave Flash"]` will return as `undefined`.

You can use the following to redirect users on browsers that do not have installed the plug-in you need:

```
if (navigator.plugins["Shockwave Flash"])
{
    window.location.replace("my_flash_enabled_page.htm");
}
else
```

```
{
   window.location.replace("my_non_flash_page.htm");
}
```

If the Flash plug-in is not installed, `navigator.plugins["Shockwave Flash"]` will be `undefined`, which JavaScript considers to be `false`, thereby causing the `else` statement to execute. If Flash is installed, `navigator.plugins["Shockwave Flash"]` will return the Flash `Plugin` object, which JavaScript treats as `true`, and the main `if` statement will execute.

The problem with this method of detection is that the name given to a plug-in may vary from operating system to operating system. For example, the name of the Windows XP version of the plug-in may vary from the name of the Mac version, which in turn may vary from the name of the Linux version. Some plug-ins, such as RealPlayer, will not work reliably at all with this detection method, because the name is not simply RealPlayer but something that contains the word "RealPlayer."

An alternative method for determining whether a plug-in is installed is to loop through the `plugins[]` array and check each `name` for certain keywords. If you find them, you can assume that the control is installed. For example, to check for RealPlayer, you may use the following:

```
var plugInCounter;
for (plugInCounter = 0; plugInCounter < navigator.plugins.length;
   plugInCounter++)
{
   if (navigator.plugins[plugInCounter].name.indexOf("RealPlayer") >= 0)
   {
      alert("RealPlayer is installed");
      break;
   }
}
```

The `for` loop goes through the `navigator.plugins` array, starting from index 0 and continuing up to the last element. Each plug-in in the array has its `name` property checked to see if it contains the text `RealPlayer`. If it does, you know RealPlayer is installed, and you break out of the loop; if not, RealPlayer is clearly not installed.

An alternative to using `navigator` object's `plugins[]` array is using the `navigator` object's `mimeTypes[]` array, which contains an array of `mimeType` objects representing the MIME types supported by the browser. You can use this array to check whether the browser supports a specific type of media, such as Flash movies.

You have already come across MIME types before — the `type` attribute of the `<embed/>` element can be used to specify a MIME type so that the browser knows which plug-in to embed. Again, using the About Plug-ins option on the Help menu, you can find out what the MIME types are for a particular plug-in. In fact, one plug-in may well support more than one MIME type. When you check for a particular MIME type, you are checking that the browser supports a particular type of file format rather than necessarily a particular plug-in.

For example, you may use the `mimeTypes` array to check for the Flash plug-in as follows:

```
if (navigator.mimeTypes["application/x-shockwave-flash"] &&
   navigator.mimeTypes['application/x-shockwave-flash'].enabledPlugin)
{
```

```
      window.location.replace("my_flash_enabled_page.htm");
   }
   else
   {
      window.location.replace("my_non_flash_page.htm");
   }
```

The if statement is the important thing here. Its condition has two parts separated by the AND operator &&.

The first part checks that the specified MIME type is supported by trying to access a specific mimeType object in the mimeTypes array. If there is no such object, then undefined is returned, which, as far as an if statement goes, means the same thing as if false had been returned.

The second part checks to see not only that the MIME type is supported, but also that a plug-in to handle this MIME type is enabled. Although unusual, it is possible for a MIME type to be supported, or recognized, by the browser, but for no plug-in to be installed. For example, if the user has Microsoft Word installed, the MIME type application/msword would be valid, but that does not mean a plug-in exists to display it in the browser! The enabledPlugin property of the mimeType object actually returns a Plugin object, but again, if it does not exist, null will be returned, which will be considered as false by the if statement.

What happens if someone browses to your page with a browser that has no support at all for plug-ins?

Well, the <embed/> elements will be basically ignored, and if the browser does support script, errors will occur if you access the plug-in through your script. To get around this, use the <noembed/> element. Anything in between the opening <noembed> tag and the closing </noembed> tag is ignored by a browser that supports the <embed/> element, so you can put a message in there telling users that the page requires a browser that supports plug-ins.

```
<noembed>
   <h2> This page requires a browser that supports plug-ins </h2>
</noembed>
```

You can also use object checking to avoid errors with different browser versions.

```
if (document.embeds && document.embeds[0])
```

Checking for and Embedding ActiveX Controls on Internet Explorer

Although IE does support plug-ins to a certain extent, its support for ActiveX controls is more complete. The main difference between an ActiveX control and a plug-in is how they are embedded into a page and how they are installed. Once they are embedded and installed, their use, as far as scripting goes, will be very similar to that for plug-ins.

ActiveX controls are a little like mini-programs, usually created in languages like C++ or Visual Basic. Unlike normal programs, like Notepad or Microsoft Word, ActiveX controls cannot run on their own; they need to be sited in a container program. Not all programs can act as containers for ActiveX controls, only those specifically designed to do so, such as Microsoft Access and, of course, Internet Explorer. When the creator of the ActiveX control compiles his code, he also assigns it a unique identification string that enables programmers like you to specify exactly which control you want to embed in your IE ActiveX container.

Adding an ActiveX Control to the Page

Adding an ActiveX control to a page for an IE browser requires the use of the `<object/>` element. Two very important attributes of the `<object/>` element are common to all controls, namely `classid` and `codebase`. The `classid` attribute is the unique ID that the creator of the control gave to it when it was compiled. The `codebase` attribute gives a URL where the ActiveX control can be found — you'll look at this attribute in more detail in the next section.

How can you find out the `classid`? Well, one way to do this is by checking the documentation that came with the control or is available on the control creator's web site. If you have the control installed, another way to do this is via IE itself, which will tell you which controls are installed on the computer and available to IE. Also, IE gives you additional information such as `classid`, though it won't inform you about any controls that were installed with the operating system. For example, Flash 3 is installed with Windows 98 and therefore won't appear.

To get this information, open up IE and select Internet Options from the Tools menu, as shown in Figure 15-4.

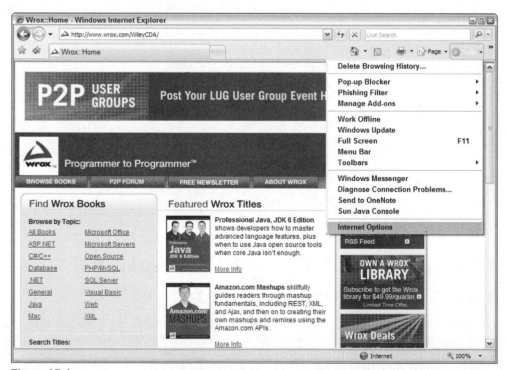

Figure 15-4

This opens up the console shown in Figure 15-5. In the Browsing history area, click the Settings button.

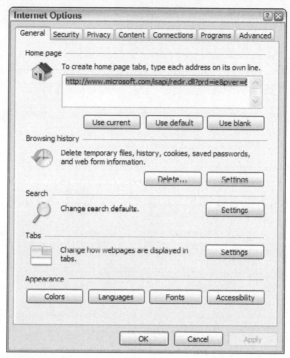

Figure 15-5

In the next console that opens, click the View objects button, shown in Figure 15-6.

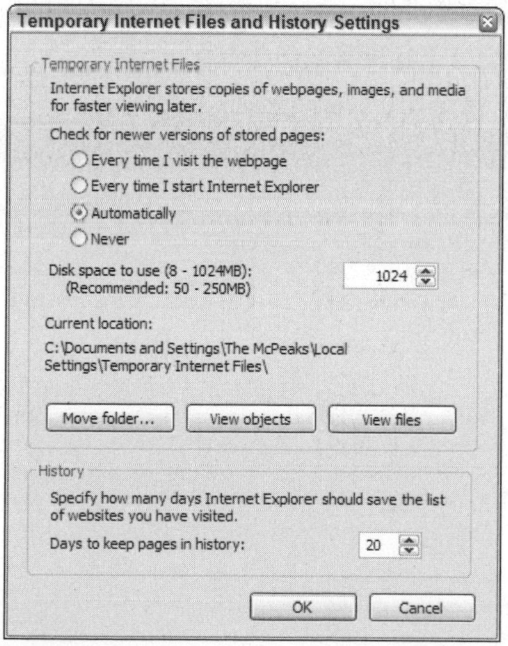

Figure 15-6

This will display a list of all the ActiveX controls IE has installed from the Internet. The list shown in Figure 15-7 will most likely be different from that on your own computer.

You can see lots of information about each control, such as when it was created and its version number. However, to find out the `classid`, you need to right-click the name of the control you're interested in and select Properties from the menu that pops up.

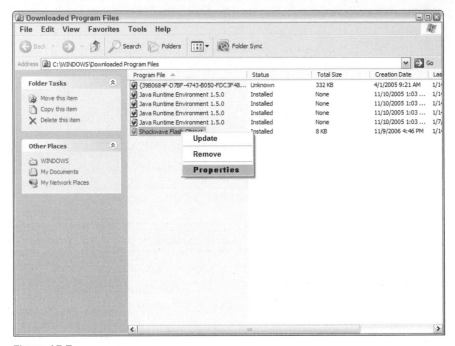

Figure 15-7

The information shown in Figure 15-8 is displayed, though this may be slightly different on your system.

You can see that the `classid` attribute, listed as just `ID`, and the `codebase` attribute, listed as `CodeBase`, are both displayed, although for `codebase` you may need to select the line and then scroll using the arrow keys to see all the information.

From this information, you see that to insert a Flash ActiveX control in your web page you need to add the following `<object/>` element:

```
<object classid="clsid:D27CDB6E-AE6D-11cf-96B8-444553540000"
    id=flashPlayer1
    width=500
    height=100>
</object>
```

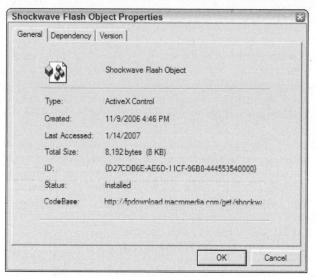

Figure 15-8

You can also set attribute or parameter values for the control itself. For example, with Flash you need to set the src attribute to point to the .swf file you want loaded, and you may also want to set the quality attribute, which determines the quality of appearance of the Flash movie. However, to set the parameters of the ActiveX control such as these (as opposed to the attributes of the <object/> element), you need to insert the <param/> element between the start <object> tag and the close </object> tag.

In each <param/> element you need to specify the name of the parameter you want to set and the value you want it set to. For example, if you want to set the src attribute to myFlashMovie.swf, you need to add a <param/> element like this:

```
<param name=src value="myFlashMovie.swf">
```

Let's add this to the full <object/> element definition and also define the quality attribute at the same time.

```
<object classid="clsid:D27CDB6E-AE6D-11cf-96B8-444553540000"
    id=flashPlayer1
    width=500
    height=100>
        <param name=src value="myFlashMovie.swf">
        <param name=quality value=high>
</object>
```

Alternatively, you can use the movie parameter instead of src parameter.

Installing an ActiveX Control

You've seen how to insert an ActiveX control into your page, but what happens if the user doesn't have that control installed on her computer?

This is where the `codebase` attribute of the `<object>` tag comes in. If the browser finds that the ActiveX control is not installed on the user's computer, it will try to download and install the control from the URL pointed to by the `codebase` attribute.

The creator of the ActiveX control will usually have a URL that you can use as a value for the `codebase` attribute. The information under the Internet Options option of the Tools menu you saw earlier provides the `codebase` for the control that was installed on your computer, though this may not necessarily be the best URL to use, particularly if it's not a link to the creator of the control.

For Flash, the `codebase` is `http://fpdownload.macromedia.com/get/shockwave/cabs/flash/swflash.cab`, so your `<object>` tag will look like this:

```
<object classid="clsid:D27CDB6E-AE6D-11CF-96B8-444553540000"
codebase="http://fpdownload.macromedia.com/get/shockwave/cabs/flash/swflash.cab "
    id="flashPlayer1"
    width=500
    height=100 >
        <param name=src value="myFlashMovie.swf">
        <param name=quality value=high>
</object>
```

Subject to license agreements, you may be able to download the `.cab` file that installs the control to your own server and point the `codebase` attribute to that.

Unfortunately, there is no easy foolproof way of checking which ActiveX controls are installed on the user's computer. However, the `Object` object of the `<object/>` element does have the `readyState` property. This returns 0, 1, 2, 3, or 4, indicating the object's operational status. The possible values are as follows:

- ❑   0 — Control is un-initialized and not ready for use
- ❑   1 — Control is still loading
- ❑   2 — Control has finished loading its data
- ❑   3 — User can interact with control even though it is not fully loaded
- ❑   4 — Control is loaded and ready for use

You need to give the control time to load before checking its `readyState` property, so any checking is best left until the window's `onload` event handler or even the `document` object's `onreadystatechange` event handler has fired.

To redirect the user to another page that doesn't need the control, you need to write this:

```
var flashPlayer1;

//code to retrieve ActiveX plug-in

if (flashPlayer1.readyState == 0)
```

```
{
    window.location.replace("NoControlPage.htm");
}
```

Attach this code to the window's `onload` event handler.

You saw that the `<noembed/>` element enables you to display a message for users with browsers that do not support plug-ins. This element works in exactly the same way with IE. Alternatively, you can place text between the `<object>` and `</object>` tags, in which case it will only be displayed if the browser is not able to display the ActiveX control.

Using Plug-ins and ActiveX Controls

When you have the plug-ins or ActiveX controls embedded into the page, their actual use is very uniform. To make life easier for you, most developers of plug-ins and controls make the properties, methods, and events supported by each plug-in and ActiveX control similar. However, it's important to check the developer's documentation because it's likely that there will be some idiosyncracies.

Inside the `<embed/>` or `<object/>` element, you give your plug-in or control a unique `id` value. You can then access the corresponding object's methods, properties, and events just as you would for any other tag. The actual properties, methods, and events supported by a plug-in or control will be specific to that control, but let's look at one of the more commonly available controls, RealNetworks RealPlayer, which comes in both plug-in form for Firefox and ActiveX control form for IE. You can find more information on this control at www.realnetworks.com/resources/index.html, and you can download a free version (RealOne Player) from www.realnetworks.com. Note that you can buy a version with more features, but if you search the web site, a no-charge basic version is available.

First you need to embed the control in a web page. Type the following into a text editor:

```
<html>
<head>
<object classid="clsid:CFCDAA03-8BE4-11CF-B84B-0020AFBBCCFA" id="real1"
  width="0" height="0">
    <param name="height" value="0">
    <param name="width" value="0">
    <embed name="real1"
        id="real1"
        border="0"
        controls="play"
        height=0
        width=0
        type="audio/x-pn-realaudio-plugin">
</object>
</head>
<body>
<noembed>
    <h2>This Page requires a browser supporting Plug-ins or ActiveX controls</h2>
</noembed>
</body>
</html>
```

Save this code as `realplayer.htm`.

The first thing to note is that the `<embed/>` element for the Firefox plug-in has been inserted between the opening `<object>` tag and the closing `</object>` tag. This is because Firefox will ignore the `<object/>` element and display only the plug-in defined in the `<embed/>` element. IE, on the other hand, will ignore the `<embed/>` element inside the `<object/>` element, but IE will display the ActiveX control.

IE does support the `<embed/>` element, though its use is discouraged. This means that if you placed the `<embed/>` element outside the `<object/>` element, IE would recognize both the `<object/>` and `<embed/>` elements and get confused — particularly over the `id` values, because both have the same `id` of `real1`.

You've placed the `<embed/>` and `<object/>` elements inside the `<head/>`. Why?

Well, for this example you don't want to display the graphical interface of the control itself; instead you want to use only its ability to play sounds. By placing it inside the head of the document, you make it invisible to the user.

Finally, you've put a `<noembed/>` element inside the body of the page for users with browsers that don't support plug-ins or ActiveX controls. This will display a message to such users, telling them why they are staring at a blank page!

You want to make sure that users without the RealPlayer plug-in or control don't see error messages when you start scripting the controls. So let's redirect them to another page if they do not have the right plug-in or control. You'll do this by adding a function to check for the availability of the plug-in or control and attaching this to the `window` object's `onload` event handler in the `<body>` tag.

```
<html>
<head>
<object classid="clsid:CFCDAA03-8BE4-11CF-B84B-0020AFBBCCFA" id="real1"
 width="0" height="0">
   <param name="height" value="0">
   <param name="width" value="0">
   <embed name="real1"
      id="real1"
      border="0"
      controls="play"
      height=0
      width=0
      type="audio/x-pn-realaudio-plugin">
</object>
<script type="text/javascript">
function window_onload()
{
   var plugInInstalled = false;
   if (navigator.appName.indexOf("Microsoft") == -1)
   {
      var plugInCounter;
      for (plugInCounter = 0; plugInCounter < navigator.plugins.length;
         plugInCounter++)
      {
```

```
            if (navigator.plugins[plugInCounter].name.indexOf("RealPlayer") >= 0)
            {
               plugInInstalled = true;
               break;
            }
         }
      }
      else
      {
         if (real1.readyState == 4)
         {
            plugInInstalled = true;
         }
      }
      if (plugInInstalled == false)    {
         window.location.replace("NoRealPlayerPage.htm");
      }
   }
</script>
</head>
<body onload="return window_onload()">
<noembed>
    <h2>This Page requires a browser supporting Plug-ins or ActiveX controls</h2>
</noembed>
</body>
</html>
```

In the `window_onload()` function, you first define a variable, `plugInInstalled`, and initialize it to `false`.

Next, since checking for plug-ins or controls is browser-dependent, you check to see if this is a Microsoft browser. If not, you assume it's Firefox, though for a real-life example you might want to do more detailed checks.

If the browser is Firefox, you use a `for` loop to go through the `navigator` object's `plugins` array, checking each installed plug-in's name for the word `RealPlayer`. If this word is found, you set the variable `plugInInstalled` to `true` and break out of the `for` loop.

If you find that this is a Microsoft browser, you use the `readyState` property of the `<object/>` element's `Object` object to see if the ActiveX control is loaded, initialized successfully, and now ready for action. If its value is 4, you know that all systems are ready to go, and you can use the control, so you set the variable `plugInInstalled` to `true`.

Finally, the last `if` statement in the function checks to see if `plugInInstalled` is `true` or `false`. If it is `false`, the user is redirected to another page, called `NoRealPlayerPage.htm`, where you can either provide alternative ways to display the content or provide a link to load the RealPlayer control. Let's create a simple page to do this.

```
<html>
<head>
    <title>No Real Player Installed</title>
</head>
```

```
<body>
    <h2>You don't have the required RealPlayer plug-in</h2>
    <p>
        You can download the plug-in from
        <a href="http://www.real.com">Real Player</a>
    </p>
</body>
</html>
```

Save this as `NoRealPlayerPage.htm`.

Finally, back in the `realplayer.htm` page, let's enable the user to select a sound file as well as to start and stop playing it. You add the following code to the top of the script block:

```
<html>
<head>
<object classid="clsid:CFCDAA03-8BE4-11CF-B84B-0020AFBBCCFA" id="real1"
 width="0" height="0">
    <param name="height" value="0">
    <param name="width" value="0">
    <embed name="real1"
        id="real1"
        border="0"
        controls="play"
        height=0
        width=0
        type="audio/x-pn-realaudio-plugin">
</object>
<script type="text/javascript">
var fileName = "";

function butPlay_onclick()
{
    document.real1.SetSource("file:///" + fileName);
    document.real1.DoPlay();
}

function butStop_onclick()
{
    document.real1.DoStop();
}

function file1_onblur()
{
    fileName = document.form1.file1.value;
}

function window_onload()
{
    var plugInInstalled = false;
    if (navigator.appName.indexOf("Microsoft") == -1)
    {
        var plugInCounter;
        for (plugInCounter = 0; plugInCounter < navigator.plugins.length;
```

```
            plugInCounter++)
        {
            if (navigator.plugins[plugInCounter].name.indexOf("RealPlayer") >= 0)
            {
                plugInInstalled = true;
                break;
            }
        }
    }
    else
    {
        if (real1.readyState == 4)
        {
            plugInInstalled = true;
        }
    }
    if (plugInInstalled == false)    {
        window.location.replace("NoRealPlayerPage.htm");
    }
}
</script>
</head>
<body onload="return window_onload()">
<noembed>
    <h2>This Page requires a browser supporting Plug-ins or ActiveX controls</h2>
</noembed>
</body>
</html>
```

You also add a form with buttons for starting, stopping, and choosing a sound file to the body of the page.

```
<html>
<head>
<object classid="clsid:CFCDAA03-8BE4-11CF-B84B-0020AFBBCCFA" id="real1"
 width="0" height="0">
    <param name="height" value="0">
    <param name="width" value="0">
    <embed name="real1"
        id="real1"
        border="0"
        controls="play"
        height=0
        width=0
        type="audio/x-pn-realaudio-plugin">
</object>
<script type="text/javascript">
var fileName = "";

function butPlay_onclick()
{
    document.real1.SetSource("file:///" + fileName);
    document.real1.DoPlay();
}

function butStop_onclick()
```

```
{
   document.real1.DoStop();
}

function file1_onblur()
{
   fileName = document.form1.file1.value;
}

function window_onload()
{
   var plugInInstalled = false;
   if (navigator.appName.indexOf("Microsoft") == -1)
   {
      var plugInCounter;
      for (plugInCounter = 0; plugInCounter < navigator.plugins.length;
         plugInCounter++)
      {
         if (navigator.plugins[plugInCounter].name.indexOf("RealPlayer") >= 0)
         {
            plugInInstalled = true;
            break;
         }
      }
   }
   else
   {
      if (real1.readyState == 4)
      {
         plugInInstalled = true;
      }
   }
   if (plugInInstalled == false)   {
      window.location.replace("NoRealPlayerPage.htm");
   }
}
</script>
</head>
<body onload="return window_onload()">
<noembed>
   <h2>This Page requires a browser supporting Plug-ins or ActiveX controls</h2>
</noembed>
<form id=form1 name=form1>
   <input type="button" value="Play Sound" id="butPlay" name="butPlay"
      onclick="return butPlay_onclick()">
   <input type="button" value="Stop Sound" id="butStop" name="butStop"
      onclick="return butStop_onclick()">
   <input type="file" id="file1" name="file1"
      onblur="return file1_onblur()">
</form>

</body>
</html>
```

You've completed your page, so let's now resave it. Load `realplayer.htm` into your browser and, as long as your browser supports plug-ins or ActiveX controls and the RealPlayer plug-in is installed, you should see something like what is shown in Figure 15-9.

Figure 15-9

Click the Browse button and browse to an MP3 sound file (`Budd_Eno.mp3` is provided with the code download, or you can create your own with Real Producer Basic, also available at `www.realnetworks.com`). Click the Play Sound and Stop Sound buttons to play and stop the sound.

So how does this work?

The form in the body of the page contains three form elements. The first two of these are just standard buttons, but the last is an `<input/>` element of `type="file"`. This means that a text box and a button are displayed. When the button is clicked, a Choose File dialog box opens, enabling you to choose the `.ra` file you want to hear. When chosen, this file's name appears in the text box.

You've connected the two buttons' `onclick` event handlers and the file control's `onblur` event handler to three functions, `butPlay_onclick()`, `butStop_onclick()`, and `file1_onblur()`, respectively, which are defined in the script block in the head of the page.

In the function `file1_onblur()`, you set a global variable, `fileName`, to the value of the file control. In other words, `fileName` will contain the name and path of the file the user has chosen to play. The `blur` event will fire whenever the user moves focus from the file control to another control or area of the page. In reality, you would perform checks to see whether the file type selected by the user is actually a valid sound file.

In the other two functions, you access the RealPlayer plug-in or control that you embedded in the page. You use one function to load the file the user selected and play it, and the other function to stop play.

In both functions, you access the RealPlayer control by using its name prefixed with `document`. The script will work with IE and Firefox, though under IE it's accessing the ActiveX control defined in `<object/>`, and in Firefox it's accessing the plug-in defined in the `<embed/>` tag.

In the `butPlay_onclick()` function, you use the `SetSource()` method of the RealPlayer object. This method takes one parameter — the file that you want the RealPlayer plug-in to load. So, in the line

```
document.real1.SetSource("file:///" + fileName);
```

you load the file the user specified. Next you use the `DoPlay()` method of the RealPlayer object, which starts the playing of the source file.

```
document.real1.DoPlay();
```

With the function `butStop_onclick()`, you stop the playing of the clip using the `DoStop()` method of the RealPlayer object.

```
document.real1.DoStop();
```

Testing Your "No Plug-in or ActiveX Control" Redirection Script

It's quite likely that if you plan to use an ActiveX control or plug-in, you're going to make sure it's installed on your computer. The problem is that while that's great for testing pages to see if they work when there is a control installed, it does make it very difficult to check redirection scripts for users without that control. You have a number of possible options:

1. Get a second computer with a clean install of an operating system and browser, then load your pages on that computer. This is the only 100 percent sure way of checking your pages.

2. Uninstall the plug-in. Depending on how the plug-in or control was installed, there may be an uninstall program for it. Windows users can use the Add/Remove programs option in the Control Panel.

3. For Firefox, install a different version of the browser. For example, if you have Firefox 2 installed, try installing an older version, say Firefox 1 or even a beta version if you can find it. The plug-ins currently installed are not normally available to a browser installed later, though this may not be true all the time.

4. With IE, you can only have one version of the browser installed at once. However, IE does make it quite easy to remove ActiveX controls. In IE 5+, choose Internet Options from the Tools menu. Click the Settings button under Temporary Internet Files (Browsing History in IE7), followed by the View Objects button. From here you need to right-click the name of the control you want removed and select Remove from the pop-up menu.

Potential Problems

Plug-ins and ActiveX controls provide a great way to extend a browser's functionality, but they do so at a price—compatibility problems. Some of the problems you may face are discussed in the following sections.

Similar but Not the Same — Differences Between Browsers

Although a plug-in for Firefox and the equivalent ActiveX control for IE may support many similar properties and methods, you will often find significant, and sometimes subtle, differences.

For example, both the plug-in and ActiveX control versions of RealPlayer support the `SetSource()` method. However, while

```
document.real1.SetSource("file:///D:\\MyDir\\MyFile.ra")
```

will work with IE, it will cause problems with the other browsers. To work with Firefox and the like, specify the protocol by which the file will be loaded. If it is a URL, specify `http://`, but for a file on a user's local hard drive, use `file:///`.

To make the code work across platforms, you must type this:

```
document.real1.SetSource("file:///D:\MyDir\MyFile.ra")
```

Differences in the Scripting of Plug-ins

When scripting the RealPlayer plug-in for Firefox, you embedded it like this:

```
<embed name="real1" id="real1"
    border="0"
    controls="play"
    height=0 width=0 type="audio/x-pn-realaudio-plugin">
```

You then accessed it via script just by typing this:

```
document.real1.DoPlay()
```

However, if you are scripting a Flash player, you need to add the following attribute to the `<embed/>` definition in the HTML:

```
swliveconnect="true"
```

Otherwise any attempts to access the plug-in will result in errors.

```
<embed name="map"
    swLiveConnect=true
    src="topmenu.swf"
    width=300 height=200

pluginspage="http://fpdownload.macromedia.com/get/shockwave/cabs/flash/swflash.cab"
    Version=ShockwaveFlash">
```

It's very important to study any available documentation that comes with a plug-in to check that there are no subtle problems like this.

Differences Between Operating Systems

Support for ActiveX controls varies greatly between different operating systems. IE for the Mac supports it, but not as well as under Win32 operating systems, such as Windows 95, 98, 2000, and XP.

You also need to be aware that an ActiveX control written for Win32 will not work on the Mac; you need to make sure a Mac-specific control is downloaded.

IE on the Mac supports plug-ins as well as ActiveX controls; so, for example, Flash is a plug-in on the Mac and an ActiveX control on Win32. Clearly, if you want to support both Mac and Windows users, you need to write more complex code.

It's very important to check which operating system the user is running (for example, using the scripts given at the end of Chapter 5) and deal with any problems that may arise.

Differences Between Different Versions of the Same Plug-in or ActiveX Control

Creators of plug-ins and controls will often periodically release new versions with new features. If you make use of these new features, you need to make sure not only that the user has the right plug-in or ActiveX control loaded, but also that it is the right version.

ActiveX Controls

With ActiveX controls, you can add version information in the `codebase` attribute of the `<object/>` element.

```
<object classid=clsid:AAA03-8BE4-11CF-B84B-0020AFBBCCFA
    id="myControl"
    codebase="http://myserver/mycontrol.cab#version=3,0,0,0">
</object>
```

Now, not only will the browser check that the control is installed on the user's system, but it'll also check that the installed version is version 3 or greater.

What if you want to check the version and then redirect to a different page if it's a version that is earlier than your page requires?

With ActiveX controls there's no easy way of using JavaScript code to check the ActiveX control version. One way is to find a property that the new control supports but that older versions don't, and then compare that to `null`. For example, imagine you have a control whose latest version introduces the property `BgColor`. To check if the installed version is the one you want, you type the following:

```
if (document.myControl.BgColor == null)
{
    alert("This is an old version");
}
```

It's also possible that the ActiveX creator has added to his control's object a `version` property of some sort that you can check against, but this will vary from control to control.

Plug-ins

With plug-ins you need to make use of the `Plugin` objects in the `navigator` object's `plugins[]` array property. Each `Plugin` object in the array has a `name`, `filename`, and `description` property, which may provide version information. However, this will vary between plug-ins.

For example, for Flash Player 4 on Win32, the description given by

```
navigator.plugins["Shockwave Flash"].description
```

is Flash 4.0 r7.

Using regular expressions, which were introduced in Chapter 8, you could extract the version number from this string:

```
var myRegExp = /\d{1,}.\d{1,}/;
var flashVersion = navigator.plugins["Shockwave Flash"].description;
flashVersion = parseFloat(flashVersion.match(myRegExp)[0]);
```

In the first line of code you define a regular expression that will match one or more digits, followed by a dot, and then one or more numbers. Next you store the description of the Flash plug-in in the variable flashVersion. Finally you search the variable for the regular expression, returning an array of all the matches made. You then use the parseFloat() function on the contents of the element in the array at index 0 (in other words, the first element in the array).

Changes to Internet Explorer 6 Service Pack 1b and ActiveX Controls

For mostly legal reasons, Microsoft is making changes to how ActiveX controls work in IE. Now whenever a user browses to a page with an ActiveX control, she gets a warning about the control, and by default it's blocked unless she chooses to unblock it. There are two ways around this:

1. Don't access any external data or have any `<param/>` elements in the definition, as the following example demonstrates:

```
<object classid="CLSID:6BF52A52-394A-11d3-B153-00C04F79FAA6"></object>
```

2. Use the new noexternaldata attribute to specify that no external access of data is used.

```
<object noexternaldata="true" classid="CLSid:6BF52A52-394A-11d3-B153-00C04F79FAA6">
    <param
        name="URL"

value="http://msdn.microsoft.com/workshop/samples/author/dhtml/media/drums.wav"/>
</object>
```

The URL parameter will be ignored, and no external data from the URL, in this case a .wav file, will be accessed.

Summary

In this chapter you looked at how you can use plug-ins and ActiveX controls to extend a browser's functionality. You saw that:

❑   Internet Explorer supports ActiveX controls, and to some extent plug-ins, on Windows operating systems. Firefox has good support for plug-ins but does not support ActiveX controls.

❑   Most creators of plug-ins also provide an ActiveX control equivalent. Internet Explorer and Firefox are incompatible as far as the installation of plug-ins and ActiveX controls goes.

❑   Plug-ins are embedded in a web page by means of the `<embed/>` element. You let Firefox know which plug-in is to be embedded by specifying either a source file or a MIME type using the src and type attributes of the `<embed/>` element. If you define a value for the `<embed/>` element's pluginspage attribute, users who don't have that plug-in installed will be able to click a link and install it.

❑   You can find detailed information about what plug-ins are installed on your Firefox browser, as well as their descriptions and types, by using the About Plug-ins option on the Help menu.

❑ To use script to check if a user has a certain plug-in, you can use the `navigator` object's `plug-ins[]` array property. For each plug-in installed, there will be a `Plugin` object defined in this array. Each `Plugin` object has the properties `name`, `description`, `filename`, and `length`, which you can use to determine if a plug-in exists on the user's computer. You can also use the `navigator` object's `mimeTypes[]` array property to check if a certain type of file is supported.

❑ Internet Explorer supports ActiveX controls as an alternative to plug-ins. These are embedded into a web page using the `<object/>` element. You specify which ActiveX control you want by using the `classid` attribute. If you want to have controls automatically install for users who don't have a particular control already installed, you need to specify the `codebase` attribute.

❑ Any parameters particular to the control are specified by means of the `<param/>` element, which is inserted between the opening and closing `<object>` tags.

❑ You can check whether a control has loaded successfully using the `readyState` property of the `Object` object, which returns a number: `0` if the control is not installed, `1` if it's still loading, `2` if it has loaded, `3` if you can interact with it, and `4` if it's installed and ready for use.

❑ Virtually every different type of plug-in and ActiveX control has its own interface, for which the control's documentation will provide the details. You looked briefly at the RealPlayer control by RealNetworks.

❑ You also saw that while plug-ins and controls are great for extending functionality, they are subject to potential pitfalls. These include differences in the way plug-ins and ActiveX controls are scripted, differences in operating systems, and differences between versions of the same plug-in or control.

In the next chapter, you change direction to cover a "new" JavaScript technique that has rekindled web application development.

Exercise Question

A suggested solution to this question can be found in Appendix A.

Question 1

Using the RealPlayer plug-in/ActiveX control, create a page with three links, so that when the mouse pointer rolls over any of them a sound is played. The page should work in Firefox and IE. However, any other browsers should be able to view the page and roll over the links without errors appearing.

Ajax and Remote Scripting

Since its inception, the Internet has used a transaction-like communication model. A browser sends a request to a server, which sends a response to the browser, on which it (re)loads the page. This is typical HTTP communication, and it was designed to be this way, but this model is rather cumbersome for developers, as it requires our web applications to consist of several pages. The resulting user experience is disjointed and interrupted.

In the early 2000s, a movement began to look for and develop new techniques to enhance the user's experience, as well as make applications easier to build and maintain. These new techniques offered performance and usability usually associated with conventional desktop applications. It wasn't long before developers began to refine these processes to offer richer functionality.

At the heart of this movement was one language: JavaScript, and its remote scripting ability.

What Is Remote Scripting?

Essentially, *remote scripting* allows client-side JavaScript to request and receive data from a server without refreshing the web page. This technique enables the developer to create an application that is uninterrupted, making only portions of the page reload with new data.

The term "remote scripting" is quite large in scope, as a variety of JavaScript techniques can be used. These techniques incorporate the use of hidden frames/iframes, dynamically adding <script/> elements to the document, and/or using JavaScript to send HTTP requests to the server; the latter has become quite popular in the last couple of years. These new techniques refresh only portions of a page, both cutting the size of data sent to the browser and making the web page feel more like a conventional application.

What Can It Do?

The concept of remote scripting opens the doors for advanced web applications—ones that mimic desktop applications in form and in function.

A variety of commercial web sites employ the use of remote scripting. These sites look and behave more like desktop applications than like web sites, but that is the whole point of remote scripting. The most notable remote scripting–enabled web applications come from the search giant Google: Google Maps and Google Suggest.

Google Maps

Designed to compete with existing commercial mapping sites (and using images from its Google Earth), Google Maps (`http://maps.google.com`) uses remote scripting to dynamically add map images to the web page. When you enter a location, the main page does not reload at all; the images are dynamically loaded in the map area. Google Maps also enables you to drag the map to a new location, and once again, the map images are dynamically added to the map area (see Figure 16-1).

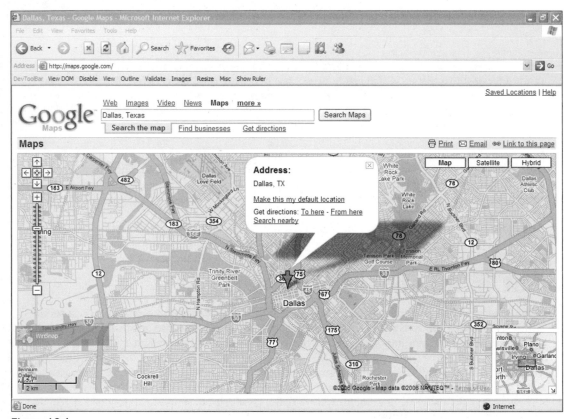

Figure 16-1

Google Suggest

Google Suggest (`http://labs.google.com/suggest/`) is another Google innovation that employs the use of remote scripting. Upon first glance, it appears to be a normal Google search page. When you start typing, however, a drop-down box displays suggestions for search terms that might interest you. To the right of the suggested word or phrase is the number of results the search term returns (see Figure 16-2).

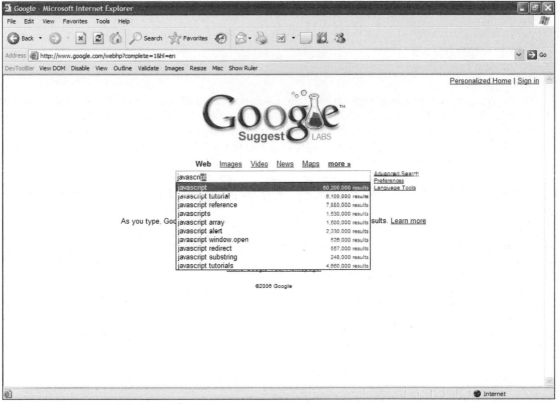

Figure 16-2

Ajax

In 2005, Jesse James Garrett wrote an article entitled "Ajax: A New Approach to Web Applications" (www.adaptivepath.com/publications/essays/archives/000385.php). In it, Garrett states that the interactivity gap between web and desktop applications is becoming smaller, and he cites Google Maps and Google Suggest as proof of this. He christened the new approach *Asynchronous JavaScript + XML*, or *Ajax*. Although the new term was coined in 2005, the underlying methodology of Ajax, which is remote scripting, has been around for many years. In fact, many developers use the terms *remote scripting* and *Ajax* interchangeably. The entire concept of Ajax can be boiled down to client-server communication—which is remote scripting.

For all intents and purposes, when Ajax is mentioned in this chapter, think of remote scripting.

Browser Support

Ajax is limited to the browser that runs the web application, and like every other advanced JavaScript concept we've covered in this book, Ajax capabilities differ from browser to browser. Thankfully, the most common forms of Ajax work in the following browsers:

❑   Internet Explorer 5+

❑   Firefox 1+

❑   Opera 9+

❑   Safari 2+

When using hidden frames, a popular Ajax approach, with these browsers, you'll notice few differences in the code, as each BOM handles frames the same way (we'll cover this approach later in the chapter). However, when you start using other forms of Ajax, the differences in code become apparent.

Ajax with JavaScript: The XMLHttpRequest Object

As stated before, there are a variety of ways that you can create Ajax-enabled applications. However, probably the most popular Ajax technique is using the JavaScript XMLHttpRequest object, which is present in IE 5+, Firefox, Opera, and Safari.

> *Despite its name, you can retrieve other types of data, like plain text, with* XMLHttpRequest.

The XMLHttpRequest object originated as a Microsoft component, called XmlHttp, in the MSXML library first released with IE 5. It offered developers an easy way to open HTTP connections and retrieve XML data. Microsoft improved the component with each new version of MSXML, making it faster and more efficient.

As the popularity of the Microsoft XMLHttpRequest object grew, Mozilla decided to include its own version of the object with Firefox. The Mozilla version maintained the same properties and methods used in Microsoft's ActiveX component, making cross-browser usage possible. Soon after, Opera Software and Apple copied the Mozilla implementation, thus bringing the easy-to-use object to all modern browsers.

Cross-Browser Issues

The XMLHttpRequest object is no different from other web standards supported by the browsers, and the differences can be divided into two camps: the IE 5 and 6 method, and the IE 7, Firefox, Opera, and Safari method. Thankfully, the two browser types only differ when you need to create an XMLHttpRequest object. After the object's creation, the remainder of the code is compatible for every browser.

IE 5 and IE 6: Using ActiveX

Because the XMLHttpRequest object originated as a part of the MSXML library, an ActiveX XML parser, instantiating an XMLHttpRequest under these browsers, requires the creation of an ActiveX object. In Chapter 14, you created ActiveX objects to traverse the XML DOM. Creating an XMLHttp object isn't much different.

```
var oHttp = new ActiveXObject("Microsoft.XMLHttp");
```

This line creates the first version of Microsoft's XMLHttpRequest. There are many other versions of Microsoft's XmlHttp, but Microsoft recommends using one of the following versions:

❑ MSXML2.XmlHttp.6.0

❑ MSXML2.XmlHttp.3.0

You want to use the latest version possible when creating an XmlHttpRequest object; the latest version contains bug fixes and enhanced performance. The downside to this is that not everyone will have the same version installed on their computer. However, you can write a function that can do this.

With the previous version information, you'll write a function called createXmlHttpRequest() to create an XMLHttpRequest object with the latest version supported by the user's computer.

```
function createXmlHttpRequest()
{
    var versions =
    [
        "MSXML2.XmlHttp.6.0",
        "MSXML2.XmlHttp.3.0"
    ];
    //more code here
}
```

This code defines the createXmlHttpRequest() function. Inside it, an array called versions is created to contain the different version names recommended by Microsoft. Notice that the version names are listed starting with the newest first. This is done because you always want to check for the newest version first and continue down the list until you find the version installed on the computer.

To decide what version to use, use a for loop to loop through the elements in the array and then attempt to create an XMLHttpRequest object.

```
function createXmlHttpRequest()
{
    var versions =
    [
        "MSXML2.XmlHttp.6.0",
        "MSXML2.XmlHttp.3.0"
    ];

    for (var i = 0; i < versions.length; i++)
    {
        try
        {
            var oHttp = new ActiveXObject(versions[i]);
            return oHttp;
        }
        catch (error)
        {
            //do nothing here
        }
    }
    //more code here
}
```

A try...catch block is used inside the loop. Unfortunately, this is the only way to determine if a version is installed on the computer. If the following line fails:

```
var oHttp = new ActiveXObject(versions[i]);
```

the code execution drops to the catch block, and since nothing happens in this block, the loop iterates to the next element in the array until a version is found to work or the loop exits. If no version is found on the computer, then the function returns null, like this:

```
function createXmlHttpRequest()
{
    var versions =
    [
        "MSXML2.XmlHttp.6.0",
        "MSXML2.XmlHttp.3.0"
    ];

    for (var i = 0; i < versions.length; i++)
    {
        try
        {
            var oHttp = new ActiveXObject(versions[i]);
            return oHttp;
        }
        catch (error)
        {
            //do nothing here
        }
    }

    return null;
}
```

Now you don't have to worry about ActiveX objects to create an object. If you call this function, it'll do all the work for you.

```
var oHttp = createXmlHttpRequest();
```

The Other Browsers: Native Support

Unlike IE 5 and IE 6, the IE 7, Firefox, Opera, and Safari browsers boast a native implementation of the XMLHttpRequest object, in that it is an object located in the window object. Creating an XMLHttpRequest object is as simple as calling its constructor.

```
var oHttp = new XMLHttpRequest();
```

This line creates an XMLHttpRequest object, which you can use to connect to, and request and receive data from, a server. Unlike the ActiveX object in the previous section, XMLHttpRequest does not have different versions. Simply calling the constructor creates the object, and it is ready to use.

Playing Together

Just as with all other cross-browser problems, a solution can be found to create an XMLHttpRequest object in a cross-browser way. You already wrote the createXmlHttpRequest() function, so you can expand it to provide cross-browser functionality.

```
function createXmlHttpRequest()
{
    if (window.XMLHttpRequest)
    {
        var oHttp = new XMLHttpRequest();
        return oHttp;

    }
    else if (window.ActiveXObject)
    {
        var versions =
        [
            "MSXML2.XmlHttp.6.0",
            "MSXML2.XmlHttp.3.0"
        ];

        for (var i = 0; i < versions.length; i++)
        {
            try
            {
                var oHttp = new ActiveXObject(versions[i]);
                return oHttp;
            }
            catch (error)
            {
                //do nothing here
            }
        }
    }

    return null;
}
```

This new code first checks to see if window.XMLHttpRequest exists. If it does, then an XMLHttpRequest object can be created with the XMLHttpRequest constructor. If this first test fails, then the code checks for window.ActiveXObject for IE 5 and 6 and tries to create an object with the latest MSXML version. If no XMLHttpRequest object can be created (both for IE 5 and 6 and the other browsers), then the function returns null.

The order in which browsers are tested is important; test for window.XMLHttpRequest *first because of IE 7, as the browser supports both* window.XMLHttpRequest *and* window.ActiveXObject.

With this function, you can create an XMLHttpRequest object easily in both browsers. For example:

```
var oHttp = createXmlHttpRequest();
```

Regardless of the user's browser, if it supports XMLHttpRequest, an object will be created.

Using the XMLHttpRequest Object

Once you create the XMLHttpRequest object, you are ready to start requesting data with it. The first step in this process is to call the open() method to initialize the object.

```
oHttp.open(requestType, url, async);
```

This method accepts three arguments. The first, requestType, is a string value consisting of the type of request to make. The values can be either GET or POST. The second argument is the URL to send the request to, and the third is a true or false value indicating whether the request should be made in asynchronous mode. We discussed synchronous and asynchronous modes in Chapter 14, but as a refresher, requests made in synchronous mode halt all JavaScript code from executing until a response is received from the server.

The next step is to send the request; do this with the send() method. This method accepts one argument, which is a string that contains the request body to send along with the request. GET requests do not contain any information, so you must pass null as an argument.

```
var oHttp = createXmlHttpRequest();
oHttp.open("GET", "http://localhost/myTextFile.txt", false);
oHttp.send(null);
```

This code uses a GET request to retrieve a file called myTextFile.txt in synchronous mode. When the send() method is called, the request is sent to the server.

> The send() **method requires an argument to be passed; even if it is** null.

Each XMLHttpRequest object has a status property. This property contains the HTTP status code sent with the server's response. If the requested file is not found, then status is 404. If the request was successful, status is 200. Consider the following example:

```
var oHttp = createXmlHttpRequest();
oHttp.open("GET", "http://localhost/myTextFile.txt", false);
oHttp.send(null);
```

```
if (oHttp.status == 200)
{
    alert("The text file was found!");
}
else if (oHttp.status == 404)
{
    alert("The text file could not be found!");
}
else
{
    alert("An error occurred while attempting to retrieve the file!");
}
```

If the request was successful (the status is 200), then an alert box tells the user that the file was found. If it could not be found (status is 404), an alert box tells the user that the file could not be found. Finally, an alert box tells the user that an error occurred if the status code happened to be something other than 200 or 404.

There are many different HTTP status codes, and checking for every code is not feasible. Most of the time, you should only be concerned with whether your request is successful. Therefore, you can cut the previous code down to this:

```
var oHttp = createXmlHttpRequest();
oHttp.open("GET", "http://localhost/myTextFile.txt", false);
oHttp.send(null);

if (oHttp.status == 200)
{
    alert("The text file was found!");
}
else
{
    alert("An error occurred while attempting to retrieve the file!");
}
```

This code performs the same basic function, but you check only for a status code of 200 and alert a generic message to the user if an error occurred.

Asynchronous Requests

The previous code samples have demonstrated synchronous requests, and the code is simple. Asynchronous requests, on the other hand, are a little more complex and require more code.

The key to asynchronous requests is the onreadystatechange event handler. In asynchronous requests, the XMLHttpRequest object exposes a readyState property, which holds a numeric value; each value refers to a specific ready state of the request.

- ❑ 0 — The object has been created, but the open() method hasn't been called
- ❑ 1 — The open() method has been called, but the request hasn't been sent
- ❑ 2 — The request has been sent
- ❑ 3 — A response has been received from the server
- ❑ 4 — The requested data have been received

Every time the readyState changes, the readystatechange event fires, calling the onreadystate-change event handler. Most of the time, you should be interested in only one state, 4, as this lets you know that the request is complete.

It is important to note that even if the request was successful, you may not have the information you wanted. An error may have occurred on the server's end of the request (a 404, 500, or some other error). Therefore, you still need to check the status code of the request.

Code to handle the readystatechange event could look like this:

```
var oHttp = createXmlHttpRequest();

function oHttp_readyStateChange()
{
    if (oHttp.readyState == 4)
    {
        if (oHttp.status == 200)
        {
            alert(oHttp.responseText);
        }
        else
        {
            alert("An error occurred while retrieving the text file!");
        }
    }
}

//more code here
```

This code first defines the oHttp_readyStateChange() function, which is assigned to the onready-statechange event handler.

First check to see if the readyState is 4, or complete. If so, you know that you can use the received data. Next, check the status property to make sure that everything's okay, and then use the responseText property, which contains the requested file in plain text format, and alert it to the user.

To use the oHttp_readyStateChange() function to handle the readystatechange event, assign it to the onreadystatechange event handler.

```
var oHttp = createXmlHttpRequest();

function oHttp_readyStateChange()
{
    if (oHttp.readyState == 4)
    {
        if (oHttp.status == 200)
        {
            alert(oHttp.responseText);
        }
        else
        {
            alert("An error occurred while retrieving the text file!");
        }
    }
}
oHttp.open("GET", "http://localhost/myTextFile.txt", true);
oHttp.onreadystatechange = oHttp_readyStateChange;
oHttp.send(null);
```

In this new code, first call the open() method, set the request type to GET, and specify the desired URL to send the request to. The call to open() differs from earlier; the final argument is set to true, specifying that you want to make an asynchronous request. Before calling send(), assign the onreadystatechange event handler to the oHttp_readyStateChange() function you previously wrote.

Asynchronous requests certainly do require more code; however, the benefits of using asynchronous communication are well worth the effort, as your other JavaScript code continues to run while the request is made. Perhaps a user-defined class that wraps an XMLHttpRequest object could make asynchronous requests easier to use and manage.

An XMLHttpRequest object also has a property called responseXML, *which attempts to load the received data into an XML DOM (whereas* responseText *just returns plain text). This is the only way Safari 2 can load XML data into a DOM.*

Creating a Remote Scripting Class

Code reuse is an important idea in programming; it is why we define functions to perform specific, common tasks. In Chapter 4, you learned that object-based and object-oriented languages have a different construct for code reuse: a class. A class contains properties that contain data, and/or methods that perform actions with those data.

In this section, you're going to wrap an XMLHttpRequest object into your own class, called HttpRequest, thereby making it easier for you to make asynchronous requests. Before getting into writing the class, we need to discuss a few properties and methods.

In the HttpRequest class, you need to keep track of only one piece of information: the underlying XMLHttpRequest object. Therefore, this class will have only one property:

❑   request—Contains the underlying XMLHttpRequest object

The methods for this class are equally easy to identify.

❑   createXmlHttpRequest()—Creates the XMLHttpRequest object in a cross-browser fashion. It is essentially a copy of the function of the same name written earlier in the chapter.

❑   send()—Sends the request to the server.

With the properties and methods identified, you can begin to write the class.

The HttpRequest Constructor

A class's constructor defines its properties and performs any logic needed in order for the class to function properly.

```
function HttpRequest(sUrl, fpCallback)
{
    this.request = this.createXmlHttpRequest();

    //more code here
}
```

629

The HttpRequest constructor accepts two arguments. The first, sUrl, is a string containing the URL the request should be sent to. The second, fpCallback, is a callback function. It will be called when the server's response is received (when the request's readyState is 4 and its status is 200). The first line of the constructor initializes the request property, assigning an XMLHttpRequest object to it.

With the request property created and ready to use, it's time to prepare the request for sending.

```
function HttpRequest(sUrl, fpCallback)
{
    this.request = this.createXmlHttpRequest();
    this.request.open("GET", sUrl, true);

    function request_readystatechange()
    {
        //more code here
    }

    this.request.onreadystatechange = request_readystatechange;
}
```

The first line of the new code uses the XMLHttpRequest object's open() method to initialize the request object. Set the request type to GET, use the sUrl parameter to specify the URL you want to request, and set the request object to use asynchronous mode. The next few lines define the request_readystate-change() function. Defining a function within a function may seem weird, but it is legal to do so. This function is called a *closure*. The request_readystatechange() function cannot be accessed outside the constructor. It, however, has access to the variables and parameters of the HttpRequest constructor. This function handles the request object's readystatechange event, and you bind it to do so by assigning it to the onreadystatechange event handler.

```
function HttpRequest(sUrl, fpCallback)
{
    this.request = this.createXmlHttpRequest();
    this.request.open("GET", sUrl, true);

    var tempRequest = this.request;
    function request_readystatechange()
    {
        if (tempRequest.readyState == 4)
        {
            if (tempRequest.status == 200)
            {
                fpCallback(tempRequest.responseText);
            }
            else
            {
                alert("An error occurred trying to contact the server.");
            }
        }
    }

    this.request.onreadystatechange = request_readystatechange;
}
```

These new lines of code may look strange. First is the `tempRequest` variable and its value. This variable is a pointer to the current object's `request` property, and it lets you get around scoping issues. Ideally, you would use `this.request` inside the `request_readystatechange()` function. However, in Firefox, `this` points to the `request_readystatechange()` function instead of to the `XMLHttpRequest` object, which would cause the code to not function properly. So when you see `tempRequest`, think `this.request`.

Inside the `request_readystatechange()` function, you see the following line:

```
fpCallback(tempRequest.responseText);
```

This line calls the callback function specified by the constructor's `fpCallback` parameter, and you pass the `responseText` property to this function. This will allow the callback function to use the information received from the server.

Creating the Methods

There are two methods in this class: one is used inside the constructor, and the other enables you to send the request to the server.

Cross-Browser XMLHttpRequest Creation...Again

The first method is `createXmlHttpRequest()`. The inner workings of cross-browser object creation were covered earlier in the chapter, so let's just see the method definition.

```
HttpRequest.prototype.createXmlHttpRequest = function ()
{
    if (window.XMLHttpRequest)
    {
        var oHttp = new XMLHttpRequest();
        return oHttp;
    }
    else if (window.ActiveXObject)
    {
        var versions =
        [
            "MSXML2.XmlHttp.6.0",
            "MSXML2.XmlHttp.3.0"
        ];

        for (var i = 0; i < versions.length; i++)
        {
            try
            {
                var oHttp = new ActiveXObject(versions[i]);
                return oHttp;
            }
            catch (error)
            {
              //do nothing here
            }
        }
    }
```

```
        }

        alert("Your browser doesn't support XMLHttp");
    }
```

In Chapter 4, you learned that class methods are assigned through the `prototype` object. This code follows that rule when writing the `createXmlHttpRequest()` method and the next method.

Sending the Request

Sending a request to the server involves the `XMLHttpRequest` object's `send()` method. This `send()` is similar, with the difference being that it doesn't accept arguments.

```
HttpRequest.prototype.send = function ()
{
    this.request.send(null);
}
```

This version of `send()` is simple in that all you do is call the request object's `send()` method and pass it `null`.

The Full Code

Now that code's been covered, open up your text editor and type the following:

```
function HttpRequest(sUrl, fpCallback)
{
    this.request = this.createXmlHttpRequest();
    this.request.open("GET", sUrl, true);

    var tempRequest = this.request;
    function request_readystatechange()
    {
        if (tempRequest.readyState == 4)
        {
            if (tempRequest.status == 200)
            {
                fpCallback(tempRequest.responseText);
            }
            else
            {
                alert("An error occurred trying to contact the server.");
            }
        }
    }

    this.request.onreadystatechange = request_readystatechange;
}

HttpRequest.prototype.createXmlHttpRequest = function ()
{
    if (window.XMLHttpRequest)
    {
```

```
            var oHttp = new XMLHttpRequest();
            return oHttp;

        }
        else if (window.ActiveXObject)
        {
            var versions =
            [
                "MSXML2.XmlHttp.6.0",
                "MSXML2.XmlHttp.3.0"
            ];

            for (var i = 0; i < versions.length; i++)
            {
                try
                {
                    var oHttp = new ActiveXObject(versions[i]);
                    return oHttp;
                }
                catch (error)
                {
                  //do nothing here
                }
            }
        }

        return null;
    }

HttpRequest.prototype.send = function ()
{
    this.request.send(null);
}
```

Save this file as `httprequest.js`. You'll use it later in the chapter.

The goal of this class was to make asynchronous requests easier to use, so let's look at a brief code-only example and see if that goal was accomplished.

The first thing you need is a function to handle the data received from the request. You'll pass this function to the `HttpRequest` constructor.

```
function handleData(sResponseText)
{
    alert(sResponseText);
}
```

Here is the definition of a function called `handleData()`: it accepts the value of `responseText` (of the `XMLHttpRequest` object) as its only argument. In this example, it merely alerts the data passed to it. Now create an `HttpRequest` object and send the request.

```
var request = new HttpRequest("http://localhost/myTextFile.txt", handleData);
request.send();
```

Pass the text file's location and the `handleData()` function to the constructor. Then send the request with the `send()` method. If the request was successful, `handleData()` is called.

This looks much easier to use (and reuse) than `XMLHttpRequest` code that you have to repeatedly rewrite. You don't have to worry about the `readyState` and `status` properties; the `HttpRequest` class does it all.

Creating a Smarter Form with XMLHttpRequest

You've probably seen it many times: registering as a user on a web site's forum or signing up for web-based e-mail, only to find that your desired user name is taken. Of course, you don't find this out until after you've filled out the entire form, submitted it, and watched the page reload with new data (not to mention that you've lost some of the data you entered). Thankfully, Ajax can soften this frustrating experience and allow the user to know if a user name is taken well in advance of the form's submission.

You can approach this solution in a variety of ways: The easiest to implement provides a link that initiates an HTTP request to the server application to check whether the user's desired information is available to use.

The form you'll build will resemble typical forms used today; it will contain the following fields:

❑ `Username` (validated) — The field where the user types her desired user name

❑ `Email` (validated) — The field where the user types her e-mail

❑ `Password` (not validated) — The field where the user types her password

❑ `Verify Password` (not validated) — The field where the user verifies her password

Note that the `Password` and `Verify Password` fields are just for show in this example. Verifying a typed password is certainly something the server application can do; however, it is far more efficient to let JavaScript perform that verification.

Next to the `Username` and `Email` fields will be a hyperlink that calls a JavaScript function to query the server with the `HttpRequest` class you built earlier in this chapter. The server application is a simple PHP file. PHP programming is beyond the scope of this book. However, we should discuss how to request data from the PHP application, as well as look at the response the application sends back to JavaScript.

Requesting Information

The PHP application looks for one of two arguments in the query string: `username` and `email`.

To check the availability of a user name, use the `username` argument. The URL to do this looks like the following:

```
http://localhost/formvalidator.php?username=[usernameToSearchFor]
```

When searching for a user name, replace [usernameToSearchFor] with the actual name.

Searching for an e-mail follows the same pattern. The e-mail URL looks like this:

```
http://localhost/formvalidator.php?email=[emailToSearchFor]
```

The Received Data

A successful request will result in one of two values:

❑   available—Means that the user name and/or e-mail is available for use

❑   not available—Signifies that the user name and/or e-mail is in use and therefore not available

These values are sent to the client in plain text format. A simple comparison will enable you to tell the user whether her user name or e-mail is already in use.

Before You Begin

This is a live-code Ajax example; therefore, your computer must meet a few requirements if you wish to run this example.

A Web Server

First, you need a web server. If you are using Windows 2000 (Server or Professional), Windows XP Professional, or Windows Server 2003, you have Microsoft's web server software, Internet Information Services, freely available to you. To install it, open Add/Remove Programs in the Control Panel and click Add/Remove Windows Components. Figure 16-3 shows the Windows Component Wizard in Windows XP Professional.

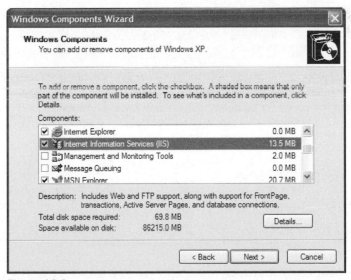

Figure 16-3

Check the box next to IIS and click Next to install. You may need your operating system's installation CD to complete the installation.

If your operating system isn't in the preceding list, or you wish to use another method, you can install Apache HTTP Server (www.apache.org). This is an open-source web server and can run on a variety of operating systems, such as Linux, Unix, and Windows, to list only a few.

PHP

PHP is a popular open source server-side scripting language and must be installed on your computer if you wish to run PHP scripts. You can download PHP in a variety of forms (binaries, Windows installation wizards, and source code) at www.php.net. The PHP code used in this example was written in PHP 4, but it should work just fine in version 5.

Try It Out   **XMLHttpRequest Smart Form**

Open your text editor and type the following:

```
<html>
<head>
    <title>Form Field Validation</title>
    <style type="text/css">
        .fieldname
        {
            text-align: right;
        }

        .submit
        {
            text-align: right;
        }
    </style>
    <script type="text/javascript" src="HttpRequest.js"></script>
    <script type="text/javascript">
        function checkUsername()
        {
            var userValue = document.getElementById("username").value;

            if (userValue == "")
            {
                alert("Please enter a user name to check!");
                return;
            }

            var url = "formvalidator.php?username=" + userValue;

            var request = new HttpRequest(url, checkUsername_callBack);
            request.send();
        }

        function checkUsername_callBack(sResponseText)
        {
```

```
            var userValue = document.getElementById("username").value;

            if (sResponseText == "available")
            {
                alert("The username " + userValue + " is available!");
            }
            else
            {
                alert("We're sorry, but " + userValue + " is not available.");
            }
        }

        function checkEmail()
        {
            var emailValue = document.getElementById("email").value;

            if (emailValue == "")
            {
                alert("Please enter an email address to check!");
                return;
            }

            var url = "formvalidator.php?email=" + emailValue;

            var request = new HttpRequest(url, checkEmail_callBack);
            request.send();
        }

        function checkEmail_callBack(sResponseText)
        {
            var emailValue = document.getElementById("email").value;

            if (sResponseText == "available")
            {
                alert("The email " + emailValue + " is currently not in use!");
            }
            else
            {
                alert("I'm sorry, but " + emailValue + " is in use by another
user.");
            }
        }
    </script>
</head>
<body>
    <form>
        <table>
            <tr>
                <td class="fieldname">
                    Username:
                </td>
                <td>
                    <input type="text" id="username" />
                </td>
```

```
                    <td>
                        <a href="javascript: checkUsername()">Check Availability</a>
                    </td>
                </tr>
                <tr>
                    <td class="fieldname">
                        Email:
                    </td>
                    <td>
                        <input type="text" id="email" />
                    </td>
                    <td>
                        <a href="javascript: checkEmail()">Check Availability</a>
                    </td>
                </tr>
                <tr>
                    <td class="fieldname">
                        Password:
                    </td>
                    <td>
                        <input type="text" id="password" />
                    </td>
                    <td />
                </tr>
                <tr>
                    <td class="fieldname">
                        Verify Password:
                    </td>
                    <td>
                        <input type="text" id="password2" />
                    </td>
                    <td />
                </tr>
                <tr>
                    <td colspan="2" class="submit">
                        <input type="submit" value="Submit" />
                    </td>
                    <td />
                </tr>
            </table>
        </form>
    </body>
</html>
```

Save this file in your web server's root directory. If you're using IIS for your web server, save it as
c:\inetpub\wwwroot\validate_form.htm. If you're using Apache, you'll want to save it inside the
htdocs folder: pathTohtdocs\htdocs\validate_form.htm.

You also need to place `httprequest.js` (the `HttpRequest` class) and the `formvalidator.php` file into the same directory as `validate_form.htm`.

Now open your browser and navigate to `http://localhost/formvalidator.php`. If everything is working properly, you should see the text "PHP is working correctly. Congratulations!" as in Figure 16-4.

Figure 16-4

Now point your browser to `http://localhost/validate_form.htm`, and you should see something like Figure 16-5.

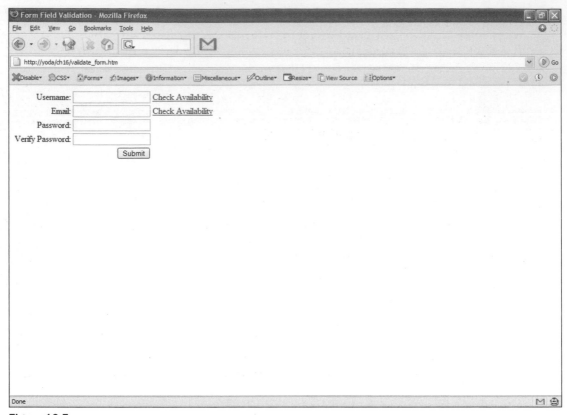

Figure 16-5

Type **jmcpeak** into the `Username` field and click the Check Availability link next to it. You'll see an alert box like the one in Figure 16-6.

Figure 16-6

Now type **someone@xyz.com** in the `Email` field and click the Check Availability link next to it. Again, you'll be greeted with an alert box stating that the e-mail's already in use. Now input your own user name and e-mail into these fields and click the appropriate links. Chances are an alert box will tell you that your user name and/or e-mail is available (the user names `jmcpeak` and `pwilton` and the e-mails `someone@xyz.com` and `someone@zyx.com` are the only ones used by the application).

How It Works

The body of this HTML page is a simple form whose fields are contained within a table. Each form field exists in its own row in the table. The first two rows contain the fields we're most interested in, the Username and Email fields.

```
<form>
    <table>
        <tr>
            <td class="fieldname">
                Username:
            </td>
            <td>
                <input type="text" id="username" />
            </td>
            <td>
                <a href="javascript: checkUsername()">Check Availability</a>
            </td>
        </tr>
        <tr>
            <td class="fieldname">
                Email:
            </td>
            <td>
                <input type="text" id="email" />
            </td>
            <td>
                <a href="javascript: checkEmail()">Check Availability</a>
            </td>
        </tr>
        <!-- HTML to be continued later -->
```

The first column contains text identifiers for the fields. The second column contains the <input/> elements themselves. Each of these tags has an id attribute, username for the Username field and email for the Email field. This enables you to easily find the <input/> elements and get the text entered into them. The third column contains an <a/> element. The hyperlinks use the javascript: protocol to call JavaScript code. In this case, the checkUsername() and checkEmail() functions are called when the user clicks the links. We'll examine these functions in a few moments.

The remaining three rows in the table contain two password fields and the Submit button (the smart form currently does not use these fields). The next two rows also contain three columns: the first is the text describing the field's function, the second contains the <input/> tag, and the third is empty.

```
        <!-- HTML continued from earlier -->
        <tr>
            <td class="fieldname">
                Password:
            </td>
            <td>
                <input type="text" id="password" />
            </td>
            <td />
        </tr>
```

```
        <tr>
            <td class="fieldname">
                Verify Password:
            </td>
            <td>
                <input type="text" id="password2" />
            </td>
            <td />
        </tr>
        <tr>
            <td colspan="2" class="submit">
                <input type="submit" value="Submit" />
            </td>
            <td />
        </tr>
    </table>
</form>
```

The final row contains two cells. The first cell spans two columns and contains the Submit button. The second cell is empty.

The CSS in this HTML page consists of only a couple of rules.

```
.fieldname
{
    text-align: right;
}

.submit
{
    text-align: right;
}
```

The style declarations used are to align the fields to give the form a clean and aligned look.

As stated earlier, the hyperlinks are key to the Ajax functionality, as they call JavaScript functions when clicked. The first function to discuss, checkUsername(), is responsible for retrieving the text the user entered into the Username field, and performing an HTTP request using that information.

```
function checkUsername()
{
    var userValue = document.getElementById("username").value;

    if (userValue == "")
    {
        alert("Please enter a user name to check!");
        return;
    }

    var url = "formvalidator.php?username=" + userValue;

    var request = new HttpRequest(url, checkUsername_callBack);
    request.send();
}
```

To retrieve the user name data, use the document.getElementById() method to retrieve the <input/> element and use the value property to retrieve the text typed into the text box. Next, check to see if the user typed any text by comparing the userValue variable to an empty string (""). If the text box is empty, the function alerts the user to input a user name and stops the function from processing further. If we didn't do this, the application would make unnecessary requests to the server.

Next, construct the URL to make the request to the PHP application. The final steps in this function are to create an HttpRequest object, pass the URL and the callback function, and send the request.

The checkUsername_callBack() function executes when the HttpRequest object receives a complete response from the server. This function uses the requested information to tell the user whether the user name is available. Remember, there are two possible values sent from the server, available and not available; therefore, you need only to check for one of these values.

```
function checkUsername_callBack(sResponseText)
{
    var userValue = document.getElementById("username").value;

    if (sResponseText == "available")
    {
        alert("The username " + userValue + " is available!");
    }
    else
    {
        alert("We're sorry, but " + userValue + " is not available.");
    }
}
```

If the server's response is available, the function tells the user that his desired user name is okay to use. If not, the alert box says that his user name is taken.

Checking the e-mail's availability is a similar process. The checkEmail() function's purpose is to retrieve the text typed in the Email field, and to pass that information to the server application.

```
function checkEmail()
{
    var emailValue = document.getElementById("email").value;

    if (emailValue == "")
    {
        alert("Please enter an email address to check!");
        return;
    }

    var url = "formvalidator.php?email=" + emailValue;

    var request = new HttpRequest(url, checkEmail_callBack);
    request.send();
}
```

The checkEmail_callBack() function is similar to checkUsername_callBack(). The function uses the same logic, but it is based on the Email field's value.

```
function checkEmail_callBack(sResponseText)
{
    var emailValue = document.getElementById("email").value;

    if (sResponseText == "available")
    {
        alert("The email " + emailValue + " is currently not in use!");
    }
    else
    {
        alert("I'm sorry, but " + emailValue + " is in use by another user.");
    }
}
```

Once again, the function checks to see if the server's response is `available`, and if so, to let the user know that the e-mail address is currently not being used. If the address is not available, a different message tells the user his e-mail is not available.

Using `XMLHttpRequest` isn't the only way to tackle this form, and we'll look at implementing this a different way in a little bit.

Creating a Smarter Form with an IFrame

One of the advantages of `XMLHttpRequest` is its ease of use. You simply create the object, send the request, and await the server's response. Unfortunately, the JavaScript object does have a downside: The browser does not log a history of requests made with the object. Therefore, `XMLHttpRequest` essentially breaks the browser's Back button.

The solution to this problem lies in an older Ajax technique: using hidden frames/iframes to facilitate client-server communication. You must use two frames in order for this method to work properly. One must be hidden, and one must be visible.

Note that when you are using an iframe, the document that contains the iframe is the visible frame.

The hidden-frame technique consists of a four-step process. The first step is taken when the user, knowingly or unknowingly, initiates a JavaScript call to the hidden frame. This can be done by the user clicking a link in the visible frame, or some other form of user interaction. This call is usually nothing more complicated than the redirection of the frame to a different web page. This redirection automatically triggers the second step: the request is sent to the server.

After the server finishes processing the request, the third step in the process happens: The server sends the response to the hidden frame. The server's response is a web page, as this response is sent to a hidden frame. When the response is completely received, the web page in the hidden frame must contact the visible frame, telling it that the response is complete. This is the fourth step, and it is sometimes accomplished with the `window.onload` event handler of the hidden frame.

The example in this section is based upon the one built in the previous section. But this time, you'll use a hidden iframe to facilitate the communication between the browser and the server. Before getting into the code, we should first talk about the data received from the server.

> The following example does not work in Safari, as it does not log the history of an iframe.

The Server Response

When we used XMLHttpRequest to get data from the server, we expected only a few words as the server's response. With this different approach, we know our response must consist of two things:

❑ The data, which must be in HTML format

❑ A mechanism to contact the parent document when the iframe receives the HTML response.

Keeping these two things in mind, you can begin to construct the response HTML page.

```
<html>
<head>
    <title>Returned Data</title>
</head>
<body>
    <script type="text/javascript">
        //more code here
    </script>
</body>
</html>
```

This simple HTML page contains a single <script/> element in the body of the document. The JavaScript code contained in this script block will be generated by the PHP application, calling either checkUsername_callBack() or checkEmail_callBack() in the visible frame and passing available or not available as their arguments. Therefore, the following HTML document is a valid response from the PHP application:

```
<html>
<head>
    <title>Returned Data</title>
</head>
<body>
    <script type="text/javascript">
        top.checkUsername_callBack("available", "some_username");
    </script>
</body>
</html>
```

In this sample response, the tested user name is available. Therefore, the HTML page calls the checkUsername_callBack() function in the parent window and passes the string available. Also, the searched user name (or e-mail) is sent back to the client. Do this, because then the client application will display the correct user name or e-mail when the Back or Forward button is pressed. With the response in this format, you can keep a good portion of our JavaScript code the same.

Try It Out   **Iframe Smart Form**

The code for this revised smart form is very similar to the code you used previously with the XMLHttpRequest example. There are, however, a few slight changes. Open up your text editor and type the following:

```
<html>
<head>
    <title>Form Field Validation</title>
    <style type="text/css">
        .fieldname
        {
            text-align: right;
        }

        .submit
        {
            text-align: right;
        }

        #hiddenFrame
        {
            display: none;
        }
    </style>
    <script type="text/javascript">
        function checkUsername()
        {
            var userValue = document.getElementById("username").value;

            if (userValue == "")
            {
                alert("Please enter a user name to check!");
                return;
            }

            var url = "iframe_formvalidator.php?username=" + userValue;

            frames["hiddenFrame"].location = url;
        }

        function checkUsername_callBack(data, userValue)
        {
            if (data == "available")
            {
                alert("The username " + userValue + " is available!");
            }
            else
            {
                alert("We're sorry, but " + userValue + " is not available.");
            }
        }

        function checkEmail()
```

```
        {
            var emailValue = document.getElementById("email").value;

            if (emailValue == "")
            {
                alert("Please enter an email address to check!");
                return;
            }

            var url = "iframe_formvalidator.php?email=" + emailValue;

            frames["hiddenFrame"].location = url;
        }

        function checkEmail_callBack(data, emailValue)
        {
            if (data == "available")
            {
                alert("The email " + emailValue + " is currently not in use!");
            }
            else
            {
                alert("We're sorry, but " + emailValue
                    + " is in use by another user.");
            }
        }
    </script>
</head>
<body>
    <form>
        <table>
            <tr>
                <td class="fieldname">
                    Username:
                </td>
                <td>
                    <input type="text" id="username" />
                </td>
                <td>
                    <a href="javascript: checkUsername()">Check Availability</a>
                </td>
            </tr>
            <tr>
                <td class="fieldname">
                    Email:
                </td>
                <td>
                    <input type="text" id="email" />
                </td>
                <td>
                    <a href="javascript: checkEmail()">Check Availability</a>
                </td>
            </tr>
            <tr>
                <td class="fieldname">
```

```
                        Password:
                </td>
                <td>
                        <input type="text" id="password" />
                </td>
                <td />
        </tr>
        <tr>
                <td class="fieldname">
                        Verify Password:
                </td>
                <td>
                        <input type="text" id="password2" />
                </td>
                <td />
        </tr>
        <tr>
                <td colspan="2" class="submit">
                        <input type="submit" value="Submit" />
                </td>
                <td />
        </tr>
    </table>
  </form>
  <iframe src="about:blank" id="hiddenFrame" name="hiddenFrame" />
</body>
</html>
```

Save this file as `validate_iframe_form.htm`, and save it in your web server's root directory. Also locate the `iframe_formvalidator.php` file from the code download and place it in the same directory.

Open your web browser (not Safari) and navigate to `http://localhost/validate_iframe_form.htm`. You should see something like what is shown in Figure 16-7.

Check for three user names and e-mail addresses. After you clear the final alert box, press the browser's Back button a few times. You'll notice that it is cycling through the information you entered. The text in the text box will not change; however, the alert box will display the names and e-mails you entered. You can do the same thing with the Forward button.

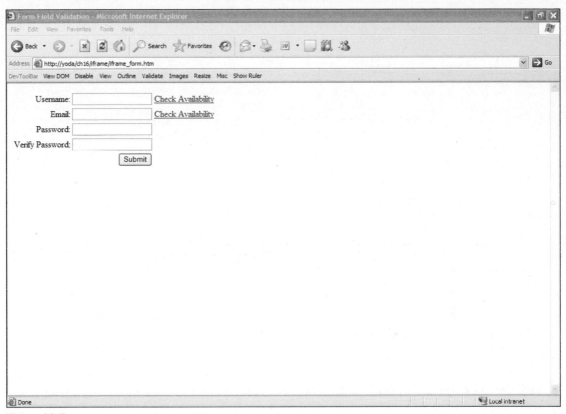

Figure 16-7

How It Works

The HTML in the body of the page remains unchanged except for the addition of the `<iframe/>` tag after the closing `<form/>` tag.

```
<iframe src="about:blank" id="hiddenFrame" name="hiddenFrame" />
```

This frame is initialized to have a blank HTML page loaded. Its `name` and `id` attributes contain the value of `hiddenFrame`. We'll use the value of the `name` attribute later to retrieve this frame from the `frames` collection in the BOM. Next, we set the CSS for the frame.

```
#hiddenFrame
{
    display: none;
}
```

This rule contains one style declaration to hide the iframe from view.

Hiding an iframe through CSS enables you to easily show it if you need to debug the server-side application.

Next up, the JavaScript.

```
function checkUsername()
{
    var userValue = document.getElementById("username").value;

    if (userValue == "")
    {
        alert("Please enter a user name to check!");
        return;
    }

    var url = "iframe_formvalidator.php?username=" + userValue;

    frames["hiddenFrame"].location = url;
}
```

The `checkUsername()` function has undergone a small change: It makes a request via the iframe instead of using `XMLHttpRequest`. It starts by retrieving the value of the `Username` text box. It then checks to see if the user typed anything into the box; if not, an alert box displays a message to the user telling her to enter a user name. If the value isn't an empty string, then the function continues and constructs the URL to send the request to. The final step is to load the URL into the hidden iframe by using the `frames` collection and the `location` property.

The second function, `checkUsername_callBack()`, has also slightly changed. It now accepts two arguments: the first will contain either `available` or `not available`, and the second will contain the user name sent in the request.

```
function checkUsername_callBack(data, userValue)
{
    if (data == "available")
    {
        alert("The username " + userValue + " is available!");
    }
    else
    {
        alert("We're sorry, but " + userValue + " is not available.");
    }
}
```

The function first checks to see if the user name is available. If so, an alert box tells the user that the user name is available. If not, the user sees an alert box stating that the user name is not available.

The functions for searching e-mail addresses are very similar to those for searching user names.

```
function checkEmail()
{
    var emailValue = document.getElementById("email").value;

    if (emailValue == "")
    {
        alert("Please enter an email address to check!");
        return;
    }

    var url = "iframe_formvalidator.php?email=" + emailValue;

    frames["hiddenFrame"].location = url;
}

function checkEmail_callBack(data, emailValue)
{
    if (data == "available")
    {
        alert("The email " + emailValue + " is currently not in use!");
    }
    else
    {
        alert("We're sorry, but " + emailValue + " is in use by another user.");
    }
}
```

The checkEmail() process follows the same pattern as checkUsername(). The function retrieves the text box's value, checks to see if the user entered data, constructs the URL, and loads the URL into the iframe.

The checkEmail_callBack() function contains changes similar to those made to checkUsername_callBack(). The function now accepts two arguments, checks to see if the e-mail is available, and displays a message accordingly.

These two examples are simple, and they were designed as such to focus on the Ajax techniques used to make them work. There are other approaches to smart forms (ones that do not include clicking a link), and while some are just as easy to implement as the ones in this chapter, others are not.

Also, keep in mind what Ajax really is: client-server communication that does not cause the page to refresh. The two key words in that definition are *client* and *server*. As these two examples have shown, a server component is required to handle data from and send data to the client. You'll need to pick up a server-side technology to perform this task in order to use Ajax to its fullest. Any server-side technology will do: PHP, ASP (classic or .NET), ColdFusion, PERL—anything that can output data in a text format.

Things to Watch Out For

Using JavaScript to communicate between server and client adds tremendous power to the language's abilities. However, this power does not come without its share of caveats.

The first two items discussed are more "for your information" than anything else. The third mini-section covers the usability issues: how Ajax breaks some aspects of web pages and how to fix them.

The Same-Origin Policy

Since the early days of Netscape Navigator 2.0, JavaScript cannot access scripts or documents from a different origin. This is a security measure that browser makers adhere to; otherwise, malicious coders could execute code wherever they wanted. The same-origin policy dictates that two pages are of the same origin only if the protocol (HTTP), port (the default is 80), and host are the same.

Consider the following two pages:

❑ Page 1 is located at `http://www.site.com/folder/mypage1.htm`

❑ Page 2 is located at `http://www.site.com/folder10/mypage2.htm`

According to the same-origin policy, these two pages are of the same origin. They share the same host (`www.site.com`), use the same protocol (HTTP), and are accessed on the same port (none is specified; therefore, they both use 80). Since they are of the same origin, JavaScript on one page can access the other page.

Now consider the next two pages:

❑ Page 1 is located at `http://www.site.com/folder/mypage1.htm`

❑ Page 2 is located at `https://www.site.com/folder/mypage2.htm`

These two pages are not of the same origin. The host is the same, and they use the same port. However, their protocols are different. Page 1 uses `HTTP` while Page 2 uses `HTTPS`. This difference, while slight, is enough to give the two pages two separate origins. Therefore, JavaScript on one of these pages cannot access the other page.

So what does this have to do with Ajax? Everything, because a large part of Ajax is JavaScript. For example, because of this policy, an `XMLHttpRequest` object cannot retrieve any file or document from a different origin. You can easily overcome this hurdle by using the server in the page's origin as a proxy to retrieve data from servers of a different origin. This policy also affects the hidden frame/iframe technique. JavaScript cannot interact with two pages of different origins, even if they are in the same frameset.

ActiveX

One of the downsides of `XMLHttpRequest` is in ActiveX, and only affects Internet Explorer on Windows; however, IE currently has the highest market share of all browsers, and it seems that isn't going to change anytime soon. Over the past few years, more security concerns have been raised with ActiveX, especially since many adware and spyware companies have used the technology to install their wares onto trusting user's computers.

Because of this rise in the awareness of security concerns, Microsoft (and users) is taking steps to make the browser more secure from hijacking attempts by restricting access to ActiveX plug-ins and objects. If a user turns off ActiveX completely, or your site is flagged for a certain security zone, ActiveX objects cannot be created, rendering your XMLHttpRequest-based Ajax applications dead in the water.

Usability Concerns

Ajax breaks the mold of traditional web applications and pages. It enables us to build applications that behave in a more conventional, non-"webbish" way. This, however, is also a drawback, as the Internet has been around for many, many years, and users are accustomed to traditional web pages.

Therefore, it is up to us to ensure that the user can use our web pages, and use them as they expect to, without causing frustration.

The Browser's Back Button

The browser's Back and Forward buttons are fundamental to how a user uses the Web. Earlier in the chapter we discussed how XMLHttpRequest breaks these buttons, and we built an Ajax-enabled form that uses a hidden iframe to ensure that the Back and Forward buttons' functionality were preserved.

There are, however, a few issues with this approach. In Internet Explorer, using the hidden frame/iframe technique works with little problem. The browser logs each request made to the server, so you can go back and forward with no problem. The other browsers, however, do have a few quirks worth mentioning.

Firefox, for example, also logs each request, as the example showed. But we added the iframe to the HTML page with the `<iframe>` tag. In some early versions of Firefox, if you dynamically add an `<iframe/>` element to an HTML page by using DOM methods, Firefox will not log the history of the iframe.

Safari is another browser we must watch for; it doesn't store the history of an iframe. A traditional frameset must be used for Safari to log the requests in the history. The hidden frame technique is almost exactly the same as the iframe technique; the only difference is that you use a frameset instead of an iframe.

Dealing with Delays

The web browser is just like any other conventional application in that user interface (UI) cues tell the user that something is going on. When a user clicks a link, the throbber animation runs, an hourglass appears next to the cursor (in Windows), and a status bar usually shows the browser's progress in loading the page.

This is another area in which Ajax solutions, and XMLHttpRequest specifically, miss the mark. This problem, however, is simple to overcome: Simply add UI elements to tell the user something is going on and remove them when the action is completed. Consider the following code:

```
function requestComplete(sResponseText)
{

    //do something with the data here

    document.getElementById("divLoading").style.display = "none";
```

```
    }

    var myRequest = new HttpRequest("http://localhost/myfile.txt", requestComplete);
    document.getElementById("divLoading").style.display = "block";//show that we're
    loading
    myRequest.send();
```

This code uses the `HttpRequest` class built earlier to request a text file. Before sending the request, retrieve an HTML element in the document with an id of `divLoading`. This `<div/>` element tells the user that data is loading. When the request is completed, hide the loading `<div/>` element, which lets the user know that the loading process is completed.

Offering this information to your users lets them know the application is performing some operation that they requested. Otherwise, they may wonder if the application is working correctly when they click something and see nothing instantly happen.

Degrade Gracefully When Ajax Fails

In a perfect world, the code you write would work every time it runs. Unfortunately, you have to face the fact that many times Ajax-enabled web pages will not use the Ajax-enabled goodness, because a user turned off JavaScript in his browser.

The only real answer to this problem is to build an old-fashioned web page with old-fashioned forms, links, and other HTML elements. Then, using JavaScript, you can disable the default behavior of those HTML elements and add Ajax functionality. As an example, consider this hyperlink:

```
    <a href="http://www.wrox.com" title="Wrox Publishing">Wrox Publishing</a>
```

This is a normal, run-of-the-mill hyperlink. When the user clicks it, it will take him to `http://www.wrox.com`. By using JavaScript, you can override this action and replace it with your own.

```
    <a href="http://www.wrox.com" title="Wrox Publishing"
       onclick="return false;">Wrox Publishing</a>
```

The key to this functionality is the `onclick` event handler and returning a value of `false`. You can execute any code you wish with the event handler; just remember to `return false` at the end. This tells the browser to not do anything when the link is clicked. If the user's JavaScript is turned off, the `onclick` event handler is ignored, and the link behaves as it normally should.

As a rule of thumb, build your web page first and add Ajax later.

Summary

In this chapter, you were introduced to the concept of Ajax, a fancy-shmancy word for an old technique called remote scripting.

❑   We discussed the `XMLHttpRequest`, and how it differed between IE 5 & 6, and IE 7, Firefox, Opera, and Safari. You learned how to make both synchronous and asynchronous requests to the server and how to use the `onreadystatechange` event handler.

❑   We built our own Ajax class to make asynchronous HTTP requests easier for us to code.

❑   We used our new Ajax class in a smarter form, one that checks user names and e-mails to see if they are already in use.

❑   We discussed how XMLHttpRequest breaks the browser's Back and Forward buttons, and addressed this problem by rebuilding the same form by using a hidden iframe to make requests.

❑   We looked at some of the downsides to Ajax, the security issues and the gotchas.

Exercise Questions

Suggested solutions for these questions can be found in Appendix A.

Question 1

Extend the HttpRequest class to include synchronous requests in addition to the asynchronous requests the class already makes. You'll have to make some adjustments to your code to incorporate this functionality.

Hint: Create an async *property for the class.*

Question 2

It was mentioned earlier in the chapter that the smart forms could be modified to not use hyperlinks. Change the form that uses the HttpRequest class so that the user name and e-mail fields are checked at form submission. The only time you need to alert the user is when the user name or e-mail is taken.

Hint: Use the new version of HttpRequest *and its new functionality.*

Exercise Solutions

In this appendix you'll find some suggested solutions to the exercise questions that appear at the end of most of the chapters in this book.

Chapter 2

In this chapter you looked at how JavaScript stores and manipulates data such as numbers and text.

Question 1

Write a JavaScript program to convert degrees centigrade into degrees Fahrenheit, and to write the result to the page in a descriptive sentence. The JavaScript equation for Fahrenheit to centigrade is as follows:

```
degFahren = 9 / 5 * degCent + 32
```

Solution

```
<html>
<body>

<script language="JavaScript" type="text/javascript">

var degCent = prompt("Enter the degrees in centigrade",0);
var degFahren = 9 / 5 * degCent + 32;

document.write(degCent + " degrees centigrade is " + degFahren +
    " degrees Fahrenheit");

</script>

</body>
</html>
```

Save this as `ch2_q1.htm`.

You get the degrees centigrade the user wants to convert by using the `prompt()` function, and store it inside the `degCent` variable.

You then do your calculation, which uses the data stored in `degCent` and converts them to Fahrenheit. The result is assigned to the `degFahren` variable.

Finally, you write the results to the web page, building it up in a sentence using the concatenation operator +. Note how JavaScript knows in the calculation that `degCent` is to be treated as a number, but in the `document.write()` it knows that it should be treated as text for concatenation. So how does it know? Simple, it looks at the context. In the calculation, `degCent` is surrounded by numbers and numerical-only operators, such as `*` and `/`. In the `document.write()`, `degCent` is surrounded by strings, hence JavaScript assumes the + means concatenate.

Question 2

The following code uses the `prompt()` function to get two numbers from the user. It then adds those two numbers together and writes the result to the page:

```
<html>
<body>
<script language="JavaScript" type="text/javascript">

var firstNumber = prompt("Enter the first number","");
var secondNumber = prompt("Enter the second number","");
var theTotal = firstNumber + secondNumber;
document.write(firstNumber + " added to " + secondNumber + " equals " +
    theTotal);

</script>
</body>
</html>
```

However, if you try the code out, you'll discover that it doesn't work. Why not?

Change the code so that it does work.

Solution

The data that the `prompt()` actually obtains is a string. So both `firstNumber` and `secondNumber` contain text that happens to be number characters. When you use the + symbol to add the two variables together, JavaScript assumes that since it's string data, you must want to concatenate the two together and not sum them.

To make it explicit to JavaScript that you want to add the numbers together, you need to convert the data to numbers using the `parseFloat()` function.

```
<html>
<body>
<script language="JavaScript" type="text/javascript">
var firstNumber = parseFloat(prompt("Enter the first number",""));
var secondNumber = parseFloat(prompt("Enter the second number",""));
var theTotal = firstNumber + secondNumber;
document.write(firstNumber + " added to " + secondNumber + " equals " +
   theTotal);

</script>
</body>
</html>
```

Save this as `ch2_q2.htm`.

Now the data returned by the `prompt()` function are converted to floating-point numbers before being stored in the `firstNumber` and `secondNumber` variables. Then, when we do the addition that is stored in `theTotal`, JavaScript makes the correct assumption that, because both the variables are numbers, we must mean to add them up and not concatenate them.

The general rule is that where we have expressions with only numerical data, the + operator means *do addition*. If there are any string data, the + will mean concatenate.

Chapter 3

In this chapter you looked at how JavaScript can make decisions based on conditions. You also looked at loops and functions.

Question 1

A junior programmer comes to you with some code that appears not to work. Can you spot where he went wrong? Give him a hand and correct the mistakes.

```
var userAge = prompt("Please enter your age");

if (userAge = 0);
{
   alert("So you're a baby!");
}
else if ( userAge < 0 | userAge > 200)
   alert("I think you may be lying about your age");
else
{
   alert("That's a good age");
}
```

Solution

Oh dear, our junior programmer is having a bad day! There are two mistakes on the following line:

```
if (userAge = 0);
```

First, he has only one equals sign instead of two in the if's condition, which means userAge will be assigned the value of 0 rather than userAge being *compared* to 0. The second fault is the semicolon at the end of the line—statements such as if and loops such as for and while don't require semicolons. The general rule is that if the statement has an associated block (that is, code in curly braces) then no semi-colon is needed. So the line should be as follows:

```
if (userAge == 0)
```

The next fault is with these lines:

```
else if ( userAge < 0 | userAge > 200)
    alert("I think you may be lying about your age");
else
```

The junior programmer's condition is asking if userAge is less than 0 OR userAge is greater than 200. The correct operator for a Boolean OR is ||, but the programmer has only used one |.

```
else if ( userAge < 0 || userAge > 200)
{
    alert("I think you may be lying about your age");
}
else
```

Question 2

Using document.write(), write code that displays the results of the 12 times table. Its output should be the results of the calculations.

```
12 * 1 = 12
12 * 2 = 24
12 * 3 = 36
.....
12 * 11 = 132
12 * 12 = 144
```

Solution

```
<html>
<body>
<script language="JavaScript" type="text/javascript">

var timesTable = 12;
var timesBy;

for (timesBy = 1; timesBy < 13; timesBy++)
```

```
{
    document.write(timesTable + " * " + timesBy + " = " + timesBy * timesTable +
       "<br>");
}
</script>
</body>
</html>
```

Save this as `ch3_q2.htm`.

You use a `for` loop to calculate from 1 * 12 up to 12 * 12. The results are written to the page with `document.write()`. What's important to note here is the effect of the order of precedence; the concatenation operator (the +) has a lower order of precedence than the multiplication operator, *. This means that the `timesBy * timesTable` is done before the concatenation, which is the result you want. If this were not the case, you'd have to put the calculation in parentheses to raise its order of precedence.

Question 3

Change the code of Question 2 so that it's a function that takes as parameters the times table required and the values at which it should start and end. For example, you might try the four times table displayed starting with 4 * 4 and ending at 4 * 9.

Solution

```
<html>
<body>
<script language="JavaScript" type="text/javascript">

function writeTimesTable(timesTable, timesByStart, timesByEnd)
{
    for (;timesByStart <= timesByEnd; timesByStart++)
    {
        document.write(timesTable + " * " + timesByStart + " = " +
            timesByStart * timesTable + "<br>");
    }
}

writeTimesTable(4,4,9);
</script>
</body>
</html>
```

Save this as `ch3_q3.htm`.

You've declared your function, calling it `writeTimesTable()`, and given it three parameters. The first is the times table you want to write, the second is the start point, and the third is the number it should go up to.

You've modified your `for` loop. First you don't need to initialize any variables, so the initialization part is left blank — you still need to put a semicolon in, but there's no code before it. The `for` loop continues while the `timesByStart` parameter is less than or equal to the `timesByEnd` parameter. You can see that, as with a variable, you can modify parameters — in this case, `timesByStart` is incremented by one for each iteration through the loop.

The code to display the times table is much the same. For the function's code to be executed, you now actually need to call it, which you do in the following line:

```
writeTimesTable(4,4,9);
```

This will write the four times table, starting at 4 times 4 and ending at 9 times 4.

Question 4

Modify the code of Question 3 to request the times table to be displayed from the user; the code should continue to request and display times tables until the user enters -1. Additionally, do a check to make sure that the user is entering a valid number; if the number is not valid, ask her to re-enter it.

Solution

```
<html>
<body>
<script language="JavaScript" type="text/javascript">

function writeTimesTable(timesTable, timesByStart, timesByEnd)
{
   for (;timesByStart <= timesByEnd; timesByStart++)
   {
      document.write(timesTable + " * " + timesByStart + " = " +
         timesByStart * timesTable + "<br>");
   }
}

var timesTable;

while ( (timesTable = prompt("Enter the times table",-1)) != -1)
{
   while (isNaN(timesTable) == true)
   {
    timesTable = prompt(timesTable + " is not a valid number, please retry",-1);
   }

   if (timesTable == -1)
   {
      break;
   }

   document.write("<br>The " + timesTable + " times table<br>");
   writeTimesTable(timesTable,1,12);

}
</script>
</body>
</html>
```

Save this as ch3_q4.htm.

The function remains the same, so let's look at the new code. The first change from Question 3 is that you declare a variable, timesTable, and then initialize it in the condition of the first while loop. This may seem like a strange thing to do at first, but it does work. The code in parentheses inside the while loop's condition

```
(timesTable = prompt("Enter the times table",-1))
```

is executed first because its order of precedence has been raised by the parentheses. This will return a value, and it is this value that is compared to -1. If it's not -1, then the while condition is true, and the body of the loop executes. Otherwise it's skipped over, and nothing else happens in this page.

In a second while loop nested inside the first, you check to see that the value the user has entered is actually a number using the function isNaN(). If it's not, then you prompt the user to try again, and this will continue until a valid number is entered.

If the user had entered an invalid value initially, then in the second while loop she may have entered -1, so following the while is an if statement that checks to see if -1 has been entered. If it has, you break out of the while loop; otherwise the writeTimesTable() function is called.

Chapter 4

In this chapter you saw that JavaScript is an object-based language and you saw how to use some of the native JavaScript objects, such as the Date and Math objects.

Question 1

Using the Date object, calculate the date 12 months from now and write this into a web page.

Solution

```
<html>
<body>
<script language="JavaScript" type="text/javascript">
var months = new Array("Jan","Feb","Mar","Apr","May","Jun","Jul","Aug",
                       "Sep","Oct","Nov","Dec");
var nowDate = new Date();

nowDate.setMonth(nowDate.getMonth() + 12);
document.write("Date 12 months ahead is " + nowDate.getDate());
document.write(" " + months[nowDate.getMonth()]);
document.write(" " + nowDate.getFullYear());

</script>
</body>
</html>
```

Save this as ch04_q1.htm.

Because the getMonth() method returns a number between 0 and 11 for the month rather than its name, an array called months has been created that stores the name of each month. You can use getMonth() to get the array index for the correct month name.

The variable nowDate is initialized to a new Date object. Because no initial value is specified, the new Date object will contain today's date.

To add 12 months to the current date you simply use setMonth(). You get the current month value with getMonth(), and then add 12 to it.

Finally you write the result out to the page.

Question 2

Obtain a list of names from the user, storing each name entered in an array. Keep getting another name until the user enters nothing. Sort the names in ascending order, and then write them out to the page, with each name on its own line.

Solution

```
<html>
<body>
<script language="JavaScript" type="text/javascript">

var inputName = "";
var namesArray = new Array();

while ( (inputName = prompt("Enter a name","")) != "" )
{
    namesArray[namesArray.length] = inputName;
}

namesArray.sort();

var namesList = namesArray.join("<br>")
document.write(namesList);

</script>
</body>
</html>
```

Save this as ch04_q2.htm.

First you declare two variables: inputName, which will hold the name entered by the user, and namesArray, which holds an Array object that stores each of the names entered.

You use a while loop to keep getting another name from the user as long as the user hasn't left the prompt box blank. Note that the use of parentheses in the while condition is essential. By placing the following code inside parentheses, you ensure that this is executed first and that a name is obtained from the user and stored in the inputName variable.

```
(inputName = prompt("Enter a name",""))
```

Then you compare the value returned inside the parentheses—whatever was entered by the user—with an empty string (denoted by ""). If they are not equal—that is, if the user did enter a value, you loop around again.

Now, to sort the array into order, you use the sort() method of the Array object.

```
namesArray.sort();
```

Finally, to create a string containing all values contained in the array elements with each being on a new line, you use the HTML <br> tag and write the following:

```
var namesList = namesArray.join("<br>")
document.write(namesList);
```

The code namesArray.join("<br>") creates the string of array elements with a <br> between each. Finally, you write the string into the page with document.write().

Question 3

You saw earlier in the chapter when looking at the pow() method how you could use it inventively to fix a number to a certain number of decimal places. However, there is a flaw in the function you created. A proper fix() function should return 2.1 fixed to three decimal places as

```
2.100
```

However, your fix() function instead returns it as

```
2.1
```

Change the fix() function so that the additional zeros are added where necessary.

Solution

```
<html>
<head>
<script language=JavaScript>

function fix(fixNumber, decimalPlaces)
{
    var div = Math.pow(10,decimalPlaces);
    fixNumber = new String(Math.round(fixNumber * div) / div);
    if (fixNumber.lastIndexOf(".")==-1)
    {
        fixNumber = fixNumber + ".";
```

```
        }

    var zerosRequired = decimalPlaces -
            (fixNumber.length - fixNumber.lastIndexOf(".") - 1);

    for (; zerosRequired > 0; zerosRequired--)
    {
        fixNumber = fixNumber + "0";
    }
    return fixNumber;
}
</script>
</head>
<body>
<script language=JavaScript>

var number1 = prompt("Enter the number with decimal places you want to fix","");
var number2 = prompt("How many decimal places do you want?","");

document.write(number1 + " fixed to " + number2 + " decimal places is: ");
document.write(fix(number1,number2));

</script>
</body>
</html>
```

Save this as ch04_q3.htm.

The function declaration and the first line remain the same as in the fix() function you saw earlier in the chapter. However, things change after that.

You create the fixed number as before, using Math.round(fixNumber * div) / div. What is new is that you pass the result of this as the parameter to the String() constructor that creates a new String object, storing it back in fixNumber.

Now you have your number fixed to the number of decimal places required, but it will still be in the form 2.1 rather than 2.100, as required. Your next task is therefore to add the extra zeros required. To do this you need to subtract the number of digits after the decimal point from the number of digits required after the decimal point as specified in decimalPlaces. First, to find out how many digits are after the decimal point, you write this:

```
    (fixNumber.length - fixNumber.lastIndexOf(".") - 1)
```

For your number of 2.1, fixNumber.length will be 3. fixNumber.lastIndexOf(".") will return 1; remember that the first character is 0, the second is 1, and so on. So fixNumber.length - fixNumber.lastIndexOf(".") will be 2. Then you subtract 1 at the end, leaving a result of 1, which is the number of digits after the decimal place.

The full line is as follows:

```
    var zerosRequired = decimalPlaces -
            (fixNumber.length - fixNumber.lastIndexOf(".") - 1);
```

You know the last bit (`fixNumber.length - fixNumber.lastIndexOf(".") - 1`) is 1 and that the `decimalPlaces` parameter passed is 3. Three minus one leaves two zeros that must be added.

Now that you know how many extra zeros are required, let's add them.

```
for (; zerosRequired > 0; zerosRequired--)
{
    fixNumber = fixNumber + "0";
}
```

Now you just need to return the result from the function to the calling code.

```
roturn fixNumber;
```

Chapter 5

This chapter dealt with how JavaScript uses the objects, methods, properties, and events made available by the BOM (Browser Object Model) of the user's browser.

Question 1

Create a page with a number of links. Then write code that fires on the window `onload` event, displaying the `href` of each of the links on the page.

Solution

```
<html>
<head>
<script language="JavaScript" type="text/javascript">
function displayLinks()
{
    var linksCounter;

    for (linksCounter = 0; linksCounter < document.links.length; linksCounter++)
    {
        alert(document.links[linksCounter].href);
    }

}
</script>
</head>
<body onload="displayLinks()">

<A href="link0.htm" >Link 0</A>
<A href="link1.htm">Link 2</A>
<A href="link2.htm">Link 2</A>


</body>
</html>
```

Save this as ch05_q1.htm.

You connect to the window object's onload event handler by adding an attribute to the <body> tag.

```
<body onload="displayLinks()">
```

On the onload event firing, this will run the script in quotes calling the displayLinks() function.

In this function you use a for loop to cycle through each A object in the document object's links array.

```
function displayLinks()
{
    var linksCounter

    for (linksCounter = 0; linksCounter < document.links.length; linksCounter++)
    {
        alert(document.links[linksCounter].href);
    }

}
```

You used the length property of the links array in your condition to determine how many times you need to loop. Then, using an alert box, you display each A object's href property. You can't use document.write() in the onload event, because it occurs when the page has finished loading.

Question 2

Create two pages, one called IEOnly.htm and the other called FFOnly.htm. Each page should have a heading telling you what page is loaded, for example:

```
<H2>Welcome to the Internet Explorer only page</H2>
```

Using the functions for checking browser type, connect to the window object's onload event handler and detect what browser the user has. Then if it's the wrong page for that browser, redirect to the other page.

Solution

The FFOnly.htm page is as follows:

```
<html>
<head>
<script language="JavaScript" type="text/javascript">

function getBrowserName()
{
    var lsBrowser = navigator.userAgent;
    if (lsBrowser.indexOf("MSIE") >= 0)
    {
        lsBrowser = "MSIE";
    }
    else if (lsBrowser.indexOf("Netscape") >= 0)
```

```
    {
        lsBrowser = "Netscape";
    }
    else if (lsBrowser.indexOf("Firefox") >= 0)
    {
        lsBrowser = "Firefox";
    }
    else if (lsBrowser.indexOf("Safari") >= 0)
    {
        lsBrowser = "Safari";
    }
    else if (lsBrowser.indexOf("Opera") >= 0)
    {
        lsBrowser = "Opera";
    }
    else
    {
        lsBrowser = "UNKNOWN";
    }
    return lsBrowser;
}


function checkBrowser()
{
    if (getBrowserName() == "MSIE")
    {
        window.location.replace("IEOnly.htm");
    }
}

</script>
</head>
<body onload="checkBrowser()">

<H2>Welcome to the Firefox only page</H2>

</body>
</html>
```

The IEOnly.htm page is very similar:

```
<html>
<head>
<script language="JavaScript" type="text/javascript">

function getBrowserName()
{
    var lsBrowser = navigator.userAgent;
    if (lsBrowser.indexOf("MSIE") >= 0)
    {
        lsBrowser = "MSIE";
    }
    else if (lsBrowser.indexOf("Netscape") >= 0)
```

```
    {
        lsBrowser = "Netscape";
    }
    else if (lsBrowser.indexOf("Firefox") >= 0)
    {
        lsBrowser = "Firefox";
    }
    else if (lsBrowser.indexOf("Safari") >= 0)
    {
        lsBrowser = "Safari";
    }
    else if (lsBrowser.indexOf("Opera") >= 0)
    {
        lsBrowser = "Opera"
    }
    else
    {
        lsBrowser = "UNKNOWN"
    }
    return lsBrowser;
}

function checkBrowser()
{
    if (getBrowserName() == "Firefox")
    {
        window.location.replace("FFOnly.htm");
    }
}

</script>
</head>
<body onload="checkBrowser()">

<H2>Welcome to the Internet Explorer only page</H2>

</body>
</html>
```

Starting with the IEOnly.htm page, first you add an onload event handler, so that on loading of the page, your checkBrowser() function is called.

```
<body onload="checkBrowser()">
```

Then, in checkBrowser(), you use your getBrowserName() function to tell you which browser the user has. If it's Firefox, you replace the page loaded with the FFOnly.htm page. Note that you use replace() rather than href, because you don't want the user to be able to hit the browser's Back button. This way it's less easy to spot that a new page is being loaded.

```
function checkBrowser()
{
    if (getBrowserName() == "Firefox")
    {
```

```
         window.location.replace("FFOnly.htm");
      }
   }
```

The `FFOnly.htm` page is identical, except that in your `if` statement you check for `MSIE` and redirect to `IEOnly.htm` if it is `MSIE`.

```
function checkBrowser()
{
   if (getBrowserName() == "MSIE")
   {
      window.location.replace("IEOnly.htm");
   }
}
```

Question 3

Insert an image in the page with the `<img>` tag. When the mouse pointer rolls over the image, it should switch to a different image. When the mouse pointer rolls out (leaves the image), it should swap back again.

Solution

```
<html>
<head>
<script language="JavaScript" type="text/javascript">

function mouseOver()
{
   document.images["myImage"].src = "Img2.jpg";
}

function mouseOut()
{
   document.images["myImage"].src = "Img1.jpg";
}
</script>
</head>
<body>

      <img src="Img1.jpg"
         name="myImage"
         onmouseover="mouseOver()"
         onmouseout="mouseOut()">

</body>
</html>
```

Save this as `ch05_q3.htm`.

At the top of the page you define your two functions to handle the onmouseover and onmouseout events.

```
function mouseOver()
{
    document.images["myImage"].src = "Img2.jpg";
}

function mouseOut()
{
    document.images["myImage"].src = "Img1.jpg";
}
```

The function names tell you what events they will be handling. You access the img object for your <img> tag using the document.images array and putting the name in square brackets. In the onmouseover event you change the src property of the image to Img2.jpg, and in the onmouseout event you change it back to img1.jpg, the image you specified when the page was loaded.

In the page itself you have your <img> tag.

```
<img src="Img1.jpg"
    name="myImage"
    onmouseover="mouseOver()"
    onmouseout="mouseOut()">
```

Chapter 6

In this chapter you looked at how to add a user interface onto your JavaScript so that you can interact with your users and acquire information from them.

Question 1

Using the code from the temperature converter example you saw in Chapter 2, create a user interface for it and connect it to the existing code so that the user can enter a value in degrees Fahrenheit and convert it to centigrade.

Solution

```
<html>
<head>
<script language="JavaScript" type="text/javascript">
function convertToCentigrade(degFahren)
{
    var degCent;
    degCent = 5/9 * (degFahren - 32);

    return degCent;
}

function butToCent_onclick()
```

```
    {
        var CalcBox = document.form1.txtCalcBox;

        if (isNaN(CalcBox.value) == true || CalcBox.value == "")
        {
            CalcBox.value = "Error Invalid Value";
        }
        else
        {
            CalcBox.value = convertToCentigrade(CalcBox.value);
        }
    }
    </script>
    </head>
    <body>

    <form name=form1>
    <P>
        <input type="text" name=txtCalcBox value-"0.0">
    </P>
        <input type="button"
            value="Convert to centigrade"
            name=butToCent
            onclick="butToCent_onclick()">
    </form>
    </body>
    </html>
```

Save this as ch06_q1.htm.

The interface part is simply a form containing a text box into which users enter the Fahrenheit value and a button they click to convert that value to centigrade. The button has its onclick event handler set to call a function called butToCent_onclick().

The first line of butToCent_onclick() declares a variable and sets it to reference the object representing the text box.

```
        var CalcBox = document.form1.txtCalcBox;
```

Why do this? Well, in your code when you want to use document.form1.txtCalcBox, you can now just use the much shorter CalcBox; it saves typing and keeps your code shorter and easier to read.

So

```
        alert(document.form1.txtCalcBox.value);
```

is the same as

```
        alert(CalcBox.value);
```

In the remaining part of the function you do a sanity check—if what the user has entered is a number (that is, it is not NotANumber) and the text box does contain a value, you use the Fahrenheit-to-centigrade conversion function you saw in Chapter 2 to do the conversion, the results of which are used to set the text box's value.

Question 2

Create a user interface that allows the user to pick the computer system of her dreams, similar in principle to the e-commerce sites selling computers over the Internet. For example, she could be given a choice of processor type, speed, memory, and hard drive size, and the option to add additional components like a DVD-ROM drive, a sound card, and so on. As the user changes her selections, the price of the system should update automatically and notify her of the cost of the system as she has specified it, either by using an alert box or by updating the contents of a text box.

Solution

```
<html>
<head>

<script language="JavaScript" type="text/javascript">
var CompItems = new Array();
CompItems[100] = 1000;
CompItems[101] = 1250;
CompItems[102] = 1500;

CompItems[200] = 35;
CompItems[201] = 65;
CompItems[202] = 95;

CompItems[300] = 50;
CompItems[301] = 75;
CompItems[302] = 100;

CompItems[400] = 10;
CompItems[401] = 15;
CompItems[402] = 25;
function updateOrderDetails()
{
   var total = 0;
   var orderDetails = "";
   var formElement;
   formElement =
      document.form1.cboProcessor[document.form1.cboProcessor.selectedIndex];
   total = parseFloat(CompItems[formElement.value]);
   orderDetails = "Processor : " + formElement.text;
   orderDetails = orderDetails + " $" + CompItems[formElement.value] + "\n";

   formElement =
      document.form1.cboHardDrive[document.form1.cboHardDrive.selectedIndex];
   total = total + parseFloat(CompItems[formElement.value]);
   orderDetails = orderDetails + "Hard Drive : " + formElement.text;
   orderDetails = orderDetails + " $" + CompItems[formElement.value] + "\n";

   formElement = document.form1.chkCDROM
```

```
      if (formElement.checked -- true)
      {
         orderDetails = orderDetails + "CD-ROM : $" +
            CompItems[formElement.value] + "\n";
         total = total + parseFloat(CompItems[formElement.value]);
      }

      formElement = document.form1.chkDVD
      if (formElement.checked == true)
      {
         orderDetails = orderDetails + "DVD-ROM : $" +
            CompItems[formElement.value] + "\n";
         total = total + parseFloat(CompItems[formElement.value]);
      }

      formElement = document.form1.chkScanner
      if (formElement.checked == true)
      {
         orderDetails = orderDetails + "Scanner : $" +
            CompItems[formElement.value] + "\n";
         total = total + parseFloat(CompItems[formElement.value]);
      }

      formElement = document.form1.radCase
      if (formElement[0].checked == true)
      {
         orderDetails = orderDetails + "Desktop Case : $" +
            CompItems[formElement[0].value];
         total = total + parseFloat(CompItems[formElement[0].value]);
      }
      else if (formElement[1].checked == true)
      {
         orderDetails = orderDetails + "Mini Tower Case : $" +
            CompItems[formElement[1].value];
         total = total + parseFloat(CompItems[formElement[1].value]);
      }
      else
      {
         orderDetails = orderDetails + "Full Tower Case : $" +
            CompItems[formElement[2].value]
         total = total + parseFloat(CompItems[formElement[2].value]);
      }

      orderDetails = orderDetails + "\n\nTotal Order Cost is $" + total;

      document.form1.txtOrder.value = orderDetails;
}

</script>
</head>

<body>
<form name="form1">
<table>
<TR>
```

```
<TD width="300">
Processor
<br>
<select name=cboProcessor>
    <option value="100">MegaPro 10ghz</option>
    <option value="101">MegaPro 12</option>
    <option value="102">MegaPro 15ghz</option>
</select>
<br><br>
Hard drive
<br>
<select name=cboHardDrive>
    <option value="200">30tb</option>
    <option value="201">40tb</option>
    <option value="202">60tb</option>
</select>
<br><br>
CD-ROM
<input type="checkbox" name=chkCDROM value="300">
<br>
DVD-ROM
<input type="checkbox" name=chkDVD value="301">
<br>
Scanner
<input type="checkbox" name=chkScanner value="302">
<br><br>
Desktop Case
<input type="radio" name=radCase checked value="400">
<br>
Mini Tower
<input type="radio" name=radCase value="401">
<br>
Full Tower
<input type="radio" name=radCase value="402">
<P>
<input type="button" value="Update" name=butUpdate onclick="updateOrderDetails()">
</P>
</TD>
<TD>
<textarea rows="20" cols="35" id=txtOrder name="txtOrder">
</textarea>
</TD>
</TR>
</table>
</form>
</body>
</html>
```

Save this as ch06_q2.htm.

This is just one of many ways to tackle this question — you may well have thought of a better way.

Here we are displaying the results of the user's selection as text in a textarea box, with each item and its cost displayed on separate lines and a final total at the end.

Each form element has a value set to hold a stock ID number. For example, a full tower case is stock ID 402. The actual cost of the item is held in arrays defined at the beginning of the page. Why not just store the price in the value attribute of each form element? Well, this way is more flexible. Currently your array just holds price details for each item, but we could modify it that so it holds more data — for example price, description, number in stock, and so on. Also, if this form is posted to a server the values passed will be stock IDs, which we could then use for a lookup in a stock database. If the values were set to prices and the form were posted, we'd have no way of telling what the customer ordered — all we'd know is how much it all cost.

This solution includes an Update button which, when clicked, updates the order details in the textarea box. However, you may want to add event handlers to each form element and update when anything changes.

Turning to the function that actually displays the order summary, updateOrderDetails(), we can see that there is a lot of code, and although it looks complex, it's actually fairly simple. A lot of it is repeated with slight modification.

To save on typing and make the code a little more readable, this solution declares a variable, formElement, which will be set to each element on the form in turn and used to extract the stock ID and, from that, the price. After the variable's declaration, we then find out which processor has been selected, calculate the cost, and add the details to the textarea.

```
formElement =
    document.form1.cboProcessor[document.form1.cboProcessor.selectedIndex];
total = parseFloat(CompItems[formElement.value]);
orderDetails = "Processor : " + formElement.text;
orderDetails = orderDetails + " $" + CompItems[formElement.value] + "\n";
```

The selectedIndex property tells us which Option object inside the select control has been selected by the user, and we set our formElement variable to reference that.

The same principle applies when we find the hard drive size selected, so let's turn next to the check boxes for the optional extra items, looking first at the CD-ROM check box.

```
formElement = document.form1.chkCDROM
if (formElement.checked == true)
{
    orderDetails = orderDetails + "CD-ROM : $" +
        CompItems[formElement.value] + "\n";
    total = total + parseFloat(CompItems[formElement.value]);
}
```

Again, we set the formElement variable to now reference the chkCDROM check box object. Then, if the check box is checked, we add a CD-ROM to the order details and update the running total. The same principle applies for the DVD and scanner check boxes.

Finally, we have the case type. Because only one case type out of the options can be selected, we've used a radio button group. Unfortunately, there is no selectedIndex for radio buttons as there is for check boxes, so we have to go through each radio button in turn and find out if it has been selected.

```
formElement = document.form1.radCase
if (formElement[0].checked == true)
```

```
{
    orderDetails = orderDetails + "Desktop Case : $" +
        CompItems[formElement[0].value];
    total = total + parseFloat(CompItems[formElement[0].value]);
}
    else if (formElement[1].checked == true)
{
    orderDetails = orderDetails + "Mini Tower Case : $" +
        CompItems[formElement[1].value];
    total = total + parseFloat(CompItems[formElement[1].value]);
}
else
{
    orderDetails = orderDetails + "Full Tower Case : $" +
        CompItems[formElement[2].value]
    total = total + parseFloat(CompItems[formElement[2].value]);
}
```

We check to see which radio button has been selected and add its details to the textarea and its price to the total. If our array of stock defined at the beginning of the code block had further details, such as description as well as price, we could have looped through the radio button array and added the details based on the CompItems array.

Finally, we set the textarea to the details of the system the user has selected.

```
orderDetails = orderDetails + "\n\nTotal Order Cost is " + total;
document.form1.txtOrder.value = orderDetails;
```

Chapter 7

In this chapter you looked at how you could put frames into your web pages and how to write JavaScript code that scripted between frames. You also learned how to open and modify new browser windows using script.

Question 1

In the previous chapter's exercise questions, you created a form that allowed the user to pick a computer system. He could view the details of his system and its total cost by clicking a button that wrote the details to a textarea. Change the example so it's a frames-based web page; instead of writing to a text area, the user should write the details to another frame.

Solution

The solution shown here involves a frameset that divides the page into two frames, left and right. In the left frame you have the form that allows the user to pick his system. The system chosen is summarized in the right frame when the user clicks an Update button.

The first page is the top frameset-defining page and is the one that needs to be loaded into the browser first.

```
<html>
<head>
</head>
<frameset cols="55%,*">
    <frame src="PickSystem.htm" name="pickSystem">
    <frame src="blank.htm" name="systemSummary">
</frameset>

</html>
```

Save this as ch7Q1TopFrame.htm.

Finally, you come to the page that's loaded into the left frame and that allows the user to choose his computer system and its components. This is very similar to the solution to Question 2 in the previous chapter, so this example will show only what's been changed. All the changes are within the updateOrderDetails() function.

```
function updateOrderDetails()
{
   var total = 0;
   var orderDetails = "<H3>Your selected system</H3>";
   var formElement;
   formElement =
      document.form1.cboProcessor[document.form1.cboProcessor.selectedIndex];
   total = parseFloat(CompItems[formElement.value]);
   orderDetails = orderDetails + "Processor : " + formElement.text
   orderDetails = orderDetails + " $" + CompItems[formElement.value] + "<br>";

   formElement =
      document.form1.cboHardDrive[document.form1.cboHardDrive.selectedIndex];
   total = total + parseFloat(CompItems[formElement.value]);
   orderDetails = orderDetails + "Hard Drive : " + formElement.text
   orderDetails = orderDetails + " $" + CompItems[formElement.value] + "<br>";

   formElement = document.form1.chkCDROM
   if (formElement.checked == true)
   {
      orderDetails = orderDetails + "CD-ROM : $" +
         CompItems[formElement.value] + "<br>";
      total = total + parseFloat(CompItems[formElement.value]);
   }

   formElement = document.form1.chkDVD
   if (formElement.checked == true)
   {
      orderDetails = orderDetails + "DVD-ROM : $" +
         CompItems[formElement.value] + "<br>";
      total = total + parseFloat(CompItems[formElement.value]);
   }

   formElement = document.form1.chkScanner
```

```
    if (formElement.checked == true)
    {
        orderDetails = orderDetails + "Scanner : $" +
            CompItems[formElement.value] + "<br>";
        total = total + parseFloat(CompItems[formElement.value]);
    }

    formElement = document.form1.radCase
    if (formElement[0].checked == true)
    {
        orderDetails = orderDetails + "Desktop Case : $" +
            CompItems[formElement[0].value] + "<br>";
        total = total + parseFloat(CompItems[formElement[0].value]);
    }
    else if (formElement[1].checked == true)
    {
        orderDetails = orderDetails + "Mini Tower Case : $" +
            CompItems[formElement[1].value] + "<br>";
        total = total + parseFloat(CompItems[formElement[1].value]);
    }
    else
    {
        orderDetails = orderDetails + "Full Tower Case : $" +
            CompItems[formElement[2].value]
        total = total + parseFloat(CompItems[formElement[2].value]);
    }

    orderDetails = orderDetails + "<P>Total Order Cost is $" + total + "</P>";

    window.parent.systemSummary.document.open();
    window.parent.systemSummary.document.write(orderDetails);
    window.parent.systemSummary.document.close();
}
```

One final optional change is to remove the text area control, as it's no longer needed.

Save this as `PickSystem.htm`, and load `ch7Q1TopFrame.htm` into your browser to try out the code.

The first difference between this and the code from Question 2 in the last chapter is that when creating the text summarizing the system, you are creating HTML rather than plain text, so rather than `\n` for new lines you use the `<br>` tag.

The main change, however, is the following three lines:

```
    window.parent.systemSummary.document.open();
    window.parent.systemSummary.document.write(orderDetails);
    window.parent.systemSummary.close();
```

Instead of setting the value of a text area box as you did in the solution to Question 2 in the last chapter, this time you are writing the order summary to an HTML page, the page contained in the right-hand frame, `systemSummary`. First you open the document for writing, then write out your string, and finally close the document, indicating that you have completed your writing to the page.

Question 2

The first example in this chapter was a page with images of books, in which clicking on a book's image brought up information about that book in a pop-up window. Amend this so that the pop-up window also has a button or link that, when clicked, adds the item to the user's shopping basket. Also, on the main page, give the user some way of opening up a shopping basket window with details of all the items he has purchased so far, and give him a way of deleting items from this basket.

Solution

This is the most challenging exercise so far, but by the end you'll see how a more complex application can be created using JavaScript. The solution to this exercise involves four pages: two that display the book's details (very similar to the pages you created in the example), a third that displays the book's images and opens the new windows, and a fourth, totally new page, which holds the shopping basket

Let's look at the main page to be loaded, called online_books.htm.

```html
<html>
<head>
<title>Online Books</title>
<script language="JavaScript" type="text/javascript">
var detailsWindow;
var basketWindow;

var stockItems = new Array();

stockItems[100] = new Array();
stockItems[100][0] = "Beginning ASP.net 2";
stockItems[100][1] = "$39.99";
stockItems[100][2] = 0;

stockItems[101] = new Array();
stockItems[101][0] = "Professional JavaScript";
stockItems[101][1] = "$46.99";
stockItems[101][2] = 0;

function removeItem(stockId)
{
    stockItems[stockId][2] = 0;
    alert("Item Removed");
    showBasket();
    return false;
}

function showDetails(bookURL)
{
    detailsWindow = window.open(bookURL,"bookDetails","width=400,height=500");
    detailsWindow.focus();
    return false;
}

function addBookToBasket(stockId)
```

```
{
    stockItems[stockId][2] = 1;
    alert("Item added successfully");
    detailsWindow.close();
}

function showBasket()
{
    basketWindow =
        window.open('ShoppingBasket.htm','shoppingBasket','width=400,height=350');
    basketWindow.document.open();
    var basketItem;
    var containsItems = false;
    basketWindow.document.write("<H4>Your shopping basket contains :</H4>");

    for (basketItem in stockItems)
    {
        if (stockItems[basketItem][2] > 0)
        {
            basketWindow.document.write(stockItems[basketItem][0] + " at ");
            basketWindow.document.write(stockItems[basketItem][1]);
            basketWindow.document.write("    ");
            basketWindow.document.write("<A href='' onclick='return " +
"window.opener.removeItem(" + basketItem + ")'>");
            basketWindow.document.write("Remove Item</A><br>");
            containsItems = true;
        }
    }

    if (containsItems == false)
    {
        basketWindow.document.write("<H4>No items</H4>");
    }
    basketWindow.document.close();
    basketWindow.focus();
}

</script>
</head>
<body>
<H2 align=center>Online Book Buyer</H2>
<form name=form1>
<input type="button" value="Show Shopping Basket" onclick="showBasket()"
name=butShowBasket>
</form>
<P>
Click any of the images below for more details
</P>
<strong>Beginning ASP.net 2</strong>
<br>
<A name="begASPLink" href="" onclick="return showDetails('beg_asp2_details.htm')">
<img src="beg_asp.gif" width-"100" height="129" border=0></A>
<br>
<br>
<strong>Professional JavaScript</strong>
```

```
<br>
<A name="profJSLink" href=""
onclick="return showDetails('prof_js_details.htm')">
<img src="prof_js.gif" border=0>
</A>
</body>
</html>
```

Please note the line basketWindow.document.write("<A href=" onclick='return " + " window.opener.removeItem(" + basketItem + ")'>"); *must be on one line. Because of the size of the page it has been split in the preceding code listing.*

The details of the books are stored in the stockItems array, which you've made a multi-dimensional array. The second dimension stores the book's title, its price, and finally the quantity the customer has in his basket.

So in the first element, you have this:

```
stockItems[100] = new Array();
stockItems[100][0] = "Beginning ASP.Net 2";
stockItems[100][1] = "$39.99";
stockItems[100][2] = 0;
```

[100][0] is the title, [100][1] is the price, and finally [100][2] is the quantity required, which starts as 0. In fact, though a customer may order more than one of a certain book, the code does not facilitate that.

The first function defined in the code is removeItem().

```
function removeItem(stockId)
{
   stockItems[stockId][2] = 0;
   alert("Item Removed");
   showBasket();
   return false;
}
```

This removes a book from the shopping basket. The parameter stockId is simply the array element index of that book, which you then use to set the quantity element of the second dimension to 0.

Next, you have the function that adds a book to the shopping basket.

```
function addBookToBasket(stockId)
{
   stockItems[stockId][2] = 1;
   alert("Item added successfully");
   detailsWindow.close();
}
```

The final function displays the contents of the shopping basket in a new window.

```
function showBasket()
{
    basketWindow =
        window.open('ShoppingBasket.htm','shoppingBasket','width=400,height=350');
    basketWindow.document.open();
    var basketItem;
    var containsItems = false;
    basketWindow.document.write("<H4>Your shopping basket contains :</H4>");

    for (basketItem in stockItems)
    {
        if (stockItems[basketItem][2] > 0)
        {
            basketWindow.document.write(stockItems[basketItem][0] + " at ");
            basketWindow.document.write(stockItems[basketItem][1]);
            basketWindow.document.write("    ");
            basketWindow.document.write("<A href='' onclick='return " +
            " window.opener.removeItem(" + basketItem + ")'>");
            basketWindow.document.write("Remove Item</A><br>");
            containsItems = true;
        }
    }

    if (containsItems == false)
    {
        basketWindow.document.write("<H4>No items</H4>");
    }
    basketWindow.document.close();
    basketWindow.focus();
}
```

A new window is opened up and its window object reference is stored in basketWindow. You then write to the new window's document. First you write a heading, and then you loop through each item in the stockItems array and check the quantity element of the second dimension, which is stockItems[basketItem][2]. If it is greater than zero, you write the book's details to the shopping list window. You also write out a link to the shopping basket that when clicked calls your removeItem() function.

Let's create the shopping basket page.

```
<html>
<head>
<title>Shopping Basket</title>
</head>
<body>
</body>
</html>
```

Save this as ShoppingBasket.htm. There's no code, but if you don't create the page and load it into the shopping basket window, you won't be able to document.write() to it.

Finally, you need to create the book description pages. First you have prof_js_details.htm. This is identical to the version you created for the example, except for the addition of the form and button inside. When clicked, the button calls the addToBasket() function in the window that opened this window — that is, your online_books.htm page.

```
<html>
<head>
<title>Professional JavaScript</title>
</head>
<body><strong>Professional JavaScript</strong>
<br>
<form name=form1>
<input type="button" value="Add to basket" name=butAddBook
      onclick="window.opener.addBookToBasket(101)">
</form>

<strong>Subjects</strong>
    ECMAScript<br>
    Internet<br>JavaScript
    <br>XML and Scripting<BR>

<HR color=#cc3333>
<P>This book covers the broad spectrum of programming JavaScript - from the core
language to browser applications and server-side use to stand-alone and embedded
JavaScript.
</P>
<P>
It includes a guide to the language - when where and how to get the
most out of JavaScript - together with practical case studies demonstrating
JavaScript in action. Coverage is bang up-to-date, with discussion of
compatibility issues and version differences, and the book concludes with a
comprehensive reference section. </P>

</body>
</html>
```

Finally, you have your beg_asp2_details.htm page. Again, it is identical to the version created in the example, with a form and button to add the book to the shopping basket, as in the preceding page.

```
<html>
<head>
<title>Beginning ASP.Net 2</title>
</head>
<body>
<strong>Beginning ASP.Net 2</strong>
<form name=form1>
<input type="button" value="Add to basket" name=butAddBook
      onclick="window.opener.addBookToBasket(100)">
</form>

<br>
Subjects
<br>
ASP
<br>
Internet
```

```
<br>

<HR color=#cc3333>

<P>ASP.Net 2 is the most recent version of ASP and this book covers it in-depth in
a clear and easy to read manner.
</P>

</body>
</html>
```

Chapter 8

In this chapter you looked at string manipulation using the string object, and the use of the RegExp object to match patterns of characters within strings.

Question 1

What problem does the code below solve?

```
var myString = "This sentence has has a fault and and we need to fix it."
var myRegExp = /(\b\w+\b) \1/g;
myString = myString.replace(myRegExp,"$1");
```

Now imagine that you change that code, so that you create the RegExp object like this:

```
var myRegExp = new RegExp("(\b\w+\b) \1");
```

Why would this not work, and how could you rectify the problem?

Solution

The problem is that the sentence has "has has" and "and and" inside it, clearly a mistake. A lot of word processors have an autocorrect feature that fixes common mistakes like this, and what your regular expression does is mimic this feature.

So the erroneous myString

"This sentence has has a fault and and we need to fix it."

will become

"This sentence has a fault and we need to fix it."

Let's look at how the code works, starting with the regular expression.

```
/(\b\w+\b) \1/g;
```

By using parentheses you have defined a group, so (\b\w+\b) is group one. This group matches the pattern of a word boundary followed by one or more alphanumeric characters — that is, characters a–z, A–Z, 0–9, and _ — followed by a word boundary. Following the group you have a space, then \1. What \1 means is "Match exactly the same characters as were matched in pattern group one." So, for example, if group one matched "has," then \1 will match "has" as well. It's important to note that \1 will match the exact previous match by group one. So when group one matches the "and," the \1 now also matches "and" and not the "has" that was previously matched.

You use the group again in your replace() method; this time the group is specified by means of the $ symbol, so $1 matches group one. It's this that causes the two matched duplicated words, "has" and "and," to be replaced by just one word in each instance.

Turning to the second part of the question, how do you change the following code so that it works?

```
var myRegExp = new RegExp("(\b\w+\b) \1");
```

Easy: Now you are using a string passed to the RegExp object's constructor, and you need to use two slashes rather than one when you mean a regular expression syntax character, like this:

```
var myRegExp = new RegExp("(\\b\\w+\\b) \\1","g");
```

Notice you've also passed a g to the second parameter to make it a global match.

Question 2

Write a regular expression that finds all of the occurrences of the word "a" in the following sentence and replaces them with "the":

"a dog walked in off a street and ordered a finest beer"

Solution

```
<html>
<body>
<script language="JavaScript" type="text/javascript">
var myString = "a dog walked in off a street and ordered a finest beer";
var myRegExp = /\ba\b/gi;
myString = myString.replace(myRegExp,"the");
alert(myString);
</script>
</body>
</html>
```

Save this as ch08_q2.htm.

With regular expressions, it's often not just what you want to match, but also what you don't want to match that is a problem. Here you want to match the letter *a*, so why not just write this?

```
var myRegExp = /a/gi;
```

Well, that would work, but it would also replace the *a* in "walked," which you don't want. You want to replace the letter *a*, but only where it's a word on its own and not inside another word. So when does a letter become a word? The answer is when it's between two word boundaries. The word boundary is represented by the regular expression special character \b, so the regular expression becomes this:

```
var myRegExp = /\ba\b/gi;
```

The gi at the end ensures a global, case-insensitive search.

Now, with your regular expression created, you can use it in the replace() method's first parameter.

```
myString = myString.replace(myRegExp,"the");
```

Question 3

Imagine you have a website with a message board. Write a regular expression that would remove barred words. (You can make up your own words.)

Solution

```
<html>
<body>
<script language="JavaScript" type="text/javascript">
    var myRegExp = /(sugar )?candy|choc(olate|oholic)?/gi;
    var myString = "Mmm, I love chocolate, I'm a chocoholic. " +
        "I love candy too, sweet, sugar candy";
    myString = myString.replace(myRegExp,"salad");
    alert(myString)
</script>
</body>
</html>
```

Save this as ch08_q3.htm.

For this example, pretend you're creating script for a board on a dieting site where text relating to candy is barred and will be replaced with references to a much healthier option, salad.

The barred words are:

❑   chocolate

❑   choc

❑   chocoholic

❑   sugar candy

❑   candy

Let's see how you can build up the regular expression to remove the offending words.

Start with the two basic words, so to match *choc* or *candy*, use this:

```
candy|choc
```

Next, add the matching for *sugar candy*. Since the `sugar` bit is optional, you group it by placing it in parentheses and adding the question mark after it. This means "Match the group zero times or one time."

```
(sugar )?candy|choc
```

Finally you need to add the optional `olate` and `oholic` end bits. You add these as a group after the "choc" word and again make the group optional. You can match either of the endings in the group by using the | character.

```
(sugar )?candy|choc(olate|oholic)?/gi
```

Finally, you declare it as follows:

```
var myRegExp = /(sugar )?candy|choc(olate|oholic)?/gi
```

The `gi` at the end means that the regular expression will find and replace words on a global, case-insensitive basis.

So, to sum up:

```
/(sugar )?candy|choc(olate|oholic)?/gi
```

reads as:

Either match zero or one occurrences of "sugar" followed by "candy." Or alternatively match "choc" followed by either one or zero occurrences of "olate" or match "choc" followed by zero or one occurrence of "oholic."

Finally, the following:

```
myString = myString.replace(myRegExp,"salad");
```

replaces the offending words with "salad" and sets `myString` to the new clean version:

"Mmm, I love salad, I'm a salad. I love salad too, sweet, salad."

Chapter 9

In this chapter you looked in more detail at the `Date` object, particularly with respect to world time and local time. You also looked at how to create timers to trigger code on a web page.

Question 1

Create a web page with an advertisement image at the top. When the page loads, select a random image for that advertisement. Every four seconds, make the image change to a different one, making sure a different advertisement is selected until all the advertisement images have been seen.

Solution

```
<html>
<head>
<script language="JavaScript" type="text/javascript">

var imagesSelected = new Array(false,false,false);
var noOfImages = 3;
var totalImagesSelected = 0;

function window_onload()
{
   setInterval("switchImage()",4000);
}

function switchImage()
{

   var imageIndex;

   if (totalImagesSelected == noOfImages)
   {
      for (imageIndex = 0; imageIndex < noOfImages; imageIndex++)
      {
         imagesSelected[imageIndex] = false;
      }

      totalImagesSelected = 0;
   }

var selectedImage = Math.floor(Math.random() * noOfImages) + 1;
while (imagesSelected[selectedImage - 1] == true)
{
      selectedImage = Math.floor(Math.random() * noOfImages) + 1;
   }
   totalImagesSelected++;
   imagesSelected[selectedImage - 1] = true;
   document.imgAdvert.src = "AdvertImage" + selectedImage + ".jpg";

}

</script>
</head>
<body onload="window_onload()">
<img src="AdvertImage1.jpg" name="imgAdvert">
</body>
</html>
```

Save this as ch09_q1.htm.

This solution is based on the example in the chapter, Adverts.htm, in which you displayed three images at set intervals, one after the other. The first difference is that you select a random image each time, rather than the images in sequence. Secondly, you make sure you don't select the same image twice in one sequence by having an array, imagesSelected, with each element of that array being true or false depending on whether the image has been selected before. Once you've shown each image, you reset the array and start the sequence of selecting images randomly again.

The final difference between this solution and the example in the chapter is that you set the timer going continuously with setInterval(). So until the user moves to another page, your random display of images will continue.

Question 2

Create a form that gets the user's date of birth. Then, using that information, tell her on what day of the week she was born.

Solution

```
<html>
<head>
<script language="JavaScript" type="text/javascript">

var days = new Array();
days[0] = "Sunday";
days[1] = "Monday";
days[2] = "Tuesday";
days[3] = "Wednesday";
days[4] = "Thursday";
days[5] = "Friday";
days[6] = "Saturday";

function dayOfWeek()
{

    var form = document.form1;
    var date = parseInt(form.txtDate.value)
    var year = parseInt(form.txtYear.value)

    if (isNaN(date) || isNaN(year))
    {
        alert("Please enter a valid whole number");
    }
    else
    {
        if (date < 1 || date > 31)
        {
            alert("Day of the month must be between 1 and 31");
        }
        else
```

```
        {
           userDate = date + " ";
           userDate = userDate +
                      form.selMonth.options[form.selMonth.selectedIndex].value;
           userDate = userDate + " " + year;
           var dateThen = new Date(userDate);
           alert(days[dateThen.getDay()]);
        }
     }
}
</script>
</head>
<body>
<P>Find the day of your birth</P>
<P>
<form name="form1">
<input type="text" name="txtDate" size="2" maxlength="2">
<select name=selMonth>
   <option selected value="Jan">Jan</option>
   <option selected value="Feb">Feb</option>
   <option selected value="Mar">Mar</option>
   <option selected value="Apr">Apr</option>
   <option selected value="May">May</option>
   <option selected value="Jun">Jun</option>
   <option selected value="Jul">Jul</option>
   <option selected value="Aug">Aug</option>
   <option selected value="Sept">Sept</option>
   <option selected value="Oct">Oct</option>
   <option selected value="Nov">Nov</option>
   <option selected value="Dec">Dec</option>
</select>
<input type=text name=txtYear size=4 maxlength=4>
<br>
<input type="button" value="Day of the week"
       onclick="dayOfWeek()" name="button1">
</form>
</P>

</body>
</html>
```

Save this as ch09_q2.htm.

The solution is surprisingly simple. You create a new Date object based on the date entered by the user. Then you get the day of the week using the Date object's getDay() method. This returns a number, but by defining an array of days of the week to match this number, you can use the value of getDay() as the index to your days array.

You also do some basic sanity checking to make sure that the user has entered numbers and that in the case of the date, the number is between 1 and 31. You could have defined a select element as the method of getting the date and only have numbers from 1 to 31. Of course, for either way, you don't check whether invalid dates are entered (for example, the 31st of February). You might want to try this as an additional exercise.

Hint: To get the last day of the month, get the first day of the next month and then subtract one.

Chapter 10

In this chapter you looked at some common mistakes in JavaScript code, debugging code using the Microsoft script debugger, and ways of handling errors using the `try...catch` clause and the `throw` statement.

Question 1

The example `debug_timestable2.htm` has a deliberate bug. For each times table it creates only multipliers with values from 1 to 11.

Use the script debugger to work out why this is happening, and then correct the bug.

Solution

The problem is with your code's logic rather than its syntax. Logic errors are much harder to spot and deal with because, unlike with syntax errors, the browser won't inform you that there's such and such error at line so and so but instead just fails to work as expected. The error is with this line:

```
for (counter = 1; counter < 12; counter++)
```

You want your loop to go from 1 to 12 inclusive. Your `counter < 12` statement will be true up to and including 11 but will be `false` when the counter reaches 12; hence 12 gets left off. To correct this, you could change your code to the following:

```
for (counter = 1; counter <= 12; counter++)
```

Question 2

The following code contains a number of common errors. See if you can spot them:

```
<html>
<head>
</head>
<body>
<script language=JavaScript>
function checkForm(theForm)
{
   var formValid = true;
   var elementCount = 0;
   while(elementCount =< theForm.length)
   {
```

```
            if (theForm.elements[elementcount].type == "text")
            {
                if (theForm.elements[elementCount].value() = "")
                    alert("Please complete all form elements")
                    theForm.elements[elementCount].focus;
                    formValid = false;
                    break;
            }
        }
        return formValid;
    }
    </script>
    <form name=form1 onsubmit="return checkForm(document.form1)">
        <input type="text" ID=text1 name=text1>
        <br>
        CheckBox 1<input type="checkbox" ID=checkbox1 name=checkbox1>
        <br>
        CheckBox 2<input type="checkbox" ID=checkbox2 name=checkbox2>
        <br>
        <input type="text" ID=text2 name=text2>
        <p>
        <input type="submit" value="Submit" ID=submit1 name=submit1>
        </p>
    </form>
    </body>
    </html>
```

Solution

The bug-free version looks like this:

```
<html>
<head>
</head>
<body>

<script language="JavaScript">
function checkForm(theForm)
{
    var formValid = true;
    var elementCount  = 0;

    while(elementCount < theForm.length)
    {
        if (theForm.elements[elementCount].type == "text")
        {
            if (theForm.elements[elementCount].value == "")
            {
                alert("Please complete all form elements")
                theForm.elements[elementCount].focus();
                formValid = false;
                break;
```

```
            ]
        }

        elementCount++;
    }

    return formValid;

}

</script>

<form name="form1" onsubmit="return checkForm(document.form1)">
    <input type="text" id="text1" name="text1">
    <br>
    CheckBox 1<input type="checkbox" id="checkbox2" name="checkbox2">
    <br>
    CheckBox 1<input type="checkbox" id="checkbox1" name="checkbox1">
    <br>
    <input type="text" id="text2" name="text2">
    <P>
    <input type="submit" value="Submit" id="submit1" name="submit1">
    </P>
</form>

</body>
</html>
```

Let's look at each error in turn.

The first error is a logic error.

```
while(elementCount =< theForm.length)
```

Arrays start at 0 so the first Form object is at index array 0, the second at 1, and so on. The last Form object has an index value of 4. However, theForm.length will return 5 because there are five elements in the form. So the while loop will continue until elementCount is less than or equal to 5, but as the last element has an index of 4, this is one past the limit. You should write either this:

```
while(elementCount < theForm.length)
```

or this:

```
while(elementCount <= theForm.length - 1)
```

Either is fine, though the first is shorter.

You come to your second error in the following line:

```
if (theForm.elements[elementcount].type == "text")
```

On a quick glance it looks fine, but it's JavaScript's strictness on case sensitivity that has caused your downfall. The variable name is `elementCount`, not `elementcount` with a lowercase *c*. So this line should read as follows:

```
if (theForm.elements[elementCount].type == "text")
```

The next line with an error is this:

```
if (theForm.elements[elementCount].value() = "")
```

This has two errors. First, `value` is a property and not a method, so there is no need for parentheses after it. Second, you have the all-time classic error of one equals sign instead of two. Remember that one equals sign means "Make it equal to," and two equals signs mean "Check if it is equal to." So with the changes, the line is:

```
if (theForm.elements[elementCount].value == "")
```

The next error is your failure to put your block of `if` code in curly braces. Even though JavaScript won't throw an error since the syntax is fine, the logic is not so fine, and you won't get the results you expect. With the braces, the `if` statement should be as follows:

```
if (theForm.elements[elementCount].value == "")
{
    alert("Please complete all form elements")
    theForm.elements[elementCount].focus;
    formValid = false;
    break;
}
```

The penultimate error is in this line:

```
theForm.elements[elementCount].focus;
```

This time you have a method but with no parentheses after it. Even methods that have no parameters must have the empty parentheses after them. So, corrected, the line is as follows:

```
theForm.elements[elementCount].focus();
```

Now you're almost done; there is just one more error. This time it's not something wrong with what's there, but rather something very important that should be there but is missing. What is it? It's this:

```
elementCount++;
```

This line should be in your `while` loop, otherwise `elementCount` will never go above 0 and the `while` loop's condition will always be `true`, resulting in the loop continuing forever: a classic infinite loop.

Chapter 11

In this chapter you looked at storing small amounts of information, called cookies, on the user's computer and using that information to customize your web site for the user.

Question 1

Create a page that keeps track of how many times the page has been visited by the user in the last month.

Solution

```
<html>
<head>
<script language="JavaScript" type="text/javascript">

function getCookieValue(cookieName)
{
    var cookieValue = document.cookie;
    var cookieStartsAt = cookieValue.indexOf(" " + cookieName + "=");

  if (cookieStartsAt == -1)
  {
      cookieStartsAt = cookieValue.indexOf(cookieName + "=");
  }

  if (cookieStartsAt == -1)
  {
      cookieValue = null;
  }
  else
  {

      cookieStartsAt = cookieValue.indexOf("=", cookieStartsAt) + 1;
      var cookieEndsAt = cookieValue.indexOf(";", cookieStartsAt);
      if (cookieEndsAt == -1)
      {
          cookieEndsAt = cookieValue.length;
      }
      cookieValue = unescape(cookieValue.substring(cookieStartsAt,
          cookieEndsAt));
  }

  return cookieValue;
}

function setCookie(cookieName,cookieValue, cookiePath, cookieExpires)
{
   cookieValue = escape(cookieValue);
   if (cookieExpires == "")
   {
      var nowDate = new Date();
      nowDate.setMonth(nowDate.getMonth() + 6);
      cookieExpires = nowDate.toGMTString();
   }

   if (cookiePath != "")
   {
      cookiePath = ";Path=" + cookiePath;
   }
```

```
        document.cookie = cookieName + "=" + cookieValue + ";Expires=" +
           cookieExpires + cookiePath;
   }

var pageViewCount = getCookieValue("pageViewCount");
var pageFirstVisited = getCookieValue("pageFirstVisited");

if (pageViewCount == null)
{
   pageViewCount = 1;
   pageFirstVisited = new Date();
   pageFirstVisited.setMonth(pageFirstVisited.getMonth());
   pageFirstVisited = pageFirstVisited.toGMTString();
   setCookie("pageFirstVisited",pageFirstVisited,"","")
}
else
{
   pageViewCount = Math.floor(pageViewCount) + 1;
}

setCookie("pageViewCount",pageViewCount,"","")

</script>
</head>
<body>
<script>
var pageHTML = "You've visited this page " + pageViewCount;
pageHTML = pageHTML + " times since " + pageFirstVisited;
document.write(pageHTML);
</script>
</body>
</html>
```

Save this as ch11_q1.htm.

We discussed the cookie functions in Chapter 11, so let's turn straight to the new code.

In the first two lines we get two cookies and store them in variables. The first cookie holds the number of visits, the second the date the page was first visited.

```
var pageViewCount = getCookieValue("pageViewCount");
var pageFirstVisited = getCookieValue("pageFirstVisited");
```

If the pageViewCount cookie does not exist, it's either because the cookie expired (remember that we are counting visits for the last month) or because the user has never visited our site before. Either way we need to set the pageViewCount to 1 and store the date the page was first visited plus one month in the pageFirstVisited variable. We'll need this value later when we want to set the expires value for the pageViewCount cookie we create because there is no way of using code to find out an existing cookie's expiration date.

```
if (pageViewCount == null)
{
   pageViewCount = 1;
```

```
        pageFirstVisited = new Date();
        pageFirstVisited.setMonth(pageFirstVisited.getMonth() + 1)
        pageFirstVisited = pageFirstVisited.toGMTString();
        setCookie("pageFirstVisited",pageFirstVisited,"","")
    }
```

In the `else` statement we increase the value of `pageViewCount`.

```
    else
    {
        pageViewCount = Math.floor(pageViewCount) + 1;
    }
```

We then set the cookie keeping track of the number of page visits by the user.

```
    setCookie("pageViewCount",pageViewCount,"","")
```

Finally, we write out the number of page visits and the date since the counter was reset.

```
    var pageHTML = "You've visited this page " + pageViewCount;
    pageHTML = pageHTML + " times since " + pageFirstVisited;
    document.write(pageHTML);
```

Question 2

Use cookies to load a different advertisement every time a user visits a web page.

Solution

```
    <html>
    <head>
    <script language="JavaScript" type="text/javascript">

    function getCookieValue(cookieName)
    {
        var cookieValue = document.cookie;
        var cookieStartsAt = cookieValue.indexOf(" " + cookieName + "=");

        if (cookieStartsAt == -1)
        {
            cookieStartsAt = cookieValue.indexOf(cookieName + "=");
        }

        if (cookieStartsAt == -1)
        {
            cookieValue = null;
        }
        else
        {

            cookieStartsAt = cookieValue.indexOf("=", cookieStartsAt) + 1;
```

```
            var cookieEndsAt = cookieValue.indexOf(";", cookieStartsAt);
            if (cookieEndsAt == -1)
            {
                cookieEndsAt = cookieValue.length;
            }
            cookieValue = unescape(cookieValue.substring(cookieStartsAt, cookieEndsAt));

        }

        return cookieValue;
    }

    function setCookie(cookieName,cookieValue, cookiePath, cookieExpires)
    {
        cookieValue = escape(cookieValue);
        if (cookieExpires == "")
        {
            var nowDate = new Date();
            nowDate.setMonth(nowDate.getMonth() + 6);
            cookieExpires = nowDate.toGMTString();
        }

        if (cookiePath != "")
        {
            cookiePath = ";Path=" + cookiePath;
        }
        document.cookie = cookieName + "=" + cookieValue + ";Expires=" +
            cookieExpires + cookiePath;
    }

</script>
</head>
<body>
<img src="AdvertImage1.jpg" name="imgAdvert">
<script>

var imageNumber = getCookieValue("displayedImages");
var totalImages = 3;

if (imageNumber == null)
{
    imageNumber = "1";
}
else
{
    imageNumber = Math.floor(imageNumber) + 1;
}

if (totalImages == imageNumber)
{
    setCookie("displayedImages","","","Mon, 1 Jan 1970 00:00:00");
}
else
{
```

```
        setCookie("displayedImages",imageNumber,"","");
    }

    document.imgAdvert.src = "AdvertImage" + imageNumber + ".jpg";
    </script>
    </body>
    </html>
```

Save this as ch11_q2.htm.

This solution is based on similar questions in previous chapters, such as Chapter 9 where we displayed a randomly selected image. In this case we display a different image in the page each time the user visits it, as far as our selection of images allows.

We've seen the cookie setting and reading functions earlier in the chapter, so let's look at the new code.

We store the number of the previously displayed images in a cookie named displayedImages. The next image we display is that image number plus one. Once all of our images have been displayed, we start again at 1. If the user has never been to the web site, no cookie will exist so null will be returned from getCookieValue(), in which case we set imageNumber to 1.

Most of the code is fairly self-explanatory, except perhaps these lines:

```
    if (totalImages == imageNumber)
    {
        setCookie("displayedImages","","","Mon, 1 Jan 1970 00:00:00")
    }
```

What this bit of code does is delete the cookie by setting its expiration date to a date that has already passed.

Chapter 12

In this chapter you were introduced to Dynamic HTML (DHTML), in which you used JavaScript to manipulate web pages after they were loaded into the browser to enhance user interaction.

Question 1

Create a web page that contains two links. The first link should say Show First Box and the second Show Second Box. Then add two <div/> elements and set their id attributes to boxOne and boxTwo. Give them a height, width, background color, and position, and then hide them. Next, set up the links so that when you click the first one, only the first box shows, and when you click the second one, only the second box shows.

Solution

```html
<html>
<head>
    <title>Chapter 12, Question 1</title>
    <style type="text/css">
        #boxOne {
            position: absolute;
            top: 125px;
            left: 231px;
            width: 100px;
            height: 100px;
            background-color: navy;
            visibility: hidden;
        }

        #boxTwo {
            position: absolute;
            top: 100px;
            left: 400px;
            width: 200px;
            height: 200px;
            background-color: red;
            visibility: hidden;
        }
    </style>
    <script type="text/javascript">
        function showBoxOne() {
            var boxOne = document.getElementById("boxOne");
            var boxTwo = document.getElementById("boxTwo");

            boxOne.style.visibility = "visible";
            boxTwo.style.visibility = "hidden";
        }

        function showBoxTwo() {
            var boxOne = document.getElementById("boxOne");
            var boxTwo = document.getElementById("boxTwo");

            boxOne.style.visibility = "hidden";
            boxTwo.style.visibility = "visible";
        }
    </script>
</head>
<body>
    <a href="#" onclick="showBoxOne(); return false;">Show First Box</a>
    <a href="#" onclick="showBoxTwo(); return false;">Show Second Box</a>

    <div id="boxOne"></div>
    <div id="boxTwo"></div>
</body>
</html>
```

Let's look at this page in more detail, starting with the style sheet. There are two rules in this style sheet, one for each <div/> element in the body of the page. These rules position the elements and assign their height, width, background-color, and visibility properties.

In the body of the page, you find two `<a/>` elements and two `<div/>` elements. The `<a/>` elements are set to handle the `click` event with the `onclick` attribute. The first link calls the `showBoxOne()` JavaScript function, and the second link calls `showBoxTwo()`. Both `onclick` event handlers return a value of `false`, which tells the browser not to navigate to the URL specified in the `href` attribute.

```
<a href="#" onclick="showBoxOne(); return false;">Show First Box</a>
<a href="#" onclick="showBoxTwo(); return false;">Show Second Box</a>
```

Next are the `<div/>` elements, which contain no content. The only attribute specified is their `id` attributes.

```
<div id="boxOne"></div>
<div id="boxTwo"></div>
```

In the `<script/>` element, two functions can be found: `showBoxOne()` and `showBoxTwo()`. Their purpose is to show one `<div/>` element while hiding the other. The first, `showBoxOne()`, shows the first box.

```
function showBoxOne() {
    var boxOne = document.getElementById("boxOne");
    var boxTwo = document.getElementById("boxTwo");

    boxOne.style.visibility = "visible";
    boxTwo.style.visibility = "hidden";
}
```

The first step in this process is to retrieve the two `<div/>` elements by using `document.getElementById()`. Next, the `visibility` property for `boxOne` is set to `visible`, while the same property for `boxTwo` is set to `hidden`. This shows the first box while hiding the other.

The `showBoxTwo()` function follows the same idea, and for the most part, uses the same code as `showBoxOne()`.

```
function showBoxTwo() {
    var boxOne = document.getElementById("boxOne");
    var boxTwo = document.getElementById("boxTwo");

    boxOne.style.visibility = "hidden";
    boxTwo.style.visibility = "visible";
}
```

The only difference in this function is the values assigned to the two element's `visibility` properties. In this case, `boxOne` is set to `hidden` while `boxTwo` is set to `visible`.

Question 2

Create a `<div/>` element that floats around the page. Use the edges of the browser's viewport as a boundary.

Solution

```
<html>
<head>
<style type="text/css">
    #floatingDiv {
        position: absolute;
        left: 0px;
        top: 0px;
        width: 50px;
        height: 50px;
        background-color: navy;
    }
</style>
<script type="text/javascript">

var floatingDiv;
var screenWidth;
var screenHeight;

var horizontalMovement = Math.ceil(Math.random() * 5);
var verticalMovement = Math.ceil(Math.random() * 5);

function startTimer() {
    floatingDiv  = document.getElementById("floatingDiv");
    screenWidth  = document.body.clientWidth;
    screenHeight = document.body.clientHeight;

    window.setInterval("moveDiv()", 10);
}

function moveDiv() {
    var currentLeft = floatingDiv.offsetLeft;
    var currentTop  = floatingDiv.offsetTop;

    if (currentTop < 0) {
        verticalMovement = Math.ceil(Math.random() * 5);
    } else if ( ( currentTop + floatingDiv.offsetHeight ) > screenHeight ) {
        verticalMovement = -(Math.ceil(Math.random() * 5));
    }

    if (currentLeft < 0) {
        horizontalMovement = Math.ceil(Math.random() * 5);
    } else if ( ( currentLeft + floatingDiv.offsetWidth) > screenWidth ) {
        horizontalMovement = -(Math.ceil(Math.random() * 5));
    }

    floatingDiv.style.left = currentLeft + horizontalMovement + "px";
    floatingDiv.style.top = currentTop + verticalMovement + "px";
}
</script>

</head>
<body onload="startTimer()">
```

```
        <div id="floatingDiv"></div>
    </body>
</html>
```

Let's see how the page works. When the page is loaded, the window's onload event handler calls the function startTimer(). This starts a timer going at regular 10-millisecond intervals. Each time the timer fires, it calls the function moveDiv(), which moves a <div/> element about the page.

The style sheet in this page consists of only one rule, which is for the floatingDiv <div/> element.

```
#floatingDiv {
    position: absolute;
    left: 0px;
    top: 0px;
    width: 50px;
    height: 50px;
    background-color: navy;
}
```

This rule sets the element to be positioned absolutely at 0, 0. It also sets the height and width to 50 pixels, and gives the element a navy background color.

Now let's look at the code. At the top of the script block, five global, page-level variables are defined. These variables are accessible from any JavaScript function used in the web page.

```
var floatingDiv;
var screenWidth;
var screenHeight;

var horizontalMovement = Math.ceil(Math.random() * 5);
var verticalMovement = Math.ceil(Math.random() * 5);
```

The floatingDiv variable will reference the <div/> element. The screenHeight and screenWidth variables will contain the height and width of the browser's viewport, respectively. These values are used to determine if the element has reached the edge of the viewport. The final two global variables are horizontalMovement and verticalMovement. These contain random numbers and are between 1 and 5. These hold the amount that the <div/> element should be moved each time the timer calls moveDiv().

The first function, startTimer(), is called when the page loads. Its job is to populate the floatingDiv, screenHeight, and screenWidth variables with their values. It also starts the animation.

```
function startTimer() {
    floatingDiv  = document.getElementById("floatingDiv");
    screenWidth  = document.body.clientWidth;
    screenHeight = document.body.clientHeight;

    window.setInterval("moveDiv()", 10);
}
```

The `floatingDiv` variable gets its value by using the `document.getElementById()` method to retrieve the `<div/>` element in the page's body. By using the `clientWidth` and `clientHeight` properties of the `document.body` object, the `screenWidth` and `screenHeight` variables get their values. The final line of this function uses `window.setInterval()` to repeatedly call `moveDiv()` every 10 milliseconds.

The real workhorse of this example is the `moveDiv()` function, which moves the element around on the page. The first task is to find the element's current top and left positions.

```
function moveDiv() {
    var currentLeft = floatingDiv.offsetLeft;
    var currentTop  = floatingDiv.offsetTop;

    //more code here
}
```

You do this by using the `offsetLeft` and `offsetTop` properties of `floatingDiv`. Next, the function needs to determine where the element should be moved. This is done in two sections.

The first section decides whether or not the element has reached the top or bottom of the page.

```
function moveDiv() {
    var currentLeft = floatingDiv.offsetLeft;
    var currentTop  = floatingDiv.offsetTop;

    if (currentTop < 0) {
        verticalMovement = Math.ceil(Math.random() * 5);
    } else if ( ( currentTop + floatingDiv.offsetHeight ) > screenHeight ) {
        verticalMovement = -(Math.ceil(Math.random() * 5));
    }

    //more code here
}
```

If the top of the element has reached the top of the page, then the `<div/>` needs to move downward. Therefore, the `verticalMovement` variable is set to a random positive number between 1 and 5 that moves the element toward the bottom of the page. If the bottom of the page has been reached by the element's bottom, then the element needs to start moving back toward the top. Therefore, `verticalMovement` is assigned a negative random number between 1 and 5.

The second section determines whether or not the element has reached the right or left edge of the browser's viewport.

```
function moveDiv() {
    var currentLeft = floatingDiv.offsetLeft;
    var currentTop  = floatingDiv.offsetTop;

    if (currentTop < 0) {
        verticalMovement = Math.ceil(Math.random() * 5);
    } else if ( ( currentTop + floatingDiv.offsetHeight ) > screenHeight ) {
        verticalMovement = -(Math.ceil(Math.random() * 5));
```

```
    }

    if (currentLeft < 0) {
        horizontalMovement = Math.ceil(Math.random() * 5);
    } else if ( ( currentLeft + floatingDiv.offsetWidth) > screenWidth ) {
        horizontalMovement = -(Math.ceil(Math.random() * 5));
    }

    //more code here
}
```

This new code follows the same principles as the top/bottom code. First, it checks to see whether the element has reached the left edge of the viewport. If so, horizontalMovement is assigned a random positive number to move the element to the right. When the right edge of the element reaches the right edge of the page, horizontalMovement is set to a random negative number, which moves the element back to the left.

The final step is to move the element to its new location.

```
function moveDiv() {
    var currentLeft = floatingDiv.offsetLeft;
    var currentTop  = floatingDiv.offsetTop;

    if (currentTop < 0) {
        verticalMovement = Math.ceil(Math.random() * 5);
    } else if ( ( currentTop + floatingDiv.offsetHeight ) > screenHeight ) {
        verticalMovement = -(Math.ceil(Math.random() * 5));
    }

    if (currentLeft < 0) {
        horizontalMovement = Math.ceil(Math.random() * 5);
    } else if ( ( currentLeft + floatingDiv.offsetWidth) > screenWidth ) {
        horizontalMovement = -(Math.ceil(Math.random() * 5));
    }

    floatingDiv.style.left = currentLeft + horizontalMovement + "px";
    floatingDiv.style.top = currentTop + verticalMovement + "px";
}
```

This code uses the style object and left and top properties to set the new left and top positions for the <div/> element. The new left position is set to the element's current left plus the number contained in horizontalMovement, and the new top position is set to the element's current top plus verticalMovement. At the end of both statements, the string px is appended to the value, making sure that the browser will position the element correctly.

Chapter 13

In this chapter you looked at the DOM and how the standard method for accessing objects on the HTML document can be applied in JavaScript and used to create web pages that will work in both major browsers.

Appendix A: Exercise Solutions

Question 1

Here's some HTML code that creates a web page. Re-create this page, using JavaScript to generate the HTML using only DOM objects, properties, and methods. Test your code in IE, Firefox, Opera, and Safari (if you have it) to make sure it works in them.

Hint: Comment each line as you write it to keep track of where you are in the tree structure, and create a new variable for every element on the page (for example, not just one for each of the TD cells, but nine variables).

```html
<html>
<head>
</head>
<body>
    <table>
        <thead>
            <tr>
                <td>Car</td>
                <td>Top Speed</td>
                <td>Price</td>
            </tr>
        </thead>
        <tbody>
            <tr>
                <td>Chevrolet</td>
                <td>120mph</td>
                <td>$10,000</td>
            </tr>
            <tr>
                <td>Pontiac</td>
                <td>140mph</td>
                <td>$20,000</td>
            </tr>
        </tbody>
    </table>
</body>
</html>
```

Solution

It seems a rather daunting example, but rather than being difficult, it is just a conjunction of two areas, one building a tree structure and the other navigating the tree structure. You start by navigating to the `<body/>` element and creating a `<table/>` element. Now you can navigate to the new `<table/>` element you've created and create a new `<thead/>` element and carry on from there. It's a lengthy and repetitious process, so that's why it's a good idea to comment your code to keep track of where you are.

```html
<html>
<head>
</head>
<body>
<script language="JavaScript">
var TableElem = document.createElement("table")
```

```
var THElem = document.createElement("thead")
var TRElem1 = document.createElement("TR")
var TRElem2 = document.createElement("TR")
var TRElem3 = document.createElement("TR")
var TDElem1 = document.createElement("TD")
var TDElem2 = document.createElement("TD")
var TDElem3 = document.createElement("TD")
var TDElem4 = document.createElement("TD")
var TDElem5 = document.createElement("TD")
var TDElem6 = document.createElement("TD")
var TDElem7 = document.createElement("TD")
var TDElem8 = document.createElement("TD")
var TDElem9 = document.createElement("TD")
var TBODYElem = document.createElement("TBODY")
var TextNodeA1 = document.createTextNode("Car")
var TextNodeA2 = document.createTextNode("Top Speed")
var TextNodeA3 = document.createTextNode("Price")
var TextNodeB1 = document.createTextNode("Chevrolet")
var TextNodeB2 = document.createTextNode("120mph")
var TextNodeB3 = document.createTextNode("$10,000")
var TextNodeC1 = document.createTextNode("Pontiac")
var TextNodeC2 = document.createTextNode("140mph")
var TextNodeC3 = document.createTextNode("$14,000")


docNavigate = document.documentElement;        //Starts with HTML document
docNavigate = docNavigate.lastChild;           //Moves to body element
docNavigate.appendChild(TableElem);            //Adds the table element
docNavigate = docNavigate.lastChild;           //Moves to the table element
docNavigate.appendChild(THElem);               //Adds the thead element
docNavigate = docNavigate.firstChild;          //Moves to the thead element
docNavigate.appendChild(TRElem1);              //Adds the TR element
docNavigate = docNavigate.firstChild;          //Moves the TR element
docNavigate.appendChild(TDElem1);              //Adds the first TD element in the
                                               // heading
docNavigate.appendChild(TDElem2);              //Adds the second TD element in the
                                               // heading
docNavigate.appendChild(TDElem3);              //Adds the third TD element in the
                                               // heading
docNavigate = docNavigate.firstChild;          //Moves to the first TD element
docNavigate.appendChild(TextNodeA1);           //Adds the second text node
docNavigate = docNavigate.nextSibling;         //Moves to the next TD element
docNavigate.appendChild(TextNodeA2);           //Adds the second text node
docNavigate = docNavigate.nextSibling;         //Moves to the next TD element
docNavigate.appendChild(TextNodeA3);           //Adds the third text node

docNavigate = docNavigate.parentNode;          //Moves back to the TR element
docNavigate = docNavigate.parentNode;          //Moves back to the thead element
docNavigate = docNavigate.parentNode;          //Moves back to the table element
docNavigate.appendChild(TBODYElem);            //Adds the tbody element
docNavigate = docNavigate.lastChild;           //Moves to the tbody element
docNavigate.appendChild(TRElem2);              //Adds the second TR element
docNavigate = docNavigate.lastChild;           //Moves to the second TR element
docNavigate.appendChild(TDElem4);              //Adds the TD element
docNavigate.appendChild(TDElem5);              //Adds the TD element
docNavigate.appendChild(TDElem6);              //Adds the TD element
```

```
docNavigate = docNavigate.firstChild;        //Moves to the first TD element
docNavigate.appendChild(TextNodeB1);         //Adds the first text node
docNavigate = docNavigate.nextSibling;       //Moves to the next TD element
docNavigate.appendChild(TextNodeB2);         //Adds the second text node
docNavigate = docNavigate.nextSibling;       //Moves to the next TD element
docNavigate.appendChild(TextNodeB3);         //Adds the third text node
docNavigate = docNavigate.parentNode;        //Moves back to the TR element
docNavigate = docNavigate.parentNode;        //Moves back to the tbody element
docNavigate.appendChild(TRElem3);            //Adds the TR element
docNavigate = docNavigate.lastChild;         //Moves to the TR element
docNavigate.appendChild(TDElem7);            //Adds the TD element
docNavigate.appendChild(TDElem8);            //Adds the TD element
docNavigate.appendChild(TDElem9);            //Adds the TD element
docNavigate = docNavigate.firstChild;        //Moves to the TD element
docNavigate.appendChild(TextNodeC1);         //Adds the first text node
docNavigate = docNavigate.nextSibling;       //Moves to the next TD element
docNavigate.appendChild(TextNodeC2);         //Adds the second text node
docNavigate = docNavigate.nextSibling;       //Moves to the next TD element
docNavigate.appendChild(TextNodeC3);         //Adds the third text node
</script>
</body>
</html>
```

Question 2

Augment your DOM web page so that the table has a border and only the headings of the table (that is, not the column headings) are center-aligned. Again, test your code in both IE, Firefox, Opera, and Safari (if you have it).

Hint: Add any extra code to the end of the script code you have already written.

Solution

Add these lines to the bottom of the script code to add a border:

```
docAttr = document.getElementsByTagName("table").item(0);
docAttr.setAttribute("border", "1");
```

Add these lines to the bottom of the script code to center-align headings:

```
docNewAttr = document.getElementsByTagName("thead").item(0);
docNewAttr.setAttribute("align", "center");
```

Chapter 14

In this chapter you took a very brief look at XML, created your first XML document (a DTD), and then formatted the XML document using CSS and XSL.

Question 1

Create an XML document that logically orders the following data for a school:

❑   Child's name

❑   Child's age

❑   Class the child is in

Use the following data:

Bibby Jones	13	1B
Beci Smith	12	1B
Jack Wilson	14	2C

Solution

```
<?xml version="1.0" encoding="iso-8859-1"?>

<school>
  <child>
    <name>Bibby Jones</name>
    <age>13</age>
    <class>1B</class>
  </child>
  <child>
    <name>Beci Smith</name>
    <age>12</age>
    <class>1B</class>
  </child>
  <child>
    <name>Jack Wilson</name>
    <age>14</age>
    <class>2C</class>
  </child>
</school>
```

Save this file as school.xml.

Question 2

Using JavaScript, load the information from the XML file into a page and display it when the user clicks a link.

Solution

```
<html>
<head>
    <title>Chapter 14 Question 2</title>
```

```
<script type="text/javascript" language="javascript">
function createDocument()
{
    //Temporary DOM object.
    var xmlDoc;

    //Create the DOM object for IE
    if (window.ActiveXObject)
    {
        var versions =
        [
            "Msxml2.DOMDocument.6.0",
            "Msxml2.DOMDocument.3.0"
        ];

        for (var i = 0; i < versions.length; i++)
        {
            try
            {
                xmlDoc = new ActiveXObject(versions[i]);
                return xmlDoc;
            }
            catch (error)
            {
                //do nothing here
            }
        }
    }
    //Create the DOM for Firefox and Opera
  else if (document.implementation && document.implementation.createDocument)
    {
        xmlDoc = document.implementation.createDocument("","",null);
        return xmlDoc;
    }

    return null;
}

var xmlDoc = createDocument();
xmlDoc.load("school.xml");

function writeTableOfSchoolChildren()
{
    var xmlNode = xmlDoc.getElementsByTagName('child');
    var newTableElement = document.createElement('table');
    newTableElement.setAttribute('cellPadding',5);

    var tempElement = document.createElement('tbody');
    newTableElement.appendChild(tempElement);
    var tableRow = document.createElement('TR');

    tempElement.appendChild(tableRow );

    for (var i = 0; i < xmlNode.length; i++)
    {
```

```
            var tableRow = document.createElement('TR');
            for (var iRow= 0; iRow < xmlNode[i].childNodes.length; iRow++)
            {
                if (xmlNode[i].childNodes[iRow].nodeType != 1)
                {
                    continue;
                }
                var tdElement = document.createElement('TD');
                var textData = document.createTextNode(xmlNode[i].childNodes[iRow]
.firstChild.nodeValue);
                tdElement.appendChild(textData);
                tableRow.appendChild(tdElement);
            }

            tempElement.appendChild(tableRow);
        }

        document.getElementById('displaySchoolInfo').appendChild(newTableElement);
    }
</script>

</head>

<body>

<p>
    <a href="javascript: writeTableOfSchoolChildren()">
        Show Table of Children At The School
    </a>
</p>
<p id="displaySchoolInfo"></p>

</body>
</html>
```

Chapter 15

In this chapter you saw how you could extend the functionality of the browser by using plug-ins and ActiveX controls, and how you could use these plug-ins within web pages.

Question 1

Using the RealPlayer plug-in/ActiveX control, create a page with three links, so that when the mouse pointer rolls over any of them a sound is played. The page should work in Firefox and IE. However, any other browsers should be able to view the page and roll over the links without errors appearing.

Solution

```
<html>
<head>
    <script type="text/javascript">
    function play(fileName)
    {
        document.real1.SetSource(fileName);
        document.real1.DoPlay();
    }


    function window_onload() {
        var plugInInstalled = false;

        if (navigator.appName.indexOf("Microsoft") == -1)
        {
            var plugInCounter;

            for (plugInCounter = 0; plugInCounter < navigator.plugins.length;
                 plugInCounter++)
            {
                if (navigator.plugins[plugInCounter].name.indexOf("RealPlayer") >= 0)
                {
                    plugInInstalled = true;
                    break;
                }
            }
        }
        else
        {
            if (real1.readyState == 4)
                plugInInstalled = true;
        }

        if (plugInInstalled == false)
            window.location.replace("NoRealAudioPage.htm");
    }
    </script>
    <object classid="clsid:CFCDAA03-8BE4-11CF-B84B-0020AFBBCCFA" id="real1"
viewastext>
        <param name="height" value="0">
        <param name="width" value="0">
        <embed name="real1" id="real1" border="0" controls="play" height="0"
width="0" type="audio/x-pn-realaudio-plugin">
    </object>
</head>
<body onload="window_onload()">
    <a onmouseover="play('Evil_Laugh.ra')" onmouseout="document.real1.DoStop();"
href="#">
        Evil Laugh
    </a>  
    <a onmouseover="play('Whoosh.ra')" onmouseout="document.real1.DoStop();"
href="#">
        Whooosh!
    </a>  
```

```
      <a onmouseover="play('Explosion.ra')" onmouseout="document.real1.DoStop();"
href="#">
         Kaboom!
    </a>
</body>
</html>
```

Save this as ch15_q1.htm.

This solution is based on the RealPlayer example in the chapter. Note that the three sound files, Evil_Laugh.ra, Whoosh.ra, and Explosion.ra, can be found in the code download for this book.

Verify that the user has the ability to play RealAudio files in the window onload event handler, which calls the window_onload() function.

Just as the IE and Firefox support for plug-ins is different, so therefore are the means of checking for plug-ins. For Firefox, go through the navigator object's plugins array and check each installed plug-in for the name RealPlayer; if it's found, you know the user has the RealAudio player installed.

With IE, simply use the real1 ActiveX control's readyState property to see if it's installed and initialized correctly.

To play the sounds, a function called play() is defined whose parameter is the name of the .ra (or .rm) sound file to be played.

```
function play(fileName)
{
    document.real1.SetSource(fileName);
    document.real1.DoPlay();
}
```

The function makes use of the RealAudio player's setSource() method to set the sound file to be played and the DoPlay() method to actually start playing the clip. You have used different sounds for each link by simply specifying a different file name each time as the parameter for the play() function.

Use the onmouseover and onmouseout event handlers to start playing the sound when the mouse pointer is over the link and to stop it when the mouse pointer moves out of the link, respectively. The mouseout event starts playing the audio clip by calling the play() function, and the mouseout event stops playing it by calling the RealPlayer's DoStop() method.

```
<a onmouseover="play('audiosig.ra')" onmouseout="document.real1.DoStop()" href="#">
    Evil Laugh
</a>
```

Chapter 16

This chapter introduced you to the concept of remote scripting. You wrote a JavaScript class to easily perform asynchronous HTTP requests and created two forms that used Ajax to validate their fields.

Question 1

Extend the HttpRequest class to include synchronous requests in addition to the asynchronous requests the class already makes.

Solution

```
function HttpRequest(sUrl, fpCallback)
{
    this.url = sUrl;
    this.callBack = fpCallback;
    this.async = true;
    this.request = this.createXmlHttpRequest();
}

HttpRequest.prototype.createXmlHttpRequest = function ()
{
    if (window.XMLHttpRequest)
    {

        var oHttp = new XMLHttpRequest();
        return oHttp;

    }
    else if (window.ActiveXObject)
    {

        var versions =
        [
            "MSXML2.XmlHttp.6.0",
            "MSXML2.XmlHttp.3.0"
        ];

        for (var i = 0; i < versions.length; i++)
        {
            try
            {
                oHttp = new ActiveXObject(versions[i]);
                return oHttp;
            }
            catch (error)
            {
               //do nothing here
            }
        }
    }
    return null;
}

HttpRequest.prototype.send = function()
{
    this.request.open("GET", this.url, this.async);

    if (this.async)
```

```
        {
            var tempRequest = this.request;
            var fpCallback = this.callBack;

            function request_readystatechange()
            {
                if (tempRequest.readyState == 4)
                {
                    if (tempRequest.status == 200)
                    {
                        fpCallback(tempRequest.responseText);
                    }
                    else
                    {
                        alert("An error occurred while attempting to contact the
server.");
                    }
                }
            }

            this.request.onreadystatechange = request_readystatechange;
        }

        this.request.send(null);

        if (!this.async)
        {
            this.callBack(this.request.responseText);
        }
    }
```

It's possible to add synchronous communication to your HttpRequest class in a variety of ways. The approach in this solution refactors the code to accommodate a new property called async, which contains either true or false. If it contains true, then the class uses asynchronous communication to retrieve the file, and if it contains false, the class uses synchronous communication. In short, this property resembles an XML DOM's async property for determining how an XML document is loaded.

The first change made to the class is in the constructor itself. The original constructor initializes and readies the XMLHttpRequest (XHR) object to send data. This will not do for this new version, however. Instead, the constructor merely initializes all the properties.

```
function HttpRequest(sUrl, fpCallback)
{
    this.url = sUrl;
    this.callBack = fpCallback;
    this.async = true;
    this.request = this.createXmlHttpRequest();
}
```

There are three new properties to the class. The first, url, contains the URL that the XHR object should attempt to request from the server. The callBack property contains a reference to the callback function, and the async property determines the type of communication the XHR uses. Setting async to true in the constructor gives the property a default value. Therefore, you can send the request without setting the property externally.

The new constructor and class properties are actually desirable, as they enable you to reuse the same `HttpRequest` object for multiple requests. If you wanted to make a request to a different URL, all you would need to do is assign the `url` property a new value. The same can be said for the callback function as well.

The `createXmlHttpRequest()` method remains untouched. This is a helper method and doesn't really have anything to do with sending the request. For completeness, however, here is its definition:

```
HttpRequest.prototype.createXmlHttpRequest = function ()
{
    if (window.XMLHttpRequest)
    {

        var oHttp = new XMLHttpRequest();
        return oHttp;

    }
    else if (window.ActiveXObject)
    {
        var versions =
        [
            "MSXML2.XmlHttp.6.0",
            "MSXML2.XmlHttp.3.0"
        ];

        for (var i = 0; i < versions.length; i++)
        {
            try
            {
                oHttp = new ActiveXObject(versions[i]);
                return oHttp;
            }
            catch (error)
            {
              //do nothing here
            }
        }
    }
    return null;
}
```

The majority of changes to the class are in the `send()` method. It is here that the class decides whether to use asynchronous or synchronous communication. Both types of communication have very little in common when it comes to making a request; asynchronous communication uses the `onreadystatechange` event handler, and synchronous communication allows access to the XHR object's properties when the request is complete. Therefore, code branching is required.

```
HttpRequest.prototype.send = function()
{
    this.request.open("GET", this.url, this.async);

    if (this.async)
    {
```

```
        //more code here
    }

    this.request.send(null);

    if (!this.async)
    {
        //more code here
    }
}
```

The first line of this method uses the open() method of the XHR object. The async property is used as the final parameter of the method. This determines whether or not the XHR object uses asynchronous communication. Next comes an if statement, which tests to see if this.async is true; if it is, the asynchronous code will be placed in this if block. Next, the XHR object's send() method is called, sending the request to the server. The final if statement checks to see whether this.async is false. If it is, synchronous code is placed here to execute.

```
HttpRequest.prototype.send = function()
{
    this.request.open("GET", this.url, this.async);

    if (this.async)
    {
        var tempRequest = this.request;
        var fpCallback = this.callBack;

        function request_readystatechange()
        {
            if (tempRequest.readyState == 4)
            {
                if (tempRequest.status == 200)
                {
                    fpCallback(tempRequest.responseText);
                }
                else
                {
                    alert("An error occurred while attempting to contact the
server.");
                }
            }
        }

        this.request.onreadystatechange = request_readystatechange;
    }

    this.request.send(null);

    if (!this.async)
    {
        this.callBack(this.request.responseText);
    }
}
```

This new code finishes off the method. Let's start with the first `if` block. A new variable called `fpCallback` is assigned the value of `this.callBack`. This is done for the same reasons as with the `tempRequest` variable — scoping issues — as `this` points to the `request_readystatechange()` function instead of the `HttpRequest` object. Other than this change, the asynchronous code remains the same. The `request_readystatechange()` function handles the `readystatechange` event and calls the callback function when the request is successful.

The second `if` block is much simpler. Because this code executes only if synchronous communication is desired, all you have to do is call the callback function and pass the XHR's `responseText` property.

Using this newly refactored class is quite simple. The following code makes an asynchronous request for a fictitious text file called `test.txt`.

```
function request_callback(sResponseText)
{
    alert(sResponseText);
}

var oHttp = new HttpRequest("test.txt", request_callback);

oHttp.send();
```

Nothing has really changed for asynchronous requests. This is the exact same code used earlier in the chapter. If you want to use synchronous communication, simply set `async` to `false`, like this:

```
function request_callback(sResponseText)
{
    alert(sResponseText);
}

var oHttp = new HttpRequest("test.txt", request_callback);

oHttp.async = false;

oHttp.send();
```

You now have a class that requests information in both asynchronous and synchronous communication!

Question 2

It was mentioned earlier in the chapter that the smart forms could be modified to not use hyperlinks. Change the form that uses the `HttpRequest` class so that the user name and e-mail fields are checked at form submission. The only time you need to alert the user is when the user name or e-mail is taken.

Solution

```
<html>
<head>
    <title>Form Field Validation</title>
    <style type="text/css">
```

```
      .fieldname
      {
          text-align: right;
      }

      .submit
      {
          text-align: right;
      }
</style>
<script type="text/javascript" src="HttpRequest.js"></script>
<script type="text/javascript">
    var isUsernameTaken;
    var isEmailTaken;

    function checkUsername_callBack(sResponseText)
    {
        if (sResponseText == "available")
        {
            isUsernameTaken = false;
        }
        else
        {
            isUsernameTaken = true;
        }
    }

    function checkEmail_callBack(sResponseText)
    {
        if (sResponseText == "available")
        {
            isEmailTaken = false;
        }
        else
        {
            isEmailTaken = true;
        }
    }

    function form_submit()
    {
        var request = new HttpRequest();
        request.async = false;

        //First check the username
        var userValue = document.getElementById("username").value;

        if (userValue == "")
        {
            alert("Please enter a user name to check!");
            return false;
        }

        request.url = "formvalidator.php?username=" + userValue;
```

```
            request.callBack = checkUsername_callBack;
            request.send();

            if (isUsernameTaken)
            {
                alert("The username " + userValue + " is not available!");
                return false;
            }

            //Now check the email
            var emailValue = document.getElementById("email").value;

            if (emailValue == "")
            {
                alert("Please enter an email address to check!");
                return false;
            }

            request.url = "formvalidator.php?email=" + emailValue;
            request.callBack = checkEmail_callBack;
            request.send();

            if (isEmailTaken)
            {
                alert("I'm sorry, but " + emailValue + " is in use by " +
                    "another user.");
                return false;
            }

            //If the code's made it this far, everything's good
            return true;
        }
    </script>
</head>
<body>
    <form onsubmit="return form_submit()">
        <table>
            <tr>
                <td class="fieldname">
                    Username:
                </td>
                <td>
                    <input type="text" id="username" />
                </td>
            </tr>
            <tr>
                <td class="fieldname">
                    Email:
                </td>
                <td>
                    <input type="text" id="email" />
                </td>
            </tr>
            <tr>
```

```
                        <td class="fieldname">
                            Password:
                        </td>
                        <td>
                            <input type="text" id="password" />
                        </td>

                    </tr>
                    <tr>
                        <td class="fieldname">
                            Verify Password:
                        </td>
                        <td>
                            <input type="text" id="password2" />
                        </td>

                    </tr>
                    <tr>
                        <td colspan="2" class="submit">
                            <input type="submit" value="Submit" />
                        </td>
                    </tr>
                </table>
            </form>
        </body>
    </html>
```

Let's begin with the HTML. The links were removed, as well as the third column of the table. The key difference in this new HTML is the onsubmit event handler in the opening <form> tag. Ideally, the form should submit its data only when the form fields have been validated. Therefore, the onsubmit event handler is set to return form_submit(). The form_submit() function returns either true or false, making the browser submit the form's data if everything is okay and not submit if a field is not validated.

The JavaScript code holds the most changes, so let's get started there. In this new implementation, two global variables, called isUsernameTaken and isEmailTaken, are declared. These variables hold true or false values: true if the user name or e-mail is taken, and false if it is not.

```
var isUsernameTaken;
var isEmailTaken;

function checkUsername_callBack(sResponseText)
{
    if (sResponseText == "available")
    {
        isUsernameTaken = false;
    }
    else
    {
        isUsernameTaken = true;
    }
}

function checkEmail_callBack(sResponseText)
```

```
{
    if (sResponseText == "available")
    {
        isEmailTaken = false;
    }
    else
    {
        isEmailTaken = true;
    }
}
```

The first two functions, checkUsername_callBack() and checkEmail_callBack(), are somewhat similar to their original versions. Instead of alerting information to the user, however, they simply assign the isUsernameTaken and isEmailTaken variables their values.

The function that performs most of the work is form_submit(). It is responsible for making the requests to the server and determines if the data in the form fields are ready for submission.

```
function form_submit()
{
    var request = new HttpRequest();
    request.async = false;

    //more code here
}
```

This code creates the HttpRequest object and sets it to synchronous communication. There are times when synchronous communication is appropriate to use, and during form validation is one of those times. Validating fields in a form is a sequential process, and its submission depends upon the outcome of the onsubmit event handler. Using synchronous communication forces the function to wait for information to be retrieved from the server before attempting to validate the field. If you used asynchronous communication, form_submit() would attempt to validate the Username and Email fields before it had the appropriate information for each field. Also note that the HttpRequest constructor received no arguments. This is because you can explicitly set the url and callBack properties with the new version.

The first field to check is the Username field.

```
function form_submit()
{
    var request = new HttpRequest();
    request.async = false;

    //First check the username
    var userValue = document.getElementById("username").value;

    if (userValue == "")
    {
        alert("Please enter a user name to check!");
        return false;
    }

    request.url = "formvalidator.php?username=" + userValue;
```

```
request.callBack = checkUsername_callBack;
request.send();

if (isUsernameTaken)
{
    alert("The username " + userValue + " is not available!");
    return false;
}

//more code here
}
```

This code retrieves the value of the Username field and checks to see whether any information was entered. If none was entered, a message is alerted to the user informing her to enter data. If the user entered information in the Username field, then code execution continues. The url and callBack properties are assigned their values and the request is sent to the server. If it turns out that the user's desired user name is taken, an alert box tells her so. Otherwise, the code continues to execute and checks the e-mail information:

```
function form_submit()
{
    var request = new HttpRequest();
    request.async = false;

    //First check the username
    var userValue = document.getElementById("username").value;

    if (userValue == "")
    {
        alert("Please enter a user name to check!");
        return false;
    }

    request.url = "formvalidator.php?username=" + userValue;
    request.callBack = checkUsername_callBack;
    request.send();

    if (isUsernameTaken)
    {
        alert("The username " + userValue + " is not available!");
        return false;
    }

    //Now check the email
    var emailValue = document.getElementById("email").value;

    if (emailValue == "")
    {
        alert("Please enter an email address to check!");
        return false;
    }

    request.url = "formvalidator.php?email=" + emailValue;
    request.callBack = checkEmail_callBack;
```

```
        request.send();

        if (isEmailTaken)
        {
            alert("I'm sorry, but " + emailValue + " is in use by another user.");
            return false;
        }

        //If the code's made it this far, everything's good
        return true;
    }
```

The e-mail-checking code goes through the same process that was used to check the user name. The value of the Email field is retrieved and checked to determine whether the user typed anything into the text box. Then that value is used to make another request to the server. Notice again that the url and callBack properties are explicitly set. If isEmailTaken is true, an alert box shows the user that another user has taken the e-mail address and the function returns false. If the address is available, the function returns true, thus making the browser submit the form.

Index

SYMBOLS AND NUMERICS

coding explanation